FORECASTING:
METHODS AND APPLICATIONS

FORECASTING:
METHODS AND APPLICATIONS

SECOND EDITION

SPYROS MAKRIDAKIS
European Institute of Business Administration (INSEAD)

STEVEN C. WHEELWRIGHT
Graduate School of Business, Stanford University

VICTOR E. McGEE
Amos Tuck School of Business Administration, Dartmouth College

---

JOHN WILEY & SONS
NEW YORK
CHICHESTER
BRISBANE
TORONTO
SINGAPORE

Library of Congress Cataloging in Publication Data:

Makridakis, Spyros G.
    Forecasting, methods and applications.

    (Wiley series in management, ISSN 0271-6046)
    Includes bibliographies and index.
    1. Forecasting—Statistical methods. I. Wheelwright,
Steven C., 1943–   . II. McGee, Victor E.   III. Title.
IV. Series.

HD30.27.M34   1983   338.5′442   82-23858
ISBN 0-471-08610-X

Printed in the United States of America

10

ABOUT THE AUTHORS

Spyros Makridakis

Spyros Makridakis, Professor of Management Science, has been on the faculty at INSEAD, the European Institute of Business Administration, since 1970. He received his M.B.A. and Ph.D. degrees from New York University Graduate School of Business Administration. He has been a consultant to many organizations and has held teaching or research positions with several European and American institutions. He was an ICAME fellow at Stanford University and a visiting scholar at Massachusetts Institute of Technology and Harvard University. He regularly contributes articles to professional journals and his work has appeared in several books on forecasting. He is the founding and chief editor of the *Journal of Forecasting*.

Steven C. Wheelwright

Steven C. Wheelwright received a B.S. in mathematics from the University of Utah and an M.B.A. and Ph.D. from the Graduate School of Business, Stanford University. He taught for one year at INSEAD and for seven years at the Harvard Business School before joining the Stanford faculty in 1979. He currently teaches M.B.A. and executive courses in the areas of business policy and manufacturing strategy. His research interests are primarily in the areas of facilities and technology planning and manufacturing strategy. He has done extensive consulting and teaching for major manufacturing firms in the United States, Europe, and the Far East. His recent publications include numerous articles in the *Harvard Business Review* and *Sloan Management Review* and such books as *Forecasting Methods for Management* (3rd ed.), *Handbook of Forecasting: A Manager's Guide*, and *Competing Through Manufacturing*.

Victor E. McGee

Victor E. McGee is currently a professor of applied statistics at the Amos Tuck School of Business Administration at Dartmouth College, where he has been on the faculty since 1962. He received his B.S. in mathematics from the University of Natal (South Africa), his B.A. and M.A. in Geodesy from Cambridge University, and his Ph.D. in psychometrics from Princeton University. His current teaching assignments in both the M.B.A. and executive programs are in the areas of information systems, forecasting, and statistical analysis of management problems. His research interests include the application of statistical techniques to a variety of organization problems and the application of computers in information system management. He has done extensive consulting for state and regional governments, as well as for business firms. His articles have appeared in such publications as the *Journal of Marketing Research, Journal of the American Statistical Association,* and *Journal of Accounting and Public Policy.* His book *Principles of Statistics: Traditional & Bayesian* has been translated into French, and his user manual *The Multivariate Package of BASIC Programs* is in its third edition.

TO
Aris and Petros
Margaret
      and Marie
Whose patience and support make such a project possible
and worthwhile

PREFACE

The past four decades have witnessed a number of developments in estimation and prediction that have direct relevance and applicability in organizational forecasting. These advances in both theory and practice have been necessitated by the increasing complexity, competitiveness, and rates of change in the environment. Organizations of all sizes find it essential to make future forecasts aimed at reducing the uncertainty of the environment and taking full advantage of the opportunities available to the organization. As with the development of most management science techniques, the *application* of forecasting methodologies has lagged behind their theoretical formulation and verification. Although many managers and students are aware of the need for improved forecasting, few are familiar with the full range of existing techniques and their characteristics and few have the knowledge required to select and successfully apply the most appropriate methods in a specific situation.

The forecasting literature is only now beginning to focus on translating what is theoretically possible and computationally feasible into a form that can be easily understood and applied. There are several excellent books and a plethora of research articles on forecasting, but these have generally been written by the specialists who have performed the theoretical formulation and verification of specific techniques and who are seeking to convey state-of-the-art knowledge to a group of specialists. For example, the works of Brown and of Box and Jenkins do a superb job in developing and proving the statistical properties of specific classes of forecasting methods but provide little information on the full range of techniques and the selection of an appropriate forecasting method in practice. Consequently, the person seeking to understand the alternatives available must first be a mathematical expert and, second, read not a single book but several books, each describing only a single method or a narrow class of methods for forecasting. In addition, the literature describing these individual methods is generally more concerned with their theoretical development and verification than with their practical application. Most users of forecasting are not directly concerned with these theoretical aspects (there are experts in the academic world who can examine each method's validity), and they do not have the time or inclination to study in depth the theoretical development of each alternative forecasting method.

Preparation of the first edition resulted from our view that the book should: (1) cover the full range of forecasting methods, (2) give a complete description of their essential characteristics, (3) outline the steps needed for their application in practice, and (4) not get bogged down in the theoretical issues underlying their development. Fortunately, that assessment proved to be shared by many. The first edition did well, and other authors began to prepare manuscripts that sought to follow some of the same guidelines.

On the basis of our own experience and that of many others—both academics and practitioners—as well as a number of further developments in the fields of forecasting, planning, and computers, we decided that a significantly better book could be prepared. While market experience indicated that the broad purposes outlined above were very appropriate, we decided that our second edition, unlike many that revise only selected chapters, should include major revisions in more than 80 percent of the chapters in order to capture as many of the recent developments and first edition experiences as possible.

The first step was to add as a third author a first-rate statistician. We have sought to maintain the original objective of presenting alternative forecasting methods in such a form that a minimum of technical background would be required, yet the increasing statistical capabilities of practitioners, the further development of certain methodologies, and the widespread availability of computers and programmable calculators indicated that a text such as this needed to be complete, thorough, and wholly accurate in its descriptions and examples. Vic McGee has provided exactly what was needed in this area. The chapters on quantitative methods have all been rewritten, and, while technical details have continued to be placed in appendixes, additional statistics and more precise language have been used throughout.

A second step was to respond to the suggestions of those teaching from the first edition to expand some materials and contract others. Increased interest in Box-Jenkins, multivariate time series, and econometric methods and in business cycle forecasting has led us to expand those sections and to add many more examples, while updating and tightening somewhat the chapters on organizational issues of forecasting. In addition, requests for supplementary materials have led us to add exercises to all chapters and to greatly expand the Teacher's Manual by including solutions to all exercises, chapter teaching plans, additional exercises, and masters for overhead transparencies for in-class lectures.

A third step was to include as many incremental improvements as possible in the final manuscript and to be certain that the entire manuscript was carefully checked for consistency and accuracy before its submission for publishing. For the latter, our special thanks go to the second-year MBA students at Tuck who took Vic McGee's course on forecasting and planning during the spring of 1982. For the former, a number of colleagues at other institutions who used the first edition have provided invaluable suggestions, corrections, and motivation for this second edition. We appreciate all of their help and wish to thank them for it. Several provided detailed reviews that proved most helpful as we prepared this edition, and we extend to them special thanks: J. Scott Armstrong (University of Pennsylvania), Vernon G. Lippitt (University of Rochester), John H. Ristroph, Bert M. Steece (UCLA), and Harold J. Steudel (Marquette University).

The final step taken in this second edition has been to refine the structure and format of individual chapters and the book's six major parts so that the materials would be useful not only in a classroom setting, but also for the practitioner faced with preparing a forecast for a specific situation and purpose. Each chapter provides an overview, the basic materials, several illustrations, and general guidelines for applications. In addition, technical appendixes are included as further background, and each chapter contains a bibliography and list of selected references for follow-on study. Finally, the exercises illustrate the variety of situations in which specific methods can be used, and the questions suggest the sequence of steps to be followed in such situations.

As noted above, the book is divided into six parts. Part One contains two introductory chapters: the first provides a conceptual framework for existing methodologies and the tasks for which they can be used. Chapter 2 gives an overview of the quantitative computations, statistics, and performance measures commonly used in forecasting and provides basic quantitative notation for the entire book.

Parts Two, Three, and Four focus on quantitative techniques of forecasting. In Chapters 3 and 4, those methods commonly referred to as smoothing and decomposition approaches to time-series analysis are examined. The causal regression methods—simple regression, multiple regression, and econometric methods—are discussed in Chapters 5 through 7. Next, the Box-Jenkins autoregressive/integrated/moving average (ARIMA) time-series methods are described in Chapters 8 through 10. The ARIMA methods covered include multivariate time-series analysis (transfer functions), as well as univariate analysis.

Part Five describes several judgmental issues and more qualitative approaches to forecasting. Chapter 11 deals with data handling concerns, Chapter 12 with predicting cycles (turning points), and Chapter 13 describes the most commonly used judgmental, exploratory, and normative approaches of qualitative and technological forecasting.

Finally, Part Six deals with the organizational and management tasks of integrating forecasting and planning. Chapter 14 describes elements of a practical framework that can be used to integrate the forecasting function into existing planning and budgeting processes. In Chapter 15 the approaches most commonly suggested for comparing and evaluating forecasting methods are described and a framework found to be particularly useful in selecting a method for a specific situation is summarized. Chapter 16 describes empirical work on the implementation and management of forecasting in organizations and suggests approaches that can overcome many of the organizational and behavioral problems commonly surrounding fore-casting applications. Finally, Chapter 17 examines recent evidence on the linking of management judgment with more quantitative forecasting methods.

Two appendices present additional material that will be useful to managers and forecasters. Appendix I contains statistical tables for the various tests of significance used in evaluating those quantitative forecast-ing methodologies for which statistics have been developed. Appendix II is a Glossary of Forecasting Terms covering the techniques, concepts, and tools that are the essential components of forecasting. This glossary can serve as a dictionary and reference for terms that may be new to the reader or whose meaning may be unclear.

As an additional aid to both the teaching and practice of forecasting, we have developed an interactive forecasting system for use on a time-shared computer. This system, referred to as SIBYL/RUNNER, is a com-prehensive set of computer programs covering the full range of quantitative forecasting methods described in Chapters 3 through 12. It is designed to facilitate their application in a timely and straightforward manner. The programs are available on several national and international time-sharing services or can be obtained for commercial or educational use in either FORTRAN or BASIC from Applied Decision Systems (a division of Temple, Barker and Sloane), 33 Hayden Avenue, Lexington, Massachusetts 02173.

Spyros Makridakis
Fontainebleau, France

Steven C. Wheelwright
Stanford, California

Victor E. McGee
Hanover, New Hampshire

CONTENTS

PART ONE
BACKGROUND AND PERSPECTIVE

Part One has two main purposes: first, to relate forecasting theory and technical knowledge to the practical problems of planning and decision making. Thus, in Chapter 1, a number of the basic concepts about the practice of forecasting and its value to managers and administrators are reviewed. While many of these topics will be discussed in more detail in later chapters, the aim in Chapter 1 is to provide an overview and rationale for the elements of forecasting that the practical user must understand and to illustrate some of the situation-specific considerations, as opposed to methodology-specific ones, that must be understood in applying forecasting methods.

The second purpose of Part One is to present an overview of those concepts that will be used as building blocks in examining and presenting several different quantitative forecasting methodologies. Thus, Chapter 2 is somewhat technique oriented and strives to identify those concepts that relate to many different forecasting methodologies and that provide the vocabulary and basis for understanding a wide range of forecasting techniques. In addition, a number of the descriptive statistics and performance measures that can be used in comparing different forecasting methods and models are also described.

1/INTRODUCTION

1/1   Needs and Uses of Forecasting

Frequently there is a time lag between awareness of an impending event or need and occurrence of that event. This lead time is the main reason for planning and forecasting. If the lead time is zero or very small, there is no need for planning. If the lead time is long, and the outcome of the final event conditional on identifiable factors, planning can perform an important role. In such situations forecasting is needed to determine when an event will occur or a need arise, so that appropriate actions can be taken.

In management and administrative situations the need for planning is great because the lead time for decision making ranges from several years (for the case of capital investments) to a few days or even a few hours (for transportation or production schedules). Forecasting is an important aid in effective and efficient planning.

Perspectives on forecasting are probably as diverse as views on any set of scientific methods used by decision makers. The lay person may question the validity and efficacy of a discipline aimed at predicting an uncertain future. However, it should be recognized that substantial progress has been made in forecasting over the past several centuries. There are a large number of phenomena whose outcomes can now be predicted easily. The sunrise can be predicted, as can the speed of a falling object, the onset of hunger, thirst or fatigue, rainy weather, and a myriad of other events. However, that was not always the case.

The evolution of science has increased the understanding of various aspects of the environment and consequently the predictability of many events. For example when the Ptolemaic system of astronomy was developed almost nineteen hundred years ago, it could predict the movement of any star with an accuracy unheard of before that time. Even then, however, systematic errors were common. Then came the emergence of Copernican astronomy, which was much more accurate than its Ptolemaic predecessor and could predict the movement of the stars to within hundredths of a second. Today, modern astronomy is far more accurate than Copernican astronomy. The same increase in accuracy is shown in the theory of motion, which Aristotle, Galileo, Newton, and Einstein each improved.

The ability to predict many types of events seems as natural today as will the accurate forecasting of weather conditions in a few decades. The trend in being able to accurately predict more events, particularly those of an economic nature, will continue providing a better base from which to plan. Formal forecasting methods are the means by which this improvement will occur.

Regardless of these improvements, two important comments must be kept in view. The first is that successful forecasting is not always directly useful to managers and others. More than 100 years ago, Jules Verne correctly predicted such developments as submarines, nuclear energy, and travel to the moon. Similarly, in the mid-1800s, Charles Babbage not only predicted the need for computers, but also proposed the design for one. In spite of the accuracy of these forecasts, they were of little value in helping organizations to realize those possibilities or achieve greater success.

A second important point is the distinction between uncontrollable external events (originating with the national economy, governments, customers, and competitors) and controllable internal events (such as marketing or manufacturing decisions within the firm). The success of a company depends on both types of events, but forecasting applies directly to the former, while decision making applies directly to the latter. Planning is the link that integrates them.

For the important areas of sales forecasting, planning, and decision making, these relationships are shown in Figure 1-1. Recognizing the role of forecasting in its organizational and managerial context is usually as important as selecting the forecasting method itself, and thus it will be addressed throughout this book.

A wide variety of forecasting methods are available to management (Chambers et al., 1971; Makridakis and Wheelwright, 1980). These range from the most naive methods, such as use of the most recent observation as a forecast, to highly complex approaches such as econometric systems of simultaneous equations. In addition, the widespread introduction of computers has led to readily available software for quantitative forecasting techniques. Complementing such software and hardware achievements has been the development of data describing the state of economic events (GNP, consumption, etc.) and natural phenomena (temperature, rainfall, etc.). These data in conjunction with organizational statistics (sales, prices, advertising, etc.) and technological know-how provide the base of past information needed for quantitative and technological methods of forecasting.

As suggested above, forecasting is an integral part of the decision-making activities of management. An organization establishes goals and objectives, seeks to predict environmental factors, then selects actions that it hopes will result in attainment of the goals and objectives. The need for forecasting is increasing as management attempts to decrease its dependence on chance and becomes more scientific in dealing with its environment. Since each area of an organization is related to all others, a good or bad forecast can affect the entire organization. Some of the areas in which forecasting currently plays an important role are:

1. *Scheduling existing resources.* Efficient use of resources requires the scheduling of production, transportation, cash, personnel, and so on. Forecasts of the level of demand for product, material, labor, financing, or service are an essential input to such scheduling.
2. *Acquiring additional resources.* The lead time for acquiring raw materials, hiring new personnel, or buying machinery and equipment can vary from a few days to several years. Forecasting is required to determine future resource requirements.

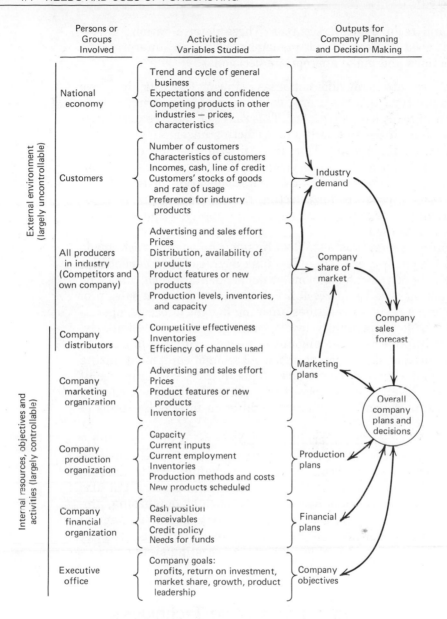

FIGURE 1-1   INFORMATION FLOWS IN SALES FORECASTING AND BUSI-
NESS PLANNING (ADAPTED FROM LINNITT, 1969. USED BY
PERMISSION.)

3. *Determining what resources are desired.* All organizations must
determine what resources they want to have in the long term.
Such decisions depend on market opportunities, environmental
factors, and the internal development of financial, human, prod-

uct, and technological resources. These determinations all require good forecasts and managers who can interpret the predictions and make appropriate decisions.

Although there are many different areas requiring forecasts, the above three categories are typical of the short-, medium-, and long-term forecasting requirements of today's organizations. This range of needs requires that a company develop multiple approaches to predicting uncertain events and build up a system for forecasting. This, in turn, requires that an organization possess knowledge and skills covering at least four areas: identification and definition of forecasting problems; application of a range of forecasting methods; procedures for selecting the appropriate methods for a specific situation; and organizational support for applying and using formalized forecasting methods.

A forecasting system must establish linkages among forecasts made by different management areas. There is a high degree of interdependence among the forecasts of various divisions or departments, which cannot be ignored if forecasting is to be successful. For example, errors in sales projections can trigger a series of reactions affecting budget forecasts, operating expenses, cash flows, inventory levels, pricing, and so on. Similarly, budgeting errors in projecting the amount of money available to each division will affect product development, modernization of equipment, hiring of personnel, and advertising expenditures. This in turn, will influence, if not determine, the level of sales, operating costs, and cash flows. Clearly there is a strong interdependence among the different forecasting areas in an organization.

In simplified terms, the interrelationships of sales and other forecasting areas in a business can be summarized schematically as shown in Figure 1-2. A major aim of this book is not only to examine the techniques available for meeting an organization's forecasting requirements, but also to consider the interdependence of needs in areas such as purchasing, production, marketing, finance, and general management. The final chapters focus on these interdependencies and the organizational steps that are most likely to lead to the development of a successful forecasting system.

1/2   Current Status of Forecasting Techniques

Since the early 1960s, organizations of all types have shown an increasing desire to obtain better forecasts and to make better use of forecasting resources. Commitment to forecasting has grown as a result of several factors. The first has been the increasing complexity of organizations and organizations' environments; it has become more and more difficult for decision makers to weigh all factors satisfactorily. Second, with the increasing sizes of organizations, the magnitude and importance of decisions have in-

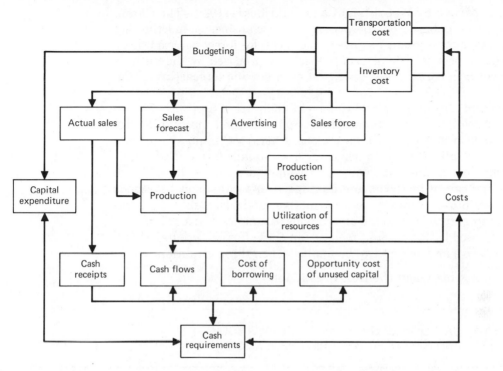

FIGURE 1-2   RELATED ELEMENTS IN AN ORGANIZATION'S FORECAST-
ING SYSTEM

creased; many more decisions warrant special forecasting studies and complete analyses. Third, the environments of most organizations have been changing rapidly. The relationships that organizations must understand have not remained stable, and forecasting enables organizations to learn new relationships more quickly. Fourth, organizations have moved toward more systematic decision making that involves explicit justifications of individual actions; formalized forecasting is one way in which actions can be supported. Fifth, and perhaps most important, is the development of forecasting methods and knowledge concerning their applications that allows their direct application by practitioners rather than solely by expert technicians.

Given the wide range of available forecasting methods, a problem for practitioners is understanding how the characteristics of a forecasting method fit a decision-making situation. Much of the published literature on forecasting does not address this problem, either because most works focus on a narrow range of methods or because many writers infer that the set of methods in which they have expertise can handle most situations.

Two comprehensive schemes for aiding practitioners in matching available methods to specific situations are those developed by Chambers et al. (1971, 1974) and by Wheelwright and Makridakis (1980). The Chambers et al. scheme is based on the product life-cycle concept and the fact that various stages of a product's development call for forecasting methods with different properties. The alternative scheme proposed by the authors considers several important dimensions of each specific forecasting situation.

Forecasting situations vary widely in their time horizons, factors determining actual outcomes, types of data patterns and many other respects. To deal with such diverse applications, several techniques have been developed. These fall into two major categories—quantitative, and qualitative or technological methods. Quantitative methods can be divided into times series and causal methods, and qualitative or technological methods can be divided into exploratory and normative methods. Table 1-1 summarizes this categorization scheme and provides examples of situations that might be addressed by forecasting methods in these further subdivisions.

Quantitative forecasting can be applied when three conditions exist:

1. Information about the past is available.

TABLE 1-1 CATEGORIES OF FORECASTING METHODS AND EXAMPLES OF THEIR APPLICATION

Type of Forecasting Situation	Type of Information Available				
	Sufficient Quantitative Information is Available		Little or No Quantitative Information is Available, but Sufficient Qualitative Knowledge Exists		Little or No Information is Available
	Time-Series Methods	Explanatory or Causal Methods	Exploratory Methods	Normative Methods	
Forecasting continuation of patterns or relationships	Predicting the continuation of growth in sales or gross national product	Understanding how prices and advertising affect sales	Predicting the speed of transportation around the year 2000	Predicting how automobiles will look in the year 1990	Predicting the effects of interplanetary travel; colonization of the earth by extraterrestrial beings; the discovery of a new, very cheap form of energy that produces no pollution
Forecasting changes—or when changes will occur—in existing patterns or relationships	Predicting the next recession or how serious it will be	Understanding how the effects of price controls, or the banning of advertising on TV, will affect sales	Forecasting how a large increase in oil prices will affect the consumption of oil	Having predicted the oil embargo which followed the Arab-Israeli war	

2. This information can be quantified in the form of numerical data.
3. It can be assumed that some aspects of the past pattern will continue into the future.

This last condition is known as the *assumption of continuity;* it is an underlying premise of all quantitative and many technological forecasting methods, no matter how sophisticated they may be.

Quantitative forecasting techniques vary considerably, having been developed by diverse disciplines for different purposes. Each has its own properties, accuracies, and costs that must be considered in choosing a specific method. Quantitative forecasting procedures fall on a continuum between two extremes: naive and intuitive methods, and formal quantitative methods based on statistical principles. The first type uses horizontal, seasonal, or trend extrapolation, and is based on empirical experience that varies widely from business to business, product to product, and forecaster to forecaster. Naive methods are simple and easy to use but not always as accurate as formal quantitative methods. Because of this limitation, their use has declined as formal methods have gained in popularity. Many businesses still use these methods, either because they do not know about simple formal methods or because they prefer a judgmental approach to forecasting instead of more objective approaches.

Formal statistical methods can also involve extrapolation, but it is done in a standard way using a systematic approach that attempts to minimize the forecasting errors. There are several formal methods, often with only limited statistical measures, that are inexpensive and easy to use and that can be applied in a mechanical manner. These methods are useful when forecasts are needed for a large number of items and when forecasting errors on a single item will not be extremely costly.

Persons unfamiliar with quantitative forecasting methods often think that the past cannot describe the future accurately because everything is constantly changing. After some familiarity with data and forecasting techniques, however, it becomes clear that although nothing remains the same, history does repeat itself in a sense. Application of the right method can often identify the relationship between the factor to be forecasted and time itself (or several other factors), making improved forecasting possible.

An additional dimension for classifying quantitative forecasting methods is to consider the underlying model involved. There are two major types of forecasting models: time-series and regression (causal) models. In the first type, prediction of the future is based on past values of a variable and/or past errors. The objective of such time-series forecasting methods is to discover the pattern in the historical data series and extrapolate that pattern into the future.

Causal models on the other hand assume that the factor to be forecasted exhibits a cause-effect relationship with one or more independent variables. For example, sales = f (income, prices, advertising, competition, etc.). The purpose of the causal model is to discover the form of that relationship and use it to forecast future values of the dependent variable.

Both time-series and causal models have advantages in certain situations. Time-series models can often be used more easily to forecast, whereas causal models can be used with greater success for policy and decision making. Whenever the necessary data are available, a forecasting relationship can be hypothesized either as a function of time or as a function of independent variables, and tested. An important step in selecting an appropriate time-series method is to consider the types of data patterns, so that the methods most appropriate to those patterns can be tested. Four types of data patterns can be distinguished: horizontal (or stationary), seasonal, cyclical, and trend.

1. A *horizontal* (H) pattern exists when data values fluctuate around a constant mean. (Such a series is "stationary" in its mean.) A product whose sales do not increase or decrease over time would be of this type. Similarly, a quality control situation involving sampling from a continuous production process that theoretically does not change would also be of this type. Figure 1-3 shows a typical pattern of such horizontal or stationary data.
2. A *seasonal* (S) pattern exists when a series is influenced by seasonal factors (e.g., the quarter of the year, the month, or day of the week). Sales of products such as soft drinks, ice creams, and heating oil all exhibit this type of pattern. For a quarterly seasonal pattern the data might be similar to Figure 1-4.
3. A *cyclical* (C) pattern exists when the data are influenced by longer-term economic fluctuations such as those associated with the business cycle. The sales of products such as automobiles, steel, and major appliances exhibit this type of pattern as shown in Figure 1-5. The major distinction between a seasonal and a cyclical pattern is that the former is of a constant length and recurs on a regular periodic basis, while the latter varies in length and magnitude.
4. A *trend* (T) pattern exists when there is a long-term secular increase or decrease in the data. The sales of many companies, the gross national product (GNP) and many other business or economic indicators follow a trend pattern in their movement over time. Figure 1-6 shows one such trend pattern.

Many data series include combinations of the above patterns. Forecasting methods that are capable of distinguishing each of the patterns must be employed if a separation of the component patterns is needed. Similarly, alternative methods of forecasting can be used to identify the pattern and to best fit the data so that future values can be forecasted.

Qualitative or technological forecasting methods, on the other hand, do not require data in the same manner as quantitative forecasting meth-

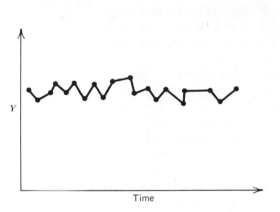

FIGURE 1-3   HORIZONTAL DATA PATTERN

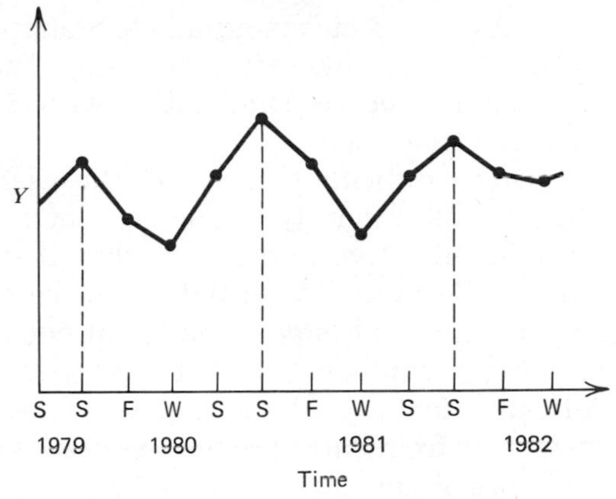

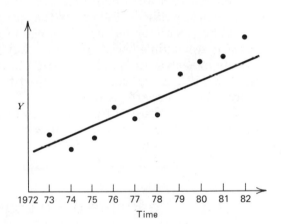

FIGURE 1-4   SEASONAL DATA PATTERN

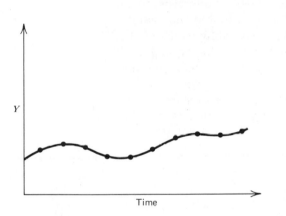

FIGURE 1-5   CYCLICAL DATA PATTERN

FIGURE 1-6   TREND DATA PATTERN

ods. The inputs required depend on the specific method and are mainly the product of intuitive thinking, judgment, and accumulated knowledge. (See Table 1-1.) Technological approaches often require inputs from a number of specially trained people. Technological methods fall into the two subdivisions of exploratory and normative methods. Exploratory methods (such as Delphi, S-curves, analogies, and morphological research) begin with the past and present as their starting point and move toward the future in a heuristic manner, often looking at all available possibilities. Normative methods (such as decision matrices, relevance trees, and system analysis) start with the future by determining future goals and objectives, then work backwards to see if these can be achieved, given the constraints, resources, and technologies available.

As with their quantitative counterparts, technological techniques vary widely in cost, complexity, and value. They can be used separately but are more often used in combination with each other or in conjunction with quantitative methods.

It is difficult to measure the usefulness of technological forecasts. They are used mainly to provide hints, to aid the planner, and to supplement quantitative forecasts, rather than to provide a specific numerical forecast. Because of their nature and cost, they are used almost exclusively for medium- and long-range situations such as formulating strategy, developing new products and technologies, and developing long-range plans. Although doubts are often expressed about the value of technological forecasting, it frequently provides very useful information for managers. It is a premise of the authors that technological methods can be used successfully in conjunction with quantitative methods in such areas as product development, capital expenditures, goal and strategy formulation, and mergers, by even medium and small organizations. Whatever the shortcomings of technological methods, frequently the only alternative is no forecast at all.

The forecaster has a wide range of methods available that vary in accuracy, scope, time horizon, and cost. Key tasks are deciding which method to apply in each situation, how much reliance to place on the method itself, and how much modification is required to incorporate personal judgment before predictions are used as a basis for planning future actions. These issues will be addressed throughout as individual methods for forecasting are introduced, and then as organizational settings for integrating forecasting and planning are considered.

1/3   The Future of Forecasting

It seems only appropriate in a book on forecasting to include some of our own predictions concerning the future of the field. Perhaps the best starting point for such a prediction is a review of the recent history of the field, starting with the evolution of the closely related fields of decision sciences, computers, and planning.

Operations research and management science emerged in the late 1940s and early 1950s. These fields sought to solve organizational problems by means of scientific methods. Techniques such as linear programming, queueing theory, network theory, and simulation were developed to handle particular classes of problems. Many companies and nonprofit organizations formed special groups of operations researchers to apply these techniques. By the late 1960s, it was apparent that these operations-research groups, although working on diverse problems, were having only minimal impact on decisions and actions. By the early 1970s, many of these groups were being disbanded, and people with skills in operations research were being distributed throughout organizations to work more directly with managers in solving their particular problems. By the early 1980s, increasing numbers of managers and planners were developing their own skills in these disciplines.

At the same time that operations research was developing, computers were also being adopted. Initially, computers were used only by scientific researchers and by payroll and accounting groups. During the 1960s, computer usage spread, and many operations researchers stressed applications of computers as an integral part of their work. Successes in computer applications for management were limited. However, by the early 1970s, time-shared computer systems had become widely available in organizations, and many schools of management included computer applications in their core curricula, and the number of people who were familiar with computers grew rapidly. Such knowledge and skills were further expanded as relatively low-priced, sophisticated hand-held calculators and personal computers became widely adopted in the late 1970s and early 1980s.

A third important development was the growth in formal planning as a specialized activity in its own right. During the late 1960s, many large organizations created formal planning groups and charged them with predicting future environments and the organizations' performances in those environments. Even though many of these early groups had only modest successes, a sufficient number of them had impacts such that formal planning departments became widespread and financially secure. Since planning involves forecasting, this gave substantial impetus to studies of forecasting methods and development of staff who were familiar with such methods. By the early 1980s, such planning functions were being integrated with other line functions, placing forecasting in much closer proximity to line managers. Increasingly, such managers found themselves preparing their own forecasts or having them prepared by members of their own staffs.

Given the broad range of forecasting methods currently available and the developments cited above, we think the greatest gains in the practice of forecasting in the decade of the 1980s will come from more and better applications and implementation, not new methods. While there undoubtedly will be some improvements in available methodologies, it is management's knowledge and use of existing methods, in their specific organizational context, that hold the greatest promise.

It is this view that has led us to prepare this text and structure it in its current format. Our hope is to provide a broad-based knowledge of a variety of methods, to relate them to management settings, and explicitly to consider the integration of forecasting with planning and decision making.

REFERENCES AND SELECTED BIBLIOGRAPHY

Armstrong, J. S. 1978. *Long-Range Forecasting: From Crystal Ball to Computer*. New York: John Wiley & Sons.

Asher, W. 1978. *Forecasting: An Appraisal for Policy Makers and Planners*. Baltimore: Johns Hopkins University.

Bails, D. G., and L. C. Pepper. 1982. *Business Fluctuations: Forecasting Techniques and Applications*. Englewood Cliffs, N.J.: Prentice-Hall.

Bright, J. R. 1978. *Practical Technological Forecasting*. Austin, Tex.: Industrial Management Center.

Chambers, J. C., S. K. Mullick, and D. D. Smith. 1971. "How to Choose the Right Forecasting Technique," *Harvard Business Review,* July-August, pp. 45-57.

———. 1974. *An Executive's Guide to Forecasting*. New York: John Wiley & Sons.

Clark, A. C. 1971. *Profiles of the Future*. New York: Bantam Books.

Cleary, J. P., and H. Levenbach. 1982. *The Professional Forecaster: The Forecasting Process Through Data Analysis*. Belmont, Calif.: Lifetime Learning Publications.

Lippitt, V. G. 1969. *Statistical Sales Forecasting*. New York: Financial Executives Institute.

Makridakis, S., and S. C. Wheelwright. 1981. "Forecasting an Organization's Futures," in *Handbook of Organizational Design,* Vol. 1, P. C. Nystrom and W. H. Starbuck, eds. Oxford: Oxford University Press, pp. 122–138.

———. 1979. "Forecasting"—*TIMS Studies in Forecasting,* Vol. 12. Amsterdam: North-Holland.

Steiner, G. A. 1979. *Strategic Planning*. New York: The Free Press.

Thomopoulos, N. T. 1980. *Applied Forecasting Methods*. Englewood Cliffs, N.J.: Prentice-Hall.

Wheelwright, S. C., and S. Makridakis. 1980. *Forecasting Methods for Management,* 3rd ed. New York: John Wiley & Sons.

2/FUNDAMENTALS OF QUANTITATIVE FORECASTING

To develop an understanding of the field of quantitative forecasting requires some basic notation and terminology. This chapter presents such fundamentals. In Appendix 2-A the notation used throughout the book is presented, and in the body of this chapter the following topics are discussed: the difference between explanatory (causal) and time-series modeling (Section 2/1), the least squares procedure for estimating parameters of a model (Section 2/2), the identification of relationships or patterns in the data (Section 2/3), the most important summary statistics (Section 2/4), and the various measures of forecasting accuracy that are used to help judge the appropriateness of a model (Section 2/5).

2/1 Explanatory versus Time-Series Forecasting[1]

In the previous chapter two major approaches to forecasting were identified: explanatory (or causal) and time series. These approaches are complementary and are intended for different types of applications. They are also founded on different philosophical premises.

Explanatory forecasting assumes a *cause and effect relationship* between the inputs to the system and its output, as shown in Figure 2-1.

The *system* can be anything—a national economy, a company's market, or a household. According to explanatory forecasting, any change in inputs will affect the output of the system in a predictable way, assuming the cause and effect relationship is constant. The first task of forecasting is to find the cause and effect relationship by observing the output of the system (either through time or by studying a cross section of similar systems) and relating that to the corresponding inputs. For example, one might seek to determine the cause and effect relationships in a system in order to predict outputs such as GNP, company sales, or household expenses. Such a process, if carried out correctly, will allow estimation of the type and extent of the relationship between the inputs and output. This relationship can then be used to predict future states of the system, provided the inputs are known for those future states.

The determination and application of cause and effect relationships

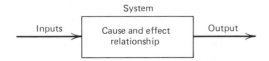

FIGURE 2-1 EXPLANATORY OR CAUSAL RELATIONSHIP

---

[1]This chapter is intended for those with little or no background in statistics. Others can skim Sections 2/1 through 2/5 without losing continuity.

can be illustrated by using a well-known physical relationship, Boyle's law. This law states:

$$P = \Theta \frac{N}{V},$$

(2-1)

where P is pressure,

N is the number of molecules,

V is the volume, and

Θ is a proportionality factor.

Assuming for a moment that (2-1) is known, it can be viewed as an example of Figure 2-1. For each value of the inputs N and V, and a value for Θ, there will be a corresponding output value P, pressure. Equation (2-1) is of value because with known inputs, the output can be predicted. Needless to say, there are almost infinite causal or explanatory relationships in the real world. A question of extreme importance to the forecaster, however, is whether or not specific relationships can be estimated. The best procedures for doing so will be discussed later in this chapter.

Unlike explanatory forecasting, time-series forecasting treats the *system* as a black box and makes no attempt to discover the factors affecting its behavior. As shown in Figure 2-2, the system is simply viewed as an unknown generating process.

There are two main reasons for wanting to treat a system as a black box. First, the system may not be understood, and even if it were understood it may be extremely difficult to measure the relationships assumed to govern its behavior. Second, the main concern may be only to predict what will happen and not to know why it happens. During the eighteenth, nineteenth, and twentieth centuries, for example, there were several people concerned with the magnitude of sunspots. There was little known at that time as to the reasons for the sunspots or the sources of energy of the sun. This lack of knowledge, however, did not hinder many investigators who collected and analyzed the frequency of sunspots. Schuster (1906) found that there was a regular pattern in the magnitude of sunspots, and he and several others were able to predict their continuation through time-series analysis.

Quite often it is possible to forecast by using either causal or time-series approaches. Economic activity, for example, can be forecasted by discovering and measuring the relationship of GNP (gross national product)

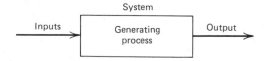

FIGURE 2-2   TIME-SERIES RELATIONSHIP

to several factors that influence it, such as monetary and fiscal policies, inflation, capital spending, and imports and exports. This will require that the form and parameters of the relationship be specified:

$$\text{GNP} = f(\text{monetary and fiscal policies, inflation,} \qquad (2\text{-}2)$$
$$\text{capital spending, imports, exports}).$$

The procedure for selecting an appropriate functional form of equation (2-2) and estimating its parameters will be discussed in detail later on. At this point it should be emphasized that according to (2-2), GNP depends upon, or is determined by, the factors on the right-hand side of the equation. As these factors change, GNP will vary in the manner specified by (2-2).

If the only purpose is to forecast future values of GNP without concern as to why a certain level of GNP will be realized, a time-series approach would be appropriate. It is known that the magnitude of GNP does not change drastically from one month to another, or even from one year to another. Thus the GNP of next month will depend upon the GNP of the previous month and possibly that of the months before. Based on this observation, GNP might be expressed as follows:

$$\text{GNP}_{t+1} = f(\text{GNP}_t, \text{GNP}_{t-1}, \text{GNP}_{t-2}, \text{GNP}_{t-3}\ldots), \qquad (2\text{-}3)$$

where t is the present month,

$t + 1$ is the next month,

$t - 1$ is the last month,

$t - 2$ is two months ago,

and so on.

Equation (2-3) is similar to (2-2) except that the factors on the right-hand side are previous values of the left-hand side. This makes the job of forecasting easier once (2-3) is known, since it requires no special input values as (2-2) does. However, one major problem with both equations (2-2) and (2-3) is that the relationship between the left- and right-hand sides of the equations must be discovered and measured.

2/2 Least Squares Estimates

Because physical and natural science relationships are usually exact, they are often called laws. For example, equation (2-1) will always hold under certain conditions. The same is true for Kepler's first two laws of planetary motion, which can specify precisely the position of planets as a function of time. However, high levels of precision disappear when one moves from physical or natural systems to social systems. The GNP relationship of equations (2-2) or (2-3) will never be exact. There will always

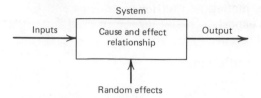

FIGURE 2-3   EXPLANATORY OR CAUSAL RELATIONSHIP WITH RANDOM
NOISE

be changes in GNP that will not be accounted for by variations in the right-hand side of (2-2) or (2-3), and thus some part of GNP changes will remain unpredictable. Therefore, to be complete, Figures 2-1 and 2-2 must be modified to include random causes that affect the GNP figures. These can be represented as shown in Figures 2-3 and 2-4. Equations (2-2) and (2-3) should be modified also to include a random term, usually denoted by u, accounting for that part of the system's behavior that cannot be explained through the causal or time-series relationship.

$$GNP = f(\text{monetary and fiscal policies, inflation,} \qquad (2\text{-}4)$$
$$\text{capital spending, imports, exports, } u) \text{ (see (2-2))}$$

and

$$GNP_{t+1} = f(GNP_t, GNP_{t-1}, GNP_{t-2}, GNP_{t-3}, \ldots, u_t) \text{ (see (2-3)).} \qquad (2\text{-}5)$$

What is observed as the output of the system is dependent on two things: the functional relationship governing the system (or the pattern, as it will be called from now on) and randomness (or error). That is,

$$\text{data} = \text{pattern} + \text{error.} \qquad (2\text{-}6)$$

The critical task in forecasting is to separate the pattern from the error component so that the former can be used for forecasting.

The general procedure for estimating the pattern of a relationship, whether causal or time series, is through fitting some functional form in such a way as to minimize the error component of equation (2-6). One form of this estimation is least squares. This approach is very old (developed first by Gauss in the 1800s) and is the one most widely used in classical statistics.

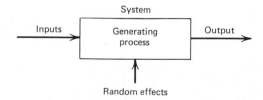

FIGURE 2-4   TIME-SERIES RELATIONSHIP WITH RANDOM NOISE

The name *least squares* is based on the fact that this estimation procedure seeks to minimize the sum of the squared errors in equation (2-6). The example shown below illustrates the basis of the least squares method. Its application to all types of functional forms (i.e., linear or nonlinear) is analogous to that shown here.

Suppose that the manager of a supermarket wants to know how much a typical customer spends in the store. The manager might start by taking a sample of say 12 clients, at random, obtaining the results shown in Table 2-1.

From Table 2-1, it is clear that not all customers spend the same amount. Some of the variation might be explained through factors such as time of the day, day of the week, discounts offered, maximum or minimum amount of checks cashed, and so on, while part of the variation may be random or unexplainable. For purposes of this illustration, it will be assumed that no variation can be explained through causal or time-series relationships. In such a case, the store manager faced with finding an appropriate estimator to describe the data may take a fixed value as an estimate. Having made this decision, the manager might decide to select an estimate in such a way as to minimize the mean (average) squared error. This could be done by trial and error. Suppose the manager chooses an estimate of 7, and then tries estimates of 9, 10, and 12. The resulting mean squared errors are shown in Table 2-2.

From Table 2-2 it is clear that the squared error is least when the manager chooses 10 as the estimate. However, there may be a better estimate. Figure 2-5 shows the resulting MSEs for all estimates from 0 through 20, and it can be seen that the MSEs form a parabola. Furthermore, the

TABLE 2-1 SAMPLE EXPENDITURES FOR SUPERMARKET CLIENTS

Client	Amount Spent
1	$9
2	8
3	9
4	12
5	9
6	12
7	11
8	7
9	13
10	9
11	11
12	10

TABLE 2-2 MEAN SQUARED ERRORS FOR ESTIMATES OF CLIENT EXPENDITURES

Client	Amount Spent	Estimate of Value: 7		Estimate of Value: 9		Estimate of Value: 10		Estimate of Value: 12	
		Error[a]	Error Squared	Error	Error Squared	Error	Error Squared	Error	Error Squared
1	9	2	4	0	0	−1	1	−3	9
2	8	1	1	−1	1	−2	4	−4	16
3	9	2	4	0	0	−1	1	−3	9
4	12	5	25	3	9	2	4	0	0
5	9	2	4	0	0	−1	1	−3	9
6	12	5	25	3	9	2	4	0	0
7	11	4	16	2	4	1	1	−1	1
8	7	0	0	−2	4	−3	9	−5	25
9	13	6	36	4	16	3	9	1	1
10	9	2	4	0	0	−1	1	−3	9
11	11	4	16	2	4	1	1	−1	1
12	10	3	9	1	1	0	0	−2	4
SSE (sum of squared errors)			144		48		36		84
MSE[b] (mean squared error)			12		4		3		7

[a]Error = amount spent − estimated value.

[b]MSE = sum of squared errors/12.

minimum value on this parabola is indeed at the point where the estimate is 10. Thus, the minimum MSE will be achieved when the value of the estimate is 10, and we say that 10 is the least squares estimate of customer spending.

Because Figure 2-5 is a mathematical function whose properties can be found exactly, it is not necessary to use trial and error to find the estimator that minimizes the MSE. Rather, this value can be found mathematically with the help of differentiation. The first step is to rewrite equation (2-6) so as to isolate the error on the left-hand side:

error = data − pattern.   (2-7)

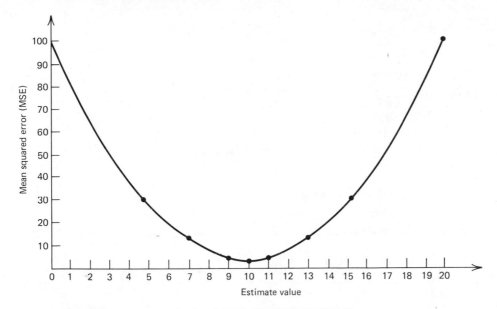

FIGURE 2-5 RELATING MSE TO ESTIMATE VALUE

For convenience, the error will be denoted by e, the data by X and the pattern by $\overline{X}$. In addition, the subscript $i(i = 1,2,3, \ldots, 12)$ will be added to denote the ith customer. Using this notation, equation (2-7) becomes:

$$e_i = X_i - \overline{X}. \tag{2-8}$$

To examine the squared error, both sides of (2-8) must be squared, giving:

$$e_i^2 = (X_i - \overline{X})^2. \tag{2-9}$$

Summing these values (squared errors) for all 12 customers yields:

$$\phi = \sum_{i=1}^{12} e^2 = \sum_{i=1}^{12} (X_i - \overline{X})^2 \tag{2-10}$$

Now initially the value $\overline{X}$ will not be known, but the store manager wants that value of $\overline{X}$ which will minimize the sum of the squared errors. This can be found by taking the derivative of ϕ, setting it equal to zero, and solving for $\overline{X}$, as follows:

$$\frac{d\phi}{d\overline{X}} = -2\sum_{i=1}^{12} (X_i - \overline{X}) = 0$$

so that

$$\sum_{i=1}^{12} (X_i - \overline{X}) = 0$$

or

$$\sum_{i=1}^{12} X_i - 12\overline{X} = 0$$

which implies

$$\overline{X} = \frac{1}{12} \sum_{i=1}^{12} X_i. \tag{2-11}$$

Solution (2-11) is easily recognized as a formula that gives the average of 12 numbers, and it gives a value that minimizes the sum of the squared errors. Applying (2-11) to the store manager's data of Table 2-1 gives

$$\overline{X} = \frac{\sum_{i=1}^{12} X_i}{12} = \frac{120}{12} = 10.$$

This value is the minimum point of Figure 2-5. As a single point estimate of the pattern of the data, the mean fits the data as closely as possible, given the criterion of minimizing the MSE.[2] While the mean is a somewhat simple estimate of the data in most situations, the procedure of least squares that was used to determine a MSE estimate can be applied no matter how complex or sophisticated the estimation situation is.

It is of course possible to minimize Σe_i, Σe_i^3, or Σe_i^4 instead of minimizing the MSE. However, minimizing the MSE is the most popular for several reasons. For one, attempting to minimize Σe_i will involve extra complications because some e_i values will be positive and some will be negative. To avoid having errors cancelling each other, one might minimize the absolute errors, $\Sigma |e_i|$. Computationally, this is not as easy as minimizing the Σe_i^2. Choosing to minimize Σe_i^4 or Σe_i^6 is unattractive because each has more than one minimum, which again adds to the computational and practical problems. On the other hand, increasing the power of the error term does magnify, or give more weight to, extreme values, and this result is attractive because large errors are less desirable than small errors. However, it should not be overdone. Additionally, many cost relationships are quadratic in nature, suggesting the appropriateness of squaring. The use of Σe_i^2 is a compromise between giving too much weight to extreme errors and giving the same weight to all values (using $\Sigma |e_i|$).

---

[2] Note that minimizing SSE (the sum of squared errors) is the "least squares" procedure. Dividing by n (which is 12 in the example above) gives the MSE. Thus minimizing the MSE is an exactly equivalent procedure.

2/3 Discovering and Describing Existing Relationships or Patterns

If the measurable output of a system is viewed as data that include a pattern and some error, a major consideration in forecasting, whether causal or time series, is to identify and fit the most appropriate pattern (functional form) so as to minimize the MSE. The basic procedure is illustrated in the next two sections.

2/3/1 Time-Series Pattern

Table 2-3 gives the population of France (in millions) for the years 1961 to 1970 and the resulting errors when the mean is used as the estimate for the pattern. If the mean is used to fit the population data following the approach outlined in the last section, the MSE will be minimized. The result is shown in Figure 2-6.

Even a casual examination of Table 2-3 or Figure 2-6 indicates that

TABLE 2-3 THE MEAN AS AN ESTIMATE OF FRENCH POPULATION

Year	Population of France (in millions)	Mean Value	Error	Squared Error
1901	46.163	48.776	−2.613	6.828
1962	46.998	48.776	−1.778	3.161
1963	47.816	48.776	−0.960	0.922
1964	48.311	48.776	−0.465	0.216
1965	48.758	48.776	−0.018	0.000
1966	49.164	48.776	0.388	0.151
1967	49.548	48.776	0.772	0.596
1968	49.915	48.776	1.139	1.297
1969	50.315	48.776	1.539	2.369
1970	50.768	48.776	1.992	3.968

$$\sum_{i=1}^{10} X_i = 487.756$$

$$\overline{X} = \frac{\sum_{i=1}^{10} X_i}{10} = \frac{487.756}{10} = 48.776.$$

$$\text{SSE} = \sum_{i=1}^{10} e_i^2 = 19.508$$

$$\text{MSE} = 1.951$$

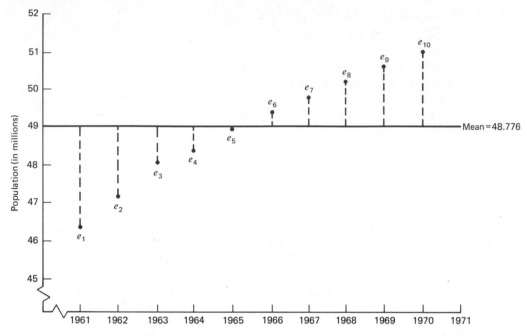

FIGURE 2-6   RESULTING ERRORS USING THE MEAN AS THE ESTIMATE
OF POPULATION

there is something wrong with using the mean as the estimate of the pattern. What is labeled as the error is not random, but exhibits some systematic variation. This systematic variation could perhaps be included as part of the pattern. Since the errors go from negative to positive, an estimate of the pattern in the form of a trend line as shown in Figure 2-7 will give much smaller errors than using the mean as an estimate.

One possible trend line is of the form

$$\text{Population} = 46.133 + .48X, \tag{2-12}$$

where X is the number of the year. The mechanics of how equation (2-12) was found are not important at this point. (They will be examined in detail in Chapter 5.) However, this particular trend line was determined in such a way that the MSE was minimized. As can be seen in Figure 2-7 and Table 2-4, a trend line does describe the data better than using the mean as an estimate.

There is no way that a statistical method can automatically determine the best pattern to describe a given set of data. Rather, this decision must be based on judgment. Then a statistical method can be used to fit the specified pattern in such a way as to minimize the MSE. There are, however, several guidelines that can be applied to determine whether the selected pattern is appropriate. One of these is that the errors must be

Minimizing MSE w/a trend line.

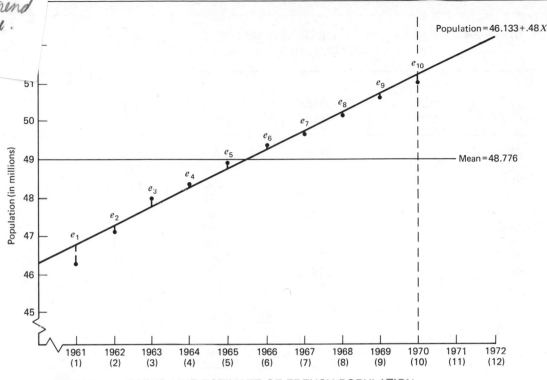

FIGURE 2-7   TREND LINE ESTIMATE OF FRENCH POPULATION

random. If they are not, as is the case in Figure 2-6, an alternative pattern should be considered.

For forecasting purposes, either Figure 2-6 or 2-7 can be used to predict the population for the year 1971. In terms of Figure 2-6, the forecast is 48.776 million. From Figure 2-7, the forecast is 51.4 million. From historical data, one would expect the actual population value to be closer to 51.4 million than to 48.776. (The actual 1971 population was 51.25 million.) Thus in practice it is clear that Figure 2-7 will be chosen, since it fits the pattern of the data much better than Figure 2-6.

The use of Figure 2-7 for forecasting is an example of a time-series approach using a trend pattern. This time-series approach is not concerned with the factors determining future population levels. Its purpose is simply to provide forecasts that are as accurate as possible, which in this case seems to have been achieved.

2/3/2   Explanatory or Causal Patterns

Time-series forecasting requires data on only one variable, namely, the output of the system. The forecast is then based on past values of that

TABLE 2-4   TREND LINE ESTIMATE OF FRENCH POPULATION
(Trend Value = 46.133 + .48X)

Year	Population of France (in millions)	Trend Value	Error	Squared Error
1961	46.163	46.613	−0.450	0.202
1962	46.998	47.093	−0.095	0.009
1963	47.816	47.573	0.243	0.059
1964	48.311	48.053	0.258	0.067
1965	48.758	48.533	0.225	0.051
1966	49.164	49.013	0.151	0.023
1967	49.548	49.493	0.055	0.003
1968	49.915	49.973	−0.058	0.003
1969	50.315	50.453	−0.138	0.019
1970	50.768	50.933	−0.165	0.027

$$SSE = \sum_{i=1}^{10} e_i^2 = 0.463$$

$$MSE = 0.046$$

variable as described above. Functionally, this can be represented as

$$P_{1971} = f(P_{1970}, P_{1969}, \ldots, P_{1961}, u), \tag{2-13}$$

where P is population and u is a random variable that represents the combined effect of influences other than past values of population on the population of 1971. The decision was then made to use as a specific linear form of this function,

$$P_{1971} = 46.133 + .48(11) = 51.4 \text{ million},$$

where 11 refers to the eleventh year (1971)(see Figure 2-7).

In this section we will attempt to determine the pattern of an output variable using a causal relationship involving at least one other variable. The annual gross national product of France will be used as the output variable in this example. Table 2-5 and Figure 2-8 shows the GNP of France (in billions of francs) during the years 1961 through 1970. This is the same time span shown in Table 2-3 for the population in France. Like population, GNP is not accurately estimated using the mean value, as illustrated in Table 2-5. Rather, a trend line is required to best describe the pattern as a function of time. As shown in Figure 2-8, a trend line gives a time-series forecast for the year 1971 of 817.2 billion francs.

TABLE 2-5   FORECASTING FRENCH GNP—MEAN ESTIMATE

Year	GNP of France (billions of francs)	Mean GNP Value	Error
1961	328.327	534.54	−206.21
1962	367.172	534.54	−167.37
1963	411.989	534.54	−122.55
1964	456.669	534.54	−77.87
1965	489.834	534.54	−44.71
1966	532.529	534.54	−2.01
1967	574.770	534.54	40.23
1968	630.012	534.54	95.47
1969	733.959	534.54	199.42
1970	820.150	534.54	285.61

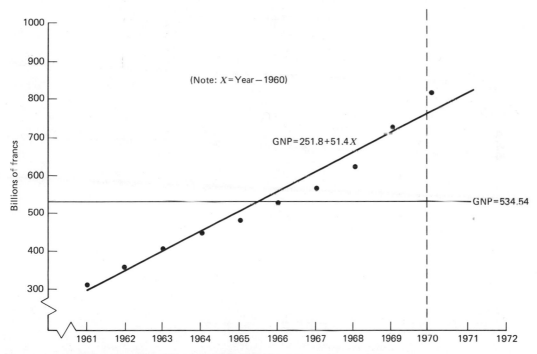

(Note: $X = \text{Year} - 1960$)

$GNP = 251.8 + 51.4X$

$GNP = 534.54$

Billions of francs

FIGURE 2-8   FORECASTING FRENCH GNP—TIME-SERIES TREND ESTI-
MATE

In order to obtain an even better estimate of French GNP, the factors that affect GNP might be considered explicitly. One such determining variable would be the number of people in the population. Functionally, this relationship can be stated as follows:

$$GNP = f(\text{population}, u) \tag{2-14}$$

To determine the appropriateness of this relationship, the pattern needs to be specified and the parameters measured. As in the previous illustrations, the objective is to decide on some pattern, then fit a functional form of that to the data in such a way as to minimize the MSE. If the errors that result from this approach are random and reasonably small, it is generally assumed that the pattern is adequate.

In order to proceed, GNP and population can be plotted on the same graph in order to represent the pair of values that occurred for each of the available ten years. This eliminates time as a determining factor of the output variable, GNP, replacing it with population. The results are shown in Figure 2-9.

Two different patterns have been fitted to the data in Figure 2-9. One is linear (a straight line) of the form

$$GNP = -4478.92 + 102.79P, \tag{2-15}$$

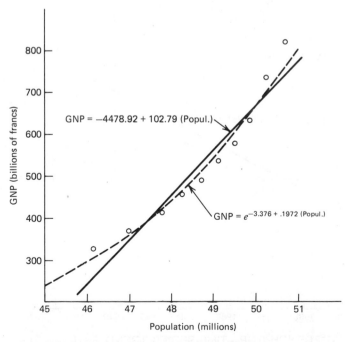

FIGURE 2-9   FORECASTING FRENCH GNP USING FRENCH POPULATION

where P is population. The second is a nonlinear one called an exponential pattern (see dotted line on Figure 2-9), and is of the form

$$GNP = e^{-3.376 + .1972P} \tag{2-16}$$

The details concerning the fitting of the two patterns, (2-15) and (2-16), and the determination of their parameters will be covered in Chapters 5 and 6. It should be clear that the two quantities GNP and population, can be related by deciding on some pattern of relationship between them, then fitting this pattern to the available data (the pairs of values for GNP and population for the years 1961 through 1970) in such a way as to minimize the MSE.

An examination of Figure 2-9 shows that the dotted line representing equation (2-16) describes the relationship between the output (GNP) and the input (population) better than the straight line representing equation (2-15). Thus for forecasting purposes, (2-16) would provide better estimates of GNP, assuming population values are available. For example, the GNP forecast for 1971 would be

$$GNP_{1971} = 2.718^{-3.376 + .1972(P_{1971})}$$
$$= 862.7.$$

This is based on the estimated value of the population for 1971 of 51.4 million that was obtained from Figure 2-7. The actual GNP value for 1971 was 904.16, which means the percentage error of this forecast was 4.8 percent.

The forecast from the linear relationship (2-15) would have been

$$GNP_{1971} = -4478.92 + 102.79(P_{1971})$$
$$= 804.486.$$

This represents a forecast error of 11 percent, much worse than 4.8 percent.

Since only 10 data points were used in this illustration, the causal model is a modest one. With more data, other GNP-related factors, and more carefully defined functional relationships, there is a chance of developing a more useful forecasting model.

2/4 Useful Descriptive Statistics

Equation (2-1) defines a deterministic physical relationship. There are no errors or random variations to consider, and, in such instances, the job of prediction is straightforward. Unfortunately, in economic and behavioral systems there is always uncertainty (randomness), and we must turn to the field of statistics for help in describing such random variables.

For a single data set (univariate data)—or a single time series—the most common descriptive statistics are the mean, the standard deviation, and the variance. We would also like to mention a measure of skewness (especially in connection with Chapters 5 and 6 on regression). Section 2/4/1 deals with these univariate statistics.

For a pair of random variables (bivariate data)—or for paired time-series data—it is of interest to describe how the two series relate to each other. The most widely used summary numbers (statistics) for this purpose are the covariance and the correlation, and these will be defined in Section 2/4/2.

Then for a single time series, it is very useful to compare the observation at one time period with the observation at another time period. For example, if we compare X_t (the observed measure at time t) with X_{t-1}, then we can decide how the series relates to itself *lagged one period*. Similarly, it is possible to compare the series with itself lagged two periods, three periods, and so on. The two most common statistics here are the autocovariance and the autocorrelation, which are defined in Section 2/4/3. These measures will be used extensively in Chapters 8 through 10.

2/4/1 Univariate Data

Consider the data set in Table 2-6, representing the age of 10 employees in a firm. Using the letter A to denote age and a subscript i ($i = 1,2,3, \ldots , 10$) to denote the ith employee, the mean age can be written

$$\overline{A} = \frac{1}{10} \sum_{i=1}^{10} A_i = 30.5 \text{ years.}$$

TABLE 2-6   THE AGE (IN YEARS) OF 10 EMPLOYEES IN A FIRM

Person (i)	Age (A_i)
1	25
2	20
3	25
4	30
5	25
6	55
7	30
8	25
9	40
10	30

Next, for each employee it is possible to find out how far their age is from the mean age. The mean $\overline{A}$ is subtracted from each A_i to give the ith deviation from the mean, $(A_i - \overline{A})$. Note that it is conventional to use lowercase letters to designate the deviation data, as follows:

$$a_i = (A_i - \overline{A}).$$

The sum of the deviations will always equal zero (as shown under column 3 of Table 2-7). Therefore, to develop a useful descriptive statistic from these deviations, they are either squared (as in column 5 of Table 2-7), or, occasionally, the absolute value is taken (as in column 4). The mean of the absolute deviations is denoted MAD, and for the age data

$$\text{MAD} = \frac{1}{10} \sum_{i=1}^{10} |A - \overline{A}| = \frac{1}{10} \sum_{i=1}^{10} |a_i| = 6.8 \text{ years},$$

where $a_i = (A_i - \overline{A})$.

If the squared deviations are summed, we get what is often designated SS (or SSD, for sum of squared deviations):

$$\text{SS} = \sum_{i=1}^{10} (A_i - \overline{A})^2 = 922.50 \text{ years}^2$$

and the mean of these squared deviations is designated MS (or MSD, for mean squared deviation):

$$\text{MS} = \frac{1}{10} \sum (A_i - \overline{A})^2 = \frac{1}{10} \sum a_i^2 = 92.25 \text{ years}^2.$$

Closely related to the mean squared (MS) deviation is the *variance*, which is defined as the sum of squared deviations divided by the *degrees of freedom*[3] (abbreviated d.f.). For the age data the variance of age is

$$S^2 = \frac{1}{9} \sum_{i=1}^{10} a_i^2 = \frac{922.50}{9} = 102.5 \text{ years}^2.$$

Note that since the variance formula uses 9 in the denominator and the mean square formula uses 10, S^2 is larger than MS.[4]

The deviations, $a_i = (A_i - \overline{A})$, are defined in units of years. Therefore, the squared deviations are in units of squared years (years^2) and so the mean square, MS, and the variance, S^2, are also defined in units of

---

[3]The degrees of freedom can be defined as the number of data points (10 in the age data) minus the number of parameters estimated (1 in the age data, because the mean, $\overline{A}$, had to be estimated using the data). So the d.f. for the variance of age = $10 - 1 = 9$.

[4]In statistics, a distinction is made between a biased estimator and an unbiased estimator. For sample data, the MS is a biased estimator of population variance and the variance S^2 is an unbiased estimator of the population variance. See Neter, Wasserman, and Whitmore (1973), pp. 195, 232–233 for a definition of unbiasedness.

squared years. By taking the square root of these two summary numbers, we get two additional summary statistics, as follows:

$$\text{RMS} = \sqrt{\tfrac{1}{10} \Sigma a_i^2} = 9.604 \text{ years,}$$

$$\text{S} = \sqrt{\tfrac{1}{9} \Sigma a_i^2} = 10.124 \text{ years,}$$

where RMS = *root mean square* and S = *standard deviation*. Note that

TABLE 2-7   COMPUTATION OF THE UNIVARIATE STATISTICS
FOR THE AGE OF EMPLOYEES

(1) Person i	(2) Age A_i	(3) $(A_i - \bar{A})$	(4) $|a_i|$	(5) a_i^2	(6) a_i^3
1	25	−5.5	5.5	30.25	−166.37
2	20	−10.5	10.5	110.25	−1157.62
3	25	−5.5	5.5	30.25	−166.37
4	30	−0.5	0.5	0.25	−0.12
5	25	−5.5	5.5	30.25	−166.37
6	55	24.5	24.5	600.25	14706.12
7	30	−0.5	0.5	0.25	−0.12
8	25	−5.5	5.5	30.25	−166.37
9	40	9.5	9.5	90.25	857.37
10	30	−0.5	0.5	0.25	−0.12
Sums:	305	0.0	68.0	922.50	13740.00

MEAN
$$\bar{A} = (\text{col 2 sum}) / 10 = 30.5 \qquad \text{using (2-17)}$$

MEAN ABSOLUTE DEVIATION
$$\text{MAD} = (\text{col 4 sum}) / 10 = 6.8 \qquad \text{using (2-18)}$$

MEAN SQUARE
$$\text{MS} = (\text{col 5 sum}) / 10 = 92.25 \qquad \text{using (2-20)}$$

VARIANCE
$$S^2 = (\text{col 5 sum}) / 9 = 102.50 \qquad \text{using (2-21)}$$

ROOT MEAN SQUARE
$$\text{RMS} = \sqrt{\text{MS}} = 9.605 \qquad \text{using (2-22)}$$

STANDARD DEVIATION
$$S = \sqrt{S^2} = 10.124 \qquad \text{using (2-23)}$$

SKEWNESS
$$\text{Skew} = ((\text{col 6 sum})/9)/S^3 = 1.47 \qquad \text{using (2-24)}$$

these statistics are closely related and that the standard deviation is greater than the root mean square.

Finally, in many contexts it is useful and important to examine the *skewness* of a univariate data set,[5] and to do this, the third powers (cubes) of the deviations from the mean are used. Column 6 of Table 2-7 shows the cubed deviations for the age data. Note that these cubed deviations preserve the sign of the deviations but greatly magnify the magnitude of large (positive or negative) deviations. A definition of skewness is as follows:

$$\text{Skew} = \frac{\frac{1}{9} \Sigma a_i^3}{S^3} = \frac{(13740/9)}{(10.124)^3} = 1.47.$$

Note that this definition uses the sum of the cubed deviations divided by degrees of freedom in the numerator, and the cubed standard deviation in the denominator. Since the units in both the numerator and the denominator are in cubed years (years[3]), the skewness measure ends up being a dimensionless number. The age data shows *positive* skewness (Skew = 1.47) because the positive deviations, when cubed, dominate the negative deviations, when cubed.

If a univariate data set is symmetric, then the skewness measure will be zero. If a set of employees is largely composed of young workers but there are one or two older ones, as in Table 2-6, then these older ages skew the age distribution positively (in the positive direction). If the employees were mostly old and there were one or two young workers, then the skewness measure would be negative; that is, the distribution of ages would be skewed in the negative direction.

To summarize, the univariate statistics (summary numbers) that will be used in this text are defined (generally) as follows:

MEAN

$$\overline{X} = \frac{1}{n} \Sigma X_i \qquad\qquad\qquad\qquad (2\text{-}17)$$

MEAN ABSOLUTE DEVIATION

$$\text{MAD} = \frac{1}{n} \Sigma |X_i - \overline{X}| \qquad\qquad\qquad\qquad (2\text{-}18)$$

SUM OF SQUARED DEVIATIONS
$$\text{SS} = \Sigma (X_i - \overline{X})^2 \qquad\qquad\qquad\qquad (2\text{-}19)$$

MEAN SQUARED DEVIATION

$$\text{MS} = \frac{1}{n} \Sigma (X_i - \overline{X})^2 \qquad\qquad\qquad\qquad (2\text{-}20)$$

---

[5]This is especially important in the context of correlation and regression analysis, where skewness can dramatically affect the size of the correlation coefficient. See Chapter 5 for details.

VARIANCE

$$S^2 = \frac{1}{n-1} \Sigma (X_i - \overline{X})^2 \tag{2-21}$$

ROOT MEAN SQUARE

$$\text{RMS} = \sqrt{\frac{1}{n} \Sigma (X_i - \overline{X})^2} \tag{2-22}$$

STANDARD DEVIATION

$$S = \sqrt{\frac{1}{n-1} \Sigma (X_i - \overline{X})^2} \tag{2-23}$$

SKEWNESS

$$\text{Skew} = \frac{\dfrac{1}{n-1} \Sigma (X_i - \overline{X})^3}{S^3} \tag{2-24}$$

All summations are over the index i from 1 through n.

2/4/2 Bivariate Data

Table 2-8 shows the heights (in inches) and the weights (in pounds) for 10 employees of a firm. When these data are plotted, as in Figure 2-10, it is clear that there is a positive relationship between these two measures. By *positive* relationship we mean that as height increases, weight tends to

---

TABLE 2-8 HEIGHT IN INCHES AND WEIGHT IN POUNDS
FOR 10 EMPLOYEES

Person i	Height H_i	Weight W_i
1	61	163
2	59	114
3	63	161
4	63	144
5	64	145
6	60	118
7	65	156
8	68	160
9	69	167
10	61	141

increase. (A negative relationship would be similar to the price versus demand relationship—as price increases demand decreases.) Whenever we are dealing with two paired measures (e.g., height and weight for one individual, price and demand for one community), it is of interest to examine the extent of the relationship between the two measures. A statistic which indicates how two variables "co-vary" is called the *covariance* and is defined as follows:

$$Cov_{XY} = \frac{1}{n-1} \Sigma (X_i - \overline{X})(Y_i - \overline{Y})$$

$$= \frac{1}{n-1} \Sigma x_i y_i, \tag{2-25}$$

where X and Y are the two variables

$\overline{X}$ and $\overline{Y}$ are the means of X and Y, respectively,

x_i and y_i are the respective deviations for X and Y, and

n is the number of paired observations.

For the height and weight data in Table 2-8 the computations necessary for determining the covariance (Cov_{HW}) between height (H) and weight (W) are shown in Table 2-9. First, the mean height ($\overline{H}$) and the mean weight ($\overline{W}$) are computed using columns 2 and 3, respectively. Then deviations from the mean are calculated in columns 4 and 5, and column 8 gives the product of these two deviations. Summing the deviation products (column 8) and dividing by the degrees of freedom, $n - 1 = 9$, yields the desired covariance,

$$Cov_{HW} = 400.3/9 = 44.48 \text{ inches-pounds.}$$

Note that the units of covariance are problematic. It is difficult to interpret *inches-pounds*. Hence the value of computing the correlation coefficient, described below. Note that the covariance between height and weight is positive, as expected, but the magnitude of Cov_{HW} clearly depends on the units involved. If the heights were converted to centimeters and the weights to kilograms, the plot (Figure 2-10) would look the same but the covariance would be quite different.

The *correlation coefficient*, designated r, is a special covariance measure that takes care of the scale problem just mentioned. If the covariance (Cov_{XY}) is divided by the two standard deviations (S_X and S_y), then the units in the numerator and the denominator cancel out, leaving a dimensionless number, which is the correlation coefficient between X and Y. This is written as follows:

$$r = \frac{Cov_{XY}}{S_X S_y} = \frac{\Sigma(X_i - \overline{X})(Y_i - \overline{Y})}{\sqrt{\Sigma(X_i - \overline{X})^2} \sqrt{\Sigma(Y_i - \overline{Y})^2}}. \tag{2-26}$$

TABLE 2-9 COMPUTATIONS FOR DETERMINING THE COVARIANCE AND THE CORRELATION FOR THE HEIGHT AND WEIGHT DATA OF TABLE 2-8

(1) OBS	(2) H	(3) W	(4) $H - \overline{H}$	(5) $W - \overline{W}$	(6) $(H - \overline{H})^2$	(7) $(W - \overline{W})^2$	(8) $(H - \overline{H})(W - \overline{W})$
1	61	163	−2.3	16.1	5.29	259.21	−37.03
2	59	114	−4.3	−32.9	18.49	1082.41	141.47
3	63	161	−0.3	14.1	0.09	198.81	−4.23
4	63	144	−0.3	−2.9	0.09	8.41	0.87
5	64	145	0.7	−1.9	0.49	3.61	−1.33
6	60	118	−3.3	−28.9	10.89	835.21	95.37
7	65	156	1.7	9.1	2.89	82.81	15.47
8	68	160	4.7	13.1	22.09	171.61	61.57
9	69	167	5.9	20.1	32.49	404.01	114.57
10	61	141	−2.3	−5.9	5.29	34.81	13.57
Sums	633	1469	0.0	0.0	98.10	3080.90	400.30

Mean Height $\overline{H} =$ 633/10 = 63.3 inches

Mean Weight $\overline{W} =$ 1469/10 = 146.9 pounds

Variance of H: $S_H^2 =$ 98.1/9 = 10.9

Variance of W: $S_W^2 =$ 3080.9/9 = 342.3

Covariance between H and W: $Cov_{HW} =$ 400.3/9 = 44.48

Correlation between H and W: $r_{HW} = \dfrac{Cov_{HW}}{S_H S_W} = \dfrac{44.48}{(3.30)(18.50)} = .73$

The effect of this scaling (dividing Cov_{XY} by S_X and S_Y) is to restrict the range of r to the interval −1 to +1. No matter what the units of measurement for X and Y the correlation coefficient, r, is always restricted to lie within that interval.

For the data in Table 2-8 the computations involved in getting to the correlation coefficient are included in Table 2-9. Columns 6 and 7 are the squared deviations for height and weight, respectively, and can be used to determine the standard deviations S_H and S_W, using equation (2-23). Then the covariance between H and W can be divided by S_H and S_W to yield the correlation between height and weight,

$$r_{HW} = \frac{44.48}{(3.30)(18.50)} = 0.73$$

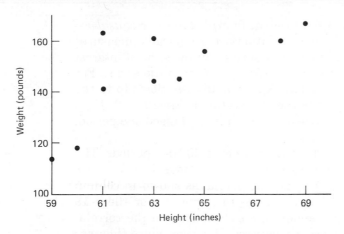

FIGURE 2-10 A PLOT OF THE HEIGHTS AND WEIGHTS OF TEN EMPLOYEES

or

$$r_{HW} = \frac{400.30}{\sqrt{98.10}\ \sqrt{3080.90}} = 0.73 \quad [\text{using } (2\text{-}26)]$$

This summary number is readily interpretable. There is a correlation of 0.73 between height and weight, which is positive and substantial. There is a strong positive association between height and weight.

Covariance and especially correlation are the bread-and-butter statistics for bivariate data sets, and for more extensive multivariate data sets. Care should be taken, however, to remember that these are measures of *linear* association between two variables, so that it is not appropriate (meaningful) to apply the correlation measure when there is a pronounced curvilinear relationship between the two variables. This point is amplified in Chapter 5.

In summary, the two "vital" statistics for bivariate data sets are

$$\text{Cov}_{XY} = \frac{1}{n-1} \Sigma\ (X_i - \overline{X})(Y_i - \overline{Y})$$

and

$$r_{XY} = \text{Cov}_{XY}/(S_X S_Y).$$

2/4/3   A Single Time Series Lagged on Itself

The covariance and correlation coefficient are statistics (summary measures) that measure the extent of the linear relationship between two variables. As such, they can be used to identify *explanatory* or *causal relationships*. Autocovariance and autocorrelation are comparable measures that serve the same purpose for a single time series. The question of interest for a single time series refers to any *time-related pattern* in the series. For example, does the observation at time t, X_t, have any relationship to the observation at time $t - 1$, X_{t-1}, or to the observation at time $t - 2$, X_{t-2}, and so on. We compare the single time series with itself, lagged one period, two periods, three periods, and so forth.

In Table 2-10 there is a single time series over 20 time periods. The observations X_1, X_2, . . . , X_{20} are observed at time periods 1, 2, . . . , 20, respectively. If we lag the series on itself one period, as shown in column 3, then there will be 19 pairs of observations to compare. For these 19 overlapping observations we can compute the covariance and the correlation, just as if they were two separate measures. However, since they are

TABLE 2-10 A TIME SERIES SHOWING RANDOM FLUCTUATION
OVER 20 PERIODS

(1) Period t	(2) Time Series X_t	(3) Time Series X_{t-1}
1	52	—
2	41	52
3	88	41
4	67	88
5	53	67
6	75	53
7	40	75
8	49	40
9	82	49
10	75	82
11	80	75
12	26	80
13	39	26
14	40	39
15	69	40
16	39	69
17	63	39
18	49	63
19	21	49
20	42	21
Sums	1037	1047
Mean	54.58	55.11

one and the same series (with a lag of one period) the summary measures are called *auto*covariance and *auto*correlation. The formulas are the same [as in equations (2-25) and (2-26)], but the subscripts are now different in important ways, and the limits of summation on the summation signs must be stated explicitly, as in equations (2-27) and (2-28) below:

$$\text{Auto-Cov} \atop \text{(lag } k) = \frac{1}{n - k - 1} \sum_{t=k+1}^{n} (X_t - M_1)(X_{t-k} - M_2), \tag{2-27}$$

$$\text{where } M_1 = \frac{1}{n - k} \sum_{t=k+1}^{n} X_t,$$

$$M_2 = \frac{1}{n - k} \sum_{t=1}^{n-k} X_t,$$

$$k = 1, 2, 3, \ldots,$$

$$\text{auto-}r \atop \text{(lag } k) = \frac{\displaystyle\sum_{t=k+1}^{n} (X_t - M_1)(X_{t-k} - M_2)}{\sqrt{\displaystyle\sum_{t=k+1}^{n} (X_t - M_1)^2} \sqrt{\displaystyle\sum_{t=1}^{n-k} (X_t - M_2)^2}}. \tag{2-28}$$

Note two minor difficulties with these formulas. The means M_1 and M_2 are not quite the same because they are based on only $(n - k)$ data points that are not quite the same, and the denominator in equation (2-28) involves two standard deviations that are not quite the same for similar reasons. Since it is one and the same time series we are dealing with, it is usual to simplify these formulas by making two assumptions:

1. that the two means M_1 and M_2 can be estimated well by using the conventional mean of all n data points [i.e., using equation (2-7)], and
2. that the two standard deviations can be estimated well by computing the standard deviation of all n data points in the conventional manner [i.e., using equation (2-23)].

With these simplifying assumptions the two formula become easier to read, as follows:

$$\text{auto-Cov} \atop \text{(lag } k) = \frac{1}{n - k - 1} \sum_{t=k+1}^{n} (X_t - \overline{X})(X_{t-k} - \overline{X}), \tag{2-29}[6]$$

$$\text{auto-}r \atop \text{(lag } k) = \frac{\displaystyle\sum_{t=k+1}^{n} (X_t - \overline{X})(X_{t-k} - \overline{X})}{\displaystyle\sum_{t=1}^{n} (X_t - \overline{X})^2}. \tag{2-30}$$

---

[6]Note that in Chapters 8, 9, and 10 we will make one more simplification; namely, all autocovariances will use $1/n$ instead of $1/(n-k-1)$ in equation (2-29).

By way of illustration, consider the data in Table 2-10 and the calculations of autocovariance and autocorrelation in Table 2-11. The first three columns in Table 2-11 are the same as in Table 2-10. The mean of *all* the data points in column 2 is $\overline{X} = 54.45$, and the deviations in columns 4 and 5 are deviations from $\overline{X}$. Column 6 is the squared deviations from column 4 and the sum of these squares is the denominator in equation

TABLE 2-11 COMPUTING THE AUTOCOVARIANCE AND THE AUTOCORRELATION FOR THE DATA IN TABLE 2-10, USING EQUATIONS (2-29) AND (2-30), AND A LAG OF ONE PERIOD.

(1) t	(2) X_t	(3) X_{t-1}	(4) $(X_t - \overline{X})$	(5) $(X_{t-1} - \overline{X})$	(6) $(X_t - \overline{X})^2$	(7) $(X_t - \overline{X})(X_{t-1} - \overline{X})$
1	52.00		−2.45		6.00	
2	41.00	52.00	−13.45	−2.45	180.90	32.95
3	88.00	41.00	33.55	−13.45	1125.60	−451.25
4	67.00	88.00	12.55	33.55	157.50	421.05
5	53.00	67.00	−1.45	12.55	2.10	−18.20
6	75.00	53.00	20.55	−1.45	422.30	−29.80
7	40.00	75.00	−14.45	20.55	208.80	−296.95
8	49.00	40.00	−5.45	−14.45	29.70	78.75
9	82.00	49.00	27.55	−5.45	759.00	−150.15
10	75.00	82.00	20.55	27.55	422.30	566.15
11	80.00	75.00	25.55	20.55	652.80	525.05
12	26.00	80.00	−28.45	25.55	809.40	−726.90
13	39.00	26.00	−15.45	−28.45	238.70	439.55
14	40.00	39.00	−14.45	−15.45	208.80	223.25
15	68.00	40.00	13.55	−14.45	183.60	−195.80
16	39.00	68.00	−15.45	13.55	238.70	−209.35
17	63.00	39.00	8.55	−15.45	73.10	−132.10
18	49.00	63.00	−5.45	8.55	29.70	−46.60
19	21.00	49.00	−33.45	−5.45	1118.90	182.30
20	42.00	21.00	−12.45	−33.45	155.00	416.45
Sums	1089.00				7022.95	628.45

$$\text{Mean } \overline{X} = \frac{1089}{20} = 54.45$$

$$\text{Auto-Cov (lag 1)} = \frac{628.45}{18} = 34.914$$

$$\text{Auto-}r\text{ (lag 1)} = \frac{628.45}{7022.95} = 0.089$$

(2-30). Column 7 is the column of deviation products (column 4 times column 5). The calculation of autocovariance, with lag one period, using equation (2-29) is as follows:

$$\text{auto-Cov} \atop \text{(lag 1)} = \frac{1}{(20-1-1)} (628.45) = 34.91 \qquad \text{[using (2-29)],}$$

and the autocorrelation, for lag one, is computed as follows:

$$\text{auto-}r \atop \text{(lag 1)} = \frac{(628.45)}{(7022.95)} = 0.09 \qquad \text{[using (2-30)].}$$

Note that if formulas (2-27) and (2-28) had been used instead, the autocovariance and autocorrelation would have been 32.99 and 0.09, respectively—not a great deal of difference in this case.

Using exactly similar procedures, the autocorrelations for lags two, three, and four could be obtained, and the results for the data in Table 2-10 are as follows:

$$\text{auto-}r \text{ (lag 2)} = -0.07,$$

$$\text{auto-}r \text{ (lag 3)} = -0.11,$$

$$\text{auto-}r \text{ (lag 4)} = -0.13.$$

From these low autocorrelations (values close to zero) it is clear that the original time series does not have a lot of pattern to it. The data were in fact generated using a random number series. In the exercises at the end of this chapter are some data sets that display various kinds of pattern (trend, seasonality, and cyclicality) and the autocorrelations for these series will be very helpful in verifying the pattern.

To sum up, much is to be learned about a single time series by examining the autocorrelations of the series with itself, lagged one period, two periods, and so on. The practical formula for computing this statistic is given in equation (2-30). Autocorrelation plays a very important role in time-series forecasting.

2/5 The Accuracy of Forecasting Methods

We now turn to another fundamental concern—namely, how to measure the suitability of a particular forecasting method for a given data set. In most forecasting situations, accuracy is treated as the overriding criterion for selecting a forecasting method. In many instances, the word "accuracy" refers to "goodness-of-fit," which in turn refers to how well the forecasting model is able to reproduce the data that are already known. In explanatory (causal) modeling, goodness-of-fit measures predominate. In time-series modeling it is possible to use a subset of the known data to forecast the rest of the known data, enabling one to study the accuracy of the *forecasts* more directly. To the consumer of forecasts, it is the accuracy of the *future* forecast that is most important. To the modeler, it is the goodness-of-fit of the model to the known facts (quantitative and qualitative) that must be addressed. The kinds of questions that are often asked are as follows:

1. What additional accuracy can be achieved in a given situation through use of a formal forecasting technique? (How inaccurate will the forecasts be if they are based on a very simple or naive approach rather than on a more mathematically sophisticated technique?)
2. For a given situation, how much improvement can be obtained in the accuracy of the forecasts? (How close can one come to achieving perfect forecasts?)
3. If the opportunity for achieving greater accuracy in a given situation is understood, how can that knowledge help in selecting the most appropriate forecasting technique?

In this section, a variety of measures of forecasting (or modeling) accuracy will be defined and in subsequent chapters these measures will be used in the context of worked examples.

To illustrate the computations involved, refer to Table 2-12, which contains a set of observed sales values, X_i, for each of ten time periods ($i = 1, 2, \ldots, 10$), and the forecasted (or fitted) values, F_i, for the same periods.

2/5/1 Standard Statistical Measures

If X_i is the actual datum for time period i and F_i is the forecast (or fitted value) for the same period, then the error is defined as

$$e_i = X_i - F_i.$$

If there are observations and fitted values for n time periods, then there will be n error terms, and the following standard statistical measures can be defined:

MEAN ERROR

$$\text{ME} = \sum_{i=1}^{n} e_i \,/\, n \tag{2-31}$$

MEAN ABSOLUTE ERROR

$$\text{MAE} = \sum_{i=1}^{n} |e_i| \,/\, n \tag{2-32}$$

TABLE 2-12   A TIME SERIES SHOWING SALES FOR A PRODUCT
OVER 10 PERIODS, AND THE CORRESPONDING
FORECASTS FOR EACH PERIOD

Period i	Observation X_i	Forecast F_i
1	22	24
2	23	28
3	39	32
4	37	36
5	38	40
6	47	44
7	43	48
8	49	52
9	61	56
10	63	60

SUM OF SQUARED ERRORS

$$SSE = \sum_{i=1}^{n} e_i^2 \qquad\qquad (2\text{-}33)$$

MEAN SQUARED ERROR

$$MSE = \sum_{i=1}^{n} e_i^2 \, / \, n \qquad\qquad (2\text{-}34)$$

STANDARD DEVIATION OF ERRORS

$$SDE = \sqrt{\sum e_i^2 \, / \, (n-1)} \qquad\qquad (2\text{-}35)$$

Table 2-13 illustrates the computation of these standard statistical measures.

A skilled forecaster may well wish to see all of the above measures routinely, but it is also important to recognize the limitations of each. For example, the objective of statistical optimization is very often to choose a model so as to minimize MSE (or SSE), but this measure has two drawbacks. First, it refers to fitting a model to historical data. Such fitting does not necessarily imply good forecasting. An MSE of zero can always be obtained in the fitting phase by using a polynomial of sufficiently high order or an appropriate Fourier transformation. Overfitting a model to a data series, which is equivalent to including randomness as part of the generating process, is as bad as failing to identify the nonrandom pattern in the data. Com-

TABLE 2-13 COMPUTATIONS OF THE STANDARD STATISTICAL
MEASURES FOR A SET OF ERRORS
(DATA FROM TABLE 2-12)

Period i	Observation X_i	Forecast F_i	Error $X_i - F_i$	Absolute Error $\lvert X_i - F_i \rvert$	Squared Error $(X_i - F_i)^2$
1	22	24	−2	2	4
2	23	28	−5	5	25
3	39	32	7	7	49
4	37	36	1	1	1
5	38	40	−2	2	4
6	47	44	3	3	9
7	43	48	−5	5	25
8	49	52	−3	3	9
9	61	56	5	5	25
10	63	60	3	3	9
Sums			2	36	160

where $e_i = X_i - F_i$

$ME = 0.2$ [using equation (2-31)]

$MAE = 3.6$ [using equation (2-32)]

$SSE = 160$ [using equation (2-33)]

$MSE = 16$ [using equation (2-34)]

$SDE = \sqrt{\dfrac{160}{9}} = 4.22$ [using equation (2-35)]

parison of the MSE developed during the fitting phase of forecasting may give little indication of the accuracy of the model in forecasting.

A second drawback of the MSE as a measure of accuracy is related to the fact that different methods use different procedures in the fitting phase. For example, smoothing methods are highly dependent upon initial forecasting estimates, decomposition methods include the trend-cycle in the fitting phase as though it were known; regression methods minimize the MSE by giving equal weight to all observations; and Box-Jenkins methods minimize the MSE of a nonlinear optimization procedure. Thus, comparison of such methods on a single criterion—namely, MSE—is of limited value.

In the forecasting phase, the use of MSE as a measure of accuracy can also create problems. It does not facilitate comparison across different time series and for different time intervals, since the MSE is an absolute measure. Furthermore, its interpretation is not intuitive even for the specialist because it involves the squaring of a range of values.

2/5/2   Relative Measures

For reasons mentioned above in connection with the limitations of the MSE as a measure of forecasting accuracy, alternative measures have been proposed, among which are those dealing with percentage errors. The following three measures are frequently used:

PERCENTAGE ERROR

$$\text{PE}_t = \left(\frac{X_t - F_t}{X_t}\right)(100) \tag{2-36}$$

MEAN PERCENTAGE ERROR

$$\text{MPE} = \sum_{i=1}^{n} \text{PE}_i / n \tag{2-37}$$

MEAN ABSOLUTE PERCENTAGE ERROR

$$\text{MAPE} = \sum_{i=1}^{n} |\text{PE}_i| / n \tag{2-38}$$

Equation (2-36) can be used to compute the percentage error for any time period. These can then be averaged as in equation (2-37) to give the mean percentage error. However, the MPE is likely to be small since positive and negative PEs tend to offset one another. Hence the MAPE is defined using absolute values of PE in equation (2-38). Table 2-14 shows how to compute the PE, MPE, and MAPE measures.

From the point of view of the ultimate user of forecasting, knowing that the MAPE of a method is 5 percent means a great deal more than simply knowing that the MSE is 183. However, even the MAPE itself does not give a good basis of comparison as to the gains in accuracy made by applying a specific forecasting method. One basis for making such a comparison is to define some very simple naive methods against which the performance of more sophisticated methods can be compared.

The authors have found it useful to define two different naive methods of forecasting for use as a basis in evaluating other methods in a given situation. The first is referred to as Naive Forecast 1 or NF1. This method uses as a forecast the most recent information available concerning the actual value. Thus, if a forecast is being prepared for a time horizon of one period, the most recent actual value would be used as the forecast for the

TABLE 2-14   COMPUTATIONS OF THE RELATIVE MEASURES
FOR A SET OF ERRORS (DATA FROM TABLE 2-12)

Period i	Observation X_i	Forecast F_i	Error $X_i - F_i$	PE $\left(\dfrac{X_i - F_i}{X_i}\right) 100$	APE $\left\|\dfrac{X_i - F_i}{X_i}\right\| 100$
1	22	24	-2	-9.09	9.09
2	23	28	-5	-21.74	21.74
3	39	32	7	17.95	17.95
4	37	36	1	2.70	2.70
5	38	40	-2	-5.26	5.26
6	47	44	3	6.38	6.38
7	43	48	-5	-11.63	11.63
8	49	52	-3	-6.12	6.12
9	61	56	5	8.20	8.20
10	63	60	3	4.76	4.76
Sums			2	-13.85	93.84

where APE = absolute percentage
error

$$\text{MPE} = \frac{-13.85}{10} = -1.385\% \qquad \text{[using equation (2-37)]}$$

$$\text{MAPE} = \frac{93.84}{10} = 9.384\% \qquad \text{[using equation (2-38)]}$$

next period. When this is done, the MAPE of this method can be expressed as follows:

$$\text{NF1} = \frac{\displaystyle\sum_{i=2}^{n} \left|\frac{(X_i - X_{i-1})}{X_i}\right|}{n-1} (100). \tag{2-39}$$

Only $n-1$ terms are included in computing the MAPE of this naive forecast, since forecasting begins with period 2 rather than period 1. The difference between the MAPE obtained from a more formal method of forecasting and that obtained using NF1 provides a measure of the improvement attainable through use of that formal forecasting method. This type of comparison is much more useful than simply computing the MAPE of the formal method or the MSE, since it provides a basis for evaluating the relative accuracy of those results.

Table 2-15 shows how to compute the MAPE for the Naive Forecast 1 (NF1) method.

A second naive method of forecasting has also been found to be extremely useful as a basis for evaluating more formal forecasting methods. This method is referred to as Naive Forecast 2 or NF2 and goes beyond NF1 in that it considers the possibility of seasonality in the series. Since seasonality often accounts for a substantial percentage of the fluctuation in a series, this method can frequently do much better than NF1 and yet is still a very simple straightforward approach. The procedure is to remove seasonality from the original data in order to obtain seasonally adjusted data. Once the seasonality has been removed, NF2 is comparable to NF1 in that it uses the most recent seasonally adjusted value as a forecast for the next seasonally adjusted value. When NF2 is applied, the MAPE can be computed as follows:

$$\text{NF2} = \frac{\sum_{i=2}^{n} \left| \dfrac{(X_i' - X_{i-1}')}{X_i'} \right|}{n - 1} (100), \tag{2-40}$$

where X_i' is the seasonally adjusted value of X_i.

TABLE 2-15   COMPUTATIONS INVOLVED IN DETERMINING THE MAPE OF THE NAIVE FORECAST 1 (NF1) METHOD

Period i	Observation X_i	Naive Forecast $F_i = X_{i-1}$	Relative Error $\left\| \dfrac{X_i - X_{i-1}}{X_i} \right\|$
1	22		
2	23	22	0.04
3	39	23	0.41
4	37	39	0.05
5	38	37	0.03
6	47	38	0.19
7	43	47	0.09
8	49	43	0.12
9	61	49	0.20
10	63	61	0.03
Sum			1.17

$$\text{NF1} = \left(\frac{1.17}{9} \right) 100 = 13.0\% \text{ [using equation (2-39)]}$$

In practice, NF2 allows one to decide whether or not the improvement obtained from going beyond a simple seasonal adjustment of the data is worth the time and cost involved.

2/5/3   Theil's *U*-Statistic

The relative measures in the previous section all give equal weight to all errors in contrast to the MSE, which squares the errors and thereby emphasizes large errors. It would be helpful to have a measure that considers both the disproportionate cost of large errors and provides a relative basis for comparison with naive methods. One measure that has these characteristics is the *U*-statistic developed by Theil (1966).

This statistic allows a relative comparison of formal forecasting methods with naive approaches and also squares the errors involved so that large errors are given much more weight than small errors. The positive characteristic that is given up in moving to Theil's *U*-statistic as a measure of accuracy is that of intuitive interpretation. This difficulty will become more apparent as the computation of this statistic and its application are examined. Mathematically, Theil's *U*-statistic is defined as

$$U = \sqrt{\frac{\sum_{i=1}^{n=1} (FPE_{i+1} - APE_{i+1})^2/(n-1)}{\sum_{i=1}^{n=1} (APE_{i+1})^2/(n-1)}}, \qquad (2\text{-}41)$$

where

$$FPE_{i+1} = \frac{F_{i+1} - X_i}{X_i} \quad \text{(This is the forecasted relative change.)}$$

and

$$APE_{i+1} = \frac{X_{i+1} - X_i}{X_i}. \quad \text{(This is the actual relative change.)}$$

Equation (2-41) is actually very straightforward, as can be seen by simplifying it to the form shown in (2-42). When the values of FPE_{i+1} and APE_{i+1} are substituted into equation (2-41), the result is

$$U = \sqrt{\frac{\sum_{i=1}^{n-1} \left(\frac{F_{i+1} - X_i - X_{i+1} + X_i}{X_i}\right)^2 \bigg/ (n-1)}{\sum_{i=1}^{n-1} \left(\frac{X_{i+1} - X_i}{X_i}\right)^2 \bigg/ (n-1)}}$$

$$= \sqrt{\frac{\displaystyle\sum_{i=1}^{n-1}\left(\frac{F_{i+1}-X_{i+1}}{X_i}\right)^2}{\displaystyle\sum_{i=1}^{n-1}\left(\frac{X_{i+1}-X_i}{X_i}\right)^2}}. \tag{2-42}$$

Comparing the numerator of equation (2-42) with equation (2-38) shows that it is similar to what was defined previously as the MAPE of a given forecasting method. Also, the denominator is very similar to equation (2-39)—namely, the MAPE of NF1. Thus, the U-statistic is an accuracy measure that incorporates both concepts.

Table 2-16 shows how to compute Theil's U-statistic for the data in Table 2-12.

Theil's U-statistic can be better understood by examining its interpretation. The value of the U-statistic given by equation (2-41) will be 0 only if $FPE_{i+1} = APE_{i+1}$. That in turn occurs only when the forecasts are exact (give 0 error). Alternatively, the U-statistic will have a value of 1 only when FPE_{i+1} is equal to 0. That would be the case only if the errors

TABLE 2-16   COMPUTATIONS INVOLVED IN DETERMINING THEIL'S
U-STATISTIC AND McLAUGHLIN'S BATTING AVERAGE

Period i	Observation X_i	Forecast F_i	Numerator $\left(\dfrac{F_{i+1}-X_{i+1}}{X_i}\right)^2$	Denominator $\left(\dfrac{X_{i+1}-X_i}{X_i}\right)^2$
1	22	24	0.052	0.002
2	23	28	0.093	0.484
3	39	32	0.001	0.003
4	37	36	0.003	0.001
5	38	40	0.006	0.056
6	47	44	0.011	0.007
7	43	48	0.005	0.019
8	49	52	0.010	0.060
9	61	56	0.002	0.001
10	63	60		
Sums			0.183	0.633

Theil's $U = \dfrac{.183}{.633} = .54$ [using equation (2-42)]

McLaughlin's Batting Average $= (4 - .54)100 = 346$

in the forecasting method were the same as those that would be obtained by forecasting no change at all in the actual values. That is comparable to assuming an NF1 approach. If FPE_{i+1} is in the opposite direction of APE_{i+1}, the U-statistic will be greater than unity since the numerator will be larger than the denominator. The ranges of the U-statistic can thus be summarized as follows:

> $U = 1$: the naive method is as good as the forecasting technique being evaluated.

> $U < 1$: the forecasting technique being used is better than the naive method. The smaller the U-statistic, the better the forecasting technique is relative to the naive method.

> $U > 1$: there is no point in using a formal forecasting method, since using a naive method will produce better results.

An alternative accuracy measure to the U-statistic and yet one that is very similar in concept to it is that suggested by McLaughlin (1975). McLaughlin refers to his measure of accuracy as a batting average. This measure is not normally squared although it can be. The score of the batting average ranges between 200 and 400 with a value of 300 having a similar interpretation to Theil's U-statistic at a value of unity. McLaughlin's batting average can actually be found from the U-statistic by subtracting it from 4 and multiplying the result by 100. This correspondence in values is shown in Table 2-17.

2/5/4 Other Measures

One other measure needs to be mentioned. The Durbin-Watson statistic (designated D-W here) is a very useful measure that will be discussed in greater depth in Chapter 6. For the moment, it should be noted that it is not an accuracy measure per se, but rather can be used to indicate whether

TABLE 2-17 RELATIVE MEASURES OF FORECASTING ACCURACY

Theil's U-Statistic	McLaughlin's Batting Averages	
0	$(4 - 0) \times 100$	400
.5	$(4 - .5) \times 100$	350
1.0	$(4 - 1) \times 100$	300
1.5	$(4 - 1.5) \times 100$	250
2.0	$(4 - 2) \times 100$	200

there is any remaining pattern in the errors (or residuals) after a forecasting model has been applied. For example, in Figure 2-7 a straight line function was fitted to the French population data and the errors of fit are shown in Table 2-4. Note that there is a pattern remaining in these errors— the first two are negative, then there are five positive errors in a row, and then three negative errors. Clearly, there is not what would be called a random set of errors. The D-W statistic (see Section 6/1/6 for details) is sensitive to such patterns and the formula is straightforward:

$$\text{D-W} = \frac{\sum_{t=2}^{n} (e_t - e_{t-1})^2}{\sum_{t=1}^{n} e_t^2} .$$

(2-43)

Note that the numerator is the sum of squared differences between *successive* errors and the denominator is merely the sum of the squared errors (SSE). For the French population data the computation of the D-W statistic is shown in Table 2-18. Column 5 gives the successive error differences and column 7 squares these successive differences. The sum of the entries in

TABLE 2-18 COMPUTATION OF THE DURBIN-WATSON STATISTIC FOR THE ERRORS AFTER FITTING A STRAIGHT LINE TO THE FRENCH POPULATION DATA IN TABLE 2-4.

(1) Year	(2) French Population (millions)	(3) Trend Value	(4) Error e_t	(5) $(e_t - e_{t-1})$	(6) e_t^2	(7) $(e_t - e_{t-1})^2$
1961	46.163	46.613	−0.450		0.203	
1962	46.998	47.093	−0.095	0.355	0.009	0.126
1963	47.816	47.573	0.243	0.338	0.059	0.114
1964	48.311	48.053	0.258	0.015	0.067	0.000
1965	48.758	48.533	0.225	−0.033	0.051	0.001
1966	49.164	49.013	0.151	−0.074	0.023	0.005
1967	49.548	49.493	0.055	−0.096	0.003	0.009
1968	49.915	49.973	−0.058	−0.113	0.003	0.013
1969	50.315	50.453	−0.138	−0.080	0.019	0.006
1970	50.768	50.933	−0.165	−0.027	0.027	0.001
Sums					0.463	0.276

$$\text{D-W} = \frac{.276}{.463} = .596$$

column 7 is divided by the sum of the squared errors in column 6 to give the D-W statistic, which in this case is .596.

If, after fitting a forecasting model, the errors are essentially random, then the D-W statistic is around 2. If there is positive autocorrelation in the set of errors—for example, if there is a relatively smooth pattern in the errors—then the D-W statistic will be less than 2. If there is negative autocorrelation left in the errors—for example, as would be caused by sawtooth oscillations in the errors, from plus to minus, minus to plus, and so on—then the D-W statistic will be greater than 2. The range of D-W is from 0 to 4, and the theoretical underpinnings of this statistic are complex, so that in practice, reference is made to tables for approximate significance tests. For the French population data the D-W of .596 indicates that there is definite positive autocorrelation left in the errors after fitting a straight line. It is left as an exercise for the reader to use equation (2-30) to compute the autocorrelation of lag one for the errors in Table 2-4.

APPENDIX 2-A
NOTATION FOR QUANTITATIVE FORECASTING

Quantitative forecasts are based on data, or observations, that describe some factor of interest. In this book a single observed value will be represented by X_i. (See Table 2.19.) This variable can be the actual number of units sold, the cost of production, the advertising budget, price per unit, gross national product, or any other event of interest, as long as it can be quantified. The objective of forecasting is to predict future values of X. The individual forecasts will be denoted by F_i, or $\hat{X}_i$, and the error by e_i, where the error is the difference between the actual value and the forecast value for observation i:

$$e_i = X_i - \hat{X}_i \text{ or } e_i = X_i - F_i.$$

In time-series forecasting and in causal forecasting when the data are taken at equal time intervals, t will denote the present time period, $t - 1$ last period, $t - 2$ two periods ago, and so on. A period can be a day, a week, a month, quarter, year, and so forth. The forecasts usually will be for future time periods such as $t + 1$.

TABLE 2-19   NOTATION USED IN TIME-SERIES FORECASTING

									Forecasted Values				
Observed values	X_1	X_2	X_3	X_4	...	X_{t-2}	X_{t-1}	X_t	F_{t+1}	F_{t+2}	F_{t+3}	...	F_{t+m}
Period i	1	2	3	4	...	$t-2$	$t-1$	t	$t+1$	$t+2$	$t+3$	...	$t+m$
Estimated values	$\hat{X}_1$	$\hat{X}_2$	$\hat{X}_3$	$\hat{X}_4$	...	$\hat{X}_{t-2}$	$\hat{X}_{t-1}$	$\hat{X}_t$	$\hat{X}_{t+1}$	$\hat{X}_{t+2}$	$\hat{X}_{t+3}$	...	$\hat{X}_{t+m}$
or	F_1	F_2	F_3	F_4	...	F_{t-2}	F_{t-1}	F_t					
Error	e_1	e_2	e_3	e_4	...	e_{t-2}	e_{t-1}	e_t					

Present

APPENDIX 2-B
SUMMATION SIGN Σ

In order to simplify the manipulation of expressions involving the adding of many numbers, it is convenient to use a summation sign, Σ. The use of this sign and the elements of notation mentioned previously can be demonstrated using the data in Table 2-20.

Based on Table 2-20,

X_i is the actual sales value,

$\hat{X}_i$ or F_i is the forecast values for sales, and

e_i is the error, or the difference between the actual (X_i) and forecast $(\hat{X}_i)$ value of sales.

If one wants the sum of the errors, it can be obtained from

$$e_1 + e_2 + e_3 + \cdots + e_{23} = \sum_{i=1}^{23} e_i$$

TABLE 2-20   USE OF QUANTITATIVE FORECASTING NOTATION

Year	Period i	No. of Units Sold Actual	No. of Units Sold Forecasted	Error	Year	Period i	No. of Units Sold Actual	No. of Units Sold Forecasted	Error
1950	1	123	120	3	1961	12	175	173	2
1951	2	125	128	-3	1962	13	176	177	-1
1952	3	133	135	-2	1963	14	192	188	-4
1953	4	140	138	2	1964	15	199	195	-4
1954	5	144	148	-4	1965	16	210	215	5
1955	6	158	157	3	1966	17	225	230	5
1956	7	161	155	6	1967	18	230	236	-6
1957	8	160	168	-6	1968	19	238	242	-4
1958	9	163	168	-5	1969	20	251	248	3
1959	10	171	171	0	1970	21	259	255	4
1960	11	175	176	-1	1971	22	275	263	12
					1972	23	283	290	-7

or

$$3 - 3 - 2 - \cdots - 7 = -2.$$

The cumulative sales for the years 1960 through 1969 can be obtained from

$$\sum_{i=11}^{20} X_i = X_{11} + X_{12} + X_{13} + \cdots + X_{20}$$

$$= 175 + 175 + 176 + \cdots + 251$$

$$= 2071.$$

The following rules apply to the use of summation signs:

1. $\sum_{i=1}^{n} \overline{X} X_i = \overline{X} \sum_{i=1}^{n} X_i,$

   where $\overline{X}$ is the sampling mean (therefore a constant) of the variable X_i.

2. $\sum_{i=1}^{n} \overline{X} = n\overline{X}.$

   For example suppose $\overline{X} = 10$ and $n = 5$, then

   $$\sum_{i=1}^{n} 10 = 10 + 10 + 10 + 10 + 10 = 50$$

   $$\text{or } 5(10) = 50.$$

3. $\sum_{i=1}^{n} (X_i - \hat{X}_i) = \sum_{i=1}^{n} X_i - \sum_{i=1}^{n} \hat{X}_i.$

4. $\sum_{i=1}^{n} (X_i - \overline{X}) = \sum_{i=1}^{n} X_i - \sum_{i=1}^{n} \overline{X}$

   $$= \sum_{i=1}^{n} X_i - n\overline{X}.$$

5. $\sum_{i=1}^{n} (X_i - \overline{X})^2 = \sum_{i=1}^{n} (X_i^2 - 2\overline{X}X_i + \overline{X}^2)$

   $$= \sum_{i=1}^{n} X_i^2 - 2\overline{X}\Sigma X_i + n\overline{X}^2.$$

   $$= \sum_{i=1}^{n} X_i^2 - n\overline{X}^2$$

   $$= \sum_{i=1}^{n} X_i^2 - (\Sigma X_i)^2/n$$

REFERENCES AND SELECTED BIBLIOGRAPHY

Bierman, H., C. P. Bonini, and W. H. Hausman. 1983. *Quantitative Analysis for Business Decisions,* 6th ed. Homewood, Ill.: Richard D. Irwin.

Cogger, K. O. 1979. "Time Series Analysis and Forecasting with an Absolute Error Criterion," in *TIMS Studies—Volume 12—Forecasting,* S. Makridakis, and S. C. Wheelwright, eds. Amsterdam: North-Holland, pp. 89–102.

Freund, J. E. 1962. *Mathematical Statistics.* Englewood Cliffs, N.J.: Prentice-Hall.

Holloway, C. A. 1979. *Decision Making Under Uncertainty.* Englewood Cliffs, N.J.: Prentice-Hall.

Koosis, D. J. 1972. *Business Statistics.* New York: John Wiley & Sons.

Locke, F. M. 1972. *Business Mathematics.* New York: John Wiley & Sons.

McLaughlin, R. L. 1975. "The Real Record of the Economic Forecasters." *Business Economics*, Vol. 10, No. 3, pp. 28–36.

Montgomery, D. C., and L. A. Johnson. 1976. *Forecasting and Time Series Analysis.* New York: McGraw-Hill.

Neter, J., W. Wasserman, and G. A. Whitmore. 1973. *Fundamental Statistics for Business and Economics,* 4th ed. Boston: Allyn & Bacon.

Schuster, R. 1906. "On the Periodicity of Sunspots." *Philosphical Transactions,* Series A, **206,** p. 69–100.

Spurr, W. A., and C. P. Bonini. 1959. *Statistical Analysis for Business Decisions.* Homewood, Ill.: Richard D. Irwin.

Steece, B. M. 1982. "The Evaluation of Forecasts," in *Handbook of Forecasting,* S. Makridakis and S. C. Wheelwright, eds. New York: John Wiley & Sons, pp. 457–68.

Theil, H. 1966. *Applied Economic Forecasting.* Amsterdam: North-Holland Publishing Co., pp. 26–32.

EXERCISES

1. The following data are the median reading scores of grades 2 and 5 in different public schools in the areas of Brooklyn and Queens, New York (*New York Times,* January 12, 1976, p. 20).

    a. Is there a relationship between the reading scores of grades 2 and 5 in the Brooklyn schools?
    b. Is there a relationship between the reading scores of grades 2 and 5 in the Queens schools?
    c. Is there a relationship between the grade 2 reading scores of the Brooklyn and Queens schools?
    d. Is there a relationship between the grade 5 reading scores of the Brooklyn and Queens schools?

	Brooklyn District 13 (Brooklyn Heights, Bedford-Stuyvesant)			Queens District 24 (Maspeth, Middle Village)		
P.S.	Grade 2 Median Score	Grade 5 Median Score	P.S.	Grade 2 Median Score	Grade 5 Median Score	
3	2.5	5.3	12	3.2	6.7	
8	3.0	5.7	13	3.7	7.1	
9	3.3	5.7	14	3.3	6.3	
11	2.4	4.4	19	2.8	6.3	
20	2.9	5.5	49	3.5	7.6	
44	3.0	5.8	68	2.5	6.3	
46	2.5	5.0	71	2.9	6.3	
54	2.9	5.0	81	3.3	5.7	
56	2.9	4.9	87	4.1	5.9	
67	2.5	5.0	88	4.5	6.8	
93	3.1	4.9	89	3.7	7.0	
133	3.2	5.1	91	4.5	5.8	
256	2.3	5.7	102	4.0	6.9	
270	3.3	5.8	113	4.0	7.6	
282	2.7	5.7	128	3.6	6.8	
287	3.2	5.2	143	3.0	5.4	
305	2.6	5.0	153	3.5	7.0	
307	3.1	5.0	199	4.0	6.8	

Source: © 1976 by The New York Times Company. Reprinted by Permission.

2. The following table gives average monthly temperatures in Paris.
   a. What is your best estimate of the average temperature in June 1975?
   b. Is there any time pattern in the temperature readings?

AVERAGE MONTHLY TEMPERATURE IN PARIS (CENTIGRADE)

1974	Jan.	7.6	1974	Oct.	8.9
	Feb.	7.1		Nov.	8.5
	Mar.	8.3		Dec.	8.5
	Apr.	11.5	1975	Jan.	7.7
	May	13.7		Feb.	6.9
	June	17.2		Mar.	6.1
	July	18.5		Apr.	10.5
	Aug.	19.7		May	12.9
	Sept.	15.1			

3.   Several approaches have been suggested by those attempting to predict stock market movements. Three of them are described briefly below. How does each relate to the different approaches to forecasting described in this chapter?

a. Dow Theory: There are support and resistance levels for stock prices both for the overall market and for individual stocks. These levels can be found by plotting prices of the market or stock over time.

b. Random Walk Theory: There is no way to predict future movements in the stock market or individual stocks, since all available information is quickly assimilated by the investors and moves market prices in the appropriate direction.

c. The prices of individual stocks or of the market in general are largely determined by earnings.

4.   Column 1 below is the actual demand for product E15 over 20 months. Columns 2 and 3 are the one-month ahead forecasts according to two different forecasting models (which are examined in chapter 3).

a. For column 1 compute the autocorrelation coefficient for one lag using equation (2-30).

b. Using columns 1 and 2 compute the mean error, mean absolute error, sum of squared errors, mean squared error, standard deviation of errors, mean percentage error, and mean absolute percentage error using equations (2-31) through (2-38).

c. Repeat part b using columns 1 and 3 below.

d. Which forecasting method appears to be better?

Period	(1) Actual Demand	(2) Method 1 Forecast	(3) Method 2 Forecast
1	139	153	170
2	137	148	171
3	174	144	169
4	142	156	176
5	141	152	172
6	162	148	167
7	180	154	168
8	164	165	172
9	171	166	172
10	206	170	173
11	193	186	183
12	207	192	189
13	218	202	198
14	229	213	208
15	225	224	220
16	204	230	229
17	227	225	230
18	223	230	236
19	242	232	239
20	239	240	245

5. Consider the following three sets of errors and compute:
    a. the Durbin-Watson statistic for each of them using equation (2-43), and
    b. the autocorrelation of lag one for each of them using equation (2-30).
    c. Is there any relationship between the D-W statistic and the autocorrelations?

Period	Set 1	Set 2	Set 3
1	−6	26	47
2	−9	0	−39
3	−3	31	46
4	32	−21	−105
5	−61	−61	96
6	−54	−79	−33
7	13	−113	82
8	−81	−69	7
9	−22	68	−46
10	3	155	31
11	13	126	28
12	49	50	30
13	−40	13	−43
14	−4	71	2
15	12	−37	30

Hint: Make a plot of these errors to see the characteristics of each set.

6. For the height and weight data in Table 2-8, convert the height to centimeters and the weight to kilograms and recompute the correlation coefficient using equation (2-26). Note: one inch = 2.54 centimeters and one kilogram = 2.2 pounds.

PART TWO
SMOOTHING AND DECOMPOSITION TIME-SERIES METHODS

Part Two describes a variety of smoothing and decomposition time-series methods. Frequently, these are intuitively appealing because their development has been empirically based. Although both categories of methods lack some of the statistical underpinnings and theoretical mathematical development of the methods described in Parts Three and Four, they have been accepted very well by practitioners who find them easy to use and fairly accurate for the costs involved.

The basis of the smoothing methods described in Chapter 3 is the simple weighting or smoothing of past observations in a time series in order to obtain a forecast for the future. In smoothing these historical values, random errors are averaged providing a "smooth" forecast that seems to work well in certain situations. The major advantages of smoothing methods are their low cost, the ease with which they can be applied, and the speed with which they can be adopted. These characteristics make them particularly attractive when a large number of items are to be forecasted, such as would be the case in many inventory situations, and when the time horizon is relatively short (less than 1 year). Given the variety of smoothing methods available, an important part of Chapter 3 is the description of a comprehensive classification scheme (Pegels') and comparisons of alternative methods.

The decomposition methods described in Chapter 4 apply many of the concepts of smoothing, but use a somewhat different structural framework in doing so. Decomposition approaches seek to decompose or break a time series into its major subcomponents. Thus, rather than trying to predict a single pattern, a separate effort is made at predicting the seasonal pattern, the trend pattern, and the cycle pattern, and at smoothing randomness. Forecasting using such methods involves extrapolating each of these component patterns separately and recombining them into a final forecast. Decomposition methods are often useful not only in providing forecasts, but also in providing information regarding the components of a time series and the impact of various factors, such as seasonality and cyclicality, on observed results. Generally, these methods are characterized by an absence of statistical language, having been developed empirically, rather than being based on theoretical constructs.

In both chapters the aim is to present the fundamental concepts involved for each class of methodology, to focus on what the authors have found to be the most commonly used methods in that class, and to thoroughly describe their application. Finally, variations of some of the methodologies are presented and practical considerations as to when specific variations should be used and how that selection can be made are discussed.

3/SMOOTHING METHODS

3/1 Introduction

In the previous chapter the mean was discussed as an estimator that minimizes the mean squared error (MSE) of actual-minus-fitted-values, and it could have been shown (as is done in most statistics books) that the mean is an *unbiased* estimator. If the mean is used as a forecasting tool, then, as with all forecasting methods, optimal use requires a knowledge of the conditions that determine its appropriateness. For the mean, the condition is that the data must be *stationary,* a term meaning that the process generating the data is in equilibrium around a constant value (the underlying mean) and that the variance around the mean remains constant over time.

Thus, if a time series is generated by a constant process subject to random error (or noise), then the mean is a useful statistic and can be used as a forecast for the next period(s). In terms of data requirements only two numbers need to be stored—the latest mean and the number of data periods used to compute the mean. However, if the time series involves a trend (in an upward or downward direction), or a seasonal effect (strong sales of paper cups for hot drinks in winter months, for example), or both a trend and a seasonal effect, then the simple average is no longer able to capture the data pattern. In this chapter we consider a variety of smoothing methods that seek to improve upon the mean as the forecast for the next period(s).

To set the stage consider Figure 3-1, which presents the forecasting scenario. On the time scale we are standing at a certain point—called the point of reference—and we look backward over past observations and forward into the future. Once a forecasting model has been selected, we fit the model to the known data (by judicious choice of parameters and initializing procedures) and obtain the *fitted values*. For the known observations this allows calculation of *fitted errors*—a measure of goodness-of-fit of the model— and as new observations become available we can examine *forecasting errors*. The smoothing methods to be discussed in this chapter are mostly *recursive* in nature—moving through the known data period by period, as opposed to using all the past data in one "fitting" exercise.

Figure 3-2 describes a strategy for appraising any forecasting methodology. In stage 1, the time series of interest is identified. This may be a real data series (e.g., sales of a product) or, for learning purposes, it may be an artificially generated time series. (See Figure 3-4 for a variety of useful artificial data sets that can be used.) The data set is then divided into two parts—an "initialization set" and a "test set"—so that an appraisal (evaluation) of a forecasting method can be conducted. In stage 2, a forecasting method is chosen from the list of smoothing methods. The menu of selections available in this chapter is shown in Figure 3-3. Stage 3 makes use of the initialization data set to get the forecasting method started. Estimates of any trend components, seasonal components, and parameter values are made at this stage. In stage 4 the method is applied to the test set to see how well it does. After each forecast, the forecasting error is deter-

FIGURE 3-1   THE FORECASTING SCENARIO

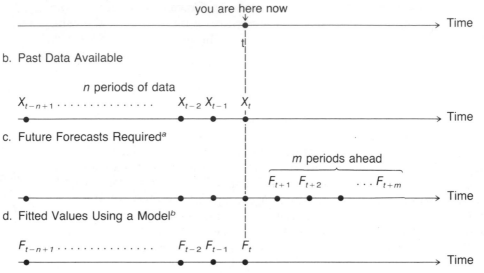

a. Point of Reference

b. Past Data Available

c. Future Forecasts Required[a]

d. Fitted Values Using a Model[b]

e. Fitting Errors

$$(X_{t-n+1} - F_{t-n+1}), \ldots, (X_{t-1} - F_{t-1}), (X_t - F_t)$$

f. Forecasting Errors (when X_{t+1}, X_{t+2}, etc., become available)

$$(X_{t+1} - F_{t+1}), (X_{t+2} - F_{t+2})$$

[a]F_{t+1}, F_{t+2}, etc., refer to forecasted values of X_{t+1}, X_{t+2}, etc.

[b]A fitted value, such as F_{t-1}, could be represented as $\hat{X}_{t-1}$ (estimated value of X_{t-1}), and can arise in two distinctly different ways. (1) In regression procedures (see Chapters 5 and 6) all values of F and F_{t-n+1} through F_t are estimated at one time using one regression equation. (2) In exponential smoothing methods, the "fitted values" are actually "forecast values," and are estimated sequentially.

mined, and over the complete test set certain measures of forecasting success will be determined, as described in the previous chapter. Stage 5 is really an iterative phase. Since there is no guarantee that the initial parameter values are optimal, this stage requires modification of the initialization process and/or searching for the optimum values of parameters in the model. Finally, in stage 6 the forecasting method is appraised as to its suitability for various kinds of data patterns (e.g., those shown in Figure 3-4) and the application potential is thereby made clearer.

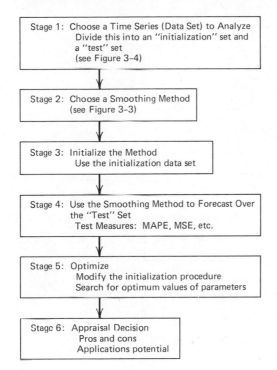

Stage 1: Choose a Time Series (Data Set) to Analyze
        Divide this into an "initialization" set and
        a "test" set
        (see Figure 3-4)

Stage 2: Choose a Smoothing Method
        (see Figure 3-3)

Stage 3: Initialize the Method
        Use the initialization data set

Stage 4: Use the Smoothing Method to Forecast Over
        the "Test" Set
        Test Measures: MAPE, MSE, etc.

Stage 5: Optimize
        Modify the initialization procedure
        Search for optimum values of parameters

Stage 6: Appraisal Decision
        Pros and cons
        Applications potential

FIGURE 3-2 A STRATEGY FOR APPRAISING ANY OF THE SMOOTHING
METHODS OF FORECASTING

It is helpful to classify the smoothing methods discussed in this chapter. This is done in Figure 3-3 where two distinct groupings are evident. The group called "averaging methods" conform to the conventional understanding of what an average is—namely, equally weighted observations. The initial method in this set is the simple average of all past data (as discussed in Chapter 2). The next method is a single moving average of the latest n observations. Double moving averages, or moving averages of moving averages, end up being *unequally* weighted averages, and can be used within a forecasting method sometimes known as "linear" moving averages. Various higher-order moving averages can be created but are not often used in practical forecasting situations.

The second group of methods applies an unequal set of weights to past data, and because the weights typically decay in an exponential manner from the most recent to the most distant data point, the methods are known as exponential smoothing methods. All methods in this group require that certain parameters be defined,[1] and these parameter values lie between 0 and 1. Analogous to the single moving average is the single

---

[1]These parameters will determine the unequal weights to be applied to past data.

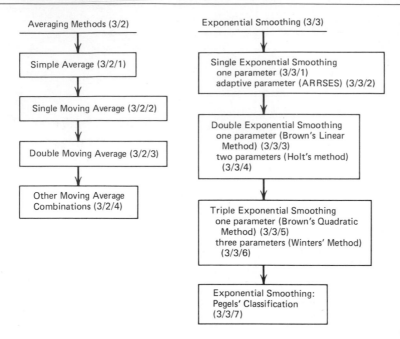

FIGURE 3-3 A CLASSIFICATION OF SMOOTHING METHODS

exponential smoothing (SES) method, for which just one parameter needs to be defined. We can choose a starting value for this single parameter and run through stages 4 and 5 of Figure 3-2 to find an optimal value of the parameter. Another possibility is to allow the value of the parameter to change over time in response to changes in the data pattern. This is known as *adaptive* SES and one variety to be discussed in Section 3/3/2 is known as Adaptive Response Rate Simple Exponential Smoothing (ARRSES). Again, analogous to double moving averages there are two double exponential smoothing methods[2]—involving two exponential smoothing equations. Brown's linear method requires the use of one and the same parameter for each of the two smoothings, whereas Holt's method makes use of two different parameters for the two separate exponential smoothings involved. In the triple exponential methods,[2] the same parameter can be used in all three exponential smoothings (as in Brown's quadratic method) or three separate parameters can be used for three separate smoothings—smoothing the data, smoothing the trend, and smoothing the seasonal index (as in Winters' method). Finally, Pegels' classification of exponential smoothing methods serves as a useful summary of the methods in practical use at this time.

Figure 3-4 portrays a set of data patterns that have been used extensively in evaluating the performance of various forecasting methods. For

---

[2]The words "double" and "triple" are somewhat ambiguous, but are convenient to describe methods that involve two and three exponential smoothing equations, respectively.

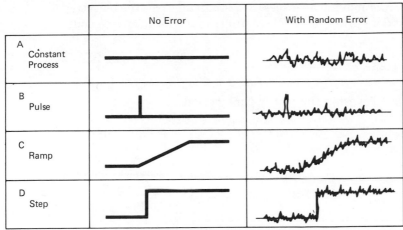

(a) Some Basic Patterns

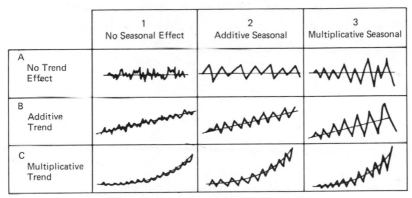

(b) Patterns Based on Pegels' (1969) Classification

FIGURE 3-4 TEST PATTERNS FOR TESTING FORECASTING PROCE-
DURES

the student of forecasting methodology these data sets can be of considerable value, and for the practitioner of the art of forecasting, the identification of the appropriate data pattern in the data series to be forecast, is
of vital importance. Clearly, an inappropriate forecasting model, even when
optimized, will be inferior to a more appropriate model.

3/2 Averaging Methods

The "past history" data can be smoothed in many ways. In this section we consider several straightforward averaging methods, including the
mean (3/2/1), simple moving averages (3/2/2), double moving averages

(3/2/3), and higher-order moving averages (3/2/4). In all cases the objective is to make use of past data to develop a forecasting system for future periods.

3/2/1   The Mean

Given a data set covering the last N time periods:

$$X_1\ X_2\ X_3\ \ldots \qquad\qquad X_{N-1}\ X_N$$

and a decision to use the first T data points as "the initialization set" and the rest as a "test set"

$$X_1\ X_2\ \ldots \qquad X_T \mid X_{T+1}\ \ldots \qquad X_N$$

INITIALIZATION SET   TEST SET

the method of simple averages is to take the average of all data in the initialization set

$$\overline{X} = \sum_{i=1}^{T} X_i/T = F_{T+1} \tag{3-1}$$

as the forecast for period $(T + 1)$. Then as period $(T + 1)$'s data becomes available it is possible to compute an error:

$$e_{T+1} = X_{T+1} - F_{T+1}. \tag{3-2}$$

For period $(T + 2)$ the situation is

$$X_1\ X_2\ \ldots \qquad X_T \qquad X_{T+1} \mid X_{T+2}\ \ldots \qquad X_N$$

INITIALIZATION SET   TEST SET

There is one more data point in the past history set, the new mean is

$$\overline{X} = \sum_{i=1}^{T+1} X_i/(T + 1) = F_{T+2} \tag{3-1'}$$

and the new error term, when X_{T+2} becomes available, is

$$e_{T+2} = X_{T+2} - F_{T+2}. \tag{3-2'}$$

When is this very simple method appropriate? Referring to the nine cells in Pegels' classification—Figure 3-4b—it is clear that only if the process underlying the observed X values (i) has no noticeable trend, and (ii) has no noticeable seasonality will this simple averaging process produce good results. As the mean becomes based on a larger and larger past history data set, it becomes more stable (from elementary statistical theory), assuming the underlying process is stationary.

What about data storage? It might seem that a lot of data needs to be stored for this procedure; but, in fact, only two items need be stored as time moves on.

Time	Stored from Last Period	Input at This Time	Output
T		$X_1, \ldots, X_T$	$F_{T+1} = \sum_{i=1}^{T} X_i/T$
$T + 1$	T, F_{T+1}	X_{T+1}	$F_{T+2} = \dfrac{(T \times F_{T+1} + X_{T+1})}{(T + 2)}$
$T + 2$	$T + 1, F_{T+2}$	X_{T+2}	$F_{T+3} = \dfrac{((T + 1) \times F_{T+2} + X_{T+2})}{(T + 2)}$
.	.	.	.
.	.	.	.
.	.	.	.

The major impediment in using this simple method is the unlikelihood that business time series are really based on an underlying "constant" process (cell A-1 in Pegels' table). As Figure 3-5 shows, when the underlying process is a step function (which is another way of saying the data undergo a sudden change at some point), then the mean used as a forecast for the next period is unable to catch up. Similarly, as will be shown in Section 3/3/6, when the data series exhibits trend and seasonality, the mean as a forecast is inappropriate.

3/2/2   Single Moving Averages

One way to modify the influence of past data on the mean-as-a-forecast is to specify at the outset just how many past observations will be included in a mean. The term *moving average* is used to describe this procedure because as each new observation becomes available, a new average can be computed by dropping the oldest observation and including the newest one. This *moving* average will then be the forecast for the next period. Note that the number of data points in each average remains constant and includes the most recent observations.

Given N data points and a decision to use T observations for each average—called a moving average of order T, or $MA(T)$ for short—the situation is as follows:

INITIALIZATION SET   TEST SET

$X_1 X_2 \ldots X_T$	$X_{T+1} \ldots X_N$

Time	Moving Average	Forecast
T	$\bar{X} = \dfrac{X_1 + X_2 + \cdots + X_T}{T}$	$F_{T+1} = \bar{X} = \sum_{i=1}^{T} X_i / T$
$T + 1$	$\bar{X} = \dfrac{X_2 + \cdots + X_{T+1}}{T}$	$F_{T+2} = \bar{X} = \sum_{i=2}^{T+1} X_i / T$
$T + 2$	$\bar{X} = \dfrac{X_3 + \cdots + X_{T+2}}{T}$	$F_{T+3} = \bar{X} = \sum_{i=3}^{T+2} X_i / T$
	etc.	

Compared with the simple mean (of *all* past data) the moving average of order T has the following characteristics:

- it deals only with the latest T periods of known data,
- the number of data points in each average does not change as time goes on.

Time	Data	Forecast	Error
1	106.74		
2	103.01	106.74	−3.72
3	102.14	104.88	−2.74
4	100.24	103.96	−3.72
5	91.45	103.03	−11.58
6	98.73	100.72	−1.99
7	94.06	100.39	−6.32
8	157.50	99.48	58.02
9	152.33	106.73	45.60
10	149.20	111.80	37.40
11	149.04	115.54	33.50
12	142.90	118.59	24.31
13	151.62	120.61	31.01
14	144.96	123.00	21.96
15	152.85	124.57	28.28
16	151.08	126.45	24.63
17	143.33	127.99	15.34
18	150.81	128.89	21.92
19	153.24	130.11	23.13
20	144.95	131.33	13.62
21		132.01	

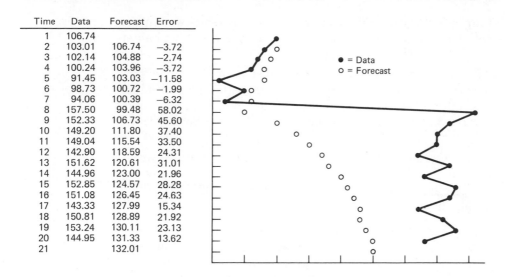

● = Data
○ = Forecast

Analysis of Errors from Period 2 to Period 20
18.35 = Mean Error
21.52 = Mean Absolute Error
14.89 = Mean Absolute Percentage Error (MAPE)
19.23 = Standard Deviation of Error (Unbiased)
687.23 = Mean Square Error (MSE)
.39 = Durbin-Watson Statistic
1.29 = Theil's U Statistic
271.07 = McLaughlin's Batting Average

FIGURE 3-5 THE MEAN OF ALL PAST DATA AS A FORECAST

But it also has the following disadvantages:

- it requires more storage because all of the T latest observations must be stored, not just the average,
- it cannot handle trend or seasonality very well, although it can do better than the total mean.

Since a forecaster must choose the number of periods (T) in a moving average, it is worth pointing out some aspects of this choice.

$MA(1)$—that is, a moving average of order 1—the last known data point (X_T) is taken as the forecast for the next period ($F_{T+1} = X_T$). An example of this is "the forecast of tomorrow's closing price of IBM stock is today's closing price." This was called the naive forecast (NF1) in Chapter 2.

$MA(4)$—for quarterly data, a four-period moving average effectively smooths out seasonal effects (especially if they are *additive* seasonal effects), but, if used as a forecast for the next period, will not be able to accommodate trend or the seasonality itself. In this situation the $MA(4)$ would be helpful if it were used as a *centered* moving average (rather than a forecast) to help examine the components within the time series. This aspect will be examined more carefully in Chapter 4.

$MA(12)$—again, for monthly data, this would smooth seasonal effects out of the series and could be helpful in decomposing the series into trend, seasonal, and other components (see next chapter), but would not be effective on its own as a forecasting tool for data showing trend and seasonality.

MA(big)—in general, the larger the *order* of the moving average— that is, the number of data points used for each average, the greater the smoothing effect. Used as a forecast, MA(big) pays little attention to fluctuations in the data series.

Table 3-1 and Figure 3-6 illustrate the application of the technique of moving averages to the series of values for electric can opener shipments using both a three- and five-month moving average.

In Table 3-1 the $MA(3)$ values in column 4 are based on the values for the previous three months. For example, the forecast for April (the fourth month) is taken to be the average of January, February, and March shipments.

$$\text{April's forecast} = 176.7 = (200 + 135 + 195)/3$$

The last figure in column 4 is December's $MA(3)$ forecast of 244.2 and is the average for September, October and November.

Similarly, in column 5, the $MA(5)$ averages are shown as forecasts for the next month ahead. The June forecast of 207.5 is the average of shipments made from January through May, and the December forecast of 203.5 is the average of months 7, 8, 9, 10, and 11. Clearly, as new values for shipments become known, the moving average can be easily recomputed.

From Figure 3-6 it can be seen that the more observations included in the moving average, the greater the smoothing effect. It is left as an exercise to consider the two extreme cases of moving averages in this example—that is, $T = 1$, in which case the most recent observation is used as the forecast for the next period, and $T = 11$, in which case the mean of all known shipments is used as the forecast for December. Note that use of a small value for T will allow the moving average to follow the pattern, but these MA forecasts will nevertheless trail the pattern, lagging behind by one or more periods.

Algebraically, the moving average can be written as follows:

$$F_{T+1} = \frac{X_1 + X_2 + \cdots + X_T}{T} = \frac{1}{T} \sum_{i=1}^{T} X_i, \qquad (3\text{-}3)$$

$$F_{T+2} = \frac{X_2 + \cdots + X_T + X_{T+1}}{T} = \frac{1}{T} \sum_{i=2}^{T+1} X_i. \qquad (3\text{-}4)$$

TABLE 3-1 FORECASTING ELECTRIC CAN OPENER SHIPMENTS USING MOVING AVERAGES

(1) Month	(2) Time Period	(3) Observed Values (shipments)	(4) Three-Month Moving Average	(5) Five-Month Moving Average
Jan.	1	200.0	—	—
Feb.	2	135.0	—	—
Mar.	3	195.0	—	—
Apr.	4	197.5	176.7	—
May	5	310.0	175.8	—
June	6	175.0	234.2	207.5
July	7	155.0	227.5	202.5
Aug.	8	130.0	213.3	206.5
Sept.	9	220.0	153.3	193.5
Oct.	10	277.0	168.3	198.0
Nov.	11	235.0	209.2	191.4
Dec.	12	—	244.2	203.5

Test Periods

Analysis of Errors	4-11	6-11
Mean Error	17.71	−1.17
Mean Absolute Error	71.46	51.00
Mean Absolute Percentage Error (MAPE)	34.89	27.88
Standard Deviation of Error (Unbiased)	83.37	60.12
Mean Square Error (MSE)	8395.66	3013.25
Durbin-Watson Statistic	1.60	.87
Theil's U Statistic	1.15	.81
McLaughlin's Batting Average	284.97	318.98

Comparing F_{T+1} and F_{T+2}, it can be seen that F_{T+2} requires dropping the value X_1 and adding the value X_{T+1} as it becomes available, so that another way to write F_{T+2} is

$$F_{T+2} = F_{T+1} + \frac{1}{T}(X_{T+1} - X_1). \qquad (3\text{-}5)$$

It can be seen from (3-5) that each new forecast (F_{T+2}) is simply an adjustment of the immediately preceding forecast (F_{T+1}). This adjustment is $(1/T)$th of the difference between X_{T+1} and X_1. Clearly if T is a big

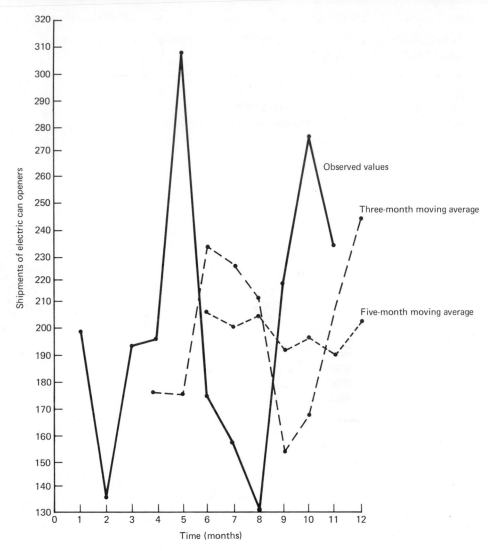

FIGURE 3-6 SHIPMENTS OF ELECTRIC CAN OPENERS—ACTUAL AND MOVING AVERAGE VALUES

number, this adjustment is small, so that moving averages of high order provide forecasts that do not change very much.

In summary, a $MA(T)$ forecasting system will require T data points to be stored at any one time. If T is small (say 4), then the storage requirements are not severe although for many thousands of time series (say for inventories involving thousands of stockkeeping units) this can be a problem. However, in practice, the technique of moving averages as a forecasting procedure is not used often because the methods of exponential smoothing (examined in Sections 3/3) are generally superior.

3/2/3 Double Moving Averages

In the two previous sections it was stated that both the mean (of all past data) and the moving average (of the most recent T values), when used as forecasts for the next period, are unable to cope with significant trend. Here we describe a variation on the moving average procedure that is intended to do a better job of handling trend.

Consider Table 3-2 in which the observed data are a steadily increasing series with no random error imposed on the linear upward trend. Using a $MA(3)$ as a forecast for the next period, it can be seen that there is a systematic error of 4 units. (As an exercise, check that a $MA(4)$ forecasting procedure would have resulted in a systematic error of 5 units.)

To mitigate against the systematic error that occurs if moving averages are applied to data with trend, the method of *linear moving averages* has been developed. The basis of this method is to calculate a second moving average. This "double" moving average is a moving average of a moving average, and in symbols it would be denoted $MA(M \times N)$ where we mean an M-period MA of an N-period MA. Table 3-3 shows an example of an $MA(3 \times 3)$—a 3-period moving average of a 3-period moving average.

Note that the placement of the moving averages in Table 3-3 is different from the placement in Table 3-2. When considering the method of linear moving averages the first 3-period moving average is known as soon as the third data point (X_3) is known. Thus we place the first MA (in column 3) opposite time period 3. Similarly, as soon as the fifth data point (X_5) is known there will be three single $MA(3)$ values available (4, 6, and 8), and so the first $MA(3 \times 3)$ can be computed (in column 5) and placed against time period 5. The differences in column 4 and column 6 are identical (for this special data set) and so by the judicious use of the single moving av-

---

TABLE 3-2 FORECASTING A SERIES WITH TREND USING
A MOVING AVERAGE OF ORDER 3

Period	Observed Value	Forecast ($N = 3$)	Error
1	2	—	—
2	4	—	—
3	6	—	—
4	8	4	4
5	10	6	4
6	12	8	4
7	14	10	4
8	16	12	4
9	18	14	4
—	—	16	4

TABLE 3-3   FORECASTING A SERIES WITH TREND USING A LINEAR MOVING AVERAGE

(1) Period	(2) Actual Value	(3) Single Moving Average ($N = 3$)	(4) Error Difference (2) − (3)	(5) Double Moving Average ($N = 3$)	(6) Error Difference (3) − (5)	(7) Forecast (3) + (6) + Trend	(8) Error Difference (2) − (7)
1	2						
2	4						
3	6	4	2				
4	8	6	2				
5	10	8	2	6	2		
6	12	10	2	8	2	12	0
7	14	12	2	10	2	14	0
8	16	14	2	12	2	16	0
9	18	16	2	14	2	18	0
10	20	18	2	16	2	20	0
11						22	

erage (column 3) and the difference between single and double moving averages (column 6), a forecast for the next period can be derived. For example, assume we know the data up to period 5 and wish to forecast period 6.

$$F_6 = (MA(3) \text{ at period 5})$$
$$+ ((MA(3) - MA(3 \times 3)) \text{ at period 5}) \tag{3-6}$$
$$+ (\text{trend from period 5 to period 6})^3$$
$$= (8) + (2) + (2) = 12.$$

The linear moving average forecasting procedure thus involves three aspects:

1. The use of a single moving average at time t (denoted S'_t),
2. an adjustment, which is the difference between the single and the double moving average at time t (denoted $S'_t - S''_t$), and
3. an adjustment for trend from period t to period $t + 1$ (or to period $t + m$ if we want to forecast m periods ahead).

Adjustment 2 is most effective when the trend is linear and the random error component is not strong. It effectively adjusts for the fact that the single MA lags behind a data series showing trend.
     The lesson to be learned from the above exercise is that when the

---

[3] The trend in this example is exactly 2 (see column 2 in Table 3-3). In practice, an estimate of trend would have to be determined.

data series shows trend, the single *MA* forecast will result in something like a systematic error, and this systematic error can be mitigated by using the difference between a double moving average value and the single moving average value. (Note that when significant random error is present it is *not* always possible to improve on the single *MA* forecast by going to a linear *MA* forecast. See Table 3-4 later in this section.)

The discussion may be generalized as follows: The general linear moving average procedure may be described by the following equations:

$$S'_t = \frac{X_t + X_{t-1} + X_{t-2} + \cdots + X_{t-N+1}}{N}, \qquad (3\text{-}7)$$

$$S''_t = \frac{S'_t + S'_{t-1} + S'_{t-2} + \cdots + S'_{t-N+1}}{N}, \qquad (3\text{-}8)$$

$$a_t = S'_t + (S'_t - S''_t) = 2S'_t - S''_t, \qquad (3\text{-}9)$$

$$b_t = \frac{2}{N-1}(S'_t - S''_t) \qquad (3\text{-}10)$$

$$F_{t+m} = a_t + b_t m. \qquad (3\text{-}11)$$

Equation (3-7) assumes that we are standing at time period t and looking over the last N known values. The single $MA(N)$ is denoted S'_t. Equation (3-8) assumes that all the single moving averages (S') have been computed and we compute the N-period moving average of the S' values. The double moving averages are denoted S''. Equation (3-9) refers to the adjustment of the single *MA*, S'_t, by the difference $(S'_t - S''_t)$, and equation (3-10) defines the estimate of trend from one time period to the next. Finally, equation (3-11) shows how to obtain forecasts for m periods ahead of t. The forecast for m periods ahead is a_t—which is the adjusted smoothed value for period t—plus m times the trend component b_t.

Note that b_t involves a factor $2/(N-1)$ in equation (3-10). This arises because an N period moving average should really be centered at a time period $(N+1)/2$ and the moving average is computed at time period N (for the *first* moving average), making a difference of

$$N - \frac{N+1}{2} = \frac{N-1}{2} \qquad \text{periods.}[4]$$

1 2 3 4 5 6   (e.g., for $N = 6$)

MA(6) should   MA(6) is
be centered   computed
here   here

$$\text{difference is } \frac{N-1}{2} = \frac{5}{2} = 2.5 \text{ periods.}$$

---

[4]This is sometimes called the "correction for lag."

TABLE 3-4   APPLICATION OF LINEAR MOVING AVERAGES

	Period	(1) Inventory Balance of Product E12	(2) Four-Month Moving Average of (1)	(3) Four-Month Moving Average of (2)	(4) Value of a	(5) Value of b	(6) Value of $a + b(m)$ When $m = 1$
	1	140.00					
	2	159.00					
	3	136.00					
	4	157.00	148.00				
	5	173.00	156.25				
	6	131.00	149.25				
	7	177.00	159.50	153.25	165.75	4.166	
	8	188.00	167.25	158.06	176.43	6.125	169.91
	9	154.00	162.50	159.62	165.37	1.916	182.56
	10	179.00	174.50	165.93	183.06	5.708	167.29
	11	180.00	175.25	169.87	180.62	3.583	188.77
T	12	160.00	168.25	170.12	166.37	−1.250	184.20
E	13	182.00	175.25	173.31	177.18	1.291	165.12
S	14	192.00	178.50	174.31	182.68	2.791	178.47
T	15	224.00	189.50	177.87	201.12	7.750	185.47
	16	188.00	196.50	184.93	208.06	7.708	208.87
P	17	198.00	200.50	191.25	209.75	6.166	215.77
E	18	206.00	204.00	197.62	210.37	4.250	215.91
R	19	203.00	198.75	199.93	197.56	−0.791	214.62
I	20	238.00	211.25	203.62	218.87	5.083	196.77
O	21	228.00	218.75	208.18	229.31	7.041	223.95
D	22	231.00	225.00	213.43	236.56	7.708	236.35
	23	221.00	229.50	221.12	237.87	5.583	244.27
	24	259.00	234.75	227.00	242.50	5.166	243.45
	25	273.00	246.00	233.81	258.18	8.125	247.66
	26						266.31

MAPE for periods 10 through 25 = 8.61.

MSE for periods 10 through 25 = 431.6.

Note: MAPE for periods 10 through 25 = 7.46 when using single *MA* of order 4.

Similarly, the time difference between when a double moving average is computed and where it should be centered, is $(N - 1)/2$ for a $MA(N \times N)$ system. So the difference $(S'_t - S''_t)$ represents the difference for $(N - 1)/2$ time periods, and the difference (or trend) *per period* is

$$\frac{(S'_t - S''_t)}{(N - 1)/2}$$

or

$$\frac{2}{N - 1} (S'_t - S''_t) = b_t. \tag{3-12}$$

As an illustration of the method of the linear moving averages, Table 3-4 presents data on a series of 25 inventory values. Using a value of $N = 4$, columns 2 through 6 show the results obtained. Figure 3-7 illustrates these same results in graphic form. The computational steps are:

Column 2: the four-period moving averages   [using (3-7)]

Column 3: the double moving averages   [using (3-8)]
(frequently called 4×4 averages)

Column 4: the values of a [using (3-9)]

Column 5: the values of b [using (3-10)]

Column 6: the forecasts for one period ahead $(m = 1)$ [using (3-11)]

As an example of the calculations required for Table 3-4 consider the forecast for period 24 that would be made in period 23.

$$F_{24} = a_{23} + b_{23}(1) = 237.875 + 5.583(1) = 243.5,$$

where $a_{23} = 2S'_{23} - S''_{23} = 2(229.5) - 221.125$
$$= 237.875,$$

$$b_{23} = \frac{2}{4 - 1} (S''_{23}) = \frac{2}{3} (229.5 - 221.125) = 5.583,$$

$$S'_{23} = \frac{X_{23} + X_{22} + X_{21} + X_{20}}{4}$$

$$= \frac{221 + 231 + 228.75 + 238}{4} = 229.5,$$

and

$$S''_{23} = \frac{S'_{23} + S'_{22} + S'_{21} + S'_{20}}{4}$$

$$= \frac{229.5 + 225 + 218.75 + 211.25}{4}$$

$$= 221.125.$$

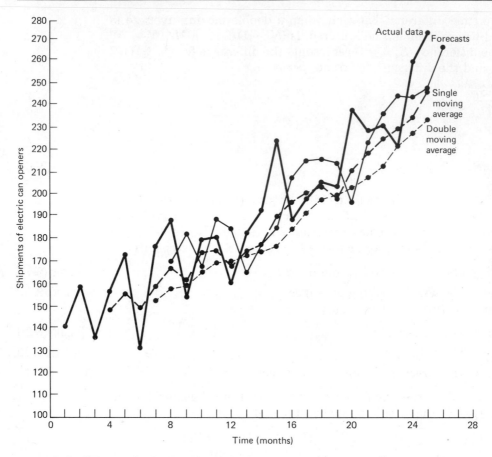

FIGURE 3-7 APPLICATION OF LINEAR MOVING AVERAGES TO THE INVENTORY DATA IN TABLE 3-4

Similarly, the forecast for period 25 is:

$$F_{25} = a_{24} + b_{24}(1) = 242.5 + 5.1667(1) = 247.667,$$

since

$$a_{24} = 242.5 \quad \text{and} \quad b_{24} = 5.1667.$$

The forecast for period 26 is:

$$F_{26} = a_{25} + b_{25}(1) = 258.187 + 8.125(1) = 266.31,$$

while for periods 27 and 28, the forecasts use the most recent values of a and b (period 25) as follows:

$$F_{27} = a_{25} + b_{25}(2) = 258.187 + 8.125(2) = 274.437,$$

$$F_{28} = a_{25} + b_{25}(3) = 258.187 + 8.125(3) = 282.562.$$

3/2/4   Other Moving Average Combinations

It is possible to conceive of an endless variety of higher-order moving average combinations. The method of linear moving averages described in the previous section used the same *order* for both the single and the double moving averages. For example Table 3-4 was a 4×4 *MA* system—that is, a $MA(4)$ of a $MA(4)$. But there is no reason not to try a 3×4 system (a three period *MA* of a 4-period *MA* of a data series), or a $3 \times 4 \times 5$ system (a 3-period *MA* of a 4-period *MA* of a 5-period *MA*), and so on. For example, in Chapter 4, in the discussion of the Census II method, reference will be made to Spencer's $5 \times 5 \times 4 \times 4$ moving average system.

The point to observe about all moving average procedures is that they all imply a set of *weights* for past observations. This is the key consideration and allows for comparison with exponential smoothing methods in the next section and various other general linear models.

By way of example, the straightforward mean of the past N observations, implies equal weights for all N data points.

$$\overline{X} = \left(\frac{1}{N}\right)X_1 + \left(\frac{1}{N}\right)X_2 + \cdots + \left(\frac{1}{N}\right)X_N.$$

(equal weights)

$$(3\text{-}13)$$

This, of course, applies to all single moving average systems as well.

For a double moving average the implied weights are determined as follows: For example, $MA(3 \times 3)$,

$$S_1' = (X_1 + X_2 + X_3)/3,$$

$$S_2' = (X_2 + X_3 + X_4)/3,$$

$$S_3' = (X_3 + X_4 + X_5)/3,$$

$$S_1'' = (S_1' + S_2' + S_3')/3,$$

$$= (\tfrac{1}{9})X_1 + (\tfrac{2}{9})X_2 + (\tfrac{3}{9})X_3 + (\tfrac{2}{9})X_4 + (\tfrac{1}{9})X_5.$$

(unequal weights)

$$(3\text{-}14)$$

In the method of linear moving averages (LMA) the forecast, for period $t + 1$ [equation (3-11)] is

$$F_{t+1} = a_t + b_t$$

$$= 2S_t' - S_t'' + \frac{2}{N-1}(S_t' - S_t'')$$

$$= \left(\frac{2N}{N-1}\right)S_t' - \left(\frac{N+1}{N-1}\right)S_t''.$$

$$(3\text{-}15)$$

If $N = 3$, the forecast for period $t + 1$ implies the following weights on the past five values:

$$F_{t+1} = (-\tfrac{2}{9})X_{t-4} + (\tfrac{4}{9})X_{t-3} + (\tfrac{3}{9})X_{t-2} + (\tfrac{5}{9})X_{t-1} + (\tfrac{7}{9})X_t. \qquad (3\text{-}16)$$

(unequal weights with generally increasing emphasis
on the latest data)

(It is left as an exercise to verify the above result.)

The conclusion is that double, triple, and other moving average combinations, on their own, imply a weighting of past data, where the largest weights are given to the middle values of the set of past data. As such they are useful for *smoothing* (as opposed to *forecasting*) data series and will most often be used as *centered* moving averages. However, when used in the forecasting context—as in LMA—the implied weighting system places more emphasis on the most recent data. In Census II the Spencer $5 \times 5 \times 4 \times 4$ moving average is used for smoothing not forecasting.

3/3   Exponential Smoothing Methods

Figure 3-8 indicates the weights implied by various procedures described in the previous section. In this section we describe a class of methods that imply *exponentially decreasing* weights as the observations get older. Thus they are called exponential smoothing procedures. As in the case of moving averages there are single, double, and more complicated exponential smoothing methods. They all have in common the property that recent values are given relatively more weight in forecasting than the older observations. (The general problem of estimation in this context will be explored in more detail in Chapter 9.)

In the case of moving averages, the weights assigned to observations are a by-product of the particular *MA* system adopted. In exponential smoothing, however, there are one or more *smoothing parameters* to be determined explicitly, and these choices determine the weights assigned to observations, as will be indicated below.

3/3/1   Single Exponential Smoothing

The simplest case of single exponential smoothing (SES) can be developed from equation (3-5), or, more specifically, from a variation on that equation, as follows:

$$F_{t+1} = F_t + \left(\frac{X_t}{N} - \frac{X_{t-N}}{N}\right). \qquad (3\text{-}5')$$

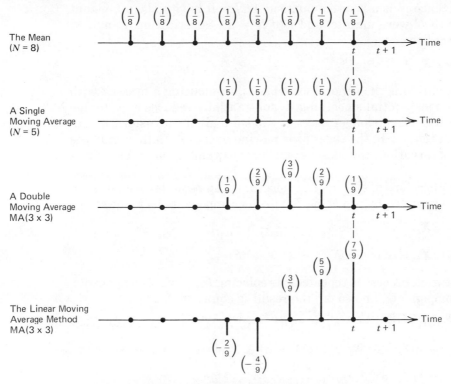

FIGURE 3-8   IMPLIED WEIGHTS GIVEN TO PAST DATA WHEN A FORE-
CAST IS MADE AT TIME t FOR THE NEXT PERIOD, USING
VARIOUS FORECASTING PROCEDURES

Suppose that the old observation X_{t-N} is not available so that in its place
an approximate value must be used. One possible replacement would be the
previous period's forecast F_t. Making this substitution equation (3-5′) becomes equation (3-17), and can be rewritten as (3-18):

$$F_{t+1} = F_t + \left(\frac{X_t}{N} - \frac{F_t}{N} \right), \tag{3-17}$$

$$F_{t+1} = \left(\frac{1}{N} \right) X_t + \left(1 - \frac{1}{N} \right) F_t. \tag{3-18}$$

(Note that if the data are stationary, the above substitution is a fairly good
approximation, but when trend is present the SES method explained here
is inadequate.)

From equation (3-18) it can be seen that this forecast (F_{t+1}) is based
on weighting the most recent observation with a weight value $(1/N)$ and
weighting the most recent previous forecast (F_t) with a weight of

$[1 - (1/N)]$. Since N is a positive number, $1/N$ will have to be a constant between zero (if N were infinite) and 1 (if $N = 1$). Substituting α for $1/N$, equation (3-18) becomes

$$F_{t+1} = \alpha X_t + (1 - \alpha)F_t. \qquad (3\text{-}19)$$

This equation is the general form used in computing a forecast with the method of exponential smoothing. It substantially reduces any storage problem, because it is no longer necessary to store all of the historical data or a subset of them (as in the case of the moving average). Rather, only the most recent observation, the most recent forecast, and a value for α must be stored.

The implications of exponential smoothing can be better seen if equation (3-19) is expanded by replacing F with its components as follows:

$$F_{t+1} = \alpha X_t + (1 - \alpha)[\alpha X_{t-1} + (1 - \alpha)F_{t-1}]$$

$$= \alpha X_t + \alpha(1 - \alpha)X_{t-1} + (1 - \alpha)^2 F_{t-1}. \qquad (3\text{-}20)$$

If this substitution process is repeated by replacing F_{t-1} by its components, F_{t-2} by its components, and so on, the result is equation (3-21):

$$F_{t+1} = \alpha X_t + \alpha(1 - \alpha)X_{t-1} + \alpha(1 - \alpha)^2 X_{t-2} + \alpha(1 - \alpha)^3 X_{t-3}$$

$$+ \alpha(1 - \alpha)^4 X_{t-4} + \alpha(1 - \alpha)^5 X_{t-5} + \cdots + \alpha(1 - \alpha)^{N-1} X_{t-(N-1)}$$

$$+ (1 - \alpha)^N F_{t-(N-1)}. \qquad (3\text{-}21)$$

Suppose $\alpha = .2, .4, .6,$ or $.8$. Then the weights assigned to past observations would be as follows:

Weight Assigned to:	$\alpha = .2$	$\alpha = .4$	$\alpha = .6$	$\alpha = .8$
X_t	.2	.4	.6	.8
X_{t-1}	.16	.24	.24	.16
X_{t-2}	.128	.144	.096	.032
X_{t-3}	.1024	.0864	.0384	.0064
X_{t-4}	$(.2)(.8)^4$	$(.4)(.6)^4$	$(.6)(.4)^4$	$(.8)(.2)^4$

If these weights are plotted it can be seen that they decrease exponentially, hence the name exponential smoothing. (It should be pointed out that even though the objective may be to find an α value that minimizes the MSE over a test set, the estimation involved in exponential smoothing is a nonlinear problem.)

An alternative way of writing equation (3-19) is the following re-arrangement:

$$F_{t+1} = F_t + \alpha(X_t - F_t). \tag{3-22}$$

This is simply

$$F_{t+1} = F_t + \alpha(e_t), \tag{3-22'}$$

where e_t is the forecast error (actual minus forecast) for period t. From these two forms for F_{t+1} it can be seen that the forecast provided by SES is simply the old forecast plus an adjustment for the error that occurred in the last forecast. In this form it is evident that when α has a value close to 1, the new forecast will include a substantial adjustment for the error in the previous forecast. Conversely, when α is close to 0, the new forecast will include very little adjustment. Thus, the effect of a large and small α is completely analogous (in an opposite direction) to the effect of including a small or a large number of observations when computing a moving average. It should also be observed that a single exponential smoothing will always trail any trend in the actual data, since the most it can do is adjust the next forecast for some percentage of the most recent error.

Equation (3-22) involves a basic principle of negative feedback, since it works much like the control process employed by automatic devices such as thermostats, automatic pilots, and so on. The past forecast error is used to correct the next forecast in a direction opposite to that of the error. There will be an adjustment until the error is corrected. It is the same principle that directs an automatic pilot device to an equilibrium course once a deviation (error) has taken place. This principle, simple as it may appear, plays an extremely important role in forecasting. If properly applied, it can be used to develop a self-adjusting process that corrects for forecasting error automatically.

The application of single exponential smoothing can be illustrated by using the example given in Section 3/2/2. Table 3-5 shows the exponential smoothing results from electric can opener shipments using α values of .1, .5, and .9.

One can forecast with single exponential smoothing by using either equation (3-19) or (3-22). For example, in Table 3-5 the forecast for period 12 (December) when $\alpha = .1$ is computed as follows:

$$F_{12} = \alpha X_{11} + (1 - \alpha)F_{11}$$

$$= (.1)(235.0) + (.9)(202.3)$$

$$= 205.6.$$

Similarly, when $\alpha = .9$, equation (3-19) gives for period 12

$$F_{12} = (.9)(235.0) + (.1)(270.9) = 238.6.$$

TABLE 3-5　FORECASTING ELECTRIC CAN OPENER SHIPMENTS USING EXPONENTIAL SMOOTHING

Month	Time Period	Observed Values (shipments)	Exponentially Smoothed Values		
			$\alpha = .1$	$\alpha = .5$	$\alpha = .9$
Jan.	1	200.0	—	—	—
Feb.	2	135.0	200.0	200.0	200.0
Mar.	3	195.0	193.5	167.5	141.5
Apr.	4	197.5	193.7	181.3	189.7
May	5	310.0	194.0	189.4	196.7
June	6	175.0	205.6	249.7	298.7
July	7	155.0	202.6	212.3	187.4
Aug.	8	130.0	197.8	183.7	158.2
Sept.	9	220.0	191.0	156.8	132.8
Oct.	10	277.5	193.9	188.4	211.3
Nov.	11	235.0	202.3	233.0	270.9
Dec.	12	—	205.6	234.0	238.6

Analysis of Errors	Test Periods		
	2-11 $\alpha = .1$	2-11 $\alpha = .5$	2-11 $\alpha = .9$
Mean Error	5.56	6.80	4.29
Mean Absolute Error	47.76	56.94	61.32
Mean Absolute Percentage Error (MAPE)	24.58	29.20	30.81
Standard Deviation of Error (Unbiased)	61.53	69.13	74.69
Mean Square Error (MSE)	3438.33	4347.24	5039.37
Durbin-Watson Statistic	1.57	1.84	2.30
Theil's U Statistic	.81	.92	.98
McLaughlin's Batting Average	319.12	307.84	301.79

Note that the choice of α has considerable impact on the December forecast and the MAPE values for periods 2 through 11 range from 24.6 percent (for $\alpha = .1$) to 30.8 percent (for $\alpha = .9$).

Single exponential smoothing requires little storage and few computations. It is therefore attractive when a large number of items require forecasting. One point of concern relates to the initializing phase of SES. For example, to get the SES forecasting system started we need F_1 because

$$F_2 = \alpha X_1 + (1 - \alpha)F_1.$$

Since the value for F_1 is not known, we can use the first observed value (X_1) as the first forecast $(F_1 = X_1)$ and then proceed using equation (3-19). This is one method of initialization. Another possibility would be to average the first four or five values in the data set, and use this as the initial forecast. Note from equation (3-21) that the *initial* forecast plays a role in *all* subsequent forecasts. The last term in equation (3-21) is

$$(1 - \alpha)^N F_{t-(N-1)}.$$

Suppose $N = 5$ and F_{t-4} is the *initial* forecast. Then it is clear that F_{t-4} plays a role in the forecast F_{t-1}. Consider the following:

F_{t-4}	F_{t-3}	F_{t-2}	F_{t-1}	F_t	F_{t+1}
X_{t-4}	X_{t-3}	X_{t-2}	X_{t-1}	X_t	

$$
\begin{aligned}
t-4 \quad t-3 \quad t-2 \quad t-1 \quad t \quad t+1 \qquad \text{Time}
\end{aligned}
$$

$$
\begin{aligned}
F_{t+1} = {} & \alpha X_t + \alpha(1 - \alpha)X_{t-1} + \alpha(1 - \alpha)^2 X_{t-2} \\
& + \alpha(1 - \alpha)^3 X_{t-3} + \alpha(1 - \alpha)^4 X_{t-4} \\
& + (1 - \alpha)^5 F_{t-4}. \\
& \qquad\qquad \uparrow \\
& \text{(the initial forecast)}
\end{aligned}
\tag{3-21'}
$$

When $\alpha = .1$ the weight for F_{t-4} is .59049.

When $\alpha = .5$ the weight for F_{t-4} is .03125.

When $\alpha = .9$ the weight for F_{t-4} is .00001.

Clearly, when a small value of α is chosen, the initial forecast plays a more prominent role than when a larger α is used.

The smoothing effect of α can be seen in Figure 3-9. A large value of α (.9) gives very little smoothing in the forecast, whereas a small value of α (.1) gives considerable smoothing. Refer to equations (3-22) for an explanation of this effect.

Simple as exponential smoothing is, it does have its problems. One of these arises in trying to find an optimal value for α. Should we optimize to minimize MSE, MAPE, or some other measure? Suppose we try to minimize MSE. Unlike the mean, where this minimization occurs any time the average of a set of numbers is calculated, for exponential smoothing the minimum MSE must be determined through trial and error. A value for α is chosen, the MSE is computed over a test set, and then another α value is tried. The MSEs are then compared to find the α value that gives the minimum MSE. In the example of Table 3-5, using periods 2 through 11 as the test set,

$$\text{MSE} = 3438 \text{ when } \alpha = .1,$$

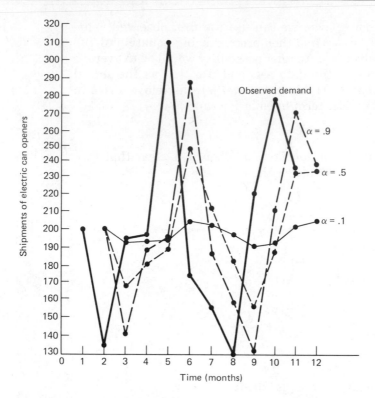

FIGURE 3-9 SHIPMENTS OF ELECTRIC CAN OPENERS—ACTUAL AND EXPONENTIAL SMOOTHING VALUES

MSE = 4347 when α = .5, and

MSE = 5039 when α = .9.

This wide range of MSE values indicates the important role of α in determining the resulting errors. Finding an α value that is close to the best possible generally requires only a few trials, since its value can be approximated by simply comparing a few MSE and α values. For the series in Table 3-5 it can be seen that the MSE decreases as α approaches 0. In fact,

α = .05 gives MSE = 3301 and

α = .01 gives MSE = 3184.

The reason for this is that the data are almost random, so the smaller the value of α, the smaller the MSE.

In the calculations above, the optimum α could be different if the objective had been to minimize the MAPE. It was also assumed that the forecast horizon was just one period ahead. Interested readers should check Dalrymple and King (1981) for more on the issues relating to forecast horizon.

3/3/2   Single Exponential Smoothing: An Adaptive Approach

The SES forecasting method requires the specification of an α value and it has been shown that the MAPE and MSE measures depend on this choice. Adaptive-response-rate single exponential smoothing (ARRSES) has an apparent advantage over SES in that it allows the value of α to change, in a controlled manner, as changes in the pattern of data occur. This characteristic seems attractive when several hundreds or even thousands of items require forecasting. ARRSES is adaptive in the sense that the value of α will change automatically when there is a change in the basic data pattern, as in some of the cases in Figure 3-4, for example.

The basic equation for forecasting with the method of ARRSES is similar to equation (3-19) except that α is replaced by α_t:

$$F_{t+1} = \alpha_t X_t + (1 - \alpha_t)F_t, \tag{3-23}$$

where

$$\alpha_{t+1} = \left| \frac{E_t}{M_t} \right|, \tag{3-24}[5]$$

$$E_t = \beta e_t + (1 - \beta)E_{t-1}, \tag{3-25}$$

$$M = \beta|e_t| + (1 - \beta)M_{t-1}, \tag{3-26}$$

$$e_t - X_t \quad F_t, \tag{3-27}$$

α and β are parameters between 0 and 1 and $\|$ denotes absolute values.

Equation (3-24) indicates that the value of α to be used for forecasting period $(t + 2)$ is defined as an absolute value of the ratio of a smoothed error term (E_t) and a smoothed *absolute error* term (M_t). These two smoothed terms are obtained using SES as shown in equations (3-25) and (3-26).

Initialization of an ARRSES process is a little more complicated than for SES. As already indicated (in the footnote to a previous page in this section) ARRSES is often too responsive to changes in the data pattern. For example, for the electric can opener shipments, if we initialize as follows:

---

[5]Instead of α_{t+1} we could have used α_t in equation (3-24). We prefer α_{t+1} because ARRSES is often too responsive to changes, thus using α_{t+1} we introduce a small lag of one period, which allows the system to "settle" a little and forecast in a more conservative manner.

$$F_2 = X_1,$$

$$\alpha_2 = \alpha_3 = \alpha_4 = \beta = .2, \qquad\qquad\qquad\qquad (3\text{-}28)$$

$$E_1 = M_1 = 0,$$

then forecasts using the ARRSES method are as shown in Table 3-6.

The forecast for period 10, for example, is

$$F_{10} = \alpha_9 X_9 + (1 - \alpha_9)F_9$$

$$= .438(220) + .562(187.3) = 201.6.$$

Once the actual value for period 10 becomes known, α can be updated and used for the next period's calculations. This entails computing e_{10}, E_{10}, and M_{10} as follows:

$$e_{10} = 277.5 - 201.6 = 75.9, \qquad\qquad\qquad \text{[using (3-27)]}$$

$$E_{10} = .2(75.9) + .8(-10.3) = 7, \qquad\qquad \text{[using (3-25)]}$$

$$M_{10} = .2|(75.9)| + .8(45) = 51.1, \qquad\qquad \text{[using (3-26)]}$$

TABLE 3-6 FORECASTING ELECTRIC CAN OPENER SHIPMENTS USING ADAPTIVE-RESPONSE-RATE SINGLE EXPONENTIAL SMOOTHING

Period	Observed Value (Shipments) (X)	Forecast (F)	Error (e_t)	Smoothed Error (E_t)	Absolute Smoothed Error (M_t)	α_t Value
1	200					
2	135	200.0	-65.0	-13.0	13.0	.200
3	195	187.0	8.0	-8.8	12.0	.200
4	197.5	188.6	8.9	-5.3	11.4	.200
5	310	190.4	119.6	19.7	33.0	.462
6	175	245.7	-70.7	1.6	40.6	.597
7	155	203.5	-48.5	-8.4	42.1	.040
8	130	201.5	-71.5	-21.0	48.0	.199
9	220	187.3	32.7	-10.3	45.0	.438
10	277.5	201.6	75.9	7.0	51.1	.228
11	235	218.9	16.1	8.8	44.1	.136
12	—	221.1	—	—	—	.199

and

$$\alpha_{11} = \left| \frac{7}{51.1} \right| = .136. \qquad\qquad \text{[using (3-24)]}$$

Similarly, the forecast for period 11 is:

$$F_{11} = \alpha_{10}X_{10} + (1 - \alpha_{10})F_{10}$$

$$= .228(277.5) + .772(201.6) = 218.9.$$

This forecast value can then be used to update the value of α_{t+1}.

$$e_{11} = 235 - 218.9 = 16.1,$$

$$E_{11} = .2(16.1) + .8(7) = 8.8,$$

$$M_{11} = .2|(16.1)| + .8(51.1) = 44.1,$$

$$\alpha_{12} = \left| \frac{8.8}{44.1} \right| = .199.$$

Finally, the forecast for period 12 can be computed using equation (3-23)

$$F_{12} = .136(235) + .864(218.9) = 221.1.$$

Note that the α values fluctuate quite significantly and, if a different initializing procedure had been adopted, a different series of α values would have been generated. One way to control the changes in α is to change the value of β. Summing up, the ARRSES method is an SES method with a difference; namely, the α value is systematically, and automatically, changed from period to period to allow for changes in the structure of the data. It can be useful for a forecasting system involving a large number of items, but care should be taken in evaluating the fluctuations in α—and maybe curbing these changes by putting on some controls.[6] Consult Gardner and Dannenbring (1980) for less favorable results using ARRSES.

3/3/3   Double Exponential Smoothing: Brown's One-Parameter Linear Method

In a manner analogous to that used in going from single moving averages to single exponential smoothing (see Section 3/3/1) it is possible to go from linear moving averages to linear exponential smoothing. Such a move may be attractive because one of the limitations of single moving

---

[6]One way to do this is to put an upper bound on how much α is allowed to change from one period to the next. For example, the maximum allowable change can be set to 0.3, or 0.5, or some other value.

averages—the need to save the last N values—still exists with linear moving averages except that the number of data points required is now $2N - 1$. Linear exponential smoothing can be computed with only three data values and a single value for α. This approach also gives decreasing weights to past observations. For these reasons it is preferred to linear moving averages as a method of forecasting in the great majority of cases.

The underlying rationale of Brown's linear exponential smoothing is similar to that of linear moving averages: since both the single and double smoothed values lag the actual data when a trend exists (as shown in Figure 3-10), the difference between the single and double smoothed values can be added to the single smoothed values and adjusted for trend. The equations used in implementing Brown's one-parameter linear exponential smoothing are shown below as (3-29) through (3-33) and their application is illustrated in Table 3-7.

Column 2
$$S'_t = \alpha X_t + (1 - \alpha)S'_{t-1}, \tag{3-29}$$

Column 3
$$S''_t = \alpha S'_t + (1 - \alpha)S''_{t-1}, \tag{3-30}$$

where S'_t is the single exponential smoothed value and S''_t is the double exponential smoothed value.

Column 4
$$a_t = S'_t + (S'_t - S''_t) = 2S'_t - S''_t, \tag{3-31}$$

Column 5
$$b_t = \frac{\alpha}{1 - \alpha}(S'_t - S''_t), \tag{3-32}[7]$$

Column 6
$$F_{t+m} = a_t + b_t m, \tag{3-33}[7]$$

where m is the number of periods ahead to be forecast.

---

[7]Equation (3-32) has a factor $\alpha/(1 - \alpha)$ for the same reason that equation (3-10) has the factor $2/(N - 1)$. The average age of data in an N-period moving average is

$$\frac{1}{N}\sum_{j=0}^{N-1} j = \frac{N - 1}{2}$$

and the average age of data in simple exponential smoothing is given by:

$$\alpha \sum_{j=0}^{\infty} (1 - \alpha)^j j = \frac{1 - \alpha}{\alpha}.$$

See Montgomery and Johnson (1976), p. 52, for details.

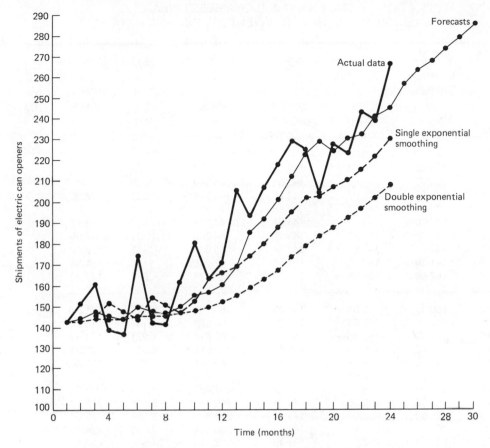

FIGURE 3-10 APPLICATION OF BROWN'S ONE-PARAMETER LINEAR EX-
PONENTIAL SMOOTHING TO INVENTORY DATA IN TABLE
3-7

The calculations in Table 3-7 are based on an $\alpha = .2$ and a forecast for one period ahead. For example, in period 23 the forecast for period 24 is as follows:

$$F_{24} = a_{23} + b_{23}(1) = 239.855 + 4.654(1) = 244.51,$$

where

$$a_{23} = 2S'_{23} - S''_{23} = 239.855,$$

$$b_{23} = \frac{.2}{.8}(S'_{23} - S''_{23}) = \frac{1}{4}(18.616) = 4.654,$$

$$S'_{23} = .2X_{23} + .8S_{22} = .2(239) + .8(216.798) = 221.238,$$

$$S''_{23} = .2S'_{23} + .8S''_{22} = .2(221.238) + .8(197.968) = 202.622.$$

TABLE 3-7 APPLICATION OF BROWN'S ONE-PARAMETER LINEAR EXPONENTIAL SMOOTHING TO INVENTORY DEMAND DATA

	Period	(1) Inventory Demand for Product E15	(2)[a] Single Exponential Smoothing	(3)[a] Double Exponential Smoothing	(4) Value of a [2(2) − (3)]	(5) Value of b [see (3-22)]	(6) Forecast Value $a + b(m)$ [(4) + (5)]
	1	143.00	143.00	143.00			
	2	152.00	144.80	143.36	146.240	.360	
	3	161.00	148.04	144.30	151.784	.936	146.60
	4	139.00	146.23	144.68	147.781	.387	152.72
	5	137.00	144.39	144.62	144.148	−.060	148.17
	6	174.00	150.31	145.76	154.856	1.137	144.09
	7	142.00	148.65	146.34	150.956	.577	155.99
	8	141.00	147.12	146.49	147.741	.156	151.53
	9	162.00	150.09	147.21	152.974	.720	147.90
	10	180.00	156.08	148.99	163.164	1.772	153.69
	11	164.00	157.66	150.72	164.599	1.735	164.94
	12	171.00	160.33	152.64	168.014	1.921	166.33
T	13	206.00	169.46	156.01	182.919	3.364	169.94
E	14	193.00	174.17	159.64	188.701	3.633	186.28
S	15	207.00	180.74	163.86	197.614	4.219	192.33
T	16	218.00	188.19	168.72	207.653	4.866	201.83
	17	229.00	196.35	174.25	218.452	5.525	212.52
S	18	225.00	202.08	179.82	224.346	5.566	223.98
E	19	204.00	202.46	184.35	220.584	4.530	229.91
T	20	227.00	207.37	188.95	225.793	4.605	225.11
	21	223.00	210.50	193.26	227.735	4.309	230.40
	22	242.00	216.80	197.97	235.628	4.708	232.04
	23	239.00	221.24	202.62	239.855	4.654	240.34
	24	266.00	230.19	208.14	252.246	5.514	244.51
	25						257.76 ($m = 1$)
	26						263.27 ($m = 2$)
	27						268.78 ($m = 3$)
	28						274.30 ($m = 4$)
	29						279.81 ($m = 5$)
	30						285.33 ($m = 6$)

Analysis of Errors from Period 10 to Period 24

7.99 = Mean Error	273.47 = Mean Square Error (MSE)
12.73 = Mean Absolute Error	1.33 = Durbin-Watson Statistic
6.04 = Mean Absolute Percentage Error (MAPE)	.98 = Theil's U Statistic
14.99 = Standard Deviation of Error (Unbiased)	302.48 = McLaughlin's Batting Average

[a]The value of α was set at 0.2.

The forecast for period 25 is:

$$F_{25} = a_{24} + b_{24}(1) = 252.246 + 5.514(1) = 257.76,$$

where a_{24} and b_{24} are calculated as before.
The forecast for period 26 is

$$F_{26} = a_{24} + b_{24}(2) = 252.246 + 5.514(2) = 263.274,$$

while the forecast for period 30 will be

$$F_{30} = a_{24} + b_{24}(6) = 252.246 + 5.514(6) = 285.33,$$

since the most recent values available for a and b are from period 24.

In order to apply formulas (3-29) and (3-30), values of S'_{t-1} and S''_{t-1} must be available. However, when $t = 1$ no such values exist. Thus, these values will have to be specified at the outset of the method. This can be done by simply letting S'_t and S''_t be equal to X_t or by using some average of the first few values as a starting point.

This type of initialization problem exists in all exponential smoothing methods. If the smoothing parameter α is not close to zero, the influence of the initialization process rapidly becomes of less significance as time goes by. However, if α *is* close to zero, the initialization process can play a significant role for many time periods ahead.

3/3/4 Double Exponential Smoothing: Holt's Two-Parameter Method

Holt's linear exponential smoothing method is similar in principle to Brown's except that it does not apply the straightforward double smoothing formula. Instead, it smooths the trend values separately. This provides greater flexibility, since it allows the trend to be smoothed with a different parameter than that used on the original series. The forecast for Holt's linear exponential smoothing is found using two smoothing constants (with values between 0 and 1) and three equations:

$$S_t = \alpha X_t + (1 - \alpha)(S_{t-1} + b_{t-1}), \tag{3-34}$$

$$b_t = \gamma(S_t - S_{t-1}) + (1 - \gamma)b_{t-1}, \tag{3-35}$$

$$F_{t+m} = S_t + b_t m. \tag{3-36}$$

Equation (3-34) adjusts S_t directly for the trend of the previous period, b_{t-1}, by adding it to the last smoothed value, S_{t-1}. This helps to eliminate the lag and brings S_t to the approximate base of the current data value. Equation (3-35) then updates the trend, which is expressed as the difference between the last two smoothed values. This is appropriate because if there is a trend in the data, new values should be higher or lower than the previous ones. Since there may be some randomness remaining, it is modified by smoothing with γ (gamma) the trend in the last period $(S_t - S_{t-1})$, and adding that to the previous estimate of the trend multiplied by $(1 - \gamma)$. Thus, (3-35) is similar to the basic form of single smoothing given by equation (3-19) but applies to the updating of the trend. Finally, equation (3-36) is used to forecast ahead. The trend, b_t, is multiplied by the number of periods ahead to be forecast, m, and added to the base value, S_t.

Using the data shown in Table 3-7, Table 3-8 shows the application of Holt's linear smoothing to a series with trend. The calculations involved can be illustrated by first looking at a forecast for period 23, using $\alpha = .2$ and $\gamma = .3$:

$$F_{23} = S_{22} + b_{22}(1), \qquad \text{[using (3-36)]}$$

where

$$
\begin{aligned}
S_{22} &= .2X_{22} + .8(S_{21} + b_{21}) &&\text{[using (3-34)]}\\
&= .2(242) + .8(233.11 + 5.43) = 239.23,\\
b_{22} &= .3(S_{22} - S_{21}) + .7b_{21} &&\text{[using (3-35)]}\\
&= .3(239.23 - 233.11) + .7(5.43) = 5.63.
\end{aligned}
$$

Thus,

$$F_{23} = 239.23 + 5.63(1) = 244.87.$$

Similarly the forecast for period 24 is

$$F_{24} = 243.70 + 5.28(1) = 248.98,$$

since

$$S_{23} = .2(239) + .8(239.23 + 5.63) = 243.70$$

and

$$b_{23} = .3(243.70 - 239.23) + .7(5.63) = 5.28.$$

Finally, the forecasts for periods 25, 26, and 30 can be computed as

$$F_{25} = 252.39 + 6.30(1) = 258.69,$$

$$F_{26} = 252.39 + 6.30(2) = 264.99,$$

$$F_{30} = 252.39 + 6.30(6) = 290.19.$$

The initialization process for Holt's linear exponential smoothing requires two estimates—one to get the first smoothed value for S_1 and the other to get the trend b_1. The first is easy. Choose $S_1 = X_1$. The trend estimate is sometimes more of a problem. We need an estimate of trend from one period to another. Here are some possibilities:

$$b_1 = X_2 - X_1,$$

TABLE 3-8 APPLICATION OF HOLT'S TWO-PARAMETER LINEAR EXPONENTIAL SMOOTHING ($\alpha = .2$, $\gamma = .3$) USING DATA FROM TABLE 3-7

	Period	(1) Inventory Demand for Product E15	(4) Smoothing of Data (3-34)	(5) Smoothing of Trend (3-35)	(6) Forecast When $m = 1$ (3-36)	
	1	143.00	143.00	9.00		
	2	152.00	152.00	9.00		
	3	161.00	161.00	9.00	161.00	
	4	139.00	163.80	7.14	170.00	
	5	137.00	164.15	5.10	170.94	
	6	174.00	170.20	5.38	169.25	
	7	142.00	168.87	3.37	175.59	
	8	141.00	165.99	1.49	172.24	
	9	162.00	166.39	1.16	167.49	
	10	180.00	170.05	1.91	167.56	
	11	164.00	170.37	1.43	171.96	
	12	171.00	171.64	1.38	171.80	
T	13	206.00	179.62	3.36	173.03	
E	14	193.00	184.99	3.96	182.99	
S	15	207.00	192.56	5.04	188.96	
T	16	218.00	201.69	6.27	197.61	
	17	229.00	212.17	7.53	207.96	
S	18	225.00	220.76	7.85	219.70	
E	19	204.00	223.69	6.37	228.61	
T	20	227.00	229.45	6.19	230.06	
	21	223.00	233.11	5.43	235.64	
	22	242.00	239.23	5.63	238.54	
	23	239.00	243.70	5.28	244.87	
	24	266.00	252.39	6.30	248.98	
	25				258.69	($m = 1$)
	26				264.99	($m = 2$)
	27				271.31	($m = 3$)
	28				277.61	($m = 4$)
	29				283.92	($m = 5$)
	30				290.19	($m = 6$)

Analysis of Errors From Period 10 to Period 24

5.71	= Mean Error	248.53	= Mean Square Error (MSE)
13.04	= Mean Absolute Error	1.28	= Durbin-Watson Statistic
6.16	= Mean Absolute Percentage Error (MAPE)	.90	= Theil's U Statistic
15.21	= Standard Deviation of Error (Unbiased)	310.45	= McLaughlin's Batting Average

$$b_1 = \frac{(X_2 - X_1) + (X_3 - X_2) + (X_4 - X_3)}{3},$$

b_1 = an "eyeball" slope estimate after plotting the data.

When the data are well behaved it will not matter much, but the inventory data in Table 3-8 shows a dramatic *drop* from period 3 to 4. If this change, $(X_4 - X_3)$, is involved in an initial slope estimate, it could take the forecasting system a long time to overcome the influence of such a large downward shift when the overall trend is upwards.

3/3/5   Triple Exponential Smoothing: Brown's One-Parameter Quadratic Method

Just as linear exponential smoothing can be used to predict data with a basic trend pattern, higher forms of smoothing can be used when the basic underlying pattern of the data is quadratic, cubic, or higher order. To go from linear to quadratic smoothing, the basic approach is to incorporate an additional level of smoothing (triple smoothing) and to deal with a quadratic forecasting equation. (Similarly, one could go from quadratic to cubic and so on for higher orders of smoothing.)

The equations for quadratic smoothing are

$$S'_t = \alpha X_t + (1 - \alpha)S'_{t-1} \quad \text{(first smoothing)}, \tag{3-37}$$

$$S''_t = \alpha S'_t + (1 - \alpha)S''_{t-1} \quad \text{(second smoothing)}, \tag{3-38}$$

$$S'''_t = \alpha S''_t + (1 - \alpha)S'''_{t-1} \quad \text{(third smoothing)}, \tag{3-39}$$

$$a_t = 3S'_t - 3S''_t + S'''_t \tag{3-40}$$

$$b_t = \frac{\alpha}{2(1 - \alpha)^2} [(6 - 5\alpha)S'_t - (10 - 8\alpha)S''_t + (4 - 3\alpha)S'''_t], \tag{3-41}$$

$$c_t = \frac{\alpha^2}{(1 - \alpha)^2} (S'_t - 2S''_t + S'''_t), \tag{3-42}$$

and

$$F_{t+m} = a_t + b_t m + \tfrac{1}{2}c_t m^2. \tag{3-43}$$

The equations required for quadratic smoothing are considerably more complicated than those for single and linear smoothing. However, the approach is the same in seeking to adjust the forecast values so they will follow changes in quadratic trends. The detailed derivation of equations (3-37) through (3-43) are given in Brown (1963, pp. 140–42).

As an application of quadratic smoothing the same data used in Tables 3-7 and 3-8 are presented in Table 3-9. The calculations required to

TABLE 3-9 APPLICATION OF BROWN'S QUADRATIC EXPONENTIAL SMOOTHING USING DATA FROM TABLE 3-7

	Period	Inventory Demand Product E15	Single Smoothing (3-37)	Double Smoothing (3-38)	Triple Smoothing (3-39)	Value of a (3-40)	Value of b (3-41)	Value of c (3-42)	Forecast (3-43)
	1	143.00	143.00	143.00	143.00				
	2	152.00	144.35	143.20	143.03	146.47	.561	.030	
	3	161.00	146.84	143.74	143.13	152.43	1.463	.077	147.05
	4	139.00	145.67	144.03	143.27	148.17	.608	.027	153.93
	5	137.00	144.37	144.08	143.39	144.24	−.101	−.012	148.79
	6	174.00	148.81	144.79	143.60	155.65	1.750	.088	144.13
	7	142.00	147.79	145.24	143.85	151.49	.873	.035	157.45
	8	141.00	146.77	145.47	144.09	147.99	.199	−.002	152.38
	9	162.00	149.05	146.01	144.38	153.51	1.058	.044	148.18
	10	180.00	153.69	147.16	144.80	164.40	2.689	.129	154.59
	11	164.00	155.24	148.37	145.33	165.93	2.621	.119	167.15
	12	171.00	157.60	149.76	146.00	169.53	2.889	.127	168.61
T	13	206.00	164.86	152.02	146.90	185.42	5.109	.240	172.49
E	14	193.00	169.08	154.58	148.05	191.55	5.496	.248	190.65
S	15	207.00	174.77	157.61	149.49	200.96	6.357	.281	197.17
T	16	218.00	181.25	161.16	151.24	211.53	7.296	.316	207.46
	17	229.00	188.41	165.24	153.34	222.85	8.238	.350	218.98
S	18	225.00	193.90	169.54	155.77	228.84	8.198	.329	231.26
E	19	204.00	195.42	173.42	158.42	224.39	6.454	.217	237.21
T	20	227.00	200.15	177.43	161.27	229.43	6.424	.204	230.95
	21	223.00	203.58	181.36	164.28	230.95	5.819	.160	235.95
	22	242.00	209.34	185.55	167.47	238.84	6.301	.177	236.85
	23	239.00	213.79	189.79	170.82	242.82	6.089	.156	245.23
	24	266.00	221.62	194.56	174.38	255.55	7.308	.214	248.99
	25								262.97

Analysis of Errors from Period 10 to Period 24

3.36 = Mean Error	251.81 = Mean Square Error (MSE)
12.13 = Mean Absolute Error	1.53 = Durbin-Watson Statistic
5.77 = Mean Absolute Percentage Error (MAPE)	.92 = Theil's U Statistic
16.05 = Standard Deviation of Error (Unbiased)	307.50 = McLaughlin's Batting Average

develop Table 3-9 can be illustrated through preparation of a forecast for period 24. The first step is to compute a_{23}, b_{23} and c_{23}, which requires values for S'_{23}, S''_{23}, and S'''_{23}. Assuming $\alpha = .15$, these are computed as

$$S'_{23} = .15(239) + .85(209.3) = 213.8, \qquad \text{[using (3-37)]}$$

$$S''_{23} = .15(213.8) + .85(185.6) = 189.8, \qquad \text{[using (3-38)]}$$

$$S'''_{23} = .15(189.8) + .85(167.5) = 170.8, \qquad \text{[using (3-39)]}$$

and a_t, b_t, and c_t are computed as

$$a_{23} = 3(213.8) - 3(189.8) + 170.8 = 242.8, \qquad \text{[using (3-40)]}$$

$$b_{23} = \frac{.15}{2(.85)^2}([6 - 5(.15)]\,213.8 - [10 - 8(.15)]\,189.8$$

$$+ [4 - 3(.15)]\,170.8)$$

$$= 1.038[(6 - .75)\,213.8 - (10 - 1.2)\,189.8 + (4 - .45)\,170.8]$$

$$= .1038(1122.45 - 1670.24 + 606.34) = 6.07, \qquad \text{[using (3-41)]}$$

$$c_{23} = \frac{.15^2}{.85^2}(213.8 - 2(189.8) + 170.8) = .1557. \qquad \text{[using (3-42)]}$$

Thus

$$F_{24} = 242.8 + 6.07(1) + \tfrac{1}{2}(.1557)(1^2) = 248.99. \qquad \text{[using (3-43)]}$$

Similarly, the forecast for period 25 is computed as

$$F_{25} = 255.6 + 7.3(1) + \tfrac{1}{2}(.2)(1^2) = 262.97,$$

since $a_{24} = 255.6$, $b_{24} = 7.3$, and $c_{24} = 2$ (from Table 3-9). Finally, forecasts for periods 26 and 30 can be computed as

$$F_{26} = 255.6 + 7.3(2) + \tfrac{1}{2}(.2)(2^2) = 270.60,$$

$$F_{30} = 255.6 + 7.3(6) + \tfrac{1}{2}(.2)(6^2) = 303.26.$$

The initialization process for Brown's quadratic exponential smoothing process can be very simple. Setting

$$S'_1 = S''_1 = S'''_1 = X_1$$

is all that is necessary to start forecasting from period 2 onwards. That is to say, at period 2, the values of S'_2, S''_2, and S'''_2 can be computed using equations (3-37), (3-38), and (3-39), from which values of a_2, b_2, and c_2 can be calculated using equations (3-40), (3-41), and (3-42), and then the forecast, F_3, can be obtained using equation (3-43). However, with this method, it is not a simple matter to follow the impact of the initialization process on future forecasts.

3/3/6   Triple Exponential Smoothing: Winters' Three-Parameter Trend and Seasonality Method

The set of moving average and exponential smoothing methods examined thus far in this chapter can deal with almost any type of stationary or nonstationary data as long as the data are nonseasonal. When seasonality does exist, however, these methods may do a poor job of forecasting.

As an illustration, consider applying the methods of single and linear exponential smoothing to the seasonal data in Table 3-10. These data are for quarterly exports of a French company from 1970 through 1976, and they are plotted in Figure 3-11. Note the pronounced seasonality.

Table 3-11 shows the forecasts and the errors (actual minus forecast) that result, and it is easy to see that a systematic error pattern exists. The errors are all positive, except for negative values that occur every fourth period. (There is an exception at period 21, due to randomness.) Clearly such a data series requires the use of a seasonal method if the systematic pattern in the errors is to be eliminated. Winters' trend and seasonal smoothing is such a method.

The example in Table 3-11 raises the important concern of selecting the best smoothing method for a given data series. Using single exponential smoothing with an optimal parameter, $\alpha = .35$, the MAPE and MSE measures are 13.05 percent and 9359, respectively, for the test set 10–24. If Brown's one-parameter linear exponential smoothing is used with an optimal parameter value, $\alpha = .20$, the MAPE and MSE values are 12.14 percent and

TABLE 3-10   QUARTERLY SALES DATA

	Quarter	Period	Sales (thousands of francs)		Quarter	Period	Sales (thousands of francs)
1970	1	1	362	1973	1	13	544
	2	2	385		2	14	582
	3	3	432		3	15	681
	4	4	341		4	16	557
1971	1	5	382	1974	1	17	628
	2	6	409		2	18	707
	3	7	498		3	19	773
	4	8	387		4	20	592
1972	1	9	473	1975	1	21	627
	2	10	513		2	22	725
	3	11	582		3	23	854
	4	12	474		4	24	661

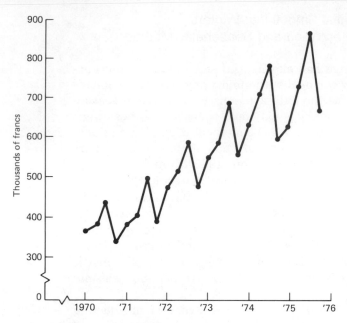

FIGURE 3-11   GRAPH OF QUARTERLY SALES DATA

7540, respectively. There is some advantage to using a method such as Brown's, which explicitly takes trend into account, but there is clearly room for improvement.

If the data are stationary, then moving averages or single exponential smoothing methods are appropriate. If the data exhibit a linear trend, either Brown's or Holt's linear models are appropriate. But if the data are seasonal, these methods, on their own, cannot handle the problem well.[8] Winters' method, however, can handle seasonality directly.[9]

The Winters method is based on three smoothing equations—one for stationarity, one for trend, and one for seasonality. It is similar to Holt's method, with one additional equation to deal with seasonality. The basic equations for Winters' method are as follows:

OVERALL SMOOTHING

$$S_t = \alpha \frac{X_t}{I_{t-L}} + (1 - \alpha)(S_{t-1} + b_{t-1}), \qquad (3\text{-}44)$$

---

[8]Of course, the data could be deseasonalized first by some other procedure. See Chapter 4 for details.

[9]Note that in the next section (3/3/7), Winter's method is just one of several exponential smoothing methods that can handle seasonality. See Table 3-13 and note that Winter's method refers to Pegel's B-3 cell: that is, it handles additive (linear) trend and multiplicative (nonlinear) seasonality.

TABLE 3-11   APPLICATION OF SINGLE AND LINEAR EXPONENTIAL SMOOTHING TO SEASONAL DATA

		Actual	(α = .35) Single Smoothing		(α = .2) Linear Smoothing	
	Period	Actual	Forecast	Error	Forecast	Error
	1	362.00				
	2	385.00	362.00	23.00		
	3	432.00	370.05	61.95	371.20	60.80
	4	341.00	391.73	−50.73	396.44	−55.44
	5	382.00	373.98	8.02	377.62	4.38
	6	409.00	376.78	32.22	380.50	28.50
	7	498.00	388.06	109.94	393.21	104.79
	8	387.00	426.54	−39.54	437.58	−50.58
	9	473.00	412.70	60.30	423.99	49.01
	10	513.00	433.81	79.19	448.21	64.79
	11	582.00	461.52	120.48	480.70	101.30
	12	474.00	503.69	−29.69	530.39	−56.39
T	13	544.00	493.30	50.70	521.06	22.94
E	14	582.00	511.04	70.96	541.20	40.80
S	15	681.00	535.88	145.12	569.40	111.60
T	16	557.00	586.67	−29.67	627.56	−70.56
	17	628.00	576.29	51.71	617.31	10.69
S	18	707.00	594.39	112.61	636.75	70.25
E	19	773.00	633.80	139.20	680.43	92.57
T	20	592.00	682.52	−90.52	735.85	−143.85
	21	627.00	650.84	−23.84	700.41	−73.41
	22	725.00	642.49	82.51	687.39	37.61
	23	854.00	671.37	182.63	715.84	138.16
	24	661.00	735.29	−74.29	786.02	−125.02
	25		709.29		756.45	

Analysis of Errors from Period 10 to Period 24

	Single	Linear
Mean Error	52.47	14.76
Mean Absolute Error	85.54	77.33
Mean Absolute Percentage Error (MAPE)	13.05	12.14
Standard Deviation of Error (Unbiased)	84.13	88.57
Mean Square Error (MSE)	9359.21	7539.65
Durbin-Watson Statistic	1.59	2.07
Theil's *U* Statistic	1.01	.86
McLaughlin's Batting Average	299.05	313.73

TREND SMOOTHING

$$b_t = \gamma(S_t - S_{t-1}) + (1 - \gamma)b_{t-1}, \tag{3-45}$$

SEASONAL SMOOTHING

$$I_t = \beta\frac{X_t}{S_t} + (1 - \beta)I_{t-L}, \tag{3-46}$$

FORECAST

$$F_{t+m} = (S_t + b_t m)I_{t-L+m}. \tag{3-47}$$

where L is the length of seasonality (e.g., number of months or quarters in a year), b is the trend component, I is the seasonal adjustment factor, and F_{t+m} is the forecast for m periods ahead.

Equation (3-46) is comparable to a seasonal index that is found as a ratio of the current values of the series, X_t, divided by the current single smoothed value for the series, S_t. If X_t is larger than S_t, the ratio will be greater than 1, while if it is smaller than S_t, the ratio will be less than 1. Important to understanding this method is realizing that S_t is a smoothed (average) value of the series that does not include seasonality. The data values X_t, on the other hand, do contain seasonality. It must also be remembered that X_t includes any randomness in the series. In order to smooth this randomness, equation (3-46) weights the newly computed seasonal factor with β and the most recent seasonal number corresponding to the same season with $(1 - \beta)$. (This prior seasonal factor was computed in period $t - L$, since L is the length of seasonality.)

Equation (3-45) is exactly the same as Holt's equation (3-35) for smoothing the trend. Equation (3-44) differs slightly from Holt's equation (3-34) in that the first term is divided by the seasonal number I_{t-L}. This is done to deseasonalize (eliminate seasonal fluctuations from) X_t. This adjustment can be illustrated by considering the case when I_{t-L} is greater than 1, which occurs when the value in period $t - L$ is greater than average in its seasonality. Dividing X_t by this number greater than 1 gives a value that is smaller than the original value by a percentage just equal to the amount that the seasonality of period $t - L$ was higher than average. The opposite adjustment occurs when the seasonality number is less than 1. The value I_{t-L} is used in these calculations because I_t cannot be calculated until S_t is known from (3-44).

The data of Table 3-10 can be used to illustrate the application of Winters' method. With parameter values of $\alpha = .2$, $\beta = .05$ and $\gamma = .1$, forecasts and related smoothed values are as shown in Table 3-12.

The computations involved in this method can be illustrated for Period 24 as follows:

$$F_{24} = [S_{23} + b_{23}(1)]I_{20} \qquad \text{[using (3-47)]}$$

$$= (726.41 + 17.17).89 = 668.94$$

TABLE 3-12 APPLICATION OF WINTERS' LINEAR AND SEASONAL EXPONENTIAL SMOOTHING TO SEASONAL DATA ($\alpha = .2$, $\beta = .05$, $\gamma = .1$) IN TABLE 3-10

	Period	Actual	Single Smoothing (3-44)	Seasonal Smoothing (3-46)	Trend Smoothing (3-45)	Forecast when $m = 1$ (3-47)
	1	362.00		.95		
	2	385.00		1.01		
	3	432.00		1.13		
	4	341.00	394.62	.89	9.75	
	5	382.00	403.69	.95	9.68	
	6	409.00	411.44	1.01	9.48	418.82
	7	498.00	424.35	1.13	9.83	478.53
	8	387.00	433.60	.89	9.77	389.62
	9	473.00	454.03	.95	10.83	422.23
	10	513.00	473.26	1.01	11.67	470.54
	11	582.00	490.17	1.14	12.20	552.19
	12	474.00	507.57	.89	12.72	450.69
T	13	544.00	529.94	.96	13.68	497.80
E	14	582.00	549.49	1.01	14.27	552.22
S	15	681.00	570.37	1.14	14.93	643.32
T	16	557.00	592.16	.90	15.61	526.16
	17	628.00	617.02	.96	16.54	583.63
S	18	707.00	645.75	1.02	17.76	644.94
E	19	773.00	665.98	1.14	18.00	758.90
T	20	592.00	678.59	.89	17.46	616.31
	21	627.00	687.05	.96	16.56	670.41
	22	725.00	704.80	1.02	16.68	718.96
	23	854.00	726.41	1.14	17.17	825.81
	24	661.00	741.82	.89	17.00	668.94
	25			.96		728.94
	26			1.02		793.00
	27					908.70
	28					728.18

Analysis of Errors from Period 10 to Period 24

21.27 = Mean Error		1200.77 = Mean Square Error (MSE)
31.36 = Mean Absolute Error		.55 = Durbin-Watson Statistic
5.13 = Mean Absolute Percentage Error (MAPE)		.40 = Theil's U Statistic
28.31 = Standard Deviation of Error (Unbiased)		360.15 = McLaughlin's Batting Average

$$S_{24} = .2\frac{X_{24}}{I_{20}} + .8(S_{23} + b_{23}) \qquad \text{[using (3-44)]}$$

$$= .2\frac{661}{.89} + .8(726.41 + 17.17) = 741.82$$

$$b_{24} = .1(S_{24} - S_{23}) + .9b_{23} \qquad \text{[using (3-45)]}$$

$$= .1(741.82 - 726.41) + .9(17.17) = 17.00$$

$$I_{24} = .05\frac{X_{24}}{S_{24}} + .95I_{20} \qquad \text{[using (3-46)}$$

$$= .05\frac{661}{741.82} + .95(.89) = .89$$

Forecasts for periods 25, 26, 27, and 28, would then be:

$$F_{25} = [741.82 + 17.00(1)](.96) = 728.94,$$

$$F_{26} = [741.82 + 17.00(2)](1.02) = 793.00,$$

$$F_{27} = [741.82 + 17.00(3)](1.14) = 908.70,$$

$$F_{28} = [741.82 + 17.00(4)](.89) = 728.18.$$

One of the problems in using Winters' method is determining those values for α, β, and γ that will minimize MSE or MAPE. The approach for determining these values is usually trial and error, although it might be possible to use nonlinear optimization algorithms to give optimal parameter values. Since either approach is time-consuming and costly, this method may not be applied as often as it should be. This is especially true if there are many data sets to handle.

To initialize the Winters forecasting method described above, we need to use at least one complete season's data (i.e., L periods) to determine initial estimates of the seasonal indices, I_{t-L}, and we need to estimate the trend factor from one period to the next. To do the latter it is convenient to use two complete seasons (i.e., $2L$ periods) as follows:

$$b = \frac{1}{L}\left[\frac{(X_{L+1} - X_1)}{L} + \frac{(X_{L+2} - X_2)}{L} + \cdots + \frac{(X_{L+L} - X_L)}{L}\right]. \qquad (3-48)$$

(each of these terms is an estimate of the trend over one complete season, and the initial estimate of b is taken as the average of L such terms)

Other methods for initializing can be created and their influence on later forecasts will depend on the length of the time series and the values of the three parameters.

Refer to Section 3/3/8 to see a comprehensive comparison of methods applied to the seasonal data in Table 3-10.

3/3/7 Exponential Smoothing: Pegels' Classification

An important consideration in dealing with exponential smoothing methods that deal with separate trend and seasonal aspects is whether or not the model should be additive (linear) or multiplicative (nonlinear). Pegels has provided a simple but useful framework for discussing these matters (as already indicated in Figure 3-4) and his two-way classification is as follows:

		Seasonal Component		
		1 (none)	2 (additive)	3 (multiplicative)
Trend Component	A (none)	$A - 1$	$A - 2$	$A - 3$
	B (additive)	$B - 1$	$B - 2$	$B - 3$
	C (multiplicative)	$C - 1$	$C - 2$	$C - 3$

Converting Pegels' notation to that of this chapter note that all nine exponential smoothing models can be summarized by the formula:

$$S_t = \alpha P + (1 - \alpha)Q, \tag{3-49}$$

where P and Q vary according to which of the cells this smoothed value S_t belongs to. Table 3-13 shows the appropriate P and Q values, and the definitions of the additive trend component (A_t), the multiplicative trend component (B_t), the additive seasonal component (C_t), and the multiplicative seasonal component (D_t).

In order to forecast ahead m periods using the Pegels' classification the formulas are as shown in Table 3-14. Note that, with a couple of notational changes, cell B-3 describes the Winters model, which was explained in detail in Section 3/3/6.

To work through an example of one of the other cells, consider cell C-3, which refers to an exponential smoothing model that allows for mul-

TABLE 3-13 THE SYMBOLS USED IN EQUATION (3-49)
AND THEIR DEFINITIONS

		Seasonal Component		
		1 (none)	2 (additive)	3 (multiplicative)
A (none)	$P =$ $Q =$	X_t S_{t-1}	$X_t - C_{t-L}$ S_{t-1}	X_t/D_{t-L} S_{t-1}
B (additive)	$P =$ $Q =$	X_t $S_{t-1} + A_{t-1}$	$X_t - C_{t-L}$ $S_{t-1} + A_{t-1}$	X_t/D_{t-L} $S_{t-1} + A_{t-1}$
C (multiplicative)	$P =$ $Q =$	X_t $S_{t-1}B_{t-1}$	$X_t - C_{t-L}$ $S_{t-1}B_{t-1}$	X_t/D_{t-L} $S_{t-1}B_{t-1}$

Trend Component

where X_t = actual data
S_t = smoothed data [equation (3-49)] $= \alpha P + (1 - \alpha)Q$
A_t = $\beta(S_t - S_{t-1}) + (1 - \beta)A_{t-1}$ (additive trend)
B_t = $\gamma(S_t/S_{t-1})$ $+ (1 - \gamma)B_{t-1}$ (multiplicative trend)
C_t = $\delta(X_t - S_t)$ $+ (1 - \delta)C_{t-L}$ (additive seasonal)
D_t = $\theta(X_t/S_t)$ $+ (1 - \theta)D_{t-L}$ (multiplicative seasonal)
α, β, γ, δ, and θ are all restricted to lie between 0 and 1.

tiplicative trend and multiplicative seasonality. Equation (3-49) says the smoothed value S_t is given by

$$S_t = \alpha P + (1 - \alpha)Q.$$

Table 3-13 identifies the proper P and Q values:

$$P = X_t/D_{t-L},$$

$$Q = S_{t-1}B_{t-1},$$

and the expressions for B and D are also identified. Putting these all together yields the C-3 model equations, as follows:

$$S_t = \alpha(X_t/D_{t-L}) + (1 - \alpha)\, S_{t-1}B_{t-1}, \tag{3-50}$$

$$B_t = \gamma(S_t/S_{t-1}) + (1 - \gamma)\, B_{t-1}, \tag{3-51}$$

$$D_t = \theta(X_t/S_t) + (1 - \theta)\, D_{t-L}, \tag{3-52}$$

TABLE 3-14 FORECASTING m PERIODS AHEAD USING THE PEGELS'
CLASSIFICATION SCHEME[a]

	Seasonal Component		
	1 (none)	2 (additive)	3 (multiplicative)
A (none)	S_t	$S_t + C_{t-L+m}$	$S_t D_{t-L+m}$
B (additive)	$S_t + mA_t$	$S_t + mA_t + C_{t-L+m}$	$(S_t + mA_t)D_{t-L+m}$
C (multiplicative)	$S_t B_t^m$	$S_t B_t^m + C_{t-L+m}$	$S_t D_{t-L+m} B_t^m$

Trend Component (row label spanning A, B, C)

[a]The cell entries are values of F_{t+m}.

and if we wish to forecast m periods ahead, Table 3-14 shows that the
forecast is:

$$F_{t+m} = S_t D_{t-L+m} B_t^m. \tag{3-53}$$

By way of illustration, Table 3-15 shows three error measures—MAPE,
MSE, and Theil's U—for each of Pegels' nine models, when applied to the
seasonal data in Table 3-10. In all cases, the parameter values were set to
.2 (arbitrarily)—that is, no attempt was made to optimize the models. Note
in passing that cell B-3 (Winters' method) shows improved MAPE, MSE,
and U measures over those seen in Table 3-12. Clearly, the choice of .2 for
all three parameters is a better choice than .2, .15, and .1 for the random,
trend, and seasonal smoothings, respectively. Optimal parameter values for
all methods will be given in section 3/5.

3/4 Other Smoothing Methods

In addition to the smoothing methods discussed so far, many others
have been proposed. Some of these involve extensive computations and are
mathematically complicated, so they have not been adopted as practical
methods. What follows is a brief look at a few of these other methods.

TABLE 3-15 APPLICATION OF THE NINE MODELS IN PEGELS'
CLASSIFICATION TO THE DATA OF TABLE 3-10

		Seasonal Component		
		1 (none)	2 (additive)	3 (multiplicative)
Trend Component	A (none)	MAPE = 14.40 MSE = 13416 U = 1.24	MAPE = 11.71 MSE = 6751 U = .91	MAPE = 11.80 MSE = 6143 U = .87
	B (additive)	MAPE = 10.15 MSE = 6065 U = .75	MAPE = 5.66 MSE = 1687 U = .44	MAPE = 4.56 MSE = 1049 U = .37
	C (multiplicative)	MAPE = 10.33 MSE = 6380 U = .76	MAPE = 5.54 MSE = 1978 U = .46	MAPE = 4.78 MSE = 1308 U = .40

Note: For all models, the value of all parameters was set (arbitrarily) to .2 for this illustration.

3/4/1 Chow's Adaptive Control Method

Chow's method is similar in philosophy to ARRSES described in Section 3/3/2 but has the additional feature that it can be used for nonstationary data. However, the way that α_t is adjusted in Chow's method is not at all similar to that used in the ARRSES equation (3-24). Rather, α_t is "adapted" by small increments (usually .05) so as to minimize the MSE. The equations of Chow's adaptive smoothing are

$$S_t = \alpha_t X_t + (1 - \alpha_t)S_{t-1}, \tag{3-54}$$

$$b_t = \alpha_t(S_t - S_{t-1}) + (1 - \alpha_t)b_{t-1}, \tag{3-55}$$

and

$$F_{t+1} = S + \frac{(1 - \alpha_t)}{\alpha_t}\, b_t. \tag{3-56}$$

3/4/2 Brown's One-Parameter Adaptive Method

Brown's one-parameter adaptive method involving a single smoothing constant (with a value between 0 and 1) is very general and has given satisfactory performance in practical situations (Brown, 1959). The computations used in this method are as follows:

$$S_t = S_{t-1} + b_{t-1} + (1 - \delta^2)e_t, \qquad (3\text{-}57)$$

$$b_t = b_{t-1} + (1 - \delta)^2 e_t, \qquad (3\text{-}58)$$

where $e_t = X_t - F_t$, δ is the smoothing constant, and

$$F_{t+m} = S_t + b_t m. \qquad (3\text{-}59)$$

Equation (3-57) differs from the computations used by many other methods in that it does not smooth previous values of S_t, but rather it smooths the current value of the errors. This approach is a different way of formulating the forecasts, which can be combined with that of formulating the forecast based on previous values of the series. As will be shown in Part Four, the combination of these two approaches provides a complete range of possible methodologies.

3/4/3   Box-Jenkins Three-Parameter Smoothing

This smoothing method developed by Box and Jenkins (1962) is based on the principle of smoothing errors—both present and past—as is Brown's adaptive method. Values of three parameters—θ_{-1}, θ_0, and θ_1—are determined so as to minimize the MSE. The Box and Jenkins three-parameter model is optimal, in the linear least squares sense, and can be used for either stationary or nonstationary data. However, its main weakness is that it requires considerable computing for forecasting. The single equation needed is

$$F_{t+m} = F_t + \theta_{-1}(e_t - e_{t-1}) + \theta_0 e_t + \theta_1 \sum_{t=1}^{n} e_t. \qquad (3\text{-}60)$$

3/4/4   Harrison's Harmonic Smoothing Method

Harrison's harmonic smoothing (HHS) method is an attempt to introduce additional mathematical sophistication into the smoothing field while maintaining most of the conceptual simplicity of smoothing methods. HHS is based on the use of Fourier transformations,[10] a methodology used by

---

[10]Equally spaced time-series observations can be closely approximated by fitting Fourier functions of the following form:

$$Y_i = \frac{a_0}{2} + \sum_{j=1}^{n} (a_j \cos jt_i + b_j \sin jt_i),$$

where $t_i = 2\pi i/(2n + 1)$ and $i = 0, 1, 2, \ldots, 2n$. Here we assume that the number of observations is an odd number, $2n + 1$, and effectively we are fitting n sine waves to the time series. See Chapter 8 for some further details.

many early statisticians in their attempts to forecast. Harrison's method avoids the original shortcomings of Fourier transformations, by averaging several of them and using this average for forecasting purposes.

The HHS method requires considerable computation at the outset and requires a knowledge of Fourier transformations to be understood. However, once the original computations are done, their updating is fairly easy. An advantage of the method is that it optimizes the parameters automatically, and thus can be used with no outside interference. Its disadvantage is that the computational costs are considerable and its data requirements significant. Additional background information can be found in Harrison (1967) and completed examples are shown in Makridakis and Wheelwright (1977).

3/4/5   Trigg's Monitoring System (Tracking Signal)

A final smoothing method that should be mentioned is Trigg's monitoring system (tracking signal). While not a forecasting method by itself, it has value as a means of monitoring forecasting errors and determining when the errors are no longer random. Trigg's method is based on three equations very similar to those for calculating α_t in the ARRSES approach (Section 3/3/2). These equations are

$$E_t = \beta e_t + (1 - \beta)E_{t-1}, \tag{3-61}$$

$$M_t = \beta|e_t| + (1 - \beta)M_{t-1}, \tag{3-62}$$

and

$$T_t = \frac{E_t}{M_t}, \tag{3-63}$$

where $e_t = X_t - F_t$, and T_t is the tracking signal at period t.

The tracking signal indicates nonrandom errors (with a 95 percent confidence) when the value of T_t exceeds .51 for a β of .1 or .74 for a β of .2. These values were developed by Trigg (1964); Batty (1969) subsequently developed somewhat different values.

The major characteristic of Trigg's monitor is that when used in conjunction with a forecasting method in a routine manner, it can indicate when something has gone wrong. When forecasts of a great number of items are required, this is a considerable advantage, since the calculations of equations (3-61), (3-62), and (3-63) are easily performed with only three stored values.

3/5   A Comparison of Methods

A variety of methods has been presented in this chapter, and a pragmatic question remains: How can a forecaster choose the "right" model for a data set? Human judgment has to be involved, but there are also some useful suggestions to make. A main objective is to decide on the nature of trend (if any) and seasonality (if any). If these can be identified, then the random component is not dominating. If the data are quarterly, for example, a plot of the raw data might show the nature of trend and seasonality (as in Figure 3-11). By plotting the four-month moving averages of the data, seasonality is removed, and the analyst can concentrate on trend—or maybe a combination of trend and a longer term business cycle. These matters are discussed more fully in Chapter 4.

Another approach for determining the patterns in the data is to study autocorrelations, a procedure that will be studied in detail in Chapter 8.

To round out the discussion of the major smoothing methods, consider Table 3-16, which presents the results of 15 different analyses of the same data set (see Table 3-10).

The eight column headings indicate particular measures of "fit" (as described in Chapter 2) and the following points should be noted. First, the ME (mean error) is not a very useful measure since positive and negative errors can cancel one another, as in LMA (row 3), which has the lowest ME but is clearly not a very good model for the data. Second, the MAE (mean absolute error) is a more useful measure than ME. Third, the minimum MAPE is obtained for Pegels' cell C-3 method (row 15) when optimum values for the three parameters are determined. However, parameter values that optimize MAPE do not necessarily optimize (minimize) MSE (see row 12 for instance). Fourth, the SDE (std. dev. of error) is useful but does not yield the same information as MAE. For example, compare rows 1 and 4. The SDE in row 1 is less than the SDE in row 4, but the MAEs are reversed. Since the method in row 1 yields more consistently large negative errors, the SDE is not as high as might be expected, but the MAE is large. Fifth, the MSE (mean square error) is a useful indicator but gives *absolute* information as opposed to the *relative* information in MAPE. Sixth, the Durbin-Watson statistic (D-W) is a pattern indicator—it refers to the pattern of the errors. If the pattern is random, D-W will be around 2. If there are runs of positive errors alternating with runs of negative errors, then D-W is much less than 2 (approaching a lower limit of 0). If there are rapid oscillations in errors (from positive to negative), then D-W is much greater than 2 (e.g., approaching an upper limit of 4). Note that a value near 2 is not necessarily "best." For example, row 12 shows a very good fit for the Winters model, but the D-W value is 1.23, meaning there remains some definite pattern in the errors, even though the errors themselves are small. Seventh, Theil's U measure (a compromise between absolute and relative measures) is very useful. In row 1, $U = 1.81$, indicting a poor fit, far worse than the "naive model," which would simply use last period's datum as the forecast for the next period. In row 7 the SES model is seen to be about as good as the naive model. Row 15 shows Pegels' cell C-3 model to be far superior ($U = .31$).

TABLE 3-16 A COMPARISON OF VARIOUS SMOOTHING METHODS APPLIED TO THE DATA IN TABLE 3-10[a]

	Mean Error (ME)	Mean Absolute Error (MAE)	Mean Abs. Percentage Error (MAPE)	Std. dev. of Error (SDE)	Mean Square Error (MSE)	Durbin-Watson Statistic (D-W)	Theil's U Statistic (U)	McLaughlin's Batting Average (MBA)
1. Mean of all past data	157.31	157.31	23.78	78.83	30546	.37	1.81	218.73
2. Moving Average MA(4)	47.08	72.25	10.92	74.27	7365	1.54	.90	310.27
3. Linear Moving Average LMA(4)	.73	63.83	9.94	79.64	5920	2.14	.75	325.44
4. Brown's Linear Method (α = .2)	14.76	77.33	12.14	88.57	7539	2.07	.86	313.73
5. Brown's Quad. Method (α = .12)	6.51	74.40	11.78	88.94	7425	2.03	.85	314.82
6. Holt's Method (α = .06, γ = .36)	.41	59.04	9.15	73.72	5072	2.27	.69	331.07
7. Pegels, Cell A-1 (and SES) (α = .35)	52.47	85.54	13.05	84.13	9359	1.59	1.01	299.05
8. Pegels, Cell A-2 (α = .69, δ = .85)	23.69	37.64	5.69	40.07	2060	1.29	.47	353.02
9. Pegels, Cell A-3 (α = .99, θ = .01)	13.19	25.87	4.11	31.70	1112	1.49	.38	362.31
10. Pegels, Cell B-1 (and Holt's) (α = .06, β = .36)	.41	59.04	9.15	73.72	5072	2.27	.69	331.07
11. Pegels, Cell B-2 (α = .46, β = .13, δ = .99)	5.71	22.81	3.46	35.37	1200	1.42	.35	365.01
12. Pegels, Cell B-3 (and Winters) (α = .27, β = .38, θ = .25)	−.79	20.62	3.27	30.62	876	1.23	.32	368.49
13. Pegels, Cell C-1 (α = .05, γ = .86)	−1.35	60.77	9.46	75.25	5286	2.21	.70	329.51
14. Pegels, Cell C-2 (α = .43, γ = .07, δ = .99)	3.28	22.27	3.43	35.18	1166	1.37	.35	365.03
15. Pegels, Cell C-3 (α = .38, γ = .18, θ = .33)	−4.34	20.36	3.23	30.67	897	1.28	.31	368.58

[a]Note that all these error measures refer to a "test set" defined as periods 10 through 24.

Eighth, McLaughlin's batting average (MBA) is simply a linear transformation of Theil's U, but it has the appeal of ready interpretability—the higher the batting average the better the model. Ninth, there is little to choose between cells B-3 and C-3 for the data in Table 3-10, but note that optimal values for cells B-2 and C-2 have to have essentially "naive" values (almost 1) for the smoothing constant associated with additive seasonality. Note finally that Pegels' cell A-1 is merely the SES model, cell B-1 is Holt's model, and cell B-3 is Winters' model.

3/6   General Aspects of Smoothing Methods

The major advantages of widely used smoothing methods are their simplicity and low cost. There is little doubt that better accuracy can usually be obtained using the more sophisticated methods of autoregressive/moving average schemes examined in Part Four or the intuitively appealing decomposition methods discussed in Chapter 4. However, when forecasts are needed for thousands of items, as is the case in many inventory systems, smoothing methods are often the only acceptable methods.

In instances of large forecasting requirements, even small things count. For example, having to store four values instead of three for each item can mean a great deal in terms of total storage requirements when forecasts for 30,000 items are required on a monthly basis. Furthermore, the computer time needed to make the necessary calculations must be kept at a reasonable level, and the method must run with a minimum of outside interference. For these reasons, exponential smoothing methods are preferable to moving average methods, and methods with fewer parameters are preferable to those with more.

If the data series is stationary, the adaptive-response-rate single exponential smoothing is often preferred to single exponential smoothing, because the latter method requires specification of α in such a way as to minimize the MSE. This takes extra computer and management time. More importantly, the optimal α will change when there is a basic change in the pattern of the data. Thus, an additional system such as the one proposed by Trigg (see Section 3/4/5) to monitor for possible changes in the pattern of data would be required. Otherwise there would be a risk of serious forecasting errors.

Adaptive-response-rate exponential smoothing, on the other hand, adjusts itself by changing the value of α to follow basic changes in the data. Although it may take one or two periods for α to catch up with changes in the data pattern, it will eventually do so. Thus, even if the forecasts from this method are somewhat inferior to those of single exponential smoothing with an optimal α, it is often preferable because it reduces the risk of serious errors and provides a system with minimal administrative worries. The fact that adaptive-response-rate exponential smoothing is completely automatic, in addition to having the other advantages of single exponential smoothing, makes it a favored method for practical use when the data are stationary and nonseasonal.

Brown's one-parameter linear exponential smoothing (Section 3/3/3) is the method preferred for nonstationary, nonseasonal data, largely because the method has only one parameter (versus Holt's two). In addition, this parameter in practice takes on only a restricted range of values, even though theoretically α can assume any value between 0 and 1. Experience suggests that the optimal value lies in the range of .1 to .2. (See Brown 1963, pp. 106–22, 145–57.) An α of .1 makes the forecasts conservative, while an α of .2 gives a more responsive system. Given this narrowed set of choices for α, this method is usually viewed as being easier to apply.

Chow's adaptive control method (Section 3/4/1) is often described as performing the same role for linear exponential smoothing as the ARRSES (Section 3/3/2) performs for single exponential smoothing. However, this is not strictly the case because (1) Chow's method is more difficult to use and (2) α, in Brown's linear smoothing method, can be almost fixed in value.

Brown's quadratic smoothing (Section 3/3/5) is easy to use, too. It has only one parameter whose value is usually close to .1. In addition, it can predict turning points better than the linear smoothing method because it is quadratic. A weakness of quadratic smoothing is that it can overreact to random changes by assuming that they represent quadratic trends. This disadvantage can be reduced by setting α equal to a value below .1.

For seasonal data series, Winters' method is the only smoothing approach that is widely used. There are other seasonal smoothing approaches available (for example, see Groff, 1973), but there is little evidence of their use in practice.

A major weakness of Winters' method that inhibits its wider applicability is that it requires three smoothing parameters. Since each of these parameters can take on any value between 0 and 1, many combinations must be tried before the optimal values for α, β, and γ can be determined. There are alternative methods (see Roberts and Reed, 1969) that can identify the optimal parameter values, but they require considerable computations. Furthermore, once the optimal values have been found, there is no easy way to modify them when a basic change in the data has taken place. An alternative to worrying about optimal values is to find good initial estimates for equations (3-44), (3-45), and (3-46), then specify small values for α, β, and γ (around .1 to .2). The forecasting system will then react slowly but steadily to changes in the data. The disadvantage of this strategy is that it gives a low response system. However, this price is often worth paying to achieve long-term stability and to provide a general, low-cost method for forecasting all types of data.

In summary, there are many different smoothing methods, and at least one of these is usually capable of dealing with any given data pattern when that basic pattern is known. If the pattern is not known, general methods such as Pegels' cells B-2, B-3, C-2, or C-3, which can deal with a range of patterns, are required.

3/7 Development of the Mathematical Basis of Smoothing Methods

Smoothing methods were first developed in the late 1950s by operations researchers. It is unclear whether Holt (1957) or Brown (1956) was the first to introduce exponential smoothing (see Cox, 1961, p. 414), or if perhaps it was Magee (see Muth, 1960, pp. 299). Most of the important development work on exponential smoothing was completed in the late 1950s and published by the early 1960s. This work included that done by Brown (1956) and Holt (1957) and subsequent work by Magee (1958), Brown (1959), Holt et al. (1960), Winters (1960), Brown and Meyer (1961), and Brown (1963). Since that time, the concept of exponential smoothing has grown and become a practical method with wide application, mainly in the forecasting of inventories.

The basic work on exponential smoothing had two purposes: first to introduce the method to a wide audience of academicians and practitioners and persuade them of its usefulness, and second to show the theoretical soundness of the method. Support for this latter purpose was launched by Brown and Meyer (1961) and continued through the work of Nerlove and Wage (1964), Theil and Wage (1964), and several others.

The fundamental theorem of exponential smoothing was proved by Brown and Meyer (1961). It states that for any time series, X_t ($t = 0$, $1, \ldots, n$), there exists at time t a unique polynomial representing the time series:

$$F_{t+m} = a_t + b_t m + \frac{C_t}{2} m^2 + \cdots + \frac{g_t}{K'} m^K. \tag{3-64}$$

Furthermore, the coefficients of equation (3-64) can be estimated as linear combinations of the values resulting from the first $K + 1$ degrees (i.e., single, double, triple, etc.) of smoothing applied to the X_t values. The detailed proof of this theorem can be found in Brown and Meyer (1961, pp. 683–85) and Brown (1963, pp. 132–34). Estimating the values of a_t, b_t, $C_t, \ldots, g_t$ requires expressing F_{t+m} as a Taylor series expansion around t and taking K derivatives to obtain K simultaneous equations, each expressing one degree of smoothing. All smoothing methods can be derived from this fundamental theorem as special cases of multiple exponential smoothing.

An additional property of multiple exponential smoothing identified by D'Esopo (1961) is that it provides an "exponentially discounted least squares" best fit to the observed series. In Part Four it will be shown that exponential smoothing is a special case of the general class of autoregressive/moving average methods.

APPENDIX 3-A
INITIAL VALUES FOR EXPONENTIAL SMOOTHING APPROACHES

Need for Initialization

The reason initial values for the exponential smoothing methods are needed can be seen by examining the equation of single exponential smoothing:

$$F_{t+1} = \alpha X_t + (1 - \alpha)F_t, \tag{1}$$

where X_t is the most recent actual value, F_t is the latest forecast, F_{t+1} is the forecast for the next period and α is the smoothing constant.

When $t = 1$, equation (1) becomes

$$F_2 = \alpha X_1 + (1 - \alpha)F_1. \tag{2}$$

In order to get a value for F_2, F_1 must be known.

The value of F_1 should have been:

$$F_1 = \alpha X_0 + (1 - \alpha)F_0 \tag{3}$$

It can be easily seen from (3) that X_0 does not exist and F_0 cannot be found. This is precisely the problem. The value of F_1 in (2) must be known to compute F_2 but it cannot be found from the existing data. Therefore, some alternative approach is needed to estimate the initial value of F_1 in (2). In an analogous way, initial values are needed for any type of exponential smoothing; the number and type of values depend upon the particular exponential smoothing approach being used.

To some extent, the problem of an initial forecast value is academic. In practice, it arises only *once* for any series—when exponential smoothing is used for the very first time. But even the very first time that an exponential smoothing method is used the problem is more theoretical than real. When such a method is first applied, most managers will not think to use its forecasts immediately. Rather, the method will be used in parallel operation with whatever system, or manual approach, existed before. During this time, no matter what the initial values, there generally will be enough history built up for the method, that self-adjustment will take place and good values will result independent of the starting value used.

For reasons of completeness we will describe the major approaches commonly used to initialize the values of exponential smoothing methods. These approaches assume that past data are available in sufficient number to do one of the following:

1. *Separate the data into two parts:* Use the first part to estimate initial values and the second to estimate optimal parameter values. As a rule of thumb, 8 to $3(L)$ data points are adequate for initial estimation purposes (where L is the length of seasonality). Thus if sufficient data are available (i.e., more than 16 to $6(L)$, use half the data for initial estimation and half for optimal parameter estimation.

2. *Use backforecasting:* This is a method used extensively by the Box-Jenkins methodology (see Box and Jenkins, 1976, pp. 199–200), which also can be applied to exponential smoothing methods. What it involves is to invert the data series and start the estimation procedure from the latest (most recent) value and finish with the first (oldest) value. Doing so will provide forecasts and/or parameter estimates for the beginning of the data, which can be used as initial values when the data are forecast in the usual sequence, that is, from the beginning to the end.

3. *Use least squares estimates:* Initial values can also be calculated using ordinary least squares. For instance in single exponential smoothing, F_t can be found by averaging, say, 10 past values. In linear exponential smoothing, a_1 and b_1 can be found by solving the normal equations in such a way that the intercept (a_1) and the slope (b_1) can be found. In higher forms of smoothing the parameters of the corresponding higher-order polynomial can be similarly estimated by least squares.

4. *When past data do not exist:* In such cases the above mentioned approaches are not applicable. Then, the only alternative is either to wait for some values to become available, or arbitrarily to specify some initial values that make some sense and start right away with the estimation. The following values can be used when no past data are available:

   a. Single and adaptive response rate exponential smoothing

   $$F_1 = X_1.$$

   b. Brown's linear exponential smoothing

   $$S_1'' = S_1' = X_1,$$

   $$a_1 = X_1,$$

   $$b_1 = \frac{(X_2 - X_1) + (X_4 - X_3)}{2}.$$

c. Holt's linear exponential smoothing,

$$S_1 = X_1,$$

$$b_1 = \frac{(X_2 - X_1) + (X_4 - X_3)}{2}.$$

d. Brown's quadratic exponential smoothing

$$S_1''' = S_2'' = S_1' = X_1,$$

$$a_1 = X_1,$$

$$b_1 = \frac{(X_2 - X_1) + (X_3 - X_2) + (X_4 - X_3)}{3},$$

$$c_1 = \frac{X_3 - X_1}{2}.$$

e. Winters' linear and seasonal exponential smoothing,

$$S_{L+1} = X_{L+1},$$

where L is the length of seasonality

$$I_1 = X_1/\overline{X},$$

$$I_2 = X_2/\overline{X},$$

$$I_3 = X_3/\overline{X},$$

.

.

.

$$I_L = X_L/\overline{X}$$

where

$$\overline{X} = \sum_{i=1}^{L} \frac{X_i}{L}$$

$$b_{L+1} = \frac{(X_{L+1} - X_1) + (X_{L+2} - X_2) + (X_{L+3} - X_3)}{3(L)}.$$

A useful procedure when using 1. or 4. above is to specify high values for the smoothing parameters for the first part of the data in 1, or for the first 8 to 3(L) data points in 4. This will result in a fast adjustment in the various parameters and forecasts, and therefore the effect of not having optimal initial values will be minimal.

REFERENCES AND SELECTED BIBLIOGRAPHY

Batty, M. 1969. "Monitoring an Exponential Smoothing Forecasting System." *Operational Research Quarterly,* **20,** No. 3, pp. 319–23.

Box, G. E. P., and G. M. Jenkins. 1962. "Some Statistical Aspects of Adaptive Optimization and Control." *Journal of the Royal Statistical Society,* Series B, **24,** pp. 297–343.

Brown, R. G. 1956. "Exponential Smoothing for Predicting Demand." Presented at the Tenth National Meeting of the Operations Research Society of America, San Francisco, November 16, 1956.

——. 1959. *Statistical Forecasting for Inventory Control.* New York: McGraw-Hill.

——. 1963. *Smoothing, Forecasting and Prediction.* Englewood Cliffs, N.J.: Prentice-Hall.

——, and R. F. Meyer, 1961. "The Fundamental Theorem of Exponential Smoothing." *Operations Research,* **9,** No. 5, pp. 673–85.

Cox, D. R. 1961. "Prediction by Exponentially Weighted Moving Averages and Related Methods." *Journal of the Royal Statistical Society,* Series B, **23,** No. 2, pp. 414–22.

Dalrymple, D. J., and B. E. King. 1981. "Selecting Parameters for Short-term Forecasting Techniques." *Decision Sciences,* **12,** pp. 661–69.

D'Esopo, D. A. 1961. "A Note of Forecasting by the Exponential Smoothing Operator." *Operations Research,* **9,** No. 5, pp. 667–86.

Gardner, Jr., E. S., and D. G. Dannenbring. 1980. "Forecasting with Exponential Smoothing: Some Guidelines for Model Selection." *Decision Sciences,* **11,** pp. 370–83.

Geurts, M. D., and I. B. Ibrahim. 1975. "Comparing the Box-Jenkins Approach with the Exponentially Smoothed Forecasting Model Application to Hawaii Tourists." *Journal of Marketing Research,* **12,** pp. 182–88.

Groff, G. K. 1973. "Empirical Comparison of Models for Short-Range Forecasting." *Management Science,* **20,** No. 1, pp. 22–31.

Harrison, P. J. 1965. "Short-Term Sales Forecasting." *Applied Statistics,* **14,** pp. 102–39.

——. 1967. "Exponential Smoothing and Short-Term Sales Forecasting." *Management Science,* **13,** No. 11, pp. 821–42.

Holt, C. C. 1957. "Forecasting Seasonal and Trends by Exponentially Weighted Moving Averages." Office of Naval Research, Research Memorandum No. 52.

Holt, C. C., F. Modigliani, J. F. Muth, and H. A. Simon. 1960. *Planning Production Inventories and Work Force.* Englewood Cliffs, N.J.: Prentice-Hall.

Lewis, C. D. 1970. "Abbreviated Notes on Short-Term Forecasting." Birmingham, England. The University of Aston Management Centre.

——. 1975. *Demand Analysis and Inventory Control.* Lexington, Mass.: D. C. Heath & Co.

Magee, J. F. 1958. *Production Planning and Inventory Control.* New York: McGraw-Hill.

Makridakis, S., and S. Wheelwright. 1977. *Interactive Forecasting,* 2nd ed. San Francisco: Holden-Day.

Mathieu, A. 1970. "Technique de Controle de Prevision a Court Terme." *Revue Francaise d'Automatique, Informatique et Recherche Opérationnelle,* V-1, pp. 29–47.

Montgomery, D. C., and L. A. Johnson. 1976. *Forecasting and Time Series Analysis.* New York: McGraw-Hill.

Muth, J. F. 1960. "Optimal Properties of Exponentially Weighted Forecasts," *Journal of American Statistical Association,* **55,** No. 290, pp. 299–306.

Nerlove, M., and S. Wage. 1964. "On the Optimality of Adaptive Forecasting." *Management Science,* **10,** No. 2, pp. 207–24.

Pegels, C. C. 1969. "Exponential Forecasting: Some New Variations." *Management Science,* Vol. 12, No. 5, pp. 311–15.

Roberts, S. D., and R. Reed. 1969. "The Development of a Self-Adaptive Forecasting Technique." In *AIIE Transactions,* **1,** No. 4, pp. 314–22.

Theil, H., and S. Wage. 1964. "Some Observations on Adaptive Filtering." *Management Science,* **10,** No. 2, pp. 198–224.

Trigg, D. W. 1964. "Monitoring a Forecasting System." *Operational Research Quarterly,* **15,** pp. 271–74.

Trigg, D. W., and D. H. Leach. 1967. "Exponential Smoothing with an Adaptive Response Rate." *Operational Research Quarterly,* **18,** pp. 53–59.

Winters, P. R. 1960. "Forecasting Sales by Exponentially Weighted Moving Averages." *Management Science,* **6,** pp. 324–42.

Wood, D., and R. Fildes. 1976. *Forecasting for Business.* London: Longman.

EXERCISES

1. The Canadian unemployment rate as a percentage of the civilian labor force (seasonably adjusted) between 1974 and the third quarter of 1975 is shown below.

	Quarter	Unemployment Rate
1974	1	5.4
	2	5.3
	3	5.3
	4	5.6
1975	1	6.9
	2	7.2
	3	7.2

What is your estimate for unemployment in the fourth quarter of 1975? (Prepare an estimate using a single moving average with $N = 3$ and single exponential smoothing with $\alpha = .7$.)

2. The following data reflect the sales of electric knives for the period Jan. 1981 through April 1982:

1981		1982	
Jan.	19.0	Jan.	82.0
Feb.	15.0	Feb.	17.0
Mar.	39.0	Mar.	26.0
Apr.	102.0	Apr.	29.0
May	90.0		
June	29.0		
July	90.0		
Aug.	46.0		
Sept.	30.0		
Oct.	66.0		
Nov.	80.0		
Dec.	89.0		

Management wants to use both moving averages and exponential smoothing as methods for forecasting sales. Answer the following questions:

a. What will the forecasts be for May 1982 using a 3-, 5-, 7-, 9-, and 11-month moving average?

b. What will the forecasts be for May 1982 for exponential smoothing with α values of .1, .3, .5, .7, and .9?

c. Assuming that the past pattern will continue into the future, what N and α values should management select in order to minimize the errors?

3. How do the α values of .1, .3, .5, .7, and .9 weight the past observations in forecasting with single exponential smoothing? How do they do it in Brown's linear exponential smoothing? What conclusions can you make by comparing the weights of single and linear exponential smoothings?

4. Using the single randomless series 2, 4, 6, 8, 10, 12, 14, 16, 18, and 20, compute a forecast for period 11 using:

a. the method of single exponential smoothing,

b. Brown's method of linear exponential smoothing,

c. Holt's method of linear exponential smoothing.

Which of the three methods is more appropriate? Why? What value of α would you use in (a) above? How can you explain it in light of equation (3-22)? What value of α and γ do you use in (b) and (c) above? Why?

5. Using the simple randomless series 3, 6, 9, 12, 3, 6, 9, 12, 3, 6, 9, 12, apply simple exponential smoothing and Brown's quadratic exponential smoothing to forecast the 13th period. Discuss the performance of these two methods on data such as these.

6. With reference to Table 3-4, compute the MAPE over the test period 10–25 when a single moving average forecast is made. Check that the footnote to Table 3-4 is accurate.

7. The Paris Chamber of Commerce and Industry has been asked by several of its members to prepare a forecast of the French index of industrial production for its monthly newsletter. Using the monthly data given below:
   a. Compute a forecast using the methods of single and linear moving averages with 12 observations in each average.
   b. Compute the error in each forecast. How accurate would you say these forecasts are?
   c. Which is better, the single or linear moving averages?
   d. Now compute a new series of single and linear moving averages using 6 observations in each average. Compute the errors as well.
   e. Which is better, the single or linear moving averages?
   f. How do these four moving average forecasts compare? Which seems most accurate? Why?

Period	French Index of Industrial Production	Period	French Index of Industrial Production
1	108	15	98
2	108	16	97
3	110	17	101
4	106	18	104
5	108	19	101
6	108	20	99
7	105	21	95
8	100	22	95
9	97	23	96
10	95	24	96
11	95	25	97
12	92	26	98
13	95	27	94
14	95	28	92

8. The data in column 2 in the following table show the daily sales of paperback books at a bookstore, and column 3 shows the daily sales of hardcover books at the same store. The task is to forecast the next four days' sales for paperbacks and hardcover books.

DAILY SALES OF PAPERBACKS (COLUMN 2) AND HARDCOVER BOOKS
(COLUMN 3) OVER 30 DAYS AT A BOOKSTORE

(1) Day	(2) Paperbacks	(3) Hardcovers
1	199	139
2	172	128
3	111	172
4	209	139
5	161	191
6	119	168
7	195	170
8	195	145
9	131	184
10	183	135
11	143	218
12	141	198
13	168	230
14	201	222
15	155	206
16	243	240
17	225	189
18	167	222
19	237	158
20	202	178
21	186	217
22	176	261
23	232	238
24	195	240
25	190	214
26	182	200
27	222	201
28	217	283
29	188	220
30	247	259

a. Use the method of linear moving averages and compute the measures of forecasting accuracy over the test periods 11–30.
b. Repeat using the method of linear exponential smoothing (Holt's method).
c. Compare the error statistics and discuss the merits of the two forecasting methods for these data sets.
d. Compare the forecasts for the two methods and discuss their relative merits.
e. Study the Durbin-Watson statistics for the two methods applied to the two data series. Is there any noticeable pattern left in the data?

9. Using the data in Table 3-6 examine the influence of different starting values for α and different values for β, on the final value for α in period 12. Try using $\alpha = .1$ and $\alpha = .3$ in combination with β values of .1, .3, and .5. What role does β play in ARRSES?

10. Using the data in Table 3-10, use Pegels' cell C-3 to model the data. First, examine the equations that go along with this method (see Tables 3-13 and 3-14), then pick specific values for the three parameters, and compute the one-ahead forecasts. Check the error statistics for the test period 10–24 and compare with the optimal results shown in Table 3-16. If you have access to a computer program to develop optimal values for the parameters, see if you can vindicate the data in Table 3-16, for the appropriate method.

4/DECOMPOSITION METHODS

4/1 Introduction

The forecasting methods outlined in the previous chapter are based on the concept that when an underlying pattern exists in a data series, that pattern can be distinguished from randomness by smoothing (averaging) past values. The effect of this smoothing is to eliminate randomness so the pattern can be projected into the future and used as the forecast. Smoothing methods make no attempt to identify individual components of the basic underlying pattern. In many instances the pattern can be broken down (decomposed) into subpatterns that identify each component of the time series separately. Such a breakdown can frequently facilitate improved accuracy in forecasting and aid in better understanding the behavior of the series.

Decomposition methods usually try to identify three separate components of the basic underlying pattern that tend to characterize economic and business series. These are the trend, the cycle, and the seasonal factors. The trend represents the long-run behavior of the data, and can be increasing, decreasing, or unchanged. The cyclical factor represents the ups and downs of the economy or of a specific industry and is common to series such as Gross National Product (GNP), index of industrial production, demand for housing, sales of industrial goods such as automobiles, stock prices, bond rates, money supply, and interest rates. The seasonal factor relates to periodic fluctuations of constant length that are caused by such things as temperature, rainfall, month of the year, timing of holidays, and corporate policies. The distinction between seasonality and cyclicality is that seasonality repeats itself at fixed intervals such as a year, month, or week, while cyclical factors have a longer duration that varies from cycle to cycle.

Decomposition assumes that the data are made up as follows:

data = pattern + error

$$= f(\text{trend, cycle, seasonality}) + \text{error}.$$

Thus in addition to the components of the pattern, an element of error or randomness is also assumed to be present. This error is assumed to be the difference between the combined effect of the three subpatterns of the series and the actual data.

Decomposition methods are among the oldest forecasting approaches. They were used in the beginning of this century by economists attempting to identify and control the business cycle. The basis of current decomposition methods was established in the 1920s when the concept of ratio-to-trend was introduced. Since that time decomposition approaches have been used widely by both economists and businessmen.

There are several alternative approaches to decomposing a time series, all of which aim at isolating each component of the series as accurately as possible. The basic concept in such separation is empirical and consists of first removing seasonality, then trend, and finally cycle. Any residual is assumed to be randomness which, while it cannot be predicted, can be identified. From a statistical point of view there are a number of theoretical weaknesses in the decomposition approach. Practitioners, however, have largely ignored these weaknesses and have used the approach with considerable success.

The general mathematical representation of the decomposition approach is:

$$X_t = f(I_t, T_t, C_t, E_t),$$
(4-1)

where X_t is the time series value (actual data) at period t,

I_t is the seasonal component (or Index) at period t,

T_t is the trend component at period t,

C_t is the cyclical component at period t, and

E_t is the error or random component at period t.

The exact functional form of (4-1) depends on the decomposition method actually used. Several of these methods will be examined in this chapter. For all such methods the process of decomposition is similar and consists of the following steps:

1. For the actual series, X_t, compute a moving average whose length, N, is equal to the length of seasonality. The purpose of this moving average is to eliminate seasonality and randomness. Averaging as many periods as the length of the seasonal pattern (e.g., 12 months, 4 quarters, or 7 days) will eliminate seasonality by averaging seasonally high periods with seasonally low periods. Since random errors have no systematic pattern, this averaging reduces randomness as well.

2. Separate the N period moving average (step 1 above) from the original data series to obtain trend and cyclicality.

3. Isolate the seasonal factors by averaging them for each of the periods making up the complete length of seasonality.

4. Identify the appropriate form of the trend (linear, exponential, S-curve, etc.) and calculate its value at each period, T_t.

5. Separate the outcome of step 4 from that of step 2 (the combined value of trend and cycle) to obtain the cyclical factor.

6. Separate the seasonality, trend, and cycle from the original data series to isolate the remaining randomness, E_t.

These steps in the decomposition procedure can be illustrated using the simple series shown in Table 4-1. This series contains trend, seasonality, and randomness. It can be seen from the last column of Table 4-1 that the observed values for the series represent the three components combined in

TABLE 4-1 DECOMPOSITION PROCEDURE FOR SERIES WITH TREND, SEASONALITY, AND RANDOMNESS

Period	T_t Trend	I_t Seasonality	E_t Randomness	$X_t = T_t + I_t + E_t$ Time Series
1	2	3	−.3	4.7
2	4	5	0	9.0
3	6	7	0	13.0
4	8	3	.3	11.3
5	10	5	.9	15.9
6	12	7	.6	19.6
7	14	3	−.3	16.7
8	16	5	−.3	20.7
9	18	7	0	25.0
10	20	3	.6	23.6
11	22	5	0	27.0
12	24	7	.3	31.3

an additive form. Thus the six steps outlined above will perform best if equation (4-1) is assumed to have the form:

$$X_t = I_t + T_t + C_t + E_t. \tag{4-2}$$

Since no cyclical component exists in these data, C_t has a value of zero.

In applying step 1 of the above procedure, the initial task is to determine the length of seasonality of the data so that number of periods can be used in the moving average. From Table 4-1, it is clear that the seasonal pattern is 3, since the same values (3, 5, and 7) repeat themselves every 3 periods. Thus a moving average of 3 periods, $N = 3$, should be computed and centered in the middle of the 3 numbers being averaged. The centering is appropriate because the concern at this point is not forecasting, as it was in Section 3/2, but rather finding the average of the 3 values surrounding each period's value. Table 4-2 shows the resulting moving average values.

The 3-period moving average values represent trend and cycle only, since randomness and seasonality have been eliminated. Step 2 is then to subtract the moving average values from the time series values (column 3). The resulting difference (column 5) is seasonality and randomness. Table 4-2 has therefore separated the original time series, X_t, into two parts—one including the trend-cycle components and the other the seasonal-random components. Step 3 separates the randomness from the seasonality by averaging all available values referring to the same season (i.e., I, II, and III). Using this procedure, one finds that the random elements will cancel each

TABLE 4-2 DECOMPOSITION COMPUTATIONS FOR MOVING AVERAGES

(1) Period	(2) Season	(3) $X_t = I_t + T_t + C_t + E_t$ X_t (Time Series)	(4) $M_t = T_t + C_t$ M_t (Moving Average)	(5) $I_t + T_t + C_t + E_t - (T_t + C_t)$ $= I_t + E_t$ $I_t + E_t = X_t - M_t$
1	I	4.7	—	—
2	II	9.0	8.9	.1
3	III	13.0	11.1	1.9
4	I	11.3	13.4	−2.1
5	II	15.9	15.6	.3
6	III	19.6	17.4	2.2
7	I	16.7	19.0	−2.3
8	II	20.7	20.8	−.1
9	III	25.0	23.1	1.9
10	I	23.6	25.2	−1.6
11	II	27.0	27.3	−.3
12	III	31.3	—	—

other, since some values will be positive and some negative. This averaging is done in Table 4-3, where the basic data are the seasonal-random components found in column 5 of Table 4-2.

The averaged seasonal factors, -2, 0, and $+2$, indicate that if season II (i.e., periods 2, 5, 8, and 11) is considered the base point for seasonality, then season I (periods 1, 4, 7, and 10) is 2 units below the base, and season III (periods 3, 6, 9, and 12) is 2 units above the base. This is so because the series was generated this way in Table 4-1.

Steps 4 and 5 in the decomposition process are to separate the trend and the cycle. In this example this separation is not necessary because the cycle is zero and therefore the trend-cycle component is all trend. In general, however, some type of trend curve would be assumed, its value found for each period, and that value subtracted from the trend-cycle value (the moving average values).

The final step (6) isolates the randomness in the series by simply subtracting from the original time series the component values found above for trend, cycle, and seasonal factors.

Before discussing the range of variations available for applying the decomposition approach to forecasting, the topic of trend fitting will be introduced in Section 4/2. Although this is a basic method of forecasting in its own right, trend fitting will not be discussed in detail until Chapter 5, in the context of regression.

TABLE 4-3 DECOMPOSITION PROCEDURE FOR SEASONAL INDICES

	Seasons	
I	II	III
—	.1	1.9
−2.1	.3	2.2
−2.3	−.1	1.9
−1.6	−.3	—

Sums of Seasonal Factors		
−6	0	6

Average Seasonal Factor		
−2	0	2

Section 4/3 presents the classical approach to decomposition—the ratio-to-moving averages procedure—which is still commonly used. Then, Section 4/4 will describe variations in the types of moving averages that are used in decomposition methodology. The discussion in Section 4/4 will help pave the way for a detailed examination of the most widely used decomposition method, Census II. This method, which lies behind many, many basic economic series used in the private and public sectors, will be studied in Section 4/5. Finally, the FORAN system will be presented briefly in Section 4/6.

4/2 Trend Fitting

Section 2/2 demonstrated that fitting a straight line to stationary (horizontal) data could be done in a way to minimize the MSE using:

$$\overline{X} = \frac{\sum\limits_{i=1}^{n} X_i}{n}.$$

(4-3)

In graphic terms, equation (4-3) represents a horizontal straight line and is specified by one parameter, X. A trend line requires two parameters, a and b, for specification. The values of a and b can be found in a manner similar to that used for $\overline{X}$. Values for a and b can be found by minimizing the MSE where the errors are the differences between the data values of the time series and the corresponding trend line values. This procedure is known as simple regression and will be examined in detail in Chapter 5. However, at this point two things need to be made clear:

1. A trend line such as that shown in Figure 4-1 can be described by two parameters, a and b, in the form

$$X_t = a + bt.$$
(4-4)

2. The values of a and b that minimize the MSE can be found using (4-5) and (4-6):

$$b = \frac{n\Sigma tX - \Sigma t\Sigma X}{n\Sigma t^2 - (\Sigma t)^2},$$
(4-5)

$$a = \frac{\Sigma X}{n} - b\frac{\Sigma t}{n}.$$
(4-6)

There are several alternative trend curves that are nonlinear that can be fit to a data series (e.g., exponential, S-curve, quadratic, logarithmic). For purposes of this chapter, only a linear trend will be considered, although

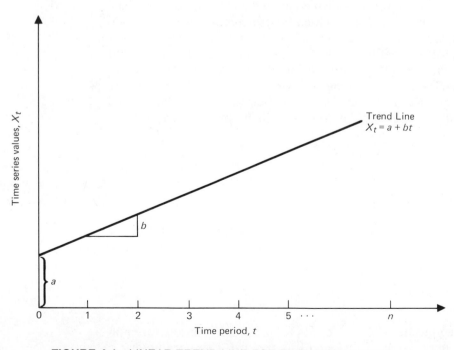

FIGURE 4-1   LINEAR TREND LINE FOR TIME-SERIES DATA

alternative forms could be used as part of a decomposition method wherever appropriate.

4/3   The Ratio-to-Moving Averages Classical Decomposition Method

Decomposition methods can assume an additive or multiplicative model and can be of varying forms. For example, the decomposition method of simple averages assumes the additive model:

$$X_t = (I_t + T_t + C_t) + E_t. \tag{4-7}$$

The ratio-to-trend method uses a multiplicative model of the form:

$$\tag{4-8}$$

$$X_t = (I_t * T_t * C_t) * E_t.$$

The decomposition methods of simple averages and ratio-to-trend were used in the past mainly because of their computational simplicity. However, they have lost most of their appeal with the widespread introduction of computers, which has made application of variations of the ratio-to-moving averages method a much preferable approach.

Developed in the 1920s, the ratio-to-moving averages method was for many years the most commonly used decomposition procedure. This approach formed the basis for Census II decomposition, which is examined in Section 4/5. This method assumes a multiplicative model of the form:

$$X_t = I_t \times T_t \times C_t \times E_t. \tag{4-9}$$

The ratio-to-moving averages method first isolates the trend-cycle of the data by calculating a moving average whose number of terms is equal to the length of seasonality. A moving average of this length contains no seasonal effects and little or no randomness. The resulting moving averages, M_t, represent

$$M_t = T_t \times C_t. \tag{4-10}$$

Equation (4-10) includes only the trend and cyclical factors, since seasonality and randomness are eliminated with the appropriate averaging. Equation (4-9) can be divided by (4-10) to obtain

$$\frac{X_t}{M_t} = \frac{I_t \times T_t \times C_t \times E_t}{T_t \times C_t} = I_t \times E_t. \tag{4-11}$$

Equation (4-11) is the ratio of actual-to-moving averages (thus the name of the method) and isolates the additional two components of the time series. Table 4-4 shows the actual time-series data, X_t, given by equation

TABLE 4-4 MOTORCYCLE REGISTRATIONS: RATIO-TO-MOVING
AVERAGES DECOMPOSITION

Year		Data	Moving Averages	Ratio of Actual-to-Moving Averages[a]
1971	Jan.	894.00	—	—
	Feb.	667.00	—	—
	Mar.	858.00	—	—
	Apr.	865.00	—	—
	May	989.00	—	—
	June	1093.00	—	—
	July	1191.00	1023.083	116.413
	Aug.	1159.00	1026.167	112.945
	Sept.	1046.00	1043.417	100.248
	Oct.	1191.00	1050.000	113.429
	Nov.	1203.00	1057.250	113.786
	Dec.	1121.00	1057.917	105.963
1972	Jan.	931.00	1065.000	87.418
	Feb.	874.00	1082.750	80.720
	Mar.	937.00	1096.750	85.434
	Apr.	952.00	1113.500	85.496
	May	997.00	1122.750	88.800
	June	1178.00	1122.917	104.905
	July	1404.00	1132.333	123.992
	Aug.	1327.00	1129.750	117.460
	Sept.	1247.00	1128.500	110.501
	Oct.	1302.00	1127.667	115.460
	Nov.	1205.00	1134.833	106.183
	Dec.	1234.00	1139.917	108.254
1973	Jan.	900.00	1158.167	77.709
	Feb.	859.00	1164.167	73.787
	Mar.	927.00	1169.667	79.253
	Apr.	1038.00	1175.417	88.309
	May	1058.00	1179.667	89.686
	June	1397.00	1184.833	117.907
	July	1476.00	1190.333	123.999
	Aug.	1393.00	1197.250	116.350
	Sept.	1316.00	1188.750	110.705
	Oct.	1353.00	1190.667	113.634
	Nov.	1267.00	1192.167	106.277
	Dec.	1300.00	1205.083	107.876

[a]As percentages.

TABLE 4-4 MOTORCYCLE REGISTRATIONS: RATIO-TO-MOVING AVERAGES DECOMPOSITION (*Continued*)

Year		Data	Moving Averages	Ratio of Actual-to-Moving Averages[a]
1974	Jan.	983.00	1199.417	81.957
	Feb.	757.00	1199.417	63.114
	Mar.	950.00	1206.083	78.767
	Apr.	1056.00	1210.417	87.243
	May	1213.00	1215.917	99.760
	June	1329.00	1234.750	107.633
	July	1476.00	1220.000	120.984
	Aug.	1473.00	1230.167	119.740
	Sept.	1368.00	1244.667	109.909
	Oct.	1419.00	1251.583	113.376
	Nov.	1493.00	1239.583	120.444
	Dec.	1123.00	1234.667	90.956
1975	Jan.	1105.00	1229.833	89.850
	Feb.	931.00	1235.083	75.380
	Mar.	1033.00	1243.583	83.066
	Apr.	912.00	1240.000	73.548
	May	1154.00	1240.333	93.040
	June	1271.00	1240.250	102.479
	July	1539.00	1257.250	122.410
	Aug.	1575.00	1245.167	126.489
	Sept.	1325.00	1247.083	106.248
	Oct.	1423.00	1244.000	114.389
	Nov.	1492.00	1267.500	117.712
	Dec.	1327.00	1288.083	103.021
1976	Jan.	960.00	1292.833	74.256
	Feb.	954.00	1311.250	72.755
	Mar.	996.00	1312.333	75.895
	Apr.	1194.00	1323.667	90.204
	May	1401.00	1341.750	104.416
	June	1328.00	1337.333	99.302
	July	1760.00	1351.000	130.274
	Aug.	1588.00	—	—
	Sept.	1461.00	—	—
	Oct.	1640.00	—	—
	Nov.	1439.00	—	—
	Dec.	1491.00	—	—

TABLE 4-5   SEASONAL INDICES FOR RATIO-TO-MOVING AVERAGES DECOMPOSITION METHOD

Year	Jan.	Feb.	Mar.	Apr.	May	June	July	Aug.	Sept.	Oct.	Nov.	Dec.	Total
1971	—	—	—	—	—	—	116.4	112.9	100.2	113.4	113.8	106.0	
1972	87.4	80.7	85.4	85.5	88.8	104.9	124.0	117.5	110.5	115.5	106.2	108.3	
1973	77.7	73.8	79.3	88.3	89.7	117.9	124.0	116.4	110.7	113.6	106.3	107.9	
1974	82.0	63.1	78.8	87.2	99.8	107.6	121.0	119.7	109.9	113.4	120.4	91.0	
1975	89.9	75.4	83.1	73.5	93.0	102.5	122.4	126.5	106.2	114.4	117.7	103.0	
1976	74.3	72.8	75.9	90.2	104.4	99.3	130.3	—	—	—	—	—	—
Medial[a] average	82.36	73.97	80.36	87.02	93.16	105.00	122.85	117.85	108.89	113.82	112.59	105.62	1204.49
Seasonal index[b]	82.05	73.70	80.06	86.69	93.81	104.61	122.39	117.41	108.48	113.39	112.17	105.23	1200.00

[a]The column average excluding the highest and lowest values.
[b]An adjustment of the medial average so that the total is equal to 1200. The adjustment factor is 1200/1204.492 = .99627.

(4-9), the moving average values, M_t, given by equation (4-10), and the ratio of the two, given by equation (4-11).[1] The ratio values vary around 100, indicating the effects of seasonality on the average deseasonalized values.

The next step in this method is to eliminate the randomness from the values given by (4-11) by using some form of averaging of the same months. That is similar to the approach used in the decomposition methods discussed previously. Classical ratio-to-moving averages decomposition uses an approach called the method of medial average at this point.

To compute the medial average the ratios of actual-to-moving averages (last column of Table 4-4) are arranged by month for all years in Table 4-5. The medial average is the mean value for each month after the largest and smallest values have been excluded. The January medial average, for example, is 82.36. This value is found by excluding January 1975 (the highest of all Januaries) and January 1976 (the lowest of all Januaries). The remaining 3 January values are summed, 87.4 + 77.7 + 82.0 = 247.1, and divided by 3 to obtain the medial average of 82.36. Seasonal indices can be obtained from the medial averages by multiplying each medial average by .99627 (1200/1204.492), which adjusts them so their average value is 100.

The final step in this method is to separate the trend from the cycle

---

[1]Throughout this text, ratio values are multiplied by 100 so that they are easier to read as percentages, and to conform with other published works on decomposition.

using (4-10). The linear trend line for these data was previously identified as

$$T_t = 975.37 + 6.035(t).\tag{4-12}$$

If equation (4-10) is divided by (4-12), the result is

$$\frac{M_t}{T_t} = \frac{T_t \times C_t}{975.37 + 6.035(t)} = C_t.\tag{4-13}$$

The resulting values are shown in the last column of Table 4-6. These ratio values fluctuate around 100, indicating cyclical factors higher than average (greater than 100) or lower than average (less than 100).

To prepare a forecast, the trend value for the period to be forecast is multiplied by the appropriate seasonal index and by the appropriate cyclical factor. Calculating the trend and identifying the appropriate seasonal factor are straightforward matters, but estimating the cyclical factor may not be. (Chapter 12 discusses this problem in detail.) Estimating the cyclical factor requires some knowledge of the level of economic or industry activity during the period to be forecast and such knowledge can frequently be based only on judgment.

If the cyclical values for January and February 1977 are assumed to be 98.2 and 98.6 respectively, the forecasts for these months will be

$$F_{J1977} = [975.37 + 6.035(73)](.8205)(.982) = 1140.85$$

and

$$F_{F1977} = [975.37 + 6.035(74)](.7370)(.986) = 1033.31.$$

These forecasts[2] are based on the fact that January 1977 is month 73 and February is month 74, and the seasonal factor for January is 82.05 and for February is 73.70.

4/4 Different Types of Moving Averages

As illustrated in the previous sections, moving averages are used to eliminate seasonality and randomness from data series. In this sense moving averages are the backbone of decomposition methods. In the methods described thus far the single moving average equal to the length of season-

---

[2]Throughout this chapter, the ratios have been multiplied by 100. Thus in computing these forecasts, they would need to be divided by 100, or for January 1977:

$$F_{J1977} = [975.37 + 6.035(73)](.8205)(.982) = 1140.85.$$

TABLE 4-6 CYCLICAL FACTORS FOR RATIO-TO-MOVING AVERAGES DECOMPOSITION METHOD

Year		Data	12-Month Moving Averages	Trend	Cyclical Factor (moving average/ trend)[a]
1971	Jan.	894.00	—	—	—
	Feb.	667.00	—	—	—
	Mar.	858.00	—	—	—
	Apr.	865.00	—	—	—
	May	989.00	—	—	—
	June	1093.00	—	—	—
	July	1191.00	1023.083	1017.61	100.54
	Aug.	1159.00	1026.167	1023.65	100.25
	Sept.	1046.00	1043.417	1029.69	101.33
	Oct.	1191.00	1050.000	1035.72	101.38
	Nov.	1203.00	1057.250	1041.75	101.49
	Dec.	1121.00	1057.917	1047.79	100.97
1972	Jan.	931.00	1065.000	1053.82	101.06
	Feb.	874.00	1082.750	1059.86	102.16
	Mar.	937.00	1096.750	1065.90	102.89
	Apr.	952.00	1113.500	1071.93	103.88
	May	997.00	1122.750	1077.97	104.15
	June	1178.00	1122.917	1084.00	103.59
	July	1404.00	1132.333	1090.03	103.88
	Aug.	1327.00	1129.750	1096.07	103.07
	Sept.	1247.00	1128.500	1102.10	102.39
	Oct.	1302.00	1127.667	1108.14	101.76
	Nov.	1205.00	1134.833	1114.18	101.85
	Dec.	1234.00	1139.917	1120.21	101.76
1973	Jan.	900.00	1158.167	1126.25	102.83
	Feb.	859.00	1164.167	1132.28	102.81
	Mar.	927.00	1169.667	1138.31	102.75
	Apr.	1038.00	1175.417	1144.35	102.71
	May	1058.00	1179.667	1150.38	102.54
	June	1397.00	1184.833	1156.42	102.46
	July	1476.00	1190.333	1162.46	102.40
	Aug.	1393.00	1197.250	1168.49	102.46
	Sept.	1316.00	1188.750	1174.52	101.21
	Oct.	1353.00	1190.667	1180.56	100.85
	Nov.	1267.00	1192.167	1186.59	100.47
	Dec.	1300.00	1205.083	1192.63	101.04

[a]As percentages

TABLE 4-6 CYCLICAL FACTORS FOR RATIO-TO-MOVING AVERAGES
DECOMPOSITION METHOD (*Continued*)

Year		Data	12-Month Moving Averages	Trend	Cyclical Factor (moving average/ trend)[a]
1974	Jan.	983.00	1199.417	1198.67	100.06
	Feb.	757.00	1199.417	1204.70	99.56
	Mar.	950.00	1206.083	1210.74	99.61
	Apr.	1056.00	1210.417	1216.77	99.48
	May	1213.00	1215.917	1222.80	99.43
	June	1329.00	1234.750	1228.84	100.48
	July	1476.00	1220.000	1234.87	98.79
	Aug.	1473.00	1230.167	1240.91	99.13
	Sept.	1368.00	1244.667	1246.95	99.82
	Oct.	1419.00	1251.583	1252.98	99.89
	Nov.	1493.00	1239.583	1259.02	98.45
	Dec.	1123.00	1234.667	1265.05	97.60
1975	Jan.	1105.00	1229.833	1271.08	96.75
	Feb.	931.00	1235.083	1277.12	96.71
	Mar.	1033.00	1243.583	1283.16	96.91
	Apr.	912.00	1240.000	1289.19	96.18
	May	1154.00	1240.333	1295.23	95.76
	June	1271.00	1240.250	1301.26	95.31
	July	1539.00	1257.250	1307.29	96.17
	Aug.	1575.00	1245.167	1313.33	94.81
	Sept.	1325.00	1247.083	1319.36	94.52
	Oct.	1423.00	1244.000	1325.40	93.86
	Nov.	1492.00	1267.500	1331.44	95.20
	Dec.	1327.00	1288.083	1337.47	96.31
1976	Jan.	960.00	1292.833	1343.51	96.23
	Feb.	954.00	1311.250	1349.54	97.16
	Mar.	996.00	1312.333	1355.57	96.81
	Apr.	1194.00	1323.667	1361.61	97.21
	May	1401.00	1341.750	1367.65	98.10
	June	1328.00	1337.333	1373.68	97.35
	July	1760.00	1351.000	1379.72	97.92
	Aug.	1588.00	—	—	—
	Sept.	1461.00	—	—	—
	Oct.	1640.00	—	—	—
	Nov.	1439.00	—	—	—
	Dec.	1491.00	—	—	—

ality was used. Census II, a much more sophisticated decomposition method, uses more elaborate moving averages of different lengths and high orders (double, triple, etc.). The purpose of this section is to review the different types of moving averages in general and those used in Census II and to discuss the advantages and shortcomings of each of them. The Census II decomposition method will then be described in the next section.

4/4/1 Centered Moving Averages

To obtain more precise results, a moving average (MA) should be centered at the middle of the data values averaged. That presents no problem when the number of averaged terms is odd, since the middle value will be $(N + 1)/2$. Thus, the 3-term moving averages (denoted 3 MA) of the 8 values shown in Table 4-7 will be those given in column 3. To calculate a 4-term moving average (4 MA) the question arises as to whether to place the MA at period 2 or at period 3, since $(4 + 1)/2 = 2.5$. Placing it at period 2 makes it half a period late and placing it at period 3 makes it half a period early. In Table 4-7 the 4 MA is placed opposite period 3 (column 5) and the ratios of actual to 4 MA are shown in column 6. Given the linear trend, it would be desirable to have these ratios equal to one. The fact that the MA is not centered in this case can create problems. Such problems are usually overcome by taking an additional 2-period MA of the 4-period moving average. This double moving average is denoted as $2 \times N$. Since $N = 4$ in the example given in Table 4-7, the result of this procedure is a 2×4. The results of following this centering procedure are shown in Table 4-8, where column 4 is simply the average of 2 successive values of the 4 MA of column

TABLE 4-7   CENTERED MOVING AVERAGES—3- AND 4-TERM

(1) Period	(2) Value	(3) 3 MA	(4) Ratio of (2)/(3)	(5) 4 MA	(6) Ratio of (2)/(5)
1	3	—	—	—	—
2	5	5	1	—	—
3	7	7	1	6	1.167
4	9	9	1	8	1.125
5	11	11	1	10	1.1
6	13	13	1	12	1.083
7	15	15	1	14	1.071
8	17	—	—	—	—

TABLE 4-8 CENTERED MOVING AVERAGES—2 × 4 MA

(1) Period	(2) Value	(3) 4 MA	(4) 2 × 4 MA	(5) Ratio of (2)/(4)
1	3	—	—	—
2	5	—	—	—
3	7	6	7	1
4	9	8	9	1
5	11	10	11	1
6	13	12	13	1
7	15	14	—	—
8	17	—	—	—

3. Since the center of the 4 MA is at periods 2.5, 3.5, 4.5, 5.5, and 6.5, the center of the additional 2 MA is at periods 3, 4, 5, and 6. Thus the 2 × 4 MA overcomes the centering problem.

A double moving average like the one described above can be expressed as a single but weighted moving average, where the weights for each period are unequal. A 2-month MA of a 12-month moving average, for example, is equivalent to a 13-month weighted moving averge (often called a 12-months centered moving average). This type of centered moving average is used in Census II rather than a single moving average of 12 periods.

The following notation is useful in discussing weighted and centered moving averages:

$$M_{6.5} = (X_1 + X_2 + \cdots + X_{12})/12, \tag{4-14}$$

$$M_{7.5} = (X_2 + X_3 + \cdots + X_{13})/12. \tag{4-15}$$

Equations (4-14) and (4-15) are not centered on integer values because 12 is an even number. However, centering can be achieved by averaging (4-14) and (4-15), which involves simply taking an additional 2-month MA of the 12-month moving averages. The result is a *centered* moving average:

$$M_7'' = \frac{M_{6.5} + M_{7.5}}{2}. \tag{4-16}$$

Substituting (4-14) and (4-15) into this equation gives

$$M_7'' = \left(\frac{X_1 + X_2 + \cdots + X_{12}}{12} + \frac{X_2 + X_3 + \cdots + X_{13}}{12} \right) \Big/ 2, \tag{4-17}$$

$$= (X_1 + 2X_2 + 2X_3 + \cdots + 2X_{11} + 2X_{12} + X_{13})/24. \tag{4-18}$$

From (4-18), it can be seen that the first and last terms in the average have weights of $1/24 = .04167$, and all other terms have weights of double that value, $.0833$.

4/4/2   A 3 × 3 Moving Average

A 3 × 3 moving average is a 3 MA of a 3 MA. It is equivalent to a 5-period weighted moving average as shown by equations (4-19) through (4-24).

$$M_2 = (X_1 + X_2 + X_3)/3, \qquad \text{[A 3-months moving average of months} \tag{4-19}$$
1, 2, and 3 (centered at period 2)]

$$M_3 = (X_2 + X_3 + X_4)/3, \qquad \text{(like } M_2 \text{ but for months 2, 3, and 4)} \tag{4-20}$$

$$M_4 = (X_3 + X_4 + X_5)/3, \tag{4-21}$$

$$M_5 = (X_4 + X_5 + X_6)/3, \tag{4-22}$$

etc.

$$M_3'' = (M_2 + M_3 + M_4)/3. \qquad \text{[a 3-months moving average of the mov-} \tag{4-23}$$
ing averages (centered at period 3)]

Substituting (4-19), (4-20), and (4-21) into (4-23) gives

$$M_3'' = \left(\frac{X_1 + X_2 + X_3}{3} + \frac{X_2 + X_3 + X_4}{3} + \frac{X_3 + X_4 + X_5}{3} \right) \Big/ 3$$

$$= (X_1 + 2X_2 + 3X_3 + 2X_4 + X_5)/9,$$

or

$$M_3'' = \frac{1}{9}(X_1 + 2X_2 + 3X_3 + 2X_4 + X_5). \tag{4-24}$$

Equation (4-24) is a 5-month weighted MA with weights of $.1111$, $.2222$, $.3333$, $.2222$, $.1111$ for the first, second, third, fourth, and fifth terms, respectively.

4/4/3   A 3 × 5 Moving Average

A 3 × 5 MA is similar to the 3 × 3 MA except that the number of terms averaged the first time is 5 and then 3. This results in a 7-term weighted moving average with weights of $.067$, $.133$, $.200$, $.200$, $.200$, $.133$, and $.067$.

4/4/4 Spencer and Henderson Moving Averages

Spencer (1904) and Henderson (see Shiskin et al.) moving averages are of still higher order than those examined above. Spencer's MA is a $5 \times 5 \times 4 \times 4$, or quadruple, MA. Or, equivalently, it is a 15-point weighted moving average as shown by equations (4-25) through (4-35):

$$M_{2.5} = (X_1 + X_2 + X_3 + X_4)/4, \tag{4-25}$$

$$M_{3.5} = (X_2 + X_3 + X_4 + X_5)/4, \quad \text{(4-month moving averages of the} \tag{4-26}$$

$$M_{4.5} = (X_3 + X_4 + X_5 + X_6)/4, \quad \text{original data)} \tag{4-27}$$

$$M_{5.5} = (X_4 + X_5 + X_6 + X_7)/4, \tag{4-28}$$

$$M_4'' = (M_{2.5} + M_{3.5} + M_{4.5} + M_{5.5})/4 \quad \text{(a 4 MA of the 4 MA).} \tag{4-29}$$

Substituting (4-25), (4-26), (4-27), and (4-28) into (4-29) gives

$$M_4'' = (X_1 + 2X_2 + 3X_3 + 4X_4 + 3X_5 + 2X_6 + X_7)/16 \quad \text{(a 7-month weighted moving average).} \tag{4-30}$$

Using this 7-month weighted MA, a 5-month moving average can be computéd.

$$M_6''' = (M_4'' + M_5'' + M_6'' + M_7'' + M_8'')/5 \quad \text{(a 5-month MA of the 7-month weighted MA).} \tag{4-31}$$

Substituting (4-30) into (4-31) gives

$$M_6''' = (X_1 + 3X_2 + 6X_3 + 10X_4 + 13X_5 + 14X_6 + 13X_7 + 10X_8 + 6X_9 + 3X_{10} + X_{11})/80.$$

(an 11-month weighted MA). $\tag{4-32}$

The final moving average applied to the 11-month moving average of (4-32) is a 5-term moving average, which is weighted as follows:

$$M_8'''' = \frac{-3}{4} M_6''' + \frac{3}{4} M_7''' + M_8''' + \frac{3}{4} M_9''' - \frac{3}{4} M_{10}''' \quad \text{(the final averaging).} \tag{4-33}$$

Substituting (4-32) into (4-33) gives (after considerable algebra)

$$M_8'''' = (-3X_1 - 6X_2 - 5X_3 + 3X_4 + 21X_5 + 46X_6 + 67X_7 + 74X_8 + 67X_9$$
$$+ 46X_{10} + 21X_{11} + 3X_{12} - 5X_{13} - 6X_{14} - 3X_{15})/320. \tag{4-34}$$

Of course the data values will be different for moving averages centered on different periods. For example, M_9'''' will include the periods:

$$M_9'''' = (-3X_2 - 6X_3 - 5X_4 + \cdots - 6X_{15} - 3X_{16})/320. \tag{4-35}$$

For a data series with n observations, M_t'''' can be computed for periods 8 to $n - 7$. Each average will include 15 terms whose weights will be $-.009$, $-.019$, $-.016$, $.009$, $.066$, $.144$, $.209$, $.231$, $.209$, $.144$, $.066$, $.009$, $-.016$, $-.019$, and $-.009$.

Another Spencer's MA that is commonly used is the 21-point weighted moving average. Its weights can be derived in the manner shown above for Spencer's 15-point formula.

In addition to Spencer's moving averages, some recent versions of Census II and X-11 also use Henderson's 5-, 9-, 13-, and 23-point weighted moving averages. The selection of a specific moving average is based upon the randomness present in the series—the greater the randomness, the larger the number of terms in the average.

4/4/5   Selecting the Appropriate Length Moving Average

Determining the appropriate length of a moving average is an important task in decomposition methods. As a rule, a larger number of terms in the moving average increases the likelihood that randomness will be eliminated. That argues for using as long a length as possible. However, the longer the length of the moving average, the more terms (and information) are lost in the process of averaging, since N data values are required for an N-term average.

The $[(N - 1)/2]$ terms lost in the beginning of the data are usually of little consequence, but those $[(N - 1)/2]$ lost in the end are critical, since they are the starting point for forecasting the cycle. Not only must the cyclical values for periods $t + 1$, $t + 2$, and so on, be estimated, but the values for periods t, $t - 1$, $t - 2, \ldots, t - (N - 1)/2 + 1$ must also be estimated. To overcome the problem of missing values at the end of the data series, a shorter length moving average can be used. This may not completely eliminate randomness however. Clearly a tradeoff must be made in selecting the appropriate length moving average.

The latest versions of Census II, notably X-11, use various length moving averages depending upon the amount of randomness in the data—the more randomness, the longer the moving average. This method is practical with Census II because it goes through several iterations of decomposition, each one further refining the component estimates. It is thus possible to obtain preliminary estimates of randomness to be used in subsequent decomposition steps to select the appropriate length moving average.

Another innovation in Census II is that rather than applying the final moving averages to the original data, they are applied to the seasonally adjusted data. Since the fluctuations in the seasonally adjusted data are small, a shorter moving average can be used. Furthermore, since the seasonally adjusted data include trend-cycle and randomness, determining the importance of the trend-cycle relative to the randomness allows the moving average to be chosen that results in the trend-cycle just dominating the randomness. This is done in Census II by calculating what is called the *months for cyclical dominance*—or MCD. The MCD is then used to set the length of the moving average applied to the seasonally adjusted data. In most cases, the final moving average is of length 3, 4, or 5, which means that only one or two values are lost at the end of the data. (Even for those few values, there are ways to estimate their magnitude, as will be seen in Chapter 12.)

4/5   The Census II Decomposition Method

The Census II method has been developed by the Bureau of the Census of the U.S. Department of Commerce. Julius Shiskin is considered the main contributor in the development of this method. Census II has been used widely by the bureau, other government agencies in the United States and elsewhere, and by an ever increasing number of businesses. Census II has gone through several variations since 1955 when the first version was developed.

The Census II method consists of four different phases. In the first phase an attempt is made to adjust the data for trading day variations. The second phase is the preliminary estimation of seasonal factors and the preliminary adjustment of the series for seasonality. The third phase refines the adjustments so that more accurate seasonal factors can be calculated. In addition, an estimation of the trend-cycle and random or irregular component is made. The final phase prepares summary statistics that can be used to determine how successful the adjustments for seasonality have been and provides information needed to estimate the trend-cycle in the data for purposes of forecasting.

To illustrate the application of Census II, 8 years of monthly data representing international airline passenger travel (in thousands) from 1949 through 1956 will be used. The actual values for this data series are shown in Table 4-9.

4/5/1   Trading Days Adjustments

Trading days adjustments are often necessary because a given month may not have the same number of working, or trading, days in different years. In some industries such as retail sales and banks, this factor becomes very important, since it can have a significant influence on the level of sales. In the airline data of Table 4-9, trading days are not an important factor because their effects on airline schedules are largely random, owing to the fact that holidays vary from country to country. However, to illustrate

TABLE 4-9 ACTUAL DATA FOR INTERNATIONAL AIRLINE PASSENGER TRAVEL

Year	Jan.	Feb.	Mar.	Apr.	May	June	July	Aug.	Sept.	Oct.	Nov.	Dec.
1949	112	118	132	129	121	135	148	148	136	119	104	118
1950	115	126	141	135	125	149	170	170	158	133	114	140
1951	145	150	178	163	172	178	199	199	184	162	146	166
1952	171	180	193	181	183	218	230	242	209	191	172	194
1953	196	196	236	235	229	243	264	272	237	211	180	201
1954	204	188	235	227	234	264	302	293	259	229	203	229
1955	242	233	267	269	270	315	364	347	312	274	237	278
1956	284	277	317	313	318	374	413	405	355	306	271	306

the procedure for making trading day adjustments, the process will be applied below.

The first step is to determine the number of trading days for each of the months of the years of interest. Next, the average number of working days in each month are calculated. Table 4-10 shows the number of trading days for the United States for 1949 through 1956. It can be seen that any given month can have a substantially different number of trading days over such an 8-year span. Once the number of trading days for each month is known, a set of monthly averages is calculated. The appropriate average is then used to divide the actual values of the corresponding month.

An example of the trading days adjustment for the month of April is given in Table 4-11. The average number of trading days for April, 21.25, is divided into each one of the actual number of trading days for April for

TABLE 4-10 NUMBER OF U.S. TRADING DAYS

Year	Jan.	Feb.	Mar.	Apr.	May	June	July	Aug.	Sept.	Oct.	Nov.	Dec.
1949	20	20	23	21	21	22	20	23	21	21	21	21
1950	21	20	23	20	22	22	20	23	20	22	21	20
1951	22	20	22	21	22	21	21	23	19	23	21	20
1952	22	21	21	22	21	21	22	21	21	23	19	22
1953	21	20	22	22	20	22	22	21	21	22	20	22
1954	20	20	23	22	20	22	21	22	21	21	21	22
1955	20	20	23	21	21	22	20	23	21	21	21	21
1956	21	21	22	21	22	21	21	23	19	23	21	20
Average	20.875	20.25	22.375	21.25	21.125	21.625	20.875	22.375	20.375	22.0	20.625	21.0

TABLE 4-11   CALCULATION OF TRADING DAYS ADJUSTMENT
FOR APRIL

Year	Trading Days	Trading Days Coefficient of Adjustment	Data (April)	Data Adjustment for Trading Days[a]
1949	21	21/21.25 = .9882	129	129/.9882 = 130.54
1950	20	20/21.25 = .9412	135	135/.9412 = 143.44
1951	21	21/21.25 = .9882	163	163/.9882 = 164.95
1952	22	22/21.25 = 1.0353	181	181/1.0353 = 174.83
1953	22	22/21.25 = 1.0353	235	235/1.0353 = 226.99
1954	22	22/21.25 = 1.0353	227	227/1.0353 = 219.26
1955	21	21/21.25 = .9882	269	269/.9882 = 272.21
1956	21	21/21.25 = .9882	313	313/.9882 = 316.74
	170/8 = 21.25			

[a]See Table 4-12 for a complete set of adjusted data.

the 8 years. The resulting coefficient of adjustment is then divided into the original data to obtain a set of data adjusted for trading days. This same procedure would then be applied for the other 11 months of the year. The complete set of data adjusted for trading days is shown in Table 4-12. These data would then normally be used as the input for Census II and would be referred to as the original data adjusted for trading days. In the example that follows the adjusted data of Table 4-12 will not be used because the adjustment does not improve the results of decomposition in this case.

TABLE 4-12   AIRLINE DATA ADJUSTED FOR TRADING DAYS

Year	Jan.	Feb.	Mar.	Apr.	May	June	July	Aug.	Sept.	Oct.	Nov.	Dec.
1949	116.9	119.5	128.4	130.5	121.7	132.7	154.5	144.0	132.0	124.7	102.1	118.0
1950	114.3	127.6	137.2	143.4	120.0	146.5	177.4	165.4	161.0	133.0	112.0	147.0
1951	137.6	151.9	181.0	164.9	165.2	183.3	197.8	193.6	197.3	155.0	143.4	174.3
1952	162.3	173.6	205.6	174.8	184.1	224.5	218.2	257.8	202.8	182.7	186.7	185.2
1953	194.8	198.5	240.0	227.0	241.9	238.9	250.5	289.8	229.9	211.0	185.6	191.9
1954	212.9	190.4	228.6	219.3	247.2	259.5	300.2	298.0	251.3	239.9	199.4	218.6
1955	252.6	235.9	259.7	272.2	271.6	309.6	379.9	337.6	302.7	287.0	232.8	278.0
1956	282.3	267.1	322.4	316.7	305.4	385.1	410.5	394.0	380.7	292.7	266.2	321.3

4/5/2   Preliminary Seasonal Adjustment

The second phase of Census II is aimed at making a preliminary separation of the seasonality from the trend-cycle and then isolating the randomness. Using the monthly airline passenger data of Table 4-9 as an example, the steps in this phase are as outlined below.

Calculation of a 12-month Centered Moving Average

A 12-month moving average applied to the original data will eliminate most of the seasonality and randomness that is in the series. The problem of centering a 12-month moving average is avoided by averaging the moving averages of 2 successive months and placing that value opposite the 7th month in the data being averaged (see Section 4/4/1).

The calculations necessary to obtain a 12-month centered MA are shown in columns 2 and 3 of Table 4-13. The ratios of these MA values to the original data are shown at the bottom of Table 4-13. Mathematically, these computations accomplish the following:

$$X_t = I_t T_t C_t E_t, \tag{4-36}$$

$$M_t = T_t C_t, \tag{4-37}$$

$$\frac{X_t}{M_t} = R_t = \frac{I_t T_t C_t E_t}{T_t C_t} = I_t E_t. \tag{4-38}$$

The values for R_t that contain seasonality and randomness are those shown at the bottom of Table 4-13. It should be pointed out that there are six values missing at the beginning and six at the end because of the averaging procedure used.

Replacement of Extreme Values

The ratios of Table 4-13 include such random or unusual events as strikes and wars. The next task in Census II is to exclude such extreme values before eliminating the randomness. This process has two stages.

1. Calculate a 3×3 month moving average. A 3×3 MA is applied to the centered ratios of Table 4-13. (This double moving average is the equivalent to a 5-month weighted moving average. See Section 4/4/2.) The purpose of this step is to eliminate as much of the randomness as possible. However, calculating a 3×3 moving average results in the loss of 2 values at the beginning of the data and 2 at the end. To avoid this loss, Census II estimates values for the beginning 2 months and the ending 2 months. Table 4-14 illustrates this procedure for the month of April. The two missing values are set equal to the average of the 2 following values. (The last 2 values are averaged to fill in the 2 months at

TABLE 4-13   PRELIMINARY SEASONALITY COMPUTATIONS
FOR CENSUS II

		(1) Original Data	(2) 12-Month Uncentered Moving Average (MA)	(3) 2-Month MA of the 12-Month MA (13-month weighted MA or 12-month centered MA)	(4) $\dfrac{(1)}{(3)}$ = Centered 12-Month Ratios
1949	Jan.	112	—	—	☐
	Feb.	118	—	—	☐
	Mar.	132	—	—	☐
	Apr.	129	—	—	☐
	May	121	—	—	☐
	June	135	—	—	☐
	July	148	126.667 ⎫	126.792	116.727
	Aug.	148	126.916 ⎭	127.252	116.305
	Sept.	136	127.587	127.960	106.283
	Oct.	119	128.333	128.583	92.547
	Nov.	104	128.833	—	(see values in
	Dec.	118	—	—	bottom portion
1950	Jan.	115	—	—	of this table)
	Feb.	l26	—	—	
	Mar.	141	—	—	
	Apr.	135	—	—	
	May	125	—	—	

Centered 12-Month Ratios (original/moving average)

Year	Jan.	Feb.	Mar.	Apr.	May	June	July	Aug.	Sept.	Oct.	Nov.	Dec.
1949	0	0	0	0	0	0	116.7	116.3	106.3	92.5	80.6	90.9
1950	87.6	94.7	104.5	99.0	91.0	107.4	120.6	118.7	108.4	89.6	75.2	90.5
1951	92.3	94.0	110.0	99.3	103.2	105.3	116.2	114.6	104.9	91.6	82.0	92.1
1952	93.4	96.7	102.1	94.6	94.5	111.3	116.1	121.2	103.4	92.6	81.7	90.9
1953	90.8	89.7	106.8	105.4	102.2	108.1	117.2	120.7	105.4	94.0	80.2	89.1
1954	89.5	81.6	101.2	97.0	99.3	111.0	125.6	120.1	104.8	91.5	80.1	89.1
1955	92.4	87.4	98.5	97.7	96.9	111.7	127.4	119.9	106.4	92.2	78.7	91.0
1956	91.6	88.1	99.5	97.3	98.0	114.3	0	0	0	0	0	0

TABLE 4-14   CALCULATION OF A 3 × 3 MOVING AVERAGE (APRIL)

	Centered Ratios (from bottom of Table 4-13, column 4)	Introduction of 2 Extra Values in Beginnning and 2 Extra Values at End	3 × 3 Moving Average	
			3 MA	3 × 3 MA
1949		$\dfrac{99 + 99.3}{2} = \begin{cases} 99.15 \\ 99.15 \end{cases}$	— 99.1	— —
1950	99	99	99.15	98.63
1951	99.3	99.3	97.63	98.85
1952	94.6	94.6	99.77	98.8
1953	105.4	105.4	99	99.68
1954	97.0	97.0	100.27	98.95
1955	97.7	97.7	97.57	98.45
1956	97.3	97.3	97.5	97.5
		$\dfrac{97.7 + 97.3}{2} = \begin{cases} 97.3 \\ 97.5 \\ 97.5 \end{cases}$	97.43 — —	— —

the end of the series.) This gives 4 more values, so that after taking the 3 × 3 moving average, there are still as many values as there were before doing so.

2. Calculate the standard deviation. After the 3 × 3 moving averages are calculated, their differences from the centered ratios shown in Table 4-13 are found for each one of the months as illustrated in Table 4-15. The standard deviation is used to construct control limits that identify extreme values. For the month of April, the limits can be set at the 3 × 3 MA plus or minus 2 standard deviations. There is only 1 value (1953) that is outside these control limits. The value for this month of April 1953 is then replaced by taking the average of the preceding and the following period. If the values to be replaced are the first or last, the average of the 3 preceding or the 3 following months is taken. Table 4-16 indicates the values replaced for the airline data assuming that the control limits are the 3 × 3 MA ± 2 standard deviations. If the limit is raised to the 3 × 3 MA ± 2.5 standard deviations, then none of the values needs replacing.

Preliminary Seasonal Factors

After the extreme values have been replaced, the ratios of Table 4-13 are adjusted and used to calculate the preliminary seasonal factors. The adjustments to be performed are the following:

TABLE 4-15   CALCULATION OF STANDARD DEVIATION AND
REPLACEMENT VALUES (APRIL)

	(1) Centered Ratios (Table 4-13)	(2) 3 × 3 MA (Table 4-14)	(3) (1) − (2) Deviations	(4) Deviations Squared
1949	—	—	—	—
1950	99	98.63	.37	.1369
1951	99.3	98.85	.45	.2025
1952	94.6	98.8	−4.2	17.64
1953	105.4	99.68	5.72	32.72
1954	97.0	98.95	−1.95	3.80
1955	97.7	98.45	−.75	.56
1956	97.3	97.5	−.2	.04
				55.1

$$Var = \frac{55.1}{7} = 7.871$$

$$SD - \sqrt{7.871} = 2.81$$

1. The 6 months at the beginning of the ratios (see Table 4-13) and the 6 months at the end are lost because of the 12-month centered moving average. These observations are replaced with the corresponding values of the following or preceding year as shown in Table 4-17.

2. The ratios of each year are adjusted so they add to 1200 by summing up the values of each of the years separately and dividing the sum by 12. The value obtained is the average of all months for each year. This value is divided into each month for the appropriate year, giving an average monthly figure of 100. This procedure is illustrated in Table 4-18.

Several adjustments have now been made to the centered ratios of Table 4-13 as part of this preliminary stage. First, the extreme values were replaced. Second, values for the missing first and last 6 observations were estimated and filled in. And third, the ratios were adjusted to sum to 1200. The objective has been to eliminate the effect of unusual events and to adjust the series for effects caused by computational procedures. The next step is to eliminate randomness by taking a 3 × 3 MA of each month of the year individually. This moving average is analogous to the one described in Table 4-14 except that the modified data with replaced extreme values, estimates for missing values, and adjusted ratios is used. Table 4-19 shows the results, the preliminary seasonal adjustment factors.

TABLE 4-16 REPLACEMENT OF EXTREME VALUES (APRIL)

	3 × 3 MA (Table 4-14)	Plus or Minus 2 * SD	Greater or Smaller Than Corresponding Control Limits (Table 4-13)		Substitute in Table 4-13
1949	—	—	—	—	—
1950	98.63	±5.62	99	No	—
1951	98.85	±5.62	99.3	No	—
1952	98.8	±5.62	94.6	No	—
1953	99.68	±5.62	105.4	Greater	(94.6 + 97.0)/2 = 95.8
1954	98.95	±5.62	97.0	No	—
1955	98.45	±5.62	97.7	No	—
1956	97.5	±5.62	97.3	No	—

Replaced Extreme Values

Year	Month	Value
1954	Feb.	88.5386
1953	Apr.	95.8314
1951	Aug.	119.947
1950	Nov.	81.3118

TABLE 4-17 ESTIMATING VALUES FOR THE FIRST AND LAST 6 OBSERVATIONS

1949	87.6	94.7	104.5	99.0	91.0	107.4	116.7	116.3	106.3	92.5	80.6	90.9
1950	87.6	94.7	104.5	99.0	91.0	107.4	120.6	118.7	108.4	89.6	81.3	90.5
1951	·	·										
1952	·	·										
1953	·	·										
1954	·	·										
1955	92.4	87.4	98.5	97.7	96.9	117.7	127.4	119.9	106.4	92.2	78.7	91.0
1956	91.6	88.1	99.5	97.3	98.0	114.3	127.4	119.9	106.4	92.2	78.7	91.0

TABLE 4-18   ADJUSTING THE MONTHLY RATIOS SO THAT THEIR
AVERAGE IS 100 (1950)

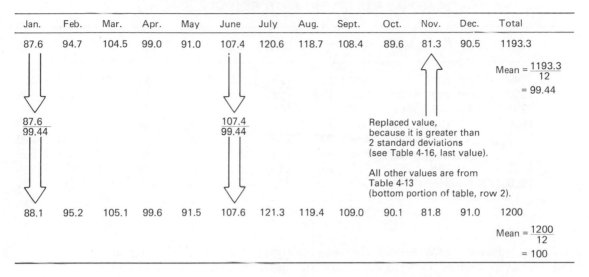

Jan.	Feb.	Mar.	Apr.	May	June	July	Aug.	Sept.	Oct.	Nov.	Dec.	Total
87.6	94.7	104.5	99.0	91.0	107.4	120.6	118.7	108.4	89.6	81.3	90.5	1193.3

Mean = $\dfrac{1193.3}{12}$ = 99.44

$\dfrac{87.6}{99.44}$ $\dfrac{107.4}{99.44}$

Replaced value, because it is greater than 2 standard deviations (see Table 4-16, last value).

All other values are from Table 4-13 (bottom portion of table, row 2).

Jan.	Feb.	Mar.	Apr.	May	June	July	Aug.	Sept.	Oct.	Nov.	Dec.	Total
88.1	95.2	105.1	99.6	91.5	107.6	121.3	119.4	109.0	90.1	81.8	91.0	1200

Mean = $\dfrac{1200}{12}$ = 100

The last step of this preliminary phase is to divide the preliminary seasonal factors of Table 4-19 into the original data to obtain the preliminary seasonally adjusted series of Table 4-20. This series constitutes the basis for further refining the estimates of seasonality, trend-cycle, and randomness performed as the third stage of Census II.

Table 4-13 gives values equivalent to equation (4-38) and these include seasonality and randomness. Since randomness was eliminated by replacing extreme values and smoothing (4-38) through a 3×3 moving

TABLE 4-19   PRELIMINARY SEASONAL ADJUSTMENT FACTOR

Year	Jan.	Feb.	Mar.	Apr.	May	June	July	Aug.	Sept.	Oct.	Nov.	Dec.
1949	89.0	95.0	106.2	99.5	94.1	107.4	118.4	118.4	107.2	91.8	81.5	91.5
1950	89.7	95.0	105.9	98.8	94.7	107.5	118.3	119.0	106.7	91.5	81.6	91.3
1951	90.8	94.3	106.0	97.7	97.0	107.6	117.3	119.6	105.5	91.7	81.4	91.0
1952	91.4	93.3	105.0	96.6	98.2	108.7	117.8	120.3	104.8	92.2	81.2	90.5
1953	91.4	91.2	103.9	96.4	99.3	109.5	119.8	120.5	104.8	92.6	80.5	90.0
1954	91.1	89.4	101.8	96.7	98.8	111.0	123.3	120.3	105.3	92.4	79.9	89.9
1955	91.2	88.1	100.3	97.2	98.3	111.7	125.7	120.0	105.8	92.2	79.2	90.2
1956	91.3	87.8	99.4	97.2	97.8	112.6	126.8	119.8	105.9	91.9	78.9	90.4

TABLE 4-20   PRELIMINARY SEASONALLY ADJUSTED SERIES
[ACTUAL DATA (TABLE 4-9)/PRELIMINARY
SEASONAL ADJUSTMENT FACTORS (TABLE 4-19)]

Year	Jan.	Feb.	Mar.	Apr.	May	June	July	Aug.	Sept.	Oct.	Nov.	Dec.
1949	126	124	124	130	129	126	125	125	127	130	128	129
1950	128	133	133	137	132	139	144	143	148	145	140	153
1951	160	159	168	167	177	165	170	166	174	177	179	182
1952	187	193	184	187	186	201	195	201	199	207	212	214
1953	214	215	227	244	231	222	220	226	226	228	224	223
1954	224	210	231	235	237	238	245	244	246	248	254	255
1955	265	265	266	277	275	282	290	289	295	297	299	308
1956	311	315	319	322	325	332	326	338	335	333	343	338

average, what remains is only the seasonal component. If this seasonal component is divided into the original data, only the trend-cycle and the irregular fluctuations in the data remain. These are the values shown in Table 4-20, and they can be written mathematically as:

$$PI_t = \frac{X_t}{I_t} = \frac{I_t T_t C_t E_t}{I_t} = T_t C_t E_t, \tag{4-39}$$

where the PI_t are the preliminary seasonally adjusted values.

4/5/3   Final Seasonal Adjustments

In this stage of Census II the preliminary seasonally adjusted series is processed further by using moving averages to eliminate any seasonal and irregular effects not detected previously. This result is achieved through a sequence of steps similar to those applied in the preliminary phase described in the last section.

Isolating the Trend-Cycle

Using the seasonally adjusted data as a starting point, one removes the randomness by applying Spencer's 15-month weighted moving average. The rationale for applying this average is that the data given by equation (4-39) include trend-cycle and randomness. This moving average eliminates the randomness, providing a smooth curve that highlights the existence of a trend-cycle in the data. Table 4-21 illustrates this, showing the results obtained with equation (4-40). When the original data are divided by the

TABLE 4-21   CALCULATING SPENCER'S 15-MONTH WEIGHTED
                 MOVING AVERAGE

Weights for Spencer's
15-point MA (see
Section 4/4/4)

				Weights		
Added Values	1	$\dfrac{504}{4} = 126$		$126 * (-.009)$		
	2			$126 * (-.019)$		
	3			$126 * (-.016)$		
	4			$126 * (\ .009)$		
	5			$126 * (\ .066)$		
	6			$126 * (\ .144)$		
	7			$126 * (\ .209)$		
1949	Jan.	$504 =$		$126 * (\ .231)$	$= 126$	First value in
	Feb.			$124 * (\ .209)$		Spencer's 15-MA (see
	Mar.			$124 * (\ .144)$		bottom portion of this table)
	Apr.			$130 * (\ .066)$		
	May			$129 * (\ .009)$		
	June			$126 * (-.016)$		
	July			$125 * (-.019)$		
	Aug.			$125 * (-.009)$		
	Sept.			127		
	Oct.			130		
	—					
	—					

Spencer's 15-Month Weighted Moving Averages (preliminary seasonally adjusted series)

Year	Jan.	Feb.	Mar.	Apr.	May	June	July	Aug.	Sept.	Oct.	Nov.	Dec.
1949	126	126	126	126	127	126	126	126	127	127	128	129
1950	130	131	133	134	137	139	141	143	144	146	148	152
1951	156	161	165	168	169	170	170	171	173	176	180	183
1952	185	187	188	189	191	193	196	200	203	206	209	213
1953	218	222	226	228	229	228	226	225	224	224	223	222
1954	222	224	227	231	235	239	242	244	247	249	253	257
1955	261	265	269	273	277	282	286	290	294	298	302	306
1956	310	315	319	322	325	328	331	333	335	337	338	338

Spencer 15-point moving averages only the seasonal and random factors remain. This result is called the final seasonal-irregular ratios and is given mathematically by equation (4-41):

$$M'_t = T_t C_t, \tag{4-40}$$

$$FIE_t = \frac{X_t}{M'_t} = \frac{I_t T_t C_t E_t}{T_t C_t} = I_t E_t, \tag{4-41}$$

where M'_t is Spencer's 15-point MA and FIE_t is the final seasonal irregular ratio.

Applying the Spencer 15-point formula would normally cause the loss of 7 values at the beginning of the series and 7 at the end. To avoid this loss, each of the missing values is replaced by an estimated value. The first 7 values are set equal to the average of the 4 following observations and the last 7 are set equal to the average of the 4 preceding observations. An illustration of this adjustment and computation of the Spencer 15-month moving average is given in Table 4-21.

Newer versions of Census II do not always use Spencer's 15-point formula. Instead, Henderson's weighted averages are used with the number of terms determined by the randomness in the series. (The greater the randomness, the longer the length of the moving average used.)

Final Seasonal-Irregular Ratios

The final seasonal-irregular ratios are calculated by dividing the values given by Spencer's 15-point formula into the original data. The result is the series of values represented by (4-41). (See Table 4-22.) These values serve as the starting point for replacing extreme values and adjusting the ratios so they sum to 1200. These steps are identical to those applied in Tables 4-14, 4-16, and 4-18.

The outcome is the set of final seasonal-irregular ratios presented in Table 4-22. The bottom portion of Table 4-22 gives the *stable factors*. These factors are the averages for each month and show the extent of the seasonality existing in the original airline data. They are equivalent to the seasonal indices calculated in the classical decomposition method. The only difference is that they have been found through two iterations of decomposition.

Final Seasonal Factors

The final seasonal factors are derived by applying a 3×3 moving average (or a 5×5 moving average if significant randomness is present) to the data of Table 4-22. The 3×3 moving average is computed as shown in Table 4-14. The 2 observations at the beginning and the 2 observations at the end that would normally be lost are estimated before the moving average is calculated. (When a 5×5 moving average is used, the 4 obser-

TABLE 4-22   FINAL SEASONAL-IRREGULAR RATIOS

Year	Jan.	Feb.	Mar.	Apr.	May	June	July	Aug.	Sept.	Oct.	Nov.	Dec.
			Centered Ratios (original/15 months moving average)									
1949	89.7	94.3	105.8	100.4	95.6	106.6	118.4	117.7	107.9	92.4	79.8	91.5
1950	90.1	94.7	105.8	99.4	95.6	107.1	118.4	118.1	107.4	92.1	79.7	91.5
1951	90.9	93.9	105.5	98.6	97.2	107.5	117.8	118.6	106.3	92.3	80.4	91.1
1952	91.3	92.3	104.6	98.3	97.9	108.7	118.1	119.6	105.2	92.5	80.8	90.7
1953	91.5	89.5	103.6	99.0	98.8	109.1	119.7	120.0	105.0	92.8	80.7	90.3
1954	91.6	87.6	102.2	98.9	98.5	110.5	122.6	120.3	105.2	92.3	80.1	90.1
1955	91.8	86.9	101.0	98.5	98.2	111.3	124.7	120.2	105.6	91.8	79.6	90.2
1956	91.9	87.1	100.3	97.8	97.9	112.3	125.5	120.4	105.7	91.4	79.6	90.2
			Stable Factors—Seasonal Indices									
	91.1	90.8	103.6	98.9	97.4	109.1	120.7	119.4	106.0	92.2	80.1	90.7

vations at each end are estimated.) The result is the set of final seasonal adjustment factors shown in Table 4-23. These factor values are projected out one year by multiplying the factor in the last row by 3, subtracting the factors of the preceding row and dividing the result by 2. For example, the one-year-ahead forecast for April of 98.1 is calculated as

$$[(98.3 \times 3) - 98.5]/2 = 98.1.$$

Mathematically, this step is equivalent to computing the expected values in order to remove any randomness that is still present.

$$FA'_t = \varepsilon\,(I_t E_t) = I_t, \tag{4-42}$$

where FA'_t is the final seasonal adjustment factor for period t and ε denotes expected value.

Final Seasonally Adjusted Series

The final seasonally adjusted series is found by dividing the final seasonal adjustment factors of Table 4-23 into the original data. The results for the international airline data are shown in Table 4-24. If the adjustment has been complete, fluctuations in the original data caused by seasonality will have been completely removed, and only the trend-cycle and randomness will remain. Mathematically, that is given by (4-43). Since seasonal

TABLE 4-23 FINAL SEASONAL ADJUSTMENT FACTORS

Year	Jan.	Feb.	Mar.	Apr.	May	June	July	Aug.	Sept.	Oct.	Nov.	Dec.
				Final Seasonal Adjustment Factors								
1949	90.1	94.3	105.7	99.6	95.9	107.0	118.2	118.0	107.4	92.3	79.9	91.4
1950	90.3	94.1	105.6	99.3	96.3	107.2	118.2	118.3	107.0	92.3	80.0	91.3
1951	90.7	93.3	105.2	98.9	97.0	107.8	118.3	118.7	106.3	92.4	80.3	91.0
1952	91.2	91.8	104.4	98.7	97.7	108.5	118.9	119.4	105.6	92.5	80.5	90.7
1953	91.5	89.9	103.4	98.7	98.2	109.4	120.3	119.8	105.3	92.5	80.4	90.4
1954	91.6	88.3	102.3	98.6	98.3	110.4	122.3	120.1	105.3	92.2	80.1	90.2
1955	91.8	87.4	101.4	98.5	98.2	111.1	123.8	120.3	105.5	91.9	79.9	90.2
1956	91.8	87.1	100.9	98.3	98.1	111.6	124.6	120.3	105.6	91.7	79.7	90.2
				One-Year-Ahead Forecasted Seasonal Factors								
	91.9	87.0	100.7	98.1	98.0	111.8	125.0	120.4	105.6	91.6	79.6	90.2

adjustments tend to smooth the series, the result is a clearer and more refined estimate of the trend-cycle pattern mixed with randomness.

$$FA_t = \frac{X_t}{\varepsilon(I_t E_t)} = \frac{I_t T_t C_t E_t}{I_t} = T_t C_t E_t. \tag{4-43}$$

The preparation of the final seasonally adjusted series completes this major phase of Census II. An important characteristic of this phase is that the task of isolating randomness and seasonal factors is not done simultaneously as it is in most decomposition methods. The division of this task enlarges the computational requirements, but it also generally improves the accuracy.

Before proceeding with the final phase of Census II, two additional sets of values for the time series are needed—a final estimate of trend-cycle values and a final estimate of the random component. The first of these is calculated by applying a 15-month weighted moving average to the final seasonally adjusted data of Table 4-24. The results are as shown in Table 4-25. Mathematically, this calculation is equivalent to computing the expected value of equation (4-43).

$$(FA_t) = \varepsilon(T_t C_t E_t), \tag{4-44}$$

$$FA_t' = T_t C_t. \tag{4-45}$$

TABLE 4-24   FINAL SEASONALLY ADJUSTED SERIES

Year	Jan.	Feb.	Mar.	Apr.	May	June	July	Aug.	Sept.	Oct.	Nov.	Dec.
1949	124	125	125	129	126	126	125	125	127	129	130	129
1950	127	134	134	136	130	139	144	144	148	144	143	153
1951	160	161	169	165	177	165	168	168	173	175	182	182
1952	188	196	185	183	187	201	193	203	198	207	214	214
1953	214	218	228	238	233	222	219	227	225	228	224	222
1954	223	213	230	230	238	239	247	244	246	248	253	254
1955	264	267	263	273	275	284	294	289	296	298	297	308
1956	309	318	314	319	324	335	331	337	336	334	340	339

Equation (4-45) is a much better estimate of the trend-cycle than either (4-37) or (4-40) because it is derived using (4-43) which is applied to the seasonally adjusted series.

Finally, equation (4-45) can be divided into (4-43) to obtain:

$$RC_t = \frac{FA_t}{FA_t'} = \frac{T_t C_t E_t}{T_t C_t} = E_t. \qquad (4\text{-}46)$$

Equation (4-46) provides the estimate of the random component. The results of this step applied to the international airline passenger series are shown in Table 4-26.

TABLE 4-25   FINAL ESTIMATE OF TREND-CYCLE COMPONENT

Spencer's 15-Point Weighted Average (seasonally adjusted series)

Year	Jan.	Feb.	Mar.	Apr.	May	June	July	Aug.	Sept.	Oct.	Nov.	Dec.
1949	125	126	126	126	126	126	126	126	127	128	129	129
1950	130	131	132	134	136	138	141	142	144	146	149	153
1951	157	162	166	168	169	169	169	170	173	176	180	184
1952	186	187	188	189	191	193	196	199	203	206	210	214
1953	218	223	226	228	229	228	226	225	224	224	223	222
1954	222	223	226	230	235	239	243	245	247	249	253	256
1955	260	264	268	272	277	283	287	291	295	298	301	305
1956	309	313	317	321	325	329	332	335	336	337	337	338

TABLE 4-26 FINAL ESTIMATE OF IRREGULAR (RANDOM) COMPONENT

Random Component (seasonally adjusted series/Spencer's 15-point formula)

Year	Jan.	Feb.	Mar.	Apr.	May	June	July	Aug.	Sept.	Oct.	Nov.	Dec.
1949	99.2	99.6	99.2	102.7	100.0	100.1	99.3	99.3	99.8	101.0	101.3	99.7
1950	97.6	102.0	100.9	101.4	95.4	100.4	102.3	100.9	102.4	98.6	95.7	100.5
1951	101.7	99.4	102.2	98.1	105.0	97.7	99.4	98.4	100.2	99.5	101.0	99.3
1952	100.8	104.7	98.2	97.0	98.3	104.1	98.7	101.7	97.6	100.3	102.0	100.1
1953	98.2	97.9	100.9	104.3	102.0	97.6	97.0	100.8	100.3	101.9	100.4	100.2
1954	~100.5	95.5	101.7	99.9	101.2	99.9	101.9	99.6	99.6	99.5	100.3	99.1
1955	101.6	101.1	98.3	100.3	99.1	100.3	102.4	99.1	100.4	100.0	98.5	101.0
1956	100.1	101.5	99.0	99.2	99.6	101.8	99.7	100.6	100.1	99.0	100.8	100.5

It may well seem that the Census II method is very complicated because of the number of steps involved up to this point. However, the basic idea is really quite straightforward—to isolate the seasonal, trend-cycle, and irregular components one by one. This process has two major phases. First, a preliminary estimate of the seasonality is made so that the seasonal component can be removed from the data. The remaining two components (trend-cycle and irregular) are therefore easier to identify and isolate. Second, refined estimates of seasonality, trend-cycle, and randomness are prepared. A summary diagram of the steps followed is given in Figure 4-2.

4/5/4 Tests and Summary Statistics

After phase III has been completed and the basic components of time series have been estimated, in phase IV a series of tests are used to determine whether or not the decomposition has been successful. These tests are not statistical in the rigorous mathematical sense, but are based on intuitive considerations. The four types of tests most commonly used are described below.

Adjacent Month Test

Calculating the ratio of a given month to the average of the preceding and following months gives an indication of how that particular month varies from the preceding and following months. If the data are nonseasonal, such variations should be small. However, when strong seasonality exists, the variations will be considerable, reflecting the pattern that exists between successive months. If the ratios of all the years are averaged for each of the individual months, the results will give an even better indication of the variability of the series. Table 4-27 shows the ratios of the preceding and following months of the original airline passenger data. These ratios vary considerably from month to month, suggesting that the original series is strongly seasonal.

If the same calculations are performed on the seasonally adjusted data the resulting ratios should be much smaller if the seasonal adjustment has been successful. The seasonal adjustment which gives these ratios for data shows that the seasonality has been removed. If some values of the average ratios in Table 4-28 had been below 95 or above 105, it would indicate that the seasonal adjustment process had not been adequate in removing the seasonal variation. Since the adjacent month ratios in Table

TABLE 4-27   ADJACENT MONTH TEST (ORIGINAL DATA)

Ratios of Preceding and Following Month[a]

Year	Jan.	Feb.	Mar.	Apr.	May	June	July	Aug.	Sept.	Oct.	Nov.	Dec.
1949	0	96.7	106.9	102.0	91.7	100.4	104.6	104.2	101.9	99.2	87.8	107.8
1950	94.3	98.4	108.0	101.5	88.0	101.0	106.6	103.7	104.3	97.8	83.5	108.1
1951	100.0	92.9	113.7	93.1	100.9	96.0	105.6	103.9	101.9	98.2	89.0	104.7
1952	98.8	98.9	106.9	96.3	91.7	105.6	100.0	110.3	96.5	100.3	89.4	105.4
1953	100.5	90.7	109.5	101.1	95.8	98.6	102.5	108.6	98.1	101.2	87.4	104.7
1954	104.9	85.6	113.3	96.8	95.3	98.5	108.4	104.5	99.2	99.1	88.6	102.9
1955	104.8	91.6	106.4	100.2	92.5	99.4	110.0	102.7	100.5	99.8	85.9	106.7
1956	102.3	92.2	107.5	98.6	92.6	102.3	106.0	105.5	99.9	97.8	88.6	0

Averages

	Jan.	Feb.	Mar.	Apr.	May	June	July	Aug.	Sept.	Oct.	Nov.	Dec.
	100.8	93.4	109.0	98.7	93.6	100.2	105.5	105.4	100.3	99.2	87.5	105.8

[a]*Sample computations* (values taken from Table 4-9): The first ratio is 0 because there is no preceding month's value for month 1;

the second ratio is

$$\frac{118}{(112 + 132)/2} = .967 \text{ or } 96.7\%;$$

the third ratio is

$$\frac{132}{(118 + 129)/2} = 1.069 \text{ or } 106.9\%;$$

and so on.

4-28 are all close to 100, one would conclude in this case that the deseasonalizing had been successful.

The January Test

Dividing the final seasonally adjusted series by the corresponding values of each preceding January gives a set of standardized values with January as the base. Examining these values of the standardized ratios could identify any constant pattern of longer than one month's duration. If such patterns exist, it suggests that seasonality has not been properly removed from the data. The January test reveals any intrayear seasonality

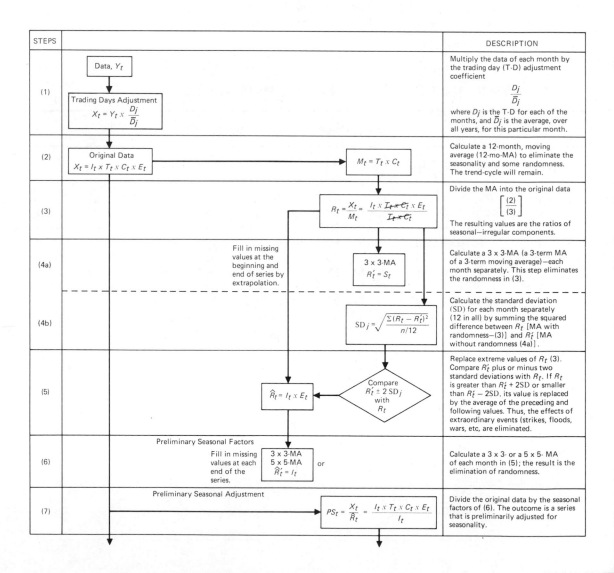

STEPS			DESCRIPTION
(1)	Data, Y_t Trading Days Adjustment $X_t = Y_t \times \dfrac{D_j}{\overline{D}_j}$		Multiply the data of each month by the trading day (T-D) adjustment coefficient $\dfrac{D_j}{\overline{D}_j}$ where D_j is the T-D for each of the months, and $\overline{D}_j$ is the average, over all years, for this particular month.
(2)	Original Data $X_t = I_t \times T_t \times C_t \times E_t$	$M_t = T_t \times C_t$	Calculate a 12-month, moving average (12-mo-MA) to eliminate the seasonality and some randomness. The trend-cycle will remain.
(3)		$R_t = \dfrac{X_t}{M_t} = \dfrac{I_t \times \cancel{I_t \times C_t} \times E_t}{\cancel{I_t \times C_t}}$	Divide the MA into the original data $\left[\dfrac{(2)}{(3)} \right]$ The resulting values are the ratios of seasonal—irregular components.
(4a)	Fill in missing values at the beginning and end of series by extrapolation.	3 x 3-MA $R'_t = S_t$	Calculate a 3 x 3-MA (a 3-term MA of a 3-term moving average)—each month separately. This step eliminates the randomness in (3).
(4b)		$SD_j = \sqrt{\dfrac{\Sigma (R_t - R'_t)^2}{n/12}}$	Calculate the standard deviation (SD) for each month separately (12 in all) by summing the squared difference between R_t [MA with randomness—(3)] and R'_t [MA without randomness (4a)].
(5)		$\hat{R}_t = I_t \times E_t$ ← Compare $R'_t \pm 2\,SD_j$ with R_t	Replace extreme values of R_t (3). Compare R'_t plus or minus two standard deviations with R_t. If R_t is greater than $R'_t + 2SD$ or smaller than $R'_t - 2SD$, its value is replaced by the average of the preceding and following values. Thus, the effects of extraordinary events (strikes, floods, wars, etc, are eliminated.
(6)	Preliminary Seasonal Factors Fill in missing values at each end of the series.	3 x 3-MA 5 x 5-MA or $\hat{R}'_t = I_t$	Calculate a 3 x 3- or a 5 x 5- MA of each month in (5); the result is the elimination of randomness.
(7)	Preliminary Seasonal Adjustment	$PS_t = \dfrac{X_t}{\hat{R}_t} = \dfrac{I_t \times T_t \times C_t \times E_t}{I_t}$	Divide the original data by the seasonal factors of (6). The outcome is a series that is preliminarily adjusted for seasonality.

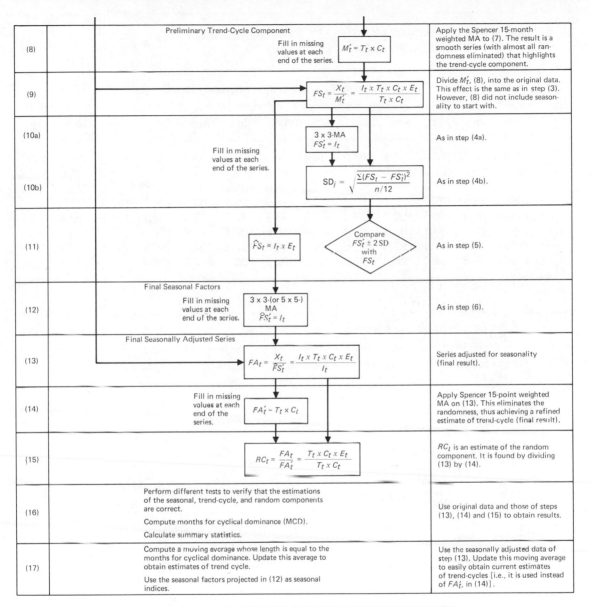

(8)	Preliminary Trend-Cycle Component Fill in missing values at each end of the series. $M'_t = T_t \times C_t$	Apply the Spencer 15-month weighted MA to (7). The result is a smooth series (with almost all randomness eliminated) that highlights the trend-cycle component.
(9)	$FS_t = \dfrac{X_t}{M'_t} = \dfrac{I_t \times T_t \times C_t \times E_t}{T_t \times C_t}$	Divide M'_t, (8), into the original data. This effect is the same as in step (3). However, (8) did not include seasonality to start with.
(10a)	Fill in missing values at each end of the series. $3 \times 3\text{-MA}$ $FS'_t = I_t$	As in step (4a).
(10b)	$SD_j = \sqrt{\dfrac{\Sigma(FS_t - FS'_t)^2}{n/12}}$	As in step (4b).
(11)	$\widehat{FS}_t = I_t \times E_t$ Compare $FS'_t \pm 2\,SD$ with FS_t	As in step (5).
(12)	Final Seasonal Factors Fill in missing values at each end of the series. $3 \times 3\text{-(or } 5 \times 5\text{-)}$ MA $\widehat{FS}'_t = I_t$	As in step (6).
(13)	Final Seasonally Adjusted Series $FA_t = \dfrac{X_t}{\widehat{FS}'_t} = \dfrac{I_t \times T_t \times C_t \times E_t}{I_t}$	Series adjusted for seasonality (final result).
(14)	Fill in missing values at each end of the series. $FA'_t = T_t \times C_t$	Apply Spencer 15-point weighted MA on (13). This eliminates the randomness, thus achieving a refined estimate of trend-cycle (final result).
(15)	$RC_t = \dfrac{FA_t}{FA'_t} = \dfrac{T_t \times C_t \times E_t}{T_t \times C_t}$	RC_t is an estimate of the random component. It is found by dividing (13) by (14).
(16)	Perform different tests to verify that the estimations of the seasonal, trend-cycle, and random components are correct. Compute months for cyclical dominance (MCD). Calculate summary statistics.	Use original data and those of steps (13), (14) and (15) to obtain results.
(17)	Compute a moving average whose length is equal to the months for cyclical dominance. Update this average to obtain estimates of trend cycle. Use the seasonal factors projected in (12) as seasonal indices.	Use the seasonally adjusted data of step (13). Update this moving average to easily obtain current estimates of trend-cycles [i.e., it is used instead of FA'_t, in (14)].

FIGURE 4-2   MAJOR STEPS IN CENSUS II DECOMPOSITION METHOD

that might remain, while the adjacent month test reveals any interyear seasonality that might remain. The adjacent month and January tests should be used in combination to be sure that the removal of seasonality has been successful. Table 4-29 illustrates the January test for the final seasonally adjusted airline data. The only apparent pattern in the ratios is trend, indicating that seasonality has been effectively removed.

TABLE 4-28   ADJACENT MONTH TEST (FINAL SEASONALLY
ADJUSTED DATA)

Ratios of Preceding and Following Month[a]

Year	Jan.	Feb.	Mar.	Apr.	May	June	July	Aug.	Sept.	Oct.	Nov.	Dec.
1949	0	100.4	98.1	103.2	98.6	100.5	99.5	99.6	99.6	100.4	100.9	100.3
1950	96.8	102.7	99.0	103.2	94.5	101.5	101.8	98.6	102.6	99.3	95.8	101.5
1951	101.7	97.7	104.0	95.1	107.5	95.6	101.1	98.2	100.9	98.8	101.7	98.7
1952	99.1	105.3	97.4	98.6	97.5	105.5	95.8	103.6	96.7	100.3	101.7	99.9
1953	99.3	98.5	100.1	103.2	101.3	98.2	97.7	102.1	98.9	101.6	99.4	99.6
1954	102.3	94.1	103.8	98.4	101.4	98.6	102.3	98.9	100.0	99.5	100.9	98.2
1955	101.4	101.1	97.6	101.5	98.7	99.7	102.8	97.8	100.9	100.6	97.9	101.7
1956	98.8	102.0	98.7	99.8	99.2̄	102.3	98.7	100.8	100.4	98.6	101.1	0

Averages

	Jan.	Feb.	Mar.	Apr.	May	June	July	Aug.	Sept.	Oct.	Nov.	Dec.
	99.9	100.2	99.8	100.4	99.8	100.2	100.0	100.0	100.0	99.9	99.9	100.0

[a]*Sample computations* (values taken from Table 4-24): The first ratio is 0 because there is no preceding month's value for month 1;

the second ratio is

$$\frac{125.1}{(124.3 + 124.9)/2} = 100.4\%;$$

the third ratio is

$$\frac{124.9}{(125.1 + 129.5)/2} = 98.1\%.$$

Equality Test

In applying a decomposition method such as Census II, over-adjustment is a concern just as under-adjustment is. One test to determine whether over-adjustment has taken place is obtained by dividing the 12-month moving average of the original data into the 12-month moving average of the seasonally adjusted data. The 12-month moving average of the original data should have eliminated the seasonality without altering the volume of the data. The 12-month moving average of the final seasonally adjusted data should also have eliminated seasonality, but in addition should make other adjustments such as the elimination of randomness, replacement of extremes, and so on. As a result, the final seasonally adjusted data may have

TABLE 4-29   JANUARY TEST

Standardized Ratios to Preceding January (seasonally adjusted series)[a]

Year	Jan.	Feb.	Mar.	Apr.	May	June	July	Aug.	Sept.	Oct.	Nov.	Dec.
1949	100.0	100.6	100.4	104.2	101.5	101.5	100.7	100.9	101.9	103.7	104.8	103.9
1950	100.0	105.2	104.9	106.8	102.0	109.1	113.0	112.9	116.0	113.2	112.0	120.5
1951	100.0	100.7	105.9	103.1	111.0	103.4	105.3	104.9	108.3	109.7	113.8	114.1
1952	100.0	104.6	98.5	97.8	99.8	107.1	103.1	108.1	105.5	110.1	114.0	114.0
1953	100.0	101.7	106.5	111.1	108.8	103.7	102.4	105.9	105.0	106.5	104.4	103.7
1954	100.0	95.6	103.2	103.4	106.9	107.5	111.0	109.6	110.5	111.5	113.8	114.0
1955	100.0	101.1	99.9	103.6	104.2	107.5	111.5	109.4	112.2	113.0	112.5	116.9
1956	100.0	102.8	101.6	103.0	104.8	108.4	107.2	108.8	108.7	107.9	109.9	109.7

[a]*Sample computations* (values taken from Table 4-24): The first ratio is

$$\frac{124.3}{124.3} = 100\%;$$

the second ratio is

$$\frac{125.1}{124.3} = 100.6\%;$$

the third ratio is

$$\frac{124.9}{124.3} = 100.4\%;$$

the thirteenth ratio is

$$\frac{127.3}{127.3} = 100\%;$$

the fourteenth ratio is

$$\frac{133.9}{127.3} = 105.2\%.$$

included some of the irregular components as part of the seasonality. The ratios between these two averages can be used to identify any over-adjustment for seasonality that may have taken place. If the ratios are close to 100, it indicates there is no over-adjustment. However, if the ratios are below 90 or above 110, it indicates that the seasonal adjustment may have been overzealous in eliminating fluctuations in the data. Table 4-30 illustrates the calculations of the equality test for the passenger airline data. For these data there does not appear to have been any over-adjustment.

TABLE 4-30   EQUALITY TEST

Ratios (12-month MA seasonally adjusted data/12-month MA original data)[a]

Year	Jan.	Feb.	Mar.	Apr.	May	June	July	Aug.	Sept.	Oct.	Nov.	Dec.
1949	101.9	100.1	98.5	97.7	98.1	99.6	99.5	99.8	100.8	100.3	100.0	100.9
1950	101.8	101.5	100.4	99.2	98.3	99.3	99.4	99.8	100.9	100.3	100.1	101.0
1951	101.7	101.4	100.3	99.1	98.4	99.5	99.6	99.9	101.1	100.6	100.5	101.3
1952	101.9	101.7	100.3	99.2	98.3	99.5	99.6	99.7	101.0	100.5	100.5	101.3
1953	102.0	101.7	100.4	99.3	98.4	99.3	99.4	99.3	100.5	100.2	100.2	101.1
1954	101.9	101.5	100.1	99.0	98.1	99.1	99.4	99.3	100.6	100.4	100.4	101.4
1955	102.2	101.5	99.9	98.8	98.0	99.1	99.4	99.2	100.5	100.3	100.3	101.4
1956	102.3	101.6	100.1	98.9	98.1	99.1	99.4	99.0	99.8	100.4	101.0	102.8

[a]Sample computations:

	(1)	(2) Final Seasonally Adjusted Data		(3) Original Data		(4)
	Period	Data	12-Month MA	Data	12-Month MA	Ratio (2)/(3)
	1	125.95		122.75		
	2	125.95		122.75		
	3	125.95	= 125.95	122.75		
	4	125.95		122.75		
	5	125.95		122.75		
	6	125.95		122.75		
1949	Jan.	124.3	126.0	112	123.6	101.9%
	Feb.	125.1	125.9	118	125.7	100.1%
	Mar.	124.9	Average = 125.95	132	127.8	98.5%
	Apr.	129.5		129	Average = 122.75	
	May	126.1		121		(See
	June	126.2		135		upper
	July	125.2		148		portion of
	Aug.	125.4		148		this table.)
	Sept.	126.7		136		
	Oct.	128.9		119		
	Nov.	130.2		104		
	etc.					
		(from Table 4-24)		(from Table 4-9)		

Percentage Change Tests

There are several percentage change tests each of which involves finding the percentage of change to each value from that of the previous month. Four percentage change tests are commonly used—one for the original data and one for each of the major components of the time series (seasonality, trend-cycle, and randomness).

Original Data The percentage change test for the original data is used as a comparison guide for evaluating the other percentage change tests. The values for the airline data are shown in Table 4-31. The values of the percentage change tests for these original data should be larger than those obtained from the other three percentage change tests.

TABLE 4-31   PERCENTAGE CHANGE TEST (ORIGINAL DATA)

Percentage Change from Previous Month[a]

Year	Jan.	Feb.	Mar.	Apr.	May	June	July	Aug.	Sept.	Oct.	Nov.	Dcc.
1949	0	5.4	11.9	−2.3	−6.2	11.6	9.6	0	−8.1	−12.5	−12.6	13.5
1950	−2.5	9.6	11.9	−4.3	−7.4	19.2	14.1	0	−7.1	−15.8	−14.3	22.8
1951	3.6	3.4	18.7	−8.4	5.5	3.5	11.8	0	−7.5	−12.0	−9.9	13.7
1952	3.0	5.3	7.2	−6.2	1.1	19.1	5.5	5.2	−13.6	−8.6	−9.9	12.8
1953	1.0	0	20.4	−.4	−2.6	6.1	8.6	3.0	−12.9	−11.0	−14.7	11.7
1954	1.5	−7.8	25.0	−3.4	3.1	12.8	14.4	−3.0	−11.6	−11.6	−11.4	12.8
1955	5.7	−3.7	14.6	.7	.4	16.7	15.6	−4.7	−10.1	−12.2	−13.5	17.3
1956	2.2	−2.5	14.4	−1.3	1.6	17.6	10.4	−1.9	−12.3	−13.8	−11.4	12.9

Overall average = 8.90942.

[a]*Sample computations* (values taken from Table 4-9). The first percentage is 0, because there is no preceding month's value for month 1;

the second percentage is

$$\frac{(118 - 112)}{112} = 5.4\%;$$

the third percentage is

$$\frac{(132 - 118)}{118} = 11.9\%;$$

and so on. The overall average of all the percentage changes in Table 4-31 is computed as

$$\frac{\sum_{t=2}^{n} |PC_t|}{n - 1} = \frac{846.40}{95} = 8.909\%.$$

Final Seasonally Adjusted Series   The seasonally adjusted series does not include seasonal effects. Applying the percentage change test to this series and comparing it to the percentage change of the original data can reveal the amount of variation in the original data caused by seasonality (see Table 4-32).

Random Component   The irregular component of the series is used as the basis for computing the percentage change of the random component. Thus for the airline passenger series, the data of Table 4-26 is used as illustrated in Table 4-33. The overall average of the random component is particularly useful as a guide to the minimum amount of forecasting error that can be expected.

The overall average of 2.1% indicates that the maximum accuracy that can be expected in forecasting is 2.1%, the amount of randomness from

TABLE 4-32   PERCENTAGE CHANGE TEST (FINAL SEASONALLY ADJUSTED DATA)

Percentage Change from Previous Month[a]

Year	Jan.	Feb.	Mar.	Apr.	May	June	July	Aug.	Sept.	Oct.	Nov.	Dec.
1949	0	.6	−.2	3.7	−2.6	.1	−.8	.2	1.0	1.8	1.0	−.9
1950	−1.4	5.2	−.2	1.8	−4.5	7.0	3.5	−.1	2.7	−2.4	−1.1	7.6
1951	4.2	.7	5.3	−2.7	7.7	−6.9	1.9	−.4	3.3	1.3	3.7	.2
1952	2.9	4.6	−5.7	−.8	2.1	7.3	−3.7	4.8	−2.4	4.4	3.5	0
1953	.2	1.7	4.7	4.3	−2.1	−4.7	−1.3	3.5	−.8	1.4	−1.9	−.7
1954	.1	−4.4	8.0	.1	3.4	.5	3.3	−1.3	.9	.9	2.0	.2
1955	3.9	1.1	−1.2	3.7	.6	3.1	3.7	−1.9	2.5	.7	−.4	3.9
1956	.3	2.8	−1.2	1.4	1.8	3.4	−1.1	1.5	−0.1	−.8	1.9	−.2

Overall average = 2.38334.

[a]*Sample computations* (values taken from Table 4-24): The first percentage is 0 because there is no preceding month's value for month 1; the second percentage is

$$\frac{(125.1 - 124.3)}{124.3} = .6;$$

the third percentage is

$$\frac{(124.9 - 125.1)}{125.1} = -.2.$$

The overall average of the absolute values of the percentage changes is 2.383%. The difference between 8.909 and 2.383, that is, 6.526%, is the amount of variation in the original series attributable to seasonality.

TABLE 4-33   PERCENTAGE CHANGE TEST (RANDOM COMPONENT)

Percentage Change from Previous Month

Year	Jan.	Feb.	Mar.	Apr.	May	June	July	Aug.	Sept.	Oct.	Nov.	Dec.	Yearly Average
1949	0	.4	−.4	3.5	−2.6	.1	−.8	0	.6	1.2	.3	−1.6	1.1
1950	−2.1	4.4	−1.1	.6	−5.9	5.3	1.9	−1.4	1.5	−3.7	−2.9	5.0	3.0
1951	1.2	−2.2	2.9	−4.0	7.1	−7.0	1.7	−1.0	1.9	−.7	1.5	−1.7	2.7
1952	1.5	3.8	−6.2	−1.3	1.3	6.0	−5.2	3.1	−4.0	2.7	1.8	−1.9	3.2
1953	−1.9	−.4	3.0	3.4	−2.2	−4.3	−.6	4.0	−.5	1.6	−1.5	−.2	2.0
1954	.3	−4.9	6.5	−1.8	1.3	−1.3	1.9	−2.3	0	0	.8	−1.2	1.9
1955	2.5	−.4	−2.7	2.0	−1.2	1.3	2.0	−3.2	1.3	−.4	−1.6	2.6	1.8
1956	−.9	1.5	−2.5	.1	.5	2.2	−2.1	.8	−.5	−1.1	1.8	−.3	1.2

Overall average = 2.10951.

month to month. Since the seasonal variation accounted for 6.526% of the 8.909% variation in the original data, and the random component accounts for 2.110%, the balance of 0.273% (8.909 − 2.110 − 6.526) must be accounted for by trend-cycle variation. The conclusion that can be drawn for the airline data is that seasonality accounts for the bulk of the variation in the original data. The overall average of the absolute values of the percentage change is 2.11%. No smaller forecasting error than 2.11% can be expected. This is, therefore, the optimal or minimum percentage error for the specific data being used.

Trend-cycle Component   The final percentage change test is applied to the trend-cycle component. It represents the month-to-month changes in the trend-cycle. For the airline data, these values are shown in Table 4-34. When combined with the values for the percentage change in the random component, these two tests provide one of the most important measures used in Census II—the month for cyclical dominance (MCD). The MCD is the time span for which the ratio of the two averages becomes greater than one.

4/5/5   Month for Cyclical Dominance (MCD)

Tables 4-33 and 4-34 show the percentage change of each month from that of the previous month for the random and trend-cycle components, respectively. The ratio of the average percentage change for all months (without regard to sign) of the random component to that of the trend-cycle component indicates the relative variation of each component. For the airline data the ratio is 1.9(2.11/1.12), which indicates that the random component dominates the cyclical component 1.9 times.

Using the same computational procedures applied in developing Tables 4-33 and 4-34, percentage changes for 2, 3, 4, and 5 months can be obtained. The ratios of the random and trend-cycle component changes for longer than 1 month's duration can then be used to determine for how many durations the random component variation exceeds that of the trend-cycle. As the time span increases, the changes in the trend-cycle component tend to become greater, while those of the irregular component become less because of the averaging of random terms. At some point the changes in the random component will about equal the changes in the trend-cycle component. The monthly span for which this occurs is called the month for cyclical dominance (MCD). In the airline data, MCD is 2 (see Table 4-36) because between a time span of 1 month and a time span of 2 months, the fluctuations in the trend-cycle become stronger than the fluctuations in the random component. This relationship can be seen by examining the ratio for a 1-month span (1.9) and a ratio for a 2-month span (.88). It means that over 2 months the trend-cycle dominates the fluctuations of the irregular component.

The MCD provides information that can be used to calculate a series of trend-cycle values with loss of a minimal number of values at the end of the series. Knowing that the MCD is 2 months for the airline data indicates that a 2-month MA of the final seasonally adjusted data should illustrate

TABLE 4-34 PERCENTAGE CHANGE TEST (TREND-CYCLE COMPONENT)

Percentage Change from Previous Month

Year	Jan.	Feb.	Mar.	Apr.	May	June	July	Aug.	Sept.	Oct.	Nov.	Dec.	Yearly Average
1949	0	.2	.2	.2	0	0	0	.2	.4	.6	.7	.7	.3
1950	.7	.7	.9	1.2	1.5	1.6	1.6	1.4	1.2	1.4	1.9	2.5	1.4
1951	3.0	3.0	2.3	1.4	.6	.1	.1	.6	1.4	2.0	2.2	2.0	1.6
1952	1.3	.7	.4	.5	.8	1.2	1.6	1.7	1.7	1.6	1.7	1.9	1.3
1953	2.1	2.1	1.6	.9	.1	−.4	−.6	−.5	−.3	−.3	−.4	−.5	.8
1954	−.1	.6	1.4	2.0	2.1	1.8	1.3	1.0	.9	1.0	1.2	1.4	1.2
1955	1.4	1.5	1.6	1.7	1.9	1.8	1.6	1.4	1.2	1.1	1.2	1.3	1.5
1956	1.3	1.3	1.3	1.3	1.3	1.2	1.0	.7	.4	.3	.1	.1	.8

Overall average = 1.11759.

the movement in the trend-cycle component, since it will eliminate the greatest part of the irregular component. Table 4-35 illustrates this, although in this case a 3-month MA was used in order to center the average. Table 4-35 is similar to Table 4-25 except that Table 4-35 has only 1 value missing and it is very easy to update. In practice, the MCD is usually less than 6, which results in a short moving average with only 1 or at most 2 values missing at the end. Furthermore, to calculate the moving average as new data become available is computationally very easy. That is not true of Table 4-25, which is calculated using Spencer's 15-point formula.

The MCD moving average is the basis for forecasting the trend-cycle. A graphical plot of the moving averages of Table 4-35 is extremely useful in identifying changes in the level of economic activity, the trend-cycle. For the airline series, the graph is shown in Figure 4-3. The last value given in that graph, 340.135, is a rough estimate of the trend-cycle found by averaging the last 2 values of the final seasonally adjusted data of Table 4-24; that is, periods 95 and 96 were averaged $[(340 + 339)/2 = 339.5]$. Since that average corresponds to period 95.5, it is half a period behind period 96. Therefore, it can be adjusted by adding to it half the trend change occurring between periods 94 and 95 $[(338. - 337.)/2 = .5]$. This procedure yields an estimate for the trend-cycle for period 96 of $339.5 + .5 = 340$. The final output of Census II (see Table 4-36) is a set of dummy statistics.

TABLE 4-35   3-MONTH MOVING AVERAGE (FINAL SEASONALLY ADJUSTED SERIES): ESTIMATE OF TREND-CYCLE COMPONENT

Moving Average of Adjusted Series, MCD Period Centered

Year	Jan.	Feb.	Mar.	Apr.	May	June	July	Aug.	Sept.	Oct.	Nov.	Dec.
1949	0	125	126	127	127	126	126	126	127	129	129	129
1950	130	132	134	133	135	138	142	145	145	145	147	152
1951	158	163	165	170	169	170	167	170	172	177	180	184
1952	189	190	188	185	190	194	199	198	202	206	211	214
1953	215	220	228	233	231	225	223	224	227	226	225	223
1954	219	222	224	233	236	241	243	246	246	249	252	257
1955	261	265	268	270	277	284	289	293	294	297	301	305
1956	312	314	317	319	326	330	334	335	335	337	338	0

Overall average (of their percentage change) = 1.43676.

Overall average of percentage changes without regard to signs is 1.44. This is found as:

$$\sum_{t=2}^{n} \frac{(|FA'_t - FA'_{t-1}|)}{FA'_{t-1}} \bigg/ (n - 1) = 1.44.$$

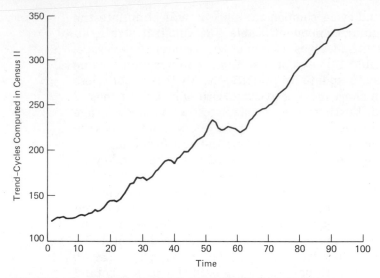

FIGURE 4-3 TREND-CYCLES COMPUTED IN CENSUS II

4/5/6 Forecasting

In order to forecast, estimates of the trend-cycle must be found. These can be obtained from Figure 4-3 then multiplied by the corresponding one-year-ahead forecasts of seasonality obtained from Table 4-23. Thus, the forecasts for January, February, and March 1957 (assuming trend-cycles of 342, 345, 347) are

$$F_{J1957} = 342(.919) = 314.3,$$

$$F_{F1957} = 345(.87) = 300.15,$$

$$F_{M1957} = 347(1.007) = 349.43.$$

4/6 Developments in Decomposition Methods

Decomposition methods originated around the beginning of this century and were initiated from two different directions. First, it was recognized that to study the serial correlation within or between variable(s), any spurious correlation that might exist because of trend must be eliminated. As early as 1884 Poynting attempted to eliminate trend and some seasonal fluctuations by averaging prices over several years. Hooker (1901) followed Poynting's example, but was more precise in his methods for eliminating trend. His work was followed by Spencer (1904) and Anderson and Nochmals (1914), who generalized the procedure of trend elimination to include higher-order polynomials.

TABLE 4-36   SUMMARY STATISTICS FROM CENSUS II

Average % Change

Original	Trend-cycle	3-M MA	Random	seas. adj. series
8.90942	1.11759	1.43676	2.10951	2.38334

$\dfrac{\text{Random}}{\text{Trend-cycle}}$	$\dfrac{\text{Random}}{\text{Season}}$	$\dfrac{\text{Season}}{\text{Trend-cycle}}$
1.88755	.885107	2.13257

$\dfrac{\text{Random}}{\text{Original}}$	$\dfrac{\text{Trend-cycle}}{\text{Original}}$	$\dfrac{\text{Season}}{\text{Original}}$
.236774	.12544	.267508

Average Duration of Positive and Negative Signs

Original	Random	Trend-cycle	3-months MA
2.5	1.31944	23.75	1.82692

Random/Trend-Cycle
Span in months

1	2	3	4	5
1.88755	.877671	.665565	.407453	.303543

Months for cyclical dominance (MCD) = 2

A second direction for work in this area originated with economists who worried about the impact of depressions and sought ways to predict them. They felt that the elements of economic activity should be separated so that changes in the business cycle could be isolated from seasonal and other changes. France appointed a committee that in 1911 presented a report analyzing the causes of the 1907 economic crisis. This group introduced the idea of leading and coincidental indicators and attempted to separate the trend from the cycle so that the movement of the latter could be followed.

In the United States this idea was expanded and the concept of constructing barometers of business activity was developed. Furthermore, an attempt to separate the seasonal fluctuation from the rest of the components was made as early as 1915 (Copeland). The process of decomposition, as it is known today, was introduced by Macauley (1930), who in the 1920s introduced the ratio-to-moving averages method that forms the basis of Census II. (For a summary article, see Burman, 1979.)

An impetus in the development of decomposition came with the introduction and widespread use of computers. Shishkin (1957) developed a computer program that could perform the needed computations easily and quickly. This gave rise to Census II, which has become the most widely used of the decomposition methods.

More recently, the advantages of decomposition approaches have been recognized and efforts are being made to upgrade these approaches (see proceedings of NBER-Census Conference, 1976). These efforts have been in the direction of introducing statistical rigor into the approach without losing its intuitive appeal. (See Dagum, 1982.)

4/6/1   The FORAN System

Another forecasting method based on the principle of decomposition is the FORAN system developed by McLaughlin in the 1960s. The FORAN system has certain advantages over the Census II approach. It can deal with more than one variable simultaneously (it can use any independent variable in addition to time), and it is oriented toward the forecasting needs of business organizations rather than towards the macroseries of government related data.

The FORAN system decomposes a time series into seasonal, cyclical and trend, and irregular elements and provides a summary of the importance or contribution of each of them. One of the strongest points of FORAN is its ability to summarize a number of forecasting results together with descriptions of their accuracy over the last year (12 months). It is then up to the user to determine which forecast, or combination of forecasts, should be used for the final predictions. FORAN extends alternative forecasts for time horizons of 1, 2, and 3 months and provides summary measures of the accuracy of each.

FORAN must be used in conjunction with some other decomposition method because it does not provide the seasonal indices required as inputs to the program. FORAN concentrates on the remaining components of a time series—the trend-cycle and randomness.

According to its developers, FORAN has four main objectives (McLaughlin and Boyle, 1968, pp. 15–16):

1. To evaluate recent trends caused mainly by cyclical factors.
2. To analyze and evaluate the forecasting results of several forecasting methods.
3. To anticipate forthcoming turning points by analyzing the changes of the isolated cyclical component and/or by using leading indicators.
4. To forecast using a number of probabilistic and/or deterministic models as well as subjective predictions. An eclectic approach is employed in which the forecasts of different methods are compared and then combined using a weighting procedure.

In 1977, McLaughlin introduced FORAN II. This system includes a full range of the major approaches to forecasting and facilitates their comparison as a means to deciding where and when each is most appropriate.

REFERENCES AND SELECTED BIBLIOGRAPHY

Anderson, O., and U. Nochmals. 1914. "The Elimination of Spurious Correlation Due to Position in Time or Space," *Biometrica*, **10**, pp. 269–76.

Burman, J. P. 1979. "Seasonal Adjustment—A Survey," *TIMS Studies in Management Sciences,* **12**, pp. 45–57.

Copeland, M. T. 1915. "Statistical Indices of Business Conditions," *Quarterly Journal of Economics*, **29**, pp. 522–62.

Dagum, E. B. 1982. "Revisions of Time Varying Seasonal Filters," *Journal of Forecasting*, **1**, No. 2, pp. 20–28.

Freund, J. E. and F. J. Williams. 1969. *Modern Business Statistics*. Englewood Cliffs, N.J.: Prentice-Hall.

Hadley, G. 1968. *Introduction to Business Statistics*. San Francisco: Holden-Day.

Hooker, R. H. 1901. "The Suspension of the Berlin Produce Exchange and Its Effect upon Corn Prices," *Journal of the Royal Statistical Society,* **64**, pp. 574–603.

Macauley, F. R. 1930. *The Smoothing of Time Series*. National Bureau of Economic Research.

McLaughlin, R. L. 1962. *Time Series Forecasting*. Marketing Research Technique, Series No. 6. American Marketing Association.

McLaughlin, R. L., and J. J. Boyle. 1968. *Short Term Forecasting*. American Marketing Association Booklet.

NBER, 1976. "NBER-Census Conference Report." New York.

Poynting, J. H. 1884. "A Comparison of the Fluctuations in the Price of Wheat and in the Cotton and Silk Imports into Great Britain," *Journal of the Royal Statistical Society,* **47**, pp. 345–64.

"Rapport sur les Indices des Crises Economiques et sur les Mesures Résultant de ces Crises." 1911. Ministry of Planning, Paris, France (Government Report)

Shiskin, J. 1957. "Electronic Computers and Business Indicators." *National Bureau of Economic Research,* Occasional Paper 57.

——. 1961. "Tests and Revisions of Bureau of the Census Methods of Seasonal Adjustments." Bureau of the Census, Technical Paper No. 5.

Shiskin, J., A. H. Young, and J. C. Musgrave. "The X-11 Variant of the Census II Method Seasonal Adjustment Program." Bureau of the Census, Technical Paper No. 15.

Spencer, J. 1904. "On the Graduation of the Rates of Sickness and Mortality." *Journal of the Institute of Actuaries,* **38**, p. 334.

Spurr, W. A., and C. P. Bonini, 1967. *Statistical Analysis for Business Decisions*. Homewood, Ill.: Richard D. Irwin.

EXERCISES

1. The following data represent the monthly sales of product A for a plastics manufacturer from 1972 through 1976.

MONTHLY SALES (IN 1000s)					
	1972	1973	1974	1975	1976
Jan.	742	741	896	951	1030
Feb.	697	700	793	861	1032
Mar.	776	774	885	938	1126
Apr.	898	932	1055	1109	1285
May	1030	1099	1204	1274	1468
June	1107	1223	1326	1422	1637
July	1165	1290	1303	1486	1611
Aug.	1216	1349	1436	1555	1608
Sept.	1208	1341	1473	1604	1528
Oct.	1131	1296	1453	1600	1420
Nov.	971	1066	1170	1403	1119
Dec.	783	901	1023	1209	1013

a. Plot the time series of sales of product A. Can you identify seasonal fluctuations and/or a trend?

b. Compute the monthly seasonal indices for these data. Do the results support the graphical interpretation of the seasonal pattern?

2. The following are the seasonal indices for Exercise 1 calculated by the ratio-to-moving averages method.

	Seasonal Indices		Seasonal Indices
Jan.	79.14	July	117.81
Feb.	70.36	Aug.	122.59
Mar.	77.03	Sept.	123.02
Apr.	91.03	Oct.	118.84
May	104.40	Nov.	98.13
June	114.71	Dec.	82.93

The trend in the data is $T_t = 894.11 + 8.85(t)$, where $t = 1$ is Jan. 1972, and $t = 60$ is Dec. 1976. Prepare forecasts for the 12 months of 1977 assuming that the cycle will be equal to 100 for the entire year.

3. The following table shows the monthly road casualties (in thousands) in the United Kingdom for the years 1964 through 1971.

	1964	1965	1966	1967	1968	1969	1970	1971
Jan.	26.0	29.0	27.0	27.5	23.9	27.6	26.9	28.4
Feb.	24.5	24.7	26.3	27.2	24.7	23.4	26.6	25.5
Mar.	27.9	31.3	29.8	30.2	27.5	25.0	27.6	26.6
Apr.	29.1	32.4	32.6	28.6	26.7	26.0	27.1	26.2
May	34.7	33.9	35.1	34.1	28.7	31.0	29.8	29.3
June	33.1	35.0	34.4	30.9	30.3	29.3	29.1	28.8
July	36.0	36.4	35.7	34.7	31.3	31.7	32.6	31.2
Aug.	37.5	36.5	33.6	33.7	32.1	32.0	31.6	31.9
Sept.	34.8	34.4	31.9	33.6	31.2	30.0	31.1	28.5
Oct.	35.5	33.9	35.1	31.0	31.4	31.8	33.2	32.2
Nov.	33.4	33.9	33.4	28.9	30.8	33.6	33.6	31.7
Dec.	32.9	36.4	37.6	29.7	30.6	31.6	34.0	31.8

a. Using the data for 1964 through 1970, calculate the seasonal indices of the data using the ratio-to-moving averages method.
b. What is the behavior of the cyclical factor? Does it vary each year?
c. What is the trend in the data?
d. Prepare forecasts for each month of 1971.
e. If a Census II program is available, apply it to the first seven years of data. How do the results compare with those of (a) above?
f. Use the Census II results to prepare forecasts for 1971. How do those compare with the results found in (d) above? Which method is the more accurate?

4. a. Using the data of Table 3-12, compute the seasonal indices using the classical decomposition method. How do these indices compare with those given in column 4 of Table 3-12?
b. Find the trend in the data. How does that compare to the trend found in column 5 of Table 3-12?
c. Forecast the next four quarters using classical decomposition. How do these forecasts compare to the forecasts provided by Winters' model?
d. What conclusions, if any, can you make concerning the behavior and accuracy of the results obtained in Table 3-12 and those obtained above from classical decomposition?

5. The following values represent a cubic trend pattern mixed with some randomness. Apply a single 5-period moving average, a single 7-period moving

average, a double 3×3 moving average, and a double 5×5 moving average. Which type of moving average seems most appropriate to you in identifying the cubic pattern of the data?

Period	Shipments	Period	Shipments
1	42	9	180
2	69	10	204
3	100	11	228
4	115	12	247
5	132	13	291
6	141	14	337
7	154	15	391
8	171		

PART THREE
REGRESSION AND ECONOMETRIC METHODS

Techniques of forecasting that are based on regression analysis are substantially different in their underlying concepts and theory from the techniques of time-series analysis, smoothing and decomposition, described in Part Two. Regression techniques are generally referred to as causal, or explanatory, approaches to forecasting. They attempt to predict the future by discovering and measuring the effect of important independent variables on the dependent variable to be forecast. Oftentimes, discovering and measuring the relationships of interest are even more beneficial than using them to obtain forecasts. Because of their greater costs, these methods are generally used in long-range planning and in situations where the value of increased accuracy warrants the additional expense.

Chapter 5 describes the techniques of simple regression that deal with one independent variable and one dependent variable. The basic concepts of estimation procedures and fitting the simple regression model to historical data are presented. Applications of simple regression are also provided.

In Chapter 6 the concepts of simple regression are extended to include multiple independent variables in what is called multiple regression analysis. Again, the basic concepts, procedures for application, and statistical measures used in evaluating multiple regression models are described. A number of extensions and limitations of this methodology are also illustrated.

Chapter 7 presents a further extension of regression analysis to the concept of econometric modeling. In econometrics, one or more multiple regression equations that are interrelated in terms of the independent variables and therefore require joint estimation of individual equations and parameters, are used. Some of the methodologies proposed for applying econometric models, as well as specific applications of those techniques, are described in this chapter.

5/SIMPLE REGRESSION

5/1 Introduction to Regression Methods

In Part Two, two major classes of time-series methods were examined: exponential smoothing and decomposition. Various models within each class were presented—models appropriate for different patterns of data and different conditions. The exponential smoothing methods were suggested to be appropriate for immediate or short-term forecasting when large numbers of forecasts are needed, such as at the operating level of a company. On the other hand, the decomposition methods were found to require many more computations. In addition, they require the personal attention of the user, who must predict the cycle with only indirect help from information provided by the method. Thus the decomposition approach to forecasting requires more time and is therefore restricted to forecasting fewer items than the simpler smoothing models.

In this and the following two chapters, another approach available to forecasters—that of causal or explanatory methods—will be examined. It is one thing to fit a recursive model (such as an exponential smoothing model) to a single time series. It is quite another to come up with other variables that relate to the data series of interest and to develop a model that expresses the functional interdependence of all the variables.

Thus Part Three introduces a new concept in the attempt to forecast: A forecast will be expressed as a function of a certain number of factors that determine its outcome. Such forecasts will not necessarily be time dependent. In addition, developing an explanatory or causal model facilitates a better understanding of the situation and allows experimentation with different combinations of inputs to study their effect on the forecasts. In this way, causal models can, by their basic formulation, be geared toward intervention, influencing the future through decisions made today.

To set the stage for the next three chapters, consider Figure 5-1. Sometimes the forecaster will be dealing with one dependent measure (e.g., sales) and one independent measure (e.g., advertising expenditure). The objective is to develop an explanatory model relating these two measures. Figure 5-1a shows this situation—a case of *simple regression of Y on X*. This is the subject of the present chapter. Sometimes there will be one dependent measure (Y) and several independent measures ($X_1, X_2, \ldots, X_k$) and the objective will be to find a function that relates Y to all of the independent (or explanatory) variables. This is *multiple regression of Y on X_1 through X_k*, and will be handled in Chapter 6. Figure 5-1b indicates what the data sets look like in this case. Finally, in many situations there will be more than one dependent variable and more than one independent variable, as indicated in Figure 5-1c, and indeed, sometimes the forecaster will even want to let some variables be both dependent *and* independent variables. Regression models that handle such situations often call for a set of equations (rather than a single equation) which are solved simultane-

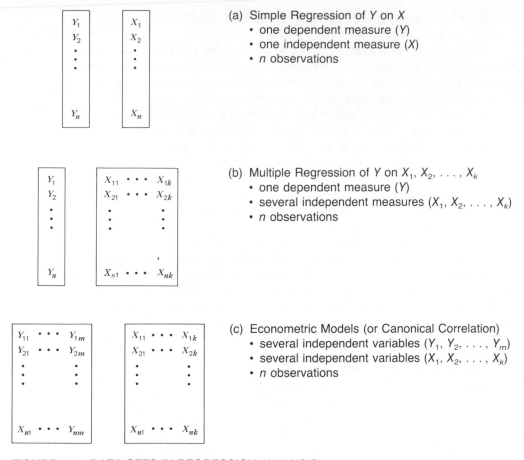

(a) Simple Regression of Y on X
- one dependent measure (Y)
- one independent measure (X)
- n observations

(b) Multiple Regression of Y on $X_1, X_2, \ldots, X_k$
- one dependent measure (Y)
- several independent measures ($X_1, X_2, \ldots, X_k$)
- n observations

(c) Econometric Models (or Canonical Correlation)
- several independent variables ($Y_1, Y_2, \ldots, Y_m$)
- several independent variables ($X_1, X_2, \ldots, X_k$)
- n observations

FIGURE 5-1   DATA SETS IN REGRESSION ANALYSIS

ously, and this is known as *econometric modeling.* Chapter 7 will deal with this topic.

An important technical distinction needs to be made between linear and nonlinear regression models. All regression models are written as equations linking the dependent and the independent variables. For example, $Y = 1.5 + 2.5X$ expresses Y as a function of X and involves two coefficients (1.5 and 2.5). When this equation is written in its general form, $Y = a + bX$, where a and b are the two coefficients, we can make two statements about it. First, Y is a linear function of X—because if we plot Y against X it will turn out to be a straight line—and second, this equation is linear in the coefficients.

The reason for making this distinction between linear and nonlinear in the coefficients is of computational interest. It is relatively easy to solve for the coefficients of a regression equation when it is linear in the coefficients. It is much more difficult if the equation is not linear *in the coeffi-*

cients. Whether it is linear or nonlinear *in the variables* is of less importance. (We will return to this topic in Section 5/2/3.)

The forecaster, then, must decide on how many variables to deal with, which one(s) will be dependent and which will be independent, and which functional form will be chosen. If the data are measured over time, then it will be called *time-series regression.* If there is no time index it will be referred to as *cross-sectional regression.* Even though cross-sectional regression does not deal with time explicitly, many important decisions affecting the future are made on the basis of such studies. In that sense it is proper to consider cross-sectional regression in a book on forecasting.

Single equation models are more restrictive than multiple (simultaneous) equation models; they are also simpler to deal with and may be sufficient for many applications. In the hands of a skilled forecaster, there are many variations on the conventional regression technique that can be used to good effect. For example, in time-series regression, some consideration is usually given to lagged relationships—for example, end of month savings deposits in a bank may be related to triple AAA bond rates one and two months ago. Some of the independent variables can be dichotomous variables (often called dummy variables) to indicate the presence or absence of some significant event (such as a strike) or to denote seasonality. For example, one dummy variable can be used to denote first quarter effects. This dummy variable is given the value one if it is first quarter data and zero otherwise. These and other techniques will be discussed in Chapter 6.

Finally, in attempting to model the relationships within one set of variables it might seem wise to remove another set of variables that interfere with (or affect) the measures of interest. This process is called "partialling out a set of variables," and really means trying to remove the influence of these variables on the underlying relationships being explored. A simple example would be examining the relationship between height and weight, and partialling out age first. There is a close analogy here to the notion of deseasonalizing, as discussed in Chapter 4.

5/2 Simple Regression

In this section the term "simple regression" will refer to any regression of a single Y measure (the dependent variable) on a single X measure (the independent variable). The general situation will involve a set of n paired observations (see Table 5-1) to be denoted:

$\{X_i, Y_i\}$ for $i = 1, 2, 3, \ldots, n$.

Each pair can be plotted as a point, and by convention, Y values are plotted against the vertical axis (ordinate) and X values against the horizontal axis (abscissa) as shown in Figure 5-2.

TABLE 5-1   SALES DATA OVER 10 TIME PERIODS

(X_i) Period	(Y_i) Sales	(X_i, Y_i) Paired Data
1	30	(1 , 30)
2	20	(2 , 20)
3	45	(3 , 45)
4	35	(4 , 35)
5	30	(5 , 30)
6	60	(6 , 60)
7	40	(7 , 40)
8	50	(8 , 50)
9	45	(9 , 45)
10	65	(10 , 65)

We will consider a linear relationship between Y and X and the problem of determining a "best fitting" straight line through the plotted points. Section 5/2/1 first considers X to be a time variable, and therefore the model relating Y to X is not causal or explanatory. Section 5/2/2 deals with the general case, where X and Y are both economic measures, for example, so that in some sense, Y might be able to be "explained" by X.

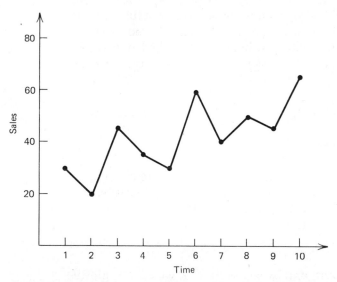

FIGURE 5-2   A PLOT OF SALES VERSUS TIME (USING DATA IN TABLE 5-1)

Then Section 5/2/3 discusses how to deal with functional forms other than straight lines.

5/2/1 Simple Regression of Y on Time

Table 5-1 and Figure 5-2 present the data and a plot of sales over time. As a way of introducing regression, consider fitting two different straight lines through the points, as in Figure 5-3. Line AA does not seem to do as well as line BB in "fitting" the observed data. How can different lines be appraised in terms of *goodness of fit*? Figure 5-4 indicates some of the different ways of evaluating goodness of fit (or badness of fit). For the point P in the plot and the fitted line CC, the error of fit can be defined as:

a. the perpendicular distance from P to CC (i.e., line PP_1),
b. the horizontal departure of the known point P from the line CC (i.e., line PP_3),
c. the vertical departure of P from CC (i.e., line PP_2),
d. the absolute value of the departure from P to the line (horizontally or vertically),
e. the squared departure from P to the line (horizontally, vertically, perpendicularly),
f. the weighted variations of any of the above (i.e., the departure for every point such as P is given a separate weight or "importance").

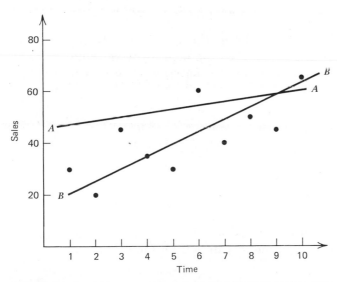

FIGURE 5-3 FITTING STRAIGHT LINES THROUGH (OR TO) THE SALES DATA

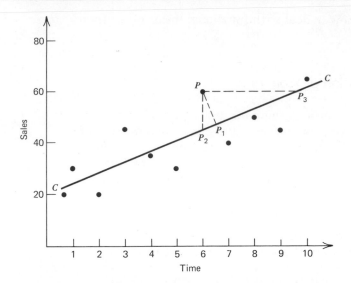

FIGURE 5-4   HOW TO MEASURE THE "FIT" OF A LINE: HORIZONTAL, VER-
TICAL, OR PERPENDICULAR "ERRORS"

Without belaboring the issue, it is clear that "goodness of fit" requires a selection from the various meanings given to the word "error" (or "departure"). There is a regression procedure known as MAD (mean absolute deviation) regression,[1] and there are many variations known as discounted or weighted LS (least squares) procedures. However, we will concentrate on the conventional form, known simply as ordinary least squares (OLS)— or just LS, for short.

The principle is straightforward and the mathematical details are presented in Appendix 5-A. If we are using Y as the dependent variable and $X = t$ as the independent variable, then the objective is to find a straight line

$$\hat{Y}_t = a + b(t)$$

(intercept)(slope)   (5-1)

such that, for a given value of time, t, the squared errors

$$(Y_t - \hat{Y}_t)^2 = e_t^2,$$ (5-2)

when summed, yield a minimum total. This is an LS procedure and the errors are the vertical departures of the known points from the fitted line $(a + bt)$.

---

[1]Which refers to mean absolute deviations in a vertical sense, or PP_2 in Figure 5-4.

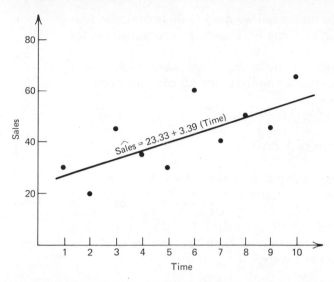

FIGURE 5-5   THE LEAST-SQUARES (LS) LINE RELATING SALES TO TIME

In the case of the data in Table 5-1, the LS solution in Figure 5-5 is

$$\hat{Y} = 23.33 + 3.39\ t,$$

and what we are saying is that the observed values of Y are modeled in terms of a pattern and an error:

$$\left.\begin{array}{l} Y = \boxed{\text{pattern}} + \text{error,} \\[2mm] Y = \boxed{a + bt} + e, \\[2mm] Y = \hat{Y} \qquad\quad + e. \end{array}\right\} \tag{5-3}$$

Note that the pattern is denoted $\dot{Y}$.

How did we get the LS solution in equation (5-3)? The formula[2] for determing the slope, b, in a simple linear regression—as in equation (5-1)—is as follows:

$$b = \frac{N\Sigma XY - (\Sigma X)(\Sigma Y)}{N\Sigma X^2 - (\Sigma X)^2}, \tag{5-4}$$

and the formula for determining the intercept, a, in equation (5-1) is:

$$a = \frac{\Sigma Y}{N} - b\frac{\Sigma X}{N}. \tag{5-5}$$

---

[2]See Appendix 5-A for a derivation of equations (5-4) and (5-5). It should be remembered that these equations provide the coefficients that minimize the sum of the squared vertical departures (equation 5-2) of the known points from the fitted line, and thus the name "least squares."

Note that in order to use these formulas, all we need to do is compute four basic sums: ΣX, ΣY, ΣX^2, and ΣXY. Table 5-2 shows the computations for the sales data in Table 5-1.

Such computations are seldom done by hand any more. Many hand calculators can perform simple regression analysis and all computer centers offer a variety of regression packages.

5/2/2   Simple Regression of Y on X

Now consider a data set consisting of n paired values (Y_i, X_i) for $i = 1, 2, \ldots, n$, where Y_i is the demand for natural gas and X_i is the price of natural gas. Table 5-3 shows actual data for 20 towns in Texas. The situation is not time dependent. It is cross-sectional data. But if a relationship between demand and price can be determined, then this can be useful in making decisions that impact on the future.

TABLE 5-2   DETERMINING THE LEAST SQUARES COEFFICIENTS FOR THE SIMPLE LINEAR REGRESSION OF SALES ON TIME

	Y Sales	X Time	X^2	XY
	30	1	1	30
	20	2	4	40
	45	3	9	135
	35	4	16	140
	30	5	25	150
	60	6	36	360
	40	7	49	280
	50	8	64	400
	45	9	81	405
	65	10	100	650
Sums	420	55	385	2590

Slope: $b = \dfrac{10(2590) - (420)(55)}{10(385) - (55)(55)}$ [using (5-4)]

$= 3.394$

Intercept: $a = \dfrac{(420)}{10} - (3.394)\dfrac{(55)}{10}$ [using (5-5)]

$= 23.333$

TABLE 5-3 PRICE AND PER CAPITA CONSUMPTION OF NATURAL GAS IN 20 TOWNS IN TEXAS

City	Average Price (cents per thousand cubic feet)	Consumption per Customer (thousand cubic feet)
Amarillo	30	134
Borger	31	112
Dalhart	37	136
Shamrock	42	109
Royalty	43	105
Texarkana	45	87
Corpus Christi	50	56
Palestine	54	43
Marshall	54	77
Iowa Park	57	35
Palo Pinto	58	65
Millsap	58	56
Memphis	60	58
Granger	73	55
Llano	88	49
Brownsville	89	39
Mercedes	92	36
Karnes City	97	46
Mathis	100	40
La Pryor	102	42

Source: Sixty-first Annual Report of the Railroad Commission of Texas, Gas Utilities Division. (See Clark and Schkade, 1969, p. 620.)

Clearly the plot in Figure 5-6 shows that a straight line function (regressing demand linearly on price) is not the best functional form to use. However, for illustrative purposes, we'll consider using the simple linear model, as follows:

Consumption = (intercept) + (slope)(price) + (error)

$$C = a + bP + e$$

$$= \hat{C} + e.$$

The four basic sums needed to compute a and b are

$$\Sigma C = 1380, \quad \Sigma P = 1260, \quad \Sigma P^2 = 90048, \quad \Sigma PC = 75161,$$

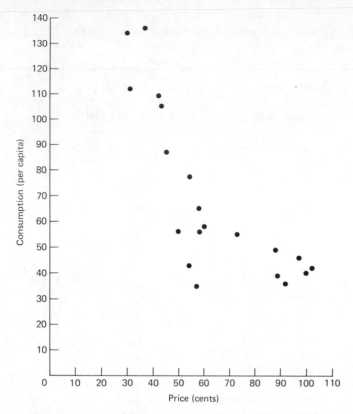

FIGURE 5-6   A PLOT OF THE NATURAL GAS DATA SHOWING PER CAPITA CONSUMPTION ON THE ORDINATE AND PRICE ON THE ABSCISSA

and thus the slope and intercept are computed to be

$$b = \frac{20(75161) - (1380)(1260)}{20(90048) - (1260)^2} \quad \text{[using (5-4)]}$$

$$= -1.104,$$

$$a = \frac{1380}{20} - (-1.104)\frac{1260}{20} \quad \text{[using (5-5)]}$$

$$= 138.561.$$

In other words, the regression equation is

$$\hat{C} = 138.561 - 1.104(P),$$

where $\hat{C}$ is the estimated value of consumption. Figure 5-7 indicates that this line fits reasonably well, but in the error analysis (often called the analysis of residuals) shown in Table 5-4, it is clear that some pattern remains in the errors. They are not random—the first few are all positive,

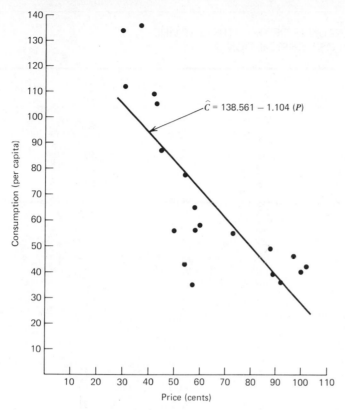

$$\widehat{C} = 138.561 - 1.104\ (P)$$

FIGURE 5-7   THE BEST FITTING (IN A VERTICAL LEAST-SQUARES SENSE) STRAIGHT LINE RELATING CONSUMPTION OF NATURAL GAS TO PRICE

then they are negative for several consecutive values, then they are back to being positive at the end—and this is obviously because the linear functional form cannot do justice to the nonlinear shape of the data plot.

Using the strategy outlined in Chapter 3, an analysis of these errors yields the following results:

-0.01 = Mean Error

15.53 = Mean Absolute Error

26.85 = Mean Absolute Percentage Error (MAPE)

20.30 = Standard Deviation of Error (Unbiased)

391.61 = Mean Square Error (MSE)

0.91 = Durbin-Watson Statistic

0.85 = Theil's U Statistic

314.56 = McLaughlin's Batting Average

TABLE 5-4 AN ERROR ANALYSIS OF THE STRAIGHT LINE
REGRESSION OF CONSUMPTION ON PRICE

Town	P	C	$\hat{C}^a$	e
Amarillo	30	134	105.4	28.6
Borger	31	112	104.3	7.7
Dalhart	37	136	97.7	38.3
Shamrock	42	109	92.2	16.8
Royalty	43	105	91.1	13.9
Texarkana	45	87	88.9	−1.9
Corpus Christi	50	56	83.4	−27.4
Palestine	54	43	78.9	−35.9
Marshall	54	77	78.9	−1.9
Iowa Park	57	35	75.6	−40.6
Palo Pinto	58	65	74.5	−9.5
Millsap	58	56	74.5	−18.5
Memphis	60	58	72.3	−14.3
Granger	73	55	58.0	−3.0
Llano	88	49	41.4	7.6
Brownsville	89	39	40.3	−1.3
Mercedes	92	36	37.0	−1.0
Karnes City	97	46	31.5	14.5
Mathis	100	40	28.2	11.8
La Pryor	102	42	26.0	16.0

[a]Based on the line: $\hat{C} = 138.561 - 1.104(P)$, where C = consumption and P = price in cents.

Later we will see how an alternative regression model for the natural gas data will improve the goodness of fit.

5/2/3 Different Forms of Functional Relationships

The fact that GNP changes over time can be expressed in shorthand notation as follows:

$$\text{GNP} = f(\text{time}). \tag{5-6}$$

Expression (5-6) states that the level of GNP is a function of time, and that future values of GNP may be forecast by identifying this time relationship. As we have seen, a functional form that relates two variables (GNP and time) does not necessarily have to include time. It can be generalized to include explanatory variables. In economics, for example, the demand for a product (quantity sold) has frequently been found to depend upon the price of the product.

Demand of product $X = f$(price of product X).   (5-7)

Expression (5-7) states that as the price of product X changes, the demand of product X will change too. For most products, an increase in price will decrease the amount sold, while a decrease in price will increase the level of demand.

When only two variables are involved (Y and X), the shape of the relationship between them can often be discovered via a simple plot. It becomes increasingly difficult to extend this principle as the number of variables increases. Figure 5-8 shows a variety of functional relationships that could exist between Y and X. Having selected a particular function, it becomes necessary to estimate, from the known data pairs, the values of the parameters in the function. This estimation task is not always easy. However, if the function is *linear in the parameters*, the principle of LS can be applied directly and the parameter estimates can be obtained deterministically. In Figure 5-8 functions a, c, and d are linear in the parameters.[3] Figure 5-8b, if it is not transformed in any way, would pose difficulties in solving for a and b (since these parameters occur in the exponent of e). It *is* possible to solve such a problem by nonlinear LS, but the methodology is *iterative* and often cannot guarantee that the global LS error fit will be obtained.

However, it should be noted that many nonlinear functions[4] can be transformed into linear functions. A few simple cases can illustrate the point. Consider

$W = AB^X$.   (5-8)

Equation (5-8) relates variable W to variable X and a plot of W versus X would be nonlinear. Our concern is with the parameters A and B, which appear as a product (therefore not linear) and B is raised to a power other than 1 (therefore not linear). To fit this curve to a set of data pairs (W, X)

---

[3]"Linear in the parameters" (or "linear in the coefficients") means that once you give values to Y and X, the parameters occur as variables raised to power 1, and in additive form only. For example,

$Y = a + bX$

is linear in the coefficients a and b, but

$Y = ce^{bX+a}$

is not linear in the coefficients.

[4]It should be stressed here that by "nonlinear functions" we mean "nonlinear in the *parameters*."

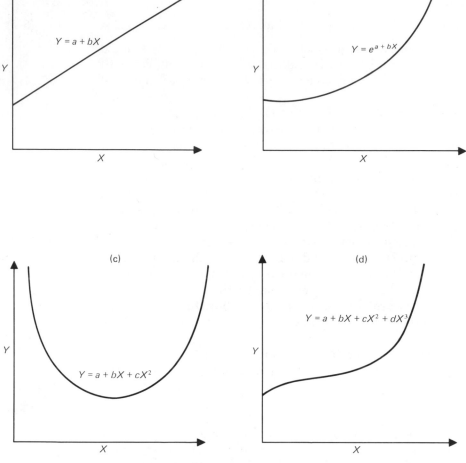

FIGURE 5-8   DIFFERENT FORMS OF FUNCTIONAL RELATIONSHIPS CON-
NECTING Y AND X: (a) LINEAR, (b) EXPONENTIAL, (c) QUAD-
RATIC, AND (d) CUBIC

would require an iterative procedure, unless logarithms are taken of both
sides:

$$(\log W) = (\log A) + (\log B)X. \tag{5-9}$$

Substituting $Y = \log W$, $a = \log A$, and $b = \log B$ gives

$$Y = a + bX. \tag{5-10}$$

Equation (5-10) is now a simple linear relationship (Y is linear on X, and
the function is linear in a and b). Thus we can use simple LS regression on
equation (5-10), solve for a and b deterministically, and then recover A and
B via antilogarithms to get the parameters for equation (5-8).

A second example of a nonlinear function of parameters is that of Figure 5-8b:

$$W = e^{a+bX}. \tag{5-11}$$

Taking logarithms to base e of both sides yields

$$\log_e W = (a + bX) \log_e e$$

$$= a + bX \text{ (since } \log_e e = 1). \tag{5-12}$$

Substituting

$$Y = \log_e W$$

gives

$$Y = a + bX, \tag{5-13}$$

which is now in linear form, so that a and b can be determined directly. Using these values in equation (5-11) allows W to be predicted (estimated) for any known value of X.

Further examples of such transformations are given as exercises at the end of the chapter.

Figure 5-9 and Table 5-5 illustrate the use of equation (5-11) to fit the natural gas data of Table 5-2. The approach (based on economic theory) was as follows:

$$\text{Demand} = e^{\alpha + \beta(\text{Price})} \tag{5-14}$$

Therefore, taking logarithms of both sides gives:

$$\log_e(\text{Demand}) = \alpha + \beta(\text{Price}).$$

With this theory in mind, the regression analyst fits a model to log(C) and P, as follows:

$$\log(C) = \boxed{a + b(P)} + e$$

$$= \widehat{\log(C)} + e.$$

Computing the four basic sums

$$\Sigma \log(C), \qquad \Sigma P, \qquad \Sigma P^2, \qquad \Sigma P \log(C)$$

and using equations (5-4) and (5-5), the fitted regression equation is

$$\widehat{\log(C)} = 5.0978 - .0153(P).$$

Now, taking antilogarithms of both sides, the functional form used to forecast natural gas consumption would be

$$\hat{C} = e^{5.0978 - .0153(P)}.$$

Comparing Figures 5-9 and 5-7, it is apparent that the nonlinear form of

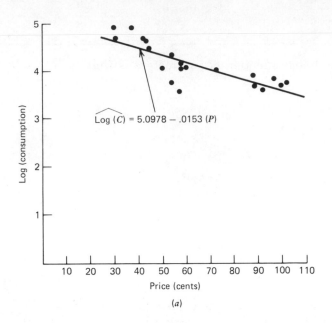

$$\widehat{\text{Log}\,(C)} = 5.0978 - .0153\,(P)$$

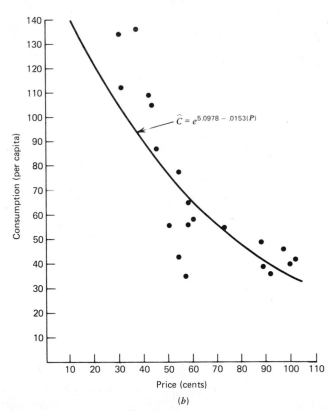

$$\widehat{C} = e^{5.0978 - .0153(P)}$$

FIGURE 5-9 THE NATURAL GAS DATA—SHOWING (a) A PLOT OF LOG (CONSUMPTION) VERSUS PRICE, AND (b) CONSUMPTION VERSUS PRICE AFTER USING THE REGRESSION, LOG (CONSUMPTION) = 5.0978 − .0153 (PRICE)

the relationship between consumption and price is more appropriate than the original linear fit. The summary statistics for the error analysis are:

2.76 = Mean Error

13.82 = Mean Absolute Error

21.73 = Mean Absolute Percentage Error (MAPE)

18.48 = Standard Deviation of Error (unbiased)

331.91 = Mean Square Error (MSE)

1.05 = Durbin-Watson Statistic

0.65 = Theil's U Statistic

334.52 = McLaughlin's Batting Average

5/3   The Correlation Coefficient

It often occurs that two variables are related to each other, even though it might be incorrect to say that the value of one of the variables depends upon, or is caused by, changes in the value of the other variable. In any event, a relationship can be stated by computing the correlation between the two variables. The coefficient of correlation, r, is a relative measure of the (linear) association between these two variables. It can vary from 0 (which indicates no correlation) to ± 1 (which indicates perfect correlation). When the correlation coefficient is greater than 0, the two variables are said to be positively correlated, and when it is less than 0, they are said to be negatively correlated.

The correlation coefficient plays an important role in multivariate data analysis (that is, whenever there are two or more variables involved) and has particularly strong ties with regression analysis. The reader is urged to develop an intuitive understanding of this coefficient. With this in mind, we consider first how to compute the correlation coefficient, r, in Section 5/3/1. Then several ways of interpreting the correlation will be given in Section 5/3/2, and some cautions in using r will be discussed in Section 5/3/3.

5/3/1   Calculation of the Correlation Coefficient

The correlation between two variables X and Y is designated r_{XY} and for n paired observations (X_i, Y_i), $i = 1, 2, \ldots, n$, the following formulas are relevant:

Mean of X

$$\overline{X} = \frac{1}{n} \sum_{i=1}^{n} X_i \qquad\qquad (5\text{-}15)$$

TABLE 5-5   NATURAL GAS DATA—RESULTS OF FITTING
LOG(CONSUMPTION) = 5.098 − .0153(PRICE) AND THEN
ANTILOGGING TO GET ESTIMATED CONSUMPTION

(a) First consider $\widehat{\log(C)}$ regressed on P.

Town	P_i	$\log(C_i)$	$\widehat{\log(C_i)}$	e_i
Amarillo	30	4.90	4.64	0.26
Borger	31	4.72	4.62	0.09
Dalhart	37	4.91	4.53	0.38
Shamrock	42	4.69	4.46	0.24
Royalty	43	4.65	4.44	0.21
Texarkana	45	4.47	4.41	0.06
Corpus Christi	50	4.03	4.33	−0.31
Palestine	54	3.76	4.27	−0.51
Marshall	54	4.34	4.27	0.07
Iowa Park	57	3.56	4.23	−0.67
Palo Pinto	58	4.17	4.21	−0.04
Millsap	58	4.03	4.21	−0.19
Memphis	60	4.06	4.18	−0.12
Granger	73	4.01	3.98	0.03
Llano	88	3.89	3.75	0.14
Brownsville	89	3.66	3.74	−0.07
Mercedes	92	3.58	3.69	−0.11
Karnes City	97	3.83	3.61	0.21
Mathis	100	3.69	3.57	0.12
La Pryor	102	3.74	3.54	0.20

where $\widehat{\log(C_i)}$ = 5.0978 − .0153 (P_i) and $e_i = \log(C_i) - \widehat{\log(C_i)}$

Mean of Y

$$\overline{Y} = \frac{1}{n} \sum_{i=1}^{n} Y_i \tag{5-16}$$

Covariance between X and Y

$$\text{Cov}_{XY} = \frac{1}{n} \sum_{i=1}^{n} (X_i - \overline{X})(Y_i - \overline{Y}) \tag{5-17}$$

Variance of X

$$\text{Cov}_{XX} = \text{Var}_X = \frac{1}{n} \sum_{i=1}^{n} (X_i - \overline{X})^2 = S_X^2 \tag{5-18}$$

TABLE 5-5   NATURAL GAS DATA—RESULTS OF FITTING
LOG(CONSUMPTION) = 5.098 − .0153(PRICE) AND THEN
ANTILOGGING TO GET ESTIMATED CONSUMPTION (*Continued*)

(b) Second, take antilogarithms of the $\widehat{\log(C)}$ values to get $\hat{C}$ values.

Town	P_i	C_i	$\hat{C}_i$	e_i
Amarillo	30	134	103.4	30.6
Borger	31	112	101.8	10.2
Dalhart	37	136	92.9	43.1
Shamrock	42	109	86.1	22.9
Royalty	43	105	84.8	20.2
Texarkana	45	87	82.2	4.8
Corpus Christi	50	56	76.2	−20.2
Palestine	54	43	71.6	−28.6
Marshall	54	77	71.6	5.4
Iowa Park	57	35	68.4	−33.4
Palo Pinto	58	65	67.4	−2.4
Millsap	58	56	67.4	−11.4
Memphis	60	58	65.4	−7.4
Granger	73	55	53.6	1.4
Llano	88	49	42.6	6.4
Brownsville	89	39	41.9	−2.9
Mercedes	92	36	40.1	−4.1
Karnes City	97	46	37.1	8.9
Mathis	100	40	35.4	4.6
La Pryor	102	42	34.4	7.6

where $\hat{C}_i = e^{5.0978 - .0153(P_i)}$ and $e_i = C_i - \hat{C}_i$

Variance of Y

$$\text{Cov}_{YY} = \text{Var}_Y = \frac{1}{n} \sum_{i=1}^{n} (Y_i - \overline{Y})^2 = S_Y^2 \tag{5-19}$$

Correlation between X and Y

$$r_{XY} = \frac{\text{Cov}_{XY}}{\sqrt{\text{Cov}_{XX}\,\text{Cov}_{YY}}} \tag{5-20}$$

$$= \frac{\text{Cov}_{XY}}{S_X\,S_Y} \tag{5-21}$$

where $S_X = \sqrt{\text{Cov}_{XX}}$ and $S_Y = \sqrt{\text{Cov}_{YY}}$ are the standard deviations
of X and Y, respectively.

Note that in these formulas, all summations have been divided by n rather than $n-1$. This is a matter of convenience here. If the divisor had been $n-1$ in the equations for covariance and the two variances [i.e., equations (5-17), (5-18), and (5-19)], there would be no change in the formula for the correlation in equations (5-20) and (5-21).

To illustrate the computation of the correlation coefficient using the above equations, we return to the Texas natural gas data. Table 5-6 shows

TABLE 5-6 COMPUTATION OF THE CORRELATION BETWEEN PRICE AND CONSUMPTION FOR THE NATURAL GAS DATA : USING THE COVARIANCE APPROACH

	(1) P	(2) C	(3) $(P - \bar{P})$	(4) $(C - \bar{C})$	(5) $(P - \bar{P})^2$	(6) $(C - \bar{C})^2$	(7) $(P - \bar{P})(C - \bar{C})$
Amarillo	30	134	-33	65	1089	4225	-2145
Borger	31	112	-32	43	1024	1849	-1376
Dalhart	37	136	-26	67	676	4489	-1742
Shamrock	42	109	-21	40	441	1600	-840
Royalty	43	105	-20	36	400	1296	-720
Texarkana	45	87	-18	18	324	324	-324
Corpus Christi	50	56	-13	-13	169	169	169
Palestine	54	43	-9	-26	81	676	234
Marshall	54	77	-9	8	81	64	-72
Iowa Park	57	35	-6	-34	36	1156	204
Palo Pinto	58	65	-5	-4	25	16	20
Millsap	58	56	-5	-13	25	169	65
Memphis	60	58	-3	-11	9	121	33
Granger	73	55	10	-14	100	196	-140
Llano	88	49	25	-20	625	400	-500
Brownsville	89	39	26	-30	676	900	-780
Mercedes	92	36	29	-33	841	1089	-957
Karnes City	97	46	34	-23	1156	529	-782
Mathis	100	40	37	-29	1369	841	-1073
La Pryor	102	42	39	-27	1521	729	-1053
Sums	1260	1380	0	0	10668	20838	-11779
Means	$\bar{P} = 63$	$\bar{C} = 69$	0	0	533	1042	-589

533.40   Variance of price
1041.90 Variance of consumption
-588.95 Covariance between price and consumption
-0.79 Correlation between price and consumption

price (P) in column 1 (in cents per 1000 cubic feet) and consumption (C) in column 2 (in 1000 cubic feet per customer). The first two column sums are used to compute the two means,

$$\overline{P} = 63 \quad \text{and} \quad \overline{C} = 69 \quad \text{[using (5-15) and (5-16)]}$$

and these means are used to get the deviations from the mean in columns 3 and 4. Columns 5 and 6 are the squared deviations from the mean for P and C, respectively, and column 7 shows the deviation cross-product terms. The covariance between P and C is computed as follows:

$$\text{Cov}_{PC} = \frac{1}{20}(-11779) = -588.95 \quad \text{[using (5-17)]}$$

and the two variances are computed as follows:

$$\text{Var}_P = \frac{1}{20}(10668) = 533.40 \quad \text{[using (5-18)]},$$

$$\text{Var}_C = \frac{1}{20}(20838) = 1041.90 \quad \text{[using (5-19)]}$$

From these two variances we get the two standard deviations,

$$S_P = \sqrt{\text{Var}_P} = 23.10 \quad \text{and} \quad S_C = \sqrt{\text{Var}_C} = 32.26.$$

Now the correlation between P and C can be computed as follows:

$$r_{PC} = \frac{-588.95}{(23.10)(32.26)} = -.79 \quad \text{[using (5-21)]}.$$

Looking at the plot of price versus consumption in Figure 5-6 and from what we know about price and quantity in economics, this r value of $-.79$ is plausible. There is a negative relationship between P and C for the natural gas data.

Another common formula for computing the correlation coefficient is as follows:

$$r_{XY} = \frac{n\Sigma XY - (\Sigma X)(\Sigma Y)}{\sqrt{n\Sigma X^2 - (\Sigma X)^2}\sqrt{n\Sigma Y^2 - (\Sigma Y)^2}}. \tag{5-22}$$

The appeal of this formula is that for any set of paired observations, just five basic quantities must be computed

$$\Sigma X, \quad \Sigma Y, \quad \Sigma X^2, \quad \Sigma Y^2, \quad \text{and} \quad \Sigma XY.$$

To illustrate the use of this formula examine Table 5-7. Columns 3 and 4 give the squared price and consumption values, respectively, and column 5 gives the cross products of P and C. Note that all these calculations use the raw data, not deviations from the mean. The five column sums give the five basic quantitites needed to use equation (5-22), as follows:

TABLE 5-7 COMPUTATION OF THE CORRELATION BETWEEN PRICE AND CONSUMPTION FOR THE NATURAL GAS DATA: USING FIVE BASIC SUMS

	(1) P	(2) C	(3) P^2	(4) C^2	(5) PC
Amarillo	30	134	900	17956	4020
Borger	31	112	961	12544	3472
Dalhart	37	136	1369	18496	5032
Shamrock	42	109	1764	11881	4578
Royalty	43	105	1849	11025	4515
Texarkana	45	87	2025	7569	3915
Corpus Christi	50	56	2500	3136	2800
Palestine	54	43	2916	1849	2322
Marshall	54	77	2916	5929	4158
Iowa Park	57	35	3249	1225	1995
Palo Pinto	58	65	3364	4225	3770
Millsap	58	56	3364	3136	3248
Memphis	60	58	3600	3364	3480
Granger	73	55	5329	3025	4015
Llano	88	49	7744	2401	4312
Brownsville	89	39	7921	1521	3471
Mercedes	92	36	8464	1296	3312
Karnes City	97	46	9409	2116	4462
Mathis	100	40	10000	1600	4000
La Pryor	102	42	10404	1764	4284
Sums	1260	1380	90048	116058	75161
Means	63	69	4502	5803	3758

$$r_{PC} = \frac{20(75161) - (1260)(1380)}{\sqrt{20(90048) - (1260)^2} \, \sqrt{20(116058) - (1380)^2}}$$

$$= -.79.$$

One other form of the correlation coefficient is worth noting. It involves the conversion of all X and Y measures into their standardized form. To convert X_i to its standardized form, we first subtract the mean and then divide by the standard deviation of the X values, as follows:

$$z_{x_i} = \text{standardized } X_i = \frac{(X_i - \overline{X})}{S_X}. \tag{5-23}$$

The symbol z is often used to identify standardized values. The correlation coefficient can be expressed in terms of standardized values by doing a little rearranging in equation (5-21), as follows:

$$
r_{XY} = \frac{\mathrm{Cov}_{XY}}{S_X S_Y}
$$

$$
= \frac{1}{n} \sum_{i=1}^{n} \frac{(X_i - \overline{X})}{S_X} \frac{(Y_i - \overline{Y})}{S_Y}
$$

$$
= \frac{1}{n} \sum_{i=1}^{n} z_{X_i} z_{Y_i} . \tag{5-24}
$$

In words, this last expression defines the correlation coefficient succinctly as the average standardized cross product. Table 5-8 shows how the com-

TABLE 5-8 COMPUTATION OF THE CORRELATION BETWEEN PRICE AND CONSUMPTION FOR THE NATURAL GAS DATA: USING THE STANDARDIZED VALUE APPROACH

	(1) P	(2) C	(3) $(P - \overline{P})$	(4) $(C - \overline{C})$	(5) $\dfrac{(P - \overline{P})}{S_P}$	(6) $\dfrac{(C - \overline{C})}{S_C}$	(7) $\left(\dfrac{P - \overline{P}}{S_P}\right)\left(\dfrac{C - \overline{C}}{S_C}\right)$
Amarillo	30	134	−33	65	−1.43	2.01	−2.88
Borger	31	112	−32	43	−1.39	1.33	−1.85
Dalhart	37	136	−26	67	−1.13	2.08	−2.34
Shamrock	42	109	−21	40	−0.91	1.24	−1.13
Royalty	43	105	−20	36	−0.87	1.12	−0.97
Texarkana	45	87	−18	18	−0.78	0.56	−0.43
Corpus Christi	50	56	−13	−13	−0.56	−0.40	0.23
Palestine	54	43	−9	−26	−0.39	−0.81	0.31
Marshall	54	77	−9	8	−0.39	0.25	−0.10
Iowa Park	57	35	−6	−34	−0.26	−1.05	0.27
Palo Pinto	58	65	−5	−4	−0.22	−0.12	0.03
Millsap	58	56	−5	−13	−0.22	−0.40	0.09
Memphis	60	58	−3	−11	−0.13	−0.34	0.04
Granger	73	55	10	−14	0.43	−0.43	−0.19
Llano	88	49	25	−20	1.08	−0.62	−0.67
Brownsville	89	39	26	−30	1.13	−0.93	−1.05
Mercedes	92	36	29	−33	1.26	−1.02	−1.28
Karnes City	97	46	34	−23	1.47	−0.71	−1.05
Mathis	100	40	37	−29	1.60	−0.90	−1.44
La Pryor	102	42	39	−27	1.69	−0.84	−1.41
Sums	1260	1380	0	0	0.00	0.00	−15.81
Means	63	69	0	0	0.00	0.00	−0.79

putations can be performed using this equation. Columns 3 and 4 are the deviations from the respective means for price and consumption. These quantities are then divided by S_P and S_C, respectively, to give columns 5 and 6. Columns 5 and 6 are now the standardized values for P and C. Finally, column 7 shows the cross products of the standardized P and C values. The sum of these standardized cross products is -15.81 and the average is $-.79$, which is the correlation coefficient between P and C:

$$r_{PC} = \frac{(-15.81)}{20} = -.79 \quad [\text{using (5-24)}] .$$

5/3/2 Interpretation of the Correlation Coefficient

The correlation coefficient can range from an extreme value of -1 (perfect negative correlation) through zero to an extreme value of $+1$ (perfect positive correlation). The paired numbers (1,1), (2,2), (3,3), (4,4), and (5,5) are perfectly correlated—that is, $r = +1$—and the paired numbers (1,5), (2,4), (3,3), (4,2), (5,1) are perfectly negatively correlated—that is, $r = -1$. The natural gas data yielded a correlation of $-.79$, indicating a strong negative relationship between price and consumption. As price increased, consumption declined—not perfectly so, but there was a strong tendency for this to happen. Figure 5-10a plots some artificial data—20 paired values of X and Y—that show a positive correlation of .603. In other words, as X increases there is a tendency for Y to increase, but the relationship is not perfect. Figure 5-10b shows another set of artificial data. Here the correlation between X and Y is .033, essentially zero, and looking at the scatterplot it is clear that there is no relationship between these measures.

Intuitively, the correlation coefficient can be interpreted in two ways: (i) as the *direction* of the relationship between two measures—meaning do they tend to increase and decrease together (positively related), one increases while the other decreases (negatively related), or move their separate ways (not correlated); and (ii) as the *strength of the association*—meaning that as the absolute value of the correlation moves away from zero, the two measures are more strongly associated. Note, however, that there are some cautions that need to be observed, as described in the next section.

5/3/3 Some Cautions in Using Correlation

The correlation coefficient is widely used in statistical analysis and can be a very useful statistic. However, certain cautions need to be observed. First, the correlation is a measure of *linear* association between two measures. If two measures are related in a nonlinear manner, the correlation coeffi-

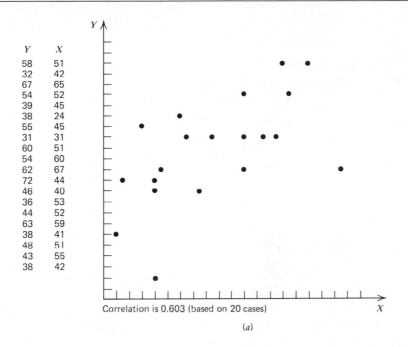

Y	X
58	51
32	42
67	65
54	52
39	45
38	24
55	45
31	31
60	51
54	60
62	67
72	44
46	40
36	53
44	52
63	59
38	41
48	51
43	55
38	42

Correlation is 0.603 (based on 20 cases)

(a)

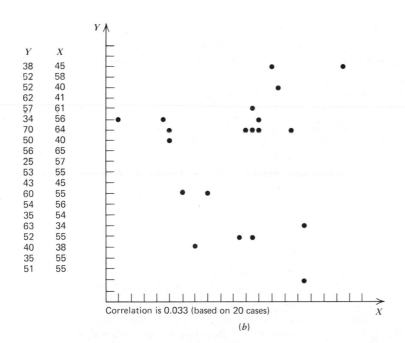

Y	X
38	45
52	58
52	40
62	41
57	61
34	56
70	64
50	40
56	65
25	57
53	55
43	45
60	55
54	56
35	54
63	34
52	55
40	38
35	55
51	55

Correlation is 0.033 (based on 20 cases)

(b)

FIGURE 5-10 SOME ILLUSTRATIONS OF CORRELATIONS AND THEIR RELATED SCATTERPLOTS

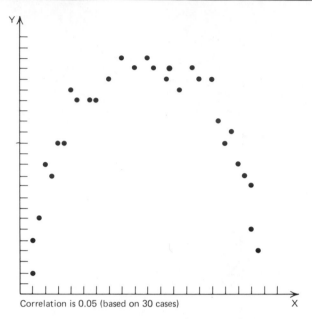

Correlation is 0.05 (based on 30 cases)

FIGURE 5-11   THE CORRELATION COEFFICIENT DOES NOT HELP DE-
FINE A NONLINEAR RELATIONSHIP

cient will not be able to do justice to the strength of the relationship. For example, in Figure 5-11, two variables X and Y are plotted to show that they have a very strong *nonlinear* relationship, but their correlation coefficient is essentially zero.

Second, when the sample size is small—meaning there are only a few pairs of data to use in computing the correlation—the sample r value is notoriously unstable. For example, if we consider the population of all adults in the world and have it in mind that the correlation between height and weight is significantly positive, say r_{HW} = .60, then we can be surprised if we take a sample of n = 10 people and compute the correlation between height and weight for them. The sample r value can range widely over the interval from −1 to +1. Figure 5-12 indicates the sampling distribution of the correlation coefficient for various population parameter values, when the sample size is only 10. Note that if the population correlation parameter is zero and the sample size is n = 10, the sample correlation values range widely on either side of zero. Similarly, even when the population correlation parameter is quite strong, for example, ρ = .8—a small sample size can yield r values a long way from .8. The message to the forecaster is that correlations based on small samples should be recognized as having a large standard error (i.e., they are unstable) and only when the sample size approaches n = 50 do they become reasonably stable.

A third point about the correlation coefficient concerns the presence

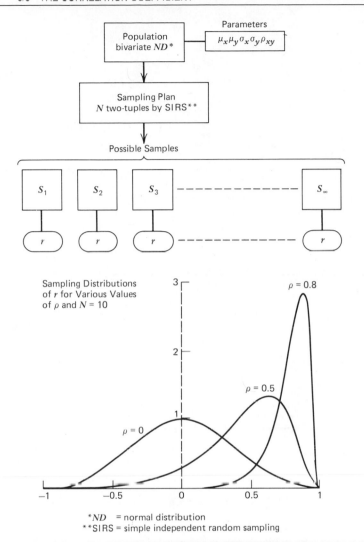

FIGURE 5-12   THE SAMPLING DISTRIBUTION OF THE CORRELATION
              COEFFICIENT (r) WHEN THE SAMPLE SIZE $N = 10$ AND
              THE TRUE POPULATION PARAMETER (ρ) IS ZERO

of extreme values. The value of r can be seriously affected by the presence
of just one outlier. We illustrate this important caution by referring to the
"King Kong" effect in Figure 5-13. Suppose we are examining the relationship between height and weight for monkeys and we take a sample of size
$n = 20$. Figure 5-13a shows a scatterplot for the height-weight pairings
and the correlation turns out to be .527. Now if one extra monkey, King
Kong, is added to the sample, there is one large height and one large weight
to add to the scatterplot, and the correlation increases to .940. Technically,

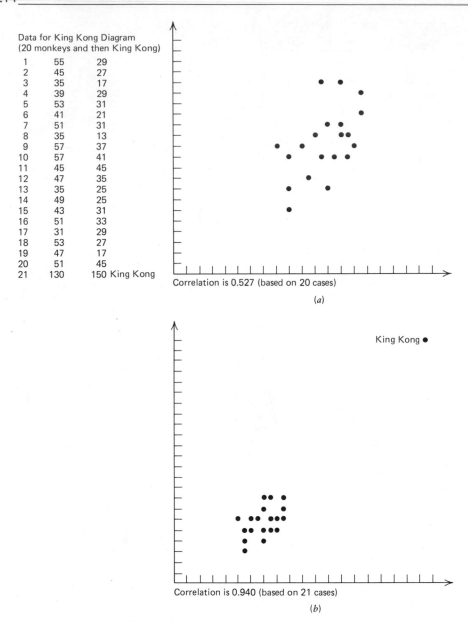

Data for King Kong Diagram
(20 monkeys and then King Kong)

1	55	29
2	45	27
3	35	17
4	39	29
5	53	31
6	41	21
7	51	31
8	35	13
9	57	37
10	57	41
11	45	45
12	47	35
13	35	25
14	49	25
15	43	31
16	51	33
17	31	29
18	53	27
19	47	17
20	51	45
21	130	150 King Kong

Correlation is 0.527 (based on 20 cases)

(a)

King Kong ●

Correlation is 0.940 (based on 21 cases)

(b)

FIGURE 5-13 THE KING KONG EFFECT ON r

what has happened here is that the height measures and the weight measures have become very *skew* distributions, and skewness has a profound effect on the correlation coefficient. Sometimes, an outlier will make only one distribution skew, and then an r value of .5 might shift to an r value of .05.

In the context of forecasting, the correlation coefficient is used very frequently. For example, in Chapters 8, 9, and 10 the notion of autocorrelation forms the very basis for the time series methods discussed there. It is well to bear in mind that r values (whether they be regular correlations, autocorrelations or cross-correlations) are unstable in small samples, are measures of linear association, and are seriously influenced by extreme values.

5/4 Simple Regression and the Correlation Coefficient

If there is a negative relation between price and consumption of natural gas (that is, r_{PC} is negative), then we know that if we raise the price we will tend to lower the consumption, and vice versa. If we regress consumption on price, choose a functional form (say linear), and solve for the best coefficients, then we will be able to estimate what the consumption will be for a given price. Clearly, the better the regression fit, the better will be the estimate so obtained, and the linear regression fit will be better if there is a strong linear relationship (correlation) between price and consumption. So we see that correlation and regression are intimately connected.

5/4/1 Computational Considerations

On a purely numerical level, this relationship between correlation and regression can be established by examining the formulas used to determine the slope and the intercept of a simple linear regression—see equations (5-4) and (5-5)—and the formula used for computing the correlation coefficient—equation (5-22). They are repeated here for ease of reference.

REGRESSION MODEL

$$Y_i = a + bX_i + e_i$$

where

$$b = \frac{n\Sigma XY - (\Sigma X)(\Sigma Y)}{n\Sigma X^2 - (\Sigma X)^2} = \frac{\text{Cov}_{XY}}{\text{Var}_X}$$

and

$$a = \frac{\Sigma Y}{n} - b\frac{\Sigma X}{n} = \overline{Y} - b\overline{X}$$

CORRELATION

$$r_{XY} = \frac{n\Sigma XY - (\Sigma X)(\Sigma Y)}{\sqrt{n\Sigma X^2 - (\Sigma X)^2}\ \sqrt{n\Sigma Y^2 - (\Sigma Y)^2}} = \frac{\text{Cov}_{XY}}{\sqrt{\text{Var}_X}\ \sqrt{\text{Var}_Y}}$$

Notice that the slope coefficient is the covariance between X and Y divided by the variance of X, and the correlation coefficient is the covariance between X and Y divided by the product of two standard deviations. It is a simple matter to write an equation linking the slope and the correlation coefficient, as follows:

$$b = \frac{\text{Cov}_{XY}}{\text{Var}_X} = \frac{r_{XY} S_X S_Y}{S_X^2} = r_{XY} \frac{S_Y}{S_X}. \tag{5-25}$$

Thus, the slope of the simple regression of Y on X is the correlation between X and Y multiplied by the ratio S_Y/S_X. (In passing, note that if we had been regressing X on Y, the slope of this regression line would be r_{XY} multiplied by the ratio S_X/S_Y.)

Given a set of paired measurements on (X,Y), it is straightforward to compute the five basic sums (ΣX, ΣY, ΣX^2, ΣY^2, and ΣXY) and to compute the slope and the intercept for the simple regression line—using equations (5-4) and (5-5)—and the correlation coefficient—using equation (5-22).

There is another important correlation to consider in regression. Once the regression model has been estimated—that is, the least squares (LS) estimates of the regression coefficients have been obtained—then all the known Y values can be compared with all the estimated Y values, using the regression line. The estimated Y values are designated $\hat{Y}$ and we have the identity

$$Y_i = (a + bX_i) + e_i$$

$$= (\hat{Y}_i) + e_i .$$

There are now n pairs of values $(Y_i, \hat{Y}_i)$ and it is of great interest to know how these two values relate to each other. In regression, the correlation between Y and $\hat{Y}$ is usually designated R. Furthermore, it is customary to present this correlation in squared form, R^2, and this statistic is known as the *coefficient of determination*. R^2 is thus the squared correlation between the dependent variable Y and its estimated value, $\hat{Y}$.

For the natural gas data, we could form two columns of data, one for consumption and one for estimated consumption—based on the regression line $\hat{C}_i = 138.561 - 1.104(P)$—as indicated in Table 5-3, and then could use any of the three methods indicated in Tables 5-6, 5-7, or 5-8 to compute the correlation between C and $\hat{C}$. It is left as an exercise for the reader to show that

$$r_{C\hat{C}} = r_{CP} = -.79$$

so that $R^2 = r_{C\hat{C}}^2$ will be .624. The correlation between C and $\hat{C}$ is *exactly* the same as the correlation between C and P. In the case of simple regression this will always be true.

5/4/2 Interpretation of the Coefficient of Determination

The coefficient of determination, R^2, will always be positive, and the intuitive meaning can be stated as follows: R^2 tells the proportion of variance in Y that can be explained by X. The dependent variable Y has a certain amount of variability, defined by its variance. The estimated $\hat{Y}$ values also have a certain amount of variance. The ratio of these two variances is R^2:

$$R^2 = \frac{\text{variance of the } \hat{Y} \text{ values}}{\text{variance of the } Y \text{ values}}.$$

Since the $\hat{Y}$ values are defined with reference to the estimated regression equation, this is often expressed as follows:

$$R^2 = \frac{\text{explained variance of } Y}{\text{total variance of } Y}.$$

In addition, there are some technical details relating to degrees of freedom in numerator and denominator in these expressions,[5] so that it is more correct to state that

$$R^2 = \frac{\text{explained sum of squares}}{\text{total sum of squares}}.$$

Table 5-9 indicates how the explained and total sum of squares are determined. Columns 1 and 2 are the true consumption (C) and the estimated consumption ($\hat{C}$) of natural gas—based on the simple linear regression $\hat{C} = 138.561 - 1.104(P)$—and these data are taken from Table 5-3. Note that the mean of the C values equals the mean of the $\hat{C}$ values. This is a fact of LS regression. Then columns 3 and 4 show the deviations from the mean for C and $\hat{C}$, and columns 5 and 6 show the squares of these deviations. The sum of the squared deviations in column 6 divided by the sum of the squared deviations in column 5 yields R^2, as follows:

$$R^2 = \frac{\text{explained SS}}{\text{total SS}} = \frac{13006}{20838} = .624.$$

where SS = sum of squared deviations. In general, R^2 can be defined as follows:

$$R^2 = \frac{\Sigma(\hat{Y}_i - \overline{Y})^2}{\Sigma(Y_i - \overline{Y})^2} = r_{Y\hat{Y}}^2, \tag{5-26}$$

---

[5]When degrees of freedom are taken into account, a *corrected* R^2 is defined, and called $\overline{R}^2$ (R-bar-squared). This will be discussed in Chapter 6.

TABLE 5-9 NATURAL GAS DATA: SHOWING HOW THE TOTAL
DEVIATION IS PARTITIONED INTO EXPLAINED
AND UNEXPLAINED DEVIATIONS

	(1)	(2)	(3) Total Deviation	(4) Explained Deviation	(5)	(6)	(7) Unexplained Deviation	(8)
	C	$\hat{C}$	$C - \overline{C}$	$\hat{C} - \overline{C}$	$(C - \overline{C})^2$	$(\hat{C} - \overline{C})^2$	$C - \hat{C}$	$(C - \hat{C})^2$
Amarillo	134	105	65	36	4225	1328	29	816
Borger	112	104	43	35	1849	1248	8	59
Dalhart	136	98	67	29	4489	824	38	1466
Shamrock	109	92	40	23	1600	538	17	283
Royalty	105	91	36	22	1296	488	14	194
Texarkana	87	89	18	20	324	395	−2	4
Corpus Christi	56	83	−13	14	169	206	−27	748
Palestine	43	79	−26	10	676	99	−36	1291
Marshall	77	79	8	10	64	99	−2	4
Iowa Park	35	76	−34	7	1156	44	−41	1650
Palo Pinto	65	75	−4	6	16	30	−10	91
Millsap	56	75	−13	6	169	30	−19	343
Memphis	58	72	−11	3	121	11	−14	205
Granger	55	58	−14	−11	196	122	−3	9
Llano	49	41	−20	−28	400	762	8	58
Brownsville	39	40	−30	−29	900	824	−1	2
Mercedes	36	37	−33	−32	1089	1025	−1	1
Karnes City	46	31	−23	−38	529	1409	15	211
Mathis	40	28	−29	−41	841	1669	12	141
La Pryor	42	26	−27	−43	729	1854	16	258
Sums	1380	1380	0	0	20838	13006	0	7832
Means	69	69	0	0	1042	650	0	392

where Y is the dependent variable with mean $\overline{Y}$. Figure 5-14 helps to make this clearer. For any Y_i value there is a total deviation, $(Y_i - \overline{Y})$—showing how far Y_i is from the mean of the Y values. This total deviation can be partitioned into two pieces, (i) an unexplained deviation, $(Y_i - \hat{Y}_i)$, showing how far Y_i is from the regression line value, $\hat{Y}_i$, and (ii) an explained deviation, $(\hat{Y}_i - \overline{Y})$, showing how far the regression value $\hat{Y}_i$ is from the mean of the Y values. In symbols, this partition is as follows:

$$(Y_i - \overline{Y}) \quad = \quad (Y_i - \hat{Y}_i) \quad + \quad (\hat{Y}_i - \overline{Y}). \qquad (5\text{-}27)$$

$$\underset{\substack{\text{total} \\ \text{deviation}}}{\uparrow} \qquad \underset{\substack{\text{unexplained} \\ \text{deviation}}}{\uparrow} \qquad \underset{\substack{\text{explained} \\ \text{deviation}}}{\uparrow}$$

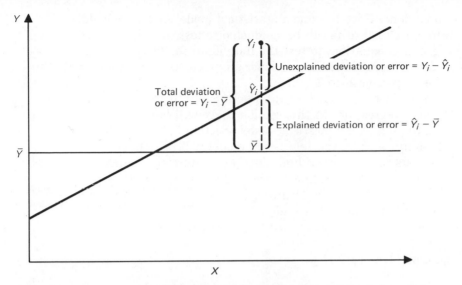

FIGURE 5-14   EXPLANATION OF THE PARTITIONING OF TOTAL DEVIA-
TION INTO EXPLAINED AND UNEXPLAINED DEVIATIONS—
IN THE CASE OF SIMPLE REGRESSION

In Table 5-9, the 7th and 8th columns show the unexplained deviations
(namely, the errors) and their squares, respectively, and the reader should
note that the sums for columns 5, 6, and 8 form an identity, as follows:

$$\begin{array}{ccccc}
\text{(column 5 sum)} & = & \text{(column 8 sum)} & + & \text{(column 6 sum)} \\
\updownarrow & & \updownarrow & & \updownarrow \\
SS_{total} & = & SS_{unexplained} & + & SS_{explained} \\
\updownarrow & & \updownarrow & & \updownarrow \\
20838 & = & 7832 & + & 13006
\end{array}$$

In a regression study, if the explained SS is very nearly equal to the total
SS, then the relationship between Y and X must be very nearly perfectly
linear. To the extent that the unexplained (error) SS is large relative to the
explained (regression) SS, the regression line is less useful.

5/5   The Significance of a Regression Equation

When we make a scatterplot of Y (dependent measure) against X
(independent measure) and decide to define an equation relating Y to X,
we can do this (i) as a purely mechanical *fitting* operation (that is, finding
the least squares fit), or (ii) as a *statistical estimation* problem. If we are
merely fitting a "best" (LS) curve to the data, then there is no further testing

of significance to be done. If we assume a statistical model underlying the data, then certain statistical tests can be conducted to test the significance of the overall regression equation, to test the individual coefficients in the equation, and to develop confidence intervals for any predictions that might be made using the regression model.

The Appendices in this chapter contain details of the statistical underpinnings of simple regression. In this section there will be only a brief introduction to regression as a statistical model (Section 5/5/1), then the F-test for overall significance of the regression model will be defined (Section 5/5/2), the t-tests for the individual slope and intercept coefficients will be defined (Section 5/5/3), and finally, the regression equation will be used to forecast (Section 5/5/4). The natural gas data (consumption versus price) will be used to illustrate each section.

5/5/1   A Little Theory

In a nutshell, the simple linear regression model may be defined precisely as follows:

REGRESSION MODEL IN THEORY

$$Y = \boxed{\alpha + \beta X} + \varepsilon,$$

where α and β are fixed (but unknown) parameters, X is assumed measured without error, and ε is a random variable that is normally distributed around zero (the mean of ε) and having a variance V_ε. Specific values of ε are obtained by simple independent random sampling (SIRS) from the parent population $ND(0, V_\varepsilon)$[6].

(5-28)

Note the formalities in a model of this type. The part in the little rectangle, $\alpha + \beta X$, is the *shape* of the regression relationship—in this case a straight line—and α and β are called parameters (which are unknown, but if they were known they would be fixed numbers). The X values are assumed to be measured without error,[7] so that, in the model, $\alpha + \beta X$, is a fixed part—

---

[6]$ND(0, V_\varepsilon)$ is a shorthand description of a normal distribution with mean zero and variance V_ε.

[7]This unrealistic assumption is often relaxed in econometric work. (See Johnston, 1966.)

not a statistical part. It is the ε term that makes this model a statistical model, because ε is defined as a random variable having a specifically identified probability distribution—the normal distribution—with specified parameters 0 (for the mean) and V_ε (for the variance).

By way of contrast to the theoretical regression model, consider the regression model in practice. All the unknown parameters in the theoretical model have to be estimated. In place of α and β (unknown parameters) we have to find a and b (estimated statistics), and in place of V_ε (variance parameter for the theoretical error term) we have to determine $\hat{V}_e$ (estimated variance of empirically defined errors). The final form of the pragmatic regression model is as follows:

REGRESSION MODEL IN PRACTICE

$$Y_i = \boxed{a + bX_i} + e_i \quad \text{for } i = 1, 2, \ldots, n,$$

where a and b are estimates of α and β, and *are both random variables now*, X is unlikely to be measured without error, e_i is an estimated error for the ith observation and is a random variable.

Note: The part in the rectangle is no longer fixed, as in the theoretical model, but represents a statistical family of lines

(5-29)

By convention, it is usual to express that part of the regression model that is enclosed in a rectangle, as $\hat{Y}$, so that we can write:

$$Y_i = \hat{Y}_i + e_i \quad \text{for } i = 1, 2, \ldots, n.$$

For the natural gas data, the simplest theoretical model to be entertained is

$$C = \boxed{\alpha + \beta P} + \varepsilon.$$

The practical model developed for this case was

$$C_i = 138.561 - 1.104P_i + e_i.$$

Now this is one line (not a family of lines), but if we sampled the same towns on the same measures over a different time period, we would not expect to get exactly the same estimated regression line. So this one line is just one member of the family of lines that could have been developed for this problem.

5/5/2   The *F*-Test for Overall Significance

The simple regression model, $Y = a + bX + e$, has slope coefficient b. If this slope were zero, the regression line would be $Y = a + e$. In other words, knowing the X values would be of no consequence at all. Even if the estimated regression model showed $b = .75$, say, it is possible that the error term may be large enough to obscure the relationship between Y and X. The F-test allows us to test the significance of the overall regression model—to be able to answer the statistical question: Is there a significant relationship between Y and X?

Consider Figures 5-15, 5-16, and 5-17. From Figure 5-15 it is clear that a linear relationship exists between sales and time. From Figure 5-16 it is clear that variable unit cost does not depend on how many units are produced. From Figure 5-17 there is a slight rising trend in consumption over time, but the variation around this trend is substantial. It would be helpful to have a statistical test that would aid the forecaster in deciding on the significance of the relationship between Y and X. The F-test is such a test.

Leaving the details to Appendix 5-C, the F statistic is defined as follows:

$$F = \frac{\mathrm{MS}_{\text{explained}}}{\mathrm{MS}_{\text{unexplained}}}$$

$$= \frac{(\mathrm{SS}_{\text{explained}})/(\mathrm{df}_{\text{explained}})}{(\mathrm{SS}_{\text{unexplained}})/(\mathrm{df}_{\text{unexplained}})}$$

$$= \frac{\Sigma(\hat{Y} - \overline{Y})^2/(k-1)}{\Sigma(Y - \hat{Y})^2/(n-k)}, \tag{5-30}$$

where MS = mean square,

  SS = sum of squares,

  df = degrees of freedom,

  k = number of parameters (coefficients) in the regression equation.

Thus the F statistic is the ratio of two mean squares.[8] The numerator refers to the variance that is explained by the regression, and the denominator refers to the variance of what is not explained by the regression, namely, the errors.

For the case of simple regression, the number of parameters is $k =$

---

[8]Statisticians define variance as an MS (mean square), which is an SS (sum of squares) divided by df (degrees of freedom).

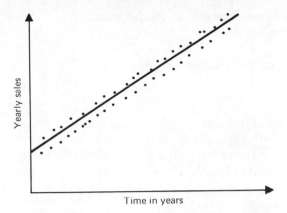

FIGURE 5-15   SIGNIFICANT REGRESSION EQUATION

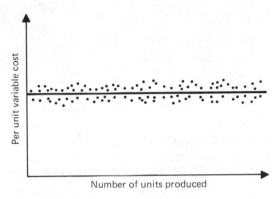

FIGURE 5-16   REGRESSION EQUATION NOT SIGNIFICANT

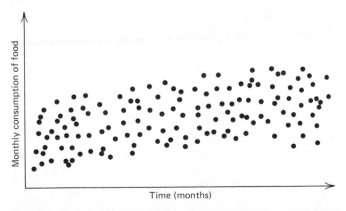

FIGURE 5-17   SIGNIFICANCE OF REGRESSION EQUATION UNCERTAIN

2, and so for the natural gas data, the linear regression model relating consumption to price would yield the following F ratio:

$$F_{(1,18)} = \frac{(13006)/(2-1)}{(7832)/(20-2)} \quad \text{(using data from Table 5-9)}$$

$$= 29.89.$$

Note that it is customary to put the degrees of freedom as subscripts on the letter F. Looking up the F tables (Table C in Appendix I), it is found that only 1 percent of the distribution is to the right of the value $F = 8.28$. In other words, our observed value of $F = 29.89$ is highly significant. There is a very significant linear relationship between C (consumption) and P (price)—even though we know that a nonlinear relation is better.

The F statistic in (5-30) is intimately connected to the definition of the coefficient of determination in (5-26). Thus it is easy to develop another computational formula for F, as follows:

$$F = \frac{R^2/(k-1)}{(1-R^2)/(n-k)}. \tag{5-31}$$

For the natural gas data, using the computed $R^2 = .624$, we get:

$$F_{(1,18)} = \frac{(.624)/(2-1)}{(.376)/(20-2)} = 29.897,$$

which, except for rounding error, is the same as before.

One point can be noted here concerning the F-test for overall significance of the regression line. In the case of simple regression, the F-test is really the same as testing the significance of the slope coefficient. In multiple regression (Chapter 6), the overall F-test is *not* the same as any one of the tests of significance for individual coefficients.

5/5/3   The *t*-Tests for Individual Coefficients

In Section 5/5/1 it was pointed out that in the practical process of estimating the coefficients a and b, they must both be considered random variables. In other words, the pair of values (a,b) fluctuates from sample to sample. They have a joint sampling distribution, and, in fact, there is a very strong negative correlation between a and b.[9] To study the stability of a and b, separately, we have to look at the marginal distributions, which we shall do here. To study the joint impact of sampling fluctuation of the (a,b) pair, we have to look at the joint distribution, which we will do in Section 5/5/4.

Again leaving the details to Appendix 5-B in this chapter, the sam-

---

[9]If you increase the slope (b), you automatically decrease the intercept (a) and vice versa.

pling distribution of a (the intercept coefficient) is a normal distribution with mean α and standard error as follows:

$$se_a = \hat{\sigma}_e \left\{ \frac{\Sigma X_i^2}{n\Sigma(X_i - \overline{X})^2} \right\}^{1/2}, \tag{5-32}$$

and the sampling distribution of b (the slope coefficient) is a normal distribution with mean β and standard error, as follows:

$$se_b = \hat{\sigma}_e \sqrt{\frac{1}{\Sigma(X_i - \overline{X})^2}}. \tag{5-33}$$

In both these equations, the estimate of the standard deviation of the errors is given by

$$\hat{\sigma}_e = \sqrt{\frac{\Sigma(Y_i - \hat{Y}_i)^2}{n - 2}}. \tag{5-34}$$

Using the natural gas data (see Table 5-9), the following values are obtained:

$$\hat{\sigma}_e = \sqrt{\frac{7832}{20 - 2}} = 20.86 \quad \text{[using (5-34)]},$$

$$se_a = (20.86)\sqrt{\frac{1}{20} + \frac{63}{10668}} \quad \left[\begin{array}{l}\text{using (5-32) and} \\ \text{data from Table 5-6}\end{array}\right]$$

$$= 4.93,$$

$$se_b = (20.86)\sqrt{\frac{1}{10668}}$$

$$= .20.$$

Consider the intercept value in the regression line $\hat{C} = 138.561 - 1.104(P)$. The standard error of this intercept is found to be 4.93 so that without too much imagination we can argue that the estimated intercept value (138.561) is significantly different from zero! The slope coefficient is -1.104 and its standard error is computed to be .20. Is -1.104 significantly different from zero?

Using the standard error formulas in equations (5-32) and (5-33), two t-tests can be set up to test the intercept and slope values, as follows:

t-VALUE FOR INTERCEPT

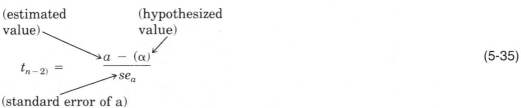

$$\text{(estimated value)} \qquad \text{(hypothesized value)}$$

$$t_{n-2)} = \frac{a - (\alpha)}{se_a} \tag{5-35}$$

$$\text{(standard error of a)}$$

t-VALUE FOR SLOPE

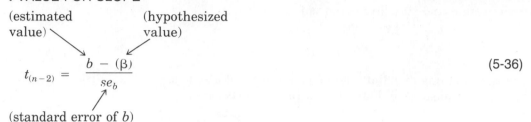

$$t_{(n-2)} = \frac{b - (\beta)}{se_b}$$ (5-36)

(estimated value) (hypothesized value)

(standard error of b)

where the subscript on t indicates the degrees of freedom. Usually, the hypothesized values being tested are zero, but they do not need to be. For the natural gas data, consider testing to see if the intercept is significantly different from 130 and the slope is significantly different from zero.

INTERCEPT TEST

$$t_{(18)} = \frac{(138.561) - (130)}{(4.93)} = 1.74$$

SLOPE TEST

$$t_{(18)} = \frac{(-1.104) - (0)}{(.20)} = -5.52$$

The subscript on t indicates degrees of freedom, and looking up the tables for t (Appendix I, Table B) we note that for df = 18 the one-tail probability that t is greater (in absolute value) than 2.552 is .01. So clearly, the slope test shows that the slope of the regression line relating consumption to price of natural gas, is highly significant—meaning significantly different from zero. For the intercept, the observed t value of 1.74 lies close to the .05 t-value (1.734) in the tables. Here the forecaster must make a judgment. There is about 5 percent chance that, with sampling fluctuation, a computed intercept value could be larger than the hypothesized value of 130 by as much as was observed. Is this significant or not? The forecaster must decide.

5/5/4   Forecasting Using the Simple Regression Model

This is a book about forecasting. How does one use a regression model to forecast Y values? This translates into using new X values and asking what Y values are implied by these X values. We can determine point estimates for Y (that is, single values, $\hat{Y}$) or interval estimates (confidence intervals). Given a particular new X value, designated X_0, the estimated regression model yields

$$\hat{Y}_0 = a + bX_0$$

as the expected value of Y given X_0. However, since a and b are both random variables (fluctuating from sample to sample) having a joint probability distribution, the standard error of $\hat{Y}_0$ can be determined (see Appendix 5-B in this chapter) as follows:

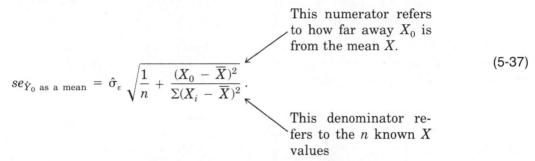

This numerator refers to how far away X_0 is from the mean X.

$$se_{\hat{Y}_0 \text{ as a mean}} = \hat{\sigma}_\varepsilon \sqrt{\frac{1}{n} + \frac{(X_0 - \overline{X})^2}{\Sigma(X_i - \overline{X})^2}}.$$

(5-37)

This denominator refers to the n known X values

Note in equation (5-37) that the only item to change on the right-hand side is X_0, the new X value. If this value equals the mean of the n known X values, then equation (5-37) yields the lowest possible value for the *standard error of the mean forecast*. As X_0 moves away from $\overline{X}$, the standard error increases.

Equation (5-37) deals with the forecast $\hat{Y}_0$ as if it were a mean (expected value). In practice, we may wish to determine how far an individual forecast may vary from the actual value. This variation can be found by combining the effects of (1) the joint variation of a and b and, (2) the historical pattern of dispersion around the regression line—namely $\hat{\sigma}_\varepsilon$. Equation (5-38) gives the *standard error of an individual forecast:*

$$se_{\text{individual } \hat{Y}_0} = \hat{\sigma}_\varepsilon \sqrt{1 + \frac{1}{n} + \frac{(X_0 - \overline{X})^2}{\Sigma(X_i - \overline{X})^2}}.$$

(5-38)

Note that when $X_0 = \overline{X}$, the mean of the known X values, equations (5-37) and (5-38) reduce to $\hat{\sigma}_\varepsilon \sqrt{1/n}$ and $\hat{\sigma}_\varepsilon \sqrt{1 + 1/n}$, respectively.

To illustrate the points made above, consider the natural gas example once again. The data in Table 5-3 are plotted in Figures 5-6 and 5-9, and show that a curved regression line is more appropriate than a straight line. However, we consider the linear regression first, for simplicity. The LS regression solution is

$$\widehat{\text{Consumption}} = 138.561 - 1.104 \text{ (price in cents)}$$

and the F-test ($F = 29.89$, with 1 and 18 df) was highly significant. The linear regression equation significantly improves upon the use of the mean alone as a forecast of consumption, or, in other words, knowing the price helps to estimate consumption much better than if price were ignored.

Now suppose that decision makers in Texas have to forecast what the consumption of natural gas would be if the price per 1000 cubic feet were 90¢, $1.00, or $1.10. The first thing they could do is substitute these values into the regression equation and get estimates of consumption as follows:

39.20 cubic feet ($\times 1000$)   when the price is   90¢,

28.15 cubic feet ($\times 1000$)   when the price is $1.00,

17.11 cubic feet ($\times 1000$)   when the price is $1.10.

Now if they were interested in estimating consumption on *average* for, the whole state, let's say, they would use equation (5-37) to estimate the standard error of the mean forecast, as follows:

$$se_{\text{mean } \hat{C}} = (20.86) \sqrt{\frac{1}{20} + \frac{(P - 63)^2}{10668}} \, .$$

The only item on the right-hand side that is not specified is the price (P). For the three prices of interest the standard errors are

$se_{\text{mean } \hat{C}} = $ 7.18   when the price is   90¢,

$se_{\text{mean } \hat{C}} = $ 8.81   when the price is $1.00,

$se_{\text{mean } \hat{C}} = $ 10.58   when the price is $1.10.

To get 90 percent confidence intervals for these estimates, refer to the *t*-tables with df = 18, and find that for $t = 1.734$, there is 5 percent of the area in the right tail of the *t*-distribution. Therefore, for $-1.734 \leq t \leq 1.734$ the area under the *t*-distribution is 90 percent (or .90). To get a 90 percent confidence interval for the consumption forecasts, the appropriate standard error is multiplied by plus or minus 1.734 and we get:

90 PERCENT CONFIDENCE INTERVAL

$(\hat{C} - 1.734 \, se_{\text{mean } \hat{C}})$ to $(\hat{C} + 1.734 \, se_{\text{mean } \hat{C}})$.

Substituting the appropriate standard errors and the estimates $\hat{C}$, yields the following 90 percent confidence intervals for the three prices of interest:

$P = 90$¢: $39.20 \pm (1.734)(7.18)$ or 39.20 ± 12.45,

$P = \$1.00$: $28.15 \pm (1.734)(8.81)$ or 28.15 ± 15.28,

$P = \$1.10$: $17.11 \pm (1.734)(10.58)$ or 17.11 ± 18.35.

In exactly similar manner, equation (5-38) can be used to determine the standard errors of forecast for individual values,[10] to yield the general formula:

$$se_{\text{indiv } \hat{C}} = (20.86) \sqrt{1 + \frac{1}{20} + \frac{(P - 63)^2}{10668}} \, ,$$

---

[10]Think of an individual value as referring to a specific town in Texas, or a specific instance of consumption at a given price.

where the only item to be defined is the new price (P) of interest. For the three prices under consideration, the standard errors are

$se_{\text{indiv } \hat{C}} = 22.06$ when the price is 90¢,

$se_{\text{indiv } \hat{C}} = 22.64$ when the price is $1.00,

$se_{\text{indiv } \hat{C}} = 23.39$ when the price is $1.10.

The point estimates of consumption at the three prices will be the same as before (namely, 39.20, 28.15, and 17.11), but the confidence intervals are now much wider, as expected. The 90 percent confidence intervals for the individual forecasts are as follows:

$P = 90$¢: 39.20 ± 38.25,

$P = \$1.00$: 28.15 ± 39.26,

$P = \$1.10$: 17.11 ± 40.56.

Looking at these two sets of confidence intervals (for mean estimates and individual estimates of consumption) it is obvious that the statistical model doesn't know that negative consumption is not allowed! The confidence intervals are symmetric about the point estimates and the range of the confidence interval increases as the new X_0 value (price in this instance) moves away from the mean. This is reasonable. However, we know that the linear regression does not do justice to the curvilinear relationship between consumption and price, so that the confidence intervals for consumption at high prices (or low prices for that matter) are not very meaningful.

One of the exercises for this chapter is to pursue the problem of forecasting consumption of natural gas when the more appropriate nonlinear regression model is used. [See equation (5-14).]

APPENDIX 5-A
DETERMINING THE VALUES
OF a AND b IN $\hat{Y} = a + bX$

Assuming n data points denoted by Y_i, the regression equation, $\hat{Y}_i = a + bX_i$, can be estimated so as to minimize the sum of the squared deviations. Defining

$$e_i = Y_i - \hat{Y}_i,$$

then

$$e_i^2 = (Y_i - \hat{Y}_i)^2$$

and

$$\Sigma e_i^2 = \Sigma(Y_i - \hat{Y}_i)^2.$$

By substitution,

$$\Sigma e_i^2 = \Sigma(Y_i - a - bX_i)^2.$$

Applying calculus,

$$\frac{\partial \Sigma e_i^2}{\partial a} = -2\Sigma(Y_i - a - bX_i) = 0, \tag{5-39}$$

$$\frac{\partial \Sigma e_i^2}{\partial b} = -2\Sigma X_i(Y_i - a - bX_i) = 0. \tag{5-40}$$

From (5-39)

$$- \Sigma Y_i + na + b\Sigma X_i = 0. \tag{5-41}$$

From (5-40)

$$- \Sigma X_i Y_i + a\Sigma X_i + b\Sigma X_i^2 = 0. \tag{5-42}$$

Equations (5-41) and (5-42) can be solved simultaneously to obtain the values of a and b. Solving (5-41) for a gives

$$a = \frac{\Sigma Y_i}{n} - b\frac{\Sigma X_i}{n}, \tag{5-43}$$

which substituted into (5-42) yields

$$b = \frac{n\Sigma X_i Y_i - \Sigma X_i \Sigma Y_i}{n\Sigma X_i^2 - (\Sigma X_i)^2}.$$ (5-44)

Thus, the values of a and b in (5-43) and (5-44) correspond to the points where the first derivatives of (5-41) and (5-42) are zero; that is, where the sum of the squared errors is at a minimum.

Since the value of b is known through (5-44), it can be substituted into (5-43) to get a. The solution point for a and b is indeed where Σe_i^2 is at a minimum, as can be verified by computing the second derivatives, and showing that

$$\frac{\partial \Sigma e_i^2}{\partial a^2} > 0 \quad \text{and} \quad \frac{\partial \Sigma e_i^2}{\partial b^2} > 0.$$

A convenient way of expressing the regression equation is in terms of deviations from the mean values of X and Y. The data are transformed by substituting

$$x_i = X_i - \overline{X} \quad \text{or} \quad X_i = x_i + \overline{X},$$

and

$$\hat{y}_i = \hat{Y}_i - \overline{Y} \quad \text{or} \quad \hat{Y}_i = \hat{y}_i + \overline{Y}.$$

The regression equation, $\hat{Y} = a + bX$, then becomes

$$\hat{y}_i + \overline{Y} = a + b(x_i + \overline{X}),$$

which simplifies to

$$\hat{y}_i = a + bx_i + b\overline{X} - \overline{Y}.$$

But, since

$$a = \overline{Y} - b\overline{X},$$ (5-45)

$$\hat{y}_i = \overline{Y} - b\overline{X} + bx_i + b\overline{X} - \overline{Y}$$

and

$$\hat{y}_i = bx_i.$$

Similarly, by substitution

$$\Sigma e_i^2 = \Sigma(y_i - \hat{y})^2$$

$$= \Sigma(y_i - bx_i)^2,$$

$$\frac{d\Sigma e_i^2}{db} = -2\Sigma x_i(y_i - bx_i)$$

$$= -2\Sigma x_i y_i + 2b\Sigma x_i^2 = 0,$$

$$b = \frac{\Sigma x_i y_i}{\Sigma x_i^2} .$$
(5-46)

Equation (5-46) is similar to (5-44) except that it is expressed in terms of deviations. Equation (5-43), on the other hand, is not needed because the value of a in (5-45) is zero.

APPENDIX 5-B
VARIANCES AND COVARIANCES
IN SIMPLE REGRESSION

As explained in Section 5/5/1, equation (5-28), the formal model for simple regression, states that $Y_i = \alpha + \beta X_i + u_i$, where α and β are fixed constants (parameters), the X_i are assumed measured without error, and the error terms, u_i, are independent of one another and have a normal distribution with mean zero and variance σ_u^2. Then, following (5-29), when we determine the LS estimates a and b, for α and β, respectively, it turns out that a and b are now random variables having a joint (or bivariate) normal distribution. For this joint distribution we can determine the variance of a, the variance of b, and the covariance between a and b, and we do so in what follows.

Variance in a

The variance of a is stated mathematically as $E(a - \alpha)^2$, where α is the true value in the regression equation, $Y_i = \alpha + \beta X_i + u_i$.

Remembering that

$$a = \overline{Y} - b\overline{X},$$

substituting for b from equation (5-46),

$$a = \overline{Y} - \frac{\Sigma x_i y_i}{\Sigma x_i^2} \overline{X}.$$

Thus

$$a = \frac{\Sigma Y_i}{n} - \overline{X} \frac{\Sigma x_i}{\Sigma x_i^2} (Y_i - \overline{Y})$$

$$= \Sigma \left(\frac{1}{n} - \overline{X} \frac{x_i}{\Sigma x_i^2} \right) Y_i,$$

since

$$\overline{X}\,\overline{Y} \frac{\Sigma x_i}{\Sigma x_i^2} = 0,$$

(inasmuch as $\Sigma x_i = \Sigma(X_i - \overline{X}) = 0$).
Thus

$$a = \Sigma \left(\frac{1}{n} - \overline{X} \frac{x_i}{\Sigma x_i^2} \right) (\alpha + \beta X_i + u_i)$$

$$= \alpha \Sigma \left(\frac{1}{n} - \overline{X} \frac{x_i}{\Sigma x_i^2} \right) + \beta \Sigma \left(\frac{1}{n} - \overline{X} \frac{x_i}{\Sigma x_i^2} \right) X_i + \Sigma \left(\frac{1}{n} - \overline{X} \frac{x_i}{\Sigma x_i^2} \right) u_i$$

$$= \alpha - 0 + \Sigma \left(\frac{1}{n} - \overline{X} \frac{x_i}{\Sigma x_i^2} \right) u_i \; .$$

$$\left[\text{Note that } \frac{\Sigma x_i X_i}{\Sigma x_i^2} = 1, \text{ since} \right.$$

$$\left. 1 = \frac{\Sigma x_i^2}{\Sigma x_i^2} = \frac{\Sigma x_i x_i}{\Sigma x_i^2} = \frac{\Sigma x_i (X_i - \overline{X})}{\Sigma x_i^2} = \frac{\Sigma x_i X_i}{\Sigma x_i^2} - \frac{\Sigma x_i \overline{X}}{\Sigma x_i^2} = \frac{\Sigma x_i X_i}{\Sigma x_i^2} - 0. \right]$$

Thus

$$a = \alpha + \Sigma \left(\frac{1}{n} - \overline{X} \frac{x_i}{\Sigma x_i^2} \right) u_i,$$

or

$$(a - \alpha) = \Sigma \left(\frac{1}{n} - \overline{X} \frac{x_i}{\Sigma x_i^2} \right) u_i, \tag{5-47}$$

and

$$E(a - \alpha) = E \left[\Sigma \left(\frac{1}{n} - \overline{X} \frac{x_i}{\Sigma x_i^2} \right) u_i \right]$$

$$= \Sigma \left(\frac{1}{n} - \overline{X} \frac{x_i}{\Sigma x_i^2} \right) E(u_i), \tag{5-48}$$

since

$$\left(\frac{1}{n} - \overline{X} \frac{x_i}{\Sigma x_i^2} \right) \text{ is a constant.}$$

Thus $E(a - \alpha) = 0$, since $E(u_i)$ is by definition equal to 0. This shows that a is an unbiased estimator of the true theoretical value of α.

The variance of a is

$$\sigma_a^2 = E(a - \alpha)^2 = E\left[\Sigma\left(\frac{1}{n} - \overline{X}\frac{x_i}{\Sigma x_i^2}\right)(u_i)\right]^2 \quad \text{(from (5-48))}$$

$$= \Sigma\left(\frac{1}{n^2} - \frac{2}{n}\overline{X}\frac{x_i}{\Sigma x_i^2} + \overline{X}^2\frac{x_i^2}{(\Sigma x_i^2)^2}\right)E(u_i^2).$$

Since by definition $E(u_i u_j) = 0$ for $i \neq j$,

$$\sigma_a^2 = E(a - \alpha)^2 = \left(\frac{n}{n^2} - \frac{2}{n}\overline{X}\frac{\Sigma x_i}{\Sigma x_i^2} + \overline{X}^2\frac{\Sigma x_i^2}{(\Sigma x_i^2)^2}\right)E(u_i^2)$$

$$= \left(\frac{1}{n} - 0 + \frac{\overline{X}^2}{\Sigma x_i^2}\right)E(u_i^2),$$

but

$$E(u_i^2) = \sigma_u^2$$

or the variance of the error terms.

Then

$$\sigma_a^2 = \left(\frac{1}{n} + \frac{\overline{X}^2}{\Sigma x_i^2}\right)\sigma_u^2,$$

and

$$\sigma_a = \sigma_u\sqrt{\frac{1}{n} + \frac{\overline{X}^2}{\Sigma x_i^2}}. \qquad (5\text{-}49)$$

Variance in b

From equation (5-46),

$$b = \frac{\Sigma x_i(\beta x_i + u_i)}{\Sigma x_i^2},$$

$$= \beta\frac{\Sigma x_i^2}{\Sigma x_i^2} + \frac{\Sigma x_i u_i}{\Sigma x_i^2},$$

$$= \beta + \frac{\Sigma x_i u_i}{\Sigma x_i^2}, \text{ since } \frac{\Sigma x_i^2}{\Sigma x_i^2} = 1.$$

Then

$$b - \beta = \frac{\Sigma x_i u_i}{\Sigma x_i^2},$$

(5-50)

$$E(b - \beta) = E\left(\frac{\Sigma x_i u_i}{\Sigma x_i^2}\right),$$

(5-51)

and

$$E(b - \beta) = \frac{\Sigma x_i}{\Sigma x_i^2} E(u_i), \text{ since } \frac{\Sigma x_i}{\Sigma x_i^2} \text{ is a constant.}$$

Thus $E(b - \beta) = 0$, since by definition $E(u_i) = 0$. Therefore, b is an unbiased estimator of the true population parameter, β.

If equation (5-51) is squared, one obtains

$$E(b - \beta)^2 = E\left[\left(\frac{\Sigma x_i u_i}{\Sigma x_i^2}\right)\right]^2$$

$$= E\left[\left(\frac{x_i}{\Sigma x_i^2}u_1\right)^2 + \left(\frac{x_2}{\Sigma x_i^2}u_2\right)^2 + \cdots + \left(\frac{x_n}{\Sigma x_i^2}u_n\right)^2\right.$$

$$+ 2\left(\frac{x_1 x_2}{\Sigma x_i^2}u_1 u_2\right) + 2\left(\frac{x_1 x_3}{\Sigma x_i^2}u_1 u_3\right) + \cdots + 2\left(\frac{x_1 x_n}{\Sigma x_i^2}u_1 u_n\right)$$

$$\left. + \cdots + 2\left(\frac{x_{n-1} x_n}{\Sigma x_i^2}u_{n-1} u_n\right)\right]$$

$$= E\left(\frac{\Sigma x_i^2 u_i^2}{(\Sigma x_i^2)^2} + \frac{2\underset{i>j}{\Sigma} x_i x_j}{\Sigma x_i^2}u_i u_j\right)$$

$$= \frac{1}{\Sigma x_i^2} E(u_i^2), \text{ since } E(u_i u_j) = 0 \text{ for } i \neq j,$$

and

$$E(b - \beta)^2 = \frac{\sigma_u^2}{\Sigma x_i^2} \text{ since } E(u_i^2) = \sigma_u^2.$$

That is,

$$\sigma_b^2 = \frac{1}{\Sigma x_i^2} \sigma_u^2.$$

(5-52)

Covariance between a and b

Using equations (5-47) and (5-50), the covariance between a and b can be defined:

$$\text{Cov}(a,b) = E[(a - \alpha)(b - \beta)]$$

$$= E\left[\left(\frac{1}{n}\Sigma u_i - \frac{\overline{X}}{\Sigma x_i^2}\Sigma x_i u_i\right)\left(\frac{1}{\Sigma x_i^2}\Sigma x_i u_i\right)\right]$$

$$= E\left[\frac{1}{n\Sigma x_i^2}(\Sigma u_i)(\Sigma x_i u_i) - \frac{\overline{X}}{(\Sigma x_i^2)^2}(\Sigma x_i u_i)^2\right]$$

$$= \frac{\Sigma x_i \sigma_u^2}{n\Sigma x_i^2} - \frac{\overline{X}\,\Sigma x_i^2}{(\Sigma x_i^2)^2}\sigma_u^2 \quad [\text{because } E(u_i u_j) = 0$$

$$\text{when } i \neq j \text{ and } E(u_i^2) = \sigma_u^2]$$

$$= -\frac{\overline{X}}{\Sigma x_i^2}\sigma_u^2 \quad [\text{because } \Sigma x_i = 0]. \tag{5-53}$$

Variance of $\hat{Y}$ (The Mean Forecast)

Since $Y = \hat{Y} + e$ in the practical regression model (5-28), we can study the variance of $\hat{Y}$ and the variance of Y. The variance of $\hat{Y}$ is often referred to as the variance of "a *mean* forecast" and the variance of Y is referred to as the variance of "an individual forecast." First consider the variance of the mean forecast $\hat{Y}_o$, corresponding to a specific value X_0:

$$\sigma_{\hat{Y}_0}^2 = E(\hat{Y}_0 - E(\hat{Y}_0))^2$$

$$= E[a + bX_0 - E(a) - X_0 E(b)]^2$$

$$= E[(a - \alpha) + X_0(b - \beta)]^2 \quad [\text{because } E(a) = \alpha \text{ and } E(b) = \beta]$$

$$= E[(a - \alpha)^2 + X_0^2(b - \beta)^2 + 2X_0(a - \alpha)(b - \beta)]$$

$$= \sigma_a^2 + X_0^2 \sigma_b^2 + 2X_0 \,\text{Cov}(a,b). \tag{5-54}$$

Using equations (5-49), (5-52), and (5-53), we have

$$\sigma_{\text{mean forecast}}^2 = \left(\frac{1}{n} + \frac{\overline{X}^2}{\Sigma x_i^2}\right)\sigma_u^2 + X_0^2 \frac{1}{\Sigma x_i^2}\sigma_u^2 - \frac{2\overline{X}X_0}{\Sigma x_i^2}\sigma_u^2$$

$$= \left[\frac{1}{n} + \frac{(X_0 - \overline{X})^2}{\Sigma x_i^2}\right]\sigma_u^2. \tag{5-55}$$

This is the formula used in equation (5-37).

Variance of Y (The Individual Forecast)

Turning now to Y, which equals $\hat{Y} + e$ in the practical regression model, we can define the variance of Y as follows:

$$\sigma_{Y_0}^2 = E[Y_0 - E(Y_0)]^2$$

$$= E[a + bX_0 + e_0 - E(a) - X_0E(b) - E(e_0)]^2$$

$$= E[(a - \alpha) + X_0(b - \beta) + (e_0 - E(e_0))]^2$$

$$= \sigma_a^2 + X_0\sigma_b^2 + \sigma_u^2 + 2X_0 \, \text{Cov}(a,b) \quad [\text{because } E(e_0 - E(e_0))^2 = \sigma_u^2$$

and all other cross-product terms are zero]

$$= \sigma_{Y_0}^2 + \sigma_u^2 \quad [\text{using (5-54)}]$$

$$= \left[1 + \frac{1}{n} + \frac{(X_0 - \overline{X})^2}{\Sigma x_i^2}\right]\sigma_u^2 . \tag{5-56}$$

This is the formula used in equation (5-38).

APPENDIX 5-C
PARTITIONING THE TOTAL VARIANCE INTO EXPLAINED AND UNEXPLAINED VARIANCE

In equation (5-27) a partition of $(Y_i - \overline{Y})$ into two parts was described, as follows:

$$(Y_i - \overline{Y}) = (Y_i - \hat{Y}_i) + (\hat{Y}_i - \overline{Y}),$$

where $\hat{Y}_i = a + bX_i$. The left-hand side of the equation is called the *total deviation*, and the two parts on the right-hand side are the *unexplained deviation* and the *explained deviation*, respectively.

Summing the squares of the total deviations yields

$$\Sigma(Y_i - \overline{Y})^2 = \Sigma[(Y_i - \hat{Y}_i) + (\hat{Y}_i - \overline{Y})]^2$$

$$= \Sigma(Y_i - \hat{Y}_i)^2 + \Sigma(\hat{Y}_i - \overline{Y})^2$$

$$+ 2\Sigma(Y_i - \hat{Y}_i)(\hat{Y}_i - \overline{Y}). \tag{5-57}$$

The cross-product term turns out to be zero for the following reasons:

$$\Sigma(Y_i - \hat{Y})(\hat{Y}_i - \overline{Y}) = \Sigma(Y_i - a - bX_i)(bX_i - b\overline{X}) \quad [\text{because } \hat{Y}_i = a + bX_i$$

$$\text{and } \overline{Y} = a + b\overline{X}]$$

$$= \Sigma b[Y_iX_i - Y_i\overline{X} - a(X_i - \overline{X}) - bX_i^2 + b\overline{X}X_i]$$

$$= b\left[\left(\Sigma X_iY_i - \frac{\Sigma X_i \Sigma Y_i}{n}\right) + 0 - b\left(\Sigma X_i^2 - \frac{(\Sigma X_i)^2}{n}\right)\right]$$

$$[\text{because } \Sigma(X_i - \overline{X}) = 0]$$

$$= b\left[nC_{XY} - \frac{C_{XY}}{C_{XX}}(nC_{XX})\right] = 0,$$

where C_{XY} = covariance between X and Y,

$\qquad C_{XX}$ = variance of X,

$\qquad\quad b = C_{XY}/C_{XX}$ (see (5-25)).

Thus, we have

$$\Sigma(Y_i - \overline{Y})^2 \;=\; \Sigma(Y_i - \hat{Y})^2 \;+\; \Sigma(\hat{Y}_i - \overline{Y})^2.$$

$$\underset{\text{SS}_{\text{total}}}{\uparrow} \qquad\qquad \underset{\text{SS}_{\text{unexplained}}}{\uparrow} \qquad\qquad \underset{\text{SS}_{\text{explained}}}{\uparrow}$$

The corresponding degrees of freedom for each of these parts are

$$\text{df}_{\text{total}} = n - 1,$$

$$\text{df}_{\text{unexplained}} = n - (\text{number of parameters estimated})$$

$$= n - 2,$$

$$\text{df}_{\text{explained}} = (\text{number of parameters}) - 1$$

$$= 2 - 1 = 1.$$

Dividing each SS by its appropriate df gives the mean squares (MS), as follows:

$$\text{MS}_{\text{total}} = \frac{\text{SS}_{\text{total}}}{\text{df}_{\text{total}}},$$

$$\text{MS}_{\text{explained}} = \frac{\text{SS}_{\text{explained}}}{\text{df}_{\text{explained}}},$$

$$\text{MS}_{\text{unexplained}} = \frac{\text{SS}_{\text{unexplained}}}{\text{df}_{\text{unexplained}}}.$$

The ratio of explained to total SS is the coefficient of determination:

$$R^2 = \frac{\text{SS}_{\text{explained}}}{\text{SS}_{\text{total}}} = r_{XY}^2 \quad [\text{see equation (5-26)}],$$

and the ratio of explained MS to unexplained MS is the F-ratio used to test the significance of the regression model:

$$F = \frac{\text{MS}_{\text{explained}}}{\text{MS}_{\text{unexplained}}} \quad [\text{see equation (5-30)}].$$

Given the relationship between MS and SS it is easy to reformulate the F-ratio in terms of the coefficient of determination, as follows:

$$F = \frac{\text{SS}_{\text{explained}}/\text{df}_{\text{explained}}}{\text{SS}_{\text{unexplained}}/\text{df}_{\text{unexplained}}}$$

$$= \frac{\text{SS}_{\text{explained}}/\text{df}_{\text{explained}}}{(\text{SS}_{\text{total}} - \text{SS}_{\text{explained}})/\text{df}_{\text{unexplained}}}$$

$$= \frac{R^2/\text{df}_{\text{explained}}}{(1 - R^2)/\text{df}_{\text{unexplained}}} \quad [\text{see equation (5-31)}].$$

REFERENCES AND SELECTED BIBLIOGRAPHY

Clark, C. T., and L. L. Schkade. 1969. *Statistical Methods for Business Decisions.* Cincinnati, Ohio: South-Western Publishing Co.

Cooley, W. W., and P. R. Lohnes. 1971. *Multivariate Data Analysis.* New York: John Wiley and Sons, Inc.

Intriligator, M. D. 1978. *Econometric Methods, Techniques, and Applications.* Englewood Cliffs, N.J.: Prentice-Hall.

Johnston, J. 1966. *Econometric Methods,* Englewood Cliffs, N.J.: Prentice-Hall.

Klein, L. R. 1968. *An Introduction to Econometrics.* Englewood Cliffs, N.J.: Prentice-Hall.

Pindyck, R. S., and D. L. Rubenfeld. 1976. *Econometric Models and Economic Forecasts.* New York: McGraw-Hill.

"Regression as a Forecasting Aid." 1973. Boston: Intercollegiate Case Clearing House, 9-173-147.

Spurr, W. A., and C. P. Bonini. 1967. *Statistical Analysis for Business Decisions,* Homewood, Ill.: Irwin.

EXERCISES

1. Suppose the following data represent the total costs (Y) and the number of units produced (X) by Company XYZ.

Y Total Cost	X Units Produced
25	5
11	2
34	8
23	4
32	6

a. Determine the linear regression line relating Y to X.

b. Compute the overall F-test value, and the t-tests for the slope and intercept.

c. Calculate r_{XY}, $r_{Y\hat{Y}}$, and $r^2_{Y\hat{Y}}$.

d. Figure 5-18 shows the confidence intervals corresponding to the above data. Interpret the meaning of the different lines.

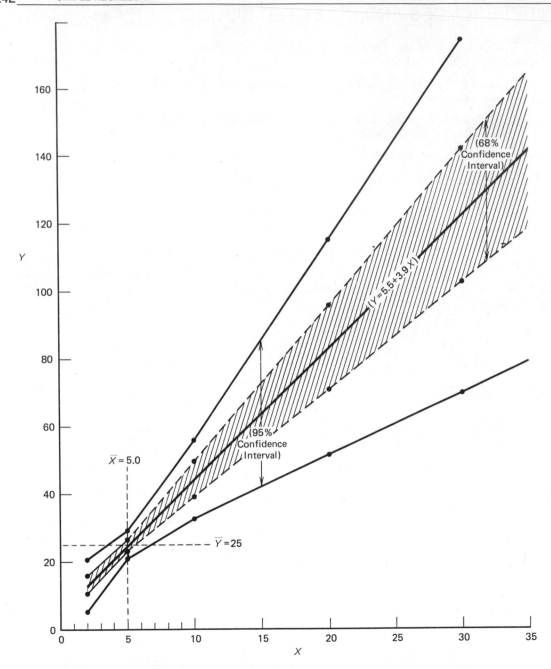

FIGURE 5-18   CONFIDENCE INTERVALS

2. Data on the test scores of various workers and their subsequent production ratings are shown in the table below.

SCORES ON MANUAL DEXTERITY TEST AND PRODUCTION RATINGS
FOR 20 WORKERS

Worker	Test Score X	Production Rating Y
A	53	45
B	36	43
C	88	89
D	84	79
E	86	84
F	64	66
G	45	49
H	48	48
I	39	43
J	67	76
K	54	59
L	73	77
M	65	56
N	29	28
O	52	51
P	22	27
Q	76	76
R	32	34
S	51	60
T	37	32

a. Plot these data on a graph with test score as the X-axis and production rating as the Y-axis.

b. Compute the coefficients of the linear regression of Y on X, and examine the significance of the relationship.

c. If a test score was 80, what would be your forecast of the production rating? What would be the standard error of this forecast if you treated it (i) as a mean, or (ii) as an individual forecast? Use equations (5-37) and (5-38) here.

d. Determine the 95 percent confidence interval for the slope coefficient in the regression equation.

e. Determine the 95 percent confidence interval for the $\hat{Y}$ values corresponding to X values of 20, 40, 60, and 80—using equation (5-37)—and construct a graph similar to that in Figure 5-18.

3. For the natural gas problem (in Table 5-3 and Figures 5-6 and 5-7) continue the analysis started in this chapter, as follows:

    a. For prices P = 20, 40, 60, 80, 100, and 120 cents per 1000 cubic feet, compute the forecasted per capita demand using the regression relationship:

    $$\hat{C} = 138.561 - 1.104(P).$$

    b. First thinking of these forecasts as mean values, compute the 95 percent confidence intervals for each of the forecasts using equation (5-37).

    c. Then thinking of each forecast as an individual value, compute the 95 percent confidence intervals for each of the forecasts, using equation (5-38).

    d. Make a graph of these confidence intervals and discuss their significance.

4. Natural gas consumption in Texas (see Table 5-3) has a curvilinear relationship to price, as shown in Figure 5-9b. The regression model actually used in Figure 5-9a was

    $$\log(C_i) = 5.0978 - .0153(P_i)$$

    and the residuals shown in Table 5-5 are actually $[\log(C_i) - \widehat{\log(C_i)}]$.

    a. Using the logged data, compute the forecasts for $\log(C)$ when the price P = 20, 40, 60, 80, 100, and 120 cents per 1000 cubic feet.

    b. Now determine the 95 percent confidence intervals for these forecasts (still on the logarithmic scale) using equations (5-37) and (5-38)—that is, thinking of the forecast as a mean, and then as an individual item. Make a table of the upper and lower confidence limits.

    c. Next convert all these upper and lower confidence limits (which are still on the logarithmic scale) to antilogarithms, to create equivalent confidence limits on the original C scale (per capita consumption).

    d. Make a graph of these confidence limits to see how the width of the confidence interval varies from P = 20 to P = 120.

    e. Comparing the confidence intervals obtained in parts b and c above, which ones are symmetric about the forecast values and which are not? Explain why.

5. For the natural gas problem two regression models were tried:

    $$\hat{C} = 138.561 - 1.104\,P \quad \text{(linear)},$$

    $$\hat{C} = e^{5.0978 - .0153P} \quad \text{(nonlinear)}.$$

    a. Using the linear model, the coefficient of determination, R^2, was computed to be .624 in Section 5/4/2. Verify that $R^2_{C\hat{C}} = r^2_{CP}$ in this case.

    b. Using the nonlinear model, compute the coefficient of determination, R^2, using (i) the data in Table 5-5(a) and (ii) the data in Table 5-5(b). Why are they different? Why are these R^2 values not the same as r^2_{CP}?

6. Figure 5-13 presents the King Kong data set and shows how strong the influence of one outlier can be in determining the correlation coefficient.

    a. Imagine that the King Kong data added to the 20 normal monkeys were $H = 130$ and $W = 45$ (a very skinny King Kong!) and recompute r_{HW}.

    b. Imagine that the King Kong data were $H = 40$ and $W = 150$ (a short, fat King Kong!) and recompute r_{HW}.

    c. Discuss the significance of the impact of such outliers on r.

6/MULTIPLE REGRESSION

6/1 Introduction to Multiple Linear Regression

Simple regression, as examined in Chapter 5, is a special case of multiple regression. In multiple regression there is one dependent variable (e.g., sales) to be predicted, but there are two or more independent variables. The general form of multiple regression is

$$Y = b_0 + b_1X_1 + b_2X_2 + \cdots + b_kX_k + \varepsilon. \tag{6-1}$$

Thus if sales were the variable to be forecast, several factors such as GNP, advertising, prices, competition, R&D budget, and time could be tested for their influence on sales by using regression. If it is found that these variables do influence the level of sales, they can be used to predict future values of sales.

To illustrate the application of multiple regression in a forecasting context, data from a mutual savings bank study will be examined throughout the chapter. These data refer to a mutual savings bank in a large metropolitan area. In 1973 there was considerable concern within the mutual savings banks because monthly changes in deposits were getting smaller and monthly changes in withdrawals were getting bigger. Thus it was of interest to develop a short-term forecasting model to forecast the changes in end-of-month (EOM) balance over the next few months. Table 6-1 shows 60 monthly observations (February 1968 through January 1973) of end-of-month balance (in column 2) and a plot of these EOM values is shown in Figure 6-1. Note that there was strong growth in early 1971 and then a slowing down of the growth rate since the middle of 1971.

Also presented in Table 6-1 are the composite AAA bond rates (in column 3) and the rates on U.S. Government 3-4 year bonds (in column 4). It was hypothesized that these two rates had an influence on the EOM balance figures in the bank.

Now of interest to the bank was the *change* in end-of-month balance and so *first differences* of the EOM data in Table 6-1 are shown as column 2 of Table 6-2. These differences, denoted D(EOM) in subsequent equations, are plotted in Figure 6-2, and it is clear that the bank was facing a volatile situation in the last 2 years or so. The challenge to the forecaster is to forecast these rapidly changing EOM measures.

In preparation for some of the regression analyses to be done in this chapter, Table 6-2 designates D(EOM) as Y, the dependent variable, and shows three independent variables X_1, X_2, and X_3. Variable X_1 is the AAA bond rates from Table 6-1, but they are now shown *leading* the D(EOM) measures. Similarly, variable X_2 refers to the rates on 3-4 year government bonds and they are shown *leading* the D(EOM) measures by one month. Finally, variable X_3 refers to the first differences of the 3-4 year government bond rates, and the timing for this variable *coincides* with that of the D(EOM)

TABLE 6-1   BANK DATA: END-OF-MONTH BALANCE, AAA BOND RATES, AND RATES FOR 3-4 YEAR GOVERNMENT BOND ISSUES OVER THE PERIOD FEBRUARY 1968 THROUGH JANUARY 1973

(1) Month	(2) (EOM)	(3) (AAA)	(4) (3-4)	
1	360071	5.94	5.31	
2	361217	6.00	5.60	
3	358774	6.08	5.49	
4	360271	6.17	5.80	
5	360139	6.14	5.61	
6	362164	6.09	5.28	
7	362901	5.87	5.19	
8	361878	5.84	5.18	
9	360922	5.99	5.30	
10	361307	6.12	5.23	
11	362290	6.42	5.64	
12	367382	6.48	5.62	
13	371031	6.52	5.67	
14	373734	6.64	5.83	
15	373463	6.75	5.53	
16	375518	6.73	5.76	
17	374804	6.89	6.09	
18	375457	6.98	6.52	
19	375423	6.98	6.68	
20	374365	7.10	7.07	
21	372314	7.19	7.12	
22	373765	7.29	7.25	
23	372776	7.65	7.85	
24	374134	7.75	8.02	
25	374880	7.72	7.87	
26	376735	7.67	7.14	
27	374841	7.66	7.20	
28	375622	7.89	7.59	
29	375461	8.14	7.74	
30	377694	8.21	7.51	
31	380119	8.05	7.46	
32	382288	7.94	7.09	
33	383270	7.88	6.82	
34	387978	7.79	6.22	
35	394041	7.41	5.61	
36	403423	7.18	5.48	
37	412727	7.15	4.78	
38	423417	7.27	4.14	
39	429948	7.37	4.64	

TABLE 6-1 BANK DATA: END-OF-MONTH BALANCE, AAA BOND RATES, AND RATES FOR 3-4 YEAR GOVERNMENT BOND ISSUES OVER THE PERIOD FEBRUARY 1968 THROUGH JANUARY 1973 (*Continued*)

(1) Month	(2) (EOM)	(3) (AAA)	(4) (3-4)
40	437821	7.54	5.52
41	441703	7.58	5.95
42	446663	7.62	6.20
43	447964	7.58	6.03
44	449118	7.48	5.60
45	449234	7.35	5.26
46	454162	7.19	4.96
47	456692	7.19	5.28
48	465117	7.11	5.37
49	470408	7.16	5.53
50	475600	7.22	5.72
51	475857	7.36	6.04
52	480259	7.34	5.66
53	483432	7.30	5.75
54	488536	7.30	5.82
55	493182	7.27	5.90
56	494242	7.30	6.11
57	493484	7.31	6.05
58	498186	7.26	5.98
59	500064	7.24	6.00
60	506684	7.25	6.24

variable. Referring to the numbers in the first row of Table 6-2, they are explained as follows:

1146 = (EOM balance March 1968) - (EOM balance February 1968)

5.94 = AAA bond rate for February 1968

5.31 = 3-4 year government bond rate for February 1968

0.29 = (3-4 rate for March 1968) - (3-4 rate for February 1968)

(Note that the particular choice of these independent variables is not arbitrary, but rather based on an extensive analysis that will not be presented in detail here.)

For the purpose of illustration in this chapter, the last six rows in Table 6-2 will be ignored in all the analyses that follow, so that they may

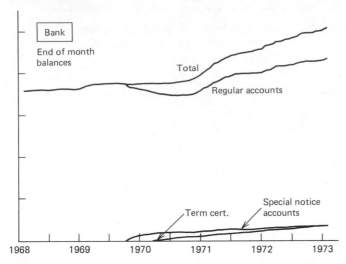

FIGURE 6-1   A PLOT OF END-OF-MONTH BALANCES IN A
MUTUAL SAVINGS BANK

be used to examine the success or otherwise of the various forecasting models
to be employed. By the end of the chapter we will forecast the D(EOM)
figures for periods 54–59, and will be able to compare them with the known
figures.

The bank could forecast Y—the D(EOM) measure—on the basis of
X_1 alone, or on the basis of a combination of the X_1, X_2, and X_3 measures
shown in columns 3, 4, and 5 (or, as we shall see later, on the basis of other
possible combinations of variables). Formally and briefly, such relationships
can be written as follows:

$$Y = f(X_1),$$

$$Y = g(X_1, X_2, X_3),$$

$$Y = h(X_1, X_2, \ldots, X_k),$$

where f, g, and h stand for "functions" of some particular form. These
equations simply say that Y, the dependent variable, is a *function* of one
or more independent variables (also called *regressors* in the context of this
chapter). Although several different forms of the function could be written
to designate the relationships among these variables, a straightforward one
that is linear and additive is

TABLE 6-2   BANK DATA: MONTHLY CHANGES IN BALANCE
AS DEPENDENT MEASURE AND THREE
INDEPENDENT VARIABLES

T Month	Y D(EOM)	X_1 (AAA)	X_2 (3-4)	X_3 D(3-4)	
1	1146	5.94	5.31	0.29	
2	−2443	6.00	5.60	−0.11	
3	1497	6.08	5.49	0.31	
4	−132	6.17	5.80	−0.19	
5	2025	6.14	5.61	−0.33	
6	737	6.09	5.28	−0.09	
7	−1023	5.87	5.19	−0.01	
8	−956	5.84	5.18	0.12	
9	385	5.99	5.30	−0.07	
10	983	6.12	5.23	0.41	
11	5092	6.42	5.64	−0.02	where:
12	3649	6.48	5.62	0.05	
13	2703	6.52	5.67	0.16	D(EOM) = change in end-of-month
14	−271	6.64	5.83	−0.30	balance (first datum is
15	2055	6.75	5.53	0.23	for March 1968-Feb.
16	−714	6.73	5.76	0.33	1968)
17	653	6.89	6.09	0.43	
18	−34	6.98	6.52	0.16	(AAA) = triple A bond rates
19	−1058	6.98	6.68	0.39	(Feb. 1968 is first
20	2051	7.10	7.07	0.05	datum)
21	1451	7.19	7.12	0.13	
22	−989	7.29	7.25	0.60	(3-4) = rates for 3-4 year
23	1358	7.65	7.85	0.17	Government issues
24	746	7.75	8.02	−0.15	(Feb. 1968 is first
25	1855	7.72	7.87	−0.73	datum)
26	−1894	7.67	7.14	0.06	
27	781	7.66	7.20	0.39	D(3-4) = first differences of (3-4)
28	−161	7.89	7.59	0.15	rates (first datum is
29	2233	8.14	7.74	−0.23	March 1968-Feb. 1968)
30	2425	8.21	7.51	−0.05	
31	2169	8.05	7.46	−0.37	
32	982	7.94	7.09	−0.27	
33	4708	7.88	6.82	−0.60	
34	6063	7.79	6.22	−0.61	
35	9382	7.41	5.61	−0.13	
36	9304	7.18	5.48	−0.70	
37	10690	7.15	4.78	−0.64	
38	6531	7.27	4.14	0.50	
39	7873	7.37	4.64	0.88	

TABLE 6-2   BANK DATA: MONTHLY CHANGES IN BALANCE
AS DEPENDENT MEASURE AND THREE
INDEPENDENT VARIABLES (*Continued*)

T Month	Y D(EOM)	X_1 (AAA)	X_2 (3-4)	X_3 D(3-4)	
40	3882	7.54	5.52	0.43	
41	4960	7.58	5.95	0.25	
42	1301	7.62	6.20	−0.17	
43	1154	7.58	6.03	−0.43	
44	116	7.48	5.60	−0.34	
45	4928	7.35	5.26	−0.30	
46	2530	7.19	4.96	0.32	
47	8425	7.19	5.28	0.09	
48	5291	7.11	5.37	0.16	
49	5192	7.16	5.53	0.19	
50	257	7.22	5.72	0.32	
51	4402	7.36	6.04	−0.38	
52	3173	7.34	5.66	0.09	
53	5104	7.30	5.75	0.07	
54	4646	7.30	5.82	0.08	
55	1060	7.27	5.90	0.21	
56	−758	7.30	6.11	−0.06	To be ignored in all analyses and
57	4702	7.31	6.05	−0.07	then used to check forecasts
58	1878	7.26	5.98	0.02	
59	6620	7.24	6.00	0.24	

$$Y = \boxed{b_0 + b_1X_1 + b_2X_2 + b_3X_3} + e, \tag{6-2}$$

where $Y = $ D(EOM),

   $X_1 = $ AAA bond rates,

   $X_2 = $ 3-4 year rates,

   $X_3 = $ D(3-4) year rates,

   $e = $ error term.

From equation (6-2) it can readily be seen that if two of the X variables were omitted, the equation would be like those handled previously with simple linear regression (Chapter 5). Just as the method of least squares was used in Chapter 5 to estimate the coefficients b_0 and b_1 in simple regression, so may it be used to estimate b_0, b_1, b_2, and b_3 in the equation above.

Change in End-of-Month Bank Balances

1	1146.00
2	−2443.00
3	1497.00
4	−132.00
5	2025.00
6	737.00
7	−1023.00
8	−956.00
9	385.00
10	983.00
11	5092.00
12	3649.00
13	2703.00
14	−271.00
15	2055.00
16	−714.00
17	653.00
18	−34.00
19	−1058.00
20	−2051.00
21	1451.00
22	−989.00
23	1358.00
24	746.00
25	1855.00
26	−1894.00
27	781.00
28	−161.00
29	2233.00
30	2425.00
31	2169.00
32	982.00
33	4708.00
34	6063.00
35	9382.00
36	9304.00
37	10690.00
38	6631.00
39	7873.00
40	3882.00
41	4960.00
42	1301.00
43	1154.00
44	116.00
45	4928.00
46	2530.00
47	8425.00
48	5291.00
49	5192.00
50	257.00
51	4402.00
52	3173.00
53	5104.00

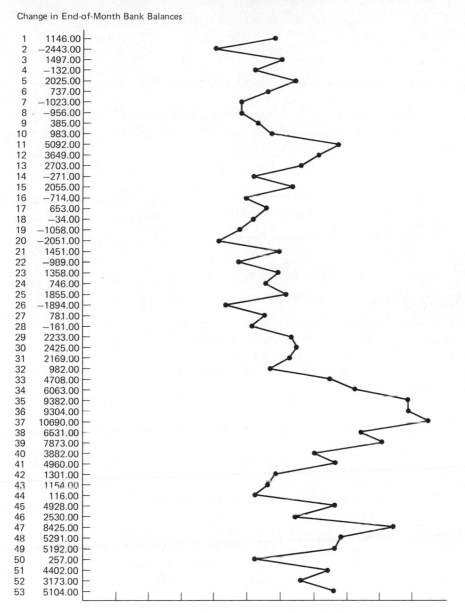

FIGURE 6-2 A PLOT OF THE FIRST DIFFERENCES OF END-OF-MONTH
BALANCES AT A MUTUAL SAVINGS BANK

(See Appendix 6-A for details.) Simple regression is thus a special case of multiple regression.

6/1/1 The Multiple Regression Model: Theory and Practice

In Section 5/5, simple linear regression was presented as a formal statistical model. We do so now for the general multiple linear regression model.

REGRESSION MODEL (THEORY)

$$Y = \boxed{\beta_0 + \beta_1 X_1 + \cdots + \beta_k X_k} + \varepsilon, \qquad (6\text{-}3)$$

where $\beta_0, \beta_1, \beta_2, \ldots, \beta_k$ are fixed parameters,

$X_1, X_2, \ldots, X_k$ are measured without error,

ε is a random variable that is normally distributed around zero (the mean of ε), and has a variance of V_ε. Specific values of ε are obtained by SIRS (simple independent random sampling) from the parent distribution $ND(0, V_\varepsilon)$.

Note in (6-3) that the form of the regression model (that is, the part enclosed by the small rectangle) is *linear in the coefficients*. The exponent of every β coefficient is 1—that is, linear—and this means that estimates of the β coefficients can be obtained efficiently using the least squares (LS) method. The shape of the function relating Y to the several X variables is no longer quite so easy to describe. If there is only one X variable in (6-3), then the shape of the underlying function is a straight line. If there are two variables, then Y is mapped into a *plane* (the plane formed by the two X variables). If there are more than two independent variables in (6-3), then we say Y is mapped into a *hyperplane* (meaning a higher dimensional surface).

Now in practice, the task of regression modeling is to estimate the unknown parameters of the model (6-3)—namely, $\beta_0, \beta_1, \ldots, \beta_k$ and V_ε. From a known data set (such as in Table 6-2), the LS procedure can be applied to determine $b_0, b_1, b_2, \ldots, b_k$ and an estimate of V_ε. The square root of this last estimate is often called the *standard error of estimate* (see). Thus the pragmatic form of the statistical regression model is as follows:

REGRESSION MODEL (IN PRACTICE)

$$Y_i = \boxed{b_0 + b_1 X_{1i} + b_2 X_{2i} + \cdots + b_k X_{ki}} + e_i \qquad (6\text{-}4)$$

$$\text{for } i = 1, 2, \ldots, N$$

where $X_1, X_2, \ldots, X_k$ are assumed measured without error,

$b_0, b_1, b_2, \ldots, b_k$ are LS estimates of $\beta_0, \beta_1, \beta_2, \ldots, \beta_k$ and are all random variables now, with a joint normal distribution.

e_i $(i = 1, 2, \ldots, N)$ is an estimated error term, for the ith observation, and is assumed to be sampled independently from a normal distribution.

Note that the coefficients in the model are no longer fixed as they were in (6-3). From sample to sample the b-coefficients fluctuate, giving rise to a statistical family of regression surfaces.

For the bank data in Table 6-2—using only the first 53 rows—the model in equation (6-2) can be solved using a least squares procedure to give

$$\hat{Y} = -4295.1 + 3363.7(X_1) - 2828.7(X_2) - 1965.7(X_3). \qquad (6\text{-}5)$$

Note that a "hat" is used over $\hat{Y}$ to indicate that this is an *estimate* of Y, not the *observed* Y. This estimate $\hat{Y}$ is based on the three independent measures only. The difference between the observed Y and the estimated $\hat{Y}$ tells us something about the "fit" of the model, and this discrepancy is called the residual (or error):

$$\text{residual} = \underset{\substack{\uparrow \\ \text{(observed)}}}{Y} - \underset{\substack{\uparrow \\ \text{(estimated using the} \\ \text{regression model)}}}{\hat{Y}}$$

6/1/2 Solving for the Regression Coefficients

A computer program would normally be used to solve for the coefficients in a multiple regression model. However, it is important to get a good understanding of what is behind the method. The practitioner proposes a model; for example,

$$Y = \boxed{\beta_0 + \beta_1 X_1 + \beta_2 X_2} + \varepsilon$$

and either explicitly or implicitly makes various assumptions about the coefficients (that they are fixed but unknown constants), the X measures (that they are measured without error), and the error term (that it is normally distributed). The pragmatic form of this theory is

$$Y = \boxed{b_0 + b_1 X_1 + b_2 X_2} + e,$$

and, for any one observation vector—say the ith observation—we add a subscript i, as follows:

$$Y_i = \boxed{b_0 + b_1 X_{1i} + b_2 X_{2i}} + e_i$$

$$= \boxed{\hat{Y}_i} + e_i. \tag{6-6}$$

Rewriting the error term, we have

$$e_i = Y_i - \hat{Y}_i \tag{6-7}$$

and the method of least squares (LS) is used to find the minimum sum of squares of these error terms—that is,

$$\text{minimize } \phi = \sum_{i=1}^{n} e_i^2$$

$$= \sum_{i=1}^{n} (Y_i - \hat{Y}_i)^2$$

$$= \sum_{i=1}^{n} (Y_i - b_0 - b_1 X_{1i} - b_2 X_{2i})^2. \tag{6-8}$$

Readers with a calculus background will recognize that this problem is solved by taking partial derivatives of ϕ with respect to each of the unknown coefficients, b_0, b_1, and b_2, setting these derivatives equal to zero, and solving a set of three equations in three unknowns to get estimated values for b_0, b_1, and b_2. (See Appendix 6-A.)

The solution to the bank data has already been shown as:

$$\text{D(EOM)} = -4295.1 + 3363.7(\text{AAA}) - 2828.7(3\text{-}4) - 1965.7(\text{D}(3\text{-}4)). \tag{6-9}$$

Consider the first observation vector in Table 6-2:

$$Y_1 = 1146, \qquad X_{11} = 5.94, \qquad X_{21} = 5.31, \qquad X_{31} = 0.29.$$

Then

$$\hat{Y}_1 = -4295.1 + 3363.7(5.94) - 2828.7(5.31) - 1965.7(0.29)$$

$$= 92 \quad \text{[using (6-9)]},$$

$$e_1 = Y_1 - \hat{Y}_1 = 1146 - 92$$

$$= 1054 \quad \text{[using (6-7)]}.$$

We have found the residual error for the first Y value. Proceeding in this manner through all of the first 53 rows of Table 6-2 we can determine the sum of the squared errors to be

$$\phi = \sum_{i=1}^{53} e_i^2 = 499,986,100 \quad \text{[using (6-8)]}.$$

This rather large number is in fact the lowest it can be when Y is regressed linearly on X_1, X_2, and X_3. It is the LS solution for these regressors. Details of this computation are shown in Table 6-3, along with other information to be used later.

The information in this table is rounded to whole numbers for convenience. Column 2 shows the original Y values, D(EOM). Column 3 gives the $\hat{Y}$ values based on equation (6-9), and column 4 is the list of errors of fit. Note three things: (1) the column sums for columns 2 and 3 are the same—which also indicates that the means of Y and $\hat{Y}$ are the same; (2) the sum of the residuals in column 4 is zero—as it will always be for LS fitting of linear regression models; and (3) because of the first two observations, it will also be true that the sums on columns 5 and 6 will be zero.

6/1/3 Multiple Correlation and the Coefficient of Determination

In Table 6-3, column 2 gives the observed Y values and column 3 gives the estimated values $\hat{Y}$, based on the fitted regression model (6-9). The correlation between Y and $\hat{Y}$ can be computed using equation (5-22) and turns out to be $R_{Y\hat{Y}} = .748$. The square of this correlation is called the *coefficient of determination:*

$$R_{Y\hat{Y}}^2 = (.748)^2 = .560 \qquad \text{(Coefficient of Determination)}.$$

R itself is known as the *multiple correlation* coefficient, and is the correlation between a dependent variable Y and an estimate of Y based on multiple independent variables. Hence it is often written as

$$R_{YX_1X_2 \cdots X_k}.$$

TABLE 6-3   BANK DATA: SHOWING THE ORIGINAL Y, THE FITTED $\hat{Y}$,
AND THE RESIDUAL $(Y - \hat{Y})$, BASED ON EQUATION (6-9)

(1) Period	(2) Y	(3) $\hat{Y}$	(4) $Y - \hat{Y}$	(5) $\hat{Y} - \overline{Y}$	(6) $Y - \overline{Y}$	(7)[a] $(Y - \hat{Y})^2$	(8)[a] $(\hat{Y} - \overline{Y})^2$	(9)[a] $(Y - \overline{Y})^2$
1	1146	92	1054	−2332	−1278	1111	5439	1633
2	−2443	273	−2716	−2151	−4867	7377	4626	23686
3	1497	14	1483	−2410	−927	2199	5806	859
4	−132	409	−541	−2014	−2556	293	4058	6532
5	2025	1128	897	−1296	−399	805	1680	159
6	737	1418	−681	−1006	−1687	464	1012	2846
7	−1023	796	−1819	−1628	−3447	3307	2651	11881
8	−956	467	−1423	−1956	−3380	2026	3828	11424
9	385	996	−611	−1428	−2039	373	2039	4157
10	983	694	289	−1729	−1441	83	2991	2076
11	5092	1386	3706	−1038	2668	13737	1078	7119
12	3649	1490	2159	−934	1225	4663	873	1501
13	2703	1287	1416	−1137	279	2006	1293	78
14	−271	2149	−2420	−275	−2695	5855	76	7262
15	2055	2302	−247	−122	−369	61	15	136
16	−714	1398	−2112	−1026	−3138	4459	1053	9846
17	653	823	−170	−1601	−1771	29	2564	3136
18	−34	409	−443	−2014	−2458	197	4058	6041
19	−1058	−492	−566	−2916	−3482	320	8502	12123
20	−2051	−516	−1535	−2940	−4475	2355	8645	20024
21	1451	−522	1973	−2946	−973	3894	8681	946
22	−989	−1447	458	−3871	−3413	210	14987	11648
23	1358	−1105	2463	−3529	−1066	6067	12454	1136
24	746	−627	1373	−3051	−1678	1886	9310	2815
25	1855	856	999	−1568	−569	998	2457	324
26	−1894	1193	−3087	−1230	−4318	9532	1514	18644
27	781	345	436	−2079	−1643	190	4323	2699
28	−161	497	−658	−1927	−2585	433	3713	6682
29	2233	1647	586	−777	−191	343	603	36
30	2425	2166	259	−258	1	67	67	0
31	2169	2398	−229	−26	−255	53	1	65
32	982	2902	−1920	478	−1442	3686	228	2079
33	4708	4102	606	1678	2284	367	2817	5217
34	6063	5516	547	3093	3639	299	9564	13243
35	9382	5013	4369	2590	6958	19084	6706	48416
36	9304	5728	3576	3304	6880	12788	10917	47336
37	10690	7499	3191	5075	8266	10181	25760	68329

[a]Columns 7, 8, and 9 have been divided by 1000.

TABLE 6-3 BANK DATA: SHOWING THE ORIGINAL Y, THE FITTED $\hat{Y}$,
AND THE RESIDUAL $(Y - \hat{Y})$, BASED ON EQUATION (6-9) *(Continued)*

(1) Period	(2) Y	(3) $\hat{Y}$	(4) $Y - \hat{Y}$	(5) $\hat{Y} - \overline{Y}$	(6) $Y - \overline{Y}$	(7)[a] $(Y - \hat{Y})^2$	(8)[a] $(\hat{Y} - \overline{Y})^2$	(9)[a] $(Y - \overline{Y})^2$
38	6531	7472	−941	5049	4107	886	25488	16869
39	7873	5634	2239	3210	5449	5013	10305	29693
40	3882	4615	−733	2191	1458	537	4799	2126
41	4960	3870	1090	1446	2536	1188	2091	6432
42	1301	4123	−2822	1699	−1123	7963	2886	1261
43	1154	5004	−3850	2580	−1270	14821	6656	1613
44	116	5690	−5574	3266	−2308	31069	10668	5326
45	4928	6129	−1201	3705	2504	1443	13729	6271
46	2530	5244	−2714	2820	106	7368	7955	11
47	8425	4764	3661	2340	6001	13400	5478	36014
48	5291	4106	1185	1683	2867	1403	2831	8220
49	5192	3760	1432	1336	2768	2051	1784	7663
50	257	3189	−2932	765	−2167	8595	585	4695
51	4402	4124	278	1700	1978	77	2889	3913
52	3173	4204	−1031	1780	749	1063	3169	561
53	5104	3854	1250	1430	2680	1562	2046	7183
Sums	128465	128465	0	0	0	220238	279748	499986

To compute R^2, note that the form is the same as for simple regression:

$$R^2 = \frac{\Sigma(\hat{Y}_i - \overline{Y})^2}{\Sigma(Y_i - \overline{Y})^2} = \frac{\text{(explained SS)}}{\text{(total SS)}}, \tag{6-10}$$

where SS means sum of squared deviations.[1]

---

[1]Note that $\overline{Y} = \overline{\hat{Y}}$.

$$E(Y) = E(b_0 + b_1 X_1 + \cdots + b_k X_k + \varepsilon)$$

$$= E(b_0 + b_1 X_1 + \cdots + b_k X_k) + E(\varepsilon)$$

$$= E(\hat{Y}) + 0$$

So

$$E(Y) = E(\hat{Y}), \text{ or } \overline{Y} = \overline{\hat{Y}}.$$

This point can also be observed with reference to Table 6-3.

For the bank data, referring to Table 6-3, the R^2 value can be computed using equation (6-10) as follows:

$$R^2 = \frac{279748}{499986} = 0.560.$$

However, statisticians have some cause for concern in calculating R^2 this way because equation (6-10) does not take into account degrees of freedom. To overcome this problem, a corrected R^2 is defined, as follows:

$$\overline{R}^2 = 1 - (1 - R^2) \frac{(\text{total df})}{(\text{error df})}$$

(6-11)

$$= 1 - (1 - R^2) \frac{(N - 1)}{(N - k - 1)}.$$

The "total df" refers to the degrees of freedom in column 6 of Table 6-3, and the "error df" refers to the degrees of freedom in column 4 of Table 6-3.[2] For the bank data,

$$\overline{R}^2 = 1 - (1 - 0.560) \frac{(53 - 1)}{(53 - 3 - 1)}$$

$$= 0.533.$$

Note that $\overline{R}^2$ is referred to as "R-bar-squared," or sometimes as "R^2, corrected for degrees of freedom."

The value R, merely the square root of R^2, is sometimes reported in regression results, but it is R^2 (or $\overline{R}^2$) that has the greater significance in interpreting regression analyses. $\overline{R}^2$ is the proportion of variance accounted for (explained) by the regressors $X_1, X_2, \ldots, X_k$.[3]

6/1/4 The F-Test for Overall Significance

After estimating the coefficients of a regression model to determine the $\hat{Y}$ values, there will be a set of errors of fit—such as $e_i = (Y_i - \hat{Y}_i)$ for the ith observation. Figure 5-14 and equation (5-27) show that one way to

---

[2]Column 6 in Table 6-3 is a set of N values for $(Y - \overline{Y})$, which sum to zero, and therefore the df are $N - 1$. Column 4 is a set of values for $(Y - \hat{Y})$ and $\hat{Y}$ values are based on $(k + 1)$ estimated values $(b_0, b_1, b_2, \ldots, b_k)$ so there are $(N - (k + 1))$ df.

[3]Uncorrected R^2, defined in equation (6-10), is not quite a proportion of variance, since it does not involve degrees of freedom. Therefore, its proper interpretation is proportion of "explained SS" relative to "total SS" (where SS is sum of squared deviations), or, said in another way, the proportion of "total SS in Y" that can be explained by the regressors. Corrected $\overline{R}^2$ does take into account the df and therefore can be interpreted as the proportion of Y variance explained by the regressors.

discuss errors of fit is to partition the discrepancy $(Y_i - \overline{Y})$ into two parts:

$$(Y_i - \overline{Y}) \equiv (Y_i - \hat{Y}_i) + (\hat{Y}_i - \overline{Y}). \tag{6-12}$$

In Appendix 5-C it was shown that if such a partition is made for all Y_i values, and if each part in the partition is squared, then the following relation among the sums of squared deviations holds:

$$\sum_{i=1}^{N} (Y_i - \overline{Y})^2 = \sum_{i=1}^{N} (Y_i - \hat{Y}_i)^2 + \sum_{i=1}^{N} (\hat{Y}_i - \overline{Y})^2. \tag{6-13}$$

$$\underset{\text{(total SS)}}{\uparrow} \qquad \underset{\substack{\text{(unexplained} \\ \text{SS)}}}{\uparrow} \qquad \underset{\text{(explained SS)}}{\uparrow}$$

Furthermore, the degrees of freedom for this partition satisfy the relation

$$\text{df}_{\text{total}} = \text{df}_{\text{unexplained}} + \text{df}_{\text{explained}}. \tag{6-14}$$

If we are dealing with k regressors, X_1 through X_k, then there will be $(k + 1)$ coefficients, b_0 through b_k, and the degrees of freedom for each part of the partition are calculated as follows:

$$\left. \begin{aligned} \text{df}_{\text{total}} &= N - 1 &&\text{(no. observations minus 1),} \\ \text{df}_{\text{explained}} &= (k + 1) - 1 &&\text{(no. coefficients minus 1),} \\ \text{df}_{\text{unexplained}} &= N - (k + 1) &&\text{(no. observations minus no.} \\ &&&\text{of coefficients).} \end{aligned} \right\} \tag{6-15}$$

It is now possible to construct an overall F-test to check on the statistical significance of the regression model. Since an F statistic is defined as the ratio of two variances (or "mean squares" as statisticians often call them), we have to convert "sums of squares" to "mean squares" as follows.

$$\left. \begin{aligned} \text{MS}_{\text{total}} &= \text{SS}_{\text{total}}/(N - 1), \\ \text{MS}_{\text{explained}} &= \text{SS}_{\text{explained}}/(k), \\ \text{MS}_{\text{unexplained}} &= \text{SS}_{\text{unexplained}}/(N - k - 1). \end{aligned} \right\} \tag{6-16}$$

The F-ratio that tests the significance of the regression model is

$$F = \frac{\text{MS}_{\text{explained}}}{\text{MS}_{\text{unexplained}}} \text{ with } (k, N - k - 1) \text{ df}$$

$$= \frac{\Sigma(\hat{Y} - \overline{Y})^2/(k)}{\Sigma(Y - \hat{Y})^2/(N - k - 1)}. \tag{6-17}$$

Note that this F-test is sensitive to the relative strengths of the numerator and denominator. If the unexplained MS (the variance of the errors) is large, then the regression model is not doing well, and F becomes smaller. If the explained MS is large relative to the unexplained MS, then F becomes larger. Looking up tables of F values for specific degrees of freedom, we can make a decision as to the significance of the regression model.

As mentioned in Section 5/5/2 and equation (5-31), there is a close connection between R^2 and F, so that in the case of multiple regression we can write

$$F = \frac{[R^2/(k)]}{[(1 - R^2)/(N - k - 1)]} .$$ (6-18)

For the bank problem (see Table 6-3[4]) the above theory can be put into practice, as follows:

$$SS_{total} \quad = 499986 \qquad \text{(column 9 sum in Table 6-3)},$$
$$SS_{unexplained} \quad = 220238 \qquad \text{(column 7 sum in Table 6-3)},$$
$$SS_{explained} \quad = 279748 \qquad \text{(column 8 sum in Table 6-3)},$$

and

$$df_{total} \quad = 53 - 1 \quad = \quad 52,$$
$$df_{unexplained} \quad = 53 - (3 + 1) = \quad 49, \quad \text{[using (6-15)]}$$
$$df_{explained} \quad = (3 + 1) - 1 = \quad 3.$$

Thus,

$$MS_{total} \quad = 499986/52 \quad = \quad 9615,$$
$$MS_{explained} \quad = 279748/3 \quad = \quad 93249, \quad \text{[using (6-16)]}$$
$$MS_{unexplained} \quad = 220238/49 \quad = \quad 4495,$$

and

$$F = \frac{93249}{4495} \quad = \quad 20.75 \qquad \text{[using (6-17)]}$$

with (3,49) df. And this value could also be obtained as

$$F = \frac{(.560)/(3)}{(1 - .560)/(53 - 3 - 1)} = 20.75 \quad \text{[using (6-18)]} .$$

Looking up the F tables for (3, 49) df, it is found that only .01 (or 1 percent) of the area under the F distribution lies to the right of $F = 4.22$. Since the computed F value for the bank data is 20.75, we can conclude that this is a highly significant regression model. That is, the regressors explain a sig-

---

[4]*Note:* Columns 7, 8, and 9 in Table 6-2 have to be multipled by 1000 to be appropriate.

nificant amount of the variability in the change in end-of-month deposits at this mutual savings bank. And we can also say that the coefficient of determination (R^2) is highly significant.

6/1/5 The Significance of Individual Coefficients: the *t*-Tests

Before getting into this section it is well to appreciate the merits of computing:

1. the simple correlation coefficients between all pairs of regressors (i.e., independent variables $X_1, X_2, \ldots, X_k$),
2. the simple correlation coefficients between the dependent variable Y and each of the X variables in turn, and
3. the coefficient of determination R^2 and its corrected value $\overline{R}^2$, for the linear regression model.

The first set of correlations is helpful in selecting appropriate independent variables for a regression model (see Section 6/2) and, at a deeper level of analysis, is critical for examining multicollinearity (see Section 6/3). The second set indicates how each independent variable, on its own, relates to Y, and the third set, R^2 and $\overline{R}^2$, indicates the extent to which a linear combination of the X variables can explain the variability in Y.

After examining the overall significance of the regression model it is sometimes useful to study the significance of individual regression coefficients. There is one very important point to bear in mind.

A *t*-test on an individual coefficient is a test of its significance *in the presence of all other regressors* (independent variables).

Multiple regression makes use of the interdependence of the regressors to model Y. It is improper to treat individual coefficients as if they could stand alone.[5]

Nevertheless, for each regression coefficient b_j we can determine a standard error (a measure of the stability of the coefficient) and, given the normality assumptions in the regression model, it is known that t, defined

---

[5]Except in the very special case where all regressors are independent of one another.

by the following equation, has a t-distribution with $(N - k - 1)$ df.:

$$t = \frac{b_j - (\beta_j)}{\text{se}_{(b_j)}},$$

(6-19)

where b_j = estimated jth coefficient,

$\quad\quad \beta_j$ = hypothesized jth parameter,

$\quad\quad \text{se}_{(b_j)}$ = standard error of b_j (see footnote 6).

Thus, using equation (6-19) for each regression coefficient, we can do a formal statistical test of the significance of that coefficient—by which is usually meant that the estimated coefficient is tested against the value zero (which would mean the independent variable in question is not helping at all in the prediction of Y—*in the presence of the other regressors*).

In the case of the bank data and the linear regression of D(EOM) on (AAA), (3-4), and D(3-4), the full output from a regression program included the following information:

The regression equation is:

$\widehat{\text{D(EOM)}}$ =	se of b	t-value	prob(1-tail)	coeff.
-4295.10	3261.94	-1.317	0.0955	(b_0)
$+3363.74$*(AAA)	556.49	6.045	0.0000	(b_1)
-2829.69*(3-4)	390.05	-7.252	0.0000	(b_2)
-1965.69*D(3-4)	863.99	-2.275	0.0130	(b_3)

(6-20)

Note that for each estimated coefficient, there is a standard error, a t-value, and a one-tailed probability for the appropriate t-distribution. Consider the coefficient b_1 for the variable (AAA).

$$b_1 = 3363.74,$$

$$\text{se}_{(b_1)} = 556.49,$$

$$t_{(b_1)} = \frac{(3363.74 - 0)}{556.49} \quad \text{[using (6-19)]}$$

$$= 6.045.$$

The degrees of freedom for this t-value are $(N - k - 1)$, or 49, and, instead of asking us to look up t-tables, this computer program computes the area in one tail of the t-distribution with 49 df. In this case it is the right tail, and the area is very small indeed—to four decimal places it is

---

[6]See Appendix 6-A for the definition of $\text{se}_{(b_j)}$.

essentially zero. From this we conclude that the estimated b_1-coefficient is very significantly different from zero. The (AAA) measure is a significant regressor *in the presence of the other two regressors.*

Similarly, the coefficients b_2 and b_3, for (3-4) and D(3-4), respectively, are highly significant, in the presence of the other regressors.

Since the overall F-test indicated a significant regression line (in Section 6/1/4), it was to be expected that at least one of the t-tests would also be significant. (However, the converse is not necessarily true.) In the case of the bank data, D(EOM) has a significant relationship to (AAA), (3-4), and D(3-4), but as we shall see, there is room for considerable improvement still.

There are two additional aspects to consider in dealing with tests of individual coefficients. First, *the stability of the regression coefficients* depends upon the intercorrelation among the independent variables. Given two regressors, X_1 and X_2, the higher the correlation between them the more unstable will be the two coefficients (b_1 and b_2) determined for these variables. Figures 6-3 and 6-4 illustrate this point by showing two sets of simulation runs for a regression model relating Y to X_1 and X_2. In Figure 6-3 the correlation between X_1 and X_2 is simulated to be 0.10 and the successive simulations[7] show that the estimated b_1 and b_2 are relatively stable. In Figure 6-4, where the simulated model is exactly the same, except for the fact that the correlation between X_1 and X_2 is set at 0.95, the successive simulations show clearly that the estimated values for b_1 and b_2 are much less stable. In the case of more than two regressors (independent variables) the situation is similar but more subtle—in the sense that even without large correlations it is possible to have very unstable coefficients—and Section 6/3 will go into this matter somewhat more deeply.

The second aspect to consider is the *estimated correlations among the regression coefficients* themselves. It will be remembered that in the practical regression model the coefficients, b_0 through b_k, are all random variables—that is, they fluctuate from sample to sample and have a joint probability distribution. Hence it is possible to determine the correlations among the coefficients. Many computer programs do not automatically provide this information, but it is very helpful. For example, in the previous chapter (Section 5/5/3) it was shown that the slope and the intercept are always going to be negatively correlated because a LS regression line goes through the mean of Y and the mean of X, and an increase in slope automatically means a decrease in intercept, and vice versa. In multiple regres-

---

[7]The simulations reported here were based on the following procedures: (a) 100 pairs of (X_1, X_2) values were sampled from a bivariate normal distribution with a specified correlation parameter and arbitrary means and standard deviations. (b) One set of $\hat{Y}$ values was then determined according to the fixed equation $2 + 2X_1 + 2X_2$. (c) Then many sets of Y values were generated by adding error terms to $\hat{Y}$, according to a normal distribution with mean 0 and variance 10.

Lower Boundary	Freq.	
1.00	0	
1.10	0	
1.20	0	
1.30	0	
1.40	0	
1.50	0	
1.60	1	*
1.70	4	* * * *
1.80	9	* * * * * * * * *
1.90	35	* *
2.00	34	* *
2.10	16	* * * * * * * * * * * * * * * *
2.20	1	*
2.30	0	
2.40	0	
2.50	0	
2.60	0	
2.70	0	
2.80	0	
2.90	0	
3.00	0	

Model

$$\hat{Y} = 2 + 2X_1 + 2X_2$$
ε is ND (0,10)

Coefficient b_1

Sample Size = 100

1.9995	Mean
0.1063	Std Dev
−0.5504	Skewness
1.6487	Minimum
2.2334	Maximum

Lower Boundary	Freq.	
1.00	0	
1.10	0	
1.20	0	
1.30	0	
1.40	0	
1.50	0	
1.60	1	*
1.70	8	* * * * * * * *
1.80	12	* * * * * * * * * * * *
1.90	30	* *
2.00	31	* *
2.10	13	* * * * * * * * * * * * *
2.20	5	* * * * *
2.30	0	
2.40	0	
2.50	0	
2.60	0	
2.70	0	
2.80	0	
2.90	0	
3.00	0	

Coefficient b_2

Sample Size = 100

1.9897	Mean
0.1274	Std Dev
−0.1160	Skewness
1.6296	Minimum
2.2837	Maximum

FIGURE 6-3 SIMULATION RESULTS: HISTOGRAMS OF 100 VALUES OF b_1 AND b_2 WHEN THE CORRELATION BETWEEN X_1 AND X_2 IS 0.10

Lower Boundary	Freq.	
1.00	1	*
1.10	1	*
1.20	1	*
1.30	2	* *
1.40	3	* * *
1.50	4	* * * *
1.60	10	* * * * * * * * * *
1.70	15	* * * * * * * * * * * * * * *
1.80	7	* * * * * * *
1.90	9	* * * * * * * * *
2.00	14	* * * * * * * * * * * * * *
2.10	7	* * * * * * *
2.20	8	* * * * * * * *
2.30	5	* * * * *
2.40	2	* *
2.50	6	* * * * * *
2.60	2	* *
2.70	2	* *
2.80	1	*
2.90	0	
3.00	0	

Model

$$\hat{Y} = 2 + 2X_1 + 2X_2$$
ε is ND(0,10)

Coefficient b_1

Sample Size = 100

1.9741	Mean
0.3646	Std Dev
0.0732	Skewness
0.9556	Minimum
2.8807	Maximum

Lower Boundary	Freq.	Coefficient b_2
1.00	1	*
1.10	1	*
1.20	1	*
1.30	1	*
1.40	5	* * * * *
1.50	6	* * * * * *
1.60	7	* * * * * * *
1.70	7	* * * * * * *
1.80	7	* * * * * * *
1.90	11	* * * * * * * * * * *
2.00	9	* * * * * * * * *
2.10	13	* * * * * * * * * * * * *
2.20	12	* * * * * * * * * * * *
2.30	5	* * * * *
2.40	8	* * * * * * * *
2.50	2	* *
2.60	0	
2.70	1	*
2.80	3	* * *
2.90	0	
3.00	0	

Coefficient b_2

Sample Size = 100

2.0078	Mean
0.3683	Std Dev
−0.1094	Skewness
1.0945	Minimum
2.8723	Maximum

FIGURE 6-4   SIMULATION RESULTS: HISTOGRAMS OF 100 VALUES OF b_1 AND b_2 WHEN THE CORRELATION BETWEEN X_1 AND X_2 IS 0.95

sion, the situation is more complicated, but, if for instance, two coefficients b_3 and b_5, are found to be significantly correlated (positive or negative), then the investigator should be warned that individual t-tests on b_3 and b_5 should *not* be considered in isolation of each other. The two coefficients are dependent on each other.

Table 6-4 shows the correlations among the independent and dependent variables in the bank example. None of the regressors has a particularly high correlation with the Y value D(EOM), and the regressors themselves do not correlate very highly ($r_{X_1 X_2} = .587$ is the biggest). We suspect no multicollinearity problem (see Section 6/3) and the correlations $r_{X_1 Y}$, $r_{X_2 Y}$, and $r_{X_3 Y}$ would tend to suggest that these three regressors together will not be able to explain a lot of the variance in Y. They *do* combine to explain 53 percent ($\overline{R}^2$), it *is* a significant contribution (F-test), and all three coefficients are significantly different from zero (t-tests), but more can be done, since $\overline{R}^2$ is only 53 percent.

Finally, Table 6-5 shows how the regression coefficients themselves are interrelated. Note how all three coefficients b_1, b_2, and b_3, correlate negatively with the intercept b_0. There is an analogy here to the simple regression case—tilt a hyperplane "up" and the intercept goes "down." Note, too, that b_1 and b_2 correlate $-.569$. The variables X_1 and X_2 correlate $.587$ and their coefficients correlate $-.569$. Thus it is necessary to interpret these two variables *jointly*. Increase b_1 and there would, in general, be a decrease in b_2, and vice versa. These considerations are obviously very important in forecasting.

6/1/6   Examining the Residual Errors

The study of residuals (or errors of fit) is very important for deciding on the appropriateness of a given forecasting model. If the errors are es-

---

TABLE 6-4   BANK DATA: THE CORRELATIONS AMONG THE
DEPENDENT AND INDEPENDENT MEASURES

	The Correlation Matrix			
	Y D(EOM)	X_1 (AAA)	X_2 (3-4)	X_3 D(3-4)
Y = D(EOM)	1.000	.256	−.391	−.195
X_i = (AAA)	.256	1.000	.587	−.204
X_2 = (3-4)	−.391	.587	1.000	−.201
X_3 = D(3-4)	−.195	−.204	−.201	1.000

TABLE 6-5 BANK DATA: THE INTERRELATEDNESS AMONG
THE REGRESSION COEFFICIENTS

The intercorrelations among the b coefficients are as follows:

	b_0	b_1	b_2	b_3
b_0	1.000	−.798	−.035	−.208
b_1	−.798	1.000	−.569	.108
b_2	−.035	−.569	1.000	.103
b_3	−.208	.108	.103	1.000

For the regression:

$$\widehat{D(EOM)} = b_0 + b_1(AAA) + b_2(3\text{-}4) + b_3[D(3\text{-}4)]$$
$$\text{where } b_0 = -4295.10$$
$$b_1 = 3363.74$$
$$b_2 = -2828.69$$
$$b_3 = -1965.69$$

sentially random, then the model may be a good one. If the errors show any kind of pattern, then the model is not taking care of all the systematic information in the data set. Among the possible analyses of errors are the following:

a. plot the errors for visual inspection;
b. study the autocorrelation of the residuals (see Chapter 8 for details);
c. compute the Durbin-Watson statistic.

In this section we examine options a and c.

First, for the bank example, Figure 6-5 shows the plot of the errors after fitting the model,

$$D(EOM) = -4925.10 + 3363.74(AAA) - 2828.69(3\text{-}4) - 1956.69\,[D(3\text{-}4)].$$

At first glance it appears that (i) the errors are often quite large, and (ii) they are essentially random. To dig a little deeper, consider a summary number—the Durbin-Watson statistic—that is sensitive to certain kinds of patterns in a set of errors.

Table 6-6 introduces three sets of errors that are plotted for visual inspection in Figure 6-6. Set a was generated by a random process, and the errors are therefore "random" (or "unpatterned"). Note that we may well see "pattern" in Figure 6-6a, especially when successive points are joined, but this perception is clearly stronger for set b. The errors tend to stay

TABLE 6-6 COMPUTATION OF THE DURBIN-WATSON STATISTIC
FOR THREE SETS OF RESIDUALS (ERRORS)

	Set a			
	(1) Error	(2) Squared	(3)	(4)
Time	e	Error	$(e_t - e_{t-1})$	$(e_t - e_{t-1})^2$
1	−0.60	0.36		
2	−0.90	0.81	−0.30	0.09
3	−0.30	0.09	0.60	0.36
4	3.20	10.24	3.50	12.25
5	−6.10	37.21	−9.30	86.49
6	−5.40	29.16	0.70	0.49
7	1.30	1.69	6.70	44.89
8	−8.10	65.61	−9.40	88.36
9	−2.20	4.84	5.90	34.81
10	0.30	0.09	2.50	6.25
11	1.30	1.69	1.00	1.00
12	4.90	24.01	3.60	12.96
13	−4.00	16.00	−8.90	79.21
14	−0.40	0.16	3.60	12.96
15	1.20	1.44	1.60	2.56
SS		193.40		382.68

$$\text{Durbin-Watson} = 1.995 = \frac{382.68}{193.40}$$

Set b		Set c	
Time	Error	Time	Error
1	2.60	1	4.70
2	0.00	2	−3.90
3	3.10	3	4.60
4	−2.10	4	−10.50
5	−6.10	5	9.60
6	−7.90	6	−3.30
7	−11.30	7	8.20
8	−6.90	8	0.70
9	6.80	9	−4.60
10	15.50	10	3.10
11	12.60	11	2.80
12	5.00	12	3.00
13	1.30	13	−4.30
14	7.10	14	0.20
15	−3.70	15	3.00
Durbin-Watson =	0.703	Durbin-Watson =	3.130

Residuals after D(EOM) was Regressed on Three Variables

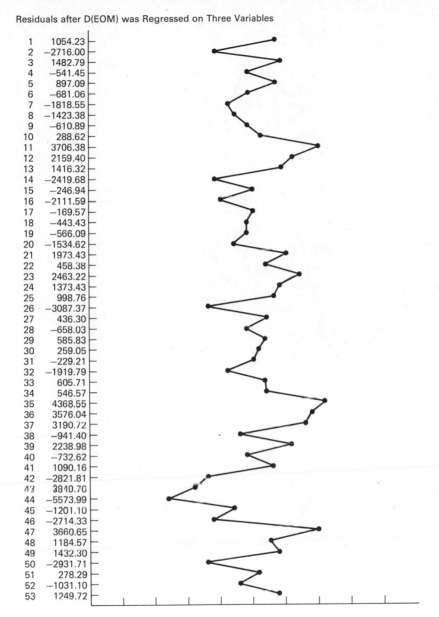

1	1054.23
2	−2716.00
3	1482.79
4	−541.45
5	897.09
6	−681.06
7	−1818.55
8	−1423.38
9	−610.89
10	288.62
11	3706.38
12	2159.40
13	1416.32
14	−2419.68
15	−246.94
16	−2111.59
17	−169.57
18	−443.43
19	−566.09
20	−1534.62
21	1973.43
22	458.38
23	2463.22
24	1373.43
25	998.76
26	−3087.37
27	436.30
28	−658.03
29	585.83
30	259.05
31	−229.21
32	−1919.79
33	605.71
34	546.57
35	4368.55
36	3576.04
37	3190.72
38	−941.40
39	2238.98
40	−732.62
41	1090.16
42	−2821.81
43	3810.70
44	−5573.99
45	−1201.10
46	−2714.33
47	3660.65
48	1184.57
49	1432.30
50	−2931.71
51	278.29
52	−1031.10
53	1249.72

FIGURE 6-5 BANK DATA: A PLOT OF THE RESIDUALS WHEN D(EOM) IS REGRESSED AGAINST THE THREE INDEPENDENT VARIABLES—(AAA), (3-4), AND D(3-4)

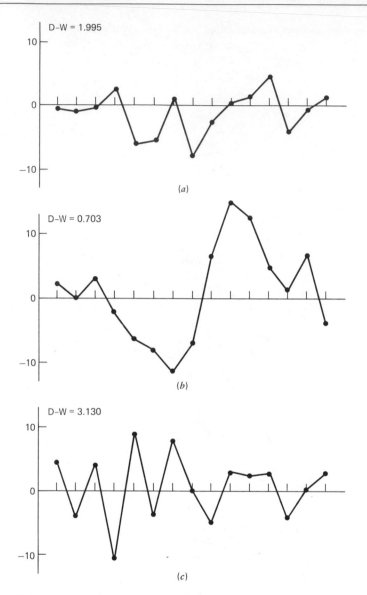

FIGURE 6-6   PLOTS OF THE THREE SETS OF RESIDUALS IN TABLE 6-5
AND THE DURBIN-WATSON STATISTICS

negative longer than expected (if they were truly random) and then stay
positive longer than expected. The third set c shows another residual pattern—a see-saw or zigzag effect. The errors seem to flip back and forth
between being positive and negative.

The following (Durbin-Watson) statistic is sensitive to the kinds of patterns just mentioned:

$$D\text{-}W = \frac{\displaystyle\sum_{t=2}^{N} (e_t - e_{t-1})^2}{\displaystyle\sum_{t=1}^{N} e_t^2} \quad \text{(Durbin-Watson statistic)}. \tag{6-21}$$

The numerator takes a look at differences between successive errors, squares these differences, and adds them up. The denominator is simply the sum of the squared errors. Table 6-6(a) indicates how these calculations can be made. Column 2 is the squared error. Column 3 is the successive error differences. For example, the first column 3 entry is determined as follows:

$$e_2 - e_1 = (-.9) - (-.6) = -.3,$$

$$D\text{-}W = (\text{col. 4 SS})/(\text{col. 2 SS})$$

$$= (382.68)/(193.40) = 1.995.$$

Similarly, for data sets b and c in Table 6-6 the D-W statistic is computed to be 0.703 and 3.130, respectively. Note the following:

   i.   When there is a distinct slow-moving pattern to the errors—as in case b—successive error differences tend to be small and the D-W statistic will be small.
   ii. When there is a distinct fast-moving (zigzag) pattern—as in case c—successive error differences tend to be large and the D-W statistic will be large.

As a matter of fact, the D-W statistic ranges in value from 0 through 4, with an intermediate value of 2. The theory behind this statistic is complicated (see Appendix 6-C for some details), but it is readily usable in a practical setting.[8] For the random errors in Table 6-6(a) the D-W statistic is near 2. For set b the D-W value is less than 1—indicating positive autocorrelation (that is, successive errors tend to have a positive relationship). And for set c, D-W = 3.13, indicating negative autocorrelation (that is, successive errors tend to be negatively related). There is some pattern left in the errors of sets b and c.

Returning now to the bank example and the set of residuals in Figure 6-5, the Durbin-Watson statistic is computed to be

$$D\text{-}W = 1.48 \quad \text{(for Figure 6-5 residuals)}.$$

---

[8]Note that when cross-sectional data are being analyzed and there is no particular order to the observations, the D-W statistic is of little value. However, even in this case, if Y is being regressed on X, and the observations are ordered according to the X-values, the D-W statistic can be helpful in deciding if an incorrect model has been fitted.

This value is less than 2, and indicates the possibility of positive autocorrelation remaining in the errors. There is still some pattern in residuals, and we will improve on the bank forecasting model in Section 6/2.

6/1/7   The Assumptions Behind Multiple Linear Regression Models

The theoretical regression model described in Section 6/1/1 makes certain assumptions, so that the practical application of such a model requires the user to examine these assumptions in the context of the problem at hand. There are four basic assumptions:

1. linearity
2. independence of residuals
3. homoscedasticity
4. normality of residuals

The full implications of each assumption can only be appreciated in conjunction with a thorough understanding of the statistical theory behind regression, but the following practical points can be made.

1. With regard to "linearity," the assumption refers to "linearity in the *coefficients*," and it relates directly to the development of the *F*-test and the *t*-tests. In other words, if the assumption is violated, then the *F*-test and *t*-tests are not strictly valid any longer. It is useful to be able to "linearize" certain nonlinear functions, and thus allow the use of the *F*- and *t*-tests, but this advantage is gained at some cost—namely, a nonlinear fit will fit the *raw* data better than a linearized fit can. (See the natural gas example in Section 6.6.)

2. The "independence of residuals" assumption is also directly tied to the validity of the *F*- and *t*-tests. If the residuals are not independent, the use of the *F*- and *t*-tests is not strictly valid. In Section 6/1/6 the Durbin-Watson statistic was discussed as a way of examining this assumption, and if positive or negative autocorrelation is discovered in the residuals, steps can be taken to remove such autocorrelation.

3. Homoscedasticity is a word used for "the constant variance" assumption. The regression model assumes an error distribution that is normally distributed around a mean of zero and having a variance, V_ε. So the variance is one value. Figure 6-7 illustrates what is meant by homoscedasticity and heteroscedasticity. For many time series (e.g., passenger traffic on airlines, monthly withdrawals at a savings bank) the raw data itself shows multiplicative trend and/or seasonality, and if regression models are used in such cases, the equal variance assumption for residuals

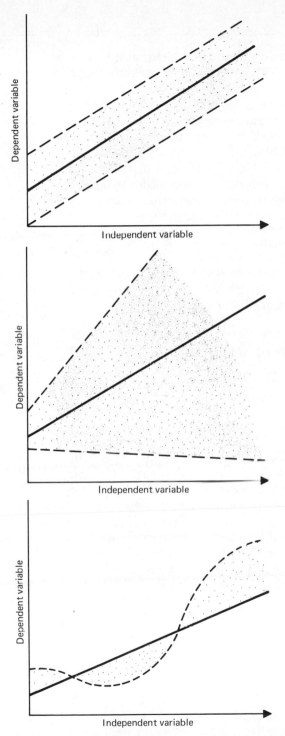

FIGURE 6-7 THE CONSTANT VARIANCE ASSUMPTION IN A REGRESSION MODEL

might well be violated. Once again the impact of this assumption is on the validity of the statistical tests (F and t) associated with the formal regression model.

4. Many regression models assume a normal distribution for the error term. This is not such a serious assumption in that residuals are the result of many unimportant factors acting together to influence the dependent variable, and the net effect of such influences is reasonably well modeled by a normal distribution.[9] Again, this assumption of normality allows the model to deduce appropriate F- and t-tests, so that, if the assumption is seriously violated, it is not appropriate to do the significance testing.

One assumption of the regression model that has not been treated above is the statement that the independent variables are fixed—that is, measured without error. This is patently false in real-world settings. Econometricians have dealt with this subject in great detail and the interested reader should pursue the topic in Johnston's excellent book (1963).

6/2 Selecting Independent Variables and Model Specification

Developing a regression model for a real problem is never a simple 1-2-3 step process, but some guidelines can be given. Whatever the problem is (and we shall illustrate this section with the bank data), experts in the general area will have to be called upon for counsel. For a defined dependent variable, Y, it will be necessary to draw up a "long list" of variables that impact on Y—this will be a set of potential independent variables. The "long list" will usually be reduced to a "short list" by various means, and a certain amount of creativity is essential. The shape of the model (or the functional form for the regression model) will gradually be decided upon in conjunction with the development of the "short list," and finally, the parameters of the model will be estimated using data collected for that purpose. In this section, we describe briefly how the bank problem was handled.

6/2/1 The Long List

Based on (i) hunches of experts and nonexperts, (ii) availability of data (see Chapter 11), and (iii) practical time and cost constraints, it was

---

[9]There is a very important probability theorem known as the Central Limit Theorem, which says: If N values are sampled independently from a population having mean μ and standard deviation σ, then the mean of these N values will tend to have a normal distribution with mean μ and standard deviation $\sigma/\sqrt{n}$, regardless of the shape of the original population distribution.

decided that end-of-month balances in a mutual savings bank were conceivably related to (or depended on) the following 19 economic variables:

1. U.S. Gross Demand Deposits
2. First Gross Demand Deposits
3. U.S. Personal Income
4. Northeast Personal Income
5. Massachusetts Personal Income
6. N.H. Personal Income
7. Rates for Three-Month Bills
8. Rates for 3-4 Year Government Issues
9. Rates for AAA Bonds
10. U.S. Negotiable CDs
11. First Negotiable CDs
12. U.S. Mutual Savings Bank Savings
13. First Mutual Savings Bank Savings
14. Massachusetts Mutual Savings Bank Savings
15. N.H. Mutual Savings Bank Savings
16. U.S. Consumer Price Index
17. U.S. Savings and Loan Index
18. First Savings and Loan Index
19. National Personal Income

In addition, since the EOM data set (Table 6-1) was a monthly time series, some other variables were being kept in mind—namely, "time" and "seasonal indices." The model "shape" was to be a simple linear (in the coefficients) function, with the possibility that a nonlinear trend line would have to be accommodated.

6/2/2   The Short List

There are many proposals regarding how to select appropriate variables for a final model. Some of these are straightforward, but not recommended:

- Plot a particular independent variable (X_j) against Y and if it shows no noticeable relationship, drop it, because X_j will not be of much help in explaining Y.
- Look at the intercorrelations among the regressors (all of the potential candidates) and every time a large correlation is encountered, remove one of the two variables from further consideration; otherwise you might run into multicollinearity problems (see Section 6/3).
- Do a multiple linear regression on all the regressors (so long as this is feasible—see Section 6/3) and disregard all variables whose t-values are very small (say $|t| < .5$).

Some proposals are more complicated, and more justifiable:

- Do stepwise regression (see Draper and Smith, 1981).
- Do a principal components analysis of all the variables (including Y) to decide on which are key variables (see Cooley and Lohnes, 1971).
- Do a distributed lag analysis to decide which leads and lags are most appropriate for the study at hand.

Quite often, a combination of the above will be used to reach the final short list of regressors and the functional form that seems most justified.

For the bank forecasting problem, the 19 potential candidates for independent variables (see Figure 6-8) were reduced to a short list of just four (see footnote 10):

1. (#7)   Rates for Three-Month Bills
2. (#8)   Rates for 3-4 Year Government Issues
3. (#9)   Rates for AAA Bonds
4. (#10) U.S. Consumer Price Index

Next, to study the relevance of lags or leads, the data matrix ($N = 60$ rows and 5 columns now—Y, X_1, X_2, X_3, X_4) was shifted one period ahead of Y and one period behind Y, as indicated in Figure 6-9. The original data matrix is designated A. The data block labeled B is the data for the regressors shifted up one line (that is, one time period)—so that "lags" can be evaluated—and data block C shows how data for the regressors can be shifted down one period—so that "leads" can be evaluated. If necessary, further leads and lags can be built up in this manner.

Note that first differences can also be built into the data blocks A, B, and C in Figure 6-9. For the bank data, since the Y variable was itself a first difference, D(EOM), it was proper to consider first differences of the chosen (short-list) regressors. Thus instead of just four regressors in data-block A, eight regressors were used:

(3 month)   (3-4 yr)   (AAA)   (CPI)

and

D(3 month)   D(3-4 yr)   D(AAA)   D(CPI).

Clearly the problem can get out of hand without some help. For example, with these eight regressors, and leads and lags of 1 and 2 periods, the total number of candidates for independent variables is 40.

---

[10]The method used was a principal components analysis (refer to Cooley and Lohnes, 1971) and Figure 6-8 shows the two-dimensional solution. It was clear that the 19 original candidates really reduced to an essential two-space (since 94.7 percent of the total variance was accounted for in two dimensions). Plotting the two-space principal component solution showed that the three rates (for three-month bills, 3-4 year issues, and AAA bonds) were separated clearly from the rest, that the Negotiable CDs separated themselves, and the remaining 12 variables were tightly clustered.

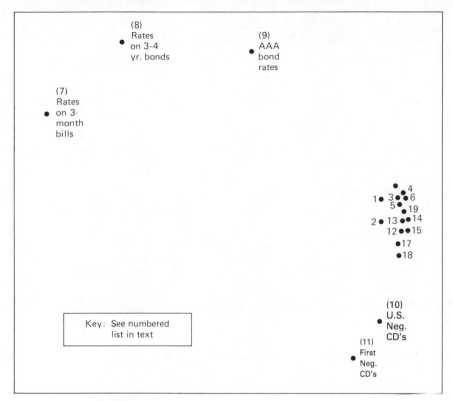

FIGURE 6-8 BANK DATA: A TWO-DIMENSIONAL PLOT OF THE 21 ECO-NOMIC INDICATORS AFTER PRINCIPAL COMPONENTS ANALYSIS

In the next section, we consider the method called stepwise regression, which can be used to help sort out the relevant regressors from the following larger set (created from the short list):

1. The four short-list regressors
2. The four first differences from (1)
3. The 1-period leads on the eight variables in (1) and (2)
4. The 2-period leads on the eight variables in (1) and (2)
5. The 1-period lags on the eight variables in (1) and (2)
6. The 2-period lags on the eight variables in (1) and (2)

6/2/3 Stepwise Regression

The book by Draper and Smith (1981) has an excellent treatment of the main kinds of stepwise regression in use today. Three such approaches are:

1. Stepwise forward regression,
2. Stepwise backward regression,

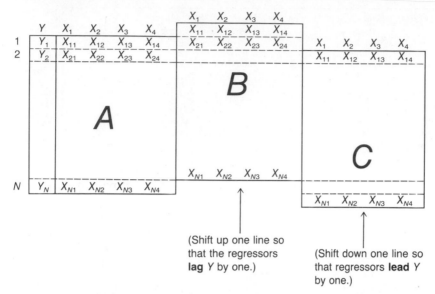

(Shift up one line so that the regressors **lag** Y by one.)

(Shift down one line so that regressors **lead** Y by one.)

FIGURE 6-9   INTRODUCING LEADS AND LAGS INTO THE REGRESSION MODEL

3.   Stepwise forward-with-a-backward-look regression.

The first method has several variations of its own, one of which is as follows. From among the potential regressors, pick the one that has the highest correlation with Y. Determine the residuals from this regression, and think of these residuals as a new set of Y values. From among the remaining regressors, pick the one that correlates most highly with these residuals. Continue this process until no remaining regressor has a significant relationship with the last set of residuals.

The stepwise backward method also has several variations. One is to start with a regression including all the variables—assuming this is possible—and weeding out that variable that is least significant in the equation (as measured by the t-value). Then, with this variable out, another regression solution is run, and the next variable to remove is determined, and so on.

Neither the stepwise forward nor the stepwise backward method is guaranteed to produce the *optimal* pair of regressors, or triple of regressors, and so on. There is, in fact, only one sure way of doing this—do all possible regressions! Since this is impractical[11] we often have to rely on less than perfect answers, and the third method is of considerable value.

The reason for the name "stepwise forward-with-a-backward-look" is explained below.

---

[11]If there are k regressors, the total number of possible regressions involving 1, 2, 3, . . . , k regressors is $(2^k - 1)$. For $k = 10$, this is 1023. For the bank example, where $k = 40$, the number is astronomical.

Step 1: Find the best single variable (X_{1*}).

Step 2: Find the best pair of variables (X_{1*} together with one of the remaining regressors—call it X_{2*}).

Step 3: Find the best triple of regressors (X_{1*}, X_{2*} plus one of the remaining regressors—call the new one X_{3*}).

Step 4: From this stage on the procedure checks to see if any of the earlier introduced variables might conceivably have to be removed. For example, the regression of Y on X_{2*} and X_{3*} might give better $\overline{R}^2$ results than if all three variables, X_{1*}, X_{2*}, and X_{3*} had been included. At stage 2, the best pair of regressors *had* to include X_{1*}, but by stage 3, X_{2*} and X_{3*} could actually be superior to all three variables.

Step 5: The process of (a) looking for the next best regressor to include, and (b) checking to see if a previously included variable should be removed, is continued until certain criteria are satisfied. For example, in running a stepwise regression program, the user is asked to enter two "tail" probabilities:
1. the probability, P_1, to "enter" a variable, and
2. the probability, P_2, to "remove" a variable.

When it is no longer possible to find any new variable that contributes at the P_1 level to the $\overline{R}^2$ value, or if no variable needs to be removed at the P_2 level, then the iterative procedure stops.

We will defer an illustration of stepwise regression (applied to the bank data) until Section 6/2/5.

6/2/4 Dummy Variables and Seasonality

In Section 6/1/3 [equation (6-9)] only three measures (regressors) were used to make up the multiple linear regression model, and $\overline{R}^2$ was 0.533. Thus there was room for improvement. It is useful to consider adding seasonality. One way to do this in the regression context is to introduce dummy variables (each of which has only two allowable values, 0 or 1) as follows:

D_1 = 1, if the month is January, say, and zero otherwise.

D_2 = 1, if the month is February, and zero otherwise.

.

.

.

D_{12} = 1, if the month is December, and zero otherwise.

Each of these dummy variables is equivalent to a new regressor. Note, however, that if we use 12 dummy variables for 12 monthly periods, we encounter the problem of multicollinearity (discussed in Section 6/3), so the rule is:

Use $(P - 1)$ dummy variables to denote P different periods.

For $P = 12$ (monthly data) we therefore use only 11 dummy variables, as shown in Table 6-7. Note that, since Y here is D(EOM), and the first datum is for March 1968–Feb. 1968, dummy variable D_1 really refers to a (March.–Feb.) change, not a specific month. Note, too, that for the twelfth data row, all eleven dummy variables have the value zero—so this set of *11* dummy variables does a good job of identifying all *12* change periods.

Running a regression model on the data in Table 6-7 shows a dramatic improvement over the simpler model analyzed previously. The results are as follows:

The Regression Equation is:[12]

Y-hat D̂(EOM) =	se_b	t-value	Prob(1-tail)
−2167.00	1989.66	−1.09	0.1415
+3295.89 *(AAA)	324.95	10.14	0.0000
−2752.43 *(3-4)	229.17	−12.01	0.0000
−1727.93 *D(3-4)	554.13	−3.12	0.0018
−451.59 *(Mar-Feb)	821.99	−0.55	n.s.
−4530.88 *(Apr-Mar)	833.20	−5.44	0.0000
−1321.10 *(May-Apr)	856.07	−1.54	0.0636
−3160.09 *(Jun-May)	838.70	−3.77	0.0003
−1392.23 *(Jul-Jun)	827.84	−1.68	0.0485
−3037.35 *(Aug-Jul)	868.40	−3.50	0.0007
−3719.42 *(Sep-Aug)	865.90	−4.30	0.0001
−4709.23 *(Oct-Sep)	864.86	−5.45	0.0000
−1871.68 *(Nov-Oct)	864.30	−2.17	0.0174
−2495.40 *(Dec-Nov)	884.30	−2.82	0.0037
+1436.50 *(Jan-Dec)	870.37	1.65	0.0516

(6-22)

[12]Note that when all dummy variables are zero (as in the rows 12, 24, 36, and 48 of Table 6-7) the regression equation (6-22) reduces to D(EOM) = −2167 + 3295(AAA) − 2752(3-4) − 1727 [D(3-4)]. In other words, the 12th months serve as a base. If some other month had been chosen as base period, the regression values would look different, but still tell the same story.

TABLE 6-7 BANK DATA: SHOWING THE ADDITION OF 11 DUMMY VARIABLES TO HANDLE SEASONALITY

Change in End-of-Month Deposits at a Mutual Savings Bank

	D(EOM)	(AAA)	(3-4)	D(3-4)	D_1	D_2	D_3	D_4	D_5	D_6	D_7	D_8	D_9	D_{10}	D_{11}
1	1146.00	5.94	5.31	0.29	1	0	0	0	0	0	0	0	0	0	0
2	−2443.00	6.00	5.60	−0.11	0	1	0	0	0	0	0	0	0	0	0
3	1497.00	6.08	5.49	0.31	0	0	1	0	0	0	0	0	0	0	0
4	−132.00	6.17	5.80	−0.19	0	0	0	1	0	0	0	0	0	0	0
5	2025.00	6.14	5.61	−0.33	0	0	0	0	1	0	0	0	0	0	0
6	737.00	6.09	5.28	−0.09	0	0	0	0	0	1	0	0	0	0	0
7	−1023.00	5.87	5.19	−0.01	0	0	0	0	0	0	1	0	0	0	0
8	−956.00	5.84	5.18	0.12	0	0	0	0	0	0	0	1	0	0	0
9	385.00	5.99	5.30	−0.07	0	0	0	0	0	0	0	0	1	0	0
10	983.00	6.12	5.23	0.41	0	0	0	0	0	0	0	0	0	1	0
11	5092.00	6.42	5.64	−0.02	0	0	0	0	0	0	0	0	0	0	1
12	3649.00	6.48	5.62	0.05	0	0	0	0	0	0	0	0	0	0	0
13	2703.00	6.52	5.67	0.16	1	0	0	0	0	0	0	0	0	0	0
14	−271.00	6.64	5.83	−0.30	0	1	0	0	0	0	0	0	0	0	0
15	2055.00	6.75	5.53	0.23	0	0	1	0	0	0	0	0	0	0	0
16	−714.00	6.73	5.76	0.33	0	0	0	1	0	0	0	0	0	0	0
17	653.00	6.89	6.09	0.43	0	0	0	0	1	0	0	0	0	0	0
18	−34.00	6.98	6.52	0.16	0	0	0	0	0	1	0	0	0	0	0
19	1058.00	6.98	6.68	0.39	0	0	0	0	0	0	1	0	0	0	0
20	−2051.00	7.10	7.07	0.05	0	0	0	0	0	0	0	1	0	0	0
21	1451.00	7.19	7.12	0.13	0	0	0	0	0	0	0	0	1	0	0
22	−989.00	7.20	7.25	0.60	0	0	0	0	0	0	0	0	0	1	0
23	1358.00	7.65	7.85	0.17	0	0	0	0	0	0	0	0	0	0	1
24	746.00	7.75	8.02	−0.15	0	0	0	0	0	0	0	0	0	0	0
25	1855.00	7.72	7.87	−0.73	1	0	0	0	0	0	0	0	0	0	0
26	−1894.00	7.67	7.14	0.06	0	1	0	0	0	0	0	0	0	0	0
27	781.00	7.66	7.20	0.39	0	0	1	0	0	0	0	0	0	0	0
28	−161.00	7.89	7.59	0.15	0	0	0	1	0	0	0	0	0	0	0
29	2233.00	8.14	7.74	−0.23	0	0	0	0	1	0	0	0	0	0	0
30	2425.00	8.21	7.51	−0.05	0	0	0	0	0	1	0	0	0	0	0
31	2169.00	8.05	7.46	−0.37	0	0	0	0	0	0	1	0	0	0	0
32	982.00	7.94	7.09	−0.27	0	0	0	0	0	0	0	1	0	0	0
33	4708.00	7.88	6.82	−0.60	0	0	0	0	0	0	0	0	1	0	0
34	6063.00	7.79	6.22	−0.61	0	0	0	0	0	0	0	0	0	1	0
35	9382.00	7.41	5.61	−0.13	0	0	0	0	0	0	0	0	0	0	1
36	9304.00	7.18	5.48	−0.70	0	0	0	0	0	0	0	0	0	0	0
37	10690.00	7.15	4.78	−0.64	1	0	0	0	0	0	0	0	0	0	0
38	6531.00	7.27	4.14	0.50	0	1	0	0	0	0	0	0	0	0	0

TABLE 6-7   BANK DATA: SHOWING THE ADDITION OF 11 DUMMY
VARIABLES TO HANDLE SEASONALITY (*Continued*)

Change in End-of-Month Deposits at a Mutual Savings Bank

	D(EOM)	(AAA)	(3-4)	D(3-4)	D_1	D_2	D_3	D_4	D_5	D_6	D_7	D_8	D_9	D_{10}	D_{11}
39	7873.00	7.37	4.64	0.88	0	0	1	0	0	0	0	0	0	0	0
40	3882.00	7.54	5.52	0.43	0	0	0	1	0	0	0	0	0	0	0
41	4960.00	7.58	5.95	0.25	0	0	0	0	1	0	0	0	0	0	0
42	1301.00	7.62	6.20	−0.17	0	0	0	0	0	1	0	0	0	0	0
43	1154.00	7.58	6.03	−0.43	0	0	0	0	0	0	1	0	0	0	0
44	116.00	7.48	5.60	−0.34	0	0	0	0	0	0	0	1	0	0	0
45	4928.00	7.35	5.26	−0.30	0	0	0	0	0	0	0	0	1	0	0
46	2530.00	7.19	4.96	0.32	0	0	0	0	0	0	0	0	0	1	0
47	8425.00	7.19	5.28	0.09	0	0	0	0	0	0	0	0	0	0	1
48	5291.00	7.11	5.37	0.16	0	0	0	0	0	0	0	0	0	0	0
49	5192.00	7.16	5.53	0.19	1	0	0	0	0	0	0	0	0	0	0
50	257.00	7.22	5.72	0.32	0	1	0	0	0	0	0	0	0	0	0
51	4402.00	7.36	6.04	−0.38	0	0	1	0	0	0	0	0	0	0	0
52	3173.00	7.34	5.66	0.09	0	0	0	1	0	0	0	0	0	0	0
53	5104.00	7.30	5.75	0.07	0	0	0	0	1	0	0	0	0	0	0
54	4646.00	7.30	5.82	0.08	0	0	0	0	0	1	0	0	0	0	0
55	1060.00	7.27	5.90	0.21	0	0	0	0	0	0	1	0	0	0	0
56	−758.00	7.30	6.11	−0.06	0	0	0	0	0	0	0	1	0	0	0
57	4702.00	7.31	6.05	−0.07	0	0	0	0	0	0	0	0	1	0	0
58	1878.00	7.26	5.98	0.02	0	0	0	0	0	0	0	0	0	1	0
59	6620.00	7.24	6.00	0.24	0	0	0	0	0	0	0	0	0	0	1

Comparing this equation (6-22) with the solution in equation (6-9), the following contrasts are obtained:

	Current Model with Seasonal Dummies	Earlier Model without Seasonal Dummies
R^2	0.887	0.560
$\overline{R}^2$	0.845	0.533
SEE[13]	1222	2120
F	21.22 with (14,38) df	20.75 with (3,49) df
D-W	0.72	1.48

The proportion of variance in Y, explained by regressing on these 14 regressors, is now 84.5 percent ($\overline{R}^2$), instead of just 53.3 percent. The standard error of estimate (see) has dropped considerably, from 2120 to 1222. The F-values, in an absolute sense, are not very different, but there has been a shift in the degrees of freedom (from denominator to numerator), which makes the numerator more stable. Thus for (14,38) df, the F-value at the 0.01 level is about 2.70, whereas for (3,49) df the 0.01 level F-value would have to be about 4.20. In other words, the F-value for the current model (with seasonal dummy variables) is more significant than the earlier model.

Also note that the Durbin-Watson statistic gives more cause for concern now (D-W = 0.72) than it did earlier (D-W = 1.48). There is not nearly as much unexplained error left in the current model, but what there is, is patterned. There is strong evidence of positively autocorrelated errors. This point will be elaborated on in the next section.

The use of dummy variables to denote seasonality has resulted in a significantly improved bank model. This method can also be used to denote special events of any kind—for example, war periods. A single dummy variable can be introduced, set equal to zero for all war periods, and set equal to one otherwise. However, the analyst should beware of using too many dummy variables, for two reasons:

1. four seasonal dummy variables for four quarters will result in perfect multicollinearity, and
2. each new dummy variable is a new regressor, requiring another regression coefficient to be estimated and thereby losing one degree of freedom for the error term (SS for errors). Eventually this could result in lowering $\overline{R}^2$ rather than increasing it.

6/2/5   A Final Model for the Bank Data

With all the procedures mentioned in the preceding sections, a forecaster can spend a lot of time trying various combinations of variables— original measures, first differences, lags, leads, and so on—and there really is no substitute for a little creativity and a lot of "feeling" for the subject matter under consideration. To complete the bank example, consider one last stepwise regression run on the following measures:

$Y \quad = \text{D(EOM)}$ [as in Table 6-2]

$X_1 \quad = (\text{AAA})_{-1}$ [as in Table 6-2]

$X_2 \quad = (3\text{-}4)_{-1}$ [as in Table 6-2]

$X_3 \quad = \text{D}(3\text{-}4)_0$ [as in Table 6-2]

---

[13]"SEE" refers to standard error of estimate and is defined as $\sqrt{\text{SSE/df}}$, where SSE = sum of squared errors and df = degrees of freedom (N − number parameters fitted).

X_4 = dummy variable for a (Mar-Feb) change

X_5 = dummy variable for a (Apr-Mar) change

.

.

.

X_{14} = dummy variable for a (Jan-Dec) change

X_{15} = time ⎫

X_{16} = $(\text{time})^2$ ⎬ These three to allow for up to cubic trend

X_{17} = $(\text{time})^3$ ⎭

The stepwise results are given in Table 6-8. For this run the probability to enter and remove a variable was set at 0.10. Note that as the procedure unfolds, the $\overline{R}^2$ values steadily increase—*even when a variable is removed at step 5.* At the end of the analysis $\overline{R}^2 = 0.851$.

TABLE 6-8   BANK DATA: A FINAL STEPWISE REGRESSION ANALYSIS OF 17 REGRESSORS

SETUP
• Prob (to enter a variable) = Prob (to remove a variable) = 0.10
• 17 potential regressors ($X_1, \ldots, X_{17}$)
Results

Step Number	Variable	Entered/Removed	R^2	$\overline{R}^2$
1	X_{15}	entered	0.277	0.263
2	X_2	entered	0.415	0.392
3	X_{14}	entered	0.521	0.491
4	X_1	entered	0.622	0.590
5	X_{15}	(removed)	0.619	0.596
6	X_5	entered	0.677	0.650
7	X_{11}	entered	0.725	0.696
8	X_3	entered	0.778	0.749
9	X_{10}	entered	0.808	0.778
10	X_7	entered	0.831	0.800
11	X_9	entered	0.853	0.823
12	X_{13}	entered	0.867	0.836
13	X_{17}	entered	0.877	0.844
14	X_{12}	entered	0.886	0.851

The regression equation resulting from the stepwise regression run is as follows:

The Regression Equation is:

Y-hat $\widehat{D(EOM)}$ =	se_b	t-value	Prob(1-tail)
−4184.42	2026.77	−2.07	0.0216
+3845.64 *(1 (AAA)$_{-1}$)	446.13	8.62	0.0000
−3125.34 *(2 (3-4)$_{-1}$)	297.12	−10.52	0.0000
−2061.05 *(3 (3-4)$_0$)	510.61	−4.04	0.0001
−3758.98 *(5 Apr-Mar)	605.64	−6.21	0.0000
−2252.68 *(7 Jun-May)	606.63	−3.71	0.0004
−2336.27 *(9 Aug-Jul)	664.78	−3.51	0.0006
−2973.85 *(10 Sep-Aug)	664.15	−4.48	0.0000
−3961.77 *(11 Oct-Sep)	662.74	−5.98	0.0000
−1175.46 *(12 Nov-Oct)	668.40	−1.76	0.0413
−1717.10 *(13 Dec-Nov)	665.94	−2.58	0.0066
+2226.83 *(14 Jan-Dec)	658.88	3.38	0.0009
−0.0107 *(17 Time 3)	0.0056	−1.92	0.0294

(6-23)

Eight of the 11 seasonal dummy variables were entered and all but one show very significant t-values. Since these variables do not correlate very highly with one another, the individual t-tests can be interpreted readily.

Clearly there is a lot of significant seasonality in the D(EOM) measures. How do we isolate the seasonality effects? Suppose we concentrate on the (April-March) change, which means rows 2, 14, 26, 38, and 50. For each of these rows the second dummy variable $D_2 - 1$ and all others are zero. Putting these values into the regression equation (6-23), we get

$$\widehat{D(EOM)} = -4184.42 + 3845.64(AAA)_{-1} - 3125.34\,(3\text{-}4)_{-1}$$

$$-2061.05[D(3\text{-}4)]_0 - 3758.98(1) - .0107(time)^3 \qquad (6\text{-}24)$$

Note that the dummy variable D_2 has the effect of changing the *intercept term only.* The new intercept is

INTERCEPT

−4184.42 − 3758.98 = −7943.40 (for April-Mar)

Repeating this procedure systematically for all 12 possible changes, we could determine the seasonality indices for each change. This will be an exercise at the end of the chapter.

The F-value (with 12 and 40 df) for this analysis is 25.82, which is again very significant, as expected, and the standard error of estimate is

1195.5, which is the lowest yet obtained. Additional improvements in the model are unlikely to come easily.

Figure 6-10 plots the residuals for this final model, on the same scale as was used in Figure 6-5 so that a comparison can be made. The improvement is clear. Perhaps the only remaining bothersome aspect of the model is the obvious presence of positive autocorrelation in the residuals. The D-W statistic has a value 0.89, which indicates positive autocorrelation. Figure 6-10 also gives evidence of the pattern remaining in the residuals. Underlying many economic time series is the presence of business cycles of one kind or another, and often such cycles are established by default. In other words, after everything reasonable is done to model systematic aspects of a Y variable, the residual pattern may be "random noise" plus a "business cycle aspect." Chapter 12 deals with business cycles in greater depth.

6/3   Multicollinearity

If two vectors (columns of data) point in the same direction, they can be called collinear. In regression analysis, *multicollinearity* is the name given to any one or more of the following conditions:

a. Two independent variables are perfectly correlated (and therefore, the vectors representing these variables are collinear).

b. Two independent variables are nearly perfectly correlated (i.e., the correlation between them is very close to $+1$ or -1).

c. A linear combination of some of the independent variables is perfectly correlated (or nearly so) with another independent variable.

d. A linear combination of one subset of independent variables is perfectly correlated (or nearly so) with a linear combination of another subset of independent variables.

The reason for concern about this issue is first and foremost a computational one. If perfect multicollinearity exists in a regression problem, it is simply not possible to carry out the LS solution. (Appendix 6-A explains why this is so.) If nearly perfect multicollinearity obtains, the LS solutions can be affected by round-off error problems in some calculators (and some computers), but this is not really a significant problem nowadays. (Appendix 6-A refers to computational methods that are robust enough to take care of all but perfect multicollinearity problems.)

The other major concern is that the stability of the regression coefficients is affected by near multicollinearity. This point is suggested in Figures 6-3 and 6-4, where it is shown that the standard error of the coefficients, b_1 and b_2, are affected by the correlation between X_1 and X_2. As

Residuals after D(EOM) was (Stepwise) Regressed on 17 Variables

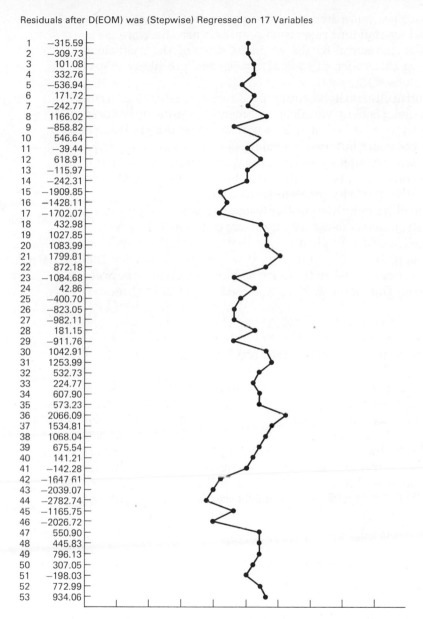

1	−315.59
2	−309.73
3	101.08
4	332.76
5	−536.94
6	171.72
7	−242.77
8	1166.02
9	−858.82
10	546.64
11	−39.44
12	618.91
13	−115.97
14	−242.31
15	−1909.85
16	−1428.11
17	−1702.07
18	432.98
19	1027.85
20	1083.99
21	1799.81
22	872.18
23	−1084.68
24	42.86
25	−400.70
26	−823.05
27	−982.11
28	181.15
29	−911.76
30	1042.91
31	1253.99
32	532.73
33	224.77
34	607.90
35	573.23
36	2066.09
37	1534.81
38	1068.04
39	675.54
40	141.21
41	−142.28
42	−1647.61
43	−2039.07
44	−2782.74
45	−1165.75
46	−2026.72
47	550.90
48	445.83
49	796.13
50	307.05
51	−198.03
52	772.99
53	934.06

FIGURE 6-10   BANK DATA: A PLOT OF THE RESIDUALS WHEN D(EOM) IS (STEPWISE) REGRESSED AGAINST 17 POTENTIAL RE-GRESSORS

multicollinearity becomes more and more nearly perfect, the regression coefficients computed by standard regression programs are therefore going to be (a) unstable—as measured by the standard error of the coefficient, and (b) unreliable—in that different computer programs are likely to give different solution values.

The word "multicollinearity" is often used (erroneously) to describe the condition when independent variables are merely significantly correlated—for example, $r_{X_2 X_4} = 0.7$—but this is not an issue unless attempts are made to isolate the contribution of variable X_2 to Y, *without* the influence of X_4. So long as regression coefficients are analyzed in the context of all the independent variables present, the mere fact of intercorrelated regressors is not a multicollinearity problem.

Another misleading definition of the term suggests that an examination of the intercorrelations among the regressors can reveal the presence or absence of multicollinearity. While it is true that a correlation very close to $+1$ or -1 *does* suggest multicollinearity, it is *not* true[14] to infer that multicollinearity does *not* exist when there are no high correlations between any pair of regressors. This point will be examined in the next three sections.

6/3/1 Multicollinearity When There are Two Regressors

If Y is being regressed on X_1 and X_2, multicollinearity[15] means that the correlation between X_1 and X_2 is perfect (or very nearly so). Thus, in this case, multicollinearity *can* be detected by looking at the correlation between the independent variables and making a decision as to what constitutes nearly perfect multicollinearity. From a computational point of view $r_{X_1 X_2} = .99$ may give no trouble, but from a pragmatic point of view this would undoubtedly be viewed as a serious case of multicollinearity.

The practical concern is with the standard error of the two regression coefficients, b_1 and b_2. The formula for the calculation of the standard errors of b_1 and b_2 has the following form:

$$se_b = \frac{v_e^*}{(1 - r_{X_1 X_2}^2)} \longleftarrow \begin{pmatrix} \text{a term related to} \\ \text{error variance} \end{pmatrix}$$

Clearly, as $r_{X_1 X_2}$ approaches $+1$ or -1, the denominator approaches the value zero. Dividing by a number that approaches zero means exploding the standard error, as when $(1 - r^2)$ is very close to zero. If the standard error of a coefficient is very large, then the analyst cannot put much faith in the value of the coefficient.

---

[14]Unless there are only two independent variables. The point is being made for the general case of several regressors.

[15]When there are only two regressors there is no need to use the word "*multicollinearity*." Two regressors are merely "collinear" or not.

6/3/2 Multicollinearity When There Are More than Two Regressors

As mentioned in the introduction to this section, multicollinearity becomes increasingly difficult to detect as the number of regressors increases. To illustrate the point, consider Table 6-9, which presents a data matrix for a dependent measure Y (quarterly sales) and four seasonal dummy variables, D_1 through D_4. (We can disregard the fact that these are dummy variables—they are simply four independent variables.) The lower part of Table 6-9 also gives the correlation matrix for all the variables. Concentrating on the correlations among the four regressors themselves, notice that they are all the same and all reasonably small (-0.333)—certainly not big enough to make anyone think of multicollinearity. Yet, if a regression run is attempted, for the model

$$\hat{Y} = b_0 + b_1 D_1 + b_2 D_2 + b_3 D_3 + b_4 D_4,$$

the computer program will either reject the data (as it should) or produce very strange results—as it did in a standard program.

The Regression Equation is:

Y-hat	($\hat{Y}$) =	se of b	t-value	Prob(1-tail)
+117.0333	*(constant)	28032.412	0.004	n.s.
−16.1979	*(D1)	28032.410	−0.001	n.s.
+24.4531	*(D2)	28032.411	0.001	n.s.
+68.3854	*(D3)	28032.411	0.002	n s
30.9739	*(D4)	28032.411	−0.001	n.s.

Note the unreasonable values for the standard error of the b-coefficients. This run even gave an R^2 value of 0.874. Now it happens to be true that the set of four dummy variables represents *perfect* multicollinearity, since

$$1 - (D_1 + D_2 + D_3) = D_4,$$

so that it is theoretically impossible to compute the regression solution. In the fallacious output above, at least the standard errors indicate that something is odd.

By way of comparison, if the regression model for the data in Table 6-9 is chosen to be

$$\hat{Y} = b_0 + b_1 D_1 + b_2 D_2 + b_3 D_3,$$

that is, leaving out one dummy variable, then the solution is:

Y-hat ($\hat{Y}$) =	se_b	t-value	Prob(1-tail)
+76.6	6.20	12.35	0.0000
+21.0 *(D1)	8.77	2.39	0.0140
+63.6 *(D2)	8.77	7.25	0.0000
+113.8 *(D3)	8.77	12.97	0.0000

TABLE 6-9   QUARTERLY DATA AND SEASONAL DUMMY VARIABLES
SHOWING THE CORRELATIONS AMONG THE DUMMY
VARIABLES AND Y

Time	Y	D_1	D_2	D_3	D_4
1	86	1	0	0	0
2	125	0	1	0	0
3	167	0	0	1	0
4	65	0	0	0	1
5	95	1	0	0	0
6	133	0	1	0	0
7	174	0	0	1	0
8	73	0	0	0	1
9	96	1	0	0	0
10	140	0	1	0	0
11	186	0	0	1	0
12	74	0	0	0	1
13	104	1	0	0	0
14	148	0	1	0	0
15	205	0	0	1	0
16	84	0	0	0	1
17	107	1	0	0	0
18	155	0	1	0	0
19	220	0	0	1	0
20	87	0	0	0	1

The Correlation Matrix

	Y	D_1	D_2	D_3	D_4
Y	1.000	−0.364	0.178	0.818	−0.632
D_1	−0.364	1.000	−0.333	−0.333	−0.333
D_2	0.178	−0.333	1.000	−0.333	−0.333
D_3	0.818	−0.333	−0.333	1.000	−0.333
D_4	−0.632	−0.333	−0.333	−0.333	1.000

$R^2 = 0.93$ and $\overline{R}^2 = 0.91$, and the overall F-value is 65.8, with (3,16) df, showing a highly significant relationship between Y and the first three dummy variables.

A second example that does not involve dummy variables will help to establish the importance of detecting multicollinearity. Table 6-10 presents data for Y and four regressors and the correlation table shows that the highest correlation between any two regressors is 0.7 (between X_1 and X_2). To interpret this correlation, simply square it, and we will be able to say that X_1 and X_2 have less than 50 percent (0.49) overlap in their variances.[16] This is hardly enough to make a claim for collinearity. In addition, this is not a case of four dummy variables for four seasons. Thus, on the surface, there does not seem to be any problem in doing a regression analysis on the data shown in Table 6-10.

An attempt to do so should be rejected by the computer program, or, as one library program would have it, the following output is obtained:

F-VALUE IS NEGATIVE—CHECK THE DATA CAREFULLY

This time the message is clearer. There is something wrong with the data.

The data in Table 6-10 were rigged in such a way that X_4 was a perfect linear combination of X_1, X_2, and X_3. Hence, the four regressors, instead of defining a four-dimensional hyperplane, actually defined a three-dimensional hyperplane of regressors. The regressor (X_4) lay perfectly in the space defined by the other three regressors. This is perfect multicollinearity and the usual regression procedure cannot get a solution.

The above illustration is not a mere exercise in subterfuge. In many financial analyses, a large number of financial ratios and indices are used, and many of them depend on one another in various ways. The fact of the matter is that cases of perfect (or nearly so) multicollinearity *have* occurred, and will continue to occur, as analysts depend more and more on large data bases with literally thousands of potential variables to choose from.

6/3/3 Special Cases in Regression

Theoreticians can have endless fun generating special or anomalous cases in the field of regression analysis, and some of these cases have important lessons for the forecaster. For example, Table 6-11 shows 15 observations on Y and two regressors, X_1 and X_2. The correlations among all pairs of variables are also shown.

From the correlation matrix we learn that Y and X_1 are not related ($r_{YX_1} = 0.015$), that Y and X_2 are not related ($r_{YX_2} = -0.062$), and that X_1 and X_2 are practically collinear ($r_{X_1X_2} = 0.997$). Thus, on the basis of what

---

[16]If X_1 is regressed on X_2, 49 percent of the variance of X_1 could be explained by knowing X_2 (and vice versa, too).

TABLE 6-10 AN EXAMPLE OF PERFECT MULTICOLLINEARITY

Obs.	Y	X_1	X_2	X_3	X_4
1	42.96	10.20	11.28	11.23	10.25
2	28.91	7.74	6.71	4.81	9.64
3	43.61	9.38	12.43	9.01	12.80
4	46.62	10.58	12.73	13.32	9.98
5	50.17	14.79	10.30	13.54	11.54
6	29.15	6.73	7.84	14.03	0.54
7	38.50	8.53	10.72	11.58	7.67
8	31.39	9.18	6.52	10.92	4.77
9	20.67	5.18	5.15	5.48	4.86
10	25.07	5.59	6.95	10.22	2.31
11	29.05	7.71	6.82	7.96	6.56
12	32.83	6.69	9.72	4.60	11.82
13	37.35	10.26	8.41	6.05	12.62
14	29.21	8.49	6.11	6.54	8.07
15	36.76	8.57	9.81	9.64	8.74
16	22.48	5.00	6.24	3.89	7.34
17	41.76	11.71	9.17	11.13	9.75
18	62.28	17.52	13.62	17.09	14.05
19	47.88	13.32	10.62	10.06	13.88
20	43.22	11.00	10.61	9.12	12.49

Correlation (R) Matrix ($n = 20$)

	Y	X_1	X_2	X_3	X_4
Y	1.000	0.942	0.900	0.695	0.736
X_1	0.942	1.000	0.700	0.660	0.688
X_2	0.900	0.700	1.000	0.618	0.669
X_3	0.695	0.660	0.618	1.000	0.025
X_4	0.736	0.688	0.669	0.025	1.000

has been said in this chapter, it would be reasonable to reach one or more of the following conclusions:

- There is a serious collinearity problem.
- The standard errors for the coefficients b_1 and b_2 in

$$\hat{Y} = b_0 + b_1 X_1 + b_2 X_2$$

  will be large (b_1 and b_2 will be unstable).
- Since X_1 and X_2, separately, have no noticeable relationship to Y, there is no point in putting them together.

TABLE 6-11 AN ANOMALOUS DATA SET FOR REGRESSION ANALYSIS

	Y	X_1	X_2
1	6.36	6.34	5.63
2	3.90	4.80	4.92
3	4.56	5.40	5.21
4	6.47	4.55	4.73
5	4.18	8.05	6.54
6	3.81	4.27	4.66
7	5.79	3.32	4.14
8	8.19	6.14	5.48
9	8.77	4.76	4.78
10	5.05	4.68	4.84
11	2.89	5.31	5.21
12	4.23	4.42	4.73
13	4.30	4.99	5.01
14	6.18	5.46	5.20
15	5.42	4.15	4.56

Correlation Matrix

	Y	X_1	X_2
Y	1.000	0.015	−0.062
X_1	0.015	1.000	0.997
X_2	−0.062	0.997	1.000

- If a stepwise regression analyses were run on the data, neither X_1 nor X_2 would be allowed to enter.

If a regression run is, in fact, performed, the following results are obtained:

$$\hat{Y} = 100.154 + 18.98(X1) - 38.034(X2)$$

$$(se_b) \longrightarrow \quad (0.465) \quad (0.929)$$

$$(t\text{-values}) \rightarrow \quad (40.85) \quad (-40.92)$$

The t-values for b_1 and b_2 are 40.85 and −40.92, respectively. R^2 turns out to be 0.993 and $\bar{R}^2 = 0.992$. In other words, X_1 and X_2, in combination, almost perfectly predict Y, in spite of all the signals that they could not. Again, in practice, when analysts use data services supplying an overload of possible regressors, and when the variables themselves are functionally related, the chances of obtaining anomalous data sets are far from negligible.

6/4 Multiple Regression and Forecasting

The main objective of this book is to examine forecasting models and then to critique their practical value. Regression models can be very useful in the hands of a creative forecaster, but there are two distinct phases to consider. The first is actually developing and fitting a model (which has been the subject matter of the current chapter so far), and the second is to do some actual forecasting with the model. We now concentrate on this second phase.

In Chapter 5, equations (5-37) and (5-38) defined the standard error of forecast for $\hat{Y}$ as a mean and $\hat{Y}$ as a single point, respectively. For the general case of multiple linear regression, the standard error formulas have to be given in matrix algebra terms, as follows:

$$se_{(\hat{Y} \text{ as a mean})} = \hat{\sigma}_\varepsilon \sqrt{c'(X'X)^{-1}c}, \tag{6-25}$$

$$se_{(\hat{Y} \text{ as a point})} = \hat{\sigma}_\varepsilon \sqrt{1 + c'(X'X)^{-1}c}, \tag{6-26}$$

where c is the vector $[1 \quad X_1^* \quad X_2^* \cdots X_k^*]$
     of new values
     for the regressors,

X is the matrix of order N-by-$(k+1)$, where the first

column is a set of ones (see Appendix 6-B for details).

For any forecast to be made, a set of values for the regressors has to be provided (the $X_1^*, X_2^*, \ldots, X_k^*$ values above). These are then put into the regression equation and a predicted value, $\hat{Y}$, is obtained. To decide how much faith to put in this value of $\hat{Y}$, equations (6-25) and (6-26) are used to evaluate the standard error of the forecast.

For the bank example (see Table 6-2) and the simple regression model (see Equation 6-9), the data setup is as follows:

Period	D(EOM)	(AAA)	(3-4)	D(3-4)
52	June 1972–May 1972	May 1972	May 1972	June 1972–May 1972
53	July 1972–June 1972	June 1972	June 1972	July 1972–June 1972
	(Data for D(EOM) assumed unknown from here on)			
54	Aug. 1972–July 1972	July 1972	July 1972	Aug. 1972–July 1972
55	Sept. 1972–Aug. 1972	Aug. 1972	Aug. 1972	Sept. 1972–Aug. 1972
.				
.		. . . etc. . . .		
.				

The objective is to forecast D(EOM) for periods 54, 55, . . . , 59 (six-month forecast). It becomes crucial to consider the *timing* of the availability of data. For example, *when* will the value of D(EOM) for (July 1972–June 1972) be known? Maybe after the first few days into August 1972. *When* will the June 1972 rates be known for (AAA) and (3-4)? And *when* will D(3-4) for (July 1972–June 1972) be available? Answers to these questions will determine how difficult it will be to forecast D(EOM) for period 54.

The equation for forecasting D(EOM) for period 54 is

$$\widehat{D(EOM)}_{54} = -4295.10 + 3363.74(AAA)_{54} - 2828.69(3\text{-}4)_{54} - 1965.69(D(3\text{-}4))_{54}.$$

Therefore, if the time point of reference is say August 5, 1972, the data

$(AAA)_{54}$ for (July 1972) will already be known,

$(3\text{-}4)_{54}$ for (July 1972) will already be known,

$D(3\text{-}4)_{54}$ for (Aug. 1972–July 1972) will not be known.

The last datum, $D(3\text{-}4)_{54}$, will have to be forecast. Any of the methods in Chapter 3 might well be tried until a "best" forecast for (3-4) rates for August 1972 can be obtained. Then D(3-4) for period 54 will be calculable.

For period 55, none of the three regressor values will be known as of August 5, 1972. They will all have to be forecast. Similarly, for any future time period, the values of (3-4) and (AAA) will have to be forecast first, and only then can the regression equation be used. Perhaps the key point to make here is this:

> *Equations (6-25) and (6-26) [and similarly, equations (5-37) and (5-38)] are based on the assumption that the regressors are measured without error. When forecasts of* $\hat{Y}$ *are made, they often depend on* forecasts *of the regressors,* $X_1, X_2, ..., X_k$*, so that these regressor values are definitely subject to error, and the standard error formulas* underestimate *the actual forecast errors.*

This is particularly relevant in the case of regression models for time-series data. In the next two sections, regression models will be used to forecast in both a cross-sectional and a time-series context.

6/4/1 Cross-sectional Regression and Forecasting

When cross-sectional data are used in a regression analysis, the estimated regression equation can be used to predict $\hat{Y}$ values for·new values of the regressors. As example 1, consider the Texas natural gas example (see Chapter 5) where one regression equation was

(consumption/capita) = 138.561 − 1.104(price in cents)

and the standard error of estimate was 20.86. What would the consumption be if the price was $1.10 per 1000 cubic feet? The new vector of regressor values, in this case, would be

$$c = [1 \quad 110]$$

and the regression equation would yield

$$\hat{Y} = (\text{consumption/capita}) = 138.561(1) - 1.104(110)$$

$$= 17.105 \ (1000 \ \text{cubic feet}).$$

The standard error of this prediction would be

$$\text{se}_{(\hat{Y} \text{ as a mean})} = 10.572 \quad [\text{using (5-37) or (6-25)}],$$

$$\text{se}_{(\hat{Y} \text{ as a point})} = 23.388 \quad [\text{using (5-38) or (6-26)}].$$

Thus, if a 95 percent confidence interval is to be established for the prediction, the following upper and lower limits would obtain:

$\hat{Y}$ AS A MEAN

lower limit: $\hat{Y} - (2.1)*(10.576) = -5.105$

upper limit: $\hat{Y} + (2.1)*(10.576) = 39.315$

$\hat{Y}$ AS A POINT

lower limit: $\hat{Y} - (2.1)*(23.388) = -32.009$

upper limit: $\hat{Y} + (2.1)*(23.388) = 66.220$

$$\uparrow$$

$$\left(\begin{array}{l} \text{2.1 standard errors on} \\ \text{either side of the mean} \\ \text{of a } t\text{-distribution with} \\ \text{18 df encloses 95 percent of} \\ \text{the area under the curve} \end{array} \right)$$

Example 2 is a multiple linear regression example involving the data shown in Table 6-12. Here the intrinsic interest is meteorological—the objective is to find out if upper atmosphere water vapor content is related to measurements that can be made on the ground. It is expensive to send weather balloons aloft to get direct measurement of Y (water vapor), so that if the regressors (X_1, X_2, X_3, X_4, and X_5) can "explain" a significant amount of the variation in Y, a useful model will be provided. The regressors in this instance are pressure (X_1), temperature (X_2), dew point (X_3), and the wind vector is resolved into an east-west component (X_4) and a north-south component (X_5). Using $N = 299$ daily observations on these six variables, a multiple linear regression model was estimated, as follows:

$$\hat{Y} = 23.725 - 0.228(X_1) - 0.024(X_2) + 0.182(X_3)$$

$$- 0.006(X_4) - 0.006(X_5)$$

$$(6\text{-}27)$$

and the standard error of estimate was 0.622.

TABLE 6-12 METEOROLOGICAL DATA: WATER VAPOR IN THE UPPER
ATMOSPHERE IS THE DEPENDENT MEASURE

Day	(X_1) Pressure	(X_2) Temp.	(X_3) Dew Pt.	(X_4) Wind E-W	(X_5) Wind N-S	(Y) Water Vapor
1	1013.3	24.7	15.0	0.00	−25.00	2.65
2	1011.6	24.8	17.0	12.86	15.32	2.63
3	1009.4	26.5	19.4	−7.87	−21.61	4.95
4	1003.1	29.6	20.1	20.78	12.00	4.49
5	1006.6	25.7	19.5	0.00	−7.00	3.17
6	1006.5	25.0	20.1	−8.21	−22.55	3.88
7	1016.9	21.6	16.3	0.00	−12.00	3.90
8	1011.8	24.7	18.0	9.58	26.31	3.51
9	1010.3	25.9	18.3	0.00	−20.00	3.90
10	1013.6	25.6	18.7	6.89	−5.79	3.47
11	1005.4	27.9	21.9	5.81	15.97	5.53
12	1013.4	25.8	20.0	−3.13	−17.73	3.48
13	1009.6	26.2	20.2	11.28	4.10	4.35
14	1013.0	24.8	21.5	0.00	−26.00	4.38
15	1009.8	27.7	20.6	10.00	17.32	4.39
16	1005.9	26.2	22.0	−3.13	−17.73	5.02
17	1011.0	23.9	22.0	−1.03	−2.82	4.77
18	1003.7	28.1	23.4	12.21	14.55	5.36
19	1001.4	23.0	18.5	5.36	−4.50	3.85
20	1007.4	27	20.9	16.45	9.50	5.37
21	1013.5	22		7.66	−6.43	3.64
22	1002.8	2			−12.00	2.64
	1003.6					3.91
289	101					
290	101			2.95		
291	1017.5	2		2.60	−14.7	
292	1020.4	23.8		5.91	1.04	2.31
293	1011.3	26.0	16.4	6.16	16.91	2.94
294	1012.4	23.6	21.0	6.93	−4.00	4.28
295	1013.0	22.4	15.0	−1.56	−8.86	4.14
296	1013.3	22.6	19.4	0.00	0.00	4.31
297	1015.6	23.4	20.3	3.08	−8.46	4.13
298	1007.2	27.5	22.0	14.78	17.62	3.64
299	1003.0	32.0	19.4	−3.13	−17.73	3.42

Suppose now that a prediction is to be made on the basis of the following set of ground control values:

$$X_1 = 1005, \quad X_2 = 22.0, \quad X_3 = 13.0, \quad X_4 = 10, \quad X_5 = 10.$$

Substituting these values in equation (6-27) gives a prediction $\hat{Y}$ (of water vapor content) of 2.595. Using equations (6-25) and (6-26), the standard error of this prediction will be

$$\text{se}_{(\hat{Y} \text{ as a mean})} = 0.133 \quad [\text{using (6-25)}],$$

$$\text{se}_{(Y \text{ as a point})} = 0.636 \quad [\text{using (6-26)}].$$

In order to give 95 percent confidence limits on the $\hat{Y}$ prediction, we add and subtract 1.96 times the standard error to 2.595, as follows

$\hat{Y}$ AS A MEAN

95 percent confidence interval is $2.595 \pm (1.96)(0.133)$

$$= 2.595 \pm 0.261$$

$\hat{Y}$ AS A POINT

95 percent confidence interval is $2.595 \pm (1.96)(0.636)$

$$= 2.595 \pm 1.247$$

The regression run gave an $\overline{R}^2$ of 0.665, so that it is not surprising to find a large confidence interval for $\hat{Y}$ as a point. A lot of the variance in Y is not being explained by the regression.

6/4/2   Time-Series Regression and Forecasting

Consider the bank data (Table 6-7) and the estimated model in equation (6-23). The objective is to forecast D(EOM) (change in end-of-month balance) for periods 54 through 59 (so that comparisons can be made with the known values in Table 6-2). The situation is as follows:

Forecasts are needed for the following:

D(EOM)	(AAA)	(3-4)
Aug. 1972-July 1972	Aug. 1972	Aug. 1972
Sept. 1972-Aug. 1972	Sept. 1972	Sept. 1972
Oct. 1972-Sept. 1972	Oct. 1972	Oct. 1972
Nov. 1972-Oct. 1972	Nov. 1972	Nov. 1972
Dec. 1972-Nov. 1972	Dec. 1972	Dec. 1972
Jan. 1973-Dec. 1972	(footnote 17)	Jan. 1973

[17]Note: it will not be necessary to forecast Jan. 1973 (AAA) bond rates because equation (6-24) has (AAA) leading D(EOM) by one month.

All the dummy variables and the (time)^3 variable in equation (6-23) give no problem. They are constants.

Table 6-13 shows what forecasts are needed. In column 1, the coefficients of the regression model are shown next to their labels (in column 2). Columns 3 through 8 are the time periods 54 through 59, for which forecasts of D(EOM) are required. In the first row of the table, the constant will be 1 for each future period. In row 2, dealing with $(AAA)_{-1}$—that is, AAA bond rates lagged one period—the regression equation will require values for periods 54 through 59. The $(AAA)_{-1}$ value for period 54 is already known (it is 7.298) because $(AAA)_{-1}$ *leads* D(EOM) by one period. The other values for $(AAA)_{-1}$ have to be estimated (forecast). To do this, Holt's method of double exponential smoothing (see Section 3/3/4) was used and the 5-period ahead forecasts using this method are shown in Table 6-13.[18]

Similarly, for row 3, dealing with $(3-4)_{-1}$—that is, rates for 3-4 year government issues—the value for period 54 is already known (it is 5.82) and the other values have to be forecast. Again using Holt's method to provide these forecasts, we determine the values shown in the rest of row

---

[18]Note that no attempt has been made to do the best job of forecasting (AAA) or (3-4). It is one of the exercises to improve upon the procedure illustrated in this section.

TABLE 6-13 BANK DATA: FORECASTING CHANGES IN END-OF-MONTH BALANCE 6 PERIODS AHEAD

	(1) Regression Coefficient	(2) Label	(3) Period 54	(4) Period 55	(5) Period 56	(6) Period 57	(7) Period 58	(8) Period 59
1	−4184.42	Constant	1	1	1	1	1	1
2	3845.64	(AAA)-1	7.298	7.305	7.307	7.309	7.311	7.313
3	−3125.34	(3-4)-1	5.820	5.848	5.883	5.918	5.952	5.987
4	−2061.05	(D(3-4))0	0.028	0.035	0.035	0.034	0.035	0.034
5	−3758.98	April-March	0	0	0	0	0	0
6	−2252.68	June-May	0	0	0	0	0	0
7	−2336.27	Aug-July	1	0	0	0	0	0
8	−2973.85	Sept.-Aug.	0	1	0	0	0	0
9	−3961.77	Oct.-Sept.	0	0	1	0	0	0
10	−1175.46	Nov.-Oct.	0	0	0	1	0	0
11	−1717.10	Dec.-Nov.	0	0	0	0	1	0
12	2226.83	Jan.-Dec.	0	0	0	0	0	1
13	−0.01070	Time^3	157464	166375	175616	185193	195112	205397
		$\widehat{D(EOM)}$	1612.74	804.79	−383.70	2200.50	1452.10	5186.53

3. The row 4 data in Table 6-13 is the set of first differences for the (3-4) data. Note that it was actually necessary to forecast 6 periods ahead for the (3-4) data so as to get the last D(3-4) value of .034 in row 4 of Table 6-13.

The rows dealing with the dummy variables are straightforward. For example, the (April-March) dummy variable (chosen in the stepwise procedure leading to equation (6-23)) takes on the value 0 for all periods 54 through 59. Similarly, the dummy variable dealing with (June-May) is also zero for periods 54 through 59. All other dummy variables have one value that is 1 and all other values zero, as shown in Table 6-13.

Finally, for the cubic trend term, the values in Table 6-13 are simply $(54)^3$, $(55)^3$, ..., $(59)^3$. That is, the time index is cubed for the 13th row of Table 6-13.

In the very last row of Table 6-13 are the desired forecasts for D(EOM) for periods 54 through 59. For example, under column 3, for period 54 (which refers to the change period Aug. 1972 minus July 1972) the forecast of D(EOM) is 1612.74. This is obtained by multiplying corresponding terms in columns 1 and 3, and summing, as follows:

$$1612.74 = (-4184.42)(1) + (3845.64)(7.298) + (-3125.34)(5.82)$$
$$+ (-2061.05)(.028) + 0 + 0 + (-2336.27)(1)$$
$$+ 0 + 0 + 0 + 0 + 0 + (-.0107)(157464).$$

From the bank's point of view, if it is August 5, 1972 and the value of D(EOM) for (July 1972-June 1972) is known, then they can expect an increase of \$1612.74 in end-of-month balance by the end of August. This is what the forecast says.

Similarly, the other forecasts can be used to get an idea of the changes in (EOM) that can be expected in future months. Since the regression method allows the forecaster to provide confidence intervals around any given forecast, we now use equations (6-25) and (6-26) to obtain the 90 percent confidence intervals for the forecasts. Table 6-14 shows the results. Note that the intervals are larger when the forecast is considered an individual realization, rather than as a mean, and that the width of the interval increases the further ahead we forecast. Both of these facts are expected. Note also that four out of the six actual values (from Table 6-2) for these periods fall within the intervals for $\hat{Y}$, and five out of the six fall within the intervals for Y.

6/4/3   Recapitulation

From the previous section it is clear that if a regression model involved a regressor that *leads* the dependent variable by 2 periods, say, then two forecasts of $\hat{Y}$ can be made *without* having to forecast the regressor values. There are two values of the regressor in hand already. Whenever

TABLE 6-14 CONFIDENCE INTERVALS FOR THE BANK FORECASTS
FOR PERIODS 54 THROUGH 59 USING THE REGRESSION
MODEL IN EQUATION (6-23)

Period	$\hat{Y}$ Forecast	$\hat{Y}$ as a mean[a] Confidence Interval	$\hat{Y}$ as a point[b] Confidence Interval
54	1613	202 to 3025	−808 to 4034
55	805	−649 to 2243	−1631 to 3241
56	−384	−1883 to 1115	−2857 to 2089
57	2201	610 to 3791	−329 to 4730
58	1452	−227 to 3131	−1134 to 4038
59	5187	3464 to 6909	2572 to 7801

[a]Using equation (6-25)

[b]Using equation (6-26)

Y is being forecast further ahead, then the regressor values must also be forecast, and the forecast values ($\hat{Y}$) are subject to additional uncertainty.

Dummy variables can be used effectively to handle seasonality or special events or both. In the cases mentioned above, the dummy variables affected only the constant term (the intercept), but they can be used to influence the slope coefficients as well.

Regression packages exist in all computer centers, so that the computational grind is minimal, but forecasters should be aware that not all computer programs are equally good. Some are robust with respect to round-off errors—others are not. Some are sensitive to near-collinearity problems—others are not. Some provide information on the correlations among the regressors and the correlations among the regression coefficients—others do not. Some allow for graphical output—others do not. In our opinion, it is worthwhile making sure a comprehensive regression package is available for the model-building process described in this chapter.

Since independent variable values often have to be forecast before dependent variable values can be forecast, it is important to get good forecasts for these independent variables. Many firms buy the services of forecasting houses to get such forecasts, and, often, corporate planners will buy econometric forecasts (see next chapter) which will then be passed down to the business units of the company for their forecasting and planning models. Much has been written on the relative merits of econometric forecasts—and the performance of such forecasts over time—but the fact is, most major companies make use of them as feeders for other models (e.g., regression models at the business unit level).

Regression analysis is a powerful method of estimation and the most commonly used causal approach to forecasting.

APPENDIX 6-A
SOLVING FOR THE COEFFICIENTS IN MULTIPLE LINEAR REGRESSION

The method indicated in Appendix 5-A can be extended readily to solve for the coefficients of any multiple linear regression equation but the algebra becomes tedious. So for the general case we shall use matrix algebra. For the general regression equation[19]

$$\mathbf{Y} = b_1 + b_2 X_2 + b_3 X_3 + \ldots + b_k X_k + e \tag{6-28}$$

the matrix expression is

$$\mathbf{Y} = \mathbf{Xb} + \mathbf{e}, \tag{6-29}$$

where

$$\mathbf{Y} = \begin{bmatrix} Y_1 \\ Y_2 \\ Y_3 \\ \cdot \\ \cdot \\ \cdot \\ Y_n \end{bmatrix} \qquad \mathbf{X} = \begin{bmatrix} 1 & X_{21} & X_{31} & \cdots & X_{k1} \\ 1 & X_{22} & X_{32} & \cdots & X_{k2} \\ 1 & X_{23} & X_{33} & \cdots & X_{k3} \\ \cdot & \cdot & \cdot & \cdots & \cdot \\ \cdot & \cdot & \cdot & \cdots & \cdot \\ \cdot & \cdot & \cdot & \cdots & \cdot \\ 1 & X_{2n} & X_{3n} & \cdots & X_{kn} \end{bmatrix}$$

$$\mathbf{b} = \begin{bmatrix} b_1 \\ b_2 \\ b_3 \\ \cdot \\ \cdot \\ \cdot \\ b_k \end{bmatrix} \qquad \text{and} \qquad \mathbf{e} = \begin{bmatrix} e_1 \\ e_2 \\ e_3 \\ \cdot \\ \cdot \\ \cdot \\ e_n \end{bmatrix}$$

---

[19]Note that for convenience, we deal here with only $(k - 1)$ regressors, labeling them X_2 through X_k. If you think of X_1 as being the column of ones in matrix X, then there will be k coefficients to solve for, but really only $(k - 1)$ regressors. When it comes to calculating degrees of freedom for the F-test, it is important to ask, "How many coefficients are we dealing with?"

where $\mathbf{Y}$ is an $n \times 1$ matrix,

$\quad$ $\mathbf{X}$ is an $n \times k$ matrix,

$\quad$ $\mathbf{b}$ is a $k \times 1$ matrix,

$\quad$ $\mathbf{e}$ is a $k \times 1$ matrix.

(For the remainder of this section, Y, X, b, and e will be used to denote matrices.)

To obtain the values of b, the sum of squared deviations must be minimized:

$$\Sigma e_i^2 = e'e = (Y - Xb)'(Y - Xb), \tag{6-30}$$

where $e' = (Y - Xb)'$, is the transpose of e. Thus

$$e'e = (Y' - b'X')(Y - Xb)$$
$$= Y'Y - Y'Xb - b'X'Y + b'X'Xb$$
$$= Y'Y - 2b'X'Y + b'X'Xb,$$

since $b'X'Y$ is a scalar and is therefore equal to its transpose, $Y Xb$.

$$\frac{\partial e'e}{\partial b} = -2X'Y + 2X'Xb = 0, \tag{6-31}$$

$$X'Y = X'Xb, \tag{6-32}$$

and

$$b = \boxed{(X'X)^{-1}X'Y} \tag{6-33}$$

where $(X'X)^{-1}$ is the inverse of $(X'X)$.

This approach is fine as long as $X'X$ has an inverse, but when multicollinearity is present, the computation of matrix inverses becomes dubious.

The Choleski Decomposition Method

A very stable and accurate method of computing regression coefficients is discussed in Martin *et al* (1965). It is known as Choleski decomposition and is illustrated here for the data in Table 6-11. The regression equation to be solved is $Y = b_0 + b_1X_1 + b_2X_2$ and it is known that $r_{X_1X_2} = .997$. The key to the Choleski method is the decomposition of $X'X$ in (6-32) into a product LL', where L is a lower triangle matrix. For Table 6-11 we have

$$X'X = \begin{bmatrix} 15 & 76.64 & 75.64 \\ 76.64 & 409.082 & 395.194 \\ 75.64 & 395.194 & 385.802 \end{bmatrix}$$

$$= \begin{bmatrix} 3.8730 & 0 & 0 \\ 19.7884 & 4.1837 & 0 \\ 19.5302 & 2.0854 & 0.1614 \end{bmatrix} \begin{bmatrix} 3.8730 & 19.7884 & 19.5302 \\ 0 & 4.1837 & 2.0854 \\ 0 & 0 & 0.1614 \end{bmatrix} = LL'$$

Now equation (6-32) can be rewritten as

$$LL'b = X'Y \tag{6-34}$$

and the next step is to solve for

$$Z = L'b \quad \text{in the equation} \quad LZ = X'Y \tag{6-35}$$

$$\begin{bmatrix} 3.8730 & 0 & 0 \\ 19.7884 & 4.1837 & 0 \\ 19.5302 & 2.0854 & 0.1614 \end{bmatrix} \begin{bmatrix} z_1 \\ z_2 \\ z_3 \end{bmatrix} = \begin{bmatrix} 80.1 \\ 409.646 \\ 403.121 \end{bmatrix}$$

Using the first row of L, we have

$$3.8730z_1 + 0z_2 + 0z_3 = 80.1$$

so that $z_1 = 80.1/3.8730 = 20.682$. Then proceed to solve for z_2 using the second row of L:

$$19.7884z_1 + 4.1837z_2 + 0z_3 = 409.646$$

Since z_1 is known, it is easy to solve for z_2. Similarly, using the third row of L, we solve for z_3.

Now that the elements of Z are known, we solve for b using

$$L'b = Z \tag{6-36}$$

To get b_3 start with the third row of L'. Then use the second row of L' to get b_2, and finally use the first row of L' to solve for b_1.

The following BASIC subprogram can be adapted to solve any linear regression equation by the Choleski method:

```
100  SUB "CHOLESKI": N, A(,), B(,), X(,)
110      ' REF: "SYMMETRIC DECOMPOSITION OF A POSITIVE DEFINITE MATRIX"
120      '     MARTIN, PETERS, WILKINSON NUMERISCHE MATHEMATIK
130      '     7,362-383(1965) SEE ALGOL PROGRAMS HERE
140      ' TO SOLVE FOR X IN AX = B
150      ' N = NO. OF ROWS (& COLS) IN A(N,N)
160      ' A(N,N) COULD BE X'X AS IN EQUATION (6-32)
170      ' B(N,1) COULD BE X'Y AS IN EQUATION (6-32)
180      ' X(N,1) WILL BE RETURNED AS THE SOLUTION VECTOR
```

```
190
200      ' (1) RESOLVE A INTO LL' WHERE L IS LOWER TRIANGLE
210      DIM P(50)
220      FOR I = 1 TO N
230       FOR J = 1 TO N
240         LET X = A(I,J)
250          FOR K = I−1 TO 1 STEP −1
260           LET X = X − A(J,K)*A(I,K)
270          NEXT K
280          IF J<>I THEN 310
290           LET P(I) = 1/SQR(X)
300           GO TO 320
310          LET A(J,I) = X*P(I)
320       NEXT J
330      NEXT I
340      ' MATRIX L IS NOW IN LOWER TRIANGLE OF A AND ITS
350      ' DIAGONAL ELEMENTS ARE RECIPROCALS OF P
360
370      ' (2) SOLVE FOR Y IN LY = B (WHERE Y = L'X)
380      FOR I = 1 TO N
390       LET Z = B(I,1)
400        FOR K = I−1 TO 1 STEP −1
410          LET Z = Z − A(I,K)*X(K,1)
420        NEXT K
430       LET X(I,1) = Z*P(I)
440      NEXT I
450
460      ' (3) SOLVE FOR X IN UX = Y
470      FOR I = N TO 1 STEP −1
480       LET Z = X(I,1)
490       FOR K = I+1 TO N
500         LET Z = Z − A(K,I)*X(K,1)
510       NEXT K
520       LET X(I,1) = Z*P(I)
530      NEXT I
540
550      ' (UNNECESSARY PART : COMPLETING L IN A)
560      FOR I = 1 TO N
570       LET A(I,I) = 1/P(I)
580        FOR J = I TO N
590         IF I = J THEN 610
600            LET A(I,J) = 0
610        NEXT J
620      NEXT I
630
640 SUBEND
```

APPENDIX 6-B
THE JOINT DISTRIBUTION OF THE b-COEFFICIENTS

Substituting $Y = X\beta + u$, where β is the matrix (vector) of the true population values of the regression parameters, into equation (6-33) gives

$$b = (X'X)^{-1}X'(X\beta + u)$$
$$= (X'X)^{-1}X'X\beta + (X'X)^{-1}X'u$$
$$= \beta + (X'X)^{-1}X'u.$$

Taking expected values gives

$$E(b) = E(\beta) + (X'X)^{-1}X'E(u),$$
$$E(b - \beta) = (X'X)^{-1}X'E(u) = 0,$$
$$E[(b - \beta)(b - \beta)'] = E[(X'X)^{-1}X'u][(X'X)^{-1}X'u]'$$
$$= E[(X'X)^{-1}X'uu'X(X'X)^{-1}]$$
$$= (X'X)^{-1}X'E(uu')X(X'X)^{-1}.$$

Now $E(uu')$ is the variance-covariance matrix of the error terms in the regression model, and it is defined as follows:

$$E(uu') = \sigma_u^2\, I,$$

where I is the identity matrix. In other words, the errors are identically and independently distributed with common (homoscedastic) variance σ_u^2. Thus

$$E[(b - \beta)(b - \beta)'] = \sigma_u^2(X'X)^{-1}X'X(X'X)^{-1}$$
$$= \sigma_u^2(X'X)^{-1}.$$

(6-37)

This gives the variance-covariance matrix for the regression coefficients. Down the diagonal will be the marginal variances for each coefficient. Off the diagonal will be the covariances between all pairs of coefficients.

Since a variance-covariance matrix is hard to interpret directly, it makes sense to convert it to a correlation matrix. Every cell (i,j) in (6-37) is converted to a correlation by dividing by two standard deviations, as follows:

$$\text{cell } (i,j): \quad r_{b_i b_j} = \frac{\text{Cov}_{(b_i b_j)}}{S_{(b_i)} S_{(b_j)}}, \tag{6-38}$$

where

$$S_{(b_i)} = \sqrt{\text{cell } (i,i) \text{ in } (6\text{-}37)},$$

$$S_{(b_j)} = \sqrt{\text{cell } (j,j) \text{ in } (6\text{-}37)}.$$

In matrix algebra, the complete correlation matrix for the b's is given by

$$R_{(b)} = D(X'X)^{-1}D, \tag{6-39}$$

where

$$D = \begin{bmatrix} 1/S_{(b_1)} & 0 & 0 & \cdots & 0 \\ 0 & 1/S_{(b_2)} & 0 & \cdots & 0 \\ \vdots & & & & \vdots \\ \vdots & & & & \vdots \\ 0 & 0 & & & 1/S_{(b_k)} \end{bmatrix}$$

Equation (6-37) is used to determine the standard error of forecasts when the forecast is treated both as a mean and as an individual forecast. Equations (6-40) and (6-41) give these standard errors for the multivariate case.

$$\text{se}_{\hat{Y} \text{ as a mean}} = \sigma_u^2 \sqrt{c'(X'X)^{-1}c}, \tag{6-40}$$

$$\text{se}_{\hat{Y} \text{ as an individual forecast}} = \sigma_u^2 \sqrt{1 + c'(X'X)^{-1}c}, \tag{6-41}$$

where $c = (1 \quad X_2^* \quad X_3^* \quad X_4^* \quad \cdots \quad X_k^*)$ is the vector of new observations on the regressors.

APPENDIX 6-C
THE DURBIN-WATSON STATISTIC

The Durbin-Watson (D-W) statistic tests the hypothesis that there is no autocorrelation present in the residuals. Like the F-test and t-tests, the computed value ($D\text{-}W_c$) of the Durbin-Watson test is compared with the corresponding values from Table D of Appendix I. The two values ($D\text{-}W_L$ and $D\text{-}W_u$) are read from a D-W table that corresponds to the degrees of freedom of the data. The D-W distribution is symmetrical around 2, its mean value. Thus confidence intervals can be constructed involving the five regions shown in Figure 6-11 and using $D\text{-}W_L$ and $D\text{-}W_u$. The five intervals are:

1. less than $D\text{-}W_L$
2. between $D\text{-}W_L$ and $D\text{-}W_u$
3. between $D\text{-}W_u$ and $4 - D\text{-}W_u$

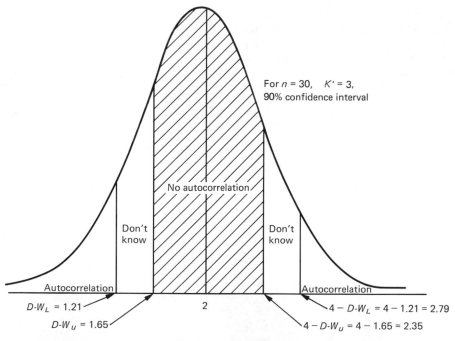

FIGURE 6-11 GRAPH OF DURBIN-WATSON DISTRIBUTION

4. between $4 - D\text{-}W_u$ and $4 - D\text{-}W_L$

5. more than $4 - D\text{-}W_L$

If the computed $D\text{-}W_c$ is either in interval 1 or 5, the existence of autocorrelation is indicated. If $D\text{-}W_c$ is in interval 3, no autocorrelation is present. If it is in either 2 or 4, the test is inconclusive as to whether autocorrelation exists.

For example, if there are three independent variables and 30 observations, then

$$D\text{-}W_L = 1.21 \quad \text{and} \quad D\text{-}W_u = 1.65.$$

If $D\text{-}W_c$ is less than 1.21 or more than

$$4 - D\text{-}W_L = 4 - 1.21 = 2.79,$$

there is autocorrelation. If $D\text{-}W_c$ is between 1.65 and $4 - D\text{-}W_u = 2.35$, there is *no* autocorrelation.

If $D\text{-}W_c$ is between 1.21 and 1.65 or between 2.35 and 2.79, the test is inconclusive.

It should be noted that when there is no prior knowledge of the sign of the serial correlation, two-sided tests may be made by combining single-tail tests. Thus by using the 5% values of d_l and d_u from Table D (page 888), a two-sided test at the 10% level is obtained.

REFERENCES AND SELECTED BIBLIOGRAPHY

Cooley, W. W., and P. R. Lohnes. 1971. *Multivariate Data Analysis.* New York: John Wiley & Sons, Inc.

Daniel, C., and F. S. Wood. 1980. *Fitting Equations to Data: Computer Analysis of Multifactor Data,* 2nd ed. New York: John Wiley & Sons, Inc.

Draper, N. R., and H. Smith. 1981. *Applied Regression Analysis,* 2nd ed. New York: John Wiley & Sons, Inc.

Goldberger, A. S. 1964. *Econometric Theory.* New York: John Wiley & Sons, Inc.

Johnston, J. 1972. *Econometric Methods.* Englewood Cliffs, N.J.: Prentice-Hall.

Klein, L. R. 1968. *An Introduction to Econometrics.* Englewood Cliffs, N.J.: Prentice-Hall.

Kmenta, J. 1971. *Elements of Econometrics.* New York: The Macmillan Company.

Kubicek, M., M. Marek and E. Eckert. 1971. "Quasilinearized Regression." *Technometrics,* **13,** No. 3, pp. 601–608.

Martin, R. S., G. Peters and J. H. Wilkinson. 1965. "Symmetric Decomposition of a Positive Definite Matrix." Numerische Mathematik, **7,** pp. 362–383.

McGee, V. E., and W. T. Carleton. 1970. "Piecewise Regression." *Journal of the American Statistical Association,* **65,** No. 33, pp. 1109–1124.

Pindyck, R. S., and D. L. Rubenfeld. 1976. *Econometric Models and Economic Forecasts.* New York: McGraw-Hill.

EXERCISES

1. The table below presents the results of a regression run. What should be done next? Interpret the final regression equation, and answer the questions below.

   a. How many observations were involved?

   b. What would be the value of $\bar{R}^2$?

   c. Why is the square root of the mean square error not equal to the standard error of the regression?

   d. Which coefficients are significantly different from zero?

RESULTS OF REGRESSION RUN 1

Variable	B	Standard Error	t-Tests
Constant	357835.	30740.8	11.6404
1	1007.43	524.846	1.91947
2	−56089.2	43008.2	−1.30415
3	21165.1	34096.	.62075
4	−88410.9	35825.1	−2.46785
5	22488.2	35428.	.634759
6	−35399.5	34087.5	−1.03849
7	−21218.7	33351.4	−.636216
8	−122709.	36535.8	−3.35859
9	−3048.89	30339.1	−.100494
10	−57311.	37581.	−1.525
11	−70596.2	38493.5	−1.83398
12	−184778.	36655.7	−5.04089
13	.417727	6.84181E-02	6.1055
14	−.216098	6.53552E-02	−3.30651
15	.297009	3.34643E-02	8.87541
16	1.19271E-02	3.37776E-02	.353106
17	−6.85211E-02	3.26835E-02	−2.0965

$R^2 = 0.943$ $R = 0.971$ F-test $= 31.04$
Standard error of regression $= +3.85012E + 04$
Degrees of freedom for numer. $= 17$ For denom. $= 30$
Do you wish the residuals to be printed? No
Durbin-Watson statistic $= 2.27202$
Mean square error $= 9.26623E + 08$
Mean percentage error (absolute value) $= 6.76519$

2. Given the data in the following table (both in actual and $\log_e$ form) for the annual sales of the Multinational Company, obtain a forecast for periods 31 through 35.
   a. Regress Y on t and $t^2 - 1$ and study the error characteristics (e.g., Durbin-Watson statistic).
   b. Regress $\log Y$ on t and $t^2 - 1$ and study the error characteristics.
   c. Compute the first few autocorrelations for the sales data (e.g., for lags 1, 2, 3, 4) and see if that suggests what kind of regression relationship is most tenable.

ACTUAL AND TRANSFORMED DATA

t Period	Y Sales ($1000s)	log Y $\log_e$ of Sales ($1000s)
1	190.464	5.24946
2	182.916	5.20903
3	246.464	5.50722
4	257.848	5.55237
5	269.559	5.59679
6	345.317	5.84446
7	355.322	5.87302
8	412.509	6.02226
9	431.081	6.06630
10	488.551	6.19144
11	572.552	6.35010
12	643.672	6.46719
13	745.539	6.61411
14	793.442	6.67638
15	922.705	6.82731
16	1028.09	6.93546
17	1125.45	7.02594
18	1266.94	7.14436
19	1490.92	7.30715
20	1637.97	7.40121
21	1814.12	7.50336
22	2082.59	7.64137
23	2315.33	7.74731
24	2585.58	7.85771
25	2932.67	7.98367
26	3330.37	8.11084
27	3690.01	8.21339
28	4179.63	8.33798
29	4740.36	8.46387
30	5331.38	8.58137

3.   The Texas natural gas data in Table 5-3 show that consumption (C) is non-linearly related to price (P). In Chapter 5, two methods of regression analysis were applied to these data. The first was a linear regression of C on P. The second was a linear regression of log C on P. The results are shown in Figures 5-7 and 5-9.

a. Now try what is known as a polynomial regression of order 2—namely, $\hat{C} = b_0 + b_1 P + b_2 P^2$. See how this compares with the previous results.

Check the $\bar{R}^2$ value, the F-test, the t-tests for the coefficients, and reach a conclusion as to which of the three models makes most sense.

b. For the second-degree polynomial regression compute the confidence intervals for forecasts of consumption for various prices, for example, $P = 20, 40, 60, 80, 100$, and 120 cents per 1000 cubic feet [using (6-25) and (6-26)].

c. What is the correlation between P and P^2? Does this suggest any general problem to be considered in dealing with polynomial regressions—especially of higher orders?

d. Study the plot of the residuals based on this second-degree polynomial regression and compute the Durbin-Watson statistic. Is there any connection?

4.   The stepwise regression analysis resulting in equation (6-23) was used to forecast the change in end-of-month balance for a bank, for the next six time periods (periods 54 through 59). See Section 6/4/2 for details. However, since we originally omitted the known values for D(EOM) for these periods, it is possible to examine the usefulness of the regression model.

a. Compare the forecasts (Table 6-13) with the actuals (Table 6-2) and determine the MAPE and other summary statistics for these forecasts.

b. As indicated in Section 6/4/2, it was necessary to forecast (AAA) and (3-4) rates for future periods before it was possible to get the forecasts for D(EOM). Holt's double exponential smoothing method was used in Section 6/4/2 to do this. However, this is by no means the best choice for forecasting (AAA) and (3-4), and furthermore, no attempt was made to optimize the parameter values for Holt's method. Try using the naive forecasting method (NF1) to forecast these (AAA) and (3-4) rates, and then recompute the forecasts for D(EOM) according to the scheme laid out in Table 6-13.

c. Compare your new forecasts with the actual D(EOM) values in Table 6-2 and compute the MAPE and other statistics to show the quality of the forecasts. How well do your new forecasts match up against those in Table 6-13?

5.   Can you figure out why the data set in Table 6-11 gives anomalous results? Can you think up data sets that would give rise to such contra-intuitive results?

6.   The data set in the following table shows the dollar volume on the New York plus American stock exchange (as the regressor X) and the dollar volume on the Boston Regional Exchange (as the dependent variable Y).

a. Regress Y on X and check the significance of the results.

b. Regress Y on X and t (time) and check the significance of the results.

c. Plot the data (Y against X) and join up the points according to their timing—that is, join the point for $t = 1$ to the point for $t = 2$, and so on. Note that the relationship between Y and X changes over time. Refer to McGee and Carleton (1970) for a more detailed analysis.

7.   Equations (6-22) and (6-23) give two regression models for the mutual savings bank data. From these two equations calculate two sets of indices that represent seasonality.

MONTHLY DOLLAR VOLUME OF SALES (IN MILLIONS) ON BOSTON STOCK EXCHANGE AND COMBINED NEW YORK AND AMERICAN STOCK EXCHANGES

Number	Month (t)	New York and American Stock Exchanges (x)	Boston Stock Exchange (y)
1	Jan. 1967	10581.6	78.8
2	Feb. 1967	10234.3	69.1
3	Mar. 1967	13299.5	87.6
4	April 1967	10746.5	72.8
5	May 1967	13310.7	79.4
6	June 1967	12835.5	85.6
7	July 1967	12194.2	75.0
8	Aug. 1967	12860.4	85.3
9	Sept. 1967	11955.6	86.9
10	Oct. 1967	13351.5	107.8
11	Nov. 1967	13285.9	128.7
12	Dec. 1967	13784.4	134.5
13	Jan. 1968	16336.7	148.7
14	Feb. 1968	11040.5	94.2
15	Mar. 1968	11525.3	128.1
16	April 1968	16056.4	154.1
17	May 1968	18464.3	191.3
18	June 1968	17092.2	191.9
19	July 1968	15178.8	159.6
20	Aug. 1968	12774.8	185.5
21	Sept. 1968	12377.8	178.0
22	Oct. 1968	16856.3	271.8
23	Nov. 1968	14635.3	212.3
24	Dec. 1968	17436.9	139.4
25	Jan. 1969	16482.2	106.0
26	Feb. 1969	13905.4	112.1
27	Mar. 1969	11973.7	103.5
28	April 1969	12573.6	92.5
29	May 1969	16566.8	116.9
30	June 1969	13558.7	78.9
31	July 1969	11530.9	57.4
32	Aug. 1969	11278.0	75.9
33	Sept. 1969	11263.7	109.8
34	Oct. 1969	15649.5	129.2
35	Nov. 1969	12197.1	115.1

a. From equation (6-22) compute a set of seasonal indices by examining the constant term in the regression equation when just one dummy variable at a time is set equal to 1, with all others set to 0. Finally, set all dummy variables to 0 and examine the constant term.

b. Repeat this procedure using equation (6-23) and compare the two sets of seasonal indices.

c. The use of dummy variables requires that some time period is regarded as "base period." In the case of (6-22) and (6-23) the 12th-period was chosen as base (that is, that period for which all the dummy variables have zero value). Rerun the regression model of equation (6-22) using some other period as the base. Then recompute the seasonal indices and see if they are the same as in part a above.

8. In Table 6-7 compute the correlation between any pair of dummy variables using equation (5-22). What can be said about the dependence or independence of dummy variables in general? Can there ever be a multicollinearity problem among a set of dummy variables?

7/ECONOMETRIC MODELS AND FORECASTING

The previous two chapters have dealt with the causal approaches to fore-casting of simple and multiple regression. Applying simple regression requires little statistical knowledge, limited data, and only moderate computational effort. (Most programmable calculators are adequate for the computations.) Multiple regression, on the other hand, requires a much greater level of sophistication, considerably more data, and a computer to do the computations. While use of simple regression can be made a mechanical task that can be entrusted to a clerical level of operations, multiple regression requires a more highly qualified person. These differences are very important in the practical use of forecasting.

In the same way that simple regression is a special case of multiple regression, the latter is a special case of econometric models. While multiple regression involves a single equation, econometric models can include any number of simultaneous multiple regression equations. The term *econometric models* will be used in this book to denote systems of linear equations involving several *interdependent variables*. It should be noted that this is not the only usage of the term *econometrics,* since there are those who use it as a general term to cover simple, multiple, and systems of multiple regression equations. The more limited definition used in this chapter appears to be the most common usage at this time.

The objective of this chapter is not to provide the level of detailed information needed to fully utilize these models, but to interpret their use in a practical sense. Such a task is difficult given the mathematical and statistical level assumed in this book. However, this chapter will seek to review the main ideas and concepts underlying econometric models, present the main advantages and difficulties involved, describe the statistical methods used, and finally discuss the role of econometric methods as a forecasting tool.

7/1   The Basis of Econometric Modeling

Regression analysis assumes that each of the independent variables included in the regression equation is determined by outside factors, that is, they are exogenous to the system. In economic or organizational relationships, however, such an assumption is often unrealistic. To illustrate this point, one can assume that sales = f(GNP, price, advertising). In regression, all three independent variables are assumed to be exogenously determined; they are not influenced by the level of sales itself or by each other. This is a fair assumption as far as GNP is concerned, which, except for very large corporations, is not influenced directly by the sales of a single firm. However, for price and advertising there is unlikely to be a similar absence of influence. For example, if the per unit cost is proportional to sales volume, different levels of sales will result in different per unit costs.

Furthermore, advertising expenditures will certainly influence the per unit price of the product offered, since production and selling costs influence the per unit price. The price in turn influences the magnitude of sales, which can consequently influence the level of advertising. These interrelationships point to the mutual interdependence among the variables of such an equation. Regression analysis is incapable of dealing with such interdependence if it is to be preserved as part of the explanatory model.

The above relationship can be more correctly expressed by a system of simultaneous equations that can deal with the interdependence among the variables.

Although very simplistic, these interdependencies might be represented by the following econometric model:

$$\text{sales} = f(\text{GNP, price, advertising}),$$

$$\text{production cost} = f(\text{number of units produced, inventories, labor costs, material cost}),$$

$$\text{selling expenses} = f(\text{advertising, other selling expenses}), \qquad (7\text{-}1)$$

$$\text{advertising} = f(\text{sales}),$$

$$\text{price} = f(\text{production cost, selling expenses, administrative overhead, profit}).$$

In place of one regression equation expressing sales as a function of three independent variables, the set of five simultaneous equations in (7-1) expresses sales and the independent variables as a function of each other plus other exogenous factors. The relationship among these variables can be represented schematically as shown in Figure 7-1.

The basic premise of econometric modeling is that everything in the real world depends upon everything else. The world is becoming more aware of this interdependence, but the concept is very difficult to deal with at an operational level. Management systems, MIS, and the systems approach in general are concrete illustrations of the increasing concern of scientists for the interdependence among organizational units. Changing A not only affects A and its immediate system, but also the environment in general. The practical question is, of course, where to stop considering these interdependencies.

One could develop an almost infinite number of interdependent relationships, but data collection, computational limitations, and estimation problems restrict one in practice to a limited number of relationships. In addition, the marginal understanding, or forecasting accuracy, does not increase in proportion to the effort required to include an additional variable or equation after the first few. In econometric models, a major decision is determining how much detail to include, since more detail inevitably means more complexity.

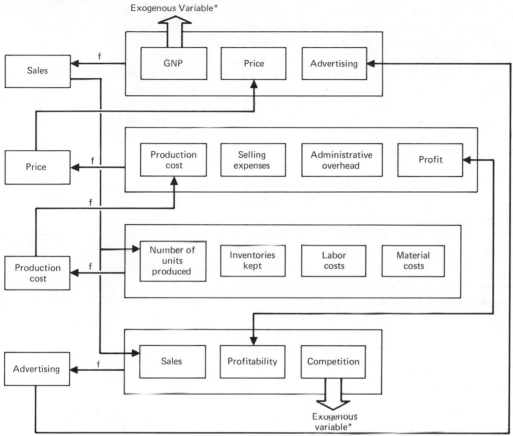

FIGURE 7-1 SIMPLE ECONOMETRIC MODEL

In an econometric model one is faced with many tasks similar to those in multiple regression analysis. These tasks include:

1. determining which variables to include in each equation (specification)
2. determining the functional form (i.e., linear, exponential, logarithmic, etc.) of each of the equations;
3. estimating in a simultaneous manner, the parameters of the equations;
4. testing the statistical significance of the results;
5. checking the validity of the assumptions involved.

Steps 2, 4, and 5 do not differ in their basic approach from those of multiple regression, and therefore will not be discussed further in this chapter. However, it should be mentioned that there is usually not much choice on Step 2, and Step 4 is seldom pursued rigorously, in practice. Furthermore, Step 3 is not often done in a simultaneous manner, in practice. Step 1 will be examined in Section 7/3 to illustrate its important aspects, and Step 3 will be addressed in Appendix 7-A. Before such a discussion, it is useful to review the advantages and disadvantages of econometric methods for forecasting.

7/2   The Advantages and Drawbacks of Econometric Methods

The main advantage of econometric models lies in their ability to deal with interdependencies. If a government, for example, would like to know the results of a 10 percent tax reduction aimed at stimulating a recessionary economy, it has few alternatives other than econometric models. A tax cut will have direct and immediate effects on increasing personal disposable income and probably decreasing government revenues. It will also tend to influence the price level, unemployment, savings, capital spending, and so on. Each of these will in turn influence personal disposable income and therefore taxes of subsequent years. Through a series of chain reactions, the 10 percent decrease will affect almost all economic factors. These interdependencies must be considered if the effect of the tax cut is to be accurately predicted. (However, it must be remembered that while an econometric model may provide useful insights, the "effects" it captures will be those built into it.)

Econometric models are invaluable tools for increasing the understanding of the way an economic system works and for testing and evaluating alternative policies. These goals, however, are somewhat different from forecasting, where the main objective is predicting rather than understanding per se. Complex econometric models do not always perform better in forecasting than simpler time-series approaches. It is important to distinguish between econometric models used for policy analysis and econometric models used for forecasting. They are two different things. In the former usage, there is little doubt as to the usefulness and uniqueness of econometric models. For forecasting usage they must be examined more carefully and in the right perspective (see Part Six).

Econometric models for forecasting are generally much simpler and involve fewer equations than those designed for policy study. The main purpose of forecasting versions is to derive values for the independent variables so that they do not have to be estimated. In the simple econometric model of equations (7-1), for example, two of the variables—price and advertising—can be estimated internally. Thus there is no need to specify their values in order to forecast sales. GNP, on the other hand, still needs to be specified because it is determined outside or exogenously.

Whether intended for policy or forecasting purposes, econometric models are considerably more difficult to develop and estimate, as will be seen in Sections 7/3 and Appendix 7-A, than using alternative statistical methods. The difficulties are of two types:

1. technical aspects, involved in specifying the equations and estimating their parameters, and
2. cost considerations, related to the amount of data needed and the computing and human resources required.

In the final analysis, the question is whether the extra burden required for developing and running an econometric model justifies the costs involved. It is the authors' experience that the answer is *yes* if the user is a government, *maybe* if it is a large organization interested in policy considerations, and *probably not* if it is a medium or small organization or if the econometric model is intended for forecasting purposes only. The above guidelines do not apply to buying the services of one of the several econometric models now available commercially (Chase Econometrics, Data Resources, Inc., General Electric Forecasting Service, Wharton Econometric Forecasting Associates, etc.). Generally, the cost of using such services is only a small fraction of that of developing and operating one's own econometric model.

One of the major weaknesses of econometric models is the absence of a set of rules that can be applied across different situations. This makes the development of econometric models highly dependent upon the specific situation and requires the involvement of a skilled and experienced econometrician. Finally, once a model is developed, it cannot be left to run on its own with no outside interference. Continuous monitoring of the results and updating for periodic changes are needed. These disadvantages have limited the application of econometrics to forecasting in medium and small organizations, although the authors are aware of such applications at a medium-sized forest products firm and at a specialty chemical firm.

7/3 Specification and Identification

An econometric model includes a number of simultaneous equations, each of which includes several variables. Specification of the right kind and number of variables is important. If a significant variable is not included in a single equation, nonrandom errors will occur because an important factor influencing the dependent variable will have been omitted. In single equations situations, misspecification can be easily understood. In econometric models the task is much more difficult because absence of an important variable will influence all equations and result in nonrandom (that is, autocorrelated) residuals but give no indication of the equation(s) generating them. Similarly, the mere fact that there are many equations increases the chances of misspecification.

Identification of the exogenous factors needed in indirect least squares (ILS) and two-stage least squares (2SLS) is not always without problems, nor is it a completely objective choice. One must decide arbitrarily on the degree of influence of the different factors (variables) involved and choose those that are least determined within the system. In the income determination example of Appendix 7-A, government spending, Z_t, was selected as the exogenous variable not because it is influenced by the level of income or consumption, but rather because the mutual dependence is less than that between income and consumption. If a more detailed model were used, it might be better to make Z_t endogenous and select some other factor such as monetary policy as the exogenous variable.

Although in practice the definition of endogenous and exogenous variables may be nontrivial, once it is done, at least one equation must be specified for each of the endogenous variables. When the number of equations is equal to the number of endogenous variables, the model is referred to as just specified. When there are fewer endogenous variables than equations, the model is underspecified and one of the variables must be arbitrarily set to some value—it must become an exogenous factor—so that estimation will be possible. If the number of endogenous variables is greater than the number of equations, the model is overspecified. This latter form is most often used for estimating the parameters of simultaneous equations.

Another point relating to specification and the choice of exogenous and endogenous variables for econometric models is that of identification. Statistical data do not represent values of a single equation but are the combined result of a number of them. For example, consider a simple demand and supply function represented by a system of two equations:

$$Q_d = a + bp + u, \tag{7-2}$$

$$Q_s = a_1 + b_1 p + u, \tag{7-3}$$

where Q_d is the quantity demanded,

Q_s is the quantity supplied,

p is the corresponding price, and

u is the error term.

The statistical data available do not represent either (7-2) or (7-3). Rather, they are the points of intersection of the two equations, since this is the only point recorded. For example, in a stock market situation, the exact range of the demand and supply is not known, but only the point of their intersection represented by a specific transaction. The same is true for most recorded data. Approaches for identifying the supply and demand functions separately must be developed.

It can be observed that some variables fluctuate more widely in value than others. This variation will have an effect on the value of u, which will be larger in those equations. For example, one could assume (or show from past data) that the supply of agricultural products varies more widely because of prevailing weather conditions than because of fluctuating demand. If a factor could be identified that correlates with the magnitude of weather variations, it could be included in the supply equation, (7-3), and varied proportionally to the supply. If an exogenous factor, such as the amount of rainfall or the number of sunny days (call it r), is important in determining variations in supply, that factor should be included in (7-3):

$$Q_s = a_1 + b_1 p + b_2 r + u. \tag{7-4}$$

The role of r in equation (7-4) is a dual one. It can identify equation (7-3) from equation (7-2), and at the same time it can be used as an exogenous variable when applying methods such as 2SLS, which use the reduced form requiring exogenous variables. Demand and supply of agricultural products are rather easy to identify and therefore specify correctly. However, this is not true in many cases where identification can become a critical issue. With sales data, for example, it is difficult to distinguish demand and supply because demand figures include sales and unfilled demand when supply is less than demand. Another difficulty arises because there are several levels of inventory between the producer and the final consumers, which distort the data and introduce true lags. All these factors make the identification of demand and supply equations and variables a difficult task.

Whatever the complications that arise in specification and identification, their solution is well documented (see Fisher, 1966), and many argue that they are not as serious as the problems arising in the estimation process. Those problems, together with the need for appropriate data, often are the biggest challenge to development and estimation of econometric models.

7/4 Development and Application of Econometric Models

Econometric models are an interesting application of interdisciplinary research involving statisticians and economists. The mixture of the two has created a new discipline known as econometrics. Econometrics is interested in measuring economic theory through statistical methods. Econometric models involving systems of simultaneous equations are the most advanced and sophisticated part of the profession. The special problems encountered in specification and identification and in estimation as well as the size and complexity of the task, make the econometrician's job a challenging one.

Econometrics is mainly concerned with macroeconomic models. It was not until the late 1960s that the econometric model approach was used for forecasting purposes. The first econometric model had been built in 1939 by Tinbergen, but it was not until 1955 and the advent of computers that a comprehensive model of the U.S. economy was constructed by Klein and Goldberger (1955). This model became the prototype for the development of most other econometric models.

Initially, econometric models used yearly data, which created a serious problem because not enough data were available. In addition, aggregation destroyed intrayear effects, such as seasonal or cyclical variations, and minimized the usefulness of the models as a forecasting tool. These flaws were corrected through development of quarterly econometric models, the best known of which is the Oxford model, developed by Klein et al. in 1961. The Oxford model has been the basis for several of the quarterly models presently used by different forecasting econometric services.

The 1960s witnessed an expansion in the size and complexity of econometric models. This was illustrated by the construction of the Brookings model, which contains more than 200 equations (see Duesenberry et al., 1965). Economic activity was divided into industrial sectors, and separate equations were included for consumption, investment, foreign trade, government transactions, and so on. Through the mid-1970s, the Brookings model was by far the biggest and most complete of all econometric models, making it particularly well suited for testing and evaluating the impact of alternative economic policies.

Simultaneously there have been efforts to construct small models that can be used with limited amounts of data at reduced cost (see von Hohenbalken and Tintner, 1962). These smaller models have also been used for forecasting purposes (see Friend and Jones, 1964). Such models tend to require the estimation of fewer exogenous factors before they can be used. This tends to make them more economical but not necessarily less accurate.

To summarize, econometric models are difficult and costly to build and operate. They are generally aimed towards policymaking and their usefulness in forecasting is somewhat controversial (see Lesser, 1966). These characteristics have limited the development of econometric models by individual companies. However, econometric forecasts, and even econometric simulations can be purchased through several services at economical rates. These professional firms market their use as an alternative or complementary procedure to the other techniques discussed in this book. In addition, a number of multistate regions maintain econometric models such as those in New England that cover Massachusetts, Connecticut, New Hampshire, and Vermont.

With three examples, the remainder of this section will illustrate the different settings for which econometric models can be developed and some of the practical issues that must be addressed in their development and use. Given the variety of approaches that can be taken, and the ongoing debate among econometric "experts" as to the best approach, the intent here is not to illustrate good or bad procedures, but rather to give the reader some appreciation of both the potential attractiveness and the computational realities of such methods.

7/4/1 Forecasting GNP and Related Macroeconomic Variables[1]

McNees, a practicing econometrician with the Federal Reserve Bank of Boston, and Perna, a practicing econometrician with the General Electric Company, have outlined an eclectic approach to forecasting GNP and related macroeconomic variables (McNees and Perna, 1982). Their approach, summarized schematically in Figure 7-2, divides the task into three stages: (1) the components of real GNP, (2) unemployment and productivity, and (3) compensation, profits, and prices. Following a brief overview of the approach, a couple of the steps will be examined in some detail to illustrate how econometric issues can be dealt with in practice and how they can be complemented with selected use of other forecasting concepts.

In forecasting GNP and other important macroeconomic variables, it is helpful to start with the more "exogenous" components—those whose behavior is tied less closely to the current performance of the economy—and proceed toward the more "endogenous" variables whose behavior depends heavily on "everything else." Thus Step 1A begins with exports and federal government purchases, where initial estimates can be taken from external sources. In addition, the relatively accurate Commerce Department survey of capital spending plans provides a good initial estimate of nonresidential fixed investment.

Next (Step 1B), time-series or autoregressive equations can provide a good starting point for short-term estimates of state and local government purchases of goods and services and changes in business inventories. It is necessary to reestimate these equations frequently and to modify the longer run forecasts with other information, such as the passage of Proposition 13 in California in the late 1970s.

In Step 1C the ASA/NBER[2] median forecast of housing starts and personal consumption expenditures for durable goods (PCD) can be analyzed to provide a rough estimate of the frequency and amplitude of the phase of the current cycle. These forecasts must be revised again to reflect prospective financial conditions and institutional changes.

Finally, in Step 1D an econometric relationship in conjunction with

---

[1]Adapted from McNees and Perna (1982). Used by permission.

[2]See Appendix 7-B for references on macroeconomic data sources that are used frequently by econometric model builders in the United States.

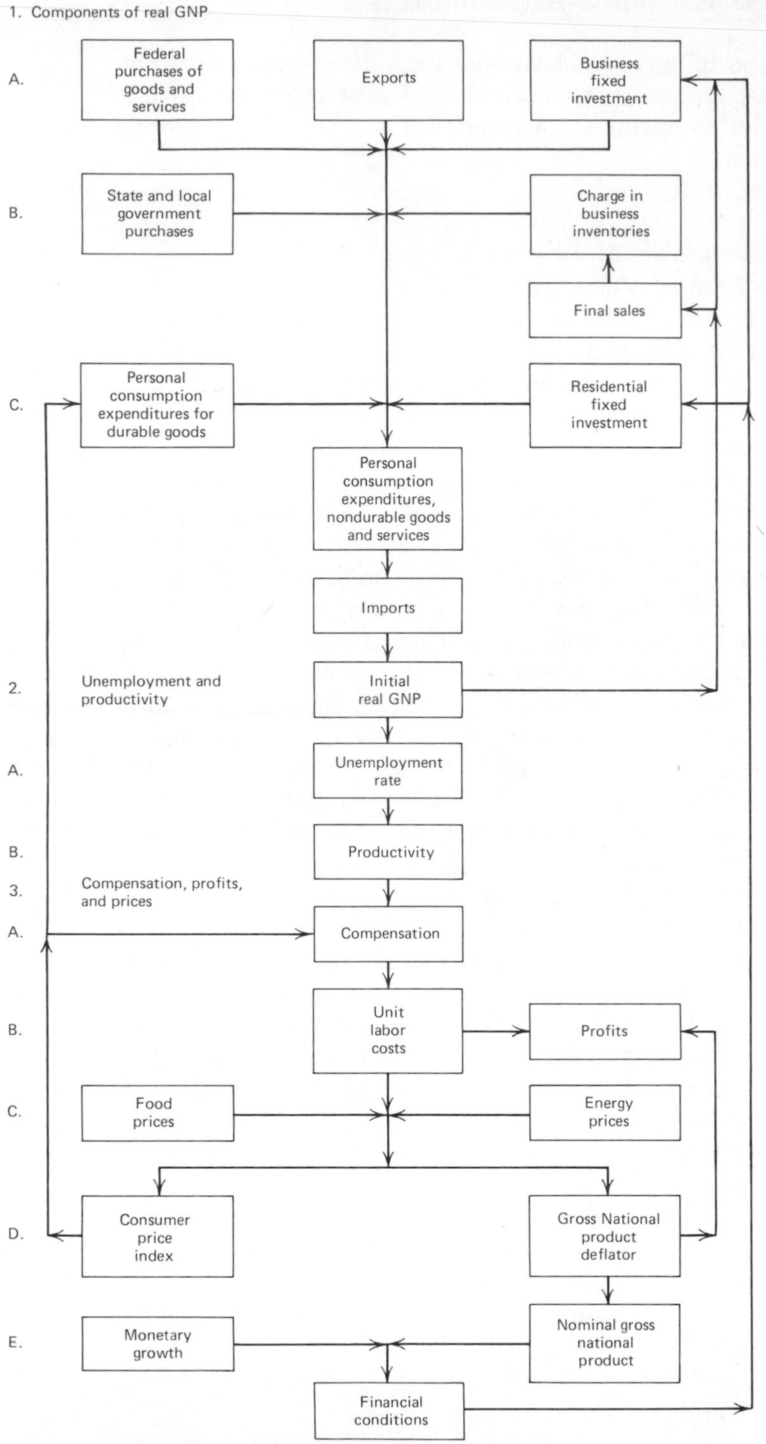

1. Components of real GNP

FIGURE 7-2 AN ECLECTIC APPROACH TO A MACROECONOMIC FORE-
CAST (McNEES AND PERNA, 1982)

some external information can be used to produce a forecast of personal consumption expenditures for nondurable goods and services and imports. Combining these steps produces an initial estimate of real GNP that should be used to go back and reassess the forecasts, especially those for business fixed and inventory investment. If these prospects are changed significantly, the whole process may have to be repeated until a consistent view emerges.

This process of a continuing series of iterations to insure consistency, both in the accounting and economic sense of the word, is common to all the stages of econometric forecasting processes. While a computer could be used to achieve some consistency in milliseconds, a key feature of the eclectic approach of Figure 7-2 is that forcing the forecaster to achieve consistency can sharpen his or her original insights.

Unemployment and Productivity

In comparison with the first stage, forecasting unemployment (Step 2A) and productivity (Step 2B) are relatively straightforward. However, once again, this stage may provide some insights that will call into question some of the forecasts generated in stage 1, and thus require one more pass through that stage.

Compensation, Profits, and Prices

Integrating the "real" forecast with the "nominal" outlook for compensation, profits, and prices is the most challenging phase of forecasting. Since the real spending decisions in stage 1 are acknowledged to depend on the rate of inflation, the results of stage 3 will probably require another pass at the preliminary forecasts generated in the earlier stages. In particular, the nominal GNP forecast combined with some assessment of the future course of monetary policy provides an important clue to prospective financial conditions. These conditions heavily influence consumer spending on durable goods and housing.

The stages outlined above and in Figure 7-2—starting with the *real* GNP and moving toward financial conditions—are probably the most appropriate approach for the production/sales decisions of nonfinancial businesses. Financial institutions and corporate treasurers would probably benefit from starting with the components of *nominal* GNP, combining these with monetary policy considerations to arrive at an impression of financial conditions, and turning then to prices in order to arrive at real GNP as a residual. More generally, the practical rule is: focus your primary attention on what you care most (and know most) about!

The nature of some of these iterative procedures can be illustrated by considering a couple of the specific steps outlined in Figure 7-2. We will look at estimating Personal Consumption Expenditures and Employee Compensation.

Personal Consumption Expenditures   The theory of consumer behavior is relatively well established: real consumer spending on services and nondurables goods (PCO) is related to its past value and some measure of income. Even though economic theory does not establish whether the effect of inflation would be positive or negative, a number of empirical studies suggest that consumption has been discouraged by inflation.

Theory also does not indicate which empirical measure of income is most appropriate. While several have been studied, they vastly complicate the forecasting process. As is often the case in forecasting, it is preferable to use a measure that is readily available (here, GNP) as a practical proxy for a theoretically ideal measure. In this case using GNP as an income measure does not reduce the accuracy of the forecast.

These considerations suggest the following econometric equation:[3]

$$\text{PCO}_t = -71.8 + .99\,\text{PCO}_{t-1} + .09\,\Delta\text{GNP}_t$$

$$+ .03\text{GNP}_{t-1} - 3.7\%\,\Delta\text{CPI}_t \tag{7-5}$$

A forecast of PCO requires projections of the right-hand side's "explanatory" variables. Typically, the explanatory variables include some of the other variables being forecasted (in this case GNP) so that the forecast must be generated iteratively. The most convenient way to begin is with some easily obtainable projections, such as those released by the CEA or the median forecast from the ASA/NBER survey. (See Appendix 7-B.)

For example, using the CEA forecast available in early 1979 for 1979 GNP (2.2 percent growth) and the Consumer Price Index, CPI (7.5 percent), the equation above implies that aggregate PCO would increase 4.1 percent in 1979, a large overestimate relative to the actual increase of 2.7 percent.

Much of the overestimate was due to incorrect forecasts of the explanatory variables in the equation. Using the actual values of GNP (1.0 percent) and the CPI (12.7 percent), the equation implies a 1.9 percent increase in PCO, an underestimate of what actually occurred. This shortfall is due partly to the influence of factors that the simple econometric equation ignores (and perhaps partly due to pure chance or bad luck!).

External factors were especially important in influencing the quarterly *pattern* of PCO. For example, the equation substantially overestimates actual consumer spending in the second quarter of 1979. The reason is now fairly obvious—the widespread gasoline shortages and lines. In this particular case, this negative factor was probably predictable in advance—the Iranian revolution occurred in late 1978. While some downward adjustment in the historical relationship was obviously necessary, the magnitude was

---

[3]The equation was fitted to real per capita data for PCO and GNP. Per capita predictions can be converted to aggregate predictions by using population projections. For a more complete discussion of the derivation and estimation of this form of consumption function, see Kuh and Schmalensee, 1973 (Chapter 3, pp. 31–49).

(as is often the case) inevitably a matter of judgment. Since the disturbance was virtually unprecedented, econometric or time-series modeling would have been of little help. The forecaster was forced to look back at the 1974 gasoline shortages and to gather anecdotal evidence in order to make an intelligent guess.

In the third quarter of 1979, PCO returned to the level that the historical econometric relationship indicated. However, in the final quarter of 1979 there was a strong surge that the equation did not predict. A wide variety of possible reasons for the spending spree were advanced—consumer sentiment, inflationary expectations, increases in personal wealth (particularly capital gains on houses), rising tax and energy burdens, and even distortions in the data.

Although virtually no forecaster identified the relevant factor and assessed in advance the magnitude of its impact, such speculation is an integral part of macroeconomic forecasting. To the extent that a forecast error can be traced to a specific external factor (rather than to purely random noise), that information can be used to improve future forecasts. If the hypothesized influence is believed to be systematic, that factor can be incorporated into the explicit econometric forecasting techniques.

On the other hand, forecasting accuracy can suffer if a forecaster "overexplains" past errors. The procedure of adding a new factor to "explain" each new large error will quickly generate so many "explanations" that attention will be drawn away from those few factors that exert a systematic, stable influence on the forecasted variable. "Correction" of recent errors can make future forecasts *worse* as well as *better*. (See Chapter 17.)

The major point of this example is that a simple econometric relationship, such as that given above for PCO, *is* useful to achieve consistency with previous historical patterns but should be used only as a benchmark for judgmental adjustments. There is no reason to think that the future will reflect only the past (indeed there are many reasons to expect that it won't), so that accurate forecasts must try to incorporate new information not captured in previous data.

At the same time, the forecaster must recognize there are few occasions when a "new" factor that will exert a *systematic* influence in the future can be identified.

Labor Compensation   The standard econometric approach links the growth in employee compensation (% ΔCOMP) to inflation (% ΔCPI) and variations in labor market conditions, as measured by changes in the unemployment rate, ΔUR. Estimated with annual data from 1955 to 1979, this equation,

$$\%\Delta\text{COMP}_t = 2.78 + 0.50\% \ \Delta\text{CPI}_t + 0.24\% \ \Delta\text{CPI}_{t-1} - 0.13 \ \Delta\text{UR}_t \tag{7-6}$$

overestimates compensation growth in 1979 by 1.5 percentage points, nearly twice its "normal" error. Two possible reasons for the overshooting are the impact of wage guidelines and the overstatement of inflation as measured by the CPI. With the personal consumption deflator, which treats home ownership differently, the 1979 error is cut in half.

To reduce such errors, procedures like those outlined for incorporating judgmental revisions could be applied. In addition, other forecasting methods might be used to estimate this same variable and to serve as a check on the econometric equation above. The exercises at the end of this chapter suggest one such alternative method.

7/4/2   Forecasting Domestic Ferrous Scrap Prices and Volumes[4]

The preceding section used a forecasting model of GNP and related macroeconomic variables to illustrate some of the realities associated with econometric methods. This section describes the overall structure and purposes of an industry-specific econometric model. The description is based on "Scrap: Prices and Issues" by Wise (1975), and illustrates the use of econometrics to predict prices and volumes (supply and demand) for iron and steel scrap.

The prices of scrap iron and steel have often behaved in unexpected ways. Since these prices and their resulting impact on supply and demand have a major effect on the profits of companies in the steel, scrap, and related industries, there are a substantial number of organizations concerned with their forecasting. As the actual values shown in Figure 7-3 indicate, domestic scrap usage (and exports) have not always moved consistently with prices, and vice versa. At times scrap prices have risen, even though scrap consumption has decreased. At other times prices have fallen, while usage has increased. These seemingly inconsistent patterns of market behavior can be explained when the full complexity of the scrap market is understood. Many important factors interact simultaneously, however, making simple analysis impossible and defying intuition. The econometric approach to predicting scrap volumes and their prices is one way of handling these complexities. Through the concepts of econometrics that have been described previously, a model can simultaneously account for the interaction of such factors as steel output, pig iron cost, exports of scrap, government policy, technological advances, and inventories.

The particular model described here was developed by Charles River Associates of Cambridge, Massachusetts, for its customers. It basically provides the following for those who use its outputs:

1.   A source of scrap prices for 1- and 2-year, and sometimes longer, profit forecasts.

---

[4]Adapted from Wise (1975). Used by permission.

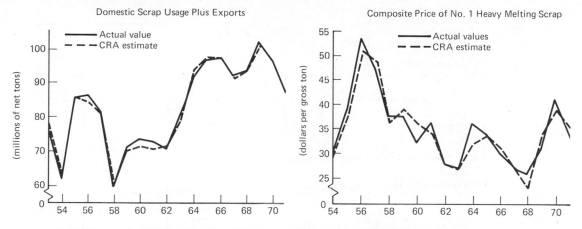

FIGURE 7-3 ECONOMETRIC MODEL FITTED VALUES VERSUS ACTUALS FOR QUANTITY AND PRICE MOVEMENTS OF FERROUS SCRAP

2. A source of market information to help top management keep tabs on their scrap purchasing operation.
3. A source of short-term price forecasts to enable inventory speculation. The model provides information corroborating that provided by scrap purchasers to treasurers and top management who must approve funds for large-scale inventory buildup.
4. Some special long-term scrap price forecasts that are suitable for use in preparing new facility plans.

In terms of the performance of this particular econometric model, Figure 7-3 summarizes actual domestic scrap usage plus exports from 1954 to 1971 and also provides actual and fitted values of the composite price of scrap for that same period. These results indicate the apparent usefulness of such an approach in this particular situation.

One of the key determinants of the success of such a forecasting use of an econometric model is the basic design of the model itself. Before an econometric model can be developed, a structural representation of the items that it represents and the various factors that it needs to include must be built. For the scrap situation such a structural representation is shown in Figure 7-4. This figure includes those items that affect scrap demand and supply, and items of general economic influence.

Once the basic structural relationship of different variables has been determined, the data can be collected. These data will be used in the same way that observations were used in estimating multiple regression coefficients in Chapter 6. In many instances these data must come from published sources or be generated for the specific model in question. As indicated previously, one of the reasons for the proprietary nature of many micro-

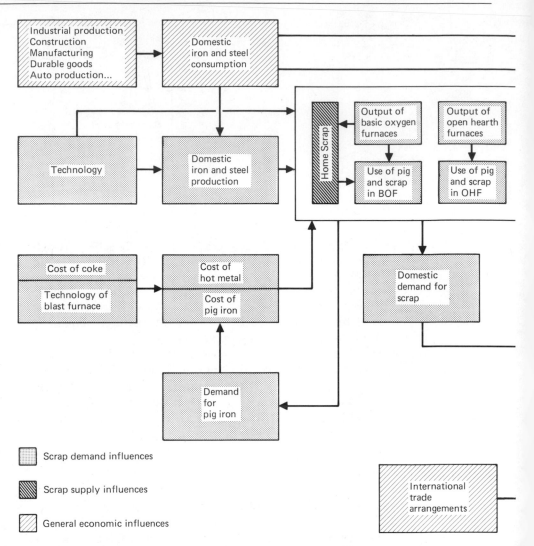

FIGURE 7-4 FACTORS INCLUDED IN THE ECONOMETRIC MODEL OF FERROUS SCRAP

econometric models, such as this one for forecasting ferrous scrap quantities and prices, is that the data are expensive to collect and are proprietary.

A major advantage claimed by those who develop econometric models for forecasting purposes is that those same models can be used to perform extensive analysis relevant to other issues of decision making. For example, in the case of the ferrous scrap model, there may be developments on the supply or demand side or changes in government legislation that will affect the quantities and price of ferrous scrap. These can be converted into assumptions suitable for incorporation in the model and tested in terms of

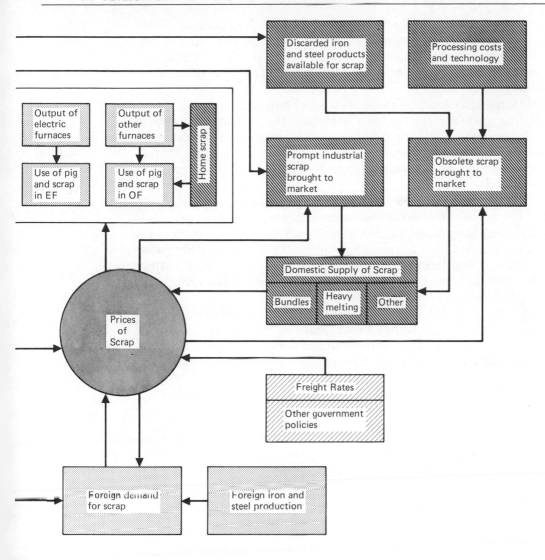

the model's sensitivity to those changes. Such a use can add substantially to the value of econometric modeling.

7/4/3 Incorporating an Econometric Model into the Practice of Corporate Forecasting, Planning, and Decision Making

In the preceding section a specific illustration of a microeconomic model was described. In that instance the outputs of the model were forecasts of prices and quantities for ferrous scrap. In many instances, additional steps in forecasting and planning can be closely tied to the use of the econometric model, especially within a single corporation. One such application reported in *Sales and Marketing Management* (1975) is illustrated in Figure 7-5.

In this particular example there are several different forecasting and decision-making models that have been linked together to more completely integrate the forecasting and planning tasks. The econometric model provides annual sales forecasts that can be used as the starting point for the planning process. (The organizational aspects of such integration are discussed further in Part Six.)

Thus, the econometric model expresses the relationship between company sales and a variety of economic indicators, such as GNP, personal consumption expenditures, and capital spending plans. A second model can be used at a more micro level to provide smooth estimates of monthly sales by product and seasonal factors for those, as well as perhaps incorporating still a third model based on a single multiple regression equation that will show the impact of past promotion on sales.

These three different forms of forecasting can then be used as the major source of input for projecting annual sales by product group. These forecasts can, in turn, serve as the basis for decisions being made at more detailed levels and for setting up performance review and evaluation procedures.

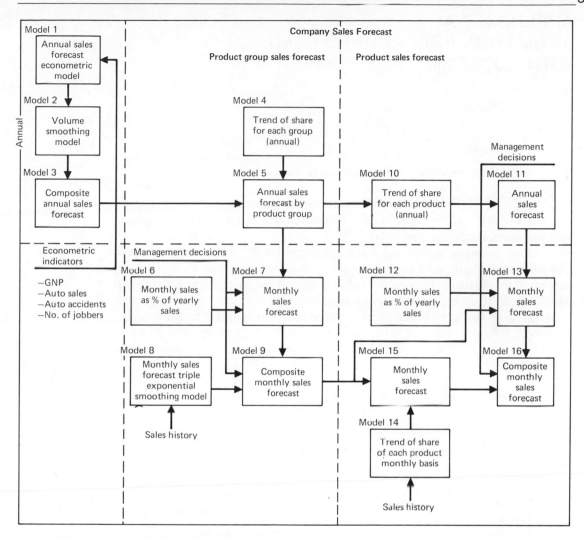

FIGURE 7-5 INTEGRATING ECONOMETRIC WITH OTHER FORECASTS WITHIN A COMPANY

APPENDIX 7-A
ESTIMATION PROCEDURES USED WITH ECONOMETRIC METHODS

In all estimating procedures it is important to obtain unbiased estimators. That means that as the sample size increases, the accuracy of the estimators must increase too. Thus, when the sample size is equal to the population size (as for a complete census), the estimates would be the values of the real population parameters.

The presence of bias in estimators can be checked by using basic procedures of statistics. The estimators of the parameters $a, b_1, b_2, \ldots, b_k$ obtained in multiple regression can be shown to be unbiased. Unfortunately, in systems of simultaneous equations, this is not the case, as can be illustrated using a classic income determination model. Consider:

$$C_t = a + bY_t + u_t, \tag{7-7}$$

$$Y_t = C_t + Z_t, \tag{7-8}$$

where C_t is consumption expenditure at period t,

Y_t is income (GNP) at period t,

Z_t is nonconsumption expenditure (such as government spending) at period t,

u_t is the error or disturbance term at period t.

Equation (7-7) states that consumption is a function of income, while equation (7-8) states that income is determined by consumption and government spending. Thus the independent variable, Y_t, of (7-3) is determined partly by the level of consumption (an endogenous variable) and partly by the outside factor, government spending (an exogenous variable). These two types of variables can be distinguished in a system of simultaneous equations—the endogenous (C_t, Y_t) and the exogenous (Z_t). A problem arises from the fact that the endogenous variables are related to each other. This relationship causes dependence between the dependent variable and the error term, u_t, which appears as a dependence among successive values of u_t. This dependence violates one of the assumptions of ordinary least squares (OLS) used in regression analysis.

The dependence between C_t and u_t in equation (7-7) can be seen by applying the OLS method to (7-7) and (7-8) and separately estimating the values of a and b.

Substituting (7-8) into (7-7),

$$C_t = a + b(C_t + Z_t) + u_t$$

or

$$C_t - bC_t = a + bZ_t + u_t,$$

$$C_t(1 - b) = a + bZ_t + u_t,$$

and

$$C_t = \frac{a}{1 - b} + \frac{b}{1 - b}Z_t + \frac{u_t}{1 - b}. \tag{7-9}$$

Letting

$$a_1 = \frac{a}{1 - b} \quad \text{and} \quad b_1 = \frac{b}{1 - b},$$

$$C_t = a_1 + b_1 Z_t + \frac{u_t}{1 - b}. \tag{7-10}$$

Equation (7-9) and its equivalent, (7-10), imply that there is a dependence between the dependent variable C_t and the error term, u_t. This dependence results in biased estimation of a_1 and b_1 in (7-10) as well as biased estimators for a and b of the original equations (7-7) and (7-8). The bias exists for both small and large sample sizes and can be predicted if one is willing to assume that the process variance is known. Its existence means that OLS cannot be used reliably to forecast when systems of simultaneous equations are involved, although in practice OLS is used extensively in such applications.

In order to avoid bias in estimation, alternative procedures have been introduced that can be applied with varying degrees of effort and success. The relative advantages and weaknesses of these methods have been debated extensively in the literature, but it is clear that their applicability depends on the characteristics of each particular situation. (See Chow, 1964 and Nager, 1959.) Several of the major alternative estimation procedures for econometric models are described below.

The full information maximum likelihood (FIML) method of estimation attacks the problem of interdependence among the different endogenous variables directly rather than in sequential steps as is done in many other methods. It constructs a matrix, W, which includes all exogenous and endogenous variables, and using a set of complex procedures based on maximum likelihood methods, solves for the parameters of the equations. The FIML estimation procedure was one of the first attempts to solve the problem of estimating the parameters of econometric models, but is one of the more difficult and expensive approaches of those currently available.

Close to FIML is the *limited information maximum likelihood* (LIML) method, which recognizes only part of the interdependence by estimating the values of each of the equations one at a time but only with respect to the exogenous variables. In each successive estimation, all previous information (estimated values) is substituted into the equation being estimated, accounting in a limited way for the existing dependence.

At the other extreme in terms of computational difficulties and theoretical rigor is the method of *indirect least squares* (ILS). It is similar to the OLS method but is applied to the reduced form of equations (7-7) and (7-8). The reduced form of a system of simultaneous equations can be obtained by successive subsituations of the original equations until all endogenous variables have been expressed as functions of only the exogenous variables. Equation (7-9) is of reduced form, since it expresses C_t, the dependent variable, in terms of the exogenous independent variable only, Z_t:

$$C_t = \frac{a}{1-b} + \frac{b}{1-b}Z_t + \frac{u_t}{1-b}. \tag{7-11}$$

Equation (7-8) can be expressed in a reduced form too by substituting (7-7) into (7-8):

$$Y_t = a + bY_t + Z_t + u_t,$$

$$Y_t(1-b) = a + Z_t + u_t,$$

and

$$Y_t = \frac{a}{1-b} + \frac{1}{1-b}Z_t + \frac{u_t}{1-b}. \tag{7-12}$$

Equations (7-11) and (7-12) are the reduced forms of (7-7) and (7-8). Through the substitutions

$$a_1 = \frac{a}{1-b}, \quad b_1 = \frac{b}{1-b}, \quad \text{and} \quad b_2 = \frac{1}{1-b}$$

in (7-11) and (7-12), the following are obtained:

$$C_t = a_1 + b_1 Z_t + \frac{u_t}{1-b}, \tag{7-13}$$

$$Y_t = a_1 + b_2 Z_t + \frac{u_t}{1-b}. \tag{7-14}$$

Equations (7-13) and (7-14) can be solved by OLS, since the only variable involved is Z, which is exogenous. The resultant estimators of a_1, b_1, and b_2 are unbiased and consistent when n, the sample size, is sufficiently large. However, the values of a and b, which will be found through a_1 and b_2, are biased but not inconsistent, an advantage over the OLS method. Even though the concept of ILS is rather simple, its computational complexities have led most researchers to use two-stages least squares in place of ILS.

The *two-stages least square* (2SLS) method lies somewhere between the FIML and the ILS. It combines some of the advantages and limitations of both, but at the same time it is practical, the estimated values are not inconsistent, and the bias is small if the sample size is sufficiently large. In practice it is used more than any other method for simultaneous equation estimation, since it performs well when n is small and does better than FIML when the equations are misspecified (see Summers, 1965).

In 2SLS one must first choose one of the endogenous variables as the independent one—Y in the previous example—then try to eliminate the dependence of C on u. This is achieved by applying OLS to the reduced form of equation (7-14) so that the values of a_1 and b_2 can be found. These are then substituted into the original equation (7-7) as follows:

$$C_t = a + bY_t + u_t, \tag{7-15}$$

$$Y_t = a_1 + b_2 Z_t. \tag{7-16}$$

Substituting Y_t of (7-16) into (7-15) gives

$$C_t = a + ba_1 + bb_2 Z_t + u_t,$$

or

$$C_t = a_3 + b_3 Z_t + u_t, \tag{7-17}$$

where

$$a_3 = a + ba_1 \quad \text{and} \quad b_3 = bb_2.$$

Equation (7-17) includes only exogenous variables and C_t is not dependent on u_t. Thus, it is an unbiased and consistent form of estimation. The problem with 2SLS is that it does not take into consideration the full extent of interdependence among the different equations, since it is applied in a sequential manner, causing some of the dependence to be lost.

Finally, one can apply *three-stages least squares* (3SLS), which is usually, although not always, more efficient than 2SLS. This method accounts for the interdependence of equations in a more holistic way than 2SLS. The advantage of greater asymptotic efficiency applies only when the sample size is very large, and the method has little practical value for all but a limited number of cases, even though computationally it is not much more involved than the 2SLS.

APPENDIX 7-B
FORECASTING TECHNIQUES AND DATA SOURCES FOR U.S. MACROECONOMIC VARIABLES[5]

Macroeconomic forecasters can draw on a large body of published projections for help in formulating and evaluating their own. Among the most important sources are the following:

1. The median forecast of 11 variables from the *Business Outlook Survey* conducted quarterly by the American Statistical Association and the National Bureau of Economic Research.
2. Export and import forecasts published semiannually in the Organization for Economic Cooperation and Development's *Economic Outlook.*
3. Quarterly surveys of business capital spending plans, published quarterly in the *Survey of Current Business.*
4. Information on automobile sales, production, inventories, and pricing published weekly in *Ward's Automotive Reports* and several newspapers.
5. The *Budget of the U.S. Government* and the *Mid-Session Review of the Budget,* for projections of federal spending and tax policies and the underlying economic assumptions.
6. Periodic forecasts of food and energy prices issued by the U.S. Departments of Agriculture and Energy, reported in major newspapers.
7. In addition, many forecasters subscribe to at least one of the major commercial forecasting services.

The relationship of these sources to various macroeconomic variables and alternative macroeconomic variables and alternative forecasting techniques is shown below. Publication addresses for each of these sources, as of 1982, are also indicated.

---

[5]Adapted from McNees and Perna (1982). Used by permission.

Macroeconomic Variable	Techniques	Sources
Personal consumption:		
Durable Goods	3,4,2	ASA/NBER
Auto Sales	3,4	WARD'S
Personal consumption, other	2	ASA/NBER
Residential investment	3,4	ASA/NBER
Housing starts	3,4	ASA/NBER
Business fixed investment	4,2	BEA,ASA/NBER
Federal government purchases	4	BEA,ASA/NBER
State and local government purchases	1	ASA/NBER
Exports	4,1	OECD
Imports	4,2	OECD
Change in business inventories	1,3	BEA
Unemployment rate	2,1,4	CEA
Productivity	2,3	CEA
Compensation	2,4,3	BLS
GNP price deflator	4,2	BLS,CEA
Consumer price index	4,2	USDA,USDE

Key to techniques: 1 = Time-series methods
                         2 = Econometric relationships
                         3 = Cyclical comparisons
                         4 = External sources

Sources:

1. *ASA/NBER:* Business Outlook Survey. *Published quarterly (March, June, September, December). Available from the American Statistical Association, 806 15th St., N.W., Washington, DC 20005. (202) 393-3253. Subscription price: $20/year.*

2. *OECD:* Economic Outlook. *Published semiannually (July and December). Available from OECD Publications and Information Center, Suite 1207, 1750 Pennsylvania Avenue, Washington, DC 20006. (202) 724-1857. Subscription price: $17.50/year.*

3. *BEA:* Survey of Current Business. *Published monthly by the Bureau of Economic Analysis of the U.S. Department of Commerce. Surveys of business capital spending plans for the current and two subsequent quarters appear in the March, June, September, and December issues. Budget information typically appears in the February issue. Available from the Superintendent of Documents, U.S. Government Printing Office, Washington, DC 20402. Subscription price (12 issues): $35/year by first class mail; $22/year by second class mail; single issue price: $1.90.*

4. *Ward's:* Ward's Automotive Reports. *Published weekly. Available from Ward's Communications Inc., 28 W. Adams Street, Detroit, MI 48225. (313) 962-4433. Subscription price: $325/year including hardbound yearbook.*

5. Budget of the U.S. Government. *Published semiannually (January and July). Available from the Superintendent of Documents, U.S. Government Printing Office, Washington, DC 20402. Price: $5.00 for fiscal year 1981 budget.*

6. *BLS:* Monthly Labor Review. *Published monthly by the Bureau of Labor Statistics of*

the U.S. Department of Labor. *Available from the Superintendent of Documents, U.S. Government Printing Office, Washington, DC 20402. Subscription price $18.00/year. Single issue price: $2.50.*

7. *CEA:* Annual Report. *Contained in the* Economic Report of the President. *Published annually in January. Available from the Superintendent of Documents, U.S. Government Printing Office, Washington, DC 20402. Price: $4.75 for 1980 report.*

8. *Department of Agriculture:* Agricultural Outlook. *Published 10 times per year. Available from the Superintendent of Documents, U.S. Government Printing Office, Washington, DC 20402. Subscription price: $19/year.*

9. *USDE:* Short-Term Energy Outlook. *Published monthly by the Energy Information Administration of the U.S. Department of Energy. Available from the Superintendent of Documents, U.S. Government Printing Office, Washington, DC 20402. Price: $13/year. Single issue price: $4.00.*

Note: Additional data sources are discussed in Chapter 11.

REFERENCES AND SELECTED BIBLIOGRAPHY

Aaker, D. 1971. *Multivariate Analysis in Marketing*. Belmont, Calif.: Wadsworth.

Bowden, R. J. 1978. *The Econometrics of Disequilibrium*. Amsterdam: North-Holland.

Chow, G. C. 1964. "A Comparison of Alternative Estimators for Simultaneous Equations." *Econometrica*, **32,** pp. 532–33.

Duesenberry, J. S., G. Fromm, L. R. Klein, and E. Kuh (eds.). 1965. *The Brookings Quarterly Econometric Model of the United States*. Chicago: Rand McNally.

Fair, R. C. 1974 and 1976. *A Model of Macroeconomic Activity*, 2 vols. Cambridge, Mass.: Lippincott, Bollinger.

Fisher, F. M. 1966. *The Identification Problem in Econometrics*. New York: McGraw-Hill.

Friend, J., and R. C. Jones. 1964. "Short-Run Forecasting Models Incorporating Anticipatory Data," in *Models of Income Determination*. New York: National Bureau of Economic Research.

Halvorsen, R. 1978. *Econometric Models of U.S. Energy Demand*. Lexington, Mass.: Lexington Books.

Johnston, J. 1972. *Econometric Methods*, 2nd ed. New York: McGraw-Hill.

Klein, L. R. (ed.). 1969–1971. *Essays in Industrial Economics*, Vols. 1–3. Philadelphia: Economics Research Unit, Wharton School of Finance and Commerce, University of Pennsylvania.

―――, and A. S. Goldberger. 1955. *An Econometric Model of the United States, 1929–1952*. Amsterdam: North-Holland.

―――, and R. M. Young. 1980. *An Introduction to Econometric Forecasting and Forecasting Models*. Lexington, Mass.: D. C. Heath.

Kuh, E., and R. L. Schmalensee. 1973. *An Introduction to Applied Macroeconomics*. Amsterdam: North-Holland.

Lambin, J. J. 1976. "Advertising," in *Competition and Market Conduct in Oligopoly Over Time: An Economic Investigation in Western Countries*. Amsterdam: North-Holland.

Lesser, C. E. V. 1966. "The Role of Macro-Models in Short-Term Forecasting." *Econometrica*, **34,** pp. 862–72.

―――. 1968. "A Survey of Econometrics." *Journal of the Royal Statistical Society*, Series A, **131,** pp. 530–66.

McNees, S. K., and N. S. Perna. 1982. "Forecasting Macroeconomic Variables," in *Handbook of Forecasting*, S. Makridakis and S. C. Wheelwright (eds.). New York: John Wiley and Sons, Inc.

Murphy, J. L. 1973. *Econometrics*. Homewood, Ill.: Richard D. Irwin.

Nager, A. L. 1959. "The Bias and Moment Matrix of the General K-Class Estimators of the Parameters in Simultaneous Equations." *Econometrica,* **27,** pp. 575–95.

Pindyck, R. S., and D. L. Rubenfeld. 1976. *Econometric Models and Economic Forecasts.* New York: McGraw-Hill.

Sales and Marketing Management. 1975. "Special Report: Forecasting for High Profits."

Summers, R. 1965. "A Capital-Intensive Approach to the Small Sample Properties of Various Simultaneous Equation Estimators." *Econometrica,* **33,** pp. 1–41.

Tinbergen, J. 1939. *Business Cycles in the United States of America, 1919–32.* Geneva: League of Nations.

von Hohenbalken, B., and G. Tintner. 1962. "Econometric Models of the O.E.E.C. Member Countries, the United States and Canada, and Their Application to Economic Policy." *Weltwirtschaftliches Archiv,* **89,** pp. 29–86.

Wise, K. T. 1975. "Scrap: Prices and Issues." *Iron and Steelmaker,* May, pp. 23–32.

Young, R. M. 1982. "Forecasting with an Econometric Model: The Issue of Judgmental Adjustment." *Journal of Forecasting,* **1,** No. 2, pp. 189–204.

EXERCISES

1. Refer to the forecasting model for GNP and related macroeconomic variables described in Section 7/4/1 and presented schematically in Figure 7-2.

    a. A major element of stage 2 of this forecasting system—estimating productivity—can be addressed using an econometric approach. Productivity, defined as the real output per hour of work in nonfinancial corporations or PROD, can be related to the annual rate of growth of real GNP (% ΔGNP), the change in the rate of growth of real GNP, and a simple time trend:

    $$\% \; \Delta \text{PROD} = 3.1 + 0.11 \; \% \; \Delta \text{ real GNP} + 0.33 \; \Delta(\%\text{real GNP}) - 0.08T.$$

    Like other cyclical variables, productivity depends on both the growth rate of GNP and changes in its growth rate. This equation provides an overly optimistic view of productivity performance. Like all of the equations in this system, it is intended as an aid in forecasting and does not attempt to unravel the causes of the mysterious slowdown in productivity.

    i. In a manner analogous to that described in 7/4/1 for Personal Consumption Expenditures, outline the steps that might be followed in revising initial estimates of this variable. How sensitive is the change in productivity to revisions in the GNP estimates? (You might relate this to the sensitivity of personal consumption expenditures to GNP estimates.)

    ii. What other variables might be included in the right-hand side of this equation? (For example, variables related to the business cycle or long-term causal variables.)

b. In forecasting employee compensation [equation (7-6)], an alternative to econometrics is a "bottom-up" approach that adds together the components of total compensation—union wages, nonunion wages, fringe benefits, and payroll taxes.

Union wages are those paid to workers covered by collective bargaining agreements. They consist of cost of living adjustments (COLAs), new settlements, and fixed (nonCOLA) deferred increases. The "average" COLA provision has a 0.6 "elasticity" with respect to increases in the CPI: a 10 percent increase in the CPI produces a 6 percent increase in wages. Escalator payments can be generated with an outside forecast of the CPI. New settlements can be estimated by examining the recent history of first year fixed increases with some modification for the government's current wage guidelines or the start of a new pattern. At the start of each year, the Bureau of Labor Statistics publishes estimates of the fixed increases in major contracts scheduled for the year. In 1979, this estimate was 5.1 percent.

The weight for each of the three components of union wages indicates the proportion of workers under collective bargaining agreements receiving each kind of increase during the year. In 1979, for example, about 60 percent of union workers were scheduled for deferred increases from previously negotiated contracts. However, these weights can add to more than 1 because many workers receive more than one type of increase in a year and the weights shift over the course of a 3-year collective bargaining cycle. A heavy bargaining year like 1979 has a higher proportion of first year increases and a smaller fraction of fixed increases from earlier contracts than 1981, a year with a light bargaining calendar.

Nonunion wages tend to move like union wages, but exhibit greater sensitivity to variations in labor market conditions. More precisely, the difference between the growth of union wages and nonunion wages has varied systematically with the unemployment rate:

(% change in union wages) − (% change in nonunion wages)
    − 2.0 + 0.5 UR.

Total Labor Compensation can be estimated using the combined estimates of union and nonunion wages, and weights based on the fact that from 1970–1979, compensation has grown about one percentage point faster than *wages* because of increases in the cost of fringe benefits and payroll taxes. Since payroll tax increases vary from year to year, the exact adjustment would have to be estimated explicitly each year. These weights can be used to obtain the following 1979 estimates.

Using the CEA's CPI and UR forecasts for 1979, both the macroeconometric wage equation and the "bottom-up" approach accurately predicted the 8.8 percent increase in compensation per hour in 1979. Even though their predictions were perfect, the techniques were right for the wrong reasons! Based on the actual 11.3 percent increase in the CPI, both approaches would have overestimated 1979 compensation growth by 1.5 percentage points, about twice their "normal" error. One reason for this overshooting may be the overstatement of domestic inflation as measured by the CPI. With the personal consumption expenditures deflator, which

	Increase (%)	Weight	Contribution
a. *Union Wages*			
Cost of living adjustments[a]	4.9	0.45	2.2
First year settlements[b]	8.0	0.40	3.2
Deferred fixed increases	5.1	0.60	3.1
Union wage change			8.5%
b. *Nonunion:* Equals union plus/minus unemployment adjustments[a]			7.5%
c. *Average of union and nonunion wages*			7.7%
d. *Further adjustments*			
Add-on for fringes and payroll taxes:			1.0%
Labor compensation: per hour			8.7%

[a]Based on January 1979 CEA forecast.

[b]Assumed equal to previous year.

treats the costs of home ownership differently, the 1979 error would have been about normal. In addition, both approaches ignored the President's 1979 wage guidelines. Even if the techniques were valid for noncontrol periods, they would need to be adjusted for wage guidelines, if those controls were effective. Further research would be needed to sort out the relative importance of each of these reasons for the overshooting.

    i. How might this macroeconometric approach be combined with a CPI equation to produce a wage and price forecast?

    ii. What are the strengths and weaknesses of each of these two approaches—econometric and bottom-up—for forecasting employee compensation? Under what circumstances would each be preferred over the other?

    iii. How might the use of both the econometric equation and the "bottom-up" approach be combined to isolate key factors underlying these numerical forecasts of employee compensation?

C. The preceding forecasts of productivity and compensation were all in terms of year-over-year percentage changes. In many situations, however, quarterly—rather than annual—forecasts are required. While the econometric equations can be estimated from quarterly data, the "bottom-up" approach to compensation is feasible only on an annual basis. There are, however, judgmental techniques available for translating annual forecasts—no matter how obtained—into a quarterly pattern.

    In recent years, most of the quarterly variability of compensation has occurred in the first quarter of the year (see Figure 7-6a). The main reason for this is the legislated increases in Social Security tax liabilities which take effect at the beginning of each year; these can be forecast from data contained in the federal budget.

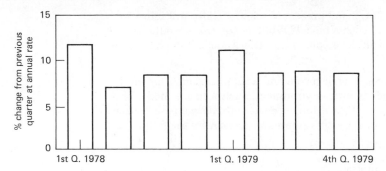

FIGURE 7-6A   U.S. EMPLOYEE COMPENSATION PER HOUR

Productivity, on the other hand, has regular quarterly movements over the course of the several (or more) years that comprise the business cycle. The 1973–1975 experience (see Figure 7-6*b*) is fairly typical. Productivity began to falter shortly before the business cycle peak, fell during much of the recession, and then began to pick up again just before the bottom of the recession. Thus, a form of the cyclical comparison technique (described in Chapter 12) can be used to fit quarterly patterns to the annual productivity forecast obtained from the economic equation.

  i. Outline a procedure for converting annual employee compensation estimates to quarterly estimates. Apply that procedure to an estimate for 1979 United States employee compensation.
 ii. Outline a procedure for converting annual productivity estimates to quarterly estimates. Apply that procedure to an estimate for 1979 United States productivity.
iii. What are the pros and cons of such procedures for obtaining quarterly estimates? How do those compare with the preparation and use of forecasting models using quarterly data directly?

2.   Refer to the econometric model of prices and quantities of steel and iron

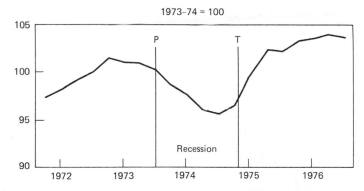

FIGURE 7-6B   OUTPUT PER HOUR—NONFINANCIAL INSTITUTIONS

scrap described in Section 7/4/2 and presented schematically in Figure 7-4. What are the possible uses of such a model? What do you think would be the major issues to be resolved in development of such a model? In the use of the results of such a model?

3.   Locate a description of an econometric model and its application. (This might be a private firm's model of its own environment, such a firm's model of a major sector of the economy, or a government model.) Prepare an evaluation of the model in the form of an executive summary that covers the following:
   a. The scope.
   b. Its purposes.
   c. Its major structural assumptions.
   d. Its input data.
   e. Its output data.
   f. The type of organization that might find it most useful.
   g. Caveats that such an organization should keep in mind when using it.
   h. The recent performance of the model (in comparison with actual outcomes).

PART FOUR
BOX-JENKINS (ARIMA)
TIME-SERIES METHODS

With the advent of widespread computer availability in organizations, the much more general and statistical based methods of time-series analysis known as Box-Jenkins or ARIMA (autoregressive/integrated/moving average) processes have been developed further and applied to forecasting. Part Four covers these more mathematically sophisticated approaches. The essence of this class of methods is similar to smoothing and decomposition in that forecasts are based on historical time-series analysis. However, the approach used in identifying the patterns in such historical time series and the methodology for extrapolating those patterns into the future are based on well-developed statistical theory.

While these autoregressive/integrated/moving average approaches are theoretically and statistically very appealing, their complexity has in many instances hindered their widespread adoption as a basis for forecasting in organizations. In order to use these methodologies, substantial analysis of historical time-series data must be performed, appropriate models must be estimated, and those models must be applied for forecasting purposes. While several useful guidelines have been developed to handle each of these tasks, there is still a substantial need for experience and some trial and error in successfully using these approaches.

Chapter 8 presents the basic elements of all autoregressive/moving average schemes for time-series analysis. This includes an introduction to the types of models that can be developed and the methodological tools found to be useful in determining the model most likely to be appropriate for a specific set of time-series data. In addition, such fundamental procedures as those for recognizing and dealing with nonstationarity and seasonality are discussed.

Chapter 9 examines the Box-Jenkins approach to ARIMA forecasting applications. Their three-phase approach of identification, estimation and testing, and application is described and the details of its use in practice are illustrated. A number of graphs are included to show how such methodologies as autocorrelations, partials, and line spectrum—described in Chapter 8—can be applied.

Chapter 10 describes the extension of the Box-Jenkins methodology to multivariate (transfer function) time-series analysis involving two or more data series. Although extremely complex, this methodology is finding increased application among forecasters, and a complete worked example is included in this chapter.

8/FUNDAMENTALS OF TIME-SERIES ANALYSIS

8/1 Introduction

As indicated in preceding chapters, application of a general class of forecasting methods involves two basic tasks: *analysis* of the data series and *selection* of the forecasting model (that is, the specific method within that class) that best fits the data series. Thus in using a smoothing method, analysis of the data series for seasonality aids in selection of a specific smoothing method that can handle the seasonality (or its absence). A similar sequence of analysis and selection is used in working with decomposition methods and regression methods. Thus, in this fourth section of the book on general time-series methods, it will come as no surprise that the same two tasks of analysis and model selection occur again. This chapter will concentrate on the former task of analysis and the subsequent two chapters will concentrate on model selection (and forecast preparation).

With regard to a general approach to time-series analysis, this chapter has four main purposes:

1. introduction of the various *concepts* useful in time-series analysis (and forecasting);
2. definition of some general *notation* (that proposed by Box and Jenkins, 1970) for dealing with time-series models;
3. description of the *statistical tools* that have proved useful in analyzing time series; and
4. illustrations of how the concepts, notation, and statistical tools can be combined to aid analysis of a wide variety of time series.

The remainder of this introduction will relate the general class of time-series forecasting methods described in this Part Four, to the three classes of methods discussed in Parts Two and Three.

In Part Two of this book, two major categories of time-series forecasting techniques were examined: smoothing and decomposition. Smoothing methods base their forecasts on the principle of averaging (smoothing) past errors by adding a percentage of the error to a percentage of the previous forecast. Mathematically, single smoothing methods are of the form:

$$F_{t+1} = F_t + \alpha(X_t - F_t)$$

$$= F_t + \alpha(e_t). \tag{8-1}$$

Equation (8-1) can be expanded by substituting

$$F_t = F_{t-1} + \alpha(X_{t-1} - F_{t-1}).$$

Thus

$$F_{t+1} = F_{t-1} + \alpha(X_{t-1} - F_{t-1}) + \alpha(X_t - F_t)$$

$$= F_{t-1} + \alpha(e_{t-1}) + \alpha(e_t). \tag{8-2}$$

And substituting for F_{t-1} in the first term of (8-2) gives

$$F_{t+1} = F_{t-2} + \alpha(e_{t-2}) + \alpha(e_{t-1}) + \alpha(e_t). \tag{8-3}$$

The results of further expanding this substitution should be clear. Given some initial forecast, call it F_{t-2}, new forecasts can be obtained by adding a percentage of the errors between the actual and forecast values (e.g., $X_{t-2} - F_{t-2}$) to this initial forecast, F_{t+1}, will be close to the actual pattern of data, on average.

Time-series decomposition methods are based on the principle of "breaking down" a time series into each of its components of seasonality, trend, cycle, and randomness and then forecasting by predicting each component separately (except randomness, which cannot be predicted) and re-combining those predictions. Both smoothing and decomposition methods express their forecasts as a function of time only.

Another approach to forecasting was discussed in Part Three. This approach included the causal or explanatory methods, with emphasis on regression. In general, regression methods attempt to forecast variations in some variable of interest, the dependent variable, on the basis of variations in a number of other factors, the independent variables. In multiple regression, for example, the causal or explanatory model is of the form:

$$Y = b_0 + b_1X_1 + b_2X_2 + \cdots + b_kX_k + e, \tag{8-4}$$

where Y is the dependent variable, X_1 through X_k are the independent variables, b_0 through b_k are the linear regression coefficients, and e is the error term.

In this chapter, the focus will be on a combination of the principles examined in Parts Two and Three. Some of the same principles used in regression will be applied to time-series methods, as indicated below.

In equation (8-4), $X_1, X_2, ..., X_k$ can represent any factors such as GNP, advertising, prices, money supply, and so on. Suppose, however, that these variables are defined as $X_1 = Y_{t-1}$, $X_2 = Y_{t-2}$, $X_3 = Y_{t-3}$, ..., $X_k = Y_{t-k}$. Equation (8-4) then becomes

$$Y_t = a + b_1Y_{t-1} + B_2Y_{t-2} + \cdots + b_kY_{t-k} + e_t. \tag{8-5}$$

Equation (8-5) is still a regression equation, but differs from (8-4) in that the right-hand side variables of (8-4) are different independent factors, while those of (8-5) are previous values of the dependent variable Y_t. These are simply time-lagged values of the dependent variable, and therefore the name *autoregression* (AR) is used to describe equations or schemes of the form of (8-5). By examining equation (3-21), which is shown below, it can be seen that the method of single exponential smoothing has a form very similar to (8-5).

$$F_{t+1} = \alpha X_t + \alpha(1 - \alpha)X_{t-1} + \alpha(1 - \alpha)^2 X_{t-2}$$

$$+ \alpha(1 - \alpha)^3 X_{t-3} + \alpha(1 - \alpha)^4 X_{t-4} + \cdots \text{ etc.} \tag{3-21}$$

In forecasting with exponential smoothing the past values are weighted by using the coefficients (parameters) α, $\alpha(1 - \alpha)$, $\alpha(1 - \alpha)^2$, $\alpha(1 - \alpha)^3$, ...

One question that arises from considering equation (8-5) is why regression that is applied to a time series (that is, autoregression) should be treated differently from ordinary least squares (OLS) regression models (Chapters 5 and 6). The answer is twofold:

1. In autoregression the basic assumption of independence of the error (residual) terms can easily be violated, since the independent (right-hand side) variables in equation (8-5) usually have a built-in dependence relationship.[1]
2. Determining the number of past values of Y_t to include in equation (8-5) is not always straightforward.

In a similar manner, equation (8-5) can be written in terms of past-error terms, as follows:

$$Y_t = a + b_1 e_{t-1} + b_2 e_{t-2} + \cdots + b_k e_{t-k} + e_t. \tag{8-6}$$

Here, explicitly, a dependence relationship is set up among the successive error terms, and the equation is called a *moving average* (MA) model.[2] Note the relation to equation (8-3).

Autoregressive (AR) models can be effectively coupled with moving average (MA) models to form a very general and useful class of time-series models called autoregressive/moving average (ARMA) schemes or processes.

In Section 8/2 some fundamentals of these general models will be discussed from the point of view of the model builder. Then, in Section 8/3 we examine some of the basic methodological tools available for analyzing

---

[1] For example, suppose $Y_t = a + bY_{t-1} + e_t$. Then

$$Y_{t+1} = a + bY_t + e_{t+1}$$

$$= a + b(a + bY_{t-1} + e_t) + e_{t+1}$$

$$= (a + ab) + b^2 Y_{t-1} + (be_t + e_{t+1}).$$

The error term at time t is e_t. The error term at time $t + 1$ is $(be_t + e_{t+1})$, which is very clearly a function of e_t. In other words, the errors at times t and $t + 1$ are not independent.

[2] The usage of the phrase *moving average* in this time-series terminology should not be confused with the use of the same phrase in the section on smoothing methods. These are very different uses of the same phrase. Throughout this and the next two chapters, *moving average* is used only in reference to a series of terms involving errors at different time periods, as shown in equation (8-6).

a given time series—with a view to selecting an appropriate model. Finally, Section 8/4 provides some illustrative examples of using these tools in time-series analysis.

8/2 Models for Time-Series Data

In Chapter 3 it was shown that smoothing methods should not be used indiscriminately, but rather that the characteristics of the time series should be identified in order to select an appropriate smoothing method. A similar phase should precede use of the ARIMA[3] models that will be discussed in the next three chapters. Identifying characteristics of a series such as stationarity, seasonality, and so on, requires a systematic approach, and it will help to have a clear picture of the basic models to be considered.

8/2/1 A Random Model: ARIMA (0,0,0)

Equation (8-7) is a simple random model where observation Y_t is made up of two parts, an overall mean, μ, and a random error component, e_t, which is independent from period to period.

ARIMA (0,0,0)

$$Y_t = \mu + e_t \tag{8-7}$$

It is classified as ARIMA (0,0,0) because there is no AR aspect to it (Y_t does not depend on Y_{t-1}), there is no differencing involved, and there is no MA process (Y_t does not depend on e_{t-1}). Figure 8-1a shows a typical ARIMA (0,0,0) data series.

8/2/2 A Nonstationary Random Model: ARIMA (0,1,0)

Equation (8-8) looks like an AR process because Y_t depends on Y_{t-1}, but when the coefficient of Y_{t-1} is unity, the equation can be rewritten as equation (8-9) to show that *first differences* of the Y_t series form a random model.

---

[3]The abbreviation ARIMA stands for "autoregressive integrated moving average model." The word "integrated" is confusing to many and refers to the "differencing" of the data series, which is explained in 8/2/2. The three numbers following ARIMA refer to the degree of the AR process, the degree of differencing, and the degree of the MA process. These terms will become clear as the various models are explained. Box and Jenkins (1976) popularized the abbreviation ARIMA.

ARIMA (0,1,0)

$$Y_t = Y_{t-1} + e_t \qquad (8\text{-}8)$$

$$Y_t - Y_{t-1} = e_t \qquad (8\text{-}9)$$

It is often convenient to redefine $(Y_t - Y_{t-1})$ as W_t, the first-difference series, so that we can then talk about W_t as a stationary series, whereas Y_t is nonstationary. This concept, stationarity, can be described in practical (non-statistical) terms as follows:[4]

1. If a time series is plotted and there is no evidence of a change in the mean over time [e.g., Figure 8-1a], then we say the series is stationary in the mean.
2. If the plotted time series shows no obvious change in the variance over time, then we say the series is stationary in the variance.
3. Figure 8-1b shows a typical ARIMA (0,1,0) data series, where the mean "wanders" (with some trend-cycle pattern) over time. This is a time-series that is nonstationary in the mean.
4. Figure 8-1c shows a time-series that is nonstationary in both mean and variance. The mean wanders (changes over time), and the variance (or standard deviation) is not reasonably constant over time.

8/2/3 A Stationary Autoregressive Model of Order One: ARIMA (1,0,0)

Equation (8-10) shows the basic form of an AR(1) model—or ARIMA (1,0,0) to be general. Observation Y_t depends on Y_{t-1}, and the value of the autoregressive coefficient ϕ_1 is restricted to lie between -1 and $+1$.[5]

ARIMA (1,0,0)

$$Y_t = \phi_1 Y_{t-1} + \mu' + e_t \qquad (8\text{-}10)$$

---

[4]For a formal definition of *stationarity,* see Box and Jenkins (1976), p. 26.

[5]Note that the term μ' in this equation (and in all subsequent equations involving AR processes) is not quite the same as the "mean" of the Y series. Rather, the development is as follows:

$$(Y_t - \mu) = \phi_1(Y_{t-1} - \mu) + e_t, \quad \text{where } \mu = \text{mean of } Y \text{ series,}$$

$$Y_t = \phi_1 Y_{t-1} + (\mu - \phi_1\mu) + e_t,$$

$$= \phi_1 Y_{t-1} + \mu' + e_t.$$

In general, the AR models involve a term of the form $(\mu - \phi_1\mu - \phi_2\mu - \cdots)$ which will be identified as μ'. Note that if we are working with first differences of the Y series, as in equations (8-8) and (8-9), then there is no μ' term because it cancels out.

(a) ARIMA(0,0,0)
- • no AR aspect
- • no differencing
- • no MA aspect

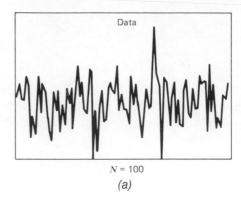

(a)

(b) ARIMA(0,1,0)
- • no AR aspect
- • needs first difference to remove non-stationarity in the mean
- • no MA aspect

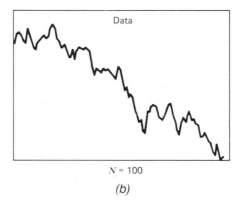

(b)

(c) ARIMA(0,1,0)
- • no AR aspect
- • "wandering-mean" and changing variance— harder to deal with
- • no MA aspect

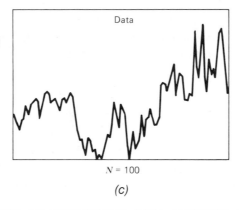

(c)

FIGURE 8-1 ILLUSTRATIONS OF TIME-SERIES DATA SHOWING (A) A RANDOM PROCESS—ARIMA(0,0,0), (B) A PROCESS THAT IS NON-STATIONARY IN THE MEAN—ARIMA(0,1,0), AND (C) A PROCESS THAT IS NON-STATIONARY IN BOTH MEAN AND VARIANCE—ARIMA(0,1,0)

Figure 8-2*a* shows an illustrative ARIMA (1,0,0) data series for the model $Y_t = .7Y_{t-1} + 30 + e_t$, where e_t is a normal, independently distributed error term.

8/2/4 A Stationary Moving Average Model of Order One: ARIMA (0,0,1)

Equation (8-11) gives an MA(1) model—or ARIMA (0,0,1) to be general. Observation Y_t depends on the error term e_t and also the previous error term e_{t-1}, with coefficient $-\theta_1$.[6]

ARIMA (0,0,1)

$$Y_t = \mu + e_t - \theta_1 e_{t-1} \qquad (8\text{-}11)$$

Figure 8-2*b* shows an example of an ARIMA (0,0,1) model:

$$Y_t = 100 + e_t - .7e_{t-1}.$$

The value of the coefficient θ_1 in equation (8-11) is again restricted to lie between -1 and $+1$.

8/2/5 A Simple Mixed Model: ARIMA (1,0,1)

The basic elements of AR and MA processes can be combined to produce a great variety of models. For example, equation (8-12) combines a first-order AR process and a first-order MA process.

ARIMA (1,0,1)

$$Y_t = \underbrace{\phi_1 Y_{t-1}}_{\text{AR(1)}} + \underset{\uparrow}{\mu'} + \underbrace{e_t - \theta_1 e_{t-1}}_{\text{MA(1)}} \qquad (8\text{-}12)$$

$$\text{AR(1)} \quad \text{constant} \quad \text{MA(1)}$$

Here, Y_t depends on one previous Y_{t-1} value and one previous error term e_{t-1}. The series is assumed stationary in the mean and in the variance. Figure 8-3*a* gives one example of an artificially generated ARIMA (1,0,1) series, where $\phi_1 = .3$ and $\theta_1 = -.7$. Figure 8-3*b* gives another example of an ARIMA (1,0,1) model, where $\phi_1 = -.8$ and $\theta_1 = .8$. Note how different the two ARIMA (1,0,1) models can be.

---

[6]The minus sign on this coefficient is a matter of convenience in the general description of ARIMA models. See Box and Jenkins (1976), Section 1.2, for an explanation.

(a) ARIMA(1,0,0) or AR(1)
$Y_t = \phi_1 Y_{t-1} + 30 + e_t,$
where $\phi_1 = .7$ and $e_t = NID(0,10)^*$

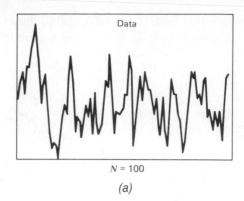

Data

$N = 100$

(a)

(b) ARIMA(0,0,1) or MA(1)
$Y_t = 100 + e_t - \theta_1 e_{t-1},$
where $\theta_1 = .7$ and e_t is $NID(0,10)^*$

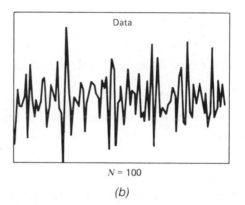

Data

$N = 100$

(b)

*NID(0,10) means "normal, independently distributed error term with mean 0 and variance 10."

FIGURE 8-2   ILLUSTRATIONS OF TIME-SERIES DATA, SHOWING (A) A FIRST ORDER AUTOREGRESSIVE PROCESS—ARIMA(1,0,0), AND (B) A FIRST ORDER MOVING AVERAGE PROCESS—ARIMA(0,0,1)

8/2/6   Higher-Order Combinations: ARIMA (p,d,q)

Clearly, there is no limit to the variety of ARIMA models. The general model, which covers all the cases mentioned above and many, many more, is known as ARIMA (p,d,q):

AR: p = order of the autoregressive process

I: d = degree of differencing involved

MA: q = order of the moving average process

In practice, it is seldom necessary to deal with values of p, d, or q that are other than 0, 1, or 2. It is perhaps remarkable that such a small range of

(a) ARIMA(1,0,1)
$Y_t = .3Y_{t-1} + 70 + e_t + .7e_{t-1}$,
where e_t is NID(0,10)

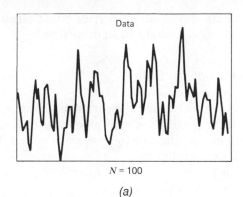

(a)

(b) ARIMA(1,0,1)
$Y_t = -.8Y_{t-1} + 180 + e_t - .8e_{t-1}$,
where e_t is NID(0,10)

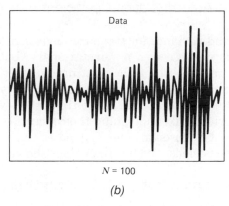

(b)

FIGURE 8-3 ILLUSTRATIONS OF TIME-SERIES DATA, SHOWING TWO VERSIONS OF AN ARIMA(1,0,1) PROCESS

values for *p, d,* or *q* can cover a tremendous range of practical forecasting situations.

The notation for writing a general ARIMA (*p,d,q*) model equation will be deferred to Chapter 9.

8/3 Methodological Tools for Analyzing Time-Series Data

The previous section was theoretical—the creation of particular models of the ARIMA family—and the main purpose was to introduce the terminology and the scope of these powerful time-series models. In this section we concentrate on certain analyses that can be applied to an empirical time series to determine its statistical properties, and thereby gain insight as to what kind of formal model might be appropriate.

8/3/1 A Plot of the Data

A good starting point for time-series analysis is a graphical plot of the data. If a plotting package is available on a computer, then it is also useful to plot various moving-average versions of the data to identify the presence of trends (wandering mean), to deseasonalize the data (e.g., plotting the four-period moving average of quarterly data), and so on.

8/3/2 The Autocorrelation Coefficient

The mean and variance (or standard deviation) of a time series may not be too helpful if the series is nonstationary, but the minimum and maximum values can be useful (for plotting purposes or as outlier candidates). However, the key statistic in time-series analysis is the autocorrelation coefficient (or the correlation of the time series with itself, lagged by 0, 1, 2, or more periods). To understand the concept, consider the following simple illustration. Suppose variable Y_t denotes the demand for Product A for the past 10 time periods, and has the values shown in Column 2 of Table 8-1.

Based on the data in Table 8-1, Y_t might be expressed as

$$Y_t = a + \phi_1 Y_{t-1} + \phi_2 Y_{t-2} + e_t. \tag{8-13}$$

Equation (8-13) is an AR model [or ARIMA (2,0,0)] expressing Y_t as a linear combination of its two immediately preceding values. Variables Y_{t-1} and Y_{t-2} are constructed easily by moving the values down the table one and two periods, respectively. This results in losing one value in the Y_{t-1} column and two values for Y_{t-2}. The autocorrelations between Y_t and Y_{t-1} and between Y_t and Y_{t-2} can be computed without difficulty. The first autocorrelation will indicate how successive values of Y relate to each other, and the second autocorrelation will indicate how Y values two periods apart relate to each other.

The simple correlation coefficient between Y_t and Y_{t-1} can be found using (2-26) or its equivalent (5-24), as restated below in (8-14)[7]:

$$r_{Y_t Y_{t-1}} = \frac{(\text{Covariance between } Y_t \text{ and } Y_{t-1})}{(\text{Std. dev. } Y_t) \times (\text{Std. dev. } Y_{t-1})}$$

---

[7]Note that equation (8-14) could be elaborated by dividing the numerator by $(n - 2)$ and the two denominator factors by $(n - 1)$ and $(n - 2)$, respectively. In practice, these degrees of freedom are not included in the calculation of autocorrelation. See Box and Jenkins (1976), p. 32.

TABLE 8-1 TIME SERIES OF DEMAND FOR PRODUCT A

(1) Time (or period) t	(2) Original Variable Y_t	(3) One Time Lag Variable Y_{t-1}	(4) Two Time Lag Variable Y_{t-2}
1	13	—	—
2	8	13	—
3	15	8	13
4	4	15	8
5	4	4	15
6	12	4	4
7	11	12	4
8	7	11	12
9	14	7	11
10	12	14	7
Sum	100		
Mean	10		

$$= \frac{\sum\limits_{t=2}^{n} (Y_t - \overline{Y}_t)(Y_{t-1} - \overline{Y}_{t-1})}{\sqrt{\sum\limits_{t=1}^{n} (Y_t - \overline{Y}_t)^2}\ \sqrt{\sum\limits_{t=2}^{n} (Y_{t-1} - \overline{Y}_{t-1})^2}}. \tag{8-14}$$

Note carefully the subscript limits in numerator and denominator here. Since this formula leads to statistical difficulties, a simplifying assumption is made. The series Y_t is assumed to be stationary (in both the mean and the variance). Thus, the two means, $\overline{Y}_t$ and $\overline{Y}_{t-1}$, can then be assumed equal (and we shall drop the subscripts, using $\overline{Y} = \overline{Y}_t = \overline{Y}_{t-1}$), and the two variances (or standard deviations) can be estimated just once, using all the known data for Y_t.

Using these simplifying assumptions, equation (8-14) becomes

$$r_{Y_t Y_{t-1}} = \frac{\sum\limits_{t=2}^{n} (Y_t - \overline{Y})(Y_{t-1} - \overline{Y})}{\sum\limits_{t=1}^{n} (Y_t - \overline{Y})^2}. \tag{8-15}$$

Note that the numerator has one fewer term than the denominator, but because of the assumption of stationarity, equation (8-15) is general, and can be used for all time lags of one period for a time series.[8] For convenience, we now write the first-order autocorrelation coefficient as r_1 (that is, autocorrelation coefficient for one time lag).

Similarly, the autocorrelations for 1, 2, 3, 4, ..., k time lags can be found and denoted by r_k, as follows:

$$r_k = \frac{\sum_{t=1}^{n-k} (Y_t - \overline{Y})(Y_{t+k} - \overline{Y})}{\sum_{t=1}^{n} (Y_t - \overline{Y})^2}. \tag{8-16}$$

In equation (8-16) the summation in the numerator has been reordered from that in (8-15). This does not affect the results, since stationarity has been assumed.

To continue the illustrative example, it is instructive to compute r_1 for the data in Table 8-1, using equation (8-16):

$$r_1 = \frac{(13-10)(8-10) + (8-10)(15-10) + (15-10)(4-10) + \cdots + (14-10)(12-10)}{(13-10)^2 + (8-10)^2 + (15-10)^2 + (4-10)^2 + \cdots + (14-10)^2 + (12-10)^2}$$

$$= \frac{3(-2) + (-2)(5) + 5(-6) + 5(-6) + (-6)(2) + \cdots + (4)(2)}{3^2 + (-2)^2 + 5^2 + (-6)^2 + \cdots + 4^2 + 2^2}$$

$$= \frac{-27}{144} = -.188.$$

Equation (8-16) is clearly a more efficient way to calculate the autocorrelations than equation (8-14).

Using equation (8-16), r_2, r_3, and so on, can also be computed. For example, the value of r_2 is

$$r_2 = \frac{(13-10)(15-10) + (8-10)(4-10) + (15-10)(4-10) + \cdots + (7-10)(12-10)}{(13-10)^2 + (8-10)^2 + (15-10)^2 + \cdots + (14-10)^2 + (12-10)^2}$$

$$= \frac{(3)(5) + (-2)(-6) + 5(-6) + \cdots + (-3)(2)}{3^2 + (-2)^2 + 5^2 + \cdots + 4^2 + 2^2}$$

$$= \frac{-29}{144} = -.201.$$

The autocorrelation coefficients for r_3 and r_4 are .181 and $-.132$, respectively.

---

[8]There are some statistical subleties underlying this sentence, and the more advanced reader should consult one of the references at the end of the chapter (e.g., Box and Jenkins, 1976, pp. 32–33).

8/3/3   The Sampling Distribution of Autocorrelations

The autocorrelation coefficient is a valuable tool for investigating properties of an empirical time series, as will become clear in the pages which follow. However, the statistical theory underlying r_k is quite complicated, and in some cases, intractable. For the special case of a stationary random series (see Section 8/2/1), the sampling theory of r_k is known and can be used to practical advantage.

There are two ways of approaching this problem. One is to study the r_k values one at a time and to develop a standard error formula to test whether a particular r_k is significantly different from zero. The second is to consider a whole set of r_k values, say the first 15 of them (r_1 through r_{15}) all at one time, and develop a test to see whether the set is significantly different from a zero set. In the first instance a simple formula that is often used is

$$se_{r_k} = 1/\sqrt{n} \qquad \text{(standard error of } r_k\text{)}$$

and the Box-Pierce portmanteau test for a set of r_k values is based on the Q statistic:

$$Q = n \sum_{k=1}^{m} r_k^2 \qquad \text{(Box-Pierce } Q \text{ statistic),}$$

where m is the maximum lag being considered.

Concerning the standard error of a single r_k value, consider the time series consisting of 36 observations in Table 8-2. This series was constructed

---

TABLE 8-2   TIME SERIES WITH 36 VALUES

Period	Value	Period	Value	Period	Value
1	23	13	86	25	17
2	59	14	33	26	45
3	36	15	90	27	9
4	99	16	74	28	72
5	36	17	7	29	33
6	74	18	54	30	17
7	30	19	98	31	3
8	54	20	50	32	29
9	17	21	86	33	30
10	36	22	90	34	68
11	89	23	65	35	87
12	77	24	20	36	44

using random numbers between 0 and 100. Suppose, however, that this fact were not known. It could be determined by applying autocorrelation analysis.

Theoretically, all autocorrelation coefficients for a series of random numbers must be zero. This, however, assumes an infinite sample. The 36 observations in Table 8-2 are only one of many possible samples of 36 random numbers. If another set of 36 random numbers had been selected, they would have somewhat different autocorrelation coefficients. If an infinite number of samples of 36 random numbers were taken and their autocorrelation coefficients for 1, 2, 3, . . ., 10 time lags were averaged, the resulting values would all be very close to zero. If ρ_k is used to denote the autocorrelation for the entire population, then autocorrelations for different samples of values should form a distribution around ρ_k. The distribution can be determined using statistical theory.

As shown by Anderson (1942), Bartlett (1946), Quenouille (1949), and others, the autocorrelation coefficients of random data have a sampling distribution that can be approximated by a normal curve with mean zero and standard error $1/\sqrt{n}$. This information can be used to develop tests of hypotheses similar to those of the F-test and the t-tests examined in Chapters 5 and 6. These can be used to determine whether some r_k comes from a population whose value is zero at k time lags. Since n is 36 in Table 8-2, the standard error is $1/\sqrt{36} = .167$. This means that 95 percent of all sample-based autocorrelation coefficients must lie within a range specified by the mean plus or minus 1.96 standard errors.[9] That is, the data series can be concluded to be random if the calculated autocorrelation coefficients are within the limits.

$$-1.96(.167) \le r_k \le +1.96(.167),$$

$$-.327 \le r_k \le .327.$$

Figure 8-4 shows the autocorrelation coefficients for the data in Table 8-2, for time lags of 1, 2, 3,..., 10. The two dashed lines are the upper and lower 95 percent confidence limits for a random series $(-.327, +.327)$. All ten autocorrelation coefficients lie within these limits, confirming what in this case was already known—the data are random.

The concept of a sampling distribution is of critical importance in time-series analysis. The autocorrelation coefficient corresponding to a time lag of seven periods in Figure 8-4 is .275. This value is empirically different from zero because of chance. The sampling distribution provides guidelines as to what is chance and what is a significant relationship. The value of .275 is not significantly different from zero. However, if this value had been obtained for 360 observations instead of 36, the standard error would have

---

[9]The value of 1.96 is found by looking at Table A, Appendix I, of areas under the normal curve. Since it is close to 2, it is often approximated by 2.

```
                    AUTOCORRELATION ANALYSIS
                    ==============================

                    -1  -.8  -.6  -.4  -.2   0   .2   .4   .6   .8   1
     LAG    VALUE   I...!...!...!...!...!...!...I...!...!...!...!...I
      1     0.103                            |         ***       |
      2     0.099                            |         ***       |
      3    -0.043                            |        **         |
      4    -0.031                            |        **         |
      5    -0.183                            |     *****         |
      6     0.025                            |         *         |
      7     0.275                            |         ******    |
      8    -0.004                            |         *         |
      9    -0.011                            |         *         |
     10    -0.152                            |     ****          |
```

FIGURE 8-4 AUTOCORRELATIONS FOR THE SERIES IN TABLE 8-2

been only .053 and the confidence limits would have been $\pm.105$, instead of $\pm.327$. In that case an r_7 of .275 would have indicated the presence of a pattern, since it falls outside the confidence limits. Of course, with 360 random values, it would be very unlikely to observe such a high r value. Owing to chance, the autocorrelation values will be slightly different from those theoretically expected, necessitating the use of such confidence limits. Success in time-series analysis depends in large part on interpreting the results from autocorrelation analysis and being able to distinguish what is pattern and what is randomness in the data.

The Box-Pierce Q statistic could also be computed for the r_k values in Figure 8-4. In effect, since the data in Table 8-2 was not modeled in any way, we are assuming an ARIMA (0,0,0) model, and the Q value is computed as follows:

$$Q = 36 \sum_{k=1}^{10} r_k^2 = 5.62.$$

This is considered to be a chi-square value with $(m - p - q)$ degrees of freedom. Since $p = 0$ and $q = 0$, we look up the chi-square value of 5.62 (in Table E of Appendix I) with 10 df and can readily see that the set of r_k values is not significantly different from a null set.

The details of this Box-Pierce Q statistic and the accompanying chi-square test are given in Appendix 8-A, and the test will be used especially in the context of transfer function modeling in Chapter 10.

8/3/4 The Periodogram and Spectral Analysis

One way to analyze a time series is to decompose it into a set of sine waves (cycles) of different frequencies. This was a very popular procedure in the days before computers and still has considerable merit. While it may appear unduly complex at this point, we shall see that it can be very helpful in identifying randomness and seasonality in a time series, and in recognizing the predominance of negative or positive autocorrelation. As we shall see in the next two chapters, such help is often needed in identifying an appropriate model for forecasting a given time series.

Leaving the details to Appendix 8-B, note simply that each sine wave has three aspects:

1. wavelength—measured from one crest to the next, and inversely related to frequency;
2. amplitude—which measures the height (or "strength") of the wave; and
3. phase—which refers to the horizontal displacement (or position) of the wave.

Figure 8-5 illustrates these features. If the phase angle is zero, then the wave starts at the origin. If the phase angle is 90 deg., then the vertical axis goes through the first maximum amplitude (as in Figure 8-5c).

Now with a discrete time series, since there are no angles to deal with, "wavelength" is translated into "time units" (or number of observations making up one wavelength), and phase is treated similarly. Without going into details here, note that any time series, composed of N equally spaced observations, can be decomposed by least-squares fitting into a number of sine waves of given frequency, amplitude, and phase, subject to the following restrictions:

- If n is an odd number, then a maximum of $(n - 1)/2$ sine waves can be fitted.
- If n is an even number, then a maximum of $(n - 2)/2$ sine waves can be fitted.

By way of example, consider the data in Table 8-2. There are 36 observations, so that 17 sine waves can be fitted. The first (or fundamental) wave has frequency one—meaning that one complete wavelength covers all 36 data points. The next two-cycle wave has two complete wavelengths in 36 observations, and so on.

Wavelength (in no. of data points)	Frequency
36	1
18	2
12	3
9	4
7.2	5

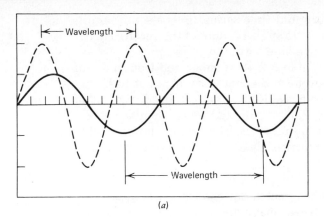

(a)

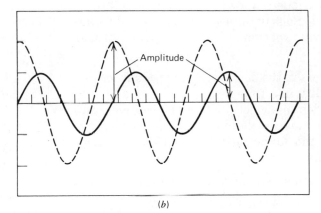

(b)

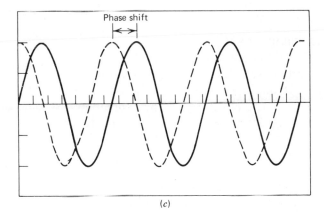

(c)

FIGURE 8-5   THE THREE ASPECTS OF A SINE WAVE: (a) WAVELENGTH;
(b) AMPLITUDE; (c) PHASE

Figure 8-6 shows (a) a plot of the original time series, (b) the set of amplitudes for all fitted frequencies from 1 through 17, and (c) the reconstructed series obtained by adding the first five sine waves together.

Note that since the data in Table 8-2 were generated from a set of random numbers (that is, from a uniform distribution), it is not to be expected that any particular sine wave would dominate. Indeed, the set of amplitudes of waves of frequency 1, 2, 3, 4, . . . , and so on, should theoretically show equal amplitudes for all frequencies. The sample data in Table 8-2 do not show equal amplitudes, but it is clear that many sine waves are contributing substantially.

Figure 8-6b will be called the *line spectrum*.

The discussion above is based on a straightforward least-squares fitting of sine waves to a time series. It was originally known as periodogram analysis (Schuster, 1898) and is variously known as harmonic analysis, Fourier analysis, or spectral analysis. Each of these terms has special meanings, but for our purposes here, the value of examining the set of amplitudes of various waves is threefold:

1. it helps identify randomness in the data series (or residual series);
2. it helps identify seasonality in a time series;
3. it helps identify the predominance of positive or negative autocorrelation (for positive autocorrelation low-frequency amplitudes should dominate, and for negative autocorrelation, high frequencies should dominate).

Although spectral analysis is not central to the ARIMA modeling process, we have found it a useful ally in the difficult task of identifying an appropriate model for a given time series.

8/3/5 The Partial Autocorrelation Coefficient

In regression analysis, if dependent variable Y is regressed on independent variables X_1 and X_2, then it might be of interest to ask how much explanatory power does X_1 have if the effects of X_2 are somehow *partialled out* first. Typically, this means regressing Y on X_2, getting the residual errors from this analysis, and regressing the residuals against X_1. In time-series analysis there is a similar concept.

Partial autocorrelations are used to measure the degree of association between X_t and X_{t-k}, when the effects of other time lags—1, 2, 3, . . ., up to $k - 1$—are somehow partialled out. Their singular purpose in time series analysis is to help identify an appropriate ARIMA model for forecasting. In fact, they have been constructed just for this use.

The partial autocorrelation coefficient of order m is defined as the last autoregressive coefficient of an AR(m) model. For example, equations (8-17) through (8-21) are used to define an AR(1), an AR(2), an AR(3), . . .,

(a) A PLOT OF THE RAW DATA

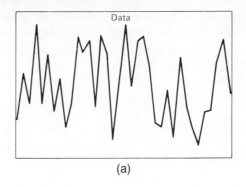

(a)

(b) THE LINE SPECTRUM RESULTS
     (also called the Periodogram)

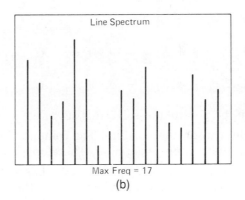

(b)

(c) THE RECONSTRUCTED SERIES
     using the first 5 waves
     (The dots are the reconstructed series.
     The solid line is the original data.)

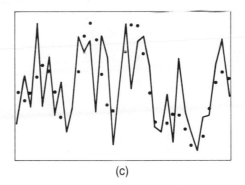

(c)

FIGURE 8-6   THE LINE SPECTRUM ANALYSIS OF THE 36 DATA POINTS
                IN TABLE 8-2

AR($m - 1$), and an AR(m) process, respectively. The last coefficient of X in each of these equations is the partial autocorrelation coefficient. That is, $\hat{\phi}_1, \hat{\phi}_2, \hat{\phi}_3, \ldots, \hat{\phi}_{m-1}$, and $\hat{\phi}_m$ are the first m partial autocorrelation coefficients for the time series:

$$X_t = \hat{\phi}_1 X_{t-1} + e_t, \tag{8-17}$$

$$X_t = \phi_1 X_{t-1} + \hat{\phi}_2 X_{t-2} + e_t, \tag{8-18}$$

$$X_t = \phi_1 X_{t-1} + \phi_2 X_{t-2} + \hat{\phi}_3 X_{t-3} + e_t, \tag{8-19}$$

.

.

.

$$X_t = \phi_1 X_{t-1} + \phi_2 X_{t-2} + \cdots + \hat{\phi}_{m-1} X_{t-m+1} + e_t, \tag{8-20}$$

$$X_t = \phi_1 X_{t-1} + \phi_2 X_{t-2} + \cdots + \phi_{m-1} X_{t-m+1} + \hat{\phi}_m X_{t-m} + e_t. \tag{8-21}$$

It would be possible to solve this set of equations for $\hat{\phi}_1, \hat{\phi}_2, \hat{\phi}_3, \ldots, \hat{\phi}_{m-1}, \hat{\phi}_m$ to determine their values. The computations required, however, would be extremely time consuming. Therefore it is more satisfactory to obtain estimates of $\hat{\phi}_1, \hat{\phi}_2, \hat{\phi}_3, \ldots, \hat{\phi}_{m-1}, \hat{\phi}_m$ based on the autocorrelation coefficients. These estimations can be made by the following method.

If both sides of (8-17) are multiplied by X_{t-1}, the result is

$$X_{t-1}X_t = \phi_1 X_{t-1}X_{t-1} + X_{t-1}e_t. \tag{8-22}$$

Taking the expected value of (8-22) yields

$$E(X_{t-1}X_t) = \phi_1 E(X_{t-1}X_{t-1}) + E(X_{t-1}e_t),$$

which can be rewritten as

$$\gamma_1 = \phi_1 \gamma_0. \tag{8-23}$$

since $E(X_{t-1}X_t) = \gamma_1$, $E(X_{t-1}X_{t-1}) = \gamma_0$, and $E(X_{t-1}e_t) = 0$ by definition.[10]

If both sides of (8-23) are divided by γ_0, the result is

$$\rho_1 = \phi_1, \tag{8-24}$$

since $\rho_1 = (\gamma_1/\gamma_0)$ is the way to define the first autocorrelation. (See Chapter

---

[10] γ_0 and γ_1 are the notations for the population autocovariances of order 0 and 1. γ_0 is thus the variance of the time series, and $\rho_k = \gamma_k/\gamma_0$ is the autocorrelation parameter for lag k.

2 for details.) Thus $\hat{\phi}_1 = \hat{\rho}_1$. That is, the first partial autocorrelation is the same as the first autocorrelation, and they will both be estimated in the sample by r_1. In general, since $\rho_k = (\gamma_k/\gamma_0)$, the operations shown in equations (8-22) through (8-24) can be extended as follows. Multiplying both sides of (8-17) by X_{t-k}, taking expected values, and dividing by γ_0 yields a set of simultaneous equations (called the Yule-Walker equations), which can be solved for $\hat{\phi}_1$, $\hat{\phi}_2$, $\hat{\phi}_3$, . . ., $\hat{\phi}_{m-1}$, and $\hat{\phi}_m$. These values can then be used as estimates of the partial autocorrelations of up to m time lags. Recursive estimation procedures do exist for obtaining a solution to these equations.

After one understands what partial autocorrelations are and how they can be obtained, the next concern is how to use them in identifying an appropriate ARMA model. If the underlying process generating a given series is an AR(1) model, it should be understood that only $\hat{\phi}_1$ will be significantly different from zero, while $\hat{\phi}_2$, $\hat{\phi}_3$, . . ., $\hat{\phi}_{m-1}$, $\hat{\phi}_m$ will not be statistically significant. If the true generating process is·AR(2), then only $\hat{\phi}_1$ and $\hat{\phi}_2$ will be significant, and the remaining estimated values will not be significant. The same can be said regarding higher-order AR processes.

In other words, because of the way in which $\hat{\phi}_1$, $\hat{\phi}_2$, $\hat{\phi}_3$, . . ., $\hat{\phi}_{m-1}$, $\hat{\phi}_m$ are constructed, they will be significantly different from zero only up to the order of the true AR process generating the data. In model identification, it is then assumed that if there are only two significant partial autocorrelations, the generating process is of second order and the order of the forecasting model should be AR(2). If there are p significant partial autocorrelations, then the order should be AR(p).

For identification purposes, therefore, if the process is an autoregressive one (its autocorrelation coefficients decline to zero exponentially), the partial autocorrelations can be examined to determine the order of the process. That order is equal to the number of significant partial autocorrelations.

If the generating process is MA rather than AR, then the partial autocorrelations will not indicate the order of the MA process, since they are constructed to fit an AR process. In fact, they introduce a dependence from one lag to the next that makes them behave in a manner like that of autocorrelations for an AR process. That is, the partial autocorrelations will decline to zero exponentially. For identification purposes, when the partial autocorrelations do not exhibit a drop to random values after p time lags but instead decline to zero exponentially, it can be assumed that the true generating process is an MA one.

In summary, when there are only p partial autocorrelations that are significantly different from zero, the process is assumed to be an AR(p). When the partial autocorrelations tail off to zero exponentially, the process is assumed to be an MA one. In the next section (8/4) the computation and use of partial autocorrelations will be illustrated.

8/4   Applications of Time-Series Analysis

Section 8/2 described briefly the general notion of an ARIMA model, showing the basic forms (random, nonstationary, AR, MA, ARMA), which are all special cases of the general model. Section 8/3 then discussed several methodological tools that are useful in the analysis of a time series. After plotting the time series for visual inspection, the major statistical tool is the autocorrelation coefficient, r_k, which describes the relationship between the time series and itself, lagged k periods. Other tools, such as the partial autocorrelation coefficient and the periodogram (amplitudes or intensities of sine waves that make up the time series), are used to aid in the identification of appropriate models. In Section 8/4 we now apply these tools to some simple illustrative time series.

8/4/1   Determining Randomness of Data (or Residuals)

Autocorrelations can be used to determine whether there is any pattern (AR, MA, ARMA, or ARIMA) in a set of data, and in the absence of any such pattern it may be argued that the data set is random. The autocorrelation coefficients for several time lags are examined to see if any of them are significantly different from zero. It is useful to plot the autocorrelation coefficients as in Figure 8-4 as one step in determining whether any pattern exists. (Those of Figure 8-4 have none.)

Once a forecasting model has been fitted, autocorrelations can be computed for the residual errors to determine whether they are random. For example, in Table 3-11 it is clear that the forecasting errors using linear exponential smoothing were not random—there is a definite pattern in the errors indicating that the model chosen was not an appropriate one. While the pattern in the errors in Table 3-11 was obvious, in many cases it is not. A standard approach for determining whether the errors are random is to compute the autocorrelations of the errors.

Figure 8-7 shows the autocorrelations for the residuals of the single exponential smoothing model of Table 3-11. It can be seen that the autocorrelation corresponding to a time lag of four periods is $r_4 = .726$, indicating that there is a pattern in the residuals. This result is expected, since the export data in Table 3-11 are seasonal and single smoothing cannot deal with seasonality. The autocorrelation for a time lag of eight periods is also large and outside the random limits suggesting a recurrence of the quarterly pattern every 2 years.

Figure 8-8 shows the autocorrelations for the residuals remaining after using Winters' linear and seasonal smoothing methods. This method has eliminated the seasonal pattern and has produced residuals for which the autocorrelations are essentially random.

```
                    AUTOCORRELATION ANALYSIS
                    ===========================================

                -1 -.8 -.6 -.4 -.2   0  .2  .4  .6  .8   1
   LAG  VALUE   I...!...!...!...!...I...!...!...!...!...I
    1  -0.233                    *****
    2  -0.375                  *********
    3  -0.219                    *****
    4   0.726                        ****************
    5  -0.177                    *****
    6  -0.256                   ******
    7  -0.177                    *****
    8   0.532                        ***********
```

FIGURE 8-7 AUTOCORRELATIONS FOR THE RESIDUAL SERIES FROM TABLE 3-11

The periodogram or line spectrum can also be used to show evidence of randomness, but it is better to have a larger number of data points in the series. In the bank regression example (Table 6-1 and Figure 6-10), after fitting the regression model in equation (6-24), the residuals can be examined to see if they are essentially random. Figure 8-9 shows the analysis as a composite of four diagrams. In the top left corner is the plot of the residuals. In the top right corner is the plot of autocorrelations. In the lower right is the plot of partial autocorrelations, and in the lower left is the plot of amplitudes of the sine waves that make up the series. Recall that the Durbin-Watson statistic computed for these residuals was 0.89 (see Section 6/2/5), which is a strong indication that the residuals show positive autocorrelation. In Figure 8-9 the autocorrelations show a distinct pattern (something called a damped sine wave), which helps corroborate the Durbin-Watson conclusion, and the line spectrum shows that the lower frequencies have the greater amplitudes, again supporting the positive autocorrelation nature of the residuals. The first partial autocorrelation is always equal to the first autocorrelation, and the standard error of the partials is computed as for the autocorrelations.[11]

In Figure 8-9 the dashed lines in the diagrams on the right indicate the 95 percent confidence limits for the autocorrelations and the partials. Since $n = 53$, the standard error is computed to be $1/\sqrt{53} = 0.1374$, and multiplying by 1.96 (for 95 percent confidence), the dashed lines are at values ± 0.263. There are several autocorrelations lying outside the 95 percent confidence bounds, and the pattern of successive values is very noticeable. In the case of the partials, the first and third are outside the bounds.

The residuals for these bank data are not random.

---

[11]Quenouille (1949) showed that if the time-series model is ARIMA $(p, 0,0)$—that is, autoregressive of order p—then the estimated partials of order $p + 1$ and higher are approximately independent and have a standard error $1/\sqrt{n}$, as discussed in Section 8/3/3.

```
                AUTOCORRELATION ANALYSIS
                =========================

                 -1 -.8 -.6 -.4 -.2   0  .2  .4  .6  .8   1
 LAG    VALUE  I...!...!...!...!...!...I...!...!...!...!...I
  1     0.395                          *********
  2     0.070                          **
  3    -0.163                      ****
  4    -0.172                      ****
  5    -0.144                      ****
  6    -0.059                        **
  7     0.063                          **
  8    -0.023                         *
```

FIGURE 8-8 AUTOCORRELATIONS FOR THE RESIDUAL SERIES AFTER
USING WINTER'S EXPONENTIAL SMOOTHING METHOD (SEE
TABLE 3-12)

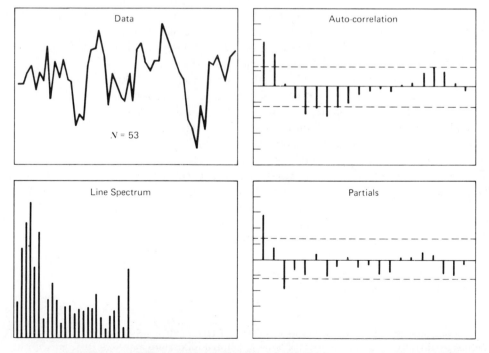

FIGURE 8-9 TIME-SERIES ANALYSIS OF THE RESIDUALS FROM THE BANK
STUDY (SEE FIGURE 6-10)

```
                    AUTOCORRELATION ANALYSIS
                    ================================

                 -1 -.8 -.6 -.4 -.2   0  .2  .4  .6  .8  1
LAG    VALUE   I...!...!...!...!...!...I...!...!...!...!...I
  1    0.889                            ******************
  2    0.765                            ****************
  3    0.631                            *************
  4    0.509                            **********
  5    0.400                            *********
  6    0.313                            *******
  7    0.230                            ******
  8    0.188                            *****
  9    0.149                            ****
 10    0.108                            ***
```

FIGURE 8-10   AUTOCORRELATION COEFFICIENTS FOR A NONSTATION-
ARY SERIES

8/4/2   Examining Stationarity of a Time Series

The visual plot of a time series is often enough to convince a forecaster that the data are stationary or nonstationary,[12] and the autocorrelation plot can also expose nonstationarity quite readily. The autocorrelations
of stationary data drop to zero after the second or third time lag, while for
a nonstationary series they are significantly different from zero for several
time periods. When represented graphically, the autocorrelations of nonstationary data show a trend going diagonally from right to left as the
number of time lags increases.

Figure 8-10 shows the graph of autocorrelations for a nonstationary
series. The autocorrelations of one to five time lags are significantly different from zero and the existence of a trend (see broken line) can be clearly
seen.

The existence of a trend (linear or nonlinear) in the data means that
successive values will be positively correlated with each other. The autocorrelation for one time lag, r_1, will be relatively large and positive. The
autocorrelation for two time lags will also be relatively large and positive,
but not as large as r_1, because the random error component has entered the
picture twice. Similarly, in general, r_k for nonstationary data will be relatively large and positive, until k gets big enough so that the random error
components begin to dominate the autocorrelation.

A classic example of a nonstationary series is the daily closing IBM
stock prices. Figure 8-11 shows the four-part analysis of $n = 369$ daily

---

[12]Recall that *stationarity* means that there is no growth or decline in the data. The
data must be roughly horizontal along the time axis. In other words the data fluctuate around
a constant mean, independent of time, and the variance of the fluctuation remains essentially
constant over time.

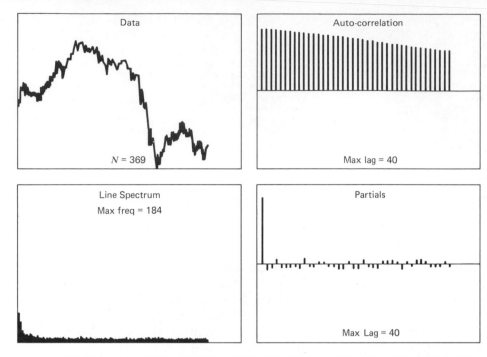

FIGURE 8-11   TIME-SERIES ANALYSIS OF N = 369 DAILY CLOSING IBM STOCK PRICES

Source: Box-Jenkins (1976, p. 526)

closing prices for IBM stock. Note from the data plot that the series is clearly nonstationary, that the autocorrelation plot shows a clear linear trend of slowly decreasing values, that the partials show one large value, and that the line spectrum verifies the dominance of low-frequency sine waves—all indicating nonstationarity.

8/4/3   Removing Nonstationarity in a Time Series

Trends of any kind result in positive autocorrelations that dominate the autocorrelation diagram, and since most of the time-series models described in Part IV assume stationarity, it is important to remove the nonstationarity before proceeding with time-series model building. This can be achieved routinely through the method of *differencing*.[13]

---

[13]In Chapter 4 an alternative method for removing trends was discussed. That method divided the trended data by the moving average to obtain a series without trend. The method of *differencing* is an alternative, more computationally efficient procedure and is better suited for ARIMA models.

Consider the simple series 2, 4, 6, 8, ..., 20, consisting of a linear trend and no randomness. Subtracting consecutive values, $4 - 2, 6 - 4, 8 - 6, \ldots, 20 - 18$, gives as the first differences, the series 2, 2, 2, ..., 2. This series is clearly stationary. Thus to achieve stationarity, a new series is created that consists of the differences between successive periods:

$$X'_t = X_t - X_{t-1}. \tag{8-25}$$

The new series, X'_t, will have $n - 1$ values and will be stationary if the trend in the original data X_t is linear (of first order).

Taking the first difference of the data used in Figure 8-10 gives a series whose autocorrelations are shown in Figure 8-12. In Figure 8-12 the first and second autocorrelation coefficients are significantly different from zero, but the rest are not, which indicates that the series of first differences has transformed the data into stationary form.

If the autocorrelations of the first differenced data do not drop to near zero after the second or third lag, this indicates that stationarity has not yet been achieved and therefore first differences of the first differenced data can be taken:

$$X''_t = X'_t - X'_{t-1}. \tag{8-26}$$

X''_t is referred to as the series of second-order differences. This series will have $n - 2$ values.

Substituting (8-25) into (8-26) yields

$$\left. \begin{array}{l} X''_t = (X_t - X_{t-1}) - (X_{t-1} - X_{t-2}), \\ X''_t = X_t - 2X_{t-1} + X_{t-2}. \end{array} \right\} \tag{8-27}$$

The process of differencing can be applied to the data of Table 8-3, which is known to include a second level (or degree) of nonstationarity. As part of this exercise, the mechanics of differencing can also be reviewed.

```
                      AUTOCORRELATION ANALYSIS
                      ========================

               -1  -.8  -.6  -.4  -.2   0   .2  .4  .6  .8   1
   LAG   VALUE  I...!...!...!...!...!...I...!...!...!...!...!...I
    1    0.625                          ***************
    2    0.284                          *******
    3   -0.045                          **
    4   -0.225                     *****
    5   -0.188                     *****
    6   -0.069                        **
    7    0.068                        **
    8    0.156                        ****
    9    0.009                        *
   10   -0.037                        **
```

FIGURE 8-12 AUTOCORRELATIONS OF FIRST DIFFERENCES OF NON-STATIONARY DATA (SEE FIGURE 8-10)

TABLE 8-3 SAMPLE TIME SERIES WITH FIRST AND SECOND DIFFERENCES

(1) Period t	(2) Time Series X_t	(3) First Differences $X'_t = X_t - X_{t-1}$	(4) Second-Order Differences $X''_t = X'_t - X'_{t-1}$
1	2.44	—	—
2	5.30	2.86	—
3	8.97	3.67	.81
4	13.88	4.91	1.24
5	19.58	5.70	.79
6	26.99	7.41	1.71
7	35.95	8.96	1.55
8	45.86	9.91	.95
9	55.70	9.84	−.07
10	67.36	11.66	1.82
11	79.63	12.27	.61
12	92.13	12.50	.23

Column 3 of Table 8-3 contains the first differences, which are found using equation (8-25):

$$X'_2 = X_2 - X_1 = 5.30 - 2.44 = 2.86,$$

$$X'_3 = X_3 - X_2 = 8.97 - 5.30 = 3.67,$$

.

.

.

$$X'_{12} = X_{12} - X_{11} = 92.13 - 79.63 = 12.50.$$

It is not possible to calculate X'_1; therefore the first differenced series has only $n - 1$ observations.

The second differences in Table 8-3, column 4, are found using equation (8-26):

$$X''_3 = X'_3 - X'_2 = 3.67 - 2.86 = .81,$$

$$X''_4 = X'_4 - X'_3 = 4.91 - 3.67 = 1.24,$$

.

.

.

$$X''_{12} = X'_{12} - X'_{11} = 12.50 - 12.27 = .23.$$

Again, it is not possible to calculate X_1'' or X_2'', resulting in the loss of two values in the series of second differences.

The values of the second differences could have been found using equation (8-27):

$$X_3'' = X_3 - 2X_2 + X_1 = 8.97 - 2(5.30) + 2.44 = .81,$$

$$X_4'' = X_4 - 2X_3 + X_2 = 13.88 - 2(8.97) + 5.30 = 1.24,$$

.

.

.

$$X_{12}'' = X_{12} - 2X_{11} + X_{10} = 92.13 - 2(79.63) + 67.36 = .23.$$

If nothing were known about the time-series data of Table 8-3, a first step in analysis would be to compute the autocorrelations for the original time-series data in column 2. These autocorrelations are shown in Figure 8-13. It is clear that the data are not stationary because of the trend in the autocorrelations. Next the differenced data of column 3 can be used and their autocorrelations calculated. The results are shown in Figure 8-14. These autocorrelations do not behave much differently from those of Figure 8-13. That is, they do not drop to zero rapidly, suggesting nonstationarity in the series of first differenced data. It is necessary, therefore, to take another difference (first difference of the first difference, or second difference) and find the autocorrelations of the second differenced data shown in column 4 of Table 8-3. The autocorrelations of the second difference are shown in Figure 8-15 and indicate stationarity at this level.

In the case of the daily closing prices of IBM stock (see Figure 8-9), notice the dramatic effect of taking first differences of this time series in Figure 8-16. The first difference date is much more nearly stationary (although there is some hint of nonstationarity in the variance), and also random, as shown by the autocorrelations and the partials. Also note that the line spectrum approximates "white noise"—equal amplitudes at all fre-

```
                     AUTOCORRELATION ANALYSIS
                     ═══════════════════════════════════════════

                   -1 -.8 -.6 -.4 -.2   0  .2  .4  .6  .8   1
      LAG  VALUE   I...!...!...!...!...I...!...!...!...!...I
       1   0.750                        ****************
       2   0.502                        ***********
       3   0.268                        ******
       4   0.056                        **
       5  -0.129                    ****
       6  -0.273                  ******
```

FIGURE 8-13 AUTOCORRELATIONS OF THE ORIGINAL DATA (SEE TABLE 8-3)

```
                AUTOCORRELATION ANALYSIS
                ==================================

              -1 -.8 -.6 -.4 -.2   0  .2  .4  .6  .8   1
LAG    VALUE   I...!...!...!...!...I...!...!...!...!...I
 1     0.751                       ****************
 2     0.475                       ***********
 3     0.213                       ****
 4    -0.010                      *
 5    -0.215                  *****
 6    -0.346                *******
```

FIGURE 8-14 AUTOCORRELATIONS OF THE FIRST DIFFERENCED DATA (SEE TABLE 8-3)

quencies—showing that the *change* in the daily stock prices is essentially a random event.

Achieving stationarity can be reduced to a rather mechanical task of taking successive differences until the autocorrelations drop to zero within two or three time lags. In practice, it is seldom necessary to go beyond second differences, because real data generally involve nonstationarities of only the first or second level.

8/4/4 Recognizing Seasonality in a Time Series

Seasonality is defined as a pattern that repeats itself over fixed intervals of time. The sales of heating oil, for example, are high in winter and low in summer, indicating a 12-month seasonal pattern. If the pattern is a consistent one, the autocorrelation coefficient of 12-month lags will have a high positive value indicating the existence of seasonality. If it were not significantly different from zero, it would indicate that months one year apart are unrelated (random) with no consistent pattern emerging from one year to the next. Such data would not be seasonal.

For stationary data, seasonality can be found by identifying those autocorrelation coefficients of more than two or three time lags that are significantly different from zero. Any autocorrelation that is significantly

```
                AUTOCORRELATION ANALYSIS
                ==================================

              -1 -.8 -.6 -.4 -.2   0  .2  .4  .6  .8   1
LAG    VALUE   I...!...!...!...!...I...!...!...!...!...I
 1    -0.202                  *****
 2    -0.217                  *****
 3     0.155                       ****
 4     0.151                       ****
 5    -0.322                *******
```

FIGURE 8-15 AUTOCORRELATIONS OF THE SECOND-ORDER DIFFERENCES (SEE TABLE 8-3)

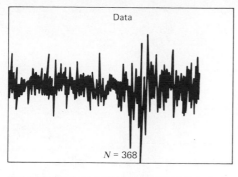

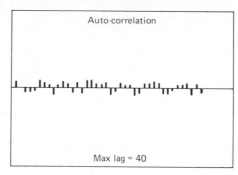

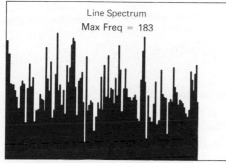

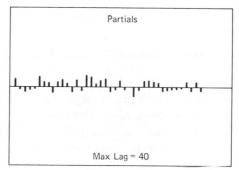

FIGURE 8-16 ANALYSIS OF FIRST DIFFERENCES FOR THE N = 369 DAILY CLOSING IBM STOCK PRICES (SEE FIGURE 8-11)

different from zero implies the existence of a pattern in the data. To recognize seasonality, one must look for such high autocorrelations.

The autocorrelation coefficients shown in Figure 8-17 indicate a clear seasonal pattern of four periods duration (four quarters). It can be seen that r_4 = .764, which is significantly different from zero. Similarly r_8 = .572 is significant and r_{12} = .417 is on the border of the limits. The periodic character of seasonality can be seen by the fact that $r_4 > r_8 > r_{12}$ and all three are significantly different from zero. Actually, the autocorrelation r_4 = .764 suffices to indicate seasonality with a length of four periods. The additional fact that r_8 and r_{12} are large confirms it.

Seasonality can easily be seen in a graph of autocorrelations or by simply looking at the autocorrelations of different time lags if it is the only pattern present. However, it is not always easy to identify when combined with other patterns such as trend. The stronger the trend, the less obvious the seasonality will be, since relatively large positive autocorrelations result from the existence of nonstationarity in the data. As a rule, the data should be transformed to a stationary series before determining seasonality.

Figure 8-18 shows a set of autocorrelations for a nonstationary data series. The trend can be seen in the autocorrelations. The autocorrelation corresponding to a four-period time lag is r_4 = .589. Its value is larger than

```
                     AUTOCORRELATION ANALYSIS
                     =============================

                    -1 -.8 -.6 -.4 -.2   0  .2  .4  .6  .8   1
       LAG   VALUE   I...!...!...!...!...!...I...!...!...!...!...!...I
        1   -0.344                  *******
        2   -0.203                  *****
        3   -0.356                  ********
        4    0.764                        *****************
        5   -0.246                  ******
        6   -0.105                    ***
        7   -0.289                  *******
        8    0.572                        ************
        9   -0.212                  *****
       10   -0.071                    **
       11   -0.234                  ******
       12    0.417                        ********
```

FIGURE 8-17 AUTOCORRELATION COEFFICIENTS OF QUARTERLY DATA

the previous two, and similarly, r_8 is larger than the one preceding it. This suggests the existence of seasonality, but does not clearly identify it. After detecting the trend, the series must be differenced and the autocorrelations of the differenced series must be calculated. The result is the graph shown previously in Figure 8-17. The differenced series is stationary, since no autocorrelation coefficients except the seasonal ones are significantly different from zero. Figure 8-17 shows a clear seasonal pattern whose length is four periods.

Not all autocorrelations for data with trend and seasonality will behave as shown in Figures 8-17 and 8-18. When the trend is much stronger in comparison to seasonality, the autocorrelations of the original data may fall on a line. On the other extreme, the seasonality may be clear and dominate the trend. Thus as a first step in autocorrelation analysis, non-

```
                     AUTOCORRELATION ANALYSIS
                     =============================

                    -1 -.8 -.6 -.4 -.2   0  .2  .4  .6  .8   1
       LAG   VALUE   I...!...!...!...!...!...I...!...!...!...!...!...I
        1    0.723                        ***************
        2    0.546                        ************
        3    0.500                        ***********
        4    0.588                        *************
        5    0.358                        ********
        6    0.191                        *****
        7    0.115                        ***
        8    0.130                        ****
        9   -0.059                      **
       10   -0.176                  *****
       11   -0.214                  *****
       12   -0.189                  *****
```

FIGURE 8-18 AUTOCORRELATION COEFFICIENTS OF QUARTERLY DATA
WITH STRONG TREND

stationarity must be removed. Once that is done, other patterns can be examined. Three cases are possible:

1. The autocorrelations may behave as those of Figure 8-4. (None is significantly different from zero.)
2. The autocorrelations may show some pattern. (The first one or two autocorrelations are significantly different from zero, or there is a distinct pattern such as the damped sine wave in Figure 8-9.)
3. The autocorrelations may indicate seasonality (as in Figure 8-17).

A clear illustration of seasonality is shown in Figure 8-19 using data on international airline passengers. Note that the 144 monthly figures show a nonlinear trend and a very pronounced (multiplicative) seasonal pattern. The autocorrelations illustrate clearly that (i) the series is nonstationary (the values of r_k stay large and positive), and (ii) the series is seasonal (the values of r_{12}, r_{24}, and r_{36} are all larger than their adjacent autocorrelations). The line spectrum confirms these otherwise obvious facts, in that the amplitudes for the 12-cycle sine wave stands out higher than its neighbors. A 12-cycle wave over $n = 144$ data points, means $144/12 = 12$ data points

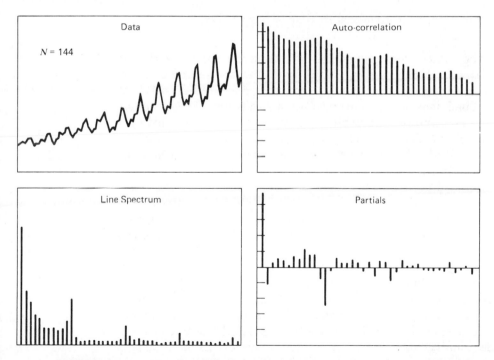

FIGURE 8-19 AN ANALYSIS OF THE AIRLINE PASSENGERS DATA (SEE BOX-JENKINS 1970, p. 531)

per wavelength; that is, there is a 12-month cycle of significant proportions. The large amplitude for the 1-cycle wave indicates the strong trend in the data.

8/5   Recapitulation

This chapter has introduced various aspects of time-series models—randomness, nonstationarity, seasonality, autoregressive processes, moving average processes, and mixtures of AR and MA processes—and makes use of the general Box-Jenkins notation ARIMA (p, d, q). Next, some useful statistical tools were examined—most notably the autocorrelation coefficient, but also the partial autocorrelation coefficient, differencing of a time series, and the line spectrum. Finally, these tools were put to use in examining a number of illustrative data sets.

It has been shown that time-series *analysis* can be performed in a fairly mechanical manner, with a minimum of human input. On the other hand, time-series *model building* is considerably more exacting and requires significant human judgment. This matter is taken up in some detail in Chapter 9.

The following steps are involved in time-series analysis:

1.   Plot the data.
2.   Find the autocorrelation and the partials of the original series. If they drop to or near zero quickly—say, after the second or third value—it indicates that the data are stationary in their original form. Then, look for any patterns (see step 4 below). If they do not drop to zero and remain positive, nonstationarity is implied (see step 3 below). Use the line spectrum to reinforce these findings. The amplitude of the lowest frequency (one cycle) will usually dominate in a nonstationary series.
3.   When the autocorrelations suggest nonstationarity, take the first differences of the original data and calculate their autocorrelations. If they indicate stationarity, look for any remaining pattern (see step 4 below). If they are still nonstationary, take the first differences again and examine their autocorrelations. For most practical purposes a maximum of two differences will transform the data into a stationary series.
4.   When stationarity has been achieved, examine the autocorrelation to see if any pattern remains (that is, other than randomly scattered around zero). There are three possibilities to consider.
     a. Seasonality may suggest itself—autocorrelations for time lags of every quarter, or every year, are large and significantly

different from zero, and amplitudes for appropriate sine waves are large.

b. AR or MA processes may be revealed—the pattern of autocorrelations, of partials, and within the line spectrum, will indicate a possible model. (This is the subject matter of Chapter 9.)

c. Mixtures of nonstationary, seasonal, AR or MA processes (that is, general ARIMA models) may be indicated. (See Chapter 9 for further information on this.)

It must be remembered that the graph of autocorrelations is completely different from the graph of the data. The graph of the data is a visual aid to help identify the behavior of the pattern. The autocorrelations and the line spectrum are a summary of the pattern existing in the data. They can reveal a great deal about the data and their characteristics. With the wide availability of computers, calculating the autocorrelations, the partials, and the line spectrum is not the cumbersome job it used to be. This makes the job of time-series analysis relatively straightforward.

APPENDIX 8-A
THE BOX-PIERCE Q STATISTIC

Box and Pierce (1970) have developed a test that is capable of determining whether a set of autocorrelations, taken as a whole, represents a departure from a null set. For any given time series the idea is first to fit an ARIMA model, say ARIMA (p,d,q). For the set of residuals so determined, it is important to test whether the autocorrelations for these residuals are significantly different from zero. If no model is fitted, then the autocorrelations can be considered to come from an ARIMA $(0,0,0)$ model.

The Q statistic is computed as follows:

$$Q = n \sum_{k=1}^{m} r_k^2, \tag{8-28}$$

where m = maximum lag considered,

$\quad\quad n = N - d$

$\quad\quad N$ = original number of observations, and

$\quad\quad r_k$ = autocorrelation for lag k

and Q is distributed approximately as a chi-square statistic with $(m - p - q)$ degrees of freedom.

By way of example consider the 6 autocorrelations in Figure 8-14 (based on the data in Table 8-3). Here the implied model is ARIMA $(0,1,0)$ and $N = 12$ to start with. The Q statistic is computed as follows:

$$Q = 11[(.751)^2 + (.475)^2 + (.213)^2 + (-.010)^2 + (-.215)^2 + (-.347)^2]$$

$$= 11(.98) = 10.78,$$

and the df are $(6 - 0 - 0) = 6$. Looking up Table E in Appendix I, note that a chi-square value of 12.5916 for 6 df leaves 5 percent of the area in the right tail of the distribution. Thus the observed Q value of 10.78 is not significant at the 5 percent level.

The same data (Table 8-3) was differenced twice and the autocorrelations for this ARIMA $(0,2,0)$ model are shown in Figure 8-15. Here there are only $m = 5$ r_k values and $n = N - d = 12 - 2 = 10$, so that the Box-Pierce Q statistic is computed as follows:

$$Q = 10[(-.202)^2 + (-.217)^2 + (.155)^2 + (.151)^2 + (-.322)^2]$$

$$= 10(.238) = 2.38.$$

This Q statistic is considered to be a chi-square value with $(m-p-q) = (5 - 0 - 0) = 5$ df. In the chi-square tables it is clear that this Q value is nowhere near significant. The set of autocorrelations in Figure 8-15 compares favorably with a null set.

The pros and cons of the Box-Pierce statistic are being debated (see, for example, McLeod, 1978) but it can provide a useful index of goodness of fit, and has the merit of simplicity. Box and Jenkins (1976, pp. 290–292, 394–395) illustrate its use in both univariate and transfer function modeling contexts.

APPENDIX 8-B
FITTING SINE WAVES TO TIME-SERIES DATA

This appendix is organized as follows. First is a brief look at the properties of a single sine wave. Next is a discussion of how sine waves can be combined to generate a wide variety of data sets. Third, it will be shown that least squares regression techniques can be used to fit a single wave to time-series data, and fourth, this notion can be extended to handle the fitting of several sine waves to time-series data. Finally, a complete Fourier analysis (line spectrum analysis) will be presented along with a short BASIC program that can perform the analysis.

Properties of a Sine Wave

A sine wave is based on the equation $Y = \sin \theta$, where θ is an angle (measured in degrees of radians). For simplicity assume that θ ranges from 0 to 360 degrees (which is the same as from 0 to 2π radians). This equation describes a wave that has a maximum value of $+1$ and a minimum value of -1. It starts at zero (at 0 deg.), ends at zero (when $\theta = 360$ deg.) and crosses zero (when $\theta = 180$ deg.).

Multiplying the right-hand side of the equation by A, the amplitude of the sine wave can be controlled. Thus, in the equation $Y = A \sin \theta$, the maximum and minimum values are $+A$ and $-A$, respectively.

If the angle θ is multiplied by a constant f, the frequency (number of waves completed in 360 deg.) can be controlled. Thus, the equation $Y = A \sin f\theta$ will complete f waves in 360 deg.

Adding a constant angle ϕ to θ allows for phase shift (horizontal displacement of the wave). In the equation $Y = A \sin(f\theta + \phi)$, when $\theta = 0$, the value of Y is $A \sin \phi$.

There are thus three properties of interest in a sine wave: amplitude (A), frequency (f), and phase (ϕ). In the context of time-series data, these concepts are expressed in a slightly different form, as follows:

$$Y_t = A \sin\left[\left(\frac{ft}{n}\right)2\pi + \phi\right],$$

(8-29)

where A is the amplitude,

f is the frequency over a span of n observations,

t is a time index,

n is the number of periods of observation, and

ϕ is the phase angle (in radians).

The fraction (ft/n), for different values of t, converts the discrete time scale of time series into a proportion of 2π.

To explore the meaning of equation (8-29) consider some special cases.

Case 1: $A = 1, n = 64, f = 1$, and $\phi = 0$

Here the amplitude is 1, the frequency is 1 (meaning one complete wave or cycle is completed in $n = 64$ periods), and the phase shift is 0. Letting t range from 0 through 64, the following values can be computed.

t	(ft/n)	$Y_t = 1 \sin\left[\left(\dfrac{1t}{64}\right)2\pi + 0\right]$
0	0	0
1	1/64	.0980
2	2/64	.1951
3	3/64	.2903
.	.	.
.	.	.
.	.	.
63	63/64	−.0980
64	64/64	0

The complete set of values is plotted in Figure 8-20. Note that saying the frequency is 1 is the same as saying that the *wavelength* is 64 periods.

Case 2: $A = 2, n = 64, f = 2$, and $\phi = 0$

Here the amplitude is doubled and the frequency is doubled. Letting t range from 0 through 64, Y_t can be computed using the equation

$$Y_t = 2 \sin\left[\left(\frac{2t}{64}\right)2\pi + 0\right]$$

and a plot of such values is shown in Figure 8-21. Note that the maximum and minimum values are $+2$ and -2, and that the Y_t values describe two complete waves in 64 periods. In other words, the wavelength in this case is 32 periods.

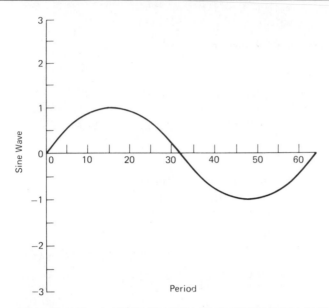

FIGURE 8-20 A PLOT OF THE SINE WAVE WITH AMPLITUDE = 1, FRE-QUENCY = 1, PHASE ANGLE = 0°, OVER N = 64 TIME PERIODS

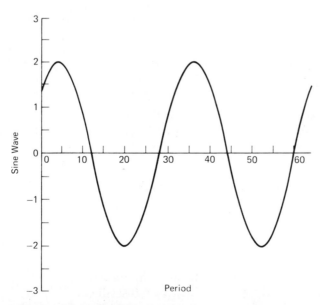

FIGURE 8-21 A PLOT OF THE SINE WAVE WITH AMPLITUDE = 2, FREQUENCY = 2, AND PHASE ANGLE = 0°, OVER N = 64 TIME PERIODS

Case 3: $A = 2, n = 64, f = 1$, and $\phi = 45$ deg. (or $\pi/4$ radians)

To show the influence of phase (horizontal displacement), this case involves computing Y_t values using the equation

$$Y_t = 2 \sin\left[\left(\frac{1t}{64}\right)2\pi + \frac{\pi}{4}\right].$$

Figure 8-22 shows that the one-cycle wave is displaced horizontally by one-eighth of a cycle.

To sum up, when sine waves are used in conjunction with time-series analysis, there are three fundamental properties of interest: (1) amplitude (or importance, or strength of the wave), (2) frequency (or its inverse, wavelength), and (3) phase (or shift of the wave—to allow for better fitting of a wave to observed data). In the next section, we consider how to fit a sine wave to empirical data.

Combining Several Sine Waves

Given equation (8-29) as the general definition of a sine wave over n time periods, it is possible to combine several such waves to create a more complicated periodic time series. For example, let there be k individual sine

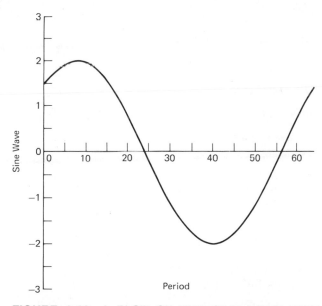

FIGURE 8-22   A PLOT OF THE SINE WAVE WITH AMPLITUDE = 2, FREQUENCY = 1, AND PHASE ANGLE = 45°, OVER N = 64 TIME PERIODS

waves, with amplitudes $A_1, A_2, \ldots, A_k$, frequencies $f_1, f_2, \ldots, f_k$, and phase angles $\phi_1, \phi_2, \ldots, \phi_k$. Then the sum of these waves is defined as follows:

$$Y_t = \sum_{i=1}^{k} A_i \sin\left[\left(\frac{f_i t}{n}\right)2\pi + \phi_i\right]. \tag{8-30}$$

It is easy to generate many such time series, but the forecaster is more interested in *fitting* sine waves to data, as will be discussed in the next two sections.

Fitting a Single Sine Wave to a Time Series

Consider $n = 48$ quarterly observations on sales. Assume there is no trend but there is a distinct seasonality. The objective is to fit a sine wave that will capture the seasonality of the data. In other words, fit a sine wave of wavelength 4 (i.e., one wave completes itself in 4 periods)—or frequency $48/4 = 12$. The other two properties of the sine wave—amplitude and phase—are to be determined in such a way as to get the "best fit."

The equation of interest is thus

$$y_t = A \sin\left[\left(\frac{ft}{n}\right)2\pi + \phi\right] + e_t, \tag{8-31}$$

where y_t is sales data in deviation form,

　　　A is the *unknown* amplitude,

　　　f is the known frequency ($f = 12$),

　　　t ranges from 1 through 48,

　　　ϕ is the *unknown* phase angle (in radians),

　　　e_t is the error of fit.

As it stands, equation (8-31) is a nonlinear regression problem and not easy to solve directly. However, there is a simple theorem in trigonometry that states the following:

　　　$\sin(U + V) = (\sin U)(\cos V) + (\cos U)(\sin V)$,

where U and V are two angles. Making use of this theorem, the task of solving equation (8-31) is made easier, as follows: Letting $U = (ft/n)2\pi$ and $V = \phi$,

　　　$y_t = A[(\sin U)(\cos V) + (\cos U)(\sin V)] + e_t,$

which, with a little rearranging, becomes

$$y_t = b_1 \sin\left[\left(\frac{ft}{n}\right)2\pi\right] + b_2 \cos\left[\left(\frac{ft}{n}\right)2\pi\right] + e_t,$$ (8-32)

where $b_1 = A \cos \phi$,

$b_2 = A \sin \phi$.

Note that equation (8-32) is now in the form of an ordinary regression equation, $y_t = b_1 X_1 + b_2 X_2 + e_t$, and there is no constant term because y_t is a deviation from the mean.

For example, the data setup for this example might be as follows:

t	y_t	$X_1 = \sin[(12t/48)2\pi]$	$X_2 = \cos[(12t/48)2\pi]$
1	12	1	0
2	46	0	−1
3	−10	−1	0
.	.	.	.
.	.	.	.
.	.	.	.
48	−7	0	1

Solving this simple linear regression problem by ordinary least squares procedures yields estimates of b_1 and b_2. How then do we recover the unknown amplitude (A) and the unknown phase (ϕ)? Using equation (8-32), the development is as follows:

$$b_1^2 + b_2^2 = (A \cos \phi)^2 + (A \sin \phi)^2$$

$$= A^2 [(\cos^2 \phi) + (\sin^2 \phi)]$$

$$= A^2$$

so that

$$A = \sqrt{b_1^2 + b_2^2},$$ (8-33)

$$\cos \phi = b_1 / \sqrt{b_1^2 + b_2^2},$$ (8-34)

$$\sin \phi = b_2 / \sqrt{b_1^2 + b_2^2}.$$ (8-35)

From equation (8-33) we determine the amplitude A, and from equations (8-34) and (8-35) we determined the phase angle ϕ. For example, suppose the estimates of b_1 and b_2 are -1.6 and $+3.1$, respectively. Then

$$A = \sqrt{(-1.6)^2 + (3.1)^2} = 3.49,$$

$$\cos \phi = (-1.6) / (3.49) = -.46,$$

$$\sin \phi = (3.1) / (3.49) = .89,$$

and the phase angle ϕ must be in the second quadrant (that is, between 90 and 180 deg.), so that

$$\phi = 180° - 62.67° = 117.33°.$$

Note that in this regression fitting procedure for one sine wave there is no requirement that the frequency f has to be an integer value.

Fitting a Set of Sine Waves to a Time Series

The procedure outlined above can be extended readily to fitting a set of sine waves, with known frequencies $f_1, f_2, \ldots, f_k$, say. The objective is to determine the amplitudes $(A_1, A_2, \ldots, A_k)$ and the phase angles $(\phi_1, \phi_2, \ldots, \phi_k)$ that would provide the "best fit" to the time series. Equation (8-32) can be generalized as follows:

$$y_t = \sum_{i=1}^{k} \left[b_{1i} \sin \left(\frac{f_i t}{n} \right) 2\pi + b_{2i} \cos \left(\frac{f_i t}{n} \right) 2\pi \right] + e_t. \tag{8-36}$$

Using LS regression techniques, we can solve for the k pairs of coefficients (b_{1i}, b_{2i}), $i = 1, 2, \ldots, k$, and can then solve for the amplitude A_i and the phase angle ϕ_i using equations (8-33), (8-34), and (8-35):

$$A_i = \sqrt{b_{1i}^2 + b_{2i}^2},$$

$$\cos \phi_i = b_{1i} / A_i,$$

$$\sin \phi_i = b_{2i} / A_i.$$

Both the fitting of a single sine wave and the fitting of multiple sine waves require that the frequencies be known ahead of time. Clearly there are many situations where the objective is to find out what these frequencies should be. In the next section, we discuss this problem.

Fourier Analysis (Line Spectrum Analysis)

Given a set of N observations (where for the moment N will be assumed an odd number) the purpose of Fourier analysis is to compute N coefficients $\alpha_0, \alpha_1, \alpha_2, \ldots, \alpha_k$ and $\beta_1, \beta_2, \ldots, \beta_k$, where $k = (N - 1)/2$, which satisfy the equations

$$Y_t = \frac{1}{2}\alpha_0 + \sum_{f=1}^{k}\left[\alpha_f \cos\left[\left(\frac{ft}{N}\right)2\pi\right] + \beta_f \sin\left[\left(\frac{ft}{N}\right)2\pi\right]\right] \qquad (8\text{-}37)$$

for $t = 1, \ldots, N$, where $k = (N - 1)/2$. An efficient solution procedure and a computer flowchart are given in Goertzel (1960), and a simple BASIC program is listed below to accomplish two things:

  i.   the determination of the Fourier coefficients α_f ($f = 0, 1, \ldots, k$) and β_f ($f = 1, 2, \ldots, k$);
  ii. the conversion of these coefficients into amplitudes and phase angles for each of the $k = (N - 1)/2$ frequencies.

This Fourier analysis (or what we have called line spectrum analysis) provides useful information as to any periodicities that might exist in a time series. To demonstrate this point consider a couple of illustrative examples.

Example 1

Here a set of $N = 21$ data points are generated according to the equation

$$Y_t = 100 + 3\sin\left[\left(\frac{2t}{21}\right)2\pi + \frac{\pi}{2}\right] \qquad (t = 1, 2, \ldots, 21).$$

In other words, this deals with a sine wave having frequency 2 (2 cycles completed in 21 periods), amplitude = 3, and phase angle = 90 degrees. Table 8-4 shows the data so generated.

TABLE 8-4 A SAMPLE DATA SET GENERATED ACCORDING TO THE EQUATION $Y_t = 100 + 3\sin\left[\left(\frac{2t}{21}\right)2\pi + \frac{\pi}{2}\right]$

Sample Data Set		Sample Data Set	
1	102.479	12	101.870
2	101.096	13	100.224
3	99.332	14	98.500
4	97.801	15	97.297
5	97.034	16	97.034
6	97.297	17	97.801
7	98.500	18	99.332
8	100.224	19	101.096
9	101.870	20	102.479
10	102.867	21	103.000
11	102.867		

Applying the FOURIER program, the Fourier coefficients are as follows:

The Fourier Coefficients

P	Alpha	Beta
0	100,000	0.000
1	0.000	0.000
2	3.000	0.000
3	0.000	0.000
4	0.000	0.000
5	0.000	0.000
6	0.000	0.000
7	0.000	0.000
8	0.000	0.000
9	0.000	0.000
10	0.000	0.000

and the line spectrum (or harmonic analysis) is shown in Figure 8-23. Note that the coefficient $\alpha_0 = 100$ (the mean of the data set), that the amplitude for the 2-cycle frequency is indeed 3, as expected, and the phase angle is 90 degrees, as expected.

```
FREQ    AMP    PHASE :
--------------------:----+----1----+----2----+----3----+----4
  1    0.00   308.45 :
  2    3.00    90.00 :*****************************************
  3    0.00   251.64 :
  4    0.00   238.35 :
  5    0.00   226.98 :
  6    0.00   219.28 :
  7    0.00   210.00 :
  8    0.00   201.67 :
  9    0.00   193.32 :
 10    0.00   183.72 :
--------------------:----+----1----+----2----+----3----+----4
```

FIGURE 8-23   THE LINE SPECTRUM ANALYSIS OF THE DATA IN TABLE 8-4

Example 2

As a second simulation example consider generating $N = 21$ data points using the equation:

$$Y_t = 100 + \sum_{j=1}^{3} A_j \sin\left[\left(\frac{f_j t}{21}\right) 2\pi + P_j\right] + e_t,$$

where $f_1 = 2, f_2 = 4, f_3 = 5,$

$\quad A_1 = 4, A_2 = 3, A_3 = 6,$

$\quad P_1 = 90$ deg., $P_2 = 0, P_3 = 100$ deg., and

$\quad e_t$ is $ND(0,6)$.

Such a data set is shown in Table 8-5. Using the FOURIER program, the Fourier coefficients are computed to be:

The Fourier Coefficients

P	Alpha	Beta
0	100.428	0.000
1	0.394	−0.820
2	3.631	−1.636
3	0.668	−0.155
4	−0.308	3.734
5	5.547	−1.875
6	1.861	−0.187
7	0.316	−0.391
8	−0.493	0.650
9	−1.359	0.867
10	−0.260	1.110

TABLE 8-5 A SAMPLE TIME SERIES GENERATED TO CONTAIN THREE FREQUENCIES (f = 2, 4, and 5) BUT WITH AN ADDED ERROR TERM

Sample Data Set		Sample Data Set	
1	106.578	12	107.576
2	92.597	13	104.658
3	99.899	14	91.562
4	97.132	15	91.661
5	93.121	16	97.984
6	95.081	17	111.195
7	102.807	18	100.127
8	106.944	19	94.815
9	100.443	20	105.009
10	95.546	21	110.425
11	103.836		

```
FREQ    AMP    PHASE :
--------------------------:----+----1----+----2----+----3----+----4
   1    0.91  154.33 :******
   2    3.98  114.25 :***************************
   3    0.69  103.07 :****
   4    3.75  355.29 :*************************
   5    5.85  108.67 :*****************************************
   6    1.87   95.74 :************
   7    0.50  141.07 :***
   8    0.82  322.84 :*****
   9    1.61  302.54 :***********
  10    1.14  346.83 :*******
--------------------------:----+----1----+----2----+----3----+----4
```

FIGURE 8-24　THE LINE SPECTRUM ANALYSIS OF THE DATA IN TABLE 8-5

And converting these to amplitudes and phase angles yields the line spectrum shown in Figure 8-24. Here, because a random error term e_t was added to the periodic values, the results are not exactly "pure." The three main frequencies showing up are 2, 4, and 5, as built into the simulated data, but other frequencies are represented too. Similarly the amplitudes for $f = 2$, $f = 4$, and $f = 6$ were built into the simulation as 4, 3, and 6, and turn out to be 3.98, 3.75, and 5.85, respectively, in the solution. The original phase angles of 90 deg., 0 and 100 deg. turn out to be 114.25 deg., 355.29 deg., and 108.67 deg., respectively, in the empirical solution.

This method of analysis is clearly useful in determining if there are any periodicities in a time series.

What if N is an Even Number?

The same program (FOURIER) can be used to solve for the Fourier coefficients and the line spectrum if N is an even number. The maximum number of frequencies that can be handled in this case is $(N/2) - 1$. Thus Figure 8-25 shows a complete analysis for $N = 10$ data points, generated to contain two waves with the following specifications:

Frequency	Amplitude	Phase Angle
1	2	50 deg.
2	3	76 deg.

Note that the analysis correctly identifies the two frequencies (2 and 3), the two phase angles (50 and 76 deg.), and that the maximum frequency that

```
INPUT N = NO. DATA POINTS
      M = NO. OF WAVES TO BE USED (UP TO 10)
      V = VARIANCE OF ERROR TERM
? 10,2,0

FOR EACH WAVE ENTER FREQUENCY, AMPLITUDE & PHASE (IN DEGREES)
WAVE  1 ? 1,2,50
WAVE  2 ? 2,3,76

SAMPLE DATA SET
================
    1     103.585
    2      99.768
    3      97.968
    4      99.725
    5     101.379
    6      99.595
    7      96.376
    8      96.469
    9     100.693
   10     104.443


THE FOURIER COEFFICIENTS
========================
   F      ALPHA        BETA
   =      =====        ====
   0     100.000      0.000
   1       1.532      1.286
   2       2.911      0.726
   3       0.000      0.000
   4       0.000      0.000


HARMONIC ANALYSIS
=================
FREQ    AMP    PHASE :
---------------------:----+----1----+----2----+----3----+----4
   1    2.00    50.00 :***************************
   2    3.00    76.00 :******************************************
   3    0.00   212.60 :
   4    0.00   195.33 :
---------------------:----+----1----+----2----+----3----+----4
```

FIGURE 8-25   SIMULATED DATA (A TIME SERIES CONTAINING ONE- AND
TWO-CYCLE PERIODICITIES) AND A LINE SPECTRUM
ANALYSIS

can be studied when $n = 10$, is

$$f_{max} = (10/2) - 1 = 4.$$

In sum, the Fourier analysis of a time series enables the forecaster to determine periodicities (if any) in the data. After examining the complete line spectrum, the investigator may wish to do a regression fit of selected frequencies—and these selected frequencies do not need to be integer valued.

Here is the listing of a simple subroutine that can perform the Fourier analysis and compute the line spectrum for a data set.

```
100 SUB "FOURIER": T, F(), E(), G(), P1
110    '   T   = NO. OF DATA POINTS
120    '   F() = DATA SERIES
130    '   E()   WILL RETURN WITH AMPLITUDES
140    '   G()   WILL RETURN WITH PHASE ANGLES (IN DEGREES)
150    '   P1    WILL RETURN AS MAXIMUM FREQUENCY
160    LET P1 = INT((T-1)/2)              'Max frequency allowed
170    LET C1 = COS(2*3.1415926/T)
180    LET S1 = SIN(2*3.1415926/T)
190    LET S = P = 0
200    LET C = 1
210    LET U1 = U2 = 0
220    LET K = T
230    LET U = F(K) + 2*C*U1 - U2
240    LET U2 = U1
250    LET U1 = U
260    LET K = K-1
270    IF K <= 0 THEN 290
280        GOTO 230
290    LET A = 2/T*(F(K) + C*U1 - U2)
300    LET B = 2/T*S*U1
310    IF P > 0 THEN 340
320        LET A = A/2
330        PRINT "P","ALPHA","BETA"
340    PRINT P, A, B
350    IF P = 0 THEN 480
360        LET E(P) = SQR(A*A+B*B)
370        LET T2 = ABS(A/B)
380        LET T2 = 360/2/3.1415926*ATN(T2)
390        IF B>0 THEN 450
400            IF A>0 THEN 430
410                LET T2 = 180+T2
420                GOTO 470
430            LET T2 = 180-T2
440            GOTO 470
450        IF A>0 THEN 470
460            LET T2 = 360-T2
470        LET G(P) = T2
480    IF P = P1 THEN 540
490        LET Q = C1*C - S1*S
500        LET S = C1*S + S1*C
510        LET C = Q
520        LET P = P+1
530        GO TO 210
540    PRINT
550    PRINT "FREQ","AMPLITUDE","PHASE"
560    FOR I = 1 TO P1
570        PRINT I,E(I),G(I)
580    NEXT I
590 SUBEND
```

REFERENCES AND SELECTED BIBLIOGRAPHY

Anderson, R. L., 1942. "Distribution of the Serial Correlation Coefficient," *Annals of Mathematical Statistics,* **13,** pp. 1–13.

Bartlett, M. S. 1946. "On the Theoretical Specification of Sampling Properties of Autocorrelated Time Series," *Journal of the Royal Statistical Society,* Series B, **8,** p. 27.

Bloomfield, Peter. 1976. *Fourier Analysis of Time Series: An Introduction.* New York: John Wiley & Sons, Inc.

Box, G. E. P., and G. M. Jenkins. 1976. *Time Series Analysis: Forecasting and Control,* Revised Edition. San Francisco: Holden-Day.

Box, G. E. P., and D. A. Pierce. 1970. "Distribution of the Residual Autocorrelations in Autoregressive-Integrated Moving-Average Time Series Models," *Journal of the American Statistical Association,* **65,** pp. 1509–26.

Goertzel, G. 1960. "Fourier Analysis," in *Mathematical Methods for Digital Computers,* edited by A. Ralston and H. S. Wilf. New York: John Wiley & Sons, Inc., pp. 258–262.

Granger, C. W. J. 1980. *Forecasting in Business and Economics.* New York: Academic Press.

Makridakis, S., and S. Wheelwright. 1978. *Interactive Forecasting,* second ed. San Francisco: Holden-Day.

McLeod, A. I. "On the Distribution of Residual Autocorrelations in Box-Jenkins Models," *Journal of the Royal Statistical Society,* Series B, 1978, **40,** No. 3, pp. 296–302.

Montgomery, D. C., and L. A. Johnson. 1976. *Forecasting and Time Series Analysis.* New York: McGraw-Hill.

Nelson, C. R. 1973. *Applied Time Series Analysis.* San Francisco: Holden-Day.

Quenouille, M. H. 1949. "The Joint Distribution of Serial Correlation Coefficients," *Annals of Mathematical Statistics,* **20,** pp. 561–71.

Wold, H. 1954. *A Study in the Analysis of Stationary Time Series.* Stockholm: Almquist & Wiksell (1st ed., 1938).

EXERCISES

1. Use the data of Table 8-1, column 2, to verify that the autocorrelation coefficients for time lags of 3 and 4 periods are .181 and $-.132$, respectively. What is the meaning of $r_3 = .181$? Of $r_4 = -.132$?

2. Using the simple noiseless series of 1, 2, 3, 4, 5, 6, 7, 8, 9, 10, calculate the autocorrelation coefficients for time lags of 1, 2, 3, 4, and 5 periods. Plot these

autocorrelations and explain why they lie on a diagonal line going from larger to smaller values as the time lag is extended.

3. Figure 8-4 shows the autocorrelations for the 36 numbers in Table 8-2.
   a. Compute the 95 percent confidence interval lines for Figure 8-4.
   b. Figure 8-26 shows the autocorrelations for 360 random numbers and Figure 8-27 shows the autocorrelation for 1000 random numbers. Explain the differences among these figures and Figure 8-4. Do they all indicate randomness in the data?
   c. Why are the confidence lines at different distances from the mean of zero? Why are the autocorrelations different in each figure when they refer to random numbers?

4. Table 8-6 shows a time series composed of 60 values. Plot this series to identify its trend. Compute the first differences and plot the resulting series. Explain why the differenced series does not have a trend. Using a computer, find the autocorrelations for time lags of 1, 2, 3, and 4 periods for both the original and the differenced series.

5. Table 8-7 shows the data for Manufacturer's stocks of Evaporated and Sweetened Condensed Milk (case goods) for the period January 1971 through December 1980. Figure 8-28 presents the analysis of this time series, showing the data plot, the line spectrum, the autocorrelations, and the partials.
   a. What is your description of the data plot?
   b. How do you interpret the line spectrum?
   c. What can you learn from the autocorrelation graph?
   d. What messages do you get out of the partials graph?

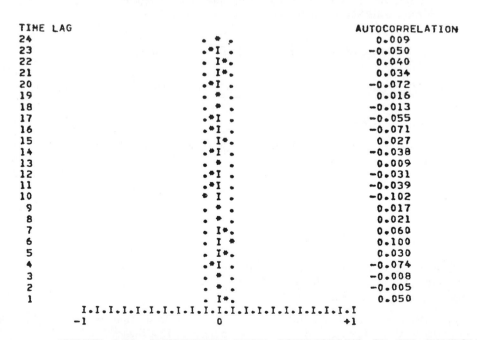

FIGURE 8-26 AUTOCORRELATION COEFFICIENTS OF 360 RANDOM NUMBERS

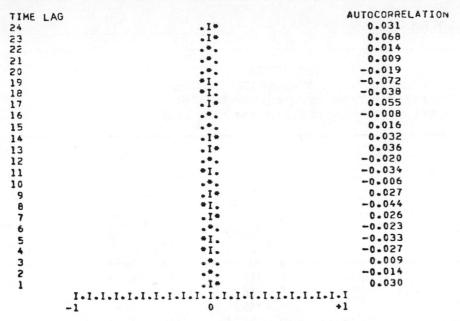

```
TIME LAG                                          AUTOCORRELATION
24                        .I*                          0.031
23                        .I*                          0.068
22                        .*.                          0.014
21                        .*.                          0.009
20                        .*.                         -0.019
19                        *I.                         -0.072
18                        *I.                         -0.038
17                        .I*                          0.055
16                        .*.                         -0.008
15                        .*.                          0.016
14                        .I*                          0.032
13                        .I*                          0.036
12                        .*.                         -0.020
11                        *I.                         -0.034
10                        .*.                         -0.006
 9                        .I*                          0.027
 8                        *I.                         -0.044
 7                        .I*                          0.026
 6                        .*.                         -0.023
 5                        *I.                         -0.033
 4                        *I.                         -0.027
 3                        .*.                          0.009
 2                        .*.                         -0.014
 1                        .I*                          0.030
       I.I.I.I.I.I.I.I.I.I.I.I.I.I.I.I.I.I.I.I.I
      -1                   0                   +1
```

FIGURE 8-27 AUTOCORRELATION COEFFICIENTS OF 1000 RANDOM NUMBERS

TABLE 8-6 TIME SERIES WITH 60 VALUES

Period	Observation	Period	Observation	Period	Observation
1	9.560	21	60.500	41	85.280
2	12.480	22	63.290	42	84.440
3	13.640	23	66.550	43	86.590
4	18.800	24	68.650	44	88.050
5	25.040	25	72.660	45	90.830
6	30.330	26	71.250	46	93.050
7	34.080	27	65.480	47	94.650
8	40.100	28	62.680	48	96.660
9	42.400	29	56.600	49	96.300
10	41.360	30	49.900	50	96.090
11	39.250	31	49.820	51	99.270
12	38.200	32	51.870	52	104.770
13	41.470	33	57.740	53	105.510
14	46.140	34	58.240	54	105.190
15	52.620	35	58.310	55	109.160
16	59.010	36	59.910	56	110.780
17	60.200	37	62.610	57	115.770
18	58.530	38	69.070	58	122.750
19	56.980	39	77.360	59	126.850
20	57.820	40	80.390	60	132.570

TABLE 8-7 STOCKS OF EVAPORATED AND SWEETENED CONDENSED
MILK FOR THE PERIOD JANUARY 1971 THROUGH
DECEMBER 1980 (Source: United States Department
of Agriculture's *Agricultural Outlook,* Vols. 1971–1980)

t	X_t	t	X_t	t	X_t	t	X_t
1	81.28	37	54.49	73	66.29	109	75.28
2	69.39	38	57.50	74	63.49	110	73.89
3	67.63	39	62.16	75	62.97	111	76.24
4	51.25	40	76.67	76	66.43	112	88.58
5	103.97	41	110.04	77	101.49	113	105.83
6	133.83	42	127.38	78	127.69	114	115.84
7	162.37	43	156.47	79	133.21	115	127.76
8	172.91	44	167.56	80	158.72	116	131.75
9	163.01	45	153.54	81	148.61	117	119.63
10	151.50	46	124.08	82	134.31	118	93.38
11	111.73	47	100.97	83	100.99	119	75.55
12	88.58	48	79.17	84	75.16	120	51.79
13	74.29	49	68.13	85	59.74		
14	63.98	50	61.77	86	52.87		
15	61.18	51	54.31	87	52.07		
16	76.48	52	60.30	88	57.38		
17	107.98	53	84.18	89	79.43		
18	124.97	54	104.05	90	101.40		
19	145.57	55	114.66	91	120.19		
20	140.20	56	105.55	92	134.38		
21	143.84	57	96.61	93	135.97		
22	138.80	58	70.94	94	113.83		
23	104.06	59	63.91	95	84.38		
24	74.70	60	58.61	96	70.28		
25	60.18	61	44.53	97	65.96		
26	55.16	62	49.58	98	56.36		
27	35.62	63	57.39	99	49.57		
28	56.18	64	76.76	100	68.33		
29	85.44	65	104.57	101	90.32		
30	114.08	66	125.41	102	117.06		
31	133.64	67	143.11	103	134.69		
32	67.14	68	136.35	104	131.67		
33	95.58	69	135.15	105	129.25		
34	89.37	70	131.70	106	118.77		
35	75.24	71	96.87	107	88.44		
36	69.18	72	70.63	108	76.79		

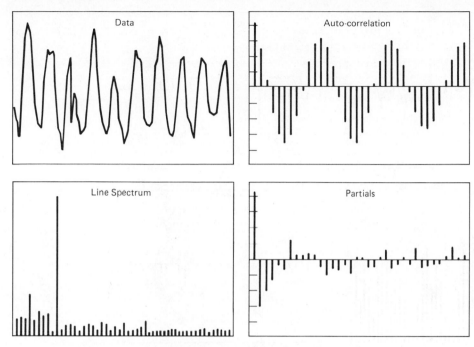

FIGURE 8-28   STOCKS OF EVAPORATED AND SWEETENED CONDENSED
MILK: AN ANALYSIS OF THE TIME SERIES SHOWING A DATA
PLOT, THE LINE SPECTRUM, THE AUTOCORRELATIONS AND
THE PARTIALS

6.   For the same data series shown in Table 8-7 (stocks of evaporated and sweet-
      ened condensed milk) Figure 8-29 shows an analysis of the differenced data
      $(1 - B)(1 - B^{12})X_t$—that is, a first-order nonseasonal differencing $(d = 1)$
      and a first-order seasonal differencing $(D = 1)$.
      a. Are there any problems in the data plot of these differences?
      b. What does the line spectrum tell you in this case?
      c. What does the autocorrelation graph tell you?
      d. What does the partial autocorrelation graph tell you?

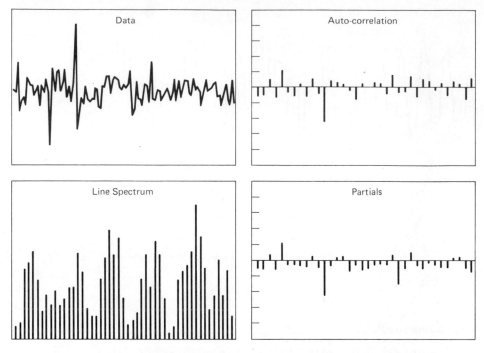

FIGURE 8-29   STOCKS OF EVAPORATED AND SWEETENED CONDENSED MILK: AN ANALYSIS OF THE NONSEASONAL AND SEASONALLY DIFFERENCED DATA SHOWING A PLOT OF THE DIFFERENCES, THE LINE SPECTRUM, THE AUTOCOR-RELATIONS, AND THE PARTIALS

9/THE BOX-JENKINS METHOD

9/1 Introduction

Autoregressive/Integrated/Moving Average (ARIMA) models have been studied extensively by George Box and Gwilym Jenkins (1976), and their names have frequently been used synonymously with general ARIMA processes applied to time-series analysis, forecasting, and control. Autoregressive (AR) models were first introduced by Yule (1926) and later generalized by Walker (1931), while moving average (MA) models were first used by Slutzky (1937). It was the work of Wold (1938), however, that provided the theoretical foundations of combined ARMA processes. Building on Wold's work, ARMA models have developed in three directions—efficient identification and estimation procedures (for AR, MA, and mixed ARMA processes), extension of the results to include seasonal time series, and the simple extension to include nonstationary processes (ARIMA).

Box and Jenkins (1976) have effectively put together in a comprehensive manner the relevant information required to understand and use univariate time series ARIMA models like those described in the last chapter. The basis of their approach is summarized in Figure 9-1 and consists of three phases: identification, estimation and testing, and application. In the remainder of this chapter, each of the three phases of Figure 9-1 will be examined and practical examples illustrating their application (the Box-Jenkins methodology) to univariate time-series analysis will be given.

The theoretical underpinnings described in Box and Jenkins (1976) are quite sophisticated, but it is possible for the nonspecialist to get a clear understanding of the essence of ARIMA methodology. The Nelson (1973) book is excellent in this regard, in that it is specifically intended for a managerial audience. Our approach in this chapter will include three aspects:

1. The notation will be established for a general ARIMA (p,d,q) model, and the various special cases of the general model will all be treated in the same notational framework.
2. Use will be made of a simulation program (called ARIMA) to *generate* time-series data, according to any specified ARIMA model.
3. The simulated data from a specified ARIMA model will be *analyzed* to see how closely the *empirical* properties of the time series match the known *theoretical* properties.

Using this approach, the reader will learn to identify properties of the time series, from a careful analysis of the autocorrelations, partials, and line spectrum.

9/2 Identification

The first thing to note is that most time series are nonstationary, and the AR and MA aspects of an ARIMA model refer only to a stationary

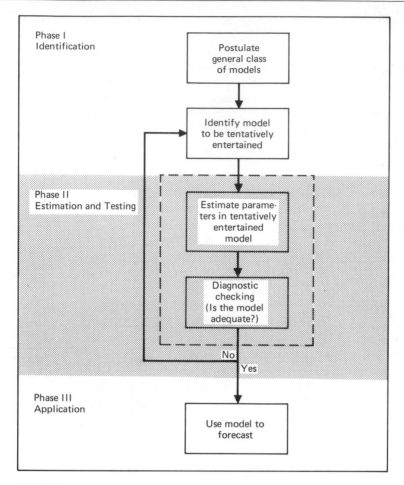

FIGURE 9-1   SCHEMATIC REPRESENTATION OF THE BOX-JENKINS
APPROACH

time series. Therefore, it is necessary to have a notational distinction between the original nonstationary time series and its stationary counterpart, after differencing.

9/2/1   Stationarity and Nonstationarity

A very useful notational device is the backward shift operator, B, which is used as follows:

$$B X_t = X_{t-1}. \tag{9-1}$$

In other words, B, operating on X_t, has the effect of shifting the data back

1 period. Two applications of B to X_t shifts the data back 2 periods, as follows:

$$B(BX_t) = B^2 X_t = X_{t-2}. \tag{9-2}$$

For monthly data, if we wish to shift attention to "the same month last year," then B^{12} is used, and the notation is $B^{12} X_t = X_{t-12}$.

The backward shift operator is convenient for describing the process of *differencing*. For example, if a time series is not stationary, then it can be made more nearly stationary by taking the first difference of the series, and equation (9-3) defines what is meant by a first difference.

FIRST DIFFERENCE

$$X_t' = X_t - X_{t-1} \tag{9-3}$$

Using the backward shift operator, equation (9-3) can be rewritten.

FIRST DIFFERENCE

$$X_t' = X_t - BX_t = (1 - B)X_t \tag{9-4}$$

Note that a first difference is represented by $(1 - B)$. Similarly, if second-order differences (that is, first differences of first differences) have to be computed, then:

SECOND-ORDER DIFFERENCE

$$
\begin{aligned}
X_t'' &= X_t' - X_{t-1}' \\
&= (X_t - X_{t-1}) - (X_{t-1} - X_{t-2}) \\
&= X_t - 2X_{t-1} + X_{t-2} \\
&= (1 - 2B + B^2)\,X_t \\
&= (1 - B)^2\,X_t.
\end{aligned}
\tag{9-5}
$$

Note that the second-order difference is denoted $(1 - B)^2$. (It is important to recognize that a *second-order difference* is not the same as a *second difference*, which would be denoted $1 - B^2$. Similarly, a twelfth difference would be $1 - B^{12}$, but a twelfth-order difference would be $(1 - B)^{12}$.)

The purpose of taking differences is to achieve stationarity, and in general, if it takes a dth-order difference to achieve stationarity, we will write

$$d\text{th-order difference} = (1 - B)^d\,X_t$$

as the stationary series, and the general ARIMA (0,d,0) model will be

ARIMA (0,d,0)

$$
\underset{\substack{\uparrow \\ (d\text{th-order difference})}}{(1 - B)^d\,X_t} = \underset{\substack{\uparrow \\ (\text{error term})}}{e_t}
\tag{9-6}
$$

Recall (from Chapter 8) that ARIMA $(0,d,0)$ means no autoregressive (AR) aspect, no moving average (MA) aspect, and a dth-order difference of the original data.

What does an ARIMA $(0,d,0)$ process look like? To answer this, we make use of the simulation program, ARIMA, which allows any ARIMA model to be specified, generates n data points from such a model, and presents graphically the theoretically expected results for such a model. By way of illustration, consider an ARIMA $(0,1,0)$ model. Figure 9-2 shows the graph of $n = 100$ data points generated according to an ARIMA $(0,1,0)$ model (which follows from equation (9-6)). The data clearly have trend (or a "wandering mean") as expected and are therefore nonstationary.

To make it stationary, we would take the first differences of the data series. For an ARIMA $(0,1,0)$ process we know that first differences would make the series stationary. And for the stationary series, so produced, the *theoretical* autocorrelations, partial autocorrelations and power spectrum (which is the theoretical counterpart of the line spectrum discussed in Chapter 8) would be as shown in Figure 9-2. The top right box shows that, theoretically, all autocorrelations should be zero. The bottom right box shows that all partials should be zero, theoretically, and the bottom left box shows

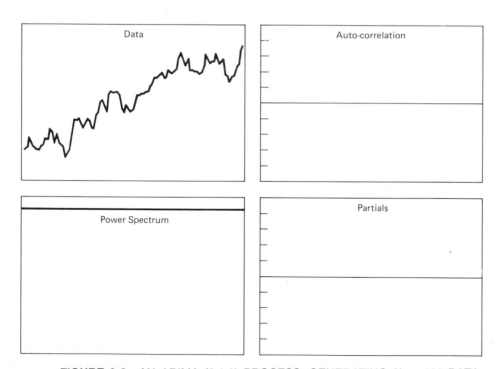

FIGURE 9-2 AN ARIMA $(0,1,0)$ PROCESS: GENERATING $N = 100$ DATA POINTS USING THE SIMULATION PROGRAM ARIMA

that the power spectrum is a continuous line, exactly horizontal, and uniformly high—indicating that all frequencies are represented in the time series with equal amplitudes.

How can we make use of this information? If, for a given time series, an analysis of first differences suggests that (i) the autocorrelations are not significantly different from zero, (ii) the partial autocorrelations are not significantly different from zero, and (iii) the line spectrum is roughly uniform, then we could be confident that the original series was similar to an ARIMA (0,1,0) process, and we would model it as such.

9/2/2 Autoregressive Processes

Section 8/2/3 described the simple ARIMA (1,0,0)—or AR(1)—model—that is, a first-order autoregressive model. In general, for a pth-order AR process, we will designate it as follows:

ARIMA (p,0,0)

$$X_t = \mu' + \phi_1 X_{t-1} + \phi_2 X_{t-2} + \ldots + \phi_p X_{t-p} + e_t, \tag{9-7}$$

where μ' = constant term,

ϕ_j = jth autoregressive parameter,

e_t = the error term at time t

and note that there are specific restrictions on the values of the autoregressive parameters.[1] In practice, the two cases most likely to be encountered are when $p = 1$ and $p = 2$, corresponding to the AR(1) and AR(2) models, respectively. These two cases are defined as follows:

ARIMA (1,0,0)

$$X_t = \mu' + \phi_1 X_{t-1} + e_t \tag{9-8}$$

ARIMA (2,0,0)

$$X_t = \mu' + \phi_1 X_{t-1} + \phi_2 X_{t-2} + e_t \tag{9-9}$$

Now, using the backward shift operator symbol, B, equations (9-8) and (9-9) can be rewritten as equations (9-10) and (9-11), respectively.

ARIMA (1,0,0)

$$\left. \begin{array}{l} X_t - \phi_1 X_{t-1} = \mu' + e_t \\[1em] \text{or} \\[1em] (1 - \phi_1 B)X_t = \mu' + e_t \end{array} \right\} \tag{9-10}$$

---

[1]Figure 9-6 should be referred to for these restrictions in the special cases where $p = 1$ and $p = 2$.

ARIMA (2,0,0)

$$X_t - \phi_1 X_{t-1} - \phi_2 X_{t-2} = \mu' + e_t$$

or

$$(1 - \phi_1 B - \phi_2 B^2)X_t = \mu' + e_t$$

(9-11)

What would an AR(1) process look like? Using the simulation program, ARIMA, we can generate $n = 100$ values according to an ARIMA (1,0,0) process—using equation (9-10) and a specific value for ϕ_1. Note that the range of permissible values for ϕ_1 in an AR(1) model are $-1 < \phi_1 < +1$. The generated data are plotted in the top left box of Figure 9-3 and it is not immediately apparent that this is a stationary series. The model behind Figure 9-3 is

$$X_t = .6 \, X_{t-1} + 40 + e_t$$

or

$$(1 - .6 \, B) \, X_t = 40 + e_t,$$

where the error term, e_t, is generated from a normal distribution with mean zero and variance 5.

Figure 9-3 shows what the theoretical autocorrelations, partials and power spectrum should be for an AR(1) model with parameter, .6. Note that the autocorrelations decay exponentially, that there is only one nonzero partial autocorrelation, and that the power spectrum indicates the predominance of low-frequency components. In order to *identify* an ARIMA (1,0,0) model for any real-world time series, we do an empirical analysis of the data and look for (i) exponentially decaying autocorrelations, (ii) a single significant partial, and (iii) dominance of low-frequency amplitudes. Figure 9-4 shows the empirical analysis of the data generated in Figure 9-3. Note that the *empirical* autocorrelations do decay exponentially, but because of the error component, they do not die out to zero. Similarly, there is one dominant partial, but also some random nonzero partials, and the line spectrum shows the tendency of low frequency amplitudes to dominate.

Figure 9-5 shows the theoretical results for a pure AR(2) process, defined as follows[2]:

ARIMA (2,0,0)

$$X_t = 1.2 \, X_{t-1} - .8 \, X_{t-2} + 60 + e_t,$$

where e_t was generated from a normal distribution with mean zero and variance 5. Note that for the second-degree AR process, the theoretical

---

[2]Consult Figure 9-6 for the restrictions on the values of the two AR parameters, ϕ_1 and ϕ_2.

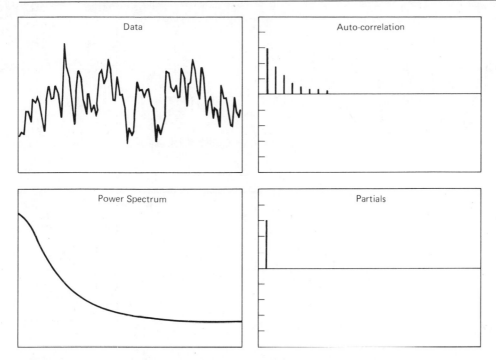

FIGURE 9-3 AN ARIMA (1,0,0) PROCESS: GENERATING $N = 100$ DATA
POINTS USING THE SIMULATION PROGRAM ARIMA AND THE
MODEL $x_t = .6x_{t-1} + 40 + e_t$

autocorrelations die out in a damped sine wave manner, that there are
exactly two (for second-order AR) partials, and that the dominant frequencies are neither high nor low.

The reader should be warned that the identification of ARIMA (2,0,0)
processes is not always cut and dried. All AR(2) processes are defined in
terms of the two parameters, ϕ_1 and ϕ_2, and the restrictions on the values
of ϕ_1 and ϕ_2 are shown in Figure 9-6. However, for different combinations
of permissible ϕ_1 and ϕ_2 values, a great variety of different data patterns
can be produced. By way of illustration, Figure 9-7 shows another pure
AR(2) process

$$X_t = .7\, X_{t-1} + .25\, X_{t-2} + 5 + e_t$$

and the shape of the data plot is entirely different from that in Figure 9-5.
The autocorrelations do not have a damped sine wave form but rather suggest dominant nonstationarity. The two significant partial coefficients give
the clue to second-order autoregressive pattern in the data. The power spectrum would suggest that first differences should be taken, since the lowest
frequencies are dominant.

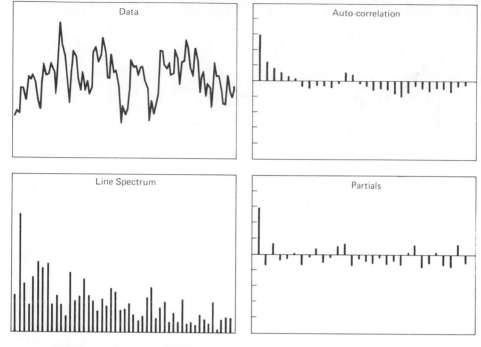

FIGURE 9-4   AN EMPIRICAL ANALYSIS OF THE DATA GENERATED IN
FIGURE 9-3

In the summary section at the end of the chapter, some other varieties of AR(2) models are discussed. For now, it suffices to point out that the process of identification of second-order ARIMA models is definitely not clear cut. Fortunately, it will become apparent that, even if a data series is modeled with two different—but equally suitable—ARIMA models, the difference in the forecasted values may not be significant.

9/2/3   Moving Average Processes

Section 8/2/4 introduced the simple MA(1), moving average process of order one, and the general MA process of order q can be written as follows:

ARIMA (0,0,q) or MA(q)

$$X_t = \mu + e_t - \theta_1 e_{t-1} - \theta_2 e_{t-2} - \cdots - \theta_q e_{t-q}, \tag{9-12}$$

where θ_1 through θ_q are the q moving average parameters (which are subject to certain restrictions in value), e_{t-k} is the error term at time $t - k$, and μ is a constant. In practice, the two cases most likely to be encountered are

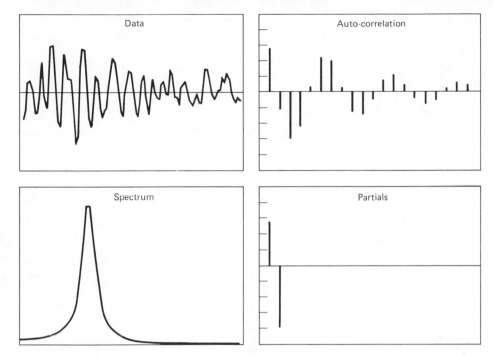

FIGURE 9-5 AN ARIMA (2,0,0) PROCESS: GENERATING N = 100 DATA POINTS USING THE SIMULATION PROGRAM ARIMA FOR THE MODEL. $x_t = 1.2x_{t-1} - .8x_{t-2} + 60 + e_t$

when q = 1 and q = 2, the MA(1) and MA(2) processes, respectively. These two cases are written as in equations (9-13) and (9-14).

ARIMA (0,0,1) or MA(1)

$$X_t = \mu + (1 - \theta_1 B)e_t \qquad\qquad (9\text{-}13)$$

ARIMA (0,0,2) or MA(2)

$$X_t = \mu + (1 - \theta_1 B - \theta_2 B^2)e_t \qquad\qquad (9\text{-}14)$$

What does a first-order MA process look like? Figures 9-8 and 9-9 illustrate the theoretical properties of two different MA(1) processes, one in which the parameter θ_1 is positive and the other in which θ_1 is negative. The simulation program ARIMA was used to generate data for the model $X_t = 100 + e_t - .6e_{t-1}$ in Figure 9-8—that is, for a positive value of θ_1 (= .6). Note that the theoretical partials decay exponentially and are all negative. Note that there is only one nonzero autocorrelation, and that the power spectrum emphasizes high-frequency waves. In Figure 9-9, the simulation program ARIMA was used to generate data for the model

FIRST-ORDER AR AND MA MODELS: ϕ_1 and θ_1 must lie between -1 and $+1$ —that is, for AR(1),

$-1 < \phi_1 < +1$

and for MA(1),

$-1 < \theta_1 < +1.$

SECOND-ORDER AR AND MA MODELS: The following conditions must be satisfied. For AR(2),

$-2 < \phi_1 < +2$ and $-1 < \phi_2 < +1,$

and for MA(2),

$-2 < \theta_1 < +2$ and $-1 < \theta_2 < +1,$

but these values must fall within the triangle shown below:

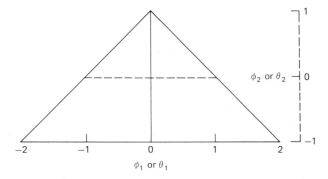

FIGURE 9-6 PERMISSIBLE VALUES FOR THE PARAMETERS OF STATIONARY AUTOREGRESSIVE AND MOVING AVERAGE MODELS

$X_t = 100 + e_t + .7e_{t-1}$—that is, for a negative value of θ_1 ($= -.7$). Note here that there is still only one autocorrelation (and it is positive), but the partials now alternate in sign. The partials still decay exponentially, but with alternating sign. The power spectrum shows that it is lower frequencies that dominate in an MA(1) process with a negative θ_1 parameter.

Summarizing these results for MA(1), we have:

	θ_1 positive	θ_1 negative
Autocorrelations	One (negative)	One (positive)
Partials	Exponential decay (all negative)	Exponential decay (alternating)
Spectrum	High frequencies dominate	Low frequencies dominate

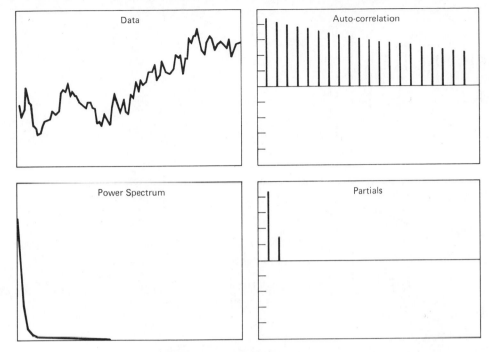

FIGURE 9-7   AN ARIMA (2,0,0) PROCESS: GENERATING $N = 100$ DATA
POINTS USING THE SIMULATION PROGRAM ARIMA FOR THE
MODEL $x_t = .7x_{t-1} + .25x_{t-2} + 5 + e_t$

Note that these are theoretical results.

Figure 9-10 shows the empirical analysis of the data in Figure 9-8. Comparing these two diagrams, note that the line spectrum shows higher frequencies to be dominant, the autocorrelations show one large negative value (the first one) and others that are not quite trivial, and the partials show two large negative values—but do not show a clear exponential decay. In other words, the MA(1) model does show up, but not unequivocally. Clearly, the more "noise" (error) in the data, the more difficult it will be to identify the underlying model.

The second-order MA process is likewise a family of processes. There are two parameters, θ_1 and θ_2, that must obey the restrictions shown in Figure 9-6, and for various combinations of values of these two parameters there will be a wide variety of MA(2) data plots, and a wide variety of theoretical properties shown in the autocorrelations, partials, and power spectrum. In the presence of "noise" (error) the identification of an MA(2) process in real data series is not always easy.

Figure 9-11 illustrates one pure MA(2) process, defined by the model

$$X_t = e_t - 1e_{t-1} + .8e_{t-2}.$$

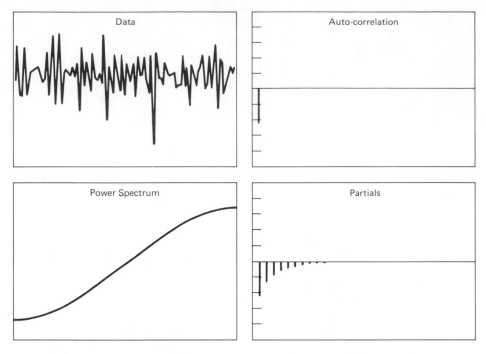

FIGURE 9-8   ARIMA (0,0,1): USING THE SIMULATION PROGRAM ARIMA
TO   GENERATE   DATA   (N = 100)   FOR   THE   MODEL
$x_t = 100 + e_t - .6e_{t-1}$

Note that the theoretical results show exactly two nonzero autocorrelations
for a second-order MA process, that the partials decay in a damped sine
wave manner, and that the spectrum indicates the dominance of high frequencies. In contrast, Figure 9-5 shows that for a pure AR(2) process there
are exactly two nonzero partials, and the autocorrelations die out in a damped
sine wave manner. The spectrum stresses lower frequencies, but not the
very lowest.

9/2/4   Mixtures: ARMA Processes

Already it has become clear that the general ARIMA (p,d,q) model
involves an enormously large family of model types. Even the simple AR
and MA processes show great variety. Thus it is to be expected that when
mixtures are considered, the complexities of identification multiply. In this
section, a general model for a mixture of a pure AR(1) process and a pure
MA(1) process would be written as follows:

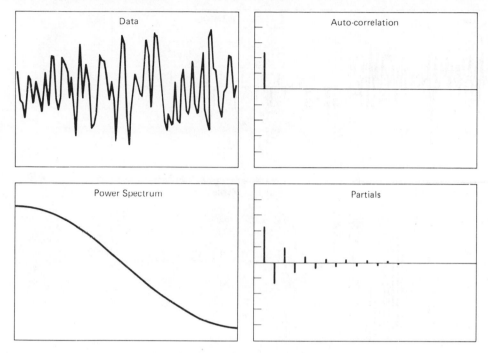

FIGURE 9-9 ARIMA (0,0,1): USING THE SIMULATION PROGRAM ARIMA TO GENERATE DATA ($N = 100$) FOR THE MODEL $x_t = 100 + e_t + .7e_{t-1}$

ARIMA (1,0,1)

$$X_t = \mu' + \phi_1 X_{t-1} + e_t - \theta_1 e_{t-1}$$

or

$$(1 - \phi_1 B)X_t = \mu' + (1 - \theta_1 B)e_t$$
$$\underset{\text{AR(1)}}{\uparrow} \qquad\qquad \underset{\text{MA(1)}}{\uparrow}$$

(9-15)

Figure 9-12 shows one special case of equation (9-15) where $\phi_1 = 0.3$ and $\theta_1 = -0.7$. The autocorrelations and partials both decay exponentially, with the partials alternating in sign.

9/2/5 Mixtures: ARIMA Processes

If nonstationarity is added to a mixed ARMA process, then the general ARIMA (p,d,q) model is implied. The equation for the simplest case,

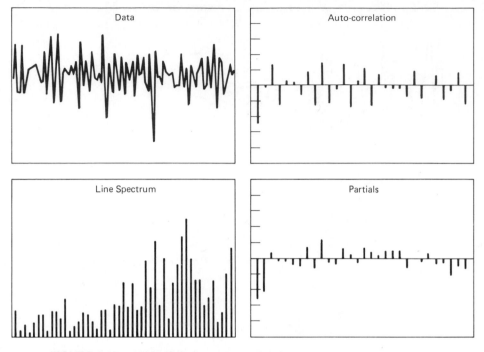

FIGURE 9-10   AN EMPIRICAL ANALYSIS OF THE DATA IN FIGURE 9-8 (DATA GENERATED BY AN MA(1) PROCESS)

ARIMA (1,1,1), is as follows:

ARIMA (1,1,1)

$$(1 - B) \; (1 - \phi_1 B)X_t = \mu' + (1 - \theta_1 B)e_t \tag{9-16}$$

First   AR(1)   MA(1)
difference

Notice the use of the backward shift operator to describe (i) the first difference, (ii) the AR(1) portion of the model, and (iii) the MA(1) aspect. The terms can be multiplied out and rearranged as follows:

$$[1 - B \, (1 + \phi_1) + \phi_1 B^2] \, X_t = \mu' + e_t - \theta_1 e_{t-1},$$

$$X_t = (1 + \phi_1) \, X_{t-1} - \phi_1 X_{t-2} \tag{9-17}$$

$$+ \; \mu' + e_t - \theta_1 e_{t-1}.$$

Note that in this form, the ARIMA model looks more like a conventional regression equation, except that there is more than one error term on the right-hand side.

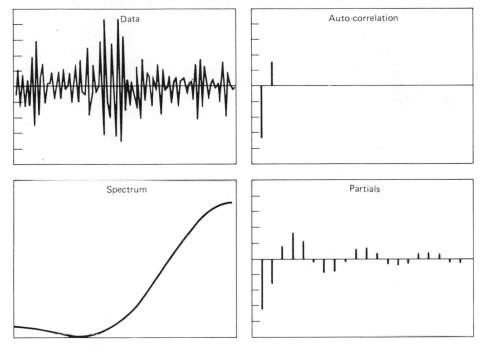

FIGURE 9-11 ARIMA (0,0,2): USING THE SIMULATION PROGRAM ARIMA TO GENERATE DATA ($N = 100$) FOR THE MODEL $x_t = e_t - 1e_{t-1} + .8e_{t-2}$

The general ARIMA (p,d,q) model with $p = q = 2$, and, say, $d = 1$, yields a tremendous variety of patterns in autocorrelations, partials, and spectra, so that it is unwise to state rules for identifying general ARIMA models. However, the simpler AR(1), MA(1), AR(2), and MA(2) models do provide some identifying features that can help a forecaster zero in on a particular ARIMA model identification.

It is also helpful to know that several different models might yield almost the same quality forecasts, so that the process of identification is not quite like looking for a needle in a haystack.

9/2/6 Seasonality and ARIMA Models

One final complexity to add to ARIMA models is seasonality. In exactly the same way that *consecutive* data points might exhibit AR, MA, mixed ARMA, or mixed ARIMA properties, so data separated by a whole season (that is, a year) may exhibit the same properties. For example, con-

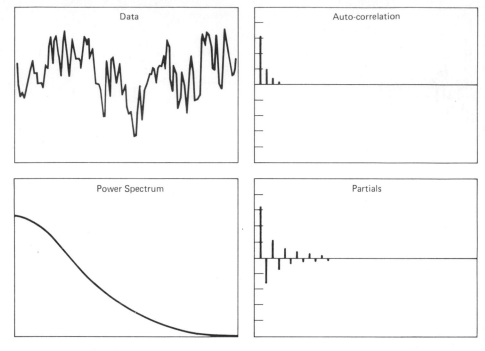

FIGURE 9-12 ARIMA (1,0,1): USING THE SIMULATION PROGRAM ARIMA TO GENERATE DATA $(N = 100)$ FOR THE MODEL: $x_t - .3x_{t-1} = e_t - (-.7)e_{t-1}$

sider a data series that is collected quarterly. Then seasonal differences could be computed as follows:

$$X'_t = X_t - X_{t-4} = (1 - B^4) X_t. \tag{9-18}$$

The new data series, represented by X'_t, would now deal with differences between one quarter's data and the data four quarters ago; that is, how different was the first quarter this year from the first quarter last year?

For data collected monthly, a full season's (year's) difference would be computed as follows:

$$X'_t = X_t - X_{t-12} = (1 - B^{12}) X_t. \tag{9-19}$$

The ARIMA notation can be extended readily to handle seasonal aspects, and the general shorthand notation is

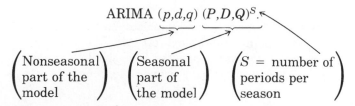

The algebra is simple but can get lengthy, so for illustrative purposes consider the following general ARIMA $(1,1,1)(1,1,1)^4$ model[3]:

$$(1 - \phi_1 B)(1 - \Phi_1 B^4)(1 - B)(1 - B^4)X_t = (1 - \theta_1 B)(1 - \Theta_1 B^4)e_t. \tag{9-20}$$

$$\begin{pmatrix} \text{Nonseasonal} \\ \text{AR(1)} \end{pmatrix} \quad \begin{pmatrix} \text{Nonseasonal} \\ \text{difference} \end{pmatrix} \quad \begin{pmatrix} \text{Nonseasonal} \\ \text{MA(1)} \end{pmatrix}$$

$$\begin{pmatrix} \text{Seasonal} \\ \text{AR(1)} \end{pmatrix} \quad \begin{pmatrix} \text{Seasonal} \\ \text{difference} \end{pmatrix} \quad \begin{pmatrix} \text{Seasonal} \\ \text{MA(1)} \end{pmatrix}$$

All the factors can be multiplied out and the general model written in what is called "unscrambled form." Multiplying out equation (9-20) yields the following:

$$\begin{aligned} X_t = &(1 + \phi_1)\, X_{t-1} + (1 + \Phi_1)\, X_{t-4} - (1 + \phi_1 + \Phi_1 + \phi_1\Phi_1)\, X_{t-5} \\ &+ (\phi_1 + \phi_1\Phi_1)\, X_{t-6} - \Phi_1 X_{t-8} + (\Phi_1 + \phi_1\Phi_1)\, X_{t-9} \\ &- \phi_1\Phi_1 X_{t-10} + e_t - \theta_1 e_{t-1} - \Theta_1 e_{t-4} + \theta_1\Theta_1 e_{t-5}. \end{aligned} \tag{9-21}$$

In this form, once the coefficients ϕ_1, Φ_1, θ_1, and Θ_1 have been estimated from the data, equation (9-21) can be used for forecasting.

The process of identification of a seasonal model depends upon the familiar statistical tools—namely, autocorrelations, partials, and the line spectrum—and a knowledge of the system (or process) under study. Examples 2 and 3 below will illustrate how to handle seasonal models in practice.

9/2/7 Example 1: A Nonseasonal Time Series

Table 9-1 contains 40 time-series observations, and Figure 9-13 shows an initial analysis of the data. The autocorrelation plot gives indications of nonstationarity, and the data plot makes this clear too. The first partial is also dominant—which in this case, refers to the nonstationarity. Similarly, the line spectrum indicates dominant slow waves (the nonstationarity of the series). So from Figure 9-13 we identify $d = 1$, for the general ARIMA (p,d,q) model. That is to say, we take first differences of the data, and reanalyze.

Figure 9-14 shows the results. Now the autocorrelations show a sine-wave pattern and there are two significant partials. This suggests an AR(2) process is operating. The line spectrum for the differenced data no longer shows dominance in the lowest frequency. Check Figure 9-5 for comparison.

---

[3]The constant term has been omitted for clarity. If X_t is replaced by $(X_t - u)$, where u is the mean of the X values, then a constant term would ultimately appear on the right-hand side of equation (9-21).

TABLE 9-1   A TIME SERIES CONTAINING $N = 40$ OBSERVATIONS

Period	X_t	Period	X_t
1	10.2	21	29.2
2	5.4	22	30.9
3	4.0	23	30.2
4	2.5	24	26.3
5	5.1	25	21.9
6	12.7	26	19.8
7	22.6	27	21.5
8	29.5	28	26.2
9	32.2	29	31.3
10	33.8	30	35.1
11	32.3	31	36.8
12	28.4	32	38.8
13	22.6	33	40.3
14	20.2	34	45.3
15	21.8	35	48.7
16	25.5	36	48.9
17	29.2	37	46.9
18	30.9	38	43.6
19	30.1	39	44.0
20	28.8	40	46.5

Putting Figures 9-13 and 9-14 together suggests that the data in Table 9-1 were generated by an ARIMA (2,1,0) process. That is, the model to be examined is of the following form:

$$(1 - \phi_1 B - \phi_2 B^2)(1 - B)X_t = e_t.$$

In terms of the Box-Jenkins stages (Figure 9-1), the *identification* of a tentative model has been completed.

9/2/8   Example 2: A Seasonal Time Series

Table 9-2 shows the monthly industry sales (in thousands of francs) for printing and writing paper between the years 1963 and 1972. Figure 9-15 shows the very clear seasonal pattern in the data plot and a general increasing trend. The autocorrelations are almost all positive, and the dominant seasonal pattern shows clearly in the large values of r_{12}, r_{24}, and r_{36}.

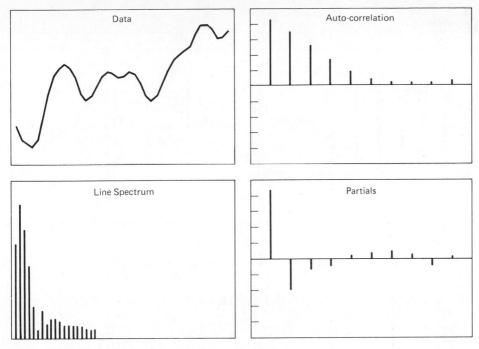

FIGURE 9-13 AN EMPIRICAL ANALYSIS OF THE DATA IN TABLE 9-1

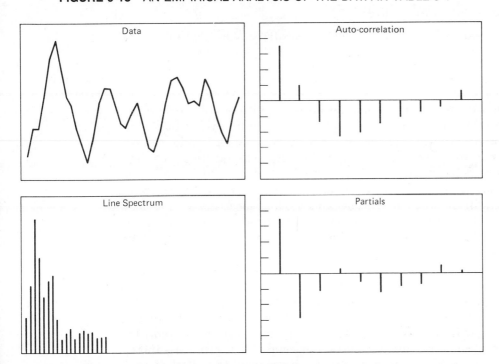

FIGURE 9-14 AN EMPIRICAL ANALYSIS OF THE FIRST DIFFERENCES OF THE TIME SERIES IN TABLE 9-1

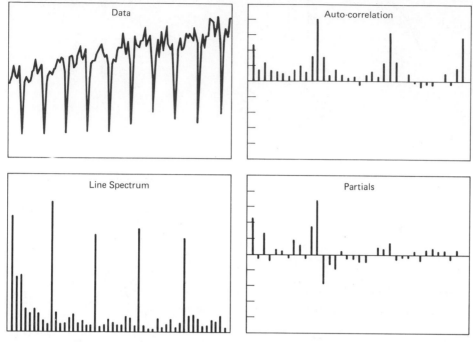

FIGURE 9-15   AN EMPIRICAL ANALYSIS OF THE SALES DATA IN TABLE 9-2

The line spectrum indicates trend (the large amplitude for the first frequency) and seasonality. (The large amplitudes for the 10-cycle wave—that is, every 12 observations—and the 20-cycle, 30-cycle and 40-cycle waves—corresponding to 6-month, 4-month, and 3-month seasonalities.) The evidence of Figure 9-15 suggests taking a nonseasonal first-difference to remove the nonstationary trend and a seasonal difference to remove the strong seasonal spikes in the autocorrelations and the line spectrum.

Figure 9-16 shows the results of examining a model of the form: ARIMA $(p,1,q)(P,1,Q)^{12}$, where values for p, q, P, and Q have not yet been identified. The differenced data appear to be stationary in the mean (maybe not quite stationary in the variance), and a lot of the dominant seasonal spikes have disappeared. From the partials, note the exponential decay of the first few lags—suggesting a nonseasonal MA(1) process—and from the line spectrum, note the relatively greater importance of higher frequencies. This suggests setting $q = 1$ and $p = 0$. In the autocorrelation plot, the value r_1 is significant—reinforcing the nonseasonal MA(1) process—and r_{12} is significant—suggesting a seasonal MA(1) process. With a little imagination the partials can be used to support this seasonal MA(1) process, and

TABLE 9-2 INDUSTRY SALES FOR PRINTING AND WRITING PAPER
(IN THOUSANDS OF FRENCH FRANCS)

Period	Observation	Period	Observation	Period	Observation
1	562.674	41	701.108	81	742.000
2	599.000	42	790.079	82	847.152
3	668.516	43	594.621	83	731.675
4	597.798	44	230.716	84	898.527
5	579.889	45	617.189	85	778.139
6	668.233	46	691.389	86	856.075
7	499.232	47	701.067	87	938.833
8	215.187	48	705.777	88	813.023
9	555.813	49	747.636	89	783.417
10	586.935	50	773.392	90	828.110
11	546.136	51	813.788	91	657.311
12	571.111	52	766.713	92	310.032
13	634.712	53	728.875	93	780.000
14	639.283	54	749.197	94	860.000
15	712.182	55	680.954	95	780.000
16	621.557	56	241.424	96	807.993
17	621.000	57	680.234	97	895.217
18	675.989	58	708.326	98	856.075
19	501.322	59	694.238	99	893.268
20	220.286	60	772.071	100	875.000
21	560.727	61	795.337	101	835.088
22	602.530	62	788.421	102	934.595
23	626.379	63	889.968	103	832.500
24	605.508	64	797.393	104	300.000
25	646.783	65	751.000	105	791.443
26	658.442	66	821.255	106	900.000
27	712.906	67	691.605	107	781.729
28	687.714	68	290.655	108	880.000
29	723.916	69	727.147	109	875.024
30	707.183	70	868.355	110	992.968
31	629.000	71	812.390	111	976.804
32	237.530	72	799.556	112	968.697
33	613.296	73	843.038	113	871.675
34	730.444	74	847.000	114	1006.852
35	734.925	75	941.952	115	832.037
36	651.812	76	804.309	116	345.587
37	676.155	77	840.307	117	849.528
38	748.183	78	871.528	118	913.871
39	810.681	79	656.330	119	868.746
40	729.363	80	370.508	120	993.733

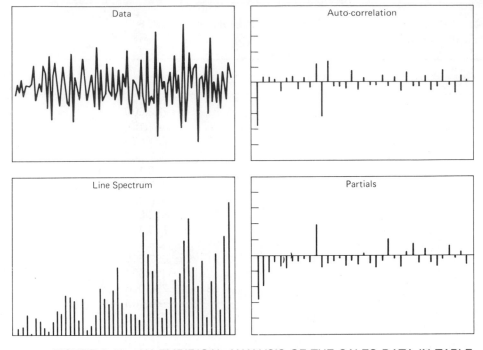

FIGURE 9-16 AN EMPIRICAL ANALYSIS OF THE SALES DATA IN TABLE 9-2, AFTER TAKING A NONSEASONAL FIRST-DIFFERENCE AND A SEASONAL FIRST-DIFFERENCE

we end up with a tentative identification as follows:

$$\text{ARIMA } (0,1,1)(0,1,1)^{12}$$

or

$$\underbrace{(1 - B)}_{\substack{\text{Nonseasonal} \\ \text{first} \\ \text{difference}}}\underbrace{(1 - B^{12})}_{\substack{\text{Seasonal} \\ \text{first} \\ \text{difference}}}X_t = \underbrace{(1 - \theta_1 B)}_{\substack{\text{Nonseasonal} \\ \text{MA}(1)}}\underbrace{(1 - \Theta_1 B^{12})}_{\substack{\text{Seasonal} \\ \text{MA}(1)}}e_t.$$

9/2/9 Example 3: A Seasonal Time Series Needing Transformation

As a final example in this section, consider the data in Table 9-3, which show the monthly shipments of a company that manufactures pollution equipment.

TABLE 9-3 MONTHLY SHIPMENTS OF POLLUTION EQUIPMENT
FROM JAN. 1966 THROUGH DEC. 1975
(IN THOUSANDS OF FRENCH FRANCS)

Period	Observation	Period	Observation	Period	Observation
1	122.640	44	459.024	87	2411.628
2	120.888	45	543.120	88	1510.224
3	164.688	46	567.648	89	1876.392
4	147.168	47	613.200	90	1792.296
5	171.696	48	791.904	91	1307.868
6	228.636	49	305.724	92	1705.572
7	124.392	50	713.064	93	1945.596
8	155.928	51	1156.320	94	2219.784
9	217.248	52	829.572	95	2528.136
10	176.076	53	865.488	96	3534.660
11	142.788	54	1318.380	97	1546.140
12	196.224	55	971.484	98	2246.064
13	228.636	56	817.308	99	2930.220
14	234.768	57	1079.232	100	2462.436
15	319.740	58	1013.532	101	2551.788
16	241.776	59	986.376	102	3140.460
17	151.548	60	1264.068	103	2437.032
18	352.152	61	997.764	104	2109.408
19	239.148	62	1415.616	105	3853.523
20	233.892	63	1709.952	106	2840.868
21	471.288	64	1443.648	107	3164.112
22	290.832	65	1619.724	108	3946.380
23	284.700	66	2120.796	109	3044.976
24	291.708	67	923.304	110	3957.768
25	287.328	68	860.232	111	4552.571
26	315.360	69	1639.872	112	3651.167
27	417.852	70	1106.388	113	3861.408
28	288.204	71	1161.576	114	5048.388
29	225.132	72	1034.556	115	2990.664
30	430.992	73	960.972	116	2677.056
31	229.512	74	1214.136	117	5566.103
32	296.964	75	1492.704	118	3661.680
33	355.656	76	991.632	119	2435.280
34	367.920	77	1025.796	120	3550.428
35	317.112	78	1399.848	121	2215.404
36	359.160	79	818.184	122	3312.156
37	249.660	80	865.488	123	4289.771
38	455.520	81	1547.892	124	3218.424
39	607.068	82	1003.020	125	3193.020
40	425.736	83	960.972	126	3542.544
41	494.064	84	1568.040	127	2169.852
42	486.180	85	1065.216	128	1536.504
43	494.064	86	1107.264	129	3454.944
				130	2351.184

The heavy line in Figure 9-17 is the plot of the actual data of Table 9-3. It can be seen clearly that the fluctuations increase as one moves from left to right on the graph. Until December 1969, the value of shipments was low and so were the fluctuations. From December 1969 until March 1971, shipments increased and so did their variations from one month to the next. The same pattern continues until 1975 when both shipments and fluctuations are largest. This variation in the magnitude of the fluctuations with time is referred to as nonstationarity in the variance of the data. It must be corrected (that is, a stationary variance achieved) before fitting an ARMA model to the series.

 The main approach for achieving stationarity in variance is through a logarithmic or power transformation of the data. The dotted line in Figure 9-17 is a logarithmic transformation of the actual data. It is plotted on the scale shown on the right side of the graph. [For example, $X_{10} = 176.076$, which corresponds to $\log_e (176.076) = 5.171$.] It is clear that the magnitude of the fluctuations in the logarithmic transformed data does not vary with time. Even the fluctuations in the very beginning of the series are not much different from those at the end. Thus one can say that the logarithmic transformation has achieved a series that is stationary in its variance. Once this stationarity in variance is achieved, the Box-Jenkins methodology of Figure 9-1 can be applied. If this is mistakenly done without first achieving stationarity in the variance, misleading results can be obtained.[4]

Achieving stationarity in variance is not a simple task in many instances. A straightforward logarithmic transformation may "over-transform" the data, necessitating a power transformation (such as square root). Unfortunately, there are no good practical methods for making such power transformations, even though on a theoretical level there are several approaches available (see Bartlett, 1947 and Box and Cox, 1964). All these methods are based on trying alternative transformations, which is often time consuming and impractical.

Figure 9-18 shows the original analysis of the raw data in Table 9-3. The autocorrelations remain high for many lags and there is a clear three-month periodicity. If a nonseasonal first difference and a seasonal first difference are taken,

$$(1 - B)(1 - B^{12})X_t,$$

then Figure 9-19 shows how the analysis changes. The plot of the differenced data shows clearly the presence of the nonstationarity in *variance,* even though stationarity in the *mean* has been achieved. Figure 9-20 shows what results if the data in Table 9-3 are first logged (that is, logarithmed),

---

[4]Chatfield and Prothero reported in a case study that the results they obtained from using the Box-Jenkins methodology were very unsatisfactory. Box and Jenkins in a discussion session following the presentation of the paper felt that the reason for the poor results was simply that the wrong transformation was used (see Chatfield and Prothero, 1973).

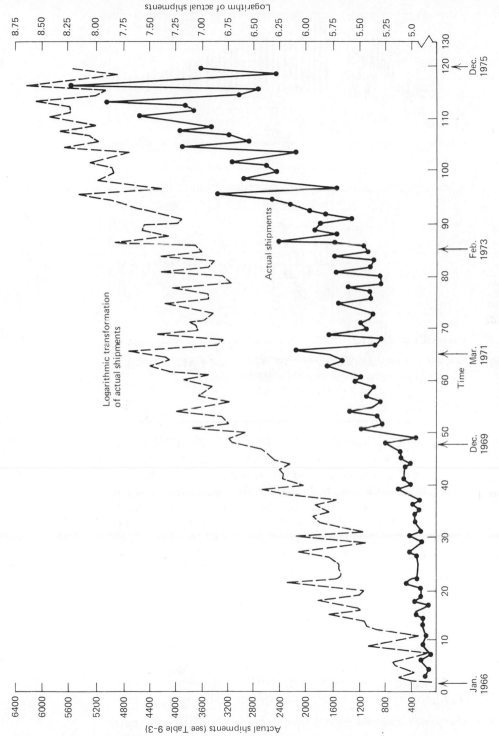

FIGURE 9-17 A PLOT OF THE ACTUAL AND LOGARITHMIC DATA FROM TABLE 9-3

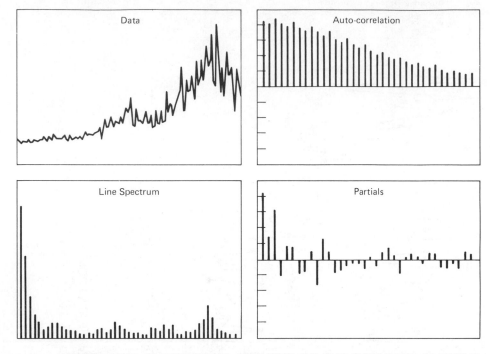

FIGURE 9-18 AN EMPIRICAL ANALYSIS OF THE RAW DATA IN TABLE 9-3 (SHIPMENTS OF POLLUTION EQUIPMENT)

and then a nonseasonal and a seasonal first difference are taken. Note how the transformed data are now stationary in both the mean and variance, how there is a suggestion of a nonseasonal MA(1) process (because the first few partials decay exponentially and because the first autocorrelation is large and significant), and, again with a little imagination, how there is the possibility of a mixed ARMA(1,1) seasonal process at work. With this interpretation of Figure 9-20, a tentative model for the shipments of pollution equipment (Table 9-3) would be:

$$\text{ARIMA } (0,1,1)(1,1,1)^{12}$$

for the logarithms of the raw data.

9/2/10 Recapitulation

The process of identifying a Box-Jenkins ARIMA model requires experience and good judgment, but there are some helpful guiding principles.

1. *Make the series stationary*. An initial analysis of the raw data

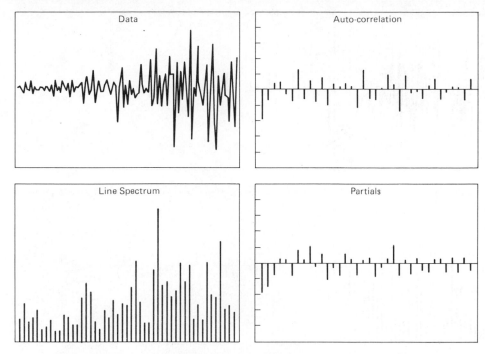

FIGURE 9-19 AN EMPIRICAL ANALYSIS OF THE DATA IN TABLE 9-3 (SHIPMENTS OF POLLUTION EQUIPMENT) AFTER TAKING A NONSEASONAL AND A SEASONAL FIRST-DIFFERENCE

can quite readily show whether the time series is stationary in the mean and the variance. First- or second-order differencing, (nonseasonal and/or seasonal) will usually take care of any non-stationarity in the mean. Logarithmic transformation of the raw data will often take care of nonstationary variance.

2. *Consider nonseasonal aspects.* An examination of the autocorrelations, partials, and line spectrum of the stationary series obtained in step 1 can reveal whether some of the following properties exist:

    AR(1)   Exponentially decaying autocorrelations, one significant partial, and line spectrum support (low frequencies if the AR coefficient ϕ_1 is positive, higher frequencies if ϕ_1 is negative).

    MA(1)   Exponentially decaying partials, one significant autocorrelation, and line spectrum support.

    AR(2)   Damped sine wave decay of autocorrelations and two significant partials.

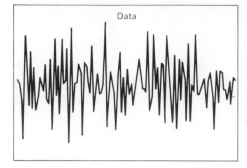

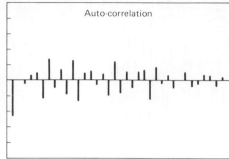

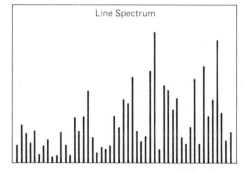

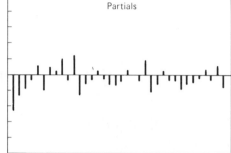

FIGURE 9-20   AN EMPIRICAL ANALYSIS OF THE DATA IN TABLE 9-3 (SHIPMENTS OF POLLUTION EQUIPMENT) AFTER TAKING THE LOGARITHMS OF THE DATA, TAKING A NONSEASONAL FIRST-DIFFERENCE, AND A SEASONAL FIRST-DIFFERENCE

MA(2)   Damped sine wave decay of partials and two significant autocorrelations.

ARMA(1,1) Exponentially decaying autocorrelations and partials.

(Note: It is to be remembered that there are many manifestations of these simple models, depending on the values of the AR and MA coefficients. See Figure 9-22 for examples.)

3. *Seasonal aspects.* An examination of the autocorrelations, partials, and line spectrum can help identify AR and MA processes for the seasonal aspects of the data, but the indications are by no means as easy to find as in the case of the nonseasonal aspects. For quarterly data, the forecaster should try to see the pattern of r_4, r_8, r_{12}, r_{16}, and so on, in the autocorrelations and the partials. For monthly data, it is seldom possible to examine very many autocorrelations for lags in multiples of 12. Thus r_{12}, r_{24}, and possibly r_{36} may be available—but these are all that can be used.

9/3   Estimating the Parameters

Having made a tentative model identification (Section 9/2), the AR and MA parameters, seasonal and nonseasonal, have to be determined in the best possible manner. For example, suppose the class of model identified is ARIMA (0,1,1). This is a family of models depending on one MA coefficient θ_1:

ARIMA (0,1,1)

$$(1 - B)X_t = (1 - \theta_1 B)e_t$$

We want the best estimate of θ_1 to fit the time series that is being modeled.

There are fundamentally two ways of getting estimates for such parameters:

1.   Trial and error—examine many different values and choose that value (or set of values, if there is more than one parameter to estimate) that minimizes the sum of squared residuals.
2.   Iterative improvement—choose a preliminary estimate and let a computer program refine the estimate iteratively.

The latter method is preferred, and a powerful algorithm (due to Marquardt, 1963) is available in many computer centers to do the computations.

9/3/1   Nonseasonal AR(1) and AR(2) Processes

The technical details relating to what follows can best be understood with reference to the Yule-Walker equations introduced in Section 8/3/5.[5] For autoregressive processes of order p, the Yule-Walker equations are defined as follows:

$$\left.\begin{array}{l} \rho_1 = \phi_1 \quad\;\; + \phi_2\rho_1 \quad + \cdots + \phi_p\rho_{p-1} \\[2mm] \rho_2 = \phi_1\rho_1 \quad + \phi_2 \qquad + \cdots + \phi_p\rho_{p-2} \\[1mm] \qquad\qquad \cdot \\ \qquad\qquad \cdot \\ \qquad\qquad \cdot \\[1mm] \rho_p = \phi_1\rho_{p-1} + \phi_2\rho_{p-2} + \cdots + \phi_p \end{array}\right\} \tag{9-22}$$

where $\rho_1, \rho_2, \ldots, \rho_p$ are the theoretical autocorrelations for lags $1, 2, \ldots, p$, respectively, and $\phi_1, \phi_2, \ldots, \phi_p$ are the p AR coefficients of the AR(p)

---

[5]The interested reader can pursue the subject in Box and Jenkins (1976), pp. 55, 60, 64, 68, and further details are also available in Appendix 9-A.

process. Since the theoretical values of ρ are not known, we replace them with their empirical counterparts, and then solve for the ϕ values.

Consider an AR(1) process. Rewriting equations (9-22) with $p = 1$ leaves just one equation:

$$\rho_1 = \phi_1. \tag{9-23}$$

Replacing the unknown ρ_1 with the known r_1 (empirical autocorrelation) gives us an estimate for the parameter ϕ_1 in the AR(1) process:

$$\hat{\phi}_1 = r_1. \tag{9-24}$$

Consider an AR(2) process. Rewriting the Yule-Walker equations for $p = 2$, yields:

$$\left.\begin{aligned}
\rho_1 &= \phi_1 + \phi_2\rho_1, \\
\rho_2 &= \phi_1\rho_1 + \phi_2.
\end{aligned}\right\} \tag{9-25}$$

Replacing ρ_1 and ρ_2 with r_1 and r_2 from the autocorrelation diagram, and solving for ϕ_1 and ϕ_2, gives preliminary estimates:

$$\left.\begin{aligned}
\hat{\phi}_1 &= \frac{r_1(1 - r_2)}{1 - r_1^2}, \\
\hat{\phi}_2 &= \frac{r_2 - r_1^2}{1 - r_1^2}.
\end{aligned}\right\} \tag{9-26}$$

9/3/2   Nonseasonal MA(1) and MA(2) Processes

The technical details for this section depend on a statistical analysis of the autocovariance function for a general MA(q) process.[6] In brief, the theoretical autocorrelations for an MA(q) process can be expressed in terms of the MA coefficients, as follows:

$$\rho_\kappa = \begin{cases} \dfrac{-\theta_\kappa + \theta_1\theta_{\kappa+1} + \cdots + \theta_{q-\kappa}\theta_q}{1 + \theta_1^2 + \cdots + \theta_q^2}, & \kappa = 1,2,\ldots,q, \\ 0, & \kappa > q. \end{cases} \tag{9-27}$$

Since the theoretical values, ρ_κ, are unknown, preliminary estimates of the coefficients, $\theta_1, \theta_2, \ldots, \theta_q$, can be obtained by substituting empirical autocorrelations, r_κ, in equations (9-27), and solving.

Consider an MA(1) process. Here $q = 1$ and equation (9-27) reduces

---

[6]See Box and Jenkins (1976), pp. 68–71, for some details, and also Appendix 9-A.

to

$$\rho_1 = \begin{cases} \dfrac{-\theta_1}{1 + \theta_1^2}, & \kappa = 1, \\ 0, & \kappa \geq 2. \end{cases} \qquad (9\text{-}28)$$

Substituting r_1 for ρ_1 and trying to solve for θ_1 yields a quadratic equation, as follows:

$$\hat{\theta}_1^2 + \left(\frac{1}{r_1}\right)\hat{\theta}_1 + 1 = 0, \qquad (9\text{-}29)$$

which has two solutions. However, θ_1 is restricted to lie between -1 and $+1$. For example, suppose the empirical autocorrelation is $r_1 = .4$. Then equation (9-29) is

$$\hat{\theta}_1^2 + 2.5\hat{\theta}_1 + 1 = 0$$

and the solutions for $\hat{\theta}_1$ are -0.5 and -2. Clearly the latter solution is unacceptable, so the preliminary estimate for θ_1 is -0.5.

Consider an MA(2) process. Now $q = 2$ and equations (9-27) become

$$\left. \begin{aligned} \rho_1 &= \frac{-\theta_1(1 - \theta_2)}{1 + \theta_1^2 + \theta_2^2}, \\ \rho_2 &= \frac{-\theta_2}{1 + \theta_1^2 + \theta_2^2}, \\ \rho_\kappa &= 0, \qquad \kappa \geq 3. \end{aligned} \right\} \qquad (9\text{-}30)$$

Substituting r_1 and r_2 for ρ_1 and ρ_2, yields two equations in two unknowns, θ_1 and θ_2, but they are by no means easy to solve. Box and Jenkins (1976), pp. 517–520, offer tables and charts to handle preliminary estimates for θ_1 and θ_2.

9/3/3 A Pragmatic Note and Example 1

Where it is possible to determine preliminary estimates for AR and MA coefficients, then do so, and follow them up with a Marquardt-type algorithm for iterative refinement. However, in practice and especially for seasonal models, the process of finding preliminary estimates can be quite time-consuming and complicated. With a little practice, it is preferable to let the Marquardt algorithm do the work. Within reason, one can start with any preliminary values for the coefficients, and the algorithm will rapidly find near-optimal values.

For example, for the data in Table 9-1, the tentative model was identified as ARIMA (2,1,0), so for the differenced data we need to estimate ϕ_1 and ϕ_2. The first two empirical autocorrelations for the differenced data (see Figure 9-14) are $r_1 = 0.617$ and $r_2 = 0.039$. Using equations (9-26), the preliminary estimated values for ϕ_1 and ϕ_2 are

$$\hat{\phi}_1 = \frac{(.617)(1 - .039)}{(1 - .617^2)} = 0.957,$$

$$\hat{\phi}_2 = \frac{(.039 - .617^2)}{(1 - .617^2)} = -0.552.$$

Starting with these values, the Marquardt algorithm takes just four iterations to reach "best" values for ϕ_1 and ϕ_2, as follows:

$$\phi_1 = \quad 1.211,$$

$$\phi_2 = -0.752,$$

sum of squared residuals = 117.472.

Now suppose we entered the Marquardt algorithm with bad starting values for ϕ_1 and ϕ_2; for example,

$$\hat{\phi}_1 = -0.957,$$

$$\hat{\phi}_2 = +0.552.$$

In eleven iterations the algorithm stabilizes as follows:

$$\phi_1 = \quad 1.210,$$

$$\phi_2 = -0.748,$$

sum of squared residuals = 117.477.

This is comforting, but, of course, the better the starting values chosen, the faster the algorithm will reach optimum values. And there is no guarantee that bad starting values will always be overcome by the algorithm.

For interest, note that the data in Table 9-1 were artificially generated by the ARIMA simulation program, for an ARIMA (2,1,0) model with $\phi_1 = 1.3$ and $\phi_2 = -0.7$.

9/3/4   Example 2 from Section 9/2/8

The tentative model for the data in Table 9-2 was

ARIMA $(0,1,1)(0,1,1)^{12}$

or

$$(1 - B)(1 - B^{12})X_t = (1 - \theta_1 B)(1 - \Theta_1 B^{12})e_t$$

so that two parameters, θ_1 and Θ_1, have to be estimated. Referring to the theoretical results for such a model,[7] only the following autocorrelations should be other than zero:

$$\rho_1 = -\theta_1(1 + \Theta_1^2)/K,$$

$$\rho_{11} = \rho_{13} = \theta_1\Theta_1/K = \rho_1\rho_{12},$$

$$\rho_{12} = -\Theta_1(1 + \theta_1^2)/K, \qquad\qquad (9\text{-}31)$$

where

$$K = (1 + \theta_1^2)(1 + \Theta_1^2).$$

As Figure 9-16 indicates, the empirical autocorrelations support this theory rather well. In fact, $r_1 = -0.552$, $r_{11} = 0.247$, $r_{12} = -0.444$, and $r_{13} = 0.279$, so that r_{11} is nearly equal to r_{13}, and r_{11} and r_{13} are nearly equal to $r_1 r_{12}$ (which is 0.245). The rest of the autocorrelations are reasonably close to zero.

Substituting the empirical autocorrelations r for the unknown theoretical values ρ in equations (9-31), produces a set of equations that can be solved for θ_1 and Θ_1, but this is not an easy solution. Therefore, relying on the power of the Marquardt algorithm, we choose as starting values

$$\hat{\theta}_1 = 0.2 \quad \text{and} \quad \hat{\Theta}_1 = 0.3$$

and after five iterations, the optimum values are found to be

$$\theta_1 = 0.862 \quad \text{and} \quad \Theta_1 = 0.766.$$

9/3/5   Example 3 from Section 9/2/9

The tentatively identified model for the data in Table 9-3 was

ARIMA $(0,1,1)(1,1,1)^{12}$ for the logarithms of the raw data.

This can be written out as

$$(1 - B)(1 - B^{12})(1 - \Phi_1 B^{12})(\ln X_t) = (1 - \theta_1 B)(1 - \Theta_1 B^{12})e_t,$$

and this time three parameters—θ_1, Φ_1, and Θ_1—are to be estimated. As might be expected, the determination of preliminary estimates is even more difficult in this case,[8] so we shall do the simple thing, namely, choose ar-

---

[7]See Box and Jenkins (1976), Appendix A9.1, p. 329.

[8]Refer again to Box and Jenkins (1976), Appendix A9.1, p. 326 ff.

bitrary starting values, as follows:

$$\hat{\theta}_1 = 0.2, \quad \Phi_1 = 0.3, \quad \text{and} \quad \Theta_1 = 0.4$$

After 10 iterations, the Marquardt algorithm produces stable parameter values,

$$\theta_1 = 0.583, \quad \Phi_1 = 0.038, \quad \text{and} \quad \Theta_1 = 0.920.$$

9/4 Diagnostic Checking

After having estimated the parameters of a tentatively identified ARIMA model, it is necessary to do diagnostic checking to verify that the model is adequate. There are basically two ways of doing this:

1. Study the residuals—to see if any pattern remains unaccounted for.
2. Study the sampling statistics of the current optimum solution—to see if the model could be simplified.

9/4/1 Studying the Residuals

The residuals (errors) left over after fitting an ARIMA model are, hopefully, just random noise. Therefore, if the autocorrelations, partials, and line spectrum of the residuals are obtained, we would hope to find (i) no significant autocorrelations, (ii) no significant partials, and (iii) consistently high amplitudes across the whole range of frequencies in the line spectrum.

For example, in Example 2 (relating to the data in Table 9-2), after fitting an ARIMA $(0,1,1)(0,1,1)^{12}$ model with optimum coefficients (as estimated in Section 9/3/5), the set of residuals was analyzed as shown in Figure 9-21. Note that the three points above are largely vindicated, so that the model appears adequate to describe the data. Since both a nonseasonal and a seasonal difference were applied to the 120 original data points, there are only 107 residuals to examine.[9]

9/4/2 Studying the Sampling Statistics

The statistical assumptions underlying the general ARIMA model allow some useful summary statistics to be computed after optimum coef-

---

[9]In general, the number of residuals will be $n - d - SD$, where n = number of observations, d and D are the degrees of nonseasonal and seasonal differencing, respectively, and S is the number of observations per season. In Example 2, $107 = 120 - 1 - (12)1$.

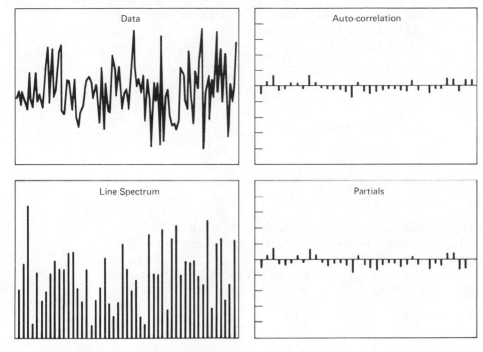

FIGURE 9-21 ANALYSIS OF THE RESIDUALS (ERRORS) AFTER FITTING AN ARIMA $(0,1,1)(0,1,1,)^{12}$ MODEL TO THE INDUSTRY SALES DATA SHOWN IN TABLE 9-2

ficient values have been estimated. For example, for each coefficient there will be a standard error for that coefficient, and since all coefficients are estimated jointly, there is a joint sampling distribution of the coefficients. This yields an intercorrelation matrix showing how the various coefficients are related to each other.

Consider Example 2 (from Table 9-2). The summary statistics are as follows:

Best Coefficient Value	Standard Error
$\theta_1 = 0.862$	0.049
$\Theta_1 = 0.766$	0.050

	Correlation Matrix	
	θ_1	Θ_1
θ_1	1.000	−0.093
Θ_1	−0.093	1.000

Assuming normality, it is clear that the optimum values of θ_1 and Θ_1 are very stable (have very small standard errors) and they are almost uncorrelated (very low correlation coefficient between them).

For Example 3 (from Table 9-3) the summary statistics after fitting the tentative model ARIMA $(0,1,1)(1,1,1)^{12}$, are as follows:

Best Coefficient Value	Standard Error
$\theta_1 = 0.583$	0.076
$\Phi_1 = 0.038$	0.089
$\Theta_1 = 0.920$	0.030

	Correlation Matrix		
	θ_1	Φ_1	Θ_1
θ_1	1.000	-0.003	0.041
Φ_1	-0.003	1.000	0.213
Θ_1	0.041	0.213	1.000

This time the second coefficient is not significantly different from zero—it is less than one standard error from zero—and one could argue that this seasonal autoregressive parameter might be dropped.

Redefining the model for Example 3 as ARIMA $(0,1,1)(0,1,1)^{12}$ yields the following summary statistics:

Best Coefficient Value	Standard Error
$\theta_1 = 0.570$	0.077
$\Theta_1 = 0.868$	0.029

	Correlation Matrix	
	θ_1	Θ_1
θ_1	1.000	-0.078
Θ_1	-0.078	1.000

There is practically no change in the sum of squared residuals for this simpler model, and an analysis of the residuals (as in Section 9/4/1) confirms that it is an adequate model for the data in Table 9-3.

9/4/3 Overfitting an ARIMA Model

One of the procedures for diagnostic checking mentioned by Box and Jenkins is called overfitting—that is, using more parameters than are necessary, or choosing a second-order AR when a first-order AR is indicated, for example. This can be a useful procedure, although it is time-consuming, and we illustrate it only with respect to Example 2 above. Suppose a tentative model is identified as ARIMA $(1,1,1)(1,1,1)^{12}$ instead of ARIMA $(0,1,1)(0,1,1)^{12}$. This means four parameters are needed: ϕ_1, Φ_1, θ_1, and Θ_1—the nonseasonal AR(1), seasonal AR(1), nonseasonal MA(1), and seasonal MA(1) coefficients, respectively. Starting with arbitrary values, the Marquardt algorithm yields the following information.

Best Coefficient Value	Standard Error
$\phi_1 = -0.119$	0.114
$\theta_1 = 0.822$	0.063
$\Phi_1 = 0.011$	0.120
$\Theta_1 = 0.793$	0.059

Correlation Matrix

	ϕ_1	θ_1	Φ_1	Θ_1
ϕ_1	1.000	0.492	0.011	-0.031
θ_1	0.492	1.000	0.069	0.009
Φ_1	0.011	0.069	1.000	0.509
Θ_1	-0.031	0.009	0.509	1.000

These statistics show clearly that coefficients ϕ_1 and Φ_1 are not significantly different from zero (with reference to their standard errors), that ϕ_1 and θ_1 are related (their correlation is 0.492), and that Φ_1 and Θ_1 are related (their correlation is 0.509). From such an overfitted model then, it would be appropriate to drop the AR coefficients, and return to the model ARIMA $(0,1,1)(0,1,1)^{12}$.

9/5 Forecasting with ARIMA Models

The notation used throughout this chapter is compact and convenient. An ARIMA $(0,1,1)(0,1,1)^{12}$ model is described as

$$(1 - B)(1 - B^{12})X_t = (1 - \theta_1 B)(1 - \Theta_1 B^{12})e_t, \tag{9-32}$$

for example. However, in order to use an identified model for forecasting, it is necessary to expand the equation and make it look like a more conventional regression equation. For the model above, the form is

$$X_t = X_{t-1} + X_{t-12} - X_{t-13} + e_t - \theta_1 e_{t-1} - \Theta_1 e_{t-12} + \theta_1 \Theta_1 e_{t-13}. \tag{9-33}$$

In order to use this equation to forecast 1 period ahead—that is, X_{t+1}—we increase the subscripts by one, throughout, as in equation (9-34)

$$X_{t+1} = X_t + X_{t-11} - X_{t-12} + e_{t+1} - \theta_1 e_t - \Theta_1 e_{t-11} + \theta_1 \Theta_1 e_{t-12}. \tag{9-34}$$

The term e_{t+1} will not be known because the expected value of future random errors has to be taken as zero, but from the fitted model it will be possible to replace the values e_t, e_{t-11}, and e_{t-12} by their empirically determined values—that is, as obtained after the last iteration of the Marquardt algorithm. Of course, as we forecast further and further ahead, there will be no empirical values for the "e" terms after a while, and so their expected values will all be zero.

For the X values, at the start of the forecasting process, we will know the values X_t, X_{t-11}, and X_{t-12}. After a while, however, the X values in equation (9-34) will be forecasted values rather than known past values.

By way of illustration, consider Example 2 (from Table 9-2). The last twelve months of data will be left off, a new ARIMA $(0,1,1)(0,1,1)^{12}$ model fitted, and then this model will be used to forecast twelve months ahead. The new optimum coefficient values are $\theta_1 = 0.864$ and $\Theta_1 = 0.803$, so that the model can be written out as equation (9-35),

$$X_t = X_{t-1} + X_{t-12} - X_{t-13} + e_t - 0.864e_{t-1} - 0.803e_{t-12} + 0.694e_{t-13}. \qquad (9\text{-}35)$$

Now in order to forecast period 109, equation (9-35) would have to be rewritten as

$$\hat{X}_{109} = X_{108} + X_{97} - X_{96} + e_{109} - 0.864e_{108} - 0.803e_{97} + 0.694e_{96}.$$

Table 9-4 shows some of the results obtained after the last iteration of the Marquardt algorithm. The period number is given in Column 1, the known observations are shown in Column 2, and the residual (or error, e_t) is given in Column 3. Using known values from this table, the forecast for period 109 can be calculated as follows:

$$\hat{X}_{109} = 880.00 + 895.22 - 807.99 + 0 - 0.864\,(18.99)$$

$$- 0.803\,(58.62) + 0.694\,(-26.63)$$

$$= 885.28.$$

Note that e has to be taken as zero.

Table 9-5 gives more complete information on the twelve-month-ahead forecasts based on $n = 108$ known observations from Table 9-2. The column numbered 1 shows one-month-ahead forecasts. For example, at period 97 the forecast for period 98 is 873.39, as shown in Column 1 opposite period 98. The columns numbered 2, 3, ..., 12 show two-month-ahead, three-month-ahead, ..., twelve-month-ahead forecasts. For example, under Column 12, if we are standing at period 108 and forecasting twelve months ahead, the forecast is 898.38, as shown in Column 12 opposite period 120.

Under each column, three different confidence bounds are shown. For example, if we are currently at period 97, then the one-month-ahead forecast (for period 98) will be

873.39 ± 68.29 for a 90 percent confidence interval,

873.39 ± 81.11 for a 95 percent confidence interval, and

873.39 ± 106.77 for a 99 percent confidence interval.

Clearly, as we forecast with a longer and longer lead-time, the confidence interval increases steadily.

TABLE 9-4 THE INDUSTRY SALES DATA (FROM TABLE 9-2) AND THE ERRORS AFTER FITTING AN ARIMA $(0,1,1)(0,1,1)^{12}$ MODEL USING MARQUARDT'S ALGORITHM

Period t	Sales X_t	Error e_t
1	562.67	−23.61
2	599.00	0.82
3	668.52	6.77
4	597.80	0.60
5	579.89	−3.09
6	668.23	25.59
7	499.23	−5.73
8	215.19	82.53
9	555.81	14.63
10	586.93	−30.74
.	.	.
.	.	.
.	.	.
94	860.00	25.26
95	780.00	−17.49
96	807.99	−26.63
97	895.22	58.62
98	856.07	−17.30
99	893.27	−52.56
100	875.00	26.87
101	835.09	−3.62
102	934.60	48.42
103	832.50	92.79
104	300.00	−96.29
105	791.44	−0.75
106	900.00	24.52
107	781.73	−48.66
108	880.00	18.99

9/6 Recapitulation

The Box-Jenkins ARIMA methodology is a powerful model-building approach to time-series analysis. It deserves careful study, but it cannot be applied meaningfully unless it is well understood. It is a remarkable fact

TABLE 9-5 TWELVE-MONTH-AHEAD FORECASTS AND STATISTICS FOR ARIMA $(0,1,1)(0,1,1)^{12}$ MODEL OF INDUSTRY SALES DATA (TABLE 9-2)

t	X_t	e_t	(1)	(2)	(3)	(4)	(5)	(6)	(7)	(8)	(9)	(10)	(11)	(12)
	90% LIMITS		68.29	68.91	69.54	70.15	70.77	71.37	71.97	72.57	73.16	73.75	74.33	74.91
	95% LIMITS		81.11	81.86	82.60	83.33	84.06	84.78	85.50	86.21	86.91	87.61	88.30	88.98
	99% LIMITS		106.77	107.76	108.73	109.70	110.65	111.60	112.54	113.48	114.40	115.32	116.23	117.13
97	895.22	58.59												
98	856.07	−17.31	873.39											
99	893.27	−52.58	945.85	948.20										
100	875.00	26.84	848.16	855.31	857.66									
101	835.09	−3.63	838.72	835.07	842.22	844.58								
102	934.60	48.40	886.19	886.69	883.04	890.19	892.54							
103	832.50	92.79	739.71	733.12	733.62	729.97	737.12	739.47						
104	300.00	−96.27	396.27	383.65	377.06	377.56	373.91	381.06	383.41					
105	791.44	−0.76	792.20	805.30	792.68	786.09	786.59	782.94	790.09	792.44				
106	900.00	24.51	875.49	875.59	888.68	876.06	869.48	869.97	866.32	873.47	875.83			
107	781.73	−48.65	830.38	827.05	827.15	840.25	827.63	821.04	821.54	817.89	825.04	827.39		
108	880.00	18.98	861.02	867.64	864.30	864.41	877.50	864.88	858.30	858.79	855.14	862.29	864.65	
109	*****	*****	885.28	882.70	889.31	885.98	886.08	899.17	886.55	879.97	880.47	876.81	883.97	886.32
110	*****	*****		900.68	898.10	904.72	901.39	901.49	914.58	901.96	895.38	895.87	892.22	899.37
111	*****	*****			968.09	965.51	972.12	968.79	968.89	981.98	969.36	962.78	963.28	959.62
112	*****	*****				891.78	889.20	895.82	892.49	892.59	905.68	893.06	886.48	886.97
113	*****	*****					873.41	870.83	877.45	874.11	874.22	887.31	874.69	868.11
114	*****	*****						931.53	928.95	935.57	932.23	932.34	945.43	932.81
115	*****	*****							788.51	785.92	792.54	789.21	789.31	802.40
116	*****	*****								397.69	395.10	401.72	398.39	398.49
117	*****	*****									822.95	820.37	826.99	823.65
118	*****	*****										911.30	908.71	915.33
119	*****	*****											849.10	846.52
120	*****	*****												898.38

that for very small values of p, d, q, P, D, and Q in the general ARIMA $(p,d,q)(P,D,Q)^S$ model, an enormous range of data sets can be comprehended. To illustrate this point and to summarize the content of this chapter, Figures 9-22, 9-23, and 9-24 give some idea of the range of possible data sets that can be modeled by the simple first- and second-order processes—AR(1) and MA(1) in Figure 9-22, AR(2) in Figure 9-23, and MA(2) in Figure 9-24. Note well, that while it is helpful to see a plot of the data, it will not be enough merely to see such a plot. The statistical properties of the series have to be examined carefully to decide on an appropriate model.

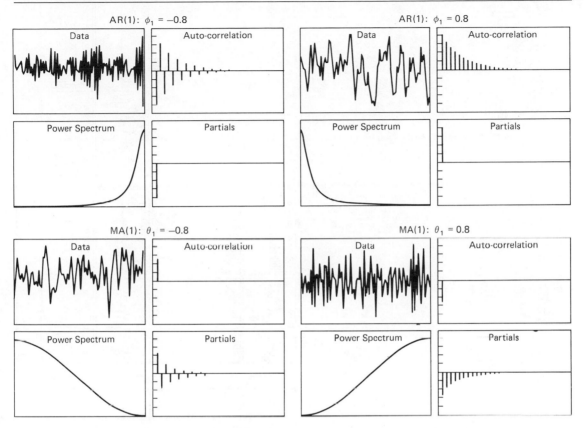

FIGURE 9-22 A SUMMARY SHOWING (a) THE KINDS OF DATA SERIES, AND (b) THE THEORETICAL PROPERTIES OF PROCESSES THAT CAN BE MODELED AS AR(1) OR MA(1)

Clearly, the Box-Jenkins methods are not suited to the handling of many hundreds of time series. It is too cumbersome for that. However, it can be used in many other situations where good data exist over a reasonable period of time and where careful forecasting is an essential part of a larger planning issue. (See McGee et al., 1979.)

Packaged computer programs exist in various forms and can be put up on most systems without unusual delays. The user of such programs should understand both the methodology and each aspect of the computer output.

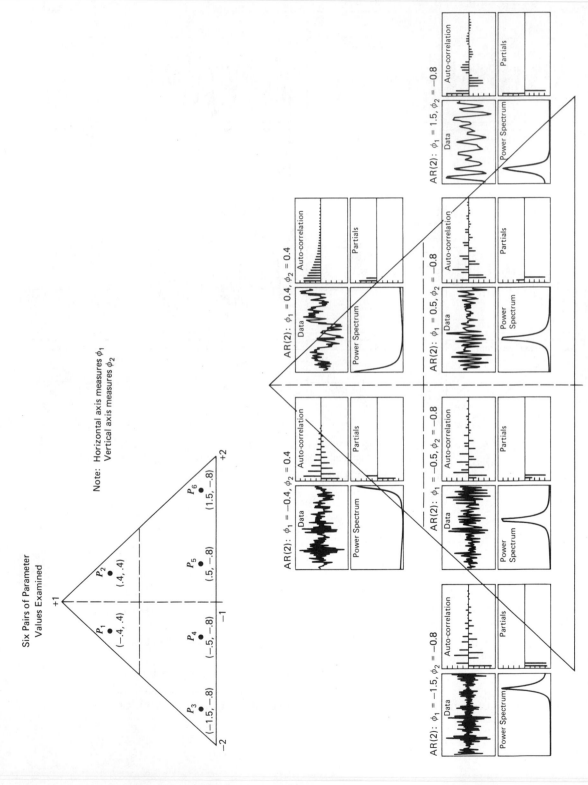

FIGURE 9-23 A SUMMARY DIAGRAM SHOWING (a) THE KINDS OF DATA
SERIES AND (b) THE THEORETICAL PROPERTIES OF PROC-

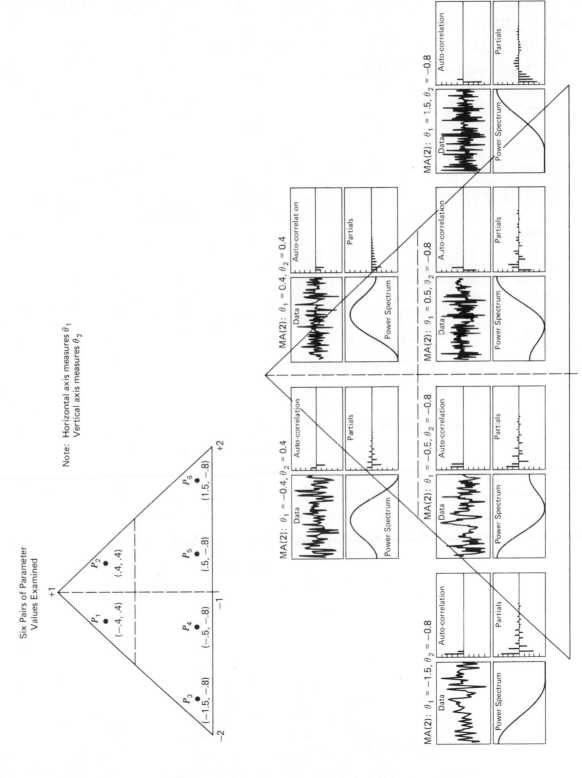

Six Pairs of Parameter
Values Examined

Note: Horizontal axis measures θ_1
Vertical axis measures θ_2

P_1 (−.4, .4) P_2 (.4, .4)

P_4 (−.5, −.8) P_5 (.5, −.8)

P_3 (−1.5, −.8) P_6 (1.5, −.8)

MA(2): $\theta_1 = -1.5, \theta_2 = -0.8$
Data   Power Spectrum

MA(2): $\theta_1 = -0.4, \theta_2 = 0.4$
Data   Auto-correlation   Power Spectrum   Partials

MA(2): $\theta_1 = -0.5, \theta_2 = -0.8$
Data   Auto-correlation   Power Spectrum   Partials

MA(2): $\theta_1 = 0.4, \theta_2 = 0.4$
Data   Auto-correlation   Power Spectrum   Partials

MA(2): $\theta_1 = 0.5, \theta_2 = -0.8$
Data   Auto-correlation   Power Spectrum   Partials

MA(2): $\theta_1 = 1.5, \theta_2 = -0.8$
Data   Auto-correlation   Power Spectrum   Partials

FIGURE 9-24 A SUMMARY DIAGRAM SHOWING (a) THE KINDS OF DATA SERIES, AND (b) THE THEORETICAL PROPERTIES OF PROCESSES THAT CAN BE MODELED AS MA(2)—ARIMA(0,0,2)

APPENDIX 9-A
INITIAL VALUES FOR THE PARAMETERS
OF AR AND MA MODELS

Finding appropriate initial parameter values for ARMA models is not a necessary condition for successful applications, since optimal parameter values will be found starting with almost any initial conditions. The purpose of this section, however, is to examine procedures for obtaining "good" initial estimates.

Initial Estimates for AR Models

In equation (9-7), the general AR(p) model was represented as

$$X_t = \phi_1 X_{t-1} + \phi_2 X_{t-2} + \phi_3 X_{t-3} + \cdots + e_3. \tag{9-36}$$

If both sides of equation (9-36) are multiplied by X_{t-k}, where $k = 1, 2, 3, \ldots, p$, the result is

$$X_{t-k}X_t = \phi_1 X_{t-k}X_{t-1} + \phi_2 X_{t-k}X_{t-2} + \phi_3 X_{t-k}X_{t-3} \\ + \cdots + \phi_p X_{t-k}X_{t-p} + X_{t-k}e_t. \tag{9-37}$$

Taking the expected value of both sides of equation (9-37) and assuming stationarity gives

$$\gamma_k = \phi_1 \gamma_{k-1} + \phi_2 \gamma_{k-2} + \phi_3 \gamma_{k-3} + \cdots + \phi_p \gamma_{k-p}, \tag{9-38}$$

where γ_k is the covariance between X_t and X_{t-k}. This is so because $E(X_{t-k}X_t)$ is, by definition the covariance between the variables X_{t-k} and X_t, where the variables are k times periods apart.[10] Similarly $E(X_{t-k}X_{t-1})$ is γ_{k-1}, since X_{t-k}, and X_{t-1} are $k-1$ periods apart, and so on. Finally $E(X_{t-k}e_t)$ is zero, since the errors are random and uncorrelated with past X_{t-k} values.

Next, both sides of equation (9-60) can be divided by the variance of X_t, which is γ_0. The result is

$$\rho_\kappa = \phi_1 \rho_{\kappa-1} + \phi_2 \rho_{\kappa-2} + \phi_3 \rho_{\kappa-3} + \cdots + \phi_p \rho_{\kappa-p}, \tag{9-39}$$

since by definition [see (8-16)]

$$\rho_\kappa = \frac{\gamma_\kappa}{\gamma_0}.$$

---

[10]This assumes X is a deviation measurement.

If $\kappa = 1, 2, 3, \ldots, p$ in (9-39), the following system of equations, known as the Yule-Walker equations, is obtained:

$$
\left.
\begin{aligned}
\rho_1 &= \phi_1 + \phi_2\rho_1 + \phi_3\rho_2 + \cdots + \phi_p\rho_{p-1}, \\
\rho_2 &= \phi_1\rho_1 + \phi_2 + \phi_3\rho_1 + \cdots + \phi_p\rho_{p-2}, \\
\rho_3 &- \phi_1\rho_2 + \phi_2\rho_1 + \phi_3 + \cdots + \phi_p\rho_{p-3}, \\
& \quad . \\
& \quad . \\
& \quad . \\
\rho_p &= \phi_1\rho_{p-1} + \phi_2\rho_{p-2} + \phi_3\rho_{p-3} + \cdots + \phi_p.
\end{aligned}
\right\}
\qquad (9\text{-}40)
$$

Since the theoretical values for $\rho_1, \rho_2, \ldots, \rho_p$ are unknown, they are replaced by their estimates $r_1, r_2, \ldots, r_p$. Equation (9-40) can then be solved for $\phi_1, \phi_2, \phi_3, \ldots, \phi_p$ to obtain initial estimates for AR models.[11] By way of example, suppose $p = 2$, and ρ_1 and ρ_2 are estimated by $r_1 = .77$ and $r_2 = .368$, respectively. Then the Yule-Walker equations (9-40) reduce to

$$
\begin{aligned}
\rho_1 &= \phi_1 + \phi_2\rho_1, \\
\rho_2 &= \phi_1\rho_1 + \phi_2.
\end{aligned}
\qquad (9\text{-}41)
$$

Solving equation (9-41) for ϕ_1 and ϕ_2 gives

$$
\hat{\phi}_1 = \frac{r_1(1 - r_2)}{1 - r_1^2}, \qquad (9\text{-}42)
$$

$$
\hat{\phi}_2 = \frac{r_2 - r_1^2}{1 - r_1^2}. \qquad (9\text{-}43)
$$

Substituting the values of r_1 and r_2 in equations (9-42) and (9-43) yields

$$
\hat{\phi}_1 = \frac{.77(1 - .368)}{1 - .77^2} = 1.1954 \doteq 1.20,
$$

$$
\hat{\phi}_2 = \frac{.368 - .77^2}{1 - .77^2} = -.5524 \doteq -.55.
$$

Following a similar procedure, one can obtain initial values for any AR(p) model. (Note that if $p = 1$, then equation (9-40) simply becomes $\rho_1 = \phi_1$, or $\hat{\phi}_1 = r_1$).

---

[11]Throughout this section, standard statistical notation is used, where ρ refers to a true population value and r is the corresponding sample estimate. For ϕ, the symbol without a hat represents a population value and $\hat{\phi}$ represents a sample estimated value.

Initial Estimates for MA Models

The MA(q) model is written as

$$X_t = e_t - \theta_1 e_{t-1} - \theta_2 e_{t-2} - \theta_3 e_{t-3} - \cdots - \theta_q e_{t-q}. \tag{9-44}$$

Multiplying both sides of equation (9-44) by X_{t-k} yields

$$X_{t-k} X_t = (e_t - \theta_1 e_{t-1} - \theta_2 e_{t-2} - \theta_3 e_{t-3} - \cdots - \theta_q e_{t-q}) \tag{9-45}$$

$$\times \ (e_{t-k} - \theta_1 e_{t-k-1} - \theta_2 e_{t-k-2} - \theta_3 e_{t-k-3} - \cdots - \theta_q e_{t-k-q}).$$

Taking expected values on both sides of equation (9-45) gives

$$\gamma_k = E[(e_t - \theta_1 e_{t-1} - \theta_2 e_{t-2} - \theta_3 e_{t-3} - \cdots - \theta_q e_{t-q})$$

$$\times \ (e_{t-k} - \theta_1 e_{t-k-1} - \theta_2 e_{t-k-2} - \theta_3 e_{t-k-3} - \cdots - \theta_q e_{t-k-q})]. \tag{9-46}$$

$$\gamma_k = E(e_t e_{t-k} - \theta_1 e_t e_{t-k-1} - \theta_2 e_t e_{t-k-2} - \cdots - \theta_q e_t e_{t-k-q}$$
$$- \theta_1 e_{t-1} e_{t-k} + \theta_1^2 e_{t-1} e_{t-k-1} + \cdots + \theta_1 \theta_q e_{t-1} e_{t-k-q}$$
$$- \theta_2 e_{t-2} e_{t-k} + \theta_2 \theta_1 e_{t-2} e_{t-k-1} + \cdots + \theta_2 \theta_q e_{t-2} e_{t-k-q}$$

$$\begin{array}{cccc} \cdot & \cdot & \cdot & \\ \cdot & \cdot & \cdot & \\ \cdot & \cdot & \cdot & \end{array} \tag{9-47}$$

$$- \theta_q e_{t-q} e_{t-k} + \theta_q e_{t-q} e_{t-k-1} + \cdots + \theta_q^2 e_{t-q} e_{t-k-q}).$$

The expected value of equation (9-47) will depend upon the value of k. **If $k = 0$,** equation (9-47) becomes

$$\gamma_0 = E(e_t e_{t-0}) + \theta_1^2 E(e_{t-1} e_{t-0-1}) + \theta_2^2 E(e_{t-2} e_{t-0-2}) + \cdots + \theta_q^2 E(e_{t-q} e_{t-0-q}). \tag{9-48}$$

All other terms of equation (9-47) drop out because by definition

$$E(e_t e_{t+i}) = 0 \text{ for } i \neq 0$$

and

$$E(e_t e_{t+i}) = \sigma_e^2 \text{ for } i = 0$$

Thus, (9-48) becomes

$$\gamma_0 = \sigma_e^2 + \theta_1^2 \sigma_e^2 + \theta_2^2 \sigma_e^2 + \theta_3^2 \sigma_e^2 + \cdots + \theta_q^2 \sigma_e^2. \tag{9-49}$$

Factoring out σ_e^2, equation (9-49) can be rewritten as

$$\gamma_0 = (1 + \theta_1^2 + \theta_2^2 + \theta_3^2 + \cdots + \theta_q^2)\sigma_e^2. \tag{9-50}$$

Equation (9-50) is the variance of the MA(q) process.
If $k = 1$, equation (9-47) becomes

$$\gamma_1 = -\theta_1 E(e_{t-1} e_{t-1}) + \theta_1 \theta_2 E(e_{t-2} e_{t-2}) + \cdots + \theta_{q-1} \theta_q E(e_{t-q-1} e_{t-q-1}),$$

$$\gamma_1 = -\theta_1 \sigma_e^2 + \theta_1 \theta_2 \sigma_e^2 + \cdots + \theta_{q-1} \theta_q \sigma_e^2.$$

All other terms are 0 because $E(e_t e_{t+i}) = 0$ for $i \neq 0$,

In general **for k = k,** equation (9-47) becomes

$$\gamma_k = -\theta_k \sigma_e^2 + \theta_1 \theta_{k+1} \sigma_e^2 + \theta_2 \theta_{k+2} \sigma_e^2 + \cdots + \theta_{q-k} \theta_q \sigma_e^2,$$

or   (9-51)

$$\gamma_k = (-\theta_k + \theta_1 \theta_{k+1} + \theta_2 \theta_{k+2} + \cdots + \theta_{q-k} \theta_q) \sigma_e^2.$$

Dividing (9-50) into (9-51) gives

$$\rho_k = \frac{\gamma_k}{\gamma_0} = \frac{(-\theta_k + \theta_1 \theta_{k+1} + \theta_2 \theta_{k+2} + \cdots + \theta_{q-k} \theta_q) \sigma_e^2}{(1 + \theta_1^2 + \theta_2^2 + \theta_3^2 + \cdots + \theta_q^2) \sigma_e^2}.$$ (9-52)

If $q = 1$, equation (9-52) becomes

$$\rho_k = \frac{-\theta_k}{1 + \theta_1^2},$$

since all other terms include indexes greater than 1, which do not exist in an MA(1) model. Thus

$$\rho_1 = \frac{-\theta_1}{1 + \theta_1^2}.$$ (9-53)

Equation (9-53) can be solved for θ_1 to obtain

$$\rho_1 + \rho_1 \theta_1^2 + \theta_1 = 0.$$

Replacing ρ_1 by its estimate, r_1, gives

$$r_1 \theta_1^2 + \theta_1 + r_1 = 0.$$ (9-54)

Solving equation (9-54) gives two values for $\hat{\theta}_1$. The one whose absolute value is smaller than 1 is chosen as the initial value of θ_1.

By way of example, suppose $q = 1$ and $r_1 = .49$. Then an initial value for θ_1 can be found using equation (9-54), as follows:

$$.4930\theta_1^2 + \theta_1 + .493 = 0.$$

But,

$$\theta_1 = \frac{-b \pm \sqrt{b^2 - 4ac}}{2a},$$

where $a = .493$, $b = 1$, and $c = .493$. Therefore

$$\hat{\theta}_1 = \frac{-1 - \sqrt{1^2 - 4(.493)(.493)}}{2(.493)} = -1.183,$$

or

$$\hat{\theta}_1 = \frac{-1 + \sqrt{1^2 - 4(.493)(.493)}}{2(.493)} = -.845.$$

The value of $\hat{\theta}_1 = .845$ is selected, since the absolute value of -1.183 is greater than 1.

For an MA(2) process, equation (9-52) becomes

$$\rho_1 = \frac{-\theta_1 + \theta_1\theta_2}{1 + \theta_1^2 + \theta_2^2} = \frac{-\theta_1(1 - \theta_2)}{1 + \theta_1^2 + \theta_2^2}, \tag{9-55}$$

$$\rho_2 = \frac{-\theta_2}{1 + \theta_1^2 + \theta_2^2}. \tag{9-56}$$

All other terms of (9-52) are 0 because they involve θ_k parameters for $k > 2$, which do not exist in an MA(2) model.

In an MA(3) process, the relevant equations are

$$\left. \begin{aligned} \rho_1 &= \frac{-\theta_1 + \theta_1\theta_2 + \theta_2\theta_3}{1 + \theta_1^2 + \theta_2^2 + \theta_3^2}, \\[2mm] \rho_2 &= \frac{-\theta_2 + \theta_1\theta_2}{1 + \theta_1^2 + \theta_2^2 + \theta_3^2}, \\[2mm] \rho_3 &= \frac{-\theta_3}{1 + \theta_1^2 + \theta_2^2 + \theta_3^2}. \end{aligned} \right\} \tag{9-57}$$

Equations (9-55) and (9-56) constitute a system of nonlinear simultaneous equations whose solution is not trivial. The same is true with (9-57), where solving for θ_1, θ_2, and θ_3 is difficult and must be done by using an iterative procedure. The estimates obtained from these equations are not as accurate as those of AR models for a variety of reasons. However, they can still be used as good initial estimates for MA models.

APPENDIX 9-B
INITIAL ESTIMATES FOR MIXED ARMA MODELS

To obtain initial estimates for mixed ARMA models, equations (9-39) and (9-46) must be combined and the expected value taken:

$$\gamma_k = \phi_1 E(X_t X_{t-k}) + \cdots + \phi_p E(X_{t-p} X_{t-k}) + E(e_t X_{t-k}) \tag{9-58}$$

$$- \theta_1 E(e_{t-1} X_{t-k}) - \cdots - \theta_q E(e_{t-q} X_{t-k}).$$

If $k > q$, the terms $E(e_t X_{t-k}) = 0$, which leaves

$$\gamma_k = \phi_1 \gamma_{k-1} + \phi_2 \gamma_{k-2} + \cdots + \phi_p \gamma_{k-p}.$$

This is simply equation (9-39).

When $k < q$, the past errors and the X_{t-k} will be correlated and the autocovariances will be affected by the moving average part of the process, requiring that it be included.

The variance and autocovariances of an ARMA (1,1) process are therefore obtained as follows:

$$X_t = \phi_1 X_{t-1} + e_t - \theta_1 e_{t-1}. \tag{9-59}$$

Multiplying both sides of (9-59) by X_{t-k} gives

$$X_{t-k} X_t = \phi_1 X_{t-k} X_{t-1} + X_{t-k} e_t - \theta_1 X_{t-k} e_{t-1}. \tag{9-60}$$

Taking the expected values of (9-60) results in

$$E(X_{t-k} X_t) = \phi_1 E(X_{t-k} X_{t-1}) + E(X_{t-k} e_t) - \theta_1 E(X_{t-k} e_{t-1}).$$

If $k = 0$, this is

$$\gamma_0 = \phi_1 \gamma_1 + E[(\phi_1 X_{t-1} + e_t - \theta_1 e_{t-1}) e_t]$$

$$- \theta_1 E[(\phi_1 X_{t-1} + e_t - \theta_1 e_{t-1}) e_{t-1}],$$

since

$$X_t = \phi_1 X_{t-1} + e_t - \theta_1 e_{t-1}, \tag{9-61}$$

$$\gamma_0 = \phi_1 \gamma_1 + \sigma_e^2 - \theta_1(\phi_1 - \theta_1)\,\sigma_e^2.$$

Similarly, if $k = 1$,

$$\gamma_1 = \phi_1 \gamma_0 - \theta_1 \sigma_e^2. \tag{9-62}$$

Solving equations (9-61) and (9-62) for γ_0 and γ_1 yields

$$\gamma_0 = \frac{1 + \theta_1^2 - 2\phi_1\theta_1}{1 - \phi_1^2}, \tag{9-63}$$

$$\gamma_1 = \frac{(1 - \phi_1\theta_1)(\phi_1 - \theta_1)}{1 - \phi_1^2}. \tag{9-64}$$

Dividing (9-64) by (9-63) gives

$$\rho_1 = \frac{(1 - \phi_1\theta_1)(\phi_1 - \theta_1)}{1 + \theta_1^2 - 2\phi_1\theta_1}. \tag{9-65}$$

Finally, if $k = 2$, the autocorrelation function, (9-39), becomes

$$\rho_2 = \phi_1\rho_1,$$

or

$$\phi_1 = \frac{\rho_2}{\rho_1}. \tag{9-66}$$

From equations (9-65) and (9-66) initial estimates can be obtained. However, solving (9-65) is not trivial and requires a time-consuming iterative procedure.

By way of illustration, suppose for an ARMA (1,1) model we have $r_1 = .77$ and $r_2 = .368$. Then ϕ_1 and θ_1 can be obtained as follows:

$$\phi_1 = \frac{r_2}{r_1} = \frac{.368}{.77} = .478.$$

Estimating θ_1 must be done iteratively by starting with a θ_1 value, seeing if it satisfies equation (9-65), and if not, trying another value. The value finally obtained is $\theta_1 = -1.09$, which satisfies (9-65) as an equality. That is,

$$.77 = \frac{(1 - .478(-1.09))(.478 - (-1.09))}{1 + (-1.09)^2 - 2(.478)(-1.09)}.$$

REFERENCES AND SELECTED BIBLIOGRAPHY

Bartlett, M. S. 1947. "The Use of Transformations." *Biometrica,* **3,** pp. 39–52.

Box, G. E. P., and D. R. Cox. 1964. "An Analysis of Transformations." *Journal of the Royal Statistical Society,* **26,** Series B, pp. 211–53.

Box, G. E. P., and G. M. Jenkins. 1976. *Time-Series Analysis, Forecasting and Control,* rev. ed. San Francisco: Holden-Day.

Chatfield, C. 1975. *The Analysis of Time Series: Theory and Practice.* London: Chapman and Hall.

Chatfield, C., and D. L. Prothero. 1973. "Box-Jenkins Seasonal Forecasting: Problems in a Case Study." *Journal of the Royal Statistical Society,* **136,** Series A, Part 3, pp. 295–336.

Cleary, J. P., and H. Levenbach. 1982. *The Professional Forecaster,* Belmont, Ca.: Lifetime Learning Publications.

Durbin, J. 1959. "Efficient Estimation of Parameters in Moving-Average Models." *Biometrica,* **46,** pp. 306–16.

Granger, C. W. J. 1980. *Forecasting in Business and Economics.* New York: Academic Press.

Granger, C. W. J., and P. Newbold. 1976. *Forecasting Economic Time Series.* New York: Academic Press.

Hannan, E. J. 1963. "The Estimation of Seasonal Variation in Economic Time Series." *Journal of the American Statistical Association,* **58,** pp. 31–44.

Jenkins, G. M., and D. G. Watts. 1968. *Spectral Analysis and its Applications.* San Francisco: Holden-Day.

Mabert, V. A. 1975. *An Introduction to Short Term Forecasting Using the Box-Jenkins Methodology.* Publication No. 2. Atlanta, Ga.: American Institute of Industrial Engineers (Production Planning and Control Division).

Makridakis, S., and S. Wheelwright. 1979. *Forecasting.* TIMS Studies in Management Science, vol. 12. Amsterdam: North-Holland.

Marquardt, D. W. 1963. "An Algorithm for Least Squares Estimation of Nonlinear Parameters." *Journal of the Society for Industrial and Applied Mathematics,* **11,** pp. 431–41.

McGee, V. E., E Jenkins, and H. M. Rawnsley "Statistical Forecasting in a Hospital Clinical Laboratory." *Journal of Medical Systems,* 1979, Vol. 3, pp. 161-174.

Montgomery, D.C., and L. A. Johnson. 1976. *Forecasting and Time Series Analysis.* New York: McGraw-Hill.

Nelson, C. R. 1973. *Applied Time Series Analysis for Managerial Forecasting.* San Francisco: Holden-Day.

Slutzky, E. 1937. "The Summation of Random Causes as the Source of Cyclic Processes." *Econometrica,* **5,** pp. 105–46.

Sorenson, H. W. 1973. "Least-Squares Estimation: from Gauss to Kalman." *IEEE Spectrum,* **7,** July, pp. 63–68.

Thomopoulos, N. T. 1980. *Applied Forecasting Methods.* Englewood Cliffs, N.J.: Prentice-Hall.

Thompson, H. E., and G. E. Tiao. 1969. "Analysis of Telephone Data: a Case Study of Forecasting Seasonal Time Series." *Proceedings of the Conference on Time Series Models for Marketing Forecasts,* University of Wisconsin, May.

Walker, A. M. 1931. "On the Periodicity in Series of Related Terms." In *Proceedings of the Royal Society of London,* A **131,** pp. 518–32.

Wold, H. 1954. *A Study in the Analysis of Stationary Time Series.* Stockholm: Almquist & Wiksell (1st ed., 1938).

Yule, G. U. 1926. "Why Do We Sometimes Get Nonsense-Correlations Between Time Series? A Study in Sampling and the Nature of Time Series." *Journal of the Royal Statistical Society,* **89,** pp. 1–64.

EXERCISES

1.   Table 9-6 gives the quarterly sales of MRAC Company for 1967 through 1975.

TABLE 9-6   QUARTERLY SALES OF MRAC COMPANY FOR THE YEARS 1967 THROUGH 1975

Period	Observation	Period	Observation	Period	Observation
1	2575.800	13	2953.430	25	3329.890
2	2606.680	14	2986.450	26	3361.130
3	2639.000	15	3017.050	27	3392.070
4	2671.000	16	3048.120	28	3423.520
5	2702.380	17	3079.180	29	3455.050
6	2733.890	18	3109.000	30	3487.140
7	2765.740	19	3143.240	31	3516.750
8	2796.710	20	3171.630	32	3550.370
9	2829.000	21	3205.110	33	3580.560
10	2859.800	22	3235.900	34	3611.470
11	2892.200	23	3266.950	35	3644.170
12	2921.900	24	3297.650	36	3674.310

Using Figures 9-25 and 9-26, answer the following questions:

a. At what level do you consider the series to be stationary?

b. What do you consider to be the most appropriate model for the series?

c. Find initial estimates for the model you identified in Part b. (See Chapter 9, Appendix 9A-2.)

d. Figure 9-27 shows the autocorrelations of the residuals from an AR model fitted to the first differenced data. Do you consider the model appropriate? If yes, why? If not, what is needed to correct any deficiencies?

e. Figure 9-28 shows the autocorrelations of the residuals from an MA model What would you propose to correct this model?

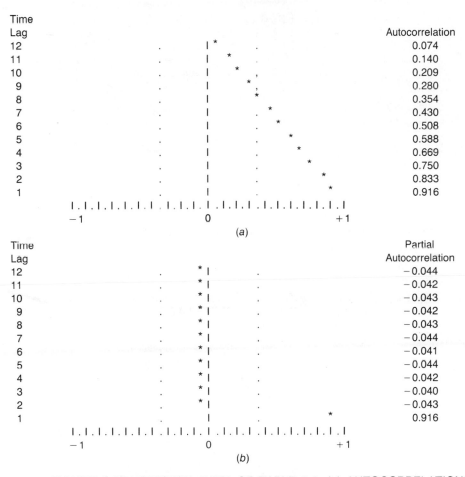

FIGURE 9-25   ORIGINAL DATA OF TABLE 9-6: (a) AUTOCORRELATIONS AND (b) PARTIAL AUTOCORRELATIONS

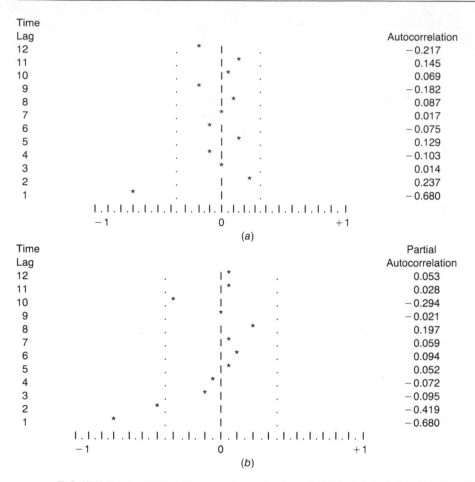

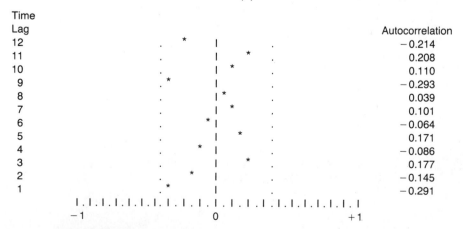

FIGURE 9-26   FIRST DIFFERENCED DATA OF TABLE 9-6: (a) AUTOCOR-
RELATIONS AND (b) PARTIAL AUTOCORRELATIONS

FIGURE 9-27   AUTOCORRELATIONS OF RESIDUALS OF AN AR MODEL

2. Table 9-7 gives U.S. car registrations for the years 1964 through 1970. Figure 9-29 gives the autocorrelations and partial autocorrelations for one long- and one short-term difference of the data in the table.

a. Using Figure 9-29, identify an appropriate model
b. Write this model in terms of the backshift operator.
c. Assume some values for the model's parameters and prepare a forecast for the next two months.
d. If you have a computerized version of the Box-Jenkins program available, run it to determine whether you have identified an appropriate model and to obtain forecasts for the next 12 months.

TABLE 9-7 REGISTRATION OF PASSENGER CARS IN THE UNITED STATES (IN THOUSANDS)

	1964	1965	1966	1967	1968	1969	1970
Jan.	613.84	667.01	606.57	616.13	657.93	657.62	619.14
Feb.	550.32	631.11	721.59	538.89	604.62	607.53	578.42
Mar.	636.88	798.66	878.80	670.78	724.98	681.21	741.13
Apr.	812.32	895.92	822.57	786.08	859.44	876.02	768.35
May	780.72	841.42	777.19	821.49	824.29	880.14	784.39
June	754.32	841.54	752.52	805.56	800.60	841.87	900.86
July	724.20	833.55	832.73	753.31	871.99	815.30	837.71
Aug.	648.68	766.72	743.62	725.73	744.38	718.84	683.15
Sept.	565.43	589.53	573.76	550.15	705.32	733.36	612.14
Oct.	658.45	745.82	766.65	710.07	880.25	955.55	719.03
Nov.	563.52	793.85	732.11	641.31	757.02	757.54	537.15
Dec.	756.71	908.71	800.32	737.37	972.98	912.49	606.67

3. Table 9-8 shows a list of normal random numbers generated with a mean of zero and a variance of one.

a. Using the normal random numbers of the table, generate an AR(1) model with $\phi_1 = .6$.
b. Generate an MA(1) model with $\theta_1 = -.6$.
c. Compare the graphs of (a) and (b). What can you say about the differences of the two models?
d. Generate an ARMA(1,1) model with $\phi_1 = .6$ and $\theta_1 = -.6$.
e. Generate an AR(2) model with $\phi_1 = -.8$ and $\phi_2 = .3$ and an MA(2) model with $\theta_1 = -.8$ and $\theta_2 = .3$. Graph the two models and compare them.

TABLE 9-8 A LIST OF 50 NORMAL RANDOM NUMBERS ($\mu = 0$, $\sigma^2 = 1$)

.01	1.38	.53	1.58	1.32
1.04	.33	−.20	1.90	.72
−.27	−1.43	−1.15	−.07	1.69
.28	−.01	.94	−2.10	.09
.91	1.76	.84	−1.13	.92
1.67	−1.03	−1.71	1.18	−.59
−.76	−.27	−.97	.59	1.55
−1.07	−1.07	1.27	−.60	.79
1.27	1.25	−.99	−.99	.15
−.94	1.37	−.00	−.57	−1.98

4. Table 9-9 shows the total generation of electricity by the U.S. electric industry (monthly for the period 1972–1980). In general there are peaks at two times of the year: in mid-summer and mid-winter.
   a. Examine the 12-month moving average of this series to see what kind of trend is involved.
   b. Are the data stationary?
   c. Examine the autocorrelations, partials and line spectrum for the data set under the following conditions: (i) no differencing, nonseasonal or seasonal; (ii) nonseasonal differencing ($d = 1$); and (iii) nonseasonal and seasonal differencing ($d = 1, D = 1$).
   d. Repeat the previous exercise using the logarithms of the data.
   e. Identify a couple of ARIMA models that might be useful in describing the time series.
   f. Estimate the parameters of your models and do diagnostic testing on the residuals, to see that no significant pattern remains in the residuals.

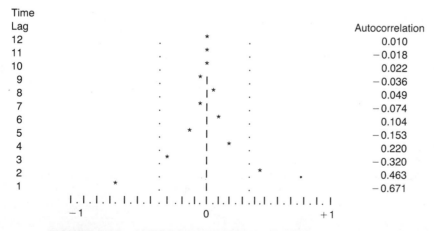

FIGURE 9-28 AUTOCORRELATIONS OF RESIDUALS OF AN MA MODEL

TABLE 9-9 THE TOTAL GENERATION OF ELECTRICITY BY THE U.S.
ELECTRIC INDUSTRY (MONTHLY DATA FOR THE PERIOD
JAN. 1972–DEC. 1980)

Time	X( )	Time	X( )	Time	X( )
1	144.58	33	155.22	65	175.24
2	137.30	34	154.94	66	188.31
3	140.06	35	152.79	67	202.68
4	132.14	36	169.35	68	206.41
5	137.75	37	178.31	69	185.57
6	145.52	38	156.67	70	175.80
7	147.85	39	164.16	71	176.17
8	162.82	40	153.15	72	191.87
9	147.36	41	157.35	73	209.69
10	143.74	42	173.36	74	186.35
11	143.87	43	186.41	75	182.85
12	154.35	44	186.38	76	169.96
13	157.24	45	164.97	77	178.07
14	142.46	46	163.63	78	186.68
15	150.02	47	168.99	79	202.25
16	142.02	48	183.09	80	204.85
17	153.49	49	196.37	81	180.75
18	156.13	50	162.73	82	179.71
19	177.91	51	169.16	83	177.50
20	173.81	52	156.85	84	188.71
21	152.16	53	169.33	85	200.00
22	151.87	54	180.79	86	188.72
23	149.73	55	198.92	87	187.47
24	159.60	56	196.09	88	168.72
25	164.33	57	176.26	89	176.73
26	147.08	58	166.39	90	189.43
27	155.48	59	167.07	91	216.78
28	146.22	60	184.21	92	215.39
29	153.23	61	197.83	93	191.48
30	162.44	62	173.50	94	178.56
31	176.82	63	173.19	95	178.55
32	179.72	64	159.74	96	195.59

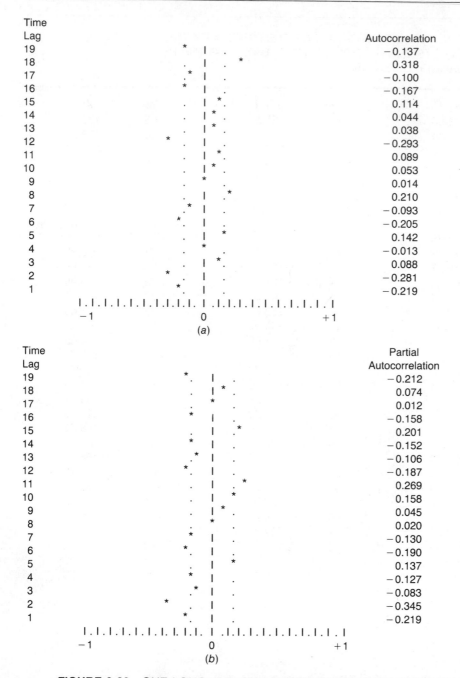

FIGURE 9-29   ONE LONG AND ONE SHORT DIFFERENCE FOR DATA OF TABLE 9-7: (A) AUTOCORRELATIONS AND (B) PARTIAL AUTOCORRELATIONS

g. Forecast the next 24 months of generation of electricity by the United States electric industry. See if you can get the latest figures from your library to check on the accuracy of your forecasts.

5. Table 9-10 shows monthly employment figures for the motion picture industry (SIC code 78) for 192 months from Jan. 1955 through Dec. 1970. This period covers the declining months due to the advent of TV and then a recovery. Answer the following questions:

a. How consistent is the seasonal pattern? Examine this question using several different techniques, including seasonal specific relatives (ratio-to-moving averages from Chapter 4), autocorrelations for lags up to 36 or 48, and examining the autocorrelations for seasonal differences (i.e., taking 12th differences, $(1 - B^{12})X_t$).

b. Split the data set into two parts, the first 8 years (96 months) and the second 8 years (96 months) and do Box-Jenkins identification, estimation and diagnostic testing for each part separately. Is there any difference between the two identified models?

c. For the first 96 months (1955 through 1962) use the ARIMA model obtained in (b) above to forecast the next 12 months ahead. How do these forecasts relate to the actuals?

d. For the last 96 months (1963 through 1970) use the ARIMA model obtained in (b) above to forecast the next 12 months ahead. Check in your library to see how close these forecasts come to the actuals for 1971.

e. In general, when there is a reasonably long time series such as this one, and there is a clear long term wave (shown by plotting a 12-month moving average, for instance) what should the forecaster do? Use all the data? Use only the last so-many years? If the object is to forecast the next 12 months ahead?

TABLE 9-10 EMPLOYMENT FIGURES IN THE MOTION PICTURE INDUSTRY (SIC CODE 78) FOR THE PERIOD JAN. 1955 THROUGH DEC. 1970

Time	X( )	Time	X( )	Time	X( )	Time	X( )
1	218.20	49	183.70	97	167.20	145	179.50
2	217.90	50	184.90	98	165.00	146	179.90
3	224.70	51	188.40	99	168.80	147	181.70
4	236.40	52	197.00	100	175.00	148	191.70
5	238.70	53	199.20	101	177.90	149	199.10
6	240.80	54	201.60	102	183.70	150	205.50
7	241.90	55	204.30	103	187.20	151	212.00
8	241.30	56	206.80	104	189.30	152	213.10
9	240.40	57	203.20	105	183.40	153	203.30
10	233.40	58	195.90	106	177.30	154	193.40
11	226.60	59	190.90	107	172.30	155	190.30
12	219.40	60	185.30	108	171.40	156	181.50
13	215.80	61	184.00	109	164.90	157	176.00
14	213.80	62	183.40	110	164.40	158	176.80
15	220.80	63	181.70	111	166.90	159	182.20
16	234.50	64	188.40	112	174.20	160	191.20
17	236.00	65	191.60	113	177.50	161	197.60
18	232.50	66	194.50	114	183.60	162	201.40
19	233.80	67	198.10	115	189.50	163	208.00
20	233.20	68	200.40	116	191.60	164	210.20
21	232.60	69	196.30	117	185.10	165	206.30
22	226.90	70	189.10	118	181.90	166	200.50
23	217.90	71	185.10	119	175.40	167	202.20
24	212.30	72	182.60	120	174.20	168	200.10
25	208.80	73	179.70	121	172.70	169	194.80
26	209.30	74	178.50	122	168.20	170	192.30
27	212.80	75	181.50	123	171.40	171	192.60
28	208.80	76	190.10	124	177.00	172	199.00
29	211.70	77	190.50	125	182.60	173	207.70
30	214.10	78	193.70	126	191.40	174	215.80
31	214.70	79	195.70	127	200.80	175	219.90
32	216.20	80	195.10	128	201.20	176	221.70
33	218.50	81	192.40	129	195.60	177	214.30
34	213.60	82	185.90	130	188.40	178	211.50
35	206.00	83	178.80	131	184.80	179	206.40
36	198.90	84	175.80	132	187.30	180	204.60
37	194.70	85	169.70	133	182.40	181	196.80
38	193.60	86	169.30	134	176.20	182	190.80
39	195.40	87	172.30	135	178.90	183	188.50
40	203.00	88	180.80	136	182.20	184	196.50
41	204.30	89	183.10	137	184.90	185	204.70
42	203.80	90	182.90	138	195.30	186	211.70
43	205.90	91	186.10	139	198.50	187	216.80
44	207.60	92	189.30	140	200.90	188	217.30
45	205.90	93	183.80	141	195.60	189	212.80
46	198.70	94	179.00	142	187.60	190	206.60
47	189.70	95	172.50	143	183.70	191	203.90
48	186.70	96	171.10	144	184.20	192	202.90

6.   Figure 9-30 shows the analysis of 108 months of housing starts for the period
      Jan. 1972 through Dec. 1980, and Figure 9-31 shows the analysis of the first
      differences of these data.
      a. What can you say about seasonality of the data?
      b. What can you say about trend in the time series?
      c. How does the line spectrum in Figure 9-30 deal with the relative strengths
         of trend, seasonality and overall business cycle?
      d. What does the one large partial suggest?
      e. Compare the autocorrelations in Figures 9-30 and 9-31. What conclusions
         can you come to?
      f. What would your next step be if you were trying to develop an ARIMA
         model for this time series? Can you identify a model on the basis of Figures
         9-30 and 9-31? Would you want to do some more analyses, and if so, what
         would they be?

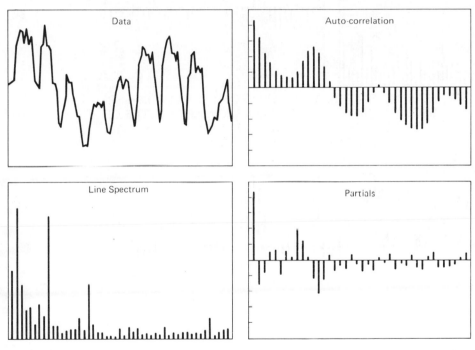

FIGURE 9-30   HOUSING STARTS DATA FOR 108 MONTHS: A PLOT OF THE
                  DATA, THE LINE SPECTRUM, THE AUTOCORRELATIONS,
                  AND THE PARTIALS

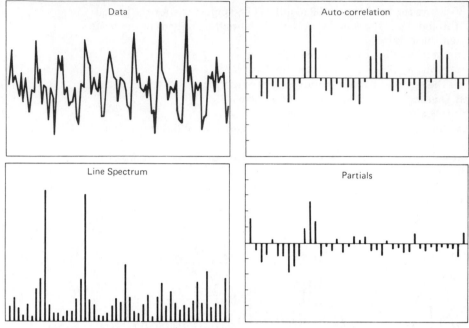

FIGURE 9-31   HOUSING STARTS: AN ANALYSIS OF THE FIRST DIFFER-
ENCES OF 108 MONTHS OF DATA SHOWING THE PLOT OF
THE FIRST DIFFERENCES, THE LINE SPECTRUM, THE AU-
TOCORRELATIONS, AND THE PARTIALS

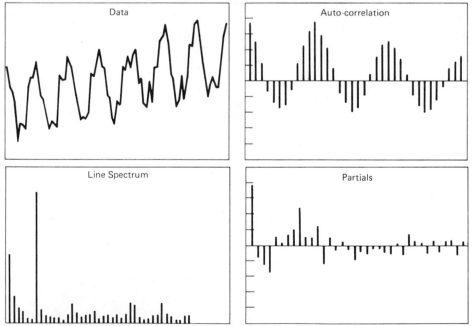

FIGURE 9-32   U.S. BEER PRODUCTION: AN ANALYSIS OF THE ORIGINAL
DATA SHOWING THE DATA PLOT, THE LINE SPECTRUM,
THE AUTOCORRELATIONS, AND THE PARTIALS

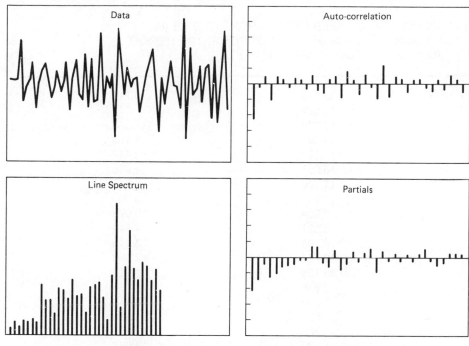

FIGURE 9-33 U.S. BEER PRODUCTION: AN ANALYSIS OF DATA AFTER NONSEASONAL AND SEASONAL DIFFERENCING, SHOWING THE PLOT OF THE DIFFERENCED DATA, THE LINE SPECTRUM, THE AUTOCORRELATIONS, AND THE PARTIALS

7.   Table 9-11 shows the United States beer production figures (in millions of 31-gallon barrels) for the period July 1970 through June 1977. The task is to forecast the next 18 months' production figures.
   a. Use Winters' method (or Pegels' Cell C-3 method) to do this forecasting first. (Alternatively, use any other method as a way of getting a base of reference for the ARIMA model to be done next.)
   b. Examine Figures 9-32 and 9-33 which show the analyses of the original data and the differenced data ($d = 1$, $D = 1$, $S = 12$) and identify an ARIMA model (or two) which seems to do justice to the time series.
   c. Estimate the best ARIMA parameters and forecast 18 months ahead.
   d. For your ARIMA model, determine the residuals and analyze the residuals for any remaining pattern.

TABLE 9-11 UNITED STATES BEER PRODUCTION FIGURES (IN MILLIONS OF 31-GALLON BARRELS) FOR THE PERIOD JULY 1970 THROUGH JUNE 1977

13.092 July 1970	12.619	10.711
11.978	12.527	11.113
11.609	13.249	12.548
10.812	14.206	11.180
8.536	13.176	12.412
9.617	13.059	14.496
9.561	11.406	14.343
9.310	11.235	15.761
11.835	9.924	16.075
12.448	9.591	14.718
12.447	10.984	13.345
13.403	10.724	12.350
12.380	13.138	11.216
11.330	12.858	12.150
11.010	13.825	12.440
10.275	13.087	11.890
9.303	13.762	11.855
9.815	14.170	13.687
9.618	12.121	15.175
9.411	12.381	15.758
12.526	10.896	16.538
12.329	10.649	16.096
12.367	12.191	14.312
13.722	10.984	13.422
13.283	13.049	11.287
12.276	13.089	11.190
11.413	14.713	11.978
10.531	15.043	11.482
9.864	15.746	16.199
10.105	14.610	16.027
9.958	12.667	16.787
10.380	12.277	16.904 June 1977

Source: *U.S. Internal Revenue Service Alcohol and Tobacco Statistics.*

10/MULTIVARIATE TIME-SERIES ANALYSIS

10/1 Introduction

The ARIMA models examined in the two previous chapters dealt with *single* time series; that is, they were univariate models. In this chapter we extend the discussion to *multiple* time series—that is, to multivariate models. Because of the increased complexity of the methodology, we will focus on the bivariate case (that is, just two time series) and will only make passing reference to more ambitious cases. The field is relatively new, but there is considerable interest at the present time[1] and, as the computer software for these approaches becomes more available, it is likely that applications will be on the increase.

In the seminal book by Box and Jenkins (1970, 1976), two chapters deal with *transfer function models,* and in an appendix to their book, the essential details of three relevant computer programs are outlined (their programs 5, 6, and 7). The first widely distributed program package (Pack, 1977) included these programs, and since that time, other software packages have included the bivariate transfer function programs. In 1975, Box and Tiao wrote an important paper on *intervention analysis,* where they applied the transfer function methodology to economic problems in which the input variable could also be a dichotomous variable (e.g., to indicate strike periods and nonstrike periods). Several studies have appeared recently using this intervention analysis procedure.

Here we shall be using the jargon of transfer function methodology (occasionally calling it multivariate ARIMA—or MARIMA) and will attempt to use notation that is consistent with the current literature. Since multivariate (transfer function) models combine some of the characteristics of the univariate ARIMA models (Chapters 8 and 9) and some of the characteristics of multiple regression analysis (Chapter 6), what we are talking about is a method that blends the *time-series* approach with the *causal* approach.

Figure 10-1 shows succinctly what the transfer function model deals with. There is an output time series, called Y_t, which is presumed to be influenced by (1) an input time series, called X_t, and (2) a lot of other inputs collectively grouped and called "noise," N_t. The whole system is a dynamic system. In other words, the input series X_t exerts its influence on the output series via a transfer function, which distributes the impact of X_t over several *future* time periods. The objective of transfer function modeling is to determine a parsimonious model relating Y_t to X_t and N_t. Note that the main objective in this kind of modeling is to identify the role of a *leading indicator* (the input series) in determining the variable of interest (the output series).

To help keep the discussion as simple as possible, we will concentrate on the bivariate case (Y_t, and just one input series, X_t), and we will resort

---

[1]See the references at the end of the chapter.

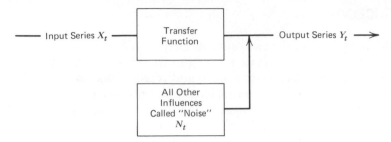

FIGURE 10-1   THE TRANSFER FUNCTION CONCEPT

to the shorthand notation that is now becoming standard in dealing with the general differencing operation. Consider the following examples:

ARIMA (2,1,1)

$$(1 - \phi_1 B - \phi_2 B^2)(1 - B)X_t = (1 - \theta_1 B)a_t$$

will be written as

$$\phi(B) \, \nabla X_t = \theta(B)a_t. \tag{10-1}$$

ARIMA (1,2,2)

$$(1 - \phi_1 B)(1 - B)^2 X_t = (1 - \theta_1 B - \theta_2 B^2)a_t$$

will be written as

$$\phi(B) \, \nabla^2 X_t = \theta(B)a_t. \tag{10-2}$$

Note that the shorthand notation $\phi(B)$ for the "phi function of backward shift operators" does not indicate the *order* of the expression. The reader must bear this in mind. All "phi functions of B" are of the same form, and once the order of the last B term is known, the whole expression can be written down. Thus, in equations (10-1) and (10-2), the orders of the phi functions are 2 and 1, respectively.

Even from this simple example it will quickly become apparent that practitioners would only apply this approach with the support of a good computer package. Thus while our approach here is to explain individual steps in some detail to aid understanding, we don't recommend pursuing applications "by hand."

One other point is worth making now. All ARIMA models are actually special cases of transfer function models. In Figure 10-1, if the input series is regarded as a_t (random disturbances), if the noise series is ignored, and the output series is called X_t, then various autoregressive (AR) and moving average (MA) processes operate on the input (a_t) to produce output (X_t). In Chapters 8 and 9 we were most interested in expressing X_t as a function of past X values and past error (random disturbance) terms—especially for the forecasting equation. The reverse process—transforming the output process (X_t) back into the input process (a_t)—is of interest in transfer function modeling, too, as we shall see in the section dealing with "prewhitening of the input."

Finally, the reader should have a concrete application in mind when going through the rather overwhelming set of computations involved in transfer function methodology. For example, the output series (Y_t) could be sales (e.g., for a soft drink concentrate) and the input series (X_t) could be advertising expenditure (e.g., dollars spent in a major marketing area). Several other applications will be noted as we proceed.

The organization of the chapter is as follows. Section 10/2 gives an overview of the foundations of transfer function model building. For pedagogic reasons, the method is described in terms of four main stages—identification, estimation, diagnostic testing, and forecasting—and various substages within these. For example, eight sub-stages are recognized for identification, and for the estimation stage, there are two sub-stages: preliminary estimation of parameters and final estimation. Section 10/3 deals with the first stage: identification. Section 10/4 deals with the second stage: estimation. Section 10/5 deals with the third stage: diagnostic testing; and Section 10/6 deals with forecasting. Section 10/7 concludes the chapter by considering other multivariate models and a prognosis for this kind of methodology.

10/2 An Overview of the Foundations of Transfer Function Modeling

10/2/1 The Concept of a Transfer Function

The key to understanding transfer function methodology is to have an intuitive feel for what a *transfer function* is. Consider the following simple example. On each of 20 successive days, you deliver to the post office a bundle of letters to be mailed. The post office system delivers these letters over the days ahead. Let the number of letters mailed on day t be X_t and the number of letters delivered on day t be Y_t. Table 10-1 gives illustrative data. For the moment, concentrate on the columns labeled "Letters mailed X_t" and "Letters delivered Y_t." The question now is this: is there a relation between Y_t and X_t? Very clearly, there should be! However, if we do the usual thing and plot Y against X as in Figure 10-2, there appears to be no obvious relationship between Y and X. Simple regression of Y on X would not help.

The reason for this situation is that the X_t values are dynamically distributed over *future* time periods, according to what is known as a trans-

TABLE 10-1   A SIMPLE ILLUSTRATION OF A TRANSFER FUNCTION RELATING LETTERS MAILED (INPUT SERIES) TO LETTERS DELIVERED (OUTPUT SERIES)

Transfer Function Weights $v_0 = 0$, $v_1 = .1$, $v_2 = .5$, $v_3 = .2$, $v_4 = .1$, $v_5 = .1$

Day	Letters Mailed ↓ X_t	1	2	3	4	5	6	7	8	9	10	11	12	13	14	15	16	17	18	19	20	Letters Delivered ↓ Y_t
1	50																					0
2	30	5																				5
3	90	25	3																			28
4	60	10	15	9																		34
5	50	5	6	45	6																	62
6	70	5	3	18	30	5																61
7	30		3	9	12	25	7															56
8	40			9	6	10	35	3														63
9	80				6	5	14	15	4													44
10	70					5	7	6	20	8												46
11	80						7	3	8	40	7											65
12	10							3	4	16	35	8										66
13	30								4	8	14	40	1									67
14	30									8	7	16	5	3								39
15	70										7	8	2	15	3							35
16	30											8	1	6	15	7						37
17	60												1	3	6	35	3					48
18	40													3	3	14	15	6				41
19	10														3	7	6	30	4			50
20	30															7	3	12	20	1		43

(Column i shows how letters mailed on day i were delivered over time.)

fer function. Thus, the 50 letters mailed on day 1 were delivered as follows:

  0 (0%) were delivered on the same day (day 1)

  5 (10%) were delivered one day later (day 2)

  25 (50%) were delivered two days later (day 3)

  10 (20%) were delivered three days later (day 4)

  5 (10%) were delivered four days later (day 5)

  5 (10%) were delivered five days later (day 6)

These deliveries are indicated in column 1 of Table 10-1. Similarly, if the transfer function remained the same, the other mailings, X_t, would be dis-

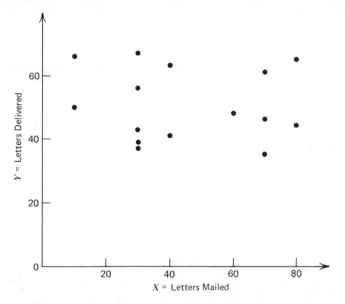

FIGURE 10-2   A PLOT OF THE OUTPUT SERIES (LETTERS DELIVERED) VERSUS THE INPUT SERIES (LETTERS MAILED) USING THE DATA IN TABLE 10-1 (FROM PERIOD 6 THROUGH PERIOD 20)

tributed according to the same percentages (called v_0, v_1, v_2, v_3, v_4, and v_5 in Table 10-1), and the details in each of the columns in Table 10-1 were so obtained. The values of v_0 through v_5 are called the *impulse response weights* (or transfer function weights). The transfer function itself can be written as follows:

$$Y_t = v_o X_t + v_1 X_{t-1} + v_2 X_{t-2} + \cdots + v_5 X_{t-5} \qquad (10\text{-}3)$$

$$= (v_0 + v_1 B + v_2 B^2 + \cdots + v_5 B^5) X_t \qquad (10\text{-}3')$$

$$= v(B) X_t. \qquad (10\text{-}3'')$$

Note the various ways in which this equation can be written, the last being the shorthand notation, where $v(B)$ is the transfer function.

The last column in Table 10-1 is merely the sum of columns 1 through 20 and represents the combined effects of the transfer function operating on the input series, X_t. The impulse response weights (the v-weights) in this instance are all positive and add up to one, but in general this need not be so. They can be positive and negative and they can sum to more than one or less than one. In engineering, the sum of the v-weights is called the *gain* and its meaning can be illustrated with Tables 10-2 and 10-3. Table

TABLE 10-2 A SIMPLE TRANSFER FUNCTION SHOWING CONSTANT
INPUT LEADING TO A STEADY-STATE OUTPUT

Transfer Function Weights: $v_0 = 0$, $v_1 = .2$, $v_3 = .6$, $v_4 = .1$, $v_5 = .1$

Time	Input Series X	1	2	3	4	5	6	7	8	9	10	Output Series Y
1	30											0
2	30	6										6
3	30	18	6									24
4	30	3	18	6								27
5	30	3	3	18	6							30
6	30		3	3	18	6						30
7	30			3	3	18	6					30
8	30				3	3	18	6				30
9	30					3	3	18	6			30
10	30						3	3	18	6		30

TABLE 10-3 A SIMPLE TRANSFER FUNCTION SHOWING CONSTANT
INPUT LEADING TO A STEADY-STATE OUTPUT WITH GAIN

Transfer Function Weights: $v_0 = 0$, $v_1 = .2$, $v_3 = .6$, $v_4 = .2$, $v_5 = .1$

Time	Input Series X	1	2	3	4	5	6	7	8	9	10	Output Series Y
1	30											0
2	30	6										6
3	30	18	6									24
4	30	6	18	6								30
5	30	3	6	18	6							33
6	30		3	6	18	6						33
7	30			3	6	18	6					33
8	30				3	6	18	6				33
9	30					3	6	18	6			33
10	30						3	6	18	6		33

10-2 shows that if the input series is constant and the transfer function is constant, then the output series will reach a steady state *with no gain* in a few periods. Table 10-3 shows a constant input series, constant impulse response weights that add up to more than one, and an eventual steady-state output *with gain*. The impact of new breeding stock (X_t) on the size of the herd (Y_t) could be modeled as a transfer function with gain. Similarly, the output (Y_t) from an extensive natural gas pipeline network might be modeled as a transfer function with loss (negative gain).

10/2/2 The Basic Forms of the Transfer Function Model

The bivariate transfer function model is written in two general forms. The first form is as follows:

$$Y_t = v(B)X_t + N_t, \tag{10-4}$$

where Y_t = the output series (e.g., sales),

$\quad\quad X_t$ = the input series (e.g., advertising expenditure),

$\quad\quad N_t$ = the combined effects of all other factors influencing Y_t (called the "noise"), and

$\quad\quad v(B)$ = $(v_0 + v_1B + v_2B^2 + \cdots + v_kB^k)$, where k is the order of the transfer function.

As will become evident in Section 10/3/1, the input and output series should be appropriately transformed (to take care of nonstationary variance), differenced (to take care of nonstationary means), and possibly deseasonalized (to make for simpler transfer function models). Thus, X_t and Y_t (and also N_t) in equation (10-4) should be thought of as transformed values rather than raw data, and we shall use lower case letters to designate such transformed values.

The order of the transfer function is k (being the highest order of differencing implied) and this can sometimes be rather large (and therefore not parsimonious). For this reason, the transfer function model is also written in the following (more parsimonious) form:

$$y_t = \frac{\omega(B)}{\delta(B)} x_{t-b} + n_t,$$

or

$$y_t = \frac{\omega(B)}{\delta(B)} x_{t-b} + \frac{\theta(B)}{\phi(B)} a_t, \tag{10-5}$$

where

$$\omega(B) = \omega_0 - \omega_1 B - \omega_2 B^2 - \cdots - \omega_s B^s,$$

$$\delta(B) = 1 - \delta_1 B - \delta_2 B^2 - \cdots - \delta_r B^r,$$

$$\theta(B) = 1 - \theta_1 B - \theta_2 B^2 - \cdots - \theta_q B^q,$$

$$\phi(B) = 1 - \phi_1 B - \phi_2 B^2 - \cdots - \phi_p B^p,$$

y_t = the transformed and differenced Y_t value,

x_t = the transformed and differenced X_t value,

a_t = a random noise value,

r, s, p, q, and b are constants.

The $\theta(B)$ and $\phi(B)$ expressions should be familiar by now. They refer to moving average and autoregressive operators, respectively, for the noise term, n_t. The other two expressions, $\omega(B)$ and $\delta(B)$, replace the $v(B)$ expression in equation (10-4). Why is equation (10-5) considered to be more parsimonious? The reason is that the values r, s, p, and q are usually going to be much smaller than the value k in equation (10-4). Consider the following identity:

$$v(B) = \frac{\omega(B)}{\delta(B)}.$$

Suppose $\omega(B) = (1.2 - .5B)$ and $\delta(B) = (1 - .8B)$. Then the right-hand side, expanded, would be as follows:

$$\text{R.H.S.} = \frac{\omega(B)}{\delta(B)} = \frac{(1.2 - .5B)}{(1 - .8B)}$$

$$= (1.2 - .5B)(1 - .8B)^{-1}$$

$$= (1.2 - .5B)(1 + .8B + .8^2 B^2 + .8^3 B^3 + \cdots)$$

$$= 1.2 + .46B + .368B^2 + .294B^3 + .236B^4 + \cdots.$$

In other words, the $v(B)$ function, corresponding to the ratio of $\omega(B)$ to $\delta(B)$, would have an infinite number of terms, and therefore an infinite number of v-weights. This is a case where $r = 1$ (the order of the δ function), $s = 1$ (the order of the ω function), and k is very large. So equation (10-5) is a more parsimonious representation.

The reader should note that the key items to concentrate on in equation (10-5) are (r,s,b) and (p,q). They are written in these two sets to emphasize the point that (r,s,b) refers to the parametrization of the transfer function model connecting y_t and x_t, and (p,q) refer to the parametrization of the noise model. Sometimes it is useful to append subscripts to (p_n,q_n) to refer to noise, n_t, so that they are not confused with similar symbols for parametrization of the input series, X_t. (See Section 10/3/2.) In the set (r,s,b), we have referred to r and s above, but have not yet referred to b. In equation (10-5), note that the subscript for x is $(t - b)$. What this means is that there is a delay of b periods before x begins to influence y. So x_t influences y_{t+b} first, or x_{t-b} influences y_t first. In an ARIMA (p,d,q) model, the purpose of the identification phase is to come up with specific values for (p,d,q). In transfer function modeling, the purpose of the identification stage is to come up with specific values for (r,s,b) and (p_n,q_n).

Before leaving this section, there is one more form of the equation that bears mentioning. Once the model has been identified, and all the parameters have been estimated, the *forecasting version* of the equation needs to be determined. If equation (10-5) is multiplied throughout by the product of $\delta(B)$ and $\phi(B)$, we get

$$\delta(B)\ \phi(B)\ y_t\ =\ \phi(B)\ \omega(B)\ x_{t-b}\ +\ \delta(B)\ \theta(B)\ a_t. \qquad (10\text{-}6)$$

The various difference operators are then multiplied together, terms are collected, and all terms except y_t are moved to the right-hand side of the equation, as shown for a simple $(1,1,b)(1,1)$ example below:

$$y_t = \frac{(\omega_0 - \omega_1 B)}{(1 - \delta_1 B)}\ x_{t-b} + \frac{(1 - \theta_1 B)}{(1 - \phi_1 B)}\ a_t,$$

$$(1 - \delta_1 B)(1 - \phi_1 B)\ y_t = (1 - \phi_1 B)(\omega_0 - \omega_1 B)\ x_{t-b}$$
$$+ (1 - \delta_1 B)(1 - \theta_1 B)\ a_t,$$

$$y_t = (\delta_1 + \phi_1)\ y_{t-1} - (\delta_1 \phi_1)\ y_{t-2} + \omega_0 x_{t-b}$$
$$- (\omega_0 \phi_1 + \omega_1)\ x_{t-b-1} + (\phi_1 \omega_1)\ x_{t-b-2}$$
$$+ a_t - (\delta_1 + \theta_1)\ a_{t-1} + (\delta_1 \theta_1)\ a_{t-2}. \qquad (10\text{-}7)$$

Knowing the values of the parameters and past values of y, x, and a, this equation can be used to determine y values for future periods.

10/2/3   The Various Stages of Transfer Function Model Building

Given an input series (X_t) and an output series (Y_t) in raw data form, there are four main stages and various sub-stages in the complete process of transfer function model building, as follows:

Stage 1: Identification of the Model Form

1-1: Preparation of the input and output series
1-2: Prewhitening of the input series

1-3: "Prewhitening" of the output series

1-4: Computing cross- and autocorrelations for the prewhitened input and output series

1-5: Direct estimation of the impulse response weights

1-6: Specifying (r,s,b) for the transfer function model relating the input and output series

1-7: Preliminary estimation of the noise series (n_t) and computation of the autocorrelations, partials, and line spectrum for this series

1-8: Specifying (p_n,q_n) for the ARIMA $(p_n,0,q_n)$ model of the noise series (n_t)

Stage 2: Estimation of the Parameters of the Transfer Function Model

2-1: Preliminary estimates of the parameters

2-2: Final estimates of the parameters

Stage 3: Diagnostic Testing of the Transfer Function Model

3-1: Computation of the autocorrelations for the residuals of the (r,s,b) model linking the input and output series

3-2: Computation of the cross-correlations between the residuals just mentioned in 3-1 and the prewhitened noise series

Stage 4: Using the Transfer Function Model for Forecasting

4-1: Forecasting future values using the transfer function model

Figure 10-3 diagrams these stages for ready reference, and in the rest of this section, we will consider briefly the mechanics of the eight sub-stages of identification. Then in Section 10/3 a complete worked example will be given to show how each of these sub-stages apply.

1-1 Preparation of the Input and Output Series

ARIMA models allow for differencing of the time series so that the AR and MA processes can be defined on stationary data. In other words, if the raw data are not stationary, then they are usually differenced (maybe first transformed by taking logarithms) in order to remove nonstationarity. This is also true for the general MARIMA models. Thus, in preparing for transfer function modeling, it will be necessary to transform and/or difference both the input and the output series, if nonstationarity exists. The transformation commonly applied is of the form:

$$X'_t = (X_t + m)^\lambda \quad \text{if } \lambda \neq 0$$

and

$$X'_t = \log(X_t + m) \quad \text{if } \lambda = 0,$$

where m is an additive constant. If $V = .5$, then a square root transformation is implied. If $V = 0$, logarithms of the data are computed and the additive constant is defined so as to ensure that $(X_t + m)$ is greater than zero.

Another useful thing to do with both the input and output series is to deseasonalize them. This is not a requirement of transfer function modeling, but it has the effect of making the (r,s,b) values much smaller than if deseasonalizing is not done.

In summary, stage 1-1 considers (i) whether transformations of the input and output series should be made, (ii) what level of differencing should be applied to both input and output series to make them stationary, and (iii) whether the input and output series should be deseasonalized. The suitably transformed series are now called x_t and y_t.

1-2 Prewhitening the Input Series (x_t)

In trying to understand the transfer function of a system that transforms an input series (x_t) into an output series (y_t), it is helpful if the input system is as simple as possible. Then we can put in a controlled input and examine the corresponding output, and repeat, until the nature of the transfer function becomes clear. For example, it would be easier to study the transfer function linking letters mailed to letters delivered using Table 10-2 where the input is constant, rather than Table 10-1 where the input is variable. In practical problems, especially in business and economics, we do not have this luxury—the input cannot be controlled. But we can make the input series more manageable by *prewhitening* it.

What this means is "remove all known pattern" in order to leave just "white noise."[2] Consider the x_t input series. If it can be modeled as an ARIMA process, say ARIMA $(p_x,0,q_x)$, then it can be defined as

$$\phi_x(B) \, x_t = \theta_x(B) \, \alpha_t, \tag{10-8}$$

where $\phi_x(B)$ is the autoregressive operator, $\theta_x(B)$ is the moving average operator, and α_t is a random shock term—that is, the white noise term. (Note that there is no need for differencing (d_x) in the ARIMA model because this was already taken care of in sub-stage 1-1.) By rearranging terms in (10-8) we can convert the x_t series into the α_t series, as follows:

$$\frac{\phi_x(B)}{\theta_x(B)} \, x_t = \alpha_t. \tag{10-9}$$

This is what is meant by prewhitening the x_t series.

---

[2]If we draw values by simple independent random sampling from a fixed probability distribution, then the resulting series if often called "white noise"—and more appropriately so by engineers dealing with physical systems.

STAGE 1: IDENTIFICATION

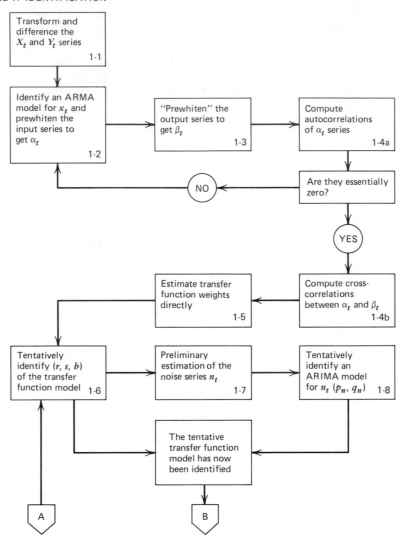

FIGURE 10-3   THE BASIC STEPS IN DEVELOPING A TRANSFER FUNC-
TION MODEL

1-3   "Prewhitening" the Output Series (y_t)

The transfer function we are trying to identify, maps x_t into y_t. If we apply a prewhitening transformation to x_t, as in equation (10-9), then we have to apply the same transformation to the y_t in order to preserve the integrity of the functional relationship. Thus we have

STAGE 2: ESTIMATION

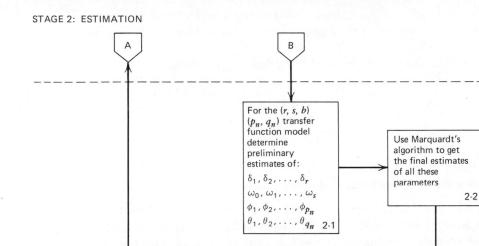

STAGE 3: DIAGNOSTIC CHECKING

STAGE 4: USAGE

FIGURE 10-3 *(Cont.)*

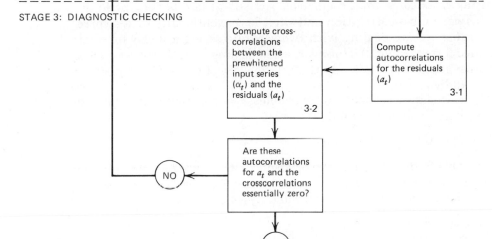

$$\text{input } (x_t) \longrightarrow \begin{array}{c} \text{transfer} \\ \text{function} \end{array} \longrightarrow \text{output } (y_t)$$

$$\text{input } \left(\frac{\phi_x(B)}{\theta_x(B)} x_t \right) \longrightarrow \begin{array}{c} \text{transfer} \\ \text{function} \end{array} \longrightarrow \text{output } \left(\frac{\phi_x(B)}{\theta_x(B)} y_t \right)$$

Now this transformation on y_t does not necessarily convert y_t to white noise, and so the word "prewhitening" is put inside quotes to remind us of this fact.

The "prewhitened" y_t series will be called the β_t series:

$$\frac{\phi_x(B)}{\theta_x(B)} y_t = \beta_t. \qquad (10\text{-}10)$$

1-4 Computing Cross- and Autocorrelations for the Prewhitened Input and Output Series

In univariate ARIMA modeling the autocorrelation coefficient was the key statistic in helping identify the form of the model. In bivariate MARIMA (or transfer function) modeling the autocorrelation plays second fiddle to the *cross-correlation* coefficient. Actually, there is very little difference between cross-correlation and what is conventionally called correlation, because we are dealing with two separate series, x and y (or their prewhitened forms, α and β). However, when dealing with time-series data, it is of great importance to study the relationship of one series *lagged* on the other, and vice versa.

The covariance between two variables X and Y (without time subscripts on them) is defined as follows:

$$C_{XY} = E\{(X - \overline{X})(Y - \overline{Y})\}.$$

We can use this form to define the two variances, C_{XX} and C_{YY}. Now putting time subscripts on the X and Y variables and letting k be the time lag, we can define the crosscovariances $C_{XY}(k)$ and $C_{YX}(k)$, as follows:

$$C_{XY}(k) = E\{(X_t - \mu_x)(Y_{t+k} - \mu_y)\}, \qquad (10\text{-}11)$$

$$C_{YX}(k) = E\{(Y_t - \mu_y)(X_{t+k} - \mu_x)\}, \qquad (10\text{-}12)$$

where $k = 0, 1, 2, 3, \ldots$, and so on. In equation (10-11) X leads Y by k periods. In equation (10-12) Y leads X by k periods.

Equations (10-11) and (10-12) are defined as expectations. In practice, the estimated crosscovariances are computed according to the following formulas:

$$C_{XY}(k) = \frac{1}{n} \sum_{t=1}^{n-k} (X_t - \overline{X})(Y_{t+k} - \overline{Y}), \qquad (10\text{-}13)$$

where $\overline{X}$ and $\overline{Y}$ are the means of the X and Y series and $k = 0, 1, 2, 3, \ldots$,

$$C_{YX}(k) = \frac{1}{n} \sum_{t=1}^{n-k} (Y_t - \overline{Y})(X_{t+k} - \overline{X}), \qquad (10\text{-}14)$$

TABLE 10-4 VALUES USED IN CALCULATING THE
CROSS-CORRELATIONS

(1) Period	(2) X_t	(3) $X_t - \bar{X}$	(4) Y_t	(5) $X_t - \bar{Y}$	(6) $Y_{t+1} - \bar{Y}$	(7) $Y_{t+2} - \bar{Y}$
1	12.77	4.37	22.00	−7.82	19.78	−6.78
2	11.56	3.16	49.60	19.78	−6.78	8.49
3	9.67	1.27	23.04	−6.78	8.49	4.87
4	8.83	.43	38.31	8.49	4.87	−.81
5	8.02	−.38	34.69	4.87	−.81	−3.34
6	12.25	3.85	29.01	−.81	−3.34	−5.77
7	4.76	−3.64	26.48	−3.34	−5.77	6.94
8	9.27	.87	24.05	−5.77	6.94	−15.54
9	3.23	−5.17	36.76	6.94	−15.54	—
10	3.66	−4.74	14.28	−15.54	—	—
	$\bar{X} = 8.40$		$\bar{Y} = 29.82$			

where $k = 0, 1, 2, 3, \ldots$. Note that $C_{XY}(k)$ is not in general equal to $C_{YX}(k)$.[3] (Note too, that these formulas can be used to define *auto*covariances—by substituting X for Y or Y for X—and simple variances—by substituting X for Y or Y for X and making $k = 0$.)

The crosscovariances can readily be converted to cross-correlations by dividing by two standard deviations, as follows:

$$r_{xy}(k) = \hat{\rho}_{XY}(k) = \frac{C_{XY}(k)}{\sqrt{C_{XX}(0)\,C_{YY}(0)}} = \frac{C_{XY}(k)}{S_X\,S_Y}, \tag{10-15}$$

where $k = 0, \pm 1, \pm 2, \pm 3, \ldots$.

The cross-correlation between X and Y defines the degree of association between values of X at time t and values of Y at time $t + k$ (where $k = 0, \pm 1, \pm 2, \pm 3, \ldots$). If X is a leading indicator of Y, then X at time t will be positively related to Y at time $t + k$, where $k = 1$ or 2 or 3, and so on. If X is a concurrent indicator of Y, then X at time t and Y at time t are going to be related significantly. If X lags Y, then Y at time t will be positively associated with X at time $t + k$, for some k greater than zero.

For a quick illustration of how to compute cross-correlations, consider the data in Table 10-4. There are just 10 observations on X and Y. The

---

[3]Although $C_{XY}(k)$ is not in general equal to $C_{YX}(k)$, it is nevertheless true that $C_{XY}(k)$ $= C_{YX}(-k)$, if we remember to adjust the limits on the summation signs in equations (10-13) and (10-14)

means are computed at the bottom of columns 2 and 4. Deviations from these means are shown in columns 3 and 5, for X and Y, respectively. Column 6 shows the Y deviations for the case where $k = 1$ and column 7 shows the Y deviations for the case where $k = 2$. Using equation (10-13), we can compute the two variances $C_{XX}(0)$ and $C_{YY}(0)$ (also denoted S_x^2 and S_y^2) as follows:

$$S_x^2 = C_{XX}(0) = \frac{1}{10}\sum_{t=1}^{10}(X_t - 8.40)^2 = \frac{109.05}{10} = 10.905,$$

$$S_y^2 = C_{YY}(0) = \frac{1}{10}\sum_{t=1}^{10}(Y_t - 29.82)^2 = \frac{928.926}{10} = 92.893.$$

Thus $S_x = 3.302$ and $S_y = 9.638$.

Computation of the crosscovariance of zero time lag (that is, $k = 0$) requires cross multiplication of columns 3 and 5 of Table 10-4. That is,

$$C_{XY}(0) = \frac{\sum_{t=1}^{10}(X_t - \overline{X})(Y_t - \overline{Y})}{10} \quad \text{[using (10-13)]}.$$

Substituting the values from columns 3 and 5 gives

$$C_{XY}(0) = \frac{(4.37)(-7.82) + 3.16(19.78) + 1.27(-6.78) + \cdots + (-4.74)(-15.54)}{10},$$

$$= \frac{63.32}{10} = 6.332.$$

Similarly, the crosscovariance of one time lag (the covariance between X_t and Y_{t+1}) is

$$C_{XY}(1) = \frac{\sum_{t=1}^{9}(X_t - \overline{X})(Y_{t+1} - \overline{Y})}{10}.$$

Substituting the values of $(X_t - \overline{X})$ and $(Y_{t+1} - \overline{Y})$ from columns 3 and 6 in Table 10-4 yields

$$C_{XY}(1) = \frac{(4.37)(19.78) + (3.16)(-6.78) + (1.27)(8.49) + \cdots + (-5.17)(-15.54)}{10}$$

$$= \frac{172.70}{10} = 17.27.$$

In like manner, using columns 3 and 7 of Table 10-4, $C_{XY}(2)$ is computed to be -5.67. Now using equation (10-15) these crosscovariances can be converted to cross-correlations as follows:

$$r_{XY}(0) = \frac{C_{XY}(0)}{S_x S_y} = \frac{6.332}{(3.302)(9.638)} = 0.199,$$

$$r_{XY}(1) = \frac{C_{XY}(1)}{S_x S_y} = \frac{17.27}{(3.302)(9.638)} = 0.543,$$

$$r_{XY}(2) = \frac{C_{XY}(2)}{S_x S_y} = \frac{-5.67}{(3.302)(9.638)} = -0.178.$$

If $k = -1$, then equation (10-14) can be used to determine $C_{YX}(1)$ as follows:

$$C_{YX}(1) = C_{XY}(-1) = .997$$

and

$$r_{XY}(-1) = .031.$$

When a reasonable number of cross-correlations have been computed, they are often presented in the form of a diagram such as shown in Figure 10-4. In this diagram, the dashed lines represent approximate 95 percent confidence limits for the cross-correlations, according to a formula by Bartlett (1955).

The sampling distribution of cross-correlations is very difficult to determine, but if we consider two independent white noise series, then the expected cross-correlation will be zero and the standard error can be approximated by $\sqrt{1/n}$. Bartlett extended this notion to the case of two uncorrelated series, one being white noise, and for cross-correlations of lag k, the standard error is approximated as follows:

$$\text{std. error of } r_{XY}(k) = \sqrt{\frac{1}{n-k}}. \tag{10-16}$$

If k is negative, simply replace k by its absolute value on the right-hand

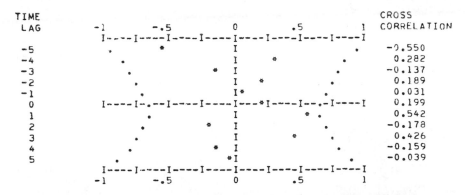

FIGURE 10-4 CROSSCORRELATIONS OF THE DATA OF TABLE 10-4

side of (10-16). As we shall see in later sections, the cross-correlations are most important in attempting to identify appropriate MARIMA models, so that this standard error formula becomes quite useful for detecting those cross-correlations that are significant.

A final point about stage 1-4 is that regular autocorrelations can be computed for the prewhitened input and output series as well. For the pre-whitened x_t series (namely the α_t series) there should not be any significant autocorrelations, but the "prewhitened" y_t series (namely the β_t series) may well include some pattern—because this is precisely what we expect from the transfer function.

1-5   Direct Estimation of the Impulse Response Weights

Having prewhitened the input series (stage 1-2), having applied the same prewhitening transformation to the output series (stage 1-3), and then computing the cross-correlations between these two prewhitened series (stage 1-4), it is a simple matter to get a direct estimate for each of the impulse response weights in equation (10-4). The formula is as follows:

$$v_k = \frac{r_{\alpha\beta}(k)\ S_\beta}{S_\alpha}. \tag{10-17}$$

In other words, the cross-correlation between α and β is multiplied by the standard deviation of the β series and divided by the standard deviation of the α series.

The theoretical rationale for this equation is straightforward. After stage 1-1 (and assuming $b = 0$) the transfer function model is written

$$y_t = v(B)\ x_t + n_t. \tag{10-18}$$

Prewhitening x_t by the transformation $\phi_x(B)/\theta_x(B)$ and carrying this trans-formation through the whole equation (10-18), yields

$$\frac{\phi_x(B)}{\theta_x(B)}\ y_t = v(B)\ \frac{\phi_x(B)}{\theta_x(B)}\ x_t + \frac{\phi_x(B)}{\theta_x(B)}\ n_t \tag{10-19}$$

or

$$\beta_t = v(B)\ \alpha_t + \varepsilon_t, \tag{10-19'}$$

where ε_t is the transformed noise series, which is presumed to be unrelated to the α_t series. Then, multiplying both sides of (10-19') by α_{t-k} and taking expectations, we get

$$E\ [\alpha_{t-k}\beta_t] = v_0\ E\ (\alpha_{t-k}\alpha_t) + v_1\ E\ (\alpha_{t-k}\alpha_{t-1})$$
$$+ \cdots + E\ (\alpha_{t-k}\varepsilon_t), \tag{10-20}$$
$$C_{\alpha\beta}(k) = v_k\ C_{\alpha\alpha}(t-k) + 0.$$

(since α and ε are assumed independent)

Note that in equation (10-20) only the v_k term appears because α_{t-k} is independent of all other α_t values.

Substituting sample values in equation (10-20), and rearranging terms, gives

$$v_k = \frac{C_{\alpha\beta}(k)}{S_\alpha^2} = \frac{r_{\alpha\beta}(k) \, S_\beta}{S_\alpha}. \qquad (10\text{-}17)$$

1-6 Specifying (r,s,b) for the Transfer Function Model

As was pointed out in Section 10/2/2, the three key parameters in a transfer function model are (r,s,b), where r refers to the degree of the $\delta(B)$ function, s refers to the degree of the $\omega(B)$ function, and b refers to the delay registered in the subscript of the x_{t-b} term in equation (10-5). It is the task of the forecaster to determine appropriate values for these three parameters, and the task is not always crystal clear.

The parameter b is perhaps the simplest to deal with. If the cross-correlations are examined and $r_{\alpha\beta}(0) = r_{\alpha\beta}(1) = r_{\alpha\beta}(2) = 0$, but $r_{\alpha\beta}(3) = .5$, then we know that $b = 3$. In other words, there is an absolute lag of 3 periods before the input series α begins to influence the output series β.

Next consider the two equations (10-4) and (10-5), and the identity

$$v(B)x_t = \frac{\omega(B)}{\delta(B)} \, x_{t-b}. \qquad (10\text{-}21)$$

If the expressions $v(B)$, $\omega(B)$, and $\delta(B)$ are expanded and coefficients are matched, we end up with the following relationships:

$$v_j = 0 \quad \text{for } j < b, \qquad (10\text{-}22a)$$

$$v_j = \delta_1 v_{j-1} + \cdots + \delta_r v_{j-r} + \omega_0 \quad \text{for } j = b, \qquad (10\text{-}22b)$$

$$v_j = \delta_1 v_{j-1} + \cdots + \delta_r v_{j-r} - \omega_{j-b} \quad \text{for } j = b+1, \ldots, b+s, \qquad (10\text{-}22c)$$

$$v_j = \delta_1 v_{j-1} + \cdots + \delta_r v_{j-r} \quad \text{for } j > b+s. \qquad (10\text{-}22d)$$

Clearly, if $b=0$, there will be no $v_j=0$ in (10-22a) above. If $s=0$, there will be no equations of the form (10-22c). And if the subscript on any v coefficient is negative, that v value is taken as zero.

Thinking intuitively about the meaning of (r,s,b), the following rules are easy to state, even though they are not at all easy to put into practice. First, the value b indicates that y is not influenced by x_t values until period $t+b$, or

$$y_t = 0x_t + 0x_{t-1} + 0x_{t-2} + \cdots + \omega_0 x_{t-b}.$$

Next, the value s indicates for how long the output series (y) continues to be influenced by *new* values of the input series (x),

$$y_t \text{ influenced by } (x_{t-b}, x_{t-b-1}, \ldots, x_{t-b-s}).$$

Finally, the r value indicates that y_t is related to its own past values as follows:

y influenced by $(y_{t-1}, y_{t-2}, y_{t-3}, \ldots, y_{t-r})$.

These facts are often summarized in the form of three guiding principles that are aimed at helping a forecaster decide on appropriate values for (r,s,b):

1. Until the bth time lag the cross-correlations will not be significantly different from zero.
2. For s further time lags the cross-correlations will not show any clear pattern.
3. For r further time lags the cross-correlations will show a clear pattern.

The truth of the matter is that it is rare to examine a cross-correlation diagram and have these three values (r,s,b) make themselves known unequivocally.

1-7   Preliminary Examination of the Noise Series

In stage 1-5, the v-weights are estimated directly, and this enables the calculation of preliminary estimates of the noise series n_t. Since

$$y_t = v(B) x_t + n_t,$$

it follows that

$$n_t = y_t - v_0 x_t - v_1 x_{t-1} - v_2 x_{t-2} - \cdots - v_g x_{t-g}, \tag{10-23}$$

where g is a practical value chosen by the forecaster. The function $v(B)$ has an infinite number of terms, but in stage 1-5 only the first 10 or 15 such v-weights will be computed, and this will be satisfactory for the preliminary analysis of the noise series.

1-8   Specifying (p_n,q_n) for the ARIMA $(p_n,0,q_n)$ Model of the Noise Series

After using equation (10-23) to estimate a noise series, the n_t values are analyzed in the conventional ARIMA manner to find out if there is an appropriate ARIMA $(p_n,0,q_n)$ model to describe them. The autocorrelations, the partial autocorrelations, and the line spectrum are determined (as in Chapters 8 and 9) and the values p_n and q_n for the autoregressive and moving average processes, respectively, are chosen. In this manner, the $\phi_n(B)$ and $\theta_n(B)$ functions for the noise series n_t in (10-5) are obtained, to give

$$\phi_n(B) n_t = \theta_n(B) a_t.$$

10/2/4   Some Illustrative Examples
of Transfer Function Models

In the field of engineering, the concept of a transfer function has been of interest for some time. It is of considerable importance to understand the operating characteristics of any physical apparatus (machinery, nuclear reactor, etc.), and it is seldom sufficient merely to understand the nature of each separate component in the system. Thus, to examine the operating characteristics, an engineer might systematically control the input to the system and measure the output response. By so doing, something can be learned about the transfer function of the system. Box and Jenkins (1976) discuss in detail the determination of the transfer function for a gas furnace, where the input series was gas rate in cu.ft./min. (sampled every 9 seconds) and the output series was percent CO_2 in the outlet gas. Their final model was written in the following form:

$$Y_t = \frac{-(.53 + .37B + .51B^2)}{(1 - .57B)} X_{t-3} + \frac{a_t}{(1 - 1.53B + .63B^2)}.$$

It is not obvious that this equation could have been generated *a priori* by simple regression considerations, although a close approximation is conceivable, and Box and Jenkins were able to use this transfer function model to do some successful forecasting.

In the field of managerial economics, applications of transfer function modeling are on the increase. For example, Umstead (1977) developed a transfer function model for the purpose of forecasting stock market prices. He used the Leading Composite Index (published by NBER) as the input series, and the S & P 500 index as the output series. Using quarterly data (104 data points starting in 1948) he developed the following transfer function model:

$$y_t = \frac{(\omega_0 - \omega_1 B - \omega_2 B^2 - \omega_3 B^3 - \omega_4 B^4)}{(1 - \delta_{16} B^{16})} x_{t-6} + n_t,$$

where y_t = first differences of logged S & P 500 index,

x_t = first differences of logged Leading Composite Index, and

n_t = the noise component.

Using this model for forecasting over a test set of data, the results were encouraging when compared with previous approaches to the problem.

Helmer and Johansson (1977) made use of the Lydia Pinkham data base and developed a transfer function model relating the sales of a vegetable compound to advertising expenditure. Their paper is a useful one in terms of learning how to go about identifying, estimating, and forecasting a transfer function model. On the same subject, Montgomery and Weatherby (1980) developed the following transfer function model to relate "soft drink concentrate" sales (y) to advertising expenditures (x):

$$y_t = \frac{(.550 + .482B)}{(1 - .847B + .286B^2)} x_{t-2} + \frac{a_t}{(1 - 1.022B + .267B^2)} .$$

In the same paper, Montgomery and Weatherby discuss other applications and give some very useful hints concerning the pragmatic aspects of identification, estimation, and forecasting with such models. Other references to practical applications are given at the end of the chapter.

10/3 Identification of a Transfer Function Model

The data in Table 10-5 will be used to illustrate the complete process of transfer function analysis. The input series (X) is monthly advertising expenditures (in thousands of dollars) and the output series (Y) is total sales (in 1000 cases). The question of interest is to what extent advertising influences sales.

Figures 10-5 and 10-6 show graphically how the input series and the output series fluctuate over time, and certain information can be picked up at a glance. The sales figures are more volatile than the advertising expenditures. The high and low points for both series occur roughly at the same periods of time, although from Table 10-5 it can be noted that the very lowest points are separated by two months. However, the low point at month 20 for advertising is seemingly related to a low point in sales at period 23—that is, three months apart.

Note in passing that if sales are regressed on advertising in simple linear regression form,

$$(\widehat{\text{sales}}) = b_0 + b_1(\text{advertising}),$$

the R^2 value turns out to be .303 and the standard error of estimate is 31.25. If allowance is made for the fact that advertising can affect sales in several future months, then a lagged regression model of the form

$$(\widehat{\text{sales}})_t = b_0 + b_1(\text{adv.})_t + b_2(\text{adv.})_{t-1} + b_3(\text{adv.})_{t-2} + b_4(\text{adv.})_{t-3}$$

yields an R^2 value of .661, and a standard error of estimate of 22.12. It is of interest to query whether the considerably more complex transfer function methodology can improve upon this result. Since the answer to the query is a resounding yes, the reader is encouraged to work through all the stages that follow.

The transfer function (TF) model that we will study for these observations is

$$y_t = \frac{\omega(B)}{\delta(B)} x_{t-b} + \frac{\theta(B)}{\phi(B)} a_t.$$

TABLE 10-5 ADVERTISING EXPENDITURES (IN $1000) AND TOTAL SALES (IN 1000 CASES) OVER A PERIOD OF 100 MONTHS

t	Advertising Input X_t	Sales Output Y_t	t	Advertising Input X_t	Sales Output Y_t
0	116.44	202.66	50	123.90	266.69
1	119.58	232.91	51	122.45	253.07
2	125.74	272.07	52	122.85	249.12
3	124.55	290.97	53	129.28	253.59
4	122.35	299.09	54	129.77	262.13
5	120.44	296.95	55	127.78	279.66
6	123.24	279.49	56	134.29	302.92
7	127.99	255.75	57	140.61	310.77
8	121.19	242.78	58	133.64	307.83
9	118.00	255.34	59	135.45	313.19
10	121.81	271.58	60	130.93	312.80
11	126.54	268.27	61	118.65	301.23
12	129.85	260.51	62	120.34	286.64
13	122.65	266.34	63	120.35	257.17
14	121.64	281.24	64	117.09	229.60
15	127.24	286.19	65	117.56	227.62
16	132.35	271.97	66	121.69	238.21
17	130.86	265.01	67	128.19	252.07
18	122.90	274.44	68	134.79	269.86
19	117.15	291.81	69	128.93	291.62
20	109.47	290.91	70	121.63	314.06
21	114.34	264.95	71	125.43	318.56
22	123.72	228.40	72	126.80	289.11
23	130.33	209.33	73	131.56	255.88
24	133.17	231.69	74	126.43	249.81
25	134.25	281.56	75	116.19	268.82
26	129.75	327.16	76	112.72	288.24
27	130.05	344.24	77	109.53	281.26
28	133.42	324.74	78	110.38	250.92
29	135.16	289.36	79	107.31	222.26
30	130.89	262.92	80	93.59	209.94
31	123.48	263.65	81	89.80	213.30
32	118.46	276.38	82	88.70	207.19
33	122.11	276.34	83	86.64	186.13
34	128.75	258.27	84	89.26	171.20
35	127.09	242.89	85	96.51	170.33
36	114.55	255.98	86	107.35	183.69
37	113.26	278.53	87	110.35	211.30
38	111.51	273.21	88	102.66	252.66
39	111.73	246.37	89	97.56	286.20
40	114.08	221.10	90	98.06	279.45

TABLE 10-5   ADVERTISING EXPENDITURES (IN $1000) AND TOTAL
SALES (IN 1000 CASES) OVER A PERIOD OF 100 MONTHS
(*Continued*)

t	Advertising Input X_t	Sales Output Y_t	t	Advertising Input X_t	Sales Output Y_t
41	114.32	210.41	91	103.93	237.06
42	115.03	222.19	92	115.66	193.40
43	124.28	245.27	93	112.91	180.79
44	132.69	262.58	94	116.89	215.73
45	134.64	283.25	95	116.84	264.98
46	133.28	311.12	96	109.55	294.07
47	128.00	326.28	97	110.63	299.08
48	129.97	322.04	98	111.32	271.10
49	128.35	295.37	99	117.09	230.56

See equation (10-5) for all the details. And we will also convert this to the
form of equations (10-6) and (10-7) for forecasting purposes.

10/3/1   Stage 1: Preparation of the Input and Output Time Series

A look at Figures 10-5 and 10-6 suggests that there is no need for
transforming the X (advertising) and Y (sales) series, but a first difference
might help to improve stationarity. Consider the input series X first. A
univariate analysis of the series is shown in Figure 10-7. The autocorrelations reduce slowly to zero, the first partial is large, and the line spectrum
is dominated by the first two frequencies—all suggesting that a first difference should be taken.

Next Figure 10-8 shows the results of analyzing the first differences
of the X (advertising) series. Note that the autocorrelations show mild signs
of a mixed ARMA process.

In sum, our examination of the input series X yields the following
decisions:

    i. Transform the data?   NO
   ii. Difference the data?   YES
 iii. Deseasonalize the data? NO

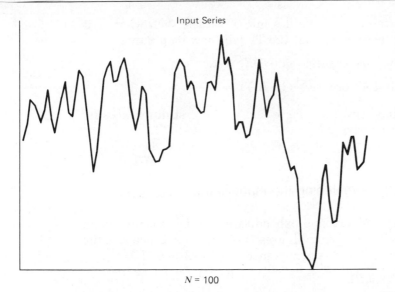

FIGURE 10-5   THE INPUT SERIES (ADVERTISING EXPENDITURES OF TA-
BLE 10-5) SHOWN GRAPHICALLY

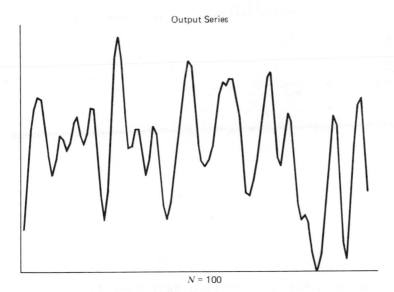

FIGURE 10-6   THE OUTPUT SERIES (TOTAL SALES OF TABLE 10-5) SHOWN
GRAPHICALLY

If a transfer function maps X values into Y values, then when X is differenced we also difference Y, so that the TF will now map x into y:

$$X_t \xrightarrow{\hspace{2cm}} \text{first difference:} \quad (1-B)X_t = x_t,$$

$$Y_t \xrightarrow{\hspace{2cm}} \text{first difference:} \quad (1-B)Y_t = y_t.$$

Table 10-6 shows the 99 observations for x_t and y_t, the first differences for advertising and sales, respectively.

10/3/2   Stage 2: Prewhitening the Input Series

The input series X_t (advertising expenditure) can be modeled as an ARIMA (1,1,1) process, after studying Figures 10-7 and 10-8. Since x_t is the differenced form of X_t, we can also say x_t is modeled as ARMA (1,1):

$$(1 - \phi_x B)x_t = (1 - \theta_x B)\alpha_t.$$

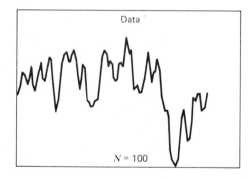
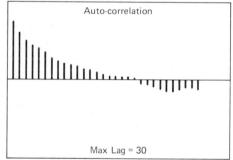
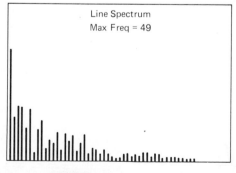
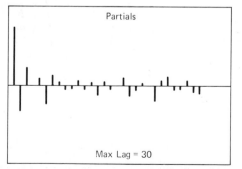

FIGURE 10-7   A UNIVARIATE ANALYSIS OF THE INPUT SERIES (ADVER-
TISING) USING THE RAW DATA FROM TABLE 10-5

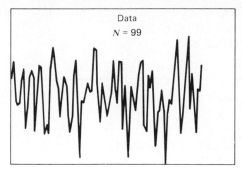

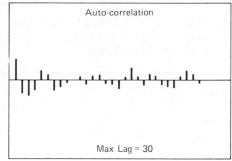

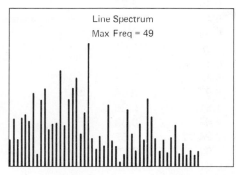

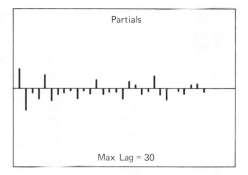

FIGURE 10-8   A UNIVARIATE ANALYSIS OF THE INPUT SERIES (ADVER-
TISING DATA OF TABLE 10-5) AFTER TAKING A FIRST DIF-
FERENCE

To estimate the parameters ϕ_x and θ_x, we run a Box-Jenkins estimation program (see Chapter 9) to get the following results:

$$\phi_x = -.301 \quad (se_{\phi_x} = .157),$$

$$\theta_x = -.789 \quad (se_{\theta_x} = .103).$$

Thus X_t is modeled as follows:

$$(1 + .301B)(1 - B)X_t = (1 + .789B)\alpha_t$$

or

$$(1 + .301B)x_t = (1 + .789B)\alpha_t,$$

and to convert the x_t series to "white noise" α_t, we use the equation

$$\frac{(1 + .301B)}{(1 + .789B)} x_t = \alpha_t \quad \text{[see equation (10-9)]}.$$

TABLE 10-6 THE FIRST DIFFERENCES OF THE INPUT (ADVERTISING) AND OUTPUT (SALES) SERIES (SEE TABLE 10-5 FOR THE RAW DATA)

t	Input X_t	Output Y_t	t	Input X_t	Output Y_t
0	0.00	0.00	50	−4.45	−28.68
1	3.14	30.25	51	−1.45	−13.62
2	6.16	39.16	52	0.40	−3.95
3	−1.19	18.90	53	6.43	4.47
4	−2.20	8.12	54	0.49	8.54
5	−1.91	−2.14	55	−1.99	17.53
6	2.80	−17.46	56	6.51	23.26
7	4.75	−23.74	57	6.32	7.85
8	−6.80	−12.97	58	−6.97	−2.94
9	−3.19	12.56	59	1.81	5.36
10	3.81	16.24	60	−4.52	−0.39
11	4.73	−3.31	61	−12.28	−11.57
12	3.31	−7.76	62	1.69	−14.59
13	−7.20	5.83	63	0.01	−29.47
14	−1.01	14.90	64	−3.26	−27.57
15	5.60	4.95	65	0.47	−1.98
16	5.11	−14.22	66	4.13	10.59
17	−1.49	−6.96	67	6.50	13.86
18	−7.96	9.43	68	6.60	17.79
19	−5.75	17.37	69	−5.86	21.76
20	−7.68	−0.90	70	−7.30	22.44
21	4.87	−25.96	71	3.80	4.50
22	9.38	−36.55	72	1.37	−29.45
23	6.61	−19.07	73	4.76	−33.23
24	2.84	22.36	74	−5.13	−6.07
25	1.08	49.87	75	−10.24	19.01
26	−4.50	45.60	76	−3.47	19.42
27	0.30	17.08	77	−3.19	−6.98
28	3.37	−19.50	78	0.85	−30.34
29	1.74	−35.38	79	−3.07	−28.66
30	−4.27	−26.44	80	−13.72	−12.32
31	−7.41	0.73	81	−3.79	3.36
32	−5.02	12.73	82	−1.10	−6.11
33	3.65	−0.04	83	−2.06	−21.06
34	6.64	−18.07	84	2.62	−14.93
35	−1.66	−15.38	85	7.25	−0.87
36	−12.54	13.09	86	10.84	13.36
37	−1.29	22.55	87	3.00	27.61
38	−1.75	−5.32	88	−7.69	41.36

TABLE 10-6 THE FIRST DIFFERENCES OF THE INPUT (ADVERTISING) AND OUTPUT (SALES) SERIES (SEE TABLE 10-5 FOR THE RAW DATA) (*Continued*)

t	Input X_t	Output Y_t	t	Input X_t	Output Y_t
39	0.22	−26.84	89	−5.10	33.54
40	2.35	−25.27	90	0.50	−6.75
41	0.24	−10.69	91	5.87	−42.39
42	0.71	11.78	92	11.73	−43.66
43	9.25	23.08	93	−2.75	−12.61
44	8.41	17.31	94	3.98	34.94
45	1.95	20.67	95	−0.05	49.25
46	−1.36	27.87	96	−7.29	29.09
47	−5.28	15.16	97	1.08	5.01
48	1.97	−4.24	98	0.69	−27.98
49	−1.62	−26.67	99	5.77	−40.54

In practice, this is done by rewriting the equation as follows:

$$x_t + .301x_{t-1} = \alpha_t + .789\alpha_{t-1},$$

$$\alpha_t = x_t + .301x_{t-1} - .789\alpha_{t-1}.$$

Setting $\alpha_t = 0$ and proceeding, we have

$$\alpha_2 = x_2 + .301x_1 - .789\alpha_1$$

$$= 6.16 + .301(3.14) - 0$$

$$= 7.11.$$

$$\alpha_3 = x_3 + .301x_2 - .789\alpha_2$$

$$= -1.19 + .301(6.16) - .789(7.11)$$

$$= -4.94.$$

The complete set of prewhitened α_t values is shown in Table 10-7.

10/3/3 Stage 3: "Prewhitening" the Output Series

As indicated in Section 10/2/3, we must apply the same prewhitening transformation to the output series in order to preserve the integrity of

TABLE 10-7   THE PREWHITENED INPUT SERIES (α_t) AND THE
PREWHITENED OUTPUT SERIES (β_t) FOR THE
ADVERTISING-SALES EXAMPLE

t	α_t	β_t	t	α_t	β_t
1	0.000	0.000	51	−1.288	−7.978
2	7.106	48.276	52	0.979	−1.760
3	−4.940	−7.387	53	5.778	4.668
4	1.339	19.644	54	−2.131	6.204
5	−3.629	−15.191	55	−0.161	15.209
6	5.088	−6.119	56	6.038	16.544
7	1.580	−24.174	57	3.518	1.807
8	−6.615	−1.052	58	−7.841	−2.000
9	−0.020	9.481	59	5.896	6.052
10	2.865	12.545	60	−8.626	−3.550
11	3.618	−8.313	61	−6.836	−8.887
12	1.881	−2.199	62	3.383	−11.065
13	−7.687	5.226	63	−2.150	−25.137
14	2.885	12.534	64	−1.561	−16.619
15	3.020	−0.448	65	0.719	2.823
16	4.415	−12.374	66	3.704	7.766
17	−3.433	−1.482	67	4.822	10.924
18	−5.700	8.502	68	4.754	13.348
19	−3.652	13.504	69	−7.622	16.590
20	−6.532	−6.320	70	−3.052	15.908
21	7.709	−21.245	71	4.008	−1.289
22	4.765	−27.611	72	−0.647	−27.077
23	5.677	−8.300	73	5.684	−20.742
24	0.353	23.162	74	−8.180	0.281
25	1.657	38.335	75	−5.332	16.959
26	−5.482	30.384	76	−2.349	11.768
27	3.269	6.850	77	−2.383	−10.413
28	0.881	−19.757	78	1.768	−24.228
29	2.060	−25.669	79	−4.209	−18.688
30	−5.371	−16.850	80	−11.324	−6.213
31	−4.459	6.056	81	1.010	4.549
32	−3.735	8.172	82	−3.039	−8.686
33	5.084	−2.651	83	0.006	−16.048
34	3.729	−15.991	84	1.994	−8.615
35	−2.601	−8.209	85	6.466	1.428
36	−10.988	14.932	86	7.923	11.971
37	3.600	14.714	87	0.015	22.191
38	−4.979	−10.133	88	−6.798	32.172
39	3.621	−20.449	89	−2.054	20.621
40	−0.441	−17.225	90	0.584	−12.912

TABLE 10-7 THE PREWHITENED INPUT SERIES (α_t) AND THE PREWHITENED OUTPUT SERIES (β_t) FOR THE ADVERTISING-SALES EXAMPLE (*Continued*)

t	α_t	β_t	t	α_t	β_t
41	1.296	−4.715	91	5.560	−34.237
42	−0.240	12.279	92	9.112	−29.423
43	9.653	16.943	93	−6.404	−2.554
44	3.581	10.898	94	8.204	33.155
45	1.659	17.288	95	−5.323	33.621
46	−2.081	20.459	96	−3.105	17.406
47	−4.048	7.417	97	1.333	0.044
48	3.572	−5.523	98	−0.036	−26.505
49	−3.845	−23.590	99	6.006	−28.060
50	−1.905	−18.105			

the TF model. Using equation (10-10), the y_t series is converted to the β_t series, as follows:

$$\frac{(1 + .301B)}{(1 + .789B)} y_t = \beta_t.$$

To do this in practice, rewrite the equation as follows:

$$y_t + .301y_{t-1} = \beta_t + .789\beta_{t-1}$$

$$\beta_t = y_t + .301y_{t-1} - .789\beta_{t-1}.$$

Setting $\beta_1 = 0$ to get things started, and proceeding to β_2, β_3, and so on, we get

$$\beta_2 = y_2 + .301y_1 - .789\beta_1$$

$$= 39.16 + .301(30.25) - 0$$

$$= 48.28,$$

$$\beta_3 = y_3 + .301y_2 - .789\beta_2$$

$$= 18.90 + .301(39.16) - .789(48.28)$$

$$= -7.39.$$

The complete "prewhitened" series β_t is shown in Table 10-7.

Next the prewhitened α_t (input) and β_t (output) will be used to identify the shape of the transfer function that maps α values into β values.

10/3/4   Stage 4: Computing the Cross- and Autocorrelations for the Prewhitened Input and Output

These are essentially $n = 98$ values[4] of α_t and β_t and the basic statistics are as follows:

	Mean	Variance
α_t	.004	22.60
β_t	−.022	288.32

To study the relation between α_t and β_t the key is to compute cross-correlations between the two series. Equations (10-13), (10-14), and (10-15) are used for this purpose, and if k is allowed range from -15 to 15 in equation (10-15), the results obtained are as shown in Figure 10-9.

How do we interpret these cross-correlations? The input series (advertising) is assumed to *lead* the output series (sales), so that we do not expect advertising in month 10, say, to influence sales in month 9, or month 8, and so on back. Note that most all the cross-correlations for $k = -1$ through -15 are essentially zero. Likewise, advertising in any given month does not appear to be related to sales in that same month or even in the next month for that matter. Then when the time gap is two months the cross-correlation is .351, and at three months it is .591. The input series has a forward (dynamic) impact on future sales. After a while the influence dies out, so that for $k = 11$ through $k = 15$ the cross-correlations are nearly zero once more.

The cross-correlations in Figure 10-9 thus indicate clearly that the input series *leads* the output series, that there is an absolute delay of 2 months (before α significantly influences β), and that after 10 months lead time, α appears to have no significant impact on β.

The same equations (10-13) and (10-15) can be used to study the α_t series and the β_t series separately.[5] Figure 10-10 graphs the first 15 autocorrelations for the prewhitened α_t (advertising) series. Note that these autocorrelations are small and we expect this, because prewhitening x_t means transforming the x_t series into essentially white noise, and theoretically the autocorrelations should be zero. This is not so for the β_t series, as seen in Figure 10-11. Whatever transfer function is operating in the input series, makes the output series have some sort of pattern in the autocorrelations.

---

[4]See Table 10-7 and ignore the first values that were set equal to zero.

[5]If in equations (10-13) and (10-15) we change Y to X, then we have formulas for computing the autocovariances and autocorrelations for X.

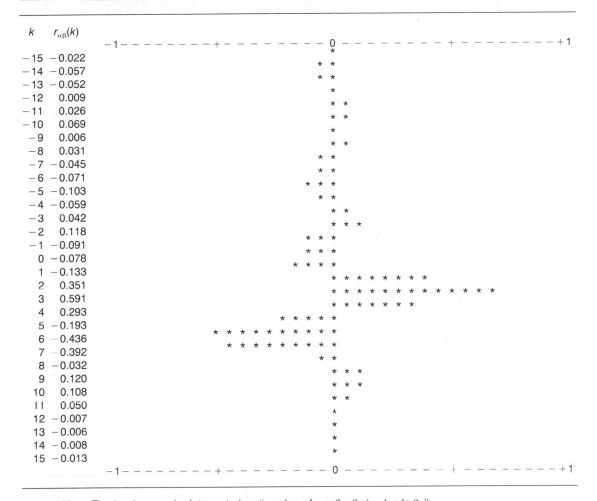

k	$r_{\alpha\beta}(k)$
−15	−0.022
−14	−0.057
−13	−0.052
−12	0.009
−11	0.026
−10	0.069
−9	0.006
−8	0.031
−7	−0.045
−6	−0.071
−5	−0.103
−4	−0.059
−3	0.042
−2	0.118
−1	−0.091
0	−0.078
1	−0.133
2	0.351
3	0.591
4	0.293
5	−0.193
6	−0.436
7	−0.392
8	−0.032
9	0.120
10	0.108
11	0.050
12	−0.007
13	−0.006
14	−0.008
15	−0.013

Note: The k value may be interpreted as "number of months that α_t leads β_t."

FIGURE 10-9 THE CROSSCORRELATIONS BETWEEN THE PRE-WHITENED INPUT SERIES (α_t) AND THE PREWHITENED OUTPUT SERIES (β_t)

10/3/5 Stage 5: Direct Estimation of the Impulse Response Weights

It has been argued that equation (10-4) is not a parsimonious representation of a transfer function because the number of impulse weights ($v_o, v_1, \ldots, v_k$) can be quite large. Nevertheless, in the process of trying to identify a TF model it is convenient to start by directly estimating the set of impulse weights.

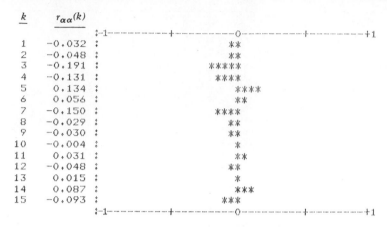

FIGURE 10-10   THE AUTOCORRELATIONS FOR THE PREWHITENED IN-
PUT SERIES (α_t)

Equation (10-17) is used to convert the cross-correlations between α and β (see Figure 10-9) into impulse response weights, as follows:

$$v_0 = r_{\alpha\beta}(0)\,\frac{s_\beta}{s_\alpha} = (-.078)\sqrt{\frac{288.32}{22.60}} = -.280,$$

$$v_1 = r_{\alpha\beta}(1)\,\frac{s_\beta}{s_\alpha} = (-.133)(3.572) = -.475,$$

$$v_2 = r_{\alpha\beta}(2)\,\frac{s_\beta}{s_\alpha} = (.351)(3.572) = 1.254.$$

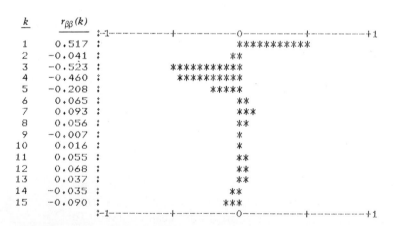

FIGURE 10-11   THE AUTOCORRELATIONS FOR THE PREWHITENED OUT-
PUT SERIES (β_t)

The first 16 impulse weights are shown in Figure 10-12. Clearly, since they are a constant multiple of the cross-correlations of Figure 10-9, the shape of the graph is the same, but note that now we consider only $k = 0, 1, \ldots, 15$. The input series is a *leading* indicator so we do not deal with negative values of k.

10/3/6 Stage 6: Identification of (r,s,b) for the Transfer Function Model

The parameter b, which deals with the absolute delay before the input series begins to influence the output series, is easy to deal with. Using the cross-correlations (Figure 10-9) or the directly estimated impulse weights (Figure 10-12) we will assert that there is a 2-month delay before advertising (input) influences sales (output). So $b = 2$.

Given the practical difficulties of interpreting the guiding principles outlined earlier (Section 10/2/3, stage 1-6) we might argue that $r + s = 6$, in that six cross-correlations (for $k = 2, 3, 4, 5, 6,$ and 7 in Figure 10-9) are significantly larger than zero. However, to decide which of these cross-correlations "do not show any clear pattern" is arbitrary. A common

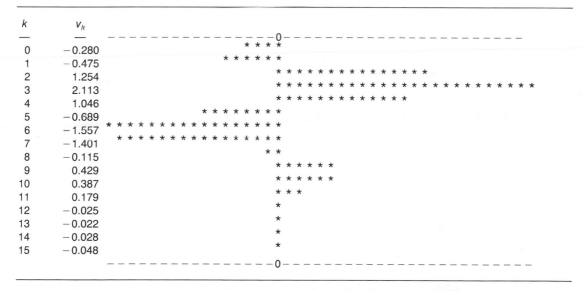

FIGURE 10-12 THE FIRST 16 IMPULSE WEIGHTS DEFINING THE TRANS-FER FUNCTION

practice in Box-Jenkins modeling is to try a few different models and make a choice amongst them at the diagnostic stage (Section 10/5).

For the advertising-sales exercise we shall choose a model with $(r,s,b) = (2,2,2)$. We are therefore implying the following equation form:

$$y_t = \frac{(\omega_0 - \omega_1 B - \omega_2 B^2)}{(1 - \delta_1 B - \delta_2 B^2)} x_{t-2} + \text{(noise model)}.$$

The noise model will be identified in the next two sections.

10/3/7   Stage 7: A Preliminary Look at the Noise Series

The estimated impulse weights shown in Figure 10-12 allow us to compute preliminary estimates of the noise component of the TF model. Using equation (10-23), we have

$$n_t = y_t - v_0 x_t - v_1 x_{t-1} - v_2 x_{t-2} - \cdots - v_{15} x_{t-15}.$$

Note that it is not necessary to use all the impulse weights. Looking at Figure 10-12, it is clear that little would be lost by omitting v_{12}, v_{13}, v_{14}, and v_{15}. If we use all 16 weights (v_0 through v_{15}), then there will be only 84 values of n_t. There are 99 values of y_t and x_t, and we lose 15 values because of the 15 time lags.

Consider n_{16}:

$$n_{16} = y_{16} - (-.280)x_{16} - (-.475)x_{15} - \cdots - (-.048)x_1.$$

Using Table 10-6, this computation is as follows:

$$n_{16} = (-14.22) + .280(5.11) + .475(5.60) - 1.254(-1.01)$$

$$-2.113(-7.20) - 1.046(3.31) - \cdots + .048(3.14)$$

$$= 4.288.$$

Similarly, the other noise values n_{17}, n_{18}, ..., n_{99}, could be determined. The full set of preliminary estimates of the noise component is shown in Table 10-8. (Note that the 84 noise values are identified in Table 10-8 as n_1 through n_{84}.)

The summary statistics for this preliminary noise series, are as follows:

mean $= .040$

variance $= 67.377$

std. dev. $= 8.208$

TABLE 10-8 PRELIMINARY ESTIMATES OF THE NOISE COMPONENTS IN THE ADVERTISING-SALES EXAMPLE

t	n_t	t	n_t
1	4.288	43	−2.286
2	13.055	44	−3.814
3	−0.372	45	−1.147
4	−8.691	46	−7.526
5	−8.430	47	−2.051
6	3.451	48	5.471
7	14.180	49	−0.642
8	5.774	50	−5.669
9	−6.167	51	−4.269
10	−11.218	52	−0.612
11	−2.260	53	6.100
12	6.535	54	7.371
13	12.770	55	−6.510
14	7.788	56	−7.069
15	−9.370	57	0.134
16	−14.318	58	6.450
17	−6.950	59	9.253
18	5.654	60	−5.187
19	15.392	61	−12.765
20	6.756	62	−0.924
21	−8.791	63	8.458
22	−20.336	64	3.488
23	−12.105	65	−13.841
24	5.243	66	−24.169
25	11.801	67	−11.018
26	−0.542	68	4.575
27	−9.726	69	8.062
28	−3.898	70	4.143
29	11.546	71	−1.385
30	15.619	72	−3.795
31	6.965	73	0.296
32	−9.209	74	−2.930
33	−8.497	75	−4.159
34	1.667	76	5.264
35	5.336	77	11.453
36	0.711	78	3.925
37	−3.978	79	−7.328
38	3.494	80	−3.143
39	7.697	81	5.398
40	5.072	82	14.049
41	2.439	83	7.495
42	1.008	84	−5.150

10/3/8   Stage 8: Identification of the ARIMA Model for the Noise Series

In order to specify the complete TF model it is now necessary to choose an ARIMA model for the noise series. Figure 10-13 shows the basic analysis of the noise data from Table 10-8. The autocorrelations show a strong second-order autoregressive aspect (a damped sine-wave shape), the partials confirm the AR(2) process (there are two strong partials to start with), and the line spectrum supports this contention (see Figure 9-5). The decision is made to model the noise series as ARIMA (2,0,1),

$$(1 - \phi_1 B - \phi_2 B^2)\, n_t = (1 - \phi_1 B)\, a_t,$$

where the MA(1) process may turn out to be unwarranted.

Thus, in the TF model

$$y_t = \frac{\omega(B)}{\delta(B)}\, x_{t-b} + n_t,$$

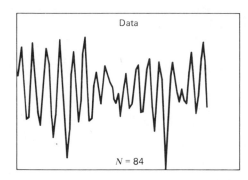

Data

$N = 84$

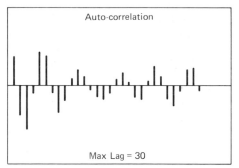

Auto-correlation

Max Lag = 30

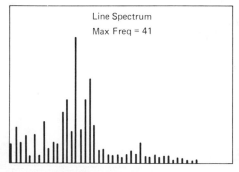

Line Spectrum
Max Freq = 41

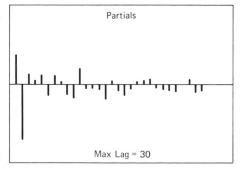

Partials

Max Lag = 30

FIGURE 10-13   A UNIVARIATE ANALYSIS OF THE PRELIMINARY NOISE SERIES (n_t) USING THE DATA OF TABLE 10-8

we may now replace n_t by

$$\frac{(1 - \theta_1 B)}{(1 - \phi_1 B - \phi_2 B^2)} a_t,$$

where a_t is a random noise process.

10/4 Estimation of the Parameters of the Model

The tentatively identified TF model is

$$y_t = \frac{(\omega_0 - \omega_1 B - \omega_2 B^2)}{(1 - \delta_1 B - \delta_2 B^2)} x_{t-2} + \frac{(1 - \theta_1 B)}{(1 - \phi_1 B - \phi_2 B^2)} a_t,$$

which could also be written as

$$y_t = v(B)x_t + n_t.$$

It is now necessary to estimate the parameters ω_0, ω_1, ω_2, δ_1, δ_2, θ_1, ϕ_1, and ϕ_2. First, preliminary estimates will be determined, and then the Marquardt algorithm described in Chapter 9 (Section 9/3) is used to proceed iteratively to better and better estimates. This involves a considerable amount of computation and is therefore done on a computer.

10/4/1 Preliminary Estimates of the Parameters

Equation (10-21) states explicitly the relationship between the impulse function, $v(B)$, and the left and right coefficient functions, $\delta(B)$ and $\omega(B)$. In expanded form, equations (10-22a) through (10-22d) spell out the details of this relationship, and for the $(r,s,b) = (2,2,2)$ TF model, the specific equations are as follows:

$$
\begin{align}
v_0 &= 0 \tag{1}\\
v_1 &= 0 \tag{2}\\
v_2 &= \delta_1 v_1 + \delta_2 v_0 + \omega_0 \tag{3}\\
v_3 &= \delta_1 v_2 + \delta_2 v_1 - \omega_1 \tag{4}\\
v_4 &= \delta_1 v_3 + \delta_2 v_2 - \omega_2 \tag{5}\\
v_5 &= \delta_1 v_4 + \delta_2 v_3 \tag{6}\\
v_6 &= \delta_1 v_5 + \delta_2 v_4 \tag{7}\\
v_7 &= \delta_1 v_6 + \delta_2 v_5 \tag{8}
\end{align}
$$

(10-24)

In stage 5, the impulse weights $v_0\, v_1, \ldots, v_{15}$ were estimated explicitly (see Figure 10-12), and these estimates may be used to solve for the unknown parameters in equation (10-24).

First solve for δ_1 and δ_2 in the 6th and 7th equations above.

$$-.689 = \delta_1(1.046) + \delta_2(2.113) \left. \begin{array}{l} \\ \\ \end{array} \right\} \begin{bmatrix} \text{using the known} \\ v \text{ weights} \end{bmatrix}$$

$$-1.557 = \delta_1(-.689) + \delta_2(1.046)$$

Solving this pair of equations yields

$$\hat{\delta}_1 = 1.01, \qquad \hat{\delta}_2 = -.83.$$

Now, letting v_0 and v_1 be zero, the 3rd equation in (10-24) yields

$$\hat{\omega}_0 = v_2 = 1.25.$$

The 4th equation is then solved for ω_1, as follows:

$$\hat{\omega}_1 = \delta_2 v_2 + \delta_2 v_1 - v_3$$

$$= (1.01)(1.25) + 0 - (2.11)$$

$$= -.85.$$

Finally the 5th equation is used to solve for ω_2, as follows

$$\omega_2 = \delta_1 v_3 + \delta_2 v_2 - v_4$$

$$= (1.01)(2.11) + (-.83)(1.25) - (1.05)$$

$$= .05.$$

This last estimate is close to zero, but is kept in because the final estimate for ω_2 may be significant.

Estimating the noise parameters, ϕ_1, ϕ_2, and θ_1, can be done in the ways mentioned in Chapter 9 (see especially the appendix). Ignoring θ_1 for the moment, we could use equations (9-42) and (9-43) to get rough estimates of ϕ_1 and ϕ_2. In Figure 10-13 the first two autocorrelations for the noise series were $r_1 = .438$ and $r_2 = -.461$, so that

$$\hat{\phi}_1 = \frac{r_1(1 - r_2)}{1 - r_1^2} = \frac{(.438)(1.461)}{1 - .192} = .79 \quad \text{[using (9-42)]},$$

$$\hat{\phi}_2 = \frac{r_2 - r_1^2}{1 - r_1^2} = \frac{-.461 - .192}{1 - .192} = -.81 \quad \text{[using (9-43)]}.$$

Finally, the MA parameter can be arbitrarily guessed as $\hat{\theta}_1 = .30$, say. The complete model is thus tentatively identified as

$$y_t = \frac{(1.25 + .85B - .05B^2)}{(1 - 1.01B + .83B^2)} x_{t-2} + \frac{(1 - .30B)}{(1 - .79B + .81B^2)} a_t.$$

TABLE 10-9 SOME RESULTS FROM THE ITERATIVE MARQUARDT
ALGORITHM WHEN TRYING TO REDUCE THE SUM OF
SQUARED RESIDUALS FOR THE ADVERTISING-SALES
EXAMPLE

Iteration	δ_1	δ_2	ω_0	ω_1	ω_2	ϕ_1	ϕ_2	θ_1	
0	1.0100	−0.8300	1.2500	−0.8500	0.0500	0.7900	−0.8100	0.3000	SSR = 4603.15
1	1.1817	−0.7659	1.3183	−0.5895	0.5576	0.8662	−0.6156	0.0890	SSR = 581.177
2	1.2121	−0.7021	1.2963	−0.5795	0.7933	0.9696	−0.4797	0.4001	SSR = 237.574
3	1.2115	−0.7092	1.3115	−0.5785	0.7789	1.2564	−0.6516	0.9483	SSR = 220.935
4	1.2084	−0.7086	1.3052	−0.5860	0.7814	1.1744	−0.6019	0.9164	SSR = 206.839
5	1.2100	−0.7080	1.3036	−0.5870	0.7906	1.1693	−0.6020	0.8917	SSR = 204.909
6	1.2102	−0.7079	1.3033	−0.5870	0.7913	1.1630	−0.5965	0.8768	SSR = 204.455
7	1.2102	−0.7079	1.3034	−0.5871	0.7911	1.1597	−0.5939	0.8677	SSR = 204.298
8	1.2102	−0.7079	1.3035	−0.5871	0.7909	1.1579	−0.5925	0.8622	SSR = 204.238
9	1.2101	−0.7078	1.3035	−0.5870	0.7907	1.1568	−0.5917	0.8590	SSR = 204.214
10	1.2101	−0.7078	1.3036	−0.5870	0.7906	1.1562	−0.5913	0.8572	SSR = 204.203
11	1.2101	−0.7078	1.3036	−0.5870	0.7905	1.1559	−0.5910	0.8562	SSR = 204.198
12	1.2101	−0.7078	1.3036	−0.5870	0.7905	1.1557	−0.5909	0.8556	SSR = 204.196
13	1.2101	−0.7078	1.3036	−0.5870	0.7904	1.1556	0.5908	0.8553	SSR = 204.194
14	1.2101	−0.7078	1.3036	−0.5870	0.7904	1.1555	−0.5908	0.8551	SSR = 204.194

⟶ Parameter corrections have gotten too small
Estimate of variance for residuals = 2.40228

10/4/2 Final Estimation of the Parameters

The Marquardt algorithm[6] can be used to solve iteratively for the
best values of the parameters, using the starting values of Section 10/4/1.
At each iteration, new values of the parameters are found and new estimates of the residuals (a_t) are computed. The sum of the squares of these
residuals (SSR) indicates how well the iterations are proceeding. Table
10-9 shows some of the details. At iteration 0, that is, using the preliminary
estimates to start with, the SSR is 4603. After just two iterations the SSR
is down to 237 and then the algorithm closes in on a minimum value for
SSR. The iterations stopped because the corrections to parameter values
became too small, and at this point the variance of the residuals was 2.40.

Table 10-10 shows the final values for the parameters together with
the appropriate standard errors. Note that all standard errors are small

---

[6]See Box and Jenkins, 1976, pp. 513–516.

TABLE 10-10   THE FINAL ESTIMATES OF THE TRANSFER FUNCTION
MODEL PARAMETERS AND THEIR STANDARD ERRORS

Left-Hand Side Parameters

Delta (1):   1.2101   See: 0.0091
Delta (2):   − 0.7078   See: 0.0083

Right-Hand Side Parameters

Omega (0):   1.3036   See: 0.0342
Omega (1):   − 0.5870   See: 0.0550
Omega (2):   0.7904   See: 0.0455

AR Parameters for Noise

Phi (1):   1.1555   See: 0.0726
Phi (2):   − 0.5907   See: 0.0675

MA Parameters for Noise

Theta (1):   0.8551   See: 0.0607

and that all parameter values are significantly different from zero. The TF model has been identified and the parameters have been estimated, to yield

$$y_t = \frac{(1.30 + .59B - .79B^2)}{(1 - 1.21B + .71B^2)}\, x_{t-2} + \frac{(1 - .86B)}{(1 - 1.16B + .59B^2)}\, a_t. \tag{10-25}$$

Note in Table 10-9 that the TF model has a residual variance of just 2.40228—a dramatic improvement over the lagged regression results mentioned in Section 10/3.

10/5   Diagnostic Checking of the Model

It is common practice in ARIMA modeling to identify more than one model form, estimate the parameters for each model, and then do a careful diagnostic check to test the validity of the model. The same is true in TF modeling. Of particular interest in this case are two items: (i) the final residual series designated a_t, and (ii) the relationship between this a_t series and the prewhitened input series, which has been designated α_t.

The α_t series has been computed in Section 10/3/2 (see Table 10-7). To compute the a_t series by hand is tedious. In abbreviated form the procedure is

$$y_t = \frac{\omega(B)}{\delta(B)} x_{t-b} + \frac{\theta(B)}{\phi(B)} a_t,$$

so that multiplying through by $\delta(B)\phi(B)$ we get

$$\delta(B)\phi(B)y_t = \phi(B)\omega(B)x_{t-b} + \delta(B)\theta(B)a_t.$$

Expanding and rearranging terms, it is possible to express a_t as a function of various y values, various x values and past a values. In particular, the equation for our worked example is

$$a_t = y_t + d_1 y_{t-1} + d_2 y_{t-2} + d_3 y_{t-3} + d_4 y_{t-4}$$

$$e_0 x_{t-b} - e_1 x_{t-b-1} - e_2 x_{t-b-2} - e_3 x_{t-b-3} - e_4 x_{t-b-4}$$

$$-f_1 a_{t-1} - f_2 a_{t-2} - f_3 a_{t-3}, \qquad\qquad (10\text{-}26)$$

where

$$d_1 = -\delta_1 - \phi_1 \qquad\qquad = -2.37$$

$$d_2 = -\delta_2 - \phi_2 + \delta_1\phi_1 \qquad = 2.70$$

$$d_3 = \delta_1\phi_2 + \delta_2\phi_1 \qquad\qquad = -1.53$$

$$d_4 = \delta_2\phi_2 \qquad\qquad = .42$$

$$e_o = \omega_o \qquad\qquad = 1.30$$

$$e_1 = -\omega_1 - \omega_0\phi_1 \qquad\qquad = -.92$$

$$e_2 = -\omega_0\phi_2 - \omega_2 + \omega_1\phi_1 \qquad = -.70$$

$$e_3 = \omega_1\phi_2 + \omega_2\phi_1 \qquad\qquad = 1.26$$

$$e_4 = \omega_2\phi_2 \qquad\qquad = -.47$$

$$f_1 = -\delta_1 - \theta_1 \qquad\qquad = -2.07$$

$$f_2 = \delta_1\phi_1 - \delta_2 \qquad\qquad = 1.74$$

$$f_3 = \theta_1\delta_2 \qquad\qquad = -.61$$

Refer to Table 10-10 for the final parameter values that are used to calculate these coefficients.

As one illustration, consider the computation of a_7, using equation (10-26) and data from Table 10-6. To get going we will have to assume previous error terms ($a_1, a_2, a_3, a_4, a_5, a_6$) to be zero.

$$a_7 = y_7 + d_1 y_6 + d_2 y_5 + d_3 y_4 + d_4 y_3$$

$$-e_0 x_5 - e_1 x_4 - e_2 x_3 - e_3 x_2 - e_4 x_1$$

$$-f_1 a_6 - f_2 a_5 - f_3 a_4$$

$$= (-23.74) + (-2.37)(-17.46) + (2.70)(-2.14) + (-1.53)(8.12)$$

$$+ (.42)(18.90) - (1.30)(-1.91) - (-.92)(-2.20)$$

$$- (-.70)(-1.19) - (1.26)(6.16) - (-.47)(3.14)$$

$$- (-2.07)(0) - (1.74)(0) - (-.61)(0)$$

$$= -1.56.$$

Similarly, we could proceed to compute a_8, a_9, ..., a_{99}. The complete set of final residuals (a_t values) is shown in Table 10-11. Note that there are (100 $- 1 - r - s - b$) = 93 of them.

10/5/1 Analysis of the Residuals: Autocorrelations

The a_t values in Table 10-11 are analyzed in Figure 10-14. The graphical plot of the residuals shows some fluctuation, but it should be remembered that all the values are reasonably small. The autocorrelations show very little in the way of pattern. The partials likewise support the contention that the a_t series is essentially random noise, although there is one noticeable partial at a lag of 15. The partial here is $-.323$. However, there is no obvious pattern in either the autocorrelations or the partials, and the line spectrum supports the notion that the residuals behave reasonably well.

It is possible to use the Box-Pierce χ^2 test (see Appendix 8-A) to determine if the set of autocorrelations in Figure 10-14 are significantly different from zero. For a stationary ARIMA (p,d,q) series, the formula is as follows:

$$\chi^2_{(df)} = n \sum_{k-1}^{m} r^2(k), \tag{10-27}$$

where n = the number of observations,

m = the largest time lag considered,

$r(k)$ = the autocorrelation for time lag k

df = degrees of freedom = $m - p - q$.

For the residuals (a_t) in the advertising-sales example, the appropriate calculations are as follows:

$$\chi^2_{(15 - p_n - q_n)} = (100 - 1 - r - s - b) \sum_{k=1}^{15} r^2_{aa}(k)$$

TABLE 10-11   THE COMPLETE SET OF FINAL RESIDUALS (a_t)
FOR THE SALES-ADVERTISING TF MODEL

t	a_t	t	a_t	t	a_t
1	−1.5593	32	−1.7738	63	−0.4226
2	−1.7704	33	1.6329	64	−0.9123
3	1.4108	34	−1.8877	65	0.7369
4	2.2523	35	−1.2880	66	−0.1640
5	0.0244	36	1.1348	67	0.0670
6	−1.1497	37	0.9398	68	3.5450
7	0.4594	38	−0.6715	69	2.0377
8	−1.4538	39	3.0067	70	−1.3976
9	0.8891	40	1.9721	71	1.4718
10	−0.4616	41	−2.6080	72	−0.2671
11	1.0335	42	1.7360	73	1.0197
12	−1.9432	43	0.1929	74	−0.0286
13	2.5377	44	0.2936	75	−1.0478
14	2.4488	45	−0.6841	76	0.5199
15	0.4256	46	−0.0710	77	−0.1463
16	1.3315	47	2.8323	78	−1.0939
17	1.4141	48	−0.2529	79	1.6146
18	−0.4120	49	0.0731	80	2.3157
19	−1.3937	50	3.9206	81	0.1798
20	−0.2245	51	3.0404	82	0.9279
21	−0.5585	52	−0.4747	83	−0.8288
22	−0.7253	53	0.0014	84	−2.0561
23	2.8435	54	1.5378	85	1.3416
24	−2.9515	55	0.9921	86	0.7126
25	0.6357	56	−0.5777	87	−1.0468
26	0.9757	57	−0.4608	88	−0.1224
27	0.4837	58	−1.1637	89	−0.7581
28	−1.9999	59	−1.1521	90	−0.7873
29	−2.9997	60	−1.8381	91	−0.4242
30	1.6628	61	−0.5490	92	−1.0444
31	−1.0884	62	−0.0129	93	−1.1685

a_7 through a_{99} have been renumbered here a_1 through a_{93}

where (r,s,b) and (p_n,q_n) are the TF model parameters. The first 15 auto-correlations are used below to compute the χ^2 value:

$$\chi^2_{(15-2-1)} = 93[(.017)^2 + (-.119)^2 + (.251)^2 + (.043)^2$$
$$+ (-.097)^2 + (-.029)^2 + (.041)^2 + (-.133)^2$$
$$+ (-.102)^2 + (-.007)^2 + (-.052) + (.007)^2$$
$$+ (-.095)^2 + (.114)^2 + (-.221)^2] = 17.95.$$

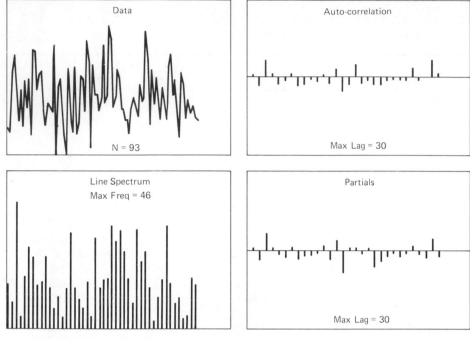

FIGURE 10-14   THE ANALYSIS OF THE SET OF RESIDUALS (a_t) FOR THE SALES-ADVERTISING MODEL

Looking up the χ^2 tables (Table E in the appendix at the end of the book), note that for 12 degrees of freedom a value of 18.5494 leaves 10 percent of the area in the right tail of the distribution. Thus we may conclude that the a_t series is essentially a random series. The TF model for the advertising-sales example fits the data well.

10/5/2   Analysis of the Residuals: Cross-Correlations

In the process of directly estimating the transfer function weights (stage 5 in Section 10/3/5) an assumption is made that the prewhitened input series (α_t) is independent of the random noise component (a_t). Thus, an important part of the diagnostic process is to vindicate this assumption. For the α_t series (Table 10-7) and the final a_t series (Table 10-11), cross-correlations are computed, as shown in Figure 10-15. There are no significant cross-correlations.

To test this conclusion formally, we may use the Box-Pierce χ^2 test once more. Using equation (10-27), the appropriate formula for testing independence of α_t and a_t, is as follows:

k	$r_{\alpha a}(k)$
1	0.046
2	0.029
3	−0.045
4	0.045
5	0.029
6	−0.005
7	−0.054
8	0.066
9	0.010
10	−0.042
11	−0.078
12	−0.010
13	−0.041
14	−0.102
15	0.120

```
 k     r  (k)
        αa
             :--1---------------+-----------------0------------------+-----------+1
 1    0.046  :                                    **
 2    0.029  :                                    **
 3   -0.045  :                                    **
 4    0.045  :                                    **
 5    0.029  :                                    **
 6   -0.005  :                                    *
 7   -0.054  :                                    **
 8    0.066  :                                    **
 9    0.010  :                                    *
10   -0.042  :                                    **
11   -0.078  :                                    ***
12   -0.010  :                                    *
13   -0.041  :                                    **
14   -0.102  :                                    ***
15    0.120  :                                    ***
             :--1---------------+-----------------0------------------+-----------+1

CHI-SQUARE TEST FOR CROSS-CORRELATIONS :   5.35267   WITH   11   D.F.
```

FIGURE 10-15 THE CROSSCORRELATION BETWEEN THE PRE-WHITENED INPUT SERIES (α_t) AND THE TF MODEL RESIDUALS (a_t)

$$\chi^2_{(m-r-s)} = (99 - n^*) \sum_{k=1}^{m} r_a^2(k),$$

where (r,s) = parameters of the TF model,

$\qquad m$ = maximum lag considered,

$\qquad n^*$ = the maximum of $(s + b + p_n)$ and (p_x), where p_x is the number of AR parameters in the ARIMA model for the input series (x_t).

The computation yields

$$\chi^2_{(15-2-2)} = (99 - 6)[(.046)^2 + (.029)^2 + (-.045)^2$$
$$+ (.045)^2 + (.029)^2 + (-.005)^2 + (-.054)^2$$
$$+ (.066)^2 + (.010)^2 + (-.042)^2 + (-.078)^2$$
$$+ (-.010)^2 + (-.041)^2 + (-.102)^2 + (.120)^2]$$
$$= 5.35.$$

There is no need to look up tables to confirm that these cross-correlations are essentially zero. Therefore, we can conclude that the TF model in equation (10-25) satisfies the assumption of independence between the α_t and a_t series.

10/6   Forecasting Using Transfer Function Models

10/6/1   The Forecasting Version of the Transfer Function Model

In Section 10/2/2, equations (10-5), (10-6), and (10-7) show how to get from the standard TF equation to the forecasting version of the equation. This is merely a matter of algebraic multiplication and rearrangement of terms. However, it is tedious to do by hand. For the advertising-sales example, we have already done the multiplication to get equation (10-26). Therefore to get the forecasting version of the TF model we simply rearrange the terms in equation (10-26), as follows:

$$y_t = -d_1 y_{t-1} - d_2 y_{t-2} - d_3 y_{t-3} - d_4 y_{t-4}$$
$$+ e_0 x_{t-b} + e_1 x_{t-b-1} + e_2 x_{t-b-2} + e_3 x_{t-b-3} + e_4 x_{t-b-4}$$
$$+ f_0 a_t + f_1 a_{t-1} + f_2 a_{t-2} + f_3 a_{t-3}, \tag{10-28}$$

where the d, e, and f coefficients are defined in equation (10-26). This equation can be used to forecast y_{t+1}, y_{t+2}, and so on. For example, the calculation needed to forecast y_{100}, is as follows:[7]

$$
\begin{aligned}
\hat{y}_{100} = \quad &-d_1 y_{99} \qquad &&\hat{y}_{100} = - \quad &&(-2.37)(-40.54) \\
&-d_2 y_{98} \qquad && - \quad &&(2.70)(-27.98) \\
&-d_3 y_{97} \qquad && - \quad &&(-1.53)(5.01) \\
&-d_4 y_{96} \qquad && - \quad &&(.42)(29.09) \\
&+e_0 x_{98} \qquad && + \quad &&(1.30)(.69) \\
&+e_1 x_{97} \qquad && + \quad &&(-.92)(1.08) \\
&+e_2 x_{96} \qquad && + \quad &&(-.70)(-7.29) \\
&+e_3 x_{95} \qquad && + \quad &&(1.26)(-.05) \\
&+e_4 x_{94} \qquad && + \quad &&(-.47)(3.98) \\
&+f_0 a_{100} \qquad && + \quad &&(1)(0) \\
&+f_1 a_{99} \qquad && + \quad &&(-2.07)(-1.17)
\end{aligned}
$$

---

[7]The relevant x_t and y_t data are found in Table 10-6, and the a_t data are in Table 10-11.

$$+ f_2 a_{98} \qquad + \quad (\quad 1.74)(\ -1.05)$$

$$+ f_3 a_{97} \qquad + \quad (\ -.61)(\quad -.43)$$

$$= \ -20.99$$

Similarly, $\hat{y}_{101}$ can be computed as 10.24.

Note that if we want to forecast $\hat{y}_{102}$, equation (10-28) will involve a term $e_0 x_{102-2}$ and there is no x_{100} datum available. Thus the input series x_t will have to be handled separately to provide forecasts for periods 100, 101, and so on.

Finally note that the y_t series is the *first difference* of sales, so that if total sales data are to be forecast, the first differences will have to be converted. Using Table 10-5 the calculations are as follows:

$$\begin{pmatrix} \text{Total Sales} \\ \text{for period 100} \end{pmatrix} = \begin{pmatrix} \text{Total Sales} \\ \text{for period 99} \end{pmatrix} + (\hat{y}_{100}),$$

$$\hat{Y}_{100} = 230.56 + (-20.99)$$

$$= 209.57,$$

$$\text{and } \hat{Y}_{101} = \hat{Y}_{100} + \hat{y}_{101}$$

$$= 209.57 + 10.24 = 219.81.$$

10/7 Other Multivariate Models

Multivariate transfer function models require a considerable amount of computation in going through the many stages of identification, estimation, diagnostic checking, and finally, forecasting. Even for the bivariate case, as illustrated in the previous pages, this is true. Thus, even though it is possible to extend the discussion to handle several independent variables (leading indicators) rather than just one, the question of costs versus benefits must be raised. Forecasters using ARIMA and MARIMA models should not fall into the same trap as econometricians who, during the 1960s, seemed to think that the more complex their forecasting models, the more accurate they would be. In the realm of Box-Jenkins ARIMA models and bivariate transfer function models, the reader should study the literature for good application studies, and weigh the pros and cons of these elegant methodologies. In the near future, there should be a number of good comparative studies emanating from the large international forecasting experiment, discussed briefly in Chapter 15.

The rest of this section will be devoted to a brief examination of two other multivariate methods—intervention analysis and Kalman filtering.

10/7/1   Intervention Analysis

Intervention analysis is an extension of MARIMA concepts. It has been made widely known through an article entitled "Intervention Analysis with Applications to Economic and Environmental Problems," in which Box and Tiao (1975) suggest an approach for recognizing the interventions (effects) of some independent variable on a dependent variable of interest. Their approach is aimed at answering questions such as "How will sales be affected if the price is increased by 20 percent?" or "How will sales be affected if a promotional campaign is started on July 1?" These types of questions are concerned, not only with the time at which the change occurred, but also with the transition period between the old equilibrium level and the new equilibrium level. The effects of the Arab oil embargo, for example, were not felt overnight. It was almost a year before their full impact was felt by many economies throughout the world.

Intervention analysis is aimed at identifying the type of response a dependent variable will exhibit, given some step change in an independent variable(s). Box and Tiao (1975) have shown the impulse response on the dependent variable for different types of changes. The objective is to identify an appropriate model similar to a transfer function model and to estimate its parameters. If the diagnostic check on the residuals of the intervention model shows no pattern, it indicates that the identified model is adequate and that the effects of the intervention (the step or other drastic change) are as postulated; otherwise, a new intervention response model must be specified. Glass, Wilson, and Gottman (1975) have written a book on the subject providing a detailed treatment of this approach and providing samples of its application.

Montgomery and Weatherby (1980) discuss the extension of intervention analysis to situations involving the combined influence of several indicator variables. Equation (10-4) is simply modified to include a summation term to represent these models, as follows:

$$Y_t = \sum_{j=1}^{k} v_j(B)X_{jt} + N_t.$$

Note that in this equation some and maybe all of the input series, $X_{jt}, j = 1, 2, 3, \ldots, k$, can be indicator series—that is, dichotomous variables. In this paper, Montgomery and Weatherby give a worked example on the effect of the Arab oil embargo.

Another interesting application of intervention analysis is to be found in the paper by Wichern and Jones (1977). They analyzed the impact of the American Dental Association's endorsement of Crest toothpaste (on August 1, 1960) on the market share of Crest and Colgate dentifrice during the period 1958–1963. Finally, Atkins (1979) considered the number of traffic accidents on the freeways in British Columbia, and used intervention analysis to tease out the influence of three changes—compulsory auto insurance (in March, 1974), a company strike (in summer of 1975), and a change in insurance companies' policies (in March, 1976)—on the number of accidents.

10/7/2   Kalman Filters

Forecasting models can be classified into two categories: (1) fixed models having fixed parameters and fixed variances, and (2) fixed models with varying parameters and variances. The first category includes all forecasting methods discussed so far with the exception of adaptive-response-rate exponential smoothing.

Fixed models with fixed parameters require stationarity of both the mean and the variance throughout the entire range of observations. That is why so much effort is spent to make the data stationary in their mean (through differencing) and in their variance (through appropriate power—logarithmic, square root, etc.—transformations). Otherwise, the results are not meaningful from a statistical point of view. Classical statistical estimation theory has not been able to deal directly with nonstationarity, and this can cause problems of significant practical consequence. For example, when the data pattern changes as with a step or trend, or when there are transient shifts, classical statistical theory will treat those as random effects or temporary shifts. If the changes are permanent, a new forecasting model will have to be specified to deal with the new equilibrium conditions. However, the model will be good for those new equilibrium conditions only when fixed patterns exist.

Classical statistical methods must be used in conjunction with other control processes (see Section 3/3/2; Page, 1957, 1961; and Barnard, 1959) if permanent or significant changes in the data are to be identified. Methods based on classical statistics cannot sense a shift by themselves and once a shift has taken place, the model will not do as well because it will still be tuned to the specification of the old set of data.

Adaptive-response-rate exponential smoothing, and adaptive filtering, on the other hand, can deal with step changes and transient situations because they update their parameters in a way that takes account of changes in pattern. Furthermore, they can deal with changes in trend better than fixed model/fixed parameter methods. However, even these two methods cannot do as well as the Kalman filters, which can deal with variable models, variable parameters, and variable variances simultaneously.

Classical statistical estimation attempts to minimize the MSE of the fitted model. This criterion is appropriate for the past, but may be inappropriate for the future. If the criterion is to minimize the MSE of the model fitted to historical data, classical estimation can provide a minimum MSE by assuming a fixed model with fixed parameters and fixed variances. However, when the MSE of the future is to be minimized, adaptive-response-rate exponential smoothing, adaptive filtering, or the Kalman filters can do as well for future periods as classical estimation procedures, even when the data pattern does not change. In addition, these methods may do much better when there are changes in the pattern of the data, since such changes will be identified and used in forecasting.

Kalman filters are the most general approach to statistical estimation and prediction. It has been shown by Harrison and Stevens (1975a) that all forecasting methods are special cases of Kalman filters. These filters can deal with changes in the model, the parameters, and the variances. The difficulty with Kalman filters is that many technical questions have not yet been answered satisfactorily. The approach itself has grown out of engineering. Consequently, many statisticians and operations researchers know little about it or find it difficult to understand because it is most often described in *state space notation*. With the exception of the work of Harrison and Stevens (1971, 1975a and 1975b), little research has been reported on the applicability of Kalman or other filters to forecasting (see Schneeweiss, 1971, Chang and Fyffe, 1971, and Mehra, 1973). Furthermore, many practical difficulties still exist as to initial estimates for parameters, variances, and covariances and for the transition matrix. In order to point out these problems and to show the substantial potential of the Kalman filters, a nontechnical introduction to the topic will be presented here. The interested reader is encouraged to examine the references suggested in the end of the chapter for an in-depth study of Kalman filters.

Kalman filtering consists of combining two independent estimates to form a weighted estimate or prediction. One estimate can be a prior prediction or an estimate based on prior knowledge, and the other a prediction based on new information (new data). The purpose of the Kalman filter is to combine these two pieces of information to obtain an improved estimate. It is similar to the Bayesian approach, which combines prior and sampling information to form a posterior distribution (see Raiffa, 1968). The name *Bayesian forecasting* is used by Harrison and Stevens as synonymous with *Kalman filters*.

In order to illustrate the Kalman filter, the simple univariate case will be examined first; then its extension to multivariate data for fixed models will be described. Finally, its application for a model of varying characteristics will be illustrated.

Univariate Data

If F_t is the forecast period t, and X_t is the latest available information, the forecast for period $t + 1$ can be expressed as a weighted sum of F_t and X_t,

$$F_{t+1} = \omega X_t + (1 - \omega)F_t. \tag{10-29}$$

Equation (10-29) is the same as equation (3-19) of single exponential smoothing. If the variance of X_t and F_t, say σ_x^2 and σ_F^2, is known, the overall variance of (10-29) can be calculated as the weighted square sum of σ_x and σ_F. That is,

$$\sigma^2 = (1 - \omega)^2 \sigma_F^2 + \omega^2 \sigma_x^2. \tag{10-30}$$

assuming independence of X_t and F_t.

Expression (10-30) can be differentiated with respect to ω to obtain the value of the parameter ω for which (10-30) is a minimum. This gives

$$\frac{d\sigma^2}{d\omega} = -2(1 - \omega)\sigma_F^2 + 2\omega\sigma_x^2 = 0. \tag{10-31}$$

Solving for ω^* gives

$$\omega^* = \frac{\sigma_F^2}{\sigma_F^2 + \sigma_x^2}. \tag{10-32}$$

If equation (10-32) is substituted into (10-29), the result is

$$F_{t+1} = \frac{\sigma_F^2}{\sigma_F^2 + \sigma_x^2} X_t + \left(1 - \frac{\sigma_F^2}{\sigma_F^2 + \sigma_x^2}\right) F_t$$

$$= \frac{\sigma_F^2}{\sigma_F^2 + \sigma_x^2} X_t + \frac{\sigma_x^2}{\sigma_F^2 + \sigma_x^2} F_t \tag{10-33}$$

$$= \frac{\sigma_F^2 X_t + \sigma_x^2 F_t}{\sigma_F^2 + \sigma_x^2}. \tag{10-34}$$

If the variance of X_t, σ_x^2, is the same as the variance of F_t, σ_F^2, then equation (10-33) will result in a constant α value of

$$\omega = \frac{\sigma_F^2}{\sigma_F^2 + \sigma_x^2} = 1/2.$$

However, if the uncertainty about the future increases, the variance of σ_x^2 will become larger relative to σ_F^2. That will increase the denominator of the right-hand side terms of (10-33) and the numerator of the second term of (10-33). Thus, relatively more weight will be given to F_t than to X_t. The opposite is true if the uncertainty about the future decreases; relatively more weight will be given to X_t and relatively less to F_t.

The ratio of the variances plays a role completely analogous to that of α_1 in adaptive-response-rate exponential smoothing [see (3-24)]. Thus, in the case of a Kalman filter, ω_t (the equivalent of α_t) is given by

$$\omega_t = \frac{\sigma_F^2}{\sigma_F^2 + \sigma_x^2}. \tag{10-35}$$

There is an operational difficulty in reconciling (10-35) and (3-24), however. Expression (3-24) can be calculated from past data, while expression (10-35) requires knowledge of the variance, σ_x^2, which is not readily available. Furthermore, the terms of (3-24) can be routinely supplied, while some provisions must be made to estimate σ_x^2 as an input to (10-35).

Furthermore, an estimate of the overall variance of F_{t+1}, σ_{F+1}^2, can be updated by substituting (10-32) into (10-30) to obtain

$$\sigma_{F+1}^2 = \left(1 - \frac{\sigma_F^2}{\sigma_F^2 + \sigma_x^2}\right)^2 \sigma_F^2 + \left(\frac{\sigma_F^2}{\sigma_F^2 + \sigma_x^2}\right)^2 \sigma_x^2$$

$$= \frac{\sigma_x^4 \sigma_F^2}{(\sigma_F^2 + \sigma_x^2)^2} + \frac{\sigma_F^4 \sigma_x^2}{(\sigma_F^2 + \sigma_x^2)^2}, \tag{10-36}$$

$$\sigma_{F+1}^2 = \frac{\sigma_x^2 \sigma_F^2}{\sigma_F^2 + \sigma_x^2}. \tag{10-37}$$

Expression (10-37) indicates that the variance at period $t + 1$ can be updated by combining the variance of up to period t, σ_F^2, with the variance of period t, σ_x^2. Expression (10-37) can be put into a more convenient form by expressing it as a function of ω^* using (10-32).

From (10-32) we get

$$(1 - \omega^*) = \frac{\sigma_x^2}{\sigma_F^2 + \sigma_x^2}. \tag{10-38}$$

Substituting (10-38) into (10-37) gives

$$\sigma_{F+1}^2 = \sigma_F^2 \frac{\sigma_x^2}{\sigma_F^2 + \sigma_x^2} = \sigma_F^2(1 - \omega^*). \tag{10-39}$$

In terms of the Kalman filters discussed so far, the following can be said:

1. An updated estimate combining new and old information can be made.
2. The weights combining new and old information are a function of the variances.
3. Both the estimates and their variances can be computed recursively (Kalman filtering is an infinite memory filter).
4. There will be some difficulties in obtaining estimates of the variance of X_t.

Multivariate Data

The multivariate Kalman filter is analogous to the univariate form and can be obtained by replacing scalars by matrices. This gives

$$\mathbf{F}_{t+1} = \mathbf{W}\mathbf{X}_t + (\mathbf{I} - \mathbf{W})\mathbf{F}_t. \tag{10-40}$$

Equation (10-40) is similar to (10-29) except that $\mathbf{F}_{t+1}$, $\mathbf{X}_t$, and $\mathbf{F}$ are vectors, $\mathbf{W}$ is the vector of weights and $\mathbf{I}$ is the identity matrix. Going from equation (10-40) to the expressions required for updating the weight vector $\mathbf{W}$ and the variance-covariance matrix (in the multivariate case the covariances between the $\mathbf{X}_t$ estimates must be estimated in addition to the variances) is not much different from the univariate case except that it involves matrix algebra.

The Kalman filter examined so far provides for varying parameters and variances, but still assumes a fixed model. This last constraint can be removed by introducing the transition matrix, $\phi_{t,t+1}$, which indicates how the parameters of the model change from period t to period $t + 1$. The forecasting error of period t is

$$\mathbf{F}_t = \mathbf{X}_t - \mathbf{e}_t.$$

The data for period t, $\mathbf{X}_t$, can be expressed as the actual pattern, $\mathbf{X}_t'$, plus the error, $\mathbf{u}_t$. Thus

$$\mathbf{X}_t = \mathbf{H}_t \mathbf{X}_t' + \mathbf{u}_t, \tag{10-41}$$

where $\mathbf{H}_t$ is the observation matrix at period t.

The best forecast of the pattern for period $t + 1$, assuming some change in the model, is given by

$$\mathbf{X}_{t+1}' = \phi_{t,t+1} \mathbf{X}_t' + \mathbf{Z}_t, \tag{10-42}$$

where $\phi_{t,t+1}$ is the transition matrix showing how the model changes from period t to $t + 1$ and $\mathbf{Z}_t$ is white noise affecting the real process generating the $\mathbf{X}_t$.

Equations (10-41) and (10-42) describe the Kalman filtering system in its most general form. They can be solved recursively using equations (10-43), (10-44), and (10-45).

Given some initial estimates, an estimate $\hat{X}_t'$ of X_t' can be made as

$$\hat{X}_t' = \phi_{t-1,t} \hat{X}_{t-1}' + K_t (X_t - H_t \phi_{t-1,t} \hat{X}_{t-1}'), \tag{10-43}$$

where the gain $\mathbf{K}_t$, is

$$\mathbf{K}_t = \mathbf{P}_{t-1,t} \mathbf{H}_t^{\mathrm{T}} (\mathbf{H}_t \mathbf{P}_{t/t-1} \mathbf{H}_t^{\mathrm{T}} + \mathbf{R}_t)^{-1} \tag{10-44}$$

(the superscript T denotes the transpose of H, and -1 denotes the inverse of the expression in the parentheses), where $\mathbf{P}_{t-1,t} = \phi_{t-1,t} \mathbf{P}_{t-1} \phi_{t-1,t}^T + \mathbf{Q}_{t-1}$, and Q_{t-1} is the covariance of Z_t in (10-42).

In addition to estimating the variance-covariance matrix, the transition matrix, $\phi_{t-1,t}$, must also be estimated. That may be difficult, but Harrison and Stevens (1971, 1975a, and 1975b) claim that the system is quite robust to the transition matrix values, and that they can therefore be set to fixed values, since they have a minimal effect on the results. However, if that is true, then the forecasting system will not be responsive to changes or it will overreact to them, depending upon the way the transition matrix is set up.

10/8   Prognosis

This chapter deals with difficult subject matter. In order to appreciate transfer function modeling (or MARIMA), a considerable amount of careful study is required, but it is our opinion that such study is warranted. As computer programs become more widely available to do the many computations swiftly, it will not be the calculations that will inhibit the use of TF methodology. It will be the level of understanding of the various steps in the process of identifying, estimating, and using a TF model—as described in this chapter.

The concept of a dynamic relationship connecting an input series (e.g., a leading indicator) to an output series, has been of interest for a long time. However, in the usual procedures for dealing with leading indicators, regression methodology has played a strong role, and, as has been pointed out in Section 10/2/1, it will not always be the preferred methodology. The Box-Jenkins transfer-function methodology can be a more powerful tool for identifying such relationships.

This chapter has dealt only with the bivariate case. Multivariate extensions are being studied in academic settings and it is to be expected that more significant use will be made of the full richness of the TF method in the near future. The Kalman filters, for all their flexibility, are sometimes criticized for being too flexible, in that so many parameters need to be estimated. At a theoretical level the Kalman filters provide a unifying feature, however, in that many other models are special cases of Kalman filters.

REFERENCES AND SELECTED BIBLIOGRAPHY

Anderson, B. D. O. 1971. "A Qualitative Introduction to Wiener and Kalman-Bucy Filters," in *Proceedings of The Institute of Radio and Electricity Engineering, Australia,* March, pp. 93–103.

Atkins, Stella M. 1979. "Case Study on the Use of Intervention Analysis Applied to Traffic Accidents," in *Journal Operations Research Society,* **30,** No. 7, pp. 651–59.

Barnard, G. A. 1959. "Control Charts and Stochastic Processes," *Journal of the Royal Statistical Society,* Series B, **21,** pp. 239–71.

Barth, J., M. Phaup, and D. A. Pierce. 1975. "Regional Impact of Open-Market Operations on Member Bank Reserves," *Journal of Economics and Business,* Fall, pp. 36–40.

Bartlett, P. S. 1955. *Stochastic Processes.* Cambridge, England: Cambridge University Press.

Box, G. E. P., and G. M. Jenkins. 1976. *Time Series Analysis Forecasting and Control,* rev. ed. San Francisco: Holden-Day (earlier edition, 1970).

Box, G. E. P., and G. C. Tiao. 1975. "Intervention Analysis with Applications to Economic and Environmental Problems," *Journal of the American Statistical Association,* **70,** No. 349, pp. 70–79.

Caines, P. E., and C. W. Keng. 1981. "Causality Analysis and Multivariate Autoregressive Modelling with an Application to Supermarket Sales Analysis," *Journal of Economic Dynamics and Control,* **3,** pp. 267–98.

Chang, S. H., and D. E. Fyffe. 1971. "Estimation of Forecast Errors for Seasonal-Style-Goods Sales," *Management Science,* **18,** No. 2, pp. B89–B96.

Cleary, J. P. 1975. "A Comparison of the Forecasting Performance of Box-Jenkins Transfer Function Models," in *Proceedings of the American Statistical Association,* August 1975, pp. 291–94.

Duncan, D. B., and S. D. Horn. 1972. "Linear Dynamic Recursive Estimation from the Viewpoint of Regression Analysis," *Journal of the American Statistical Association,* December, **67,** No. 340, pp. 815–21.

Gelb, A. 1974. *Applied Optimal Estimation.* Cambridge, Mass.: MIT Press.

Glass, G. V., V. L. Wilson, and J. M. Gottman. 1975. *Design and Analysis of Time-Series Experiments.* Colorado. Colorado University Press.

Granger, C. W. J., and A. P. Anderson. 1978. *An Introduction to Bilinear Time Series Models.* Gottingen: Vanderbroeck and Ruprecht.

Harrison, P. J., and C. F. Stevens. 1971. "A Bayesian Approach to Short-Term Forecasting," *Operational Research Quarterly,* **22,** No. 4, pp. 341–62.

—— 1975a. "Bayesian Forecasting." University of Warwick, Working Paper No. 13.

—— 1975b. "Bayesian Forecasting in Action: Case Studies." University of Warwick, Working Paper No. 14.

Helmer, R. M., and Johny K. Johansson. 1977. "An Exposition of the Box-Jenkins Transfer Function Analysis with an Application to the Advertising-Sales Relationship," *Journal of Marketing Research,* **14,** May, pp. 227–39.

Jenkins, G. M. 1979. *Practical Experience with Modelling and Forecasting Time Series.* Jersey, Channel Islands: GJ&P (overseas) Ltd.

Kalman, R. E. 1960. "A New Approach to Linear Filtering and Prediction Problems," *Journal of Basic Engineering,* **D82,** March, pp. 35–44.

Kalman, R. E., and R. S. Bucy. 1961. "New Results in Linear Filtering and Prediction Theory," *Journal of Basic Engineering,* **D83,** March, pp. 95–107.

Makridakis, S., and S. Wheelwright. 1979. *Forecasting, Time Studies in Management Science,* Vol. 12. Amsterdam: North-Holland.

Manegold, J. G. 1981. "Time Series Properties of Earnings: A Comparison of Extrapolative and Component Models," *Journal of Accounting Research,* **19,** No. 2, Autumn, pp. 360–73.

Marquardt, D. W. 1963. "An Algorithm for Least-Squares Estimation of Nonlinear Parameters," *Journal of the Society for Industrial and Applied Mathematics,* **2,** pp. 431–41.

Mehra, R. K. 1973. "A Mechanical Forecasting System for Financial Variables Using Kalman Filtering and Maximum Likelihood Estimation." Progress Report No. 1 (Feb.). New York: Baker Weeks.

Montgomery, D. C., and G. Weatherby. 1980. "Modeling and Forecasting Time Series Using Transfer Function and Intervention Methods," *AIIE Transactions,* December, pp. 289–307.

Moriarty, M., and G. Salamon. 1980. "Estimation and Forecast Performance of a Multivariate Time Series Model of Sales," *Journal of Marketing Research,* **17,** November, pp. 558–64.

Morrison, G. W., and D. H. Pike. 1977. "Kalman Filtering Applied to Statistical Forecasting," *Management Science,* **23,** No. 7, March, pp. 768–74.

Newbold, Paul. 1973. "Bayesian Estimation of Box-Jenkins Transfer Function-noise Models," *Journal of the Royal Statistical Society,* **35,** No. 2, pp. 323–36.

Pack, D. J. 1974. "Computer Programs for the Analysis of Univariate Time Series Models and Single Input Transfer Function Models Using the Methods of Box and Jenkins." Ohio State University, December.

—— 1975. "Revealing Time Series Interrelationships," *Decision Sciences,* **8,** pp. 377–402.

Page, E. S. 1957. "On Problems in Which a Change in Parameters Occurs at an Unknown Point," *Biometrica,* **4,** 1957, pp. 249–60.

—— 1961. "Cumulative Sum Charts," *Technometrics,* **3,** pp. 1–10.

Priestly, M. B. 1971. "Fitting Relationships Between Time Series," in *International Statistical Institute Proceedings.* Washington, D.C.

Quenouille, M. H. 1957. *The Analysis of Multiple Time Series*. New York: Hafner Publishing Co.

Raiffa, H. 1968. *Decision Analysis*. Reading, Mass.: Addison-Wesley.

Schneeweiss, C. A. 1971. "Smoothing Production by Inventory—An Application of the Wiener Filtering Theory," *Management Science,* **17,** No. 7, pp. 472–99.

Subba-Rao, U. V., R. Schroth, and A. Fask. 1975. "Application of Box-Jenkins Transfer Function Methodology to Marketing Problems." Presented at the 1975 Joint Institute of Management Sciences/Operations Research Society of America Conference.

Trigg, D. W., and D. H. Leach. 1967. "Exponential Smoothing with an Adaptive Response Rate," *Operational Research Quarterly,* **18,** pp. 53–59.

Umstead, David A. 1977. "Forecasting Stock Market Prices," *The Journal of Finance,* **32,** No. 2, May, pp. 427–41.

Whittle, P. 1953. "The Analysis of Multiple Stationary Time Series," *Journal of the Royal Statistical Society,* B, **15,** pp. 125–39.

Wichern, Dean W., and R. H. Jones. 1977. "Assessing the Impact of Market Disturbances Using Intervention Analysis," *Management Science,* **24,** No. 3, pp. 329–37.

Zellner, A., and F. Palm. 1974. "Time Series Analysis and Simultaneous Equation Econometric Models," *Journal of Econometrics,* **2,** pp. 17–54.

EXERCISES

1. Three sets of transfer function weights are described as follows:

	v_1	v_2	v_3	v_4	v_5	v_6	v_7
Set 1	.2	.4	.3	.1	0	0	0
Set 2	0	.2	.4	.3	.1	0	0
Set 3	0	0	.2	.5	.4	.2	.1

An input time series (X_t) is shown in Table 10-12.

a. Using equation (10-4), generate three output time series (Y_t) corresponding to the three sets of impulse (TF) weights above. How many Y_t values can you calculate for each set?

b. Consider only the last 20 pairs of observations—that is, (X_t, Y_t) for $t = 11, 12, 13, \ldots, 30$—make a plot of Y_t versus X_t for each of the three sets of data.

c. Perform the following regression runs on each set of data:
   i. Y_t regressed on X_t

TABLE 10-12 AN INPUT SERIES (X_t) FOR EXERCISES 1 AND 2

t	X_t	t	X_t
1	50	16	30
2	90	17	60
3	50	18	70
4	30	19	40
5	80	20	70
6	80	21	10
7	30	22	30
8	70	23	30
9	60	24	40
10	10	25	30
11	40	26	100
12	20	27	60
13	40	28	90
14	20	29	60
15	10	30	100

     ii. Y_t regressed on X_t, X_{t-1}

    iii. Y_t regressed on X_{t-1}, X_{t-2}, X_{t-3}

Interpret your findings, given that you know how the three sets of Y_t values were actually generated.

2.   Three sets of $(r,s,b)(p_n,q_n)$ parameters are shown below:

	r	s	b	p_n	q_n
Set 1	1	1	1	0	0
Set 2	2	2	2	1	0
Set 3	1	2	3	0	1

An input time series (X_t) is shown in Table 10-12.

a. Using equation (10-5), generate three output series (Y_t) corresponding to the three transfer function identifications $(r,s,b)(p_n,q_n)$ given above. For the error term (a_t) in equation (10-5) use random normal deviates (see Table 10-13) and, where appropriate, let the autoregressive parameter for the noise series be $\phi_1 = .8$ and the moving average parameter for the noise series be $\theta_1 = -.7$.

b. Plot Y_t versus X_t for each of the three sets, using (X_t, Y_t) for $t = 11, 12, 13, \ldots, 30$.

TABLE 10-13 A TABLE OF RANDOM NORMAL DEVIATES

1.33	−0.32	−1.24	1.25	−0.66	0.38	1.68	0.99
0.84	2.76	−0.62	−1.08	−1.27	−0.74	−0.88	0.14
0.43	−0.50	−1.80	0.60	1.57	−1.23	−1.50	0.35
0.10	1.20	−1.63	−0.75	0.23	0.18	−0.59	−0.94
−0.58	0.85	0.62	−0.50	−1.73	0.17	0.32	−0.71
−0.10	−0.84	−0.32	−1.34	−0.10	−0.18	−1.66	−1.27
0.57	−1.06	−0.48	0.78	0.84	−1.13	−0.83	−0.03
−0.04	−0.85	−1.62	−0.12	0.28	−0.70	−1.54	−0.51
−1.54	0.65	−0.66	0.55	−2.34	1.19	0.62	0.29
0.17	0.01	−1.21	−1.57	−0.54	−0.41	−0.33	1.82
−2.60	0.21	−0.52	−0.18	−1.66	−2.45	0.46	−1.20
−0.83	0.70	−1.93	−1.36	−0.34	0.16	−0.64	1.79
0.63	−2.15	0.24	−1.31	−0.25	−1.41	−0.41	1.49
−0.30	0.09	2.01	1.69	−0.55	−0.77	−0.01	0.26
−0.49	−0.33	−1.01	−0.94	−1.31	−0.10	0.27	0.20
−0.40	0.44	−0.44	−0.30	1.76	1.07	−0.83	0.77
−0.87	0.48	−0.64	−0.74	0.22	0.00	−0.58	1.09
1.54	0.44	0.80	−0.79	−1.41	0.61	0.18	−0.49
0.00	−0.30	0.16	0.12	−0.47	−0.91	−1.01	−1.05
−1.90	−1.20	0.43	−0.48	−0.28	0.19	1.36	1.06
0.19	1.07	0.06	0.16	1.17	−1.04	1.06	1.19
0.49	−1.03	−1.62	−0.73	−0.18	0.40	0.67	−0.05
−1.81	0.56	0.13	1.08	−1.00	2.57	1.79	−0.63
1.19	0.64	0.86	1.14	0.14	−2.36	0.46	−0.66
0.54	−0.47	−0.42	0.08	0.90	0.97	0.35	0.35
−0.70	−0.60	1.52	−0.45	−1.20	−1.87	−0.86	−0.06
−0.12	0.60	−0.05	−1.37	0.11	−0.09	0.39	0.75
0.61	0.31	−0.95	−0.25	−1.63	−0.90	0.22	0.99
0.26	0.04	1.64	−0.96	−0.05	0.04	−0.01	0.17
−0.84	0.69	0.30	0.07	0.87	−0.81	0.88	−1.67
−0.16	0.80	−0.30	1.24	0.78	1.69	−1.39	1.47
0.55	−0.54	−1.35	0.54	0.61	0.78	0.37	−0.80
−1.10	−0.37	0.39	−0.21	−0.76	0.63	0.86	0.41
1.27	−0.26	−1.14	−1.08	−1.10	−1.01	−2.61	0.82
−0.54	−0.80	0.61	0.61	−1.74	0.88	−0.70	0.15
0.79	−0.10	−0.91	−0.77	0.94	−0.30	0.83	1.93
−0.53	0.58	0.41	−0.89	0.84	0.95	2.38	1.58
−0.12	0.48	0.99	0.28	−0.42	−0.91	1.66	−0.94

TABLE 10-13 A TABLE OF RANDOM NORMAL DEVIATES (*Continued*)

−0.23	−1.14	−1.67	0.07	2.15	0.39	−0.29	1.17
0.11	0.80	−0.07	0.48	−0.62	−1.63	0.14	−0.60
−0.07	−1.39	0.35	−0.55	2.43	−1.29	−0.52	0.91
0.25	−1.71	−0.63	0.37	0.94	0.68	0.16	1.51
−0.36	1.94	−0.56	0.10	−1.50	0.86	1.17	1.88
−0.23	0.52	−0.72	−1.73	0.60	−0.23	0.22	−0.98
0.59	0.00	−0.62	1.53	−0.67	0.53	0.92	−2.51
−1.30	0.99	−0.02	−2.37	−0.75	0.81	−0.53	−1.19
−1.06	0.85	1.05	0.92	−0.12	0.14	−0.68	−0.77
−1.39	−1.69	−1.96	0.94	−0.06	−1.67	1.68	0.27
1.58	0.36	0.44	−1.67	−0.27	0.90	2.15	0.04
−0.80	1.33	1.22	0.64	0.24	0.49	1.16	−0.48

    c. Perform the following regression analyses for each set of data:
        i. regress Y_t on X_t,
        iii. regress Y_t on X_t, X_{t-1}, X_{t-2},
        iii. regress Y_t on $X_{t-1}, X_{t-2}, X_{t-3}, X_{t-4}$.
    Interpret your findings, given that you know how the three sets of Y_t values were generated.

3.   The input data series (X_t) in Table 10-14 was generated by the ARIMA (1,1,1) model:

$$(1 + .7B)(1 - B)X_t = (1 - .6B)a_t.$$

    a. Prewhiten this X_t series using equation (10-9) to get an α_t series.
    b. What parameter values should be used for ϕ_1 and θ_1 in the prewhitening operation performed in 3a?
    c. Plot the α_t series and find the autocorrelations (up to lag 10) for these prewhitened values. Compute the Box-Pierce chi-square statistic and decide whether the 10 autocorrelations, as a set, are significantly different from a null set.

4.   The input data series (X_t) in Table 10-15 was generated by an unknown process.
    a. Prewhiten this X_t series.
    b. Examine the prewhitened series by plotting it, computing a set of autocorrelations (up to lag 10), and applying the Box-Pierce chi-square test to see whether the X_t series had been effectively prewhitened.

5.   The worked example in this chapter deals with advertising-sales data and the model chosen was $(r,s,b) = (2,2,2)$ and $(p_n,q_n) = (2,1)$. Suppose the identification stage had arrived at another transfer function model: $(r,s,b) = (1,1,2)$ and $(p_n,q_n) = (1,1)$.
    a. Write down the appropriate equations corresponding to equations (10-24) for this new model.

TABLE 10-14   A TIME SERIES GENERATED BY AN ARIMA (1,1,1) MODEL

1	39.5	21	53.1
2	53.5	22	47.4
3	38.8	23	54.9
4	55.6	24	48.8
5	37.1	25	55.8
6	51.3	26	49.9
7	43.4	27	49.3
8	44.1	28	50.0
9	52.0	29	52.5
10	44.4	30	47.2
11	48.6	31	50.6
12	47.5	32	48.5
13	49.6	33	42.6
14	47.9	34	57.0
15	41.8	35	36.1
16	53.2	36	57.4
17	42.7	37	44.7
18	57.9	38	51.8
19	48.5	39	45.6
20	53.0	40	48.0

TABLE 10-15   A TIME SERIES GENERATED BY AN UNKNOWN ARIMA (p,d,q) MODEL

1	102.2	21	40.3
2	100.5	22	26.2
3	87.9	23	17.9
4	71.6	24	20.0
5	56.6	25	29.6
6	49.0	26	39.5
7	46.2	27	53.4
8	50.9	28	63.4
9	56.9	29	59.9
10	51.9	30	55.7
11	40.4	31	51.1
12	30.8	32	57.2
13	30.0	33	68.4
14	38.8	34	75.0
15	55.3	35	78.2
16	68.5	36	72.2
17	73.6	37	63.9
18	71.3	38	54.0
19	61.4	39	46.4
20	51.2	40	38.8

b. Using the directly estimated impulse weights as in Figure 10-12, compute preliminary estimates of the unknown transfer function parameters, δ_1, ω_0, ω_1, ϕ_1, and θ_1.

c. If you have access to a TF computer program, then use the Marquardt algorithm to get better estimates of these parameters.

d. Compute the set of transfer function residuals (a_t).

e. Compute the autocorrelations for this residual series (up to lag 10) and do a Box-Pierce test to see if they are essentially a null set.

f. Compute the cross-correlations between these residuals (a_t) and the pre-whitened input series (the α_t series in Table 10-7).

g. What is your conclusion regarding the (2,2,2)(2,1) model versus the (1,1,2)(1,1) model?

PART FIVE
INFORMATION NEEDS AND MORE QUALITATIVE METHODS

The chapters in Part Five make a transition from the focus on quantitative methods in Parts One through Four, and deal with more qualitative, or judgmental, approaches. The main distinction is that, rather than basing forecasts exclusively on historical data and the information they contain, these methodologies seek to make effective use of judgmental processes and management experience and knowledge in arriving at forecasts.

Before moving into these judgmentally based forecasting methods, Chapter 11 deals with a number of data issues related to forecasting, where considerable management judgment is also required. Such topics as deciding what to forecast, the gathering and preparation of historical data needed to apply specific forecasting methods, and the ongoing management of forecasting data are addressed in this chapter.

Chapter 12 examines the problems associated with predicting business cycles and, more generally, turning points in a data series. One of the most useful techniques developed in this area and described in Chapter 12 is the use of leading indicators. Other methods that are more subjective in nature and that seek to combine managerial judgment with the results of quantitative forecasts, such as paired indices and "pressures," are also described.

Many of the more subjective methods of forecasting are described in Chapter 13. These are frequently referred to as qualitative or technological methods and range from those methods used when an organization first approaches the forecasting function, such as sales force composites and opinion surveys, to approaches like the Delphi method, which seek to use the creative potential of experts to more thoroughly identify long-run outcomes and to aid in the long-range planning process. Additionally, normative methodologies like Relevance Trees, which seek to identify desired future outcomes and alternative plans for achieving them, are discussed.

11/DATA REQUIREMENTS FOR FORECASTING

In this chapter, several issues and concerns are examined that must be addressed in specifying, procuring, preparing, and handling data for forecasting purposes. First, the question of what to forecast is discussed. This section considers the definition and specification of the variable(s) to be forecast and important factors in those determinations. (Chapter 17 reviews some of these considerations in the context of specific forecasting situations.) Second, the question of how to procure the data (and from where) is discussed. A number of general data sources are described and the need to provide adequate data for selected forecasting methodologies is reviewed.

The third section of this chapter addresses questions of data preparation ranging from issues of data collection to possible preprocessing to adjust for missing values or trading day differences across time periods. The fourth section then considers issues of data management, including the use of database systems, data presentation concerns, and ongoing improvement in the data procurement, preparation, and handling side of forecasting.

Throughout this chapter, the authors' views are that the quality of data is important in determining the accuracy, credibility, and value of forecasts. Improvement in data quality is most often an incremental and iterative process—definitions of variables are sharpened, data collection is upgraded, and data are presented more effectively. Forecasters and decision makers must start with what they have (or can obtain) and improve from there. Thus while this chapter follows the flow of data concerns and issues associated with new forecasting applications, we have found that individual topics apply to ongoing systems as well. A major challenge to forecasters is to identify the opportunities for such applications and to pursue them on an ongoing basis to achieve continued improvement in forecasting.

11/1 Definition and Specification of Variables in Forecasting

Most work on forecasting tends to assume that the variable to be forecast is known and well defined. While that may be the case for ongoing situations in which a forecasting method has been applied in the past, in new situations it is not necessarily true. Thus a first step in forecasting is to decide just what to forecast and how best to define that variable.

The decision as to the appropriate variable to be forecast depends largely on the needs of the manager or planner. The contribution that the forecast will make to the manager or planner will determine the time span that should be covered by each value of the variable, the level of detail required, the frequency with which it is required, the most appropriate unit of measurement, the required level of accuracy, the appropriate segmentation of the variable, and the value of the forecast. Because of the importance of each of these aspects to the definition of appropriate variables for forecasting, each will be discussed briefly.

The Time Period Covered by Each Data Value

Most of the factors involved in a business situation can be viewed as taking place in a continuous manner. For example, for a large company, sales can be considered to take place continuously rather than at some instant of time each day or each month. However, for accounting purposes it is necessary to define some period of time and to summarize the value of each variable for that time period.

In some instances, the variable to be forecast relates not to a time period, but rather to the magnitude of a single observed value. For example, in the production control area one may want to forecast the number of rejects in batches of product coming off a certain machine. In such a case, the batch serves the same function as the time period in defining the span to which the variable refers.

Level of Detail Required

During the definition phase of forecasting, determining just what level of detail will be required can save substantial costs later on if management decides that its initial forecasts are too aggregated and that data will have to be re-collected at a more detailed level. It is generally best to *collect* data at the most detailed level possible, within the budget appropriate, then aggregate them as a part of the data preparation phase for forecasting, rather than aggregating them in the collection phase.

The Frequency of Data Use

The frequency with which new data are collected generally is related closely to the time period covered by each value of the variable and the frequency with which they are used. For example, a company may wish to forecast monthly sales for the next year, but it may do so only once each year. However, if the data are taken from records prepared at the close of each month, it may be best to collect them monthly rather than collecting them only once per year.

The Unit of Measurement

Historically, accounting systems have been oriented toward reporting in terms of value, such as dollars. Data collection in many accounting systems converts whatever units may naturally exist to some common monetary unit before actually storing the data. This conversion represents a loss of information and can impede the application of effective forecasting. An important step in the design and definition of forecasting situations is determining the appropriate measurement units to be used. As a rule of thumb, those units that would naturally be associated with the variable should be used for purposes of procuring and storing the raw data. Subsequent conversion to more common denominators such as monetary units can then be made as desired.

Level of Accuracy Required

Different applications of forecasting require different levels of accuracy. Two factors that determine the most suitable level of accuracy are the importance of the management situation and the role of the forecast in affecting that situation. In some cases, the forecast prepared for a very important management situation may be largely background to that situation, and thus the required level of accuracy would not be great, even though the situation is of major importance. On the other hand, a management situation of more limited importance might use as the basis for decision making the forecast for a single variable, making a high degree of accuracy in that forecast very desirable. Since increased accuracy is almost always accompanied by increased expenses, each new forecasting situation requires that appropriate trade-offs be made in selecting the most desirable level of accuracy.

Disaggregation of the Variable to be Forecast

In many instances it is possible to segment or decompose the item to be forecast and/or to use surrogate variables for that item that will greatly improve the accuracy and performance of the forecast. Frequently, spending some time identifying alternative aggregation plans can give much better results than spending that same amount of time simply collecting better data on the wrong variable or at the wrong level of detail.

One basis for disaggregating the variable to be forecast is to separate those portions that contain major uncertainties from those that are more stable and easier to forecast. For example, if a company is preparing a sales forecast, it may be best to segment the forecast into two parts, one representing those items that are stable and rather straightforward to forecast, and the other representing new products and items that are much more difficult to forecast.

Another basis for decomposing or disaggregating the item to be forecast is when underlying patterns vary. For example, when new products are being introduced, there may be exponential growth or perhaps an S-curve pattern, while the remainder of the company's products may follow a linear growth trend.

Another disaggregation scheme often used is forecasting cumulatively, for example, for a 1-year time horizon, then breaking that forecast down by percentages into monthly estimates. This scheme is particularly useful in production planning systems where the aggregate planning task looks at a 1-year time horizon but is updated monthly or quarterly.

Some additional examples of ways companies have disaggregated or decomposed their forecasting problem may help to illustrate the possibilities available. In one instance, a winery wanted to forecast its corporate sales. Its market share had been changing in recent years, and it did not have clean data on its own sales. This company chose to forecast industry sales (there was an industry association that had excellent industry-wide data), and to apply its own estimates of its market share to those industry forecasts. This provided company sales forecasts more quickly, at lower cost, and with better accuracy than management felt would have been possible using only their own in-house data.

Still another firm involved in light manufacturing chose to prepare its sales forecasts by making separate estimates for each geographical region. One reason for doing so was that the seasonal pattern was slightly different from region to region. Another more important reason was that the company was growing rapidly and felt that it would be much easier to incorporate the judgmental assessments of its sales force if it had that sales force react to quantitative sales estimates made for each geographical region rather than for the company as a whole.

Determining the Value of the Forecast

A final step in the definition and specification of the variables to be forecast is the potential value of that forecast. Clearly, this value is related to the required level of accuracy and the importance of the management situation. It also depends on the opportunity for improvement in that situation. At this initial phase of data definition, some rough estimate of the potential value of the forecast is needed so that the costs of alternative data collection procedures can be kept within the upper bound set by the value of the data.

11/2   Data Procurement

Two critical items in data procurement are understanding available data sources, their characteristics and use, and understanding the data requirements of various forecasting methods. This section will examine both questions in some detail.

11/2/1   Data Sources[1]

Primary data sources include all forms of original collection of data. Such data are more expensive to obtain than data taken from secondary

---

[1] Portions of this section were adapted from T.A. Davidson and J.L. Ayers, "Selecting and Using External Data Sources," Chapter 28 in S. Makridakis and S. Wheelwright (eds.) *Handbook of Forecasting*. New York: John Wiley and Sons, 1982.

sources, but can be designed to fit a particular forecasting requirement. Some alternative ways to collect primary data include sampling procedures, continuous surveys, or a complete census covering the items of interest. For example, the initial stages of the Delphi approach can be thought of as the collection of primary source data. Quantitative methods of forecasting can also use primary data as in the case of a survey aimed at discovering customer inventory levels.

Secondary data sources such as existing accounting records are often the easiest source of data to deal with and usually the cheapest. Their major drawback is that they are geared toward legal and financial reporting requirements and may not be directly suited for the forecasting situation.

Data collection is generally much more difficult in the initial stages of forecasting than it is later on. Initial decisions on data are of great importance because once made, organizations exhibit substantial inertia and are reluctant to change such collection procedures. Spending more time initially will make it much easier and more economical later on.

In recent years, there has been a tremendous increase in the number of published data sources available to forecasters. This increase is due in part to the realization of government and business managers that more and better information increases the effectiveness of planning and decision making. It is also due in part to the introduction of computers that substantially reduce the costs of processing and storing such data. Government sources, nonprofit institutions, and international organizations issue a host of statistical data that can be used as relevant information for forecasting. Some of the most important economic data currently available are summarized in Table 11-1. This table summarizes the type and frequency of income and expenditure measures that are reported in the United States, France, the United Kingdom and Germany. They include not only federal government sources, but also other sources such as Organization for Economic Cooperation and Development (OECD), International Monetary Fund (IMF), and the United Nations. The table includes the names and addresses of the issuing agencies from which these statistics can be obtained.

Because of the importance such national economic variables can have in an organization's forecasting function, it may be useful to describe what is represented by some of these major accounts. The national income and product accounts generally include the gross national product (GNP) and its expenditure components—personal consumption expenditures, gross private domestic investment, net exports of goods and services, inventories, and government purchases of goods and services. Such GNP figures are usually presented both in terms of constant dollar value and current dollar value. The national income and product accounts are the most comprehensive of all of the general economic data available and governments expend great effort in compiling them. In many causal models, they can be used as independent variables to indicate the level and influence of cyclical factors or to indicate the general environment and its impact on the item to be forecast.

TABLE 11-1 AVAILABLE DATA ON NATIONAL ECONOMIC INDICATORS

Type of Data	France Yr.	France Mo.	United Kingdom Yr.	United Kingdom Mo.	Germany Yr.	United States Yr.	United States Qtr.	United States Mo.	OECD[a] 6 Mo.	OECD[a] Irreg-ular	IMF[b] Yr.	IMF[b] Mo.	United Nations Yr.	United Nations Mo.
GNP	X	X	X	X	X	X	X	X	X			X	X	X
Personal income and outlays	X	X	X	X	X	X	X	X	X				X	X
Government receipts and expenses	X	X	X	X	X	X	X	X	X		X	X	X	X
Foreign transactions	X	X	X	X	X	X	X	X	X		X	X	X	X
Savings and investment	X	X	X	X	X	X	X	X						
Income and employment	X	X	X	X	X	X	X	X	X				X	X
Miscellaneous tables	X	X	X	X	X	X	X	X	X				X	X
Price deflators	X	X	X	X	X	X	X							
Index of industrial products	X	X	X	X	X			X		X			X	X
Index of general economic activity	X	X	X	X	X			X			X	X		

Data can be obtained from:
France—Institut National de la Statistique et des Etudes Economiques (INSEE), 29, Quai Branly, 75—Paris 7e.
United Kingdom—Central Statistical Office, Great George St., London SWIP 3Ad; Her Majesty's Stationery Office, P.P. Box 569, London SE7 9NH.
United States—Survey of Current Business, Supt. of Documents, U.S. Govt. Printing Office, Washington D.C. 20402.
OECD—OECD Publications, 2, Rue André Pascal, 75—Paris 16e; OECD Publications Center, Suite 1207, 1750 Pennsylvania Ave. NW, Washington D.C. 20006.
IMF—The Secretary, I.M.F., 19th & H St. NW, Washington D.C. 20431.
United Nations—Publishing Service, United Nations, New York, NY 10017.

[a]Organization for Economic Cooperation and Development.

[b]International Monetary Fund.

Most national data sources also provide price deflators for their GNP figures on both an annual and a quarterly (seasonally adjusted) basis. These can be used to remove the effects of inflation on the data and may also be used as deflator indices with other data series. For example, a company may choose to deflate its own corporate sales using such an index.

In addition to the national income and product accounts, many other forms of economic data are published at varying intervals by government institutions and private groups. Some of the most important of these series cover financial and industrial data. Many such data series are available from the Federal Reserve Board in the United States and the national banks in France, the United Kingdom, and Germany. While the majority of these data are gathered and reported on a national basis, some series are also available at regional levels and can be used in regional forecasting.

One source of data that is particularly useful to organizations doing long-range planning in the United States is the National Bureau of Economic Research (NBER—261 Madison Ave., N.Y., N.Y. 10016). This bureau (and corresponding institutions in other countries) provides data on several different business cycle indicators. These include leading, lagging, and coincidental series that can be used as the basis for predicting turning points or changes in the business cycle.

A third source of government data that has been increasing in importance for forecasting during recent years is the census. In the United States, each census provides detailed information by geographical area on many demographic characteristics. For those companies concerned with forecasting series that depend on such demographic characteristics, the census data can be extremely valuable.

For those organizations involved in international trade or import/export activities, the foreign transaction accounts can be very useful. These present data on both a quarterly and annual basis for the various account groups that make up these transactions.

Finally, the savings and investment accounts can be particularly useful in certain industries. These accounts show the sources and uses of savings in both current and constant dollars and indicate private purchases of producers durable equipment, by type. These accounts also supply a complete breakdown of annual changes in business inventories and in personal savings. They can be used in estimating interest rates, assessing fiscal policy changes, and estimating general levels of economic activity.

A number of private organizations produce macroeconomic forecasts of demographic and economic measures at little or no cost to the public. These can often supplement government data sources and serve as input to individual forecasting systems. Examples of such services are the following:

The Conference Board, *Guide to Consumer Markets,* New York. This provides statistics and graphs on consumer behavior in the marketplace. Projections of population, employment, income, expenditures, production and distribution, and prices are included.

National Planning Association, *National and Regional Economic Projection Series,* Washington, DC. This long-range forecasting service analyzes and projects population, employment, personal income, and personal consumption expenditures for the United States, states, and SMSA's.

Sales and Marketing Management, *Survey of Buying Power.* Contains short-range projections and growth rates for population, households, effective buying income, and retail sales for states, counties, and SMSA's.

Business International's *Forecasting Studies.* Cover trends and key indicators; contain some non-U.S. forecasts.

Commodity Research Bureau publishes demand, supply, and price level forecasts of all major commodities.

Business Week features in their first issue each year a forecast entitled "Industrial Outlook," projecting major industry trends in the coming year.

Trade journals produce short-term forecasts for their industry focus, such as *Electronics'* "World Market Forecasts," *Oil and Gas Journal's* "Forecast/Review," and *Iron Age's* (Chilton's) "Annual Metalworking Forecast."

For a complete list of published forecasts, see *Business Forecasting in the 1980s,* a selected annotated bibliography compiled by Lorna Daniells of Baker Library at Harvard Business School, Boston, MA. This book provides a list of books and articles providing general forecasts as well as the sources of forecasts on specific subjects. In addition, most libraries now have fee-based computerized data retrieval services that can do literature surveys and data searches for published forecast sources.

Statistics that can serve as source data in many forecasting applications are also published by commercial organizations. Fairchild Publications is one example of a firm that produces a variety of books containing data on such industries as clothing, appliances, and textiles. Financial data such as stock prices, trading volumes, dividends, company earnings ratios, bond yields, and information relating to credit can be obtained from:

Dun and Bradstreet, Inc., *Dun's Census of American Business.*

Moody's Investors Services.

Standard and Poor's Corporation Statistical Service.

The Fortune Directory by Time, Inc.

Much of these data can be accessed from computerized data bases such as Standard and Poor's *Compustat, Value Line,* and Dow-Jones' *News Retrieval Service.* A complete list of data base suppliers for all kinds of data, historical as well as forecast, can be found in:

Computer Readable Databases: A Directory and Data Source Book, 9th ed., by Martha Williams, Knowledge Industry Publications, White Plains, N.Y., 1979.

Directory of Online Databases (Quarterly), Cuadra Associates, Inc., Santa Monica, CA.

Many market research firms sell data on a subscription basis. The data provided by these organizations are sometimes subjective when dealing with consumer preferences. Other syndicated data suppliers report product movement in specific market areas or through certain channels of distribution (outlets). Much of this market research is based on a sampling (versus a census) of the population and therefore requires certain demographic adjustments to project full market size. Prominent syndicated data firms include:

Market Facts, Inc., NPD Research, Inc., National Family Opinion (NFO), and Market Research Corporation of America (MRCA) for consumer panels and mail survey.

A. C. Nielsen Company and Audits and Surveys, Inc. for retail store audits and product tracking services.

Selling Areas-Marketing, Inc. (SAMI) and Pipeline for audit services covering warehouse withdrawals.

Predicasts, Inc., which abstracts short- and long-range forecast statistics for basic economic indicators and industry forecasts from the news media, periodicals, and journals.

These private firms can often supply an organization with the data it needs for its forecasting, either on a one-time or ongoing basis. In many cases, such firms can spread the cost of primary data collection and thus provide very reliable data at much lower cost than could the individual organization.

11/2/2 Data Requirements for Various Forecasting Methods

There are two main uses of data in forecasting. First, data are used to determine the pattern of behavior of some variable based on historical observations. The various time-series approaches to forecasting are methodologies for using data in this fashion. Table 11-2 provides some rough guidelines of the data required by each of the major quantitative techniques described in this text. Increasing the amount of data will generally increase the accuracy of forecasts, but not necessarily in direct proportion to the amount of data. One of the problems in the quantity of data used is that frequently the pattern changes with time and thus using a longer time span (more data) may in fact give less accurate results than using only the minimum amount of data necessary and using that most recently available.

Second, data are used to provide future values of independent variables included in a causal model. This usage often requires that those independent variables be forecast before they can be part of the input to such

TABLE 11-2   ROUGH GUIDELINES FOR MINIMUM DATA
REQUIREMENTS OF QUANTITATIVE
FORECASTING METHODS

Method	Simple Model Nonseasonal Data (no. of data points)	Seasonal Data	Yearly (12 mo.) Seasonal Pattern (no. of data points)
Naive	1	—	—
Mean	30	—	—
Simple moving average	2–10	—	—
Simple exponential smoothing	2	—	—
Linear moving average	4–20	—	—
Linear exponential smoothing	3	—	—
Classical decomposition	—	5 times the length of the seasonal pattern	60
Census II	—	6 times the length of the seasonal pattern	72
Foran system	24	—	—
Box-Jenkins methodology	20	3 times the length of the seasonal pattern	36
Simple regression	10	—	—
Multiple regression	More than 15, depending upon the number of independent variables	5–6 times the length of the seasonal pattern; or 5–6 times the number of independent variables	60–72
Econometric models	30	—	—
Life-cycle analysis	6	—	—
Input-output analysis	A few hundred	—	—
Multivariate ARMA models	30	5–6 times the length of the seasonal pattern	60–72

a causal model. As pointed out in the chapters on regression analysis, it is often necessary to examine several alternative independent variables and to include only those that give suitable results and that can be most easily predicted in the future.

The above discussion of data relates mainly to quantitative methods of forecasting. For technological or qualitative forecasting methods, data uses and sources are somewhat different. The information or data required by technological forecasting is specialized and generally of a primary nature. Data bases and regular information updates are not so valuable for these methods. Rather data for such methods consist largely of scientific reports, intelligence data, or general information gathered from newspapers, magazines, or other publications. The data themselves are not of uniform importance in such situations. Rather it is the way the data are processed to form future alternatives that is critical. Technological forecasting involves evaluating these alternative formulations and assessing their chances of realization.

11/3   Data Preparation

In addition to identifying sources of data that meet forecasting requirements, a number of issues related to data preparation affect the accuracy of the data and their ability to meet the specific requirements of individual forecasts. These issues can be divided into two main parts. First are those related to the collection and use of data, and second are those related to data adjustments. These latter items might be thought of as preprocessing of the data after its collection but before its use in a quantitative forecasting methodology. Both aspects of data preparation will be dealt with in turn.

11/3/1   Problems with Data Collection

In a very extensive and far-reaching study, Morgenstern (1963) considered many of the major aspects of data collection and deficiencies in the resulting data. He not only considered the conceptual problem, but also examined in some detail many of the more commonly used published data sources in the United States. The results of his study are indeed revealing. For example, he concluded that the widely used statistics of GNP and private expenditures in the United States can include errors that range in magnitude from plus or minus 10 to 15 percent. This means that in addition to the forecasting error resulting from the application of the methodology itself, one must consider additional errors of 20 to 30 percent that can be built into the results simply because of the source of data being used. Morgenstern found it particularly disconcerting that those preparing such published reports have made no attempt to estimate the magnitude of the errors in their data.

Numerous sources of error influence data accuracy. Morgenstern has classified these sources as follows:

sampling methods

measurement errors

hidden information

poorly designed questionnaires

data aggregates

classification and definition

time factors

miscellaneous errors

These errors not only are important to the government or institution that gathers data for general publication, but also affect primary data collected for specific forecasting situations. Each of these sources of error deserves consideration by the forecaster in preparing data for a specific situation.

Sampling Methods

In many situations, data must be estimated from sample surveys. Sampling theory and its application are fairly well developed in statistics, but there are several problems that frequently arise because of human error or sampling bias. When the rules of sampling theory are followed explicitly, many of these errors can be avoided. The problem arises when the rules that ensure the validity and accuracy of the sample are not followed carefully. (See Williams, 1978, for an excellent critique of sampling methods and the 1971 BLS Handbook for a review of methodologies for surveys.)

Measurement Errors

Errors that occur in the actual collection and processing of data are usually called measurement errors. They may be the result of deficient measures, or they may involve reporting and processing errors. They range from collecting the wrong information to keypunching errors at the computer end. Once incorrect information has been included in the basic set of data, it is often hard to identify and eliminate it. General experience seems to suggest that the more automated the measurement, collection, and storage of data, the smaller the chances of measurement error.

Hidden Information

Often information is deliberately hidden or falsified by firms, households, or other responders for fear that it will be used for tax purposes.

Human nature is often the cause of such falsifications. For example, exaggeration of items related to prestige is not uncommon in surveys and research studies. One must also be aware that although there are general guidelines for the accounting profession, there is still tremendous flexibility as to the exact reporting of items and the way in which expenses are classified. Accounting rules for such things as profit and loss statements must be studied carefully and data should be adjusted to reflect accounting practices before being used as input for forecasting.

Poorly Designed Questionnaires

Often the data used in forecasting are collected from respondents who fill in questionnaires. For example, the anticipatory surveys of plant and equipment expenditures and those of consumer expenditures are based on data collected through questionnaires. A questionnaire should be carefully designed to communicate clearly and elicit the needed information. (See Payne, 1951.) Errors in questionnaire responses can arise for a variety of reasons ranging from the inability of the respondent to understand exactly what is wanted to his or her desire to avoid the appearance of ignorance by leaving questions blank. (See Chapter 4 on Data Collection in Boyd and Westfall, 1972.)

Data Aggregates

When aggregated data are collected from large populations, errors frequently occur as a result either of omitting part of the population or of double counting some parts. Sometimes even the time periods used in reporting in various published sources will overlap, and thus the task of fitting the data together in a meaningful time series is difficult. This problem is particularly significant in the area of financial statistics when different government agencies are involved. It is generally impossible for a corporation using these series to sort out how time periods are defined and how adjustments can be made to compensate for possible differences.

Classification and Definition

Proper classification of the items to be measured and the quantifiable variables to be used in the measurement are important aspects of data collection. This can become a particularly difficult problem in a multi-product firm where it is often impossible to allocate costs and profits to the various product lines in an exact way. Since the trend in corporations is toward larger companies of a diversified nature, it is likely that the difficulty of isolating and classifying the factors for individual products will become more difficult in the future. Also, intercompany transactions make it hard to assess and allocate overhead and other charges to various parts of the organization.

Time Factors

Data must be collected at discrete intervals, which can create problems with respect to timing. For example, organizations that use cash rather than accrual accounting methods will report financial data for a time period that does not necessarily reflect accurately their economic activity during that period. Even with an accrual accounting method, problems can arise when a physical transaction is reported in a different time period from the corresponding financial transaction. At the corporate level, these time problems can often be minimized by attempting to make all data series consistent with the accounting system. However, in using external published sources it is frequently impossible to maintain such consistency.

Miscellaneous Errors

Another source of error in the use of data for forecasting is that the characteristics of a sample or population may change over time. As a result, the observations reported for different time periods may actually represent slightly different samples or populations. All of the forecasting methods discussed thus far are based on the notion that the historical data used by a given method come from a homogeneous population. This assumption implies that when there are significant changes, substantial error may occur in the forecast.

One other factor that often causes inaccuracy in data is what Morgenstern identifies as functionally false data. A good example of this phenomenon might be the construction of price indices. These indices are generally based on published prices, but because of rebates, discounts, and so on, transactions rarely occur at published prices. In addition, the weights used to calculate price indices may change significantly over short periods of time, which again would cause functionally false data. Assuring that the variable for which the data are collected is appropriately defined initially, and taking steps to verify that the actual collected data represent that variable are often solutions to this problem.

11/3/2   Preprocessing Data for Forecasting

In many forecasting situations, it is necessary to preprocess or adjust the data after they have been collected but before they are used in a quantitative forecasting method. A number of the most common types of adjustments will be described here. It should be stressed that judgment must be exercised in determining when such preprocessing will improve the forecasting results and when it will not. Most adjustments involve modifications of the data or additions to the data base that eliminate part of the information contained in the raw data. In many instances, these adjustments make it easier to apply standardized forecasting methodologies and thus they are worthwhile. However, in other instances these adjustments may cause such a loss of information that the results of using the modified data will not be nearly as reliable as those obtained from using the raw data.

Missing Data Values

Frequently in collecting data for forecasting, data are not available for some small fraction of the observations that are desired. However, some estimate of those data values may be necessary to make application of a quantitative technique viable. The most common approach to overcoming this problem is to use a moving average estimate in place of the missing values. It will be recalled that this approach was described in Chapter 4 when decomposition methods were discussed and the twelve-month moving averages were computed as an intermediate stage of forecasting. Rather than leave six values blank at each end of the moving average series, shorter moving averages were taken to fill in all but one or two values at each end of the series.

Time Factors: Trading Day Adjustments

One problem commonly faced in business forecasting is variation in the actual number of trading days included in each time period. (See Chapter 4.) Accounting periods that are four weeks in length with thirteen periods per year partially overcome this problem. However, in companies that use the twelve calendar months for reporting periods, and even in many that use thirteen four-week periods, some kind of working day adjustment is required. This adjustment is often referred to as a *trading day* adjustment.

The first step in making a trading adjustment is to collect data on the number of working days or business days occurring in each period covered by the time series. The adjustment is made by finding the average number of working days for each period in the series and adjusting the raw data by the appropriate percentage to reflect what actual values would have been if the period had contained the average number of working days. For example, if the average number of days for a given month over the past several years had been 20 working days, but there were only 18 days in the period in question, the raw data would have to be multiplied by 20/18 so that the month would not be comparable to a 20-day month. The resulting adjusted series is then used as the input to forecasting. (Conversion to a "per day" rate is an alternative type of adjustment.)

Outlier (or Special Event) Adjustments

Another type of adjustment is often needed when special events affect the value of the variable in a given period. For example, in the restaurant business there may be individual days that are not representative of that day normally during the week because of local activities or specials offered by the restaurant. In such instances, there may be insufficient data to average out this kind of special fluctuation in the values. When that is the case, one might choose to replace those special values with a more typical value for that day. That can be done simply using a moving average or some other smoothed estimate for that day of the week. One must be cautious in this kind of data adjustment, since it eliminates fluctuations from the historical data that may in fact recur in the future.

Constant Versus Current Price Data

In many instances, accounting data are recorded in terms of current prices and thus reflect both inflation and real growth or decline in that item. Such series can be transformed into constant prices using a deflator index such as the GNP deflator or the Consumer Price Index. While this transformation allows forecasting to deal with a series that is not biased by inflation, the deflator index itself may further distort the original data. For example, a company selling a single product in a specific industry may have trouble identifying a deflator index that adequately represents that single product. When a more general index relating to the industry as a whole is used, it may overadjust for some time periods and underadjust for others simply because the inflation pattern for the company's products differs from the industry average.

Preliminary Versus Revised Data

For many national and regional economic indicators, data are often first collected in a raw form on a sample basis. These raw data are then used to estimate the actual values of the series before the time when those actual values become available. These estimates allow forecasting to respond more quickly to changes in the short-term situation than would be the case if only the final published data were used several months later. For the forecaster, the important concern is whether or not the raw estimates adequately represent the final reported values. In many instances it has been found that these raw estimates may vary by 10 percent or more from the actual values. Thus a trade-off must be made between more current, and possibly less accurate, information and older, more accurate information.

Data Transformations

Modifications in data like those described above are generally carried out independent of the actual forecasting methodology. Depending on the method being applied, additional transformations—deseasonalizing, detrending, standardizing, and transformations to linear forms—are often desired or required. Since these are most often done in conjunction with specific methods, they have been discussed in prior chapters, as appropriate. However, they could be viewed as simply further adjustments in the raw data.

Data Verification

Several types of data modification (preprocessing) are described above. It's also essential that data be checked for transcription errors (e.g., keypunch and recording). Such checks can range from simply a review of the listed data to sampling procedures to verify data records. The most appropriate procedure depends on the situation and the cost/value of such verification.

11/4 Data Management

There are several important aspects of effective data management for purposes of forecasting. These can be grouped into four categories—database systems, data manipulation, data presentation, and revisions and updates. Each of these will be discussed briefly in this section.

11/4/1 Database Systems

During the past few years, interest in establishing data bases has increased. (See Lackman, 1981.) This interest deserves special consideration in connection with forecasting. A database is a collection of data on a number of different variables that is stored in some easily accessible manner (such as a computerized data processing system) so that the data will be available when needed. There are generally three types of data that can be included in a database designed to support forecasting: (1) data that are needed for existing requirements, (2) data that are currently available but are not currently required as part of forecasting, and (3) data that may be required in the future but are not currently available.

A database that focuses only on handling existing data requirements is generally the most straightforward and least expensive system to develop. With small incremental cost, such a base can often be expanded to include the collection of available data that are not currently required but may be useful in the future. Finally, with the use of some planning and management judgment, the database can often be expanded further to include data that may be required in the future but are not currently available. The attractiveness of a database that includes all three types of data is that most forecasting applications require historical observations before a technique can be applied. Thus if the database includes a collection of several different items, it is much more likely that the required historical data will be readily available when new forecasts are desired.

The trade-off involved in developing such a general database to support forecasting is the cost of its development and maintenance. Generally, however, if a flexible database is developed, the incremental costs of collecting data on an additional variable are quite low. Key aspects in determining the value and flexibility of a proposed database system are the level of detail involved and the structure of the data actually stored there.

For maximum value, data should be gathered and stored in disaggregated form. Aggregation causes the loss of information. For example, when the daily shipments of a factory are aggregated into a total sales figure for the week, information on the daily pattern of shipments that may be valuable for inventory planning purposes is lost. Similarly, if the sales of a product sold during a special low-priced promotion are aggregated with the sales of that product at a regular price, information concerning the price-quantity relationship is lost. In predicting product volumes, such loss of information may severely limit the forecasting ability of even the most sophisticated methodologies.

One of the basic reasons for aggregation in most accounting databases is related to their presentation orientation. Most such systems have been designed to be used by people who are processing data collected by people, to produce information to be filed by people, and to provide reports for other people. The convenience of having a single unit of measure and a single system of accounts provided by summarizing transactions has historically been desirable and necessary. However, with the level of computerization available in many companies and the ability to separate data storage from presentation, such summaries are no longer necessary, nor are they attractive for forecasting purposes.

In today's businesses, machines, not people, do much of the gathering, processing, filing, and reporting of data. The capabilities and deficiencies of such computer systems are different from those of people. One of the important considerations in designing a database system for forecasting is to adequately utilize the capabilities of the computer in storing data in the form that will make it most usable for forecasting purposes. Examples of firms that have specialized in such skills will be discussed later in this section and should help illustrate what can be done.

For readers wishing to learn more about the burgeoning field of database management systems and their limitations, an excellent reference is Kroenke's Database Processing (1977). Kroenke describes the CODASYL (Conference on Data Systems Languages) group, which has played an important role in trying to develop national standards for database management systems themselves (see CODASYL references, 1969 and 1971). Kroenke classifies database *users* in terms of five dimensions:

1. Language used (query/host language)
2. Type of access (batch/interactive)
3. Form of requests (fixed/dynamic)

4. Degree of access allowed (schema/subscheme)
5. Type of data accessed (data/data structure)

The first dimension refers to whether the user interacts with the database system using a high-level query language (similar to natural language commands) or whether the user actually writes applications programs in one of the languages (for example, COBOL, PL/I, FORTRAN, PASCAL) of the host computer.

The second dimension concerns the user's access to the database. In batch mode the user has practically no control over transaction processing, whereas in the interactive mode the user controls the program and the processing, as for example in the airline reservation scheme.

The third dimension refers to the way a user can make requests of the database. If only a fixed menu of options is available, then the user must be satisfied with that menu. Dynamic systems allow users to create their own requests by using commands available in the query or host language.

The fourth dimension describes how much of the database a given user will be allowed to access. If the database serves several different user groups, it may be appropriate to limit access to that portion (subschema) of the database that is relevant to the particular user category. Only such (subschema) data would then be available for reference or modification by the user.

The last dimension refers to what kind of information can be accessed. "Data" means just single variables such as a salesperson's sales record. "Data structure" means relationships between two or more variables—for example, the relationship between salespersons and sales records. In the fifth dimension, as in the fourth, the user may be able to reference or modify data or data structures, but use of the modification privilege has to be carefully controlled.

Kroenke's Chapters 8, 9 and 10 describe the "cast of characters" in database processing, and he gives a useful summary of six of the major commercial database systems in use today—ADABAS, IDMS, IMS, MAGNUM, SYSTEM 2000, and TOTAL. All of these systems are attempts at managing the important tasks of data storage and efficient information retrieval. To understand what these systems offer to users, it is necessary to distinguish between "a database" and "a database management system (DBMS)."

A database is a collection of data stored on some mass memory device, for example, a disk. A user can write an application program that interacts directly with the data via the format of the records on the disk. This application program itself is thus tied to the particular formatting of the data on the disk. If the disk format is changed (as when a new disk replaces an old disk), then the application program must also be changed. A DBMS is designed to make the application programs *independent* of the database.

The DBMS is a software package that acts as an interface between the application programs and the database. Changes in the database structure can be accomplished without changing the applications programs. This is a tremendous advantage from the user's point of view, but of course, it comes at some significant cost. DBMS systems are expensive to install; there have been many implementation failures; and forecasts (for example, Hussain and Hussain, 1981, p. 210) of their adoption seem overly optimistic. Nevertheless, database systems of one kind or another are certain to affect the way forecasters will interact with data and with data structures, from both internal and external sources. As Sibley, chairman of CODASYL, states, "There are hardly any technical problems involved with installing a DBMS, only people problems and managerial problems."

11/4/2   Data Presentation

Depending on the specific organization setting, the requirements and characteristics desired in a data management system may vary tremendously. In one system, the emphasis may be on preparing data to be examined by the forecaster in some detail. Thus much of the emphasis would be on preliminary analysis and data manipulation so that substantial time spent on selecting the appropriate forecasting method and applying it to the data can be used most effectively.

In other settings, the emphasis may not be so much on the application of sophisticated forecasting methodologies as on meeting a number of diverse requirements for forecasts in a satisfactory manner. When the aim of the data management system is more closely related to the presentation of data for a number of different managers and administrators in a wide range of situations, the system must possess characteristics appropriate to meet those needs. One such system is that developed by Mr. T. W. Hibson, manager of forecasting for the Optical Products Division of American Optical Corporation.

The American Optical system uses a very straightforward approach to forecasting and focuses much more on the manipulation of data and its presentation for management purposes. The actual forecasting routines most commonly used by the system are simply to deseasonalize a time series of data, to apply a trend extrapolation routine to that deseasonalized data, and finally to reincorporate the seasonal factors in coming up with a final forecast. Although this is fairly straightforward as a forecasting application, the volume of different items to be forecast and the number of managers involved place special requirements on the complete system. It must be particularly flexible in presenting a wide range of forecasts and yet must present them in a consistent manner so that different managers can readily compare their own forecasts and those prepared by others.

The sequence of steps involved in forecasting and planning for the variety of product lines and geographical areas handled by American Optical starts with a tracking of actual values and a rather straightforward forecast of future values on either a monthly or annual basis. The next step seeks agreement from those managers involved as to the most appropriate final forecast for the situation and, ultimately, a tracking of performance of that agreed upon forecast against actual values. This system allows management to measure its performance against those forecasts that have been previously agreed upon. Since several managers and a variety of products and geographical areas are handled with the system, data (and forecast) presentation is particularly important. Reports are prepared in a manner that is consistent from area to area, thus facilitating management's comparison of performance in different areas. In addition, plotting routines are available that help to illustrate graphically actual versus forecast performance.

A number of studies have been done regarding data presentation and its impact. One particularly useful article along this line is that by Dickson et al. (1977). Others are cited in Chapter 18 of this text.

11/5 Summary

Once data have been specified, procedures must be designed and implemented for collecting new data as they are generated and adding them to the database. As a part of such a procedure, it is important to include a method for determining when additional data are needed and when changes might be necessary in the forecasting methods to accommodate basic changes in pattern. Such a procedure might be thought of as an early warning signal to identify potential changes in data series. One type of signal was described in Chapter 3 in connection with smoothing methods. There, a tracking signal that measures cumulative error was used to identify when the parameter values of the smoothing model should be updated so that they could more quickly accommodate changes in the basic pattern. When a forecasting system is being designed for several different items, some procedures, either formal or informal, are needed to perform the same function as a tracking signal and facilitate the periodic evaluation of the database and the forecasting methodologies being applied.

As with any management process, a forecasting system and its attendant data support efforts must be viewed as dynamic, evolving activities. They should be upgraded and improved through regular review and feedback, not installed and forgotten. This chapter has only scratched the surface of what can be done. The coming decade and its anticipated boom in computing capability should make this entire field of data support one of significant progress.

REFERENCES AND SELECTED BIBLIOGRAPHY

Biderman, A. D. 1966. "Social Indicators and Goals." In *Social Indicators,* R. A. Baner (ed.). Cambridge, Mass.: MIT Press, pp. 68, 153.

Boyd, H., and R. Westfall. 1972. *Marketing Research.* Homewood, Ill.: Richard D. Irwin.

Bureau of Labor Statistics. 1971. *Handbook of Methods for Surveys and Studies.* Washington, D.C.: U.S. Department of Labor, Bulletin 1711.

Butler, W. V., and R. A. Kavesh. 1966. *How Business Economists Forecast.* Englewood Cliffs, N.J.: Prentice-Hall.

Cochran, W. G. 1977. *Sampling Techniques,* 3rd ed. New York: John Wiley & Sons, Inc.

CODASYL. CODASYL Data Base Task Group Report. 1971. New York: ACM.

CODASYL. CODASYL Data Description Language, Journal of Development. Washington, D.C.: U.S. Department of Commerce, National Bureau of Standards Handbook 113.

Daniells, L. M. 1980. *Business Forecasting for the 1980s—And Beyond.* Boston: Baker Library, Harvard Business School.

Davidson, T. A., and J. L. Ayers. 1982. "Selecting and Using External Data Sources." Chapter 28 in *Handbook of Forecasting,* S. Makridakis and S. C. Wheelwright (eds.). New York: John Wiley & Sons, Inc.

Dickson, G. R., et al. 1977. "Research in Management Information Systems: The Minnesota Experiments," *Management Science, 23,* pp. 913–922.

Diebold Group. 1977. *Automatic Data Processing Handbook.* New York: McGraw-Hill.

Dunn, D. M., W. H. Williams, and T. L. DeChaine. 1975. "Aggregate versus Subaggregate Models in Local Area Forecasting," *Journal of the American Statistical Association, 71,* No. 353, March, pp. 68–71.

Grether, D. M., and M. Nerlove. 1970. "Some Properties of 'Optimal' Seasonal Adjustment," *Econometrica, 38,* September, pp. 682—703.

Hussain, D., and K. M. Hussain. 1981. *Information Processing Systems for Management.* Homewood, Ill.: Richard D. Irwin, Inc.

Ijiri, Y. 1967. *The Foundation of Accounting Measurement.* Englewood Cliffs, N.J.: Prentice-Hall.

Jessen, R. J. 1978. *Statistical Survey Techniques.* New York: John Wiley & Sons, Inc.

Kroenke, D. 1977. *Database Processing.* Chicago: Science Research Associates.

Lackman, C. L. 1981. "Forecasting Information Systems: The Data Base Module," *Journal of Systems Management,* January, *32,* No. 1, pp. 29–35.

Lucas, H. C. 1978. *Information Systems Concepts for Management.* New York: McGraw-Hill.

Makridakis, S., and S. C. Wheelwright. 1982. *Handbook of Forecasting*. New York: John Wiley & Sons, Inc.

McRae, T. W. 1964. *The Impact of Computers on Accounting*. London: John Wiley & Sons, Inc.

Morgenstern, O. 1963. *On the Accuracy of Economic Observations*. Princeton, N.J.: Princeton University Press.

Payne, S. L. 1951. *The Art of Asking Questions*. Princeton, N.J.: Princeton University Press.

Porter, W. T., Jr. 1966. *Auditing Electronic Systems*. Belmont, Calif.: Wadsworth.

Sims, C. A. 1974. "Seasonality in Regression," *Journal of the American Statistical Association,* **69,** No. 347, September, pp. 618–26.

Stekler, H. O., and F. W. Burch. 1968. "Selected Economic Data: Accuracy vs. Reporting Speed," *Journal of the American Statistical Association,* June, pp. 436-44.

Wheelwright, S. C., and D. G. Clarke. 1976. "Corporate Forecasting: Promise and Reality," *Harvard Business Review,* November-December.

Williams, B. 1978. *A Sampler on Sampling*. New York: John Wiley & Sons, Inc.

Zschau, E. V. W. 1968. "The Impact of Computers and Information Sciences on Accounting." Presented at the Annual Meeting of the American Accounting Association, San Diego, Calif., August.

EXERCISES

1. Deciding What to Forecast

   In the two following situations, forecasts are being prepared for the first time. What is your evaluation of the data collected for use in these situations? What variables would you recommend be forecast? What should be given to those requesting the forecasts? What other data/forecasting issues need attention in each of these situations and how should those be addressed?

   a. *Arizona Security Bank*
   With the increased level of interest in long-range planning, the Arizona Security Bank (ASB) in early 1974 had almost overnight decided to initiate an annual long-range planning exercise. The purpose of this exercise was to review important trends in the banking business and in various characteristics of ASB's performance and to project those into the future assuming no changes in management policies. It was then felt that a group of the top operating executives in the bank could spend two to three days reviewing these data and determining what changes in policy would be required in coming months and years if the bank were going to achieve its long-term goals.

Since the bank had a substantial data processing group to handle all of its accounting and financial data, top management thought it would be a relatively simple task for this group to prepare forecasts of several important variables that could serve as input to this planning exercise. Six of the specific items relating to ASB's area of competition that were felt to be important were:

1. total bank deposits for all of Arizona,
2. total loans,
3. the ratio of loans to deposits,
4. savings deposits in banks,
5. savings deposits in S&L's (Savings and Loan Associations),
6. the relative share of deposits going to banks as opposed to S&L's.

The historical data for these several variables were immediately available to the data processing group through the *Arizona Statistical Review,* an official state publication (see Table 11-3). It was the assignment of the data processing group to prepare the best forecast possible for each of these six variables and to make those available to the top operating executives who would be involved in the annual long-range planning exercise.

In the instructions provided to data processing from the long-range planning committee, a couple of important points had been highlighted. One of these was the feeling of the top management at ASB that the ratio of deposits to loans, which had been increasing over the past decade, would almost certainly level off before reaching 80 percent. (Management felt that the Federal Government would not allow that figure to rise above 80 percent in the future.) It was also the feeling of the bank's management that the banking segment of the industry would continue to grow more rapidly than the savings and loan segment and thus banks would gradually increase their share of the total market.

One of the questions raised by the long-range planning committee's memo was whether these six variables should be forecast independently of one another or if some approach that forecasted one variable and then prepared a forecast for another by simply taking the complement might be more accurate. For example, total bank and S&L deposits might be forecast, the bank's share of those might be forecast and then the actual dollar figures for both the banks and the S&L's could be projected using those two forecast items. The long-range planning committee had made it quite clear in their directives to the data processing group that it was up to data processing to determine which forecasting techniques would be most appropriate for this situation.

b. *Phoenix City Council*

In spite of the fact that it was a sunny, warm day in early April 1974, Paul Marshall was visibly concerned about the task he had recently been given by the Phoenix City Council. As a staff assistant to that group for the past 3 years he had been involved in generating a number of ideas and programs that would help the Council make better decisions. He also supplied them with any analytical and data support that they requested. In one of their recent meetings, an outside consultant had suggested that it might be very helpful to them in planning their tax levies and estimating their future tax base to have projections concerning the population of the city of Phoenix.

TABLE 11-3 ARIZONA SECURITY BANK

Deposits and Loans of All Arizona Banks[a]

Dec. 31	Deposits	Loans	Ratio
1963 (Dec. 20)	$1,732,374,000	$1,201,556,000	69.4%
1964	1,970,219,000	1,358,105,000	68.9
1965	2,096,020,000	1,452,733,000	69.3
1966	2,238,692,000	1,566,465,000	70.0
1967	2,484,924,000	1,708,776,000	68.5
1968	2,856,225,000	1,971,650,000	69.0
1969	3,110,704,000	2,324,095,000	74.7
1970	3,552,079,000	2,585,854,000	72.8
1971	4,322,060,000	3,163,440,000	73.3
1972	5,248,274,000	3,997,988,000	76.2
1973 (June 30)	5,523,727,000	4,193,845,000	75.9

Savings Deposits in Arizona[b]

Dec. 31	Banks	Savings & Loan Associations	Total
1963 (Dec. 20)	$ 728,191,000	$ 488,202,000	$1,216,393,000
1964	872,848,000	582,876,000	1,455,724,000
1965	992,231,000	619,418,000	1,611,649,000
1966	1,131,334,000	597,318,000	1,728,652,000
1967	1,293,367,000	684,833,000	1,978,200,000
1968	1,461,418,000	741,016,000	2,202,434,000
1969	1,521,213,000	791,084,000	2,312,297,000
1970	1,790,884,000	919,172,000	2,710,056,000
1971	2,260,126,000	1,231,714,000	3,491,840,000
1972	2,807,359,000	1,667,807,000	4,475,166,000
1973 (June 30)	2,996,978,000	1,862,995,000	4,859,973,000

[a]Source: Arizona Statistical Review

[b]Source: Arizona Statistical Review

The City Council had felt that was a great idea and had immediately assigned it to Paul and asked him to prepare annual forecasts for 3, 5, and 10 years. Their thought on the various number of time periods had been that some people in the city government might only be concerned with one time horizon while others might deal with very different time horizons depending on the responsibilities involved and the decisions in question.

Paul was anxious to meet the needs of the City Council but was not sure exactly where he should begin. He knew that there were several state agencies that seemed to pull population projections out of thin air whenever they needed them to support their position. However, he was not aware of any group that had systematically been projecting Phoenix city population with any consistency or any level of accuracy. Thus he felt he really needed to start from scratch in pursuing his assignment.

As a first step he gathered together the historical data published by the city's planning department (see Table 11-4). Upon reviewing these data,

TABLE 11-4 PHOENIX CITY COUNCIL—POPULATION GROWTH OF PHOENIX AND MARICOPA COUNTY

As of July 1	Phoenix City Limits	Maricopa County[a]
1950 (April Census)	106,818	331,770
1951	109,000	364,000
1952	119,000	390,000
1953	130,000	417,000
1954	140,000	446,000
1955	155,000	477,000
1956	170,000	510,000
1957	179,000	545,000
1958	242,000	583,000
1959	364,000	625,000
1960 (April Census)	439,170	663,510
1961	452,000	740,000
1962	468,000	775,000
1963	483,000	808,000
1964	494,000	833,000
1965	504,000	852,000
1966	511,000	870,000
1967	519,000	890,000
1968	528,000	914,000
1969	546,000	946,000
1970 (April Census)	582,500	969,425
1971	621,000	1,017,000
1972	674,000	1,060,000
1973	724,000	1,105,000

Source: Inter-census year figures for Maricopa County are by the Arizona Department of Economic Security in cooperation with the U.S. Bureau of the Census; all Phoenix inter-census year figures are by the Phoenix City Planning Department.

[a]Totals for the county including Phoenix

Population

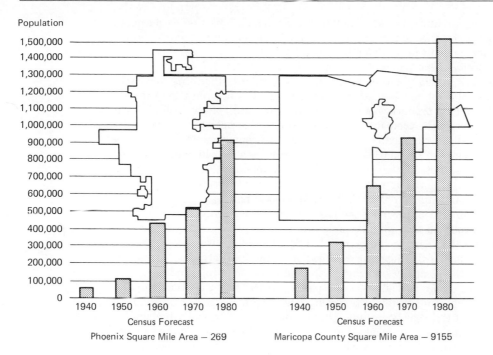

Census Forecast   Census Forecast

Phoenix Square Mile Area — 269   Maricopa County Square Mile Area — 9155

Paul decided that there were at least three questions that he needed to answer before preparing his forecast. The first revolved around the specific technique most suitable for this situation. Not having had much experience with forecasting, he really was not sure which approach should be tested and how to go about doing that.

The second question concerned whether or not he should supply identical forecasts for the first three years of the 3-, 5-, and 10-year projections. Since these were going to different people who would use them for different things, he thought there might be some argument for having them somewhat different. Of particular concern was the fact that if one of them was to be used in making projections concerning the tax base in the city, that it would be much better to underestimate future population figures rather than to overestimate them and thus create financial problems for the city in the future.

The third question concerned the use of the population data available for the county of Maricopa. While he had historical data for the county, he was not sure whether or not that would be useful to him in projecting future population in the city of Phoenix. The City Council had not expressed any particular interest in having population projections for the county as a whole since there was an entirely different government organization concerned with the county's problems.

2.   Data Adjustments for Forecasting

The three following situations involve adjustments to the data being used as a basis for forecasting, and/or adjustments in the forecasts. What is your evaluation of the adjustments that have been made/proposed? What alternatives might be considered? What recommendations would you make with regard to the issues raised in each situation and the interpretation/limitations of the resulting forecasts?

a. *Basic Metals Limited*

In early 1973 Mr. Ian McDonald, Director of Corporate Planning Research, was contemplating how best to predict the company's future sales of carbon steel alloys. This product was one of many that were bought in bulk form and processed by the company. As with most of the company's products, this was essentially a commodity item and thus the company, while having a significant share of the market, did not determine the world-wide prices for their products. Instead, they were faced with simply accepting whatever the market dictated as the appropriate price at any point in time.

The particular problem that Mr. McDonald had was taking the data shown in Table 11-5, covering the past 11 years, and trying to apply some forecasting method that would enable him to effectively predict the company's future sales. Among the points that Mr. McDonald wanted to keep in mind in preparing this forecast was first of all the marketing department's feeling that the company's market share had been changing gradually over that entire 11-year period. A second point was the fact that the company used in its reporting system alternating four- and five-week periods. Thus, the months of the year beginning with January would typically include for accounting purposes four weeks, four weeks, and five weeks and then repeat again. The month of July was when the plants typically shut down for vacation, and thus that month for the company included only two weeks of actual shipments. A final point that Mr. McDonald thought was important to keep in mind was the long term cyclical pattern that people in the industry felt applied to the product. While he wasn't sure that he had sufficient data to identify that cycle, he did feel it was important to investigate its possible existence since he knew the President would ask about it when he reviewed the final forecast.

b. *INSEAD's Restaurant*

The INSEAD restaurant is a school-run eating facility where participants of the various management programs can take their meals. Unlike the typical university dining hall in the U.S., eating in France is taken very seriously, even in a student restaurant. The quality of the food at INSEAD's restaurant is pretty good by non-French standards.

Daily food preparation starts early in the morning when the cook and his assistant visit the market to buy the ingredients needed to prepare the meals for the day. Little of the food is prepared from frozen ingredients. The restaurant has only a small freezer and limited refrigerator capacity for storing unused ingredients. Furthermore, cooked food and bread cannot be stored for use the next day.

Due to the above constraints and the need to maintain consistent high quality, predicting the number of students who will eat in the restaurant each day is a very important activity which requires the attention of the restaurant's director. He considers such things as the day of the week, weather, holidays, exam times, and so on, in attempting to forecast the number of customers desiring to be served lunch and dinner. Historically, the accuracy of his forecasts has fluctuated widely, resulting in inconvenience for those customers coming late when the number of clients has been under-

TABLE 11-5   BASIC METALS LTD. WEEKLY SHIPMENTS OF CARBON
STEEL ALLOYS (IN 1000's OF TONS)

Year	Jan.	Feb.	Mar.	Apr.	May	June	July	Aug.	Sep.	Oct.	Nov.	Dec.
1961	2079	1952	1941	2311	3035	2276	3514	2398	2734	2650	2847	2495
1962	2592	3190	2741	2806	2993	2704	2999	2640	2360	2413	2501	2391
1963	2328	2691	3045	2918	3071	2847	3141	2730	2546	2255	2536	2495
1964	2373	2734	2985	2889	3109	2638	3940	2986	3178	3122	2559	2625
1965	2584	3271	3287	3536	4042	3165	4119	3178	3449	3687	4187	3112
1966	3571	3755	4303	4651	4128	3953	4646	3622	3929	4183	3936	3758
1967	3605	3919	3526	2997	2883	2346	2773	2539	3052	3311	3836	2942
1968	3356	4070	3657	3348	3562	3335	3660	3426	3530	3263	3471	3212
1969	3600	3408	3921	3462	3408	3315	4463	3213	3195	2976	2759	2659
1970	3419	3348	3311	3488	2941	3142	2935	2440	2591	2314	2346	2252
1971	1990	2354	2639	2915	2977	3105	2994	2454	2372	2709	2833	3173
1972	2250	2831	3351	3275	3271	3218	3732	2813	2845	3036	2996	2670
Number of weeks in month:	4	4	5	4	4	5	2	4	5	4	4	5

Note: Figures are average shipments/week for each month. These were obtained by taking
accounting's record of shipments for the month and dividing by the number of weeks over
which those shipments were made.

estimated or throwing food and bread away when the number of people desiring to eat in the restaurant has been overestimated.

An INSEAD student, Mr. Dahlem, taking an elective course on forecasting decided that the quality of the food could be improved if the accuracy
of the prediction of the number of students eating could be improved. Upon
contacting the director of the restaurant, he obtained the data shown in Table
11-6.

Mr. Dahlem quickly discovered that on holidays and exam days, the
number of students eating at the restaurant varied considerably with no
apparent pattern. He therefore substituted for the number of customers on
each holiday or exam day, the average historical value for that particular
day of the week. These averages are identified with an * in Table 11-6 and
are as follows:

Mon: 294
Tue: 300
Wed: 291
Thu: 285
Fri: 242
Sat: 182
Sun: 182

TABLE 11-6 NUMBER OF STUDENTS EATING AT INSEAD'S RESTAURANT DAILY—NOVEMBER 1, 1974, TO APRIL 13, 1975

	1974				1975					
	November		December		January		February		March		April
Sat									1	132	
Sun			1	176					2	165	
Mon			2	278					3	273	
Tue			3	300					4	289	1	280
Wed			4	283	1				5	285	2	287
Thu			5	292*	2				6	267	3	294
Fri	1	242*	6	210	3				7	250	4	260
Sat	2	178	7	248	4		1	87	8	176	5	181
Sun	3	233	8	211	5		2	116	9	189*	6	172
Mon	4	294*	9	303	6		3	294	10	282	7	296
Tue	5	329	10	300	7		4	308	11	310	8	281
Wed	6	310	11	289	8	267	5	302	12	285	9	288
Thu	7	312	12	260	9	280	6	299	13	272	10	260
Fri	8	242*	13	271	10	255	7	244	14		11	220
Sat	9	133	14	285	11	281	8	245	15		12	128
Sun	10	131	15	145	12	223	9	239	16		13	146
Mon	11	294*	16	278	13	309	10	294*	17		14	
Tue	12	293	17	313	14	302	11	301	18		15	
Wed	13	290	18		15	294	12	282	19		16	
Thu	14	285	19		16	299	13	271	20		17	
Fri	15	273	20		17	257	14	206	21		18	
Sat	16	168	21		18	185	15	137	22		19	
Sun	17	130	22		19	207	16	158	23		20	
Mon	18	320	23		20	324	17	277	24		21	
Tue	19	293	24		21	304	18	287	25		22	
Wed	20	286	25		22	323	19	279	26		23	
Thu	21	289	26		23	293	20	295	27		24	
Fri	22	285	27		24	242	21	228	28	242*	25	
Sat	23	197	28		25	124	22	152	29	182*	26	
Sun	24	203	29		26	164	23	190	30	189*	27	

TABLE 11-6 NUMBER OF STUDENTS EATING AT INSEAD'S
RESTAURANT DAILY—NOVEMBER 1, 1974,
TO APRIL 13, 1975 (*Continued*)

	1974			1975						
	November		December	January		February		March		April
Mon	25	286	30	27	315	24	278	31	294*	28
Tue	26	301	31	28	309	25	280			29
Wed	27	290		29	310	26	281			30
Thu	28	284		30	273	27	295			
Fri	29	204		31	243	28	217			
Sat	30	180								

By running an autocorrelation program Mr. Dahlem discovered, as expected, that the data showed a strong seasonal pattern of 7 periods (days) duration and were stationary at zero differences. Stationarity was expected because on different days there are different numbers of students eating and because the total number of students at INSEAD did not change over the five months covered by the historical data.

By running a decomposition program, Mr. Dahlem found that Tuesday was the most popular day for eating at the restaurant while Saturday was the least popular. The seasonal coefficients identified had the following values:

Mon: 120.49
Tue: 121.62
Wed: 117.88
Thu: 115.29
Fri: 93.95
Sat: 63.19
Sun: 67.59

The results of this preliminary analysis simply increased Mr. Dahlem's interest in this forecasting situation and he decided to use several alternative forecasting techniques to address it.

c. *Shasta Timber*[2]

For the past 2 years, Bob Cohen and J.B. Sullivan have been serving as timber estimator apprentices under Al Beers, one of the two master estimators presently retained by Shasta Timber, a moderately large wood products firm in northern California. The timber estimator is a crucial link in maintaining a steady flow of logs from the forests to the mill, for based on his estimates, logging decisions are made and the flow thus established. If the flow is too low, the milling operations are disrupted and, if too high, excessive waste will result. Consequently, a good estimator is a highly valued asset to any company. Shasta will soon begin developing several new areas and a third master estimator will be required to cover these tracts. Mr. Cohen and Mr. Sullivan are prime candidates for this assignment.

A timber estimator surveys the tracts by foot and by helicopter estimating the forest density, the average height of the trees, and the average diameter. From this data and a certain feel that is developed over many years of close association with logging operations, an estimate of the number of cubic feet of usable timber is made. This estimate is given to the manager of the Forest Operations Division where it is locked and stored in his safe. The division manager is the only person in the company who has access to the estimate as well as to the actual yield from each of the surveyed tracts. The yield is roughly measured when the cut logs are transported from the tract to the mill.

The estimator works in an environment of little feedback since Shasta does not inquire as to how he made his prediction nor do they tell him the actual yield. In addition, two master estimators are never assigned to survey the same tracts. Thus the estimator does not have a standard against which he can compare his performance. In fact, the only indication that he had been performing well is that he has retained his job. When an estimator goes bad, he is transferred to another area.

The training program operates in precisely the same way except that the master estimator assists in the apprentice's estimates. For the past six months the two apprentices have been operating without Mr. Beer's assistance and the following performance has resulted:

Cohen		Sullivan	
Estimate[a]	Actual[a]	Estimate[a]	Actual[a]
1500	1410	1425	1570
1625	1940	1625	2000
1225	1660	1400	1330
1375	1140	1100	1250
1850	1200	1500	1780
1450	1550		

[a]Cubic feet per acre

On the basis of these records, the division manager must decide which apprentice is to be retained and whether that person's estimates should be systematically modified to adjust for bias.

3.   Tempo, Inc. Developing a Database for Forecasting[3]

Louis De Rosa, the president of Tempo, Inc., had just acquired a new computer for his firm's data processing needs. Tempo was a medium-sized temporary help company operating throughout the New York-New Jersey metropolitan area. The new computer was intended primarily for payroll work (a particularly complex task for Tempo, which used a large number of part-time and occasional workers) but De Rosa had read enough about the uses of computers to realize that he should also consider the potential for having the machine contribute to the business in other ways. In the past, he had personally taken charge of forecasting the demand for workers in the 25 different categories supplied by Tempo: he prepared such forecasts several days in advance. He hoped that the new computer system could simplify this forecasting task and, perhaps, take over the bulk of the forecasting work.

The Temporary Help Industry

In 1974 the U.S. temporary help industry was only about 25 years old. It had grown from a volume of $100 million in 1960 to one of a billion dollars in 1973. Initially, most of the workers provided by the temporary help agencies were clerical workers, but as the industry grew it had begun to provide a much wider range of employees, including some with specialized technical skills. The industry was dominated by Manpower, Inc., a 25-year-old company that accounted for a quarter of the industry's business in 1973. There were other large firms (Kelly Services, Inc. and Olsten Temporary Services) and also several thousand smaller (and more localized) firms in the field. Altogether, temporary workers constituted approximately 3 percent of the U.S. labor force in 1973; the fraction of temporary workers was expected to rise markedly.

Customers of these temporary help firms hired temporary workers for varied reasons. In some cases, the temporaries were used to staff once or twice a year efforts such as the mail work associated with special promotions. Other firms used temporaries to fill in for regular workers who were on vacation. Sometimes employees who had reached the mandatory retirement age of their employer company were transferred to a temporary help agency and then hired through the agency by their original employers so that they could continue to work while technically not violating the retirement rules.

The conservative business climate and the inflationary pressure in 1974 had provided a particularly good opportunity for a more widespread and more sophisticated use of temporary help. Instead of maintaining personnel at the levels needed for times of maximum or near-maximum work load, companies whose work loads varied over the year instead were beginning to maintain their permanent staffs at lower levels, nearer the minimum required levels, and to fill in during peak times with temporary help. Such temporary workers generally cost the customer companies more than would their own permanent workers on a per hour basis, but the temporaries were

---

nevertheless useful because they could be hired (and hence paid) for only the hours they worked. The customer's own permanent help, on the other hand, had to be paid both wages and fringes during both the times when they were badly needed and the times when they were largely superfluous. The *total* cost of the temporaries turned out to be lower because the temporaries were not paid when they were not needed.

Another factor aiding the growth of the temporary work industry was the fact that work weeks in many industries were being shortened at the same time that the hours of stores and banks were being extended. Part-time and sometimes temporary help was used to provide staffing for the stores and banks over their extended working days.

Competition among temporary help firms was based primarily on the quality of the workers and the ability of the agencies to respond to customer needs. Most of the agencies charged comparable rates and so price competition was not important.

In 1974 the industry had been growing at more than 20 percent a year and its firms were finding it more difficult to find high quality employees. Manpower's V.P. for marketing was quoted in *Business Week* (August 3, 1974) as saying that past marketing efforts had been concentrated on generating job orders; the current problem was to build up Manpower's pool of workers. The industry was spending more effort on recruiting and training its employees and was also working to reduce its extremely high turnover rates (75 percent each year for Manpower, with many employees working only a few months) and to establish closer ties with its customer firms.

Tempo, Inc.

Tempo operated twelve different offices scattered throughout the New York-New Jersey metropolitan area. The company prided itself on (and advertised strongly) its high quality personnel and its ability to fill many customer requests for help on extremely short notice—often within a matter of hours. Each of the twelve offices maintained a call list of workers in each of the twenty-five diverse fields in which the company claimed competence. These areas included secretarial work, typing, outdoor maintenance, janitorial work, electrical wiring, bookkeeping, drafting, driving and moving. Normally each office would receive most of the requests for workers at least one day early, although some of the requests came in at the last minute. The company was not always able to meet last minute requests for workers but, especially if the requests came from regular customers, the managers did try to provide the requested help. For orders for help placed at least a day early, the managers of the individual offices had orders to meet the demands, even if doing so involved unusual effort; for example, if there were an unusually high demand for outdoor maintenance workers, one office might exhaust its own call list in this area and might have to try to call up workers from other offices' lists.

De Rosa had established a system under which the work orders were reported from the individual offices to his office so that he could examine them as they came in. He also kept the demand figures for each office for each category of worker for the past several weeks to use in his forecasting.

With this information, he tried to anticipate the demand figures a full week in advance so that the individual offices could have early warning of abnormally high or low demand levels. In addition, he knew that the early demand estimates were important to his managers in maintaining the particularly high quality work force which was extremely important for Tempo's business. Many of the workers on Tempo's lists were particularly good workers who, for one reason or another, chose to work part time and, often, required advance warning so that they could make arrangements to work on any given day. Many of the other temporary help firms in the metropolitan area refused to hire such people because managing them required extra effort, but De Rosa's policy was to encourage such arrangements if the workers were particularly good. His theory was that they would be likely to remain with Tempo for much longer than was common in the industry, simply because the company was willing to arrange for their needs. He saw the policy as a way of making Tempo's work force significantly better in quality than were those of some of the competitors.

Tempo had a policy for all of its workers that they would be paid in full for every day for which they were called to work, even if a job did not materialize for them on some days. Thus, the company could not afford to call up enough workers to be certain to meet all of the last minute requests which came in. On the other hand, De Rosa did ask the office managers to call in a few workers for filling such requests.

De Rosa felt that the business benefited in several ways from the demand forecasts he prepared. The forecasts gave the branch managers advance warning of their labor needs so that they could call up appropriate numbers of workers; often a manager used the forecasts to call up workers before firm orders for those individuals had been received. In some cases the early warning allowed managers to call on workers who could work only on advance notice. In other cases, a manager was warned by the forecasts of an impending particularly heavy demand in time to be able to ask for names from the lists of other branch offices to fill the demand. De Rosa believed that without the forecasts his managers would have been reluctant to call up large numbers of workers to meet any anticipated heavy load of last minute requests for workers; he feared that without forecasts the managers would not have wanted to go out on a limb before substantial numbers of firm orders were received. With the forecasts, on the other hand, De Rosa had himself taken responsibility for such orders and his managers were far less reluctant to plan in anticipation of demand.

The Forecasting Problem

As a first step in setting up a forecasting system, De Rosa sat down with a consultant in the field to discuss the important characteristics of his business which any worthwhile system would have to consider. He explained:

I do my planning in half-day time periods. Full-day periods just aren't fine enough and I've never had the time to consider more than two periods per day. Actually, though, I really don't think more than two slots per day would make sense.

It's essential to keep track of the figures for the separate offices rather than to try to guess at total figures for the business. The whole pattern of demand at the office near Wall Street is fundamentally different from the one in Long Island City and also different from the various Jersey offices. The offices have different busy days, different patterns of demand for the various categories of workers—I guess I'd just call them basically different.

I have to keep the figures for the 25 different worker categories separate, too. In fact, if I had the opportunity, I'd really like to break the categories down more finely than I have in the past. I think it would help to match workers to jobs more effectively. Anyhow, the categories behave differently, in terms of demand. Some are higher at one time of the year, others higher at other times. Also, the pattern of use of the various categories over the year isn't the same at all 12 of our offices.

There are real differences in the demand pattern over the course of an individual week, too. Demand is particularly high on Mondays, for example, and there is often a rush of last minute orders at the end of the week as our customers try to finish one job or another. I don't think that the pattern within a week depends on the time of the year for any of our offices, but I'm pretty sure that the patterns at the different offices are different.

There's another set of problems which complicate the forecasting process. They're what I call special events—a bad snowstorm which raises the demand for outdoor maintenance help, for example. I can predict some of these special events (conventions, for example) but not others. And after one of those things, it's never quite clear to me how to use the demand figures which were affected by a special event.

There are, as I see it, two main sources for information for my forecasting. One is the demand information from the past few weeks. Unfortunately, I haven't kept good demand information over the years, but I do always have reasonable information from the past month or so and I use that information, together with any hunches I have based on the time of year, or special events or something, to come up with a preliminary set of demand figures a full week in advance. I use those figures to give the managers a really early indication of what to expect a week later.

There's a second set of numbers which I've decided should be used separately from the demand numbers. Those are the actual work orders as they come in. I know, for example, that work orders for a given day straggle in over the week or maybe two weeks preceding. If I see an unusually high number of orders for 5 days from now, I can do some work to try to find out whether something unusual is happening and has to be prepared for or whether there's just a fluke in the timing. I'm pretty certain that I want the forecasts prepared from the past demand kept separate from the forecasts prepared from the early orders because I wouldn't want to have to look at a single high figure, say, and try to decide which of the two factors (past demand or early orders) made it high. Also, I'd like the computer system to generate the figures based on past demand automatically. Maybe it should consider the early orders and also check whether those orders look unusual. It could send out a warning only if something strange is happening which needs my attention.

I've been assured that there is computer time available for doing some forecasting. We'll probably need to buy some extra storage space of one type

or another for the data. I'm anxious to keep the costs of the computer instal-
lation down, but I do think some kind of automated forecasting would be
worthwhile.

Assignment

Design, in some detail, a forecasting system using the past demand data. In particular, how would you consider the differences among offices and work categories? What would you do about special events? How might you set up a separate procedure for using the early order information? (For each of the two procedures, consider not only how the procedure would operate when fully implemented, but also what data would have to be collected to make such full implementation possible and how the procedures could be modified if necessary for use during the implementation stage.)

4. Gruner and Jahr AG & Co.—Integrating Data Requirements, Forecasting System Design and Planning Needs[4]

    In early 1973, Mr. Gustav Becker, head of planning and corporate development at Gruner & Jahr, was concerned with improving the company's profit performance through better matching production quantities with sales demand. Although the problem was certainly not new to either the company or the industry, Gustav felt that some of the things he had recently learned about forecasting methods and computer models might enable him to make substantial improvements in the existing procedures. As a starting point, Gustav wanted to look at the problem in the context of the company's most important magazine: *Der Stern*, a weekly magazine comparable to *Life*.

    The basic difficulty the company faced in planning production for this magazine was that only about 35 percent of the copies produced for each issue were sold through subscription. The remaining 65 percent reached the final consumer through thousands of retailers who were served by a few hundred independently owned wholesalers. Since both retailers and wholesalers could return unsold copies of any issue to the publisher for full credit and since there was clearly a cost associated with being out of stock when the final customer desired a specific issue, the problem Gustav faced was setting up a system that would forecast demand as accurately as possible and then trade off the costs of overstocking against those of understocking in coming up with the most desirable production and shipping schedule for each issue.

German Magazine Industry

The demand for magazines in the Federal Republic of Germany (West Germany) in the early seventies was in a period of general stagnation. While there was always some shifting of market positions among the major magazines, the total demand for magazines in the country did not seem to be changing very rapidly. There were about 50 magazines in Germany that had

---

[4]This case is based on a consulting project conducted by Mr. Wallace I. Stimpson and Mr. Edwin G. B. Terry of Applied Decision Systems, Inc., 33 Hayden Ave., Lexington, Mass. 02173. Copyright © 1973 by the President and Fellows of Harvard College. Used with permission.

sales in excess of 100,000 copies per issue with the largest having sales of 3.5 million copies per issue.

The most important categories of magazines in Germany were:

a. TV magazines,
b. topical illustrated magazines for the general public,
c. yellow press, and
d. women's magazines.

Four publishing houses whose aggregate sales accounted for 65 percent of the magazines sold (through 30 major titles) were the dominant factors in the German market. Gruner & Jahr ranked third in this group, with 12 percent of the country's total sold circulation. (Total sold circulation included both subscription sales and retail newsstand sales.)

In most instances, publishers obtained only 10–20 percent of their sold circulation through subscriptions, with the remainder coming from sales at retail outlets. The thousands of magazine retailers were served by a relatively small number of wholesalers. Both the wholesalers and the retailers were independent of the publishers and it was the publisher who assumed all of the risks associated with unsold copies. Thus, the motivation for accurate forecasting and ordering for individual wholesalers and retailers lay mainly with the publisher.

The Economics of Magazine Publishing

Like most German magazines, the titles published by Gruner & Jahr depended heavily on advertising for a major part of their revenues. In fact, the individual costs of production and of distribution for each issue clearly exceeded the revenue the publisher received from sale of that issue to the final customer. Thus it was necessary for the publisher to sell substantial amounts of advertising space in each issue, in order to make the magazine profitable. The sale of this advertising was generally handled through the company's direct sales force of four people who contacted the major advertising agencies in the country on a regular basis. This sales force also arranged individual contracts with a few of the larger advertisers. The price that could be charged for an advertising page depended on many factors, including the percentage of advertising in the magazine, the sold circulation (both retail and subscription sales), the quality of the magazine, the audience being reached, and the number of colors used in the ad.

Due to the high fixed costs associated with the editorial work and the production setup required for each issue, publishers were continually seeking to increase their sold circulation. One way of doing this was to increase the level of service by supplying retailers with additional copies and thus reducing the number of stockouts. This, in turn, resulted in a substantial number of unsold copies that were returned to the publisher. Gruner & Jahr was typical of the industry, having experienced about a 15–18 percent return rate over the past year for their weekly, *Der Stern*. This meant that for every five copies sold, on the average, one copy would remain unsold. (Gustav mentioned that top management of the company considered these returns "over-production," whereas he considered them a mixture of both over-production and improper allocation to individual sales outlets.) In absolute figures per year, this meant that Gruner & Jahr was printing and distributing (under six different titles) 122 million copies per year and that about 20 million of these were being returned unsold. The direct costs associated with these returns (variable production and distribution costs) amounted to DM 22 million annually.[5]

Distribution Through Wholesalers and Retailers

While the cost of these returns made unsold copies a major management concern, the fact that circulation of *Der Stern* was through 180 wholesalers, each with a delivery volume of between 1,000 and 50,000 copies per issue, made it an extremely difficult problem to deal with. It was further compounded in that these major distributors supplied magazines to a total of 60,000 retailers. The wholesalers held exclusive regional monopolies and thus distributed magazines, newspapers and newsprint novels of all publishers to retail outlets in a particular geographical region. The typical wholesaler would have a line that would include about 800 titles, although the 30 magazines published by the four leading companies in the German publishing industry would account for just over half of the wholesaler's volume.

It was the job of the wholesaler to deliver the quantity that had been arranged between him and the publisher at the right time (for each issue there was a certain "first-sales" day), in the right quantity and to the right place. For his services, Gruner & Jahr paid the wholesaler 16 percent of the retail selling price for each copy actually sold. Although there were certain norms in the industry concerning the terms of agreement between the wholesaler and the publisher, there was still considerable flexibility on the part of the publisher to set up individualized agreements wherever advantageous, as long as the wholesaler continued to receive his basic commission of 16 percent. In the past, Gruner & Jahr had not done much in the way of special agreements, but was aware that other publishers had done so with some success.

In general, German publishers were well satisfied with the physical distribution achieved by the industry wholesalers. Thanks to the transport and distribution organization of the wholesale trade, a publisher could deliver magazines to distributors in the early morning and have them placed in 60,000 retail outlets by the end of the day. However, German publishers were generally dissatisfied with the allocation of copies to individual retail outlets. Frequently, a substantial number of retailers would be sold out on a particular issue, while an equally large number of retailers would be over-stocked.

At the retail level, there were actually 80,000 individual sales outlets but only three-fourths of those handled *Der Stern*. This meant that there was roughly one retail outlet handling this magazine for every 1,000 inhabitants in Germany. Of these outlets, 60 percent were independent sole proprietors. The remaining 40 percent belonged to chains, such as food stores. For 90 percent of the retail outlets, magazine sales represented less than

---

[5]After the dollar devaluation in early 1973, the Deutsch Mark had a value of about $.35 in U.S. currency (i.e., three Marks to the dollar).

DM 2000 per month. Since the retailer was paid 20 percent of the retail price for each copy sold, the gross earnings from magazine sales for all but 10 percent of these outlets was less than DM 400 per month.

In 50 percent of these retail outlets, food items represented the major category of merchandise in terms of sales volume. In another 16 percent of the outlets, tobacco was the major sales item and in only 7 percent of these retail outlets were published products the major sales category. In terms of space utilized by the magazine line, in 75 percent of the outlets, magazines accounted for less than 10 percent of the floor space on which merchandise was displayed.

The typical sales outlet handling Gruner & Jahr publications would sell 15 copies of each issue of *Der Stern* (weekly) while returning 3 copies unsold. Because retailers as well as wholesalers had the right to return unsold copies, most retailers did not avail themselves of the possibility of continuously changing and adjusting the number of copies delivered to them. Rather, determination of the quantities to be delivered to each retailer was left in the hands of the wholesaler. (This was a common practice throughout the industry.)

Unsold Returns

In early 1973, Gustav Becker was particularly concerned with the number of unsold copies being returned. After some preliminary analysis, he had determined that returns were due to three causes:

1. Individual customers (readers) did not buy a copy of every issue.
2. Individual customers did not always buy from the same retail outlet.
3. Technical returns (damaged or soiled copies).

Gustav had determined that only 30 or 40 percent of the nonsubscription customers of Gruner & Jahr would buy a copy of every issue of a magazine. However, because of the large number of individual customers, each buying different issues, the fluctuations in total demand for each issue were not as great as would otherwise be the case. For the magazine *Der Stern*, Gustav had gathered the data in Table 11-7, which gave an indication of the range of fluctuations in total demand over the past 2 years. Gustav attributed these fluctuations in total demand to (a) trends in general demand and seasonal factors (magazine sales typically declined from January through May, increased from June through October and then dropped off again in December), (b) differences in individual issues such as cover photo, special features and total pages, (c) market factors (weather, political situation, holidays, etc.), and (d) advertising and promotion.

The fact that customers did not always buy the same magazine from a specific retail outlet was a particularly aggravating reason for unsold returns. Because of the high density of retail outlets in a given area, the copies sold through individual retail outlets could vary considerably from week to week, even though the national demand and the copies sold by individual wholesalers remained relatively constant. (Table 11-8 indicates the magnitude of these demand fluctuations at individual retail outlets.) To allow for these fluctuations, most wholesalers planned deliveries to each of their re-

TABLE 11-7   GRUNER AND JAHR—WEEKLY PRODUCTION AND SALES
OF *DER STERN* (1971–1972) (ALL FIGURES IN 1000's)

| | | | Representative Wholesalers | | | |
| | | | Wholesaler A | | Wholesaler B | |
Week	Delivery to Wholesalers	Sales of Wholesalers	Delivery	Sales	Delivery	Sales
1/71	1,247	1,025	11.600	9.318	76.850	65.480
2/71	1,239	1,031	11.600	9.867	76.850	66.875
3/71	1,230	1,062	11.680	10.161	76.850	68.090
4/71	1,226	1,040	11.705	9.896	76.852	67.377
5/71	1,242	1,044	11.700	9.883	77.140	67.235
6/71	1,239	1,065	12.000	10.431	77.350	68.250
7/71	1,240	1,055	12.000	10.406	77.350	66.885
8/71	1,239	976	12.000	9.246	77.350	62.965
9/71	1,246	975	12.000	9.218	77.550	64.194
10/71	1,244	974	12.000	9.111	77.350	63.335
11/71	1,232	967	11.500	9.101	77.350	62.705
12/71	1,231	969	11.500	9.184	77.350	61.449
13/71	1,220	947	11.000	8.609	76.350	59.711
14/71	1,203	971	10.700	8.975	75.350	62.685
15/71	1,199	888	10.700	8.078	74.050	57.780
16/71	1,184	976	10.700	9.162	72.560	62.462
17/71	1,171	928	10.700	8.782	72.335	61.795
18/71	1,163	903	10.700	8.399	71.000	59.900
19/71	1,153	920	10.595	8.734	71.001	59.541
20/71	1,142	884	10.900	8.347	71.001	58.041
21/71	1,144	943	10.706	9.036	70.750	60.870
22/71	1,139	950	10.400	8.566	69.750	63.810
23/71	1,139	949	10.400	8.793	69.750	62.225
24/71	1,125	911	10.100	8.452	68.750	58.485
25/71	1,126	900	10.010	7.984	68.500	59.000
26/71	1,127	945	10.000	8.697	68.380	59.545
27/71	1,130	924	10.102	8.704	68.542	59.618
28/71	1,135	973	10.000	9.044	68.750	61.230
29/71	1,131	975	10.200	8.822	68.000	60.988
30/71	1,113	970	10.000	8.654	67.000	58.725
31/71	1,123	970	10.200	8.651	67.150	58.342
32/71	1,127	988	10.400	9.078	67.420	60.390
33/71	1,154	1,093	10.400	9.494	67.990	65.108
34/71	1,152	1,011	10.400	9.233	68.730	61.234
35/71	1,169	1,020	10.800	9.375	70.410	62.358
36/71	1,202	1,006	11.300	9.190	72.700	63.199
37/71	1,212	995	11.600	9.015	74.500	60.787

TABLE 11-7 GRUNER AND JAHR—WEEKLY PRODUCTION AND SALES
OF *DER STERN* (1971–1972) (ALL FIGURES IN1000's)
(*Continued*)

| Week | Delivery to Wholesalers | Sales of Wholesalers | Representative Wholesalers | | | |
| | | | Wholesaler A | | Wholesaler B | |
			Delivery	Sales	Delivery	Sales
38/71	1,225	995	11.600	9.276	75.500	63.499
39/71	1,229	990	11.600	9.336	75.500	63.048
40/71	1,226	995	11.600	9.661	76.000	63.518
41/71	1,208	1,005	11.600	9.739	75.000	64.657
42/71	1,201	1,051	11.200	10.172	75.200	68.126
43/71	1,200	1,106	11.575	10.982	75.070	72.254
44/71	1,218	1,040	12.200	10.546	75.915	68.734
45/71	1,233	1,057	12.200	10.587	76.215	69.733
46/71	1,246	1,089	12.600	11.333	77.455	71.854
47/71	1,248	1,059	12.675	11.161	78.595	69.673
48/71	1,252	1,076	12.800	11.327	79.000	71.305
49/71	1,268	1,103	13.000	11.530	79.640	71.876
50/71	1,274	1,118	13.300	11.805	79.500	73.432
51/71	1,275	1,141	13.600	12.249	79.675	73.954
52/71	1,278	1,186	13.660	12.891	79.811	77.696
2/72	1,289	1,196	13.000	12.486	82.020	77.455
3/72	1,298	1,194	13.770	12.374	81.650	75.190
4/72	1,319	1,201	14.630	12.010	82.620	77.265
5/72	1,353	1,142	14.800	11.948	84.650	72.260
6/72	1,375	1,200	14.800	12.576	86.000	77.430
7/72	1,134	1,079	14.550	11.321	85.700	69.619
8/72	1,355	1,143	14.550	12.008	85.705	72.199
9/72	1,346	1,113	14.400	11.424	85.200	70.104
10/72	1,347	1,178	14.400	12.307	85.378	74.728
11/72	1,328	1,089	14.000	11.281	85.200	68.842
12/72	1,315	1,122	13.600	11.742	82.440	72.560
13/72	1,309	1,022	13.800	10.277	82.200	64.872
14/72	1,304	1,097	13.400	11.111	79.000	70.475
15/72	1,299	1,090	13.800	11.219	79.000	67.670
16/72	1,295	1,086	12.000	11.007	78.000	67.850
17/72	1,284	1,041	13.000	10.858	76.000	66.588
18/72	1,299	1,045	13.400	10.909	76.000	64.049
19/72	1,304	955	13.400	9.143	75.003	62.683
20/72	1,299	985	13.400	9.842	75.000	61.040
21/72	1,293	1,025	13.000	10.288	74.500	62.908
22/72	1,288	1,000	13.000	10.056	73.700	61.495
23/72	1,278	928	13.000	8.425	73.500	60.690

TABLE 11-7 GRUNER AND JAHR—WEEKLY PRODUCTION AND SALES OF *DER STERN* (1971–1972) (ALL FIGURES IN 1000's) (*Continued*)

Week	Delivery to Wholesalers	Sales of Wholesalers	Representative Wholesalers			
			Wholesaler A		Wholesaler B	
			Delivery	Sales	Delivery	Sales
24/72	1,245	985	12.400	9.620	72.400	61.745
25/72	1,229	960	12.000	9.185	72.200	62.775
26/72	1,224	977	11.600	9.495	71.250	60.000
27/72	1,222	1,018	11.400	9.421	71.000	62.390
28/72	1,207	1,012	11.000	9.717	71.000	61.670
29/72	1,212	1,037	11.000	9.925	70.500	61.847
30/72	1,200	1,019	11.000	9.628	69.500	58.652
31/72	1,181	1,011	11.000	9.354	69.500	58.655
32/72	1,182	991	11.000	9.072	69.800	58.750
33/72	1,187	1,003	11.000	9.083	69.890	58.545
34/72	1,195	1,013	11.000	9.240	70.300	60.275
35/72	1,196	1,023	11.500	9.244	71.200	62.150
36/72	1,208	1,005	11.500	9.281	71.695	61.720
37/72	1,214	1,019	11.500	9.548	72.500	61.560
38/72	1,234	1,075	11.500	10.267	73.500	61.595
39/72	1,218	1,027	11.500	9.858	73.500	62.540
40/72	1,220	1,030	11.500	9.778	73.008	63.777
41/72	1,224	1,009	11.800	9.765	73.002	62.872
42/72	1,224	1,026	11.800	10.282	72.504	64.344
43/72	1,225	1,025	11.800	10.309	72.504	65.020
44/72	1,223	1,031	11.950	10.266	72.510	64.385
45/72	1,230	1,029	12.000	10.433	72.750	64.370
46/72	1,219	1,037	12.000	10.381	73.001	65.392
47/72	1,191	976	11.700	9.883	71.501	64.067
48/72	1,191	956	11.700	9.539	71.180	60.974
49/72	1,210	924	12.200	9.573	73.000	59.040
50/72	1,197	1,006	12.000	10.608	72.000	63.816
51/72	1,193	987	12.000	10.320	72.015	62.174
52/72	1,156	918	11.500	9.516	70.000	57.239
53/72	1,160	968	11.500	9.715	70.000	57.230

tailers on the basis of average sales by that retailer for recent issues plus an additional complement of copies. The size of the complement of copies depended on the magazine sales volume handled by that retailer.

A final cause of unsold returns was due to technical reasons. Included here were copies used by the owner of the retail outlet, copies damaged in

TABLE 11-8   GRUNER AND JAHR DELIVERY AND SALES
FOR TYPICAL RETAILERS

	Issue 30		Issue 31		Issue 32	
	Delivery	Sales	Delivery	Sales	Delivery	Sales
Retailer A	7	4	7	5	7	5
Retailer B	10	7	10	9	10	4
Retailer C	10	10	10	3	10	7
Retailer D	9	7	6	2	6	6
Retailer E	8	5	8	7	8	3
Retailer F	19	13	19	19	19	19
Retailer G	3	2	3	3	33	2
Retailer H	18	14	18	18	18	17
Totals For Wholesaler	20,300	16,395	19,300	16,496	19,300	16,290

production or shipment, and soiled display copies. This category was generally only a small portion of total returns.

Planning Production and Delivery Quantities
After gathering historical data on production, shipment and sales quantities, Gustav turned to an examination of the current procedure used at Gruner & Jahr to determine production and delivery plans. Although a number of staff people in the company ascribed considerable sophistication to decision making in this area, most of top management and the line people saw it as a rather straightforward matter. In the latter group the consensus was that a four-step procedure was involved in planning each issue.

1. *Preparation of a forecast of total demand.* This gave a single number corresponding to the expected number of copies that would be demanded.
2. *Setting production at the forecast value of demand plus 15–20 percent.* This reflected management's past experience that around 16 percent unsold returns provided a reasonable level of service at the retail level.
3. *Allocating the total production by first meeting subscription requirements and then dividing the remaining copies among the wholesalers.* The allocation to each wholesaler was based largely on the *percentage* of wholesale distributed copies that had gone to that wholesaler for each of the last several issues. Occasionally, this was modified slightly if for the recent series of issues the number of unsold returns for that wholesaler had been unusually small or unusually large.

4. *The wholesaler would then distribute the copies he received to
    those retailers in his service area, as he thought most appropriate.*
    Management at Gruner & Jahr believed that most wholesalers
    made their allocation to each retailer based on the percentage of
    each issue generally handled by that retailer. However, Gustav's
    examination of recent data indicated that a wholesaler would
    generally react very quickly to a significant number of unsold
    returns from a given retail outlet. As a result, the number of
    copies of each issue going to a single retailer was likely to fluc-
    tuate widely over a period of a few months.

One of the things that Gustav had become aware of during his preliminary analysis of the unsold returns problem was that the 16 percent
figure used as a norm in decision making was not based on any kind of
economic analysis. Rather it had simply become an accepted standard for
unsold returns based on habit and tradition of the past few years.

Pursuing his study of the existing procedure for determining total
production and its allocation, Gustav had learned from the corporate marketing staff that the forecast of total demand for each issue of DER STERN
was based largely on subjective estimates. One week prior to the start of
each production run, the managing editor, the marketing director and a
couple of key staff people would meet and review the production quantities,
wholesale deliveries and unsold returns for the past several issues. After
discussing the reasons for possible unexpected results on recent issues, they
would consider those factors that they felt would be important determinants
of demand for the coming issue. These factors would include such things as
characteristics of the next issue, possible seasonal effects, planned advertising expenditures and holiday effects. Finally, after much discussion they
would arrive at a single estimate of total demand for the coming issue. To
this figure, 15–20 percent would be added to represent planned returns, and
this total quantity would be communicated to the production manager as the
amount to be produced.

It was not until two days before the production run that detailed plans
were made on the quantities to be shipped to each wholesaler. This task was
handled by one of the staff people in distribution and shipping. This person
would start with a set of basic percentage figures which indicated what fraction of total wholesaler shipments had been sent to each of the 180 wholesalers on the previous issue. He would then use data on the four most recent
issues to determine which wholesalers had "excessive" or "insufficient" unsold returns. Although the actual criteria used to identify "excessive" and
"insufficient" had never been stated explicitly, it was clear that "excessive"
unsold returns was a much more frequent occurrence than "insufficient"
returns. Typically only three or four wholesalers were identified as falling
into one of these two categories during the planning cycle for a single issue.
For these three or four, an adjustment would be made in the percentage of
wholesale distributed copies each was to receive. The amount of the adjustment was based on the staff person's experience in doing that kind of thing.

Although Gustav had hoped to identify the procedure(s) most commonly used by individual wholesalers in allocating copies to their retailers,
contact with half a dozen of these wholesalers had led him to believe that

each used a different method. He had also concluded that overall these procedures tended to be very unsystematic and often over-reacted to variations in unsold returns from individual retailers.

Assignment

Having become familiar with the procedures for planning allocating production, Gustav was more convinced than ever that substantial improvements could be made. Some of the areas that he thought might be particularly fruitful to investigate included:

1. Determination of the most appropriate level of planned returns. (Was it really 16 percent?)
2. Specification of the data that should be collected, so that in the future substantial improvement could be made in the planning and forecasting system.
3. Application of systematic techniques for forecasting total demand, allocation to wholesalers, and allocation to retailers.
4. Automation of a complete procedure for not only preparing forecasts but determining production quantity and delivery schedules in detail.

Although he thought it best to proceed by working on one of the company's most important magazines—the weekly *Der Stern*—he hoped that as he progressed, he would be able to apply his findings to all six of the firm's magazines.

12/PREDICTING THE CYCLE

12/1 Introduction

So far in this book we have described a full range of quantitative forecasting methods: from the simplest exponential smoothing techniques to complex econometrics and multivariable ARIMA techniques. Unfortunately, the realities of most forecasting tasks are such that technical knowledge of available quantitative methods seldom solves 100 percent of the problem. Additionally, there are many forecasting situations (see Makridakis and Wheelwright, 1982, Part 3) that cannot be dealt with as a straightforward application of such methods. Predicting the economic cycle is one of the most difficult of these forecasting challenges. The purpose of this chapter is to describe the difficulties in predicting cyclical turns and to outline available approaches to deal with such difficulties.

Economic activity generally exhibits a longer-term cyclical pattern called the *business cycle* (periods of expansion followed by periods of contraction). A noted economist, Schumpeter (1939), has claimed that there are cycles of 1 to 10 years' duration within longer cycles of about thirty years' duration. Prediction of cyclical changes is extremely critical to many organizations but is generally the component of time series that is hardest to predict accurately (see Chapter 4). This poor accuracy is due to the length and intensity of cycles, which vary radically from one cycle to the next (see, for example, Table 12-5), from one industry to another, and even for companies in the same industry.

The effect of cycles on forecasting depends upon the length and intensity of the specific cycle. However, one thing that is very clear is that forecasting accuracy deteriorates rapidly during periods of cyclical changes (see Eckstein, 1978). Some of the evidence on the behavior of macroeconomic forecasts during such cyclical swings as reported by McNees (1979), in an article entitled "Lessons from the Track Record of Macroeconomic Forecasts in the 1970's," is summarized in Table 12-1. The conclusions are straightforward: forecasts made for periods exhibiting little or no cyclical pattern have been relatively accurate; those made for periods of recession or expansion have not.

To illustrate further the importance and influence of the cycle on forecasting accuracy with micro data, the monthly sales of writing paper in France of Table 9-2 (these data extend through December of 1973) and the Box-Jenkins model described in Section 9/3/5 can be used to prepare a forecast for the twelve months of 1973.

The year 1973 was fairly normal for the French economy. There was a minor slowdown in the rate of growth in September and October, but in November the economy resumed its normal growth. Table 12-2 shows the forecasts obtained using Box-Jenkins for up to twelve months ahead. These forecasts were found using 120 data points (up through December 1972). Since the actual values for 1973 are known, a comparison can be made of

TABLE 12-1   THE IMPACT OF BUSINESS CYCLES ON THE ACCURACY
OF MACROECONOMIC FORECASTS

A—Sustained expansion: 1972: II–1973: II

Growth rate of (percent)	Forecasts			Actual
	High	Median	Low	
Real GNP	7.3	6.0	5.7	5.9
GNP deflator	3.7	3.6	3.0	5.2
GNP	10.5	9.8	9.5	11.4
Unemployment rate[a]	5.2	5.1	4.8	4.9

B—The recession: 1974: I–1975: I

Growth rate of (percent)	Forecasts			Actual
	High	Median	Low	
Real GNP	3.8	2.2	1.6	−5.6
GNP deflator	8.5	7.0	6.6	11.6
GNP	11.6	10.3	8.9	5.4
Unemployment rate[a]	6.1	5.9	5.7	8.1

C—The first year of recovery: 1975: I–1976: I

Growth rate of (percent)	Forecasts			Actual
	High	Median	Low	
Real GNP	5.3	4.4	3.4	7.3
GNP deflator	6.8	5.8	5.6	5.4
GNP	11.5	11.4	9.8	13.1
Unemployment rate[a]	8.4	8.3	7.7	7.6

[a]Level in final quarter.

Source: McNees (1979). Used by permission.

TABLE 12-2 ANALYSIS OF THE FORECASTING ERRORS FOR 1973, BASED ON AN ARIMA $(0,1,1)(0,1,1)^{12}$ MODEL FOR THE WRITING PAPER DATA OF TABLE 9-2

Month	Period	Actual Sales	Box-Jenkins Forecast	% Error
Jan.	121	946.23	946.11	.01
Feb.	122	1013.38	996.70	1.65
Mar.	123	1051.97	1029.98	2.09
Apr.	124	1019.86	981.83	3.73
May	125	1007.72	929.50	7.76
June	126	1020.73	1022.41	−.16
July	127	867.26	868.72	−.17
Aug.	128	326.12	423.36	−29.82
Sept.	129	911.28	894.53	1.84
Oct.	130	960.00	978.55	−1.93
Nov.	131	870.00	907.49	−4.31
Dec.	132	915.00	999.30	−9.21
				MAPE = 5.22%

the accuracy of the forecasts. Table 12-2 shows the percentage error and the mean absolute percentage error (MAPE). The MAPE for these twelve forecasts is 5.22 percent.

It is interesting now to see the effect of a change in the cycle on the forecasting accuracy in this situation. If one assumed that only the data up through 1973 are known (132 values), forecasts for the twelve months of 1974 can then be obtained using the Box-Jenkins approach. The results are shown in Table 12-3.

Table 12-3 indicates the model did well up through October of 1974 and then the errors increased substantially. (Through October the MAPE is 5.42 percent.) The forecasting performance deteriorates even more from an accuracy point of view, if the last four months of 1974 and the first two months of 1975 are forecast as shown in Table 12-4. The MAPE is 41.36 percent. In contrast to the 1973 performance and the first eight months of 1974, these are very inaccurate forecasts.

From previous chapters, it will be recalled that formal forecasting methods attempt to separate randomness and pattern and then extrapolate the latter. Thus at the end of 1972 (see Table 12-2) the method simply extrapolates the established pattern of the previous years. As long as the

TABLE 12-3   ANALYSIS OF THE FORECASTING ERRORS FOR 1974,
BASED ON AN ARIMA $(0,1,1)(0,1,1)^{12}$ MODEL FOR THE
WRITING PAPER DATA OF TABLE 9-2

Month	Period	Actual Sales	Box-Jenkins	
			Forecast	% Error
Jan.	133	975.00	961.98	1.33
Feb.	134	1039.59	1020.42	1.84
Mar.	135	1174.84	1054.59	10.24
Apr.	136	973.27	1014.22	−4.21
May	137	1063.44	977.20	8.11
June	138	1110.79	1038.62	6.50
July	139	834.24	884.83	−6.06
Aug.	140	381.42	398.02	−4.35
Sept.	141	965.79	917.51	5.00
Oct.	142	926.18	986.91	−6.56
Nov.	143	724.34	907.86	−25.34
Dec.	144	703.69	981.79	−39.52
				MAPE = 9.92%

TABLE 12-4   ANALYSIS OF THE FORECASTING ERRORS FOR
SEPTEMBER 1974–FEBRUARY 1975, BASED ON AN ARIMA
$(0,1,1)(0,1,1)^{12}$ MODEL FOR THE WRITING PAPER DATA
OF TABLE 9-2

Month	Period	Actual Sales	Box-Jenkins	
			Forecast	% Error
1974				
Sept.	141	965.79	934.09	3.30
Oct.	142	926.18	999.13	−7.90
Nov.	143	724.34	919.27	−26.97
Dec.	144	703.69	993.27	−41.08
1975				
Jan.	145	560.00	1011.12	−80.56
Feb.	146	570.00	1073.53	−88.39
				MAPE = 41.36%

trend-cycle continues to behave as in the past, forecasting usually will be quite accurate. However, at the end of 1973 there is no way for the typical time-series forecasting method to know that there will be a downturn in October, November, and December of 1974. Since such a downturn has not occurred in the past in a consistent manner, a time-series quantitative method cannot predict it. That accounts for the large errors at the end of 1974 and the beginning of 1975 (see Table 12-4) that were found using 140 data points and forecasting up to 6 periods ahead.

Forecasting requires two types of predictions. The first is for the continuation of existing conditions, as shown in Table 12-2. The other involves the prediction of turning points, as shown in Tables 12-3 and 12-4. In the first case, one or more of the quantitative time-series methods described in previous chapters will do well. In such cases, one simply predicts a continuation of the cyclical pattern. However, when the first signs of cyclical changes appear, additional work is required to predict those changes of the cycle. Some of the different approaches that are available to predict such turning points will be discussed in this chapter. Several things should be clear, however: forecasting will be more difficult, errors are likely to be larger, and more time and effort will be required for effecting forecasting than is the case when no cyclical changes are in sight. This is true for both macro and micro data series.

The remainder of this chapter will describe briefly business cycles and their causes and will discuss some of the methods available for predicting fluctuations in the economic cycle. Finally, one method for linking economic cycles to industry and individual company cycles will be discussed. As subjective as those methods are, they can be useful because the stakes are high when an inaccurate prediction is made of the level of economic activity.

12/2 Business Cycles

Business cycles have received attention since the early stages of the Western economic system and probably have been studied more extensively than any other economic phenomenon. The reason for such interest has been the human misery and suffering that business cycles cause when their downswings reach depression magnitudes. Classical economists have accepted the existence of cycles, feeling that they are temporary deviations from equilibrium that can correct themselves without outside interference. The classical economist's viewpoint has been expressed in Say's law, which asserts that supply creates its own demand. In other words, supply and demand are equal and deviations are only temporary.

The classical viewpoint has troubled many, mainly because depressions have appeared often during the last two centuries. The work of Keynes has probably had the most profound effect on government thinking about the causes and cures of inflation and depression cycles. Keynes advocated direct government interference through fiscal and monetary policies in order to maintain the economic equilibrium. Keynes's view has been widely adopted today and many governments actively intervene in the economic arena. It has generally been thought that Keynesian policies have been successful in averting depressions. Until the 1970s it was even believed that, modified as they were, they could avert all serious recessions. Some economists even believed that recessions were a thing of the past (see Beman, 1976). The 1974–75 recession, the most serious since the 1930s, has reopened the question and made both government officials and private citizens realize that business cycles and their effects are here to stay. Attempts to predict the cycle have received renewed attention recently.

Table 12-5 shows the economic cycles in the United States between 1850 and 1981. An examination of the table reveals the following:

1. The length of an expansion in economic activity can vary from 6 to 105 months. Even in the postwar period, which is thought to have been relatively free of major economic upheavals, the duration of expansion varies from 25 to 105 months.
2. The length of a contraction in economic activity has varied from 6 to 65 months.
3. The duration of a full cycle also varies considerably, ranging from 17 to 117 months.

Table 12-5 particularly reveals the difficulty of trying to predict the cycle mechanically, simply by analyzing the behavior of past cycles. As practitioners have long known and academicians have confirmed (see Mitchell, 1951), there may be some features common to all cycles, but at the same time each cycle is unique. It is with this background that one attempts to predict changes in the cycle. There are no quantitative approaches that will guarantee success, since cycles are unique and the length and intensity of each one vary. Subjective methods need therefore to be incorporated in the attempt to predict cyclical fluctuations. Unlike quantitative methods, the success of cyclical predictions depends on many factors often outside the control of the forecasters. Several methods are available that can provide a great deal of information about the state of economic activity and its future direction. These methods will be presented in the remainder of this chapter, and in the next chapter an approach will be described for combining the results of these methods with the subjective feelings of the decision maker to obtain a unique forecast of the cycle. In the final analysis, how-

TABLE 12-5 U.S. BUSINESS CYCLES 1850 THROUGH 1980

Business Cycle			Duration (months) of:		
Trough	Peak	Trough	Expansion	Contraction	Full Cycle
Dec. 1854	June 1857	Dec. 1858	30	18	48
Dec. 1858	Oct. 1860	June 1861	22	8	30
June 1861	Apr. 1865	Dec. 1867	46	32	78
Dec. 1867	June 1869	Dec. 1870	18	18	36
Dec. 1870	Oct. 1873	Mar. 1879	34	65	99
Mar. 1879	Mar. 1882	May 1885	36	38	74
May 1885	Mar. 1887	Apr. 1888	22	13	35
Apr. 1888	July 1890	May 1891	27	10	37
May 1891	Jan. 1893	June 1894	20	17	37
June 1894	Dec. 1895	June 1897	18	18	36
June 1897	June 1899	Dec. 1900	24	18	42
Dec. 1900	Sept. 1902	Aug. 1904	21	23	44
Aug. 1904	May 1907	June 1908	33	13	46
June 1908	Jan. 1910	Jan. 1912	19	24	43
Jan. 1912	Jan. 1913	Dec. 1914	12	23	35
Dec. 1914	Aug. 1918	Mar. 1919	44	7	51
Mar. 1919	Jan. 1920	July 1921	10	18	28
July 1921	May 1923	July 1924	22	14	36
July 1924	Oct. 1926	Nov. 1927	27	13	40
Nov. 1927	Aug. 1929	Mar. 1933	21	43	64
Mar. 1933	May 1937	June 1938	50	13	63
June 1938	Feb. 1945	Oct. 1945	80	8	88

Postwar Cycles

Oct. 1945	Nov. 1948	Oct. 1949	37	11	48
Oct. 1949	July 1953	Aug. 1954	45	13	58
Aug. 1954	July 1957	Apr. 1958	35	9	44
Apr. 1958	May 1960	Feb. 1961	25	9	34
Feb. 1961	Nov. 1969	Nov. 1970	105	12	117
Nov. 1970	Nov. 1973	Feb. 1975	33	15	48
Feb. 1975	Jan. 1980	Aug. 1980	58	6	64
July 1980[a]	Dec. 1980	Nov. 1981	6	11	17

[a]Preliminary estimates updated by the authors.

Source: National Bureau of Economic Research.

ever, business cycles are extremely difficult to predict, as reported by Makridakis (1982).

12/3   Causes of Business Cycles

There are numerous theories as to what causes cycles in economic activity. These theories cite causes ranging from random events, such as a good or bad harvest, to necessary readjustments in the economic system. Those who have studied this topic include Dauten and Valentine (1974, Parts 1 and 2), Evans (1969, Part II), Schumpeter (1939), Mitchell (1913 and 1951), Mass (1976), Forrester (1971), and DeWolf et al. (1978). In spite of the fact that cycles have been studied extensively, there is little agreement as to their real causes and the means of preventing them. For the purposes of this book, it is useful to discuss two possible causes of the business cycle—capital spending and inventory levels—because their influence on forecasting is extremely important.

12/3/1   Capital Spending

Whatever the explanation, business cycles do take place, and government officials as well as private sector managers are aware of their effects on consumer spending. When a slowdown (recession) in the economy is predicted, businesses generally cut back their capital outlays, feeling that consumer spending will be reduced in the near term. If a sufficient number of businessmen take such action, even if a slowdown in consumer spending could have been avoided, a slowdown in economic activity occurs because of a considerable reduction in capital spending that would have otherwise taken place. Thus, a recession can become a self-fulfilling prophecy. Many people believe that the 1974–75 recession was partially caused by the prediction of a depression. World leaders anticipated a depression because of the oil embargo following the 1973 Arab-Israeli war and the fourfold increase in oil prices. This is not to say that the recession was purely the result of its own anticipation, but rather that its intensity might have been much less had it not been advertised so widely. (See Forrester, 1971.)

In a similar manner, booms of economic activity can be intensified by expectations of booms among enough people. The forecaster of business cycles must, therefore, bear in mind that predictions can intensify recessions or booms and this possibility must be taken into account in the preparation of forecasts.

Government policies are generally aimed at stabilizing the economy. When there are indications of boom or bust conditions, governments through fiscal and/or monetary policies attempt to avert these extremes. As more is learned about the intricate balances of the economic system and as more accurate and timely statistics are obtained about it, governments can act promptly to minimize such swings in activity. Such actions must be considered by the forecaster, since even the best predictions can be nullified once government actions have been taken to modify the course of events. This situation creates a dilemma for the forecaster of cyclical changes: are the psychological considerations affecting recessions or booms more or less important than government actions aimed at balancing the economy? That is one reason why the prediction of cyclical change is so difficult.

12/3/2 Level of Inventories

In major world economies there is continuous adjustment of inventory levels among wholesalers and retailers in such a way that there is a rather constant ratio of demand to inventory (see Mack, 1956, and Barksdale and Hilliard, 1975). However, since neither wholesalers nor retailers can forecast cyclical changes with complete accuracy, their inventory levels require frequent adjustment to maintain a ratio with actual demand as well as predicted demand that falls within the limits that management thinks are prudent for it. These adjustments have profound effects on the cycle as well as implications for sales forecasting when the cycle changes.

The impact of inventory and sales adjustments becomes even more profound when several levels of inventories are kept between manufacturers and final consumers. The recession finds the inventories too large at all levels and by the time they are readjusted to reflect actual demand levels, the volume of orders is reduced considerably, intensifying the recession. This pattern can be easily seen in the fact that GNP may fall by 3 to 5 percent, while utilization of production capacity for individual firms may be reduced by as much as 50 percent.

It has been estimated (Barksdale and Hilliard, 1975, pp. 380–82) that it takes an average of five months for firms to realize changes in the cyclical component and react to them by adjusting their inventory levels. That is a long time, and it must be kept in mind while preparing forecasts aimed at predicting the cycle that such adjustments in inventories are a major element in determining the timing of turning points in the cycle. The timing of these adjustments in inventories is difficult to predict, even when one is using anticipatory surveys.

12/4 Anticipatory Surveys

Anticipatory surveys are aimed at collecting information concerning the intentions of consumers or businesses. There are three major types of anticipatory surveys:

1. consumer attitudes and buying plans
2. investment anticipations
3. inventory and sales anticipations

The outcome of these surveys can be used as input to the prediction of the cycle, even though the forecasting accuracy of such surveys is not necessarily better than naive approaches. The forecaster must bear in mind the characteristics and accuracy record of these surveys, each of which is described below.

12/4/1 Consumer Attitudes and Buying Plans

The survey on consumer attitudes and buying plans (CABP) is conducted by the Survey Research Center at the University of Michigan. The survey gathers information on consumer opinions about general economic conditions and consumer buying plans (Day, 1977). Although the forecasting record of CABP has been poor in several instances, their record is better than simply using last year's attitudes or sales data as a prediction for next year. When considered as one of many inputs, the survey can reveal a great deal about anticipated consumer actions.

12/4/2 Investment Anticipations

There are two widely used investment anticipation surveys. One is prepared by the McGraw-Hill Company and is published the first week of November in *Business Week*. The other is conducted by the Office of Business Economics and the Securities and Exchange Commission (OBE-SEC) of the U.S. government. Of the two, the OBE-SEC has historically been the more accurate (Okun, 1962). Its only disadvantage is that it does not appear until March of the year to which it applies. Thus, it is of little value in preparing budgets that must be completed before the end of the previous year. The McGraw-Hill survey is much more timely for such use although not as accurate. However, it can become a useful tool since its predictive power often has been satisfactory in the past (Okun, 1962, p. 221).

12/4/3 Inventory and Sales Anticipations

Besides the investment anticipation survey, the OBE-SEC also conducts inventory and sales anticipation surveys. There is general agreement that the results of the sales anticipation survey provide little help, since those surveyed are not necessarily good forecasters. [It has been shown that sales anticipations are no better than naive models (Okun, 1962, p. 219).] Anticipatory data on inventories have been more accurate and more useful than naive models. They can be used together with the investment and consumers' plans to obtain information about possibly cyclical changes. For additional information on the methods described briefly in this section, see Tobin (1959) and Juster (1964).

12/5 Leading Indicators

Leading indicators are series whose changes in pattern precede those of the specific series forecast. (Some limited use of leading indicators was seen in Chapter 10 in the discussion of multivariate time series.) There is no such thing as a *perfect* leading indicator. If there were, forecasting would be a trivial task that could be done by using only a leading indicator. There are some series that on average lead others, but they do not always do so, nor is the lead time constant. The problems of identifying a leading indicator and determining what deviation from the average lead time is likely make the use of leading series often unreliable. Evans (1969, p. 460) writes about leading indicators as follows: "The series serves as a valuable historical record and sheds light on the causes of past depressions. But as a practical method of forecasting, the leading indicators cannot be used very effectively or accurately."

As a subsequent step in the development of leading indicator approaches, multiple series have been used as leaders instead of a single series. Also, a composite leading indicator constructed by combining individual series has been suggested. These composite leading indicators have several merits, even though they should still be used with caution. By examining several leading indicators, the risks are reduced of missing a cycle or predicting one when none will occur, since some of the leading series will almost always reach a turning point before the actual series does.

McLaughlin (1975) has proposed a variation of leading indices by advocating the construction of a pyramid of leaders and coinciders and then noting the points at which each achieves its low value. This configuration allows one to better see the chances of an upturn. Figure 12-1 (McLaughlin, 1975, p. 158) illustrates the procedure and is explained as follows:

BCD#	Indicator	D	1971 J	F	M	A	M	J	J	A	S	O	N	D	1972 J	F	M	A	M	J	J	A	S	O	N	D
102	Money Supply CHG (M2)		H	$	$	$	$	$	$	$	$	$	$	$	$	$	$	$	$	$	$	$	$	$	$	$
103	Money Supply CHG (M3)		H	$	$	$	$	$	$	$	$	$	$	$	$	$	$	$	$	$	$	$	$	$	$	$
	+Fiscal Policy Index #1					H				$				$				$				$				$
	+MFP #1					H				$				$				$				$				$
85	Money Supply CHG (M1)																									H
39	Credit Delinquency													H	#	#	#	#	#	#	#	#	#	#	#	#
	+Leader: Level Pressure														H	#	#	#	#	#	#	#	#			
	+Leader: Rate of Change																							H	#	
29*	Housing Permits																									H
	+Leader: Rate Pressure																									
28	Housing Starts																									
12*	New Business Starts																									
813	Employment Composite		H - High (Peak)																							
1*	Average Workweek		L - Low (Trough)																							
21	Overtime Hours																									
32	Vendor Performance																									
5*	Unemployment Claims																									
9	Non-Res Buildings																									
	Leaders: Boston Fed																									
2	Hiring Rate																									
3	Layoff Rate																									
37	Materials Inventories																									
	+Brass Industry Orders																									
	+Brass Industry Sales																									
26	Materials Commitments																									
13	New Incorporations																									
14	Bus Failure Liabilities																									H
19*	Stock Market																									
113*	Instalment Debt CHG																									
817	Financial Composite																									
814	Investment Composite																									
8	Construction Contracts																									
245	Business Inventory CHG																									
23*	Materials Prices																									
33	Mortgage Debt CHG																									
112	Bank Loan CHG																									
110	Private Borrowing																									
10*	Plant/Eqt. Contracts																									
24	Capital Goods Orders																									
20	Inventory Value CHG																									
810	Leaders: Trend Adjust																									
811	Leaders: Not Adjusted																									
815	Purchasing Composite																									
816	Profits Composite																									
6*	Durables New Orders																									
11	Capital Appropriations																									
16*	Profits: Current $																									
18	Profits: Constant $																									
31*	Inv. Book Value CHG																									
17*	Price to Labor Cost																									

(a) 50 Leaders

FIGURE 12-1 INDICATOR PYRAMIDS: (a) 50 LEADERS AND (b) 28 COIN-CIDERS (*SOURCE:* McLAUGHLIN, 1975)

```
        1973                    1974                    1975
J F M A M J J A S O N D   J F M A M J J A S O N D   J F M A M J J A S O N D

$ $ $ $ $ $ $ $ $ $ $ $   $ $ $ $ $ $ $ $ $ $ $ Ⓛ   - - -
$ $ $ $ $ $ $ $ $ $ $ $   $ $ $ $ $ $ $ Ⓛ - - -    - - -      Monetary-Fiscal
  $     $     $     $       $     $     Ⓛ     -              -        Policy
  $     $     $     $       $     $     Ⓛ     -              -      Indicators
$ $ $ $ $ $ $ $ $ $ $ $   $ $ $ $ $ $ $ Ⓛ $ $ $ $   Ⓛ - - -

# # # # # # # # # # # #   # # # # # # # # # # # #
# # # # # # # # # # # #   # # # # # # # # # # # Ⓛ   - - -
# # # # # # # # # # # #   # # # # # # # # # # # Ⓛ -  - - -
# # # # # # # # # # # #   # # # # # # # # # # # #   Ⓛ - -
H # # # # # # # # # # #   # # # # # # # # Ⓛ - - -    - - -
H # # # # # # # # # # #   # # # # # # # # # # # Ⓛ   - - -
  H # # # # # # # # # #   # # # # # # # # # # # #   # #
    H # # # # # # # # #   # # # # # # # # # # # #   # #
    H # # # # # # # # #   # # # # # # # # # # # #   # # ⊘
    H # # # # # # # # #   # # # # # # # # # # # #   # # ⊘
      H # # # # # # # #   # # # # # # # # # # # #   # Ⓛ -      Deflated
        H # # # # # #     # # # # # # # # # # # #   # Ⓛ -
        H # # # # #       # # # # # # # # # # # #   # # #    Indicators
        H # # # # #       # # # # # # # # # # # #   Ⓛ - -
          H # #           # # # # # # # # # # # Ⓛ   - - -
          H # #           # # # # # # # # # # # #   # ⊘
          H # #           # # # # # # # # # # # #   # # ⊘
          H #             # # # # # # # # # # # #   Ⓛ - - -
                          H # # # # # # # # # # #   Ⓛ - - -
                            H # # # # # # # # # #   # # #
                              H # # # # # # # #     # #

$ $ $ $ $ $ $ $ $ $ $     $ $ $ $ $ $ $ $ $ $ $     $ $
H $ $ $ $ $ $ $ $ $ $ $   $ $ $ $ $ $ $ $ $ $ $ Ⓛ   - - - -
  H $ $ $ $ $ $ $ $ $ $   $ $ $ $ $ $ $ $ $ $ $ Ⓛ   - - -
  H $ $ $ $ $ $ $ $ $ $   $ $ $ $ $ $ $ $ $ $ $ $   Ⓛ - -
      H $ $ $ $ $ $ $ $   $ $ $ $ $ $ $ $ $ $ $ $   $ $ $
        H $ $ $ $ $ $     $ $ $ $ $ $ $ $ $ $ $ $   $ Ⓛ
                H         $     $     $     $       Ⓛ
                          H $ $ $ $ $ $ $ $         Ⓛ - - -
                          H $ $ $ $ $ $ $ Ⓛ         - -
                          H $ $ $ $ $ $ $ Ⓛ         - - -
                            H     $     $
                              H $ $ $ $ $ $           $ Ⓛ -
                              H $ $ $ $ $ $           $ $ $      Inflated
                              H $ $ $ $ $ $           $ $
                              H $ $ $ $ $ $           Ⓛ - -
                              H $ $ $ $ $ $           $ $ $   Indicators
                                H $ $ $ $ $           $ Ⓛ -
                                H $ $ $ $ $           Ⓛ - -
                                H $ $ $ $ $           $ $ $
                                H     $
                                H     $
                                H     $
                                  H $ $               $ $
                                  H $                 $ $ $
```

Month of Current Cycle ⟶ 1   10   20

BCD#	Indicator	D	1971 J F M A M J J A S O N D	1972 J F M A M J J A S O N D
59	Retail Sales (Deflated)			
46	Help-wanted Index			
41*	Unemployment Rate			
45	Insured Unemployment			
40	Married Males Unemployed			
47*	Industrial Production			
205*	GNP (1958 Dollars)			
825	Coinciders (Deflated)			
42	Employment (Non-ag)			
41*	Number on Payrolls			
48	Man-hours			
119	Federal Funds Rate			
54*	Retail Sales (Current $)			
93	Free Reserves			
114	Treasury Bill Rate			
115	Treasury Bond Yields			
116	Corporate Bond Yields			
96	Unfilled O/R (Durables)			
53	Wages & Salaries			
56*	Mfg/Trade Sales			
820	Coinciders (Current $)			
200*	GNP (Current $)			
97	Backlog: Capital Approp.			
117	Municipal Bond Yields			
58	Wholesale Prices (Mfg)			
57	GNP Final Sales			
55	Wholesale Prices (Commod)			
52*	Personal Income			

(b) 28 Coinciders

FIGURE 12-1 (*Continued*) INDICATOR PYRAMIDS: (a) 50 LEADERS AND
(b) 28 COINCIDERS (*SOURCE: MCLAUGHLIN, 1975*)

Indicator pyramids are particularly useful in identifying business cycles and the month in which a trough or turning point is reached. The data for the various indicators used by McLaughlin are taken from the monthly U.S. government publication, *Business Conditions Digest*. In McLaughlin's approach, 50 indicators that lead the bottoming out of a business cycle are broken into three general categories—those related to monetary/fiscal policy, those described as deflated indicators, and those described as inflated indicators. As shown in Figure 12-1, the indicators within each of these three groupings can be ordered according to the average number of periods lead time associated with each of these indicators over several preceding business cycles. For the current business cycle, those indicators are plotted starting with the month in which they reach their high point (indicated by an H, above) and then going out to the current month with

```
       30                     40                    50                    60

┌─────────────────────────┬─────────────────────────┬─────────────────────────┐
│          1973           │          1974           │          1975           │
│  J F M A M J J A S O N D │  J F M A M J J A S O N D │  J F M A M J J A S O N D │
├─────────────────────────┼─────────────────────────┼─────────────────────────┤
│                         │                         │                         │
│  H # # # # # # # # #     │  # # # # # # # # # # #(L)│  - - -                  │
│      H # # # #           │  # # # # # # # # # # # # │  # # #                  │
│          H # #           │  # # # # # # # # # # # # │  # # #                  │
│          H # #           │  # # # # # # # # # # # # │  # # #                  │
│          H # #           │  # # # # # # # # # # # # │  # # #                  │
│            H #           │  # # # # # # # # # # # # │  # # #        Deflated   │
│            H             │    #   #   #   #        │  #           Indicators  │
│            H #           │  # # # # # # # # # # #   │  # # #                  │
│                         │          H # # # #       │  # # #                  │
│                         │              H # #       │  # # #                  │
│                         │              H # #       │  # # #                  │
│                         │                         │                         │
│                         │      H $ $ $ $ $         │  $ $ $                  │
│                         │      H $ $ (L) -         │  - - -                  │
│                         │      H $ $ $ $           │  $ $ $                  │
│                         │      H $ $ $ $           │  $ $ $                  │
│                         │      H $ $ $ $           │  $ (L) -                │
│                         │        H $ $ $           │  $ (L) -                │
│                         │        H $ $ $           │  $ $ $                  │
│                         │          H $ $           │  $ $ $        Inflated   │
│                         │          H $ $           │  (L) -       Indicators  │
│                         │          H $ $           │  $ $ $                  │
│                         │        H                 │      $                  │
│                         │            H             │                         │
│                         │            H             │  $ (L) -                │
│                         │                         │  H $ $                  │
│                         │                         │  H                      │
│                         │                         │      H                  │
│                         │                         │      H                  │
└─────────────────────────┴─────────────────────────┴─────────────────────────┘
```

those indicators that have reached a low having an L placed in the column for the month in which the low was reached. (Those L's are circled to highlight the general pattern for the indicators.) When a majority of these leading indicators have reached their low point, that indicates the trough or turning point in the recession. While this is clearly not a foolproof approach, it can often give a good indication of what is happening to the business cycle, as suggested by Figure 12-1*a*.

McLaughlin also suggests the use of 28 coincider indicators, which can be handled in a manner analogous to that in which the leading indicators are handled. Since these indicators coincide with the business cycle, rather than leading it, they reach their high points (indicated by an H) some months after most of the leading indicators. Similarly, they reach their lows (indicated by an L) some months after most of the leading indicators. It can be seen that this approach has performed very well, since the smaller values indicate a bottoming out of the 1974–75 recession from as early as the end of 1974. (The actual bottom was July 1975 according to United States government economists.)

12/6   Paired Indices

Paired indices is another method suggested by McLaughlin and Boyle (1968) for predicting cyclical changes. It combines the concept of leading indicators with that of the percentage change in a series. The basis of the method of paired indices can be seen in Figure 12-2, which consists of three graphs, each containing a time series and a leading indicator. Figure 12-2a shows the plot of the time series and its leading indicator for the last twelve periods. This is a plot of the trend-cycle values (or just the cycle values), which are standardized so that they fluctuate around 100. (The standardization is accomplished by dividing all data by the mean, then multiplying the resulting values by 100.) Figure 12-2a is intended as a graphic presentation of the cyclical behavior of the time series and its leader from which leads can be inferred and their length determined. In the case of Figure 12-2a, the indicator series leads the time series by three periods. Figure 12-2b is merely the period-to-period percentage change of the values in Figure 12-2a. This second graph highlights changes in the rate of change. In Figure 12-2a it can be seen that the time series (or its leader) first decreases rapidly in value, then the rate of decrease slows, becomes zero, slowly increases, increases more rapidly, slows down, becomes zero, and so on. This pattern of changes is shown clearly in Figure 12-2b, where it also is seen to lead 12-2a by about two periods. That is, assuming no random-ness—which unfortunately is never the case with real life data—Figure 12-2b leads 12-2a by two periods. The trend-cycle changes in 12-2a therefore can be forecast using Figure 12-2b. Finally, Figure 12-2c shows the ratio of the leading indicator to the time series (heavy line) and the ratio of the percentage change of the leading indicator to the time series. This pattern is called a pressure by McLaughlin and leads both Figure 12-2a and 12-2b—(a) by four periods and (b) by almost two. Although one would not expect such perfect behavior of paired indices in practice as those shown in Figure 12-2, even imperfect relationships provide enough information to be helpful in predicting turning points. Often when the leader is not very good, the percentage changes and the pressures may well lead the actual series. In practice it has been found that one- to three-month leads usually can be inferred so that turning points in the time series can be predicted reason-ably well within the time horizon of one to three months.

Figures 12-3, 12-4, 12-5, and 12-6 show an application of the method of paired indices to a specific situation. This application involves the months

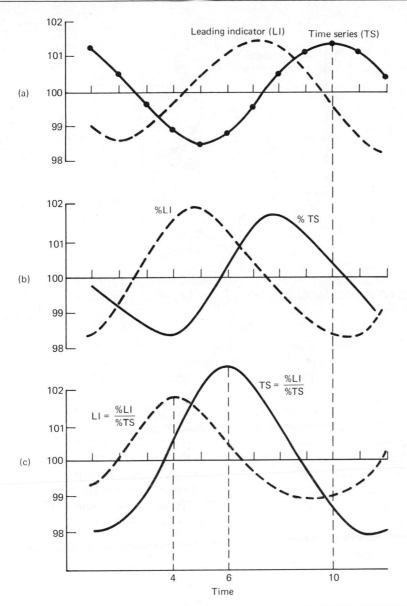

FIGURE 12-2 PAIRED INDICES: (a) INDICES, (b) RATES OF CHANGE, AND (c) PRESSURES

of June, July, August, and September 1975 when a European firm was in the midst of its worst recession in several decades. That firm was operating at 60 percent of capacity and there was a fear among the executives that the worst was yet to come. (In Europe, the 1974–75 recession bottomed

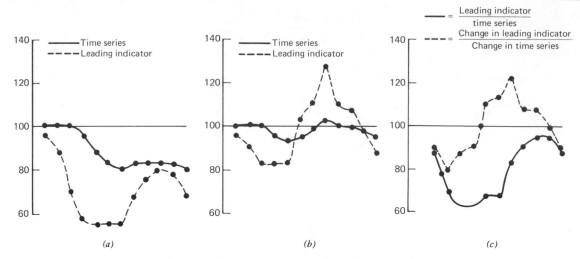

FIGURE 12-3   ENDING MONTH JUNE 1975. (a) TREND CYCLE, (b) PER-
CENTAGE CHANGE IN TREND CYCLE, AND (c) PRES-
SURES

several months later than in the United States.) The time series plotted in
Figures 12-3 through 12-6 is the set of trend-cycle values (see Chapter 4
for an explanation) of Table 9-3, while the leading indicator is sales orders
received by the company.

In June the situation was bleak, as can be seen in Figure 12-3, where
all three measures are pointing down. In July, both the time series and its
leader still point downward as shown in Figure 12-4a. The percentage changes
of the time series and its leader, however, indicate a slowing down in their
descent as shown in Figure 12-4b. Most important, the pressures show a
slight turning point [Figure 12-4c]. August and September confirm this
pattern, indicating a continuing increase in the percentage changes and
pressures, even though the trend-cycle of the shipments and orders is still
decreasing (see Figures 12-5 and 12-6).

It was not until October and November 1975 that the actual trend-
cycle values turned up and verified the evidence of the turn started in July.
Unfortunately, one can never be sure that a turn will in fact develop simply
because it is signaled by the percentage change indices or the pressures.
There are false alarms and sometimes changes take place without warning.
As a whole, however, the method of paired indices can be used quite successfully in conjunction with other evidence to signal impending changes
in the trend-cycle.

Figure 12-5 will be used as an example of how the numbers used to
plot these graphs are obtained. Figure 12-5 refers to August 1975 (period
128 in the data given in Table 9-3. One would therefore use the first 128
points of Table 9-3 in performing the following calculations:

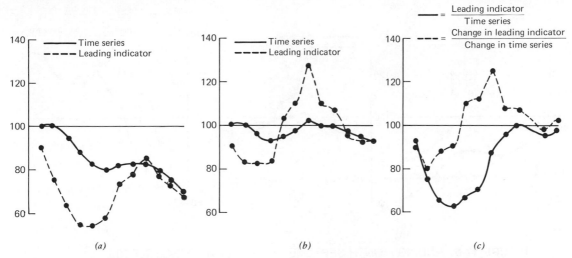

FIGURE 12-4   ENDING MONTH JULY 1975. (a) TREND CYCLE, (b) PER-
CENTAGE CHANGE IN TREND CYCLE, AND (c) PRES-
SURES

1.   Deseasonalize the time series by finding the seasonal indices (see
Chapter 4) of the data, then dividing them into the actual values
of Table 9-4. The seasonal indices are shown in Table 12-6, column 3. Thus, the seasonally adjusted value for August 1975 (period 128) is 1975.97 (1536.5/.778). The value for July (period 127)
is 2711.9 (2169.9/.800), and so on. Table 12-6, column 4, shows
these seasonally adjusted values of the time series.

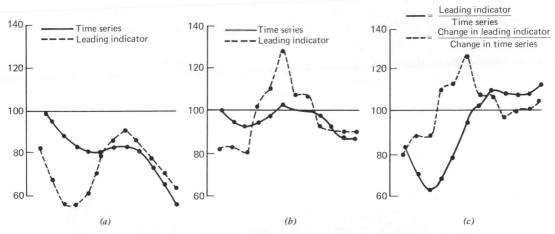

FIGURE 12-5   ENDING MONTH AUGUST 1975. (a) TREND CYCLE, (b) PER-
CENTAGE CHANGE IN TREND CYCLE, AND (c) PRESSURES

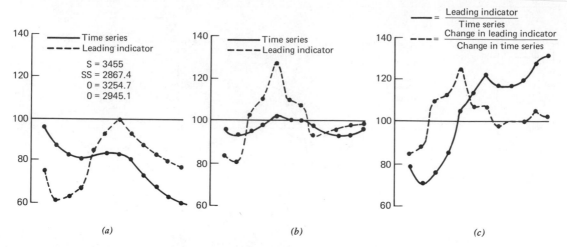

FIGURE 12-6   ENDING MONTH SEPTEMBER 1975. (a) TREND CYCLE, (b) PERCENTAGE CHANGE IN TREND CYCLE, AND (c) PRESSURES

2. Calculate the trend-cycle values by applying some form of moving average to the seasonally adjusted data of column 4. A 3 × 3 moving average (see Section 4/4) has been applied in this case. Other types of moving averages could have been applied, but a centered 3 × 3 MA was used here because it irons out irregular movements in the data while losing only two data points at the beginning and end of the series. The 3 × 3 moving values of the trend-cycle are shown in column 5 of Table 12-5. The last two values of column 5 are obtained by taking a three-point weighted moving average [.3(2813.5) + .4(2711.9) + .3(1976) = 2521.6] and a two-point weighted moving average, respectively, adjusted for trend (see Section 4/4).

3. Standardize the trend-cycle values—by dividing each trend-cycle value by the largest trend-cycle value (3902.1) and multiplying the result by 100 to obtain the values in column 8. These values are those plotted as the heavy line in Figure 12-5*a*.

4. Find the percentage change in the trend-cycle, by using

$$\%TC_t = \frac{TC_t - TC_{t-1}}{TC_{t-1}} \times 100.$$

Thus for period 117, the percentage change in trend-cycle is

$$\%TC_{117} = \frac{3902.1 - 3887}{3887} (100) = .38.$$

TABLE 12-6 RELEVANT VALUES FOR CONSTRUCTING PAIRED
INDICES OF FIGURE 12-5

(1) Period	(2) Time Series (see Table 10-4)	(3) Seasonal Index	(4) (2)/(3) Seasonally Adjusted Time Series	(5) Trend- Cycle of Time Series	(6) Percentage Change in Trend- Cycle	(7) (6) + 100 Plotted in Figure 12-5(b)	(8) (5)/3902.1 Plotted in Figure 12-5(a)
114 June	5048.1	1.259	4009.8	—	—	—	—
115 July	2990.7	.800	3738.4	—	—	—	—
116 Aug.	2677.1	.778	3441.0	3887.0	—	—	—
117 Sept.	5566.1	1.198	4647.9	3902.1	.38	100.4	100.0
118 Oct.	3661.7	.944	3877.4	3707.5	−4.99	95.0	95.0
119 Nov.	2435.3	.871	2797.6	3387.6	−8.63	91.4	86.8
120 Dec.	3550.4	1.044	3402.2	3187.4	−5.91	94.1	81.7
121 Jan.	2215.4	.767	2888.7	3099.8	−2.75	97.3	79.4
122 Feb.	3312.2	1.025	3230.6	3168.1	2.20	102.2	81.2
123 Mar.	4289.8	1.353	3169.4	3188.7	.65	100.7	81.7
124 Apr.	3218.4	.974	3303.3	3195.7	.22	100.2	81.9
125 May	3193.0	.987	3234.4	3090.9	−3.28	96.7	79.2
126 June	3542.5	1.259	2813.5	2845.8	−7.93	92.1	72.9
127 July	2169.9	.800	2711.9	2521.6	−11.39	88.6	64.6
128 Aug.	1536.5	.778	1976.0	2181.9	−13.47	86.5	55.9

Adding 100 to these values gives column 7 in Table 12-6 which
is plotted as the heavy line in Figure 12-5b.

5. Repeat steps 1, 2, 3, and 4 as above, substituting the leading
   indicator as the basic data instead of the time series. This process
   gives the values shown as the broken lines in Figure 12-5a and
   12-5b.

6. Find the pressure index by dividing the values shown in column
   8 of Table 12-6 by the corresponding values for the leading indicator. For period 128, for example, the pressure index is

$$P^*_{128} = \frac{\text{Standardized value of leading indicator}}{\text{Standardized value of time series}}$$

$$= \frac{62.6}{55.9} \times 100 = 112.01,$$

and the pressure of the percentage change is

$$P_{128} = \frac{\text{Percentage change in leading indicator}}{\text{Percentage change in time series}}$$

$$= \frac{90.15}{86.5} = 104.22.$$

Note that 86.5 is the last value (period 128) in column 7 of Table 12-6 and 90.15 is the corresponding value for the leading indicator.

12/7   Tracking the Evolution of Cycles

Tracking the evolution of cycles and comparing them to previous cyclical patterns is the final method for predicting turning points to be presented. An illustration of this method can be seen in Figure 12-7 which shows the cycles in the Federal Reserve Board Production Index between 1948 and 1980. It shows five complete major cycles (1948–49, 1953–54, 1957–58, 1960–61, and 1969–70), the cycle (1974–75), and the (1979–80) cycle.

The method for tracking the evolution of cycles is straightforward. It consists of finding the trend-cycle of the series of interest, then determining the periods in which the trend-cycle has peaked historically. The intent is to plot each complete cycle from one peak to the next (or similarly, from one trough to the next). This plotting is done in a way that overlaps each cycle by starting at its peak and then plotting all other values as "periods after the peak" (see Figure 12-7). Finally, to provide a more meaningful comparison, the data are standardized by dividing the time-series values within each cycle by the value of the series at the peak. That gives the peak period the value of 100 and the remaining periods in each cycle values smaller than 100. Following this procedure for all cycles gives an idea of how past cycles have behaved and allows the current cycle (heavy line) to be placed among the previous ones. In Figure 12-7, for example, it can be seen that the 1974–75 recession started slowly but then the level of economic activity declined more rapidly than it did during any of the other postwar cycles. This important information can help the forecaster to determine the intensity and the possible length of the current cycle.

The calculations required to prepare Figure 12-7 are shown in Table 12-7 for both the 1969–70 and 1974–75 cycles. The data used are the Federal Reserve Board's Index of Industrial Production. (The base is different for each of the two cycles, but this does not matter since the data are standardized.) The steps in preparing this calculation are as follows:

Federal Reserve Board Production Index

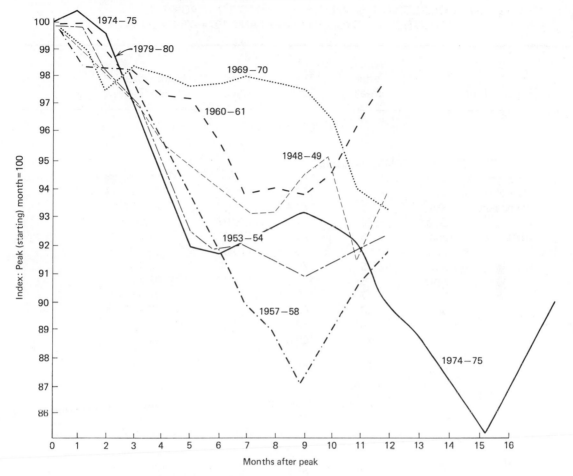

FIGURE 12-7   TRACKING THE EVOLUTION OF CYCLES USING ACTUAL
DATA

1. Calculate the trend-cycle values by applying some form of moving
    average to the time-series data. In Table 12-7, Column 3 provides
    the actual values of the series and Column 4 is a three-month
    moving average of Column 3. In this instance, the three-month
    moving average is used because the randomness in the series is
    small. However, for many less aggregated series, it may be nec-
    essary to use a longer-term moving average.
2. Standardize the trend-cycle values by dividing the smoothed trend-
    cycle values by the maximum of those values. In Table 12-7,
    Column 5 presents the standardized trend-cycle values which were

TABLE 12-7 COMPUTING THE VALUES REQUIRED TO TRACK THE
EVOLUTION OF CYCLES (1969–70 AND 1974–75 CYCLES)

Time		Months after Peak	Time Series	Trend-Cycle	Standardized Trend-Cycle
			1969–70 Recession		
(1)		(2)	(3)	(4)	(5)
1969	Sept.	—	173.9	—	—
Start of	Oct.	0	173.1	172.80	100.00
Recession	Nov.	1	171.4	171.87	99.46
	Dec.	2	171.1	170.97	98.94
1970	Jan.	3	170.4	170.67	98.77
	Feb.	4	170.5	170.67	98.77
	Mar.	5	171.1	170.60	98.73
	Apr.	6	170.2	170.10	98.44
	May	7	169.0	169.33	97.99
	June	8	168.8	169.00	97.80
	July	9	169.2	169.27	97.96
	Aug.	10	169.8	168.27	97.39
	Sept.	11	165.8	166.00	96.06
	Oct.	12	162.4	162.97	94.31
			1974–75 Recession		
(6)		(7)	(8)	(9)	(10)
1974	July	—	125.2	—	—
Start of	Aug.	0	125.2	125.27	100.00
Recession	Sept.	1	125.4	125.07	99.84
	Oct.	2	124.6	123.90	98.91
	Nov.	3	121.7	122.40	97.71
	Dec.	4	120.9	119.57	95.45
1975	Jan.	5	116.1	116.23	92.78
	Feb.	6	111.7	112.33	89.67
	Mar.	7	109.2	109.53	87.44
	Apr.	8	107.7	108.27	86.43
	May	9	107.9	107.05	85.46

obtained by dividing each of the values of Column 4 by 172.80,
the largest value or the value representing the peak of the cycle.

3. Present the standardized trend cycle values graphically, as in
Figure 12-7, so that different cycles can be more easily contrasted

and compared. Column 5 of Table 12-7 is very similar to the data plotted in Figure 12-7. (There are some slight differences between Column 5 and the corresponding plot in Figure 12-7, because Figure 12-7 uses the actual data, rather than the trend-cycles.) In making this plot of the standardized trend-cycle values, Column 2, which shows the periods (months) after the peak, is used as the X axis and Column 5 is used as the Y axis.

In Table 12-7, columns 7, 8, 9, and 10 are analogous to Columns 2, 3, 4, and 5, except that they refer to the 1974–75 cycle. Columns 6 through 10 include the whole cycle, while Figure 12-7 shows the first four months following the peak of that cycle (that is, the four months through December 1974).

In addition to the methods examined so far in this chapter, the person in charge of predicting the cycle must be continuously informed of economic trends, government initiatives, proposed legislation, and other actions. Hence that person must follow economic publications and be aware of consensus forecasts made by economists, government officials, and private forecasting services. In addition, industry trends also must be followed and analyzed using a top-down approach that starts from the total economic activity and goes down to industry activity and then to total corporate projections.

Predicting the cycle is a complex activity that requires substantial effort and reliable information. One should also bear in mind the tendency among forecasters to underestimate the magnitude of changes—underestimation of actual values in periods of booms and overestimation in periods of recession (see Theil, 1975). Table 12-8 shows some indication of this bias using a comparison taken from Modigliani and Sauerlender (1955).

12/8 Cycle Forecasting for the Individual Business

For many industries and individual companies, cycles are a fact of life. During the 1970s, a number of these firms adopted an approach to forecasting cycles based on work done by the Institute for Trend Research, Contoocook, New Hampshire. Referred to as cycle forecasting, or pressures analysis, this approach builds on several of the ideas presented earlier in this chapter. While it is not the only approach to forecasting cycles for an industry, firm, or business unit, it is one of the most widely used. This section summarizes the steps involved in applying this approach, indicates its value in some multinational manufacturing firms, and links this technique with action planning for businesses that confront business cycles as an ongoing part of their environment.

TABLE 12-8 AVERAGE PREDICTED AND ACTUAL PERCENTAGE
CHANGES IN SALES OF MANUFACTURING FIRMS
RESPONDING TO OBE-SEC SURVEYS

Asset of Firm	Number of Observations	Average Predicted Change	Average Actual Change
1948			
Above $50 million	26	7.8	14.2
$10–$50 million	58	4.4	11.9
Below $10 million	39	.5	5.8
1949			
Above $50 million	57	1.8	−2.1
$10–$50 million	208	−4.5	−8.6
Below $10 million	211	−1.9	−7.0

Source: F. Modigliani and O. H. Sauerlender, "Economic Expectations and Plans of Firms in Relation to Short-Term Forecasting," in Short-Term Economic Forecasting, *vol. 17 of* Studies in Income and Wealth *(Princeton, N.J.: Princeton University Press, 1955), pp. 288–89. Reprinted by permission.*

12/8/1 Basic Steps in Pressure Calculations

The cycle forecasting approach is relatively straightforward. Perhaps one of the best summary explanations of it is that given by Sommer (1977), relating to its application at Parker Hannifin Corporation. The starting point is monthly data on a single time series. For example, Table 12-9 presents actual monthly orders (in millions of dollars) for the United States metalworking industry. The first step in preparing the cycle analysis, or "pressures" analysis, for this data series is to compute the 12-month moving total. As indicated in Table 12-9, this is simply the sum for a 12-month span. This total is placed opposite the twelfth or final month it includes. In Table 12-9, each subsequent 12-month moving total (MMT) is formed by dropping the earliest month and adding the most recent month. Thus, the second MMT value goes from February of 1972 through January of 1973. The third MMT value goes from March of 1972 through February of 1973, and so on. The effect of using 12 months in computing the MMT is that it eliminates any seasonality in the data.

The second step is to calculate the ratio of one 12-month moving total to the 12 MMT of a year earlier (12/12). These ratios (multiplied by 100) are indicated in the final column of Table 12-9, where each 12/12 pressure is listed opposite the MMT used as the numerator in the ratio. Thus, the

TABLE 12-9 CALCULATING PRESSURES
                FOR BUSINESS CYCLE FORECASTING

	Actual Orders	12-Month Moving Total (MMT)	Ratio of 12-Month Moving Totals[a] (12/12)
1972			
Jan.	226		
Feb.	284		
Mar.	331		
Apr.	292		
May	301		
June	336		
July	315		
Aug.	277		
Sept.	332		
Oct.	314		
Nov.	335		
Dec.	362	3,705	
1973			
Jan.	370	3,849	
Feb.	407	3,972	
Mar.	498	4,139	
Apr.	411	4,258	
May	406	4,363	
June	421	4,448	
July	387	4,520	
Aug.	382	4,625	
Sept.	393	4,686	
Oct.	487	4,859	
Nov.	423	4,947	
Dec.	500	5,085	137.3
1974			
Jan.	375	5,090	132.2
Feb.	517	5,200	130.9
Mar.	628	5,330	128.8
Apr.	581	5,500	129.2
May	573	5,667	129.9
June	589	5,835	131.2
July	524	5,972	132.1
Aug.	519	6,109	132.1
Sept.	690	6,406	136.7

[a]The ratio is multiplied by 100.

12/12 for December 1973 (a value of 137.3 in Table 12-9) is obtained by taking the 12-month moving total for December 1973, dividing it by the 12-month moving total for December 1972, and multiplying by 100. The resulting 12/12 value indicates that the 12-month moving total has increased by 37.3 percent over its year earlier value.

An examination of the 12/12 pressure of monthly orders shown in Table 12-9 shows that a minimum value for that ratio was reached in March 1974, suggesting that was the bottom of the cycle, even though this did not become obvious until several months later. These 12/12 pressure values for monthly orders can also be plotted graphically to see more clearly the amplitude and length of individual cycles for a specific time series.

This same approach to calculating pressures can be used with any of a variety of time series. In addition, different ratios can be taken in order to see peaks and valleys in individual cycles more clearly. For example, it would be easy to calculate the ratio of 3-month moving totals for the data shown in Table 12-9 for one year to the next. This would be referred to as a 3/12 pressure of monthly orders. (The first value in identifying a particular pressure is the number of periods included in the numerator—such as 3 months—and the second value is the number of periods between the moving totals—such as 12 months—being compared. The values most commonly used in computing pressures are those of 1/12, 3/12, and 12/12.)

12/8/2 Cycle Forecasting Using Pressures on Multiple Data Series

In much the same fashion that leading indicators were described earlier in this chapter, pressure values for different time series can be compared to identify cycles affecting a specific company or business unit. These pressures may simply be different pressure series for the same basic time series, or they might be pressures derived from different time series. Some examples will help to illustrate how these might be calculated and used in practice.

At Parker Hannifin Corporation, one of the relationships that was observed early in the use of the pressures technique was that certain order receipt pressure series tended to lead or lag other pressures. An illustration of this is given in Figure 12-8, where the 1/12 pressures for inventories is plotted on the same graph as the 12/12 pressures for orders. (Note that the 1/12 pressure is simply the ratio of a single month's value compared with the same month a year ago. The 12/12 pressure is the ratio of the 12-month moving total up through the current month compared with the 12-month moving total a year ago.) Comparing these two pressures on the same graph suggests that inventories continued to build in late 1969 and early 1970, even though orders had peaked and were on the decline. That six-month to a year lag indicated that the company had been building inventories at the

FIGURE 12-8 USING ORDER CYCLES TO GUIDE BUSINESS INVENTORY CYCLES

wrong time, in the downswing, and had failed to build them during the upswing.

Owing in part to the use of the 1/12 pressures of inventories and comparing those with the 12/12 pressures for orders, the company was able to control inventory buildup and production levels much more successfully during the 1973–74 downturn than in 1969–70. This, in turn, aided the company in reducing its working capital requirements during calendar 1975 and repaying funds that had been borrowed to finance much of the peak of 2 years earlier.

Another application of multiple pressures to guide management action is that suggested in Figure 12-9. Management at Parker-Hannifin had noted that its orders tended to drop drastically with even a minor cutback in customers' inventories. In fact, customer inventory swings were found to be the most significant factor affecting swings in Parker Hannifin's own business activity level. As an aid to anticipating the impact of such customer inventory adjustments on an individual division's order receipts, two pressure series were compared, as in Figure 12-9. One of those was simply the 12-month moving totals for orders (the 12/12 pressure based on data readily available within the division). The other series was made up of data representing the ratio of inventories to orders for the major customer industry. In this instance, Commerce Department data gathered through trade associations were used to develop a series representing the ratio of inventory to orders for the U.S. metalworking machinery industry. Then 12/12 pressures were computed for this series, and these were plotted on the same graph as the Cylinder Division's 12/12 orders.

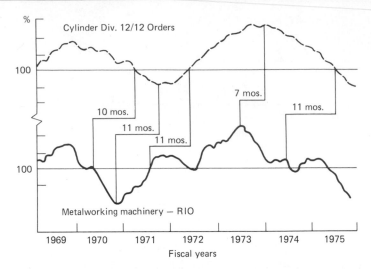

FIGURE 12-9   USING THE RATIO OF INVENTORIES TO ORDERS (RIO) AS
A LEADING INDICATOR OF THE ORDER CYCLE

It was found that the ratio of inventory to orders (RIO) for this major customer segment provided a leading indicator of the customer's business activity and thus a fairly accurate indicator of what was in store for one of Parker Hannifin's major divisions. While the lead time varied from seven to eleven months, it was consistently a leading indicator and thus provided additional guidance for management.

As a result of this RIO analysis, Parker Hannifin began to cut back steel and casting orders and long-term contracts, even in the face of growing orders for their own products. This was in anticipation of the downturn that this analysis predicted for early 1974.

One other example that illustrates the use of multiple pressures to predict individual cycles comes from the Motor Division of Reliance Electric Company. That division found that plotting the 1/12 pressure for order receipts on the same graph as the 12/12 pressure for order receipts provided them with the former as a good leading indicator of the latter. This has been particularly helpful to the Division in its budgeting, since it allows them to anticipate the general business cycle for the coming year at the time the annual budget is being prepared. This has avoided problems of predicting significant growth in a year where the cycle is on the downturn and allowed them to budget for even greater growth during a year where the cycle is clearly on the upturn. This has helped their budgets to be much more credible and has encouraged actions that are consistent both with the long-term goals of the business and the short-term realities of the cycle and the environment.

12/8/3 Planning Management Actions Based on Pressure Cycle Forecasts

In businesses that are traditionally cyclical in nature, a major concern of management is adjusting decisions to fit the stage of the business cycle in which it finds itself. In order to do this, many companies have found it useful to separate the problem of forecasting the business cycle from the problem of selecting those actions most appropriate for a given phase of the business cycle. Several companies associated with the Institute for Trend Research have identified a useful approach for guiding actions in various phases of the business cycle. This is summarized in Figure 12-10 and Table 12-10. As suggested by Figure 12-10, a business cycle can be divided into six major phases. These can be referred to in sequence in growth, prosperity, warning, recession, depression, and recovery. While many economic forecasters think of business cycles as being made up of only two phases (or possibly four phases), for most management teams the use of six phases offers a distinct advantage. The problem with using only two or four phases is that a phase will then end at a major turning point (a peak or trough). If such an ending point is used for a phase, substantial debate arises as to exactly when a turning point has been reached, and when the next phase has been entered. Using six phases where Phases 2 and 5 span the upside turning point and the downside turning point, respectively, much of this debate on turning points can be eliminated.

Once a management group has agreed that their business generally goes through cycles that can be represented adequately with these six phases, there are two separable tasks—forecasting movement through those phases and determining appropriate actions for any given phase. Again, it is extremely useful to separate those two tasks and to use pressures, leading

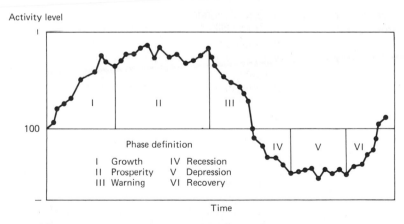

FIGURE 12-10 SIX PHASES OF A BUSINESS CYCLE

TABLE 12-10   PLANNING FOR THE SIX PHASES OF A BUSINESS CYCLE

Phase	Recognition	Suggested Responses/Actions
I. Growth	Optimistic conditions	• Expand workforce • Accelerate training • Undertake plant expansions • Examine outside manufacturing sources • Try to build inventories
II. Prosperity	Gains in cycle chart narrow for 2-3 months	• Stay in stock • Review sales forecasts • Freeze plant expansions • Spin off undesired divisions • Unload surplus equipment • Missionary work in new fields (but don't add to costs)
III. Warning	Three months of cycle decline	• Reduce inventories • Make inventory curve (1/12) • Start cuts in training and advertising • Weed out bad products • Cut hiring • Reduce long-term purchasing commitments
IV. Recession	Orders fall below year ago level	• Further inventory reductions • Layoffs • Review purchase decisions
V. Depression	Declines in cycle chart narrow for 2–3 months	• Freeze workforce • Keep skilled employees • Reduce work hours if needed • Order major capital equipment for next upswing • Enter into long-term leases and labor contracts • Prepare training programs.
VI. Recovery	Gains in cycle chart, but still below 100	• Rehire • Build inventories • Get distributors and suppliers to build inventories

indicators, and other cyclical forecasting techniques to handle the forecasting part of the problem. The conclusion of the forecasting activity is the identification of the phase in which the business now finds itself.

The second task of identifying the actions and responses appropriate for each phase of the business cycle can be clearly discussed and planned well in advance of actual entry into a given phase. Table 12-10 suggests one way that this might be done and indicates the responses and actions that might be appropriate for each of the six phases. People are frequently influenced a great deal by current events. They tend to believe that a boom or decline will go on forever. It is important, therefore, that managers agree in principle about what is appropriate for each phase. Then it becomes a matter of operationalizing and applying those general guidelines, rather than starting from scratch every time the firm finds itself in either an overcapacity or an out-of-supply situation.

REFERENCES AND SELECTED BIBLIOGRAPHY

Bails, D. G., and L. C. Peppers. 1982. *Business Fluctuations: Forecasting Techniques and Applications*. Englewood Cliffs, N.J.: Prentice-Hall.

Barksdale, H. C., and J. E. Hilliard. 1975. "A Cross-Spectral Analysis of Retail Inventories and Sales," *Journal of Business*, **48**, No. 3, pp. 365–82.

Beman, L. 1976. "The Chastening of the Washington Economists," *Fortune*, January, pp. 158–66.

Dauten, C. A., and L. M. Valentine. 1974. *Business Cycles and Forecasting*. Cincinnati: South-Western Publishing Co.

Day, R. L. (ed.). 1977. *Consumer Satisfaction, Dissatisfaction and Complaining Behavior*. Bloomington, Indiana: Division of Research, Graduate School of Business, Indiana University.

DeWolf, J. W., et al. 1978. *Early Warning Forecast*. Boston: Cahners Publishing Co.

Eckstein, O. 1978. *The Great Recession*. Amsterdam: North-Holland.

Evans, M. K. 1969. *Macroeconomic Activity*. New York: Harper & Row.

Forrester, J. W. 1971. *World Dynamics*. New York: Wright-Allen.

Juster, F. T. 1964. *Anticipation and Purchases: An Analysis of Consumer Behavior*. Princeton, N.J.: Princeton University Press.

Keynes, J. M. 1936. *The General Theory of Employment, Interest, and Money*. New York: Harcourt, Brace and World.

Mack, R. P. 1956. *Consumption and Business Fluctuations*. New York: National Bureau of Economic Research.

Makridakis, S. 1982. "Chronology of the Last Six Recessions," *Omega*, **10**, No. 1, pp. 43–50.

Makridakis, S., and S. C. Wheelwright (eds.) 1982. *The Handbook of Forecasting: A Manager's Guide*. New York: John Wiley and Sons, Inc.

Mass, N. J. 1976. *Economic Cycles: An Analysis of Underlying Causes*. New York: John Wiley & Sons, Inc.

McLaughlin, R. L. 1982. "A Model of an Average Recession and Recovery," *Journal of Forecasting*, **1**, No. 1, pp. 55–63.

—— 1975. "A New Five-Phase Economic Forecasting System," *Business Economics*, September, pp. 49–60.

——, and J. J. Boyle. 1968. *Short Term Forecasting*. American Marketing Association (booklet).

McNees, S. 1979. "Lessons from the Track Record of Macroeconomic Forecasters in the 1970s," *TIMS Studies in the Management Sciences*, **12**, pp. 227–264. Amsterdam: North-Holland.

Mitchell, W. C. 1913. *Business Cycles*. Berkeley, Calif.: University of California Press.

—— 1951. *What Happens During Business Cycles: A Progress Report.* Studies in Business Cycles. New York: National Bureau of Economic Research.

Modigliani, F., and O. H. Sauerlender. 1955. "Economic Expectations and Plans of Firms in Relation to Short-Term Forecasting." In *Short-Term Economic Forecasting,* Vol. 17 of Studies in Income and Wealth. Princeton, N.J.: Princeton University Press, pp. 288–89.

Mueller, E. 1963. "Ten Years of Consumer Attitude Surveys: Their Forecasting Record," *Journal of the American Statistical Association,* **58,** No. 4.

Okun, A. 1962. "The Predictive Value of Surveys of Business Intentions," *American Economic Review Papers and Proceedings,* **52,** No. 2.

Schumpeter, J. A. 1934. *Theory of Economic Development.* Cambridge, Mass.: Harvard University Press.

—— 1939. *Business Cycles,* Vol. 1. New York: McGraw-Hill.

Sommer, Dale W. 1977. "Cycle Forecasting Spots Trends," *Industry Week,* April 25, pp. 71+.

Theil, H. 1975. *Economic Forecasts and Policies.* Amsterdam/New York: North-Holland/American Elsevier (1st ed. 1958).

Tobin, J. 1959. "On the Predictive Value of Consumer Intentions and Attitudes," *Review of Economics and Statistics,* **41,** pp. 1–11.

U.S. Government. *Business Conditions Digest.* Washington D.C. (monthly publication).

EXERCISES

1. For many firms and industries, housing starts are an important indicator of economic activity and general business health. During the decade of the 1970s, free reserves were considered a reliable leading indicator of housing starts. Using the data in Tables 12-11 and 12-12, plot the paired indices, rates of change, and pressures in order to develop the type of graphic analysis shown in Figure 12-2. What conclusions can you draw from these graphs?

2. The following data are for new orders (per month) at an electrical equipment company.
   a. Compute the 12-month moving total, the 12/12 pressure, and the 3/12 pressure. (The form provided in Table 12-13 might be useful for this.)
   b. Graph both the 12/12 and 3/12 pressures on regular graph paper and on graph paper where the vertical scale is logarithmic (see Table 12-14). What conclusions can you draw about new orders at this firm?

	1975	1976	1977	1978
Jan.	129.9	115.2	125.7	131.9
Feb.	129.6	112.7	127.3	133.2
Mar.	130.0	111.7	128.2	135.3
Apr.	129.9	112.6	128.7	136.1
May.	131.3	113.7	129.5	137.0
Jun.	131.9	116.4	130.1	137.8
Jul.	131.8	118.4	130.7	138.8
Aug.	131.7	121.0	131.3	138.2
Sep.	131.8	122.1	130.8	138.7
Oct.	129.5	122.2	130.4	139.1
Nov.	124.9	123.5	131.7	137.3
Dec.	119.3	124.4	132.8	136.1

TABLE 12-11   U.S. HOUSING STARTS

	1970	1971	1972	1973	1974	1975	1976	1977
Jan.	69.2	114.8	150.9	147.3	86.2	56.9	72.9	81.3
Feb.	77.0	104.6	153.6	139.5	109.6	56.2	91.6	112.5
Mar.	117.8	169.3	205.8	200.0	127.2	81.1	118.4	173.6
Apr.	130.2	203.6	213.2	203.5	160.9	98.4	137.2	182.4
May	127.3	203.5	227.9	233.9	149.9	117.1	147.9	201.3
Jun.	141.6	196.8	226.2	202.6	149.5	110.9	154.2	197.6
Jul.	143.4	197.0	207.5	201.1	127.2	120.6	136.6	189.8
Aug.	131.6	205.9	228.1	193.1	114.0	117.3	145.9	194.0
Sep.	133.4	175.6	204.4	148.9	99.6	112.8	153.1	177.7
Oct.	143.4	181.7	218.2	149.5	97.2	123.6	149.8	190.9
Nov.	128.3	176.4	187.1	134.6	75.1	97.2	127.1	
Dec.	123.9	155.3	150.9	90.6	55.1	77.1	107.4	

12-Month Moving Total

	1970	1971	1972	1973	1974	1975	1976	1977
Jan.	1463.5	1512.7	2120.6	2370.2	1983.5	1322.2	1185.2	1550.5
Feb.	1445.7	1540.3	2169.6	2356.1	1953.6	1268.8	1220.6	1571.4
Mar.	1427.9	1591.8	2206.1	2350.3	1880.8	1222.7	1257.9	1626.6
Apr.	1398.2	1665.2	2215.7	2340.6	1838.2	1160.2	1296.7	1671.8
May	1367.8	1741.4	2240.1	2346.6	1754.2	1127.4	1327.5	1725.2
Jun.	1358.6	1796.6	2269.5	2323.0	1701.1	1088.8	1370.8	1768.6
Jul.	1375.5	1850.2	2280.0	2316.6	1627.2	1082.2	1386.8	1821.8
Aug.	1379.5	1924.5	2302.2	2281.6	1548.1	1085.5	1415.4	1869.9
Sep.	1380.0	1966.7	2331.0	2226.1	1498.8	1098.7	1455.7	1894.5
Oct.	1397.6	2005.0	2367.5	2157.4	1446.5	1125.1	1481.9	1935.6
Nov.	1428.5	2053.1	2378.2	2104.9	1387.0	1147.2	1511.8	
Dec.	1467.1	2084.5	2373.8	2044.6	1351.5	1169.2	1542.1	

12-Month Rate of Change

	1970	1971	1972	1973	1974	1975	1976	1977
Jan.	93.2	103.4	140.2	111.8	83.7	66.7	89.6	130.8
Feb.	91.6	106.5	140.9	108.6	82.9	64.9	96.2	128.7
Mar.	90.1	111.5	138.6	106.5	80.0	65.0	102.9	129.3
Apr.	88.5	119.1	133.1	105.6	78.5	63.1	111.8	128.9
May	85.9	127.3	128.6	104.8	74.8	64.3	117.7	130.0
Jun.	84.9	132.2	126.3	102.4	73.2	64.0	125.9	128.6
Jul.	86.8	134.5	123.2	101.6	70.2	66.5	128.1	131.4
Aug.	87.8	139.5	119.6	99.1	67.9	70.1	130.4	132.1
Sep.	88.2	142.5	118.5	95.5	67.3	73.2	132.5	130.1
Oct.	90.4	143.5	118.1	91.1	67.0	77.8	131.7	130.6
Nov.	94.3	143.7	115.8	88.5	65.9	82.8	131.8	
Dec.	97.8	142.1	113.9	86.1	66.1	86.6	131.8	

TABLE 12-12   U.S. FREE RESERVES

	1970	1971	1972	1973	1974	1975	1976	1977
Jan.	(799)	(91)	153	(823)	(790)	(441)	139	441
Feb.	(819)	(127)	91	(1388)	(980)	96	(51)	(102)
Mar.	(781)	(120)	134	(1563)	(1144)	153	386	168
Apr.	(704)	(8)	27	(1560)	(1509)	17	56	(48)
May	(795)	(18)	(15)	(1638)	(2284)	(52)	272	103
Jun.	(701)	(322)	(110)	(1653)	(2739)	278	17	(94)
Jul.	(1217)	(658)	(55)	(1605)	(2982)	276	(29)	72
Aug.	(682)	(606)	(183)	(1734)	(3008)	44	221	(771)
Sep.	(335)	(295)	(352)	(1477)	(2957)	(136)	243	(245)
Oct.	(208)	(153)	(327)	(1141)	(1585)	30	155	
Nov.	(305)	(144)	(292)	(1111)	(960)	257	301	
Dec.	(49)	58	(830)	(995)	(333)	148	122	

12-Month Moving Total + 48,000[a]

	1970	1971	1972	1973	1974	1975	1976	1977
Jan.	37234	41313	45760	45485	31345	27079	49250	50134
Feb.	37011	42005	45978	44006	31753	28154	49103	50083
Mar.	36931	42666	46232	42309	32172	29451	49336	49865
Apr.	37071	43362	46267	40722	32223	30977	49375	49761
May	37378	44139	46270	39099	31577	33209	49699	49592
Jun.	37741	44518	46702	37336	30491	36226	49438	49481
Jul.	37598	45077	47305	35785	29114	39484	49133	49582
Aug.	37862	45153	47728	34235	27840	42536	49310	48590
Sep.	38358	45193	47671	33110	26360	45357	49689	48102
Oct.	39142	45248	47497	32296	25916	46972	49814	
Nov.	39825	45409	47349	31477	26067	48189	49858	
Dec.	40605	45516	46461	31312	26729	48670	49832	

12-Month Rate of Change

	1970	1971	1972	1973	1974	1975	1976	1977
Jan.	82.9	111.0	110.8	99.4	68.9	86.4	181.9	101.8
Feb.	83.6	113.5	109.5	95.7	72.2	88.7	174.4	102.0
Mar.	84.2	115.5	108.4	91.5	76.0	91.5	167.5	101.1
Apr.	85.3	117.0	106.7	88.0	79.1	96.1	159.4	100.8
May	87.6	118.1	104.8	84.5	80.8	105.2	149.7	99.8
Jun.	90.0	118.0	104.9	79.9	81.7	118.8	136.5	100.1
Jul.	91.5	119.9	104.9	75.6	81.4	135.6	124.4	100.9
Aug.	93.9	119.3	105.7	71.7	81.3	152.8	115.9	98.5
Sep.	96.8	117.8	105.5	69.5	79.6	172.1	109.5	96.8
Oct.	100.8	115.6	105.0	68.0	80.2	181.3	106.0	
Nov.	104.6	114.0	104.3	66.5	82.8	184.9	103.5	
Dec.	108.1	112.1	102.1	67.4	85.4	182.1	102.4	

[a]This constant term is added so all 12 MMT will be positive.

TABLE 12-13 WORKSHEET FOR COMPUTING PRESSURE DATA

	19__	19__	19__	19__	19__	19__	19__	19__	19__	19__
Jan.										
Feb.										
Mar.										
Apr.										
May										
Jun.										
Jul.										
Aug.										
Sep.										
Oct.										
Nov.										
Dec.										
12-Month Moving Total										
Jan.										
Feb.										
Mar.										
Apr.										
May										
Jun.										
Jul.										
Aug.										
Sep.										
Oct.										
Nov.										
Dec.										

TABLE 12-13 WORKSHEET FOR COMPUTING PRESSURE DATA (*Continued*)

12/12 Pressure										
Jan.										
Feb.										
Mar.										
Apr.										
May										
Jun.										
Jul.										
Aug.										
Sep.										
Oct.										
Nov.										
Dec.										

__ /12 Pressure										
Jan.										
Feb.										
Mar.										
Apr.										
May										
Jun.										
Jul.										
Aug.										
Sep.										
Oct.										
Nov.										
Dec.										

TABLE 12-14 LOGARITHMIC PAPER FOR PLOTTING PRESSURES

13/QUALITATIVE AND TECHNOLOGICAL METHODS OF FORECASTING

13/1   Introduction

The terms *qualitative* and *technological* are generally used to denote forecasting techniques focused primarily on predicting the environment and technology over the longer term. In contrast to quantitative methods that are employed mainly for economic, marketing, financial, and other business forms of forecasting, technological methods are not simply an extrapolation of historical data patterns, as are many of their quantitative counterparts, nor do they assume constancy of the past pattern into the future. Even though history plays an important role in these methods of forecasting, technological techniques require imagination combined with individual talent, knowledge, foresight, and judgment to predict effectively long-run changes. A knowledge of the procedures involved in various qualitative or technological approaches can help formalize both thought processes and the prediction of the future where the prerequisites for the quantitative methods discussed in previous chapters simply are not met.

Technological methods of forecasting do not always provide a step-by-step procedure, nor do they give their forecast in terms of a single numerical answer. Use of these methods requires an understanding of the factors involved in each situation and the need to adapt the method to that situation. When technological methods are used, it is the expert who becomes the processor of facts, knowledge, and information, rather than some set of mathematical rules or mathematical model, as would be the case with quantitative methods. In his book *Profiles of the Future,* Clarke describes the environment within which the technological forecaster must operate:

> *He does not try to describe the future, but to define the boundaries within which possible futures must lie. If we regard the ages which stretch ahead of us as an unmapped and unexplored country, what he's attempting to do is to survey its frontiers and to gain some idea of its extent. The detailed geography of the interior must remain unknown until he reaches it.* [Clarke, 1973, p. xi]

In spite of the difficulties and the subjective nature of technological forecasting and its evaluation, its acceptance and application in organizations have grown rapidly. In 1969 Jantsch estimated that about 500 to 600 medium-sized and large American companies had established a technological forecasting function as a part of their operations. In that same year Ayres estimated that about half of the largest 500 companies in the United States were using such forecasting methodologies. Cetron and Ralph reported in 1971 that about 50 percent of the people responding to their survey on the use of various forecasting methods indicated they used technological approaches.

Some authors have chosen to include long-range planning activities as an integral part of technological forecasting. When such planning activities are included, the number of organizations using these methods is substantial indeed. In 1971 Gerstenfeld reported that 71 percent of the respondents in his forecasting survey were using such methodologies. Subsequent studies have indicated that between 70 and 90 percent of respondents were using such techniques, depending on the population being surveyed and the range of techniques included in this category of forecasting approaches.

The exact percentage of organizations making use of technological methodologies is not of great importance. However, the fact that these methods have gained widespread acceptance in spite of their drawbacks indicates the importance of the problems with which they deal and the need that organizations feel for improving their forecasting in such situations. It is likely that organizations in the future will feel even more need to use technological forecasting in order to cope with the rapid acceleration of technological innovation and changes in the environment.

Before describing several of the different methods included in the category of qualitative or technological forecasting, it is useful to define further these terms and the items they cover. Since these definitions vary substantially from one writer to another, it is useful to consider definitions from several different authors in order to more completely describe the area covered by these methods and some of their important characteristics.

Prehoda (1967, p. 12) provides a simple intuitive definition of technological forecasting as "the description or prediction of a foreseeable invention, specific scientific refinement or likely scientific discoveries, that promise to serve some useful function. These are functions that meet the requirements of industry and military services, government agencies, and the general needs of society." Cetron (1969, p. 4) defines these methodologies as "a basis for prediction with a level of confidence of a technological achievement in a given time frame with a specific level of support." Jantsch (1969, p. 15) uses as his definition, "the probabilistic assessment on a relatively high confidence level of future technology transfer." Other writers offer other definitions, but most seem to agree that these methodologies distinguish formal prediction with specified confidence levels from mere guesses or fiction. Technological forecasting falls into the category of formal prediction because it is systematic and provides greater confidence in the results, although these approaches are far more subjective than many other quantitative approaches to forecasting.

A question that is often raised in discussions of technological or qualitative methods of forecasting is whether or not they really represent methods at all, or whether they are simply attempts to describe what experts might do anyway. One objection to these methods is the fact that different experts using the same method do not always produce the same forecasts. Sometimes the divergence in opinion among experts is so extensive that it is hard to imagine that any substantial confidence could be placed in the results. While these are clearly important issues to consider in determining whether a specific method should be adopted, the fact remains that in many instances these methods are the only systematic approaches available. As more experience is gained in the field, other methods will be proposed; many of them will represent improvements over existing approaches. In the meantime, understanding the methods currently available can be very helpful.

In the remainder of this chapter three subcategories of qualitative and technological methods of forecasting are presented and several specific illustrations are given for each of them. The first is subjective assessment methods—jury of executive opinion, sales force composites, subjective assessment methods and surveys. These make efficient use of the human mind in processing diverse pieces of information and/or structuring resulting forecasts in formats that can be integrated easily with other planning and decision-making processes. The second is exploratory methods—scenario development, Delphi, cross impact, curve fitting, analogy, morphological research, and catastrophe theory. These start with a variety of knowledge and data about the past and judgments and predictions about various aspects of the future, and through the procedure associated with each specific method, combine into the desired forecast. The third is normative methods—relevance trees (PATTERN) and system dynamics. These first assess future goals, needs, desires, missions, and so on, and then work backwards to the present to identify those developments necessary to achieve those goals.

13/2 Subjective Assessment Methods

For a number of situations (for example, new product forecasting), management may have information that is relevant to forecasting but that may not be amenable to quantitative forecasting techniques based on historical data. In such instances, forecasts reflecting subjective assessments of the situation can often be of substantial benefit. Some of the methods commonly used for obtaining such subjective assessment forecasts include group composites, surveys, market research, and individual judgmental assessments. These approaches are discussed in this section.

Owing to the subjective nature of these methods, the reliability of their results is often questionable. Consequently, such results are frequently stated in terms of prediction intervals and ranges of outcomes, rather than as single point estimates. Managers frequently wish to incorporate explicitly the range of uncertainty associated with a forecast into their decision making. That can be done for several of the quantitative techniques discussed in previous chapters, and is not unique to subjective assessment. For example, a methodology such as regression analysis that provides confidence intervals surrounding a forecast can be thought of as providing a point estimate (the expected outcome) as well as some prediction interval around that outcome. Although many users of quantitative methods account for such variability in the forecasts either in an implicit manner or through sensitivity analysis to determine the effect of changes in the forecast value on their decisions, it is also possible to be explicit about this variability using a technique like decision analysis.

While this section does not delve into the technique of decision analysis, much of the research on subjective assessment methods has been done by those who have studied such techniques. Thus the interested reader might find references like Holloway (1979), Vatter et al. (1978), and Raiffa (1968) to be useful literature on subjective assessment methods, even though their primary focus is on decision analysis.

13/2/1   Jury of Executive Opinion

The jury of executive opinion approach has been summarized by the Conference Board (1978). Recent surveys of actual forecasting practice in business indicate that it is one of the simplest and most widely used forecasting approaches available. In its most basic form, it simply amounts to the corporate executives sitting around a table and deciding as a group what their best estimate is for the item to be forecast. One of the main drawbacks of this approach is that because it puts the estimators in personal contact with one another, the weights assigned to each executive's assessment will depend in large part on the role and personality of that executive in the organization. Thus the executives with the best information will not necessarily have the greatest weight given to their assessments.

When using this approach, a company generally brings together executives from sales, production, finance, purchasing, and administration so as to achieve broad coverage in experience and opinion. A number of companies provide the executives involved in this assessment process background data on the economy and various factors within the company that may be useful in assessing forecasts. This factual assistance can help to separate those areas for which judgment is most important from those for which historical information is very relevant. Making this separation often helps the group to move toward a more precise evaluation of the factors that affect the forecast.

In one variation of the jury of executive opinion approach, the jury is periodically requested to submit its estimates in writing. (This variation begins to look very much like the Delphi approach described below in 13/3/2.) These written estimates may then be reviewed by the president or an executive vice-president who makes a final assessment on the basis of the opinions expressed, or they may be averaged to arrive at a representative forecast. Executives often perceive that this has the advantage that the president or executive vice-president may have learned from experience which executives are generally biased in which direction and can appropriately weight each individual's estimates. As outlined in Chapter 17, the evidence on this is mixed.

The advantages most often cited for the jury of executive opinion approach to forecasting are that it provides forecasts quickly and easily, it does not require the preparation of elaborate statistics, it brings together a variety of specialized viewpoints (it pools experience and judgment), and many times it may be the only feasible means of forecasting, especially in the absence of adequate data. In addition, for some very dominant companies, like IBM, they can make their forecasts become reality. As might be expected, the disadvantages are also related to the important role of judgment in this approach. For example, it is often thought to be inferior to more factually based (quantitative) forecasting methods that do not rely so heavily on opinion. In addition, this method requires costly executive time, disperses responsibility for accurate forecasting, and may present difficulties in making breakdowns by products, time intervals, or markets for operating purposes.

13/2/2 Sales Force Composite Methods

The sales force composite approach to forecasting consists of obtaining the views of the individual sales people and sales management as to the future sales outlook. This method is frequently used and has been the focus of studies by the Conference Board and others. In describing the technique, the Conference Board (1978) has divided its use into three general categories: the grass roots approach, the sales management technique, and the distributor's approach.

In the grass roots approach, the process begins with the collection of each salesperson's estimate of probable future sales in his or her territory. These estimates may be made privately by the salesperson on forms provided for that purpose, or they may be made by the salesperson in consultation with a branch or regional manager. Oftentimes these assessments are associated with the annual budgeting and planning cycle of the company. Once the salespeople have made their individual assessments, the results for the district or region are accumulated and forwarded to the central office where a composite forecast is put together. It is commonly the practice to have the salespeople estimate demand by classes of products and often by customer so that the final composite can provide forecasts on several different dimensions—geographical area, product line, customer size, and so on. The checks generally used in application of this approach are based mainly on the judgment and assessment of district salespeople and top management as to the reasonableness of the individual salespeople's estimates. It is also common practice for a corporate staff group to make an independent estimate of demand and use that as a basis for cross-checking the composite results.

The advantages most often cited for the sales force composite approach are that it uses the specialized knowledge of those closest to the marketplace, it places responsibility for the forecasts in the hands of those who can most affect the actual results, and it lends itself to the easy break-down of the forecasts by territory, product, customer, or salesperson. The disadvantages are in many cases very similar to those found in consumer surveys. (See Section 13/2/3.) Oftentimes salespeople are poor estimators and are either overly optimistic or overly pessimistic. At other times they are unaware of broad economic patterns that may affect demand in their territory for various product lines. (Some companies have sought to over-come this weakness by giving salespeople information on general economic projections before they make their estimates.)

As an alternative to the grass roots approach to the sales force com-posite method, the sales management technique is often used. In this ap-proach, the specialized knowledge of the sales executive staff is used rather than assessments by individual salespeople. The rationale is that the sales executives generally possess almost as much information as the individual members of the sales force and the executives can be trained to make better assessments over time. Sometimes this approach involves only such high level executives that it begins to resemble the jury of executive opinion. One of the advantages claimed for using only sales executives rather than individual salespeople is that it reduces the time required to obtain such forecasts. However, it also means that the individual salespeople will not be committed to the forecast nearly as much as they would have been had they prepared their portion of it.

The wholesaler, or distributor, approach to the sales force composite method is generally used by manufacturing concerns that distribute their products through independent channels of distribution rather than through direct contact with the users of their products. In such instances, this ap-proach looks very much like the survey method described for National Lead in Section 13/2/3. Essentially, it involves asking each distributor of the product for information as to the size and quantity of the company's product lines that they expect to sell in the next quarter or the next year. To promote interest and improve validity of results, some companies who use this ap-proach give their distributors comparisons of previous sales forecasts and actual performance. Alternatively, they may provide similar data designed to encourage the cooperating distributors to evaluate their sales prospects objectively. Some companies have gone one step further: they help their distributors do their own forecasting and planning, and as a spinoff from that, the manufacturing company receives better forecasting information.

13/2/3   Formal Surveys and Market Research-Based Assessments

Both the jury of executive opinion and the sales force composite ap-proaches to forecasting rely on a type of "expert" knowledge concerning future trends and the translation of those into specific forecasts. An alternative to using a handful of experts is to sample the population whose behavior and actions will determine future trends and activity levels of the items in question. Several surveys based on a sampling of intentions are prepared on a regular basis. Two of these of particular interest to forecasters deal with business plant and equipment expenditures and purchases of consumer durables. After a review of these, the use of market research techniques to gather survey information for an organization-specific need will be discussed.

Business fixed investment consists of nonresidential structures and producer variables. Statistical series for past expenditures are usually available, but the short-term fluctuations in actual expenditures can be substantial and the pattern can change because of cyclical factors. Many planners and forecasters find it useful to consider surveys aimed at determining the intentions of business in this area, such as the U.S. Department of Commerce–Securities and Exchange Commission Survey published quarterly in the survey of current business. This survey is one of the most widely used in the area of business plant and equipment expenditures. Although the sample is not particularly large, it does provides useful information in many situations.

The *Commerce–SEC* survey is published in the third month of each quarter. At each publication date, a revised estimate of expenditures for the current quarter and the survey results for the next quarter are published. In December, the estimate for the second quarter of the next calendar year is also included, while the March issue contains estimates for the calendar year even though three months have passed. With these yearly estimates, the revised first quarter estimate and the second quarter estimate, the forecaster can project the expenditures for the last half of the calendar year.

A second survey in the area of business plant and equipment expenditures is that published by *McGraw-Hill* in *Business Week*. This survey is published twice a year and concentrates on large firms in order to pick up the big capital expenditure programs. Surveying large firms may contain some biases when business activity changes, but also may provide a useful source of data to forecasters.

McGraw-Hill conducts a preliminary survey early in the fourth quarter and releases its results in November. This date is generally late enough that most large firms have pretty well fixed their expenditures for the following year, and yet early enough to provide the forecaster with information that is generally useful in planning for the subsequent year. McGraw-Hill then resurveys during the spring of the year and publishes that result in April. Usually this second survey is much more accurate than the first, since most business budgets are operational by then. Both the fall and spring surveys prepared by McGraw-Hill contain forecasts for multiple years in advance.

Both the Commerce–SEC survey and the McGraw-Hill survey include requests for information that serves as an internal check on the firmness and validity of the responses. Essentially, these requests try to cover three questions: (1) Do expenditure plans allow for changes in the price of capital goods? (2) What is the firm's own forecast of sales or GNP? (3) What are its present and preferred rates of capacity utilization?

A third survey of business plant and equipment expenditures is that conducted by the *Conference Board.* This survey of capital appropriations is reported quarterly. It is based on a sample of 1000 manufacturing firms that account for a substantial portion of the total capital expenditures in the United States. The survey picks up plans that are reasonably firm since it reports capital appropriations that boards of directors have made commitments to. This survey has been particularly helpful to many forecasters in picking up turning points in the plant and equipment series.

A second type of survey often found useful by forecasters are those dealing with **consumer purchasing of durables.** As one might expect, individual consumers are somewhat less sophisticated in forecasting their own expenditures; thus the results of those surveys tend to be much less accurate than the results of surveys based on business intentions. Nonetheless, they can be useful in many situations. Perhaps the best known of the consumer surveys are those conducted by the *Survey Research Center* (SRC) of the University of Michigan. SRC publishes an index that contains information about consumer sentiment (what the consumer thinks about the economy) and consumer buying plans. Several studies have concluded that indices based on attitudes are more accurate in predicting consumer purchases than are indicators of buying plans. Furthermore, these attitudes seem more useful in predicting purchases of automobiles than in predicting the purchases of other durables.

Several other consumer surveys are available. These include *Consumer Reports,* published by Consumer's Union; "Consumer Buying Intentions," a survey published by the United States Bureau of the Census in its current population reports; and *Consumer Buying Prospects,* a quarterly pamphlet published by Commercial Credit Company. Unfortunately, most of these consumer surveys do not adequately record the consumer's feelings and intentions or determine the firmness of consumer attitudes. Studies evaluating the effectiveness of such surveys have found that generally they are not very adequate in predicting turning points, but they do give some indication of the rate of change in the near term.

As an alternative to published surveys, forecasters can simply survey their customers by mail, telephone, or personal interview. The method used depends on the number of companies or individuals to be surveyed and the amount of detail being sought. To increase the accuracy of customer forecasts, many of those conducting such surveys seek to obtain information from more than one source in each customer company that is surveyed. For example, the production manager as well as the purchasing agent may be questioned.

The general goal of such corporate surveys is to determine how much of a given product the consumer firm plans to use. Sometimes the inquiry is limited to the customer's expected use of the company's brand of the product, but other times it may relate to the customer's use of several related items as well.

Skill is required in designing market research studies that will discover such relationships and determine their validity. Sometimes a single factor may upset an otherwise strong correlation. The trick is to recognize and correct for such factors. For example, a chemical manufacturer found that there was an apparent relation between industrial employment and the sales of one of its products. Based on market research, however, some disturbing variations were identified. Through the appropriate design of this market research, it was discovered that one industry using exceptionally large quantities of the chemical was concentrated in a few localities. It was that high consumption in the one industry and its concentration in a few localities that was causing the distortion of the normal relationship between industrial employment and demand for the company's products. By adjusting regional figures to correct for this distortion, sales and industrial employment were very closely correlated. This correlation allowed industrial employment figures and projections to be used as the basis for forecasting the company's product sales.

In designing market research studies for purposes of forecasting it is important to be explicit as to what information is needed and what the value of that information will be once it is obtained. Frequently decision analysis can be used to shed light on this latter question. The information that might possibly be obtained from the market research study is assessed and its value in increasing the expected value for the alternative decisions is determined. Clearly the market research is only worthwhile when its value exceeds its cost. The interested reader may want to pursue some of the references cited at the end of this chapter that deal with the value of information as obtained from such market research (see Holloway, 1979, Vatter et al., 1978, Brown et al., 1974, and Raiffa, 1968).

13/2/4 Individual Subjective Probability Assessments

The use of subjective probability estimates is another method commonly used for incorporating individual judgment into forecasting. However, this approach handles the forecasting problem somewhat differently. The previously mentioned assessment procedures generally aim at a single point estimate (the expected value of a random variable) as the most likely forecast. In the case of subjective probability estimates, an attempt is made to identify the probability distribution for the uncertain event. Actually, in practice, only a finite number of outcomes of the variable are specified, and the judgmental assessment involves determining the probabilities associated with each of these outcomes. For example, the company faced with forecasting its sales for a certain product line might specify three or four different levels of sales covering the full range of possible outcomes, and might then subjectively assess the probability associated with achieving each level of outcome.

Considerable work has been done by those who have developed the technique of decision analysis in regard to alternative procedures for assessing probability distributions as an integral part of forecasting and decision making. Rather than cover all of these, this section will summarize some of the main conclusions that have been reached and suggest an approach for calibrating such individual assessments and using that calibration as the basis for developing a probability distribution. A good comprehensive summary of judgmental probability assessment methods is given by Bodily (1982), including techniques for situations with continuous possible outcomes, as well as techniques for situations with discrete outcomes.

One of the original developers of decision analysis, Robert Schlaifer (1968), has summarized some of the important aspects involved in the direct judgmental assessment of subjective probabilities along the following lines:

1. Uncertainty concerning events that individually may have a substantial effect on the item being estimated should be separated wherever possible. The decision maker should not attempt to directly assess a probability distribution for the variable in question that combines several different elements of uncertainty. Rather it is better to apply the individual's judgment and experience to the problem in smaller increments by estimating distributions for each of several different uncertain events, and then combining them through use of decision analysis.

2. An advantage of separating those individual events that may have a substantial effect on the outcome of the uncertain quantity or the variable in question is that the decision maker is likely to feel that for each individual event, the assessed probability should be unimodal and smooth.

3. If the decision maker feels that the probability distribution should be unimodal and smooth for a particular event, the distribution can be assessed by making a few separate assessments at various points on the cumulative function, plotting those points, and then fitting a smooth curve to them.

4. If only a very small probability is to be assigned to any individual value or outcome of an event, the decision maker can assess points on the cumulative function by selecting various fractiles (such as the .25, .5, and .75 fractiles) and specifying the outcome that corresponds to each of them.

Additionally, the decision maker may be able to improve the accuracy of the subjective probability assessment by relating it to historical frequency and through understanding the rules of probability assessment and the implications of various shapes in those probability distributions more fully. Generally, research in this field has found that even individuals who know a lot about the variable to be forecast may have trouble making subjective probability assessments unless they are given guidance as to how these assessments can be made. Thus an important step in this approach is to guide those making the assessments. They may need to practice by assessing the probability of various levels of the New York Stock Exchange Index or the GNP rather than starting immediately with the key item in a forecast.

A critical aspect in using subjective probability assessments as a part of forecasting is calibrating the individuals making those assessments. If the decision maker or forecaster is to use such subjective estimates developed by people either internal or external to the firm, it must be determined whether those individuals are generally optimistic or pessimistic in their assessment of probabilities and various outcomes. This, of course, cannot be done by simply looking at the after-the-fact results for one or two assessments. Rather several repeated assessments must be obtained, and an evaluation procedure for calibrating bias in them adopted.

To illustrate just how such a calibration procedure might be carried out in practice, it is useful to consider a specific example. In this case, a forest products firm faced with the task of estimating the amount of timber that can be cut from specific parcels of land will be considered. Suppose that one such company follows the procedure of sending an estimator out to examine each such parcel and to prepare an estimate of the yield per acre in thousands of board feet. Of course once the parcel is harvested, the company will know the yield exactly. The estimator's record on the last ten parcels is shown in Table 13-1. The third column of the table shows the ratio of actual to forecast (A/F) for each parcel. This ratio can be used to determine both the extent of bias in the estimator's forecasts and the distribution of the forecasting errors.

In the example shown in Table 13-1, the average A/F value is .98. This value suggests that the estimator is only slightly biased on the side of overestimating the yield of a given parcel of land. If this pattern were observed consistently, the planner might want to revise the estimator's forecast downward by 2 percent in each individual instance in order to compensate for this bias.

The dispersion in the subjective assessments shown in Table 13-1 can be determined in two different ways. First, one could compute the standard deviation of the A/F ratio, which gives a value of .06 and suggests that the estimator is quite precise. (It will be recalled from earlier chapters that for a normal distribution the values will be within plus or minus three standard deviations of the mean 99 percent of the time. That indicates the estimator will be within plus or minus 18 percent of the actual value over 99 percent of the time.)

TABLE 13-1   SUBJECTIVE ESTIMATE OF FOREST YIELD PER ACRE
(THOUSANDS OF BOARD FEET)

Forecast (estimate)	Actual	Actual/Forecast
170	175	1.03
190	178	.93
165	175	1.06
203	200	.98
169	170	1.01
183	190	1.04
190	180	.95
200	205	1.02
206	200	.97
185	160	.86

Using an alternative means of viewing the dispersion in the estimates, one could draw a cumulative probability graph of the A/F values. The A/F values could be ranked, then plotted in the manner shown in Figure 13-1. This approach has the advantage of being able to determine a distribution for any new estimate. For example, suppose the estimator gave a forecast value of 180 for a new parcel of timber (180,000 board feet per acre). The horizontal axis in Figure 13-1 shows as a second row the range

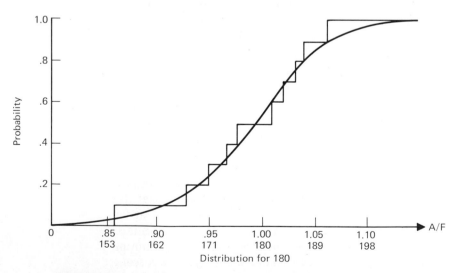

FIGURE 13-1   CALIBRATING A FORECASTER WITH A/F

of possible outcomes for the actual value based on the estimator's past record. As can be seen, there is only a 20 percent chance in this situation that the actual value will lie outside the range 162 through 193. Other probability ranges could also be estimated in the same fashion. Thus the calibration of the forecaster is a practical method for assessing expected bias and dispersion in a subjective estimating situation where individual assessments must be made repeatedly.

Owing to the wide range of approaches that have been suggested for obtaining subjective assessments as the basis for forecasting, it is not surprising that a number of studies have been conducted to estimate the relative accuracy and benefits of these alternative approaches. Several of these are compared in Chapter 15. The general conclusion, however, is that the adequacy of various methods depends more on their being tailored to the situation in question than on any inherent features of the method itself. Thus it is imperative that the forecaster adopting such methods not only know the methods, but understand the situation in which they are to be applied.

An example of the use of customer surveys is that of National Lead as reported by the Conference Board (1964). In order to obtain a 5-year forecast of its sales of titanium (a pigment used in volume in the paint, paper, rubber, and hard-surface flooring industries), the company uses a customer survey to determine the answer to three questions.

1. Will the products in which titanium is an ingredient increase in sales?
2. Is the average rate of the use of titanium expanding or contracting in each of the using industries?
3. What share of the resulting market can National Lead reasonably expect to get over the 5-year period covered by the forecast?

In conducting this survey, National Lead goes directly to executives in the customer companies that use its product, titanium. Executives of about 100 companies are interviewed in person, and as many as 300 to 500 more are surveyed by mail. National Lead considers such large samples necessary to ensure the reliability of the survey findings. Interviews are conducted by marketing research personnel trained to do this type of work.

In the case of personal interviews, three individuals are contacted in each customer company: the technical research director (or chief engineer), the sales manager (or director of marketing research), and the director of purchases. An attempt is made to elicit different types of information from each of these executives, and both specific and general questions are asked about the three topics above.

Some advantages that companies have found in customer surveys are: (1) they provide a better understanding of the customers' motivations and considerations in buying; (2) they enable the company to obtain information in the form and detail desired; and (3) they provide a basis for making a forecast in situations for which historical data either may not be available or may not be relevant. There are some disadvantages to this approach, however. It is clearly difficult to employ in markets where the final customers are hard to identify. It also depends on the judgment and cooperation of the customers, and it takes considerable time and money to complete. However, in many instances it may be the best way to proceed with forecasting and planning.

Closely related to surveys as a forecasting tool is the entire field of market research. Market research indicates not only why the consumer is or is not buying (or likely to buy), but also who the consumer is, how he or she is using the product, and what characteristics the consumer thinks are most important in the purchasing decision. Such information can often be helpful to the forecaster preparing estimates of market potential and market share for various products and services.

As an example of the role of market research, one can consider the situation described by Chambers et al. (1974) involving the picture phone. Forecasts were prepared in the late 1960s that projected sales of the picture phone as entering the rapid growth stage by 1973. It was assumed in these projections that the product features and price would be sufficiently appealing to the customer and that the method of transmission would be both feasible and sufficiently economical to ensure this rapid growth. The picture phone was subsequently introduced for market testing in Pittsburgh and New York City. The market tests showed that the demand was extremely low because of high costs and other related problems, and that significant improvements in transmission methods were needed to achieve lower cost and to make large volumes feasible. It was concluded from the tests that while a large market for picture phones was still likely, it would probably not emerge until at least the late 1970s and then—as the test indicated—the initial market would be for communications within and between corporations.

Another very important use of market research is in determining and identifying those factors that affect or can be used to predict a major variable to be forecast. In one sense, this use of market research might be compared to the initial stages of multiple regression where several independent variables that may be related to the dependent variable are identified and their correlations determined. A major use of market research is simply to identify those independent variables that might be correlated with the dependent variable to be forecast. This identification can be done effectively even when there is no intention of using regression analysis as the forecasting methodology.

An example of this approach is the manufacturer of aluminum who discovered a relationship between the sales of the industry's major product line and industrial power consumption. With the aid of power companies, the manufacturer was able to obtain power consumption figures for all of the principal markets that the company served. Applying the ratio that had been derived from the test market areas, the manufacturer estimated the total demand in each market segment. This estimate was then compared to actual past performance in order to determine market penetration in each of the markets served. Also, the manufacturer was able to obtain forecasts of probable demand for industrial power in each region and use them as the basis for predicting demand of the company's own products.

13/3   Exploratory Methods of Technological Forecasting

The methods of forecasting discussed in this section are "exploratory" in that they start with knowledge and assessments about the past and seek to forecast the future. The first two methods—scenario development and Delphi—are very similar to the subjective assessment methods described in the preceding section. The remaining methods described—cross impact, curve fitting, analogies, morphological research, and catastrophe theory—use different frameworks, concepts, and guidelines to explore what the future may hold.

13/3/1   Scenario Development Methods

Several techniques attempt to simulate reality to explore possible futures. Scenario writing, gaming or role playing, and science fiction are examples of these methods.

Scenario writing takes a well-defined set of assumptions, then develops an imaginative conception of what the future would be like if these assumptions were true. In this sense, scenarios are not future predictions by themselves. Rather they present a number of possible alternatives, each one based on certain assumptions and conditions. It is then up to the decision maker to assess the validity of the assumptions in deciding which scenario is most likely to become reality.

Much of the work on scenario writing has been done by Kahn of the Hudson Institute. Kahn (1964) and Kahn et al. (1976) developed a number of alternative scenarios for the world. In one he assumed that an arms control agreement between the United States and Russia would be reached and that China would follow only a defensive policy, not an offensive policy. Based on these and other assumptions, he developed a scenario describing a future political-social environment, following a predictable sequence of developments, constraints, and ideologies. For this set of assumptions, Kahn predicted a future environment that would be highly stable and peaceful. Under a different scenario, Kahn assumed that Russia would lose control over the world Communist movement, that the European Economic Community would become much stronger and more protectionist in its policies, and so on. The third scenario Kahn described in 1964 was based on the construction of new alliances among the countries and the development or acquisition of nuclear arms by smaller countries. This set of assumptions gives rise to a very different scenario of the world's future environment and its relative stability.

A technological approach that is very similar to that of scenario writing in concept is *gaming* or *role playing*. It consists of using either straight mathematics or combining it with individuals serving as actors to determine the effects of an action and reaction pair. For example, the role might involve various competitors, consumers, or another third party and might give some general guidelines for behavior, and then require the participants to develop their own responses to various actions by the central organization. One difficulty in such role playing or gaming can be the inability of the person or mathematical model representing the individual player to act as that party would act in reality. However, in many cases the method can suggest a number of alternatives, much as brainstorming would, that would not normally be thought of within the planning organization.

Another approach that is similar to scenario writing, but even more speculative, is that of science fiction. Many of the writers of science fiction literature are actually spinning scenarios as to alternative states of technology and the environment. Historically there have been some writers who have done fairly well at predicting the future. For example, Jules Verne, Karel Ĉapek, Aldous Huxley, and David A. Clarke seem to have been particularly successful in foreseeing future environmental states. The major problem in using such science fiction as a source of information for planning is distinguishing those writings that are pure fantasy from those that are likely to represent reality. It is also often the case that the time horizon for these scenarios is so long that they are of very limited value to an individual organization. For example, if an individual company had accepted Verne's predictions regarding atomic energy and moon flights as being accurate more than 100 years ago when Verne wrote those stories, it would have had little impact on the company's own performance and strategy.

13/3/2   The Delphi Approach

The Delphi approach is undoubtedly the most commonly used of technological or qualitative forecasting methods. This approach, originally developed at Rand Corporation, is essentially a method for obtaining a consensus from a group. In this sense, it is similar to some of the methodologies discussed in the previous chapter. However, it is more systematic in its use of individual assessments and can be used whenever a group consensus is needed, whether for a forecast or for some other type of estimate.

The objective of the Delphi approach is to obtain a reliable consensus of opinion from a group of experts that can be used as a future forecast, while at the same time minimizing the undesirable aspects of group interaction. Two of the main developers of this approach—Helmer and Rescher—have described the Delphi method as follows:

The Delphi technique eliminates committee activity altogether thus further reducing the influence of certain psychological factors, such as specious persuasion, the unwillingness to abandon publicly expressed opinions, and the bandwagon effect of majority opinion. This technique replaces direct debate by a carefully designed program of sequential individual interrogations (best conducted by questionnaires), interspersed with information and opinion feedback derived by computer consensus from the earlier parts of the program. Some of the questions directed at respondents may, for instance, inquire into the "reasons" for previous expressed opinions and a collection of such reasons may then be presented to each respondent in the group, together with an invitation to reconsider and possibly revise his or her earlier estimates.[1]

Application of the Delphi approach requires a group of experts who are willing to answer specific questions relating to problems, such as the forecasting of a new technological process and the time at which that will take place. However, these experts do not meet to debate the question, but rather are kept apart from one another so that their judgment will not be influenced by social pressure or other aspects of small-group behavior. An example of how this approach has been used will demonstrate its procedural characteristics (Helmer and Rescher, 1959).

Phase 1. The experts on the panel were asked in a letter to name inventions and scientific breakthroughs that they thought were both urgently needed and could be achieved within the next 20 years. Each expert was then asked to send his or her list back to the coordinator of the panel. From these lists, a general list of 50 items was compiled.

Phase 2. The experts were then sent a list of the 50 items and asked to place each of those items in one of the 5-year time periods into which the next 20 years had been divided. The basis for this categorization was that there would be a 50-50 probability that it would take a longer or shorter period of time for each breakthrough to occur. Again, the experts were asked to send their responses to the panel coordinator. (Throughout this procedure the

---

[1]O. Helmer and N. Rescher, "On the Epistemology of the Inexact Sciences," *Management Science,* **6,** No. 1 (1959), p. 47. Reprinted by permission.

experts were kept apart and asked not to contact any of the other members of the panel.)

Phase 3. Letters were again sent to the experts telling them on which items there was a general consensus and giving them the responses falling in the middle 50 percent, as well as in each of the higher and lower quartiles on those items where there was not a general consensus.

The experts were also asked to state their reason for any widely divergent estimates they had made. Several of the experts, as a result of this, reassessed their estimates in a narrower range.

Phase 4. To narrow the range of estimates further, the phase 3 procedure was repeated. At the end of this phase, a number of the original items on the list were grouped together as breakthroughs for which a relatively narrow time estimate of their occurrence had been obtained. Thus, the final result of such a procedure was not only information based on expert opinion as to what breakthroughs were likely to occur, but also information as to when those breakthroughs would most likely be achieved.

The individual answers obtained when the Delphi approach is applied ensure the anonymity that is needed to reduce the effect of the "socially dominant individual," and controlled feedback reduces the redundant or irrelevant noise often found in direct confrontations. Furthermore, the conformity to a majority opinion achieved by committee meetings is avoided through presentation of a statistical group (quartile) response in relation to the feedback of previous estimates. It would be possible also to consider questions of cost as well as questions of timing of breakthroughs and the nature of those breakthroughs.

The Delphi approach permits a spread of opinion so that the uncertainties surrounding a situation can be reflected. The objective is to narrow the quartile range as much as possible without pressuring the experts on the panel to the extent that deviant opinion would no longer be allowed. This can be done in part by asking deviants to justify their position.

The Delphi method, like any individual forecasting approach, has its disadvantages. The most general complaint against it are its often low level of reliability and its oversensitivity of results to ambiguity in the questionnaire. These disadvantages must be weighed against the advantages that can often be achieved through its use. These objections obviously apply to even less systematic techniques with greater force than they do to the Delphi approach.

There are a variety of situations within business and government in which the Delphi technique can be used with only minor modifications. In the corporate setting, the experts in the group generally come from both within and outside the company. An important aspect of such a group is that each expert need not be well qualified in exactly the same portion of the area of interest. Rather, the experts can be qualified in only subparts of the area, with at least one expert in every subpart. In this way, information can be processed about the entire problem area. The initial questionnaire distributed to the group of experts should seek to establish the general products or production processes for which the forecasts are to be made. The subsequent phases would then give the panel members feedback on the results of the first phase and attempt to have the panel reach a consensus on some of the kinds of products and processes likely to be developed and the timing of these developments. The final phase might seek to further detail some of the specifics of these developments and attempt to discover the most likely alternatives to be developed first.

A number of evaluative studies have been made to summarize experiences with the Delphi technique and some of its advantages and disadvantages. One of the most thorough of these is that prepared by Sackman (1975). He not only attempts to evaluate the Delphi approach, he also seeks to describe some of its variations and some of the alternative procedures that have been found to best overcome shortcomings in the method as it was originally developed. A second work, by Linstone and Turoff (1975), also has added to the descriptive literature on the Delphi approach, as well as expanding discussion of its practical applications.

13/3/3 Cross-Impact Matrices

A technological method of forecasting closely related to both the Delphi method and the use of the scenario is that of cross-impact matrices. A number of papers have appeared reporting applications of this methodology. (See Linstone and Turoff, 1975; Helmer, 1977; and Rochberg et al., 1970.) A cross-impact matrix describes two types of data for a set of possible future developments. The first type estimates the probability that each development will occur within some specified time period in the future. The second estimates the probability that the occurrence of any one of the potential developments would have an effect on the likelihood of occurrence of each of the others. In general, the data for such a matrix can be obtained using either subjective assessment procedures or a method such as the Delphi approach.

The aim of cross-impact analysis is to refine the probabilities relating to the occurrence of individual future developments and their interaction with other developments to the point that these probabilities can be used either as the basis for planning or as the basis for developing scenarios that subsequently can be used in planning. An example taken from Rochberg et al. (1970) will help to illustrate this methodology and its application in forecasting. In this example there are four developments that might occur in the next year. These developments are shown at the top of Figure 13-2.

Development D_i	Probability P_i
1. One-month reliable weather forecasts	.4
2. Feasibility of limited weather control	.2
3. General biochemical immunization	.5
4. Elimination of crop damage from adverse weather	.5

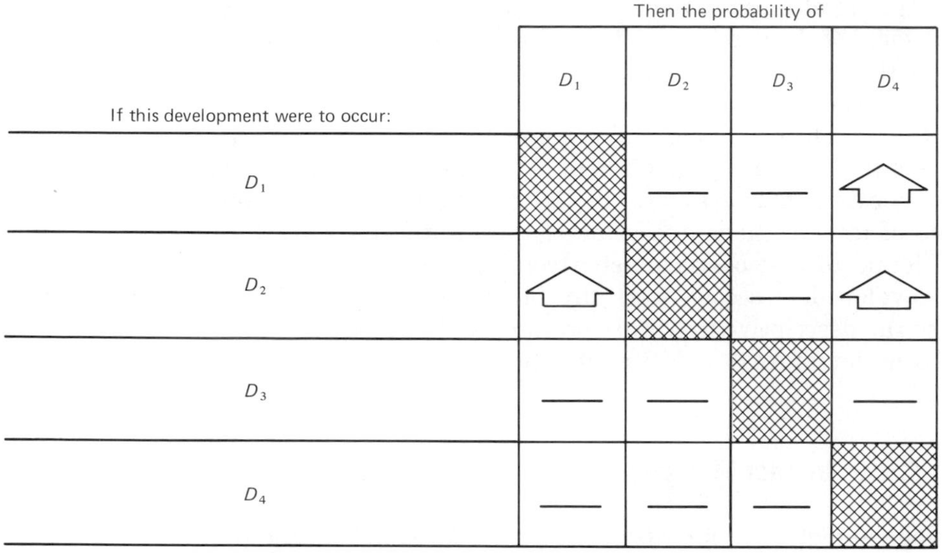

FIGURE 13-2   EXAMPLE OF A CROSS-IMPACT MATRIX

In the bottom of that figure, the cross-impact matrix is shown. The upward arrows in certain of the boxes in the matrix indicate where the occurrence of a certain development will increase the probability of one of the other developments. For example, if D-2, *Feasibility of Limited Weather Control,* were to occur, then D-1, *One-Month Reliable Weather Forecast,* would become more probable as noted by the upward arrow.

The interaction between the various potential developments shown in Figure 13-2 are, of course, complex. The arrows simply indicate the nature of the relationship. Some form of expert opinion and subjective assessment could be needed to quantify that relationship. In addition, the technique of simulation is often used to further refine these probability estimates and their overall impact on the probability that each individual development will occur in the specified time period.

Through appropriate analysis of the problem and use of the guidelines suggested by those who have developed this approach to forecasting, numerical estimates of the probabilities can be filled in for each box in a cross-impact matrix. In addition, formulas can be developed for calculating changes in probabilities that will occur as different developments become a reality. Once this has been done, the matrix can be analyzed using a computer and the technique of simulation. Rochberg (1970) describes the following set of steps for this analysis:

1. Assessing the potential interactions (the cross impacts) among individual events in a set of forecasts in terms of:
   a. direction or mode of the interaction
   b. strength of the interaction
   c. time delay of the effect of one event on another
2. Selecting an event at random and "deciding" its occurrence or nonoccurrence on the basis of its assigned probability. (This is simply an application of simulation.)
3. Adjusting the probability of the remaining events according to interactions assessed in step 1.
4. Selecting another event from among those remaining and deciding its occurrence or nonoccurrence (using its new probability) as before. (Again, this is an application of simulation.)
5. Continuing this process until all events in the set have been decided.
6. "Playing" the matrix in this way many times so that the probabilities can be computed on the basis of the percentage of times an event occurs during these repeated plays.
7. Changing the initial probability of one or more events and repeating steps 2 through 6.

Through application of this procedure, a set of probabilities can be developed that adequately represents the interaction between a number of different developments, each of which is uncertain. This analysis allows such probabilities to take into account the cross-impacts of other events. Clearly, that is of help to the forecaster and planner who must consider a number of different uncertain developments.

One of the first applications of the cross-impact method was that developed by Gordon and Hayward (1968). This application involved 28 events that were judged to be relevant to the decision concerning deployment of the Minuteman Missile System. These 28 events were arrayed in a matrix like that of Figure 13-2 and estimates were obtained for the direction, strength, and time phasing of the effects of the events on each other. The matrix was then run 1000 times on a computer according to the steps outlined above. The results were averaged in order to obtain new estimates of the probability of occurrence of each of the events in the matrix. Those probability shifts identified through this procedure provided the forecasters with some measure of the combined cross-impact effects implicit in the original matrix.

The results of this application to the Minuteman analysis problem indicated that the mutual interaction of the events increased the likelihood of the decision to deploy the system. In addition, a ranking of the events in terms of their final cross-impacted probabilities provided the ingredients for a scenario that subsequently proved to be quite descriptive of the technological and political environment of the 1950s. Thus, despite the simplifications needed to apply the methodology, the findings were consistent with what actually occurred.

While the basic concept of cross-impact matrices is straightforward, the detailed steps involved in its application are generally quite complex. In fact, Amara (1972) points out that one of the major shortcomings of the methodology is that frequently the impact of various developments on each other is sequence-dependent. That is, the probabilities for the impact of one development on another depend on sequences of activity rather than on individual activities. That, of course, greatly increases the magnitude of the problem and the difficulties associated with the application of this methodology. However, in spite of these shortcomings, it is a technique that has found a number of useful applications in both government and business. (See Linstone and Turoff, 1975; Helmer, 1977.)

13/3/4 Curve Fitting

Curve fitting is a methodology commonly discussed as a quantitative forecasting technique, but it is also an approach that can be effectively used as a technological method. However, there are considerable differences in the approaches taken in both instances. It will be recalled from previous chapters that in the quantitative methods, some form of curve fitting is often done to approximate the basic trend component of a time series. This fitting is usually based on historical data and covers only a few years in most instances. In the case of technological approaches to curve fitting, the time horizon is generally much longer, only a limited number of data points are available, some rather tenuous assumptions must be made, and an interpretation of results is required. However, in some instances, this approach can indeed be most helpful to the forecaster and planner.

The application of curve fitting in predicting the efficiency of man-made illumination (Cetron, 1969) can serve as an example of this approach. In this particular application there are only seven data points available, each representing a substantial development in technology that has occurred historically. This small number of data points makes it very tenuous to do any quantitative type of prediction. Furthermore, a simple trend cannot be extrapolated directly because the curve would increase indefinitely. Such an increase is impossible because the efficiency of man-made illumination cannot exceed the theoretical efficiency of light. Thus the trend will have to bend as shown in Figure 13-3.

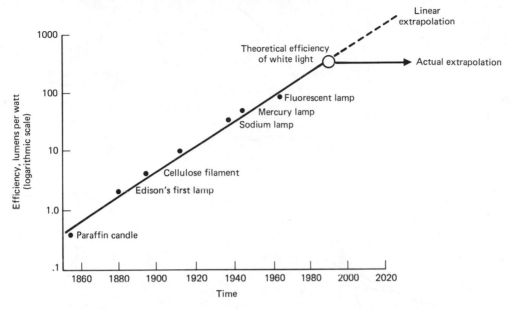

FIGURE 13-3   EFFICIENCY OF MANMADE WHITE LIGHT

Many different shapes of curves can be used in fitting historical data for technological forecasting. One of the most frequently used forms is that of the S-curve. As indicated in the example shown in Figure 13-4, this curve implies a slow start, a steep growth, and then a plateau that is characteristic of many technological capabilities. This shape of curve is often used in depicting the product life cycle. Chambers et al. (1974) report that the sales of both black and white and color TV have followed such S-patterns. Ayres (1969) and Jantsch (1969) also report a number of applications of different technologies that have followed such S-shaped curves. By connecting the tangents of individual growth curves, an envelope of S-curves can be formed that can be used to predict such things as the maximum speed of transportation. The example in Figure 13-4 shows the behavior of transportation speed from the Pony Express to the chemical rocket. This curve can be further extrapolated to predict future speeds of nuclear rockets or even currently unknown forms of energy.

Mathematically, there are many different equations that can be used to represent an S-shaped curve. The most common of these are the following:

$$Y = e^{a-(b/t)} \tag{13-1}$$

$$Y = \frac{L}{1 + ae^{-bt}} \tag{13-2}$$

$$Y = Le^{-ae^{-bt}} \tag{13-3}$$

$$Y = (1 - ae^{-bt})^3 \tag{13-4}$$

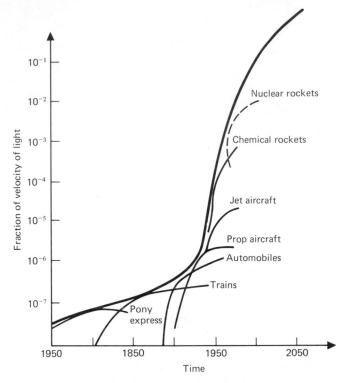

FIGURE 13-4   S-CURVE OF TRANSPORTATION SPEED

Estimating the parameters for equation (13-1) can be accomplished in a straightforward manner by taking logarithms of both sides and solving for a and b using least squares procedures. In equations (13-2) and (13-3), if $L = 1$, the equation is simplified considerably and can be estimated using the method of least squares after the appropriate transformation has been applied. In equation (13-4), the parameters cannot be estimated using simple least squares because the functional form cannot be reduced to a linear trend. However, the parameters can be estimated iteratively and through the use of other algorithms. Note that if a nonlinear regression package is available (for example, the SHARE program NLINREG), a better fit will be obtained for all equations than if some form of linearizing transformation is applied first.

A major issue when a decision has been made to apply an S-curve in technological forecasting is selecting the right form of S-curve. S-curve in technological forecasting is selecting the right form of S-curve. The solution to this problem depends on the technology or the product being forecast and its characteristics. Through previous experience one might approximate the S-curve form in order to use it for forecasting. Fortunately, the exact form of S-curve necessary for sufficient accuracy for planning is not always critical as can be seen from Figure 13-5. (The choice of one S-curve over another will result in little difference in the arrow.)

Several other functional forms can also be used in curve fitting for technological purposes—exponential, logarithmic, double exponential, and others. The problem of determining which form of curve will best fit the available data and give an accurate forecast for the future is a difficult part of such applications. One illustration of these difficulties is reported by Ayres (1969), who describes the use of S-curves by two different forecasters. In each instant a different scale was used and this change alone led strikingly different results.

13/3/5 Analogy Methods

Analogies are attempted to compare historical patterns with existing situations in order to forecast future progress and developments. These forecasts are generally technological in nature and involve changes in various technologies or the environment. There are several types of analogies, including growth analogies, historical analogies, and social physics. Each of these will be discussed in turn.

Growth Analogies

Many researchers have shown that the population growth tends to follow a pattern similar to the growth of biological organisms. The same conclusion was reached by Gompertz and Von Bertalanffy. The S-type curve described in the previous section can be used in predicting population growth pattern and its point of stability by using such analogies. The concept of analogy between biological and other kinds of growth has recently been applied to such phenomena as the growth pattern of particular technologies, transportation speeds, the life cycle of individual products, and the growth of government spending. (See Ascher, 1978.)

Growth analogies are similar to S-shaped curves except that no prediction of parameters is required, since with growth analogies the curve is considered known and the purpose is to fit the data to the curve rather than vice versa. This application allows the curve to be used in predicting time estimates for the occurrence of various events in the future. With growth curves, as with S-curves, saturation will eventually be reached and identification of when that will occur is very important in determining the appropriate growth analogy. Whether such saturation is more descriptive of the future than an increasing rate of growth, like that depicted by exponential curves, is a matter still open to debate.

Historical Analogies

Historical analogies are more intuitive than any of the other forms of this approach. In many different ways predictions can be based on what

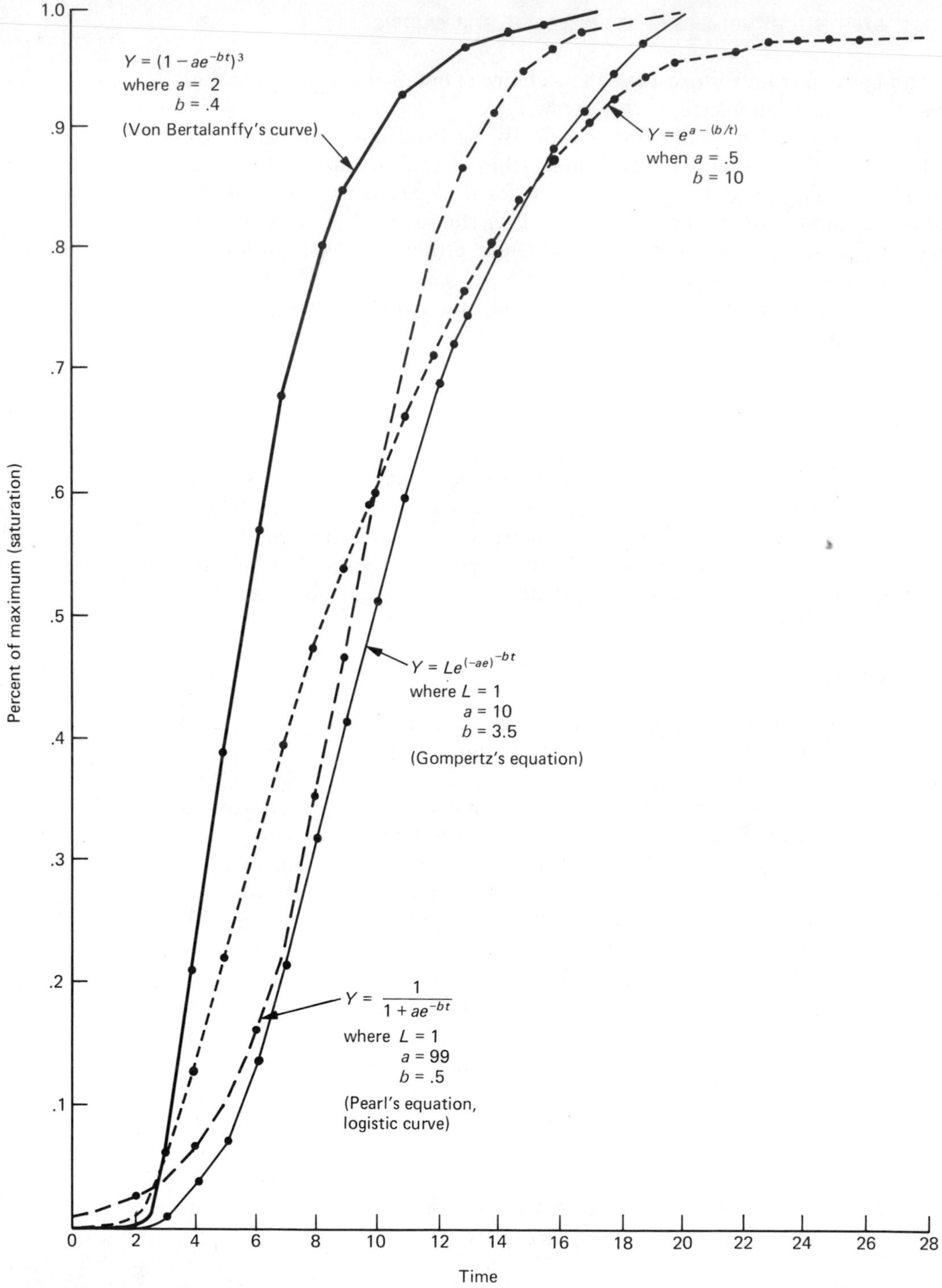

1.0
.9
.8
.7
.6
.5
.4
.3
.2
.1
0
2
4
6
8
10
12
14
16
18
20
22
24
26
28
Percent of maximum (saturation)
Time
$Y = (1 - ae^{-bt})^3$
where a = 2
b = .4
(Von Bertalanffy's curve)
$Y = e^{a - (b/t)}$
when a = .5
b = 10
$Y = Le^{(-ae)^{-bt}}$
where L = 1
a = 10
b = 3.5
(Gompertz's equation)
$Y = \frac{1}{1 + ae^{-bt}}$
where L = 1
a = 99
b = .5
(Pearl's equation,
logistic curve)

FIGURE 13-5 COMMONLY USED S-CURVES

has happened in the past. In these common forms, such as superstition or rational thinking, historical analogies are as old as civilization itself.

One attempt to formalize the use of historical analogies for predictive purposes has been made in a book edited by Mazlish (1965). This book attempts to show a number of analogies between the development of railroads and the development of the space program. The attempt is to predict the technological development and social and political implications of the space program by drawing an analogy to these aspects of the development of railroads in the last century. Unfortunately, there are a number of deficiencies in this study, as pointed out by Jantsch (1969) and Ayres (1969), that detract from Mazlish's attempt to apply this approach. However, the use of historical analogies can still be extremely important in many other instances. General Electric has been using a form of historical analogy in its TEMPO project, attempting to forecast the proportion of electrical power that will be produced by nuclear fuels through the year 2060. Estimates have been made using the consumption of fossil fuel and hydroelectric power during the period from 1800 to 1960 as a base for historical comparison.

Social Physics

In a manner analogous to physical or natural laws, there may well be social laws, which if discovered could be used as the basis for making a number of important and valuable predictions. Unfortunately, the task of identifying such social laws is sufficiently difficult that even their existence has not yet been completely verified. However, the concept holds some promise as another approach to technological forecasting.

According to Bell (1964), there may be a number of social laws upon which human behavior, development of the social environment, and development of the political system at a given time are predicated. Bell uses the law of motion of capitalism set forth by Marx as an example of an attempt to identify such a social law. The falling rate of profit on which Marx based the large armies of unemployed, the impoverishment of labor, the centralization of capital, and so on, can in fact be thought of as an analogy to a falling object that accelerates in speed and rate of fall because of gravity. The conclusion that Marx reached is that capitalism will fall in the same manner and nothing can stop or slow the rate of increased speed until it crashes. This conclusion is based on the assumption that there are natural laws that govern falling objects whether they be societies or whether they be physical items. Although Marx's specific predictions lack accuracy because he did not recognize the existence of the feedback mechanisms that could slow down or reverse such laws of motion as they apply to societies, his predictions are based on an interesting methodology that may be applicable elsewhere.

Bell refers to still another application of the effort to create a social physics in discussing the work of Rappaport as follows:

He [Rappaport] set up mathematical models for mass action and descriptive models for conflict situations. One section of the book deals with arms races and the equations that are developed seek to describe the development of actual arms races in the same way that the equations of thermodynamics are meant to describe the behavior of gases. One intention of the new social physics is to set up general probabilistic laws that govern behavior in game-like situations. [Bell, 1964, p. 850]

To what extent analogies can be used for technological forecasting is a question that has not yet been thoroughly answered. At the present time they are not used to any great extent, nor have they been used in the past by any large number of forecasters. However, they may be useful in particular situations for which data are not available or other methods simply are not suitable. One advantage of analogies is that they can be used intuitively and without much effort in many situations. Thus, they might be preferred in cases that require a tremendous amount of work before other methodologies can be applied successfully.

13/3/6 Morphological Research

The morphological approach to technological forecasting was developed by the Swiss astronomer, Zwicky, in his efforts to discover new inventions in the field of jet engines. Zwicky claims over 30 industrial applications in addition to a large number of purely theoretical uses of this technique in discovering new technological possibilities. The General Electric TEMPO Center has used a morphological approach in some of its research and the same is true for several projects conducted at the Stanford Research Institute in areas of political and social development.

Morphological research "concerns itself with the development and the practical application of basic methods that will allow us to discover and analyze the structural or morphological interrelationships among objects, phenomena, and concepts and to explore the results obtained for the construction of a sound world" (Zwicky, 1962, p. 275). This definition of the morphological method goes beyond simple forecasting applications and represents an approach to systematic thinking and problem solving. Although there may be some arguments about the universality of such an approach, the framework may be useful to those faced with technological forecasting problems. An application of this methodology will help to describe its use.

Zwicky (1962) describes five basic steps that constitute the morphological method:

Step 1. The problem must be explicitly formulated and defined.

Step 2. All parameters that may enter into the solution must be identified and characterized.

Step 3. A multidimensional matrix (the Morphological Box) containing all parameters identified in Step 2 must be constructed. This matrix will contain all possible solutions (combinations).

Step 4. All solutions of the Morphological Box should be examined for their feasibility, and analyzed and evaluated with respect to the purposes which are to be achieved.

Step 5. The best solutions identified in step 4 should be analyzed (possibly through an additional Morphological Study) as to the feasibility of carrying them out with available resources.

As an application of this approach, Zwicky mentions his attempts in the late thirties to identify possible propulsive power plants (jet engines) that could be activated by chemical energy. He distinguishes six parameters that define all possible jet engines of this form:

P_1: The medium through which the jet engine moves. There are four components related to the first parameter.
    P_{11}: denoting that the jet engine moves through a vacuum,
    P_{12}: denoting that the jet engine moves in the atmosphere,
    P_{13}: denoting that the jet engine moves in large bodies of water,
    P_{14}: denoting that the jet engine moves in the solid surface strata of the Earth.

P_2: The type of motion of the propellant relative to the jet engine, with the following four components:
    P_{21}: denoting a propellant at rest,
    P_{22}: denoting a translatory motion,
    P_{23}: denoting an oscillatory motion,
    P_{24}: denoting a rotary motion.

P_3: The physical state of the propellant, with the following three components:
    P_{31}: denoting a gaseous physical state,
    P_{32}: denoting a liquid physical state,
    P_{33}: denoting a solid physical state.

P_4: The type of thrust augmentation, with the following three parameters:
    P_{41}: denoting no thrust augmentation,
    P_{42}: denoting internal thrust augmentation,
    P_{43}: denoting external thrust augmentation.

P_5: The type of ignition, with the following two parameters:
    P_{51}: denoting a self-igniting engine,
    P_{52}: denoting an externally ignited engine.

P_6: The sequence of operations, with the following two parameters:
    P_{61}: continuous operation,
    P_{62}: intermittent operation. [Zwicky, 1962, p. 32]

From the above Morphological Box of 6 parameters, 576 combinations ($4 \times 4 \times 3 \times 3 \times 2 \times 2 = 576$) of jet engines can be identified. These can then be studied for their feasibility and analyzed and evaluated with respect to their ability to achieve a specific set of objectives. The large number of alternatives involved makes it impractical to examine all of them (step 4). Zwicky had either to pick at random some of them for study, or to discover some principle that would relate a number of possible alternatives so he could study them as a group.

Based on this use of morphological analysis, Zwicky was able to suggest several radical new inventions that were at least conceptually sound and many of which were later successfully developed in various stages of jet engine technology. He goes on to describe 16 different patents that were granted to him as a result of his study of the jet engine example and claims that those patents and the inventions they represent were obtained largely as a result of applying this morphological approach.

One of the advantages accompanying the use of morphological research stems from its assessment of the chances that a future technology will be realized. This assessment can be made based on a study of the Morphological Box and is calculated as a function of what Zwicky calls the morphological distance (the number of parameters by which the existing technology differs from a specific one inside the Morphological Box). The greater the distance the smaller will be the chances of that particular technology's being realized. In a similar fashion, technological opportunities can be evaluated as a function of the number of combinations existing within the neighborhood of a certain technology. The greater the number the higher the chances that technology will materialize, either by accident or because it will be needed before some future technological development can be realized.

It should be stressed that morphological research is a kind of checklist that in a systematic manner enumerates all possible combinations of technologies. Its advantage is that it allows the user to identify hidden or rare opportunities for technological possibilities that can be profitably developed. Both the search for new technologies and their chances of successful development can be calculated from the checklist or Morphological Box. Even though simple in nature, the morphological approach can serve as a useful tool to the forecaster in many situations.

Taylor et al. (1967) have combined the morphological approach with scenario writing. A similar combination has also been used by the Hudson Institute where a variety of different types of nuclear threats and possible future worlds have been classified in a Morphological Box. Although few applications of this approach to business situations have been reported, an exercise is included at the end of this chapter that suggests how it might be used in that setting.

13/3/7 Catastrophe Theory

Most forecasting methodologies look at average values as the basis for prediction. Generally they assume that randomness consists of a large number of unimportant factors that can take on either positive or negative values. The result of these numerous random elements is a unimodal distribution. Such random elements are generally ignored because their expected value is assumed to equal zero.

One of the main rationales for *catastrophe theory* is that such assumptions about randomness are inappropriate in a number of situations. Catastrophe theory assumes that bimodality (or, in general, multimodality) very often exists in the real world. In such instances the outcome that is observed has as much chance of moving toward one modal point as toward another, so that on average it is very unlikely that it will fall in between those two modes. In fact, the average outcome is extremely unlikely to occur in many instances because it is not one of the modes.

One of the most complete descriptions of the use of catastrophe theory in forecasting is that reported by Zeeman (1976). Using a number of graphics, and concepts from topology, he gives several different examples of phenomena that exhibit bimodality or multimodality. Much of Zeeman's work is based on the original work of Thom (1972), which reports on the initial development and exposition of this approach.

Zeeman describes five properties that characterize phenomena that can be effectively described using this set of concepts:

1. The behavior (the outcome) is always bimodal in some part of its range and sudden jumps are observed between one mode of behavior and the other.
2. The jump from the upper plane of the behavior surface to the lower plane does not take place at the same position as the jump from the bottom sheet to the top one, an effect called *hysteresis*.
3. Between the top and bottom sheets there is an inaccessible zone on the behavior axis.
4. The middle sheet representing least likely behavior is usually not important.
5. This model implies a possibility of divergent behavior. [Zeeman, 1976, p. 76].

In Zeeman's description of the theory he uses a number of examples based on behavior. These vary from situations involving self-pity and anger to those involving aggression and fear. He also includes some physical examples, such as decompression of an elastic beam that may buckle either downward or upward, depending on which mode is reached. Finally, he considers the transition of a liquid to a gaseous state, a process that is affected by the pressure, temperature, and density during the transition.

Graphically, the notion of catastrophe theory and bimodal outcome can be represented as shown in Figure 13-6. The x- and y-axes indicate the two important criteria that can be used to distinguish the two modes of likely behavior. The vertical axis represents the actual behavior that is observed. According to application of the theory, what happens is that as the various levels of x and y (for example, fear and rage) are altered, the behavior may change radically if it forces a precipitous drop from one level of the surface to another level. (A low level of fear may cause withdrawal; a high level may cause aggressive behavior.) It is also possible to interpret the implications of Zeeman's five characteristics for applying this approach.

While still a relatively new technique, this approach fills a gap in existing forecasting methodologies and has been illustrated to effectively explain a number of different outcomes in a wide range of situations suggests that it may find increasing application in the future. Undoubtedly other techniques will also be developed for use in forecasting as the base of experience in the application of existing methodologies is expanded.

13/4 Normative Approaches to Technological Forecasting

Exploratory methods of technological forecasting begin with the existing situation and in an intuitive, extrapolative, or heuristic manner move toward prediction of the future. In so doing, no explicit attempt is made to consider the objective or goal of society or the individual organization and the impact of these factors on the eventual outcome. Such goals and desires often serve an important role in determining future developments.

Two examples can help to illustrate the need for assessing goals or objectives as an integral part of forecasting. The first example is the use of the Universal Product Code (the series of bars often printed on product packages in the United States today) and its adoption by supermarkets. The aim of the Universal Product Code is to make it possible to reduce the amount of labor required in the retail food industry through fewer mistakes at the checkout stand and through having scanning devices read the product code rather than requiring the checker to type in each price and item. Part of the savings originally anticipated from the use of such codes was that marking individual prices on each item would no longer be necessary, since prices could be stored in a central computer and accessed when the product was passed over the scanner and the product code identified. Unfortunately,

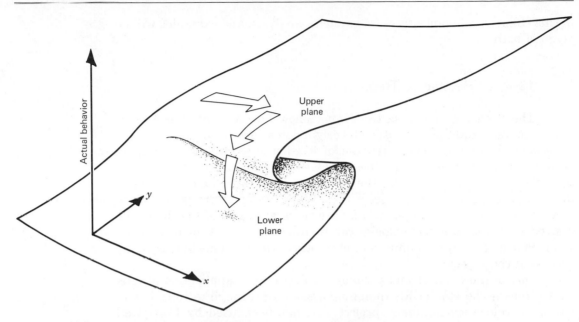

FIGURE 13-6 GRAPHIC REPRESENTATION OF PREDICTING BIMODAL BEHAVIOR WITH CATASTROPHE THEORY

very little research was done on consumer reaction to removal of individual prices on each item, and in the early seventies the industry was surprised to find that consumers were unwilling to have prices simply marked on the shelves, and insisted they be marked on individual items. This problem could have been foreseen and perhaps at least partially compensated for if the forecasting had looked not only at the development of the technical capabilities required for use of such a system, but also at the goals and objectives in adopting the system and the desires and needs of consumers.

Another example is the development of the supersonic transport (SST) in the United States. During the sixties it was repeatedly assumed that the problems of adoption of SST technology and aircraft were technical in nature and that once it became feasible and economical, the use of such aircraft would become widespread. Again, the reaction of consumers and those elements of the United States population that would be affected by the noise and pollution associated with the SST aircraft were not considered in forecasting the adoption of this technology. The SST projects of United States manufacturers were dropped by the mid-seventies and even the European SST manufacturing had been stopped by the early eighties.

In order to overcome some of the problems that can often hinder the actual adoption of technologies and to adequately forecast when such adoption will take place, many forecasters have considered the use of normative methods of technological forecasting. Two such methods will be described in this chapter: relevance trees and systems analysis, and examples will be given of both.

13/4/1   Relevance Trees

The method of relevance trees is not a new development. (See Ascher, 1978; Alderson and Sproull, 1971.) Its origin dates back to the development of decision theory and the construction of decision trees aimed at aiding the decision maker in selecting the best strategy from among a number of alternatives. Relevance trees use the concepts and methodologies of decision theory and decision trees to assess the desirability of future goals and to select those areas of development that are necessary in order to achieve the desired goals. Specific technologies can then be singled out for further development and greater commitment of resources can be made to ensure the success of those projects.

One of the earliest and perhaps the best-known application of relevance trees is the PATTERN (planning assistance through technical evaluation of relevance numbers) project that has been used by Honeywell Corporation for military, space, and medical purposes. The aim of the PATTERN approach, as with other types of relevance trees, is to aid planners in indentifying the long-range developments that are most important to the accomplishment of specific objectives. The PATTERN computer program sequences the relevance of the objectives and prints out a list of technological breakthroughs that are needed to achieve those objectives. In one sense, the results obtained from a PATTERN application often become self-fulfilling prophecies, since they identify the primary objectives and the means available for their accomplishment.

One of the first applications of PATTERN was in evaluating national objectives for military and space exploration. On the highest level three broad goals were stated: national survival, creation of a credible posture, and favorable world opinion. As a starting point in helping the planners identify the developments necessary to achieve these national objectives, a scenario was prepared identifying all levels of support needed for their successful accomplishment. This scenario was simply a brief description about the future and what the situation might possibly be surrounding related military and scientific developments. The scenario itself was developed by a group of experts involved in long-range planning for the government. The scenario served as a starting point and thus did not need to be accurate in every detail, but rather simply suggested the types of problems that had to be considered in achieving the three goals.

Based on the scenario, a panel of experts was used to develop the relevance tree shown in Figure 13-7. This relevance tree shows the relationship between the primary objectives and the subobjectives and breaks those subobjectives down to a level at which specific technological require-

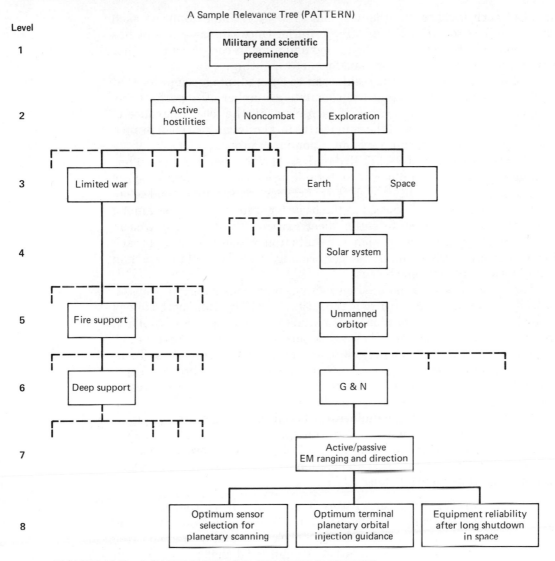

FIGURE 13-7 A SAMPLE RELEVANCE TREE (PATTERN)

ments can be identified. In the example of Figure 13-7, eight such levels have been defined. The elements of the final level represent the breakthroughs required in order to achieve the long-run objectives given in the first level.

Once the relevance tree has been constructed and the criteria for the achievement (and measurement) of the primary objectives have been identified, a panel of experts can be used to determine the relevance and importance of each element of the tree. This process involves relating each element at each level to all others at that same level and evaluating each element's ability to fulfill the existing criteria. Once this assessment has been completed, the results can be tallied and a mean computed by either averaging all answers or using some form of weighting.

Following this phase, the results can be entered into a computer that has previously been programmed to calculate a number of important factors, such as the partial relevance of each element, the local relevance of each branch at each level, and the cumulative total relevance of each branch using a top-down or bottom-up accumulation procedure.

Through this type of PATTERN analysis of objectives, Honeywell has been able to identify a number of high-ranking missions related to space and ocean exploration, military counterinsurgency, arms control, and so on. These missions could then be used as the basis for shifting resources among various programs in order to better meet existing goals. In the area of aircraft technology and field guidance, results from the use of this approach indicate that lower costs and better performance have been obtained than would otherwise have been the case.

Relevance trees can be used for evaluating a wide range of projects. However, it should be realized that the cost of applying this methodology can be significant. Like morphological research, relevance trees involve a large number of alternatives, all of which must be assessed and evaluated. This process requires considerable human and computer resources. To illustrate some of the advantages and disadvantages of this approach, a specific application developed by Alderson and Sproull (1971) in the area of automobile transportation can be considered.

Suppose that an auto manufacturer is concerned with predicting future technological innovations related to automobile transportation. Further, assume that the company selects PATTERN as the approach to using relevance trees. To facilitate this application, the total task can be divided into a number of sequential steps.

Step 1. A relevance tree structure must be developed that identifies the company's objectives, each of the functions involved, requirements to achieve these objectives and so on. The tree must be extended to a low enough level that the individual technologies and developments needed to achieve each of the higher level objectives can be identified.

Step 2. A number of criteria must be established so that priorities in ordering each of the variables can be determined in a meaningful manner. Criteria must be established for each level. For illustrative purposes, however, attention will be focused on level 1, where one might establish the following four criteria:

    a. reduced cost
    b. increased safety

  c. increased efficiency

  d. increased comfort

 Step 3. A panel of experts could be asked to weight the importance of each criterion in relation to the others. The question might be phrased as follows: "What is the relative importance (weight) of each of the following criteria in achieving the higher level objective of providing automobile transportation?"

A second set of questions could then be used to determine the importance of each element at each level in relation to all other elements at that same level. At level 1 the following elements might be considered:

  a. accommodate passengers

  b. provide an environment

  c. provide performance monitoring capabilities

  d. provide control capabilities

The comparison might take the form of weighting with regard to each of the four criteria. Thus, a typical question might be: "In order to reduce the cost of automobile transportation, what is the relative importance (weight) of each of the following elements?"

 When the experts have answered all the questions for all elements at each level, their answers can be coded and the data entered into a previously programmed computer that will calculate several useful numbers. Before doing this, however, it is useful to consider the computations involved in calculating a single relevance number. The tree itself can be summarized as shown in Figure 13-8.

 Step 4. Assuming that the average panel weights for the items assessed in step 3 are as shown in Table 13-2, the individual relevance numbers can be computed.

 The partial relevance number (PRN) is

 PRN = (criterion weight)(element weight).

Thus,

  $(.20)(.05) = .01$ is a partial relevance number;

  $(.20)(.30) = .06$ is another partial relevance number.

A local relevance number for level 1 is

  $R_L = \Sigma PRN$.

 There are as many local relevance numbers as there are elements at the level. The local relevance numbers for the first level are shown in Table 13-3.

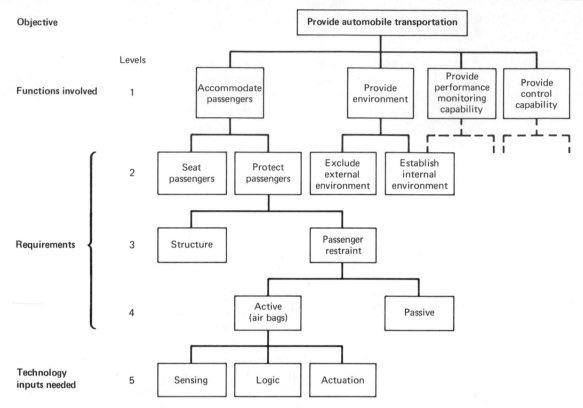

FIGURE 13-8   RELEVANCE TREE STRUCTURE

Summing the partial relevance numbers corresponding to each element, four local relevance numbers that indicate the importance of each element are obtained. From these it can be seen that *provide control capabilities* is the most important of the four functions, and *provide environment* is the least important function or characteristic of the car—as perceived or judged by the panel members. (The summation of all local relevance numbers is always 1, making such comparisons straightforward.)

Cumulative direct relevance numbers can be calculated as

$$R_D = R_{L,i}(R_{L,i+1}),$$

where $R_{L,i}$ is the local relevance number at level 1 and $R_{L,i+1}$ is the local relevance number of the related (continued) element(s) of the next level. For example, if the local relevance numbers for level 2 are as follows (calculated exactly as for level 1):

seat passengers—.12,

protect passengers—.23,

TABLE 13-2 WEIGHTS FOR CRITERIA AND ELEMENTS
OF RELEVANCE TREES

	Criteria				
	Reduced Cost	Increased Safety	Increased Efficiency	Increased Comfort	
Criterion weight	.20	.50	.20	.10	= 1.0
	Element Weights (based on specific criterion)				
Elements of level 1					
Accommodate passenger	.05	.25	.40	.35	
Provide environment	.30	.05	.15	.50	
Provide performance monitoring capabilities	.60	.10	.40	.05	
Provide control capabilities	.05	.60	.05	.10	
	1.00	1.00	1.00	1.00	

exclude external environment—.08,

establish internal environment—.15,

then the cumulative direct relevance number will be as shown in Table 13-4.

In the second level, the most important of the four elements is *protect passengers* (local relevance number .23), followed by *establish internal environment*. Looking at the cumulative direct relevance numbers, which show the importance of an element up to the level of calculation, *protect passengers* is still the most important element and the second is *seat passengers*.

In a similar manner, the cumulation of relevance numbers can be achieved for each of the levels until the lowest level is reached. The cumulative direct relevance number of the lowest level will become the total direct relevance number indicating the importance of each of the final technological requirements if the higher-level objectives are to be realized.

In the Alderson and Sproull illustration, the element at the last level that has the highest total direct relevance number is that of sensing (see

TABLE 13-3   LOCAL RELEVANCE NUMBERS FOR LEVEL 1

| | | Elements of Level 1 | | | | | | | |
| | | Accommodate Passengers | | Provide Environment | | Provide Performance Monitoring Capabilities | | Provide Control Capabilities | |
Criterion	Criterion Weight	W[a]	PRN[b]	W	PRN	W	PRN	W	PRN
Reduced costs	.20	.05	.01	.30	.06	.60	.12	.05	.01
Increased safety	.50	.25	.125	.05	.025	.10	.05	.60	.30
Increased efficiency	.20	.40	.08	.15	.03	.40	.08	.05	.01
Increased comfort	.10	.35	.035	.50	.05	.05	.005	.10	.01
Local relevance number for level 1			.250		1.65		.255		.330

[a]Weights.
[b]Partial relevance number.

Figure 13-8), with a total direct relevance number of .052. It is followed in importance by a response element (not shown in Figure 13-8) with .0375 relevance and an information transmission element (not shown in Figure 13-8) with .0358 relevance. The first number implies that there will be a high demand for technological break-throughs, so that an air bag protecting passengers can be developed. The most critical element will be the sensing device to operate that air bag. In the same manner, the other relevant numbers can be interpreted and used as a basis for selecting future areas of technological pursuit. Through R&D investments and other commitments of resources, these areas can then be developed in order to realize the higher level objectives and missions.

Generally, the computer printout of a PATTERN application provides substantially more information than the few relevance numbers described in this example. This information includes the variance of each element, the weights voted by each of the panel members (and the distribution of those weights), selected ratios permitting the display of the relationship between relevance rankings, measures of dispersion, and so on. All of these are aimed at facilitating the identification of future technological needs and concentrating efforts on those areas that are most important.

It is interesting to compare the weighting of criteria developed by United States car manufacturers with those developed by some European

TABLE 13-4 CUMULATIVE DIRECT RELEVANCE NUMBERS FOR LEVELS 1 AND 2

Corresponding Element of Level 1	Local Relevance Number (level 1)	Element of Level 2	Local Relevance Number (level 2)	Cumulative Direct Relevance Number
Accommodate passengers	.25	Seat passengers	.12	(.25)(.12) = .03
Accommodate passengers	.25	Protect passengers	.23	(.25)(.23) = .05
Provide environment	.165	Exclude external environment	.08	(.165)(.15) = .013
Provide environment	.165	Establish internal environment	.15	(.165)(.15) = .024

auto manufacturers for the example shown in Figure 13-8. Reducing cost and increasing efficiency tend to be more important than safety and comfort in the priorities assigned by these European auto companies. As a result, there may be substantial differences in the ranking of technological requirements for the United States and European companies. In recent years government legislation and other social changes have made it necessary for all auto manufacturers to move closer together in their product design and specifications than had previously been the case. Thus, U.S. auto manufacturers have moved toward smaller and more efficient cars, while European manufacturers have tended to incorporate additional safety equipment in their autos. However, differences in objectives still play an important role in selecting those technologies to which resources are going to be committed. Relevance trees are one approach for handling such differences and systematically integrating forecasting and planning in regard to them.

13/4/2 Systems Dynamics

Systems analysis or the systems approach, as it is commonly called, is aimed at considering the interrelationships among the components of an organization or environment rather than looking at each component in isolation. In such applications it is the mutual interaction of each unit with other units that is of interest. Better understanding of the complex pattern of interactions among the elements composing the system often results in better predictions of future behavior of the system.

An example of this approach is system dynamics, which originated at MIT under Forrester (1958), and was initially called industrial dynamics. The goals of this methodology are:

1. To develop a better understanding of *time-varying behavior*.
2. To show *interrelationships* among the major aspects of a system.
3. To help *predict the future* course of an existing system.
4. To help *improve the prospects* for the future.

Instead of defining a system as a set of separate functions, system dynamics views it as a system of *flows*—of information, of materials, of manpower, of capital equipment, and of money—which set up forces that determine tendencies toward growth, fluctuation, and decline. Successful problem solving in system dynamics, therefore, urges the following philosophy:

- Use explicit, formal models.
- Do not look for perfect models.
- Do not try to tell what will actually happen, but rather start making conditional statements.
- Look for policies that increase the probability of more desirable outcomes.

The development of a system dynamics model follows several guidelines, which can be presented in the form of a hierarchical list (see Forrester, 1968), as follows:

Closed Boundary. Define the boundary of the problem (that is, what will be internal to the system and what will be external), and within the boundary, define:
Feedback Loops. "The structural setting within which all decisions are made," feedback loops imply "the circularity of cause and effect." Within feedback loops are *levels* and *rates*.
Levels. Often referred to as "state variables" or "stocks," levels can be treated as static (that is, can be measured or counted at any instant of time).
Rates. Representing the system activity (or dynamics), these are the policy variables that influence "levels" and constitute decision possibilities. A statement of system policy has an important substructure built into it, as follows:
There is a *goal*.
There is an *observed condition*.
There is a *discrepancy* between these two, which suggests a *desired action*.

System dynamics modeling has been applied to a variety of complex problem areas, and practitioners of this analysis are a dedicated fraternity. They believe that (1) economic instability (at the corporate, national, or international level) is caused by *micro* decision-making—in other words, that *macro* behavior is generated by the *micro* structure; (2) individuals (for example, forecasters) are good at specifying *structure* but bad at anticipating the *dynamic consequences* implied by the structure; and (3) there is generally too much information available for model-building exercises, rather than too little.

The implications of this approach for a forecaster are direct. Since cause and effect are often widely separated in time and space, and since policy-making is often directed at handling short-term problems, there is no guarantee that the long-term response of the system will be acceptable. System dynamics deals explicitly with the delay structures built into feedback loops, and a special programming language (DYNAMO) is available to examine the dynamic consequences of interacting feedback loops within a system.

Initially, system dynamicists were reluctant to use the word "forecasting" to describe what their simulation models accomplished. However, in recent years there has been a positive interest in dealing with the forecasting issue. In the crucial area of future energy scenarios, several system dynamics models have been developed, including Gross and Ware (1975), Naill (1977), and a recent thesis by Marshall (1981). This latter study makes use of a system dynamics model to examine the feasibility and likelihood of extensive wood-energy use in New England, 1970–2000.

From a system dynamics point of view the traditional management paradigm views organization as an *effect,* that is, external forces such as GNP, energy prices, and so on, result in organizational performance of a particular kind. This leads to the traditional prescription: forecast the external forces and then design an "optimal" response based on the forecast. If accurate forecasts are possible and if management knows what to do to achieve desired results, then the traditional approach is satisfactory. System dynamicists do not believe this to be the case. Rather, organization is viewed as a *cause,* that is, external forces and internal organizational performance result in organizational policies, which cause organizational performance to be what it is. This leads to a system dynamics prescription: gain an understanding of how organizational policies are determining performance and then redesign policies to make the organization resilient in the face of uncontrollable external forces.

In summary, system dynamics and traditional forecasting methods should be seen as complementary, one focusing more on internal dynamics and the other on external forces. The internal focus, with its emphasis on dynamic feedback loops and their inherent delay structure, is especially useful in order to avoid "policy insensitivity," that is, the failure of a system to respond in the manner intended by the policy initiative.

REFERENCES AND SELECTED BIBLIOGRAPHY

Alderson, R. C., and W. C. Sproull. 1971. "Requirement Analysis, Need Forecasting and Technology Planning, Using the Honeywell PATTERN Technique," in *Industrial Applications of Technological Forecasting,* M. Cetron (ed.). New York: John Wiley & Sons, Inc.

Amara, R. C. 1972. "Methodology: A Note on Cross-Impact Analysis," *Futures,* September, pp. 267–71.

Ament, R. H. 1970. "Comparison of Delphi Forecasting Studies in 1964 and 1969," *Futures,* March, pp. 35–44.

Ascher, W. 1978. *Forecasting an Appraisal for Policy Makers and Planners.* Baltimore, Md.: The John Hopkins University Press.

Ayres, R. U. 1969. *Technological Forecasting and Long-Range Planning.* New York: McGraw-Hill.

Bell, D. 1964. *Daedalus, Journal of the American Academy of Arts and Sciences,* Summer, pp. 848–80.

Blohm, H., and K. Steinbuch. 1973. *Technological Forecasting in Practice.* Lexington, Mass.: Lexington Books.

Bodily, S. E. 1982. "Judgmental and Bayesian Forecasting," in *Handbook of Forecasting,* S. Makridakis and S. C. Wheelwright, (eds.). New York: John Wiley & Sons, Inc.

Bright, J. R. 1978. *Practical Technological Forecasting.* Austin, Tex.: The Industrial Management Center.

——, and M. E. F. Schoeman (eds.). 1973. *A Guide to Practical Technological Forecasting.* Englewood Cliffs, N.J.: Prentice-Hall.

Brown, R. V., A. S. Kahr, and C. Peterson. 1974. *Decision Analysis for the Manager.* New York: Holt, Rinehart & Winston.

Cetron, M. 1971. *Industrial Applications of Technological Forecasting.* New York: John Wiley & Sons.

Cetron, M., and C. A. Ralph. 1971. *Industrial Application of Technological Forecasting.* New York: John Wiley & Sons, Inc.

Chambers, J. C., S. K. Mullick, and D. D. Smith. 1974. *An Executive's Guide to Forecasting.* New York: John Wiley & Sons, Inc.

Clarke, A. C. 1973. *Profiles of the Future: An Enquiry into the Limits of the Possible,* rev. ed. New York: Harper & Row.

The Conference Board. 1964. "Sales Forecasting," in *Studies in Business Policy No. 106.* New York.

——. 1978. *Sales Forecasting.* New York.

Dalrymple, D. J. 1975. "Sales Forecasting: Methods and Accuracy." Papers from the Marketing Department, Indiana University, Bloomington, Indiana.

Forrester, Jay W. 1958. "Industrial Dynamics—A Major Breakthrough for Decision Makers," *Harvard Business Review*, **36**, July-August, pp. 37–66.

——. 1968. "Market Growth as Influenced by Capital Investment," *Industrial Management Review*, Winter, **9**, pp. 83–105.

Gerstenfeld, A. 1971. "Technological Forecasting," *Journal of Business*, **44**, No. 1, January, pp. 10–18.

Gordon, T. J., and H. Hayward. 1968. "Initial Experiment with the Cross-Impact Matrix Method of Forecasting," *Futures*, **1**, No. 2, December.

Gross, A. C., and W. W. Ware. 1975. "Profiles of the Future: Energy Prospects in 1990," *Business Horizons*. June, pp. 5–18.

Hahn, W. A., and K. F. Gordon (eds.). 1973. *Assessing the Future and Policy Planning*. New York: Gordon & Breach.

Harrison, P. J., and C. F. Stevens. 1976. "Bayesian Forecasting," *Journal of the Royal Statistical Society*, **38B**, pp. 205–247.

Helmer, O. 1979. "The Utility of Long Term Forecasting," *TIMS Studies in the Management Sciences, Forecasting*, **12**, pp. 141–147.

——. 1977. "Problems in Futures Research—Delphi and Causal Cross-Impact Analysis," *Futures*, **9**.

——. 1966. *The Use of the Delphi Technique—Problems of Educational Innovations*. Santa Monica, Calif.: The RAND Corp., December.

——, and N. Rescher. 1959. "On the Epistemology of the Inexact Sciences," *Management Science*, **6**, No. 1.

Holloway, C. A. 1979. *Decision Making Under Uncertainty*. Englewood Cliffs, N.J.: Prentice-Hall.

Howard, R. 1980. "An Assessment of Decision Analysis," *Operations Research*, February, **28**, No. 1, pp. 4–27.

Hueckel, G. 1975. "A Historical Approach to Future Economic Growth," *Science*, **197**, March, pp. 925–31.

Jantsch, E. 1969. *Technological Forecasting in Perspective*. Paris: O.E.C.D.

Jolson, M. A., and G. L. Rossow. 1971. "The Delphi Process in Marketing Decision Making," *Journal of Marketing Research*, **8**, November, pp. 443–48.

Kahn, H. 1964. "Alternative World Futures." Paper HI-342-B IV. Croton-on-Hudson: Hudson Institute.

Kahn, H. et al. 1976. *The Next 200 Years*. New York: Morrow.

Kahneman, D., and A. Tversky. 1979. "Prospect Theory," *Econometrica*, March, **47**, No. 2.

Kotler, P. 1980. *Marketing Management*, 4th ed., Englewood Cliffs, N.J.: Prentice-Hall.

Kullback, S. 1968. *Information Theory and Statistics*. New York: Dover Publications.

Linstone, H.A., and M. Turoff. 1975. *The Delphi Method: Techniques and Applications*. Reading, Mass.: Addison-Wesley.

Loye, D. 1978. *The Knowable Future*. New York: John Wiley & Sons, Inc.

Malabre, A. L. 1976. "The Future Revised," in *The Wall Street Journal,* Monday, March 15.

Marshall, N. L. 1981. "The Dynamics of Residential Wood-Energy Use in New England 1970–2000." Thesis submitted to Thayer School of Engineering, Dartmouth College. (June 1981)

Naill, R. F. 1977. *Managing the Energy Transition*. New York: Ballinger Publishing Company.

National Science Foundation. 1977. *The Study of the Future: An Agenda for Research*. Washington, D.C.: U.S. Government Printing Office (NSF/RA-770036).

Prehoda, R. W. 1967. *Designing the Future*. Philadelphia: Chilton Book Co.

————. 1975. "The Future in Retrospect," *The Futurist,* October, pp. 263–65.

Raiffa, H. 1968. *Decision Analysis*. Reading, MA: Addison-Wesley.

Roberts, E. 1969. "Exploratory and Normative Technological Forecasting: A Critical Appraisal." MIT Working Paper, No. 378–69.

Rochberg, R., T. J. Gordon, and O. Helmer. 1970. "The Use of Cross-Impact Matrices for Forecasting and Planning." Middletown, Conn.: The Institute for the Future, IFF Report R-10. April.

Sackman, H. 1975. *Delphi Critique*. Lexington, Mass.: Lexington Books.

Schlaifer, R. O. 1968. *Analysis of Decisions Under Uncertainty*. New York: McGraw-Hill.

Sigford, J. V., and R. H. Parvin. 1965. "Project PATTERN: A Methodology for Determining Relevance in Complex Decision-Making," *IEEF Transactions on Engineering Management,* **12,** No. 1, March.

Steiner, G. A. 1969. *Top Management Planning*. London: Macmillan.

Taylor, T. B., et al. 1967. "Preliminary Survey of Non-National Nuclear Threats." *Stanford Research Institute Technical Note,* SSG-TN-5205-83. September.

Tersine, R. J., and W. E. Riggs. 1976. "The Delphi Technique: A Long-Range Planning Tool," *Business Horizons,* April, pp. 51–56.

Theil, H., and R. F. Kosobud. 1968. "How Informative Are Consumer Buying Intentions Surveys?" *Review of Economics and Statistics,* **19,** February.

Thom, Rene. 1972. *Stabilitie Structurelle et Morphogenese*. Reading, Mass.: Benjamin.

Vatter, P. A. et al. 1978. *Quantitative Methods in Management*. Homewood, Ill.: Richard D. Irwin.

Wheelwright, S. C., and S. Makridakis. 1980. *Forecasting Methods for Management*. 3d ed. New York: John Wiley & Sons, Inc.

Withington, F. G. 1976. "Beyond 1984: A Technology Forecast," *Datamation,* January.

Wotruba, T. R., and M. L. Thurlow. 1976. "Sales Force Participation in Quota Setting and Sales Forecasting," *Journal of Marketing,* **40,** April, pp. 11–16.

Zeeman, E. C. 1976. "Catastrophe Theory," *Scientific American,* April, pp. 65–83.

Zwicky, F. 1962. "Morphology of Propulsive Power." *Monographs on Morphological Research,* No. 1. Pasadena, Calif.: Society of Morphological Research.

———, and G. Wilson. 1967. *New Methods of Thought and Procedure.* New York: Springer Verlag.

EXERCISES

1. Sales force composite forecasting at EX-CELL-O Corporation.

    The following description suggests one way in which a judgmentally based forecasting system can be pursued in practice. After reading this description, answer the following:

    a. What are the strengths (advantages) of this approach? The weaknesses (disadvantages)?

    b. How might this forecasting task be handled using a formal quantitative approach? What advantages and disadvantages would such an approach have over the existing judgmental one?

    c. Could this forecasting task be handled with the Delphi approach? How would that be done? What advantages and disadvantages would that have?

EX-CELLO-O Corporation.[2]

Method: Sales-force estimates of new orders for machine tools, adjusted on the basis of market and economic information.

Ex-Cell-O manufacturers diversified industrial items, including machinery, precision parts and assemblies, aerospace and electronic products, and expendable tools and accessories.

The company group that manufactures machine tools, the traditional mainstay of the company's line, produces units ranging in price from a few thousand dollars to $400,000 or more. With such high-priced units, it is necessary to forecast new orders for such machine tools as realistically and in as fine detail as possible.

In a recent company communication, sales management spelled out some of the reasons that sales forecasts must be realistic and reliable:

"New-order forecasts are needed to plan cash flow, provide adequate funding for operations, plan production, set budget, determine manpower needs, establish prices based on expected production volume costs, and for

---

[2]Adapted from *Sales Forecasting,* 1978. New York: The Conference Board. Used by permission.

other reasons." The communication added: "Accurate information helps make better use of facilities by spacing out production to avoid peaks and valleys. One indirect benefit is to keep overtime to a minimum, thus avoiding product price increases due to higher labor costs. Building standard machines in more efficient lot sizes can result in price reductions, which improve competitive position and increase share of market. Forecasts also indicate areas where additional product promotion and advertising are required."

The machine tool group has eight manufacturing units, whose product lines are sold by the group's own sales force (consisting of about 50 field sales people) and through some 100 independent distributors. The combined sales organization is divided into seven regions, each headed by a regional manager. Assisting this executive and the individual sales representatives and distributors in each region are several "product sales managers" who have specialized knowledge of the machine tools made by one or more of the manufacturing units. The product sales managers are also familiar with the technical requirements of the important industries that constitute Ex-Cell-O's market within their regions.

A Knowledgeable Sales Force Ex-Cell-O's "new order" forecast is based on four major inputs: (1) forecasting of economic trends; (2) forecasting of industrial demand for products of the kind made by the company; (3) field sales-force forecasts; and (4) Ex-Cell-O historical performance data. Sales analysts —armed with their computer storage and retrieval systems—supply the first two of these inputs. The headquarters marketing staff, aided by information from distributors and the company's own sales personnel, is primarily responsible for the last two. The foundation of the forecasting process, however, is the third input, which rests on the intimate market knowledge and the estimating talents of the sales personnel in the field—both the company's own sales force and its distributor network.

Each field sales manager, salesperson, and distributor is familiar with the chief customers and potential customers in his or her area. Each is supplied by the group's staff with historical data concerning past orders, by customer and machine-tool category. Each sounds out his or her customers and prospective customers periodically regarding probable purchases, during the next year and a half or so, of machinery of the type Ex-Cell-O offers. And each consults with the product sales managers in the region, and benefits from their specialized knowledge regarding technical and market developments.

Proposals vs. Firm Orders The procedure described below is concerned only with new orders for specific types of machinery manufactured by the eight units of the machine tool group.

The nature of the machine tool group's business is such that the submitting of an "open proposal" is also the initial event in the forecasting procedure. An open proposal is a quotation or bid made to a specific customer for specific types and quantities of machinery the firm plans to buy. The likelihood of any given proposal becoming a firm order cannot, of course, be known with certainty. The purchaser may change its plans or decide to buy from one of Ex-Cell-O's competitors. The company's past experience, however, provides some general guidelines.

TABLE 13-5 EXPLANATORY SAMPLE OF FORM FOR OPEN PROPOSAL FORECASTS, EX-CELL-O CORPORATION

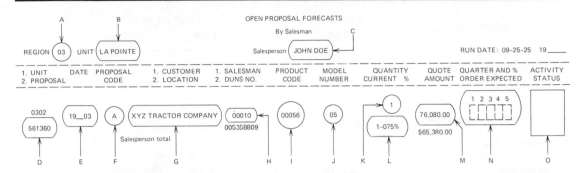

Item A = Your region number.
Item B = Name of XLO manufacturing you represent.
Item C = Your name.
Item D = Proposal number.
Item E = Year and month proposal was entered.
Item F = Proposal code for marketing department use only.
Item G = Customer's name and address.
Item H = Your XLO salesman number.
Item I = Product number.
Item J = Machine model number.
Item K = Quantity (number) of machines quoted.
Item L = Quarter and percent previously forecast for this proposal.
Item M = Amount of quote.
Item N = Quarter and percent order is expected.
Item O = Field to be used for lost order code.

Rolling Forecast for Next Five Quarters Sales-force and distributor personnel are required to forecast the open proposals that they expect will be converted to orders during each of the coming five quarters. The process is repeated every three months, so that each new forecast drops the previous first future quarter and adds a new fifth quarter.

The quarterly cycle involves four steps:

1. The machine tool marketing staff at group headquarters requests from the computer systems department a printout of all open proposals contained in the marketing information system. These proposals, grouped by representative, are then forwarded to each of the salespeople and distributors (see Table 13-5). At the same time a "recap" sheet is mailed to each regional manager, providing a consolidated record of all details contained in the proposal forecast sheets sent to the individual salespeople and distributors in the region.

TABLE 13-6   QUARTERLY FORECASTING SCHEDULE, EX-CELL-O CORPORATION

Procedure Description	Required Date	Required Date	Required Date	Required Date
1. Request open proposal printout and mail.	Dec. 16	March 17	June 18	Sept. 19
2. Salespersons and distributors return form to regional manager.	Jan. 6	April 1	July 1	Sept. 30
3. Regional mgr. reviews and returns to machine tool marketing	Jan. 13	April 11	July 14	Oct. 13
4. Summarized and mailed to unit sales manager.	Jan. 31	April 29	Aug. 1	Oct. 24

Note: Should any required date fall on a Saturday or Sunday, move date back to prior Friday.

2.   Each salesperson and distributor reviews the proposal sheet, makes any adjustments or revisions, prepares his or her proposal forecast for the next five future quarters, and then sends the revised forecast to the regional manager.

3.   The regional manager reviews these forecasts, discussing them with the individual salespeople or distributors as required, gets agreement on any necessary adjustments, and—when satisfied that all the individual forecasts in the region are as realistic as they can be—forwards them to the marketing staff at group headquarters.

4.   At group headquarters, all forecasts are processed by computer, permitting the mailing of updated forecast information to the eight manufacturing units. Table 13-6 shows the schedule for the quarterly cycle just described.

As mentioned, the salespeople and distributors bear the greatest responsibility in the company's procedure for forecasting. To make their task easier and less time-consuming, the forecasting forms are designed to require as little writing as possible, and to be speedily given his or her previous forecast figures at forecasting time to help in updating and revising them.

Forecasts of proposals that may not turn into firm orders until the third, fourth, or fifth quarter ahead are acknowledged to be far more conjectural than those likely to be resolved during the next quarter or two. This is one of the chief reasons for repeating the forecasting procedure every quarter, thus making forecasts as up-to-date as practical.

Two additional aids to realistic forecasting—helpful to both field personnel and management—are (1) estimates of the likelihood of transforming an open proposal into a firm order, and (2) postmortems on why potential orders are lost (represented, respectively, by items N and O of Table 13-5).

Estimates of Likelihood; Analysis of Lost Orders

Upon receipt of the forecast request, the salesperson settles down for a couple of hours to complete the request.

The first item on the forecast forms received direct from the company's marketing headquarters is his or her forecast, made three months previously, that the XYZ Tractor Company might make a firm order for machinery (of the type indicated in Table 13-5—see items I and J) to the value of $76,980. The salesperson had then expected and indicated a 75 percent likelihood that XYZ would place the order during the coming quarter—that is, during the one just completed. But this did not happen.

So the salesperson has two alternatives. Based on past conversations he or she has had with XYZ during the past few weeks, a specific likelihood (e.g., 10 percent, 25 percent, 100 percent) that the order *will* in fact materialize during any one of the coming five quarters can be indicated. This would be recorded in the box for the appropriate quarter. (Assignment of a percentage indicating likelihood of sale must be to a single quarter—not split between two quarters.)

The other alternative would be to indicate that the order is lost. In this event, the salesperson must give the reason for the lost order in the box labeled "Activity Status." To simplify matters, a code is used.:

Reason	Code
Competition; price	N
Delivery	J
Economy; cutback	G
Late quotation	M
Machinery capacity	K
Machine features	L
Other Ex-Cell-O unit	E
Price	F
Program dropped	H
Quote revised	R
Other	P

(If "other" applies, the salesperson is required to explain briefly what this means on a separate sheet.)

The salesperson does no further calculating on this form. The remaining task is to fill out a supplementary form covering various sales possibilities not provided for in Table 13-5. Included here are possible sales of Ex-Cell-O equipment not yet represented by formal quotations or proposals. These reflect possible purchase intentions of prospects who might well consider the company as a potential supplier.

Forecast Consolidations

Once the forecasts of salespeople and distributors are received by their regional managers, changes and adjustments can still be negotiated. When this is done, all individual forecasts are sent to corporate headquarters, and the incoming forecasts are sent to corporate headquarters, and the incoming forecasts are reviewed for processing and consolidation by computer. During the review marketing management critically examines each of the forecasts. If necessary, further discussions take place (typically by phone) with those in the field who have prepared or approved the forecasts.

It is at this point that judgments are made as to appropriate treatment of the percentage probabilities that salespeople and distributors have assigned to their current outstanding proposals. In general, conservatism prevails. Proposals whose likelihood of realization is less than 50 percent in the first two quarters will be dropped from the forecasts unless special circumstances seem to justify their retention. Forecast orders having a greater than 50 percent likelihood in quarters one or two, or *any* percentage likelihood in quarters three, four or five, are included in the forecast summary. A percentage value assigned to the likelihood of sales is regarded more optimistically when it relates to a near quarter than to a distant one.

When the review process has been completed, various forecast summaries are produced by computer. Among them are consolidated forecasts for eqch of the operating units and for each of the sales regions. The consolidations for the manufacturing units take into account forecasts received from the company's subsidiaries and distributors abroad—forecasts that have been prepared and reviewed in a manner similar to that described above. With the distribution of the various forecast summaries to the respective recipients, the marketing staff at group headquarters has now completed its forecast responsibility for this cycle. It now becomes the unit manager's responsibility to combine this material with his own knowledge of business conditions to plan future workforce and manufacturing requirements.

2.   Delphi Forecasts at Bell Canada[3]

Background

Bell Canada is an operating telecommunications company serving the provinces of Ontario and Quebec in Canada. In addition to offering voice, data, and visual telecommunications services, Bell Canada owns a large manufacturing subsidiary (Northern Electric) and an R & D subsidiary (Bell-Northern Research). There are also several other subsidiaries in the telephone, directory, and electronic components manufacturing fields. The Business Planning Group in Bell has the responsibility for identification of corporate opportunities (or threats) that will arise through changes in society and/or technology in the next decade or two.

The communications field is in the midst of rapid change which will have a significant impact on its intermediate and long term future. Highlights of these changes include:

- merging computer and communications technologies
- regulatory changes introducing new competitive elements
- emerging visual telecommunications markets

---

[3]Adapted from "Delphi Research in the Corporate Environment," by L. H. Day. Reprinted in *The Delphi Method,* H. A. Linstone and M. Turoff (eds.). 1975. Reading, Mass.: Addison-Wesley. Used by permission.

- perceived and projected social changes
- decreasing costs of investment options

The Business Planning Group surveyed these various pressures in the late 1960s as it was developing a study plan to evaluate future trends in the visual and computer communications fields. There was a distinct lack of qualitative data on potential futures for these fields, especially in the Canadian environment. An examination of various potential technological forecasting techniques indicated that the Delphi technique would fill the perceived information gap.

Bell Canada Delphi Study Development

The individuals involved in designing, conducting and managing the Business Planning Delphi efforts have generally had a marketing background. This background includes both academic training and professional experience. These background factors were important determinants of the approach followed.

Initial steps relied upon the basic marketing approach of defining the "market segments" that will have the most important impact on future applications of visual and data communications. These segments were chosen after preliminary studies of potential segments and taking account of the time and resources available. The final choices were future applications in the educational, medical, information systems, and residential markets.

The basic philosophy in the studies was to examine the future applications in these segments from a user point of view, not from the direction of technological imperatives. The initial questionnaires were prepared after extensive literature reviews of potential developments in each of the chosen areas. The approach in questionnaire design was to guide the discussions in some basic areas of interest in a segment rather than start with blank paper and ask the experts to suggest the most important areas of interest. Since the panelists were actively encouraged to suggest new questions or modifications to existing ones, the potential for significant study bias by the designers was low. This approach also helped reduce the number of rounds required for the studies and hence saved time for the participants and study managers alike.

Next, initial questionnaires were pretested with groups of readily available experts. This proved to be a very valuable step, as poorly worded questions or confusing questionnaire design were largely eliminated before the errors could be inflicted upon the Delphi panel. This step adds time to the study and may be somewhat ego deflating at times for the study managers; however, it pays good dividends in higher quality, less ambiguous results, and happier panelists.

Delphi Study Results—Education, Medicine, and Business

The initial studies in education, medicine, and business followed a similar format. The first part of the questionnaire asked the panelists to project their views on the long-term (30 years) future of some basic North American values. The purpose in asking these questions was more to help the panelists get in a societal frame of mind when answering the rest of the questionnaire than to obtain the societal trend data itself. When the social trend views of the various groups of experts, as shown in the following table, were compared after all these studies were completed, it was interesting to note how similar the results were, considering the diverse background of the 165 individuals in the various panels (there was no interpanel communication during the studies).

Other areas of each study also explored nontechnological developments as well as the adoption of systems to serve various applications. Some of these nontechnical factors considered in the three studies are illustrated below:

NONTECHNOLOGICAL FACTORS CONSIDERED
IN THE BELL CANADA DELPHI STUDIES

Education	Medicine	Business
1. Value trends 2. Evolution in school design 3. Changing role of the teacher	1. Value trends 2. Trends in the medical profession 3. Changes in the medical environment	1. Value trends 2. Changes in business procedures 3. Trends in business physical environment

The Education Delphi examined potential adoption of three basic types of educational technologies: Computerized Library Systems (CLS), Computer Aided Instruction Systems (CAI), and Visual Display Systems (including IRTV—Instant Retrieval Television). In both areas, threshold market penetration values of 20 percent and/or 55 percent were used for the technologies. This gives the panelists and readers some feeling for the scope of service acceptance in the markets under consideration.

The Medical Delphi explored acceptance of a number of developing medical technologies. These included: Multiphasic Screening, Computer-Assisted Diagnosis, Remote Physiological Monitoring, Computerized Medical Library Systems, and Terminal Usage. The format and adoption thresholds were similar to those in the Education Delphi.

The Business Information Processing Technology study examined trends in Management Information Systems, Mini and Small Computers, Terminals and Data Processing. Panelists were sometimes split into "schools of thought" on various issues. These opinion splits were often not reflected in graphic presentation of the results. In these cases the panelists were encouraged to debate their differences in writing through the rounds of the various studies. These differences are reflected in the reports along with supporting assumptions and comments of the panelists. It was found that the panelists' comments and their analyses were often very important modifications of the statistical projections developed.

a. Using an approach like that suggested above, identify the set of factors that might be examined in a Bell Canada Delphi study dealing with future home services that might be of interest to the company.

b. What type of experts might you assemble to pursue this study?

    c. Develop a questionnaire that could be used in the first round of inquiry with these experts.

    d. Outline the remaining steps (round 2, etc.) that could be taken to complete this Delphi study.

3.   Developing and implementing a Delphi application.

    a. Select a topic for which a long-term forecast might be prepared using the Delphi approach. (This might be the development of a new technology, a breakthrough in medical research, or a significant social or economic development.)

    b. Define the Delphi procedure to be used in preparing forecasts for this topic. This should include defining what is to be forecast (that is, an event *and* its timing), who will participate, the steps to be followed, and the desired final results.

    c. Using a group of your peers as the "experts," carry out your procedure and plan.

    d. Evaluate the results of this exercise. For example, consider how the design might have been improved, how useful the forecasts would be, how you would update them over time, and so on.

4.   Long-Term Energy Demand at Duke Power Company[4]

       In 1975, Duke Power Company was a fully integrated public utility that generated, transmitted, and sold electricity in central North Carolina and western South Carolina. Its service area, approximately two-thirds of which was in North Carolina, covered about 20,000 square miles with an estimated population of 3.8 million. It included a number of cities, the largest of which were Charlotte, Greensboro, Winston-Salem, and Durham, North Carolina, and Greenville and Spartanburg, South Carolina. The company's 1974 electric revenues were approximately $823 million—about 70 percent came from North Carolina and 30 percent from South Carolina.

       The preceding year, 1974, had been unique in the company's planning experience. Because of reduced industrial and commercial activity, energy conservation, and mild weather, the company's regular sales in 1974 were 2.3 percent below those for 1973—approximately 41.7 billion kilowatt hours (kwh). The company normally experienced seasonal peak loads in summer and winter which were more or less the same from year to year. The 1974 peak load of 8,057,625 kilowatts (kw) occurred on August 28, 1974; it represented a decrease of 2.15 percent below the 1973 peak load, which also occurred in late August. The 1973 peak load, by contrast, was 10.55 percent higher than the 1972 peak.

       As Duke Power's Manager of Forecasting and Budgets, Burt Raymond spent much of his time trying to identify the best approach for preparing intermediate-term demand forecasts and collecting the data necessary to implement that approach. Unfortunately, he had little county-level economic data to permit close correlation of local economic trends with either energy or demand growth trends for electricity. Nor did he have any useful information regarding price elasticities of demand in different customer classes.

---

[4]Adapted from S. C. Wheelwright, 1977, "Duke Power Company." Boston: Harvard Business School Case Service, #9-677-147. Reprinted by permission.

TABLE 13-7   DUKE POWER COMPANY: FORECAST OF BASE LOAD AND
WEATHER-RESPONSIVE LOAD—SUMMER 1974

A. Regression Model for Forecasting
   Standard error of estimate[a] = 65.611
   Multiple correlation coefficient[b] = 0.976
   Constant term[c] = 5628.0430

Variable	Coefficient[d]	Standard Deviation of coefficient[e]	t-Value[f]
1	13.6521	0.6530	20.9083

B. Forecast Performance

Observation	Actual	Estimate	Residual[f]
1	6766.00	6802.12	−33.12
2	7010.00	6993.25	16.75
3	7356.00	7348.20	7.80
4	6931.00	6884.03	46.97
5	7099.00	7061.51	37.49
6	6845.00	6870.38	−25.38
7	6384.00	6433.86	−49.52
8	6703.00	6733.86	−30.86
9	6755.00	6774.82	−19.82
10	7075.00	7075.16	−0.16
11	6787.00	6856.73	−69.73
12	6862.00	6911.34	−49.34
13	6928.00	7006.90	−78.90
14	6306.00	6324.30	−18.30
15	7059.00	7088.81	−29.81
16	5960.00	5942.04	17.96
17	6805.00	6802.12	2.88
18	6667.00	6597.34	69.66
19	6732.00	6761.16	−29.16
20	7038.00	6938.64	99.36
21	7176.00	7034.21	141.79
22	6770.00	6638.30	131.70
23	6803.00	6802.12	0.88
24	6745.00	6884.03	−139.03

[a]The standard error of estimate is used to indicate the level of uncertainty surrounding forecasts based on the regression model. As an approximation, it can be assumed that less than 10 percent of the time, the actual value will differ from the estimated (forecast) value by more than two times the standard error of estimate.

[b]The squared multiple correlation coefficient, sometimes referred to as the coefficient of determination, indicates the amount of the variation in total peak electric energy demand

Available 1974 demand data suggested that the elasticity of demand for peak usage was lower than that for off-peak usage, and monthly aggregate load factors showed that sales had been off more than demand for every month of 1974.

Duke Power had already determined that any new capacity to be added in the next several years should be base-load capacity. Because capacity planning must be based upon peak-load forecasts and because the highest peak loads had occurred during the summer, Raymond directed his efforts toward predicting future summer peak loads.

Raymond's initial problem was to separate summer peak demand into two components: a base-load component, and a weather-responsive (WR) component. Raymond first examined a scatter plot of degree-hours[5] between noon and 4 p.m. on Monday through Thursday from early June through early September. This permitted him to identify weekday afternoons with unusual characteristics, the "outliers" in the scatter plot. These he examined individually to see if they were special weather-related phenomena such as a local thunderstorm in the vicinity of one of the three reporting stations from which degree-hour data were collected. He eliminated such days from further consideration.

For the summer of 1974, this data-screening procedure gave Raymond 36 observations which he used to estimate a regression equation of the form:

$$MW = a + b(\text{d. hr.})$$

where MW was the actual value of the system peak for that particular summer and (d. hr.) was the corresponding degree-hours.

Raymond interpreted the constant term a as the base-load component of demand for that summer. The WR component was obtained by multiplying the coefficient b by the 20-year average value of degree-hours for a particular day. (See Table 13-7.)

---

[5]Degree-hours are the weighted average of the difference of the recorded hourly temperature from 67°F over the period in consideration—in this case, 12 noon to 4 p.m., Monday–Thursday.

(the item being forecast) that is explained by variation in summer afternoon temperature (the causal factor). In this model, 95.3 percent of the variation in peak summer demand is explained by variation in the afternoon temperature.

[c]The constant term is determined during the estimation of the regression model. In this instance, it is interpreted as the base-load requirement. (See 1974 Base Load in Exhibit 9.)

[d]The coefficient term is also determined during the estimation of the regression model. This coefficient is multiplied by the degree-hours (degrees above average for noon to 4:00 p.m.) and added to the constant term to provide the model's forecast of peak energy demand.

[e]This standard deviation is used in conjunction with the t-test to determine whether the estimated value of the coefficient, 13.6521, is statistically significantly different from zero. In this case, it is.

[f]Actual value minus estimated value.

TABLE 13-8 DUKE POWER COMPANY: SUMMER PEAK LOADS (ESTIMATED AND ACTUAL) AND GENERATING CAPABILITY

| Year | Estimated (using Regression) | | | Actual | |
	Base Load	Weather-Responsive Load	Total	Summer Peak Load (mw)	Generating Capability (mw)
1963	2,130	451.2	2,581.2	3,239	3,542
1964	2,463	459.2	2,922.2	3,538	4,070
1965	2,571	467.2	3,038.2	3,878	4,418
1966	2,773	500.0	3,273.0	4,346	4,914
1967	2,991	646.0	3,637.0	4,547	5,031
1968	3,569	670.9	4,239.9	5,364	5,757
1969	3,807	695.7	4,502.7	5,614	6,427
1970	4,116	1,008.5	5,124.5	6,284	6,719
1971	4,419	1,246.9	5,665.9	6,585	7,371
1972	4,718	1,500.2	6,218.2	7,450	8,168
1973	5,267	1,625.2	6,892.2	8,236	9,110
1974	5,628	1,750.2	7,378.2	8,058	9,531

This same approach separated the base-load and *WR* components for the years from 1963 to 1973, using the appropriate data sets for each year. (See Table 13-8.)

a. Assume that Raymond has decided that the next step is to project the base-load component and the weather-responsive load component (WR) for the next 10 years (1975–1984) using a curve-fitting approach. What type of curve should he use for each component? What results do you obtain from those?

b. What alternative approaches are there for making this 10-year forecast? As Raymond, which, if any, of these would you use? Be specific as to how you would reach a final set of forecasts.

5. Step-Function Patterns and Trend Extrapolation[6]

In studying the actions of the Canadian and United States chemical firms on new plant capacity, prices, and so on, relative to total demand, Clive Simmonds observed distinct patterns or "step functions" in the building of new factilities. Further research led him to conclude that these patterns were not merely mechanistic displays but actually revealed how this industry tended to think and respond. Coupling this idea to the suggestions of Robert

---

[6]For a complete discussion, see W. H. C. S. Simmonds, "The Analysis of Industrial Behavior and Its Use in Forecasting," in Bright & Schoeman, *Guide to Practical Technological Forecasting* (Englewood Cliffs, N.J.: Prentice-Hall, Inc., 1973).

Ayres, he hypothesized that industries could be classified in a manner relevant to forecasting:

> *Performance-maximizing industries compete on the basis of highest performance per unit price. They include the aerospace, computer, defense, electronic, nuclear, petro-chemical, scientific instrument, and tanker industries and are typically science- and technology-based.*
>
> *The performance-maximizing industries contrast with the sales-maximizing industries which compete for the consumers' dollar through intensive advertising. Examples of these industries include the auto, cosmetic, detergent, food and beverage, and apparel industries. Cost-minimizing industries compete to produce standardized products at lower prices. They include utilities, communication, transportation, metals, glass, cement, concrete, and petroleum products.*
>
> *The thesis is therefore advanced that it is the common pattern of behavior of industries grouped in this fashion which is relevant for technological forecasting.*

Each type of industry responds to its own manner as constrained and driven by its special combination of forces. Market demand, technological innovation, and scale of facility are dominant in the performance-maximizing chemical industry.

Simmonds argues that analysis of these patterns facilitates forecasting with some accuracy, subject, of course, to major changes that limit or alter the patterns.

Since developing his original thesis, Simmonds has expanded and refined his classification system several times and added new insights. For example, the chemical industry's pattern of building ethylene plants in jumps of 200 to 300 percent every 5 years or so led to cycles of over and under capacity, proportional sudden price changes, profit losses, and cycles of management optimism and pessimism. These impacts, he claims, can be approximately forecasted, resulting in better management decisions.

a. Plot the data given in Table 13-9 against time on semilog paper. (The data should be plotted as "steps" to show the size of the largest unit as constant until the next larger unit is built.)

b. Consider the following for your plot of the ethylene manufacturing data:

> Is there a relation between the size of the largest operating unit in existence and the size of the market for which it is competing?
>
> If so, what will be the size of the next largest ethylene plant, and when will it come on stream according to the plot?
>
> The extrapolation is, of course, merely mechanistic. Consider (i) what factors will tend to *advance* timing and/or size and (ii) what factors will tend to *delay* timing and/or limit size.
>
> On the basis of this information, what could you say about the future cost/price relationship of ethylene? What other information would be pertinent?

Estimate, very roughly, the future market for ethylene in 1985 and 1995.

TABLE 13-9   MANUFACTURE OF ETHYLENE

Year	Production (billion lb/yr)	Capacity of Largest Plant (billion lb/yr)	Estimated Selling Price (U.S. cents/lb)
1940	0.3 Est.	0.03	N.A.
1941	0.35	0.03	N.A.
1942	0.4	0.03	N.A.
1943	0.5	0.03	N.A.
1944	0.6	0.10	N.A.
1945	0.7	0.10	N.A.
1946	0.07	0.10	N.A.
1947	0.8	0.10	N.A.
1948	1.0	0.10	N.A.
1949	1.2	0.10	N.A.
1950	1.45	0.10	4¼
1951	1.65	0.10	4¼
1952	1.9	0.10	4¼
1953	2.1	0.18	4¼
1954	2.3	0.22	4½
1955	3.0	0.22	4½
1956	3.6	0.22	4½
1957	3.9	0.22	4½
1958	4.1	0.22	4½
1959	5.1	0.22	5
1960	5.4	0.22	5¼
1961	5.7	0.38	5¼
1962	6.3	0.55	5
1963	7.5	0.55	4¾
1964	8.6	0.55	4¾
1965	9.6	0.55	4
1966	11.2	0.55	4
1967	11.8	0.75	3¼
1968	13.3	1.00	3
1969p	15.7	1.20	2¾
1970 Est.	17.3	1.20	3

1976 Notes:

1. CDF-Chimie (France) proposed a 500,000-ton plant to be built in 1977. Project stalled because Qatar failed to come up with 40 percent of financing.

2. Italy's 1980 plan for 500,000-ton cracker to serve large ethylene plant pushed back to 1985.

3. Great Britain's ICI planned to open 500,000-ton plant at Billingham in 1977.

6.   Morphological Matrix for Domestic Timepieces
           A morphological matrix for domestic timepieces outlined by Blohm
       and Steinbuch (1973) is summarized in Table 13-10.
       a. Trace the two existing systems described in the footnote to Table 13-10.
       b. Construct and outline the particular morphological structure for the fol-
          lowing time-keeping systems:

              Grandfather clock

              Battery-powered, quartz crystal watch with stepping motor-actuated
              hands

              Digital electronic, quartz crystal, battery-powered watch with liquid
              crystal display

       c. Consider completely new combinations of the given alternates in the ma-
          trix that might form the basis of new clock systems. Are there any shorter
          (more compact) systems that appear feasible? Evaluate these systems in
          terms of their potential advantages, limitations, and requirements for
          further R&D work to support their development.

7.   Development of a Morphological Box for Food Production and Processing
           Suppose that a food company is concerned with its future expansion
       and technological possibilities in the areas of food production and processing.
       One approach to planning and forecasting in such a company might be that
       of morphological research. As a first step the following six classes of param-
       eters might be identified.

              P_1: Market
              P_2: Market territory
              P_3: Type of food
              P_4: Materials used
              P_5: Location of sources of materials
              P_6: Manner of obtaining and/or processing materials

       Develop a Morphological Box that describes four or five parameters
       under each of these headings. How many combinations of parameters from
       each of these six classes does this give? How might one decide which com-
       binations to pursue in order to make this analysis feasible?

8.   Relevance Tree Analysis for Evaluating Future Family Transportation
       Systems[7]

---

[7]This problem was originally prepared by Maurice Esch at the Technology Forecasting
Short Course conducted by the Industrial Management Center, Inc., in 1968. It proved so
useful that it was successively refined for these semiannual courses by Bright and Dennis
Meadows, then supplemented by Ronald Jablonski in 1972 and 1976. It has been rewritten
for use in France, Norway, Israel, South Africa, Japan, Italy, Australia, England, and Brazil.
It seems to be universally effective for rapid learning of the concepts if cultural setting and
technical data are appropriately altered. Adapted from Bright (1978). Used by permission.

TABLE 13-10 MORPHOLOGICAL MATRIX FOR DOMESTIC TIMEPIECES

Alternates	1	2	3	4	5	6	7	8	9
A Energy input	Manual wind	Vibration or movement	Expansion wind	Pressure fluctuation	Temperature fluctuation	Hydraulic	Galvanic reaction	Light rays	External power supply (electric)
B Energy storage	Weight	Spring	Bimetallic coil	Pressure container	Electric accumulator or battery	Volume container	Expansion bar	Solar cell	No store
C Motor or power transmission	Spring	Electric	Pneumatic	Hydraulic	None				
D Regulator	Balance wheel	Pendulum	Armature	Centrifugal governor	Tuning fork	Inching pendulum	Electric mains frequency	Crystal resonance (quartz crystal)	Capacitor-phasing circuit
E Information transmission	Pinion gear	Chain	Worm gear	Magnetic coupling	Lever system	Fluid coupling	Counter/decoder		
F Indicator	Hands and dial	Plates and marks	Roller and window	Slide and marks	Digital display (mechanical)	Moving figures	Light-emitting diodes	Liquid crystal display	Sound effects

Note: Morphology sequence for standard spring-wound wristwatch is *A1-B2-C1-D1-E1-F1*. Morphology sequence for battery-powered wristwatch of 1950s is *A7-B5-C2-D5-E1-F1*.

Source: *H. Blohm and K. Steinbuch (eds.). **Technical Forecasting in Practice**. London: Saxon House, 1973.* (**Note:** *This matrix has been heavily modified by author.*)

The Family Transportation Scenario—1977

Jack Daniels is a senior project engineer who works for the Department of Defense of the United States government at a downtown Washington, D.C., location. He is in his mid-thirties and lives with his wife and two children, a boy age 12 and a girl age 11, in Falls Church, Virginia, a suburban community located about twelve miles from downtown Washington.

Jack's automobile was recently damaged beyond repair, and he is now faced with the problem of replacing it. As the car has no trade-in value, it will be scrapped. Jack has, however, received the money from the settlement of the insurance claims. The Daniels have been a one-car family and intend to remain so. Thus, any car that Jack purchases will have to satisfy all of the family's transportation needs.

To ease the strain of commuting, Jack and two other men in the neighborhood have formed a car pool. Usually, Jack drives the participants two or three times a week. As there are no government-furnished parking facilities in the vicinity, the pool participants have arranged for parking at one of the nearby private parking facilities.

The family generally takes an automobile trip once a year to visit relatives in the Midwest—a round-trip distance of about 2,000 miles. They also take a vacation trip each year, which involves another 2,000 miles of cross-country driving. Three or four times during the summer the family drives to the mountains or to the Atlantic shore, a round-trip distance of approximately 300 miles.

The Daniels also use their automobile to provide family transportation for such normal tasks as shopping, transporting the children, and dining out. School busses are available to transport the children to and from school during normal classroom hours, but the family must furnish transportation for the children to special after-hour school events. They average a total of about 15,000 miles of driving per year. Jack plans to keep any car for 3 years and feels that he can get a relatively good measure of "expected cost of ownership for 3 years," which he has computed. However, he and his wife are fully aware that "cost" is not the only consideration. His dilemma is how to evaluate all the subjective reactions to the merits of various cars (technical systems) for their particular situation. Furthermore, he appreciates that his wife (a "colleague" with different interests) is involved.

After consulting several publications of consumer groups, reports from the Environmental Protection Agency (EPA), and various automotive magazines, Jack has narrowed his choice of replacement vehicles to four models. The data he has assembled on each of these were derived from these sources as well as official price guides and manufacturers' suggested preventive maintenance schedules. In his calculations Jack used a figure of 65 cents per gallon for gasoline and $15.00 per hour for automotive mechanics' time charges. Jack believes these to be minimum estimates of costs. They are likely to go higher over the lifetime of his purchase in light of recent petroleum and wage price movements, he assumes.

Operating expenses include such items as fuel, lubrication, tires, suggested preventive maintenance (tune-ups, bearing repacking, etc.), estimated repair expense based upon previous year's experience of the particular model, insurance, license fees, and depreciation. (The latter was estimated by subtracting from the purchase price the current market value of a similarly equipped three-year-old model of the same vehicle.) Freight and dealer preparation charges, where applicable, are included in the original cost.

The four vehicles under consideration are as follows[8]:

1. **Datsun B-210:** A four-door subcompact; manual four-speed transmission, AM/FM radio, all other accessories are standard. "Best features are EPA mileage (29 mpg city, 41 mpg highway, 33 mpg avg.) and handling and steering in normal and emergency situations . . . comfort fair in front and poor in rear with interior noise levels fairly high . . . expected repairs to be much lower than average." Costs $3,200; expected cost of ownership is $2,600 for 3 years.

2. **Dodge Aspen Special Edition:** A four-door mid-size station wagon with two seats, six-cylinder engine with standard power disc brakes; "Easy Order Accessory Package" includes automatic transmission, power steering, AM/FM radio, and trim; also, manual-controlled air conditioning . . . "good ride in front and rear with normal and full loads . . . noise levels fairly low . . . good handling in normal conditions but only fair in emergency situations . . . average on repairs." Costs $5,600; expected ownership cost is $4,700. Other possible appearance and performance options could add from $25 to $1,000 to cost. EPA gas mileage: 18 mpg city, 23 mpg highway, 20 mpg average.

3. **Mercury Marquis:** A four-door full-size sedan, eight-cylinder engine with standard accessories as power steering, power brakes, automatic transmission, deluxe AM/FM/stereo sound package, steel-belted radial tires, air conditioning. "Good comfort and ride in both front and back with low interior noise levels . . . good handling in normal driving but fair in emergency maneuvers . . . lower than average expected incidence of repair." EPA gas mileage: 13 mpg city, 17 mpg highway, 14 mpg average. Costs $6,200; expected ownership cost is $6,200; other available options individually cost from $30 to $500.

4. **Chevrolet Sport Van:** G-10 series, 110-inch wheel base, seats eight (two bench seats plus two front seats), six-cylinder engine with standard power disc brakes, custom appearance package, automatic transmission, AM/FM radio, air conditioning (serves primarily the driver's and forward areas, full air conditioning would add additional $370 to cost). "Steering and handling similar to full-size car, but with improved visibility due to elevated and forward position of driver . . . interior noise fairly high . . . repair incidence average on mechanical equipment, worse than average on body work . . . very high resale value." Costs $5,100; expected ownership cost is $4,200; other appearance and performance options range from $50 to $900 each. EPA gas mileage: 16 mpg city, 20 mpg highway, 17 mpg average.

The additional options for the various cars would not materially affect the operating costs or the resale value of the car, as those options having the major effect on resale and operating performance have already been included in Jack's calculations.

---

[8]This information was valid in mid-1977. Due to inflation and rapidly changing automobile designs, it may be desirable to provide current data for these (or other) vehicles.

a. On the basis of the scenario above, what conclusions can be drawn about the choices Jack and his wife will consider?

b. The following relevance tree shows the first two levels—missions and systems—for this situation.

RELEVANCE TREE FOR FIRST TWO LEVELS
OF FAMILY TRANSPORTATION PROBLEM

Objective	Family Transportation			
Missions (Level 1)	Vacation	Professional	Household	Social
Systems (Level 2)	Datsun Aspen Marquis Sport Van	Datsun Aspen Marquis Sport Van	Datsun Aspen Marquis Sport Van	Datsun Aspen Marquis Sport Van

For each of the four missions, list the types of transportation activities included from the scenario above.

For each of the four systems, list the relevant costs—both original and 3-year cost of ownership.

c. What decision criteria should be used in establishing the mission weights? The system weights?

d. Outline a procedure for assigning the required weights. Implement that procedure (the type of formats outlined in Table 13-11 might be helpful.)

e. What are your conclusions from this analysis? What are its strengths and weaknesses? Would you recommend that its conclusions be followed? Why or why not?

TABLE 13-11 FORMATS FOR ORGANIZING RELEVANCE TREE
WEIGHTS AND CALCULATIONS[a]

A. Calculation of Mission Weights

Objective: Family Transportation		Mission				Totals
Criteria	Weight	1. Vacation	2. Professional	3. Household	4. Social	
Self						
Wife						
Mission Weights						

B. Calculation of System Relative Weights for Mission 1 (or 2, 3, or 4)

Mission 1: Vacation	Wt.	System				Totals
Criteria	Weight	Datsun	Aspen	Marquis	Sport Van	
Utility						
Prestige						
Relative System Weights						

C. Calculation of System Relevance Number

Objective: Family Transportation	Mission Weight (From table A) × System Weight (From table noted)				System Relevance Number	Benefit/$ of System Cost for 3 years
System	Vacation (From table B)	Professional (From table C)	Household (From table D)	Social (From table E)		
Datsun						
Aspen						
Marquis						
Sport Van						
Totals						

[a]Adapted from Bright (1978). Used by permission.

PART SIX
INTEGRATING FORECASTING AND PLANNING IN PRACTICE

The authors believe that while understanding forecasting methodologies and their use is interesting for academic purposes, the real test comes in their applicability in practice and their impact on planning and decision making. The purpose of Part Six is to describe some of the most important issues surrounding effective utilization of forecasting in the organization and some of the empirical results reported in the published literature.

In Chapter 14 the nature of the planning function is described, and the requirements of planning are related to the characteristics of forecasting. This chapter seeks to integrate many of the advantages and disadvantages of individual forecasting methods that were described in earlier chapters with the requirements of specific planning situations.

A number of studies reporting on the application and performance of various forecasting methodologies are described in Chapter 15. The purpose of this chapter is to suggest a framework for comparing alternative forecasting methods and to provide guidelines for selecting those methods most appropriate in a given situation.

In Chapter 16 some of the behavioral and organizational problems that often hinder effective use of forecasting resources are examined. A number of structures are presented for tackling these common problems, and empirical results showing the need for placing major attention on these topics are presented.

The hope is that by the end of Part Six not only will the forecasting methodologies and their applications have been described and understood, but the initial steps required for effectively using them in the organization will also have been presented.

14/FORECASTING AND PLANNING

This chapter begins the final segment of the book—the integration of forecasting into planning and decision making in the organization. The aim in this chapter is to provide background on the role of planning in organizations and to illustrate the role of forecasting as it can be effectively integrated into the management and administrative tasks of planning and decision making.

The chapter is organized into four main sections. The first examines the concept of planning and defines the opportunities and problems of forecasting in connection with planning. Current trends relating to planning and its use by organizations are also examined. These topics are covered first at a conceptual level. In the second section they are dealt with on a much more practical basis by looking at the adaptation required to fit forecasting and planning to specific organizations. Two examples of the roles of forecasting in the firm are described: one for the B.F. Goodrich Company and one for the Armstrong Cork Company.

The third segment of this chapter deals in some detail with specific areas in an organization where forecasting can serve as an input to planning and decision making. The time horizon of planning is used as a criterion for categorizing such needs. Several examples of applications are included in this section.

The final section of the chapter examines the contribution that forecasting can make to the analysis and understanding of administrative and management problems. This section looks beyond obtaining a forecast for a given variable and points out some of the learning that is possible when formalized forecasting procedures are applied. These benefits often can be of significant value in planning and decision making, further enhancing the contribution of forecasting.

14/1 The Role of Forecasting in Planning

Thus far it has been assumed that the purpose of forecasting has been relatively simple to define. However, it should be clear to the reader who anticipates becoming a practical user of forecasting that this is not always the case. Although one can focus direct attention on what is to be forecast and the best way to approach that, it is perhaps more instructive to deal first with the topic of planning and its role in the organization. A basic understanding of planning can aid the forecaster in determining what types of forecasts would be most useful and how one might proceed to define them.

Most writers tend to agree that the concept of planning deals with some form of decision making involving the future. The Random House dictionary, for example, defines planning as a method of thinking out acts and purposes beforehand. Drucker (1959, p. 238) describes planning "as the conscious recognition of the futurity of present decisions," while Ackoff (1970, p. 2) talks about planning as a task that is performed in advance of taking actions. Ackoff continues his description by saying that planning is actually anticipatory decision making, even though not all forms of decision making are planning.

Because both forecasting and planning concern themselves with the future, it is important to integrate these two functions within the organization. A knowledge of forecasting techniques is of little value unless they can be effectively applied in the organization's planning process. That requires an examination of the planning activities within an organization so that the types of forecasts required and the techniques available for providing them can be tailored to the organization's needs.

The manner in which organizations and managers plan has received considerable attention in the management literature, and books have been written about both the theory and practice of planning. Mockler (1970) and Naylor and Schauland (1976) give a good overview of some of the concepts used in planning. Most of the planning literature has concerned itself with the various aspects of the planning process—establishing goals, objectives, strategies, and so on—and has largely assumed that forecasting, while important, is readily available.

Emphasis is placed on planning for several reasons. First, when needs and opportunities arise, they should be met without delay. For example, a manufacturer whose product experiences high seasonal demand in the summer months does not want to wait until summer to start producing products for that season. Rather some lead time is needed so that appropriate products can be manufactured in advance and be immediately ready for purchase by consumers. A second impetus for planning is that frequently the future environment can be influenced if certain actions are taken beforehand. For example, the manufacturer can advertise or open new retail outlets in order to increase sales. However, such action is most effective when plans are based on accurate predictions about the future.

Planning not only allows actions to be taken that will meet lead time requirements and that will influence the future environment, but also has by-products that can create a more efficient and effective mode of operation. One such by-product is increased motivation of individuals in the organization. Many companies have found that morale has improved when individuals are involved in planning the future course of the organization, and that organization goals are more likely to be achieved when people understand them and are committed to them. Planning also aids in the coordination of several diverse activities and enables the organization to meet its objectives with a minimum amount of resources.

Some of the reasons commonly given for the adoption of formal planning procedures include the following (Steiner, 1979, pp. 35–43):

1. Focuses attention on asking and answering questions of importance to the company.
2. Introduces a set of decision-making forces and tools into a business:
   —simulates the future
   —applies the systems approach
   —forces the setting of objectives
   —reveals and clarifies future opportunities and threats
   —provides a uniform decision framework throughout the firm
   —encourages performance measurement
   —links a variety of management functions
   —raises strategic issues to higher levels of management.
3. Provides behavioral benefits by establishing communication channels, managerial training, and a sense of participation.

14/2 Relating Forecasting and Planning in the Organization

In discussing the role of forecasting in planning, it is important to distinguish between two forecasting situations. In one the forecaster will also prepare the plans and make the decisions; in the other the forecasters are generally part of a staff function and the decision makers and/or planners are in line positions located elsewhere in the organization. The latter is probably the most frequently encountered situation in forecasting because as organizations grow and develop, the need for increased specialization arises. Many of the techniques that have been described in this book require substantial resources and skills to apply. As a result, they tend to be most useful when the planning activity to which they are related has a major impact on and value to the organization. In many such cases the forecasters and possibly the planners are not the same individuals as the decision makers and line managers.

To illustrate the alternative ways in which forecasting as a staff function can be integrated with line management's decision making and planning, forecasting/planning organizations in two firms will be examined: the B. F. Goodrich Company and the Armstrong Cork Company. Although several other variations in organization have been followed in practice, these examples can indicate some of the problems involved in integrating forecasting and planning and some alternative procedures for effectively handling these problems.

14/2/1 Putting Forecasting to Work at the B. F. Goodrich Company[1]

At the B. F. Goodrich Company, forecasting is organized as an integral part of the business research department. The group has had an outstanding reputation over the past several years, as indicated by the positions that some of its members have attained in the organization (including chairman and chief executive officer, group vice-president, vice-president, and senior division vice-president), and the fact that requests from outside the company for the industry forecasts prepared by this department greatly exceed requests for information about the company itself.

As a key to understanding the use of forecasts in planning and management at B. F. Goodrich, it is helpful to consider the company's organization, which is shown in Figure 14-1. The vice-president of planning reports to the group vice-president of corporate services. This vice-president of planning is responsible for both the planning and development division as well as the corporate communication division. In addition, he or she serves as a secretary of the management committee. The operations of the company are handled by six operating divisions under two executive vice-presidents.

At B. F. Goodrich, planning is the major use of forecasting. The company has formalized part of its planning procedures into a planning cycle that produces a completed corporate plan in the fourth quarter of each year. This plan states the goals, missions, and objectives of the company and of all the divisions in broad terms—outlining businesses that fall into the categories of harvest, expand, or hold. These categories are based upon the forecasts of the markets that have been made by the company's economists and the forecast of the company's own strengths and weaknesses made by the operating divisions and the corporate support groups.

In the first quarter of each year, the operating divisions receive guidance in the form of market forecasts and a reminder of their portion of the previous corporate plan. In addition, the controller's office provides forecasts of profit and loss statements and sources and uses of funds statements. These latter are used by the treasurer to forecast whether or not the company has the financial capability to carry out the plan.

The vice-president of planning, the treasurer, and the controller then work with various combinations of each division's plan to find one that appears to be workable. When such a plan is developed, it is presented to the management committee and guidelines are released to the division for development of additional strategic plans. The divisions then prepare the next year's detailed operating budget for submission in the fourth quarter.

---

[1]This description is adapted from an article prepared by T. W. Blazey, Vice-President and Controller, B. F. Goodrich Company. That article appeared in *Business Economics* (January 1976), pp. 41–44.

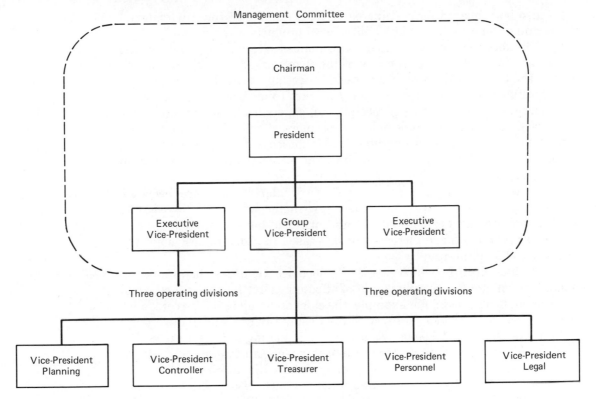

FIGURE 14-1 B.F. GOODRICH COMPANY—ORGANIZATION

That completes a full cycle in the planning process, which includes both a revision of the corporate plan and development of division operating budgets.

Forecasting has an important role in this cycle. Two factors whose forecasts are particularly critical are those of market size and market share, since they determine such things as capacity requirements, size of sales staff, and methods of distribution. Considerable justification is required of individual divisions when they project changes in growth rates or other assumptions that are not completely consistent with the forecasts prepared by the planning division.

Attempts are continually made to upgrade the forecasting in the planning cycle and its value to the individual divisions. One refinement recently made is switching from using constant dollars to current dollars for the last 4 years of the 5-year plan. Previously, they had used a rather simplistic assumption that price increases would offset cost increases. Since that rarely had been found to be the case, a switch to current dollars seemed to be a substantial improvement. This switch, however, required that forecasts also be prepared for cost increases for a number of the raw material items and other inputs to the manufactured products.

The forecasts of the company's economists are used not only in the planning process but also in many of the firm's other operations. For example, the treasury division has a weekly meeting at which the company's economists review and forecast money market conditions. These forecasts are combined with forecasts of receipts and expenditures so that maturity dates of financial paper to be sold can be more effectively planned. Similarly, since the firm has considerable funds exposed to movements in foreign exchange rates, forecasting is also involved in determining how best to hedge and handle those foreign obligations.

Other areas in which forecasts are particularly useful are feedstock prices, transportation costs, and basic raw materials. Depending on the economists' forecasts of both supply and prices of basic commodities, raw material inventories are increased or decreased in order to best meet the firm's needs at minimum cost.

A final area in which the B. F. Goodrich Company has found an important role for forecasting is that of affecting policy for the industry and the economy as a whole. For example, the chief economist and the controller at B. F. Goodrich worked closely with the Cost of Living Council during the early 1970s. It was the company's feeling that existing indices for tires and inner tubes and productivity for the industry were misleading and incomplete. Through the company's efforts in working with the Bureau of Labor Statistics, an improved new tire and inner tube wholesale price index has been established and is being published as of 1976. These are just a few of the uses that B. F. Goodrich has made of forecasting in both its short- and long-range planning.

14/2/2   Forecasting and Planning at the Armstrong Cork Company[2]

The Armstrong Cork Company is one of the leading producers of interior furnishings for residences as well as commercial and institutional buildings in the United States. With annual sales approaching a billion dollars, Armstrong and its subsidiaries employ some 23,000 people and operate more than 50 plants worldwide.

Armstrong is involved in four principal markets—home improvement and refurbishing, new residential building, commercial and institutional building, and specialty industrial products. The company has chosen to organize its manufacturing activities into six divisions or profit centers.

---

[2]This description is adapted from an article prepared by George F. Johnston, Vice-President and Chief Planning Officer, Armstrong Cork Company. That article appeared in *Business Economics* (January 1976), pp. 35–40.

These profit centers are supported by more than a dozen centralized staff departments including a corporate planning department and a corporate economist's office.

Even though the corporate planning and chief economist groups are separated at Armstrong, the two work closely together to coordinate their various functions. Both are concerned with the future, but from differing points of view. The chief economist department is involved in predicting what is likely to happen with a focus on trends and implications for the company's various businesses. The corporate planning group, on the other hand, is involved in helping managers identify opportunities and problems so that they can achieve a measure of control over what will happen and direct their businesses accordingly.

To better understand the integration of planning and forecasting at Armstrong, it is useful to consider the basic concepts and objectives that it holds for its planning operations. The ultimate goal is the development of both operational plans (2-year time horizon) and strategic plans (5-year time horizon) for each operation and subsidiary and for the company as a whole. These plans are aimed at coordinating marketing, production, personnel, and financial requirements in achieving a predetermined set of goals.

The starting point for initiating the planning process is the concept of business unit planning. This concept provides the framework that is used by general managers to involve a wide range of middle managers in the planning process. The concept of business unit planning focuses on the smallest practical unit for which planning can be performed. That is a single business or collection of related businesses that has its own unique mission, product lines, markets, distribution, competitors, and so on, and whose planning and managing generally can be focused on one individual.

The corporate planning development provides a format for the company's general managers to use in the preparation of their business unit plans. The execution of that format involves four distinct phases.

Phase I.   In this phase the business unit data base is prepared. The intent is to bring together as much factual data as is available on that specific business unit. Data both external and internal to the firm are included and are generally collected through marketing, marketing research, the controller, and the economic research departments. The economic research department actually provides information that represents a historical analysis of the business unit as well as an analysis of the industry and markets that it serves.

Phase II. This phase involves the assessment of the business unit. Essentially, it is aimed at determining what can realistically be done by the business unit during that planning period. Key elements for success are identified and the competitive constraints and relevant aspects of the environment are recognized. The business unit manager and his staff do much of this work.

Phase III. In this phase objectives, strategies, and action plans are established. As such it is the most crucial step in business unit planning. Essentially, the unit manager is specifying his goals and his plans for achieving them.

During this phase the economic research department makes valuable contributions by providing forecasts of basic assumptions for operational planning purposes, and later in the cycle by providing forecasts of long-range assumptions for strategic planning purposes. These basic assumptions cover general economic forecasts as well as specific market forecasts. In addition, the economic research department provides forecasts of the potential of each individual market segment. For example, general forecasts are developed for a market such as the resilient flooring industry, then for Armstrong's resilient flooring operation, and then for the sheet flooring business unit within that operation. Finally the focus is narrowed further as specific forecasts are developed for individual market segments such as the builder market, the installed residential replacement market, the do-it-yourself market, and the commercial market.

To give business unit managers a perspective for the 5-year plan, the economic research department publishes long-range assumptions that are more general in nature than the shorter-range assumptions used in the 2-year operating plan. These include forecasts for some of the basic markets and industries served by Armstrong on inflation factors, prices, raw material supplies, and capital expenditures as well as forecasts of economic, social, political, and international factors.

Because of the emphasis that Armstrong puts on this third phase in its planning cycle, it encourages management to allow substantial time to study the assumptions and to prepare specific statements on objectives, strategies, and action plans for both the 2-year operational and 5-year strategic recommendations. The concept for business unit planning is based on managers developing the most likely plan after reviewing various alternatives. However, it also emphasizes the need to consider contingency planning given today's business climate and the uncertainty in the environment. Here the economic research department again makes a contribution by forecasting alternative paths that the economy might take and the probability of occurrence of each of those alternatives.

Phase IV. This final phase in business unit planning deals with the financial and resource implications of the selected strategic plan. In essence, it is aimed at getting the managers to describe the resources that their plans will require and to assess the availability of these resources and their costs. Much of the input for this phase comes from the business unit manager working with staff departments such as

purchasing, production planning, engineering, and finance. At the completion of this phase, all business unit
plans are accumulated and adjusted to accommodate the
priorities at the division level within the operation or
subsidiary and finally within the entire corporation.

Planning at Armstrong has become essentially a year-round activity
with operational plans covering sales, profits, and expenses for a 2-year
time horizon being developed during the September through December
months. Those plans then serve as the base for the 5-year strategic plans
that are developed and consolidated from March through June.

One of the key elements of Armstrong's planning process is the development of contingency plans and the integration of them at the corporate
level. An example of how the economist's office plays a role in helping the
chief executive officer deal with contingencies is provided by the situation
in January of 1975. With a tight corporate operational plan for 1975, the
chief executive was faced with several questions concerning uncertainties
about the economy and about the specific segments in which Armstrong
was involved. As an aid to the chief executive officer in these considerations,
the economist's office described three possible economic paths in terms of
the recession, inflation rates, unemployment rates, real GNP, and the impact on Armstrong's markets. Once contingency plans were developed for
each of these three scenarios, trigger points were identified and the economy
was monitored continually against these alternative paths. When it became
apparent early in 1975 that the path the economy was taking was not
consistent with the corporate operational plan, a predetermined contingency plan was put into effect. This change helped to minimize disruptions
at the corporate level as well as in the individual operating units.

By way of summary, it can be noted that at Armstrong Cork Company the economic research department provides forecasts and other information for developing business unit data bases, then publishes basic
assumptions and long-range assumptions for use in the preparation of operational, strategic, and contingency plans. Essentially, it focuses on preparing forecasts of uncontrollable, external influences on the business. Next
the corporate planning group concerns itself with helping to systematize,
guide, and assist the business unit managers in their planning process. The
aim is to help them identify opportunities and threats and prepare plans
that are realistic, challenging, and achievable. Once specific operational
and strategic plans have been developed and agreed upon for individual
business units, divisions, and subsidiaries, the president's office reviews the
results and synthesizes them into a total plan for using the resources of the
corporation.

In practice this integration of forecasting and planning is much more
difficult than it may sound in this description. The Armstrong Cork Company has been making substantial progress in both of these areas. The
people at Armstrong feel that forecasting is one of the most valuable tools

they have and that as they learn to use it better, it will improve both their strategic and operational planning and decision making.

14/3   Forecasting as Input to Planning and Decision Making

The previous sections have shown that forecasting and planning are closely interrelated areas. One of the main challenges to be met in accomplishing the integration of forecasting and planning is helping forecasters understand the opportunities for their services in planning. In this section, several specific areas of planning will be examined, and a partial list will be developed of the areas where forecasting has been found to be most beneficial. It is hoped that this discussion will help forecasters (and planners) understand the opportunities for integrating their viewpoints. However, since each organization is distinct in terms of its environment, its structure, and its existing strategies and plans, these guidelines would have to be adapted for each new situation.

From a *management process* point of view, the linkage between forecasting, planning, and decision making can be summarized as shown from left to right in Figure 14-2. The essential elements of this representation are that environmental forecasting generally precedes planning, which in turn precedes organization forecasting decision making. However, a number of important interactions exist between each of these three activities and several related activities. While most managers would find Figure 14-2 consistent with their own views in this field, it is not sufficiently specific to serve as a guide to forecasters seeking to better understand the opportunities for their services in developing specific types of plans within an organization. As suggested in both the B. F. Goodrich and the Armstrong Cork examples of planning and forecasting, an important dimension used to classify individual situations is the time horizon. This dimension can be thought of either in terms of strategic versus operational or, as suggested in earlier chapters, as ranging from immediate term (less than one month) to short term (one to three months) to medium term (three months to 2 years) to long term (2 years or more). While this dimension may be useful in thinking about the needs for forecasting in a range of organizational environments, the specific characteristics of each situation largely dictate which of these decisions will fall into each of these four time horizons. For example, in one company, a 2-year time horizon may be very long range, while in another it may be short- or medium-range (Steiner, 1963, pp. 44–45). For individual managers, the meaning of these terms may depend on their positions in the organization. For a foreman, immediate-term planning or forecasting may be related to the next hour or the current shift, and long-range planning or forecasting may involve only a three-month horizon. For

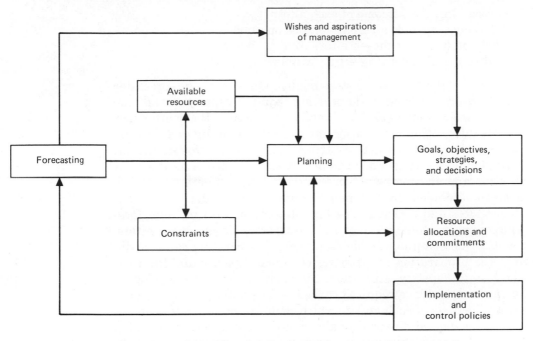

FIGURE 14-2 LINKING FORECASTING, PLANNING, AND DECISION MAK-
ING

top management, on the other hand, planning for the coming month may
be immediate term, and long-term planning may span several years or even
a decade.

To understand the nature of the linkages among forecasting, planning, and decision making, it is useful to consider a specific functional area
and the dimension of the time horizon suggested above. The remainder of
this section will consider the production operations area and the specific
roles that forecasting can fulfill in that function. The comparable roles in
other functions, as well as the general management role of forecasting, will
then be summarized.

Consider the set of decisions that management must make in capacity planning. The management tasks that are usually associated with capacity planning decisions are the following:

1. Assessing the company's situation and environment
2. Determining available capacity
3. Forecasting required capacity
4. Developing alternative plans to achieve required capacity
5. Making quantitative and financial analyses of capacity alternatives
6. Analyzing qualitative issues for each alternative

7. Forecasting the outcome of each alternative
8. Selecting a specific alternative to be pursued
9. Implementing the chosen alternative
10. Auditing and reviewing actual results

A cursory review of these 10 steps might suggest that the forecaster need be involved only in step 3—forecasting required capacity—and step 7—forecasting the outcome of each alternative. Assuredly, these are major focal points for integrating forecasting into capacity planning and decision making, but almost every other step of the process also involves significant requirements for forecasting. For example, in step 1—assessing the company's situation and environment—forecasting can play a very useful role in projecting the economic environment and its impact on demand for the company's products and services. The first step might also include "forecasting" the competitive environment and the capacity plans of competitors.

In step 2—determining available capacity—forecasting can contribute through the preparation of estimates of usable capacity and the relationship of cost to capacity utilization. Similarly, in step 4—developing alternative plans to achieve required capacity—forecasting can contribute by estimating the costs of each option, which could lead directly to step 5—making quantitative and financial analyses of capacity alternatives. Step 5 might include forecasting lead times for new construction and relocation, as well as lead times for hiring and training new workers and procuring materials associated with changes in output levels. Even in the final step—auditing and reviewing actual results—forecasting can upgrade existing procedures and develop skills and capabilities that will help in future production operations decision making and planning.

Forecasting's contributions can also be related to the time horizon of capacity planning situations. Figure 14-3 splits capacity planning tasks into a long-range portion (usually part of the 5-year or 10-year plan), an annual capacity plan (usually part of the current operating budget), and then into shorter planning periods, such as those for scheduling and dispatching.

Most of the decisions typically associated with each of these subsegments of capacity planning, and thus linked directly to forecasting needs, are summarized in Table 14-1. When forecasters consider their input, recognizing the interaction of these various time horizons, the subfunctions involved, and the resources affected, they can greatly leverage their contribution to the production and operations function. Similar potential exists for linking forecasting with planning and decision making in the other functional areas. Space does not permit an extensive elaboration of those, but some of the major areas where forecasting contributions can generally be made are summarized in Table 14-2. As suggested in this table, forecasting can be viewed as an information source for managers faced with specific tasks of planning and decision making for the four time horizon categories used above. This table is meant to suggest the nature of the opportunities that

TABLE 14-1   PLANNING DECISIONS IN OPERATIONS[a]

	Types of Decisions—By Time Horizon			
Capacity, Determining Resources	Long-Range Capacity Planning (Long Term)	Annual Capacity Planning (Medium Term)	Scheduling (Short Term)	Dispatching (Immediate Term)
Acquiring and deploying physical space and capital equipment	Selection of capabilities Location decisions Timing decisions Quantity Capital spending	Minor additions Subcontracting Product mix	Allocation of facilities to products in specific time periods	
Acquiring and deploying human resources	Hiring and layoff policies Skill requirements Timing Quantity Training and development	Number of shifts Overtime Hire-fire Line balancing	Overtime (allocation of manpower to products (jobs) in specific time periods	Rescheduling Expediting and detailed coordination of all three factors of production
Acquiring and deploying materials	Material requirements Long-term contracts Vendor selection Warehouse requirements Timing Quantity	Short-term purchase commitments Shipping schedules Inventory planning	Ordering materials Marshalling materials Inventory control Allocation of materials	

[a]See: Wheelwright, 1982.

TABLE 14-2   INFORMATION NEEDS FOR PLANNING

	Time Horizon			
Organization Unit	Immediate Term (less than 1 mo)	Short Term (1–3 mo)	Medium Term (3 mo–2 yr)	Long Term (2 yr or more)
	Quantitative Forecasting			
Business Marketing	Sales of each product type, sales by geographical area, sales by customer, competition, prices, inventory levels	Total sales, product categories, major products, product groups, prices	Total sales, product categories, prices, general economic conditions	Total sales, major product categories, new product introduction, saturation points of existing products, customers' preferences and tastes
Production	Demand of each product, plant loading	Total demands, demand of product categories and product groups, scheduling employment level, costs	Costs, budget allocations, buying or ordering equipment and machinery, employment level	Costs, facility investments, expansion of plant and equipment, ordering of heavy machinery and equipment, demand of production facilities, new technologies
Inventory	Demand of each product, production, demand for material, demand for semifinished products, weather conditions	Demand for materials, demand for semifinished products, demand for products, possible strikes	Possible strikes in suppliers or transportation facilities	Total sales, expansion of warehouses
Finance	Sales revenue, production costs, inventory costs, leading indicators, cash inflows, cash outflows	Total demand, inventory levels, cash flows, short-term borrowing, prices	Budget allocations, cash flows	Total sales, investment selections, capital expenditure, allocations of resources, capital programs, cash flows

TABLE 14-2   INFORMATION NEEDS FOR PLANNING (*Continued*)

Organization Unit	Time Horizon			
	Immediate Term (less than 1 mo)	Short Term (1–3 mo)	Medium Term (3 mo–2 yr)	Long Term (2 yr or more)
	Quantitative Forecasting			
Purchasing	Production, cash availability, purchasing of supplies and materials	Demand for products, demand for materials, lead time for purchasing	Demand for products, demand for raw and other materials	Contracts for buying raw materials, customers' preferences and tastes
R&D			New product introduction, R&D selections	Total sales; technological, social, political, and economic conditions of future; new product development
Top management		Total sales, sales breakdowns, pricing	Demand for sales, costs and other expenses, cash position, general economic conditions, control objectives	Total sales; costs and other expenses, social and economic trends; goals, objectives and strategies; new products; pricing policies
Economic Economic unit		Level of economic activity	General economic conditions, turning points in economy, level of economic activity	State and type of economy, level of economic activity, sales of industry

TABLE 14-2   INFORMATION NEEDS FOR PLANNING (*Continued*)

Organization Unit	Time Horizon			
	Immediate Term (less than 1 mo)	Short Term (1–3 mo)	Medium Term (3 mo–2 yr)	Long Term (2 yr or more)
		Technological Forecasting		
Environment Technological unit			Available technologies	Areas of technological innovation, R&D selections, available technological opportunities
Business environment forecasting unit			Social attitudes	Social trends, tastes, areas of social concern
		Availability of money, interest rates	Fiscal and monetary policies	Trends in the rate of taxation, depreciation, and concept of free market
	Prices, sales promotions	Prices, advertising selections, sales promotions, new product introduction	New product development	Capital investment, new technologies, R&D selections of competitors
	Weather conditions	Weather conditions	Crops	General environmental constraints (pollution level, availability of raw materials, etc.)

might be identified and pursued; it is not an exhaustive list of them. The task of selecting the most appropriate forecasting approach for this range of situations will be discussed in Chapter 15.

14/4 Contribution of Forecasting to Analysis and Understanding

In each of the chapters that deals with specific methods of forecasting, the aim has been to provide a forecast or range of forecasts for a specific variable or item. Although that is most often the direct application of forecasting as suggested in the preceding sections of this chapter, there are frequently other substantial benefits to analysis and understanding that accompany the application of forecasting methodologies. The extent and potential for these benefits depend upon the type of forecasting model applied (causal or time series) and the statistical parameters provided by that technique. In this respect, regression methods have a much higher potential contribution in regard to analysis and understanding than many of the other methodologies. The remainder of this chapter will look at several of the specific areas where significant benefits can arise from the application of a formal forecasting methodology.

14/4/1 The Variance as a Measure of Risk

As shown previously, statistical forecasting methods can use the statistical properties of the data to construct confidence intervals and test different hypotheses about the forecasts and their means and variances. In addition to its use in constructing a confidence interval for a forecast, the variance of a forecast can help to measure risk. It provides an indication of the degree of uncertainty associated with predicting that variable, and as such can be useful in the preparation of contingency plans for optimistic and pessimistic outcomes. In the short run, this measure of risk can be utilized for inventory and cash management purposes, since its magnitude will be reflected in the extent of over- or under-prediction. Decision models for managing inventory and cash levels in an optimal way can be built based on a knowledge of the magnitude of the variance.

A tremendous amount of work has been done on financial portfolio analysis (Markowitz, 1959) involving the covariance as a basis for minimizing the risk in a set of investments, or optimizing the return for a given level of risk. In a similar manner, forecasting models can be built to minimize the effects of forecasting errors when a number of items or areas of management are involved. In other words, it may be possible to decrease the total risk of inaccurate forecasts by examining in a global fashion the variance and covariance of the predictions made on different items. This technique can decrease substantially the effects of over- or under-estimation for the total organization by grouping the forecasts in such a way that their covariance will be as small as possible.

14/4/2   Marginal Analysis

In many forecasting situations, the parameter(s) of the forecasting model contain useful information. In the case of a time-series model of the form

$$Y = a + bt$$
where t is time,

(the change in Y caused by a unit change in t is $b(dY/dt)$. Since successive values of t correspond to successive periods, the value of b indicates the change in Y for each time period. For example, if the model is

$$Y = 10 + 250t$$

where t represents months, and Y represents the sales of product A, then the first derivative is

$$\frac{dY}{dt} = 250.$$

This means that, on the average, there is an increase of 250 units in the sales of product A every month.

Oftentimes the relationship of a variable to time is nonlinear. In such instances, simple transformations can provide information on the growth rate (in terms of units) as well as improving forecasting performance. If the values of Y are transformed to their natural logarithms, the result is

$$\log_e Y = a + bt. \tag{14-1}$$

The values of a and b in this equation can be easily estimated using regression analysis or some form of time-series analysis. The parameter b, the slope of the line, can then be shown to be a good estimate of the growth rate (measured as a percentage).

As an example of how this estimate of the growth rate might be obtained, suppose the following functional form is applied to a set of data:

$$Y = ab^t. \tag{14-2}$$

Taking logs (either natural or common) of both sides of equation (14-2) gives

$$\log Y = \log a + t(\log b). \tag{14-3}$$

This means that if the data of both the dependent and independent variables are transformed into logarithms, estimates for $\log a$ and $\log b$ could be obtained and used as the parameters of equation (14-3). It can then be shown that a will be the value of Y at period $t = 0$, while $(b - 1)$ will be the growth rate.

As a specific example, suppose one has a quantity of Y_0 units that are increasing at a constant rate of r per period. This can be expressed as

$$Y = Y_0(1 + r)^t, \tag{14-4}$$

where t is the time period $(1, 2, \ldots)$.

If $Y_0 = 100$ and $r = .10$, then equation (14-4) gives

Period	Value of Y	Increase in Y over Previous Period	Growth Rate r
$t = 0$	$Y_0 = 100$	—	—
$t = 1$	$Y_1 = 110$	$(1/100)(110 - 100) = 10/100 =$	.10
$t = 2$	$Y_2 = 121$	$(1/100)(121 - 110) = 11/110 =$	.10
$t = 3$	$Y_3 = 133.1$	$(1/121)(133.1 - 121) = 12.1/121 =$	.10
$t = 4$	$Y_4 = 146.4$	$(1/133.1)(146:4 - 133.1) = 13.3/133.1 =$	.10
etc.			

If equation (14-2) is substituted into (14-4), the result is

$$ab^t = Y_0(1 + r)^t. \tag{14-5}$$

Taking the logs of both sides of (14-5) gives

$$\log a + t(\log b) = \log Y_0 + t[\log(1 + r)],$$

$$\log a = \log Y_0,$$

$$a = Y_0. \tag{14-6}$$

Thus the initial value of Y (at time $t = 0$) will be equal to the intercept, a.

Similarly

$$\log b = \log(1 + r),$$

$$b = 1 + r,$$

$$r = b - 1.$$

This means that the growth rate of a set of data of the form $Y = ab^t$ can be found directly by applying equation (14-3) and subtracting 1 from b.

If the data cannot be expressed by equation (14-2), but can be better approximated by

$$Y = e^{a+bt}, \tag{14-7}$$

the growth rate can still be found.

This is done by first taking the logs of both sides to obtain

$$\log Y = [a + bt](\log e),$$

$$\log Y = a + bt, \tag{14-8}$$

$$\cdot Y' = a + b$$

since $\log e = 1$, and from Chapter 5,

$$b = \frac{n\Sigma XY' - \Sigma X\Sigma Y'}{n\Sigma X^2 - (\Sigma X)^2}.$$

From equation (14-8), the values of a and b can be estimated after the data of the dependent variable have been transformed to log.

The log of equation (14-4) is

$$\log Y = \log Y_0 + t[\log(1 + r)]. \tag{14-9}$$

Substituting (14-8) into (14-9) gives

$$a + bt = \log Y_0 + t[\log(1 + r)].$$

Thus,

$$a = \log Y_0,$$

$$b = \log(1 + r). \tag{14-10}$$

The antilog of equation (14-10) is

$$e^b = 1 + r,$$

which gives

$$r = e^b - 1. \tag{14-11}$$

This simply says that the constant growth rate r will be equivalent to $(e^b - 1)$. For growth rates of less than 20 percent, the estimated value of b in equation (14-7) will be very close to the actual growth rate. If expanded, (14-11) yields

$$r = e^b - 1,$$

$$r = [1 + b + \frac{b^2}{2!} + \frac{b^3}{3!} + \cdots] - 1,$$

$$r = b + \frac{b^2}{2} + \frac{b^3}{6} + \cdots.$$

When $b = .20$, this gives

$$r = .20 + \frac{(.20)^2}{2} + \frac{(.20)^3}{6} \cdots \cong .221.$$

It can thus be concluded that the coefficient b of the independent variable x provides an approximate measure of the growth rate for actual growth rates less than .20, while an exact measure of the growth rate can be found using equation (14-2).

When a causal instead of a time-series model exists, the parameters of the equation can supply marginal information. Their value can indicate the change in the dependent variable Y caused by a unit change in the independent variable corresponding to that parameter. Thus, for the causal model

$$Y = a + bX_1 + cX_2,$$

where X_1 is GNP and X_2 is advertising, b will indicate the change in Y accompanying a unit increase in GNP, and c will indicate the change in Y accompanying a unit change in advertising. In terms of policymaking, it may be very useful to know whether the change in Y corresponding to a dollar increase in advertising will cover the cost of that advertising.

14/4/3 Elasticities

Elasticity, the percentage change in one variable divided by the associated percentage change in another variable, is an important factor in many situations. It can be estimated easily after a logarithmic transformation (either natural or common) of both dependent and independent variables has taken place. For example, for the function

$$Y = aX^b, \tag{14-12}$$

taking logs of both sides gives

$$\log Y = \log a + b(\log X). \tag{14-13}$$

In equation (14-13), the values of $\log a$ and b can be calculated and the derivative found as

$$\frac{d \log Y}{d \log X} = b.$$

This indicates the change in $\log Y$ caused by a one-unit change in $\log X$. Since a logarithmic change corresponds to a percentage change in the original data, b can be interpreted as the percentage change in Y caused by a percentage change in X. As such it is a measure that is independent of the absolute value of the units involved.

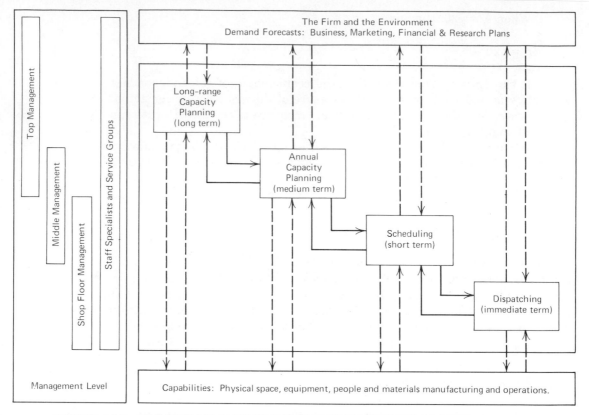

FIGURE 14-3   CAPACITY PLANNING AND THE TIME HORIZON IN OPERATIONS

In equation (14-12) three categories of values for b can be distinguished: $b < 1$, $b = 1$, and $b > 1$. The functional forms corresponding to each of these can be seen in Figure 14-3.

For $b < 1$, a 1 percent increase in X will cause less than a 1 percent increase in Y. When $b > 1$, a 1 percent increase in X will cause more than a 1 percent increase in Y. Finally, when $b = 1$, equation (14-12) becomes the equivalent of $Y = a + bX$, indicating a constant linear increase in Y for each increase in X. This behavior of Y can be seen in Figure 14-4.

The usefulness of elasticities for policymaking can be illustrated by an example. Suppose

$$\log Y = \log a + b \log X,$$

where Y is the sales of product A, and X is its price.

If $b = -1.5$, it indicates that every percentage increase in the price of product A will result in a 1.5 percent decrease in sales. In this case the

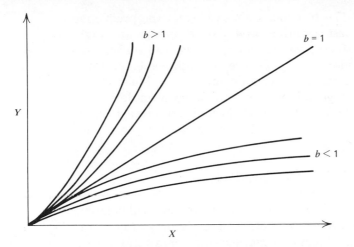

FIGURE 14-4 ALTERNATIVE VALUES FOR THE COEFFICIENT b

demand is elastic. On the other hand, if $b = -.5$, an increase in price of 1 percent will decrease demand by only .5 percent. This is commonly called inelastic demand. This type of information can provide important data upon which to base pricing decisions. Similar measures can be calculated for other factors as long as the data can be modeled by an equation like (14-12).

14/4/4 Costing

Once a cost function has been estimated, questions relating to fixed, variable, marginal, or per unit costs often can be answered. For example, suppose the estimated total cost function is cubic and of the form

$$\text{Cost} = a + bX + cX^2 + dX^3. \tag{14-14}$$

Then

$$\text{fixed cost} = a, \tag{14-15}$$

$$\text{variable cost} = bX + cX^2 + dX^3, \tag{14-16}$$

$$\text{per unit cost} = (a/X) + b + cX + dX^2, \tag{14-17}$$

$$\text{marginal cost} = b + 2(c)X + 3(d)X^2. \tag{14-18}$$

Decisions on production levels, expansion policies, pricing, and efficiency can be facilitated using the information obtained through cost functions like those above. For example, the optimal production will be at the lowest point of equation (14-17). If sales increase beyond the production level corresponding to the lowest cost, then new plant or equipment might be considered to raise the optimal level. Because of long lead times, a decision to expand must be made well in advance through combined information obtained from growth rates, elasticities, and so on. Much of this information needed by top management for long-run policy formulation can be obtained as direct and indirect output from formalized forecasting applications.

14/4/5   Seasonal and Cyclical Considerations

Forecasting methods can discover the seasonal and cyclical behavior of the data. Through such analyses, it is often possible to predict future variations in sales and attribute them to trend, seasonal, or cyclical factors.

Decomposition methods are the most direct and explicit in isolating the seasonal and cyclical part of a set of data. Their output for monthly data consists of 12 seasonal indices whose base is 100. Index values higher or lower than this base indicate expected variations attributable to the season. Similarly cyclical indices are provided that help to explain and predict the effects of cycle.

Regression methods are less explicit in isolating seasonal and cyclical elements. By defining dummy variables for each of the seasons but one, the season without a corresponding dummy variable becomes the base and the parameters of the other variables will indicate seasonal adjustments to that base. Thus a positive coefficient will denote a higher level of sales caused by seasonal effects, and a negative coefficient will denote a lower level. The effects of cyclicality can be estimated by relating the dependent variable to an independent factor, such as GNP, that can be used to explain cyclical changes.

ARMA methods are less explicit in the way they estimate the seasonal effects. These methods do not separate the trend, cyclical, or seasonal effects from each other. Thus, a total forecast is given, which includes all effects without breaking the pattern down into its various components.

Seasonal variations can cause considerable fluctuations in sales that have important policy consequences. For example, the manager making a decision to cut production when a lower level of sales is forecast will want to consider whether a few months later more favorable seasonal factors will cause the sales to pick up again. If so, it may be that inventories should be accumulated to keep a more constant production rate. Similar questions will arise with respect to predicted cyclical fluctuations. Policy questions of this type can be dealt with through knowledge of the seasonal and cyclical factors. Thus not only is the forecast important, but so too are the reasons for that forecast.

14/4/6 Simulation and Sensitivity Analysis

Causal forecasting models are not as easy to use as time-series models. The difficulty is that the values of each of the independent variables used in the model must be estimated before one can forecast. This can be a serious problem because it shifts the burden of forecasting to that of estimating the values of the independent variables. However, this very problem can present many advantages, too. First, marginal analyses can be applied and elasticities for any of the independent variables can be found. In addition, the effects of multiple changes and their influence on the dependent variable can be calculated. For example, suppose that the following model of sales has been determined:

$$\text{Sales} = 250 + .03(\text{GNP}) + 3.8(\text{Advertising}) - 4.5(\text{Price}) + 2.5(\text{R\&D}). \qquad (14\text{-}19)$$

This model could be used to predict the sales volume under varying decisions regarding advertising, prices, and R&D expenditures. Thus, more than one input can be varied to determine their effects on sales. This use of the model goes beyond forecasting in trying to shape the future, since the values of advertising, prices, and R&D are controllable. They can be set at a level that best fits the organization's plans and goals.

A forecast model like equation (14-19) is one of the most efficient ways to obtain information about the influence of changes in controllable factors (the independent variables) on the dependent variable. Actually it is a form of laboratory simulation that shows how varying the levels of advertising, price, and R&D will influence the sales. From this simulation, a desirable level of sales, advertising, price, and R&D can be selected, and the feasibility of actions needed to achieve that level examined. In this way, equation (14-19) can be used to formulate alternatives for management choice.

Significant benefits often can be obtained from forecasting techniques beyond simply a prediction about a single variable. The extent of these benefits depends upon the particular method used and the extra work put forth to extract them. As a rule, causal models provide more such information than time-series models, and statistical models more than nonstatistical ones. In the end, such advantages must be weighed against the costs in deciding how many such benefits should be sought from forecasting applications.

REFERENCES AND SELECTED BIBLIOGRAPHY

Ackoff, R. L. 1970. *A Concept of Corporate Planning*. New York: John Wiley & Sons, Inc.

———. 1981. *Creating the Corporate Future*. New York: John Wiley & Sons, Inc.

Armstrong, J. S. 1978. *Long Range Forecasting*. New York: John Wiley & Sons, Inc.

Ayres, R. U. 1969. *Technological Forecasting and Long-Range Planning*. New York: McGraw-Hill.

———. 1979. *Uncertain Futures: Challenges for Decision Makers*. New York: John Wiley & Sons, Inc.

Blazey, T. W. 1976. "Putting Forecasts to Work in the Firm," *Business Economics,* January, pp. 41–44.

Brandt, S. C. 1981. *Strategic Planning in Emerging Companies*. Reading, Mass.: Addison-Wesley.

Centron, M. 1971. *Industrial Applications of Technological Forecasting*. New York: John Wiley & Sons, Inc.

Cohen, K. J., and R. M. Cyert. 1965. *The Theory of the Firm: Resource Allocation in a Market Economy*. Englewood Cliffs, N.J.: Prentice-Hall.

Cotton, D. B. 1970. *Company Wide Planning*. London: Macmillan.

Drucker, P. F. 1959. "Long Range Planning," *Management Science,* **5,** April, pp. 238–39.

Ewing, D. C. 1968. *The Practice of Planning*. New York: Harper & Row.

Ewing, D. W. 1969. *The Human-Side of Planning—Tool or Tyrant?* London: Macmillan.

Holt, C., F. Modigliani, J. F. Muth, and H. A. Simon. 1960. *Planning Production, Inventories and Work Force*. Englewood Cliffs, N.J.: Prentice-Hall.

Hussey, D. E. 1971. *Introducing Corporate Planning*. Oxford: Pergamon Press.

Johnston, G. F. 1976. "Putting Forecasts to Work in the Corporate Planning Function," *Business Economics,* January, pp. 35–40.

Lorange, P., and R. F. Vancil. 1977. *Strategic Planning Systems*. Englewood Cliffs, N.J.: Prentice-Hall.

———. 1980. *Corporate Planning*. Englewood Cliffs, N.J.: Prentice-Hall.

Makridakis, S., and S. C. Wheelwright (eds.). 1982. *Handbook of Forecasting*. New York: John Wiley & Sons, Inc.

Markowitz, H. M. 1959. *Portfolio Selection: Efficient Diversification of Investments*. New York: John Wiley & Sons, Inc.

Meadows, D. H. 1972. *Limits of Growth*. London: Earth Island Limited.

Miller, E. C. 1971. *Advanced Techniques for Strategic Planning*. Research Study 104. New York: American Management Association.

Mockler, R. J. 1970. "Theory and Practice of Planning," *Harvard Business Review,* March-April, pp. 148–59.

Naylor, T. H. 1978. *Corporate Planning Models.* Reading, Mass.: Addison-Wesley.

Naylor, T. H., and H. Schauland. 1976. "A Survey of Users of Corporate Planning Models," *Management Science,* **22,** No. 9, pp. 927–37.

Porter, M. E. 1980. *Competitive Strategy.* New York: Free Press.

Quinn, J.B. 1980. *Strategies for Change.* Homewood, Ill.: Richard D. Irwin.

Steiner, G. A. 1963. *Managerial Long-Range Planning.* New York: McGraw-Hill.

———. 1969. *Top Management Planning.* London: Macmillan.

———. 1979. *Strategic Planning.* New York: Free Press.

Warren, E. 1966. *Long-Range Planning: The Executive Viewpoint.* Englewood Cliffs, N.J.: Prentice-Hall.

Wheelwright, S. C. 1979. *Capacity Planning and Facilities Choice.* Boston: Division of Research, Harvard Business School.

———. 1982. "Capacity Planning Forecasting Requirements," Chapter 4 in *Handbook of Forecasting,* Makridakis and Wheelwright (eds.). New York: John Wiley & Sons, Inc.

EXERCISES

1. Perkin Elmer Instrument Division[3]

The following materials describe issues related to the Instrument Division's plans and forecasts. Analyze this situation and prepare a set of recommendations that address these issues. The following questions may be helpful in guiding your work on this assignment.

a. Analyze the major elements of:
   —the forecasting and planning environment.
   —the approach used in forecasting the "basic" items.
   —the approach used in forecasting "spare parts."
   —the approach used for "management" stock orders.

b. What are the planning needs in this situation?

c. Assess the strengths and weaknesses of the forecasting approaches being used, in terms of the requirements of the situation.

d. What recommendations would you make concerning the differences in the recently prepared forecasts and plans? Regarding the overall forecasting and planning system?

In October 1974, Gaynor Kelley, Vice-President and Manager of Perkin Elmer's Instrument Division, perceived disgruntling differences among three plans central to his division's operations.

---

[3]Copyright © 1977 by the President and Fellows of Harvard College. Used with permission.

The first plan was the division's annual business plan. This plan, dated July 1974, was the result of the division's annual planning activities. It was based on a projected division sales level of $93.4 million. The second plan had just reached Kelley. It was an updated forecast of orders received made by the product managers in early October 1974. It forecast 1974/75 fiscal year orders at $103.1 million. The third plan, also recently received by Kelley, was a manufacturing plan, which forecast the sales value of the product which was to be manufactured during the 1974/75 year. This "build plan" indicated that manufacturing planned to build $111.8 million worth of product for sale in the year. Inventories had already increased by over a million dollars since August in anticipation of the increase in sales projected by the product managers.

Kelley was more troubled by the high volumes indicated by the later two plans than by the discrepancies between them. Division sales had almost doubled in the previous 3 years, but signs that the economy was weakening had long been expected and were already appearing in other major industries. Moreover, the corporate financial staff had indicated that they had not planned to provide funds to meet the unexpected surge in business predicted by the marketing and build plans, and that they would have difficulty in obtaining them economically on such short notice.

Company Background

Perkin Elmer was an international developer and producer of high technology scientific instrumentation. The company was founded in 1938 to design and produce ultra-precise optical equipment. Growth in this area was rapid as these optical instruments found wide application in defense and space programs. In the 1970s under the leadership of Chairman Chester W. Nimitz, Jr., and President Robert H. Sorensen, the company began to emphasize the development of other types of laboratory analytical instrumentation. Products were marketed to researchers in college and hospital clinical laboratories, and to research and process control groups in a variety of industries. The rapid growth of the Instrument Group, which was responsible for manufacturing and selling these nonoptical instruments, resulted in a decrease in the percentage of the company's business that went to the United States government agencies. This percentage fell to only 27 percent of total sales in 1974. By this time, Instrument Group's sales accounted for more than one-half of the sales of the total company.

The Instrument Group, under the guidance of Senior Vice-President Horace McDonell, had sales of $150 million in 1974, a 17 percent increase over 1973 sales levels. This group also emphasized research and development as an integral part of their competitive strategy. Historically, research and development expenses had averaged 8–9 percent of instrument sales. Over 70 percent of the orders taken by the group in 1974 were for products that had not existed in 1969.

The Instrument Division

The Instrument Division, headed by Gaynor Kelley, was the largest organizational entity in the Instrument Group. Kelley had profit and asset responsibility for the marketing and manufacture of eight product lines. Reporting to him were eight product managers, the director of manufacturing, and the technical director who was responsible for engineering and development. Kelley also worked closely with the vice president of the Instrument Marketing Division, which was responsible for field sales and service.

Instrument Division products were sold through the field sales and service representatives of the Instrument Marketing Division. These people called on and advised potential customers, attended trade shows, and provided spare parts and technical service advice to users of Perkin Elmer equipment.

Marketing strategy, product line selection, and promotional strategy were the responsibility of the eight product managers in the Instrument Division. Each product manager had profit responsibility for an entire line of instruments and associated accessory items.

The price of an instrument varied from $3,000–$35,000, while the price range for the accessory items used to operate the instrument was from $200–$5,000. Price was not the primary basis for competition, however. Perkin Elmer's product managers claimed that the most important selling points were the features of their products. Perkin Elmer customers tended to be highly sophisticated from a technological standpoint. Thus, new instruments that could perform new tests or measurements with a high or greater degree of accuracy and reliability were preferred by them. Most major competitors tended to compete on the same basis.

A secondary selling point was delivery time and service. In the words of Jack Kerber, product manager for the atomic absorption instrument line, "A customer may take up to a year deciding whether he needs an instrument or in obtaining funds to purchase it, but once they decide and have the money, they want immediate delivery. And a lot of times, if they can't get it, they'll turn to our competitors if they have a comparable instrument."

Because the mechanical or electrical failure of an instrument could delay the completion of a research project, or shut down the production of industrial customers, rapid customer service was also felt to be important. To respond rapidly to these customer service needs, over 60 domestic field sales and service offices were maintained by the United States Sales Division.

The Instrument Division dealt with delivery lead times in two ways. First, they maintained an informal standard delivery lead time of 4–6 weeks. In other words, they attempted to maintain enough components in parts inventory or in-process, to be able to assemble, inspect, package, and ship an instrument within 4–6 weeks after it was ordered. During 1974, the average delivery lead time had slipped to about 12 weeks, however. According to Bill Chorske, General Manager, United States Sales Division, "We just haven't been able to catch up with our orders. The purchase lead times on some of the critical parts and materials we use have gone out to 10–12 months from an average of three months. Add to that the manufacturing time required to assemble parts into an instrument and you've got an impossible planning horizon. Couple that with an unexpected increase in demand and the result is inevitable."

The second way that the Instrument Division coped with delivery lead times was to keep the field sales force constantly informed of changes in them. This was partially accomplished with a monthly "Export Instrument Shipment Schedule" for export items and sales. In the United States, delivery lead times for an item could be supplied to the field sales force almost instantaneously if they called the marketing service department at Perkin Elmer's home office in Norwalk, Connecticut. Marketing service representatives queried computerized files from the centralized production control system on video display units to determine if enough parts were on hand to assemble the item immediately, or to determine the length of time required to obtain unavailable parts. This information was relayed to the field representative. If a firm order was made, parts were reserved for that order and an assembly order issued.

The Planning Process

The total planning process at Perkin Elmer's Instrument Division involved the coordination of the plans of the four major functional entities: engineering, marketing, manufacturing, and finance. The degree of coordination in these individual efforts was most apparent in the annual business and financial planning cycle.

The Business Plan The annual business plan started off with a detailed instrument by instrument forecast of order receipts. This forecast was made from a "bottom up" sales forecast from the field sales and service personnel in the Instrument Marketing Division, and a top down forecast by the product managers. Differences between these two forecasts were resolved by further investigation and negotiation between the two groups. These forecasts specified orders by month for the two immediately following quarters, and projected orders by quarter for the last half of the fiscal year (Table 14-3).

In addition to the forecast of orders for instruments, the sales of spare parts for technical service and accessory items were also forecasted. Since these items were generally stocked in inventory for immediate delivery, sales rather than orders were forecasted. A computer program incorporating some simple smoothing methodologies was used to forecast most of these items. All in all, accessories and spare parts sales accounted for about 20 percent of the division's annual sales. Instruments accounted for only a small percentage of the total number of salable items, but made up 80 percent of sales.

Yet a third source of forecast information was Gaynor Kelley himself. He reserved the right to make "management stock orders." These were essentially hedges on major products with long lead times. For example, one new product which was still partially in the preproduction design stage was expected to be completely ready for manufacture by February 1975. Since the procurement and manufacturing lead times for this item were in excess of a year, and the company wished to be in a position to promise six weeks delivery when it was introduced, Kelley, after weighing both the market and engineering risks, might wish to forecast sales for this item in April. This would serve as an authorization to purchase or start manufacturing the long lead time parts that went into the instrument. Similarly, if a major sale to a single customer (such as the government) of a particular high value, long lead time instrument was expected (over and above regular sales), a management stock order might be placed to ensure that a reasonable delivery lead time could be offered to the prospective customer, or to make sure that the sale could be made within the current fiscal year.

TABLE 14-3 PERKIN ELMER INSTRUMENT DIVISION: INSTRUMENT ORDERS FORECASTS (FISCAL YEAR ENDS JULY 31)*

Instrument	Fiscal Year Actual/(Forecast)[a]			Fiscal Year 1975 (Forecasts)								12-Month Total[a]
	72	73	74	A	S	O	N	D	J	3rd Q	4th Q	
874X	—	—	78/(101)	19	33	51	27	29	48	133	129	469
90475Z	174/(169)	235/(214)	153/(160)	8	8	18	15	8	14	18	20	109
9903751	177/(185)	122/(111)	110/(85)	2	3	9	—	2	3	11	—	30
4753ZY	22/(15)	14/(21)	15/(15)	—	—	2	1	—	1	—	1	5
976427	3/(5)	14/(10)	18/(20)	—	—	7	1	—	2	1	3	14
274678	—	4/(0)	33/(45)	4	7	12	2	6	11	29	26	97

*Figures in parentheses in 72, 73, and 74 columns and all figures in following columns are forecasts.

[a] Annual forecasts are simply the sum of the forecasts for 6 single months plus two quarters prepared as a part of the business plan just prior to the start of each fiscal year.

Management stock orders were collected together in a special "Z" plan. In general, the Z plan served to ensure that the major risks of the division were handled and monitored by the highest levels of management. In October of 1974, the sales value of the instruments in the Z plan for fiscal year 1975 was $4.3 million, while the product manager's forecast plus the forecast for spare parts totaled $72.2 million.

The three forecasts—the product manager/marketing forecast of major instrument orders, the computer generated forecast of accessory and spare parts sales, and the "Z" plan for management stock orders—were given to manufacturing. The production planning group then proceeded to project the manufacturing function, and the business as a whole. This was accomplished with the help of a computerized material and capacity requirements planning system.

First, the forecasts were used to construct a series of master plans. At least a part of the forecast data was forecasted order receipts. To construct the "exploded" master plan, which showed forecasted shipments, the standard delivery lead times were added to the forecasted order receipt dates. For example, instrument number 874ZX had sales orders for 51 systems projected for October. The "exploded" master plan broke this monthly forecast down into a weekly forecast for 13 units in each of the four weeks of the month. Then, since the Instrument Division tried to maintain a four-week position on this part, that is, be able to deliver four weeks after an order, the forecast orders for 13 units in each week in October were translated into forecast shipments of 13 in each week of November.

Parts and accessories which were stocked for immediate shipment were transposed directly into a "sales" master plan without adding lead times. The Z plan, which already reflected delivery time hedging, was the third type of master plan used by the Instrument Division.

The business plan was formulated in the manner described above at the beginning of each fiscal year. The process was repeated at mid-year in what was called the phase II plan. Thus, the company maintained a rolling six-month plan.

Short-term Planning Between the business planning cycles, the process of forecasting and replanning was carried out on a continual basis. Sales and orders forecasts for major items were reviewed monthly by product managers. Sales and orders forecasts for less important items were reviewed bi-monthly or every quarter. These changes in forecasts meant that changes in the master plans were made monthly.

Preparing for a Business Turndown

Gaynor Kelley felt that the differences between the forecasts in the annual business plan, the product manager forecast, and the build plan were largely due to differences in the perceptions of the people involved in making these forecasts. The product managers, after having been caught short during the '74 boom, were bullish. Many manufacturing people, and especially the product planners, after having lived through a period of shortages, extended lead times, and vendor unreliability, were cautious. They were attempting to gain back the four- to six-week delivery position lost earlier in the year, and were still projecting protracted lead times for use in timing orders in the material requirements planning system.

Kelley felt that fiscal year 1975 sales would actually turn out to be very close to those projected in the original business or financial plan. The Instrument Division had generally followed a cyclical pattern close to that of the national economy. Some lead times were falling and purchase commitments for the division were rising. Order cancellations threatened in other industries. But, he was at this point undecided as to whether the Instrument Division should position themselves to handle the upside or downside risks.

The upside risks of losing sales and market position would be felt if they cut back and a recession did not materialize. The downside risks of large inventories and a high fixed cost position would be felt if they increased production and a recession did materialize.

2.   The Sea Pines Racquet Club[4]

The situation at Sea Pines involves the integration of forecasting and planning, but in a service business rather than a manufactured product business. In order to plan recreational facilities, the director of tennis at Sea Pines must first forecast future demand and then compare that with various

---

[4]Copyright © 1973 by the President and Fellows of Harvard College. Used by permission.

capacity options. The following questions may be helpful as you prepare your analysis and recommendations for this situation.

a. When do the peak demands for tennis courts occur? How many hours are available/tennis court during those peak months?
b. How many tennis court hours will be demanded during the peak months of 1973, 1974, and 1975? (Forecasts of demand might be based on projections of court hours/guest night and guest nights.)
c. How many courts are required to provide those hours demanded? Can available capacity be expanded without building new courts? How?
d. If a new court is used only during the peak months, will it be profitable?
e. Are there other options for meeting peak demand for tennis court time?
f. What recommendations would you make to the tennis director? How many courts should he build? What else should he do?

Overview

In June 1973, John Baker, having recently accepted the newly created position as Tennis Director of The Sea Pines Racquet Club, was working on his first assignment for The Sea Pines Company, Hilton Head, S.C. His initial project was to formulate a strategy for tennis operations on the Plantation.

A 1970 graduate of the University of Virginia Business School, Mr. Baker had accepted the position with The Sea Pines Company in April 1973 after 2 years as product manager for General Foods and a year as sales manager for a small real estate development firm in Boston. An avid tennis player, Mr. Baker had accepted his new position because he had felt that the combination of tennis and The Sea Pines Company represented a tremendous opportunity for him.

Sea Pines Plantation Hilton Head Island had been substantially undeveloped and sparsely populated when The Sea Pines Company, under the leadership of its president, Charles Fraser, had begun development of the 5200-acre Sea Pines Plantation in 1957. In developing Sea Pines Plantation, The Sea Pines Company had prepared and periodically had updated a comprehensive land use plan; had developed residential subdivisions, park, utilities, golf, tennis and other recreational and resort facilities, and had donated land for churches, medical facilities and other community purposes.

In 1973, the company's resort and recreational operations on Sea Pines Plantation consisted of a country club and an 18-hole golf course, which it owned (another 18-hole golf course for members only was under construction), two additional 18-hole golf courses operated by it, a 127-unit ocean-front inn leased and operated by it; three marinas; 27 tennis courts; and several food and beverage facilities. While its resort operations had not been profitable to date, the company believed that these activities were an integral part of its overall development plans and that their operation could both produce profits and benefit its real estate activities.

The company's principal business was the sale and resale of home-sites, houses, and villas for which it received brokerage fees. The company also acted as agent and received fees for renting privately owned homes and villas (apartments) in Sea Pines Plantation. Substantially all of the company's sales of homesites and villas were made by its resident sales representatives to vacationers or visitors to its properties, the majority of whom lived either on the eastern seaboard and/or in the midwestern part of the United States. In fiscal 1972, the selling price of homesites sold by the company at Sea Pines Plantation ranged from $9,000 to $52,000, with an average selling price of $16,000, and the selling price of villas ranged from $28,500 to $102,000 with an average selling price of $62,000. During fiscal 1972, the company sold 574 homesites and 93 villas.

The company typically rented to vacationers and meeting groups those vacation homes and villas under its management 20 weeks or more a year, although higher occupancy levels were experienced during 1972.[5] The company's rental department provided the housekeeping and maintenance services for homes and villas in Sea Pines Plantation when they were not occupied by the owners. These noncompany-owned rental units were an important part of the company's resort operations and real estate program, since vacationers were its primary source of real estate sales. The demographic characteristics of 38 vacation parties at Sea Pines Plantation in August 1972 are included in the Appendix.

As of March 1, 1973, approximately 350 privately owned villas and 135 private single-family homes were on the rental market within Sea Pines Plantation. Ultimately, perhaps by 1980, it was estimated that 1,650 villas and 150 or 200 homes would be on the rental market. These units would comprise about 50 percent of the total residences within the Plantation.

Past Tennis Play John Baker spent the first two months in his new position accumulating information about past usage of tennis facilities at Sea Pines Plantation. He discovered that recording of tennis play began in June 1970 on the four Plantation Club hard-surface courts and eight composition courts in Harbour Town. Nine additional courts in Harbour Town (five hard-surface[6] and four composition) were completed in the spring of 1972. Construction of an additional six composition courts at Harbour Town was begun in May 1972 and they were completed in March 1973, at a cost of $12,000 per court (excluding land).

Mr. Baker learned that monitoring of play at the Plantation Club had been discontinued because of its distance from the Harbour Town facility. The Plantation Club's courts were scheduled to be removed in late 1973 to make way for the planned expansion of the Plantation Club. Statistics on court usage at Harbour Town indicated that usage there had more than doubled each year since 1970 and that the capacity utilization of the courts had increased from 18.4 percent to 47.3 percent even though the number of courts had increased from eight to twenty-three.

---

[5]SEC regulations prohibited Sea Pines and other developers of condominia from promoting condominia by emphasizing the economic benefits of rental income.

[6]The five hard-surface courts were equipped with lights for night play. The lighting, which had an expected life of 5 years, was installed at a cost of $4,000 per court. The direct operating cost (electricity and bulbs) was $1.75 per court hour. Tokens ($4 for an hour of night play) for using these courts at night are sold at the pro shop during the day. Statistics on the use of these courts at night had not been collected on a player or court-hour basis.

Year	Harbour Town Court Usage (by Court Hour)	Percent Capacity Utilization (Act. + Pot. Crt. Hrs.)
1970	2,789	18.4
1971	6,101	25.9
1972	16,142	34.8
1973 (est.)	32,816	47.3

The potential court capacity by month is shown in Table 14-4. A monthly breakdown of guest nights and court hours for FY 1973 is included as Table 14-5. Actual revenue and expenses for FY 1973 and projections for FY 1974 are given as Tables 14-6 and 14-7.

After reviewing the information he had collected, Mr. Baker decided to tackle three related issues in greater detail: pricing structure, member policy, and overall court capacity.

Court Capacity Mr. Baker faced a major dilemma with regards to court capacity. Guest night projections revealed that the number of guests on Sea Pines Plantation would double in the next 2 years. (See Table 14-8.) In addition, the number of court hours per guest night for March (0.68), April

TABLE 14-4   SEA PINES RACQUET CLUB: MONTHLY CAPACITY OF A COMPOSITION COURT

Month	Number of Days	Days Missed Bad Weather	Daily Hours	Maintenance Hours	Total Hours Available For Play	Mid-Day Temperature
January	31	3	9–5	0	224	64.9°
February	28	3	9–5	0	200	66.8°
March	31	3	8–6	1	252	73.3°
April	30	2	8–6	1	252	80.0°
May	31	2	8–8	1	319	80.4°
June	30	2	8–8	1	308	89.0°
July	31	2	8–8	1	319	90.4°
August	31	2	8–8	1	319	89.0°
September	30	2	8–7	1	280	86.0°
October	31	2	9–7	1	261	73.3°
November	30	3	9–5	0	216	71.4°
December	31	3	9–5	0	224	64.4°

TABLE 14-5   SEA PINES RACQUET CLUB: COURT HOURS AND GUEST NIGHTS—12 MONTHS ENDING FEBRUARY 1973

Month	Total Court Hours	Guest Nights	Court Hours/ Guest Nights
March	889	22,222	.040
April	1,797	29,450	.061
May	938	20,390	.046
June	1,506	35,848	.042
July	2,824	50,434	.056
August	2,885	51,515	.056
September	1,196	20,986	.057
October	1,459	22,798	.064
November	1,090	17,298	.063
December	840	9,551	.088
January	457	9,924	.046
February	629	16,139	.039

TABLE 14-6   SEA PINES RACQUET CLUB: 12 MONTHS ENDING FEBRUARY 1973—REVENUES AND EXPENSES

	Shop	Courts	Total
Revenues	59,400	56,100	115,500
Less Cost of Sale	35,700		35,700
Gross Margin	23,700	56,100	79,800
Expenses			
Professional and clerical	12,500	11,000	23,500
Labor	1,500	22,000	23,500
Benefits	3,600	2,700	6,700
Supplies	1,800	600	2,400
Repairs and maintenance		2,000	2,000
Utilities	1,400	1,900	3,300
Misc. expenses	4,400	4,000	8,400
Rent	3,000	10,000[a]	13,000
Total Expenses	28,200	54,200	82,400
Contribution	(4,500)	1,900	(−2,600)

[a]Direct maintenance costs was estimated at $1950 for each of the 12 composition courts and zero for the five hard-surface courts.

TABLE 14-7 SEA PINES RACQUET CLUB: 12 MONTHS ENDING FEBRUARY 1974—ESTIMATED REVENUES AND EXPENSES

	Shop	Courts	Total
Revenues	98,800[a]		
Court fees		109,000	
Annual members		10,000	
Lessons		10,000	
Total Revenue	98,800	129,000	227,800
Less Cost of Sale	58,800	—	58,800
Gross Margin	40,000	129,000	169,000
Expenses			
Supervisory[b]	7,000	38,000	45,000
Clerical	9,000	9,000	18,000
Labor	3,000	10,000	13,000
Benefits	1,900	1,900	3,800
Taxes	2,100	4,000	6,100
Supplies	1,750	750	2,500
Repairs and maintenance	100	3,300	3,400
Utilities	1,500	2,000	3,500
Misc. expenses	3,500	3,600	7,100
Rent	3,000	12,000[c]	15,000
Total Expenses	32,850	84,550	117,400
Contribution	7,150	44,450	51,600

[a]Includes miscellaneous rentals.

[b]Includes director of tennis, assistant professional (base salary + 50% of lessons), and head of maintenance.

[c]Direct maintenance costs divided between 18 comp. courts estimated at $1700 in 1973–74 (assumes no maintenance for 5 hard courts).

(.082), and May (.084) revealed increases from the prior year. John felt confident that the guest night projections were accurate because many new housing units were scheduled for completion. He also was aware of the rising popularity of tennis and felt that the increase in court hours per guest night reflected a national upward trend.

However, there was space for only four additional courts at the Harbour Town location. Any expansion beyond four courts would require a duplication of facilities and staff at the new location. It was estimated that a new tennis pro shop would cost $100,000 and the annual staffing and maintenance would be similar to those incurred at Harbour Town. There was an

TABLE 14-8   SEA PINES RACQUET CLUB: GUEST NIGHT PROJECTION
SEA PINES PLANTATION

Year	Month	Projected Guest Nights
1973	March	35,526
	April	41,576
	May	33,632
	June	59,950
	July	83,887
	August	86,475
	September	34,514
	October	36,221
	November	27,180
	December	18,509
1974	January	16,293
	February	30,330
	March	57,741
	April	66,462
	May	53,992
	June	95,620
	July	130,696
	August	129,111
	September	53,218
	October	55,197
	November	38,819
	December	24,627
1975	January	21,717
	February	37,083
	March	73,580
	April	83,773
	May	68,607
	June	120,826
	July	168,797
	August	166,263
	September	66,168
	October	68,883
	November	50,435
	December	31,530

area on the master plan near the center of the Plantation with enough space for forty courts and supporting facilities.

With increased pressure for profitability from top management, John felt that a decision to increase the number of courts had to be carefully balanced against the increased costs of a new facility that might be needed only three or four months each year. On the other hand, Sea Pines Plantation had spent a great deal of effort developing its tennis image and limited court capacity during the summer months would not enhance that image. On recent days, Mr. Baker had overheard some complaints about the unavailability of courts during the prime playing hours of 9–11 a.m. and 4–6 p.m. He was also concerned by comments from visitors from the previous year that the combination of high temperatures and humidity from noon to 4 p.m. created very uncomfortable playing conditions in July and August.

Recommended Rate Structure After reviewing the available data on pricing (Table 14-9), John Baker recommended changing the rate structure for use of tennis facilities at The Sea Pines Racquet Club as follows:

1. Charge $5.00 per court hour (singles or doubles) for use of the composition courts in lieu of the present $2.00 per hour per person.

TABLE 14-9 SEA PINES RACQUET CLUB: PRESENT TENNIS PRICING STRUCTURE

Guests:
   1 hour $2.00
($2.00 per hour for the first 2 hours of play each day, and $1.00 for each additional hour of play, when courts are available.)

Students (18 years and under):
   1 hour $1.00
($1.00 per hour for the first 2 hours of play each day, and $.50 for each additional hour of play, when courts are available.)

Racquet Rental ....$1.00 per hour

Ball Machine Rental ....$7.00 per hour (includes court fee)

Lighted Courts for Evening Play ....$4.00 per hour per court

Tennis Plans (available at all times except July and August)
  A. 4-Day Tennis Plan—$13.00
      Four days of daily tennis play—one hour in the morning and one hour in the afternoon. Plan to be played within 8 days of purchase. (Additional hours at $1.00/hr.)
  B. 7-Day Tennis Plan—$23.00
      Seven days of daily tennis play—one hour in the morning and one hour in the afternoon. Plan to be played within 14 days of purchase. (Additional hours at $1.00/hr.)

2. Discontinue half rates after 2 hours of play.
3. Charge $3.00 per court hour for the use of the all-weather courts.
4. Discontinue student rates.
5. Discontinue tennis plans.

Reasons for Recommendations

A. *Per Court vs. Per Person Charge*

By encouraging and enabling more people to play more tennis, both our court revenues and importantly our merchandising revenues will increase. The present mix of singles and doubles play is 72 percent and 28 percent in favor of singles. Those who now play 1 hour of singles for $2.00 may be encouraged to play 2 hours of doubles under the proposed rates for $2.50 or double the amount of playing time for 25 percent more court fees. They will also take up no more court time by doing so.

Those people who play an hour of doubles vs. an hour of singles will obviously decrease our revenues, but more doubles play will free up court time for others. When more courts are available than can readily be filled, it may not seem so appropriate to charge on a per court basis. However, this is not the case at Harbour Town. We will be extremely close to reaching actual capacity this summer.

B. *Discontinue Half Rates After 2 Hours of Play*

As we reach higher levels of capacity, our present policy becomes more inappropriate. The majority of our guests will be willing to pay regular court fees for all hours of play.

C. *$3.00 Per Court Hour for All-Weather Courts*

From September 1972 to April 1973 the all-weather court capacity utilization was 15 percent compared to 38 percent over the same period for the composition courts. Since these courts are less desirable and cost substantially less to maintain, it seems appropriate that we charge less for their use.

D. *Discontinue Half Rates for Students*

With the reduction in rates on the all-weather courts, there is no necessity to charge less for student (under 18) play. The major complaint about all-weather courts centers around leg fatigue and younger players should be less affected by this than our older tennis guests. Students playing doubles with parents (who might insist on playing on composition courts) can still play for less even on these courts—namely, $5.00 vs. $6.00 under the present rate structure. Our younger players should be encouraged to use our all-weather courts, thus freeing up the composition courts for more play by our adult clientele who often refuse to play on the all-weather courts.

E. *Discontinue Tennis Plans*

As we reach higher levels of capacity, we are losing rather than gaining revenues by offering plans of this nature.

John Baker's Dilemma John Baker summarized his feelings on how capacity and pricing fit into the overall tennis strategy for Sea Pines:

The increase in the popularity and play of tennis at Sea Pines is common knowledge. We expect that July and August of this year will find Sea Pines Racquet Club at capacity. Since potential court hours include all hours except downtime for rain and actual maintenance time, "unbearably" hot hours are not excluded. Therefore, it may not be possible to exceed the 80 percent capacity figure by very much.

Tennis play at Sea Pines has increased at a compounded rate of over 100 percent a year. While the tennis "boom" must plateau or at least slow down its frantic momentum at some stage, it is generally considered not to have reached its peak.

The argument against building more tennis courts when the tennis operation is making little or no contribution to resort operations is valid. Table 14-5 illustrates that the court operations (as opposed to merchandising) barely covered costs last year. The high fixed costs and relatively low percent capacity utilization have prevented court operations from making a contribution in the past.

My proposed pricing structure in itself will not necessarily bring us much closer to achieving our goal of 25 percent contribution. Some of the increase will be eaten up by inflation. Our profitability in the next few years depends upon the length of time that we can reasonably hold off building additional courts at another location.

Top Management's Viewpoint Top management felt that tennis represented a great opportunity for Sea Pines. They had invested a great deal in facilities, promotion, advertising, and management time. They felt tennis operations must not only stand on its own two feet, but produce a significant contribution to resort operations. Tennis operations were now considered a profit center, not just an inducement for people to buy property.

John Baker's dilemma was not unique among operations managers at Sea Pines. Most managers faced a growing but seasonal demand for their services. For example, Donald O'quinn, golf director, could foresee a problem with golf course capacity. The members course under construction was the last course scheduled for the Plantation. In resolving the tennis capacity issue, it was hoped that an appropriate methodology could be developed to apply to the capacity planning decisions facing all operations managers.

3. Ferric Processing[7]

Richard Hansen, the Assistant to the General Manager of Ferric Processing, was preparing his presentation for the upcoming Executive Committee meeting. He wanted to present the results of his recent cost study, and propose a new way of predicting processing costs for prospective plant sites. He also wanted to suggest several possible extensions of his study that

---

he felt would help the company better understand their long-run costs, and the way these costs were influenced by several key factors.

Company Background

Ferric Processing was a subsidiary of the Metzger Machinery Company. It was organized in 1956 to capitalize upon a newly patented process for recovering iron from the waste slag of steel mills. In the last 8 years, Ferric had built 10 new slag processing plants, and compiled an enviable record of both sales and earnings growth.

As a largely unwanted by-product of steel-making in an open hearth furnace, great quantities of slag are produced. Particularly in the vicinity of the open hearth pouring pits, this slag contains small amounts of iron and iron oxides which would be potentially valuable if they could be economically recovered from the slag. Several steel companies had experimented with recovery processes that re-cycled the recovered iron to the blast furnaces, but these processes seemed to be of doubtful utility.

In the middle 1950's, an executive of the Metzger Machinery Company who was familiar with the steel industry developed and patented a new process for this recovery which promised great potential. Basically, the slag was carried along conveyor belts through a continuous cycle of alternating crushers, magnets, and screens. The crushers broke the slag into smaller and smaller pieces, the magnets recovered the iron, and the screens sorted the remaining slag with a very low iron content into various particle sizes that could be used for other industrial purposes.

Once the patents for the process seemed secure, the Metzger Machinery Company formed a new subsidiary named Ferric Processing, Inc., and negotiated contracts for two of these slag processing plants. Although there were many unexpected problems in the initial break-in period of about 2 years, these plants were eventually very successful. They were followed in succeeding years by eight other plants, all of a similar design, but modified slightly because of Ferric's experience with earlier plants.

In every instance, Ferric's plant processed the slag from a particular steel mill, and each of the plants was located as close as possible (usually within five or ten miles) to the steel mill it served. Ferric's personnel would dig the slag from the deposits in the open hearth area, and load it into large heavy duty trucks. These trucks would deliver it to the intake conveyor at Ferric's plant, where it would be fed into the recovery process. After processing, the recovered iron would be returned to the steel mill to be charged into the blast furnace, and the remaining slag would be returned to the slag operations at the steel mill. Ferric Processing was paid a flat processing charge per ton of slag it handled, and this fee was always negotiated at the time the original contract with the steel company was signed. Generally, a rather lengthy series of negotiations preceded the decision to build any new plant. As the final outcome of these negotiations, the steel company and Ferric would agree upon a contract covering at least 3 to 5 years, which stipulated both the processing charge per ton and several minimum guarantees to Ferric in terms of total tonnage processed. After the contract, Ferric would begin constructing the new plant, whose capacity was matched to the size of the particular steel mill.

Over the years, Ferric had attempted to make sure that the negotiated rate per ton was high enough to cover all their expenses, including
labor, transportation, depreciation of the capital equipment, and so on. They
found, however, that on several of their plants they had seriously under-
estimated the total processing costs per ton, and in several instances they
had renegotiated a second contract at higher rates after the first contract
expired. On the other hand, they also had overestimated these costs in several plant locations that were now producing efficiently at cost/ton rates
significantly below the negotiated processing charge.

The Cost Study

Currently, Ferric was considering three additional plant sites, and in one
case negotiations were proceeding rapidly to a final agreement. Because the
difference between the negotiated charge per ton and the average processing
costs per ton was the critical variable for Ferric's profitability, it was important to estimate future processing costs early in the stages of negotiation
for each prospective plant site.

Ferric's management had, on several earlier occasions, asked its industrial engineer to provide detailed cost estimates for various parts of their
overall process. Based upon the auditing of an individual plant's cost records
and time-and-motion studies of various functions within the plant, these
studies had provided what was considered to be a very detailed and accurate
breakdown of all costs within a plant, as well as some suggestions for cost
reduction. On the whole, however, they did not provide an adequate comparison of costs across different plants; and it was very difficult to extrapolate
cost estimates for a new plant from them.

In a recent discussion with the General Manager, his Assistant, Richard Hansen, had volunteered to make a new kind of cost study. Mr. Hansen
believed that some of the key factors influencing Ferric's costs were the
economies of scale inherent in the different plant sizes, and he believed that
the effect of these economies of scale were acknowledged but not well understood by top management. Indeed, it seemed that there could be a substantial
disagreement about the way plant size affected total costs per ton, particularly among several of Ferric's management group responsible for making
cost projections. This disagreement could be inferred from the different cost
estimates these executives had submitted for the smallest of the three prospective plant sites, although none of them had ever directly addressed the
problem of economies of scale as such. With the concurrence of the General
Manager, Mr. Hansen set aside his other duties for several days and concentrated upon this new study of average costs per ton across different plants.

As the basic data to study this problem of costs, Mr. Hansen compiled
a list of all of Ferric's plants, their processing capacity, and an estimate of
their individual average costs/ton for the last year. These data are shown
below in Table 14-10. The cost estimates were furnished by the Controller's
office. The total yearly costs attributable to each plant, including all direct
and indirect labor, materials, transportation, depreciation of capital equipment, supervisors' salaries, and so on, were already compiled as an important
part of Ferric's management control system. These costs for last year, divided

TABLE 14-10   FERRIC PROCESSING: COSTS AND CAPACITIES
OF EXISTING PLANTS

Plant No.	First Began Operations	Capacity	Average Costs/Ton in 1964
1	1956	900 tons/mo.	$21.95
2	1956	500 tons/mo.	27.18
3	1958	1750 tons/mo.	16.90
4	1959	2000 tons/mo.	15.37
5	1960	1400 tons/mo.	16.03
6	1960	1500 tons/mo.	18.15
7	1961	3000 tons/mo.	14.22
8	1962	1100 tons/mo.	18.72
9	1962	2600 tons/mo.	15.40
10	1963	1900 tons/mo.	14.69

by the number of tons actually processed last year by the plant, provided the
average costs/ton figure which the Controller's office furnished.

As a first look at his problem, Mr. Hansen constructed the graph
shown in Figure 14-5. On the basis of this plot of the data, he was convinced
that economies of scale were indeed important, and he decided to use regression analysis to study them. Employing the services of a statistical analyst
and a computer, he first obtained a simple linear regression analysis of the
average costs/ton versus plant size (capacity). The input data and results of
this regression are shown in Table 14-11. Mr. Hansen and the analyst then
jointly decided to run another regression analysis, using (1/capacity) as the
revised independent variable. The input data and results of this regression
are shown in Table 14-12.

Intrigued with the progress of his cost study, Mr. Hansen discussed
the results in general terms with several managers in the company. They
were all quite interested, but many of them objected to drawing any conclusions from studies across different plants. There were so many other important differences from plant to plant, they argued, that it was very risky to
draw conclusions using only plant capacity as a discriminating factor. In
particular, several of these managers pointed out that the costs of hauling
the slag between the steel mill and processing plant was a major factor in
Ferric's overall costs. Because some of the plants were built adjacent to the
steel mills and others were up to nine miles away, the differences in transportation mileage could cause major differences in total costs that would be
reflected in the average costs/ton figures. Several plant managers argued
that these differences could be seriously distorting the results of Hansen's
cost study.

In addition, the manager of one of the older plants argued that the
age of the plants could be one of the principal determinants of costs. More

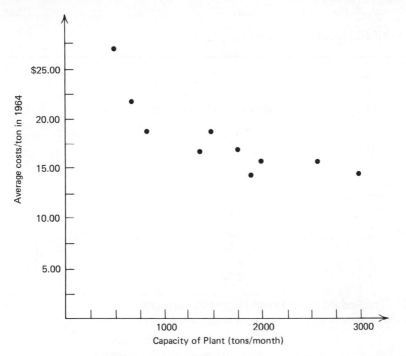

FIGURE 14-5 FERRIC PROCESSING PLOT OF COSTS/TON VERSUS CA-
PACITY FOR 10 PLANTS

recent plants incorporated several modifications made in light of previous
plants' experiences, and thus they tended to be somewhat more efficient.
Because the early plants tended to be smaller and later plants tended to be
larger, the increased efficiency of the later plants could be distorting the
results of the cost study. Furthermore, the older plants might well have
higher maintenance costs, although the newer plants might have initially
higher costs before management could get the "bugs" shaken out of the
processing unit. The manager of one of the older plants was concerned that
Hansen's study was overlooking these possible effects.

Richard Hansen sat down to prepare a brief presentation of his results
for the upcoming Executive Committee meeting. He wanted to briefly summarize and interpret the results, and discuss possible problems with the
interpretation. He also wanted to suggest several extensions of the study he
felt would help management better understand their average costs, and the
way these costs were related to various key factors.

4.   Forecasting Learning Curves for Planning Purposes
        In many situations, it has been observed empirically that labor hours
per unit and even operating costs per unit often follow what is referred to
as the *learning curve*. When the rate of growth is rapid, and the rate of
learning is also fairly rapid, the effect of the learning curve on capacity
planning can be dramatic—the labor required per unit produced declines

TABLE 14-11 FERRIC PROCESSING DATA

Part 1: The Input Data

y (Average Costs/Ton)	x (Capacity) in 000 tons/month
$27.18	.50
21.95	.90
18.72	1.10
16.03	1.40
18.15	1.50
16.90	1.75
14.69	1.90
15.37	2.00
15.40	2.60
14.22	3.00

Part 2:   The Results of the Linear Regression Analysis

Variable	B	Std. Error	t-Test	Pct Variation Explained
Constant	25.193	1.85876	13.5536	.697798
	−4.40357	1.02457	−4.29796	

R-Squared $= 0.698$ $R = 0.835$
F-Test $=$ 18.47   Std. of regr. $= 2.33$
Degrees of freedom for number $= 1$ For denumber. $= 8$

Do you want the residuals to be printed? Y

Actual	Predicted	Residuals	% Error
27.18	22.9912	4.18884	15.4115
21.95	21.2287	.720266	8.28139
18.72	20.349	−1.62902	−8.70302
16.03	19.0279	−2.99795	−18.7021
18.15	18.5876	−.437588	−2.41086
16.9	17.4867	−.586695	−3.47157
14.69	16.8862	−2.13616	−14.5416
15.77	16.3859	−1.0158	−6.60999
15.4	18.7437	1.65634	10.7555
14.22	11.9822	2.23777	15.7858

Durbin-Watson stat. $= .851989$

TABLE 14-12 FERRIC PROCESSING DATA

Part 1: The Input Data

y (Average Costs/Ton)	x (1/Capacity in 000's tons/month)
$27.18	2.00
21.95	1.11
18.72	.909
16.03	.714
18.15	.666
16.90	.571
14.69	.526
15.37	.500
15.40	.385
14.22	.333

Part 2: The Results of the Regression Analysis

Variable	B	Std. Error	t-Test	Pct. Variation Explained
Constant	11.7478	.602338	19.5036	.94517
2	7.92486	.663293	11.8534	

R-Squared = 0.845 R = 0.873
F-Test = 140.62   Std. of regr. = 0.99   For denumber. = 8
Degree of freedom for number. = 1

Do you want the residuals to be printed? Y

Actual	Predicted	Residuals	% Error
27.18	27.5875	−.417486	−1.53601
21.95	20.=444	1.40564	6.40383
18.72	18.9515	−.231462	−1.23644
16.03	17.4061	−1.37611	−3.58462
18.15	17.0257	1.12438	6.19438
16.9	16.2729	.627144	3.71091
14.69	15.9162	−1.22624	−8.34744
15.37	15.7102	−.340192	−2.21335
15.4	14.7988	.601166	3.90368
14.22	14.3867	−.166741	−1.17253

Durbin-Watson Stat. = 2.5128

significantly as additional cumulative production experience is gained. The result is that, over several years, the labor input per unit may become only a fraction of what it was initially. Thus, in forecasting floor space requirements as well as human resource requirements, estimating the learning curve may be an important first step.

The two major methods used to prepare a learning curve[8] are graphical analysis and regression analysis. The steps for each are outlined in Figure 14-6. The following two problems illustrate some of the insights for planning and decision making that can be gained through the forecasting of experience (learning) curves.

Planning a Cost Reduction Program

One company's approach to developing a cost reduction program was to base it largely on projected market requirements (price) and historical cost reductions. The six-step procedure developed for this is summarized in Figure 14-7. Step 1 involves analyzing historical data on prices and costs (both in constant dollars). Step 2 requires that marketing/sales project future prices (in constant dollars) and quantities demanded (at those prices). Step 3 involves manufacturing estimating possible future cost reductions (in constant dollars) under various assumptions about cost reduction efforts expended. Step 4 is a negotiation among all concerned, the output of which is final agreement on a plan for prices, quantities, and costs. In Step 5, manufacturing and engineering decide which cost reduction projects will be pursued to give the reductions agreed to in the preceding step. The final task, step 6, is the tracking of actual performance against plans.

During this process, an inflation index is also used so that constant dollars can be converted to current dollars and vice-versa.

The data of Table 14-13 are those gathered for a specific product during steps 1 and 2 of the cost reduction planning process. Prepare one set of forecasts that might be used as steps 3 and 4 in the process by answering the following:

a. What has been the experience curve for production costs on this product from 1971–1980? What has been the rate of learning (that is, the percent improvement in costs with each doubling of cumulative production)?

b. If the company believes that the same rate of learning can be maintained for 1981–1985, what will be the production costs at the end of each of those years? What will be the production costs in current dollars for 1981–1985?

Estimating System Manufacturing Costs

A company is planning to introduce a new product (system) that is composed of one unit of component (item) A, four units of component B, and two units of component C. Each of these components has its own history of cumulative production volume and current cost, and the company has estimated the experience curve for each component on the basis of these histories. (See Table 14-14.)

---

[8]The term "experience curve" is often used when cost/unit (in constant dollars) is used in place of labor hours/unit. The steps in estimating the curve are the same as those outlined in Figure 14-6.

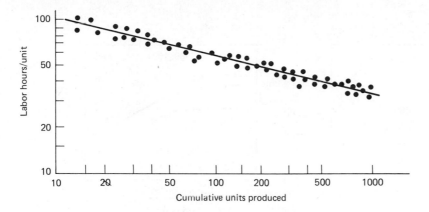

A. Graphical Approach for Estimating the Rate of Learning

1. Fit a straight line to actual data plotted on log-log paper.
2. Identify two levels of cumulative production, where one is twice the other (i.e., $J/I = 2.0$).
3. Identify the cost/unit for each of these two cumulative production volumes (i.e., Y_J and Y_I).
4. Compute the ratio Y_J/Y_I and convert to a percentage. This is the rate of learning.
5. Forecast future labor required for unit J by reading, from the fitted line, the labor/unit that corresponds to that cumulative production unit.

B. Regression Analysis Approach for Estimating the Rate of Learning

1. Convert the learning curve equation $Y_I = AI^{-B}$ to a linear form by taking logs of both sides [i.e., $\log Y_I = \log A + (-B) \log I$].
2. Transform the actual observed data to log Y_I and log I data.
3. Apply regression analysis to estimate a and b in $y = a + bx$, where $y = \log Y_I$ and $x = \log I$.
4. Transform the regression estimates of a and b to obtain $A = \log^{-1} a$ and $B = -b$.
5. Convert B to a rate of learning by computing 2^{-B}.
6. Forecast labor requirements, Y_J, for some future unit, J, by computing $Y_J = Y_I(J/I)^{-B}$.

FIGURE 14-6 FORECASTING LABOR REQUIREMENTS/UNIT USING THE LEARNING CURVE

The company wishes to estimate the future manufacturing component costs of the system as its volume grows. Assuming that past rates of learning will continue in the future, forecast the cost/unit for each component for the quantities listed in the last five columns of Table 14-14. What will be the cost of the components going into each system (final row of Table 14-14)? What percent of the total component costs for each system will be represented by each type component as the production volume builds? What conclusions can you draw about the importance of component experience curves based on the completed Table 14-14?

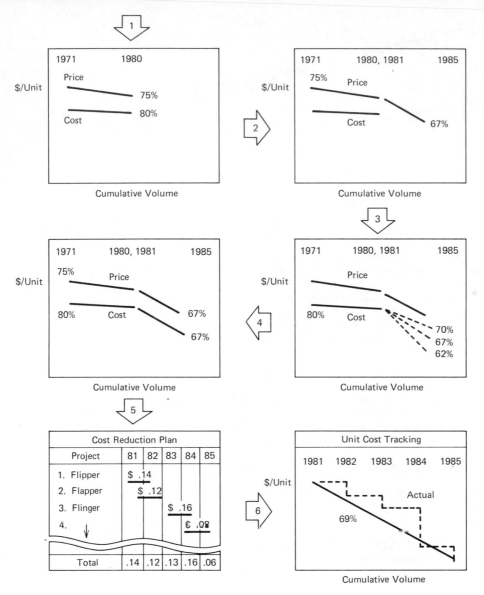

FIGURE 14-7   SIX STEPS FOR DEVELOPING A COST REDUCTION PRO-
GRAM FOR A PLANNING UNIT

TABLE 14-13   PRODUCT ABC—COST REDUCTION PROGRAM BASED
ON EXPERIENCE CURVE ANALYSIS

Year	Annual Volume	Cumulative Annual Volume	Deflation Index 1980 = 100	Selling Price/Unit Current $	Selling Price/Unit Constant (80 $)	Production Cost (Current $)	Unit Constant (80 $)
1971	7294	7294	54.6	$33.00	60.43	$20.60	37.72
1972	685	7979	57.3	34.30	59.86	19.60	34.21
1973	1035	9014	60.4	35.20	58.28	20.10	33.28
1974	1725	0739	63.2	35.63	56.38	20.20	31.96
1975	3201	13940	65.3	37.50	57.43	14.30	21.90
1976	3805	17745	68.8	39.10	56.83	14.90	21.66
1977	3852	21597	76.0	40.90	53.82	14.50	19.08
1978	2750	24373	82.6	49.00	59.33	17.40	21.06
1979	2550	26923	90.9	51.40	56.55	17.40	19.14
1980	2831	29754	100.0	52.70	52.70	18.10	18.10
1981	3255e	33009e	110.0e	55.30e	50.27e		
1982	3278e	36287e	120.8e	58.10e	48.10e		
1983	3378e	39665e	133.0e	61.00e	45.86e		
1984	3494e	43159e	146.3e	64.10e	43.81e		
1985	3605e	46764e	159.1e	67.40e	42.36e		

Note: 1981–1985 figures are all estimates.

TABLE 14-14   IMPACT OF THE UNIT OF ANALYSIS
ON EXPERIENCE CURVES

Component Items	Cumulative Volume (Experience)					
	1,000 Units	4,000 Units	16,000 Units	64,000 Units	256,000 Units	1,024,000 Units
Item A (1 per unit)						
75% curve						
Component experience	1,000	4,000	16,000	64,000	256,000	1,024,000
Cost/Unit	$80.					
Percent of total cost	24.2%					
Item B (4 per unit)						
80% curve						
Component experience	4,000	16,000	64,000	256,000	1,024,000	4,096,000
Cost/unit	$55.					
Percent of total cost	66.7%					
Item C (2 per unit)						
70% curve						
Component experience	1,002,000	1,008,000	1,032,000	1,128,000	1,512,000	3,048,000
Cost/unit	$30.					
Percent of total cost	9.11%					
Total Unit Cost	$330.					

15/COMPARISON AND SELECTION OF FORECASTING METHODS

Given the wide choice of alternative forecasting methods available (as presented in the first 13 chapters of this book), it is useful to both the forecaster and the user of forecasts to have criteria that can be used to compare and select among competing methodologies. This chapter deals with these matters from a conceptual point of view and also from an empirical base (presenting published evidence on forecasting accuracy).

The chapter will first discuss the various factors affecting the selection of one forecasting method over others. Since accuracy is the important factor in such a selection, the chapter will concentrate on the empirical results available concerning the accuracy of various methods. In addition, the cost and the ease of application of the various methods will be discussed as factors affecting method selection.

Conceptually, there are several ways in which criteria for selecting and comparing forecasting methods can be organized. A common approach is to prioritize criteria according to their order of importance in practice, and, as might be expected, *accuracy* is given top priority.

Unfortunately, forecasters often terminate the evaluation process after this first criterion—accuracy—has been examined. The authors' own experience and contacts with practitioners indicate that a number of other criteria are also very important as a part of this evaluation process. These criteria include the pattern of the data to be forecast, the type of series, the time horizon to be covered in forecasting, the cost of applying alternative methodologies, and the ease of application in organization situations.

It is helpful to start with an overview of the major criteria in this evaluation process. Such an overview is important because of the interrelationships among criteria and the need to select that forecasting method that best meets all of the dimensions of the given situation.

The *accuracy* of the forecast as a criterion seems too obvious to require comment. However, in decision analysis (see Chapter 13), a careful distinction is made between a good decision and a good outcome. If a forecaster models a situation well in the face of uncertainty, there is reason to support the forecast, regardless of the accuracy. At the time that a future forecast is made, there can be no test of that forecast's accuracy. Furthermore, once a forecast is made, it can be in the best interests of the user (client) to make every effort either (i) to make the forecast come true, or (ii) to make the forecast not come true. One of the purposes of a decision analytic approach to forecasting is to help managers decide where to focus attention (money, manpower, etc.) to enhance the probabilities of desirable outcomes.

The *pattern of the data* is important in selecting a forecasting method because, as shown in previous chapters, different methods can cope with only certain kinds of data patterns. There are, of course, methods that can cope with a very wide range of patterns, but these are usually more expensive to use and more difficult to apply; thus a trade-off is involved in using them. Generally, the pattern element can be divided into two main subparts, which can then be subdivided further. The two main subparts are patterns that repeat with time (periodic patterns such as trend and seasonal components) and patterns that represent turning points that do not repeat over fixed time intervals. These latter turning points, caused by business cycles or by other changes in the environment, are an important consideration in selecting a forecasting method, as are periodic patterns.

The *type of series* is another important factor in selecting forecasting methods because methods vary greatly in their predictive accuracy, depending upon the type of series being forecast. Empirical research has shown, for instance, that for the short term, macro economic series can be forecast as accurately by ARMA and adaptive parameter methods while micro series are best forecast by exponential smoothing methods.

The *time horizon* criterion for evaluating forecasting methods is closely related to the pattern criterion. Different planning horizons involve different pattern characteristics and make different demands in terms of the number of items to be forecast and the value of accuracy. Closely related to the time horizon to be forecast is the time that can be taken to actually prepare the forecast. In immediate- and short-term situations, a much quicker turnaround for obtaining the forecast is needed than in situations involving medium- and long-term planning.

The element of *cost* is often one of the key criteria that is traded off against such things as accuracy, ease of application, and the pattern. The costs of forecasting depend very much on the method itself and its inherent complexity as well as on its data requirements and the number of items to be forecast. In discussing this criterion later in the chapter, elements of costs associated with data requirements, computer and human resources, training of the forecasting methodology, and use of the methodology on an ongoing basis will be considered.

Ease of application might be thought of as a criterion that brings together several remaining considerations not covered by the previous four criteria. Included under this heading are such things as the complexity of the method, the timeliness of the forecasts that it provides, the level of knowledge required for application, and the conceptual basis and the ease with which it can be conveyed to the final user of the forecast. As practitioners know, one of the common stumbling blocks in adoption of appropriate forecasting techniques is making the ultimate user comfortable with the technique and its rationale so that the user can effectively judge the results of the forecasting method and their usefulness.

It should be clear from the brief description of these criteria that the assignment of priorities to them in comparing and selecting a forecasting method for a given situation will depend in part on the situation to be forecast and in part on the organization's experience with forecasting. Thus while accuracy is almost universally recognized as being the number one criterion, the relative importance of the others will depend on the situation and the organization.

15/1 The Accuracy of Forecasting Methods

In the majority of practical forecasting situations, accuracy is treated as the overriding criterion for selecting a forecasting method. Accuracy is not only important in itself, but other factors are also frequently reflected in accuracy. (For example, insufficient data or use of a technique that does not fit the pattern of the data will be reflected in less accurate forecasts.) In spite of the fact that accuracy is given prime importance as a factor in the selection process, little systematic work has been done to develop a framework for measuring and evaluating accuracy-related issues. Such a framework would be particularly useful if it could serve as a mechanism for bracketing the accuracy that is possible in a given situation and as an aid in answering the following kinds of questions:

1. For a given situation, how much improvement can be obtained in the accuracy of the forecasts? (How close can one come to achieving perfect forecasts?)
2. What additional accuracy can be achieved in a given situation through use of a formal forecasting technique? (How inaccurate will the forecasts be if they are based on a very simple or naive approach rather than on a more mathematically sophisticated technique?)
3. What is the role of judgment in forecasting accuracy? When can subjective assessments help improve the accuracy of forecasting?

In this section, a conceptual framework for applying the criterion of accuracy will be developed. Although this framework is applicable mainly in the area of quantitative forecasting methods, its extension to qualitative or technological methods should become apparent. Chapter 18 will extend this through a comparison of subjective or judgmental forecasting methods and more formal objective procedures.

15/1/1 Measuring Forecasting Accuracy

One of the difficulties in dealing with the criterion of accuracy in forecasting situations is the absence of a single universally accepted measure of accuracy. Several alternative measures have been suggested and dealt with in Chapter 2. In this chapter several accuracy comparisons will be made using these measures.

The authors have found it useful to define two different naive methods of forecasting for use as a basis in evaluating other methods in a given situation. The first is referred to as Naive Forecast 1 or NF1. This method uses as a forecast the most recent information available concerning the actual value. Thus, if a forecast is being prepared for a time horizon of one period, the most recent actual value would be used as the forecast for the next period. When this is done, the MAPE of this method can be expressed as follows:

$$\text{MAPE}_{\text{NF1}} = \frac{\sum\limits_{i=2}^{n} \left| \dfrac{(X_i - X_{i-1})}{X_{i-1}} \right|}{n-1} (100).$$

(15-1)

Only $n-1$ terms are included in computing the MAPE of this naive forecast since forecasting begins with period 2 rather than period 1. The difference between the MAPE obtained from a more formal method of forecasting and that obtained using NF1 provides a measure of the improvement attainable through use of that formal forecasting method. This type of comparison is much more useful than simply computing the MAPE of the formal method or the MSE, since it provides a basis for evaluating the relative accuracy of those results.

A second naive method of forecasting has also been found to be extremely useful as a basis for evaluating more formal forecasting methods. This method is referred to as Naive Forecast 2 or NF2 and goes beyond NF1 in that it considers the possibility of seasonality in the series. Since seasonality often accounts for a substantial percentage of the fluctuation in a series, this method can frequently do much better than NF1 and yet is still a very simple straightforward approach. The procedure is to remove seasonality from the original data in order to obtain seasonally adjusted data. Once the seasonality has been removed, NF2 is comparable to NF1 in that it uses the most recent seasonally adjusted value as a forecast for the next seasonally adjusted value. When NF2 is applied, the MAPE can be computed as follows:

$$\text{MAPE}_{\text{NF2}} = \frac{\sum\limits_{i=2}^{n} \left| \dfrac{(X_i - X'_{i-1})}{X'_{i-1}} \right|}{n-1} (100),$$

(15-2)

where X'_i is the seasonally adjusted value of X_i.

In practice, NF2 allows one to decide whether or not the improvement obtained from going beyond a simple seasonal adjustment of the data is worth the time and cost involved.

Finally, there is one other measure that has some theoretical interest as a basis for comparing the accuracy of a formal forecasting method with some standard. This standard could be referred to as the optimal forecast, OF, and the MAPE of the OF would denote the minimum possible value that could be achieved by a forecasting method. In concept, the OF would be found by isolating the randomness in the data set (that is, removing all systematic components) and calculating the MAPE of that randomness. Since this is not possible in practice, the only way to approach the OF is via some ad hoc estimating process, but in principle it represents a lower bound on the level of accuracy achievable. The MAPE of the OF can be defined as follows:

$$
\text{MAPE}_{\text{OF}} = \frac{\displaystyle\sum_{i=2}^{n} \left| \frac{(R_i - R_{i-1})}{R_i} \right|}{(n-1)} \ (100),
$$
(15-3)

where R_i is the random component of the actual value, X_i.

By way of illustration, consider Table 15-1, where the MAPE values for three hypothetical series—A, B, and C—are shown for NF1, NF2, and OF forecasts. As would be expected, the relative differences in these three comparative measures depend largely on the series being considered. For example, for series A in Table 15-1 the MAPE of NF1 is 26.5 percent. Because of seasonality in the series, this MAPE drops to 19.8 percent using NF2. The optimal forecast gives a MAPE of 8.3 percent. These differences indicate that substantial improvement over NF1 is possible with NF2, and that further improvements might also be made with more appropriate methods. However, the best that can be achieved, on average, is a MAPE of 8.3 percent.

The results for series B in Table 15-1 indicate that it has a much stronger seasonal component than series A. Thus simply applying NF2 rather than NF1 reduces the MAPE from 32.6 percent to 10.2 percent. Since the average randomness in the series gives a MAPE of 9.3 percent, there is little reason to go beyond NF2 in looking for a more sophisticated (and more accurate) forecasting methodology.

In the case of series C, it can be seen that little seasonality is present in the series and little pattern of any kind. Thus the change in MAPE obtained in going from NF1 to NF2 is only from 30.4 percent to 29.3 percent. The randomness in the series gives a MAPE of 28.7 percent, which indicates that there is not much room for improvement from using any formal forecasting methodology.

TABLE 15-1 APPLICATION OF ACCURACY CRITERIA IN EVALUATING POTENTIAL IMPROVEMENT FROM FORMAL FORECASTING TECHNIQUES

Series	Percentage of MAPE for:		
	Naive 1	Naive 2	Optimal Forecast
A	26.5	19.8	8.3
B	32.6	10.2	9.3
C	30.4	29.3	28.7

Although the procedure above for computing the mean absolute percentage error for NF1, NF2, and OF forecasts as well as for selected formalized forecasting methodologies is very useful, it still has a disadvantage in that it gives equal weight to both small and large errors. In many situations, it is particularly important to avoid large errors in forecasting, since they tend to be much more costly than small errors. The MSE measure (see Chapter 2) avoids this disadvantage by employing a quadratic loss function (it squares the errors). However, its weakness is its absolute characteristic as opposed to a relative measure of accuracy like the MAPE.

15/1/2   Forecasting Accuracy of Technological Methods

Much of what has been discussed in the previous section relates specifically to quantitative methods of forecasting. Unfortunately, it is more difficult to assess the accuracy of technological forecasting methods because they are nonstandardized procedures. In addition, they rely heavily on the forecaster since different forecasters can arrive at quite different forecasts using the same methods.

While the accuracies of various qualitative or technological methods of forecasting generally are not documented, it is useful to consider the few reported studies, since they are indicative of some of the accuracies that might be anticipated. Oftentimes the studies that are available seek to bridge the gap between quantitative and qualitative forecasting approaches in comparing the accuracy of very diverse methods.

One area that has received considerable attention in the literature is that of anticipatory surveys. In Chapter 12, some of the more common of these techniques were examined and the basic problems of accuracy discussed. In one recent study, Rippe and Wilkinson (1974) examined the forecasting accuracy of the McGraw-Hill anticipatory survey data dealing with investment, sales, and capacity. Those researchers concluded that the McGraw-Hill data were generally less accurate than the Bureau of Economic Analysis-Securities and Exchange Commission survey (now known as the BEA survey) of anticipated investments on a 1-year time horizon. However, the McGraw-Hill data were found to be more accurate than naive approaches as well as some sophisticated econometric models. In addition, the researchers report that more recent anticipatory surveys tend to be more accurate, on the average, than older surveys. Tables 15-2 and 15-3 summarize the MAPE values obtained for the McGraw-Hill surveys and compare those with the equivalent results for the BEA survey.

From Tables 15-2 and 15-3 it can be seen that the accuracy in the anticipatory surveys is generally no better than a 10 percent MAPE. Furthermore, it is clear that the accuracy deteriorates as the forecasting time horizon is lengthened. That is typical of all forecasting methods whether qualitative, technological, or quantitative.

15/1/3   Forecasting Accuracy of Quantitative Methods

Almost all of the quantitative methods discussed in Chapters 3 through 11 can be classified into one of two categories: time series or causal (regression). (Only the multivariate ARMA methods of Chapter 11 do not fall naturally into one of these two categories.) This categorization is a useful one to make in discussing the accuracy of quantitative forecasting methods, since the basis of comparison depends very much on which category is being considered.

During the decade of the 1960s and in the early 1970s, regression methods of forecasting became very popular. Many of these methods were of the econometric type dealing with several variables and several equations. Naylor et al. (1972) suggested it might be appropriate to label the 1960s "the age of the large-scale econometric model." The initial success with these econometric models generated considerable optimism about their forecasting performance over the longer term. Unfortunately, however, the 1960s turned out to be a rather special period for the economy. That period included 105 months of uninterrupted growth and prosperity, which was longer than any other similar period since 1850. The fact that many econometric models performed well during the 1960s is not a good indication of their level of accuracy when economic conditions are changing as they were in the 1970s and 1980s.

Since the early 1950s (see Christ, 1951), studies have indicated that when structural changes are taking place in the economy, econometric models are not superior to time-series approaches. Even a study conducted in the 1960s (Steckler, 1968) found that econometric models were not entirely successful in improving accuracy in forecasting. In another study, Cooper (1972) concluded that econometric models are not in general superior to purely mechanical (time-series) methods of forecasting. Naylor et al. (1972) made a more extensive and detailed comparison of alternative methods and examined the Box-Jenkins approach in contrast to the Wharton econometric model for the years 1963 through 1967. A summary of the results of this study is shown in Table 15-4. The results indicate that the accuracy of ARMA models of the Box-Jenkins methodology is considerably better than the accuracy of the Wharton econometric model.

Another study by Nelson (1972) compared econometric (regression) and time-series (ARMA) methods for an even longer time horizon. This comparison was made using the FRB-MIT-PENN econometric model. Nelson (1972, p. 915) concluded that "the simple ARMA models are relatively more robust with respect to post sample predictions than the complex FRB-MIT-PENN models. Thus if the mean squared error were an appropriate measure of loss, an unweighted assessment clearly indicates that a decision maker would have been best off relying simply on ARMA predictions in the post sample periods" (that is, in the forecasting phase).

Within the sets of time-series approaches and regression approaches,

TABLE 15-2 MEAN ABSOLUTE PERCENTAGE ERROR
OF MCGRAW-HILL ANTICIPATORY SURVEY DATA
(1948–71[a] AND 1962–72)

Industry	Anticipated Investment				Anticipated Sales		Anticipated Capacity	
	1 yr	2 yr	3 yr	4 yr	1 yr	4 yr	1 yr	4 yr
				1948–71				
Durables								
Iron and steel	12.60	17.00	22.19	31.05	7.39	22.96	1.78	4.73
Nonferrous metals	12.14	11.50	24.79	29.74	5.41	10.87	1.70	6.21
Electrical machinery	16.47	17.95	19.11	25.49	4.36	7.24	1.68	7.10
Nonelectrical machinery	10.47	17.04	23.47	32.67	5.01	23.24	2.07	4.99
Motor vehicles and parts	10.58	25.30	29.58	29.62	6.69	14.32	1.95	5.26
Other transp. equip.	20.56	30.25	45.17	50.68	3.56	18.65	2.43	9.92
Fabricated mtls. and instru.	8.42	13.99	19.56	20.18	4.29	13.90	1.22	3.75
Stone, clay, and glass	12.24	19.46	15.84	15.08	5.15	14.10	2.66	5.82
Nondurables								
Chemicals	9.54	13.79	15.01	15.40	2.61	8.23	2.93	5.21
Paper and pulp	7.94	18.92	27.93	28.63	3.98	7.68	2.56	6.83
Rubber	10.04	17.08	22.84	22.67	4.56	9.14	2.25	3.67
Petroleum	6.97	10.51	15.86	20.30	2.88	9.77	1.40	4.72
Food and beverages	7.67	12.44	19.31	27.00	2.24	6.61	1.04	3.41
Textiles	11.33	19.55	23.07	25.30	3.57	10.03	1.76	3.99
All manufacturing	6.45	11.59	19.52	24.26	2.65	8.49	1.04	3.71
All business	3.01	9.36	16.43	21.65	[b]	[b]	[b]	[b]

[a]Series begin at various years between 1948 and 1955.

studies have also been performed to compare the relative accuracy of individual techniques. In the case of regression and econometric models, both Cooper (1972) and Fromm and Klein (1973) conclude that no single econometric model is overwhelmingly superior to all others. These researchers recognize that differences may exist in the forecasting performance for single items or over a limited time horizon, but on the average, these differences in accuracy do not consistently favor one model over another.

Armstrong (1978) surveyed the published empirical studies concerning econometric models and the comparison of those with time-series methods. His conclusions were the following:

1. Econometric forecasts were not shown to be significantly better than time-series forecasts

TABLE 15-2   MEAN ABSOLUTE PERCENTAGE ERROR
OF MCGRAW-HILL ANTICIPATORY SURVEY DATA
(1948–71[a] AND 1962–72) (*Continued*)

Industry	Anticipated Investment				Anticipated Sales		Anticipated Capacity	
	1 yr	2 yr	3 yr	4 yr	1 yr	4 yr	1 yr	4 yr
				1962–72				
Durables								
Iron and steel	8.49	14.70	21.16	29.52	5.20	16.75	1.99	3.74
Nonferrous metals	6.06	10.84	21.07	26.52	5.90	9.60	1.30	4.50
Electrical machinery	6.04	12.43	16.19	24.53	4.21	7.29	1.50	7.72
Nonelectrical machinery	10.55	15.36	20.30	30.46	4.70	17.67	1.26	3.72
Motor vehicles and parts	8.40	21.70	20.47	19.69	6.26	12.01	1.29	4.18
Other transp. equip.	9.09	23.04	38.17	42.62	4.05	17.14	1.24	10.62
Fabricated mtls. and instru.	6.40	11.67	17.51	24.04	4.29	8.92	1.12	3.34
Stone, clay, and glass	14.87	20.52	16.46	15.54	4.27	9.76	3.74	7.09
Nondurables								
Chemicals	3.82	11.09	14.27	17.89	1.91	7.64	4.81	6.35
Paper and pulp	7.32	14.15	27.35	31.56	2.67	3.59	3.36	7.32
Rubber	10.31	16.68	22.12	27.80	3.67	8.41	2.13	3.05
Petroleum	4.55	7.62	10.59	17.63	3.51	13.91	1.46	4.85
Food and beverages	6.55	8.09	15.58	24.56	2.13	5.44	.84	3.56
Textiles	7.91	21.11	28.77	29.90	2.96	9.47	1.51	4.05
All manufacturing	4.17	9.57	17.29	23.53	2.21	6.03	.53	2.24
All business	2.22	9.42	18.29	25.77	[b]	[b]	[b]	[b]

[b]Data not available.

*Source: R. D. Rippe and M. Wilkinson, "Forecasting Accuracy of the McGraw-Hill Anticipatory Data," Journal of the American Statistical Association, **69**, No. 348 (1974), p. 851. Reprinted by permission.*

2. Complex econometric models did not perform better in terms of accuracy in comparison with simpler econometric models.

In a recent paper, McNees (1982) has dealt in considerable detail with the topic we have been discussing so far in this section. He considers three claims made against econometric models for which he finds no strong support from empirical evidence. These claims are:

1. forecasts from these models are generally poor and specifically inferior to judgmental forecasts;

TABLE 15-3 MEAN ABSOLUTE PERCENTAGE ERROR FOR MCGRAW-HILL AND BEA ONE-YEAR INVESTMENT ANTICIPATIONS

Industry	McGraw-Hill	BEA
Durables		
Iron and steel	11.19	10.61
Nonferrous metals	12.14	11.01
Electrical machinery	10.05	6.53
Nonelectrical machinery	9.96	8.44
Motor vehicles and parts	11.65	12.11
Other transp. equip.	14.87	10.79
Fabricated mtls. and instru.	8.42	[a]
Stone, clay, and glass	12.24	9.06
Nondurables		
Chemicals	9.20	7.17
Paper and pulp	7.94	7.49
Rubber	10.04	7.81
Petroleum	6.17	5.92
Food and beverages	5.41	6.73
Textiles	9.52	13.04
All manufacturing	6.45	3.66

[a]Data not available.

Source: R. D. Rippe and M. Wilkinson, "Forecasting Accuracy of the McGraw-Hill Anticipatory Data," Journal of the American Statistical Association, **69,** No. 348 (1974), p. 852. *Reprinted by permission.*

TABLE 15-4 COMPARISON OF THE WHARTON ECONOMETRIC MODEL WITH THE BOX-JENKINS APPROACH (1963–67)

	Wharton (average absolute error)	Box-Jenkins (average absolute error)
I_p (investment in billions)	1.09	.59
P (GNP price deflator in percentages)	.22	.11
Un (unemployment in percentages)	.186	.109
GNP (in billions)	2.51	2.01

Source: T. H. Naylor, T. G. Seaks, and D. W. Wichern, "Box-Jenkins Methods: An Alternative to Econometric Forecasting," International Statistical Review, **62,** No. 5 (December, 1972), p. 831. Reprinted by permission.

2. econometrically generated forecasts are inferior to those from time-series models;

3. existing econometric models are worthless for policy analysis.

McNees indicates that time-series forecasts may be more accurate than econometric forecasts for one period ahead predictions but, as the time horizon of forecasting increases, econometric models provide forecasts that are considerably more accurate than those of time-series models.

Finally, McNees (1982) states that none of the major forecasters dominates the others for all or even most variables and forecast horizons. Even for a specific variable and horizon, the differences in accuracy among the major forecasters is typically (though not invariably) rather small. In addition, he is not aware of any test to determine whether the differences are significant in a statistical sense.

A comparison of the relative accuracy of various time-series methods has shown the following:

In a study reported by Kirby (1966), three different time-series methods were compared—moving averages, exponential smoothing, and regression. Kirby found that in terms of month-to-month forecasting accuracy, the exponential smoothing methods did best; both moving averages and exponential smoothing gave similar results when the forecasting horizon was increased to six months. The regression model included in that study was the best method for longer-term forecasts of 1 year or more.

In a study reported by Levine (1967), the same three forecasting methods examined by Kirby were compared. Levine concluded that although there was an advantage of simplicity with the moving average method, exponential smoothing offered the best potential accuracy for short-term forecasting. Other studies reported by Gross and Ray (1965), Raine (1971), and Krampf (1972) have arrived at conclusions similar to those of Levine and Kirby. Essentially, these researchers found that exponential smoothing models were generally superior in short-term forecasting situations, although among these researchers there was not much agreement as to the specific exponential smoothing model that was best.

In another large simulation study, Gardner and Dannenbring (1981) compare the performance of regular versus adaptive exponential smoothing methods. They conclude adaptive methods did not do better in terms of accuracy mainly because of their adaptive nature, which made them overreact to random errors. Unfortunately, comparisons among alternative decomposition methods and other techniques of forecasting have not been reported in the literature. However, studies have been published that compare exponential smoothing with Box-Jenkins models. Both Reid (1971) and Newbold and Granger (1974) conclude that the Box-Jenkins approach of ARMA models gives more accurate results than exponential smoothing or step-wise regression methods. When the comparison was made for a single-period time horizon, the Box-Jenkins results were found to be the most accurate of the three in 73 percent of the cases. When the lead time for the forecast was increased to six periods, Box-Jenkins models still gave the best results of the three, but in only 57 percent of the examples. These results are summarized in Table 15-5.

The conclusion that exponential smoothing can give results as accurate as autoregressive models and sometimes compete with ARMA methods in terms of accuracy may indeed be surprising to many forecasters. However, this conclusion is further supported by Groff (1973), who concluded that the Box-Jenkins methodology gave results that were approximately equal in accuracy or slightly worse than those achieved using exponential smoothing. That same conclusion was also reached by Geurts and Ibrahim (1975). This latter study is somewhat limited, however, because it relates to only a single time-series application.

In the late seventies some additional studies dealt with comparisons of forecasting accuracy among time-series methods. Makridakis and Hibon (1979) found, for instance, that exponential smoothing methods perform quite well in comparison with ARMA models. Table 15-6 shows the mean average percentage error for the 111 series (of actual data) used in their comparison, while Table 15-7 shows the percentage of times that the Box-Jenkins method did better than the alternatives listed.

In a more recent study, Makridakis et al. (1982) compared the forecasting accuracy of up to 1001 series (of actual data) using recognized experts to model and forecast each type of forecasting method. Table 15-8 shows the mean average percentage errors (MAPE) for 111 of these series. These results indicate that simple exponential smoothing methods do relatively well compared with the more advanced statistically based time-

TABLE 15-5 COMPARISON OF FORECASTING METHODS: PERCENTAGE OF TIME FIRST METHOD OUTPERFORMS SECOND FOR VARIOUS LEAD TIMES

Methods Compared[a]	Lead Times							
	1	2	3	4	5	6	7	8
B-J : H-W	73	64	60	58	58	57	58	58
B-J : S-A	68	70	67	62	62	61	63	63
H-W : S-A	48	50	58	57	55	56	58	59

[a]B-J is Box-Jenkins; H-W is Holt-Winters; S-A is step-by-step autoregressive.

*Source: P. Newbold and C. W. J. Granger, "Experience with Forecasting Univariate Time Series and the Combinations of Forecasts," Journal of the Royal Statistical Society, Series A, **137**, pt. 2 (1974), p. 138. Reprinted by permission.*

TABLE 15-6   THE AVERAGE OF THE MEAN ABSOLUTE PERCENTAGE
ERRORS (MAPE) OF ALL SERIES (111)

Forecasting Method	Model Fit-ing	Forecasting Horizons							
		1	2	3	4	5	6	9	12
Original Data: Nonseasonal Methods									
1. Naive 1	21.9	15.5	18.4	20.4	27.9	28.8	28.6	32.2	34.1
2. Single moving average	19.5	13.8	16.4	18.7	27.2	28.2	27.8	30.7	32.3
3. Single exponential smoothing	19.5	14.4	16.6	19.0	27.3	28.1	27.9	31.3	33.3
4. Adaptive response rate exponential smoothing	21.2	13.5	15.4	18.0	25.8	26.4	26.0	28.6	30.5
5. Linear moving average	22.2	17.1	20.3	23.6	34.2	36.5	37.1	44.1	49.6
6. Brown's linear exponential smoothing	20.2	13.2	15.8	18.4	26.5	27.7	27.3	31.2	34.7
7. Holt's (2 parameters) linear exp. smoothing	20.5	13.3	15.6	18.1	26.2	27.7	27.5	30.5	32.5
8. Brown's quadratic exponential smoothing	20.8	13.6	15.9	18.1	26.2	28.4	29.0	36.4	43.3
9. Linear trend (regression fit)	22.5	19.0	19.8	22.3	30.8	31.3	30.6	34.8	38.0
Seasonal and Nonseasonal Methods									
10. Harrison's harmonic smoothing	11.0	26.4	26.3	27.6	27.4	28.0	29.3	32.2	34.2
11. Winters' linear and seasonal exp. smoothing	10.9	13.8	14.8	15.4	16.2	17.1	18.4	21.3	23.6
12. Adaptive filtering	11.7	15.6	16.7	16.8	18.9	18.7	19.5	22.9	24.5
13. Autoregressive moving average (Box-Jenkins)	10.6	14.7	15.0	15.7	16.6	17.1	18.1	21.6	24.3
Seasonally Adjusted Data: Nonseasonal Methods									
14. Naive 2	10.0	14.5	15.0	15.1	15.3	15.6	16.6	19.0	21.0
15. Single moving average	8.4	12.9	13.6	13.7	13.8	14.3	15.3	17.7	19.8
16. Single exponential smoothing	8.5	12.8	13.4	13.8	14.0	14.3	15.6	18.1	20.2
17. Adaptive response rate exponential smoothing	9.2	13.0	14.0	14.5	14.7	15.2	16.2	18.5	20.4
18. Linear moving average	9.1	15.0	15.6	16.3	16.6	17.4	18.6	22.6	26.4
19. Brown's linear exponential smoothing	8.5	12.9	14.3	14.6	14.9	15.9	17.1	20.3	23.5
20. Holt's (2 parameters) linear exp. smoothing	9.0	12.0	12.8	13.2	13.7	14.8	16.0	19.7	23.0
21. Brown's quadratic exponential smoothing	8.7	12.5	14.0	14.7	15.6	17.0	18.6	23.6	28.9
22. Linear trend (regression fit)	11.4	19.6	20.4	21.1	21.1	21.9	22.8	25.3	27.4

TABLE 15-7 PERCENTAGE OF TIME THAT THE ARMA METHOD IS
BETTER THAN OTHER METHODS LISTED (111 SERIES)

Forecasting Method	Model Fitting	Forecasting Horizons							
		1	2	3	4	5	6	9	12
Original Data: Nonseasonal Methods									
1. Naive 1	98.2	59.1	63.6	57.3	63.6	64.5	59.1	63.6	67.3
2. Single moving average	92.7	49.1	56.4	53.6	60.9	64.5	61.8	65.5	66.4
3. Single exponential smoothing	90.9	53.6	57.3	55.5	60.0	62.7	62.7	65.5	66.4
4. Adaptive response rate exponential smoothing	95.5	49.1	56.4	56.4	60.0	62.7	64.5	62.7	67.3
5. Linear moving average	97.3	63.6	63.6	63.6	69.1	70.9	70.0	70.0	70.9
6. Brown's linear exponential smoothing	92.7	42.7	51.8	50.0	53.6	59.1	59.1	67.3	70.9
7. Holt's (2 parameters) linear exp. smoothing	90.9	50.0	55.5	50.0	54.5	62.7	61.8	62.7	66.4
8. Brown's quadratic exponential smoothing	91.8	48.2	51.8	50.9	57.3	61.8	63.6	65.5	73.6
9. Linear trend (regression fit)	90.9	60.9	61.8	63.6	65.5	69.1	68.2	71.8	72.7
Seasonal and Nonseasonal Methods									
10. Harrison's harmonic smoothing	49.1	62.7	68.2	72.7	70.0	70.0	73.6	71.8	65.5
11. Winters' linear and seasonal exp. smoothing	69.1	47.3	49.1	51.8	50.0	50.0	50.9	46.4	45.5
12. Adaptive filtering	70.9	49.1	54.5	52.7	55.5	56.4	56.4	58.2	51.8
Seasonally Adjusted Data: Nonseasonal Methods									
13. Naive 2	40.9	53.6	46.4	44.5	42.7	48.2	41.8	38.2	39.1
14. Single moving average	19.1	46.4	42.7	43.6	39.1	42.7	39.1	37.3	38.2
15. Single exponential smoothing	19.1	50.0	42.7	42.7	38.2	43.6	39.1	41.8	40.0
16. Adaptive response rate exponential smoothing	30.9	44.5	46.4	42.7	40.9	47.3	48.2	44.5	41.8
17. Linear moving average	26.4	55.5	50.9	50.9	49.1	47.3	49.1	51.8	51.8
18. Brown's linear exponential smoothing	19.1	42.7	48.2	44.5	44.5	49.1	47.3	49.1	46.4
19. Holt's (2 parameters) linear exp. smoothing	20.9	41.8	43.6	42.7	40.0	46.4	44.5	46.4	45.5
20. Brown's quadratic exponential smoothing	20.0	41.8	44.5	44.5	45.5	47.3	47.3	50.9	59.1
21. Linear trend (regression fit)	41.8	63.6	59.1	62.7	60.0	59.1	57.3	53.6	50.0

TABLE 15-8 AVERAGE MAPE: ALL DATA (111)

Methods	Model Fitting	Forecasting Horizons										Average of Forecasting Horizons					
		1	2	3	4	5	6	8	12	15	18	1–4	1–6	1–8	1–12	1–15	1–18
Naive 1	14.4	13.2	17.3	20.1	18.6	22.4	23.5	27.0	14.5	31.9	34.9	17.3	19.2	20.7	19.9	20.9	22.3
Mov.Average	12.8	14.1	16.9	19.1	18.9	21.8	23.6	23.9	16.3	28.7	31.9	17.3	19.1	20.1	18.9	19.7	20.8
Single EXP	13.2	12.2	14.8	17.4	17.6	20.3	22.5	22.7	16.1	28.8	32.5	15.5	17.5	18.5	17.8	18.8	20.1
ARR EXP	15.1	13.0	17.1	18.4	18.3	20.7	22.8	22.4	16.1	29.6	32.2	16.7	18.4	19.2	18.3	19.3	20.5
Holt EXP	13.6	12.2	13.9	17.6	19.2	23.1	24.9	31.2	22.6	40.4	40.3	15.7	18.5	21.1	21.3	23.4	25.1
Brown EXP	13.6	13.0	15.1	18.6	19.5	25.2	27.1	35.0	28.0	54.0	59.6	16.5	19.7	22.8	23.6	26.8	30.3
Quad. EXP	13.9	13.2	16.1	21.9	23.2	30.3	34.1	51.5	49.0	103.1	106.0	18.6	23.1	28.4	31.7	40.4	47.7
Regression	16.6	17.9	19.9	21.1	21.2	23.2	25.0	26.2	26.1	49.5	60.2	20.0	21.4	22.5	22.9	25.4	29.5
Naive 2	9.1	8.5	11.4	13.9	15.4	16.6	17.4	17.8	14.5	31.2	30.8	12.3	13.8	14.9	14.9	16.4	17.8
D Mov.Avrg	8.1	10.7	13.6	17.3	19.4	22.0	23.1	22.7	15.7	28.3	34.0	15.4	17.8	19.0	18.4	19.1	20.6
D Sing EXP	8.6	7.8	10.8	13.1	14.5	15.7	17.2	16.5	13.6	29.3	30.1	11.6	13.2	14.1	14.0	15.3	16.8
D ARR EXP	9.8	8.8	12.1	14.0	16.4	16.7	18.1	16.5	13.7	28.6	29.3	12.9	14.4	15.1	14.7	15.8	17.1
D Holt EXP	8.6	7.9	10.5	13.2	15.1	17.3	19.0	23.1	16.5	35.6	35.2	11.7	13.8	16.1	16.4	18.0	19.7
D Brown EXP	8.3	8.5	10.8	13.3	14.5	17.3	19.3	23.8	19.0	43.1	45.4	11.7	13.9	16.2	17.0	19.5	22.3
D Quad. EXP	8.4	8.8	11.8	15.0	16.9	21.9	24.1	35.7	29.7	56.1	63.6	13.1	16.4	20.3	22.2	25.9	30.2
D Regress	12.0	12.5	14.9	17.2	18.4	19.7	21.0	21.0	23.4	46.5	57.3	15.7	17.3	18.2	18.8	21.3	25.6
WINTERS	9.3	9.2	10.5	13.4	15.5	17.5	18.7	23.3	15.9	33.4	34.5	12.1	14.1	16.3	16.4	17.8	19.5
Autom. AEP	10.8	9.8	11.3	13.7	15.1	16.9	18.8	23.3	16.2	30.2	33.9	12.5	14.3	16.3	16.2	17.4	19.0
Bayesian F	13.3	10.3	12.8	13.6	14.4	16.2	17.1	19.2	16.1	27.5	30.6	12.8	14.1	15.2	15.0	16.1	17.6
Combining A	8.1	7.9	9.8	11.0	13.5	15.4	16.8	19.5	14.2	32.4	33.3	10.8	12.6	14.3	14.4	15.9	17.7
Combining B	8.2	8.2	10.1	11.8	14.7	15.4	16.4	20.1	15.5	31.3	31.4	11.2	12.8	14.4	14.7	16.2	17.7
Box-Jenkins	N.A.	10.3	10.7	11.4	14.5	16.4	17.1	18.9	16.4	26.2	34.2	11.7	13.4	14.8	15.1	16.3	18.0
Lewandowsky	12.3	11.6	12.8	14.5	15.3	16.6	17.6	18.9	17.0	33.0	28.6	13.5	14.7	15.5	15.6	17.2	18.6
Parzen	8.9	10.6	10.7	10.7	13.5	14.3	14.7	16.0	13.7	22.5	26.5	11.4	12.4	13.3	13.4	14.3	15.4
Average	10.7	10.8	13.2	15.5	16.8	19.3	20.8	24.0	19.2	37.5	40.7	14.1	16.1	17.8	18.0	19.9	22.1

ARR = Adaptive Response Rate
MOV. = Moving
QUAD. = Quadratic
EXP. = Exponential Smoothing
SING. = Single
D = Deseasonalized
WINTERS = Holt-Winters Exponential Smoothing

series forecasting techniques. However, in this latter study exponential smoothing methods did not perform the best, although they usually did better than fixed parameter ARMA (Box-Jenkins) models.

The differences in the conclusions reached by researchers examining various time-series methods of forecasting deserve some further consideration. That is particularly true when one recognizes that exponential smoothing models are simply a special case of the general ARMA methods. The best explanation can be found in recognizing that the accuracy of a forecasting method depends upon several factors and that those factors cannot be completely summarized in a single measure of accuracy. Reid (1971) discusses several of these factors including the number of observations in the series, seasonality of the data, the number of periods in the time horizon to be forecast, the extent of randomness in the series, and others. As reported by Adam (1973), these factors have a substantial impact on the accuracy and performance of individual forecasting models.

A logical explanation for the differences in the results reported in some of these studies is simply that different factors played different roles in the specific situations examined and thus biased the results in terms of accuracy in different ways. Recent research has investigated ways to express the accuracy of a forecasting method as a function of the various factors that affect accuracy (Makridakis and Hibon, 1979; Makridakis et al., 1982). This approach, in the opinion of the authors, is the relevant one for forecasters, since differences do exist among methods which make them more or less desirable for specific forecasting situations.

Eventually, additional research will need to be done on the determinants of accuracy and on developing procedures that can be used by the forecaster in estimating the relative accuracy of different methods. That information can then be used to apply the criterion of accuracy more effectively in comparing and selecting a forecasting method.

15/2   Pattern of the Data and Its Effects on Individual Forecasting Methods

A major consideration in the selection of a forecasting method for a specific situation is the type of patterns in the data. These patterns may represent characteristics that repeat themselves with time or they may represent turning points that are not periodic in nature. As has been pointed out previously, a data series can be described as consisting of two elements—the underlying pattern and randomness. The objective of forecasting is to distinguish between those two elements using the forecasting method that can most appropriately do so. It has also been suggested in describing some of the methods such as decomposition and time-series analysis that the pattern itself can be thought of as consisting of subpatterns or components, each of which can be considered separately. The three components most frequently used in describing elements of the pattern are trend, seasonality, and cycle.

Knowledge of the types of subpatterns included in a data series can be very useful in selecting the most appropriate forecasting method, since different methods vary in their ability to cope with different kinds of patterns. The mean and the simple smoothing techniques can deal only with stationary (horizontal) subpatterns in the data, while linear or higher forms of smoothing (quadratic, cubic, etc.) can deal with linear or higher forms of subpatterns in the data. As was shown previously, a method like Winters' exponential smoothing can deal with both trend and seasonal elements of a pattern.

Single equation regression methods can deal with almost any subpattern that can be transformed into a linear relationship. Furthermore, in regression, explanatory variables can be included, allowing the user to develop causal or explanatory models. These models, in addition to forecasting, allow better understanding of the situation involved and facilitate policy or decision making when large changes take place. In regression, the ability to handle different subpatterns depends largely on the user's ability to specify the most appropriate regression model.

The decomposition and ARMA methods can deal with a wide variety of patterns involving trend, seasonal, and/or cyclical subpatterns. However, like the bulk of the quantitative forecasting techniques, these methods have much more difficulty forecasting the cyclical subpatterns and predicting turning points, than they do in dealing with seasonal, trend, and horizontal subpatterns.

Decomposition methods are clearly the strongest available for dealing with cyclical components and providing information that can be used in predicting cyclical turning points. Census II and the Foran systems in particular have been designed specifically to aid in better analyzing, understanding, and possibly predicting the cyclical component. Multiple equation regression and econometric models can deal well with both seasonal and cyclical subpatterns as long as they can be isolated in the form of a causal relationship. In some instances, the burden simply shifts from selecting a method that can handle such subpatterns to specifying the appropriate model within that method.

As pointed out in Chapter 12, the forecasting of a change in pattern and particularly of turning points in the cycle is an extremely difficult task. However, if not done adequately it can have a substantial negative impact on the organization and its performance. Researchers have investigated some methods that might more appropriately handle such turning points. These include several of the variations in basic forecasting methods that have been described previously—effective monitoring, paired indices, and catastrophe theory. This area of forecasting clearly requires additional study and development of new tools before it can offer the same assistance to users that is now available for handling more stable subpatterns such as trends and seasonal components.

15/3 Time Horizon Effects on Forecasting Methods

In the previous chapter, the interaction between forecasting and planning was discussed in some detail. There the planning task was divided into four time horizons:

immediate term—less than one month

short term—one to three months

medium term—three months to 2 years

long term—over 2 years

One of the reasons the time horizon is particularly important in selecting a forecasting method in a given situation is that the relative importance of different subpatterns changes as the time horizon of planning changes. In the very immediate term, the randomness is usually the most important element. As the time horizon lengthens to two or three months, the seasonal subpattern generally becomes dominant. Then in the medium term, the cyclical component becomes more important, and finally in the long term, the trend element dominates. Graphically, the changing importance of each of these subpatterns with a lengthening time horizon can be presented as shown in Figure 15-1.

In general, qualitative or technological methods are most appropriate for long-term forecasting requirements. Quantitative methods, however, can

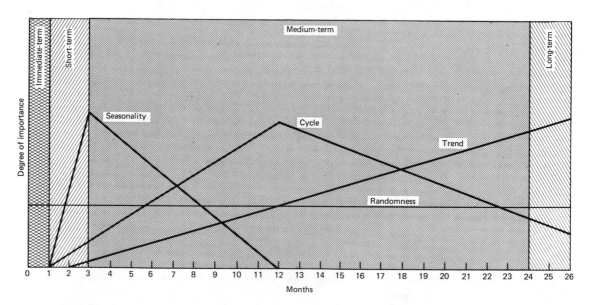

FIGURE 15-1 RELATIVE IMPORTANCE OF DATA PATTERNS FOR DIFFERENT TIME HORIZONS

be applied for all time horizons as long as patterns do not change. If they do, the appropriateness of time-series methods is reduced considerably. Smoothing methods are usually best for immediate or short term and decomposition and ARMA methods are usually better for short to medium term. Regression techniques tend to be best suited for medium- to long-term usage. It should be remembered, however, that the suitability of an individual method will depend not only on the time horizon but on the costs, accuracy, and other factors that are most heavily weighted in that particular situation. Furthermore, it is important to understand that, as the time horizon of forecasting increases, the chances of a change in established patterns or relationships increase too. Such nonrandom changes make quantitative forecasting methods less appropriate, and there is much more need, therefore, for nonquantitative or judgmental methods, when systematic changes do take place.

Since there generally is greater uncertainty as the time horizon lengthens, the forecaster is often challenged to find better ways of defining the problem in order to deal with that uncertainty. One such way that has not been studied extensively in the literature but that deserves further consideration is forecasting cumulative units rather than units per time period. Part of the difficulty in using cumulative units is that most quantitative methods assume time periods of equal length. However, it is certainly possible to forecast cumulative demand for the next 12 months rather than simply forecasting demand in each month and adding them together to get a cumulative forecast. Although not yet published, some work has been done in using cumulative units as the basis for forecasting rather than units of a shorter time period. This work indicates that more accurate results can frequently be obtained by making such cumulative forecasts. In situations such as production planning where cumulative forecasts are often what is needed for aggregate planning purposes, this may indeed be a very valuable approach that will be further developed in the future.

15/4 Impact of Type of Series on Forecasting Methods

A major factor found to affect forecasting accuracy in the Makridakis et al. (1982) study was the type of time series. With micro data, exponential smoothing methods seemed to do much better than the statistically sophisticated methodologies of ARMA, Bayesian forecasting, Parzen's method, and adaptive filtering. For instance, the overall MAPE was 13.7 percent for micro data for Lewandowski's (1979) exponential smoothing method while it was 18.2 percent for macro data. On the other hand, the MAPE for Parzen's method was 18.4 percent for micro data and 11.2 percent for macro data. Obviously, differences of this type are highly significant. Tables 15-9 and 15-10 show these differences between micro and macro data. For more

TABLE 15-9   AVERAGE MAPE: MICRO DATA (33)

Methods	Model Fitting	Forecasting Horizons										Average of Forecasting Horizons						n(max)
		1	2	3	4	5	6	8	12	15	18	1–4	1–6	1–8	1–12	1–15	1–18	
NAIVE 1	19.2	17.7	25.4	31.3	25.9	33.4	25.0	17.8	19.7	38.9	31.3	25.1	26.5	25.6	24.5	25.7	26.8	33
Mov. Average	18.1	15.0	19.9	24.7	21.6	28.3	20.7	10.8	22.0	31.1	24.5	20.3	21.7	20.7	19.8	20.5	21.4	33
Single EXP	18.4	14.8	19.0	24.0	22.7	28.5	21.6	10.7	21.1	30.1	25.4	20.4	21.8	20.6	19.8	20.5	21.5	33
ARR EXP	20.3	15.0	20.3	24.9	21.2	27.0	20.7	9.8	19.9	28.2	22.9	20.4	21.5	20.2	19.2	19.6	20.4	33
Holt EXP	20.1	15.8	20.2	26.6	22.6	32.0	22.1	15.8	22.0	41.9	33.1	21.3	23.2	23.0	22.3	23.6	25.5	33
Brown EXP	19.5	18.1	22.9	27.6	22.6	35.5	24.0	16.9	25.6	49.5	43.0	22.8	25.1	24.8	24.3	26.6	29.5	33
Quad. EXP	19.9	18.5	23.6	31.0	25.6	39.1	28.7	29.3	41.5	82.2	85.5	24.7	27.7	28.5	30.5	36.8	43.1	33
Regression	20.3	17.7	20.1	25.5	21.1	27.3	19.6	12.4	18.9	28.5	17.8	21.1	21.9	21.2	19.7	19.8	20.2	32
NAIVE 2	14.3	12.4	19.7	17.9	17.0	22.9	19.4	14.9	19.7	20.0	26.3	16.0	18.2	10.5	10.5	19.6	20.4	33
D Mov. Avrg	13.0	12.6	17.6	20.2	18.1	25.6	22.1	17.4	20.1	29.2	32.0	17.4	19.4	20.2	20.1	21.0	22.2	33
D Sing EXP	13.6	11.8	17.6	15.8	15.1	19.9	18.0	11.5	17.4	24.7	25.3	15.4	16.4	16.5	16.3	17.2	18.0	33
D ARR EXP	15.2	11.6	17.4	15.1	14.9	19.5	17.5	10.9	18.3	23.3	23.6	14.8	16.0	16.0	16.0	16.7	17.8	33
D Holt EXP	15.1	12.8	18.8	18.0	15.8	23.0	19.1	15.9	17.0	33.3	34.0	16.4	17.9	19.0	18.6	19.9	21.7	33
D Brown EXP	13.9	14.2	19.9	18.9	15.4	25.1	21.7	18.4	22.7	41.7	46.0	17.4	19.2	20.4	21.0	23.4	26.8	33
D Quad. EXP	14.2	14.8	21.5	20.0	16.0	29.8	26.6	29.6	39.4	69.4	82.7	18.4	21.5	23.8	27.0	32.5	39.0	33
D Regress	15.6	11.9	17.1	17.8	15.9	20.8	17.5	12.4	13.2	23.2	22.2	15.7	16.8	17.0	15.6	15.9	16.7	32
WINTERS	15.8	14.9	19.7	18.7	16.3	23.0	19.1	15.0	17.6	29.3	34.5	17.4	18.6	19.3	18.9	20.0	21.7	33
Autom. AEP	14.0	18.0	19.9	17.7	16.5	21.2	13.7	12.2	21.8	29.2	30.1	18.4	17.8	18.1	18.4	19.6	20.9	33
Bayesian F	18.8	13.7	19.4	17.1	15.0	20.5	18.8	18.2	22.6	36.4	37.4	16.3	17.4	18.8	18.9	20.7	22.7	33
Combining A	12.3	13.3	18.2	16.6	14.8	21.4	17.0	13.1	16.6	29.6	30.7	15.7	16.9	17.4	17.2	18.3	19.8	33
Combining B	11.6	12.9	16.9	13.5	14.8	16.6	13.9	10.3	16.1	24.2	22.4	14.5	14.8	14.9	15.0	16.0	16.6	33
Box-Jenkins	N.A.	17.1	19.8	14.1	17.4	22.7	14.5	12.6	18.6	25.9	28.7	17.4	17.6	17.7	17.7	18.9	20.2	33
Lewandowsky	20.3	13.2	14.4	12.1	11.6	13.9	13.3	10.9	12.6	17.8	13.7	12.8	13.1	13.5	13.7	13.8	13.7	33
Parzen	14.8	18.9	21.4	14.1	16.7	18.1	14.1	11.9	17.2	26.2	27.5	17.8	17.2	17.0	16.8	17.6	18.4	33
Average	15.8	14.9	19.6	20.1	18.1	24.8	19.5	15.0	20.9	34.3	33.4	18.0	19.5	19.7	19.6	21.0	22.7	

TABLE 15-10 AVERAGE MAPE: MACRO DATA (35)

Methods	Model Fitting	Forecasting Horizons										Average of Forecasting Horizons						n(max)
		1	2	3	4	5	6	8	12	15	18	1–4	1–6	1–8	1–12	1–15	1–18	
NAIVE 1	7.7	6.8	10.5	10.5	12.8	14.9	15.4	16.2	13.1	32.1	33.8	10.1	11.8	12.8	13.0	14.5	15.9	35
Mov. Average	6.2	8.5	12.4	11.8	15.8	17.3	18.6	16.6	14.9	31.5	33.4	12.1	14.1	14.7	14.3	15.5	16.7	35
Single EXP	6.5	5.9	9.9	9.5	13.2	14.6	16.1	13.7	15.6	32.0	33.8	9.6	11.5	12.1	12.4	13.9	15.8	35
ARR EXP	8.1	5.5	11.0	10.1	14.6	14.6	17.8	15.9	17.3	36.7	38.5	10.8	12.3	13.1	13.5	15.8	17.4	35
Holt EXP	5.8	5.2	8.0	6.7	10.0	11.9	13.3	14.0	16.6	32.3	34.0	7.5	9.2	10.3	10.9	12.7	14.8	35
Brown EXP	6.2	6.5	8.5	8.1	11.8	14.2	15.8	19.0	30.2	64.8	79.6	8.5	10.7	12.4	14.9	19.4	24.8	35
Quad.EXP	6.3	4.9	7.8	7.0	10.9	13.4	15.5	21.4	24.9	60.7	86.2	7.6	9.9	12.1	13.6	17.8	23.8	35
Regression	8.8	9.8	12.8	11.4	14.4	15.0	15.8	16.1	16.1	29.5	30.4	12.1	13.2	13.8	14.0	15.8	16.8	35
NAIVE 2	4.9	4.1	7.4	11.4	13.7	13.2	16.1	14.0	13.1	52.2	39.2	9.2	11.0	11.7	12.5	15.8	17.4	35
D Mov. Avrg	4.4	8.2	10.1	13.5	17.1	17.6	19.8	17.7	12.9	34.7	34.0	12.2	14.4	15.0	14.9	16.0	17.6	35
D Sing EXP	4.4	4.3	7.6	11.4	13.8	13.2	16.4	13.9	13.0	52.0	39.1	9.3	11.1	11.8	12.5	15.3	17.4	35
D ARR EXP	5.5	4.8	8.9	11.1	15.0	13.3	17.3	14.2	12.7	48.8	37.3	10.0	11.8	12.3	12.8	15.3	17.2	35
D Holt EXP	3.6	3.4	5.8	8.4	10.7	10.2	13.6	16.0	15.7	63.6	45.8	7.0	8.7	10.1	11.5	15.2	18.0	35
D Brown EXP	3.8	3.6	5.8	8.8	10.9	10.3	14.0	15.9	15.6	71.4	53.9	7.3	8.9	10.3	11.9	16.3	19.6	35
D Quad. EXP	3.9	3.5	5.9	8.5	11.2	10.9	15.1	20.3	12.1	56.5	42.8	7.3	9.2	11.3	11.9	15.2	17.6	35
D Regress	7.1	9.3	9.1	10.9	13.1	13.7	15.1	13.7	13.1	34.9	25.1	10.6	11.9	12.2	12.4	14.0	14.9	35
WINTERS	4.1	5.2	5.2	9.0	11.8	11.1	13.6	15.7	14.6	68.7	54.4	7.8	9.3	10.8	11.9	15.7	19.4	35
Autom. AEP	9.8	5.9	6.0	8.3	10.8	10.6	11.4	14.2	14.2	48.6	37.4	7.8	8.8	9.8	11.2	13.8	16.2	35
Bayesian F	8.6	6.2	7.7	9.4	10.6	12.3	13.5	12.2	13.2	31.5	22.7	8.5	9.9	10.3	10.6	12.1	12.9	35
Combining A	4.7	4.0	5.9	8.8	11.4	10.4	13.2	13.5	13.2	57.9	43.0	7.5	8.9	9.9	11.0	14.3	16.8	35
Combining B	5.8	4.8	6.8	10.1	12.1	11.2	13.4	12.5	12.4	50.9	38.6	8.5	9.7	10.4	11.1	14.1	16.1	35
Box-Jenkins	N.A.	6.0	5.7	6.5	10.5	10.3	12.4	16.0	16.2	36.3	35.5	7.2	8.6	10.0	11.6	13.5	15.3	35
Lewandowsky	6.3	6.6	10.9	11.5	14.0	11.8	15.8	14.4	16.1	61.0	36.6	10.7	11.8	12.0	12.5	16.4	18.2	35
Parzen	4.0	4.9	1.6	5.5	9.0	9.6	9.2	10.8	10.9	26.5	25.3	6.0	7.1	7.9	8.4	9.9	11.2	35
Average	5.7	5.7	8.1	9.5	12.5	12.7	14.9	15.3	15.3	46.5	40.8	8.9	10.6	11.5	12.3	14.9	17.0	

information, the reader should consult Makridakis et al. (1982) or Makridakis et al. (1983).

Although difficult to generalize from the forecasting performance of time-series methods to all forecasting methods, it seems that the type of series used influences forecasting accuracy. In general, micro series include much more randomness than macro series, making statistically sophisticated methods that often assume there is some pattern in the randomness less appropriate than exponential smoothing methods that forecast by sticking close to the average.

15/5   The Costs of Forecasting Methods

There are four main elements of cost in using a forecasting method: development costs, data storage costs, maintenance costs, and the costs of repeated applications. The importance of these various costs depend both on the method and the situation. For most qualitative or technological methods of forecasting, a separate cost estimate must be made for each situation. This cost estimate will need to consider human resource inputs and outside data acquisition requirements as a major part of the total costs of forecasting. Generally, these costs are incurred again whenever a new forecast is prepared for that specific situation. In the case of quantitative methods, however, many of the costs are fairly independent of the particular management situation. This section will concentrate on this latter type of costs, since they are the ones about which some generalizations can be made.

Most quantitative methods applied in organizations today use the computer as an integral part of their application. In fact, even in 1966, Reichard found in a survey of business use of forecasting that 68 percent of the companies surveyed were at that time using the computer in this manner. That percentage is undoubtedly even higher today. Thus in this discussion of cost, it will be assumed that the computer is being used as an integral part of quantitative forecasting applications.

The development cost, D_1, includes the cost of writing and modifying a computer program to apply a given forecasting method. It also covers the human resources required (mainly programming time) for the development of such programs and the computer time cost for establishing them in working order.

Once a computerized version of a forecasting method exists, an appropriate model for the given situation must be developed. This second stage in development can require anywhere from a few minutes, such as would be the case in a simple exponential smoothing model, to several months as would be the case with an econometric model. These development costs can be denoted by D_2 and will include both human resources and computer time expenditures. One of the differences between the costs for these two development stages is that in the first stage a substantial portion of the costs may be in computer time, whereas in the second stage the largest proportion tends to be for human resource expenditures.

In order to use the computerized version of a quantitative forecasting method, the appropriate computer program must be working on the computer system and the data must be stored in a memory device on that system. The data storage itself implies additional costs. These storage costs can be broken into two portions. The first, S_1, can represent the amount of storage required for the computer program of the forecasting method itself. The second, S_2 can represent the amount of storage space required for the data. The measure generally used for such storage is in terms of thousands of words of computer space required.

A third element of the costs for forecasting is the expense incurred when readjustments or modifications are made in the working model for a given forecasting situation. These changes will generally be made when new data become available, when basic changes in the pattern occur, or when additional runs of the model are required. These costs can be denoted by M; they are actually a subpart of the cost of repeated applications. If no modification or readjustment is needed, this element of cost will be zero.

The final portion of the cost of repeated applications is that for each run of the computerized forecasting method needed to obtain a new forecast. This cost can be denoted by R. Most of this cost is for the computer time usage (CPU—central processing unit time) required to run the program and some small amount of human resources required to supervise that run.

One way of further categorizing these costs is in terms of fixed, semifixed, and variable components. Using this scheme, the elements can be combined as follows:

$$\text{fixed costs} = D_1 + S_1,$$

$$\text{semifixed costs} = D_2 + S_2,$$

$$\text{variable costs} = R + M + S_2.$$

The total cost for a new situation can then be written as

$$\text{total cost} = \frac{D_1 + S_1}{I} + \frac{D_2}{J} + S_2 + (R + M), \tag{15-4}$$

where I is the number of items to be forecast using the same computer program, and J is the number of items that uses the same working model.

These elements of cost have been studied by the authors for several different forecasting methods. Table 15-11 summarizes the results obtained when those methods were applied to a wide range of data series in 1980. Although each situation will involve somewhat different costs, this table can serve as a benchmark for comparing different methods and the major elements of cost that each involves.

TABLE 15-11   COSTS OF QUANTITATIVE FORECASTING METHODS[a]

Methods	Number of Trials to Achieve Acceptable Working Model	Overall Development Costs	Program Storage Requirements (1000s of words)	Minimum Data Storage Requirements[b]	Frequency of Program Reruns	Cost per Run[c]
Mean	1	$300	1.8	30	Rarely needed	$.15
Simple moving average	2	300	1.8	7.5	Every time	.03
Simple exponential smoothing	2	150	1.6	2	Every time	.025
Linear moving average	2	250	2.6	15	Every time	.035
Linear exponential smoothing	2	300	2.4	3	Every time	.025
Classical decomposition	2	1200	3.8	60	Every few times	1.00
Census II	1	1800	12.0	72	Every few times	3.25
Foran system	1	1500	10.0	24	Every few times	1.00
Adaptive filtering	4	1200	5.6	60	Every few times	1.50
Box-Jenkins	3	2400	18.0	72	Every few times	4.40
Generalized adaptive filtering	5	1500	7.0	72	Every few times	3.50

TABLE 15-11 COSTS OF QUANTITATIVE FORECASTING METHODS[a]
(*Continued*)

Methods	Number of Trials to Achieve Acceptable Working Model	Overall Development Costs	Program Storage Requirements (1000s of words)	Minimum Data Storage Requirements[b]	Frequency of Program Reruns	Cost per Run[c]
Simple regression	1	900	3.4	30	Rarely needed	.50
Multiple regression	6	1800	6.8	30	Rarely needed	1.00
Econometric models	10–20	2400	.6	300	Rarely needed	3.50

[a]Based on 1980 data.

[b]Based on a 32 bit, single precision word of an IBM 370.

[c]Based on a cost of $300 an hour of CPU time.

The authors have gone one step further and tried to forecast the costs of various forecasting methodologies by using regression analysis and a single independent variable—the number of data points involved. In non-seasonal time-series forecasting methods, the results shown in Table 15-12 were obtained. These cost functions are for the computer time (CPU) required to achieve the optimal model where this is based on the model's fit to historical data. For example, in a single exponential smoothing model the data must be run for different values of α until the optimal α is found. Thus, this expense is only one element of the total costs described above. As indicated in Table 15-12, the results of trying to forecast this portion of forecasting costs were very good. Over 98 percent of the variation for different series using each model can be explained by just the simple relationship involving the number of data points.

15/6 The Ease of Application of Forecasting Methods

There are several factors that can be summarized under the heading *ease of application*. These include such things as the basic complexity of the

TABLE 15-12   COSTS OF FORECASTING METHODS (OPTIMAL MODEL)

Method	Constant Term	Coefficient of Independent Variable: Number of Data Points	R^2
Single exponential smoothing	.11	.133	.99
Trigg and Leach's adaptive-response-rate exponential smoothing	.10	.78	.99
Single moving average	.10	.335	.98
Brown's one-parameter linear exponential smoothing	.11	.18	.99
Linear moving average	.11	.5	.98
Brown's one-parameter quadratic exponential smoothing	.12	.22	.99
Trend analysis	.10	.25	.99
Holt's two-parameter linear exponential smoothing	.09	.3	.99
Naive method	.11	.008	.99

method, its timeliness in providing forecasts when they are needed, the level of expertise required to apply those different methods, and the conceptual appeal that the methods have to the ultimate user. All of these elements are important, since in the end they determine whether or not the forecasts will have an impact on management action.

In a survey conducted by Wheelwright and Clarke (1976) it was found that because of the relative complexity of various methods, organizations tend to go through evolutionary stages in their adoption of different forecasting techniques. As would be expected, they usually start with the more simple techniques, such as subjective executive estimates or simple smoothing methods, then gradually move to more complex methods. The reason often given for this evolutionary approach is the need for the increased accuracy that more complex methods seem to provide, but it was also found by Wheelwright and Clarke that the organization required certain expertise before it could effectively apply more complex methods. In the case of one methodology, Box-Jenkins, many organizations that had tried the method no longer used it simply because it was too complex. It was too difficult for the ultimate users of the forecasts to understand the conceptual basis for the method and to feel confident that it was being applied correctly.

In order to really base decisions and plans on forecasts obtained from quantitative methods, the ultimate user must either understand the conceptual basis of the method and feel comfortable that it represents a "correct" approach or put blind trust in the method feeling that it will perform uniformly well over time. Since the latter is seldom in fact the case, both individual users and the organization as a whole need to understand the basics of the methods that are going to be applied rather than wanting to apply the most sophisticated forecasting methods.

15/7 An Interactive Procedure for Selecting, Running, and Comparing Alternative Forecasting Methods

Forecasting methods are useless if they are only described but cannot be applied because of lack of computational means, or for any other reasons. To facilitate the application of quantitative forecasting methods, the authors have developed a set of interactive computer programs that include the great majority of the methods described in Chapters 3 through 11. A description of this interactive system, known as SIBYL/RUNNER, can be found in Makridakis et al. (1974), and there is a detailed explanation of all programs included and the information needed to run them in Makridakis and Wheelwright (1977).

SIBYL/RUNNER has been used extensively for teaching and actual day-to-day forecasting since it was introduced in 1973. In addition to allowing the usage of all major forecasting methods, SIBYL/RUNNER permits analysis of the data, suggests available forecasting methods, compares results, and provides several accuracy measures in such a way that it is easier for the user to select an appropriate method and forecast needed data under different economic conditions.

Another major advantage of SIBYL/RUNNER is its motivational impact on the user. Since learning to use a forecasting method takes time and effort, this package has been particularly well received because it makes effective use of the user's time and provides rapid feedback as to progress being made in that forecasting situation. In essence, one can start with very little knowledge and a set of real data, then gradually learn about different methods and their characteristics while working on that particular forecasting problem.

In other words, SIBYL/RUNNER is a set of programs designed to bring the learning and application of forecasting within the realm of a person who is not an expert in statistics or in use of the computer.

15/8   Summary

Selecting an appropriate forecasting method is a difficult task due to the variety of situations and the large number of techniques available. This chapter has provided some guidelines and information to facilitate such choice. Several criteria were proposed. Among them accuracy was considered the most important. In general, published empirical evidence suggests that there is not a direct link between the sophistication of a forecasting method and its accuracy. Simple methods can do as well in a wide variety of cases. Forecasting users should not, therefore, opt for the most difficult or mathematically sophisticated methods before they are sure that the results are better than those of simpler methods which are easier to apply and much less costly to use.

REFERENCES AND SELECTED BIBLIOGRAPHY

Adam, E. E. 1973. "Individual Item Forecasting Model Evaluation," *Decision Sciences,* **4**, October, pp. 458–70.

Armstrong, J. S. 1978. "Forecasting with Econometric Methods: Folklore versus Fact," *Journal of Business,* **S1**, pp. 549–600.

Christ, C. F. 1951. "A Test of an Econometric Model of the United States, 1921–1974," in *Conference on Business Cycles.* New York: National Bureau of Economic Research.

Cooper, R. L. 1972. "The Predictive Performance of Quarterly Econometric Models of the United States," in *Econometric Models of Cyclical Behavior,* B. C. Hickman (ed.). New York: National Bureau of Economic Research.

Cragg, J., and B. Malkiel. 1968. "The Consensus and Accuracy of Some Predictions of the Growth in Corporate Earnings," *Journal of Finance,* March, pp. 67–84.

Dalrymple, D. J. 1975. "Sales Forecasting Methods and Accuracy," *Business Horizons,* December, pp. 69–73.

Elton, E. J., and M. J. Gruber. 1972. "Earnings Estimates and the Accuracy of Expectational Data," *Management Science,* April, pp. B409–B424.

Fildes, R., and S. Howell. 1979. "On Selecting a Forecasting Model," in *TIMS Studies—Vol. 12—Forecasting,* S. Makridakis and S. Wheelwright (eds.). Amsterdam: North-Holland, pp. 297–312.

Fromm, G., and L. R. Klein. 1973. "A Comparison of Eleven Econometric Models of the United States," *American Economic Review,* May, pp. 385–401.

Gardner, E. S., Jr., and Dannenbring, D. G. 1980. "Forecasting with Exponential Smoothing: Some Guidelines for Model Selection," *Decision Sciences,* **11**, pp. 370–383.

Geurts, M. D., and I. B. Ibrahim. 1975. "Comparing the Box-Jenkins Approach with the Exponentially Smoothed Forecasting Model Application to Hawaii Tourists," *Journal of Marketing Research,* **12**, May, pp. 182–88.

Green, D., and J. Segall. 1967. "The Predictive Power of First-Quarter Earnings Reports," *Journal of Business,* **40**, January, pp. 44–55.

Groff, G. K. 1973. "Empirical Comparison of Models for Short-Range Forecasting," *Management Science,* **20**, No. 1, September, pp. 22–31.

Gross, D., and J. L. Ray. 1965. "A General Purpose Forecasting Simulator," *Management Science,* **11**, No. 6, April, pp. B119–B135.

Johnson, T. E., and T. G. Schmitt. 1974. "Effectiveness of Earnings per Share Forecasts," *Financial Management,* Summer, pp. 64–72.

Kiernan, J. D. 1970. "A Survey and Assessment of Air Travel Forecasting." Urban Mass Transportation Project. Arlington, Va., April.

Kirby, R. M. 1966. "A Comparison of Short and Medium Range Statistical Forecasting Methods," *Management Science,* No. 4, pp. B202–B210.

Krampf, R. F. 1972. "The Turning Point Problem in Smoothing Models." Unpublished Ph.D. dissertation, University of Cincinnati.

Levine, A. H. 1967. "Forecasting Techniques." *Management Accounting,* January.

Lewandowski, R. 1979. *La Prévision à Court Terme.* Dunod (pub), Paris.

Mabert, V. A. 1975. "Statistical Versus Sales Force-Executive Opinion Short Range Forecasts: A Time Series Analysis Case Study." Krannert Graduate School, Purdue University (working paper).

Makridakis, S., A. Hodgsdon, and S. Wheelwright. 1974. "An Interactive Forecasting System," *American Statistician,* November.

Makridakis, S., and H. M. Vandenburgh. 1974. "The Accuracy and Cost of Non-Seasonal Time Series Forecasting Methods." *INSEAD Research Papers*, Series No. 143, December.

Makridakis, S., and S. C. Wheelwright. 1978. *Interactive Forecasting: Univariate and Multivariate Methods*, 2nd ed. San Francisco: Holden-Day.

Makridakis, S. and Hibon, M. 1979. "Accuracy of Forecasting: An Empirical Investigation (with Discussion)," *Journal of the Royal Statistical Society*, A, **142**, Part 2, pp. 97–145.

Makridakis S., et al. 1982. "The Accuracy of Extrapolation (Time Series) Methods: Results of a Forecasting Competition," *Journal of Forecasting,* forthcoming.

Makridakis S., et al. 1983. *The Accuracy of Major Extrapolation (Time Series) Methods*. John Wiley & Sons, Inc., forthcoming.

McLaughlin, R. L. 1975. "The Real Record of the Econometric Forecasters," *Business Economics*, **10**, No. 3, pp. 28–36.

McNees, S. K. 1974. "How Accurate Are Economic Forecasts?" *New England Economic Review*, Federal Reserve Bank of Boston, Nov.–Dec., pp. 2–19.

McNees, S. K. 1982. "The Role of Macroeconometric Models in Forecasting and Policy Analysis in the United States," *Journal of Forecasting,* **1**, January.

Naylor, T. H., T. G. Seaks, and D. W. Wichern. 1972. "Box-Jenkins Methods: An Alternative to Econometric Forecasting," *International Statistical Review*, **40**, No. 2, pp. 123–37.

Nelson, C. 1972. "The Prediction Performance of the FRB-MIT-PENN Model of the U.S. Economy," *The American Economic Review,* **62**, No. 5, December, pp. 902–17.

Newbold, P., and C. W. J. Granger. 1974. "Experience with Forecasting Univariate Time Series and the Combination of Forecasts," *Journal of the Royal Statistical Society,* Series A, **137**, Part 2, pp. 131–65.

Niederhoffer, V., and D. Regan. 1972. Summarized in *Barron's* magazine, December 18, p. 9.

Parzen, E. 1982. "ARMA Models for Time Series Analysis and Forecasting." *Journal of Forecasting*, **1**, January.

Raine, J. E. 1971. "Self-Adaptive Forecasting Considered," *Decision Sciences,* April

Reid, D. J. 1971. "Forecasting in Action: A Comparison of Forecasting Techniques in Economic Time Series." Presented at the Joint Conference of Operations Research Society's Group in Long-Range Planning and Forecasting.

Richard, R. S. 1966. *Practical Techniques of Sales Forecasting.* New York: McGraw-Hill.

Rippe, R. D., and M. Wilkinson, 1974. "Forecasting Accuracy of the McGraw-Hill Anticipatory Data," *Journal of the American Statistical Association,* **69**, No. 348, December, pp. 849–58.

Steckler, H. O. 1968. "Forecasting with Econometric Models: An Evaluation," *Econometrica,* **34**, July–October, pp. 437–63.

Theil, H. 1966. *Applied Economic Forecasting.* Amsterdam: North Holland Publishing Co., pp. 26–32.

Wheelwright, S. C., and D. G. Clarke. 1976. "Corporate Forecasting: Promise and Reality," *Harvard Business Review,* November–December.

Zeeman, E. C. 1976. "Catastrophe Theory," *Scientific American,* April.

EXERCISES

1.   Develop a list of criteria that might be used in determining the characteristics of a forecasting method appropriate for a given situation. For example, one criterion might be time horizon covered by the forecast and another might be the cost of forecast preparation. Identify the possible subcategories that might be associated with each of these criteria, such as the three or four time horizons to be considered (and their definitions) or the types of costs and their ranges of values.

2.   Select a set of 10 specific forecasting methods that are addressed in previous chapters *and* that you think are most likely to be useful in practice. Characterize each method in terms of (a) the foregoing criteria and (b) the method's ability to handle situations where those criteria are present. It might be helpful to prepare a table with each row representing a criterion, each column representing a method, and the body of the table indicating where matches exist.

3.   Listed below are several types of forecasting situations. For each, describe the major characteristics that will impact the selection of a forecasting method, and indicate which methods (if any) of the 10 covered in the preceding question are likely to be most appropriate (and why).
     a. Demand forecasting for a spare parts inventory system covering 30,000 parts for a heavy construction equipment manufacturer.
     b. Annual earnings forecasts prepared for 5-12 companies in each of 15 industries by the research firm of a commercial brokerage firm.

    c. Ten-year projections of weight to horsepower ratios prepared for each of eight product families by the product-planning group of an electric motor manufacturer.

    d. Construction activity forecasts for the entire United States and for each of seven geographical territories for a construction products firm seeking to plan operating levels for the next 18 months.

    e. Projections of market share for a diversified products firm and its top four competitors in each of 17 product-markets as part of the strategic planning process.

4.   Apply the list of criteria (Exercise 1 above) and the characterization of the methods (Exercise 2 above) to the capacity planning situation described for Duke Power Company in Chapter 13, Exercise 3. What methods do you think should be considered for that situation? How do those compare with the methods actually applied by Duke Power? What leverage for improvements are there in method selection in this situation?

5.   Identify an item for which publicly available forecasts are prepared on a regular basis. (Options might include GNP, unemployment, inflation, or the money supply.)

    a. What methods are used? Why? How have those been changed over the past 5 years? Why?

    b. Analyze the performance of the forecasts. When do they do well? Poorly? Why? How do they perform on the criteria developed as part of Exercise 1 above?

16/MANAGING THE FORECASTING FUNCTION

The past two decades have seen a substantial increase in the range of forecasting methods available and in the number of statisticians, operations researchers, and management scientists trained to apply these methods. The increases in these two factors should serve as building blocks for substantial growth in the systematic and effective use of forecasting methods in the coming decade. However, the failure of the predicted rapid expansion of management science to materialize in the mid-sixties demonstrates the importance of developing an effective interface between the management scientist and the user and of developing supporting organizational efforts. Both are equally necessary to the effective growth and utilization of quantitatively based techniques.

A prerequisite for the effective management of a forecasting system and of an organization's forecasting resources is an appreciation of the role forecasting plays—or can play—in management. At the risk of some oversimplification, there are two such roles.

The first, most obvious, and most frequently cited role is to reduce the range of uncertainty confronting management. From a capital budgeting perspective, for example, forecasting's role in reducing uncertainty has the effect of lowering the "risk premium" and hence the cost of capital to the firm. Stated in this way, forecasting lowers the cost of doing business but does not, in its own right, create additional options for decision making.

Second, forecasting can effectively broaden the range of options available to managers. A forecasting system can be a tool for the systematic and relatively inexpensive generation and evaluation of options. For example, the effects of price changes, marketing programs, geographical shifts in distribution patterns, and so forth can be simulated with the objectives of aiding managerial decision making.

In sum, forecasting can serve different and simultaneous functions within the firm. This fact, in turn, dictates that managers charged with responsibility for the forecasting function be open to a broad range of possibilities. It should be remembered that the alternative to formal forecasting—human intuition and judgment—is not necessarily better and is often more expensive, as discussed in Chapter 17.

There are two key tasks in organizing, implementing, and improving the forecasting function in an organization. The first deals with identifying, evaluating, and implementing an overall approach to forecasting in an organization. The second involves effectively applying forecasting methods and resources to specific situations and developing a pattern of improvement in each such application over time. Both of these areas will be discussed in some detail in this chapter.

As a starting point, the initial section of this chapter reviews some recent studies on the status of forecasting in United States businesses and some of the explanations for that current state of affairs. The second section deals with various approaches that can be used to make an assessment in a specific business situation in order to identify and evaluate what's currently being done and the opportunity for making significant improvements in the forecasting activity. This includes a review of audit procedures that might be used, as well as suggestions on the type of action that can generally improve the effectiveness of the forecasting function. The final section deals directly with the task of managing a forecasting system. This includes a description of the critical dimensions of any forecasting system, how those can be identified and evaluated, and the management approaches that might be used to control and improve the overall system.

16/1   A Review of Forecasting in Business Firms in the 1970s

During 1975, Dalrymple (1975a, 1975b) and Wheelwright and Clarke (1976) made two important studies of the status and success of forecasting in business organizations. These two studies (and subsequent studies by Mentzar, 1981 and The Conference Board, 1978) can serve as a useful basis for discussing the primary dimensions of the forecasting function in an organization and the opportunities and challenges generally faced by those managers charged with directing the forecasting function. Each of these two studies will be reviewed briefly and their implications for managing the forecasting function will be summarized.[1]

In the Dalrymple study, a questionnaire was mailed to 500 business managers in the midwestern United States. Responses were obtained from 35 percent of those surveyed, representing a mix of firms in terms of size, age, and industries. In the Wheelwright-Clarke study, a more detailed questionnaire was mailed to 500 companies representing a broad cross section of all United States firms. A major feature of this study was that two questionnaires were sent to each firm—one to be completed by a preparer of forecasts and the other by a user of forecasts. Approximately 15 percent of the surveyed companies returned usable responses from both a user and a preparer, and an additional 10 percent responded with one or the other, but not both.

Three findings deserve particular attention in this chapter. These deal with the actual status of forecasting in the surveyed companies (that is, the methods used and their performance), the interaction between decision makers and forecasters, and the dimensions viewed as holding the

---

[1]It should be noted that none of these studies is representative in a statistical sense of general practices regarding forecasting. However, they do provide insights as to what the surveyed firms had found to be important and where opportunities for better utilizing forecasting might be most significant.

greatest potential for making more effective use of forecasting resources. Each of these will be summarized in turn in this section.

16/1/1   The Status of Forecasting

In the Wheelwright-Clarke study, the application of forecasting in each of the respondent companies was pursued at two levels. One level examined the methodologies that had been applied in the past (as well as those currently being applied). Table 16-1A summarizes these findings.[2] The two most commonly used techniques were the jury of executive opinion and regression analysis. For all eight methods surveyed, the researchers also inquired as to why some methods might have been used at one time but were no longer in use. The major explanation given was inadequate accuracy. However, one exception to this was the Box-Jenkins technique, where complexity was most frequently given as the reason for no longer using it.

As part of their survey of techniques being used, Wheelwright and Clarke also investigated the development stages companies pass through in becoming more sophisticated and extensive users of forecasting. As summarized in Table 16-1B, the methodologies used varied considerably, depending on whether the firm viewed itself as behind its industry counterparts in the use of forecasting, average, or ahead of its counterparts in the forecasting arena. This table suggests the types of methods that make up the bulk of the forecasting efforts in the early stages of a firm's development of its forecasting capabilities and in subsequent stages of that development. In the Dalrymple study, the relative use of a variety of methods was also examined and the forecasting errors associated with the use of each of those methods was reported. These results are summarized in Table 16-2 and appear to be fairly consistent with those reported by Wheelwright and Clarke. The one exception to this consistency is the percentage of respondents never having tried some of the methods. This is not too surprising, given that the Dalrymple study was a more regional one and involved a greater percentage of smaller firms than the Wheelwright and Clarke study.

Decision Maker and Forecaster Perceptions and Interactions

Following the identification of the methodologies used, both of these studies sought to identify the important variables used in applying these forecasting techniques. While in many instances there seemed to be a range

---

[2]Throughout the Wheelwright and Clarke study, those who primarily prepare forecasts are referred to as *Preparers,* while those who primarily use forecasts are referred to as Users.

TABLE 16-1A ACCEPTANCE AND USE OF ALTERNATIVE
FORECASTING METHODS—PREPARERS' RESPONSES
(WHEELWRIGHT AND CLARKE STUDY)

Method	Familiar with the Method (Percent)	Use of the Method by Those Familiar with It (Percent)	Ongoing Use of the Method by Those Who Have Tried It (Percent)
Jury of executive opinion	94	82	89
Regression analysis	92	76	91
Time-series smoothing	87	75	84
Sales force composite	90	74	82
Index numbers	67	67	85
Econometric models	88	65	88
Customer expectations	85	57	78
Box-Jenkins	61	40	71

TABLE 16-1B DEPENDENCE OF USE OF METHODS ON FORECASTING
STATUS (WHEELWRIGHT AND CLARKE STUDY)

Percentage of Preparers Using Method Who Place Their Company

Method	Behind Industry (17%)	Average (33%)	Ahead of Industry (50%)
Jury of executive opinion	68	84	71
Regression analysis	39	71	76
Time-series smoothing	32	71	66
Sales force composite	50	65	71
Index numbers	36	41	42
Econometric models	25	53	63
Customer expectations	29	47	51
Box-Jenkins	11	18	32
Other	18	24	32

Source: Steven C. Wheelwright and Darral G. Clarke, "Corporate Forecasting: Promise and Reality," *Harvard Business Review* (November–December 1976), copyright © 1976 by the President and Fellows of Harvard College, all rights reserved. Reprinted by permission.

TAABLE 16-2   FORECASTING TECHNIQUES USED AND ERRORS
REPORTED (DALRYMPLE STUDY)

Method	Usage				Usage for Forecast Period		Percentage Errors of Firms Who Report Regular Use
	Use Regularly (Percent)	Use Occasion- ally (Percent)	No Longer Use (Percent)	Never Tried (Percent)	Short Term (year or less) (Percent)	Long Term (1 to 5 years) (Percent)	
Jury of executive opinion	52	16	1	5	27	16	7.0
Sales force composite	48	15	3	9	37	6	6.8
Trend projections	28	16	1	12	13	13	6.2
Moving average	24	15	2	15	18	7	6.2
Industry survey	22	20	2	16	17	8	6.7
Regression	17	13	1	24	8	9	6.4
Intention to buy survey	15	17	2	23	15	3	8.5
Exponential smoothing	13	13	3	26	13	7	7.3
Leading index	12	16	1	24	12	5	5.4
Life-cycle analysis	8	11	1	28	2	11	4.5
Diffusion index	8	11		30	9	6	8.1
Simulation models	8	8	1	35	5	5	6.5
Input/output model	6	8	1	34	6	3	6.2

Source: D. J. Dalrymple, "Sales Forecasting Methods and Accuracy," *Business Horizons* (December, 1975), pp. 69–73, copyright 1975 by the Foundation for the School of Business at Indiana University. Reprinted by permission.

of variables in use, the Wheelwright and Clarke study (using factor analysis) identified three general categories of variables. These were: the *user environment* (related to the user's level of forecasting knowledge and the relationship of the user of the forecast to the preparer of the forecast); *cost* (including computer costs, data costs, and the time cost of both preparers and users); and *problem-specific characteristics* (including the time horizon of the forecast, the accuracy required, and the degree of top management support).

While the Dalrymple study concentrated its attention on simply reporting the status of forecasting in the surveyed firms, the Wheelwright and Clarke study sought to identify explanations as to why the full potential of forecasting in many of the surveyed firms had not been realized. Through a comparison of the responses obtained from users and preparers, several dimensions along which the perceptions of these two groups varied significantly were identified. These responses are summarized in Table 16-3. Factor analysis was used to group these into four major areas—the abilities of those who prepare the forecasts, the technical abilities of those who use the forecasts, the interactions between the users and the preparers, and the management skills of those who use the forecasts.

16/1/2   Potential for Improved Use of Forecasting

Through their analysis, Wheelwright and Clarke identified major differences between the perceptions of forecast *users* (managers and decision makers) and the perceptions of forecast *preparers*. While this gap was reflected in part in the technical emphasis of the preparers and the managerial emphasis of the users, the need for each of these two groups to understand and respect the perspective of the other proved critical in realizing the full potential of the resources committed to forecasting. This conclusion was further supported in a series of questions asked concerning those activities whose improvement would be most beneficial to the firm's forecasting efforts. A majority of the responses highlighted communication between preparers and users. In addition, management support and data-processing support were also cited as important areas that could significantly enhance the value of the firm's forecasting efforts.

Wheelwright and Clarke concluded from their survey that while the communication problem was indeed real, it was merely a symptom of a deeper problem for many companies. The problem inherent in a number of the responding firms centered around the *definition of the responsibilities and skills of users and preparers*. It appeared that both groups had abdicated certain essential tasks and skills to their counterparts with the result that some of the basics were not being covered. This conclusion is shown graphically in Figure 16-1. Each group appeared to view its own role more narrowly than the role of its counterpart, with the consequence that some responsibilities and skills were not being picked up by either group. Wheelwright and Clarke identified a number of critical tasks where a significant number of the surveyed firms rated themselves as only adequate or less than adequate in their skills and abilities. For example, in only 15 percent of the surveyed firms did both the user and preparer rate themselves as adequate or more than adequate in understanding management's forecast-

TABLE 16-3   DIFFERENCES IN PERCEPTIONS OF USERS
AND PREPARERS OF FORECASTS

Preparer's Ability	Rating (%)
Understand sophisticated mathematical forecasting techniques	1
Understand management problems	-25^a
Provide forecasts in new situations	-42
Provide forecasts in ongoing situations	-13
Identify important issues in a forecasting situation	-30
Identify the best technique for a given situation	-56
Provide cost-effective forecasts	-33
Provide results in the time frame required	-38
User's Technical Ability	
Understand the essentials of forecasting techniques	$+27$
Understand sophisticated mathematical forecasting techniques	$+12$
Identify new applications for forecasting	$+5$
Effectively use formal forecasts	-6
Evaluate the appropriateness of a forecasting technique	$+24$
User/Preparer Interaction Skills	
Understand management problems (preparers)	-25
Work within the organization (preparers)	-10
Understand management problems (users)	5
Communicate with preparers of forecasts (users)	-1
Work within the organization in getting forecasts (users)	$+2$
User's Management Abilities	
Make the decisions required in their jobs	-3
Effectively use formal forecasts	-6
Describe important issues in forecasting situations	-8
Work within the organization in getting forecasts	$+2$

[a]25% more preparers rated themselves good or excellent than did users.

$$\text{Rating} = 100 \times \frac{\text{percentage of users rating good or excellent} - \text{percentage of preparers rating good or excellent}}{\text{percentage of preparers rating good or excellent}}$$

Source: Steven C. Wheelwright and Darral G. Clarke. "Corporate Forecasting: Promise
and Reality," *Harvard Business Review* (November–December 1976), copyright © 1976
by the President and Fellows of Harvard College, all rights reserved. Reprinted by permission.

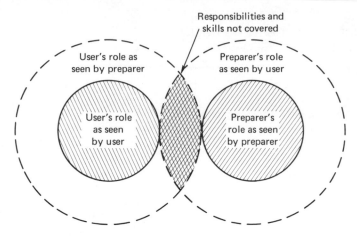

FIGURE 16-1 ROLE PERCEPTIONS OF PREPARERS AND USERS OF FORECASTS

ing problems. In only 29 percent of the firms did both users and preparers rate themselves as adequate or better at identifying the important issues in a forecasting situation.

While these results suggest some basic areas for attention by those charged with managing the forecasting function, such individuals need a mechanism for identifying what's wrong with their own situation and the types of actions most appropriate for those. The next section deals directly with procedures for handling such an audit analysis and development of an action plan.

16/2   Correcting an Organization's Forecasting Problems

Much of the authors' work in forecasting has suggested that a good starting point for improving an organization's forecasting is to audit existing problems and opportunities. While there is some literature on performing such reviews, the bulk of it concentrates on accuracy as the key problem and identifies as causes of the problem the use of poor data, the use of the wrong methods, and the lack of trained forecasters. Without much empirical basis, this literature suggests that an obvious solution to problems of accuracy would be the use of improved—by which is generally meant more sophisticated—methods. Not surprisingly, such solutions tend to require more sophisticated forecasters or additional training for those already at work. Thus, the typical solution suggested has been to replace existing methods with those that are more mathematical and to replace and upgrade existing forecasters so that they could handle those more mathematical methods. Unfortunately, empirical evidence does not support the assumption that sophisticated methods outperform simpler ones (see Chapter 15).

The results of such actions range from slight improvements to frustration and higher turnover among forecasters. Even organizations with trained statisticians and sophisticated methods are frequently disappointed with the performance and impact of their forecasting. As suggested by the Wheelwright and Clarke study reviewed in the preceding section, they often find that the problem is one of communication—the experts lack an appropriate understanding of the areas in which their forecasts are to be applied. This interaction of problem-causes-remedies-results often leads to the undesired scenario summarized in Figure 16-2.

One reason that the results are less desirable than expected is that in many organizations, forecasting is not a career. Rather, it is part of the assignment of a market planner or a group controller or it is a short-term way station on the upward route to more important positions. Recommending that such forecasters become experts in sophisticated statistical techniques has been inconsistent with organizational and personal philosophies and objectives, as well as bad advice if the goal is improved accuracy.

Additional condemnation of such a simplistic approach comes from the recognition that the application of a specific method and the obtaining of a numerical output are only one step, albeit an important one, in the process of forecasting. Concentrating on accuracy is like trying to melt an iceberg by heating the tip: when forecasting accuracy is slightly improved, other managerial problems of implementation rise to the surface to prevent the full realization of forecasting's promise.

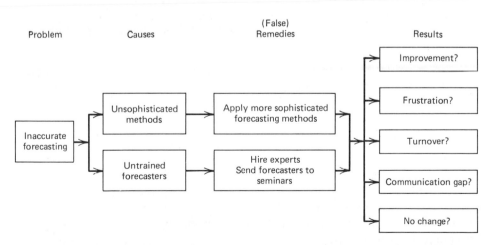

FIGURE 16-2   TRADITIONAL VIEWS OF FORECASTING PROBLEMS

16/2/1   Types of Forecasting Problems and Their Solutions

To improve forecasting, one framework that the authors have found useful has as its *first step* the characterization of problems as one of five types: bias, credibility and impact, lack of recent improvement, lack of a firm base on which to build, and recognition of flaws in the existing approach. These will be discussed below.

Bias

In many situations, there is an incentive for the forecast to represent personal, political, or self-serving organizational goals. This incentive may be systematic, such as might be caused by a reward system or some overt manipulation by those in control of forecasting. It may also be benign, such as sales-force optimism or a narrow view of the goals of a business by production. Whatever the cause, forecasting is often caught up in the middle of an organizational whirlwind and emerges biased in its representation of future outcomes, decreasing its accuracy considerably. (See Chapter 17.)

Credibility and Impact

Forecasting often has little impact on decision making. This may be caused by a lack of relevance of the forecast—in terms of what, when, how, and in what form such forecasts are provided. The problem may be interpersonal—as when those who prepare the forecasts and those who use them fail to communicate effectively—or the problem may be one of organizational structure where forecasting is performed at such a level that it is highly unlikely that it will ever have much impact on decision making. It is also the case that forecasters tend to concentrate on well-behaved situations that can be forecast with standard methods, and ignore the more dynamic (and often more interesting) change situations that decision makers most want to forecast.

Lack of Recent Improvements in Forecasting

Forecasting problems arise when forecasting is no longer improving. Sometimes the reason is simply that the resources committed to forecasting have become so stretched in maintaining ongoing forecasting procedures that no new development is possible. At other times, there may not be enough commitment to attain the next level of substantial progress. This also occurs when organizational change and managerial interface problems are not recognized. The remedies prescribed in Figure 16-2 run into barriers that they cannot overcome. Furthermore, these remedies probably are not helpful, even if accepted by the organization.

Lack of a Firm Base on which to Build

This is generally a getting-started problem. Resources or emphasis committed to forecasting may be insufficient for substantial impact. Even when the resources have been committed, knowledge of good forecasting practice and available methods may be lacking during startup. This problem may also result from an absence of any systematic strategy or plan for improving forecasting.

Recognition of Major Opportunities for Improvement in the Present Approach

Organizations frequently describe their forecasting problems in terms of opportunities for substantial improvements. They may be quite satisfied with what is being done, but feel that more could be done. This would be the case if certain areas were not being handled systematically as part of the forecasting system or if performance was not yet at the expected level. Organizations may also feel this way when they think their forecasting approach is extremely vulnerable to changes in the environment or when changes in their strategy may require (be contingent on) significant improvements in forecasting performance.

The *second step* in the author's framework for improving forecasting performance is identifying alternative remedies. Many of these are not commonly thought of as solutions; nevertheless, the authors have found it helpful to view them as basic elements or conceptual building blocks for a plan of action that will help solve an organization's major forecasting problems.

Managing the Growth of Forecasting

Over the past two decades, management scientists have learned—often by sad experience—that an organization must actively manage the introduction and development of decision-making systems, such as those represented by forecasting (Hammond, 1974). Like individuals, most organizations go through stages in improving their forecasting effectiveness, as suggested in Section 16/1. These stages can be identified by the methods applied, by the level of commitment, by the range of applications, and by expectations as to forecasting performance.

Training

Training is the most common remedy as organizations attack forecasting problems. It may also be the most overrated. The emphasis should not be on increasing the forecaster's knowledge of sophisticated methods, since doing so does not necessarily lead to improved performance. Perhaps the training should consider such issues as how to select a time horizon, how to choose the length of a time period, how judgment can be incorporated into a quantitative forecast, how large changes in the environment can be monitored, and the level of aggregation to be forecast. Users of forecasts need training in the pros and cons of alternative methods and in the identification of situations where systematic forecasting can have a major role in improving organizational decision making. Finally, training may help in refining one's approach to implementation.

Supporting the Forecasters

Support for forecasting can be divided into three areas: organizational support, including top-management attention; data processing, particularly the development of software programs that will make the forecaster's job easier; and support of data procurement and handling.

Evaluating Performance

The authors' experiences indicate that published works by statisticians often use accuracy as the single performance criterion for all forecasting situations, and many decision makers and forecasters agree with that criterion. However, few organizations measure or use accuracy as a performance criterion in practice. As staff members, most forecasters feel much more comfortable if evaluated on their process rather than on the results of their performance. When forecasters evaluate the state of their organization's forecasting, they focus on the methods used and not on the success of the forecasts (Wheelwright and Clarke, 1976). Decision makers, on the other hand, relate the state of their organization's forecasting not only to the methods used but also, just as importantly, to the accuracy of the forecasts and with their use of those forecasts. To be effective, performance criteria should be agreed on and used consistently by forecasters and by decision makers.

Defining a Forecaster's Job

A forecaster's job definition should have the traditional description of authority and responsibility and should also include the decision makers' expectations regarding forecasting. A forecaster needs to see a career path and to know the benefits and risks of accepting such an assignment.

Defining the Forecasting Function

Just as a forecaster needs to decide what to forecast and how to do that, specifying the interface of forecasting with planning and budgeting and other organizational control systems is also important. Finally, the contribution of forecasting in strategy formulation needs to be defined.

Incorporating Redundancy in Forecasts

One way to improve forecasting is to develop checks and balances within an organization by providing redundancy in forecasting. This allows double checking, which can contribute to eliminating bias and mistakes in forecasts. Furthermore, it may serve as a basis for gaining commitment from decision makers on resulting forecasts. The frequently cited top-down versus bottom-up concern might appropriately be rephrased as a question of redundancy: Who will use which approach? This ensures different approaches to what is being forecast, the level at which it is done, and the approaches used, thus providing additional reliability.

In specific instances, these seven means of solving forecasting problems may need augmentation. However, combining these elements into a plan of action can take many forms. Table 16-4 suggests one combination that some organizations have found effective in improving forecasting performance.

TABLE 16-4 A FRAMEWORK FOR MATCHING FORECASTING PROBLEMS AND SOLUTIONS

Major Classes of Problems	Major Elements of Solutions
Bias, gaming, negotiating, politics	Incentives for forecasters • Rewards • Punishments
Credibility, impact	Relevance of forecasts • When, where and how Interpersonal • Users and preparers Organizational • Positioning
Lack of improvement plateaued, stale	Resource commitment Development plan
Base of experience, data, knowledge	Getting started Good practice Forecasting strategy
Major weaknesses, opportunities to improve	Response to change • Environment Completeness

Source: Makridakis, S., and S. C. Wheelwright. 1981. "Forecasting an Organization's Futures," in *Handbook of Organizational Design,* P. C. Nystrom and W. H. Starbuck (eds.). New York: Oxford University Press. Reprinted by permission.

16/2/2 Additional Perspectives on Organizational Forecasting

While the authors have developed the preceding framework as one that they feel particularly comfortable with, there recently have been other authors who have tackled the same issues but come up with different approaches. Two of these approaches seem to have been particularly effective in practice and thus deserve mention at this point. One is that outlined by Armstrong (1978, 1982). Armstrong's approach starts with a basic audit of the existing forecasting situation. Table 16-5 summarizes the checklist that he suggests be used. (Some of the exercises at the end of this chapter describe settings where Armstrong's checklist might well be applied.)

Underlying Armstrong's audit checklist is the notion that both forecasters and the decision makers who use their forecasts tend to do a number of things "wrong," which detracts from realizing the full potential for their organization. As suggested in Table 16-5, Armstrong has identified 16 pitfalls that are characteristic of mistakes in using forecasting often seen in practice. Table 16-5 also suggests (in the form of a question) the solution for each of those mistakes. As indicated in this checklist, a firm that can answer yes to each one of those solution questions is doing an outstanding job of avoiding the mistakes and getting the most out of its forecasting applications. The larger the percentage of "no" responses for a given situation, the more things are being done incorrectly and the greater the opportunity to improve significantly the way the forecasting situation is being handled.

Another author who has suggested a checklist for guiding the realization of forecasting's full potential is Hoffman (1975). His checklist, originally developed to deal with a range of operations research applications, is particularly applicable to forecasting situations. Unlike Armstrong's approach, which starts with an audit of the existing situation, Hoffman's approach is aimed at directing major new application of forecasting and effectively guiding its marketing and selling as a project activity. The steps suggested by Hoffman are summarized in Table 16-6.

The first step in Hoffman's approach is that of market research. This involves determining what is wanted so it can be coordinated with what it is possible to deliver. Since the literature is replete with applications of technical problem-solving techniques in which either the wrong problem was solved or a problem was solved that was of little or no value to the potential user, this first step of marketing research is particularly critical. A part of this might well be an audit of existing forecasting procedures along the lines suggested by Armstrong.

The second step is that of product design—developing a forecasting product that will meet the customer's (decision maker's) wants. Central to this step is reaching agreement between the forecaster and the user as to the product to be delivered, its specifications, and the performance standards that will be used to evaluate it. It's also important to avoid what might be

TABLE 16-5 ARMSTRONG'S FORECASTING AUDIT CHECKLIST

1. *Assess the methods without the forecasts.* Most of the discussion should focus on the methods. Which forecasting methods were considered, and which ones were used? The auditor is in a good position, as an outside observer, to say whether the methods are reasonable. (See checklist items 1 through 8.)
2. Given that the methods are judged reasonable, *what assumptions and data were used in the forecast?* (This step may be difficult to separate from the previous step.) One role of the auditor is to judge whether all relevant factors have been examined. In particular, the auditors might help to ensure that key environmental factors have been assessed. (See items 9 through 11.)
3. *An assessment should be made of uncertainty.* This should include upper and lower bounds for each forecast, contingency forecasts, previous accuracy, and the arguments *against* each forecast. Interestingly, in a study on long-range metals forecasts, Rush and Page found that while 22 percent of the 27 forecasts published from 1910 to 1940 made explicit references to uncertainties, only 8 percent of the 63 studies from 1940 to 1964 did so. In other words, the concern over uncertainty *decreased* over time. (See items 12 through 15.)
4. Finally, an *assessment should be made of costs.* (See item 16.)

Forecasting Methods	No	?	Yes
1. Forecast independent of top management?	___	___	___
2. Forecast used objective methods?	___	___	___
3. Structured techniques used to obtain judgments?	___	___	___
4. Least expensive experts used?	___	___	___
5. More than one method used to obtain forecasts?	___	___	___
6. Users understand the forecasting methods?	___	___	___
7. Forecasts free of judgmental revisions?	___	___	___
8. Separate documents prepared for plans and forecasts?	___	___	___
Assumptions and Data			
9. Ample budget for analysis and presentation of data?	___	___	___
10. Central data bank exists?	___	___	___
11. Least expensive macroeconomic forecasts used?	___	___	___
Uncertainty			
12. Upper and lower bounds provided?	___	___	___
13. Quantitative analysis of previous accuracy?	___	___	___
14. Forecasts prepared for alternative futures?	___	___	___
15. Arguments listed *against* each forecast?	___	___	___
Costs			
16. Amount spent on forecasting reasonable?	___	___	___

Source: Armstrong, J. S. 1982. "The Forecasting Audit," Chapter 32, *The Handbook of Forecasting.* S. Makridakis and S. C. Wheelwright (eds.). New York: John Wiley & Sons, Inc. Reprinted by permission.

TABLE 16-6   BASIC ELEMENTS OF MARKETING FORECASTING

Market Research—Determining what the decision maker (customer) wants.
1. The customer's goal is *not* to keep the forecaster in business.
2. The customer doesn't always know what he or she wants. The customer who does know, may be unwilling to tell the forecaster what it is.
3. What the customer says is wanted and what is actually wanted may be two different things.
4. What the customer wants may not be what the customer needs.

Product Design—Developing a product that will satisfy the customer's wants. In addition to the product itself, product design includes:
1. Price
2. Delivery
3. Convenience
4. Style

Selling—Convincing the customer that the product will satisfy his or her wants at acceptable cost. The important steps in selling include:
1. Qualifying the prospective customer.
2. Establishing the forecaster's credibility.
3. Knowing the customer.
4. Knowing the product.
5. Selling benefits not features. (It should be noted that features usually increase cost, while benefits increase value.)
6. Taking the order. (One of the most prevalent failings of salespersons is not asking for the order.)

Product Creation
1. Develop the product as agreed upon.
2. Get customer input on major options identified during product development.
3. Continue to market the product actually being developed.

Delivery—Delivering a product that meets the customer's wants:
1. As specified and as expected
2. On time
3. At quoted cost

Service—Ensuring that the product continues to meet the customer's wants.
1. Maintenance
2. Postaudit of costs and benefits
3. Identification of new wants and opportunities arising from use of the product (Repeat the entire cycle.)

Source: G. M. Hoffman, "Selling Operations Research to Management," presented at TIMS/ORSA '75, Chicago, April 30–May 2, 1975. Reprinted by permission.

termed technological overkill. Woolsey (1975, p. 169) has hypothesized the following law in this regard: "A manager would rather live with a problem that he cannot tolerate than use a solution he cannot understand."

The third step is that of selling—convincing the customer that the product will satisfy the customer's needs and wants. As suggested in Table 16-6, in order to qualify the prospect, the forecaster must determine whether the customer has the authority to buy the product and whether the customer has the inclination to buy. If the latter requirement is not met, it may not be worth the effort to try to change the customer's mind, and it may be better to seek initial applications elsewhere. To establish credibility, the forecaster must rely on past successes, establish a history of fulfilling promises, and acknowledge incidents of failure when they occur.

Perhaps one of the most important aspects of selling a product is selling benefits and not features. Features include such things as the sophistication and intricacies of the model to be used in forecasting. The benefits (the manager's real concern) include the impact of the forecast in that particular decision-making situation, the kinds of risks that improved forecasting will be able to reduce, and the time that accurate forecasts may be able to save the decision maker. Other benefits might include helping the decision maker to identify a broader range of options and aiding in the implementation of specific decisions being pursued.

The final stage of the selling step—one that is usually done badly, particularly by forecasters—is taking the order. This requires getting the specifications down in writing, before the product is built. The forecaster must know when to stop selling (rather than forcing the manager to listen to a complete presentation) and when to take no for an answer.

The fourth step suggested by Hoffman is developing a product to be delivered. In many management science applications, the product development is fairly removed from the management user. However, in most forecasting situations, that is not practical. A series of interactions between the forecaster and the manager are required to effectively complete the definition of the product and insure that the manager understands the product, its use and its benefits by the time the step is completed.

The fifth step of delivering the product involves being certain that it has been adequately tested and validated before being turned over to the manager. As with any product, the forecasting application must be delivered on time and within budget if the manager is to be fully satisfied.

The final step is that of ongoing service. This involves maintaining (including debugging and making minor modifications) and performing postaudits of the application's costs and benefits. Two important aspects of this step are that the user must have solid reinforcement to support the changes in behavior required for its application, and the forecasting group must recognize the additional opportunities and needs that exist, once an initial application has been made. This final step of service often becomes the first step of market research for the next forecasting application.

16/2/3 Behavioral Change and the Implementation of Forecasting Systems

In the final analysis, the behavior of individuals within the company will determine the success or failure of any attempt to establish an effective forecasting function. Individuals involved with forecasting will have to alter their behavior to perform the tasks required and take full advantage of the results obtained. While an extensive literature exists on the accomplishment of such behavioral change, one very effective framework that has stood the test of time is that developed by Kurt Lewin (1947) and expanded by Ed Schein (1961). Lewin's and Schein's framework for behavioral change is based on a three-step model.

1. *Unfreezing*. First, the person whose behavior is to be changed must perceive a need for making that change. This need can arise either because the individual feels some aspect of his or her behavior is inadequate, or because the individual identifies the opportunity to improve that behavior.

2. *Change*. The second step in Schein's model is the change itself. Here the person must see the change as his or her own and must incorporate that change into individual behavior patterns. This step requires that the person be fully involved in implementing the change.

3. *Refreezing*. The final step is that of refreezing. The change that has been made in the second step must be personally incorporated into the individual's everyday pattern of behavior. Effective refreezing insures that the individual will not easily go back to his or her former behavioral pattern.

An example of how unfreezing, change, and refreezing applies will help to illustrate its relevance in managing the forecasting function. One such example comes from a course in speed reading called *Reading Dynamics*. This course advertises that readers can triple their reading speed within a very short period of time. To unfreeze the individual, the Reading Dynamics Institute offers free introductory sessions to demonstrate how easy it is to improve reading speed and to convince the individual of the need to make such an improvement. The Institute then offers teaching sessions on speed reading techniques in which the individual makes the behavioral changes required for faster reading. Finally, for refreezing, the Institute offers "whip" sessions or refresher sessions aimed at reinforcing the individual's use of the technique and insuring that old reading habits do not return.

This three-step process of unfreezing, change, and refreezing can be used to make the forecasting function more effective. Many of the problems outlined earlier in this chapter can be traced to a failure at one of these three stages of behavioral change. For example, the failure of a manager to use the forecast in making decisions might well be the result of a weak refreezing following the change in behavior. The manager may be well aware of the need for forecasting and may feel that the forecasting procedure is appropriate, but perhaps has not followed the procedure for a sufficient length of time (with needed support) to insure appropriate refreezing. Alternatively, a forecasting roadblock may arise in the collection of data in a timely fashion. Such a problem might occur when those implementing the forecasting system fail to make those who collect the data feel that the need to get the data on time is of personal importance. If the clerk or accountant who gathers the data does not feel personally that the required change in procedures is worth the trouble (perhaps because it was proposed by someone else and is not fully understood), the change is unlikely to be carried out effectively.

Many of the suggestions included in Hoffman's checklist, as well as the sixteen pitfalls and solutions identified by Armstrong, can be tied directly to one of these three stages in the change process. An organizational behaviorist who has recently sought to bridge the gap even more directly between organizational and behavioral change research and the practice of forecasting is Taylor (1982). Taylor's work is particularly useful to those concerned with their own skills and abilities with regard to the behavioral side of forecasting applications. This topic is pursued further in Chapter 19.

16/3 Managing a Forecasting System[3]

Like any other managment task, forecasting can benefit significantly from the development of an effective plan of action. This might well include the development of a forecasting strategy for an organization. A strategy is nothing more than a carefully developed method for marshalling limited resources to achieve specific goals. The development of a forecasting strategy requires (1) the specification of forecasting objectives, (2) the identification of the available data and scientific resources, (3) the selection of forecasting methodologies that will effectively utilize the available resources, and (4) a control or performance evaluation procedure to monitor progress toward achieving the specified goals.

These phenomena must be understood if a sophisticated forecasting system is to evolve, but they are not basically "forecasting" questions—they are important questions in their own right.

Ultimately, it is research and policy analysis, not forecasting methods and capacities, which will dictate levels of disaggregation, choice of methodology, and the variables to be forecast.

In sum, it is our conclusion that managing a forecasting system through formulation of strategic goals, identification of managerial options, and implementation of tactical decisions can do much to loosen the serious intellectual, data, organizational and methodological constraints that currently limit forecasting advances.

---

[3]Parts of this section are adapted from "Managing a Forecasting System," by Robert A. Leone and Steven C. Wheelwright, in *Applications of Management Science*, Vol. 1, Randall L. Schultz (ed.). Greenwich, Conn., JAI Press, 1981, pp. 139–60. Reprinted by permission.

In the remainder of this section, three different forecasting *systems* will be examined. These come from very different settings, but as will be seen, their development and application require that several common issues be addressed by each. These three systems will be used to illustrate some of the management concerns that must be addressed in forecasting—beyond the selection and application of a forecasting methodology—and some of the common pitfalls to be avoided.

16/3/1   Examples of Three Forecasting Systems

Labor Forecasting System[4]

Focus   This forecasting system was developed for the State of Michigan to follow up the recommendations of a "job needs" study prepared in 1973. (The job needs study had identified the importance of providing a balanced work force in a number of different sectors if the long-term growth possibilities for Michigan's industrial sector were to be realized.) This system is designed to forecast the level of demand for building and construction trade craft labor (measured in terms of number of employees in each of nine critical construction crafts); it also forecasts the number of new employees required to fill these positions based on the 1970 supply of workers in each category. The study provided these results on a statewide level and also for each of ten regions within the state. As constructed, this forecasting system typifies efforts to disaggregate economic forecasts into their component parts.

Elements of the Labor Forecasting System   The Michigan system is composed of five elements. First, an econometric model for the entire state and individual econometric models for each region, forecast employment levels for major industries. These econometric models relate aggregate employment activity to population growth, general economic activity, and, more specifically, to growth forecasts for the state's major export sectors based on exogenously determined "national demands." To account for the uncertainty present in the projections, each econometric model is evaluated using pessimistic, most likely, and optimistic input data. The results are low, medium, and high employment projections for each major industry, including construction. These econometric models ignore both seasonal and cyclical patterns in construction labor demand; rather, only long-term trends are considered.

These aggregate employment forecasts are then converted into fore-

---

[4]This description is based on the "Michigan Building and Construction Trades Craft Manpower Study," prepared for the Citizens' Research Council of Michigan by Dr. John W. Mattila, Professor of Economics, and James R. Moor, Jr., doctoral candidate in economics, both of Wayne State University, Report No. 245 (April, 1974).

casts by trade category using a top-down approach which disaggregates them into the nine crafts being considered, plus an "other" category. This disaggregation is accomplished using an industry/occupation matrix obtained from 1970 pension fund data, adjusted (based mainly on judgmental inputs) for technological change and other anticipated shifts in the mix of demand for different labor crafts.

The third element adjusts these disaggregate forecasts for the number of new laborers who will be needed due to growth in demand and attrition and retirement of the existing labor supply. This step utilizes surviving-cohort methods to adjust 1970 labor supply figures for retirements. Additionally, in three regions large power plant construction projects were anticipated during the 1970s and thus some judgmental input was made to these demand requirements.

The fourth element in this forecasting system determines disaggregated labor requirements for the years between 1970 and the forecast period by computing the average annual growth rate, based on actual 1970 supply and forecast demand.

The final step in this system compares existing levels of apprenticeship programs with forecast needs for new laborers to identify any gaps between supply and demand. Presumably, these gap forecasts can then be used to determine requirements for additional training programs.

Reliability of Findings   The designers of this system felt that determining the reliability of their findings was an important part of their overall project. They sought to establish reliability by carefully checking and evaluating each step in the forecasting system to make sure that it was statistically correct. Additionally, they sought to provide a range of forecasts for each labor category to indicate to potential users the degree of uncertainty in their projections. They also sought to test the sensitivity of their results to changes in exogenous variables in the various econometric models. Finally, their report noted a number of assumptions that might bias their results. In sum, they sought to make potential users aware of the many limitations in the approach they had taken.

Key Aspects of the Labor Forecasting System   This forecasting system has several key characteristics, each with attendant strengths and weaknesses:

- The designers used the same approach to obtain forecasts for the entire state and its component regions, thus allowing a check of the internal consistency of the forecasts for the state and its regions. It is interesting to note that while the designers of this system could have used the state projections to corroborate the combined results of the regional projection and vice versa, there is no indication that they chose to do so.

- The evaluation of the system made by the designers was based largely on the *process* they had followed and not on the accuracy or reasonableness of the resulting forecasts, although in several instances the designers altered their initial approaches in the light of untenable forecasts.
- A top-down approach was used to disaggregate total construction labor forecasts into individual trade craft forecasts.
- A top-down approach was also used to translate a single 10-year forecast into forecasts for intervening years. Such an approach can be misleading given the cyclical nature of the industry.
- The econometric models provided direct estimates of construction labor, and *did not* project the dollar value of construction. Since labor is a derived demand, it might be better to forecast directly the primary demand figure and then systematically disaggregate.
- The purpose of this study was clearly specified at the outset and was used throughout by the designers as a guide to what was worthwhile, and to determine whether they were on the right track.
- The methodologies employed were mainly econometric, although trend analysis was used to forecast the industry/occupation matrix for each region.
- The designers sought to verify input data with alternate sources and generally sought expert judgment whenever possible.
- To account for the uncertainty of their forecasts, the system designers reported forecasts for three different macroeconomic scenarios. Unfortunately, the study is unclear as to precisely what macro variables were altered and why. While it is important to include such sensitivity analysis in a longer-term forecasting effort, it is equally important that the alternative scenarios be carefully developed.

Fleet Requirements Forecasting System[5]

Focus   The purpose of this forecasting system is to provide forecasts of fleet requirements from 1975 through the year 2000 in 5-year increments by type of ship and by region. The system assumes that supply will meet demand; thus the change in supply for each ship category is calculated rather mechanistically without regard to the economics of supply.

Elements of the Fleet Requirements Forecasting System   This system is composed of five elements. The starting point is a set of shipping demand

---

See "A Methodology for Forecasting the Fleets to Service U.S. International Commercial Trade Until the Year 2000" by Henry S. Marcus, Michael L. Sclar, Randall E. Wise, and James A. Lisnyck, a paper presented to the Society of Naval Architects and Marine Engineers Annual Meeting, New York, November 11–13, 1976 (Paper No. 11).

forecasts (in dollars) by type of product. There might be as many as two to three dozen types of products included in this base forecast. The forecasts are developed by an econometric model designed expressly for that purpose.

The second element of this system allocates the national forecasts of dollar shipments by type (for the fifth year of 5-year periods) to the individual regions. This top-down approach yields regional forecasts in dollars of shipping activity.

The third element in this system converts the regional forecasts of dollar-level shipping activity into the number of ships required by each individual product category. This is done using historical conversion patterns with minor modifications for observed trends. In practice, these modifications are not significant, and essentially the same conversion factors that have held in the recent past are used through the year 2000.

The fourth element in this system estimates withdrawals from the supply of ships during each 5-year interval. Since it is assumed that all demand by category will be met, these withdrawals are sensitive to the level of demand existing in each forecast period. The supply of ships in 1975 by equipment (fleet) category is exogenous.

The final element estimates the additions to each equipment category needed to fill the forecast gap between supply and demand. These last two steps are actually performed in an iterative fashion as the time horizon is extended to the year 2000.

An important characteristic of this forecasting system is that it distinguishes three databases upon which the system is built. The first database contains the results of the initial econometric model: forecasts of shipping dollar activity for each fifth year by type of product. A second database relates requirements for individual equipment categories to dollars of activity for each type of product. The third database is the equipment supply matrix that starts with actual 1975 data and is then periodically updated.

Reliability of Findings   The designers of this forecasting system made no attempt to test the accuracy of the basic forecasts of shipping dollar activity by type of product. Rather, emphasis was placed on the disaggregation of these forecasts by region and the conversion of dollar forecasts into ship requirements. The designers did evaluate individual segments of the system, but did not do so statistically. Rather, they evaluated the process they had to use to determine whether they had used it correctly; they also relied heavily on experts to evaluate judgmentally the reasonableness of their results.

Key Aspects of the Fleet Requirements Forecasting System   This forecasting system has a number of identifying characteristics, each representing relative strengths and weaknesses:

- The designers considered the level of detail a key strength of the system. Some of that detail, however, came simply from using a top-down approach; for example, regional forecasts were merely disaggregated national forecasts. Other detail came from a bottom-up approach; for example, the disaggregated ship supply forecasts were based on detailed surviving cohort estimations.
- This system assumed that ships were perfectly mobile. Thus, while demand was projected regionally, supply was balanced at the national level and then allocated to the regions where demand occurred.
- This forecasting system used judgmental inputs to adjust trends and modify results when the latter were markedly inconsistent with what experts had expected.
- The designers of this system were also potential users. This compensated, in part, for the lack of system focus at the outset, since they adapted the system as they proceeded, based on their own assessment of forecasting needs.
- In making choices about the elements of this system, the designers opted for reasonableness and understandability, rather than sophistication.

Construction Forecasting System[6]

Focus The third forecasting system we wish to describe is a major element in the comprehensive construction labor market information system for the Kansas City standard metropolitan statistical area. The overall system includes the collection of four important data components: construction industry characteristics, past trends in the industry, labor demand, and labor supply. This system also includes established procedures for periodic updating of the information and for identifying and evaluating alternative methods for disseminating that information.

The system itself was motivated by the "national need" to control construction cost increases. Accurate forecasts of the supply and demand for labor by trade craft category were considered essential to this task. The remainder of this description relates only to the forecasting components of this overall system.

Elements of the Construction Forecasting System The forecasting approach used in this system can be divided into two unrelated parts. The

---

[6]This system is based on "Construction Labor Market Information System: Kansas City SMSA",—Vols. I, II, and III, by Dr. Darwin W. Daicoff, Professor of Economics, University of Kansas, Lawrence, Kansas, prepared for the Research and Information Department, Employment Security Division, Kansas Department of Labor and Manpower Administration, United States Department of Labor (August, 1973).

first is a short-term system for forecasting labor demand by trade craft category. That system starts with a data base containing current and proposed construction projects in terms of dollar level of activity. The data sources are the *Dodge Reports* and the *Peters Reports*. The system also provides an alternative approach to obtain those dollar values of construction activities which is based on trend forecasting using the Box-Jenkins approach (time-series analysis). These short-term dollar forecasts of construction activity by month are then converted to labor requirements by selecting an appropriate "profile" for each project. This profile shows labor requirements by craft type over the life of the project. The result is a set of monthly labor forecasts by trade craft category for each project. These are aggregated to yield regional forecasts by labor category.

The second component of this forecasting system is completely unrelated to the short-term forecast. This long-term forecasting component gives annual forecasts based on an econometric model which forecasts the dollar level of construction activity. These dollar forecasts are converted to total labor hours based on estimates of the hours of construction labor per thousand dollars of construction activity. Once total labor hours are obtained, those are broken down using a top-down approach which splits the total into individual requirements by trade craft category.

Reliability of Findings   While the system makes possible the use of alternative methodologies and approaches to obtaining the desired forecasts, there is no systematic effort to corroborate the result of any single approach. Rather, the system has been developed independent of decision making, and thus no real tests of the results appear possible. It is also clear that no major judgmental input has been included, but rather it is assumed that such judgment will be brought to bear by the decision maker using the system. The designers of this system seem to have been more concerned with establishing the feasibility of their own procedures than establishing the utility of their forecasts.

Key Aspects of the Construction Forecasting System   The characteristics of this system have a number of strengths and weaknesses:

- The system is statistically very sophisticated, as is illustrated by the use of Box-Jenkins time-series techniques.
- While the system designers have recognized a need for improvement based on experience, they limit those improvements to parameters of the system, implicitly assuming that the underlying methodological approach will not require improvements based on experience.
- While checks and balances are available, they are viewed as technical options useful for determining the internal consistency of system calculations. They are not viewed as tools for verification and validation of the system's results.

- No judgmental inputs are used in preparing the forecasts.
- The major emphasis in this system is on short-term forecasting. The long-term forecasts appear to be an afterthought or add-on to the system, rather than a major portion of the system's purpose.

16/3/2   Major Decisions in Forecasting System Design

It is clear from the examples above that there are several major decisions that must be made in designing forecasting systems. Based on the examples above and also on our own experience, we describe below six major decision areas and associated pitfalls that designers often encounter when developing a forecasting system. While some of these have been touched on individually in earlier chapters, our intent here is to illustrate how these issues arise in practice (at least in these three systems) and to show how they are related to one another.

Focus and Purpose

The initial question confronting designers of a forecasting system relates to the focus and purpose of that system. All too often this question is addressed after the system has been designed. The difficulty—and the necessity—of answering this question initially results from the fact that tradeoffs must always be made in system design and development.

As Figure 16-3 shows, in the examples outlined above, very different approaches were taken in defining the focus and purpose. In the Labor Forecasting System, focus was determined by a previous study. In the Fleet Requirements Forecasting System, the preparers of the system were also potential users, and thus the preliminary definition of focus and purpose was not as important, since they could let that definition evolve as they developed the system. In the Construction Forecasting System, system design and system use were completely separate. Only general guidelines were developed as to purpose and focus. Lack of focus, it is worth noting, did not hinder the development of a methodologically sophisticated forecasting system. In this third case, it appears that the sacrifice of a specific decision focus was the price paid to obtain a system that was ostensibly general in purpose.

The failure to understand the purpose and focus of a forecasting system may be the most common pitfall confronted by systems designers. This danger may be compounded in "general purpose" or "integrated" forecasting systems. This assertion is based on the simple premise that it is difficult for a single forecasting system to be all (or even many) things for all users. Indeed, where there are such scale economies in forecasting, the private sector often responds by providing a marketable service. Macroeconomic

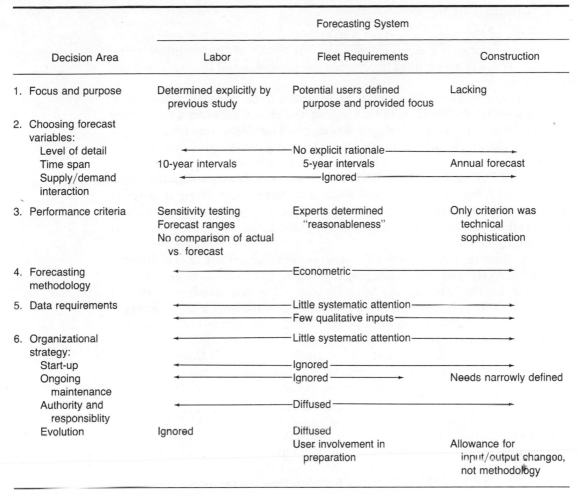

	Forecasting System		
Decision Area	Labor	Fleet Requirements	Construction
1. Focus and purpose	Determined explicitly by previous study	Potential users defined purpose and provided focus	Lacking
2. Choosing forecast variables:			
Level of detail	←————————— No explicit rationale ————————→		
Time span	10-year intervals	5-year intervals	Annual forecast
Supply/demand interaction	←—————————— Ignored ————————→		
3. Performance criteria	Sensitivity testing Forecast ranges No comparison of actual vs. forecast	Experts determined "reasonableness"	Only criterion was technical sophistication
4. Forecasting methodology	←————————— Econometric ————————→		
5. Data requirements	←————— Little systematic attention —————→		
	←————— Few qualitative inputs —————→		
6. Organizational strategy:	←————— Little systematic attention —————→		
Start-up	←————————— Ignored ————————→		
Ongoing maintenance	←————————— Ignored ————————→		Needs narrowly defined
Authority and responsiblity	←————————— Diffused ————————→		
Evolution	Ignored	Diffused User involvement in preparation	Allowance for input/output changoo, not methodology

FIGURE 16-3 MAJOR DECISION AREAS IN DEVELOPING A FORECAST-ING SYSTEM: THREE EXAMPLES

forecasts and some industry-specific forecasts fit this model. Firm-specific forecasting systems, virtually by definition, ought to reflect the unique competitive and economic situation of the firm, whether this uniqueness stems from geography, market niche, or some other firm attribute.

The interest in all-purpose systems may well result from the technical allure of such a system and not its economy or usefulness. To yield to such temptations is to acknowledge the dysfunctional division between users and forecasters. This is not to condemn large and complex forecasting models, but merely to stress that the demand for such systems should be predicated on usefulness, not availability.

Choosing the Forecast Variables

One of the most important and crucial decisions in the articulation of a sound forecasting strategy concerns the choice of the variables to be forecast. There is also a need to consider the level of detail that can usefully be forecast.

Closely related to the choice of variables to be forecast is the choice of time span of the forecast. In this regard, the choice between a period (for example, year-by-year) forecasting strategy, a long-term time horizon forecast (for example, for 10 years out, using a simple rule to split that forecast among intervening years), and a cumulative forecasting strategy are all important alternatives. Cumulative forecasts can often simplify the problem of modifying forecasts based on recent experience. Thus, it may be possible to forecast a long-term trend with some degree of accuracy and then examine cumulative deviations from that trend to identify potential near-term problems.

As Figure 16-3 shows, all three systems described above forecast demand directly and then disaggregate the results as needed. In terms of time span for the forecast, the labor forecasting system predicted demand at 10-year intervals. Forecasts for intervening years were simply interpolations of each 10-year forecast. In the Fleet Requirements System, the forecast period was 5 years. The Construction Forecasting System developed and updated an annual forecast on a periodic basis. In all three instances some forecasts were based on a top-down approach, while others were based on a bottom-up approach. There was no explicit rationale for any of these choices.

In choosing forecast variables, systems designers often ignore important interactions of key factors. Indeed, there is a common tendency to focus attention solely on issues of demand to the neglect of issues of supply. It is interesting to note, for example, that none of the three systems we examined considered supply or the *interaction* between that supply and demand.[7] It is not at all clear to us that these two factors are completely separable. Rather, it might be more useful to consider, as a subpart of the system, the way in which they interact and how that might be incorporated to affect the demand forecasts that are developed.

Specification of Performance Criteria

To be of full value, the credibility of a forecast must be determinable. Thus, a forecasting strategy must consider the set of criteria that will be

---

[7]This is not an artifact of our selection process but a common characteristic of forecasting systems.

used to measure the performance of the forecasting system. Important strategic issues in this area include the kinds of accuracy that are sought and the ways in which accuracy will be measured. There must also be some built-in cross-checks, and some redundancy so that users can calibrate the credibility of the forecast for their own individual purposes. A range of criteria was used in the three case examples to determine the reliability of the forecasts provided by each system, as Figure 16-3 shows.

When identifying performance criteria, it is important to recognize, as outlined earlier in this chapter, that there are major differences between the criteria that users of a forecasting system and the criteria designers and developers (preparers) of such a system attempt to satisfy. Recognition of these differences is important in forecasting system design. On the one hand, the final product should complement the reasonable expectations of both preparer and user; on the other hand, efforts should be made to alter unreasonable expectations before they destroy the system's credibility. This suggests the need for direct user involvement in the design and development of a forecasting system and its performance criteria.

Among the three forecasting systems described previously, the Labor and Fleet Requirements systems attempted to accommodate some user perceptions, but the Construction system took no account of user perceptions at all. In practice, the accommodation of user and preparer perceptions may require little more than an explicit consideration of the intended uses of the forecasts prior to system construction. Or, put another way, there is a need for some overlap between what the preparers consider their role in developing the forecast and the forecasting system, and what the users see as their role in using that system in decision making and planning.

Additionally, our three examples demonstrated that there is a real danger that system performance evaluations will be based on process and methodology criteria, not on the forecasting results. The exception was the Fleet Requirements System where designers did use expert opinion to evaluate the reasonableness of their results and procedures.

When specifying performance criteria, it is important to recognize that checks and balances are helpful to a forecasting system. These not only serve to validate and challenge the resulting forecasts, but also serve as the basis for user discussions of the strengths and weaknesses of the forecasts. Such checks and balances might be thought of as built-in system redundancy.

These checks and balances can be in the form of different methodological approaches to the same forecasting problem—for example, different cuts at the problem as in the case of *both* a top-down and a bottom-up approach to disaggregated forecasts. Alternatively, redundancy might come in the form of judgmental inputs which augment quantitative inputs, or it might involve the application of a similar methodology to different sets of survey data.

Choice of Forecasting Methodologies

In evaluating a forecasting strategy, there are important questions to be asked regarding the appropriateness of econometric forecasting techniques and the potential of alternative methods. For example, a cumulative forecasting strategy, if deemed desirable, might rest on time-series projections, with deviations being amenable to analysis using more mechanistic techniques, such as exponential smoothing and tracking signals. Similarly, if the long-term strategy dictates the forecasting of conversion factors, one might address this problem by examining trends using a time-series approach, estimating production relationships using an econometric approach, or examining emerging technological changes using a structural approach.

In all three of the forecasting systems presented previously, Figure 16-3 shows that the starting point was an econometric model that would provide forecasts of demand. Based on that econometric methodology and its results, all three of the systems then made some use of time-series analysis, and two of the three also made extensive use of judgmental techniques. Only the third system failed to make extensive use of more qualitative techniques and relied completely on quantitative methods.

Identification of Data Requirements

Because data collection is costly, there are often pressures to economize in this area. For example, it would seem an obvious economy to use short-term forecasting information as the basis for a long-term forecasting model. From a strategic viewpoint, it is essential to evaluate the extent to which it is productive to apply long-term forecasting methodologies to short-term data. In this regard, it is important to restate the obvious: a long-run forecast is not merely a serial repetition of a short-run forecasting model. The ability to forecast short-run movements will not lend credibility to a set of long-term forecasts. Like any system, a forecasting process is only as strong as its weakest link, so care must be taken to ensure that data quality is matched with the need of the forecast methodology.

A database designed to satisfy immediate needs may make compromises in quality and coverage not necessary—or even destructive—to a long-run forecast. Thus, someone developing a short-run forecasting model in the construction industry might opt for F. W. Dodge data, as was the case in the Construction system because they are available quickly; on the other hand, a model might opt to utilize census data, which may be acquired only with some time lag, but with offsetting advantages in detail, consistency, and coverage.

Similarly, even if data on current (and past) projections were used as the database for the long-term forecast, a number of questions remain regarding the level of aggregation appropriate when using such data and the length of history that is necessary. Also important are questions concerning the identification and use of external data sources that can complement existing databases.

In all three systems described previously, the designers say very little as to the amount of historical data necessary to validate their forecasts (see Figure 16-3). In fact, it would appear in each instance that the designers simply got as much data as they could and did not address the question as to whether that was sufficient.

Development of an Organizational Strategy

The five preceding questions relate to specific forecasting techniques and data requirements. We feel strongly that a forecasting strategy should also address the organizational issues that will arise in the development of the forecasting capability. For example, there are important decisions to be made regarding the system start-up. Since credibility is essential to any forecasting system, a superb system can be rendered valueless by a troubled start-up.

Similarly, the sophistication of any system is often limited more by the technical capabilities of those using it than by the boundaries of forecasting science. Forecasting problems are complex and entail considerable subtlety. There are major decisions to be made regarding tradeoffs between a system that may capture this complexity and subtlety, but which may sacrifice practical application. In the case of system III, for example, was it really appropriate to leave the addition of judgmental information to the discretion of individual users?

Lastly, since it appears that the ultimate objective is to develop an ongoing system, it is essential to consider the resource requirements of alternative forecasts. It is important to distinguish the operating resources required for maintenance and the resources initially required for system design and development.

In the three forecasting systems described previously, Figure 16-3 shows that the question of organizational strategy does not appear to have been addressed in any systematic fashion. Only in the instance of the Construction system was consideration given to ongoing maintenance of the forecasting system. However, even there the maintenance function was defined very narrowly and addressed only the acquisition of data and not the ongoing use of the system by potential decision makers.

Throughout this section we have stressed the need for focus. An important benefit of focus is that authority and responsibility for maintaining the system and insuring that its results will be compatible with the desired objectives can be more easily assigned to individuals in the organization.

When developing an organizational strategy, forecasting system designers often ignore the potential of evolutionary approaches to complex systems. Such an evolutionary approach allows the users and preparers to exchange information and experiences effectively and to interact while up-grading the system over time.

An evolutionary approach should encompass technical features of the forecasting system as well as database and report generation features. It will be recalled that our examples demonstrated that evolutionary changes are often limited to data inputs. In the Construction Forecasting System, the technical aspects of the system were designed at the current level of knowledge of the preparers, and allowance for evolution of the system related mainly to features of output format and to data inputs, not to technical evolution. This problem was largely overcome in the Fleet Requirements system because preparers and users were involved in the design and development of the system; as a consequence, much technical evolution took place as the system was developed.

16/4   Summary and Recommendations

In this chapter, we have raised a number of issues, considerations, and choices that must be made in first designing and then managing any forecasting system. Our analysis leads us to make several specific recommendations to management.

1. *Management should identify the users of the "ultimate" system and their needs and interests.* We believe strongly that user involvement throughout the entire process is essential. Our experience suggests that the user's viewpoint is most often under-represented.

2. *Management should distinguish the preparation of a forecast from data analysis and research.* In the instance of short-run forecasts, the limiting factor is often timely, accurate, and detailed information. In contrast, the major limitation to a truly sophisticated long-range forecasting system is often a poor understanding of important dynamic elements being forecast. In a market situation, for example, how geographically mobile are labor or other input resources in the long run? Does supply analysis require the same degree of geographic detail as demand analysis? How price-elastic is demand over time? Answers to these kinds of questions are important to the design of a useful forecasting system, but the answers themselves are necessarily the product of independent data analysis and research efforts. Indeed, the commitment to a forecasting system requires a parallel—and often more significant—commitment to a research program that will develop the understanding and knowledge needed for the forecasting capability to become more sophisticated and more useful over time.

3. *Management should consider the development of an evolutionary forecasting system.* If a research program is to be of any use, interim findings must be reflected in adaptations of the forecasting system. Indeed, the primitive nature of forecasting knowledge suggests that many firms may still be at a stage of development where ostensibly redundant, parallel systems are in order. Parallel efforts would simultaneously permit individual systems to maintain focus but not deny the advantages of multiple coordinated effort. Indeed, it is our suspicion that redundant forecasting efforts might be usefully paralleled by research programs that would yield important economies of scale and simultaneously guarantee the maintenance of communications channels on the individual forecasting efforts.

4. *Management should develop explicit forecasting system performance criteria for the system users and the system designers.* The existence of cross-checks would lend credibility to the forecasts from the perspective of users and identify areas of methodological improvement from the perspective of system designers. Additionally, they would aid in maintaining the appropriate focus for the system.

If taken, these actions would, in our view, go a long way toward satisfying the criteria for a good forecasting system, discussed earlier.

REFERENCES AND SELECTED BIBLIOGRAPHY

Armstrong, J. S. 1978. *Long-Range Forecasting: From Crystal Ball to Computer.* New York: Wiley-Interscience.

———. 1980. "The Seer-Sucker Theory: The Value of Experts in Forecasting," *Technology Review,* **83,** pp. 18–24.

———. 1982. "The Forecasting Audit," Chapter 32, in *Handbook of Forecasting.* S. Makridakis and S. C. Wheelwright (eds.). New York: John Wiley & Sons, Inc.

———, and M. C. Grohman. 1972. "A Comparative Study of Methods for Long-Range Market Forecasting," *Management Science,* **19,** No. 2, October, pp. 211–21.

Bell, E. C. 1968. "Practical Long-Range Planning," *Business Horizons,* December, pp. 45–49.

Daicoff, D. W. 1973. "Construction Labor Market Information System: Kansas City SMSA—Volumes I, II, and III," Research and Information Department, Employment Security Division, Kansas Department of Labor and Manpower Administration, United States Department of Labor, August.

Dalrymple, D. F. 1975a. "Sales Forecasting Methods and Accuracy," *Business Horizons,* December, pp. 69–73.

———. 1975b. "Sales Forecasting Methods and Accuracy." Working paper. Marketing Department, School of Business, Indiana University, Bloomington, Ind., September.

———. 1967. "Sales Forecasting: Is 5% Error Good Enough?" *Sales Management,* **99,** No. 14, pp. 41–48.

Hammond, J. S., III. 1974. "The Roles of the Manager and Management Scientist in Successful Implementation," *Sloan Management Review,* **15,** No. 2, pp. 1–24.

Hoffman, G. M. 1975a. "Selling Operations Research to Management." Presented at TIMS/ORSA, 1975, Chicago, April 30–May 2.

———. 1975b. "Selling Operations Research to Management." Working paper, Standard Oil Company of Indiana.

Hogarth, R. M. 1978. "A Note on Aggregating Opinions," *Organizational Behavior and Human Performance,* **21,** pp. 40–46.

Lewin, K. 1947. "Group Decision and Social Change," in *Readings in Social Psychology,* T. Newcomb and E. L. Hartley (eds.). New York: Holt, Rinehart and Winston.

McLaughlin, R. L., and J. J. Boyle. 1968. *Short-Term Forecasting.* New York: American Marketing Association.

Makridakis, S. 1971. "The Whys and Wherefores of the Systems Approach," *European Business,* No. 30, Summer, pp. 64–70.

———, and S. C. Wheelwright. 1976. *Interactive Forecasting.* 2nd ed. San Francisco: Holden-Day.

————, (eds.). 1982. *Handbook of Forecasting.* New York: John Wiley & Sons, Inc.

————. 1981. "Forecasting an Organization's Futures," Chapter 6, in *Handbook of Organizational Design,* Vol. I. P. C. Nystrom and W. H. Starbuck (eds.). New York: Oxford University Press.

Marcus, H. S., M. L. Sclar, R. E. Wise, and J. A. Lisnyk. 1976. "A Methodology for Forecasting the Fleets to Service the U.S. International Commercial Trade Until the Year 2000." Presented at Annual Meeting, Society of Naval Architects and Marine Engineers, New York, November (Paper No. 11).

Mattila, J. W., and J. R. Moor, Jr. 1974. "Michigan Building and Construction Trades Craft Manpower Study," Citizens' Research Council of Michigan, Detroit, Report No. 245, April.

Mentzer, J. T., and J. E. Cox. 1981. "Executive Familiarity and Usage of State-of-the-Art Sales Forecasting Techniques," *AMA Educator,* Summer.

Pan, J., D. R. Nichols, and O. M. Joy. 1977. "Sales Forecasting Practices in Large U.S. Industrial Firms," *Financial Management,* **6,** No. 3 (Fall), pp. 72–77.

Rothe, James T. 1978. "Effectiveness of Sales Forecasting Methods," *Industrial Marketing Management,* **7,** pp. 114–18.

Schein, E. H. 1961. "Management Development as a Process of Influence," *Industrial Management Review,* **2,** No. 2, May.

Taylor, R. N. 1982. "Organizational and Behavioral Aspects of Forecasting," in *Handbook of Forecasting,* Spyros Makridakis and S. C. Wheelwright (eds.). New York: John Wiley & Sons, Inc.

Wheelwright, S. C., and D. G. Clarke. 1976. "Corporate Forecasting: Promise and Reality," *Harvard Business Review,* **54,** No. 6, November-December, pp. 40ff.

Wheelwright, S. C., and S. Makridakis. 1980. *Forecasting Methods for Management,* 3rd ed. New York: John Wiley & Sons, Inc.

Woolsey, R. E. D., and H. F. Swanson. 1975. *Operations Research for Immediate Application: A Quick and Dirty Manual.* New York: Harper & Row.

EXERCISES

1. Recognizing what's wrong in a forecasting situation is an important step in pursuing an action program that will enable management to realize the full potential of forecasting. Consider the following company outlook forecast presented by the Chief Executive Officer of Ajax Corporation.[8]

---

[8]Armstrong, J. S. 1982. "The Forecasting Audit," Chapter 32, in *The Handbook of Forecasting.* S. Makridakis and S. C. Wheelwright (eds.). New York: John Wiley & Sons, Inc. Reprinted by permission.

Chairperson: *The next thing on the agenda is to hear Mr. Raft, our Chief Executive Officer, describe the forecast for our company.*

Raft: *Today, I present to you the annual forecast for our firm. It covers the next 5 years.*

We take this forecasting task seriously. Top management was actively involved. As they are the ones who use the forecasts, it was appropriate that they also be involved in making the forecasts.

Our industry is characterized by rapid change and a turbulent environment. In view of this, we realize that historical data provide a poor guide to the future. Rather, it is necessary to be forward looking and to use our judgment. As a result, the members of our top management team spent many hours in meetings with me to prepare these forecasts.

In the final analysis, forecasting is more of an art than a science; nothing can currently replace experience and good judgment. Therefore, we sought out the best judgment. We hired one of the top economic consultants and obtained his opinions on the economic future of our firm.

We sought to use the best possible method to prepare the forecasts. As I mentioned, it was essentially a judgmental procedure that we used. But we also examined the output from some highly sophisticated computer methods. Of course, we used our judgment to modify the results from these computer methods.

The judgmental procedure we used with our management team also helped to achieve commitment to the forecasts. Since those concerned have agreed, we intend to meet these forecasts!

Our most important need was to obtain more information. We spent much time and money this year to seek out whatever data were needed. This required that we obtain data from all areas of the company. In addition, we subscribed to one of the most prestigious econometric services so that we would have early access to their short-range macroeconomic forecasts.

Before presenting the forecasts, some comment about last year's forecast is in order. Sales and profits at Ajax were lower than we had forecast. Actually, we had been quite optimistic in our forecast. Also, the growth in the economy leveled off due to government policies. So the results were not surprising, after all.

The forecasts for the next 5 years are provided in the tables of the report before you. Overall, we forecast a growth in dollar sales of 12.5% for next year with an increase in profits of 16%. We believe that these figures will improve in years 2 through 5. During that time we forecast annual growth of 15% in sales and 20% in profits. Roughly half of the increase will be due to inflation and half to the growth in unit sales. These forecasts provide our best assessment of the future. We are confident of the forecasts.

For the rest of the meeting, I suggest that you examine the forecasts. They are provided in detail in the report—covering our eight major product areas for our three major geographical markets for each of the next 5 years. We believe you will find these forecasts to be reasonable and realistic.

(This report was followed by a brief discussion concluding with unanimous agreement by the board members that the forecasts looked reasonable.)

a. List the things wrong with this forecast situation. What's the cause of those mistakes (that is, why did they happen)? How serious is each? Why?
b. What recommendations would you make to this CEO regarding this forecast? If your suggestions were heeded, how might this statement be different? (Rewrite the statement so the things wrong with it are corrected.)

2. Consider the following memo prepared by a staff analyst for the Manager of Marketing Services[9]:

Date: December 15, 1985

Memo to: Mr. Peter Hardgrove, Manager
                  Marketing Services

From: Frederick Falsepoint, Analyst

Re: Sales Forecast for 1986

Demand for telephone products has been strong during the last few years and it is expected that this trend will continue into the future, at least for the near term. Undoubtedly, the strength of this demand is in large part attributable to the excellent work of our customer representatives and the ability of our inventory staff to keep our installers supplied with equipment. In view of the large number of items carried by our company, this is no small achievement.

Given the items identified above and the present inflationary experience of the country, total sales next year are projected to be $X.Y million. Naturally, this projection is subject to statistical error which makes this forecast uncertain. Thus, an updated forecast will be provided at a later date.

a. What mistakes have been made by the forecaster? How will those mistakes impact the use of the forecast? How will they impact future forecasts made by this forecaster?
b. What guidelines would you give this forecaster with regard to forecast preparation and forecast distribution?

---

[9]Remus, W., and M. G. Simkin. 1982. "Integrating Forecasting and Decision Making," in *The Handbook of Forecasting*. S. Makridakis and S. C. Wheelwright (eds.). New York: John Wiley & Sons, Inc. Reprinted by permission.

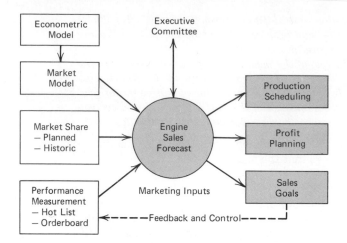

FIGURE 16-4   SALES FORECASTING SYSTEM, CUMMINS ENGINE COMPANY

3.   Consider the description of the forecasting system given below for Cummins Engine Company.[10]
      a. What is your evaluation of this system? Why?
      b. What might be done to improve the system?
      c. How would that impact its performance? How would you measure that impact?

Cummins Engine Company

Method: Econometric estimation of demand for truck engines, with company sales to individual customers forecast in the light of research department analysis and sales department feedback.

Cummins Engine Company manufactures diesel engines, parts, and accessories, and markets them internationally. Forecasting of sales for the truck market (the market dealt with in this example) is the responsibility of four executives, each of whom has an assigned role in the process: manager, economic forecasting; vice president, automotive OEM sales; director, automotive market planning; and manager, marketing services. (Sales forecasting of engines for other uses is handled separately.)

The company's forecasting system (Fig. 16-4) is an integral part of the planning and goalsetting process.[11] It rests heavily on Cummins' own market-modeling capabilities and computer facilities, but draws also on outside talent and data, chiefly for forecasts of the United States economy. The

---

    [10]The company's approach to sales forecasting, as outlined here, was previously reported on by M. C. Dietrich, executive vice president of Cummins, at a marketing conference of The Conference Board.

    [11]*Sales Forecasting.* 1978. New York: The Conference Board. Reprinted by permission.

sales force plays an indispensable role and provides up-to-date field information, which permits continuous monitoring of performance as against goals.

National Econometric Model The forecasting process begins with a macro forecast obtained from an economic consulting service—with emphasis on national production and consumption data.[12] The service's "quarterly model" results are used for Cummins' *short-term* market model, covering the next eight quarters. The service's "annual model" is used for the company's *long-term* market model, which adds 8 years (annual data only) to the 2-year horizon of the quarterly model. This provides the economic backdrop or environment within which it is assumed that Cummins, its competitors, and its customers will be operating.

Company forecasters refine these tentative economic forecasts by taking into account their own assumptions regarding changes in the economy, as well as additional data especially important in connection with the company's chief markets. Cummins' products are sold for use in heavy-duty trucks, boats, oil drilling, construction and other industrial applications. The truck market is of central interest, and the balance of this discussion deals with the development of forecasts for that market.

Truck Market Model The second step is to forecast the aggregate sales of the company's actual and potential customers—in this case, future sales of all diesel truck manufacturers. What these users of diesel engines can expect to sell, of course, will govern the size of the potential original-equipment market for engines within which Cummins will be competing for its desired share. Figure 16-5 diagrams elements of the company's short-term model of the truck market. (The long-term model is similar.)[13]

As shown, three important components of this model are:

- *Truckers' output*—This estimate of total tonnage transported by trucks is a function of production and consumption in the economy as a whole.
- *Previous demand*—This measure of earlier sales of trucks is needed to gauge the size and age of the existing stock of trucks in the country. Future sales ("shipments") will have two components: (1) sales of trucks representing a net addition to the total inventory of trucks in the country (if new demand is higher than previous), and (2) sales of trucks to replace trucks that have completed their useful life.
- *Financial environment*—This component will influence truck buyers' decisions during the forecast period (e.g., whether or not to expand the size of fleet, or merely to replace aging trucks with new ones). The financial environment is defined by a number of varia-

---

[12]The "Wharton model."

[13]In connection with these models, the company has found useful the investment theory of Dale W. Jorgenson. See, for example, an article coauthored by Jorgenson and Robert E. Hall, "Tax Policy and Investment Behavior," *The American Economic Review*, June 1967.

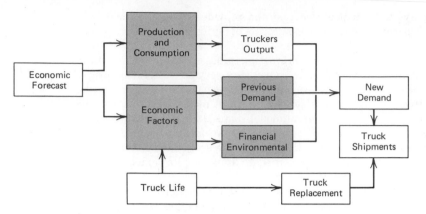

FIGURE 16-5   SHORT-TERM MODEL OF TRUCK MARKET, CUMMINS EN-
GINE COMPANY

bles, including: (1) expected freight-rate level; (2) relevant tax factors; (3) expected rate of return; (4) wholesale prices for equipment;
and (5) the useful and "depreciation" life of the equipment.

These three inputs, or components of the model, have a delayed effect
on demand for new trucks, a delay captured in the model by means of a
polynomial distributed lag structure.[14] As seen in Figure 16-5, the end result
of the model is a forecast of shipments of new trucks—trucks that can be
equipped with engines made by Cummins or its competitors.

Accuracy Achieved The procedure just described has proved to be sufficiently
accurate for the company's purposes since it was instituted several years
ago. Because the heavy-duty truck market is quite cyclical, the important
thing is to predict turning points. Figure 16-6 shows how well the quarterly
model would have worked had it been used over an 18-year historical period.
The standard error of about 1,700 trucks is 7.8 percent of quarterly volume,
and R^2 is .93. Figure 16-7 displays the historical fit of the *annual* model
applied to the period. Again the R^2 is high—.98—and the small standard
annual error of 3,600 trucks is only 3.8 percent of the average annual shipment level.

The model has also been sufficiently accurate in forecasting actual
levels of truck sales. On a quarterly basis, average errors over a recent 5-
year period have been about 1 percent for one quarter out, and only slightly
over 2 percent for five quarters out. The absolute average percentage of error,
obtained by disregarding the direction of the forecasting error (i.e., over-
forecast or under-forecast) is below 4.5 percent for one to five quarters out.

---

[14]See Elliot S. Grossman, *Capital Appropriations and Expenditures: A Quarterly Forecasting Model*, The Conference Board, Report 668, 1975; note references at end of that publication. Also see Grossman annd Takao Maruyama, "Timing the Contributions of Capital
Expansion to Recovery," *The Conference Board RECORD,* December 1975.

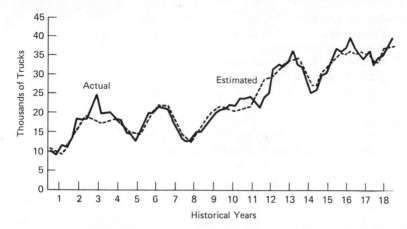

FIGURE 16-6 QUARTERLY SALES, ACTUAL VERSUS ESTIMATED, CUM-MINS ENGINE COMPANY

Cummins' Share of Market Up to now, the objective has been to forecast the demand for truck engines of the type Cummins manufactures. Step 1 was the forecast of the national economy. Step 2 was the forecast of the diesel truck market—that is, total sales by manufacturers of diesel trucks.

Now the third step is to develop a forecast of Cummins' sales to the diesel truck industry. Two approaches are used, both in terms of Cummins' share of market. If the two forecasts meet at the same figure, it is accepted. If not, the figures are restudied to see where the discrepancies lie. Thus, the two methods provide a check against each other.

The first method is called "forcing"; the implication is that the method is a sales forecast but it *also* takes on the character of a sales goal or "target"—the share of market Cummins expects and will strive to achieve. It is

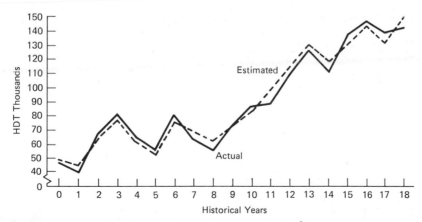

FIGURE 16-7 ANNUAL SALES, ACTUAL VERSUS ESTIMATED, CUMMINS ENGINE COMPANY

derived by multiplying the truck market forecast by the percentage representing the company's expected and intended market share. The upper portion of Figure 16-8 represents this approach.

The second approach involves an analysis of Cummins' prospects with
each manufacturer of diesel trucks (whether a present or potential customer).
This is regarded as a "bottom-up" forecasting method, in contrast to the
"forcing" approach, which is regarded as "top-down." The lower part of Figure
16-8 represents this "bottom-up" or "by account" approach.

The information inputs for the "by account" analysis come from two
chief sources. One is the company's market research department, which continuously studies the performance of each major truck manufacturer in the
United States and Canada, and develops a scenario for it, looking as far
ahead as ten years. Known expansion and new-product plans are taken into
account, along with an evaluation of the firm's competitiveness, capabilities
and financial strength. For each company thus studied, a projection of truck-
market share is made, and hence a sales forecast. In effect, the truck-market
forecast derived via the econometric approach is divided among the individual manufacturers based on the market research department's analysis.

The second source of information on individual truck manufacturers
comes from the sales department. Every month it gives the corporate forecasting group its best estimate on each company's:

- Truck production plans
- Inventory level—of both Cummins and competitors' engines
- Truck order backlog situation

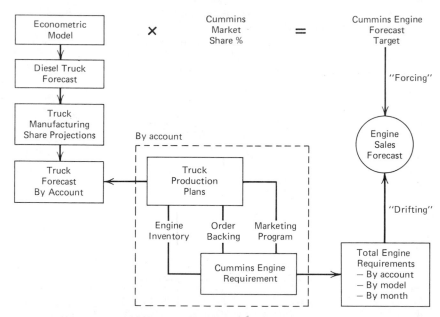

FIGURE 16-8 TWO APPROACHES TO SALES FORECASTING (FORCING
AND DRIFTING), CUMMINS ENGINE COMPANY

- Percentage of trucks on order that are equipped with Cummins engines
- Special truck sales and marketing programs.

This and other sales department information is used for two purposes. First, when sales-force projections of truck sales by individual manufacturers are added up, the total provides a test of the truck-market forecast developed by the econometric approach.

Second, truck production and sales projections by individual manufacturers are translated into engine requirements by model and by month, and Cummins' probable share of each manufacturer's engine requirements is estimated—also by model and month. As shown in Figure 16-8, this "bottom-up" forecast, heavily based on sales department feedback, is termed "drifting"; that is, it "drifts" (rises or falls) with each company's engine requirements. The individual "drifting" forecasts are totaled to yield the aggregate "engine sales forecast."

The sales forecast derived via the "bottom-up" method should coincide closely with that developed by the "top-down" method. If it does not, one or the other of the approaches must be reviewed.[15] It may be, for example, that Cummins' desired ("target") market share is too modest or too ambitious; in the latter event, extra sales effort may have to be budgeted, or perhaps sights lowered. On the other hand, it may be that faulty estimates were made of one or more individual customer's engine requirements, or the likelihood of Cummins' supplying certain percentages of them.

When the "forcing" and "drifting" forecasts have been reconciled, the result is an official engine sales forecast for the next six months. Reviewed and approved by the policy committee, it is released to production as the major input to a process known in the company as an "O.P.P." or "operations production plan." Plant management "explodes" the six-month forecast data for control and planning purposes in scheduling materials for the next six months of operation. For other planners, the approved sales forecast becomes the basis for determining cash requirements, contribution by various markets and models, and profit projections.

"Making It Happen" The fourth and final step in the company's standard procedure is the performance monitoring and measurement that show how well the forecast is being met, enabling management to adjust marketing efforts where needed. The forecast thus becomes the goal, and the object is to change it from a mere prophecy to a *self-fulfilling* prophecy. Performance measurement is the "feedback and control loop" (Figure 16-4) that helps turn the forecast into reality.

One control mechanism, illustrated in Figure 16-9, is an analysis bringing together data on orders received at each of three Cummins factories (two in England plus the home plant in Indiana), production plans, and the

---

[15]In general, the "top-down" method, based heavily on econometrics and market analysis, has been found to be the more reliable of the two methods when forecasting sales six months or more in the future. The "bottom-up" approach has been found to be somewhat more reliable when forecasting a shorter period ahead.

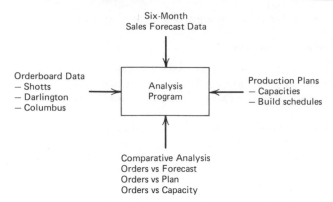

FIGURE 16-9 COMPARATIVE ANALYSIS OF ORDERS VERSUS FORE-CAST, PLAN AND CAPACITY, CUMMINS ENGINE COMPANY

six-month forecast. A weekly analysis is printed out by computer showing, for the next six months, the firm order position compared with plant capacities and forecast plan. Data on actual sales (drawn from the company's invoicing and sales bonus systems) include customer identification, distributor territory, units ordered, engine models, and application codes. No later than six days after the close of the month, a computer report is in the hands of management, showing results—last month and year-to-date—by market and by model, classified by direct and indirect engine sales, and compared with sales goals.

Assessment of Method The method has proved satisfactory both in terms of accuracy achieved (as seen above) and the close tracking and control of sales performance against forecast. It illustrates a successful blend of computer capability, continuous information input from the field, market research and executive judgment. The forecast plays an indispensable role in the tracking of marketing results and in fine-tuning marketing effort. Computer technology is essential to this system, in the company's view; the truck market model (Figure 16-5) for example, incorporates interrelated variables too numerous to solve without a computer, and the time-sharing programs in the feedback and control loop permit almost instantaneous analysis and adjustment of marketing activity.

On the other hand, the procedure described above is not considered the last word. The model is continually being refined to reflect advances in methodology and changes in the marketing environment.

17/JUDGMENTAL FACTORS IN FORECASTING

In this book we have dealt with a variety of both quantitative and qualitative or technological methods of forecasting.[1] These formal approaches have been described in detail, and several published comparisons of their performance have been summarized. However, whatever formal forecasting procedure is used, human judgment always plays an important role in preparing the forecast. Formal forecasts are rarely used without modifications based on new information, "inside knowledge," or real-time environmental "updates." Judgment is critical in determining the success or failure of forecasting, no matter what method is used for initial analysis.

This chapter considers the influence human judgment can have on organizational forecasts and forecasting. The evidence presented comes mainly from the field of judgmental psychology, which we believe bears directly on an organization's forecasting processes, and goes beyond the role of judgment in preparing or modifying specific forecasts, a topic frequently discussed in the forecasting literature. Finally, this chapter suggests ways of combining human judgment and formal forecasting methods to increase overall forecasting accuracy and effectiveness.

17/1 Empirical Evidence on Judgmental Forecasts

The performance of judgmental predictions can be illustrated using published evidence on specific forecasts. [For additional detail, interested readers can consult Armstrong (1978) and Hogarth and Makridakis (1981a and 1981b).] The difficulties associated with judgmentally based forecasts can be illustrated using an example of oil demand forecasts. Table 17-1 summarizes selected oil demand forecasts made in 1972, 1977, and 1981. This table also shows actual worldwide demand for oil and OPEC's share of that demand for those three years.

One forecasting difficulty highlighted by Table 17-1 is choosing among the many forecasts available and checking the validity of each one's assumptions. The 1972 forecast, for instance, assumed an economic growth rate of 4 percent, an energy growth rate about equal to economic growth, and a 2/3 OPEC share in meeting total demand. In the 1977 forecast, the economic growth rate was assumed to be about 2.5 percent, the energy growth was about 80 percent of economic growth, and OPEC's share of the total was significantly reduced as new oil fields were discovered outside OPEC countries. Finally, the forecasts in 1981 assumed even lower economic growth rates, lower energy growth ratios, and a lower OPEC share.

---

[1]This chapter is based on a paper by Hogarth and Makridakis (1981a and 1981b).

TABLE 17-1   OIL DEMAND IN 1972, 1977, AND 1981

Year	Actual Worldwide Demand for Oil (mbd)[a]	Demand Supplied by OPEC Oil (mbd)	Percentage of Worldwide Demand Met by OPEC Oil	Demand Forecasts for OPEC Oil in the Year 2000 (mbd)	Percentage of Demand Met by OPEC Oil in the Year 2000
1972	43	30	70	75	66.67
1977	52	31.6	60	40	55
1981	48	25	50	12	20

[a]mbd: million barrels per day
Source: Hogarth and Makridakis (1982)

Similar uncertainties and revisions can be observed in a review of oil price forecasts. In 1972 the forecasts were for continuing low prices for oil (at that time selling for less than two dollars a barrel). From 1974 to 1979 there were shortages and considerable gloom about energy costs in general and high oil prices in particular. Forecasts of oil prices of up to 100 dollars per barrel for 1990 were not uncommon. During 1979–80 and 1981–82 there was an oil glut and forecasters started talking about a drop in oil prices to 20 and even 15 dollars a barrel.

The differences in such forecasts, all made within a period of 9 years, are startling and significant. For instance, OPEC's share for the year 2000 varies from 66.67 to 20 percent—that is, from 75 million barrels a day to 12 million barrels a day, depending on the prediction used. A first step in assessing the role of judgment in forecasting is to understand that energy forecasts have changed dramatically from: (1) before 1970 when few predicted an energy crisis; (2) between 1974 and 1980 when there was little optimism about the energy outlook; and (3) since mid-1981 when a more middle-of-the-road attitude has prevailed.

The data of Table 17-1 also highlight that dramatic changes can occur within a relatively short time, no matter what the prevailing attitude or how certain forecasters may be. However, judgment in such situations is not without its problems. Human forecasters are unduly influenced by recent events, which are expected to continue to dominate the future. Considerable changes that forecasters have failed to predict often occur. This is particularly true for long-term projections where major changes and discontinuities can and do arise.

Hogarth and Makridakis (1981a and 1981b) have examined a wide range of empirical evidence dealing with predictability in the social sciences, as part of their research to evaluate forecasting and planning. Their conclusions can be summarized as follows:

1. Forecasts beyond the short term (three months) can be very inaccurate: long-established trends can change; systematic bias and errors can arise (McNees, 1979); historical data may provide contradictory clues to future trends (Dhalla and Yuspeh, 1976); and cyclical swings are unpredictable (Makridakis, 1982). Furthermore, discontinuities (such as the 1973 oil embargo or the fall of the Shah in Iran) are possible; attitudes can change (for example, the increased popularity of small cars); and new technological breakthroughs may occur. Such events can have significant impact, and yet most of them cannot be predicted with existing methods. The result is that forecasting errors for medium- to long-term projections vary from a few percent to several hundred percent (Ascher, 1978).

2. In the short term, the considerable inertia inherent in most situations makes forecasting fairly reliable, and major uncertainties frequently can be assessed and measured explicitly.

3. Objective approaches to forecasting, such as quantitative models or consistent decision rules, have performed as well or better than judgmental forecasts as measured by predictive accuracy (Dawes, 1976 and 1979; Camerer, 1981).

4. Simple quantitative models and decision rules compare favorably in their accuracy with sophisticated statistical approaches to forecasting (Armstrong, 1978; Makridakis and Hibon, 1979). One comparison of objective and judgmental forecasting approaches reported by Mabert (1976) is summarized in Table 17-2. Mabert took a situation in which sales forecasts had been based historically on opinions of the sales force and corporate executives. The accuracy of these forecasts was compared with three different quantitative forecasting methods, both in terms of mean absolute deviation (MAD) and mean absolute percentage error (MAPE). As can be seen from Table 17-2, all three quantitative methods provided more accurate results over the 5-year period covered by the study than did the judgmental (nonquantitative) forecasts. In addition, Mabert found that, in terms of timeliness and the costs of preparing forecasts, the quantitative techniques were more attractive than the subjective estimates. (It should be noted that the difference between the three quantitative methods is small and statistically not significant, though the Box-Jenkins method is much more sophisticated than the harmonic or exponential smoothing models.)

5. Although several have tried, it has not been possible to identify

TABLE 17-2 COMPARISON OF SALES FORECAST ERRORS
(MEAN ABSOLUTE DEVIATION)

| Year | Judgmental | Quantitative | | |
	Company Forecast	Exponential Smoothing	Harmonic Model	Box-Jenkins
1968	5479	5974	5408	4755
1969	3858	4470	4013	4403
1970	4013	2958	2998	3284
1971	6033	5657	5311	4785
1972	9782	8958	8384	8748
Average	5887	5603	5222	5195
MAPE	15.9%	15.1%	14.1%	14.0%

Source: V. A. Mabert. 1976. "Statistical Versus Sales-Force Executive Opinion Short Range Forecasts: A Time Series Analysis Case Study," Decision Sciences, **7**, pp. 310–318.

a single forecasting method or a single forecaster who has consistently outperformed all other methods or forecasters (Ascher, 1978; McNees, 1979; O'Carroll, 1977).

6.   Finally, forecasts based on different assumptions, models, or methods are usually available, but their predictions vary considerably. The problem of evaluating such a variety of forecasts can be as difficult and time-consuming as the task of preparing the original forecasts themselves (Ascher, 1978).

The foregoing points do not imply that forecasts are never accurate; on the contrary, they *are* in many situations. The problem is to distinguish accurate from inaccurate forecasts before outcomes are known. The problem is complicated by the fact that it is not possible to identify a single forecasting method that has consistently outperformed all others. In the final analysis, it is the uncertainty associated with predictions beyond the short term that decision makers and policy makers must understand and incorporate. This is precisely where judgment needs to concentrate, since objective or quantitative approaches can be of little help in this area.

In applying judgment to forecasting, the biases of human thought processes and their influences on predictions are of major importance. These judgmental biases will be discussed in the next section.

17/2 Judgmental Biases—Impacts and Sources

It has been the authors' experience that the vast majority of managers—both planners and decision makers—consider carefully prepared judgmental forecasts to be far superior in performance (accuracy) to unadjusted quantitative forecasts. If this were generally true, the reduction of bias in judgmental forecasts would be largely an exercise in fine tuning or incremental improvement. Unfortunately, a number of studies contradict this conventional wisdom, casting considerable doubt on the usefulness of small improvements in judgmental approaches. Such a disparity of views deserves closer analysis.

There is ample empirical evidence to support the conclusion that judgmental predictions are not necessarily better than quantitative forecasts. A review of over two dozen studies that compared both categories of forecasting approaches—judgmental and quantitative—is summarized in Table 17-3. As suggested by several of those studies, even simple quantitative models often outperform detailed judgmental approaches. Thus, while managers may find several aspects of judgmental approaches to be appealing, they should recognize that accuracy is not one of those.

The source of the performance problems of judgmental methods can be linked directly to the biases that research has identified as being frequently present in human information processing and judgmental assessments. A variety of these research studies are summarized in Table 17-4. While not all managers would be susceptible to all of these biases in a given situation, even the presence of only one or two can be sufficient to significantly alter predictions and hinder the performance of the resulting forecasts.

In order to improve judgmental forecasts, managers must first recognize the impact that biases can (and do) have. Then the specific biases present must be identified so that corrective actions can be taken. These actions will need to be significant if they are to make judgmental forecasts superior to quantitative forecasts.

17/3 Combining Judgmental and Quantitative Forecasts

From a practical point of view, forecasts can be obtained by (1) strictly judgmental or intuitive approaches, (2) strictly quantitative methods, and (3) a combination of judgmental and quantitative methods. Whereas purely judgmental approaches may suffer from a number of biases, formal quantitative forecasting methods suffer major difficulties in situations of signif-

(Text continues on page 862.)

TABLE 17-3 EMPIRICAL STUDIES OF FORECASTING AND PLANNING

Subject of Study	Area of Application[a]	Description	Main Finding(s)	Literature Sources
Forecasting Services	F	Extensive attempt to determine the validity of "expert" forecasting in the stock market.	Recommendations made by the major financial services—between 1928 and 1932—had an average record 1.4% worse than the "average" common stock annually.	Cowles, A. (1933)
			Recommendations made by *Wall Street Journal* between 1904 and 1929 achieved a result poorer than a representative sample of the average of the market.	
	F	Examination of forecasts published in the *Wall Street Journal*.	The average absolute percentage error of the forecasts was 20.1% with a range of 0 to 218.2%.	Copeland, R. M. and Marioni, R. J. (1972)
	F	Follow-up study of Cowles.	Financial services did not forecast better than the average of the market. Furthermore, 80% of all forecasts were optimistic.	Cowles, A. (1944)
	F	Examination of earning projections, of 185 companies, made by five forecasting services.	Correlation between predicted and actual earnings was very low. The careful and painstaking efforts of analysts to forecast companies' earnings did very slightly better than simple projections of past trends.	Cragg, J. G. and Malkiel, B. G. (1968)

	F	Examination of the reliability of published predictions of future earnings.	The errors occurred over a wide range (for the 1966–1970 period of the study, they ranged from −395.6 to 108.5%). The mean error was negative and overpredictions of earnings were much more frequent than underpredictions.	McDonald, C. L. (1973)
Security Analysis	F	Analysis and examination of forecasts made by security analysts.	The forecasts made by the analysts were not more accurate than simple projections.	Richards, R. M. (1976)
	F	Analysis and comparison of forecasts of earnings made by analysts and companies.	On average analysts overestimated earnings by nearly 9% (with a range of −25 to +150%), while corporate forecasts were overestimated by 6% with a range from −37.5 to 126.4%.	Basi, B. A., Carey, R. J. and Twark, R. D. (1976)
	F	Comparisons were made between analysts and a regression model (estimating future returns of 35 securities).	The results of the analysts were worse than those of the regression model.	Ebert, R. J. and Kruse, T. E. (1978)
	F	Forecasts of earnings per share made by analysts were compared with those of time-series quantitative models.	Quantitative models do as well as, or better than, forecasts provided by analysts. Analysts show a bias toward overestimating actual earnings performance. Analysts forecast better than a random walk model in 68 out of 100 companies.	Elton, E. J. and Gruber, M. J. (1972) Green, D. and Segall, J. (1967) Barefield, R. M. and Comisky, E. E. (1975)

TABLE 17-3   EMPIRICAL STUDIES OF FORECASTING AND PLANNING (*Continued*)

Subject of Study	Area of Application[a]	Description	Main Finding(s)	Literature Sources
	F & P	Study of judgmental processes of stockbrokers.	The longer a stockbroker had been in the business, the less insight he had concerning his own judgmental policy.	Slovic, P., Fleissner, D. and Bauman, W. S. (1972)
Mutual Funds	F & P	Evaluation of the performance of mutual funds to the random selected portfolio, or the average of the market.	Mutual funds have performed the same, or worse than, the average of the market.	Bauman, W. S. (1965) Fama, E. F. (1965) Jensen, M. C. (1968)
Management Forecasts	F	A comparison of management forecasts of earnings and those of Box-Jenkins method.	In cases in which management forecasts proved reasonably accurate, overall they were not more so than those generated from Box-Jenkins. Where management forecasts proved to be relatively inaccurate, those from the Box-Jenkins models were significantly less so.	Lorek, R. S., McDonald, C. L. and Patz, D. H. (1976)
	F	Comparison between sales forecasts made by management and those made by three quantitative models.	The sales forecasts of corporate executives gave less accurate results than those of quantitative models over the 5-year period of comparison.	Mabert, V. A. (1976)

Subjective Probability Forecasts (for additional references, see Exhibit 2)	F	Subjective probabilities from 23 participants were collected in an experiment involving forecasting the F. I. Share Index, dollar-sterling rate, and three oil prices.	There was a common tendency to underestimate the probability of extreme values and there were substantial differences between individuals. Thus, some participants reported distributions which were realistic and informative, but unfortunately there was no obvious means of identifying those individuals in advance. Performance does not appear to be associated with experience or academic training, and it is not noticeably correlated with performance in single-point forecasting.	O'Carroll, F. M. (1977)
Bowman's Theory of Managerial Decision Making	P	Development of decision rules for managerial decision making.	Simple decision rules may result in more accurate decisions than experienced managers. Averaging past decisions of managers may result in better performance than individual managerial decisions.	Bowman, E. H. (1963)
	P	Testing or expanding Bowman's theory on managerial decision making.	All findings have been consistent with Bowman's original findings that decision rules or averaging of past decisions of managers produces better results than individual managerial decisions.	Ebert, R. J. (1972) Kunreuther, H. (1969) Remus, W. E. (1978)

TABLE 17-3   EMPIRICAL STUDIES OF FORECASTING AND PLANNING (*Continued*)

Subject of Study	Area of Application[a]	Description	Main Finding(s)	Literature Sources
Miscellaneous	F	Experimental design to test the accuracy of intuitive judgment versus exponential smoothing models.	Winters' exponential smoothing produced forecasts which were statistically more accurate than those of human forecasters.	Adam, E. E. and Ebert, R. J. (1976)
	F	A comparative study of methods for long-range market forecasting.	"Objective" methods are more accurate than intuitive ones; causal methods are more accurate than naive ones; and the superiority of objective or over intuitive increases as the "amount of change" in the environment increases.	Armstrong, J. S. and Grohman, M. C. (1972)
	P	Testing how planning affects performance.	Amount of planning and objective measures of financial performance are not positively correlated; however, the number of informal channels of communication used, the percentage of relevant items of information received that are used in reaching decisions, and financial performance are positively correlated.	Grinyer, P. H. and Norburn, D. (1975)

| P | Simulation of the portfolio selection process of an investment officer in a bank. | Investment officer's "intuitions" were captured as witnessed by the similarity between portfolios selected by the simulation model and the investment officer. | Clarkson, G. P. E. (1962) |

[a]Area of Application is categorized as Forecasting (F) or Planning (P).

TABLE 17-4 JUDGMENTAL FORECASTING BIASES (ORGANIZED BY STAGES OF INFORMATION PROCESSING)

	Bias/Source of Bias	Description	Example	Literature Sources[a]
Acquisition of Information	Availability	Ease with which specific instances can be recalled from memory affects judgments of frequency.	Frequency of well-publicized events are over-estimated (e.g., deaths due to homicide, cancer); frequency of less well-publicized events are under-estimated (e.g., deaths due to asthma and diabetes).	Fischhoff, B. Layman, M. and Combs, B. (1978) Kunreuther H. and White, G. F. (1974) Tversky, A. (1973)
		Chance "availability" of particular "cues" in the immediate environment affects judgment.	Problem solving can be hindered/facilitated by cues perceived by chance in a particular setting (hints set up cognitive "direction").	Maier, N.R.F. (1931)
	Selective Perception	People structure problems on the basis of their own experience.	The same problem can be seen by a marketing manager as a marketing problem, as a financial problem by a finance manager, etc.	Dearborn, D.C. and Simon, H.A. (1958)
		Anticipations of what one expects to see bias what one does see.	Identification of incongruent objects—e.g., playing cards with red spades—are either inaccurately reported or cause discomfort.	Bruner, J.S. and Postman, L.J. (1949)
		People seek information consistent with their own views/hypotheses.	Interviewers seek information about candidates consistent with first impressions rather than information that could refute those impressions.	Wason, P.C. (1960) Webster, E.C. (1964)

Heuristic	Description	Example	Sources
	People downplay/disregard conflicting evidence.	In forming impressions, people will underweight information that does not yield to a consistent profile.	Anderson, N.H. and Jacobson, A. (1965)
Frequency	Cue used to judge strength of predictive relationships is observed frequency rather than observed relative frequency. Information on "non-occurrences" of an event is unavailable and ignored.	When considering relative performance (of, say, two persons), the absolute number of successes is given greater weight than the relative number of successes to successes *and* failures (i.e., the denominator is ignored). Note, the number of failures is frequently unavailable.	Estes, W.K. (1976) Smedslund, J. (1963) Ward, W.C. and Jenkins, H.M. (1965)
Concrete information (ignoring base-rate, or prior information)	*Concrete* information (i.e., vivid, or based on experience/incidents) dominates *abstract* information (e.g., summaries, statistical base-rates, etc.).	When purchasing a car, the positive or negative experience of a *single* person you know is liable to weigh more heavily in judgment than available and more valid statistical information, e.g., in *Consumer Reports*.	Bar-Hillel, M. (1973), Borgida, E. and Nisbett, R.E. (1977), Hammerton, M. (1973), Kahneman, D. and Tversky, A. (1973), Lyon, D. and Slovic, P. (1976), Nisbett, R.E. and Borgida, E. (1975, 1976)

TABLE 17-4 JUDGMENTAL FORECASTING BIASES (ORGANIZED BY STAGES OF INFORMATION PROCESSING) (*Continued*)

Bias/Source of Bias	Description	Example	Literature Sources[a]
Illusory correlation	Belief that two variables covary when in fact they do not. (Possibly related to "Frequency" above.)	Selection of an inappropriate variable to make a prediction.	Chapman, L.J. and Chapman, J.P. (1969) Golding, S.L. and Rorer, L.G. (1972) Shweder, R.A. (1977) Smedslund, J. (1963) Ward, W.C. and Jenkins, H.M. (1965)
Data presentation	Order effects (primacy/recency).	Sometimes the first items in a sequential presentation assume undue importance (primacy), sometimes the last items (recency).	Slovic, P. and Lichtenstein, S. (1971)
	Mode of presentation.	Sequential vs. intact data displays can affect what people are able to access. Contrast, for example, complete listed unit-price shopping vs. own sequential information search.	Dickson, G.W., Senn, J.A. and Chervany, N.L. (1977), Jenkins, H.M. and Ward, W.C. (1965), Ronen, J. (1973), Russo, J.E. (1977)
Data presentation	Mixture of types of information, e.g., qualitative and quantitative.	Concentration on quantitative data, exclusion of qualitative, or vice-versa.	Slovic, P. (1972)

Category	Type of bias	Description	Illustrative example	References
	Logical data displays.	Apparently complete "logical" data displays can blind people to critical omissions.		Fischhoff, B., Slovic, P. and Lichtenstein, S. (1978)
	Context effects on perceived variability.	Assessments of variability, of say, a series of numbers, is affected by the absolute size (e.g., mean level) of the numbers.		Lathrop, R.G. (1967)
Processing of Information	Inconsistency	Inability to apply a consistent judgmental strategy over a repetitive set of cases.	Judgments involving selection, e.g., personnel/graduate school admissions	Brehmer, B. (1976), Dawes, R.M. (1971), Dawes, R.M. and Corrigan, B. (1974), Goldberg, L.R. (1970), Hammond, K.R. and Brehmer, B. (1973), Meehl, P.E. (1954), Sawyer, J. (1966)
	Conservatism	Failure to revise opinion on receipt of new information to the same extent as Bayes' theorem. (Note this may be counterbalanced by the "best-guess" strategy and produce near optimal performance in the presence of unreliable data sources.)	Opinion revision in many applied settings, e.g., military, business, medicine, law.	Ducharme, W.M. (1970), Edwards, W. (1968)

TABLE 17-4   JUDGMENTAL FORECASTING BIASES (ORGANIZED BY STAGES OF INFORMATION PROCESSING) (*Continued*)

Bias/Source of Bias	Description	Example	Literature Source[a]
Non-linear extrapolation	Inability to extrapolate growth processes (e.g., exponential) and tendency to underestimate joint probabilities of several events.	Gross underestimation of outcomes of exponentially increasing processes and overestimation of joint probabilities of several events.	Bar-Hillel, M. (1973), Cohen, J., Chesnick, E.I. and Haran, D. (1971, 1972), Wagenaar, W.A. and Timmers, H. (1978), Wagenaar, W.A. (1979)
"Heuristics" used to reduce mental effort			
Habit/"rules of thumb"	Consuming an alternative because it has previously been satisfactory.	Consumer shopping; "rules of thumb" adopted in certain professions.	Knafl, K. and Burkett, G. (1975)
Anchoring and adjustment	Prediction made by anchoring on a cue or value and then adjusting to allow for the circumstances of the present case.	Making a sales forecast by taking last year's sales and adding, say, 5%.	Tversky, A. (1974)
Represent-ativeness	Judgments of likelihood of an event by estimating degree of *similarity* to the class of events of which it is supposed to be an exemplar.	Stereotyping, e.g., imagining that someone is a lawyer because he exhibits characteristics typical of a lawyer.	Kahneman, D. and Tversky, A. (1972, 1973)

Law of *small* numbers	Characteristics of small samples are deemed to be representative of the populations from which they are drawn.	Interpretation of data, too much weight given to small sample results (which are quite likely to be atypical).	Berkson, J., Magath, T.B. and Hurn, M. (1940) Tversky, A. and Kahneman, D. (1971)
Justifiability	A "processing" rule can be used if the individual finds a rationale to "justify" it.	When provided with an apparently rational argument, people will tend to follow a decision rule even if it is really inappropriate.	Slovic, P. (1975) Tversky, A. (1972)
Regression bias	Extreme values of a variable are used to predict extreme values of the next observation of the variable (thus failing to allow for regression to the mean).	Following observation of bad performance by an employee, a manager could attribute subsequent improvement to his intervention (e.g., warning to the employee). However, due to regression effects, improvement (performance closer to the mean level), is likely *without* intervention.	Campbell, D.T. (1969) Kahneman, D. and Tversky, A. (1973)
"Best-guess" strategy	Under conditions involving several sources of uncertainty, simplification is made by ignoring some uncertainties and basing judgment on the "most likely" hypothesis. (Note: people simplify by ignoring uncertainty). More generally, tendency to discount uncertainty.	Ignoring the fact that information sources are unreliable.	Gettys, C.F., Kelly, C.W. and Peterson, C.R. (1973)

TABLE 17-4 JUDGMENTAL FORECASTING BIASES (ORGANIZED BY STAGES OF INFORMATION PROCESSING) (*Continued*)

Bias/Source of Bias	Description	Example	Literature Source[a]
The decision environment:			
Complexity	Complexity induced by time pressure, information overload, distractions lead to reduced connsistency of judgment.	In decisions taken under time pressure information processing may be quite superficial.	Einhorn, H.J. (1971), Payne, J.W. (1976), Pollay, R.W. (1970), Wright, P. (1974)
Emotional stress	Emotional stress reduces the care with which people select and process information.	Panic judgments.	Janis, I.L. and Mann, L. (1977)
Social pressures	Social pressures, e.g., of a group, cause people to distort their judgments.	The majority in a group can unduly influence the judgment of minority members.	Asch, S.E. (1951)
Information sources:			
Consistency of information sources	Consistency of information sources can lead to increases in confidence in judgment but not to increased predictive accuracy.	People often like to have more information, even though it is redundant with what they already have.	Kahneman, D. and Tversky, A. (1973), Oskamp, S. (1965), Slovic, P. (1980), Slovic, P., Fischhoff, B. and Lichtenstein, S. (1977)

Data presentation:	See items under the ACQUISITION section.		
Response mode			
Question format	The way a person is required or chooses to make a judgment can affect the outcome.	Preferences for risky prospects have been found to be inconsistent with the prices for which people are willing to sell them.	Grether, D.M. and Plott, C.R. (1979), Lichtenstein, S. and Slovic, P. (1971, 1973), Slovic, P. (1975), Tversky, A. (1972).
Scale effects	The scale on which responses are recorded can affect responses.	Estimates of probabilities can vary when estimated directly on a scale from zero to one, or when "odds" or even "log-odds" are used.	Hogarth, R.M. (1975) Slovic, P. and Lichtenstein, S. (1971)
Wishful thinking	People's preferences for outcomes of events affect their assessment of the events.	People sometimes assess the probability of outcomes they desire higher than their state of knowledge justifies.	Cyert, R.M., Dill, W.R. and March, J.G. (1958), Morlock, H. (1967), Slovic, P. (1966), Armstrong, J.S. (1978)
Illusion of control	Activity concerning an uncertain outcome can by itself induce in a person feelings of control over the uncertain event.	Activities suuch as planning, or even the making of forecasts, can induce feelings of control over the uncertain future.	Langer, E.J. (1975), Langer, E.J. and Roth, J. (1975), Perlmutter, L.C. and Monty, R.A. (1977)

Output

TABLE 17-4 JUDGMENTAL FORECASTING BIASES (ORGANIZED BY STAGES OF INFORMATION PROCESSING) (Continued)

	Bias/Source of Bias	Description	Example	Literature Sources[a]
Feedback	Outcome irrelevant learning structures	Outcomes observed yield inaccurate or incomplete information concerning predictive relationships. This can lead, inter alia, to irrealistic confidence in one's own judgment.	In personnel selection you can learn how good your judgment is concerning candidates selected, but you usually have no information concerning subsequent performance of rejected candidates.	Einhorn, H.J. (1980) Einhorn, H.J. and Hogarth, R.M. (1978) For overconfidence, see Fischhoff, B., Slovic, P. and Lichtenstein, S. (1977) Lichtenstein, S., Fischhoff, B. and Phillips, L.D. (1977)
	Misperception of chance fluctuations (e.g., gambler's fallacy)	Observation of an unexpected number of similar chance outcomes leads to the expectation that the probability of the appearance of an event not recently seen increases.	So-called "gambler's fallacy"—after observing, say, 9 successive Reds in roulette, people tend to believe that Black is more likely on the next throw.	Jarvik, M.E. (1951), Wagenaar, W.A. (1970)

Success/failure attributions	Tendency to attribute success to one's skill, and failure to chance. (This is also related to the "Illusion of Control"—see above.)	Successes in one's job, e.g., making a difficult sale, are attributed to one's skill; failures to "bad luck."	Hogarth, R.M. and Makridakis, S. (1979), Langer, E.J. and Roth, J. (1975), Miller, D.T. (1976). For a review of "Attribution Theory" see Ross, L. (1977)
Logical fallacies in recall	Inability to recall details of an event leads to "logical" reconstruction which can be inaccurate.	Eyewitness testimony.	Buckhout, R. (1974) Loftus, E.F. (1975) Snyder, M. and Uranowitz, S.W. (1978)
Hindsight bias	In retrospect, people are not "surprised" about what has happened in the past. They can easily find plausible explanations.	The "Monday morning quarterback" phenomenon.	Fischhoff, B. (1975, 1977) Fischhoff, B., Slovic, P. and Lichtenstein, S. (1977)

[a]The list of references provided here cannot claim to be comprehensive; however, review papers are cited in which readers will be able to find additional references. It should also be added that individuals may vary on their susceptibility to different forms of bias. A large literature exists, for example, concerning "cognitive styles" [Pinson, C. (1978)].

icant environmental change. Approaches that combine the best elements of both categories of methods may well produce significantly improved results in comparison with those produced by using one or the other approaches alone. Although such a combined approach is a relatively new area of activity, some suggestions as to how it might improve forecasting results can be presented below.

The effective combining of judgment with quantitative forecasting models requires a clear understanding of the advantages and drawbacks of each. As indicated in Table 17-4, judgment is susceptible to a number of biases, especially that of inconsistency. This bias can cause wide fluctuations in judgmental forecasts and is a major source of forecasting errors (see Bowman, 1963; Remus, 1978; Hogarth and Makridakis, 1981b). On the other hand, formal quantitative methods are always consistent in the way they forecast and the weighting rules they use. When the situation being forecast does not change, these latter approaches have an advantage over judgment because of their consistency. However, if there is a change in the environment or the organization, these quantitative methods are less useful, since generally they have no effective way to take such changes into consideration.

A logical conclusion is that forecasts should rely more heavily on the predictions provided by formal quantitative methods, as long as there are no major changes in the environment or the organization. When such changes do occur, judgmental inputs should be given increased weight. The key question, however, is determining when such changes are present. This requires not only a forecasting system but also a monitoring system. The monitoring system provides information about external fluctuations in the environment or internal changes in the organization that are nonrandom. Thus the monitoring system would signal the need to change the relative emphasis to judgment and formal quantitative methods in forecasting.

In this respect, monitoring should be considered an early warning system that continuously tracks fluctuations in variables of interest. If these fluctuations appear nonrandom, a signal to that effect is given. The importance of a separate monitoring system can be better appreciated by recognizing that people generally are not willing to accept evidence of negative events (Wason, 1960). For instance, management might be unwilling to accept evidence of a forthcoming recession or declining sales, which would have negative repercussions for the company, until such evidence is obvious to all concerned. However, this is often too late for efficient corrective action. A monitoring system can be more objective and provide warning signals of declining sales in a manner that is difficult to ignore.

As expanded role of forecasting would include monitoring and understanding of basic changes, in addition to traditional extrapolative forecasting. One framework for this is presented in Figure 17-1 and Table 17-5. These exhibits suggest that formal methods should be used primarily when there are no systematic changes from established patterns or rela-

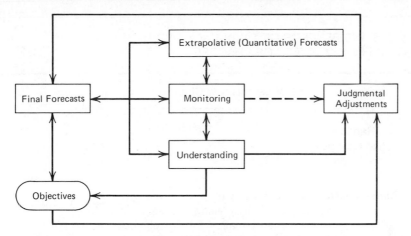

FIGURE 17-1 EXPANDED FUNCTIONS FOR FORECASTING

tionships, whereas judgment should be relied on in preparing or modifying the forecast when the presence of nonrandom changes has been identified. Finally, judgment needs to be concerned with the nature and duration of changes, since they can greatly affect organizational performance. As a decision matrix, Table 17-5 lists alternative actions that might be taken, contingent on the type of change identified by the monitoring system.

As advocated previously, no action should be taken unless the monitoring system gives a warning signal of a possible nonrandom change. In practice, the monitoring system can be set up to test for nonrandom errors at, say, a 95 percent confidence level. On average, such a system will give a false signal five times out of one hundred. While a higher confidence level, say 99 percent, would reduce considerably the chances of a false alarm, the chances of missing (not detecting) a nonrandom (systematic) fluctuation would increase. The user cannot avoid completely both types of errors and must attempt to balance them through an appropriate choice of a confidence level and the subsequent application of judgment when a signal is triggered.

If the conclusion is that the alarm is false, no action is needed. If the conclusion is that some systematic change is taking place, then a second level of decision must be made concerning the duration of the change. Will it be temporary (in which case its duration must be determined)? Or will it be permanent? These alternatives and possible follow-up actions are suggested in the body of Table 17-5. One must decide on the costs and benefits involved in each entry of the table for the particular situation in question. In the final analysis, such choices are the most crucial aspects of judgmental forecasting, and they are where the bulk of the attention must be focused.

The strengths and weaknesses of judgmental and quantitative forecasting methods need to be better understood and accepted by general management. Those responsible for forecasting must be knowledgeable enough

TABLE 17-5   COSTS AND BENEFITS OF TAKING ACTIONS
FOR DIFFERENT TYPES OF CHANGES

Action Alternatives	Random (No Change in Pattern)	Type of Deviation or Change	
		Systematic	
		Temporary	Permanent
No Action	Correct match	Opportunity or real cost of taking no systematic action; extent of cost is function of how big systematic change is	Large opportunity or real costs can result; major strategic consequences
Systematic Temporary	Cost of planning and action on assumed change; possible opportunity costs	Correct match	Important opportunity or real costs are involved; important strategic consequences
Permanent	Large costs and major strategic consequences	Strategic issues are involved; costs (opportunity or real) can be substantial	Correct match

Source: Makridakis, S. and Wheelwright, S.C., "Forecasting and Long-Range Planning," in Management Handbook (ed. Mali), John Wiley & Sons, Inc. 1981.

about both categories of approaches to avoid the weaknesses of each while exploiting their advantages. Interference with the predictions being generated by formal models should be kept at a minimum as long as the monitoring system does not indicate the development of significant nonrandom errors. If such errors are indicated, then the costs/benefits of the alternative actions must be reviewed and a decision made as to the best action to follow. When decision makers and planners are freed from the tedious task of attempting to adjust all forecasts—something that judgment does not do well anyway—they have more time to concentrate on the issues where judgment is important.

REFERENCES AND SELECTED BIBLIOGRAPHY

Adam, E. E. and Ebert, R. J. 1976. "A Comparison of Human and Statistical Forecasting," *AIEEE Trans.*, **8,** pp. 120–127.

Anderson, N. H. and Jacobson, A. 1965. "Effect of Stimulus Inconsistency and Discounting Instructions in Personality Impression Formation," *J. Personality and Social Psychology,* **2,** No. 4, pp. 531–539.

Armstrong, J. S. 1978. *Long-Range Forecasting: From Crystal Ball to Computer.* New York: Wiley-Interscience.

—— and Grohman, M. C. 1972. "A Comparative Study of Methods for Long-range Market Forecasting," *Management Sci.,* **19,** No. 2, pp. 211–221.

Asch, S. E. 1951. "Effects of Group Pressure on the Modification and Distortion of Judgments," in H. Guetzkow (ed.), *Groups, Leadership and Men.* Pittsburgh: Carnegie Institute of Technology Press.

Ascher, W. 1978. *Forecasting: An Appraisal for Policy Makers and Planners.* Baltimore: The Johns Hopkins University Press.

Barefield, R. M. and Comisky, E. E. 1975. "The Accuracy of Analysts' Forecasts of Earnings Per Share," *J. Business Res.,* **3,** No. 3, pp. 247–252.

Bar-Hillel, M. 1973. "On the Subjective Probability of Compound Events," *Organizational Behavior and Human Performance,* **9,** No. 3, pp. 396–406.

——. 1980. "The Base-Rate Fallacy in Probability Judgments," *Acta Psychologica,* **44,** No. 3, pp. 211–233.

Basi, B. A., Carey, R. J. and Twark, R. D. 1976. "A Comparison of the Accuracy of Corporate Security Analysts' Forecasts of Earnings," *Accounting Rev.,* **51,** No. 2, pp. 244–254.

Bauman, W. S. 1965. "The Less Popular Stocks versus the Most Popular Stocks," *Financial Analysts J.,* **21,** No. 1, pp. 61–69.

Berkson, J., Magath, T. B. and Hurn, M. 1940. "The Error of Estimate of the Blood Cell Count as Made with the Hemocytometer," *Amer. J. Physiology,* **128,** pp. 309–323.

Borgida, E. and Nisbett, R. E. 1977. "The Differential Impact of Abstract vs. Concrete Information on Decisions," *J. Appl. Social Psychology,* **7,** No. 3, pp. 258–271.

Bowman, E. H. 1963. "Consistency and Optimality in Managerial Decision Making," *Management Sci.,* **10,** No. 1, pp. 310–321.

Brehmer, B. 1976. "Social Judgment Theory and the Analysis of Interpersonal Conflict," *Psychological Bull.,* **83,** No. 6, pp. 985–1003.

Bruner, J. S. and Postman, L. J. 1949. "On the Perception of Incongruity: A Paradigm," *J. Personality,* **18,** pp. 206–223.

Buckhout, R. 1974. "Eyewitness Testimony," *Sci. Amer.,* **231,** No. 6, pp. 23–31.

Camerer, C. 1981. "General Conditions for the Success of Bootstrapping Models," *Organizational Behavior and Human Performance,* **27,** pp. 411–422.

Campbell, D. T. 1969. "Reforms as Experiments," *Amer. Psychologist,* **24,** No. 4, pp. 409–429.

Chapman, L. J. and Chapman J. P. 1969. "Illusory Correlation as an Obstacle to the Use of Valid Psychodiagnostic Signs," *J. Abnormal Psychology,* **74,** No. 3, pp. 271–280.

Clarkson, G. P. E. 1962. *Portfolio Selection: A Simulation of Trust Investment.* Englewood Cliffs, N.J.: Prentice-Hall.

Cohen, J., Chesnick, E. I. and Haran, D. 1971. "Evaluation of Compound Probabilities in Sequential Choice," *Nature,* **232,** No. 5310, pp. 414–416.

——. 1972. "A Confirmation of the Inertial ψ-Effect in Sequential Choice and Decision," *British J. Psychology,* **63,** No. 1, pp. 41–46.

Copeland, R. M. and Marioni, R. J. 1972. "Executives Forecasts of Earnings per Share versus Forecasts of Naive Models," *J. Business,* **45,** No. 4, pp. 497–512.

Cowles, A. 1933. "Can Stock Market Forecasters Forecast?" *Econometrica,* **1,** No. 3, pp. 309–324.

——. 1944. "Stock Market Forecasting," *Econometrica,* **12,** Nos. 3 & 4, pp. 67–84.

Cragg, J. G. and Malkiel, B. G. 1968. "The Consensus and Accuracy of Some Predictions of the Growth of Corporate Earnings," *J. Finance,* **23,** No. 1, pp. 67–84.

Cyert, R. M., Dill, W. R. and March, J. G., 1958. "The Role of Expectations in Business Decision Making," *Admin. Sci. Quart.,* **3,** pp. 307–340.

Dawes, R. M. 1971. "A Case Study of Graduate Admissions: Applications of Three Principles of Human Decision Making," *Amer. Psychologist,* **26,** No. 2, pp. 180–188.

——. 1976. "Shallow Psychology," in J. S. Carroll and J. W. Payne (eds.), *Cognition and Social Behavior.* Hillsdale, N.J.: Erlbaum.

——. 1979. "The Robust Beauty of Improper Linear Models in Decision Making," *American Psychologist,* **34,** No. 7, pp. 571–582.

—— and Corrigan, B. 1974. "Linear Models in Decision Making," *Psychological Bull.,* **81,** No. 2, pp. 95–106.

Dearborn, D. C. and Simon, H. A. 1958. "Selective Perception: A Note on the Departmental Identification of Executives," *Sociometry,* **21,** No. 2, pp. 140–44.

Dhalla, N. K. and Yuspeh, S. 1976. "Forget the Product Life Cycle Concept," *Harvard Business Rev.,* **54,** No. 1, pp. 102–112.

Dickson, G. W., Senn, J. A. and Chervany, N. L. 1977. "Research in Management Information Systems: The Minnesota Experiments," *Management Sci.,* **23,** No. 9, pp. 913–23.

DuCharme, W. M. 1970. "A Response Bias Explanation of Conservative Human Inference," *J. Experimental Psychology,* **85,** pp. 66–74.

Ebert, R. J. 1972. "Environmental Structure and Programmed Decision Effectiveness," *Management Sci.,* **19,** No. 4, pp. 435–445.

—— and Kruse, T. E. 1978. "Bootstrapping the Security Analyst," *J. Appl. Psychology,* **63,** No. 1, pp. 110–119.

Edwards, W. 1968. "Conservatism in Human Information Processing," in B. Kleinmuntz (ed.), *Formal Representation of Human Judgment.* New York: John Wiley & Sons, Inc.

Einhorn, H. J. 1971. "Use of Nonlinear, Noncompensatory Models as a Function of Task and Amount of Information," *Organizational Behavior and Human Performance,* **6,** No. 1, pp. 1–27.

—— 1980. "Learning from Experience and Suboptimal Rules in Decision Making," in T. Wallsten (ed.), *Cognitive Processes in Choice and Decision Behavior.* Hillsdale, N.J.: Erlbaum.

Einhorn, H. J. and Hogarth, R. M. 1978. "Confidence in Judgment: Persistence of the Illusion of Validity," *Psychological Rev.,* **85,** No. 5, pp. 395–476.

Elton, E. J. and Gruber, M. J. 1972. "Earnings Estimates and the Accuracy of Expectational Data," *Management Sci.,* **18,** No. 8, pp. 409–424.

Estes, W. K. 1976. "The Cognitive Side of Probability Learning," *Psychological Rev.,* **83,** No. 1, pp. 37–64.

Fama, E. F. 1965. "The Behavior of Stock Market Prices," *J. Business,* **38,** No. 1, pp. 34–105.

Fischhoff, B. 1975. "Hindsight $\neq$ Foresight: The Effect of Outcome Knowledge on Judgment under Uncertainty," *J. Experimental Psychology: Human Perception and Performance,* **1,** No. 2, pp. 288–299.

—— 1977. "Perceived Informativeness of Facts," *J. Experimental Psychology: Human Perception and Performance,* **3,** No. 2, pp. 349–358.

—— Slovic, P. and Lichtenstein, S. 1977. "Knowing with Certainty: The Appropriateness of Extreme Confidence," *J. Experimental Psychology: Human Perception and Performance,* **3,** No. 4, pp. 552–564.

—— 1978. "Fault Trees: Sensitivity of Estimated Failure Probabilities to Problem Representation," *J. Experimental Psychology: Human Perception and Performance,* **4,** No. 2, pp. 330–44.

Gettys, C. F., Kelly, C. W. and Peterson, C. R. 1973. "The Best Guess Hypothesis in Multistage Inference," *Organizational Behavior and Human Performance,* **10,** No. 3, pp. 364–73.

Goldberg, L. R. 1970. "Man versus Model of Man: A Rationale, Plus Some Evidence for a Method of Improving on Clinical Inferences," *Psychological Bull.,* **73,** No. 6, pp. 422–32.

Golding, S. L. and Rorer, L. G. 1972. "Illusory Correlation and Subjective Judgment," *J. Abnormal Psychology,* **80,** No. 3, pp. 249–60.

Green, D. and Segall, J. 1967. "The Predictive Power of First Quarter Earnings Reports," *J. Business,* **40,** No. 1, pp 44–45.

Grether, D. M. and Plott, C. R. 1979. "Economic Theory of Choice and the Preference Reversal Phenomenon," *Amer. Economic Rev.,* **69,** No. 4, pp. 623–38.

Grinyer, P. H. and Norburn, D. 1975. "Planning for Existing Markets: Perceptions of Executives and Financial Performance," *J. Roy. Statist. Soc. A,* **138,** Part 1, pp. 70–98.

Hammerton, M. 1973. "A Case of Radical Probability Estimation," *J. Experimental Psychology,* **101,** No. 2, pp. 252–254.

Hammond, K. R. and Brehmer, B. 1973. "Quasi-Rationality and Distrust: Implications for International Conflict," in L. Rappoport and D. A. Summers (eds.), (eds.), *Human Judgment and Social Interaction,* New York: Holt, Rinehart & Winston.

Hogarth, R. M. 1975. "Cognitive Processes and the Assessment of Subjective Probability Distributions," *J. Amer. Statist. Assoc.,* **70,** No. 350, pp. 271–89.

Hogarth, R. M. and Makridakis, S. 1982. "The Limits to Predictability." INSEAD Research paper, No. 133.

—— 1981a. "The Value of Decision Making in a Complex Environment: An Experimental Approach," *Management Science,* **27,** No. 1.

—— 1981b. "Forecasting and Planning: An Evaluation," *Management Science,* **27,** No. 2. 1977.

Janis, I. L. and Mann, L. 1977. *Decision Making: A Psychological Analysis of Conflict, Choice and Commitment.* New York: The Free Press.

Jarvik, M. E. "Probability Learning and a Negative Recency Effect in the Serial Anticipation of Alternative Symbols," *J. Experimental Psychology,* **41,** pp. 291–97.

Jenkins, H. M. and Ward, W. C. 1965. "Judgment of Contingency between Responses and Outcomes," *Psychological Monographs: General and Applied,* **79,** No. 1 (Whole No. 594), pp. 1–17.

Jensen, M. C. 1968. "The Performance of Mutual Funds in the Period 1945–1964," *J. Finance,* **23,** No. 2, pp. 389–416.

Kahneman, D. and Tversky, A. 1972. "Subjective Probability: A Judgment of Representativeness," *Cognitive Psychology,* **3,** No. 3, pp. 430–454.

——. 1973. "On the Psychology of Prediction," *Psychological Rev.,* **80,** No. 4, pp. 237–51.

Knafl, K. and Burkett, G. 1975. "Professional Socialization in a Surgical Specialty: Acquiring Medical Judgment," *Social Science of Medicine,* **9,** pp. 397–404.

Kunreuther, H. 1969. "Extensions of Bowman's Theory of Managerial Decision Making," *Management Sci.,* **15,** No. 8, pp. B-415–439.

Langer, E. J. 1975. "The Illusion of Control," *J. Personality and Social Psychology,* **32,** No. 2, pp. 311–328.

Langer E. J. and Roth, J. 1975. "The Effect of Sequence of Outcomes in a Chance Task of the Illusion of Control," *J. Personality and Social Psychology,* **32,** No. 6, pp. 951–55.

Lathrop, R. G. 1967. "Perceived Variability," *J. Experimental Psychology,* **73,** No. 4, pp. 498–502.

Lichtenstein, S., Fischhoff, B. and Phillips, L. D. 1977. "Calibration of Probabilities: The State of the Art," in H. Jungermann & G. de Zeeuw (eds.), *Decision Making and Change in Human Affairs.* The Netherlands: Reidel, Dordrecht.

—— and Slovic, P. 1971. "Reversals of Preference between Bids and Choices in Gambling Decisions," *J. Experimental Psychology,* **89,** No. 1, pp. 46–55.

——. 1973. "Response-Induced Reversals of Preference in Gambling: An Extended Replication in Las Vegas," *J. Experimental Psychology,* **101,** No. 1, pp. 16–20.

——, Fischhoff, B., Layman, M. and Combs, B. 1978. "Judged Frequency of Lethal Events," *J. Experimental Psychology: Human Learning and Memory,* **4,** No. 6, pp. 551–578.

Loftus, E. F. 1975. "Leading Questions and the Eyewitness Report," *Cognitive Psychology,* **7,** No. 4, pp. 560–572.

Lorek, R. S., McDonald, C. L. and Patz, D. H. 1976. "A Comparative Examination of Management Forecasts and Box-Jenkins Forecasts of Earnings," *Accounting Rev.,* **51,** No. 2, pp. 321–330.

Lyon, D. and Slovic, P. 1976. "Dominance of Accuracy Information and Neglect of Base Rates in Probability Estimation," *Acta Psychologica,* **40,** pp. 287–298.

Mabert, V. A. 1976. "Statistical versus Sales Force—Executive Opinion Short-Range Forecasts: A Time-Series Analysis Case Study," *Decision Sci.,* **7,** pp. 310–318.

Maier, N. R. F. 1931. "Reasoning in Humans: II. The Solution of a Problem and Its Appearance in Consciousness." *J. Comparative Psychology,* **12,** No. 2, pp. 181–194.

Makridakis, S. and Hibon, M. 1979. "Accuracy of Forecasting: An Empirical Investigation," *J. Roy. Statist. Soc., A,* **142,** Part 2, pp. 97–125.

Makridakis, S. 1982. "A Chronology of The Last Six Recessions," forthcoming *OMEGA.*

McDonald, C. L. 1973. "An Empirical Examination of the Reliability of Published Predictions of Future Earnings," *Accounting Rev.,* **48,** No. 3, pp. 502–510.

McNees, S. K. 1979. "Forecasting Performance in the 1970's," in *TIMS Studies in Management Sci.,* **12.**

Meehl, P. E. 1954. *Clinical versus Statistical Prediction: A Theoretical Analysis and Review of the Literature.* Minneapolis: University of Minnesota Press.

Miller, D. T. 1976. "Ego Involvement and Attributions for Success and Failure," *J. Personality and Social Psychology,* **34,** No. 5, pp. 901–906.

Morlock, H. 1967. "The Effect of Outcome Desirability on Information Required for Decisions," *Behavioral Sci.,* **12,** No. 4, pp. 296–300.

Nisbett, R. E. and Borgida, E. 1975. "Attribution and the Psychology of Prediction," *J. Personality and Social Psychology,* **32,** No. 5, pp. 932–943.

——, Borgida, E., Crandall, R. and Reed, H. 1976. "Popular Induction: Information Is Not Necessarily Informative," in J. S. Carroll and J. W. Payne (eds.), *Cognition and Social Behavior,* Hillsdale, N.J.; Erlbaum.

O'Carroll, F. M. 1977. "Subjective Probabilities and Short-Term Economic Forecasts: An Empirical Investigation," *Appl. Statist.,* **26,** No. 3, pp. 269–278.

Oskamp, S. 1965. "Overconfidence in Case-Study Judgments," *J. Consulting Psychology,* **29,** No. 3, pp. 261–265.

Payne, J. W. 1976. "Task Complexity and Contingent Processing in Decision Making: An Information Search and Protocol Analysis," *Organizational Behavior and Human Performance,* **16,** No. 2, pp. 366–387.

Perlmutter, L. C. and Monty, R. A. 1977. "The Importance of Perceived Control: Fact or Fantasy?," *Amer. Scientist,* **65** (November/December), pp. 759–65.

Pinson, C. 1978. "Consumer Cognitive Styles: Review and Implications for Marketers," in E. Topritzhofer (ed.). *Marketing, Neue Ergebnisse aus Forschung und Praxis.* West Germany: Gabler, Wiesbaden.

Pollay, R. W. 1970. "The Structure of Executive Decisions and Decision Times," *Admin. Sci. Quart.,* **15,** No. 4, pp. 459–71.

Remus, W. E. 1978. "Testing Bowman's Managerial Coefficient Theory Using a Competitive Gaming Environment," *Management Sci.,* **24,** No. 8, pp. 827–35.

Richards, R. M. 1976. "Analysts' Performance and the Accuracy of Corporate Earnings Forecasts," *J. Business,* **49,** No. 3, pp. 350–57.

Ronen, J. 1973. "Effects of Some Probability Displays on Choices," *Organizational Behavior and Human Performance,* **9,** No. 1, pp. 1–15.

Ross, L. 1977. "The Intuitive Psychologist and His Shortcomings: Distortions in the Attribution Process," in L. Berkowitz (ed.), *Advances in Experimental Social Psychology,* Vol. 10. New York: Academic Press.

Russo, J. E. 1977. "The Value of Unit Price Information," *J. Marketing Res.,* **14,** No. 2, pp. 193–201.

Sawyer, J. 1966. "Measurement *and* Prediction, Clinical *and* Statistical," *Psychological Bull.,* **66,** No. 3, pp. 178–200.

Shweder, R. A. 1977. "Likeness annd Likelihood in Everyday Thought: Magical Thinking in Judgments about Personality," *Current Anthropology,* **18,** No. 4, pp. 637–658.

Slovic, P. 1966. "Value as a Determiner of Subjective Probability," *IEEE Trans. Human Factors in Electronics*, **HFE-7**, No. 1, pp. 22–28.

——. 1972. "From Shakespeare to Simon: Speculations—and Some Evidence—About Man's Ability to Process Information," *Oregon Research Institute Research Monograph*, **12**, No. 2, Oregon Research Institute, Eugene.

——. 1975. "Choice Between Equally-Valued Alternatives," *J. Experimental Psychology: Human Perception and Performance*, **1**, No. 3, pp. 280–87.

——. 1980. "Toward Understanding and Improving Decisions," in W. Howell (ed.), *Human Performance and Productivity*, Hillsdale, N.J.: Erlbaum.

——. 1977. Fischhoff, B. and Lichtenstein, S. 1977. "Behavioral Decision Theory," *Annual Rev. of Psychology*, **28**, pp. 1–39.

——, Fleissner, D. and Bauman, W. S. 1972. "Analyzing the Use of Information in Investment Decision Making: A Methodological Proposal," *J. Business*, **45**, No. 2, pp. 283–301.

——, Kunreuther, H. and White, G. F. 1974. "Decision Processes, Rationality and Adjustment to Natural Hazards," in G. F. White (ed.), *Natural Hazards, Local, National and Global*. New York: Oxford University Press.

—— and Lichtenstein, S. 1971. "Comparison of Bayesian and Regression Approaches to the Study of Information Processing in Judgment," *Organizational Behavior and Human Performance*, **6**, No. 6, pp. 649–744.

Smedslund, J. 1963. "The Concept of Correlation in Adults," *Scandinavian J. Psychology*, **4**, No. 3, pp. 165–73.

Snyder, M. and Uranowitz, S. W. 1978. "Reconstructing the Past: Some Cognitive Consequences of Person Perception," *J. Personality and Social Psychology*, **36**, No. 9, pp. 941–50.

Tversky, A. 1969. "Intransitivity of Preferences," *Psychological Rev.*, **76**, No. 1, pp. 31–48.

——. 1972. "Elimination by Aspects: A Theory of Choice," *Psychological Rev.*, **79**, No. 4, pp. 281–99.

—— and Kahneman, D. 1971. "The Belief in the 'Law of Small Numbers'," *Psychological Bull.*, **76**, No. 2, pp. 105–110.

Tversky, A. 1973. "Availability: A Heuristic for Judging Frequency and Probability," *Cognitive Psychology*, **5**, No. 2, pp. 207–32.

——. 1974. "Judgment under Uncertainty: Heuristics and Biases," *Science*, **185** (27 September), pp. 1124–1131.

Wagenaar, W. A. 1970. "Appreciation of Conditional Probabilities in Binary Sequences," *Acta Psychologica*, **34**, Nos. 2 & 3, pp. 348–56.

—— and Timmers, H. 1978. "Intuitive Prediction of Growth," in D. F. Burkhardt and W. H. Ittelson (eds.), *Environmental Assessment of Socio-Economic Systems*. New York: Plenum.

——. 1979. "The Pond-and-Duckweed Problem: Three Experiments on the Misperception of Exponential Growth," *Acta Psychologica*, **43**, No. 3, pp. 239–51.

Ward, W. C. and Jenkins, H. M. 1965. "The Display of Information and the Judgment of Contingency," *Canad. J. Psychology*, **19**, No. 3, pp. 231–41.

Wason, P. C. 1960. "On the Failure to Eliminate Hypotheses in a Conceptual Task," *Quart. J. Experimental Psychology*, **12**, No. 3, pp. 129–40.

Webster, E. C. 1964. *Decision Making in the Employment Interview,* Industrial Relations Centre, McGill University, Montreal.

Wright P. 1974. "The Harassed Decision Maker: Time Pressures, Distractions and the Use of Evidence," *J. Appl. Psychology,* **59**, No. 5, pp. 555–61.

Exercises

1. As a basis for gaining experience concerning the relative strengths and weaknesses of judgmental and quantitative forecasting methods, prepare your own (personal) projections of the following items:
   i. The annualized national inflation rate (as measured by the price index) for the most recent month for which it has not yet been announced. For one year from now.
   ii. The average height of people in your class. The 25th and 75th percentile heights for people in the class.
   iii. Tomorrow's mean temperature for your local community. The maximum and minimum temperatures for the 24 hours beginning tonight at midnight.
   iv. The change in the Dow Jones Industrial Stock Average from its opening to its closing tomorrow.

   Having made the foregoing judgmental forecasts, prepare the following:
   a. Compare the process you used to prepare a forecast with the process that might be used by a specialist applying a quantitative forecasting method. What are the dimensions along which the two processes differ? What biases would you expect each process to exhibit when making repeated forecasts of these items?
   b. Obtain forecasts of these same items, prepared by specialists applying quantitative methods. How do your judgmental forecasts compare with these more quantitative forecasts? What explanations would you give for these performance differences?

2. Refer to the salesforce composite forecasting system used at Ex-Cell-O Corp. and described in Exercise 1 in Chapter 13. Using the list of biases given in Table 17-4, answer the following:
   a. What biases do you think exist in the Ex-Cell-O process?
   b. How might you control for those biases?
   c. Which biases are likely to remain always?
   d. How might quantitative forecasting methods be used to complement/replace part or all of the judgmental approach used at Ex-Cell-O? What further improvements would you expect as a result of such changes?

3. Refer to the information in Exercise 5 in Chapter 13 regarding step-function patterns in trend extrapolation of maximum facility size for ethylene manufacturing. What are the relative roles of judgmental methods as compared with quantitative methods of forecasting? Would use of only one or the other type of method give as good a result as the combined approach? Why or why not?

4. Jentronics, a small French manufacturing company, historically had supplied components to manufacturers of electronic games. Four years ago, an engineer on the staff of Jentronics developed an idea for a small game that would be easy to construct and cheap to produce. At that time, Jentronics was experiencing a slump in orders. It was decided to go ahead with production of the entire game, thus moving the company into a new area. Fortunately, Jentronics was very successful in marketing the new game.

    Christened "Electrack," the game consisted of an elliptical racetrack on which up to twelve "horses" could run from one to ten laps. Thus, up to twelve players could play the game, placing bets on the sequence of finishers in the race or on the winning horse.

    The sales of the game had been extremely strong in France (as shown in Table 17-6 and Figure 17-2A), and Jentronics began to wonder whether it would be worthwhile to develop a more professional marketing and distribution approach. They were also considering the possibility of extending sales efforts to other countries.

    The major question facing Jentronics' management was the market potential for the game (both in France and abroad), and the maximum sales possible before the market was saturated.

    To help with its planning problem, the management of Jentronics sought advice from a marketing consultant, who suggested carrying out a market research study to determine the game's market potential and its appropriate positioning against competitors' games. The ideas proposed and the method suggested for obtaining the information were intriguing to the president of Jentronics, and he requested that the consultant provide a firm proposal and cost estimates for the study.

    Two weeks later, both the proposal and the budget figures were on the president's desk. He and his colleagues were of the opinion that the market research study could indeed provide a great deal of valuable information, but it was felt that the cost of carrying out the study—FF150,000—was prohibitive. To break even on this cost would require that about 95,000 units of the game be sold. It was decided, therefore, to forgo the study.

    The president himself went to see the consultant and explained why Jentronics had decided not to go ahead with the proposal. During this meeting, the consultant suggested as an alternative approach the use of a simple marketing model, which had been used on other occasions to estimate sales of new products. The model required only 3 years of historical sales data, on the basis of which an estimate could be made of the total number of potential users and the number of years it would take for the saturation sales level to be reached.

    The president was given a published reference (see Table 17-7) to

TABLE 17-6   ACTUAL AND PREDICTED UNIT SALES OF "ELECTRACK"
(PREDICTIONS BASED ON BASS MODEL OF TABLE 17-7)[a]

Year	Year from Introduction	Actual Sales	Cumulative Actual Sales	Predicted Sales	Cumulative Predicted Sales
1977	0	0	0	0	0
1978	1	4,433	4,433	3,100	3,100
1979	1	60,298	64,731	59,900	63,000
1980	2	67,884	132,615	74,760	137,760
1981	3	89,512	222,127	89,120	226,880
1982	4			100,400	327,280
1983	5			105,490	432,770
1984	6			102,100	534,870
1985	7			90,440	625,310
1986	8			73,100	698,410
1987	9			53,440	751,850
1988	10			36,870	788,720
1989	11			24,100	812,820
1990	12			15,170	827,990

[a]See Figure 17-2B for a plot of actual and predicted sales.

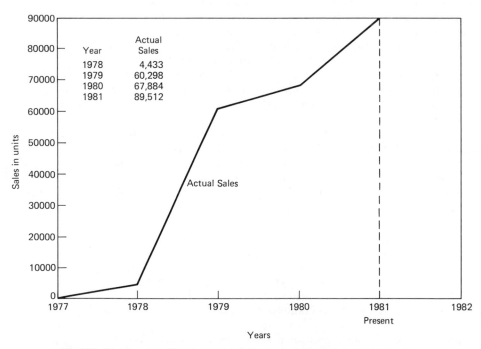

FIGURE 17-2A   JENTRONICS' ACTUAL SALES OF "ELECTRACK"

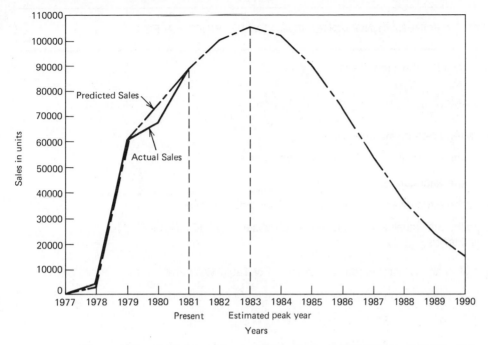

FIGURE 17-2B JENTRONICS' ACTUAL AND PREDICTED SALES OF "ELECTRACK" (USING BASS MODEL)

provide further information on the "straightforward" use of the model. Reading the article, he soon discovered that the sales of one of the products used to illustrate the model (see Figure 17-3) were very similar to the sales of "Electrack." He decided to go ahead and use the model, obtaining the numerical results shown in Tables 17-6 and 17-7 and plotted in Figure 17-2B.

a. What is your assessment of the model described in Table 17-6?
b. How applicable is it in this situation?
c. What recommendations would you make to Jentronics regarding the production and marketing of "Electrack"?

TABLE 17-7   A FORECASTING MODEL FOR NEW PRODUCT SALES

The Bass model for new products is:

$$X_t = pT + (r - p)S_t^* - \frac{r}{T} S_t^* \tag{1}$$

where X_t is the sales during period t

S_t^* is the cumulative number of adopters to date,

T is the total number of adopters

r is the effect of each adopter on each non-adopter, and

p is the individual conversion rate in the absence of the adopters' influence.

The values of X_t and S_t^* for Jentronics (using data of Table 17-7) are:

X_1 = 4433 S_1^* = 4433

X_2 = 60298 S_2^* = 64731

X_3 = 67884 S_3^* = 132615

X_4 = 89512 S_4^* = 222127

To obtain values for the parameters of the equation that represents the model (above), three values for X_t and S_t^* are needed.

The result is a system of three simultaneous equations that can be solved for T, r, and p. In addition, peak sales can be estimated.

The relevant values for Jentronics obtained by solving the equation above are:

Total sales =   more than 850,000
Predicted peak year =   1983
Predicted sales at peak =   105,500

Source: Bass, F. M. 1969. "A New Product Growth Model for Consumer Durables, "Man-agement Science, January, pp. 215–77.

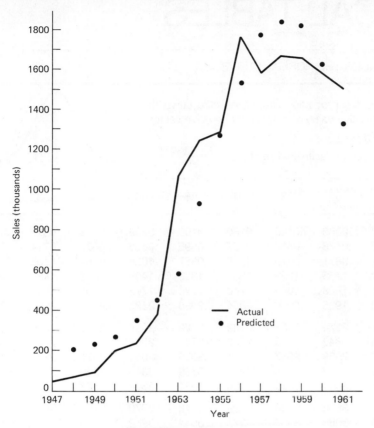

FIGURE 17-3   A NEW PRODUCT GROWTH MODEL FOR ROOM AIR CON-
DITIONERS

APPENDIX I
STATISTICAL TABLES

TABLE A AREAS UNDER THE NORMAL CURVE

An entry in the table is the proportion under the entire curve that is between $z = 0$ and a positive value of z. Areas for negative values of z are obtained by symmetry.

Second decimal place of z

z	.00	.01	.02	.03	.04	.05	.06	.07	.08	.09
0.0	.0000	.0040	.0080	.0120	.0160	.0199	.0239	.0279	.0319	.0359
0.1	.0398	.0438	.0478	.0517	.0557	.0596	.0636	.0675	.0714	.0753
0.2	.0793	.0832	.0871	.0910	.0948	.0987	.1026	.0164	.1103	.1141
0.3	.1179	.1217	.1255	.1293	.1331	.1368	.1406	.1443	.1480	.1517
0.4	.1554	.1591	.1628	.1664	.1700	.1736	.1772	.1808	.1844	.1879
0.5	.1915	.1950	.1985	.2019	.2054	.2088	.2123	.2157	.2190	.2224
0.6	.2257	.2291	.2324	.2357	.2389	.2422	.2454	.2486	.2517	.2549
0.7	.2580	.2611	.2642	.2673	.2703	.2734	.2764	.2794	.2823	.2852
0.8	.2881	.2910	.2939	.2967	.2995	.3023	.3051	.3078	.3106	.3133
0.9	.3159	.3186	.3212	.3238	.3264	.3289	.3315	.3340	.3365	.3389
1.0	.3413	.3438	.3461	.3485	.3508	.3531	.3554	.3577	.3599	.3621
1.1	.3643	.3665	.3686	.3708	.3729	.3749	.3770	.3790	.3810	.3830
1.2	.3849	.3869	.3888	.3907	.3925	.3944	.3962	.3980	.3997	.4015
1.3	.4032	.4049	.4066	.4082	.4099	.4115	.4131	.4147	.4162	.4177
1.4	.4192	.4207	.4222	.4236	.4251	.4265	.4279	.4292	.4306	.4319
1.5	.4332	.4345	.4357	.4370	.4382	.4394	.4406	.4418	.4429	.4441
1.6	.4452	.4463	.4474	.4484	.4495	.4505	.4515	.4525	.4535	.4545
1.7	.4554	.4564	.4573	.4582	.4591	.4599	.4608	.4616	.4625	.4633
1.8	.4641	.4649	.4656	.4664	.4671	.4678	.4686	.4693	.4699	.4706
1.9	.4713	.4719	.4726	.4732	.4738	.4744	.4750	.4756	.4761	.4767
2.0	.4772	.4778	.4783	.4788	.4793	.4798	.4803	.4808	.4812	.4817
2.1	.4821	.4826	.4830	.4834	.4838	.4842	.4846	.4850	.4854	.4857
2.2	.4861	.4864	.4868	.4871	.4875	.4878	.4881	.4884	.4887	.4890
2.3	.4893	.4896	.4898	.4901	.4904	.4906	.4909	.4911	.4913	.4916
2.4	.4918	.4920	.4922	.4925	.4927	.4929	.4931	.4932	.4934	.4936
2.5	.4938	.4940	.4941	.4943	.4945	.4946	.4948	.4949	.4951	.4952
2.6	.4953	.4955	.4956	.4957	.4959	.4960	.4961	.4962	.4963	.4964
2.7	.4965	.4966	.4967	.4968	.4969	.4970	.4971	.4972	.4973	.4974
2.8	.4974	.4975	.4976	.4977	.4977	.4978	.4979	.4979	.4980	.4981
2.9	.4981	.4982	.4982	.4983	.4984	.4984	.4985	.4985	.4986	.4986
3.0	.4987	.4987	.4987	.4988	.4988	.4989	.4989	.4989	.4990	.4990

Source: Donald J. Koosis. Business Statistics. New York: John Wiley & Sons, Inc., 1972.
Reprinted by permission.

TABLE B CRITICAL VALUES FOR THE t STATISTIC

The first column lists the number of degrees of freedom (k). The
headings of the other columns give probabilities (P) for t to exceed
the entry value. Use symmetry for negative t values.

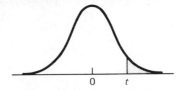

df	P .10	.05	.025	.01	.005
1	3.078	6.314	12.706	31.821	63.657
2	1.886	2.920	4.303	6.965	9.925
3	1.638	2.353	3.182	4.541	5.841
4	1.533	2.132	2.776	3.747	4.604
5	1.476	2.015	2.571	3.365	4.032
6	1.440	1.943	2.447	3.143	3.707
7	1.415	1.895	2.365	2.998	3.499
8	1.397	1.860	2.306	2.896	3.355
9	1.383	1.833	2.262	2.821	3.250
10	1.372	1.812	2.228	2.764	3.169
11	1.363	1.796	2.201	2.718	3.106
12	1.356	1.782	2.179	2.681	3.055
13	1.350	1.771	2.160	2.650	3.012
14	1.345	1.761	2.145	2.624	2.977
15	1.341	1.753	2.131	2.602	2.947
16	1.337	1.746	2.120	2.583	2.921
17	1.333	1.740	2.110	2.567	2.898
18	1.330	1.734	2.101	2.552	2.878
19	1.328	1.729	2.093	2.539	2.861
20	1.325	1.725	2.086	2.528	2.845
21	1.323	1.721	2.080	2.518	2.831
22	1.321	1.717	2.074	2.508	2.819
23	1.319	1.714	2.069	2.500	2.807
24	1.318	1.711	2.064	2.492	2.797
25	1.316	1.708	2.060	2.485	2.787
26	1.315	1.706	2.056	2.479	2.779
27	1.314	1.703	2.052	2.473	2.771
28	1.313	1.701	2.048	2.467	2.763
29	1.311	1.699	2.045	2.462	2.756
30	1.310	1.697	2.042	2.457	2.750
40	1.303	1.684	2.021	2.423	2.704
60	1.296	1.671	2.000	2.390	2.660
120	1.289	1.658	1.980	2.358	2.617
∞	1.282	1.645	1.960	2.326	2.576

Source: Donald J. Koosis, Business Statistics. New York: John Wiley & Sons, Inc. 1972.

TABLE C   CRITICAL VALUES FOR THE *F*-STATISTIC

Degrees of Freedom for Denominator (df_2)	Degrees of Freedom for Numerator (df_1)										
	1	2	3	4	5	6	7	8	9	10	11
1	161	200	216	225	230	234	237	239	241	242	243
	4052	4999	5403	5625	5764	5859	5928	5981	6022	6056	6082
2	18.51	19.00	19.16	19.25	19.30	19.33	19.36	19.37	19.38	19.39	19.40
	98.49	99.01	99.17	99.25	99.30	99.33	99.34	99.36	99.38	99.40	99.41
3	10.13	9.55	9.28	9.12	9.01	8.94	8.88	8.84	8.81	8.78	8.76
	34.12	30.81	29.46	28.71	28.24	27.91	27.67	27.49	27.34	27.23	27.13
4	7.71	6.94	6.59	6.39	6.26	6.16	6.09	6.04	6.00	5.96	5.93
	21.20	18.00	16.69	15.98	15.52	15.21	14.98	14.80	14.66	14.54	14.45
5	6.61	5.79	5.41	5.19	5.05	4.95	4.88	4.82	4.78	4.74	4.70
	16.26	13.27	12.06	11.39	10.97	10.67	10.45	10.27	10.15	10.05	9.96
6	5.99	5.14	4.76	4.53	4.39	4.28	4.21	4.15	4.10	4.06	4.03
	13.74	10.92	9.78	9.15	8.75	8.47	8.26	8.10	7.98	7.87	7.79
7	5.59	4.74	4.35	4.12	3.97	3.87	3.79	3.73	3.68	3.63	3.60
	12.25	9.55	8.45	7.85	7.46	7.19	7.00	6.84	6.71	6.62	6.54
8	5.32	4.46	4.07	3.84	3.69	3.58	3.50	3.44	3.39	3.34	3.31
	11.26	8.65	7.59	7.01	6.63	6.37	6.19	6.03	5.91	5.82	5.74
9	5.12	4.26	3.86	3.63	3.48	3.37	3.29	3.23	3.18	3.13	3.10
	10.56	8.02	6.99	6.42	6.06	5.80	5.62	5.47	5.35	5.26	5.18
10	4.96	4.10	3.71	3.48	3.33	3.22	3.14	3.07	3.02	2.97	2.94
	10.04	7.56	6.55	5.99	5.64	5.39	5.21	5.06	4.95	4.85	4.78
11	4.84	3.98	3.59	3.36	3.20	3.09	3.01	2.95	2.90	2.86	2.82
	9.65	7.20	6.22	5.67	5.32	5.07	4.88	4.74	4.63	4.54	4.46
12	4.75	3.88	3.49	3.26	3.11	3.00	2.92	2.85	2.80	2.76	2.72
	9.33	6.93	5.95	5.41	5.06	4.82	4.65	4.50	4.39	4.30	4.22
13	4.67	3.80	3.41	3.18	3.02	2.92	2.84	2.77	2.72	2.67	2.63
	9.07	6.70	5.74	5.20	4.86	4.62	4.44	4.30	4.19	4.10	4.02

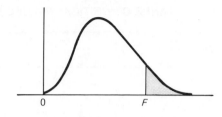

12	14	16	20	24	30	40	50	75	100	200	500	∞
244	245	246	248	249	250	251	252	253	253	254	254	254
6106	*6142*	*6169*	*6208*	*6234*	*6258*	*6286*	*6302*	*6323*	*6334*	*6352*	*6361*	*6366*
19.41	19.42	19.43	19.44	19.45	19.46	19.47	19.47	19.48	19.49	19.49	19.50	19.50
99.42	*99.43*	*99.44*	*99.45*	*99.46*	*99.47*	*99.48*	*99.48*	*99.49*	*99.49*	*99.50*	*99.50*	*99.50*
8.74	8.71	8.69	8.66	8.64	8.62	8.60	8.58	8.57	8.56	8.54	8.54	8.53
27.05	*26.92*	*26.83*	*26.69*	*26.60*	*26.50*	*26.41*	*26.30*	*26.27*	*26.23*	*26.18*	*26.14*	*26.12*
5.91	5.87	5.84	5.80	5.77	5.74	5.71	5.70	5.68	5.66	5.65	5.64	5.63
14.37	*14.24*	*14.15*	*14.02*	*13.93*	*13.83*	*13.74*	*13.69*	*13.61*	*13.57*	*13.52*	*13.48*	*13.46*
4.68	4.64	4.60	4.56	4.53	4.50	4.46	4.44	4.42	4.40	4.38	4.37	4.36
9.89	*9.77*	*9.68*	*9.55*	*9.47*	*9.38*	*9.29*	*9.24*	*9.17*	*9.13*	*9.07*	*9.04*	*9.02*
4.00	3.96	3.92	3.87	3.84	3.81	3.77	3.75	3.72	3.71	3.69	3.68	3.67
7.72	*7.60*	*7.52*	*7.39*	*7.31*	*7.23*	*7.14*	*7.09*	*7.02*	*6.99*	*6.94*	*6.90*	*6.88*
3.57	3.52	3.49	3.44	3.41	3.38	3.34	3.32	3.29	3.28	3.25	3.24	3.23
6.47	*6.35*	*6.27*	*6.15*	*6.07*	*5.98*	*5.90*	*5.85*	*5.78*	*5.75*	*5.70*	*5.67*	*5.65*
3.28	3.23	3.20	3.15	3.12	3.08	3.05	3.03	3.00	2.98	2.96	2.94	2.93
5.67	*5.56*	*5.48*	*5.36*	*5.28*	*5.20*	*5.11*	*5.06*	*5.00*	*4.96*	*4.91*	*4.88*	*4.86*
3.07	3.02	2.98	2.93	2.90	2.86	2.82	2.80	2.77	2.76	2.73	2.72	2.71
5.11	*5.00*	*4.92*	*4.80*	*4.73*	*4.64*	*4.56*	*4.51*	*4.45*	*4.41*	*4.36*	*4.33*	*4.31*
2.91	2.86	2.82	2.77	2.74	2.70	2.67	2.64	2.61	2.59	2.56	2.55	2.54
4.71	*4.60*	*4.52*	*4.41*	*4.33*	*4.25*	*4.17*	*4.12*	*4.05*	*4.01*	*3.96*	*3.93*	*3.91*
2.79	2.74	2.70	2.65	2.61	2.57	2.53	2.50	2.47	2.45	2.42	2.41	2.40
4.40	*4.29*	*4.21*	*4.10*	*4.02*	*3.94*	*3.86*	*3.80*	*3.74*	*3.70*	*3.66*	*3.62*	*3.60*
2.69	2.64	2.60	2.54	2.50	2.46	2.42	2.40	2.36	2.35	2.32	2.31	2.30
4.16	*4.05*	*3.98*	*3.86*	*3.78*	*3.70*	*3.61*	*3.56*	*3.49*	*3.46*	*3.41*	*3.38*	*3.36*
2.60	2.55	2.51	2.46	2.42	2.38	2.34	2.32	2.28	2.26	2.24	2.22	2.21
3.96	*3.85*	*3.78*	*3.67*	*3.59*	*3.51*	*3.42*	*3.37*	*3.30*	*3.27*	*3.21*	*3.18*	*3.16*

TABLE C   CRITICAL VALUES FOR THE *F*-STATISTIC (*Continued*)

Degrees of Freedom for Denominator (df_2)	Degrees of Freedom for Numerator (df_1)										
	1	2	3	4	5	6	7	8	9	10	11
14	4.60	3.74	3.34	3.11	2.96	2.85	2.77	2.70	2.65	2.60	2.56
	8.86	6.51	5.56	5.03	4.69	4.46	4.28	4.14	4.03	3.94	3.86
15	4.54	3.68	3.29	3.06	2.90	2.79	2.70	2.64	2.59	2.55	2.51
	8.68	6.36	5.42	4.89	4.56	4.32	4.14	4.00	3.89	3.80	3.73
16	4.49	3.63	3.24	3.01	2.85	2.74	2.66	2.59	2.54	2.49	2.45
	8.53	6.23	5.29	4.77	4.44	4.20	4.03	3.89	3.78	3.69	3.61
17	4.45	3.59	3.20	2.96	2.81	2.70	2.62	2.55	2.50	2.45	2.41
	8.40	6.11	5.18	4.67	4.34	4.10	3.93	3.79	3.68	3.59	3.52
18	4.41	3.55	3.16	2.93	2.77	2.66	2.58	2.51	2.46	2.41	2.37
	8.28	6.01	5.09	4.58	4.25	4.01	3.85	3.71	3.60	3.51	3.44
19	4.38	3.52	3.13	2.90	2.74	2.63	2.55	2.48	2.43	2.38	2.34
	8.18	5.93	5.01	4.50	4.17	3.94	3.77	3.63	3.52	3.43	3.36
20	4.35	3.49	3.10	2.87	2.71	2.60	2.52	2.45	2.40	2.35	2.31
	8.10	5.85	4.94	4.43	4.10	3.87	3.71	3.56	3.45	3.37	3.30
21	4.32	3.47	3.07	2.84	2.68	2.57	2.49	2.42	2.37	2.32	2.28
	8.02	5.78	4.87	4.37	4.04	3.81	3.65	3.51	3.40	3.31	3.24
22	4.30	3.44	3.05	2.82	2.66	2.55	2.47	2.40	2.35	2.30	2.26
	7.94	5.72	4.82	4.31	3.99	3.76	3.59	3.45	3.35	3.26	3.18
23	4.28	3.42	3.03	2.80	2.64	2.53	2.45	2.38	2.32	2.28	2.24
	7.78	5.66	4.76	4.26	3.94	3.71	3.54	3.41	3.30	3.21	3.14
24	4.26	3.40	3.01	2.78	2.62	2.51	2.43	2.36	2.30	2.26	2.22
	7.82	5.61	4.72	4.22	3.90	3.67	3.50	3.36	3.25	3.17	3.09
25	4.24	3.38	2.99	2.76	2.60	2.49	2.41	2.34	2.28	2.24	2.20
	7.77	5.57	4.68	4.18	3.86	3.63	3.46	3.32	3.21	3.13	3.05
26	4.22	3.37	2.89	2.74	2.59	2.47	2.39	2.32	2.27	2.22	2.18
	7.72	5.53	4.64	4.14	3.82	3.59	3.42	3.29	3.17	3.09	3.02
27	4.21	3.35	2.96	2.73	2.57	2.46	2.37	2.30	2.25	2.20	2.16
	7.68	5.49	4.60	4.11	3.79	3.56	3.39	3.26	3.14	3.06	2.98
28	4.20	3.34	2.95	2.71	2.56	2.44	2.36	2.29	2.24	2.19	2.15
	7.64	5.45	4.57	4.07	3.76	3.53	3.36	3.23	3.11	3.03	2.95
29	4.18	3.33	2.93	2.70	2.54	2.43	2.35	2.28	2.22	2.18	2.14
	7.60	5.52	4.54	4.04	3.73	3.50	3.33	3.20	3.08	3.00	2.92

12	14	16	20	24	30	40	50	75	100	200	500	∞
2.53	2.48	2.44	2.39	2.35	2.31	2.27	2.24	2.21	2.19	2.16	2.14	2.13
3.80	*3.70*	*3.62*	*3.51*	*3.43*	*3.34*	*3.26*	*3.21*	*3.14*	*3.11*	*3.06*	*3.02*	*3.00*
2.48	2.43	2.39	2.33	2.29	2.25	2.21	2.18	2.15	2.12	2.10	2.08	2.07
3.67	*3.56*	*3.48*	*3.36*	*3.29*	*3.20*	*3.12*	*3.07*	*3.00*	*2.97*	*2.92*	*2.89*	*2.87*
2.42	2.37	2.33	2.28	2.24	2.20	2.16	2.13	2.09	2.07	2.04	2.02	2.01
3.55	*3.45*	*3.37*	*3.25*	*3.18*	*3.10*	*3.01*	*2.96*	*2.89*	*2.86*	*2.80*	*2.77*	*2.75*
2.38	2.33	2.29	2.23	2.19	2.15	2.11	2.08	2.04	2.02	1.99	1.97	1.96
3.45	*3.35*	*3.27*	*3.16*	*3.08*	*3.00*	*2.92*	*2.86*	*2.79*	*2.76*	*2.70*	*2.67*	*2.65*
2.34	2.29	2.25	2.19	2.15	2.11	2.07	2.04	2.00	1.98	1.95	1.93	1.92
3.37	*3.27*	*3.19*	*3.07*	*3.00*	*2.91*	*2.83*	*2.78*	*2.71*	*2.68*	*2.62*	*2.59*	*2.57*
2.31	2.26	2.21	2.15	2.11	2.07	2.02	2.00	1.96	1.94	1.91	1.90	1.88
3.30	*3.19*	*3.12*	*3.00*	*2.92*	*2.84*	*2.76*	*2.70*	*2.63*	*2.60*	*2.54*	*2.51*	*2.49*
2.28	2.23	2.18	2.12	2.08	2.04	1.99	1.96	1.92	1.90	1.87	1.85	1.84
3.23	*3.13*	*3.05*	*2.94*	*2.86*	*2.77*	*2.69*	*2.63*	*2.56*	*2.53*	*2.47*	*2.44*	*2.42*
2.25	2.20	2.15	2.09	2.05	2.00	1.96	1.93	1.89	1.87	1.84	1.82	1.81
3.17	*3.07*	*2.99*	*2.88*	*2.80*	*2.72*	*2.63*	*2.58*	*2.51*	*2.47*	*2.42*	*2.38*	*2.36*
2.23	2.18	2.13	2.07	2.03	1.98	1.93	1.91	1.87	1.84	1.81	1.80	1.78
3.12	*3.02*	*2.94*	*2.83*	*2.75*	*2.67*	*2.58*	*2.53*	*2.46*	*2.42*	*2.37*	*2.33*	*2.31*
2.20	2.14	2.10	2.04	2.00	1.96	1.91	1.88	1.84	1.82	1.79	1.77	1.76
3.07	*2.97*	*2.89*	*2.78*	*2.70*	*2.62*	*2.53*	*2.48*	*2.41*	*2.37*	*2.32*	*2.28*	*2.26*
2.18	2.13	2.09	2.02	1.98	1.94	1.89	1.86	1.82	1.80	1.76	1.74	1.73
3.03	*2.93*	*2.85*	*2.74*	*2.66*	*2.58*	*2.49*	*2.44*	*2.36*	*2.33*	*2.27*	*2.23*	*2.21*
2.16	2.11	2.06	2.00	1.96	1.92	1.87	1.84	1.80	1.77	1.74	1.72	1.71
2.99	*2.89*	*2.81*	*2.70*	*2.62*	*2.54*	*2.45*	*2.40*	*2.32*	*2.29*	*2.23*	*1.19*	*2.17*
2.15	2.10	2.05	1.99	1.95	1.90	1.85	1.82	1.78	1.76	1.72	1.70	1.69
2.96	*2.86*	*2.77*	*2.66*	*2.58*	*2.50*	*2.41*	*2.36*	*2.28*	*2.25*	*2.19*	*2.15*	*2.13*
2.13	2.08	2.03	1.97	1.93	1.88	1.84	1.80	1.76	1.74	1.71	1.68	1.67
2.93	*2.83*	*2.74*	*2.63*	*2.55*	*2.47*	*2.38*	*2.33*	*2.25*	*2.21*	*2.16*	*2.12*	*2.10*
2.12	2.06	2.02	1.96	1.91	1.87	1.81	1.78	1.75	1.72	1.69	1.67	1.65
2.90	*2.80*	*2.71*	*2.60*	*2.52*	*2.44*	*2.35*	*2.30*	*2.22*	*2.18*	*2.13*	*2.09*	*2.06*
2.10	2.05	2.00	1.94	1.90	1.85	1.80	1.77	1.73	1.71	1.68	1.65	1.64
2.87	*2.77*	*2.68*	*2.57*	*2.49*	*2.41*	*2.32*	*2.27*	*2.19*	*2.15*	*2.10*	*2.06*	*2.03*

TABLE C   CRITICAL VALUES FOR THE *F*-STATISTIC (*Continued*)

Degrees of Freedom for Denominator (df_2)	Degrees of Freedom for Numerator (df_1)										
	1	2	3	4	5	6	7	8	9	10	11
30	4.17	3.32	2.92	2.69	2.53	2.42	2.34	2.27	2.21	2.16	2.12
	7.56	5.39	4.51	4.02	3.70	3.47	3.30	3.17	3.06	2.98	2.00
32	4.15	3.30	2.90	2.67	2.51	2.40	2.32	2.25	2.19	2.14	2.10
	7.50	5.34	4.46	3.97	3.66	3.42	3.25	3.12	3.01	2.94	2.86
34	4.13	3.28	2.88	2.65	2.49	2.38	2.30	2.23	2.17	2.12	2.08
	7.44	5.29	4.42	3.93	3.61	3.38	3.21	3.08	2.97	2.89	2.82
36	4.11	3.26	2.86	2.63	2.48	2.36	2.28	2.21	2.15	2.10	2.06
	7.39	5.25	4.38	3.89	3.58	3.35	3.18	3.04	2.94	2.86	2.78
38	4.10	3.25	2.85	2.62	2.46	2.35	2.26	2.19	2.14	2.09	2.05
	7.35	5.21	4.34	3.86	3.54	3.32	3.15	3.02	2.91	2.82	2.75
40	4.08	3.23	2.84	2.61	2.45	2.34	2.25	2.18	2.12	2.07	2.04
	7.31	5.18	4.31	3.83	3.51	3.29	3.12	2.99	2.88	2.80	2.73
42	4.07	3.22	2.83	2.59	2.44	2.32	2.24	2.17	2.11	2.06	2.02
	7.27	5.15	4.29	3.80	3.49	3.26	3.10	2.96	2.86	2.77	2.70
44	4.06	3.21	2.82	2.58	2.43	2.31	2.23	2.16	2.10	2.05	2.01
	7.24	5.12	4.26	3.78	3.46	3.24	3.07	2.94	2.84	2.75	2.68
46	4.05	3.20	2.81	2.57	2.42	2.30	2.22	2.14	2.09	2.04	2.00
	7.21	5.10	4.24	3.76	3.44	3.22	3.05	2.92	2.82	2.73	2.66
48	4.04	3.19	2.80	2.56	2.41	2.30	2.21	2.14	2.08	2.03	1.99
	7.19	5.08	4.22	3.74	3.42	3.20	3.04	2.90	2.80	2.71	2.64
50	4.03	3.18	2.79	2.56	2.40	2.29	2.20	2.13	2.07	2.02	1.98
	7.17	5.06	4.20	3.72	3.41	3.18	3.02	2.88	2.78	2.70	2.62
55	4.02	3.17	2.78	2.54	2.38	2.27	2.18	2.11	2.05	2.00	1.97
	7.12	5.01	4.16	3.68	3.37	3.15	2.98	2.85	2.75	2.66	2.59
60	4.00	3.15	2.76	2.52	2.37	2.25	2.17	2.10	2.04	1.99	1.95
	7.08	4.98	4.13	3.65	3.34	3.12	2.95	2.82	2.72	2.63	2.56
65	3.99	3.14	2.75	2.51	2.36	2.24	2.15	2.08	2.02	1.98	1.94
	7.04	4.95	4.10	3.62	3.31	3.09	2.93	2.79	2.70	2.61	2.54
70	3.98	3.13	2.74	2.50	2.35	2.32	2.14	2.07	2.01	1.97	1.93
	7.01	4.92	4.08	3.60	3.29	3.07	2.91	2.77	2.67	2.57	2.51
80	3.96	3.11	2.72	2.48	2.33	2.21	2.12	2.05	1.99	1.95	1.91
	6.96	4.88	4.04	3.56	3.25	3.04	2.87	2.74	2.64	2.55	2.48

12	14	16	20	24	30	40	50	75	100	200	500	∞
2.09	2.04	1.99	1.93	1.89	1.84	1.79	1.76	1.72	1.69	1.66	1.64	1.62
2.84	*2.74*	*2.66*	*2.55*	*2.47*	*2.38*	*2.29*	*2.24*	*2.16*	*2.13*	*2.07*	*2.03*	*2.01*
2.07	2.02	1.97	1.91	1.86	1.82	1.76	1.74	1.69	1.67	1.64	1.61	1.59
2.80	*2.70*	*2.62*	*2.51*	*2.42*	*2.34*	*2.25*	*2.20*	*2.12*	*2.08*	*2.02*	*1.98*	*1.96*
2.05	2.00	1.95	1.89	1.84	1.80	1.74	1.71	1.67	1.64	1.61	1.59	1.57
2.76	*2.66*	*2.58*	*2.47*	*2.38*	*2.30*	*2.21*	*2.15*	*2.08*	*2.04*	*1.98*	*1.94*	*1.91*
2.03	1.89	1.93	1.87	1.82	1.78	1.72	1.69	1.65	1.62	1.59	1.56	1.55
2.72	*2.62*	*2.54*	*2.43*	*2.35*	*2.26*	*2.17*	*2.12*	*2.04*	*2.00*	*1.94*	*1.90*	*1.87*
2.02	1.96	1.92	1.85	1.80	1.76	1.71	1.67	1.63	1.60	1.57	1.54	1.53
2.69	*2.59*	*2.51*	*2.40*	*2.32*	*2.22*	*2.14*	*2.08*	*2.00*	*1.97*	*1.90*	*1.86*	*1.84*
2.00	1.95	1.90	1.84	1.79	1.74	1.69	1.66	1.61	1.59	1.55	1.53	1.51
2.66	*2.56*	*2.49*	*2.37*	*2.29*	*2.20*	*2.11*	*2.05*	*1.97*	*1.94*	*1.88*	*1.84*	*1.81*
1.99	1.94	1.89	1.82	1.78	1.73	1.68	1.64	1.60	1.57	1.54	1.51	1.49
2.64	*2.54*	*2.46*	*2.35*	*2.26*	*2.17*	*2.08*	*2.02*	*1.94*	*1.91*	*1.85*	*1.80*	*1.78*
1.98	1.92	1.88	1.81	1.76	1.72	1.66	1.63	1.58	1.56	1.52	1.50	1.48
2.62	*2.52*	*2.44*	*2.32*	*2.24*	*2.15*	*2.06*	*2.00*	*1.92*	*1.88*	*1.82*	*1.78*	*1.75*
1.97	1.91	1.87	1.80	1.75	1.71	1.65	1.62	1.57	1.54	1.51	1.48	1.46
2.60	*2.50*	*2.42*	*2.30*	*2.22*	*2.13*	*2.04*	*1.98*	*1.90*	*1.86*	*1.80*	*1.76*	*1.72*
1.96	1.90	1.86	1.79	1.74	1.70	1.64	1.61	1.56	1.53	1.50	1.47	1.45
2.58	*2.48*	*2.40*	*2.28*	*2.20*	*2.11*	*2.02*	*1.96*	*1.88*	*1.84*	*1.78*	*1.73*	*1.70*
1.95	1.90	1.85	1.78	1.74	1.69	1.63	1.60	1.55	1.52	1.48	1.46	1.44
2.56	*2.46*	*2.39*	*2.26*	*2.18*	*2.10*	*2.00*	*1.94*	*1.86*	*1.82*	*1.76*	*1.71*	*1.68*
1.93	1.88	1.83	1.76	1.72	1.67	1.61	1.58	1.52	1.50	1.46	1.43	1.41
2.53	*2.43*	*2.35*	*2.23*	*2.15*	*2.06*	*1.96*	*1.90*	*1.82*	*1.78*	*1.71*	*1.66*	*1.64*
1.92	1.86	1.81	1.75	1.70	1.65	1.59	1.56	1.50	1.48	1.44	1.41	1.39
2.50	*2.40*	*2.32*	*2.20*	*2.12*	*2.03*	*1.93*	*1.87*	*1.79*	*1.74*	*1.68*	*1.63*	*1.60*
1.90	1.85	1.80	1.73	1.68	1.63	1.57	1.54	1.49	1.46	1.42	1.39	1.37
2.47	*2.37*	*2.30*	*2.18*	*2.09*	*2.00*	*1.90*	*1.84*	*1.76*	*1.71*	*1.64*	*1.60*	*1.56*
1.89	1.84	1.79	1.72	1.67	1.62	1.56	1.53	1.47	1.45	1.40	1.37	1.35
2.45	*2.35*	*2.28*	*2.15*	*2.07*	*1.98*	*1.88*	*1.82*	*1.74*	*1.69*	*1.63*	*1.56*	*1.53*
1.88	1.82	1.77	1.70	1.65	1.60	1.54	1.51	1.45	1.42	1.38	1.35	1.32
2.41	*2.32*	*2.24*	*2.11*	*2.03*	*1.94*	*1.84*	*1.78*	*1.70*	*1.65*	*1.57*	*1.52*	*1.49*

TABLE C CRITICAL VALUES FOR THE *F*-STATISTIC (*Continued*)

Degrees of Freedom for Denominator (df_2)	Degrees of Freedom for Numerator (df_1)										
	1	2	3	4	5	6	7	8	9	10	11
100	3.94	3.09	2.70	2.46	2.30	2.19	2.10	2.03	1.97	1.92	1.88
	6.90	4.82	3.98	3.51	3.20	2.99	2.82	2.69	2.59	2.51	2.43
125	3.92	3.07	2.68	2.44	2.29	2.17	2.08	2.01	1.95	1.90	1.86
	6.84	4.78	3.94	3.47	3.17	2.95	2.79	2.65	2.56	2.47	2.40
150	3.91	3.06	2.67	2.43	2.27	2.16	2.07	2.00	1.94	1.89	1.85
	6.81	4.75	3.91	3.44	3.13	2.92	2.76	2.62	2.53	2.44	2.37
200	3.89	3.04	2.65	2.41	2.26	2.14	2.05	1.98	1.92	1.87	1.83
	6.76	4.71	3.88	3.41	3.11	2.90	2.73	2.60	2.50	2.41	2.34
400	3.86	3.02	2.62	2.39	2.23	2.12	2.03	1.96	1.90	1.85	1.81
	6.70	4.66	3.83	3.36	3.06	2.85	2.69	2.55	2.46	2.37	2.29
1000	3.85	3.00	2.61	2.38	2.22	2.10	2.02	1.95	1.89	1.84	1.80
	6.66	4.62	3.80	3.34	3.04	2.82	2.66	2.53	2.43	2.34	2.26
	3.84	2.99	2.60	2.37	2.21	2.09	2.01	1.94	1.88	1.83	1.79
	6.64	4.60	3.78	3.32	3.02	2.80	2.64	2.51	2.41	2.32	2.24

12	14	16	20	24	30	40	50	75	100	200	500	∞
1.85	1.79	1.75	1.68	1.63	1.57	1.51	1.48	1.42	1.39	1.34	1.30	1.28
2.36	*2.26*	*2.19*	*2.06*	*1.98*	*1.89*	*1.79*	*1.73*	*1.64*	*1.59*	*1.51*	*1.46*	*1.43*
1.83	1.77	1.72	1.65	1.60	1.55	1.49	1.45	1.39	1.36	1.31	1.27	1.25
2.33	*2.23*	*2.15*	*2.03*	*1.94*	*1.85*	*1.75*	*1.68*	*1.59*	*1.54*	*1.46*	*1.40*	*1.37*
1.82	1.76	1.71	1.64	1.59	1.54	1.47	1.44	1.37	1.34	1.29	1.25	1.22
2.30	*2.20*	*2.12*	*2.00*	*1.91*	*1.83*	*1.72*	*1.66*	*1.56*	*1.51*	*1.43*	*1.37*	*1.33*
1.80	1.74	1.69	1.62	1.57	1.52	1.45	1.42	1.35	1.32	1.26	1.22	1.19
2.28	*2.17*	*2.09*	*1.97*	*1.88*	*1.79*	*1.69*	*1.62*	*1.52*	*1.48*	*1.39*	*1.33*	*1.28*
1.78	1.72	1.67	1.60	1.54	1.49	1.42	1.38	1.32	1.28	1.22	1.16	1.13
2.23	*2.12*	*2.04*	*1.92*	*1.84*	*1.74*	*1.64*	*1.57*	*1.47*	*1.42*	*1.32*	*1.24*	*1.19*
1.76	1.70	1.65	1.58	1.53	1.47	1.41	1.36	1.30	1.26	1.19	1.13	1.08
2.20	*2.09*	*2.01*	*1.89*	*1.81*	*1.71*	*1.61*	*1.54*	*1.44*	*1.38*	*1.28*	*1.19*	*1.11*
1.75	1.69	1.64	1.57	1.52	1.46	1.40	1.35	1.28	1.24	1.17	1.11	1.00
2.18	*2.07*	*1.99*	*1.87*	*1.79*	*1.69*	*1.59*	*1.52*	*1.41*	*1.36*	*1.25*	*1.15*	*1.00*

Note: 5 percent points for the distribution of F are presented in roman type: 1 percent points are in italic type.

Source: Donald J. Koosis. *Business Statistics.* New York: John Wiley & Sons, Inc. 1972.
Reprinted by permission.

TABLE D VALUES OF THE DURBIN-WATSON STATISTIC

5 Percent Significance Points of d_l and d_u (for one-sided test)

n	k =1 d_L	k =1 d_U	k =2 d_L	k =2 d_U	k =3 d_L	k =3 d_U	k =4 d_L	k =4 d_U	k =5 d_L	k =5 d_U
15	1.08	1.36	0.95	1.54	0.82	1.75	0.69	1.97	0.56	2.21
16	1.10	1.37	0.98	1.54	0.86	1.73	0.74	1.93	0.62	2.15
17	1.13	1.38	1.02	1.54	0.90	1.71	0.78	1.90	0.67	2.10
18	1.16	1.39	1.05	1.53	0.93	1.69	0.82	1.87	0.71	2.06
19	1.18	1.40	1.08	1.53	0.97	1.68	0.86	1.85	0.75	2.02
20	1.20	1.41	1.10	1.54	1.00	1.68	0.90	1.83	0.79	1.99
21	1.22	1.42	1.13	1.54	1.03	1.67	0.93	1.81	0.83	1.96
22	1.24	1.43	1.15	1.54	1.05	1.66	0.96	1.80	0.86	1.94
23	1.26	1.44	1.17	1.54	1.08	1.66	0.99	1.79	0.90	1.92
24	1.27	1.45	1.19	1.55	1.10	1.66	1.01	1.78	0.93	1.90
25	1.29	1.45	1.21	1.55	1.12	1.66	1.04	1.77	0.95	1.89
26	1.30	1.46	1.22	1.55	1.14	1.65	1.06	1.76	0.98	1.88
27	1.32	1.47	1.24	1.56	1.16	1.65	1.08	1.76	1.01	1.86
28	1.33	1.48	1.26	1.56	1.18	1.65	1.10	1.75	1.03	1.85
29	1.34	1.48	1.27	1.56	1.20	1.65	1.12	1.74	1.05	1.84
30	1.35	1.49	1.28	1.57	1.21	1.65	1.14	1.74	1.07	1.83
31	1.36	1.50	1.30	1.57	1.23	1.65	1.16	1.74	1.09	1.83
32	1.37	1.50	1.31	1.57	1.24	1.65	1.18	1.73	1.11	1.82
33	1.38	1.51	1.32	1.58	1.26	1.65	1.19	1.73	1.13	1.81
34	1.39	1.51	1.33	1.58	1.27	1.65	1.21	1.73	1.15	1.81
35	1.40	1.52	1.34	1.58	1.28	1.65	1.22	1.73	1.16	1.80
36	1.41	1.52	1.35	1.59	1.29	1.65	1.24	1.73	1.18	1.80
37	1.42	1.53	1.36	1.59	1.31	1.66	1.25	1.72	1.19	1.80
38	1.43	1.54	1.37	1.59	1.32	1.66	1.26	1.72	1.21	1.79
39	1.43	1.54	1.38	1.60	1.33	1.66	1.27	1.72	1.22	1.79
40	1.44	1.54	1.39	1.60	1.34	1.66	1.29	1.72	1.23	1.79
45	1.48	1.57	1.43	1.62	1.38	1.67	1.34	1.72	1.29	1.78
50	1.50	1.59	1.46	1.63	1.42	1.67	1.38	1.72	1.34	1.77
55	1.53	1.60	1.49	1.64	1.45	1.68	1.41	1.72	1.38	1.77
60	1.55	1.62	1.51	1.65	1.48	1.69	1.44	1.73	1.41	1.77
65	1.57	1.63	1.54	1.66	1.50	1.70	1.47	1.73	1.44	1.77
70	1.58	1.64	1.55	1.67	1.52	1.70	1.49	1.74	1.46	1.77
75	1.60	1.65	1.57	1.68	1.54	1.71	1.51	1.74	1.49	1.77
80	1.61	1.66	1.59	1.69	1.56	1.72	1.53	1.74	1.51	1.77
85	1.62	1.67	1.60	1.70	1.57	1.72	1.55	1.75	1.52	1.77
90	1.63	1.68	1.61	1.70	1.59	1.73	1.57	1.75	1.54	1.78
95	1.64	1.69	1.62	1.71	1.60	1.73	1.58	1.75	1.56	1.78
100	1.65	1.69	1.63	1.72	1.61	1.74	1.59	1.76	1.57	1.78

Source: J. Durbin and G. S. Watson, "Testing for Serial Correlation in Least Squares Regression," *Biometrika* **38** (1951), pp. 159–177. Reprinted by permission.

k = no. of regressors (independent variables)

TABLE E CRITICAL POINTS OF THE CHI-SQUARE (χ^2) STATISTIC

The first column lists the number of degrees of freedom. The headings of the other columns give probabilities (P) for χ^2 to exceed the entry value.

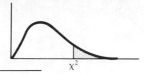

df	.050	P .025	.010	.005
1	3.84146	5.02389	6.63490	7.87944
2	5.99147	7.37776	9.21034	10.5966
3	7.81473	9.34840	11.3449	12.8381
4	9.48773	11.1433	13.2767	14.8602
5	11.0705	12.8325	15.0863	16.7496
6	12.5916	14.4494	16.8119	18.5476
7	14.0671	16.0128	18.4753	20.2777
8	15.5073	17.5346	20.0902	21.9550
9	16.9190	19.0228	21.6660	23.5893
10	18.3070	20.4831	23.2093	25.1882
11	19.6751	21.9200	24.7250	26.7569
12	21.0261	23.3367	26.2170	28.2995
13	22.3621	24.7356	27.6883	29.8194
14	23.6848	26.1190	29.1413	31.3193
15	24.9958	27.4884	30.5779	32.8013
16	26.2962	28.8454	31.9999	34.2672
17	27.5871	30.1910	33.4087	35.7185
18	28.8693	31.5264	34.8053	37.1564
19	30.1435	32.8523	36.1908	38.5822
20	31.4104	34.1696	37.5662	39.9968
21	32.6705	35.4789	38.9321	41.4010
22	33.9244	36.7807	40.2894	42.7956
23	35.1725	38.0757	41.6384	44.1813
24	36.4151	39.3641	42.9798	45.5585
25	37.6525	40.6465	44.3141	46.9278
26	38.8852	41.9232	45.6417	48.2899
27	40.1133	43.1944	46.9630	49.6449
28	41.3372	44.4607	48.2782	50.9933
29	42.5569	45.7222	49.5879	52.3356
30	43.7729	46.9792	50.8922	53.6720
40	55.7585	59.3417	63.6907	66.7659
50	67.5048	71.4202	76.1539	79.4900
60	79.0819	83.2976	88.3794	91.9517
70	90.5312	95.0231	100.425	104.215
80	101.879	106.629	112.329	116.321
90	113.145	118.136	124.116	128.299
100	124.342	129.561	135.807	140.169

Source: Donald J. Koosis, *Business Statistics.* New York: John Wiley & Sons Inc., 1972.

APPENDIX II
GLOSSARY OF FORECASTING TERMS

Accuracy
The most commonly used criterion for evaluating the performance of alternative forecasting methods and models is accuracy. It refers to the correctness of the forecast as measured against actual events. Accuracy can be measured using such dimensions as mean squared error (MSE); mean absolute percentage error (MAPE); or mean percentage error or bias (MPE).

Adaptive response rate
In many time-series forecasting methods a trade-off must be made between smoothing randomness and reacting quickly to changes in the basic pattern. Adaptive-response-rate forecasting involves using a decision rule that instructs the forecasting methodology (such as exponential smoothing) to adapt more quickly when it appears that a change in pattern has occurred and to do more smoothing of randomness when it appears that no such change has occurred.

Algorithm
A systematic set of rules for solving a particular problem. The sets of rules used in applying many of the quantitative methods of forecasting are algorithms.

Amplitude
In the context of line spectrum analysis of a time-series the amplitude of a wave is the "strength" of the wave. See chapter 8.

Applicability
Recently, applicability has gained recognition as an important criterion in selecting a forecasting method. Applicability refers to the ease with which a method can be applied to a given situation with a specific user of forecasting. Increased complexity of sophisticated forecasting methods often reduces applicability.

ARIMA
An abbreviation for autoregressive (AR)—integrated (I)—moving average (MA). This name describes a broad class of time-series models. See *Autoregressive, Differencing, Integrated,* and *Moving average.*

Autocorrelated residuals
When the residual or error terms remaining after application of a forecasting method are autocorrelated, it indicates that the forecasting method has not removed all of the pattern from the data. See also *Autocorrelation.*

Autocorrelation

This term is used to describe the association or mutual dependence between values of the same time series at different time periods. It is similar to correlation, but relates the series for different time lags. Thus there would be an autocorrelation for a time lag of 1, another autocorrelation for a time lag of 2, and so on. The pattern of autocorrelation coefficients is frequently used to identify whether or not seasonality is present in a given time series (and the length of that seasonality), to identify appropriate time-series models for specific situations, and to determine the presence of stationarity in the data.

Autoregressive (AR)

Autoregression is a form of regression, but instead of the dependent variable (the item to be forecast) being related to independent variables, it is related to past values of itself at varying time lags. Thus an autoregressive model would express the forecast as a function of previous values of that time series.

Autoregressive/moving average (ARMA) scheme

This type of time-series forecasting model can be autoregressive (AR) in form, moving average (MA) in form, or a combination of the two (ARMA). In an ARMA model, the series to be forecast is expressed as a function of both previous values of the series (autoregressive terms) and previous error values from forecasting (the moving average terms).

Back forecasting

In applying quantitative forecasting techniques based on past errors, starting values are required so certain recursive calculations can be made. One way to obtain these is to apply the forecasting method to the series starting from the end and going to the beginning of the data. This procedure is called back forecasting and provides a set of starting values for the errors that can then be used for applying that forecasting method to the standard sequence of starting from the data and forecasting through the end.

Backward Shift Operator

The letter B is used to denote a backward shift by one period. Thus B operating on X_t has the effect of shifting attention to X_{t-1}. Similarly BB or B^2 is the same as shifting attention to two periods back. A first difference for a time-series can be denoted $(1 - B)X_t$. A second order difference is denoted $(1 - B)^2 X_t$ and a second difference would be denoted $(1 - B^2)X_t$. See *Differencing*.

Bayes Theorem

A formula which defines the posterior probability of an hypothesis as the product of the prior probability and a likelihood ratio. The formula is named after its original developer, the Reverend Thomas Bayes, and is the cornerstone of inductive decision analysis. See *Prior* and *Posterior*.

Biased estimator

If a formula is defined to calculate a statistic (such as the mean) and the expected value of this statistic is not equal to the corresponding population parameter (e.g., the mean of the population), then the formula will be called a biased estimator. This definition of biasedness has nothing to do with sample size. The usual formula for the sample mean is an unbiased estimator, but the formula for variance when we divide by N (sample size) is a biased estimator.

Box-Jenkins methodology

George E. Box and G. M. Jenkins have popularized the application of auto-regressive/moving average schemes to time-series forecasting problems. While this approach was originally developed in the 1930s, it did not become widely known until Box and Jenkins published a detailed description of it in book form in 1970.* The general methodology suggested by Box and Jenkins for applying ARIMA models to time-series analysis, forecasting, and control has come to be known as the Box-Jenkins methodology for time-series forecasting.

Business cycle

Periods of prosperity generally followed by periods of depression make up what is called the business cycle. Such cycles tend to vary in length and magnitude and are often dealt with as a separate subcomponent of the basic pattern contained in a time-series.

Causal or explanatory model

This type of forecasting model assumes that the factor to be forecast exhibits a cause/effect relationship with one or more other factors. Regression models and multivariate time-series models are the most common forecasting approaches of this type.

Census II

The Census II method of forecasting is a refinement of the classical decomposition method. It attempts to decompose a time series into seasonal, trend, cycle, and random components that can be analyzed separately, then recombined for predictive purposes. This method has been developed by using the empirical results obtained from its application at the United States Bureau of Census and elsewhere.

Central limit theorem

Regardless of the shape of the population distribution, this theorem states that the sampling distribution of the mean of N independently sampled values will approach the normal distribution as the sample size increases. In practice, when the sample size is sufficiently large (say greater than 30) this theorem is invoked.

Chi-square test

Given a standard normal population (i.e., normal distribution with mean zero and variance one) and N independently sampled values, the sum of the squares of these sampled values is called a chi-square value with N degrees of freedom. The complete set of such chi-square values is called a chi-square distribution. Several statistics used in practice (e.g., the correlation coefficient) can be converted to forms

---

*G. E. Box and G. M. Jenkins, *Time Series Analysis*. San Francisco: Holden-Day, 1970, 1976.

which have approximate chi-square distributions, and then statistical tests of significance can be conducted—e.g., to see if the sample correlation is significantly different from zero. See chapters 9 and 10 for two other examples.

Classical decomposition method

This approach to forecasting seeks to decompose the underlying pattern of a time series into cyclical, seasonal, trend, and random subpatterns. These subpatterns are then analyzed individually, extrapolated into the future, and recombined to obtain forecasts of the original series.

Coefficient of determination

See R^2 and $\overline{R}^2$.

Coefficient of variation

This statistic is the ratio of the standard deviation to the mean, expressed as a percent. It is a measure of the relative dispersion of a data series.

Confidence limits

Based on statistical theory and probability distributions, a confidence interval, or set of confidence limits, can be established for future forecasts. These limits are based on the extent of variation of the data and the time horizon of forecasting.

Consistent estimator

If a formula is defined to calculate a statistic (such as the mean) and the expected value of this statistic approaches the corresponding population parameter (e.g., the mean of the population) as the sample size increases, then the formula will be called a consistent estimator. The usual formula for the sample mean and the formula for variance where we divided by N (sample size) are both examples of consistent estimators.

Correlation coefficient

A standardized measure of the relationship between two variables, say X and Y. Commonly designated as r, its values range from -1 to $+1$, indicating strong negative relationship, through zero, to strong positive association. The correlation coefficient is the covariance between a pair of standardized variables.

Correlation matrix

Most computer programs designed to perform multiple regression analysis include the computation of the simple correlation coefficients between each pair of variables. The set of these correlation coefficients is often presented in the form of a matrix, referred to as the simple correlation matrix.

Covariance

This is a measure of the joint variation between two variables, say X and Y. The range of covariance values is unrestricted (large negative to large positive). However, if the X and Y variables are first standardized (see *Standardize*), then covariance is the same as correlation and the range of covariance (correlation) values is from -1 to $+1$.

Crosscorrelation

A standardized measure of association between one time-series and the past, present and future values of another time-series. This statistic has the characteristics of a regular correlation coefficient—i.e., varies from minus one to plus one—and serves the same purpose in transfer function modeling that autocorrelation does for univariate time-series analysis.

Crosscovariance

A measure of the association between the present value of a given variable and past, present and future values of another time-series variable. Since the values do not need to be standardized, the crosscovariance values can range from large negative to large positive.

Cross-impact matrix

In technological forecasting, several future events often interact with one another in affecting the likelihood that any single event will occur. The cross-impact matrix is a technological method of forecasting that seeks to determine the net effect of the probabilities of occurrence of several interrelated items on the probability that a specific item will occur.

Cumulative distribution function (CDF)

For a random variable X, a plot of (i) any given value of X, say X^*, against (ii) the probability that X does not exceed X^*, generates the cumulative probability distribution for X. Many statistical tables are based on cumulative probability distributions.

Cumulative forecasting

Instead of forecasting values for sequential time periods of equal length, users of forecasting often prefer to forecast the cumulative level of a variable over several periods. For example, one might forecast cumulative sales for the next twelve months, rather than forecast an individual value for each of those twelve months.

Curve fitting

One approach to forecasting is simply to fit some form of curve, perhaps a polynomial, to the historical time-series data. Use of a linear trend is, in fact, a curve fitting method. Higher forms of curve fitting are also possible, and they frequently provide better results.

Cyclical data

See *Business cycle*.

Cyclical index

A cyclical index is a number, usually standardized around 100, that indicates the cyclical pattern of a given set of time-series data.

Decomposition

See *Classical decomposition method*.

Degrees of freedom (df)

Given a sample of data and the computation of some statistic (e.g., the mean), the degrees of freedom are defined as (number of observations included in the formula) minus (number of parameters estimated using the data). For example, the mean statistic for N sample data points has N d.f., but the variance formula has $(N - 1)$ df because one parameter (the mean X) has to be estimated before the variance formula can be used.

Delphi method

This qualitative or technological approach seeks to use the judgment of experts systematically in arriving at a forecast of what future events will be or when they may occur. The approach uses a series of questionnaires to elicit responses from a panel of experts.

Dependent variable

A variable that is determined by some other factor or factors is referred to as a dependent variable. In regression analysis the variable being predicted is the dependent variable.

Depression

This term is used to describe that portion of the business cycle in which production and prices are at their lowest point, unemployment is highest, and general economic activity is low.

Deseasonalized data

Removal of the seasonal pattern in a data series results in deseasonalized data. Deseasonalizing facilitates the comparison of month-to-month changes. It is used in dealing with such data as unemployment statistics, economic indicators, or product sales.

Diagnostic checking

A step in times-series model building where the estimated errors of a model are examined for independence, zero mean, constant variance, and so on.

Differencing

When a time series is nonstationary, it can often be made stationary by taking first differences of the series—i.e., creating a new time series of successive differences, $(X_t - X_{t-1})$. If first differences do not convert the series to stationary form, then first differences of first differences can be created. This is called second-order differencing. A distinction is made between a second-order difference (just defined) and a second difference $(X_t - X_{t-2})$. See *Backward shift operator*.

Double moving average

When a moving average is taken of a series of data that already represents the result of a moving average, it is referred to as a double moving average. It results in additional smoothing or the removal of more randomness than an equal-length single moving average.

Dummy variable

Often referred to as a binary variable whose value is either 0 or 1, a dummy variable is frequently used to quantify qualitative events. For example, a strike/nonstrike situation could be represented by a dummy variable. These variables are most commonly used in the application of multiple regression analysis.

Durbin-Watson test (D-W test)

The Durbin-Watson statistic, named after its creators, tests the hypothesis that there is no autocorrelation of one time lag present in the residuals obtained from forecasting. By comparing the computed value of the Durbin-Watson test with the appropriate values from the table of values of the D-W statistic (Table D of Appendix I), the significance can be determined.

Econometric forecasting

An econometric model is a set of equations intended to be used simultaneously to capture the way in which endogenous and exogenous variables are interrelated. Using such a set of equations to forecast future values of key economic variables is known as econometric forecasting. The value of econometric forecasting is intimately connected to the value of the assumptions underlying the model equations.

Economic indicator

An economic indicator is a time series that has a reasonably stable relation (it lags, leads, or is coincident) to the average of the whole economy, or to some other time series of particular interest. Leading indicators are frequently used to identify turning points in the level of general economic activity.

Elasticity

This term is used to describe the amount of change in supply or demand when there is a change in price. For a highly elastic product there would be a substantial change in quantity with any change in price. The opposite is true for an inelastic product.

Endogenous variable

An endogenous variable is one whose value is determined within the system. For example, in an econometric model the market price of a product may be determined within the model, thus making that an endogenous variable.

Error

See *Residual*.

Error cost function

An error cost function states the cost of an error as a function of the size of the error. The most frequently used functional form for this is quadratic, which assumes that the effect of an error is proportional to the square of the error.

Estimating systems of simultaneous equations

There are many alternative methods for estimating the parameters for systems of simultaneous equations. These vary in terms of complexity, cost, and statistical completeness. The most common method is probably that of two-stage least squares.

Estimation

Estimation consists of finding appropriate values for the parameters of an equation in such a way that some criterion will be optimized. The most commonly used criterion is that of mean squared error. Oftentimes, an iterative procedure is needed in order to determine those parameter values that minimize this criterion.

Ex ante forecast

A forecast that uses only information available at the time of the actual forecast. See *Ex post forecast*.

Ex post forecast

A forecast that uses some information beyond the time at which the actual forecast is prepared. See *Ex ante forecast*.

Exogenous variable

An exogenous variable is one whose value is determined outside of the model or system. For example, in an econometric model the gross national product might be an exogenous variable. In a multiple regression equation, the independent variables would be exogenous variables.

Exploratory forecasting

The general class of technological forecasting methods that seek to predict long-run outcomes are known as exploratory approaches. These contrast with the normative approaches that seek to determine how best to achieve certain long-term results.

Exponential growth

If $100 is invested in a bank at 10% compound interest, then the amount grows at an exponential rate. This is exponential growth. Similarly, populations grow exponentially if unchecked. In forecasting, some phenomena are modeled as exponential functions.

Exponential smoothing, linear (Brown's)

Single exponential smoothing cannot deal with nonstationary data. Linear exponential smoothing seeks to overcome this problem by taking the difference between the single smoothed value and the second application of smoothing to those single smoothed values, in order to adjust the results of exponential smoothing for the trend. This approach is referred to as double or linear exponential smoothing.

Exponential smoothing, linear (Holt's two-parameter method)

This approach to handling nonstationary series with exponential smoothing is similar to that of Brown's method. However, Holt's approach uses two parameters, one of which is used to add a trend adjustment to the single smoothed value.

Exponential smoothing (Pegels' classification)

Pegels has conveniently classified exponential smoothing models into a two-way table with three rows labeled A (no trend), B (linear trend) and C (multiplicative trend), and three columns labeled 1 (no seasonality), 2 (additive seasonality) and 3 (multiplicative seasonality). Cell A-1 represents simple exponential smoothing; cell B-1 represents Holt's two-parameter method; and cell B-3 represents Winters' model.

Exponential smoothing, quadratic (Brown's one-parameter method)

This approach is an extension of linear exponential smoothing that is aimed at dealing with trends that are of higher order than linear. The method uses a triple exponential smoothing form. Although frequently referred to as quadratic exponential smoothing, it is not limited to quadratic functions only, but can be used for nonstationary series of higher than first degree.

Exponential smoothing, seasonal (Winters' three-parameter method)

Winters has extended Holt's two-parameter exponential smoothing by including an extra equation that is used to adjust the smoothed forecast to reflect seasonality. This form of exponential smoothing can thus account for data series that include both trend and seasonal elements, as well as randomness.

Exponential smoothing, single

This is the most basic form of exponential smoothing. It uses the parameter alpha to smooth past values of the data and errors in forecast. It is most commonly used in inventory control systems where many items are to be forecast and low cost is a primary concern.

File

A file is a collection of data arranged in some order for future reference. When stored on a computer, files may represent actual computer programs for performing certain forecasting methods or simply historical data to be used by those computer programs.

Filter

The purpose of a filter, as developed in engineering, is to eliminate random variations (high or low frequencies) so that only the true pattern remains. As applied to time-series forecasting, filters generally involve one or more parameters that are used to weight historical values of the series, or of the residuals of the series, in some optimal way that eliminates randomness.

First difference

See *Differencing*.

Foran system

This approach to forecasting is based on the fundamental concepts of time-series decomposition. It is similar to the Census II approach, except that it tends to be more oriented to corporate forecasting problems than to government forecasting. It incorporates the notion of economic indicators as an integral part of forecasting.

Forecasting

Forecasting is the prediction of values of a variable based on known past values of that variable or other related variables. Forecasts also may be based on expert judgments, which in turn are based on historical data and experience.

Forecasting horizon

The forecasting horizon is the length of time into the future for which forecasts are to be prepared. These generally vary from short-term forecasting horizons (less than three months) to long-term horizons (more than 2 years).

Fourier analysis

See *Spectral analysis*.

F-test

In statistics the ratio of two mean squares (variances) can often be used to test the significance of some item of interest. For example, in regression the ratio of (mean square due to the regression) to (mean square due to error) can be used to test the overall significance of the regression model. By looking up F-tables, the degree of significance of the computed F-value can be determined.

Frequency

In the context of line spectrum analysis this refers to how many sine waves are completed over N observations. A frequency of 1 means one complete wave over the N observations in the time series. A frequency of 4 means four complete waves in the time span of the N observations. See *Sine Wave* and *Line Spectrum*.

Function

A function is a statement of relationship between variables. Virtually all of the quantitative forecasting methods involve a functional relationship between the item to be forecast and either previous values of that item, previous error values, or other independent variables.

Gross national product (GNP)

The most comprehensive measure of a nation's income is the gross national product. It includes the total output of goods and services for a specific economy over a specific period of time (usually 1 year).

Harmonic smoothing (Harrison's method)

This approach to smoothing time series is based on the use of sine and cosine functions. Harmonic analysis is aimed at fitting some combination of sine and cosine terms to the historical values of a time series, and then extrapolating that to prepare forecasts for the future.

Heteroscedasticity

This condition exists when the errors do not have a constant variance across an entire range of values. For example, if the residuals from a time series have increasing variance with increasing time, they would be said to exhibit heteroscedasticity.

Heuristic

A heuristic is a set of steps or procedures that uses a trial and error approach to achieve some desired objective. The word comes from Greek, meaning *to discover or find.*

Homoscedasticity

This condition exists when the variance of a series is constant over the entire range of values of that series. It is the opposite of heteroscedasticity. When a series of residuals exhibits constant variance over the entire range of time periods it is said to exhibit homoscedasticity.

Horizontal or stationary data

See *Type of data.*

Hypothesis testing

An approach commonly used in classical statistics is to formulate a hypothesis and test the statistical significance of a hypothesis. For example, a hypothesis might be that the residuals from applying a time-series method of forecasting are random. The statistical test would then be set up to determine whether or not those residuals behave in a pattern that makes them significantly different (statistically) from 0.

Identification

This is the step in time-series model building (for ARMA and ARIMA approaches) where patterns in summary statistics such as autocorrelation functions, partial autocorrelation functions, and so on are related to potential models for the data. The intent is to identify, at least tentatively, an appropriate model so that the next steps in model-building—estimating parameters followed by diagnostic checking—can be pursued. (It should be noted that this definition and use of the word bear no relationship to the same word as used in the economics literature.)

Impulse response weights

If an input time-series X exerts its influence on an output variable Y in a dynamic manner over future time periods, then the set of weights defining this relationship is called the impulse response function. The transfer function method (multivariate ARIMA modeling) estimates these impulse response weights as part of the method for estimating parameter values in the final model.

Independent variable

An independent variable is one whose values are determined outside of the system being modeled. An independent variable is used in a causal relationship to predict values of a dependent variable.

Index numbers

These numbers are frequently used as summary indicators of the level of economic activity and/or corporate performance. For example, the Federal Reserve Board Index of Industrial Production summarizes a number of factors that indicate the overall level of industrial production activity. Similar index numbers can be prepared for economic variables, as well as for corporate variables.

Input-output analysis

This approach to planning an analysis deals with the modeling of a total system in terms of the relationship among several variables. Some of the best known work in this area is that by Leontief.* His models indicate the interrelationship between the outputs of one segment of the economy and the inputs to another segment.

Integrated

This is often an element of time-series models (the I in ARIMA models) where one or more of the differences of the time series are included in the model. The term comes from the fact that the original series may be recreated from a differenced series by a process of "integration" (involving a summation in the typical discrete environment).

Interactive forecasting

This term has been used to describe forecasting packages that are run on a time-shared computer. They allow the user to interact directly with the data and with the results of alternative forecasting methods. SIBYL/RUNNER, a set of programs developed by Makridakis and Wheelwright, is one such interactive forecasting package.

Intercept

In simple regression the constant term is referred to as the intercept of the regression equation with the Y-axis. If the independent variable (X) is 0, then the value of the dependent variable will be the intercept value.

Interdependence

If two or more factors are interdependent or mutually dependent, it indicates that their values move together in some specific manner. Thus a change in the value of one of the variables would correlate with a change in the value of the other variable.

Intervention analysis

This approach to forecasting is an extension of multivariate ARMA models. It facilitates determining the effects of unusual changes in the independent variables on the dependent variable. The most important characteristic of intervention analysis is that transient effects caused by such changes can be measured and their influence on the dependent variable can be predicted.

Kalman filter

This engineering approach to estimating the parameters of a function or filter is the most general approach to estimation in time-series forecasting. Although extremely powerful, computationally they are quite complex and have not yet found widespread use in forecasting applications.

---

*Leontief. *The Structure of American Economy, 1913–1931*. New York: Oxford University Press, 1951. *Input-Output Economics*. New York: Oxford University Press, 1966.

Leading indicator

An economic indicator whose peaks and troughs during the business cycle tend to occur sooner than those of the general economy. Turning points in such an indicator "lead" subsequent turning points in the general economy or some other economic series, thus signaling the likelihood of such a subsequent turning point.

Lead time

This term refers to the time interval between two events, when one must precede the other. In many inventory and order entry systems, the lead time is the interval between the time when an order is placed and the time when it is actually delivered.

Least squares estimation

This approach to estimating the parameter values in an equation minimizes the squares of the deviations that result from fitting that particular model. For example, if a trend line is being estimated to fit a data series, the method of least squares estimation could be used to minimize the mean squared error. This would give a line whose estimated values would minimize the sum of the squares of the actual deviations from that line for the historical data.

Likelihood

The probability that a certain empirical outcome will be observed, conditional on a certain prior outcome. This term is often used in connection with Bayes' theorem and in talking about statistics that are "maximum likelihood estimators" for a population.

Linear exponential smoothing

See *Exponential smoothing, linear.*

Line spectrum

A time-series can be fitted by a set of sine waves of various frequencies (1,2,3, . . .), various amplitudes and various phase angles. In this book the graph of the amplitudes for frequencies 1,2,3, . . . etc., is called the line spectrum. See *Power spectrum.*

Logistic curve

This curve has the typical S-shape often associated with the product life cycle. It is frequently used in connection with long-term curve fitting as a technological method.

Long (seasonal) difference

In order to achieve stationarity before applying the Box-Jenkins methodology to time-series forecasting, the first or second differences of the data must often be taken. A long (or seasonal) difference refers to a difference that is taken between seasonal values that are separated by one complete season. Thus, if monthly data are used with an annual seasonal pattern, a long difference would simply compute the difference for values separated by twelve months rather than using the first difference, which is for values adjacent to one another in a series. See *differencing.*

Macrodata

This type of data describes the behavior of macroeconomic factors such as GNP, inflation, the index of industrial production, and so on. Macroeconomics deals with the study of economics in terms of whole systems, usually at national or regional levels.

Marginal analysis

This type of analysis is incremental in nature. It seeks to determine the marginal change in one variable for a marginal change in a related variable.

Marginal probability

The probability of an event, unconditional on any other event, is often referred to as the marginal probability. This term is frequently used in connection with Bayesian analysis.

Marquardt's nonlinear estimation

See *Nonlinear estimation*.

Matrix

In mathematical terminology a matrix is a rectangular array of elements arranged in rows and columns. There may be one or more rows and one or more columns in such a matrix.

Mean

The arithmetic average or mean for a group of items is defined as the sum of the values of the items divided by the number of items. It is frequently used as a measure of location for a frequency or probability distribution.

Mean absolute percentage error (MAPE)

The mean absolute percentage error is the mean or average of the sum of all of the percentage errors for a given data set taken without regard to sign. (That is, their absolute values are summed and the average computed.) It is one measure of accuracy commonly used in quantitative methods of forecasting.

Mean percentage error (MPE)

The mean percentage error is the average of all of the percentage errors for a given data set. This average allows positive and negative percentage errors to cancel one another. Because of this, it is sometimes used as a measure of bias in the application of a forecasting method.

Mean squared error (MSE)

The mean squared error is a measure of accuracy computed by squaring the individual error for each item in a data set and then finding the average or mean value of the sum of those squares. The mean squared error gives greater weight to large errors than to small errors because the errors are squared before being summed.

Medial average

The middle number of a data set is the median. It can be found by arranging the items in the data set in ascending order and identifying the middle item. The medial average includes only those items grouped around the median value. For example, the highest and lowest value may be excluded from a medial average.

Median

Frequently used as a measure of location for a frequency or probability distribution, the median of a group of items is the value of the middle item when all the items are arranged in either ascending or descending order of magnitude.

Microdata

Micro comes from the Greek word meaning small. Microdata refers generally to data collected at the level of an individual organization or a company. Microeconomics refers to the study of such data as contrasted with macroeconomics, which deals generally with a regional or national level.

Mixed process

In time-series analysis a process or model that combines moving average (MA) forms with autoregressive (AR) forms is frequently referred to as a mixed process.

Model

A model is the symbolic representation of reality. In quantitative forecasting methods a specific model is used to represent the basic pattern contained in the data. This may be a regression model, which is causal in nature, or a time-series model.

Months for cyclical dominance (MCD)

The months for cyclical dominance is computed as the ratio of the average percentage change in the random component of a series to the average percentage change in the trend-cycle component. It indicates the number of months that it takes for the trend-cycle element to dominate the random component.

Morphological research

This approach to technological forecasting seeks to enumerate the major classes of activity that will affect the successful development of a certain outcome. Those major classes can then be subdivided and used to examine different combinations of variables and the possibilities that they provide for achieving some specified technological goal.

Moving average

There are two distinct meanings to this term. First, for a time series we can define the moving average of order K as the average (mean) value of the last K observations. See chapter 3 for examples. Second, in Box-Jenkins modeling the MA in ARIMA stands for "moving average" and means that the value of the time series at time t is influenced by a current error term and (possibly) weighted error terms in the past. See chapters 8, 9 and 10 for examples.

Multicollinearity

In regression analysis a computational problem arises if two or more regressors (independent variables) are perfectly correlated with one another. This is called perfect collinearity. If the correlation between two regressors is not perfect (i.e., $+1$ or -1) but nearly so, then the regression coefficients associated with those two regressors will be very unstable. In larger sets of regressors, the condition of multicollinearity (or near multicollinearity) may not be easy to detect. If any linear combination of one subset of regressors is nearly perfectly related to a linear combination of any other subset of regressors, then a multicollinearity problem is present. See chapter 6 for details.

Multiple correlation coefficient

If a dependent measure Y is regressed against several independent measures $X_1, X_2, \ldots, X_k$, then the estimated Y value is designated $\hat{Y}$. The correlation between $\hat{Y}$ and Y is called the multiple correlation coefficient and is often designated R. It is customary to deal with this coefficient in squared form, i.e., R^2. See R^2 and $\overline{R}^2$.

Multiple regression

The technique of multiple regression is an extension of simple regression. It allows for more than one independent variable to be included in predicting the value of a dependent variable. For forecasting purposes a multiple regression equation is often referred to as a causal or explanatory model.

Multivariate autoregressive/moving average (ARMA) model

Multivariate ARMA models express future values of a time series (the output variable) as a function of both past values and/or past errors of that series and past, present, or future values of related series (the input variables). Such approaches to time-series analysis provide an alternative to regression techniques for those wishing to develop a causal model. See *Transfer function*.

Multivariate Box-Jenkins modeling

See *Transfer functions*.

Naive forecast

Forecasts obtained with a minimal amount of effort and data manipulation and based solely on the most recent information available are frequently referred to as naive forecasts. One such naive method would be to use the most recent datum available as the future forecast. A slightly more sophisticated naive method would be to adjust that most recent datum for seasonality.

Noise

The randomness often found in data series is frequently referred to as noise. This term comes from the field of engineering where a filter is used to eliminate noise so that the true pattern can be identified.

Nonlinear estimation

If parameters have to be estimated for nonlinear functions, then ordinary least squares procedures may not apply. Under these circumstances certain nonlinear techniques exist for solving the problem. Marquardt's algorithm used in chapters 9 and 10 is an example. Minimizing the sum of squared residuals is the usual criterion (as in linear estimation), but nonlinear estimation is an iterative procedure and there is no guarantee that the final solution is the global minimum.

Nonstationary

A time series exhibits nonstationarity if the underlying generating process does not have a constant mean and/or a constant variance. In practice, a visual inspection of the plotted time series can help determine if either or both of these conditions exist, and the set of autocorrelations for the time series can be used to confirm the presence of nonstationarity or not.

Observation

An observation is the value of a specific event as expressed on some measurement scale by a single data value. In most forecasting applications a set of observations is used to provide the data to which the selected model is fit.

Optimal parameter or weight value

The optimal, final parameters or weights are those values that give the best performance for a given model applied to a specific set of data. It is those optimal parameters that are then used in forecasting.

Outlier

An outlier is a data value that is unusually large or small. Such outliers are sometimes removed from the data set before fitting a forecasting model so that unusually large deviations from the pattern will not affect the fitting of the model.

Parameter

Characteristics of a population such as the mean or standard deviation are called parameters. These should be distinguished from the characteristics of a sample taken from a population, which are called statistics.

Parsimony

The concept of parsimony holds that as few parameters as possible should be used in fitting a model to a set of data. This concept is a basic premise of the Box-Jenkins approach to time-series analysis.

Partial autocorrelation

This measure of correlation is used to identify the extent of relationship between current values of a variable with earlier values of that same variable (values for various time lags) while holding the effects of all other time lags constant. Thus, it is completely analogous to partial correlation but refers to a single variable.

Partial correlation

This statistic provides a measure of the association between a dependent variable and one or more independent variables when the effect of the relationship with other independent variables is held constant.

Pattern

The basic set of relationships and the underlying process over time is referred to as the pattern in the data.

Phase

When plotting a sine wave ($Y = \sin B$), the value of Y when $B = 0$ is zero. The whole wave may be shifted horizontally (to the left or right) by adding a constant angle to the equation ($Y = \sin (B + C)$) and this constant angle C is called the phase angle or phase shift. See *Sine wave*.

Polynomial

In algebra a polynomial is an expression containing one or more terms, each of which consists of a coefficient and a variable(s) raised to some power. Thus $a + bX$ is a linear polynomial and $a + bX + cX$ is a nonlinear polynomial in X. Regression models involve linear and nonlinear polynomials.

Polynomial fitting

It is possible to fit a polynomial of any number of terms to a set of data. If the number of terms (the order) equals the number of data observations, the fit can be made perfectly.

Postsample evaluation

The practice of evaluating a time-series model or some other forecasting model using data that were collected after the set of data on which the model was estimated is often referred to as a postsample evaluation of the forecasting model. Ongoing tracking of the performance of a model is another example of this.

Posterior

In Bayesian analysis all probabilities are conditional probabilities. When we consider the probability of an hypothesis (or forecast) being true given the prior probability and given new information (data), then we are asking about "the posterior" probability. See *Prior* and *Bayes Theorem*.

Power spectrum

The theoretical equivalent of the line spectrum is a continuous curve from 0 through .5. It represents the energy of the theoretical process from the lowest frequency to the highest frequency, and is used in this book to explore the theoretical properties of the various Box-Jenkins models (AR, MA and ARIMA). See *Line Spectrum*.

Prewhitening

In transfer function modeling an input series X influences an output variable Y dynamically over future time periods. In order to study the transfer function itself, it is convenient to make X as simple as possible so that the properties in Y (the output of the system) are essentially the properties of the system itself, operating on X (the input). Since the input series X may not always be simple, attempts are made to make it more simple by removing all possible pattern features in X. This process of removing "pattern" is called prewhitening, and the prewhitened X is as close as possible to white noise. See *Noise*.

Prior

In Bayesian analysis all probabilities are conditional probabilities. Thus when we start an investigation of a particular hypothesis (or forecast), the probability that the hypothesis is true given all we know at this time, but "prior" to the examination of new information (data), is called "the prior." See *Bayes Theorem*.

Probability

The probability of an event is expressed as a number from 0 through 1. An impossible event has probability zero. A certain event has probability 1. Classical probability is defined in terms of long-run relative frequency—in a long series of identical trials the relative frequency of occurrence of the event approaches a fixed value called the probability of the event. In Bayesian analysis, probability is defined more subjectively as the "encoding of my knowledge about that event." It is the degree of plausibility of the event given all that I know at this time, and is expressed as a number between 0 and 1.

Product life cycle

The concept of the product life cycle is particularly useful in forecasting and analyzing historical data. It presumes that demand for a product follows an S-shaped curve growing slowly in the early stages, achieving rapid and sustained growth in the middle stages, and slowing again in the mature stage.

Quadratic exponential smoothing

See *Exponential smoothing, quadratic*.

Qualitative or technological forecasting

Qualitative or technological methods of forecasting are appropriate when the assumption of constancy is invalid (the pattern contained in past data cannot be assumed to continue into the future), when information about the past can not be obtained, or when the forecast is about unlikely or unexpected events in the future.

Quantitative forecasting

Quantitative forecasting methods can be applied when information about the past is available, if that information can be quantified and if the pattern included in past information can be assumed to continue into the future.

R Squared (R^2)

In regression the square of the correlation between Y (the dependent variable) and $\hat{Y}$ (the estimated Y value based on the set of independent regressors) is denoted R^2. This statistic is often called the coefficient of determination. See $\overline{R}^2$.

R-bar squared ($\overline{R}^2$)

Since the computation of R^2 does not involve the degrees of freedom for either the SS (sum of squares) of deviations due to the regression or the SS of deviations in the original Y data, a corrected R^2 is defined and designated $\overline{R}^2$ (R-bar squared). See R^2. This statistic can be interpreted as the proportion of variance in Y that can be "explained" by the regressors.

Randomness

The noise or random fluctuations in a data series are frequently described as the randomness of that data series.

Random sampling

This statistical sampling method involves selecting a sample from a population in such a way that every unit within that population has the same probability of being selected as any other unit.

Regression

A term that dates back to Sir Francis Galton and his work with the heights of siblings in different generations. The heights of children of exceptionally tall (or short) parents "regress" to the mean of the population. Regression analysis today means any modeling of a dependent variable Y as a function of a set of independent variables X_1 through X_k.

Regression coefficients

When a dependent measure Y is regressed against a set of independent measures X_1 through X_k, the analyst specifies a particular functional form—linear or nonlinear—and solves for the values of the unknown coefficients by least squares procedures. The properties of these regression coefficients can be used to understand the importance of each independent variable (as it relates to Y) and the interrelatedness among the independent variables (as they relate to Y).

Relative frequency curve

A picture of a probability distribution where the uncertain quantity is displayed on the horizontal axis and relative frequency is displayed on the vertical axis.

Relevance tree

This normative approach to technological forecasting specifies top-level goals and objectives, then subdivides them to lower-level goals until the current level of technology is reached. Probabilities can then be assigned to determine the likelihood of various goals and objectives being reached and to identify those areas where major resources will need to be expended in order to accomplish certain goals.

Residual

In forecasting this term is commonly used as a synonym for error. It is calculated by subtracting the forecast value from the actual value to give a "residual" or error value for each forecast period.

Sample

A sample is a finite or limited number of observations or data values selected from a universe or population of such data values

Sampling error

The sampling error is an indication of the magnitude of difference between the true values of a population parameter and the estimated value of that parameter based on a sample

S-Curve

An S-curve is most frequently used to represent the product life cycle. Several different mathematical forms, such as the logistics curve, can be used to fit an S-curve to actual observed data.

Seasonal data
See *Type of data*.

Seasonal exponential smoothing
See *Exponential smoothing, seasonal*.

Seasonal index
A seasonal index is a number that indicates the seasonality for a given time period. For example, a seasonal index for observed values in July would indicate the way in which that July value is affected by the seasonal pattern in the data. Seasonal indices are used to obtain deseasonalized data.

Seasonal variation
The change that seasonal factors cause in a data series is frequently called seasonal variation.

Serial correlation
See *Autocorrelation*.

Short (nonseasonal) difference
A short difference is aimed at removing nonstationarity that is caused by period-to-period trends—that is, $(X_t - X_{t-1})$. It is often used in conjunction with long differences.

Significance
See *Hypothesis testing*.

Simple regression
Simple regression is a special case of multiple regression involving a single independent variable. As with multiple linear regression it assumes a linear relationship between the independent variable and the dependent variable. That relationship is estimated using the method of least squares and a set of observed values.

Sine wave
The equation $Y = A \sin (B + C)$ represents a wave with amplitude A, frequency and wavelength related to angle B, and phase angle (or shift in a horizontal sense) C. See *Amplitude*, *Wavelength*, *Frequency*, *Phase*, and *Line spectrum*.

Slope
The slope of a curve at a given point indicates the amount of change in the dependent variable for a one-unit change in the independent variable. In simple regression the coefficient of the independent variable indicates the slope of the regression line.

Smoothing
Combining two or more observations taken from periods during which the same causal factors were in effect provides a smoothed value, or estimate. The term smoothed is used because such combinations tend to reduce randomness by allowing positive and negative random effects to partially offset each other.

Specification error

A type of error often caused either by the incorrect choice of a functional form of a forecasting model or the failure to include important variable in that functional form or model.

Spectral analysis

The decomposition of a time series into a set of sine waves (or cosine waves) with differing amplitudes, frequencies, and phase angles, is variously known as spectral analysis, harmonic analysis, Fourier analysis, and so on. Each method has specific features but in general they all look for periodicities in the data.

Spencer's weighted moving average

The Spencer's weighted moving average is an approach to computing a moving average that will compensate for a cubic trend in the data. It consists of two averages, one for 15 periods and the other for 21 periods. Both have been used widely in many decomposition methods.

Standard deviation

A summary statistic (parameter) for a sample (population). It is usually denoted S (σ) for a sample (population), and is the square root of variance. It is the square root of the average squared-deviation-from-the-mean.

Standard error

Given a population distribution (say a normal distribution), a sampling plan (say a simple independent random sampling plan), and a specific statistic (say the mean), then the sampling distribution of the mean is a probability distribution with an expected value, a standard deviation, and various other properties. The standard deviation of the sampling distribution of a statistic is called the standard error of that statistic.

Standardize

Given a sample set of values for X, where the mean is X and the standard deviation is S, the i-th value in the set, X_i, is standardized by subtracting the mean and dividing by the standard deviation. The standardized values are often designated by the letter z.

Stationary

If the underlying generating process for a time series is based on a constant mean and a constant variance, then the time series is stationary. More formally, a series is stationary if its statistical properties are independent of the particular time period during which it is observed.

Statistic

Given a sample consisting of N values, a statistic is any summary number that captures a property of the sample data. For example, the mean is a statistic, and so are the variance, the skewness, the median, the standard deviation, etc. For a pair of variables sampled jointly the correlation coefficient is a statistic and so is the covariance. The values of a statistic vary from sample to sample, and the complete set of values is called the sampling distribution of the statistic.

Structural stability

A model for which both the parameter values and the functional form are constant over time is often referred to as having the property of structural stability.

Technological forecasting

See *Qualitative or technological forecasting.*

Time series

An ordered sequence of values of a variable observed at equally spaced time intervals is referred to as a time series.

Time-series model

A time-series model is a function that relates the values of a time series to previous values of that time series, its errors, or other related time series. See *ARIMA.*

Tracking signal

Since quantitative methods of forecasting assume the continuation of some historical pattern into the future, it is often useful to develop some measure that can be used to determine when the basic pattern has changed. A tracking signal is the most common such measure. One frequently used tracking signal involves computing the cumulative error over time and setting limits so that when the cumulative error goes outside those limits, the forecaster can be notified and a new model can be considered.

Trading day

A trading day is an active day. In many business time series the number of business days in a month or some other specified period of time may vary. Frequently trading-day adjustments must be made to reflect the fact that every January (or similar period) may not include the same number of trading days.

Transfer functions

The multivariate Box-Jenkins modeling procedures are described in their book as transfer function models. A typical situation would be the determination of that function which "transferred" the input series (say a leading indicator) through the system and out as the output series (economic consequence). By modeling the transfer function in such a situation the forecaster can predict what will happen to the output series if the input series changes.

Transformation

Transformation involves changing the scale of measurement in variable(s). For example, data can be transformed from a linear to a logarithmic scale, or from a linear to a square root scale. Transformations play two roles: (1) in time series they are used to achieve stationarity in variance and (2) in regression they are used to make the relationship linear or to improve the fit of the model.

Trend analysis

Trend analysis is a special form of simple regression in which time is the independent variable. It consists of fitting a linear relationship to a past series of values, with time as the independent variable.

t-test

The t-test is a statistical test used extensively in regression analysis to test the hypothesis that the individual coefficients are significantly different from 0. It is computed as the ratio of the coefficient to the standard error of that coefficient.

Turning point

Any time a data pattern changes direction it can be described as having reached a turning point. For seasonal patterns these turning points are usually very predictable and can be handled by many different forecasting methods because the length of a complete season remains constant. In many cyclical data patterns the length of the cycle varies as does its magnitude. Here the identification of turning points is a particularly difficult and important task.

Type of data

In many forecasting methods, such as decomposition, data is classified as having one or more subpatterns. These include a seasonal pattern, a trend pattern, and a cyclical pattern. Frequently, when forecasters refer to the type of data they mean the specific forms of subpatterns that are included in that data.

Unbiasedness

A statistic is referred to as an unbiased estimator of a population parameter if the sampling distribution of the statistic has a mean equal to the parameter being estimated.

Updated forecast

Revisions of original forecasts in light of data that subsequently become available after the time period in which the original forecasts were made are often referred to as updated forecasts. This concept is analogous to posterior distributions, although the updating is often much more subjective than in Bayesian analysis and the calculation of posterior distributions.

Validation

The process of testing the degree to which a model is useful for making forecasts. The sample data are often split into two segments, one being used to estimate the parameters of the model, and the other being used as a "holdout" sample to test the forecasts made by the model. There are many variations on this process of validation.

Variance

A summary statistic (parameter) for a sample (population). It is denoted S_x, V_x, and sometimes COV_{xx} (to identify it with covariance). It is the average of squared deviations from the mean.

Wavelength

In the context of line spectrum analysis of a tie-series the wavelength of a sine wave is the number of time periods it takes to complete one wave. See chapter 8.

Weight

The term weight indicates the relative importance given to an individual item included in forecasting. In the method of moving averages all of those past values included in the moving average are given equal weight. In more sophisticated methods of time-series analysis, the problem of model identification involves determining the most appropriate values of those weights.

White noise

When there is no pattern whatsoever in the data series, it is said to represent white noise. Thus, it is analogous to a series that is completely random.

Winters' exponential smoothing

See *Exponential smoothing, seasonal.*

INDEX